Rest easy and save!

AAA Members: Save 10% - 30%* at 72 Days Inn® hotels in Texas.

Just book and save at any of the AAA-approved Days Inn locations listed in this TourBook®. Your room comes with an AM/FM clock radio and hair dryer. You'll also get a free continental breakfast and free *USA Today* newspaper. Not to mention special bonus offers for AAA Members all year long! Pets are welcome at more than 900 Days Inn locations worldwide. For specific locations and reservations, call **1-800-432-9755** or visit **daysinn.com**.

Show Your Card & Save

AAA. Every Day.®

DAYS INN®

There you go.

*Discount off published Tour...
other discounts or special...
Some restrictions may ap...

Texas

TourBook Navigator

Follow our simple guide to make the most of this member benefit

Comprehensive City Index

Alphabetical list for the entire book

■ Texas

Have you ever celebrated when you've seen your exit sign?

AAA MEMBERS SAVE 10%

Every day should come with a smile. And at Hampton®, we're committed to making you smile. That's why we offer our Stay and Save™ rates for AAA members. That's 10% off the best available room rates when you book a room with your AAA card. And with over 1,000 locations nationwide, we're sure to be close to wherever you're traveling. Plus, we'll make sure you start the day right with our free breakfast bar and leave completely satisfied. It's why we have our 100% Satisfaction Guarantee. It's also why you get both Hilton HHonors® hotel points and airline miles for each stay. So book your next trip at Hampton today. Just call 1-800-456-7793 for reservations.

We're with you all the way.

The Hilton Family

Look for our Partners in Savings!

*W*hen selecting a AAA Approved lodging, look for properties that participate in our various partnership programs. In addition to actively soliciting AAA business, many of them also offer discounts to AAA members.

* Properties that advertise in the TourBook® guide understand the value of AAA member business and want to provide members with a more complete picture of their property. Please refer to their ads for more details on what these properties have to offer.

* A red (SAVE) icon in their TourBook guide listing indicates an **Official Appointment** property that offers a minimum 10% discount off published TourBook standard room rates or the lowest public standard room rate, at the time of booking, for the dates of stay.

* A black (SAVE) icon indicates a chain hotel that participates in the **Show Your Card & Save®** program. SYC&S partners offer a satisfaction guarantee and savings up to 50% on over 1.5 million hotel rooms throughout North America.

Participating Chains:

Sleep Inn, Comfort Inn, Comfort Suites, Quality Inn, Clarion, Econo Lodge, Rodeway Inn, Mainstay Suites, Days Inn, Hilton Hotels & Resorts, Hilton Garden Inn, Hampton Inn, Hampton Inn & Suites, Embassy Suites, Doubletree Hotels, Homewood Suites, Hyatt Hotels & Resorts, La Quinta Inn, La Quinta Inn & Suites, Marriott Hotels & Resorts, Renaissance Hotels & Resorts, Courtyard by Marriott, Fairfield Inn, Residence Inns, SpringHill Suites, TownePlace Suites, Best Western

Valid membership card needed time of resservation.

Visit	Over 1,100 AAA Offices	Click	aaa.com	Call	866-AAA-SAVE

All discounts are off full rates and vary by location and time of year. The 50% discount is not available at all times.

6

Crossword Puzzle

DOWN

ACROSS

11

2

12

4

13

5

8

9

14

1

3 FLORIDA AAA 12B

6

7

10

Which two are the same?

Towty is a trademark of AAA

8

Special People Get Special Treatment

Want to be sure you'll be treated right on your next travel adventure?

*L*ook for establishments that advertise in the AAA TourBook® guides. These are the businesses that cater to AAA members. They value the business they receive from AAA members, and are willing to go the extra mile to get it. And in turn, they pass value on to you.

Trust

the AAA TourBook® guide for objective travel information. Follow the pages of the TourBook Navigator to thoroughly understand this unique member benefit.

Making Your Way Through the AAA Listings

Attractions, lodgings and restaurants are listed on the basis of merit alone after careful evaluation, approval and rating by one of our full-time, professionally trained Tourism Editors. Annual evaluations are unannounced to ensure that our Tourism Editors see an establishment just as our members would see it.

Those lodgings and restaurants listed with an (fyi) icon have not gone through the same evaluation process as other rated properties. Individual listings will typically denote the reason why this icon appears. Bulleted recreational activity listings are not inspected but are included for member information.

An establishment's decision to advertise in the TourBook guide has no bearing on its evaluation or rating. Advertising for services or products does not imply AAA endorsement.

How the TourBook is

Organized

Geographic listing is used for accuracy and consistency. This means attractions, lodgings and restaurants are listed under the city in which they physically are located—or in some cases under the nearest recognized city. The Comprehensive City Index located in the back of the book contains an A-to-Z list of cities. Most listings are alphabetically organized by state or province, city, and establishment name. A color is assigned to each state or province so that you can match the color bars at the top of the page to switch from ❶ Points of Interest to ❷ Lodgings and Restaurants.

Destination Cities and Destination Areas

The TourBook guide also groups information by destination city and destination area. If a city is grouped in a destination vicinity section, the city name will appear at its alphabetical location in the book, and a handy cross reference will give the exact page on which listings for that city begin. Maps are placed at the beginning of these sections to orient you to the destinations.

❸ Destination cities, established based on government models and local expertise, are comprised of metropolitan areas plus nearby vicinity cities.

Destination areas are regions with broad tourist appeal. Several cities will comprise the area.

All information in this TourBook guide was reviewed for accuracy before publication. However, since changes inevitably occur between annual editions, we suggest you contact establishments directly to confirm prices and schedules.

Points of Interest Section

Orientation maps

near the start of each Attractions section show only those places we call points of interest. Coordinates included with the city listings depict the locations of those cities on the map. A GEM symbol (☞) accents towns with "must see" points of interest which offer a *Great Experience for Members*. And the black ovals with white numerals (22 for example) locate items listed in the nearby Recreation Areas chart.

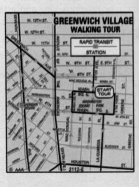

Destination area maps

illustrate key travel areas defined by local travel experts. Communities shown have listings for AAA approved attractions.

National park maps

represent the area in and around the park. Some campground sites and lodges spotted on the maps do not meet AAA/CAA criteria, but are shown for members who nevertheless wish to stay close to the park area.

Walking or self-guiding tour maps

correspond to specific routes described in TourBook guide text.

City maps

show areas where numerous points of interest are concentrated and indicate their location in relation to major roads, parks, airports and other landmarks.

Lodgings & Restaurants Section

Destination area maps illustrate key travel areas defined by local travel experts. Communities shown have listings for AAA-RATED® lodgings and/or restaurants.

Spotting maps show the location of lodgings and restaurants. Lodgings are spotted with a black background (**22** for example); restaurants are spotted with a white background (**23** for example). Spotting map indexes have been placed immediately after each map to provide the user with a convenient method to identify what an area has to offer at a glance. The index references the map page number where the property is spotted, indicates if a property is an Official Appointment and contains an advertising reference if applicable. It also lists the property's diamond rating, high season rate range and listing page number.

Downtown/city spotting maps are provided when spotted facilities are very concentrated. GEM points of interest also appear on these maps.

Vicinity spotting maps spot those properties that are outside the downtown or city area. Major roads, landmarks, airports and GEM points of interest are shown on vicinity spotting maps as well. The names of suburban communities that have AAA-RATED® accommodations are shown in magenta type.

Featured Information Section

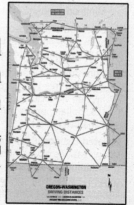

Driving distance maps are intended to be used only for trip-distance and driving-time planning.

Sample Attraction Listing

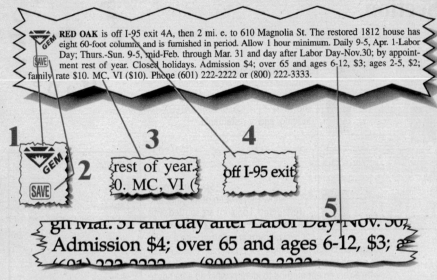

RED OAK is off I-95 exit 4A, then 2 mi. e. to 610 Magnolia St. The restored 1812 house has eight 60-foot columns and is furnished in period. Allow 1 hour minimum. Daily 9-5, Apr. 1-Labor Day; Thurs.-Sun. 9-5, mid-Feb. through Mar. 31 and day after Labor Day-Nov.30; by appointment rest of year. Closed holidays. Admission $4; over 65 and ages 6-12, $3; ages 2-5, $2; family rate $10. MC, VI ($10). Phone (601) 222-2222 or (800) 222-3333.

rest of year. 0. MC, VI (

off I-95 exit

gh Mar. 31 and day after Labor Day-Nov. 30;
Admission $4; over 65 and ages 6-12, $3;

1 This attraction is of exceptional interest and quality and therefore has been designated a AAA GEM—offering a *Great Experience for Members.*

2 Participating attractions offer AAA/CAA, AAA MasterCard or AAA Visa cardholders a discount off the attraction's standard admission; members should inquire in advance concerning the validity of the discount for special rates. Present your card at the admission desk. A list of participating points of interest appears in the Indexes section of the book. The SAVE discount may not be used in conjunction with other discounts. Attractions that already provide a reduced senior or child rate may not honor the SAVE discount for those age groups. All offers are subject to change and may not apply during special events, particular days or seasons or for the entire validity period of the TourBook. Shopping establishments preceded by a SAVE icon also provide discounts and/or gift with purchase to AAA/CAA members; present your card at the mall's customer service center to receive your benefit.

3 AX=American Express   DS=Discover   MC=MasterCard
CB=Carte Blanche   JC=Japan Credit Bureau   VI=VISA
DC=Diners Club
Minimum amounts that may be charged appear in parentheses when applicable.

4 Unless otherwise specified, directions are given from the center of town, using the following highway designations: I (interstate highway), US (federal highway), Hwy. (Canadian highway), SR (state route), CR (county road), FM (farm to market road), FR (forest road), MM (mile marker).

5 Admission prices are quoted without sales tax. Children under the lowest age specified are admitted free when accompanied by an adult. Days, months and age groups written with a hyphen are inclusive. Prices pertaining to points of interest in the United States are quoted in U.S. dollars; prices for Canadian province and territory points of interest are quoted in Canadian dollars.

Bulleted Listings: Casino gambling establishments are visited by AAA personnel to ensure safety; casinos within hotels are presented for member information regardless of whether the lodging is AAA approved. Recreational activities of a participatory nature (requiring physical exertion or special skills) are not inspected. Wineries are inspected by AAA Tourism Editors to ensure they meet listing requirements and offer tours. All are presented in a bulleted format for informational purposes.

Attraction Partners

These Show Your Card & Save® partners provide the listed member benefits. Admission tickets that offer greater discounts may be available for purchase at the local AAA/CAA club. A maximum of six tickets is available at the discount price.

SeaWorld/Busch Gardens

[SAVE] Save at SeaWorld, Busch Gardens, Sesame Place, Water Country USA and Adventure Island

[SAVE] Save 10% on general admission

Six Flags Adventure Parks

[SAVE] Save $4 per adult on general admission at the gate

[SAVE] Save $12 per adult on general admission at the gate each Wednesday

[SAVE] Save 10% on selected souvenirs and dining (check at main gate for details)

Universal Orlando

[SAVE] Save $4 on a 2-day/2-park pass or $5 on a 3-day/2-park pass at Universal Orlando's theme parks (savings apply to tickets purchased at the gate)

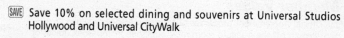

[SAVE] Save 10% on select dining and souvenirs at both Universal Orlando theme parks and at all Universal CityWalk Orlando restaurants (except Emeril's)

Universal Studios Hollywood

[SAVE] Save $3 on a 1-day Universal Hollywood pass (savings applies to tickets purchased at the gate)

[SAVE] Save 10% on selected dining and souvenirs at Universal Studios Hollywood and Universal CityWalk

Gray Line

[SAVE] Save 10% on sightseeing tours of 1 day or less

Restaurant Partners

Landry's Seafood House, The Crab House, Joe's Crab Shack

[SAVE] Save 10% on food and non-alcoholic beverages at Landry's Seafood House, The Crab House and Joe's Crab Shack and 10% on merchandise at Joe's Crab Shack. Savings applicable to AAA/CAA members and up to six people

Hard Rock Cafe

[SAVE] Save 10% on food, beverage, and merchandise at all U.S., Canada, and select international locations

Visit aaa.com to discover all the great Show Your Card & Save® restaurants in your area.

Sample Lodging Listing

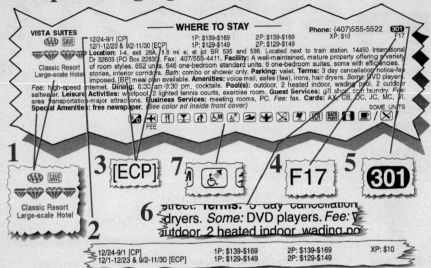

WHERE TO STAY

VISTA SUITES
(AAA) (SAVE)
Classic Resort
Large-scale Hotel

Phone: (407)555-5522 **301**
XP: $10 **F17**

12/24-9/1 [CP]   1P: $139-$169   2P: $139-$169
12/1-12/23 & 9/2-11/30 [ECP]   1P: $129-$149   2P: $129-$149
Location: I-4, exit 26A, 1.8 mi e; at jct SR 535 and 536. Located next to train station. 14450 International Dr 32603 (PO Box 22830). Fax: 407/555-4411. **Facility:** A well-maintained, mature property offering a variety of room styles. 652 units. 646 one-bedroom standard units. 6 one-bedroom suites, some with efficiencies. 3 stories, interior corridors. *Bath:* combo or shower only. **Parking:** valet. **Terms:** 3 day cancellation notice-fee imposed, [BP] meal plan available. **Amenities:** voice mail, safes (fee), irons, hair dryers. *Some:* DVD players. *Fee:* high-speed internet. **Dining:** 6:30 am-9:30 pm, cocktails. **Pool(s):** outdoor, 2 heated indoor, wading pool, 2 outdoor saltwater. **Leisure Activities:** whirlpool, 2 lighted tennis courts, exercise room. **Guest Services:** gift shop, coin laundry. *Fee:* area transportation-major attractions. **Business Services:** meeting rooms, PC. *Fee:* fax. **Cards:** AX, CB, DC, JC, MC, VI. **Special Amenities:** free newspaper. *(See color ad inside front cover)*

SOME UNITS

1 (AAA) (SAVE)
Classic Resort
Large-scale Hotel

2

3 [ECP]

7 (icon)

4 F17

5 301

6 street. **Terms:** 3 day cancellation dryers. *Some:* DVD players. *Fee:* outdoor, 2 heated indoor, wading po...

12/24-9/1 [CP]   1P: $139-$169   2P: $139-$169   XP: $10
12/1-12/23 & 9/2-11/30 [ECP]   1P: $129-$149   2P: $129-$149

1 (AAA) or (CAA) indicates our Official Appointment (OA) lodgings. The OA program permits properties to display and advertise the (AAA) or (CAA) emblem. We highlight these properties with red diamonds and classification. Some OA listings include special amenities such as free continental breakfast; early check-in/late check-out; free room upgrade or preferred room, such as ocean view or poolside (subject to availability); free local phone calls; and free daily newspaper. This does not imply that only these properties offer these amenities. The (AAA) or (CAA) sign helps traveling members find accommodations that want member business.

(diamonds) or (diamonds) The number of diamonds—not the color—informs you of the overall level of quality in a lodging's amenities and service. More diamond details appear on page 16.

Classic Resort Large-scale Hotel or Classic Resort Large-scale Hotel: Diamond ratings are applied in the context of lodging type, or classification. See pages 22-23 for details about our Lodging Classifications and Subclassifications.

Member Values

SAVE Official Appointment properties guarantee members a minimum 10% discount off the standard room rates published in TourBook guides or the lowest public rate available at the time of booking for the dates of stay, for standard rooms.

SAVE AAA's Show Your Card & Save® chain partners provide AAA's best rates and a satisfaction guarantee to our members: Select from Best Western, Choice Hotels, Hyatt Hotels, Days Inn, most Hilton brands, La Quinta Inn and most Marriott brands. Individual properties appearing in the TourBook guides have been evaluated and approved by AAA. Reservations can be made by calling the AAA member toll-free reservation number 866-AAA-SAVE (have your membership card available), or refer to page 20 for details and a complete listing of participating lodging chains.

S/D Establishments offer a minimum senior discount of 10% off the listed rates. This discount is available to members 60 or older.

ASK Many properties offer discounts to members even though the lodgings do not participate in a formal discount program. The **ASK** is another reminder to inquire about available discounts when making your reservations or at check-in.

> Discounts normally offered at some lodgings may not apply during special events or holiday periods. Special rates and discounts may not apply to all room types.

To obtain published rates or discounts, you must identify yourself as a AAA or CAA member, request AAA rates when making reservations and have written confirmation sent to you. The SAVE or senior discount may not be used in conjunction with other discounts. At registration, show your membership card and verify the room rate.

The rates listed for approved properties are provided to AAA by each lodging and represent the regular (rack) rate for a standard room. Printed rates, based on rack rates and last room availability, are rounded to the nearest dollar. Rates do not include taxes and discounts. U.S. rates are in U.S. dollars; rates for Canadian lodgings are in Canadian dollars.

2 Rate Lines
Shown from left to right: dates the rates are effective; meal plan provided with rates (see Meal Plan Indicators-if no plan noted, rate includes room only); rates for 1 person or 2 persons; extra person charge (XP); and any applicable family plan indicator.

Rates Guaranteed
AAA/CAA members are guaranteed that they will not be charged more than the maximum regular rate printed in each rate range for a standard room. Rates may vary within the range depending on season and room type. Listed rates are based on last standard room availability. Rates for properties operating as concessionaires for the National Park Service are not guaranteed due to governing regulations.

Exceptions
Lodgings may temporarily increase room rates, not recognize discounts or modify pricing policies during special events. Examples of special events range from Mardi Gras and Kentucky Derby (including pre-Derby events) to college football games, holidays, holiday periods and state fairs. Although some special events are listed in AAA/CAA TourBook guides, it is always wise to check, in advance, with AAA travel professionals for specific dates.

Discounts
Member discounts will apply to rates quoted, within the rate range, applicable at the time of booking. Special rates used in advertising, and special short-term, promotional rates lower than the lowest listed rate in the range, are not subject to additional member discounts.

3 Meal Plan Indicators
The following types of meal plans may be available in the listed room rate:
AP = American Plan of three meals daily
BP = Breakfast Plan of full hot breakfast
CP = Continental Plan of pastry, juice and another beverage
ECP = Expanded Continental Plan, which offers a wider
    variety of breakfast items
MAP = Modified American Plan of two meals daily
See individual listing "Terms" section for additional meal plans that may be offered.

> **Check-in times are shown in the listing only if they are after 3 p.m.; check-out times are shown only if they are before 10 a.m.**

4 Family Plan Indicators
F = Children stay free
D = Discounts for children
F17 = Children 17 and under stay free (age displayed will reflect property's policy)
D17 = Discount for children 17 and under

5 Lodging Locators
Black ovals with white numbers are used to locate, or "spot," lodgings on maps we provide for larger cities.

6 Unit Types
Unit types, amenities and room features preceded by the word "Some" indicate the item is available on a limited basis, potentially within only one unit.

7 Lodging Icons
A row of icons is included with each lodging listing. These icons represent the member values, member services, and facilities offered by that lodging. See page 19 for an explanation of each icon.

The Lodging Diamond Ratings

AAA Tourism Editors evaluate and rate each lodging based on the overall quality, the range of facilities and the level of services offered by a property. The size, age and overall appeal of an establishment are considered as well as regional architectural style and design.

While guest services are an important part of all diamond ratings, they are particularly critical at the four and five diamond levels. A property must provide a high level of service, on a consistent basis, to obtain and support the four and five diamond rating.

These establishments typically appeal to the budget-minded traveler. They provide essential, no-frills accommodations. They meet the basic requirements pertaining to comfort, cleanliness, and hospitality.

These establishments appeal to the traveler seeking more than the basic accommodations. There are modest enhancements to the overall physical attributes, design elements, and amenities of the facility typically at a modest price.

These establishments appeal to the traveler with comprehensive needs. Properties are multifaceted with a distinguished style, including marked upgrades in the quality of physical attributes, amenities and level of comfort provided.

These establishments are upscale in all areas. Accommodations are progressively more refined and stylish. The physical attributes reflect an obvious enhanced level of quality throughout. The fundamental hallmarks at this level include an extensive array of amenities combined with a high degree of hospitality, service, and attention to detail.

These establishments reflect the characteristics of the ultimate in luxury and sophistication. Accommodations are first-class. The physical attributes are extraordinary in every manner. The fundamental hallmarks at this level are to meticulously serve and exceed all guest expectations while maintaining an impeccable standard of excellence. Many personalized services and amenities enhance an unmatched level of comfort.

The lodging listings with **fyi** in place of diamonds are included as an "information only" service for members. The icon indicates that a property has not been rated for one or more of the following reasons: too new to rate; under construction; under major renovation; not evaluated; or may not meet all AAA requirements. Those properties not meeting all AAA requirements are included for either their member value or because it may be the only accommodation available in the area. Listing prose will give insight as to why the **fyi** designation was assigned.

Guest Safety

Room Security

In order to be approved for listing in AAA/CAA TourBook guides for the United States and Canada, all lodgings must comply with AAA's guest room security requirements.

In response to AAA/CAA members' concern about their safety at properties, AAA-RATED® accommodations must have dead-bolt locks on all guest room entry doors and connecting room doors.

If the area outside the guest room door is not visible from inside the room through a window or door panel, viewports must be installed on all guest room entry doors. Bed and breakfast properties and country inns are not required to have viewports. Ground floor and easily accessible sliding doors must be equipped with some other type of secondary security locks.

Tourism Editors view a percentage of rooms at each property since it is not feasible to evaluate every room in every lodging establishment. Therefore, AAA cannot guarantee that there are working locks on all doors and windows in all guest rooms.

Fire Safety

Because of the highly specialized skills needed to conduct professional fire safety inspections, AAA/CAA Tourism Editors cannot assess fire safety.

Properties must meet all federal, state and local fire codes. Each guest unit in all U.S. and Canadian lodging properties must be equipped with an operational, single-station smoke detector. A AAA/CAA Tourism Editor has evaluated a sampling of the rooms to verify this equipment is in place.

For additional fire safety information, read the page posted on the back of your guest room door, or write:

National Fire Protection Association
1 Batterymarch Park / P.O. Box 9101 / Quincy, MA 02269-9101.

Golden Passports

Golden Passports, available in two types, offer a significant savings to individuals who meet certain guidelines.

Citizens or permanent residents of the United States who are 62 and older can obtain Golden Age Passports for a one-time $10 fee. Proof of age is required.

Golden Access Passports are free to citizens or permanent residents of the United States (regardless of age) who are medically blind or permanently disabled.

Both cover entrance fees for the holder and accompanying private party to all national parks, historic sites, monuments, battlefields, recreation areas and wildlife refuges within the U.S. national park system, plus half off camping and other fees. Apply in person at a federally operated area where an entrance fee is charged.

National Parks Pass

The National Parks Pass, valid for 1 year from the month of purchase, allows unlimited admissions to all U.S. national parks. The $50 pass covers all occupants of a private vehicle at parks where the entrance fee is per vehicle. At parks with individual entry fees, the pass covers the pass holder, spouse, parents and children.

As a result of a partnership with the National Park Service, AAA members may purchase the pass for $48, either through AAA's internet site (www.aaa.com) or by visiting a participating AAA office. Members may also phone the National Park Foundation at (888) 467-2757. Non-members may purchase the pass through AAA for the full $50 price.

For an upgrade fee of $15, a Golden Eagle hologram sticker can be added to a National Parks Pass. The hologram covers entrance fees not just at national parks, but at any federal recreation area that has an admission fee. Valid for the duration of the National Parks Pass to which it is affixed, the Golden Eagle hologram is available at National Park Service, Fish and Wildlife Service and Bureau of Land Management fee stations.

Access for Mature Travelers and Travelers with Disabilities

Qualified properties listed in this guide are shown with symbols indicating they meet the needs of the hearing-impaired or offer some accessible features for mature travelers or travelers with disabilities.

 Hearing Impaired

Indicates a property has the following equipment available for hearing-impaired travelers: TDD at front desk or switchboard; visual notification of fire alarm, incoming telephone calls, door knock or bell; closed caption decoder; text telephone or TDD for guest room use; telephone amplification device, with shelf or electric outlet next to guest room telephone.

 Accessible Features

Indicates a property has some accessible features meeting the needs of mature travelers and travelers with disabilities. Lodging establishments will provide at least one guest room meeting the designated criteria as well as accessible restrooms and parking facilities. Restaurants provide accessible parking, dining rooms and restrooms.

AAA/CAA strongly urges members to call the property directly to fully understand the property's exact accessibility features. Some properties do not fully comply with AAA/CAA's exacting accessibility standards but may offer some design standards that meet the needs of some guests with disabilities.

AAA/CAA does not evaluate recreational facilities, banquet rooms, or convention or meeting facilities for accessibility.

Service Animals

No fees or deposits, even those normally charged for pets, may be charged for service animals. Service animals fulfill a critical need for their owners—they are *not* pets.

The Americans With Disabilities Act (ADA) prohibits businesses that serve the public from discriminating against persons with disabilities. Some businesses have mistakenly denied access to persons who use service animals. ADA, a federal mandate, has priority over all state and local laws, as well as a business owner's standard of business, which might bar animals from the premises. Businesses must permit entry to guests and their service animals, as well as allow service animals to accompany guests to all public areas of a property. A property is permitted to ask whether the animal is a service animal or a pet, and whether the guest has a disability. The property may not, however, ask questions about the nature of the disability, the service provided by the animal or require proof of a disability or certification that the animal is a service animal.

What The Lodging Icons Mean

Member Values
(see p. 14)

AAA or **CAA** Official Appointment

SAVE Offers minimum 10% discount or lowest public rate (see p. 14)

SAVE Show Your Card & Save lodging partners

ASK May offer discount

SD Offers senior discount

fyi Informational listing only

Member Services

Airport transportation

Pets allowed

Restaurant on premises

Restaurant off premises (walking distance)

24 24-hour room service

Cocktail lounge

Child care

Accessibility Features
(see p. 18)

M Accessible features

Roll-in showers

Hearing impaired

Leisure Activities

Full service casino

Pool

Health club on premises

Health club off premises

Recreational activities

In-Room Amenities

Designated non-smoking rooms

AC No air conditioning

TV No TV

CTV No cable TV

VCR VCR

Movies

DATA PORT Data port/modem line

No telephones

Refrigerator

Microwave

Coffee maker

Availability

If an in-room amenity is available only on a limited basis (in one or more rooms), the term "SOME UNITS" will appear above those icons.

SOME UNITS

&M VCR / DATA PORT /

Additional Fees

Fees may be charged for some of the services represented by the icons listed here. The word "FEE" will appear below each icon when an extra charge applies.

SOME UNITS

&M VCR / DATA PORT /
FEE FEE   FEE

Preferred Lodging Partners

AAA. Every Day.

SAVE UP TO 50% ON OVER 1,500,000 ROOMS - When contacting one of the partners listed, you will be given AAA's best rates for your dates of stay. Your valid membership card must be presented at check-in.

SATISFACTION GUARANTEE - If you are not satisfied with any part of your stay, you must provide the property the opportunity to correct the situation during your stay. If the matter cannot be resolved, you will be entitled to recompense for a portion of, or your entire, stay. Satisfaction guarantee varies by chain.

Select the chain you want and have your membership card available when making a reservation and checking in.

| Visit | Over 1,100 AAA Offices | Click | aaa.com | Call | 866-AAA-SAVE |

Making Reservations

When making reservations, you must identify yourself as a AAA or CAA member. Give all pertinent information about your planned stay. Ask about the lodging's pet policy, or the availability of any other special feature that is important to your stay. Request written confirmation to guarantee: type of room, rate, dates of stay, and cancellation and refund policies. At registration, show your membership card. Note: Age restrictions may apply.

Confirm Deposit, Refund and Cancellation Policies

Most establishments give full deposit refunds if they have been notified at least 48 hours before the normal check-in time. Listing prose will note if more than 48 hours notice is required for cancellation. However, when making reservations, confirm the property's deposit, cancellation and refund policies. Some properties may charge a cancellation or handling fee.

When this applies, "cancellation fee imposed" will appear in the listing. If you cancel too late, you have little recourse if a refund is denied.

When an establishment requires a full or partial payment in advance, and your trip is cut short, a refund may not be given.

When canceling reservations, phone the lodging immediately. Make a note of the date and time you called, the cancellation number if there is one, and the name of the person who handled the cancellation. If your AAA/CAA club made your reservation, allow them to make the cancellation for you as well so you will have proof of cancellation.

Review Charges for Appropriate Rates

When you are charged more than the maximum rate listed in the TourBook guide for a standard room, question the additional charge. If management refuses to adhere to the published rate, pay for the room and submit your receipt and membership number to AAA/CAA within 30 days. Include all pertinent information: dates of stay, rate paid, itemized paid receipts, number of persons in your party, the room number you occupied, and list any extra room equipment used. A refund of the amount paid in excess of the stated maximum will be made if our investigation indicates that unjustified charging has occurred.

Get the Room You Reserved

When you find your room is not as specified, and you have written confirmation of reservations for a certain type of accommodation, you should be given the option of choosing a different room or finding one elsewhere. Should you choose to go elsewhere and a refund is refused or resisted, submit the matter to AAA/CAA within 30 days along with complete documentation, including your reasons for refusing the room and copies of your written confirmation and any receipts or canceled checks associated with this problem.

How to Get the Best Room Rates

You'll find the best room rate if you book your reservation in advance with the help of a travel professional or agent at your local AAA/CAA office.

If you're not yet ready to make firm vacation plans or if you prefer a more spontaneous trip, take advantage of the partnerships that preferred hotel chains have arranged with AAA. Phone the toll-free number on the previous page that has been set up exclusively for members for the purpose of reserving with these Show Your Card & Save® chain partners.

Even if you were unable to make a reservation, be sure to show your membership card at the desk and ask if you're being offered the lowest rate available for that time. Many lodgings offer reduced rates to members.

Lodging Classifications

AAA Tourism Editors evaluate lodgings based on classification, since all lodging types by definition do not provide the same level of service and facilities. Thus, hotels are rated in comparison to other hotels, resorts to other resorts—and so on. A lodging's classification appears beneath its diamond rating in the listing.

Large-scale Hotel
A multistory establishment with interior room entrances. A variety of guest unit styles is offered. Public areas are spacious and include a variety of facilities such as a restaurant, shops, fitness center, spa, business center, or meeting rooms.

Small-scale Hotel
A multistory establishment typically with interior room entrances. A variety of guest unit styles is offered. Public areas are limited in size and/or the variety of facilities available.

Motel
A one- to three-story establishment typically with exterior room entrances facilitating convenient access to parking. The standard guest units have one bedroom with a bathroom and are typically similar in décor and design throughout. Public areas are limited in size and/or the variety of facilities available.

Country Inn
Similar in definition to a bed and breakfast, but usually larger in scale with spacious public areas and offers a dining facility that serves at least breakfast and dinner.

Bed & Breakfast
Small-scale properties emphasizing a high degree of personal touches that provide guests an "at home" feeling. Guest units tend to be individually decorated. Rooms may not include some modern amenities such as televisions and telephones, and may have a shared bathroom. Usually owner-operated with a common room or parlor separate from the innkeeper's living quarters, where guests and operators can interact during evening and breakfast hours. Evening office closures are normal. A continental or full, hot breakfast is served and is included in the room rate.

Condominium
Vacation-oriented or extended-stay, apartment-style accommodations that are routinely available for rent through a management company. Units vary in design and décor and often contain one or more bedrooms, living room, full kitchen, and an eating area. Studio-type models combine the sleeping and living areas into one room. Typically, basic cleaning supplies, kitchen utensils and complete bed and bath linens are supplied. The guest registration area may be located off-site.

Cabin/Cottage

Vacation-oriented, small-scale, freestanding houses or cabins. Units vary in design and décor and often contain one or more bedrooms, living room, kitchen, dining area, and bathroom. Studio-type models combine the sleeping and living areas into one room. Typically, basic cleaning supplies, kitchen utensils, and complete bed and bath linens are supplied. The guest registration area may be located off-site.

Ranch

Typically a working ranch with an obvious rustic, Western theme. In general, equestrian-related activities are featured, but ranches may include other animals and activities as well. A variety of guest unit styles is offered in a family-oriented atmosphere.

Vacation Home

Vacation-oriented or extended-stay, large-scale, freestanding houses that are routinely available for rent through a management company. Houses vary in design and décor and often contain two or more bedrooms, living room, full kitchen, dining room, and multiple bathrooms. Typically, basic cleaning supplies, kitchen utensils, and complete bed and bath linens are supplied. The guest registration area may be located off-site.

Lodging Subclassifications

The following are subclassifications that may appear along with the classifications listed above to provide a more specific description of the lodging.

Casino

Extensive gambling facilities are available such as blackjack, craps, keno, and slot machines. **Note:** This subclassification will not appear beneath its diamond rating in the listing. It will be indicated by a dice icon and will be included in the row of icons immediately below the lodging listing.

Classic

Renowned and landmark properties, older than 50 years, well-known for their unique style and ambience.

Historic

These properties are typically over 75 years of age and exhibit many features of a historic nature with respect to architecture, design, furnishings, public record, or acclaim. Properties must meet one of the following criteria:
- Maintained the integrity of the historical nature
- Listed on the National Register of Historic Places
- Designated a National Historic Landmark
- Located in a National Register Historic District

Resort

Recreation-oriented, geared to vacation travelers seeking a specific destination experience. Travel packages, meal plans, theme entertainment, and social and recreational programs are typically available. Recreational facilities are extensive and may include spa treatments, golf, tennis, skiing, fishing, or water sports, etc. Larger resorts may offer a variety of guest accommodations.

Sample Restaurant Listing

WHERE TO DINE

KINGSTON'S RESTAURANT Classic · **Dinner:** $16-$35 · **Phone:** 555/987-1600 ⑱
Location: I-459, exit 13 (US 31); adjacent to Riverchase Galleria; in The Wynfrey Hotel. 1000 Riverchase Galleria 35244. **Hours:** 6 pm-10 pm. Closed major holidays; also Sun. **Reservations:** suggested. **Features:** Boasting an upscale atmosphere and excellent American cuisine, the fine dining establishment is the ideal setting for a special, intimate dinner. Its newly renovated dining rooms offer an elegant setting for a truly memorable meal. Dressy casual; cocktails. **Parking:** on-site. **Cards:** AX, DC, DS, MC, VI.

1 American

5 Classic

2 Dinner: $16-$35

3 Cards: AX, DC, DS, MC, VI.

6 ⑱

4

1 ⚑ or ⚑ indicates our Official Appointment (OA) restaurants. The OA program permits properties to display and advertise the ⚑ or ⚑ emblem. We highlight these properties with red diamonds and cuisine type. The ⚑ or ⚑ sign helps traveling members find restaurants that want member business.

◆◆◆ or ◆◆◆ The number of diamonds—not the color—informs you of the overall level of quality for food and presentation, service and ambience.

A cuisine type is assigned for each restaurant listing. AAA currently recognizes more than 90 different cuisine types.

2 Prices represent the minimum and maximum entree cost per person. Exceptions may include one-of-a-kind or special market priced items.

3 AX = American Express
CB = Carte Blanche
DC = Diners Club

DS = Discover
JC = Japan Credit Bureau

MC = MasterCard
VI = VISA

4 These three icons are used in restaurant listings. When present, they indicate: the presence of a cocktail lounge, the lack of air conditioning, and/or that the restaurant has a designated non-smoking section or is entirely smoke-free.

5 If applicable, restaurants may be further defined as:

Classic—renowned and landmark properties, older than 25 years, known for unique style and ambience.

Historic—properties must meet one of the following criteria:
- Listed on the National Register of Historic Places
- Designated a National Historic Landmark
- Located in a National Register Historic District

6 These white ovals with black numbers serve as restaurant locators and are used to locate, or "spot," restaurants on maps we provide for larger cities.

The Restaurant Diamond Ratings

AAA Tourism Editors are responsible for determining a restaurant's diamond rating based on established criteria.

These criteria were established with input from AAA trained professionals, members, and restaurant industry experts. They are purposely broad to capture what is typically seen throughout the restaurant industry at each diamond rating level.

These establishments appeal to a diner seeking good, wholesome, no-nonsense eating at an affordable price. They typically provide simple, familiar, and unadorned foods served in a sensible, casual or self-service style. Often quick service and family oriented.

Examples include coffee shops, diners, cafeterias, short order, and modest full service eateries.

These establishments provide for dining needs that are increasingly complex, but still reasonably priced. They typically exhibit noticeable efforts in rising above the ordinary in many aspects of food, service and decor. Service is typically functional yet ambitious, periodically combining informal style with limited self-service elements. Often well-suited to traditional, special occasion, and family dining.

Examples include a varied range of specific concept (theme) and multi-purpose establishments.

These establishments impart an increasingly refined and upscale, adult-oriented experience. This is the entry level into fine dining. Creative and complex menus offer a blend of traditional and trendy foods. The service level is typically semi-formal with knowledgeable and proficient staff. Routinely these restaurants appeal to the diner in search of an experience rather than just a meal.

Examples include high-caliber, chic, boutique, and conventional restaurants.

These establishments impart a luxurious and socially refined experience. This is consistent fine dining. Menus typically reflect a high degree of creativity and complexity, featuring elaborate presentations of market-driven or traditional dishes. A cultured, professional, and highly proficient staff consistently demonstrates a profound desire to meet or exceed guest expectations. Restaurants of this caliber are geared to individuals with an appetite for an elite, fine-dining experience.

Examples include dining rooms associated with luxury lodgings, or exclusive independent restaurants often found in metropolitan areas.

Often renowned, these establishments impart a world-class and opulent, adult-oriented experience. This is "haute cuisine" at its best. Menus are often cutting edge, with an obvious dedication to use of only the finest ingredients available. Even the classic dishes become extraordinary under the masterful direction of highly acclaimed chefs. Presentations are spectacular, reflecting impeccable artistry and awareness. An expert, formalized staff continuously anticipates and exceeds guest expectations. Staff members' unfailing attention to detail appears effortless, well-rehearsed and unobtrusive. Undoubtedly, these restaurants appeal to those in search of the ultimate dining experience.

Examples include renowned dining rooms associated with luxury lodgings, or exclusive independent restaurants often found in metropolitan areas.

The restaurants with [fyi] in place of diamonds are included as an "information only" service for members. These listings provide additional dining choices but have not yet been evaluated.

Savings for all Seasons

Hertz rents Fords and other fine cars. ® REG. U.S. PAT. OFF. © HERTZ SYSTEM INC., 1999/2006-99.

No matter the season, Hertz offers AAA members exclusive discounts and benefits.

Operating in 140 countries at over 7,000 locations, Hertz makes traveling more convenient and efficient wherever and whenever you go. Hertz offers AAA members discounts up to 20% on car rentals worldwide.

To receive your exclusive AAA member discounts and benefits, mention your AAA membership card at time of reservation and present it at time of rental. In addition, to receive a free one car class upgrade, in the United States mention PC# 929714, in Canada mention PC# 929725 and in Puerto Rico mention PC# 929736 at the time of reservation. Offer available through 12/31/04.

For reservations and program details, call your AAA travel office or the Hertz/AAA Desk at **1-800-654-3080**.

Texas

Panhandle Plains

A vibrant palette creates the colors in pastures of wildflowers

Floating Down the Rio Grande

River canyons provide scenic views for raft travelers

South of the Border

The state's proximity to Mexico shapes its culture and commerce

Legions of Longhorns

The distinctive cattle still roam and graze in parts of Texas

Hot and Spicy

Tex-Mex dishes and five-alarm chili put tears in diners' eyes

lone
star
shining

Texans ain't Texans if they aren't willing to boast about the state they call home.

And why not?

Texas is diverse enough that its geography can appeal to all kinds of folks. You like mountains? Got 'em. Beaches? Plenty, and their white sands and temperate waters are pure solace for the soul. Deserts? Yep, look out for tumbleweeds. Plains?

Heavens, yes! Oh, and fields of flowers splash blue, yellow and red for miles upon miles upon miles.

History buffs can surrender themselves to the abandoned forts of west Texas, the peaceful old missions of the Rio Grande Valley or the battlefield of San Jacinto.

If you're into adventure, you can pit the theme parks' roller coasters against

each other, learn the ins and outs of a dude ranch, rappel down the face of a rock or taste-test chili hot enough to blow holes in the toes of your socks.

Most of all, Texans invoke their bragging rights when it comes to the issue of size. The state's impressive land area exceeds the total acreage covered by all of New England, New York, Pennsylvania, Ohio and Illinois combined.

With all the Lone Star State has to offer, Texans would reckon they have every right to swagger.

With one visit, you'd reckon they're right.

If you're fixin' to head to Texas, you'd best study up on what it means to be tough. The quickest way to round up respect in the Lone Star State is to demonstrate that you've got true grit.

The state's pioneers had gumption galore. Initially conquistadors, Estevanico and Álvar Núñez Cabeza de Vaca took a lesson from the Indians and transformed themselves into healers and savvy traders. And although most of the rest of his expedition had returned to Mexico after finding no trace of treasure, Francisco Vásquez de Coronado plugged on despite mounting disappointments.

René-Robert Cavelier, Sieur de La Salle, survived a perilous journey from France and established a promising settlement, only to be killed shortly thereafter at the hands of his own men. Stephen F. Austin's unassuming presence gained him widespread regard, thereby allowing him to greatly advance the Americans' cause during the Texas Revolution.

Almost everything about Texas reveals some trademark of an iron will.

Plants are hardy. Tumbleweeds roll across the landscape, seemingly oblivious to the searing sun, coarse sand and swirling winds. Wildflowers, most notably the ubiquitous bluebonnet and Indian paintbrush, spread out like colorful carpets across fields throughout the state. The prickly pear cactus gives a painful poke to anyone who wanders too close.

Spiders, Snakes and Scorpions

Animals seem to give some credence to Charles Darwin's "survival of the fittest" theory. With one sting, scorpions and tarantulas can take down an enemy many times larger than themselves. The distinctive horns of longhorn cattle contributed significantly to the breed's longevity.

Rattlesnakes have the upper hand in nearly any confrontation. But although sturdy armor shields it from many natural foes, a sluggish gait too often renders the armadillo defenseless against its primary man-made enemy: the automobile.

You've got to have pluck and a stomach of steel just to tackle the food for which the state is most noted. Tamales sear away layers from the lining of the digestive tract. Jalapeños bring the most strapping of men to tears.

Chili packs a wallop stronger than a spurned lover sending a four-knuckle message to his romantic rival. If Texas had a

Alonso Álvarez de Piñeda is the first Spanish explorer to reach Texan shores.

1519

René-Robert Cavelier, Sieur de La Salle, founds a French colony at Matagorda Bay.

1685

Stephen F. Austin builds an American settlement on the Brazos River.

1822

1716
Spaniards establish Catholic missions in the region.

1836
Texas wins its independence from Mexico at the Battle of San Jacinto; statehood is granted in 1845.

Texas Historical Timeline

state condiment, it would no doubt be Tabasco.

And what better to wash it all down than a sinus-clearing, throat-torching prairie fire—a shot of tequila blended with a minimum of three drops of hot sauce and garnished with a dash of black pepper?

Equally hard to swallow is the lingering image of the stereotypical Texan: the cowboy. Sure, you still can find a genuine cowboy at home on the range if you're willing to search, but he probably won't be the spitting image of the Marlboro man.

There is a good chance, however, that he'll don at least one component of the full-fledged standard uniform—10-gallon hat, neckerchief, snap-button shirt, bolo tie, mighty belt buckle, Wrangler jeans, chaps and boots (spurs optional).

Aerospace and High-Technology

It's easier finding a true Texan in big business: manufacturing, aerospace, finance, insurance and real estate. Workers also contribute to the state's reputation as a booming center for high-technology and biotechnology.

The state's ample natural resources provide jobs in the cotton fields and timber forests.

Texans also find work sustaining a thriving tourism business or contributing to the significant force of trade.

The importance of a once-dominant petroleum industry has waned over time; now only a few still operate the derricks in search of "black gold, Texas tea."

Contributing to the state's economy as well as to its diverse culture is the Hispanic community. Comprising a quarter of the populace, Hispanics touch all areas of Texas life. Their influence—so prevalent due to the state's proximity to the Mexican border—adds depth to the visual arts, Tejano to the music scene and the exotic Spanglish to the list of spoken languages.

When you're ready to ride off into the spectacular sunset, you probably won't be on one of the saddled steeds that once were key modes of transportation here. Many Texans nowadays prefer the versatile pickup truck—among the hardiest of vehicles—and they like it American made. So hop behind the wheel, give the engine a rev and leave a cloud of dust trailing in your wake.

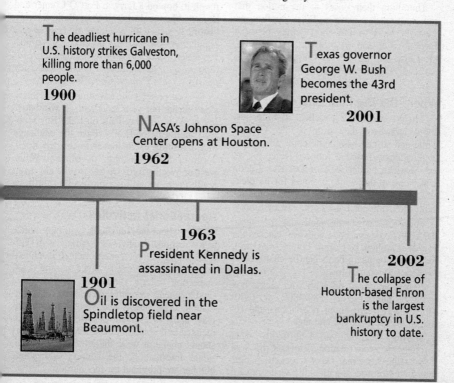

The deadliest hurricane in U.S. history strikes Galveston, killing more than 6,000 people.
1900

Texas governor George W. Bush becomes the 43rd president.
2001

NASA's Johnson Space Center opens at Houston.
1962

1963
President Kennedy is assassinated in Dallas.

1901
Oil is discovered in the Spindletop field near Beaumont.

2002
The collapse of Houston-based Enron is the largest bankruptcy in U.S. history to date.

Recreation

The variety of ways in which you can play in Texas is as vast as the acreage on which you can do it.

Boating, swimming and other water sports abound on such impoundments as the immense Toledo Bend Reservoir, on the Louisiana border; Lake Texoma, on the Oklahoma border; Sam Rayburn Lake, north of Jasper; Lake Tawakoni, south of Greenville; and Lake Livingston, west of Livingston.

For a varied **canoeing** run that offers shallow floats, long pools and sporadic, turbulent rapids, visit Devil's River, north of Del Rio. To really unwind, go **tubing** on the Guadalupe or Frio rivers. Settle into a tube in Guadalupe River State Park in Spring Branch or in Garner State Park, north of Concan, respectively.

Scuba diving is but one way to enjoy the sparkling waters of Lake Travis, the southernmost body of water in the Highland Lakes chain, a 150-mile-long stretch of reservoirs on the Colorado River northwest of Austin. Offshore diving is spectacular at Flower Garden National Marine Sanctuary, 110 miles south of the Texas-Louisiana border.

Thumbing their noses at the notion that you can't catch a wave in Texas, **surfing** enthusiasts head to the short jetties between Flagship Pier and 61st Street in Galveston; J.P. Luby Surfing Pier in Corpus Christi; or the South Padre Island jetty.

Where the Big Fish Bite

Anglers will find excellent **fishing** just about anywhere they drop a line. Catfish, white and striped bass and crappie are among the challenges posed at Amistad Reservoir, on the Mexican border west of Del Rio. Caddo Lake, east of Jefferson, is noted for its pickerel and sunfish. Trophy largemouth bass inhabit the depths of Lake Fork, east of Emory.

For a saltwater battle, pick your spot along the Gulf Coast and hope your bait catches the eye of a wahoo, red drum bonito, mackerel, marlin or pompano; boats can be chartered at nearly every coastal town.

Before you head off with your tackle box in tow, phone (512) 389-4800 or (800) 792-1112 to learn about regulations and required licenses, stamps and tags.

Hiking trails of varied difficulty wind through the four national forests of east Texas—the Angelina, Davy Crockett, Sabine and Sam Houston. Breathtaking vistas reward hikers who navigate the rugged gorge in Pedernales Falls State Park, east of Johnson City. No less majestic is the colorful mountain and desert scenery of Big Bend and Guadalupe Mountains national parks in west Texas.

For a tough **bicycling** ride with plenty of roots, branches and tight wooded stretches, take on the terrain at Jack Brooks Park, southeast of Houston. If you're content to pass on Mother Nature's surprises, the paved trail at McKinney Falls State Park, southeast of Austin, may be more to your liking.

To view the countryside from high in the saddle, visit Hill Country State Natural Area, southwest of Bandera, where 36 miles of multiuse trails are prime real estate for **horseback riding.** Several adjacent ranches offer horse rentals. Ten miles of trails through the semirough terrain of Palo Duro Canyon State Park, southeast of Amarillo, also are worth exploring; riders of all levels of experience can rent horses from stables on the canyon floor.

Sleeping Beneath the Stars

You can pitch a tent for a **camping** adventure at most state parks. If you're prepared to rough it, hop on a ferry in Port O'Conner and head to Matagorda Island State Park, a richly historical area with a widely diverse animal population. The park has no electricity, drinking water, concessions or telephones. *For additional information about camping sites, see the AAA South Central CampBook.*

Do you prefer your adventure on the hairy side? Shake out your sails and go **windsurfing** at Windsurf Bay Park on Lake Ray Hubbard, northeast of Dallas. Face the challenge of a **climbing** excursion at Enchanted Rock, north of Fredericksburg; or Mineral Wells, west of Weatherford. Or take to the sky from South Padre Island for a **parasailing** thrill.

Recreational Activities

Throughout the TourBook, you may notice a Recreational Activities heading with bulleted listings of recreation-oriented establishments listed underneath. Since normal AAA inspection criteria cannot be applied, these establishments are presented only for information. Age, height and weight restrictions may apply. Reservations often are recommended and sometimes are required. Visitors should phone or write the attraction for additional information; the address and phone number are provided for this purpose.

Fast Facts

POPULATION: 20,851,820.

AREA: 275,416 square miles; ranks 2nd.

CAPITAL: Austin.

HIGHEST POINT: 8,749 ft., Guadalupe Peak.

LOWEST POINT: Sea level, Gulf of Mexico.

TIME ZONE(S): Central/Mountain. DST.

MINIMUM AGE FOR DRIVERS: 15 with approved driver education course; restricted hours under 16 years, 6 months; 18 without driver education.

SEAT BELT/CHILD RESTRAINT LAWS: Seat belts required for all front-seat occupants and back-seat occupants under 16; child restraints under age 4 or under 36 inches tall.

HELMETS FOR MOTORCYCLISTS: Required under 21. Optional for 21 and over with sanctioned training safety course or proof of medical insurance (minimum $10,000 coverage).

RADAR DETECTORS: Permitted.

FIREARMS LAWS: Vary by state and/or county. Contact the Texas Department of Public Safety, 5805 N. Lamar Blvd., P.O. Box 4087, Austin, TX 78752; phone (512) 424-2000. For more information, contact the U.S. Treasury Department, Bureau of Alcohol, Tobacco and Firearms, 9009 Mountain Ridge Dr., Austin, TX 78759; phone (512) 349-4545.

HOLIDAYS: Jan. 1; Martin Luther King Jr. Day, Jan. (3rd Mon.); Confederate Heroes' Day, Jan. 19; Presidents' Day, Feb. (3rd Mon.); Texas Independence Day, Mar. 2; San Jacinto Day, Apr. 21; Memorial Day, May (last Mon.); Emancipation Day, June 19; July 4; Lyndon Baines Johnson Day, Aug. 27; Labor Day, Sept. (1st Mon.); Veterans Day, Nov. 11; Thanksgiving, Nov. (4th Thurs.); Dec. 24-25; Boxing Day, Dec. 26.

TAXES: Texas' statewide sales tax is 6.25 percent. Cities and/or counties may impose additional rates up to 2 percent for a maximum rate of 8.25 percent. Counties may impose lodgings taxes of up to 7 percent.

STATE INFORMATION CENTERS: Centers are on I-40 in Amarillo; on I-10W in Anthony; in the Capitol complex in Austin; on US 75/69 in Denison; on I-35 at US 77 in Gainesville; on US 83, just w. of US 77 in Harlingen; on US 90 Loop 25 in Langtry; on I-35 at US 83 in Laredo; on I-10E in Orange; on I-30 in Texarkana; on I-20 in Waskom; and on I-44 in Wichita Falls. The Capitol complex center is open daily 9-5. All others are open daily 8-6, Memorial Day-Labor Day; 8-5, rest of year. Phone (512) 463-8586 or (800) 452-9292.

NATIONAL FOREST INFORMATION:
U.S. Forest Service
701 N. First St.
Lufkin, TX 75901
(936) 639-8501

FISHING & HUNTING INFORMATION:
Texas Parks & Wildlife Department
4200 Smith School Rd.
Austin, TX 78744
(512) 389-4800
(800) 792-1112

FURTHER INFORMATION FOR VISITORS:
Travel Division
Texas Department of Transportation
P.O. Box 149248
Austin, TX 78714-9248
(512) 486-5800
(800) 452-9292 (travel and road conditions)

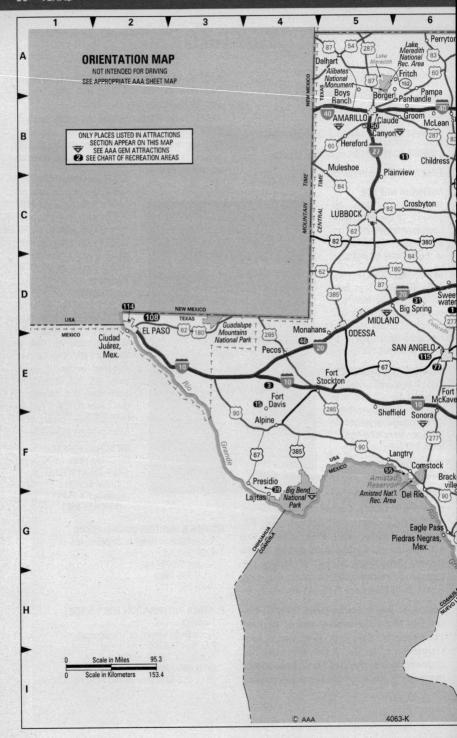

ORIENTATION MAP
NOT INTENDED FOR DRIVING
SEE APPROPRIATE AAA SHEET MAP

ONLY PLACES LISTED IN ATTRACTIONS
SECTION APPEAR ON THIS MAP
▽ SEE AAA GEM ATTRACTIONS
❷ SEE CHART OF RECREATION AREAS

Perryton
Lake Meredith National Rec. Area
Dalhart
Lake Meredith
Fritch
Alibates National Monument
Pampa
Boys Ranch
Borger
Panhandle
AMARILLO
Claude
Groom
McLean
Canyon
Hereford
Childress
Muleshoe
Plainview
Crosbyton
LUBBOCK
Big Spring
Sweetwater
MIDLAND
ODESSA
Monahans
Pecos
SAN ANGELO
Fort McKavett
Fort Stockton
Sheffield
Sonora
Guadalupe Mountains National Park
EL PASO
Ciudad Juárez, Mex.
USA
MEXICO
NEW MEXICO
TEXAS
MOUNTAIN TIME
CENTRAL TIME
Fort Davis
Alpine
Langtry
Comstock
Brackettville
Amistad Reservoir
Amistad Nat'l. Rec. Area
Del Rio
Rio Grande
Presidio
Lajitas
Big Bend National Park
Eagle Pass
Piedras Negras, Mex.
CHIHUAHUA
COAHUILA
NUEVO

Scale in Miles   0   95.3
Scale in Kilometers   0   153.4

© AAA   4063-K

7   8   9   10   11   12

N

TEXAS

Vernon
3
WICHITA
FALLS
OKLAHOMA
TEXAS
Lake
Texoma
Pat
Mayse
Lake
66   68   Paris
Denison
Sherman   62   259
TEXARKANA
ARKANSAS
OKLAHOMA
ARKANSAS
LOUISIANA
283
82   29   287   81
114
277   283
Jacks-
boro   82   Bedford
Justin
Plano
Farmers
Branch
75
McKinney
Parker,
105
Sulphur
Springs
109
14   59
Jefferson
67
82
2
17   99
35
Newcastle
Fort
Griffin   34
52
20
6
Albany   59
41   ABILENE
20
283
Buffalo
Gap
84
75
87
67   377
Brownwood
183
Paint
Rock
190
103
85
84
Lake
Buchanan
87
60   27
Burnet
81   Georgetown
Fredericks-
burg   106   L.B.J.
Nat'l. Hist.
40   Park
281
79
78   AUSTIN
290
10
7
Kerrville   6
28   Stonewall
Boerne   74
38   107
23   Bandera
Castroville
90
Uvalde
57
83
35
83
37
Laredo
Nuevo
Laredo,
Mex.
MEXICO
83
19   Falcon
281   77
Edinburg
Mission
McALLEN
Pharr
Reynosa,
Mex.
Alamo   Matamoros,
Mex.
5
Rio Hondo
Harlingen
South Padre Island
Port Isabel
BROWNSVILLE
TAMAULIPAS
NUEVO LEON
FORT
WORTH
DALLAS
University Park
Irving
820
35E
86
87
ARLING-
TON
Mesquite
Grand
Prairie
111   Canton
TYLER
Waxahachie
Cresson   58
Granbury   67
64   16
12
Cleburne
35W
Glen Rose   44
281   6
94
35
Hillsboro
35E   84
83   89
104   18
84
WACO   21
Marlin   72
77
47
Temple
Killeen   76
92
Independence
Brenham
8
290
Round Top
Columbus   56
Katy
La Porte
22
Galveston
45
Pasadena
Anahuac
Alvin   73
Richmond
Wharton   El Campo
Victoria   36   35
Goliad   24
West
Columbia
25   Austwell
96
Rockport
48
Port Aransas
CORPUS CHRISTI
Kingsville
Padre
Island
National
Seashore
GULF
OF
MEXICO
Bonham
7
Lake
Crook
30
82
McKinney
63
116
DALLAS
69   LONGVIEW
Henderson   259   96
Kilgore   71
20
79
Rusk   95
Alto   45
Nacogdoches
Angelina
Nat'l.
Forest
Palestine
Davy
Crockett
Nat'l.
Forest
Lufkin   70
42   93
Woodville
69   96   98   Orange
BEAUMONT
HOUSTON   10   Port
113   Arthur
69
53
54
Conroe
Spring
Sam
Houston
Nat'l.
Forest
33
Huntsville
26
College
Station
Bryan
Independence
Washington
110
Sam
Rayburn
Reservoir
59
Toledo Bend
Reservoir
Sabine
Nat'l.
Forest
Sabine
Angelina
Nat'l.
Forest
Big Thicket
Nat'l. Preserve
116
Red
Red
Brazos
Colorado
49
Seguin
San
Marcos
Gonzales   77
59
SAN
ANTONIO
101
32
61   59
Sulphur
Springs
Marshall
10
65
61
48
Lake Jackson
Johnson
City
43
4
9
La
Grange
New Braunfels
80
San   La
Antonio
117
290
Waco
Corsicana
LONGVIEW
Canton
Rusk
San Marcos
4
9

Points of Interest Offering A *Great Experience for Members*

Amarillo (B-5)

AMERICAN QUARTER HORSE HERITAGE CENTER & MUSEUM—Multimedia presentations, artwork and interactive exhibits chronicle the history of this distinctive breed. See p. 57.

Arlington (D-9)

SIX FLAGS OVER TEXAS—A turn-of-the-20th-century train winds through the park, which features more than 100 rides, attractions and shows. See p. 58.

Austin (F-8)

BOB BULLOCK TEXAS STATE HISTORY MUSEUM—This 34,000-square-foot complex is a monument to the spirit, determination and pride that makes Texans unique. See p. 61.

LYNDON BAINES JOHNSON LIBRARY AND MUSEUM—Sculptures of Johnson and the first lady, gifts from

diplomats and papers of the Johnson presidency are among the museum's displays. See p. 63.

TEXAS STATE CAPITOL—Modeled after the U.S. Capitol, the edifice boasts sunset-red Texas granite as its main building material. See p. 62.

Austwell (G-9)

ARANSAS NATIONAL WILDLIFE REFUGE—Alligators, armadillos, javelinas and a huge flock of whooping cranes coexist in the 59,700-acre refuge. See p. 63.

Big Bend National Park (G-4)

BIG BEND NATIONAL PARK—Mountain and desert scenery supplement unusual geological structures in this adventurist wonderland. See p. 64.

Brownsville (I-9)

GLADYS PORTER ZOO—The more than 1,500 animal inhabitants of the zoo, many of which are endangered species, are grouped according to their native regions. See p. 68.

Canyon (B-5)

PALO DURO CANYON STATE PARK—Geological formations more than 250 million years old and traces of pre-Pueblo habitation are the park's primary draws. See p. 71.

PANHANDLE-PLAINS HISTORICAL MUSEUM—One highlight of the museum, which details the history of northwest Texas, is a recon-

structed pioneer town that features buildings filled with period artifacts. See p. 72.

College Station (E-9)

GEORGE BUSH PRESIDENTIAL LIBRARY AND MUSEUM—Artifacts, films, photographs and interactive exhibits trace the life of the 41st president. See p. 73.

Corpus Christi (H-9)

TEXAS STATE AQUARIUM—Among the aquarium's notable draws is an artificial reef community that is home to moray eels, stingrays and sharks. See p. 74.

Texas State Aquarium

Dallas (D-9)

BIBLICAL ARTS CENTER—In this collection of non-denominational religious art are paintings, sculptures, icons and clerical artifacts. See p. 80.

DALLAS ZOO—A 67-foot giraffe statue greets visitors at the entrance of the zoo, which is noteworthy for its gorilla conservation center and its

chimpanzee forest exhibit. See p. 81.

FAIR PARK—Site of the 1936 Texas Centennial Exhibition, the park features *moderne* buildings as well as murals and sculptures of  mermaids and winged horses. See p. 81.

THE SIXTH FLOOR MUSEUM AT DEALEY PLAZA—The memorial in the Texas School Book Depository, the site from which the shots that killed  John F. Kennedy were fired, pays tribute to the popular president. See p. 83.

Fort Worth (D-8)

FORT WORTH MUSEUM OF SCIENCE AND HISTORY—Museum exhibits center on such themes as medicine, the human body, geology and technology. See p. 97.

FORT WORTH ZOO—Among the zoo's habitats are Raptor Canyon, Asian Rhino Ridge, World of Primates and Penguin Island. See p. 97.

KIMBELL ART MUSEUM—The museum collection features 18th-century British portraits and late European Renaissance art. See p. 97.

Fredericksburg (E-7)

NATIONAL MUSEUM OF THE PACIFIC WAR—The museum is dedicated to the men and women who served in the Pacific Theater and on the home front during World War II. See p. 99.

Galveston (F-11)

MOODY GARDENS—A 10-story Rainforest Pyramid features streams, waterfalls, exotic plants and varied animals and insects. See p. 100.

Harlingen (I-8)

THE IWO JIMA WAR MEMORIAL—In addition to the original sculpture of the Iwo Jima flag-raising, the memorial includes displays of battle artifacts. See p. 105.

Houston (F-10)

BAYOU BEND COLLECTION AND GARDENS—Decorative arts are displayed in rooms that trace the evolution in American style from the Colonial period to the mid-19th century. See p. 107.

THE MENIL COLLECTION—Changing exhibits draw from a diverse collection of more than 15,000 works of art. See p. 111.

MINUTE MAID PARK—Tours of this state-of-the-art baseball stadium take visitors to historic Union Station, the press area, luxury suites, the club level, the dugout and center field. See p. 112.

SIX FLAGS ASTROWORLD—The park's roller coasters—such as the loop-to-loop Ultra Twister, the Texas Cyclone and a stand-up ride—are among its most popular attractions. See p. 113.

SPACE CENTER HOUSTON—A full-size space shuttle, live demonstrations, computer simulators and tram tours educate visitors about  space exploration. See p. 113.

Huntsville (E-10)

SAM HOUSTON MEMORIAL MUSEUM COMPLEX—Two of Houston's houses as well as his law office and a museum of his belongings comprise the complex. See p. 118.

Kilgore (D-10)

EAST TEXAS OIL MUSEUM—Pioneers of the Texas oil industry are honored in exhibits, audiovisual presentations and photographs. See p. 119.

La Porte (F-10)

SAN JACINTO BATTLEGROUND STATE HISTORIC SITE—The battle that resulted in Texas' independence from Mexico was fought on this 1,200-acre site. See p. 116.

SAN JACINTO MONUMENT AND MUSEUM OF HISTORY—Spectacular panoramas are enjoyed from the top  of the 50-story masonry obelisk. See p. 116.

Lyndon B. Johnson National Historical Park (F-8)

LYNDON B. JOHNSON NATIONAL HISTORICAL PARK—Bus tours through the LBJ Ranch include the ranch and the Johnson family cemetery, where the former president is buried. See p. 124.

Midland (D-5)

THE PETROLEUM MUSEUM—Artifacts, interactive exhibits and works of art tell the story of the oil and gas industry in the Permian Basin of western Texas. See p. 126.

San Antonio (F-8)

THE ALAMO—A symbol of Texas' pride and independent spirit, the outpost now houses exhibits and artifacts from the era of the Texas Revolution. See p. 139.

INSTITUTE OF TEXAN CULTURES—Exhibits illustrate the customs, dress and skills of early Texas residents. See p. 141.

THE McNAY ART MUSEUM—In addition to works by renowned masters, the museum includes a collection of American Indian arts and crafts. See p. 141.

MISSION SAN JOSÉ Y SAN MIGUEL DE AGUAYO—The restored compound features a Spanish Colonial gristmill and outer walls with  American Indian dwellings. See p. 144.

NATURAL BRIDGE CAVERNS—The caverns are a showcase for magnificent limestone formations created by dripping water. See p. 143.

NATURAL BRIDGE WILDLIFE RANCH—The drive-through safari lets visitors come face-to-face with more than 60 varieties of exotic animals. See p. 143.

PASEO DEL RÍO (RIVERWALK)—A few steps below the business district, tree-lined footpaths follow the river past galleries, craft shops and terraces. See p. 143.

SAN ANTONIO BOTANICAL GARDENS—Adobe houses, a log cabin and a lake supplement native wildflowers to reflect the  rural color of the Hill Country. See p. 143.

SAN ANTONIO MUSEUM OF ART—Regional materials and art of the Americas are key focuses of the museum, a former brewhouse. See p. 144.

SAN ANTONIO ZOO—Scenic limestone cliffs surround the zoo, where rare snow leopards, white rhinos and whooping cranes thrive. See p. 140.

SEAWORLD SAN ANTONIO—Exhibits and shows at the marine-life park—famous for its killer whale Shamu and its performing sea lions, ot-  ters and walruses—are designed to educate and entertain. See p. 144.

SIX FLAGS FIESTA TEXAS—The park is home to The Rattler, reputed to be the world's tallest and fastest wooden roller coaster. See p. 145.

WITTE MUSEUM—Interactive exhibits pertain to Texas history, natural science and anthropology. See p. 140.

Sonora (E-6)

CAVERNS OF SONORA—Colorful stalagmites, stalactites and helictites adorn the floor, ceiling and walls of the cave. See p. 152.

Tyler (D-10)

CALDWELL ZOO—The zoo features elephant and giraffe houses, a monkey island and a native Texas exhibit. See p. 154.

Look for a SAVE Place to Stay!

When selecting a AAA Approved lodging, look for properties that participate in our SAVE programs. These properties understand the value of AAA business and many offer discounts to AAA members.

- A red **SAVE** icon in their TourBook® guide listing indicates an **Official Appointment** property that offers a minimum 10% discount off published TourBook standard room rates or the lowest public standard room rate, at the time of booking, for the dates of stay.

- A black **SAVE** icon indicates a chain hotel that participates in the **Show Your Card & Save®** program. SYC&S partners offer a satisfaction guarantee and AAA's best rate for your dates of stay. Reservations must be made by calling the exclusive AAA member toll-free number:

AAA and CAA members save up to 50% on over 1.5 million hotel rooms throughout North America.

Participating Chains:
Sleep Inn, Comfort Inn, Comfort Suites, Quality Inn, Clarion, Econo Lodge,
Rodeway Inn, Mainstay Suites, Days Inn, Hilton Hotels & Resorts,
Hilton Garden Inn, Hampton Inn, Hampton Inn & Suites, Embassy Suites, Doubletree Hotels,
Homewood Suites, Hyatt Hotels & Resorts,
La Quinta Inn, La Quinta Inn & Suites, Marriott Hotels & Resorts,
Renaissance Hotels & Resorts, Courtyard by Marriott, Fairfield Inn,
Residence Inns, SpringHill Suites, TownePlace Suites, Best Western

Valid membership card needed at time of reservation.

Visit	Over 1,100 AAA Offices	**Click**	aaa.com	**Call**	866-AAA-SAVE

All discounts are off full rates and vary by location and time of year. The 50% discount is not available at all times.

RECREATION AREAS

	MAP LOCATION	CAMPING	PICNICKING	HIKING TRAILS	BOATING	BOAT RAMP	BOAT RENTAL	FISHING	SWIMMING	PETS ON LEASH	BICYCLE TRAILS	SKIN/SCUBA	VISITOR CENTER	LODGE/CABINS	FOOD SERVICE
NATIONAL PARKS *(See place listings)*															
Big Bend (G-4) 801,163 acres. Horse rental.		•	•	•	•			•		•			•	•	•
Guadalupe Mountains (D-3) 86,416 acres.		•	•	•						•			•		
NATIONAL FORESTS *(See place listings)*															
Angelina (E-10) 153,179 acres. East Texas.		•	•	•	•	•		•	•	•					
Davy Crockett (E-10) 161,500 acres. East Texas.		•	•	•	•	•	•	•	•	•					•
Sabine (E-11) 160,609 acres. East Texas.		•	•	•	•	•		•	•	•					
Sam Houston (E-10) 161,654 acres. East Texas.		•	•	•	•	•		•	•	•	•				
NATIONAL PRESERVES *(See place listings)*															
Big Thicket (E-11) 97,000 acres.		•	•	•	•	•		•	•				•		
NATIONAL RECREATION AREAS *(See place listings)*															
Amistad (G-5) 67,000 acres.		•	•	•	•	•	•	•	•	•		•			
Lake Meredith (A-6) 16,504 acres. Water skiing.		•	•		•	•		•	•	•					
NATIONAL SEASHORES *(See place listings)*															
Padre Island (H-9) 130,697 acres.		•	•		•	•		•	•	•			•		•
ARMY CORPS OF ENGINEERS															
Aquilla Lake (D-9) 3,280 acres 9.5 mi. s.w. of Hillsboro via I-35 and FM 310.	83			•	•			•	•	•					
B.A. Steinhagen Lake (E-11) 13,700 acres 15 mi. e. of Woodville via US 190.	93	•	•	•	•	•		•	•	•					
Bardwell Lake (D-9) 3,570 acres 4 mi. s.w. of Ennis via SR 34.	84	•	•	•	•	•		•	•	•					
Belton Lake (E-8) 12,300 acres 4 mi. n.w. of Belton via SR 317 and FM 439.	85	•	•		•	•	•	•	•	•		•			•
Benbrook Lake (D-8) 3,770 acres 12 mi. s.w. of Fort Worth on US 377. Horse rental.	100	•	•		•	•		•	•	•					
Canyon Lake (F-8) 8,240 acres 16 mi. n.w. of New Braunfels via SR 306.	80	•	•		•	•		•	•	•		•			
Granger Lake (E-8) 4,400 acres 10 mi. n.e. of Taylor via SR 95 and FM 971.	81	•	•	•	•	•		•	•	•					
Grapevine Lake (C-9) 7,280 acres n.e. of Grapevine on SR 121.	86	•	•	•	•	•		•	•	•			•		•
Hords Creek Lake (D-7) 510 acres 8 mi. w. of Coleman on FM 153.	75	•	•	•	•	•		•	•	•					
Joe Pool Lake (D-8) 7,470 acres 2 mi. s. of Grand Prairie off I-20 on Great South Pkwy.	87	•	•		•	•		•	•	•					•
Lake Georgetown (E-8) 1,310 acres 4 mi. w. of Georgetown via I-35 and CR 2338.	76	•	•	•	•	•		•	•	•					
Lake Lavon (C-9) 21,400 acres 3 mi. e. of Wylie on SR 78. Water skiing.	63	•	•		•	•		•	•	•					
Lake O' the Pines (C-10) 19,780 acres 25 mi. n.e. of Longview off FM 729. *(See Longview p. 122)*	65	•	•		•	•		•	•	•					
Lake Texoma (C-9) 195,326 acres. *(See Denison p. 88)*	66	•	•		•	•	•	•	•	•				•	•
Lake Wright Patman (C-10) 33,750 acres 9 mi. s.w. of Texarkana on US 59.	67	•	•	•	•	•		•	•	•					
Lewisville Lake (C-9) 28,980 acres in Lewisville.	88	•	•		•	•		•	•	•			•		•
Navarro Mills Lake (D-9) 5,070 acres 18 mi. w. of Corsicana via SR 31 and FM 667.	89	•	•		•	•			•	•					
O.C. Fisher Lake (E-6) 5,440 acres 3 mi. n.w. of San Angelo off FM 2288.	77	•	•	•	•	•		•	•	•		•			
Pat Mayse Lake (C-9) 8,000 acres 10 mi. n. of Paris off US 271.	68	•	•		•	•		•	•	•			•		
Proctor Lake (D-7) 4,610 acres 3.5 from Hasse via US 377 and FM 2861.	90	•	•		•	•		•	•	•					
Sam Rayburn Reservoir (E-11) 114,500 acres 20 mi. n. of Jasper via US 96 and FM 1007. *(See Angelina National Forest p. 58)*	70	•	•		•	•	•	•	•	•					

RECREATION AREAS	MAP LOCATION	CAMPING	PICNICKING	HIKING TRAILS	BOATING	BOAT RAMP	BOAT RENTAL	FISHING	SWIMMING	PETS ON LEASH	BICYCLE TRAILS	SKIN/SCUBA	VISITOR CENTER	LODGE/CABINS	FOOD SERVICE
Somerville Lake (F-9) 11,460 acres in Somerville.	35	•	•	•	•	•		•	•	•					
Stillhouse Hollow Lake (E-8) 6,430 acres 4 mi. s.w. of Belton US 190 and FM 1670.	92	•	•	•	•	•		•	•	•					•
Waco Lake (E-8) 7,270 acres in Waco.	94	•	•		•	•	•	•	•	•					
STATE															
Abilene (D-6) 621 acres 16 mi. s.w. of Abilene via FM 89 near Buffalo Gap.	1	•	•	•	•			•	•	•					•
Atlanta (C-10) 1,475 acres 12 mi. n.w. of Atlanta off US 59.	2	•	•	•	•			•	•	•					
Balmorhea (E-4) 43 acres .1 mi. n.e. of Balmorhea on FM 3078. Spring-fed swimming pool.	3	•	•	•					•	•				•	
Bastrop (F-8) 3,500 acres 1 mi. n.e. of Bastrop off SR 21. Scenic. Golf.	4	•	•	•				•	•	•				•	•
Bentsen-Rio Grande Valley (I-8) 588 acres 6 mi. s.w. of Mission off US 83. Scenic.	5	•	•	•	•	•		•		•					
Big Bend Ranch (G-4) 287,000 acres 4 miles s.e. of Presidio on River Road (FM 170). Historic. *(See Presidio p. 131)*	39	•	•	•				•				•	•	•	•
Blanco (F-7) 105 acres 1 mi. s. of Blanco off US 281.	6	•	•	•				•	•	•					
Bonham (C-9) 261 acres 3.5 mi. s.e. of Bonham on FM 271.	7	•	•		•	•	•	•	•	•					
Brazos Bend (F-10) 4,897 acres 20 mi. s.w. of Richmond on FM 762. *(See Richmond p. 117)*	73	•	•	•				•		•	•		•		
Buescher (F-9) 1,016 acres 3 mi. n.w. of Smithville off SR 71. Scenic.	9	•	•	•	•			•	•	•					
Caddo Lake (D-10) 484 acres 15 mi. n.e. of Marshall off SR 43. Historic. Scenic.	10	•	•	•	•	•	•	•		•				•	
Caprock Canyons (B-6) 13,960 acres 3.5 mi. n. of Quitaque off SR 86. Horse trails, rock climbing.	11	•	•	•	•	•		•	•	•	•				
Cedar Hill (D-9) 1,810 acres on FM 1382 near Cedar Hill.	58	•	•		•	•		•		•			•		
Choke Canyon (H-8) e. of Calliham on SR 72.	101														
Cleburne (D-8) 529 acres 12 mi. s. of Cleburne via US 67 and Park Rd. 21. *(See Cleburne p. 73)*	12	•	•	•	•	•	•	•	•	•	•				•
Colorado Bend (E-8) s. of Bend on FM 501.	103	•	•	•	•	•		•	•	•					
Confederate Reunion Grounds (D-9) 7 mi. n. of Mexia on SR 14. Historic.	104	•	•	•				•		•					
Cooper Lake (C-10) s. of Cooper off SR 24. Horse trails.	105	•	•	•	•	•		•	•	•				•	
Copper Breaks (C-7) 1,889 acres 12 mi. s. of Quanah on SR 6. Horse trails.	13	•	•	•	•	•		•	•	•			•		
Daingerfield (C-10) 551 acres 2 mi. s.e. of Daingerfield on SR 49.	14	•	•	•	•	•	•	•	•	•			•	•	•
Davis Mountains (E-4) 2,678 acres 4 mi. n.w. of Fort Davis off SR 118. Scenic. *(See Fort Davis p. 94)*	15	•	•	•				•		•			•	•	•
Dinosaur Valley (D-8) 1,274 acres 5 mi. w. of Glen Rose off US 67. Historic. Horse trails.	16	•	•	•				•	•	•	•				
Eisenhower (C-9) 423 acres off US 75, 2 mi. n. on FM 1310 at Lake Texoma.	17	•	•	•	•	•	•	•	•	•					
Enchanted Rock (F-7) 18 mi. n. of Fredericksburg on FM 965. Rock climbing.	106	•	•	•						•					
Fairfield Lake (D-9) 1,460 acres 4.5 mi. n. of Fairfield off FM 2570.	18	•	•	•	•	•	•	•	•	•		•			
Falcon (I-7) 572 acres from US 83, 3.5 mi. n.w. on FM 2098 to Park Road 46.	19	•	•	•	•	•		•	•	•		•			
Fort Griffin (D-7) 506 acres 15 mi. n. on US 283. Historic. Horse trails. *(See Fort Griffin p. 94)*	20	•	•	•				•		•			•		
Fort Parker (E-9) 1,459 acres 7 mi. s. of Mexia on SR 14.	21	•	•	•	•	•	•	•	•	•					
Fort Richardson (C-8) 396 acres 1 mi. s. off US 281. Historic. *(See Jacksboro p. 118)*	82	•	•	•				•		•			•		

RECREATION AREAS

	MAP LOCATION	CAMPING	PICNICKING	HIKING TRAILS	BOATING	BOAT RAMP	BOAT RENTAL	FISHING	SWIMMING	PETS ON LEASH	BICYCLE TRAILS	SKIN/SCUBA	VISITOR CENTER	LODGE/CABINS	FOOD SERVICE
Franklin Mountains (D-2) 24,000 acres 3.8 mi. e. of El Paso on I-10 at McKelligon Canyon Rd.	114	•	•	•						•	•				
Galveston Island (G-10) 1,950 acres. Historic. Summer outdoor musical drama. *(See Galveston p. 99)*	22	•	•	•	•	•		•	•	•					
Garner (F-7) 1,420 acres 5 mi. e. of Concan on Hwy. 1050.	23	•	•	•				•	•	•				•	•
Goliad (G-8) 178 acres .2 mi. s. on US 77A/183. Historic. *(See Goliad p. 102)*	24	•	•	•				•	•	•					
Goose Island (G-9) 314 acres 12 mi. n.e. of Rockport off SR 35.	25	•	•	•	•	•		•	•	•					
Guadalupe River/Honey Creek (F-7) 1,938 acres 13 mi. e. of Boerne on SR 46.	74	•	•	•				•	•	•					
Hill Country (F-7) 5,369 acres 4 mi. n.e. of Tarpley on FM 470. Horse trails.	107	•		•				•	•	•	•				
Hueco Tanks (D-2) e. of El Paso on US 180/62, then 8 mi. n. on FM 2775. Rock climbing. *(See El Paso p. 92)*	108	•	•	•						•					
Huntsville (E-10) 2,083 acres 10 mi. s. of Huntsville off I-45. Miniature golf.	26	•	•	•	•	•		•	•	•					•
Inks Lake (E-7) 1,200 acres 9 mi. w. off SR 29. Canoeing, golf (nine holes), water skiing. *(See Burnet p. 71)*	27	•	•	•	•	•	•	•	•	•		•			
Kerrville-Schreiner (F-7) 517 acres 3 mi. s.w. of Kerrville off SR 16 on FM 173.	28	•	•	•	•	•		•	•	•					
Lake Arrowhead (C-7) 524 acres 15 mi. s.e. of Wichita Falls via US 281 and FM 1954. Horse trails.	29	•	•	•	•	•		•	•	•					
Lake Bob Sandlin (C-10) 9 mi. w. of Mount Pleasant on FM 127.	109	•	•	•	•	•		•	•	•					
Lake Brownwood (D-7) 537 acres 22 mi. n.w. of Brownwood off SR 279.	30	•	•	•	•	•		•	•	•				•	•
Lake Casa Blanca (H-7) 371 acres 1 mi. e. of Laredo off Lake Casa Blanca Rd.	61	•	•		•	•		•	•	•					
Lake Colorado City (D-6) 500 acres 10 mi. w. of Colorado City on I-20.	31	•	•	•	•	•		•	•	•					
Lake Corpus Christi (G-8) 288 acres 4.5 mi. s. of Mathis on SR 359, then 2 mi. n.w. on Park Road 25.	32	•	•	•	•	•		•	•	•					
Lake Houston (F-10) 3 mi. e. of New Caney on FM 1485.	110	•	•	•						•	•				
Lake Livingston (E-10) 82,600 acres 5 mi. s.w. of Livingston off US 190. Horse trails.	33	•	•	•	•	•		•	•	•			•		•
Lake Mineral Wells (D-8) 3,004 acres 4 mi. e. of Mineral Wells on US 180. Horse trails, rock climbing.	34	•	•	•	•	•	•	•	•	•					
Lake Somerville (F-9) 2,600 acres 15 mi. n.w. of Brenham on SR 36. Horse trails.	8	•	•	•	•	•		•	•	•					
Lake Tawakoni (D-9) 376 acres 4 mi. n. of Wills Point on FM 2475.	116	•	•	•	•	•		•	•	•					
Lake Texana (G-9) 575 acres 6 mi. s.e. of Edna on SR 111. Water skiing.	36	•	•	•				•	•	•					
Lake Whitney (D-8) 23,560 acres 4 mi. w. of Whitney on SR 22.	37	•	•	•	•	•	•	•	•	•		•			
Lockhart (F-8) 263 acres 45 mi. s. of Austin off US 183. Golf.	91	•	•					•	•	•					
Lost Maples (F-7) 2,200 acres 5 mi. n. of Vanderpool on FM 187. Natural area.	38	•	•	•				•	•	•	•				
Lyndon B. Johnson (F-7) 733 acres e. of Stonewall on US 290. Historic. *(See Stonewall p. 152)*	40		•	•						•			•		
Martin Creek Lake (D-10) 287 acres 8 mi. n.e. of Henderson off SR 43.	71	•	•	•	•	•		•	•	•					•
Martin Dies Jr. (E-11) 705 acres 15 mi. e. of Woodville on US 190.	42	•	•	•	•	•		•	•	•					
Matagorda Island (G-9) 7,328 acres off SR 60 at Port O'Connor.	96	•	•	•				•	•	•	•				
McKinney Falls (F-8) 641 acres 7 mi. s.e. of Austin off US 183.	43	•	•	•				•	•	•			•		
Meridian (D-8) 503 acres 3 mi. s.w. of Meridian off SR 22.	44	•	•	•	•	•	•	•	•	•					

RECREATION AREAS

RECREATION AREAS	MAP LOCATION	CAMPING	PICNICKING	HIKING TRAILS	BOATING	BOAT RAMP	BOAT RENTAL	FISHING	SWIMMING	PETS ON LEASH	BICYCLE TRAILS	SKIN/SCUBA	VISITOR CENTER	LODGE/CABINS	FOOD SERVICE
Mission Tejas (E-10) 363 acres just n. of Weches on Park Rd. 44. Historic. *(See Davy Crockett National Forest p. 88)*	45	•	•	•				•	•						
Monahans Sandhills (E-4) 3,840 acres 5 mi. e. off I-20 to Park Rd. 41. Horse trails. *(See Monahans p. 126)*	46	•	•	•						•			•		•
Mother Neff (E-8) 259 acres 9 mi. w. of Moody on SR 236.	47	•	•	•				•	•						
Mustang Island (H-8) 3,954 acres 14 mi. s. of Port Aransas on SR 361. *(See Port Aransas p. 130)*	48	•	•					•	•	•					
Palmetto (F-8) 265 acres 6 mi. s.e. of Luling off US 183.	49	•	•	•	•			•	•						
Palo Duro Canyon (B-5) 16,402 acres 12 mi. e. on SR 217. Scenic. Horse rental, outdoor drama. *(See Canyon p. 71)*	50	•	•	•				•		•			•	•	•
Pedernales Falls (F-8) 5,212 acres 9 mi. e. of Johnson City via FM 2766. Horse trails. *(See Johnson City p. 119)*	51	•	•	•				•	•	•					
Possum Kingdom (D-7) 1,528 acres 17 mi. n.e. of Caddo via Park Rd. 33.	52	•	•		•	•	•	•	•	•				•	•
Purtis Creek (D-9) 1,533 acres 4 mi. n. of Eustace on FM 316.	111	•	•	•	•	•		•	•						
Ray Roberts Lake (C-8) 29,350 acres 15 mi. n. of Denton via I-35 and FM 455. Horse trails.	99	•	•	•	•	•		•	•	•					
Rusk and Palestine (D-10) 136 acres 3 mi. w. of Rusk on US 84. Tennis.	95	•	•	•	•			•	•						
Sabine Pass Battleground (F-11) 56 acres 1.5 mi. s. of Sabine Pass on FM 3322. Historic.	53	•	•					•		•					
San Angelo (E-6) 7,677 acres n. of San Angelo on US 87 to FM 2288.	115	•	•	•	•	•		•	•	•	•				
Sea Rim (F-11) 15,109 acres 10 mi. s. of Sabine Pass off SR 87. Water skiing; canoe trails.	54	•	•	•	•			•	•	•			•		
Seminole Canyon (F-5) 2,172 acres 8 mi. w. on US 90. Historic. *(See Comstock p. 73)*	55	•	•	•						•	•		•		
Sheldon Lake (F-10) w. of Sheldon on US 90 Bus. Rte.	113		•	•	•	•		•							
South Llano River (F-7) 2,640 acres 5 mi. s. on FR 134, off Park Road 2N.	97	•	•	•				•	•	•	•				
Stephen F. Austin (F-9) 667 acres 6 mi. e. of Sealy via I-10 and FM 1458. Historic. Golf.	56	•	•	•				•	•	•					
Tyler (D-10) 986 acres 2 mi. n. of Tyler off FM 14.	57	•	•	•	•	•	•	•	•	•					•
Village Creek (F-11) 986 acres 2.5 mi. s.e. of Lumberton.	98	•	•	•	•	•		•	•						
OTHER															
Falls on the Brazos (E-9) 22 acres 3 mi. s. of Marlin on FM 712.	72	•	•		•	•		•	•						•
Hubbard Creek Lake (D-7) 15,250 acres 4 mi. w. of Breckenridge on US 180. Water skiing.	59	•	•		•	•		•	•			•		•	•
Lake Buchanan (E-7) 10 acres 9 mi. w. of Burnet on SR 29 and 15 mi. e. of Llano. *(See Burnet p. 71)*	60	•	•		•	•		•	•				•	•	•
Lake Crook (C-10) 2,717 acres about 5 mi. n.w. of Paris off US 271.	62	•	•		•	•		•							
Lake Fort Phantom Hill (D-7) 4,246 acres about 10 mi. n.e. of Abilene via FM 600.	41	•	•		•	•		•							
Lake Leon (D-7) 50 acres 6 mi. s. of Ranger off FM 2461.	64	•	•		•	•	•	•	•					•	•
Pace Bend (E-8) 1,520 acres 27 mi. n.w. of Austin via SR 71.	79	•	•		•	•		•	•						
Sabine Lake (F-11) e. of Port Arthur via SR 82 and Gulfgate Bridge. Water skiing.	69	•	•	•	•	•		•				•			•
Zilker (F-8) 351 acres 1.5 mi. s.w. on Barton Springs Rd (FM 2244). *(See Austin p. 63)*	78		•	•	•			•	•	•	•				

Texas Temperature Averages
Maximum / Minimum
From the records of the National Weather Service

	JAN	FEB	MAR	APR	MAY	JUN	JUL	AUG	SEP	OCT	NOV	DEC
Abilene	56 / 33	61 / 36	68 / 42	77 / 51	83 / 60	92 / 69	94 / 72	94 / 72	87 / 64	79 / 54	65 / 41	58 / 34
Amarillo	49 / 24	53 / 27	60 / 32	70 / 42	78 / 52	89 / 62	92 / 66	91 / 65	83 / 57	73 / 46	59 / 32	51 / 26
Austin	60 / 41	64 / 44	71 / 49	78 / 57	85 / 65	92 / 72	95 / 74	96 / 74	90 / 69	82 / 60	70 / 48	63 / 43
Brownsville	71 / 52	73 / 55	77 / 59	82 / 66	87 / 71	91 / 75	93 / 76	93 / 75	90 / 73	85 / 67	77 / 58	72 / 54
Corpus Christi	67 / 47	70 / 51	74 / 56	80 / 63	85 / 69	91 / 74	94 / 75	94 / 75	90 / 71	85 / 65	74 / 54	69 / 50
Dallas-Fort Worth	56 / 36	60 / 39	67 / 45	75 / 55	83 / 63	91 / 72	95 / 75	95 / 75	88 / 67	79 / 57	66 / 44	58 / 38
El Paso	56 / 32	62 / 37	68 / 41	77 / 50	86 / 58	94 / 67	94 / 69	92 / 68	88 / 62	79 / 52	66 / 38	58 / 33
Galveston	60 / 48	63 / 51	67 / 56	74 / 64	81 / 71	87 / 77	89 / 79	89 / 79	85 / 75	79 / 68	69 / 57	63 / 51
Houston	62 / 46	66 / 50	71 / 54	78 / 61	85 / 67	90 / 74	92 / 75	93 / 75	89 / 71	82 / 63	71 / 53	64 / 47
San Antonio	62 / 42	66 / 45	72 / 50	79 / 58	85 / 65	92 / 72	94 / 74	94 / 73	89 / 69	82 / 60	70 / 49	65 / 42

Exploring Texas

For descriptions of places in bold type, see individual listings.

Central Texas

Stretching from just north of **San Antonio** to the outskirts of **Waco** and then west to **San Angelo,** central Texas is the geographic axis around which Texas' other major regions revolve. Unlike the generally flat terrain of its neighbors, much of central Texas is dominated by the eroded features of the Edwards Plateau and the Balcones Escarpment.

Known as "Hill Country," central Texas is characterized by broken terrain covered with grasses shaded by pecan, oak and sumac. Rocky outcroppings punctuate the landscape of the sparse, arid region, where riches lie in the many rivers and colorful displays of spring wildflowers.

Despite the number of roads running through central Texas, this was an isolated area even into the 20th century. The area's insularity was compounded by the close-knit nature of the German settlers, whose politics and way of life ran contrary to those of other Texans.

Although distinctions between these German settlers and their neighbors since have faded, many of their traditions survive in **Fredericksburg** and **New Braunfels.** German tradition also is apparent in the crescent-shaped pattern of old-world

houses and orderly fields trimmed with stone walls that pepper the countryside north of San Antonio.

Forming an irregular "V" converging on San Antonio, Interstates 10 and 35 are the principal routes through central Texas. Interstate 10 begins ascending into the "Hill Country" near **Boerne,** which with Comfort and Sister-

Deep in the Heart of Texas!

dale, was settled by German groups who spoke only Latin. Despite such anomalies the romance and traditions of Texas can still be seen in **Kerrville's** popular Cowboy Artists of America collection at the National Center for American Western Art.

West of the interstate and south of Kerrville SR 173 twists through rugged terrain suitable only for sheep and goat ranches.

At **Bandera** SR 173 meets SR 16 and parallels the Medina River as it meanders through country sprinkled with dude ranches and apple orchards. Near Vanderpool is a pocket-size remnant of maples, a reminder of an era when such trees were common in a less-arid Texas.

Bisecting the two interstates, US 281 runs north to south through some of the more scenic areas of central Texas. As the highway nears **Burnet** from Lampasas it passes Lake Buchanan, the last of the Highland Lakes—a series of lakes formed behind a staircase of dams that begin in **Austin.**

Lying just west of US 281 from Burnet, Lake Buchanan interrupts a rocky landscape covered with live oaks, cedars and cacti that shelter wild goats, deer, turkeys and other wildlife. In the spring, especially along SR 29, bluebonnets, Indian paintbrush, primrose and other wildflowers carpet the hillsides. From SR 29 you can rejoin US 281 in Marble Falls by following FR 1431, which offers views of the Colorado River and Lake Lyndon Johnson.

A little farther south, **Johnson City** has preserved a slice of 19th- and early 20th-century life in the **Lyndon B. Johnson National Historical Park.** Eastward, waterfalls can be seen on the Pedernales River.

As beautiful as the Pedernales, Colorado and Blanco rivers are, perhaps the most scenic river is the Guadalupe. Just west of US 281 on SR 46, Guadalupe River State Park captures nearly 2,000 acres of this cypress-lined river and its nearby hills dotted with juniper thickets. Heading east on SR 46 visitors can roughly follow the course of the Guadalupe River as it descends through ever-green hillsides near Canyon Lake to New Braunfels.

From historic New Braunfels with its German heritage I-35 roughly follows the Old San Antonio Road and then the Chisholm Trail as it heads northeastward to **Fort Worth.** .The Balcones Fault, which parallels this route, is the source of many springs, one of the largest of which feeds the San Marcos River in **San Marcos.**

Austin, the state capital, straddles the Colorado River at the foot of the Balcones Escarpment and the Blackland prairie. In the city, Town Lake is the first of the Highland Lakes, which trend northwestward into the Hill Country. From Austin, I-35 follows a succession of old rail stops—Round Rock, **Georgetown** and **Temple**—as central Texas fades into the east Texas prairie.

East Texas

Historically the east Texas boundary includes the Red River on the north and the Sabine River on

the east. Excluding the narrow coastal strip from Beaumont to Victoria, the boundary follows the earliest pattern of settlement as far west as Bastrop. Running northeasterly through the middle of the region is the Old San Antonio Road (SR 21).

This route was a natural corridor of prairie, 5 miles wide and almost 100 miles long, through the forests that once covered east Texas. Over this route marched key figures of Texas history, from the Spanish missionaries to the defenders of the Alamo. Little of this is apparent along SR 21 as most of the countryside is open pastureland, but as you travel east, especially beyond I-45, trees again crowd the landscape.

Originally the southern coniferous forest reached roughly as far west as I-45 and gave rise to the popular name for east Texas, the "Piney Woods." By the mid-19th century cotton plantations had supplanted this mixture of pine and hardwoods. In an unusual reversal the pine forest has returned as commercial tree farms.

Running north to south through the heart of the "Piney Woods," US 59 strings together many of the region's major cities and smaller towns. On either side of this thoroughfare, side roads lead to Texas' four national forests, many lakes and **Big Thicket National Preserve.**

Nacogdoches, at the intersection of US 59 and SR 21, was the historic center of east Texas. The town, which was a remote outpost at the edge of the Spanish Empire, and east Texas were pawns in the empire-building schemes of Spain and of France, which controlled neighboring Louisiana.

When Louisiana changed hands, the United States became the chief conspirator, both officially and unofficially, in the plot to secure Texas. Numerous American plotters raised

private armies and tried unsuccessfully several times to oust the Spanish, and one even went so far as to establish a short-lived state called Fredonia.

Matters of international intrigue disappeared in the aftermath of the Civil War, and economic survival become paramount. The plantation culture was ruined. In its place east Texas turned to its greatest natural resource, as logging camps and mills sprang up all over the area. The South's first paper mill was founded in **Lufkin,** and the city remains the center of the region's timber industry.

On either side of Lufkin are **Davy Crockett** and **Angelina** national forests. These areas were heavily logged in the 1920s but have made a dramatic comeback, offering a variety of woodlands and recreation. East of Angelina National Forest, **Sabine National Forest** includes a narrow strip of woodlands along the Toledo Reservoir on the Louisiana border.

Southwest of Lufkin fragments of the country's most diverse and unusual natural area are preserved in several scattered sections of the Big Thicket National Preserve. This biological crossroads, a storehouse of plants and animals, embraces species native to areas as far north as Newfoundland and as far south as the tropics.

In **Marshall** US 59 meets I-20, which links Marshall with east Texas' two other major cities, **Tyler** and **Longview.** The discovery of huge oil reserves in this region in 1930 made boomtowns of Longview and Tyler. Both cities remain major petroleum centers, but in Tyler a more delicate treasure holds an equally prominent position. The city is one of the largest producers of rose bushes.

In the rolling red hills north of I-20, US 59 enters country that once was dotted with cotton plantations. The best example of this period is the wealth of historic structures in **Jefferson.** Many of the buildings were erected when the city was a major cotton port from which

steamers rode the Big Cyprus Bayou and the Red River to New Orleans. Dams have since enlarged the size of Caddo Lake on Big Cyprus Bayou and have created another popular recreation area, Lake O' the Pines, west of Jefferson.

North of Jefferson US 59 skirts the edge of Lake Wright Patman, one of the many manmade lakes that dot east Texas. **Texarkana** straddles the Arkansas-Texas border at a centuries-old crossroads of American Indian trails between the Mississippi Valley and the Southwest.

Gulf Coast

More than 300 miles long, the Texas Gulf Coast describes a narrow arc from Louisiana to Mexico. This shoreline gradually surrenders to the sea first as marsh, then as shallow bays opening onto the Gulf. Despite its length and several large bays, the Texas coast proved inhospitable to early explorers and settlers. Those who did not perish in shipwrecks in the treacherously narrow passages to the few natural harbors often were killed by marauding cannibals or vanquished by hurricanes.

The promise of Texas' unknown riches continued to inspire both pirates and entrepreneurs; by the late 19th century a number of ports dotted the coastline. Some of these survived, and those that did not became footnotes to the development that has made the area a playground for beach-hungry city dwellers.

Because of the nature of this coast, its major highway, actually parts of I-10, US 59 and US 77, is an inland route. For a closer look at Texas' early history and the popular resorts along the coast, SRs 35 and 87 are better routes.

The countryside around the cities of **Beaumont, Port Arthur** and **Orange** little resembles the bayous and salt marshes or the Spanish moss-draped woodlands of pine, magnolia and oaks that once dominated this area. The discovery of oil at the turn of the 20th century transformed this agricultural region of rice plantations and lumber mills into industrial boomtowns of refineries and chemical plants. Vestiges of the area's earlier landscape linger in Sea Rim State Park, which preserves 5,000 acres of saltwater marshes and beachfront along SR 87.

There are other refuges scattered along this section of the coast. At a point roughly midway down SR 87 and a few miles inland Anahuac National Wildlife Refuge offers sanctuary to waterfowl as well as the endangered red wolf, once common to Louisiana and east Texas. Beyond Crystal City the beach widens and remains relatively undeveloped except for a few houses and fishing camps.

From Port Bolivar a ferry crosses to **Galveston,** once known as the "Wall Street of the South." Galveston was Texas' wealthiest city until the hurricane of 1900 virtually destroyed it. Although the city was rebuilt, it never regained its position as a leading financial center and seaport, a role quickly filled by neighboring **Houston.** Galveston's restored historical structures and miles of beaches have transformed the city into a resort.

South of Galveston along SR 35 you travel through country whose rivers and creeks were once lined with cotton plantations. At the end of SR 288 and the intersection with SR 35 is Brazosport, a cluster of nine towns noted both for a large industrial complex and as a beach resort. Austin's colonists first entered Texas at this spot, many of them claiming the fertile lands along the Brazos River. These tracts and their wealthy cotton plantations became the envy of antebellum Texas.

So influential was this region that Texas' first capital was established at **West Columbia.** Little of that period remains except in such places as the Varner-Hogg Plantation State Historic Site and Brazos Bend State Park. The latter contains almost 5,000 acres of woodlands and Brazos River bottomlands, which closely resemble the country first settled by Austin's pioneers.

Beyond Bay City the level coastal prairie along SR 35 still feeds cattle as it did when such large spreads as the Pierce Ranch dominated the area. East of this route the little community of Matagorda was the first official port of entry for the Austin colony but since has faded to a quiet beach resort.

Across the bay only historical markers remain of Indianola, a port of immigration and supply depot for the Army until a hurricane in 1886 leveled the community. Misfortune also dogged the French explorer René-Robert Cavelier, Sieur de La Salle, who established a settlement in this vicinity in the late 17th century. La Salle died during an expedition into the interior, and the small fort he left behind soon was wiped out by American Indians.

South of Port Lavaca is Aransas National Wildlife Refuge, home to the endangered whooping crane and more species of birds than any other refuge along the coast. Bird-watching here and at other local refuges has made the nearby fishing village of **Rockport** a favorite colony for artists and tourists.

A scenic route off SR 35 crosses to **Port Aransas** and then follows a park road through Mustang Island State Park. At the south end of the park is the entrance to **Padre Island National Seashore,** which protects 65 miles of this barrier island. This long finger of sand stretches almost to the Mexican border, and only its northern and southern ends are developed. To reach South Padre Island you must retreat to **Corpus Christi** and

continue the journey through the open rangelands of south Texas.

North-central Texas

Dallas and Fort Worth are the urban links between east and west Texas. Drawing in highways from all directions, these twin metropolitan magnets hold sway over all of north-central Texas, giving rise to the term "Metroplex." From the Red River to Waco and from just west of Tyler to Mineral Wells this is a region of rolling wheat fields, woodlands and dazzling skyscrapers.

Although they appear to be stranded in a desert of grass, Fort Worth and Dallas both lie on a natural thoroughfare as important as the Mississippi River. Known as the Blackland Prairie, this relatively narrow corridor once was separated by two fingers of woodland and formed a grass highway that extended from San Antonio through Fort Worth and Dallas to the Red River. It was over this avenue that the legendary cattle drives moved from south Texas to the railheads of Kansas, bringing eventual prosperity to the two cities.

South of Fort Worth, I-35 roughly follows the earlier cattle trails as it travels across the level wheat fields of the Grand Prairie. West of **Hillsboro**

on SR 22 is Lake Whitney, one of the more popular of the many man-made lakes that encircle the Fort Worth and Dallas area.

Farther north near **Glen Rose** is Dinosaur Valley State Park, where dinosaur tracks are imprinted in stone on the bottom of the Paluxy River. Eons ago this area was a coastal swampland, and the footprints left behind by these animals have changed many of the traditional theories of paleontology.

Paralleling the Red River Valley along the Oklahoma border, US 82 is the small-town Main Street of north-central Texas. At its eastern end is **Paris,** one of the region's earliest settlements. Numerous small farms and towns are strung along this route as it moves west over the Blackland Prairie.

Northeast of **Bonham** you can see some of the open prairie that once dominated this region in the Caddo National Grassland. Farther west just north of **Sherman** the Hagerman National Wildlife Refuge straddles part of the huge Lake Texoma reservoir. The oil pumps that dot the refuge's uplands and marshes do not seem to bother the thousands of migratory waterfowl that stop at the reservoir every year.

Beyond Gainesville and the intersection with I-35 cultivation and irrigation have vanquished the waist-high grasses and herds of buffalo that once filled this landscape. Forty-niners in their rush for California were among the first to travel through this area, opening the way for eventual settlement.

Panhandle-Plains

The rolling grasslands of the Great Plains flow mile after mile from the Great Lakes and Canada deep into the heart of Texas. Covering the northern quarter of the state from the Oklahoma border to just south of **Abilene** and east to **Wichita Falls,** the Panhandle-Plains area could easily swallow almost all of the New England states.

In this region the prairie is broken into two general areas— the North Central, or Osage, Plains and the Llano Estacado.

Unlike the Llano Estacado the Osage Plains are gently rolling expanses dotted with mesquite. The Llano Estacado is an area so flat and devoid of landmarks that the Spanish explorer Francisco Vasquez de Coronado marked his passage with piles of bones and dung so he could find his way back through the sea of grass.

Running through the heart of the Llano from north to south is I-27. After leaving Amarillo it crosses SR 217, which heads east to Palo Duro Canyon. For centuries this canyon provided shelter and water for the Comanches, who used the vastness of the Llano as a sanctuary from pursuing enemies. The Army under Ronald Mackenzie finally defeated the Comanches in Palo Duro Canyon, opening the way for ranchers whose holdings covered millions of acres.

Today none of the terror that this immense tableland held for early explorers and settlers is apparent from I-27. Yet less than 120 years ago only the Comanches knew how to navigate the emptiness of this plain and where to find its few waterholes. Now the land unfolds in a rich pattern of irrigated wheat and cotton fields dotted with farmhouses and an occasional oil pump.

The interstate joins several other major highways in **Lubbock,** the commercial center of this region. One such road, US 84, runs in almost a straight line from northwest to southeast. After crossing the New Mexico/ Texas border it passes by one of the Panhandle's more unusual sights, the Muleshoe National Wildlife Refuge. Lying 20 miles south of **Muleshoe** on SR 214, it is one of the major refuges for majestic sandhill cranes that gather by the thousands from October to March.

A few miles beyond Lubbock, US 84 crosses FR 1729, which leads to colorful Yellowhouse Canyon and Buffalo Springs Lake. Descending the caprock onto the central plains US 87 meets I-20 just west of **Sweetwater.**

Although not readily apparent the central plains along this transcontinental link present subtle differences. To the south you can discern the low hills of the Callahan Divide. An opening in this barrier, Buffalo Gap, was a funnel for the buffalo and later the numerous cattle drives that converged on Abilene.

Heading east you will notice that the landscape becomes more

populated with frequent towns and cattle ranches. Beyond Abilene I-20 intersects US 283, which roughly traces the arc of the post-Civil War frontier.

Following US 283 north you come to Fort Griffin State Historic Site. In the 1870s as the Comanches and the Kiowas were displaced, a volatile mixture of buffalo hunters, outlaws and embittered Confederates took their place. The town they formed became one of Texas' wildest. Only a few stone ruins testify to its brawling past.

Farther north US 283 meets US 277, which travels through an area once known as the Mustang Prairie. In the late 19th century mustangers rounded up great herds of wild horses for northern markets. As US 283 draws closer to **Vernon** it crosses several rivers, some of which have been dammed to form large lakes.

Once in Vernon US 283 meets US 287, which follows the Red River Valley for most of its journey from **Amarillo** to Fort Worth. The valley provides a lush contrast to most of the Panhandle-Plains area. Shaded by trees and set off in the spring by a carpet of wildflowers, US 287 from Vernon to **Childress** travels through rich fields of wheat and cotton.

Beyond Childress the road rises slowly to meet the High Plains. Such legendary 19th-century cattle ranches as the Diamond Tail, JA and Mill Iron made Estelline a prosperous railhead.

On the eastern outskirts of Amarillo US 287 joins I-40. Many travelers' only glimpse of Texas is from this east-west interstate. To most, reaching Amarillo is a relief from the monotony of the prairie. A short distance north of Amarillo US 287 crosses the Canadian River, which has transformed the featureless plains into a series of colorful buttes and mesas known as the Canadian Breaks.

One of the surprises of this arid region is Lake Meredith **National Recreation Area.** Adjoining the lake is **Alibates Flint**

Quarries National Monument, where for centuries American Indians mined flint for tools and weapons. Beyond the breaks US 287 re-enters terrain that some say is the flattest in the country.

South Texas

Between San Antonio and the Rio Grande River lies a thorny pocket known as "brush country," a nettlesome assortment of bunch grass, prickly pear and other shrubs. Because of the aversion people have for this spiky landscape, south Texas, except for its perimeters along the Rio Grande and the coastal prairie north of the Nueces River, remains almost as sparsely settled as it was more than 300 years ago. Nevertheless, cattle have flourished since the Spanish laid out the first ranches in the 18th century.

Although not at the center of south Texas, San Antonio is the area's heart. Just as spokes radiate from the center of a wheel, so the earlier trails and modern interstates scatter to all directions from San

governors was the linchpin between Texas and Mexico; it extended as far north as the Nueces River. Presently the city is a rich mixture of cultures and history and a gateway to south Texas.

Three major highways leave San Antonio for south Texas, US 90 and Interstates 35 and 37. Heading almost directly west US 90 roughly follows the weathered features of the Balcones Escarpment. This geologic formation runs from **Del Rio** through San Antonio and forms the boundary between the western plains of the Edwards Plateau and the east.

Outside of San Antonio the highway passes through hills dotted with pecan and oak. Urbanization has changed much of the area, but **Castroville** still reflects the Old World influence of its early European settlers. Farther west the country becomes brush-covered hills that nurture a thriving population of sheep and goats. Besides goats and sheep the area also attracted Hollywood producers, who chose **Brackettville** for filming

thickets of prickly pear, chaparral and mesquite.

During the 18th century missions and haciendas brought thousands of cattle to this empty range, where they thrived on the sweet grass and the prickly pear. The Spanish *vaqueros* who tended these cattle were rarely equaled in their riding skill and ability to track these longhorns. Though Anglo-Americans displaced the Mexican cowboys in movie westerns, the brush country remains more Spanish than Anglo in its traditions and spirit.

In part this was due to the volatile mix of outlaws, cattle barons and self-proclaimed liberators that made the country below the Nueces River a no-man's land. Perhaps no one personified this better than Juan Cortina. Considered a cattle thief and outlaw by the Texas Rangers and the Army, Cortina frustrated all attempts to end his daring exploits.

Such feats as his capture of **Brownsville** and his raids on Anglo ranches made him a hero to his countrymen, whose ancient land grants were being usurped by the Anglos. Today Cortina would not recognize the stretch of the Rio Grande between Del Rio and Brownsville.

The dusty border towns of **Laredo** and Brownsville have become cities wedded to their Mexican counterparts, Nuevo Laredo and Matamoros.

Antonio. The city is a natural crossroads where three distinct geographic regions intersect. To the north is the central Texas Hill Country, to the east the fertile prairies of east Texas, and to the south the level chaparral country.

Partly because of this intersection of trails, the San Antonio of the Spanish missionaries and

the 1959 epic "The Alamo."

The Hollywood matinee idol in a white 10-gallon hat bears little resemblance to his real-life counterpart and would be out of place in this rugged environment. The region's heart unfurls in a gently rolling plain from either side of I-35 and is covered with

Shoppers looking for bargains have replaced the border raiders—both Anglo and Mexican—who once looked for a few untended cows or a fight.

Another change is the transformation of the alluvial plain below the Falcon Dam into acres and acres of citrus groves, pastureland and palm-lined fields of vegetables. Remnants of the junglelike lushness that once characterized this region along the Rio Grande survive in Bentsen-Rio Grande Valley State Park and Santa Ana National Wildlife Refuge. Lying just south of US 83, these two areas are considered by many to be the best areas in the country for birdwatching.

Skirting the edge of the coastal plain, US 281 heads north from the Rio Grande Valley over rolling grasslands dotted with mesquite and live oak. Despite the occasional oil well, cattle ranches still rule the range. One of the largest—so large it measures its holdings in Rhode Islands (3) rather than acres—is the King Ranch. The ranch lies east of the highway and north of Falfurrias.

Near Three Rivers and the Choke Canyon Reservoir US 281 crosses the Nueces River and joins I-37. The area between I-10 and I-37 once was some of the land grants ceded to Texas' first immigrants, among them Austin's settlers and a colony of Irish at San Patricio. This area of rolling farmland and small towns also was a battleground. Of the many battles fought in the area it was the ruthless execution of Col. James Fannin Jr.'s Texans at **Goliad** that spawned the legendary and victorious battle cry of independence at San Jacinto, "Remember Goliad!"

West Texas

If you asked a Texan where west Texas begins, you might get the simple reply, "where the east ends." Exactly where that might be is debatable, but one thing is certain—the familiar lushness of the east begins to dissolve slowly and then dramatically once you cross the 100th meridian. Beyond this invisible barrier, rainfall becomes more scarce and the landscape becomes more harsh as oaks and prairie grasses give way to greasewood and yucca.

From Del Rio to the south through San Angelo and **Big Spring** on the north and then west to New Mexico and the Rio Grande, west Texas is a world of

contrasts. It is a source of wealth as well as a place the Spanish christened *El Despoblado*, the place of desolation.

Lying just east of the 100th meridian the Concho River valley, paralleled by US 87, is a buffer between the more bounti-

ful east and the arid west. This area of broken hills dotted with pecan and oak once was a rich hunting ground for the American Indians, who found buffalos, wild turkeys and waterfowl in abundance. After the Civil War its plentiful water and grass made it a frontier crossroads.

Cattle trails heading north and wagon roads heading west converged on the confluence of the three forks of the Concho River. The Army had built Fort Concho as its forward base for raids against the Comanche. The restored fort currently lies in the midst of downtown San Angelo, a major wool market for the outlying sheep ranches.

North and west of San Angelo are the Twin Buttes and O.C. Fisher reservoirs, expanses of water unknown to early travelers, who depended on the few springs scattered across west Texas. One of these waterholes was in Big Spring, at the junction of I-20 and US 87. Originally the spring was a halfway

point on the Comanche War Trail, which swept down off the High Plains in a long arc to the Mexican border near Big Bend.

Until 20th-century oil strikes brought prosperity to Big Spring, efforts to capitalize on the area's wealth of short-grass prairie failed.

During the late 19th century English investors built ranches covering thousands of acres, but they soon foundered on a west Texas fact of life—drought.

Traveling west at night from Big Spring on I-20, you will see what appears to be the Emerald City, as the lights from refineries and the burning gas wells give **Midland** a fantastic appearance. Together with **Odessa,** some 20 miles farther west, these two cities sit atop the Permian Basin, a prehistoric sea now producing an ocean of oil. Unlike the short-lived dreams of the earlier cattle barons, the discovery of oil has made many Texans millionaires.

Leaving the forest of wellheads behind, I-20 soon enters the Chihuahuan Desert, which is rarely what you would expect. There are, of course, the expanses of sand dunes north of the interstate at Monahans Sandhills State Park. However, due to overgrazing, there also are huge stretches of tumbleweed, yucca and greasewood that have displaced much of the earlier short-grass prairie.

There also are surprises in this area. Forests of diminutive Harvard oak known as "shinnery" live along the desert's margin. Rich fields of cantaloupes are grown along the arid reaches of the the Pecos River, and groves of walnuts and maples can be found in the recesses of **Guadalupe Mountains National Park.**

Lying north of I-20 on the New Mexico border, the Guadalupe

water for travelers and animals as they journeyed across the desert expanses of the Trans-Pecos.

Modern I-10, as it rolls across arid rangeland from **Sonora** to Balmorhea, roughly connects many of west Texas' widely scattered waterholes. Some of the springs are now dry. Others have been diverted to irrigate fields, and the one at Balmorhea feeds an immense public swimming pool.

From Balmorhea SR 17 heads into the the Davis Mountains. Mountain wildflower-carpeted

midst of the latter are the roof-less adobes and crumbling walls of Shafter, once Texas' silver-mining capital.

Beyond Shafter the highway descends to a grassy tableland that drops quickly to the rock-strewn desert below. From Presidio to **Lajitas** FR 170 passes through scenic canyons of volcanic rock sculpted by the twisting course of the Rio Grande River. Crumbling Terlingua, once a booming mining town, has revived somewhat as the gateway to **Big Bend National Park.**

From Terlingua and Lajitas outfitters offer raft trips through the park's three major river canyons. Besides the spectacle of the canyons, the park encompasses a stunning variety of woodlands, desert plants and wildflowers that bloom in profusion from February through April. Park roads follow the earlier Comanche War Trail, now US 385, as it heads north over the Chisos Mountains and desert flats to Persimmon Gap in the Santiago Range.

Some miles from the gap in Marathon, US 385 joins US 90. This highway roughly follows the path of early settlers and Spanish explorers as they moved westward from Del Rio to El Paso. West of Marathon the road climbs steadily to **Alpine** in the Davis Mountains, finally joining I-10 in Van Horn.

Mountain range is one of several alpine oases rising out of the desert. From nearby US 180/62 the majestic bulk of El Capitan dominates the peaks in this range. This 8,000-foot sentinel is an uplifted coral reef that was once part of the same ocean that lies buried beneath Odessa and Midland.

Despite their barren appearance the mountains shelter a rich variety of hardwoods, evergreens and flowers. To the south, where I-20 and I-10 join, rise the Davis Mountains. Like the Guadalupes, the Davis Mountains were a vital source of

slopes, verdant grasslands and the cool waters of Limpia Creek offer a vivid contrast to the desert below. Beginning at the carefully preserved ruins of **Fort Davis,** SR 116 follows an indirect route over and around the canyons and mountains.

Descending from the Davis Mountains, SR 17 and US 67 follow a centuries-old trading route to **Presidio.** South of Marfa the road climbs through a jumble of broken terrain as it rises into the Cuesta del Burro and Chinati Mountains. In the

Heading east from Marathon, US 90 drops through a series of canyons and open rangeland sprinkled with sheep ranches. For most of the journey mountains hang on the southern horizon until the road enters the Pecos River Canyon. Once across the Pecos River, you have again crossed the mythical barrier between east and west.

Points of Interest

ABILENE (D-7) pop. 115,930, elev. 1,726′

For centuries the Central Plains around Abilene were filled only with buffalo. In the late 1870s cattle replaced the buffalo and a tent city soon took shape. The efforts of Col. C.W. Merchant convinced Jay Gould's Texas and Pacific Railway to route its tracks through the settlement, which was named Abilene after the Kansas cattle boomtown. Abilene soon became a major shipping point for cattle.

Livestock still plays a role in the economy of this city, which has grown into an urban center supporting such diverse industries as petroleum refining, manufacturing and the production of musical instruments. The city also has three universities, a symphony orchestra and a medical cultural center.

Nearby recreational and historic areas include the ruins of Fort Phantom Hill, 10 miles northeast on FM 600, and 621-acre Abilene State Park, 16 miles southwest via FM 89 (see Recreation Chart and the AAA South Central CampBook). The guardhouse, commissary, powder magazine and several chimneys are all that remain of Fort Phantom Hill, once part of a string of forts along the Texas frontier.

Abilene Convention and Visitors Bureau: 1101 N. First St., P.O. Box 2281, Abilene, TX 79601-2281; phone (325) 676-2556 or (800) 727-7704.

ABILENE ZOO is at 2070 Zoo Ln. in Nelson Park, SR 36 and Loop 322. Animals of the North American Plains are compared to those of similar habitat in Africa. The zoo houses more than 500 amphibians, birds, mammals and reptiles. Allow 1 hour minimum. Daily 9-5 (also Thurs. 5-9, Memorial Day-Labor Day); closed Jan. 1, Thanksgiving and Dec. 25. Admission $3; over 59 and ages 3-12, $2. DS, MC, VI. Phone (325) 676-6085.

[SAVE] **GRACE MUSEUM** is at 102 Cypress St. Three museums are housed at the former Grace Hotel, including a fine arts collection, local history exhibits and hands-on activities for children Tues.-Sat. 10-5 (also Thurs. 5-8:30); closed major holidays. Admission $3; ages 4-12, $1; free to all Thurs. 5-8:30. MC, VI. Phone (325) 673-4587.

ALAMO (I-8) pop. 14,760, elev. 101′

Incorporated in 1924 and named for the Alamo Land and Sugar Co., Alamo produces vegetables and citrus.

SANTA ANA NATIONAL WILDLIFE REFUGE is 7 mi. s. on FM 907, then .25 mi. e. on US 281. This 2,000-acre refuge harbors birds rare to southern Texas, including the great kiskadee, chachalaca, hook-billed kite and green jay. Twelve miles of walking trails weave through the refuge, and an interpretive 90-minute tram ride is offered. Visitor center daily 8-4. Trails dawn-dusk. Tram runs three times daily, late Nov.-late Apr. Closed Thanksgiving and Dec. 25. Entrance fee $3 per private vehicle. Tram $3; under 12, $1. Phone (956) 784-7500.

ALBANY (D-7) pop. 1,921, elev. 1,412′

Settled on the north fork of Hubbard Creek, Albany was a supply point on the Western Trail to Dodge City. The surrounding area is known as the home of the Herefords. The town also is the home of the Albany News, which was established in 1883 and contains a frontier news file open for public inspection. The 1883 courthouse is the oldest still in use in Texas. Ledbetter Picket House, 24 S. Main St., is a dog-run cabin that was a site for supplying salt to the Confederacy.

Albany Chamber of Commerce: P.O. Box 185, Albany, TX 76430; phone (325) 762-2525.

THE OLD JAIL ART CENTER is at 201 S. Second St. Housed in a former 1877 jail, the center features pre-Columbian displays; an Asian collection that includes Chinese tomb figures; and works by American and European artists. Allow 1 hour minimum. Tues.-Sat. 10-5, Sun. 2-5; closed major holidays. Donations. Phone (325) 762-2269.

ALIBATES FLINT QUARRIES NATIONAL MONUMENT (A-5)

Alibates Flint Quarries National Monument is 34 miles northeast of Amarillo off SR 136 on the south shore of Lake Meredith (see place listing p. 121). The land at this 1,000-acre site is rich in flint, which occurs in a variety of colors and was used

---

DID YOU KNOW

The name Texas derives from the Native American word "tejas" meaning friendship.

for toolmaking and barter by prehistoric cultures up to 12,000 years ago. The area around the monument was the source of many ancient implements discovered throughout the Southwest and Great Plains.

Park headquarters in Fritch open daily 8-4:30, Memorial Day-Labor Day; Mon.-Fri. 8-4:30, rest of year. Closed holidays. Flint quarries can be visited only on a 1-mile ranger-guided walking tour; reservations are required. Free. For more information contact Alibates Flint Quarries National Monument, 419 E. Broadway, P.O. Box 1460, Fritch, TX 79036; phone (806) 857-3151.

ALPINE (F-4) pop. 5,786, elev. 4,481'

Alpine, with its valley location in the heart of Big Bend, resembles the towns and villages dotting European mountain regions. The Texas Alps, like their namesake, attract throngs of outdoor enthusiasts who use Alpine as a base for mountain and desert exploration.

Recreational opportunities range from hiking in the area's large parks to hunting in nearby canyons. Big Bend National Park *(see place listing p. 64)* is a 2-hour drive to the south.

Kokernot Springs, on the Kokernot Lodge grounds, is the site of the Burgess Water Hole, which was used by pioneers, immigrants, stagecoach passengers and others to quench their thirst during desert passages.

Alpine Chamber of Commerce: 106 N. 3rd St., Alpine, TX 79830; phone (432) 837-2326 or (800) 561-3735.

MUSEUM OF THE BIG BEND is on the Sul Ross State University campus facing US 90. Exhibits present the artifacts and history of the Big Bend region, including a reconstructed general store and a children's discovery center. Tues.-Sat. 9-5, Sun. 1-5. Donations. Phone (432) 837-8143.

ALTO (D-10) pop. 1,190, elev. 433'

In the heart of the tomato-growing redland belt, Alto, derived from the Spanish word for "high," is the highest point between the Angelina and Neches rivers.

CADDOAN MOUNDS STATE HISTORIC SITE is 6 mi. s.w. on SR 21. The southwesternmost ceremonial center of the Moundbuilder culture, this settlement was occupied approximately A.D. 800-1200. An interpretive center offers exhibits about the site, which now consists of a burial mound, two temple mounds and a borrow pit. Guided tours are available. Allow 1 hour, 30 minutes minimum. Thurs.-Mon. 9-4; closed Thanksgiving and Dec. 24-25. Admission $2, over 65 and students with ID $1. DS, MC, VI. Phone (936) 858-3218.

ALVIN (F-10) pop. 21,413, elev. 51'

Founded in 1876 as a stop along the railroad route connecting Galveston and Richmond, Alvin is named for its founder Alvin Morgan. The city survived despite hurricanes in 1900 and 1915 and a devastating fire in 1902. Diversified industries sustain the city's economy.

Alvin Tourist and Visitor Information Center: 105 W. Willis, P.O. Box 2028, Alvin, TX 77512; phone (281) 331-3944 or (800) 331-4063.

[SAVE] **BAYOU WILDLIFE PARK** is 3 mi. e. of SR 35 on FM 517. The 86-acre park features a tram ride that lets visitors view and feed rare and endangered animals in natural settings. A petting zoo and picnic facilities are on the grounds. Allow 2 hours minimum. Daily 10-4, Mar.-July; Tues.-Sun. 10-4, rest of year. Closed Dec 25. Last tram leaves 30 minutes prior to closing. Hours may vary; phone ahead. Admission (Mar.-July) $9.95; ages 3-11, $5.50. Admission (rest of year) $8.95; ages 3-11, $5. Phone (281) 337-6376.

AMARILLO (B-5) pop. 173,627, elev. 3,672'

Amarillo was settled in 1887 as cattle raisers, buffalo hunters and pioneers pushed west across the Texas panhandle. The name, which means "yellow" in Spanish, comes from the gold-colored soil along Amarillo Creek. Situated at the intersection of the Fort Worth & Denver Railroad and the Atchison, Topeka & Santa Fe, Amarillo was a railhead for the great cattle drives of the late 1800s. Cattle feeding and shipping remain major industries. The Amarillo Livestock Auction, held every Tuesday, is one of the nation's largest cattle auctions.

West of the city, Cadillac Ranch consists of 10 cars found nose-down in a working grain field along I-40. The roadside sculpture, called the "Hood Ornament of Route 66," constitutes a pop-art homage to the fins that characterized automobile design in the 1950s. The undulation of the wheat reminded the artist of ocean waves; hence the Cadillacs completed the picture with what resembled dolphin fins. The work is part of the collection of Amarillo's millionaire art fancier Stanley Marsh III, noted for his patronage of the pop-art movement of the late 1960s and early 1970s.

The flavor of the West can be sampled on Cowboy Mornings/Evenings, along with breakfast from a chuck wagon after a ride across the plains to the rim of Palo Duro Canyon or dinner with a wagon ride, cowboy roping and branding, from April through October; phone (800) 658-2613.

Amarillo Convention & Visitors Council: 1000 S. Polk St., P.O. Box 9480, Amarillo, TX 79101; phone (806) 374-1497 or (800) 692-1338.

Shopping areas: Major shopping centers include Westgate, off I-40W on the south side of the city between Coulter and Soncy streets; and Wolflin, at the southeast corner of I-40W and Georgia Street. Antiques can be found along historic Route 66 and Sixth Street between Georgia and Western sts.

AMARILLO BOTANICAL GARDEN is off I-40 Bus. Loop (Coulter exit) at 1400 Streit Dr., next to Don Harrington Discovery Center. The garden covers 4 acres of the 51-acre Medical Center Park and includes fragrance plantings and changing exhibits. Blooming season is mid-May to late October. Tues.-Fri. 10-5, Sat.-Sun. 1-5. Free. Phone (806) 352-6513.

AMARILLO MUSEUM OF ART is at 2200 S. Van Buren St. on the Amarillo College campus. Six galleries are devoted to changing exhibits of the visual arts. Tues.-Fri. 10-5, Sat.-Sun. 1-5. Free. Phone (806) 371-5050.

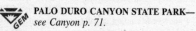 **AMERICAN QUARTER HORSE HERITAGE CENTER & MUSEUM** is off I-40 exit 72A to Quarter Horse Dr. Interactive exhibits, artwork, a multimedia presentation and live demonstrations tell the story of the American Quarter Horse from its early racing days in Colonial Virginia to modern ranching in the Southwest. Allow 1 hour minimum. Mon.-Sat. 9-5, Sun. noon-5, Mar.-Nov.; Mon.-Sat. 9-5, rest of year. Closed Jan. 1, Thanksgiving and Dec. 24-25. Admission $4; over 55, $3.50; ages 6-18, $2.50. AX, DS, MC, VI. Phone (806) 376-5181 or (888) 209-8322.

DON HARRINGTON DISCOVERY CENTER is off I-40 Bus. Loop (Coulter exit) in Harrington Regional Medical Center Park at 1200 Streit Dr. The center has hands-on exhibits, aquariums and a planetarium with changing presentations. **Note:** Exhibits will be closed for renovation through Sept. 2003; planetarium will remain open. Displays Tues.-Sat. 10-5, Sun. 1-5. Planetarium shows are given on the hour Tues.-Sat. at 11 and 1-3, Sun. 1-3. Closed Jan. 1, Easter, Thanksgiving and Dec. 25. Admission (includes planetarium) $5. During renovation, free planetarium shows will be offered Sat.-Sun. at 1 and 3. Phone (806) 355-9547.

International Helium Centennial Time Columns Monument is on the grounds of the Don Harrington Discovery Center. This 60-foot stainless steel monument commemorates the discovery of helium in 1868. Erected in 1968, the monument contains sealed time capsules filled with data related to helium as well as a $10 savings account deposit that will be worth $1 quintillion when the capsule is opened in the year 2968. Free.

FIREWATER WATER PARK is off I-40 exit 74 (Whittaker Rd.), then .3 mi w. to 1415 Sunrise Dr. Visitors to this 14-acre park can race down Sensational Sidewinder and Speed Slides, surf at Whitewater Waves, float down the Lazy River and play in the interactive Kiddie Pool. The Bucket Dump Tower holds 750 gallons of water. Beach and grass volleyball courts, an arcade, picnic facilities and food are available.

Allow 5 hours minimum. Mon.-Sat. 11-7, Sun. noon-6, June 1 to mid-Aug.; Sat. 11-6, Sun. noon-6 in May and late Aug. Admission $16.95; under 55 inches tall, $14.95; ages 3-5, $9.95; over age 60, $8.95. MC, VI. Phone (806) 342-3473 or (866) 234-3473.

PALO DURO CANYON STATE PARK— see Canyon p. 71.

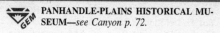 **PANHANDLE-PLAINS HISTORICAL MUSEUM**—see Canyon p. 72.

THOMPSON PARK is off US 287N exit 24th Ave. to 2600 Dumas Dr. Encompassing 610 acres, the park includes a children's zoo, a 36-hole golf course, a small lake, picnic areas, ball parks and a section for flying model airplanes. Allow 2 hours minimum. Dawn-midnight. Phone (806) 378-3036.

Amarillo Zoo is at 2400 N. Polk St. in Thompson Park. Herds of bison graze on a 14-acre range in the zoo, which displays animals indigenous to the area. A small playground is at the center of the zoo. Tues.-Sun. 9:30-5:30. Donations. Phone (806) 381-7911.

[SAVE] **Wonderland Park** is at 2601 Dumas Dr. in Thompson Park. More than 30 rides and attractions are featured, including the Texas Tornado double-loop roller coaster and the Shoot the Chute water ride. Other amusements include an 18-hole miniature golf course, arcades, children's rides, a pirate ship and the Fantastic Journey haunted house. Food is available.

Mon.-Fri. 7-10:30 p.m., Sat.-Sun. 1-10, June-Aug.; Sat.-Sun. 1-8, Apr.-May. Regular admission $3, tickets $1.50 (all rides require one ticket except the Texas Tornado, which requires two tickets). Miniature golf $3.50. Semi-inclusive admission (excluding Texas Tornado, Fantastic Journey and miniature golf) Sat.-Sun. $16.95, Mon.-Fri. $10.95. Phone (806) 383-3344 or (800) 383-4712.

AMISTAD NATIONAL RECREATION AREA (G-5)

Amistad National Recreation Area is northwest of Del Rio via US 90. The 67,000-acre area and reservoir are an outgrowth of the Amistad Dam water-storage project, a joint venture of the United States and Mexico. The boundaries of the area extend 74 miles up the Rio Grande and portions of the Pecos and Devils rivers. More than 6 miles long, the dam creates 85-mile-long Lake Amistad.

This tract of land and water was the prehistoric home of American Indians. Excavations have uncovered more than 300 sites. Primitive campsites are at San Pedro Flats on Spur 454, Governor's Landing on Spur 349 and at two other points, one along US 277N and one along Spur 406. Houseboats can be rented from Lake Amistad Resort and Marina; phone (830) 774-4157 or (800) 255-5561.

Fishing is possible all year. A Mexican license must be obtained for fishing in Mexican waters. Hunting is permitted only in designated areas. Shotgun hunting for rabbits, dove and quail as well as ducks and other waterfowl is permitted. Other hunting is only by bow and arrow and is restricted to deer, javelinas and turkeys. Rifles and pistols are not permitted.

The recreation area is open all year. The park headquarters on US 90, west of Del Rio, is open Mon.-Fri. 8-5; closed holidays. For further information write the Superintendent, Amistad National

Recreation Area, National Park Service, HCR 3, Box 5J, Del Rio, TX 78840; phone (830) 775-7491. *See Recreation Chart and the AAA South Central CampBook.*

ANAHUAC—*see Houston p. 116.*

ANGELINA NATIONAL FOREST (E-10)

Elevations in the forest range from 100 ft. on the Neches River below the Sam Rayburn Reservoir Dam to 406 ft. at Moss Hill. Refer to AAA maps for additional elevation information.

Angelina National Forest surrounds Sam Rayburn Reservoir in east Texas, off US 69 east of Lufkin. The forest's 153,179 acres encompass fragments of the "Pineywoods" region, which was heavily logged early in the 20th century. Towering pines and hardwoods have returned, sheltering deer, squirrels and occasional turkeys.

Sam Rayburn Reservoir is the largest reservoir wholly within the state, and its 560-mile shoreline is dotted with campgrounds and marinas. Plentiful bass and catfish make it popular with anglers.

Relics of the region's logging days can be seen along the 5.5-mile Sawmill Trail. The trail, connecting Bouton Lake Recreation Area with Boykin Springs Recreation Area, follows the Neches River past vestiges of an old tram line, logging camps and ruined bridges. Two other notable areas are the Turkey Hill and Upland Island wilderness areas.

For information contact the district ranger station; phone (936) 897-1068, or write the Forest Supervisor, 701 N. First St., Lufkin, TX 75901. *See Recreation Chart.*

ARLINGTON (D-9) pop. 332,969, elev. 617'

The city of Arlington grew out of a trading post established at Marrow Bone Springs in accordance with the Indian Peace Council of 1843. Originally named Hayter, the town was renamed for Robert E. Lee's hometown in Virginia. Upon the arrival of the Texas and Pacific Railway in 1876, Arlington became a market center for surrounding towns, remaining an agricultural community until after World War II. The construction of a General Motors assembly plant in 1951 spurred commercial expansion; city population increased by more than 75 percent during the 1970s. Alcohol prohibition went into effect in 1902, and Arlington is still a dry town today.

Arlington Visitor Center: 1905 E. Randol Mill Rd., Arlington, TX 76011-8214; phone (817) 461-3888 or (800) 342-4305.

[SAVE] **LEGENDS OF THE GAME BASEBALL MUSEUM & LEARNING CENTER** is off I-30 exit 28B (eastbound) or exit 29 (westbound), then s. following signs to 1000 Ballpark Way. The museum is part of the 270-acre metroplex at The Ballpark in Arlington, home of the Texas Rangers.

Baseball artifacts dating to the late 1800s include equipment, cards, uniforms, and photographs. Interactive exhibits demonstrate the legacy and science of baseball. Guided 50-minute tours of The Ballpark are available.

Allow 1 hour minimum. Museum open Mon.-Sat. 9-5:30, Sun. 11-4, Apr.-Oct.; Tues.-Sat. 9-4, Sun. 11-4, rest of year. Ballpark tours are offered Mon.-Sat. 9-4, Sun. noon-4 on non-game days; Mon.-Sat. 9-1 on game days. Museum admission $6; over 61 and college students with ID $5; ages 4-18, $4. Combination ticket (including Ballpark tour) $10; over 61 and college students with ID $8; ages 4-18, $6. Phone (817) 273-5098.

RIVER LEGACY LIVING SCIENCE CENTER is 1.5 mi. n. of I-30 on Cooper St., then e. to 703 N.W. Green Oaks Blvd. Interactive exhibits challenge visitors to explore and discover. Two animal rehabilitation compounds are home to reptiles, amphibians, mammals, arachnids and fish. Allow 1 hour, 30 minutes minimum. Tues.-Sat. 9-5, Sun. 1-5; closed major holidays. Admission $2; ages 2-18, $1. MC, VI. Phone (817) 860-6752.

[SAVE] **SIX FLAGS HURRICANE HARBOR** is at 1800 Lamar Blvd. just n. of I-30 between exits SR 360 and FM 157. Among the activities at this 47-acre water theme park are a wave pool and numerous waterslides, such as Black Hole, Sea Wolf and Shotgun Falls. Visitors can explore the treasures of Hooks Lagoon, a five-story interactive treehouse; catch a wave on Surf Rider, a surfboarding experience in the Boogie Beach area; or float on park-supplied inner tubes on the Lazy River, which flows at 2 mph.

Allow 6 hours minimum. Park open daily at 10:30, late May to mid-Aug.; Sat.-Sun. and holidays at 10:30, mid-Aug. through Labor Day. Closing times vary; phone ahead. Admission $27.99, over 54 and under 48 inches tall $17.99, under age 3 free. Phone ahead to confirm rates. Parking $7. Preferred parking $10. Glass containers and alcohol are prohibited. AX, DS, MC, VI. Phone (817) 265-3356.

[GEM] [SAVE] **SIX FLAGS OVER TEXAS** is s.w. at jct. I-30 and SR 360 exit 30, following signs. The 205-acre landscaped theme park depicts Texas under the flags of the Confederate States of America, France, Mexico, the Republic of Texas, Spain and the United States. Each area has food and entertainment in keeping with its theme.

More than 100 rides, attractions and shows include Titan, a steel coaster that reaches speeds of up to 85 mph as the bright orange trains zip through spirals, plunges, helixes and a 120-foot-long, totally dark tunnel; Mr. Freeze, which thrills riders in forward and reverse; a 200-foot parachute drop; the Texas Giant, a 14-story roller coaster; Roaring Rapids, a river-rafting adventure; Wildcatter, offering the sensation of a 10-story free fall; and Runaway Mountain, a roller coaster that travels in the dark. Gotham City is the appropriate home of

Batman the Ride supercoaster. Space Shuttle America provides the opportunity to experience space travel on a simulated shuttle trip to the moon, including the excitement of warp speed and meteor attacks.

Music Mill features big-name entertainment in season. Looney Tunes USA is an area devoted to children and their parents. The Silver Star Carousel is restored in period. The park can be seen via a turn-of-the-20th-century-style train; a 300-foot oil derrick tower also provides a good view. Picnic facilities, food and air-conditioned kennels are available.

Allow 8 hours minimum. Park open daily, June 1 to mid-Aug. and mid-Dec. to late Dec.; Sat.-Sun. and Labor Day, late Mar.-May 31, mid-Aug. through Oct. 31 and early Dec. to mid-Dec. Hours vary; phone ahead to confirm schedule. All-inclusive admission $39.99, over 54, physically impaired and under 49 inches tall $24.99, under age 3 free. Two-day pass $44.99, over 54, physically impaired and under 49 inches tall $40.99. Parking $9; preferred parking $12. AAA members save 10 percent on select in-park dining and merchandise. Check at the park's Guest Relations window for details. AX, DS, MC, VI. Phone (817) 530-6000.

ATHENS—see Dallas p. 85.

AUSTIN (F-8) pop. 656,562, elev. 511′

See map page 60.

In the fall of 1839, Republic of Texas president Mirabeau Lamar charged a delegation of five horsemen with finding the best place for the capital. Their choice was the small, remote community of Waterloo on the north bank of the Colorado where the river cascades down the Balcones Escarpment. The next year the legislature confirmed the selection and renamed it in honor of Stephen F. Austin, colonizer of the first American settlement in Texas.

Growth during Austin's first decade was sporadic. A Mexican invasion, the danger of American Indian raids and the town's isolation discouraged many settlers. More important than these risks was Sam Houston's opposition to Austin. During his presidency he moved the capital to Houston and later to Washington-on-the-Brazos.

The people of Austin didn't take all this capital-moving lying down. In late 1842 Sam Houston sent a contingent of Texas Rangers to retrieve government documents still being housed in Austin. A hotel keeper named Angelina Eberly saw the men loading a wagon and fired a cannon in their direction, which didn't stop them but did alert the rest of the town. A group of determined citizens caught up with Houston's men and took back the papers without bloodshed, thus concluding an episode in Texas history known as the Archive War.

It took two statewide voter referendums to finally settle the matter in Austin's favor. After the Civil War, the city's struggles as a frontier capital ended with the coming of the railroad and the subsequent founding of the University of Texas.

Although the city's skyline today is dominated by contemporary glass-and-steel office towers and high-rise hotels, two longtime landmarks still stand tall: the 1888 Texas State Capitol *(see listing p. 62)*, the dome of which rises higher than even the U.S. Capitol's, and the picturesque University of Texas Clock Tower.

Authorized in 1882 and completed in 1888, the Capitol was plagued by controversy from the beginning, not the least of which was the issue of who actually owned it. In fact, the state still has no clear title to the grounds, despite having paid for the land three times.

Rising above the sprawling University of Texas campus *(see listing p. 62)* just a few blocks north of the Capitol, the U.T. Clock Tower serves as helpful point of reference to new students navigating the streets of this virtual city within a city. The Beaux Arts skyscraper was completed in the late 1930s and contains a 56-bell carillon, which is played on Mondays, Wednesdays and Fridays. The tower's observation deck is open to visitors but only by way of guided tours; reservations can be made at the university's Union Building.

Among the city's other architectural landmarks are the Lester E. Palmer Events Center, a premier facility for meetings and exhibits in Town Lake Park; the State Archives and Library Building, with its displays of rare documents and an immense mural chronicling Texas history; and the 17,000-seat Frank Erwin Special Events Center.

The city bills itself as "live music capital of the world," no idle boast considering the numerous musical events held year-round. What's more, downtown's East Sixth Street is packed with bars, restaurants and intimate music venues where everything from blues to country to punk rock can be heard. The Warehouse District, which is bounded roughly by Sixth and Third streets on the north and south, Guadalupe Street on the west and Congress Avenue on the east, is another entertainment hotspot.

Although downtown Austin is compact and can be traversed on foot, the free 'dillo (short for armadillo) trolley makes sightseeing even easier. The service links the Capitol Complex, University of Texas campus and downtown commercial areas with free park-and-ride lots; phone (512) 474-1200 for route information.

Winged creatures have found the city hospitable as well; Austin is home to one of the largest urban bat populations in North America. More than 1.5 million Mexican free-tailed bats have taken up residence beneath the Congress Avenue Bridge since its 1980 restoration. Emerging each night, they eat up to 30,000 pounds of insects, including agricultural pests. Bat flights can be observed just before sunset from March through November, with peak viewing in late summer. An observation area is south of the bridge; phone (512) 416-5700, ext. 3636 for flight times.

In the shadow of the "bat bridge" is a recreation trail that stretches more than 10 miles along both shores of Town Lake. Popular with bicyclists and joggers, the path is lined with benches, shelters and water fountains and even has its own bridge spanning the lake. Other recreation options immediately at hand include canoes, kayaks and paddleboats, which are available for rent along the lakefront. Visitors are likely to notice teams sculling across Town Lake, which is a popular training spot for collegiate crews.

Somewhat farther afield are the other Highland Lakes. Austin's Town Lake is just the first in a 163-mile chain formed by a series of dams on the Colorado River. Outside of the city's core are lakes Austin, Travis, Marble Falls, LBJ, Inks and Buchanan. Boating and water skiing are two of the many activities possible there.

Another outdoor activity frequently recommended by locals is a dip in Barton Springs Pool within Zilker Metropolitan Park *(see listing p. 63)*, which can be especially pleasant on a summer day in Texas. For views of the city and the surrounding hill country, Mount Bonnell, 1 mile past the west end of 35th Street, can't be beat. But be prepared for a bit of a climb: it takes 99 steps to reach the top.

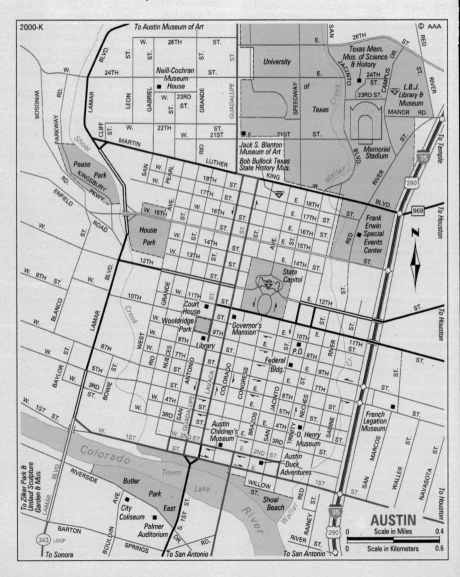

Austin Convention and Visitors Bureau: 201 E. 2nd St., Austin, TX 78701; phone (512) 474-5171 or (800) 926-2282.

Self-guiding tours: Brochures outlining historic areas are available from the convention and visitors bureau.

Shopping areas: The west end of Sixth Street contains shops, galleries and restaurants. Of historical interest is the Old Bakery and Emporium at 1006 Congress Ave. Area malls include the Arboretum, 10000 Research Blvd.; Barton Creek Square, 2901 Capital of Texas Hwy.; and Highland Mall, 6001 Airport Blvd.

[SAVE] **AUSTIN CHILDREN'S MUSEUM** is at 201 Colorado St. This hands-on museum for preschool and grade school children offers activity galleries, changing and touring exhibits, workshops, performances and demonstrations. Visitors can shop in a pint-sized grocery store, climb an indoor playscape or step onto the Austin Kiddie Limits Stage and sing with their favorite Texas musicians. Allow 1 hour minimum. Tues.-Sat. 10-5 (also Wed. 5-8), Sun. noon-5; closed Jan. 1, July 4, Thanksgiving and Dec. 25. Admission $4.50, under 2 free; free to all Wed. 5-8 and Sun. 4-5. MC, VI. Phone (512) 472-2499.

AUSTIN DUCK ADVENTURES departs from the Austin Visitors Center at 201 E. 2nd St. This 75-minute narrated tour aboard an amphibious military landing vehicle includes the Texas State Capitol, the Governor's Mansion, The University of Texas at Austin, Sixth Street and historic Congress Avenue and a cruise on Lake Austin.

Tours are given Mon.-Tues. at 2, Wed.-Fri. at 11 and 2, Sat. at 10:15, noon, 2 and 4, Sun. at 11, 2 and 4; closed holidays. Schedule may change; phone for departure times. Admission $18.50; over 64 and students with ID, $16.50; ages 3-12, $13. AX, DS, MC, VI. Phone (512) 477-5274.

AUSTIN MUSEUM OF ART includes the downtown site at 823 Congress Ave. and the Laguna Gloria site at 3809 W. 35th St. The museum's downtown site, the interim location until a permanent facility is completed in 2004, presents traveling exhibitions, hands-on educational activities and public programs. Street parking is limited.

Visitors to the museum's original home, Laguna Gloria, can stroll the 12-acre grounds overlooking Lake Austin. **Note:** Driscoll Villa, the Italianate-style estate, is closed for renovation; the sculpture garden and art school will remain open.

Allow 1 hour minimum. Tues.-Sat. 10-6 (also Thurs. 6-8), Sun. noon-5; closed holidays. Admission $5, over 55 and students with ID $4, under 12 free; $1 to all Thurs. AX, MC, VI. Phone (512) 495-9224 for downtown or (512) 458-8191 for Laguna Gloria.

AUSTIN STEAM TRAIN EXCURSIONS departs from the Cedar Park Depot, 15 mi. n. on I-35 to exit 256, 8 mi. w. on FM 1431, then s. on Quest Blvd. Sightseeing excursions include the Hill Country Flyer, a 7-hour round trip through the hill country to the town of Burnet (*see place listing p. 71*), where shopping and dining are available; the 3-hour Bertram Flyer; and themed trips aboard the Twilight Flyer. The River City Flyer, boarding at Austin's Plaza Saltillo at E. Fifth and Comal streets, offers a 90-minute train ride through historic East Austin.

Hill Country Flyer departs Sat.-Sun. at 10, Mar.-May; Sat.-Sun. at 1:30 in Dec.; Sat. at 10, Jan.-Feb. and Oct.-Nov. Closed Dec. 25. Bertram Flyer departs Sat. at 10, June-Sept. River City Flyer departs from Plaza Saltillo Sun. at 1, June-Nov. Hill Country Flyer fare $25-$40; over 62, $22-$36; ages 3-13, $15-$24. Bertram Flyer $15-$30; over 62, $12-$27; ages 3-13, $10-$22. River City Flyer $12-$26; over 62, $11-$23; ages 3-13, $8-$16. Reservations are recommended. Twilight Flyers run throughout the year; phone for schedule and fares. AX, DS, MC, VI. Phone (512) 477-8468.

[GEM] **BOB BULLOCK TEXAS STATE HISTORY MUSEUM** is off I-35 exit Martin Luther King Jr. Blvd., then w. to 1800 Congress Ave. This sprawling complex explores three themes: Land, Identity and Opportunity. Three floors of interactive exhibits chronicle the region's first inhabitants and early explorers; the fight for independence and statehood; and 20th-century contributions to space, industry and technology.

The Texas Spirit Theater re-creates the Galveston hurricane, an oil gusher and a rocket launch at Johnson Space Center, complete with such special effects as moving seats, wind and smoke. A 400-seat IMAX theater presents large-format films. Food is available.

Allow 3 hours minimum. Mon.-Sat. 9-6, Sun. noon-6; closed Jan. 1, Easter, Thanksgiving and Dec. 24-25. Admission $5; over 64, $4.25; under 19 free. Combination ticket (including IMAX and Texas Spirit theaters) $12.50; over 64, $10; under 19, $6. Parking $3. AX, DS, MC, VI. Phone (512) 936-8746 or (866) 369-7108.

ELISABET NEY MUSEUM is at 304 E. 44th St. near the Ave. H intersection. The home and studio of the 19th-century sculptor now contains collections of her plaster and marble portrait sculptures and statuary. Allow 30 minutes minimum. Wed.-Sat. 10-5, Sun. noon-5; closed holidays. Free. Phone (512) 458-2255.

[SAVE] **FRENCH LEGATION MUSEUM** is 1 blk. e. of I-35 at E. Seventh and San Marcos sts. This restored 1841 structure, said to be the only building in Texas erected by a foreign government, features period antiques and an authentic early French kitchen complete with copper pots and period pewter utensils. Allow 1 hour minimum. Tues.-Sun. 1-5. Admission $4, senior citizens $3, teachers and students with ID $2. Phone (512) 472-8180.

GOVERNOR'S MANSION is at 1010 Colorado St. This 1856 Southern mansion, with its white-columned facade, occupies an entire city block.

Tours depart every 20 minutes Mon.-Thurs. 10-noon, except during events; closed holidays. Hours may vary; phone ahead. Free. Phone (512) 463-5516 for recorded information.

SAVE **LADY BIRD JOHNSON WILDFLOWER CENTER** is 10 mi. s. on Loop 1, then e. to 4801 La Crosse Ave. Dedicated to promoting education about the environmental necessity, economic value and natural beauty of native plants, this 179-acre botanical garden features a rooftop rainwater-collection system. Highlights include a visitors gallery, observation tower, nature trails and display gardens. The blooming season peaks in April and May. Food is available, and picnicking is permitted.

Allow 1 hour, 30 minutes minimum. Grounds open daily 9-5:30, mid-Mar. to Apr. 30; Tues.-Sun. 9-5:30, rest of year. Visitors gallery open Tues.-Sat. 9-4, Sun. 1-4. Guided tours are available by reservation. Admission Apr.-May $7, senior citizens and students with ID $5.50, under 5 free. Admission rest of year $5, senior citizens and students with ID $4, under 5 free. AX, DS, MC, VI. Phone (512) 292-4200.

NEILL-COCHRAN MUSEUM HOUSE is at 2310 San Gabriel St. The furniture in this restored 1855 Greek Revival house reflects 19th century eclectic tastes. Allow 30 minutes minimum. Wed.-Sun. 2-5; closed Jan. 1, Easter, July 4, Thanksgiving and Dec. 25. Admission $2. Phone (512) 478-2335.

O. HENRY MUSEUM is 3 blks. w. of I-35 at 409 E. Fifth St. This Queen Anne-style cottage was the 1893-95 residence of William Sydney Porter, the short story writer known as O. Henry. Many of the author's personal effects are displayed. Allow 30 minutes minimum. Wed.-Sun. noon-5; closed Jan. 1, July 4, Thanksgiving and Dec. 25. Free. Phone (512) 472-1903.

TEXAS MEMORIAL MUSEUM OF SCIENCE & HISTORY is at 2400 Trinity St. on the University of Texas at Austin campus. The museum contains fossils and archeological, biological, geological and historical exhibits. Allow 1 hour minimum. Mon.-Fri. 9-5, Sat. 10-5, Sun. 1-5; closed major holidays. Free. Phone (512) 471-1604.

GEM **TEXAS STATE CAPITOL** is at the n. end of Congress Ave. Construction began in 1882 and continued for more than 6 years on the state building, which was influenced by the U.S. Capitol in Washington, D.C. The original plans called for a limestone structure, but native limestone proved unsuitable. When the builder suggested limestone from Indiana, the governor of Texas vetoed the plan. Finally, Texas granite in shades of sunset red was chosen as the primary building material. Housed within the 1857 General Land Office Building on 11th Street, the Capitol Complex Visitors Center features history exhibits as well as displays describing the life of author O. Henry (William S. Porter), who worked as a draftsman in the building 1887-91.

Allow 1 hour minimum. Mon.-Fri. 7 a.m.-10 p.m., Sat.-Sun. 9-8. Guided tours depart every 15 minutes Mon.-Fri. 8:30-4:30, Sat.-Sun. 9:30-4:30, depending on legislative sessions and other official functions. Closed Jan. 1, Easter, Thanksgiving and Dec. 24-25. Free. Phone (512) 463-0063.

UMLAUF SCULPTURE GARDEN & MUSEUM is 1.5 mi. n.w. on Barton Springs Rd., then s. to 605 Robert E. Lee Rd. More than 130 sculptures by internationally-known sculptor Charles Umlauf belong to the museum collection. Ranging from detailed realism to lyrical abstractions, the sculptures of different mediums are situated throughout a wood and water hillside setting as well as inside the museum.

Allow 1 hour minimum. Wed.-Fri. 10-4:30, Sat.-Sun. 1-4:30; closed Jan. 1, July 4, Thanksgiving and Dec. 24-25. Admission $3.50, senior citizens $2.50, students with ID $1, under 6 free. Phone (512) 445-5582.

UNIVERSITY OF TEXAS AT AUSTIN is bounded by W. 19th, Guadalupe and Red River sts. Chartered in 1883, the University of Texas at Austin is the keystone campus of the statewide University of Texas system. It boasts one of the largest endowments of any public university and is a noted national research center with several Nobel laureates on its faculty. Campus walking tours are offered daily through the Texas Union Information Center, and tours of the U.T. Clock Tower observation deck are available by reservation. Tower tours $3. Phone (512) 475-6636 or (877) 475-6633 for tour information.

Jack S. Blanton Museum of Art is in the Art Building at 23rd and San Jacinto. The museum features changing exhibits from a 17,000-piece permanent collection that includes European art from the Renaissance and Baroque periods, 19th- and 20th-century American art, contemporary Latin American art and prints and drawings from the 15th through 20th centuries. Allow 1 hour minimum. Mon.-Fri.

DID YOU KNOW

Women's clubs founded 85 percent of the public libraries in Texas.

9-5 (also Thurs. 5-9), Sat.-Sun. 1-5; closed holidays. Free. Phone (512) 471-7324.

Lyndon Baines Johnson Library and Museum is at 2313 Red River St. Papers of the Johnson presidency are preserved at the complex, which also includes sculptures of President and Mrs. Johnson, gifts from foreign heads of state, Johnson's 1968 Lincoln limousine, a collection of American political memorabilia and changing exhibits about American history.

Displays chronicle Johnson's life, from his boyhood along the Pedernales River to retirement at his ranch as well as his Great Society program. A ⅛-scale replica allows visitors to enter the Oval Office of Johnson's administration (1963-69). A 20-minute multimedia program about Johnson's life is shown every 45 minutes. The First Lady's Gallery highlights Lady Bird Johnson's life from the time she met Lyndon Johnson to the present. Allow 1 hour minimum. Daily 9-5; closed Dec. 25. Free. Phone (512) 916-5137.

ZILKER METROPOLITAN PARK is 1.5 mi. s.w. on Barton Springs Rd. bordering Town Lake. The centerpiece of the 351-acre park is Barton Springs, a former watering hole that is now a spring-fed 1,000-foot-long swimming pool with a constant temperature of 68 F. A large natural area offers opportunities for bicycling, canoeing, hiking and picnicking; canoe rentals are available. A 20-minute train ride aboard the Zilker Zephyr is offered.

Allow 4 hours minimum. Park open daily 5 a.m.-10 p.m. Barton Springs open Fri.-Wed. 5 a.m.-10 p.m.; Thurs. 5-9 a.m. and 7-10 p.m. (weather permitting). Train operates daily 10-6. Park admission free. Barton Springs $2.75; ages 12-17, $1; under 12, 50c. Train $2.75; over 65 and ages 2-11, $1.75. Parking Sat.-Sun. $2-$3. Phone (512) 478-0905 for the park or (512) 476-9044 for Barton Springs. *See Recreation Chart.*

Austin Nature & Science Center is off Stratford Dr. at 301 Nature Center Dr. Visitors can explore the animals, plants and geology of central Texas through interactive outdoor exhibits and nature trails. The Dino Pit features reproductions of local fossils, dinosaur tracks and archeological finds. Wildlife exhibits include native Texas mammals, birds and reptiles that have been injured or orphaned. Allow 1 hour minimum. Mon.-Sat. 9-5, Sun. noon-5; closed July 4, Thanksgiving and Dec. 25. Donations. Phone (512) 327-8181.

Zilker Botanical Gardens is at 2220 Barton Springs Rd. Oriental, rose, butterfly, growgreen, cactus and herb gardens are featured. The Hartman Prehistoric Garden recreates a Cretaceous habitat with plants, ponds, a waterfall and dinosaur tracks. On the grounds is the Austin Area Garden Center. Allow 1 hour minimum. Daily dawn-dusk. Free. Phone (512) 477-8672.

AUSTWELL (G-9) pop. 192, elev. 24′

Austwell was founded in 1911 by Preston Rose Austin, a cotton grower and land developer who owned 20,000 acres along the lower Guadalupe River. Austin combined his name and business partner Jesse McDowell's to create a town designation. Hotels, stores, lumberyards and cotton gins were among Austin's financial stakes in the community; he also donated a school, a church and land for a train station. In 1914, he dredged Hynes Bay to create a shipping channel. Five years later, the town was badly damaged by a storm, and it never recovered from a second deluge in 1942.

ARANSAS NATIONAL WILDLIFE REFUGE is 7 mi. s.e. on FM 2040. This 70,500-acre refuge encompasses the tidal flats and salt marshes of the Blackjack Peninsula on San Antonio Bay. Inhabitants of the refuge include alligators, armadillos, white-tailed deer, raccoons and javelinas. Among the 300 species of birds that winter at the site are roseate spoonbill, crested caracara, sora rail, a variety of ducks and endangered whooping cranes. The best viewing times are the early morning and late afternoon, November through March.

The Wildlife Interpretive Center features mounted specimens, wildlife literature and a whooping crane videotape. The refuge includes a 40-foot observation tower, several miles of walking trails and a self-guiding tour along 16 miles of paved road; register at the center. Picnicking is permitted. Refuge open daily dawn-dusk. Interpretive center open daily 8:30-4:30; closed Thanksgiving and Dec. 25. Admission $5 per vehicle, $3 per person. Phone (361) 286-3559.

BANDERA (F-7) pop. 957, elev. 1,258′

The cypress trees that line the Medina River brought settlers to Bandera in 1853 to establish a lumber mill. In the 1870s the town was a staging area for large cattle drives through Bandera Pass and along the Western Trail to Montana and Kansas, earning the town the title of "Cowboy Capital of the World."

Modern Bandera is surrounded by dude ranches, and the cypress trees shade visitors canoeing or tubing down the Medina River. Nearby Medina Lake offers water sports and excellent year-round fishing. Hill Country State Natural Area, west near Tarpley, is popular with equestrians, while Lost Maples State Natural Area, northwest near Vanderpool, offers exceptional wildlife viewing and autumn foliage. *See Recreation Chart and the AAA South Central CampBook.*

Bandera County Convention and Visitors Bureau: 1134A Main St., P.O. Box 171, Bandera, TX 78003; phone (830) 796-3045 or (800) 364-3833.

BEAUMONT (F-10) pop. 113,866, elev. 21′

The early economy of Beaumont, which was settled around 1824, was based on cattle, lumber and rice. Then on Jan. 10, 1901, in the nearby Spindletop Oil Field, the first great Texas oil well blew.

The Beaumont area currently forms one of the largest concentrations of petroleum refineries in the nation. Agriculture also contributes to the economy of this thriving deep-water Neches River port.

Visitor information is available at the Babe Didrikson Zaharias Museum and Visitors Center *(see attraction listing)*. The Edison Plaza Museum, 350 Pine St., chronicles the theories and inventions of Thomas Alva Edison; phone (409) 981-3089.

Beaumont Convention and Visitors Bureau: 801 Main St., Suite 100, P.O. Box 3827, Beaumont, TX 77704; phone (409) 880-3749 or (800) 392-4401.

Shopping areas: Beaumont's Old Town, bordered by Harrison, Laurel, Third and 11th streets, recaptures the boomtown spirit with stately Victorian houses that are now shops and restaurants.

ART MUSEUM OF SOUTHEAST TEXAS is at 500 Main St. Permanent and changing exhibits are offered at the museum, which displays American paintings, graphics, drawings, decorative arts and photography as well as a contemporary folk art exhibit and an outdoor sculpture garden. Allow 1 hour minimum. Mon.-Fri. 9-5, Sat. 10-5, Sun. noon-5; closed holidays. Donations. Phone (409) 832-3432.

BABE DIDRIKSON ZAHARIAS MUSEUM AND VISITORS CENTER is off I-10 exit 854. This museum displays golfing trophies, artifacts and memorabilia honoring Babe Zaharias, a woman considered to be one of the great athletes of the 20th century. Daily 9-5; closed Dec. 25. Donations. Phone (409) 880-3749 or (800) 392-4401.

FIRE MUSEUM OF TEXAS is at Walnut and Mulberry sts. in the Beaumont Fire Headquarters Station. A 24-foot-tall fire hydrant greets visitors to this museum, which displays firefighting paraphernalia such as hats, extinguishers, alarm systems and fire trucks. A fire-safety activity area has hands-on exhibits for children. Guided 1-hour tours are available. Mon.-Fri. 8-4:30; closed holidays. Donations. Reservations are required for guided tours. Phone (409) 880-3927.

JOHN JAY FRENCH HISTORIC HOUSE MUSEUM is off US 69/96/287 exit Lucas, then e. on access rd. to 3025 French Rd. This simple 1845 Greek Revival house is one of the area's first two-story, painted dwellings. The museum chronicles rural life in east Texas during the mid-19th century. The grounds include the Heritage Hall, a smokehouse, laundry shed, tannery, blacksmith shop and cemetery. Tours of Beaumont's historic sites can be arranged. Allow 30 minutes minimum. Tues.-Sat. 10-4; closed holidays. Last tour begins at 3. Admission $3, senior citizens $2, students $1. Phone (409) 898-0348 or (409) 898-3267.

McFADDIN-WARD HOUSE is at 1906 McFaddin Ave. Wealthy businessman W.P.H. McFaddin built this Beaux Arts Colonial-style mansion in 1906. The furnishings, collected by the family over a 60-year period and reflecting an elegant lifestyle, include silver, porcelain and Oriental rugs. A carriage house contains servants' quarters, stables, garages and a hayloft. Tickets are available at the visitor center on Calder Avenue at Third Street, where a videotape presentation begins the 1-hour guided tour of the house. The carriage-house tour is self-guiding.

Tues.-Sat. 10-3, Sun. 1-3; closed holidays. All-inclusive admission $3. Under age 8 are not permitted on house tour and must be accompanied by adult on carriage-house tour. Reservations are recommended for guided tours. Phone (409) 832-2134.

SPINDLETOP-GLADYS CITY BOOMTOWN MUSEUM is 5 mi. s. on US 69 to University Dr. on the campus of Lamar University. An oil-field boomtown has been re-created at the museum, which features 15 buildings and equipment of the era that led to the liquid-fuel age. Tues.-Sat. 10-5, Sun. 1-5; closed major holidays. Admission $3; over 60, $2; ages 6-12, $1. AX, DS, MC, VI. Phone (409) 835-0823.

TEXAS ENERGY MUSEUM is at 600 Main St. Lifelike robots describe the evolution of the petroleum industry and the history of the Spindletop Gusher. Allow 1 hour, 30 minutes minimum. Tues.-Sat. 9-5, Sun. 1-5; closed holidays. Admission $2; over 65 and ages 6-12, $1. Phone (409) 833-5100.

BEDFORD (C-8) pop. 47,152, elev. 598'

Bedford was named for a county in Tennessee, the original home of many of its early settlers. A general store and gristmill built by Weldon Bobo in the 1870s established the town as a gathering place for area farmers. The 229-acre Bedford Boys Ranch, a home for wayward boys, opened in 1949. The ranch is now a city park.

OLD BEDFORD SCHOOL is off SR 183 exit Bedford Rd., then .5 mi. n. to 2400 School Ln. Visitors to the restored 1915 school can view a classroom furnished in period. A videotape presentation is offered. Allow 1 hour minimum. Tues.-Fri. 9-5, Sat.-Sun. 1-5; closed major holidays. Donations. Phone (817) 952-2290.

▼ BIG BEND NATIONAL PARK
(G-4)

Elevations in the park range from 1,840 ft. along the Rio Grande River as it leaves Big Bend to 7,835 ft. on Emery Peak. Refer to AAA maps for additional elevation information.

Big Bend National Park is southeast of Alpine on SR 118 and US 385. The park derives its name from a U-shaped bend of the Rio Grande bordering the park. This last great wilderness area of Texas offers mountain and desert scenery and a variety of unusual geological structures within its 801,163 acres.

The park encompasses the entire range of the Chisos Mountains. Three river canyons—Santa Elena, Mariscal and Boquillas—channel the Rio Grande as it forms the international border. Santa Elena Canyon's cliffs rise 1,513 feet above the river. The region is rugged, with volcanic rock formations, abrupt pinnacles, dry channels and deep-cut canyons. It was here that the fossilized bones of a pterosaur, a soaring reptile with a wingspan of 38 feet, were discovered in 1971.

Big Bend's scenery and wildlife are more typical of Mexico than of the United States. When conditions are right, the lowlands bloom with desert flowers, shrubs and cacti. Piñon woodlands are found on the mountain slopes. High in the mountain canyons are forests of Arizona cypress, Douglas fir, juniper and oak.

Desert mule deer live in the area, and small white-tailed deer inhabit the Chisos Mountains. Coyotes, foxes and collared peccary or javelina also can be seen. More than 400 species of birds have been identified in the park.

General Information and Activities

Big Bend National Park is open all year. Summer temperatures in the desert and valley are usually high and afternoon thunderstorms are frequent July through September, but the mountains are pleasant in summer.

A trip from Marathon by way of park headquarters at Panther Junction and the Chisos Mountains Basin to Alpine provides a scenic 187-mile circle tour of the park. Hard-surfaced roads lead to Santa Elena and Boquillas canyons.

Many miles of trails are available for hiking. One of the more interesting hikes is along the self-guiding nature trail to Lost Mine Peak. The round-trip hike lasts about 3 hours. Other trips include the South Rim, the Window and a variety of desert hikes.

Guided walks and interpretive programs are given throughout the park; information is available at visitor centers. Illustrated talks by park interpreters are given year round.

Visitors can get assistance and information about planning back-country trips from the Panther Junction Visitor Center at the park headquarters. The visitor center, which also has exhibits, is open daily 8-6.

Reservations for accommodations at Chisos Mountains Lodge should be made well in advance. Write P.O. Box 129, Big Bend National Park, TX 79834; phone (432) 477-2251. *See Recreation Chart and the AAA South Central CampBook.*

ADMISSION is $5 per person or $10 per private vehicle (7-day pass). The park is open daily 24 hours. Motorists should fill their gas tanks before leaving US 90; service stations in the park close at 6 p.m.

PETS must be on a leash or otherwise physically restricted and are not permitted in public buildings, the river or on trails.

ADDRESS inquiries to the Superintendent, Big Bend National Park, TX 79834; phone (432) 477-2251.

BIG SPRING (D-6) pop. 25,233, elev. 2,397'

The west Texas town of Big Spring was named for the spring that served as a watering place for buffaloes, antelopes, deer, mustangs and people. The spring is now part of 400-acre Big Spring City Park, which offers a swimming pool; an 18-hole golf course; tennis courts; playgrounds; hiking, bicycling and nature trails; an amphitheater and overnight camper parking. Since the discovery of oil in 1927, Big Spring has been a refining center and a distribution point for locally manufactured oil-well machinery.

Big Spring Area Convention and Visitors Bureau: 215 W. 3rd St., P.O. Box 1391, Big Spring, TX 79721; phone (432) 263-7641 or (800) 734-7641.

BIG SPRING STATE PARK is off I-20 exit 174 (eastbound) or 181A (westbound) on FM 700. Named for the only watering place for bison, antelopes and wild horses within a 60-mile radius, the park is atop a 200-foot mesa at the south city limits. Highlights of the 382-acre park include a prairie-dog town, jogging and nature trails, a playground, camping and picnic sites and a panorama from a 3-mile scenic drive around the mountain.

Daily 8 a.m.-10 p.m., Apr.-Sept.; 8-8, rest of year. Admission $2. Camping $6 per night. RV reservations are recommended. DS, MC, VI. Phone (432) 263-4931 or (800) 792-1112.

HERITAGE MUSEUM is at 510 Scurry St. Photographs and artifacts chronicle the development of this area from the 1880s through World War II. Noteworthy are a collection of rare phonographs from the late 1800s to the 1920s and a display of longhorn steer horns. Allow 1 hour minimum. Tues.-Fri. 9-5, Sat. 10-5; closed July 4, Thanksgiving and Dec. 24-25. Admission (includes the Potton House) $2; over 65 and under 12, $1. Phone (432) 267-8255.

Potton House is 1.5 mi. s. of I-20 on US 87 to 200 Gregg St. This 1901 red sandstone Victorian house reflects turn-of-the-20th-century living and features period furniture. Built for an Englishman who worked for the Texas and Pacific Railroad, the house contains many items original to the family. Guided tours are available. Tues.-Sat. 1-5, Feb.-Dec.; closed July 4, Thanksgiving and Dec. 24-25.

BIG THICKET NATIONAL PRESERVE (E-11)

Big Thicket National Preserve encompasses 13 units in southeast Texas. The 97,000-acre park protects one of the country's most biologically diverse wilderness areas. Until the 19th century, this region was a vast and almost impenetrable combination of woodlands and swamps.

The preserve's thicket of woods resulted from the unusual intermixing of elements from four major habitats—Southeastern swamps, Eastern forests, Central plains and the Appalachians. Within the remnants of this once-vast wilderness is an uncommon mix of plants and animals—Eastern bluebirds nest near road runners, and lush bogs border cactus and yucca-dotted sandhills.

Big Thicket includes nine land units and four water corridors. Only the Turkey Creek, Beech Creek, Big Sandy and Hickory Creek Savannah units have hiking trails. Most other units include visitor day-use areas near unit boundaries. Walking is the best way to see the preserve, which offers trails varying in length from .2 to 18 miles. Naturalist programs are offered throughout the year. Another popular activity is canoeing on the Neches River, Pine Island Bayou and Village Creek.

The Roy E. Larsen Sandyland Sanctuary, in Hardin County off SR 327, offers numerous trails where nature lovers can view flora and fauna indicative of both desert and bog.

The Big Thicket Visitor Center is about 7 miles north of Kountze at the junction of US 69 and FM 420. For more information contact the Superintendent, Big Thicket National Preserve, 3785 Milam, Beaumont, TX 77701. Visitor center open daily 9-5; closed Jan. 1 and Dec. 25. Phone (409) 246-2337. *See Recreation Chart.*

BOERNE (F-7) pop. 6,178, elev. 1,405′

Boerne's beginnings are evident in its old stone buildings with narrow windows, steep gables, outside stairways and gardens. Members of the idealist German colony of Bettina, students of the classics who founded several "Latin settlements" in Texas, first settled in the area in 1849. The immigrants designed their farm after Cicero's country home, Tusculum, and laid out the town to resemble the communities they had known in Europe.

Boerne was the home of George Wilkins Kendall, one of the founders of the *New Orleans Picayune*. At the outbreak of the Mexican War in 1846, Kendall organized a system of pony-express riders and ships to carry stories to his newspaper. So efficient was this method of reporting that the *Picayune* printed the text of the Treaty of Guadalupe before the U.S. government received a copy. Kendall's ranch, where he spent the last years of his life, encompassed most of what is modern Kendall County.

Situated along Cibolo Creek, the Cibolo Wilderness Trail offers hiking trails, a boardwalk and a nature center; phone (830) 249-4616.

Boerne Chamber of Commerce: 126 Rosewood, Boerne, TX 78006; phone (830) 249-8000.

BONHAM (C-9) pop. 9,990, elev. 568′

Named for James B. Bonham, a hero of the Alamo siege, Bonham is in the heart of the fertile Blacklands. Hamlets with names such as Telephone and Bug Tussle attest to the "down-homeness" of the area. During the Civil War the town was headquarters of the Texas Confederate forces.

In a park next to Sam Rayburn Library *(see attraction listing)* is Fort Inglish Museum and Village. Structures include three original, restored log cabins dating from the 1830s and a replica of the 1837 fort.

Bonham Area Chamber of Commerce: 110 E. First, Bonham, TX 75418; phone (903) 583-4811.

FANNIN COUNTY MUSEUM OF HISTORY is at 1 Main St. Twelve rooms of the restored 1900 Texas and Pacific Railroad Depot display collections of vintage clothing and furniture, antique farm implements, documents and photographs, American Indian artifacts, railroad memorabilia and tools relating to the history of the area since its settlement in 1836. A pioneering exhibit features a mid-19th-century weaving loom and 100-year-old quilts. A World War II exhibit includes a pilot training base that features a restored Fairchild PT19 airplane. A fire museum also is featured.

Allow 1 hour minimum. Tues.-Sat. 10-4, Apr. 1-Labor Day; Tues.-Sat. noon-4, rest of year. Closed Jan. 1, July 4, Thanksgiving and Dec. 25. Donations. Phone (903) 583-8042.

SAM RAYBURN HOUSE MUSEUM is 2.2 mi. w. on US 82/56. The 12-room country house of the former Speaker of the House of Representatives contains family furnishings and belongings. Guided tours interpret the life and work of this powerful, long-term Congressional leader. Allow 30 minutes minimum. Tues.-Fri. 8-5, Sat. 9-5; closed state holidays. Free. Phone (903) 583-5558.

SAM RAYBURN LIBRARY is 4 blks. w. on US 56 at 800 W. Sam Rayburn Dr. The site was established to preserve books, papers and historical mementos collected by Speaker of the House Rayburn during a half-century of public service, and to provide a place for study and research. A replica of the speaker's office at the United States Capitol contains the silver and crystal chandelier that hung in the White House from the terms of President Ulysses S. Grant to those of Theodore Roosevelt. Allow 1 hour minimum. Mon.-Fri. 9-5, Sat. 1-5, Sun. 2-5; closed holidays. Free. Phone (903) 583-2455.

BORGER (B-6) pop. 14,302

In 1926 the Panhandle Oil Field was discovered, and a boomtown of 40,000 people mushroomed on the site of Borger. The town remains a major petrochemical center. Before the oil boom, the area's most significant events were the Battles of Adobe Walls, which took place about 37 miles northeast of Borger in 1864 and 1874.

Borger Chamber of Commerce: 613 N. Main St., P.O. Box 490, Borger, TX 79008; phone (806) 274-2211.

HUTCHINSON COUNTY MUSEUM is at 618 N. Main St. Exhibits trace the history of the county and the town of Borger, depicting the Spanish exploration, the Plains Indians, the American frontier and the discovery of oil, when Borger's population grew from 15 to 35,000 in 3 months. An authentic cable tool drilling rig is displayed. Allow 30 minutes minimum. Mon.-Fri. 9-5, Sat. 11-4:30; closed holidays. Donations. Phone (806) 273-0130.

BOYS RANCH (B-5) elev. 3,202'

CAL FARLEY'S BOYS RANCH is on FM 1061. An Amarillo businessman founded the 120-acre ranch for wayward boys in 1939 on the site of the 1870s town of Tascosa. Today, the 10,700-acre ranch is home to more than 250 at-risk boys and girls ages 5-17. The ranch includes a museum with Old West memorabilia and a barbed-wire collection. Guided tours are available; reservations are recommended. A rodeo is held Labor Day weekend. Ranch open daily 8-5. Free. A fee is charged for special events. Phone (806) 373-6600, ext. 635, or (800) 687-3722.

BRACKETTVILLE (F-6) pop. 1,876

Established in 1852 as a supply center for Fort Clark, Brackettville became a trade center as the region filled with ranches and farms. This historic fort has been transformed into a resort with many of its original buildings serving as lodges and residences.

Kinney County Chamber of Commerce: P.O. Box 386, Brackettville, TX 78832; phone (830) 563-2466.

SAVE **ALAMO VILLAGE MOVIE LOCATION** is 7 mi. n. of US 90 on FM 674. Built for the 1959 John Wayne epic "The Alamo,"this permanent outdoor movie set re-creates the 1836 Alamo and a western town. The village, with dozens of full-scale buildings, and the John Wayne Museum are open to the public. Entertainment is offered in summer. Food is available. Allow 2 hours, 30 minutes minimum. Daily 9-6, Memorial Day-Labor Day; 9-5, rest of year. Closed Dec. 21-26. Admission Memorial Day weekend-Labor Day $8; over 65, $7.50; ages 6-11, $4. Admission rest of year $7; over 65, $6.50; ages 6-11, $3. AX, DS, MC, VI. Phone (830) 563-2580.

BRENHAM (F-9) pop. 13,507, elev. 332'

Brenham retains much of its mid-19th-century grandeur. The Main Street District contains restored 19th-century buildings that house restaurants and shops.

The city is the county seat for Washington County, which is home to some 120 historic sites and markers, many from the Texas Revolution. Brenham is home to Blinn College, the state's first county-owned junior college which was founded in 1883.

Chappell Hill, 10 miles east, is the first town in Texas planned and laid out by a woman. Many of the original 19th-century structures remain, including the 1850s Stagecoach Inn, the 1869 Old Rock Store and the Browning Plantation of about 1857. The Masonic Cemetery contains the graves of Col. William Travis' family and Confederate soldiers. A museum and visitor center displays area artifacts.

Nearby a cloistered order of nuns operates the Monastery of St. Clare Miniature Horse Farm, a renowned breeding farm for horses that stand less than 34 inches high at the shoulder. The farm is 9 miles east via SR 105; self-guiding tours of the facilities are available year-round; phone (979) 836-9652. The Nueces Canyon Equestrian Center offers weekend horse shows; phone (979) 289-5600.

Blue Bell Creameries, 2 miles southeast on FM 577, is open Monday through Saturday. Tours of the ice-cream plant with a film about the history of the creamery are offered on weekdays except holidays. Samples are served following the tour; phone (979) 830-2197 or (800) 327-8135.

Washington County Convention and Visitors Bureau: 314 S. Austin, Brenham, TX 77833; phone (979) 836-3695 or (888) 273-6426. *See ad.*

Self-guiding tours: Visitors to the area can view the bluebonnets and other wildflowers that bloom in profusion along country roads in the spring. The visitors center at 314 S. Austin provides a free map outlining the most scenic routes.

RECREATIONAL ACTIVITIES

Horseback Riding

• **Shiloh Ranch** is at 12009 FM 1155, Brenham, TX 77833. Horseback riding and trail rides are offered Mon.-Sat. by appointment. Phone (979) 836-0599.

BROWNSVILLE (I-9) pop. 139,722, elev. 45'

Brownsville is historically and economically intertwined with Matamoros, its sister city on the Mexican side of the border. As a major seaport and railhead, Brownsville exports the agricultural products of the Rio Grande Valley as well as a large percentage of Mexican commerce. Locally, both cities are often thought of as one. Brownsville is a bilingual city with strong Spanish cultural ties, and residents frequently cross the three international bridges to shop, visit and work.

During the 19th century, wars and banditry marked relations between the two communities. Brownsville began as Fort Brown, built to support the United States' claim to the Rio Grande as its southern border. The two battles at Palo Alto and Resaca de la Palma successfully defended that claim and started the Mexican-American War.

During the Civil War, Brownsville prospered as the Confederacy's chief cotton port, shipping materials out of Mexico to dodge the Union blockade. One of the last land battle of the Civil War was fought near Brownsville at Palmito Ranch; the Confederate troops had not heard of Gen. Robert E. Lee's surrender 1 month earlier. The dissent along the border did not end with the Civil War, however, as plots and counterplots by revolutionaries across the border kept Fort Brown busy during the rest of the 19th century and into the next.

Local monuments remind visitors of the strife that occurred in Brownsville during the Mexican-American War. Battle sites include the Palo Alto

---

DID YOU KNOW

Farms and ranches cover approximately 132 million acres, nearly 80 percent of the state's land area.

Battlefield Monument, at jct. FM 1847 and FM 511; the Resaca de la Palma Battlefield Marker, on FM 1847 between Price and Coffee Port roads; and the Palmito Hill Battlefield Marker, 12 miles east on SR 4. The Charro Days Fiesta in late February celebrates the charro horsemen of Mexico with a grand ball, street dances, parades, a carnival and a traditional Mexican rodeo; phone (956) 542-4245.

The city is known for its shrimp fleet and its dual-frontier *maquiladora* manufacturing program, which includes *Fortune* 500 companies in both Brownsville and Matamoros. Nearby are the wide sandy beaches of South Padre Island *(see place listing p. 152 and Padre Island National Seashore p. 128)*, which are reached via SRs 48 and 100 to Port Isabel, then over Laguna Madre Bay via the Queen Isabella Causeway.

Birdwatchers can find a variety of the winged species in the Brownsville area, including wild parrots and Brown Pelicans. More than 470 bird species call the area home.

Brownsville Convention and Visitors Bureau: 650 FM 802, P.O. Box 4697, Brownsville, TX 78523; phone (956) 546-3721 or (800) 626-2639.

BROWNSVILLE MUSEUM OF FINE ART is e. of the International Bridge on E. Elizabeth St. to Ringold St., then s. to 230 Neale Dr. The museum offers a variety of permanent and changing exhibits. Allow 1 hour minimum. Tues.-Fri. 10-2:30, Sat. 10-4; closed major holidays. Donations. Phone (956) 542-0941.

FORT BROWN is e. of the International Bridge on Elizabeth St. to 600 International Blvd. Established in 1846 on the north bank of the Rio Grande River, this fortification provoked an attack by the Mexican army and began the Mexican War. Today several of the fort's original buildings are part of the campus shared by Texas Southmost College and University of Texas at Brownsville. Highlights include the post hospital (college administration building), the guardhouse (fine arts center) and the post headquarters. A cannon and earthworks can be seen near the Fort Brown Memorial. Phone (956) 544-8231.

GLADYS PORTER ZOO is 2 mi. n. at 500 Ringgold St. Moats, streams, rocks and cavelike structures provide natural enclosures for more than 1,500 animals at the 31-acre zoo. Some 400 species are represented, including nearly 50 endangered.

Jaguars, Galapagos tortoises, spider monkeys and Cuban crocodiles inhabit Tropical America. Indo-Australia is home to orangutans, grey kangaroos, kookaburras and wallabies. The Asia environment features Sumatran tigers, gibbons, Indian blue peafowl and Bactrian camels. Popular residents of the Africa area include reticulated giraffes, elephants, zebras, lions, gorillas, chimpanzees and the rare Jentink's duiker antelope.

The Herpetarium and Aquatic Wing contains lizards, turtles, snakes and freshwater and saltwater fish. The zoo also offers a free-flight aviary, bear grottoes and an exhibit of California sea lions. The children's zoo lets youngsters interact with Nigerian dwarf goats, miniature mules and domestic chickens.

Mon.-Fri. 9-5:30, Sat.-Sun. 9-6. Train rides are available Sun. 1:30-3:30 (weather permitting). Admission $7; over 65, $5.50; ages 2-13, $3.75. Train $2; ages 2-13, $1. Phone (956) 546-2177.

HISTORIC BROWNSVILLE MUSEUM is off SR 77/83 6th St. exit, then e. to 641 E. Madison. Housed in a 1928 Southern Pacific Railroad Depot, the museum offers interpretive exhibits from Brownsville's past, including the area's earliest military fort and the arrival of French teaching nuns. Displays include agricultural and ranching tools, artifacts and pictures from the battles of the Mexican-American War and a restored Baldwin wood-burning, narrow-gauge railroad locomotive. Allow 30 minutes minimum. Mon.-Fri. 10-4:30, Sat. 10-4; closed major holidays. Admission $2; under 16, 50c. Phone (956) 548-1313.

RIO GRANDE VALLEY WING FLYING MUSEUM is s. of the airport terminal at 955 S. Minnesota Ave. World War II military aircraft, antique vehicles, military uniforms and models are displayed. A 30-minute videotape features military aircraft operated and restored by the Commemorative Air Force. Allow 30 minutes minimum. Mon.-Sat. 9-4; closed Jan. 1, Thanksgiving and Dec. 25. Admission $5; over 65, $4; ages 12-18, $3. Phone (956) 541-8585.

STILLMAN HOUSE MUSEUM is at 1305 E. Washington St. Charles Stillman, the founder of Brownsville, built the house in 1850. Historic items are displayed in the house and at the adjacent Brownsville Heritage Museum. Tues.-Sat. 10-noon and 1-4. Admission $4; under 13, $1; students with ID 50c. Phone (956) 542-3929.

Matamoros, Mexico

Main port of entry to Mexico from the lower Rio Grande Valley, Matamoros (mah-tah-MOH-rohs) is connected with Brownsville. The city is the commercial center for the surrounding cotton-producing and cattle-raising region and also serves as a crafts and housewares emporium for border-hopping tourists.

Matamoros is the most historically significant of the Rio Grande border towns. Settled around 1700, burned twice and pillaged several times, it is known as the "Thrice Heroic" city. It derived much of its wealth during the U.S. Civil War, when the Confederates smuggled contraband cotton across the border for shipment to European markets.

The center of this trade was the short-lived Mexican town known as Bagdad, or Washington Beach, about 8 miles (12 km) north of Playa Lauro Villar at the mouth of the Rio Grande, where weapons were channeled to the Confederate Army in exchange for cotton. The city, which once boasted 6,000 residents, died out after suffering floods, hurricanes and military attacks; old artifacts can often be found by digging into the sand that now buries much of the site.

While Bagdad crumbled into the Rio Grande, Matamoros began to lure tourists with bargains on housewares, glass items, basketry, pottery, papiermâché items and table linens. Also of interest is Casamata Museum which is housed in a small fort. The beaches of Playa Lauro Villar are a popular escape, 24 miles (38 km) east of the city.

The Mexican customs and immigration office is open 24 hours daily; baggage must be inspected for visitors who plan to go beyond Matamoros. U.S. customs offices at the B & M and Gateway bridges are open daily 24 hours; the office at Veterans Bridge is open 6 a.m.-midnight.

U.S. and Canadian visitors must carry proof of citizenship. A valid U.S. or Canadian passport is the most convenient since it serves as a photo ID and facilitates many transactions, such as cashing traveler's checks. The U.S., Canadian and Mexican governments also recognize a birth certificate, which must be a certified copy from the government agency that issued it. A driver's license, voter registration card or baptismal certificate is **not** proof of citizenship.

All who plan to visit the interior or stay in the border area more than 72 hours also must obtain a Mexican government tourist card. Tourist cards are available, with proof of citizenship, from Mexican government tourism offices, Mexican consulates in the U.S. and Canada or immigration offices at official points of entry.

For a more detailed explanation of border-crossing procedures and the requirements for temporary importation of vehicles, *see the Arriving in Mexico section in the AAA Mexico TravelBook.*

Mexico collects a visitor entry fee of 185 pesos (at press time, about $19) from each person entering the country. The fee must be paid in order to have your tourist card validated if you plan to remain anywhere in Mexico for more than 72 hours, or stay less than 72 hours and travel beyond the 16-mile (26-kilometer) border zone. If arriving by land, the fee is paid at a branch of any bank operating in Mexico. Upon payment your tourist card is stamped with an official "Fee paid" designation. All visitors are required to produce verification of payment by showing the "Fee paid" stamp on their tourist card upon departing Mexico. If arriving by air, the fee is included in the price of the ticket charged by the airline.

Visitors who limit their travel to destinations within the border zone, regardless of length of stay, are exempt. An exemption also applies to visitors staying more than 72 hours but limiting their visit to the following destinations/tourist routes: Ciudad Juárez to Paquime, Chihuahua; Piedras Negras to Santa Rosa, Coahuila; or Reynosa to China, Nuevo Leon, and Reynosa to Presa Cuchillo, Tamaulipas.

Brownsville Chamber of Commerce: 1600 E. Elizabeth St., Brownsville, TX 78520; phone (956) 542-4341. The office is one block from the Gateway Bridge.

Shopping areas: The most popular shopping districts include Mercado Juárez, an enclosed marketplace that covers several blocks; the shops along Avenida Obregón; and the Centro Artesanal, the government-run arts and craft center.

BROWNWOOD (E-8) pop. 18,813, elev. 1,342'

A cotton-buying center in its early days, Brownwood now relies on industry to sustain its economy. Structures of native sandstone reflect city history.

Brownwood Chamber of Commerce: 600 E. Depot St., P.O. Box 880, Brownwood, TX 76804; phone (325) 646-9535.

DOUGLAS MacARTHUR ACADEMY OF FREEDOM is 1 mi. s. on the Howard Payne University campus at Austin and Coggin aves. The museum chronicles the evolution of Western civilization. Featured are a 3,500-square-foot mural, a large electric map of Gen. Douglas MacArthur's Pacific campaigns and some of his mementos. Allow 1 hour minimum. Guided tours are given Mon.-Sat. at 1, 2 and 3, June-July; by appointment rest of year. Closed school vacations. Free. Phone (325) 649-8700.

BRYAN (E-9) pop. 65,660, elev. 367'

Bryan is the county seat of Brazos County and a major educational and commercial center. Many of its first settlers were colonists who arrived with Stephen F. Austin, but not until the Houston & Texas Central Railroad arrived in 1860 did Bryan begin to take shape. The city has prospered with an economy based upon diversified agriculture and industry.

Bryan-College Station Convention and Visitors Bureau: 715 University Dr. E., College Station, TX 77840; phone (979) 260-9898 or (800) 777-8292.

Self-guiding tours: A brochure about the historic district is available from the convention and visitors bureau.

WINERIES

- **Messina Hof Wine Cellars** is 2 mi. n.e. off SR 6/Old Reliance Rd. exit, following signs to 4545 Old Reliance Rd. Tours are given Mon.-Fri. at 1, 2:30 and 5:30, Sat. at 11, 12:30, 2:30, 4 and 5:30, Sun. at 12:30 and 2:30; closed Jan. 1, Thanksgiving and Dec. 25. Phone (979) 778-9463.

BUFFALO GAP (D-7) pop. 463

Buffalo Gap is at the site of a natural pass in the Callahan Divide through which buffalo traveled for

many years. The town was a point on the Dodge Cattle Trail.

BUFFALO GAP HISTORICAL VILLAGE is s. on SR 89, then 2 blks. w. on Elm St. This collection of late 19th-century buildings includes an 1875 log cabin, stores and the original county courthouse and jail that now houses a museum. Allow 2 hours minimum. Mon.-Sat. 10-6, Sun. noon-6, Mar. 15-Nov. 15; Fri.-Sat. 10-5, Sun. noon-5, rest of year. Closed Thanksgiving and Dec. 25. Admission $5; over 65, $4; ages 6-18, $2. AX, DS, MC, VI. Phone (325) 572-3365.

BURNET (E-8) pop. 4,735, elev. 1,304′

The town grew around Fort Croghan, established by ranchers in 1849 as part of a string of outposts on the Texas frontier. The region's many immense granite outcroppings proved a hindrance for early settlers. G.W. Lacy of nearby Marble Falls tried and failed to trade his granite mountain for a saddle horse. Later he deeded part of it to the state, which used the stone in the construction of the Texas Capitol. These outcroppings, some of the oldest in the world, are now prized by rockhounds and geologists.

Two other resources, water and wildflowers, have helped make Burnet a popular recreation center. Nine miles west via SR 29 is Inks Lake State Park *(see Recreation Chart and the AAA South Central CampBook)*, whose 1,200 acres of woodlands and wildflowers border Lake Inks. The visitor center at nearby Lake Buchanan offers a panoramic view. *See Recreation Chart and AAA South Central CampBook.*

Burnet Convention and Visitors Bureau: 703 Buchanan Dr., Burnet, TX 78611; phone (512) 756-4297.

FORT CROGHAN MUSEUM is at 703 Buchanan Dr. On the grounds are six restored 19th-century stone and log buildings, including a powder house. Thurs.-Sat. 10-4, first weekend in Apr.-Labor Day; closed holidays. Donations. Phone (512) 756-8281.

LONGHORN CAVERN STATE PARK is 6 mi. s. on US 281, then 6 mi. w. on Park Rd. 4. One mile of the cave is lighted. The temperature is a constant 68 F. Of interest are the Cathedral Room and two rooms of transparent crystal. Rubber-soled shoes are recommended. Allow 1 hour, 30 minutes minimum. Tours depart on the hour Mon.-Fri. 10-4, Sat.-Sun. 10-5. Closed Dec. 24-25. Admission $8; senior citizens $7; ages 5-12, $4.50. AX, DS, MC, VI. Phone (830) 598-2283, (512) 756-6976 or (877) 441-2283.

VANISHING TEXAS RIVER CRUISE is 3 mi. w. on SR 29, then 16.5 mi. n. on FM 2341, following signs. The narrated cruise offers a 2.5-hour tour of the Colorado River as it cuts through hill country. In the event of low water on the river, a 36-mile round-trip cruise of Lake Buchanan is substituted. Of interest are the spring-blossoming wildflowers

and cactuses, and the bald eagles that winter in the area November through March. A 4-hour Ultimate Eagle tour focuses on the majestic birds. A sunset dinner cruise is offered May through October.

Sightseeing cruise departs Wed.-Mon. at 11 (weather permitting). Eagle cruise departs Sat. at 9, Nov.-Mar. Sightseeing cruise $15; over 60 and students with ID $13; ages 6-12, $10. Eagle cruise (includes lunch) $26.95. Reservations are recommended. AX, DS, MC, VI. Phone (512) 756-6986 or (800) 474-8374.

CANTON (D-9) pop. 3,292

Canton and its First Monday Trade Days are legendary in northern Texas. The tradition started in the 1850s when farmers began bringing horses, hunting hounds and other dogs to Canton to trade or sell on the first Monday of each month. Originally called Hoss Monday, the event has continued uninterrupted over the years, growing into a huge trading bazaar and flea market that starts the Friday before the first Monday of each month. About 7,000 exhibition stalls attract up to 250,000 people each month.

Canton Chamber of Commerce: 315 First Monday Ln., Canton, TX 75103; phone (903) 567-2991.

CANYON (B-5) pop. 12,875, elev. 3,566′

Cattle ranches and the railroad sparked Canyon's commercial development at the turn of the 20th century. Agriculture and the campus of West Texas A&M University are the basis of the town's economy.

Canyon Chamber of Commerce: 1518 Fifth Ave., Canyon, TX 79015; phone (806) 655-7815 or (800) 999-9481.

BUFFALO LAKE NATIONAL WILDLIFE REFUGE is about 12 mi. s.w. via US 60, then 2 mi. s. on FM 168. A winter refuge for ducks and geese, the 7,677-acre refuge no longer contains the lake for which it is named. Facilities for picnicking, camping and birdwatching are available. For information write the Refuge Manager, Box 179, Umbarger, TX 79091. Entrance open daily 8-8, Apr.-Sept.; 8-6, rest of year. Admission $2 per private vehicle per day. Phone (806) 499-3382.

PALO DURO CANYON STATE PARK is 12 mi. e. on SR 217. The canyon exposes geological formations more than 250 million years old. There are 16 miles of scenic drives that descend to the canyon floor, some 1,000 feet below the rim. There also are 35 miles of bridle paths and bicycling and hiking trails. Camping facilities and cabins are available.

Daily 7 a.m.-10 p.m., June-Aug.; 8 a.m.-10 p.m., rest of year. Admission $3, under 12 free. DS, MC, VI. Phone (806) 488-2227. *See Recreation Chart and the AAA South Central CampBook.*

"Texas" is held in the Pioneer Amphitheatre in Palo Duro Canyon State Park. The base of a 600-foot cliff serves as the backdrop for this outdoor musical drama by Pulitzer Prize winner Paul Green. The production features 140 company members, horses, light and sound effects and fireworks. Food is available. Inquire about weather policies. Tickets are available at the theater and at the "TEXAS" Information Office at 1514 5th Ave., Canyon, TX 79015.

Allow 2 hours, 30 minutes minimum. Performances are given Thurs.-Tues. at 8:30 p.m., early June to mid-Aug. Tickets $8-$23; under 12, $4-$23. Park admission free to theater patrons after 5:30 p.m. Reservations are recommended. AX, DS, MC, VI. Phone (806) 655-2181 or (877) 588-3927.

PANHANDLE-PLAINS HISTORICAL MUSEUM is on the campus of West Texas A&M University at 2503 Fourth Ave., e. of US 87 on SR 217. The museum—finished in Texas limestone and with a facade of decorative stone work and carvings—presents the cultural, geological and economic history of northwest Texas.

Major exhibits are dedicated to western heritage, petroleum, paleontology and geology, furniture and decorative arts, textiles and fine art. Highlights include a reconstructed pioneer town whose shops, houses and other buildings are filled with period artifacts. One of the Panhandle's oldest buildings, the T-Anchor Ranch headquarters, stands outside. The People of the Plains exhibit traces 14,000 years of human habitation; American Indian artifacts include weavings, pottery, baskets and clothing.

Chippendale furniture, dinosaur and mastodon skeletons, windmills, oil rigs, saddles, guns and quilts are among the many items on display. A 1903 Model A Ford is reputed to be the oldest known assembly-line car. The museum's art collection includes works from the Taos and Santa Fe art colonies as well as a permanent gallery for Texan art.

Allow 1 hour minimum. Mon.-Sat. 9-6, Sun. 1-6, June-Aug.; Mon.-Sat. 9-5, Sun. 1-6, rest of year.

DID YOU KNOW

Longhorn cattle outnumbered people nine to one in the 1860s.

Closed Jan. 1, Thanksgiving and Dec. 24-25. Admission $4; over 64, $3; ages 4-12, $1. AX, DS, MC, VI. Phone (806) 651-2244.

CASTROVILLE (F-7) pop. 2,664

On Sept. 3, 1844, Henri Castro led Alsatian emigrants to this tranquil, tree-shaded area along the Medina River. Castro was consul general for the Republic of Texas in France and contracted with the French government to establish the settlement. With a guarantee of a town lot and 40 acres to farm, French settlers transformed the area into an independent farming center with its own gristmill and cotton gin.

Castroville Chamber of Commerce: 802 London St., P.O. Box 572, Castroville, TX 78009; phone (830) 538-3142 or (800) 778-6775.

Self-guiding tours: Information about a walking tour of historic homes and buildings is available from the chamber of commerce.

LANDMARK INN is .5 mi. e. on US 90 to jct. Florence and Florella sts. This restored, 1849 plastered limestone structure includes eight rooms furnished in period. An exhibit room contains memorabilia of the area. On the grounds are an 1850s two-story gristmill and dam and the old bathhouse. Allow 30 minutes minimum. Daily 8-5. Admission $1, under 12 free. Reservations are required. Phone (512) 389-8900 or (830) 931-2133.

CHILDRESS (B-6) pop. 6,778, elev. 1,877'

The economy of Childress is sustained by agriculture, particularly in the form of cotton, grains and livestock, as well as by small, diversified industry. The town is named for George Campbell Childress, author of the Texas Declaration of Independence.

CHILDRESS COUNTY HERITAGE MUSEUM is at 210 Third St. N.W. Housed in the old post office, the museum displays late 19th-century furniture, maps, photographs and other artifacts chronicling the history of Childress and the region. Transportation exhibits include automobiles, buggies and a train. Mon.-Fri. 9-5, Sat.-Sun. by appointment; closed holidays. Donations. Phone (940) 937-2261.

CLAUDE (B-5) pop. 1,313, elev. 3,407'

Armstrong City was established in 1887 as a stop on the Fort Worth and Denver City Railroad. The Panhandle settlement soon was renamed for Claude Ayers, the engineer who brought the first passenger train into town. Dr. W.A. Warner arrived in Claude in 1897 and is credited with founding one of the first Boy Scout troops west of the Mississippi.

ARMSTRONG COUNTY MUSEUM is 1 block n. of US 287 at 120 N. Trice St. Three historic downtown buildings are dedicated to the history of the Panhandle region. Exhibits chronicle the Red River

Indian Wars, the founding of the 1.3-million-acre JA Ranch and the relocation of the Southern buffalo herd. A musical revue is presented every first Saturday in the Gem Theater. An art gallery features local artists. Allow 30 minutes minimum. Tues.-Fri. 10-4, Sat.-Sun. 1-4; closed holidays. Donations. Phone (806) 226-2187.

CLEBURNE (D-8) pop. 26,005, elev. 764'

Established in 1854 as Camp Henderson and renamed in 1867 after Confederate general Pat Cleburne, the town has large railroad construction and repair shops. Cleburne State Park, 12 miles south on US 67, contains a wildlife refuge and 116-acre Cedar Lake. *See Recreation Chart and the AAA South Central CampBook.*

Cleburne Chamber of Commerce: 1511 W. Henderson St., P.O. Box 701, Cleburne, TX 76033; phone (817) 645-2455.

LAYLAND MUSEUM is at 201 N. Caddo St. on the ground floor of the 1905 Carnegie Building. This museum traces early settlement through the 20th century. An American Indian exhibit traces the history of North America's natives. Other displays include a 12-foot mammoth tusk and a caboose with railroad memorabilia. Mon.-Fri. 9-5, second and fourth Sat. 10-4; closed major holidays. Free. Phone (817) 645-0940.

COLLEGE STATION (E-9)
pop. 67,890, elev. 330'

College Station is the home of Texas A&M University, the state's oldest public institution of higher education. The Agricultural and Mechanical College opened in 1876 with 106 students. The university is now the nation's fourth-largest with an enrollment of 45,000.

Bryan-College Station Convention and Visitors Bureau: 715 University Dr. E., College Station, TX 77840; phone (979) 260-9898 or (800) 777-8292.

GEORGE BUSH PRESIDENTIAL LIBRARY AND MUSEUM is .8 mi. w. of Wellborn Rd. (FM 2154) on the west campus of Texas A&M University at 1000 George Bush Dr. W. The 90-acre complex preserves an extensive collection of photographs, official and personal papers and videotaped footage. Some 60,000 artifacts include gifts of state and personal items. An orientation film chronicles the 42nd president's life. Highlights of the museum include a World War II Avenger torpedo bomber, a 1947 Studebaker, a slab of the Berlin Wall and replicas of Bush's offices at Camp David and on *Air Force One.* Changing exhibits also are presented.

Allow 1 hour, 30 minutes minimum. Mon.-Sat. 9:30-5, Sun. noon-5; closed Jan. 1, Thanksgiving and Dec. 25. Admission $5; students and military with ID $4; over 62, $3.50; under 17 free. AX, DS, MC, VI. Phone (979) 260-9552 or TTY (979) 260-3770.

COLUMBUS (F-9) pop. 3,916, elev. 200'

Once the site of an American Indian village called Montezuma, Columbus was settled in 1823 by members of the Stephen F. Austin colony— groups of settlers led by pioneer Austin, who founded the first American settlements in Texas.

In 1836 Gen. Sam Houston deliberately burned the town to the ground in hopes of deterring Mexican general Antonio López de Santa Anna during the Texas Revolution. By the following year, Columbus citizens began to rebuild; many of those 19th-century structures can be seen in the downtown area. The restored 1886 Stafford Opera House, 425 Spring St., offers tours and family entertainment; phone (979) 732-5135 or (877) 444-7339.

The 1891 Colorado County Courthouse, on Milam St., features a stained-glass dome in the district courtroom and a four-face Seth Thomas clock. On the east side of Courthouse Square is the Courthouse Oak, where the first district court was held in 1836. A 75-foot tree at 1218 Walnut St. is purported to be the second largest live oak in Texas.

Historically, Beason Park marks the spot where Beason's ferry, operated by the Texas Army, once crossed the Colorado River. Today, the park offers camping, picnicking, fishing and ball fields.

Columbus Convention and Visitors Bureau: P.O. Box 98, Columbus, TX 78934; phone (979) 732-5135 or (877) 444-7339.

Self-guiding tours: Maps outlining a back-road bluebonnet tour, a talking house tour and a historical walking tour are available from the convention and visitors bureau.

COMSTOCK (F-6) elev. 1,550'

Settled in the 1880s along the Galveston, Harrisburg and San Antonio Railway, Comstock was named for a railroad dispatcher.

SEMINOLE CANYON STATE HISTORIC SITE is 9 mi. w. on US 90. The 2,100-acre archeological preserve contains hundreds of pictographs made by prehistoric inhabitants 2,000-8,000 years ago. Rock paintings on the walls of Fate Bell Shelter, a huge cliff overhang, may be viewed on a 90-minute guided hiking tour. A visitor center displays artifacts from the site's limestone shelters as well as dioramas of early man. Daily 8-5. Guided tours are given Wed.-Sun. at 10 and 3 (weather permitting). Admission $2, under 12 free. Guided tour $3; ages 6-12, $1. DS, MC, VI. Phone (432) 292-4464. *See Recreation Chart and the AAA South Central CampBook.*

CONROE (F-10) pop. 36,811, elev. 213'

On the southern edge of Big Thicket National Preserve, Conroe offers beautiful vistas of rolling hills, woodland lakes and tall pines. An oil field southeast of the city continues to produce.

Southern Empress Cruises, I-45 exit 87, then 7.5 mi. w. on SR 105, offers cruises around Lake Conroe on an 1800s paddlewheeler; phone (936) 588-3000.

Lake Conroe Convention and Visitors Bureau: 505 W. Davis St., P.O. Box 2347, Conroe, TX 77305; phone (936) 756-6644 or (800) 283-6645.

Shopping areas: Prime Outlets at Conroe, I-45 and League Line Rd., features such designer outlets as Liz Claiborne, Mikasa and Nike.

CORPUS CHRISTI (H-9)
pop. 277,454, elev. 27'

Although first explored by Europeans in 1519, for more than 300 years Corpus Christi remained just the name of a landlocked bay. In 1839 Col. Henry Kinney established a trading post in the area, aggressively marketed his dusty settlement, and the town soon became a trade center for the nearby cattle ranches and the Mexican border towns.

Corpus Christi's transformation into an international port occurred when the Army Corps of Engineers dug a new ship channel in the mid-1920s. The completion of this project made the city the deepest port on the Texas coast and attracted many of the businesses that form its industrial base.

The city's importance was enhanced further with the addition of the Naval Air Station and its advanced flight-training school. This facility is one of the area's major employers and includes the Army Depot, the primary repair facility for Army helicopters.

Ironically, the city's metamorphosis into a booming cosmopolitan tourist mecca of hotels and palm-lined boulevards has fulfilled Henry Kinney's extravagant portrayal of this former patch of sand and sea at the end of nowhere as a resort area.

Despite its big-city stature, Corpus Christi has retained its earlier small-town flavor—a quality best expressed by the 2-mile seawall in the heart of the business district. Unlike other similar barricades, this seawall opens onto the bay, with stairs leading into the water. By adding this feature, Gutzon Borglum, its builder and the sculptor of Mount Rushmore, joined the vistas of blue water with the cityscape.

If the bay is Corpus Christi's front yard, then the more than 100 miles of beaches on nearby Padre and Mustang islands are its back yard. Hotels, condominiums and other resort facilities characterize North Padre Island, which mirrors the development at the south end of the island near Brownsville. Between these two extremes are almost 80 miles of beach in the Padre Island National Seashore *(see place listing p. 128).*

Nearby Mustang Island State Park *(see Port Aransas p. 130)* preserves many of the barrier beaches north of Padre Island. A freshwater alternative to these coastal areas is Lake Corpus Christi Recreation Area, 30 miles northwest of the city. *See Recreation Chart.*

Corpus Christi Area Convention and Visitors Bureau: 1823 N. Chaparral St., Corpus Christi, TX 78401; phone (361) 561-2000 or (800) 766-2322.

[SAVE] **ART MUSEUM OF SOUTH TEXAS** is at 1902 N. Shoreline Blvd. in Bayfront Arts and Science Park. Changing exhibits of prints, paintings, sculpture, photography and folk art are presented. Tues.-Sat. 10-5 (also first Thurs. of the month 5-9), Sun. 1-5; closed Jan. 1, Easter, Thanksgiving and Dec. 25. Admission $3; over 60 and ages 13-19, $2; under 12 free; free to all Thurs. AX, MC, VI. Phone (361) 825-3500.

ASIAN CULTURES MUSEUM AND EDUCATIONAL CENTER is in Bayfront Arts and Science Park at 1809 N. Chaparral St. Life in the Orient is portrayed through exhibits of pottery, kimonos, bronzeware, watercolors, Japanese dolls, masks, funerary and ancient Hindu art as well as objects from the Tang, Sung and Ming dynasties. A Buddhist art exhibit contains a large bronze Buddha made in 1766. Tues.-Sat. 10-5. Admission $5; students $2; under 13, $1. AX, MC, VI. Phone (361) 882-2641.

CORPUS CHRISTI MUSEUM OF SCIENCE AND HISTORY is in Bayfront Arts and Science Park at 1900 N. Chaparral St. Natural science and natural history are the focus of interpretive exhibits and hands-on activities. Visitors can explore a Spanish shipwreck of 1554, identify local shells and birds, view live alligators and other South Texas reptiles, walk among native plants and play in the Children's Wharf exhibit.

The Seeds of Change commemorates the impact of Christopher Columbus' voyages on the world. Replicas of Columbus' 15th-century ships the *Pinta* and *Santa Maria* are moored outside the museum. Allow 1 hour, 30 minutes minimum. Tues.-Sat. 10-5, Sun. noon-5; closed Jan. 1, Thanksgiving and Dec. 25. Admission $9; over 60, $7; students and military with ID $6; ages 5-12, $5. AX, MC, VI. Phone (361) 883-2862.

[GEM] **TEXAS STATE AQUARIUM** is at 2710 N. Shoreline Blvd. on Corpus Christi Beach. Whales, stingrays, dolphins and sharks [SAVE] adorn the entrance to the aquarium, which is dedicated to the aquatic inhabitants and habitats of the Gulf of Mexico. Visitors pass under a waterfall representing a full submersion into the Gulf.

The Islands of Steel habitat, a replica of an offshore oil platform, features a 132,000-gallon tank with more than 150 marine animals. Moray eels, angelfish and a barracuda live in the Flower Gardens Coral Reef. Other habitats are home to otters, alligators, sea turtles, marsh birds, hermit crabs, sea urchins and jellyfish. The aquarium also offers changing exhibits, dive shows, feeding demonstrations and hands-on experiences with sharks and stingrays. Guides are available to explain exhibits and answer questions about the aquarium's programs for education, conservation and wildlife rehabilitation.

Allow 1 hour, 30 minutes minimum. Mon.-Sat. 9-6, Sun. 10-6, Memorial Day-Labor Day; Mon.-Sat. 9-5, Sun. 10-5, rest of year. Closed Thanksgiving and Dec. 25. Admission $9.25; over 60 and military with ID $7.75; ages 4-12, $5.50. Parking $3. AX, MC, VI. Phone (361) 881-1200 or (800) 477-4853.

USS *LEXINGTON* MUSEUM ON THE BAY is docked at 2914 N. Shoreline Blvd. This floating naval museum features tours of the wartime aircraft carrier commissioned in 1943. Because the ship was navy blue and was reported sunk no less than four times during World War II, it was nicknamed "The Blue Ghost" by the Japanese. Self-guiding tours of the 910-foot carrier offer views of the flight deck, bridge, sick bay, captain's quarters and hangar deck, complete with several planes and engines. Tours involve climbing up steep stairways; comfortable walking shoes are recommended.

A multi-media presentation is offered in a large-screen theater aboard the ship. Allow 1 hour, 30 minutes minimum. Daily 9-6, Memorial Day-Labor Day; 9-5, rest of year. Closed Dec. 25. Admission $10; over 60 and military with ID $8; ages 4-12, $5. Combination ticket (includes theater) $13; over 60 and military with ID $11; ages 4-12, $8; under 4, $4. AX, DS, MC, VI. Phone (361) 888-4873 or (800) 523-9539.

CORSICANA (D-9) pop. 24,485, elev. 328'

Corsicana's officials were disappointed when oil was struck in 1894 during an attempt to locate a water supply for the town. Within a year not only water but also an abundance of oil had been discovered, and Corsicana became one of the first commercial oil-well and refinery sites west of the Mississippi. The rotary drill bit, used in drilling operations for commercial wells, was developed in Corsicana.

Corsicana Area Chamber of Commerce: 120 N. 12th St., Corsicana, TX 75110; phone (903) 874-4731 or (877) 376-7477.

PIONEER VILLAGE is 1 mi. n.w. at 912 W. Park Ave., just n. of SR 22. This restored log cabin village includes an American Indian trading post, a smithy, a general store and slave quarters. Early Texas furniture, documents and pre-Civil War artifacts are displayed. The carriage house contains an early iron-wheeled tractor.

The log cabin Melton Kitchen includes a pioneer kitchen with Texana furnishings while the McKie Playhouse is complete with early children's toys. Western and Civil-War items are displayed in the Sam Roberts Museum and the Lefty Frizzell Museum honors the Corsicana-born country singer. The Peace Officers Museum displays pictures and artifacts from the careers of law enforcement legends and outlaws. Mon.-Sat. 9-5, Sun. 1-5; closed Jan. 1, Easter, Mother's Day and Dec. 25. Admission $2; ages 12-18, $1; ages 6-11, 50c. Phone (903) 654-4846.

CRESSON (D-8) elev. 1,054'

Founded circa 1887, Cresson was named for an official of the Fort Worth & Rio Grande Railway Co.

PATE MUSEUM OF TRANSPORTATION is 3 mi. n. on US 377. Antique automobiles, airplanes, helicopters, a mine sweeper and a railroad car are featured. Tues.-Sat. 9-5, Sun. 11-5. Free. Phone (817) 396-4305.

CROSBYTON (C-6) pop. 1,874

Once the site of the Two Buckle Ranch, Crosbyton is an agricultural community. Associated Cotton Growers, reputedly the world's largest cotton-processing plant producing stripped cotton, serves 520 producers in a 50-mile radius.

Crosbyton Chamber of Commerce: 114 W. Aspen, Crosbyton, TX 79322; phone (806) 675-2261.

CROSBY COUNTY PIONEER MUSEUM is at 101 W. Main St. Pioneer life is depicted through replicas of houses and collections of household articles, crafts and equipment. Exhibits also include American Indian artifacts and ecological displays. Allow 1 hour, 30 minutes minimum. Tues.-Sat. 9-noon and 1-5; closed holidays. Donations. Phone (806) 675-2331.

DALHART (A-5) pop. 7,237, elev. 3,984'

First known as Twist, Dalhart grew from a junction of Denver City and Rock Island Railroad lines that crossed here in 1901. It was later named Denroc, a melding of the two railroad names, and finally its present Dalhart, a syllable combination of the two counties in which it resides, Dallam and Hartley. Dalhart now serves as a shipping point for cattle, grains and other agricultural products.

The Empty Saddle Monument north of US 87 was commissioned in 1940 to honor an XIT cowhand who died on his way to Dalhart for a reunion; the statue of a riderless horse has come to symbolize all pioneers who helped build the town.

Dalhart Chamber of Commerce: 102 E. Seventh St., Dalhart, TX 79022; phone (806) 244-5646.

XIT MUSEUM is at 108 E. Fifth St. across from the courthouse. The XIT Ranch was once a working ranch of more than 3 million acres. Museum exhibits include a 1900 chapel, parlor, bedroom and kitchen; a chuck wagon, an antique switchboard, an antique gun collection, works of Texas artists and a revolving American Indian artifacts exhibit. Guided tours are available. Allow 30 minutes minimum. Tues.-Sat. 9-5; closed major holidays and Dec. 25-Jan. 1. Donations. Phone (806) 244-5390.

Dallas

To outsiders Dallas represents Texas, displaying the characteristics associated with the state—individualism, affluence and sheer size, almost larger than life. Through a combination of big thinking and swashbuckling free enterprise, a dusty river crossing with no discernible assets was transformed into modern Dallas, a leading commercial and financial center and the country's eighth largest city.

The town began slowly. John Neely Bryan chose the site in 1841 and erected a single cabin. He believed that the Trinity River was navigable for trade all the way to the Gulf of Mexico. He was mistaken, and 3 years later the site consisted of only two cabins. Bryan then realized that he would have to settle for ferrying emigrants across the river. A steamboat reached Dallas from Galveston in 1868, but the journey took more than a year, and Bryan's new settlement languished until after the Civil War.

In 1872, through bribes and gifts of land, Dallas' leaders convinced the Texas Central Railroad to divert its tracks to the community. A year later the Texas Pacific arrived, and because of a nationwide financial panic the town became the temporary railhead for both lines. The effect was immediate. The population doubled to 6,000, and soon wagonloads of wheat, wool and other products crowded in to be shipped via the railroad.

By 1900 Dallas was a regional banking center for north Texas farmers and one of the world's largest inland cotton markets. Its financial role was enhanced when many insurance firms, prompted by a 1908 Texas law requiring them to keep a major part of their reserves in the state, established headquarters in the city.

The catalyst for modern Dallas was the 1930 oil strike in east Texas. The city became a conduit for the wealth generated by the nearby oil fields. Many Dallas citizens became millionaires as the community became more affluent. Persuasion and occasional machinations brought such prestigious commercial plums as the regional Federal Reserve Bank and the 1936 Texas Centennial Exhibition to Dallas. The latter provided the city with a windfall of buildings as well as the lucrative Texas State Fair.

As early as 1908 congestion and the frequent flooding of the Trinity River had forced city fathers to consider rebuilding. George Kessler, a planning engineer, proposed straightening the Trinity River, removing the railroad tracks beyond the city limits, widening the streets and developing business and residential zones. To many these proposals were too radical, but over time Kessler's plan was carried out.

Kessler's ideas are visible in the modern cityscape, where the largest buildings are concentrated in the downtown area. One Dallas Center, the Plaza of the Americas

and the Reunion Complex are mixed-use buildings incorporating offices, hotels and retail outlets. To balance these forbidding structures, an ambitious 20-block arts district draws residents to downtown after dark. Such nearby oases of calm as the John Fitzgerald Kennedy Memorial at Main and Market streets, and Thanks-Giving Square at Pacific and Bryan avenues *(see attraction listings p. 83 and 83, respectively)* offer a chance to escape and reflect amid the frenetic inner city.

Many historic buildings have been preserved as well. The West End Historic District, bounded by Elm, Record and Lamar streets and the Woodall Rodgers Freeway, preserves a turn-of-the-20th-century business district that is now a lively retail area. Another such area is the Swiss Avenue Historic District, where Georgian, Prairie, Spanish and other architectural styles are reflected in the 200 houses concentrated in several blocks of Bryan Parkway, Swiss Avenue and La Vista, Live Oak and Bryan streets.

One of the city's outstanding individual historic restoration projects is Union Station at Houston Street between Wood and Young. Vaulted ceilings and a glazed terra-cotta walk are highlights of this 1914 building, which houses the Amtrak station.

Although Dallas was home to such blues musicians as Blind Lemon Jefferson and Huddie Leadbetter (Leadbelly), its most prominent cultural contributions are its buildings. Some of the country's leading architects have lent their skills to shaping the city. I.M. Pei designed the distinctive City Hall, an immense triangle balancing on one edge; Frank Lloyd Wright inspired the Dallas Theatre Center, the only theater built to his design; and William D. Cook, designer of Beverly Hills, laid out the fashionable suburb of Highland Park.

The educational and cultural resources of Southern Methodist University, the University of Texas at Dallas, the University of Texas at Arlington and nearby Baylor as well as other colleges, enhance Dallas' entrepreneurial ability and enrich the lives of its citizens.

T.R. Fehrenbach, noted Texas historian, once suggested a Texas motto: "We chose this land; we took it; we made it bear fruit." Fehrenbach was speaking about Texas in general, but his quote could apply equally well to Dallas. On the remote prairie, in the shadow of a cattle boomtown, John Neely Bryan staked his land claim. Now Bryan's reconstructed one-room cabin sits neatly in Historic Square in the shadow of a towering skyscraper in the cosmopolitan heart of Dallas.

Approaches
By Car

Major highways provide quick access to the city. US 75 (North Central Expressway) and the Dallas North Tollway approach from the north, I-45 (South Central Expressway) from the southeast, I-20 and I-30 (R.L. Thornton Freeway) from the east, and I-30 from the west. I-35 runs northwest to southwest.

(continued on p. 80)

The Informed Traveler

City Population: 1,188,580

Elevation: 434 ft.

Sales Tax: Municipalities may impose additional rates of up to 2 percent on the statewide 6.25 percent sales tax. Sales tax in the city of Dallas is 8.25 percent; rates vary in the suburbs.

WHOM TO CALL

Emergency: 911

Police (non-emergency): (214) 670-3011

Fire: (214) 670-3011

Time: (214) 844-1111

Weather: (214) 787-1111

Hospitals: Baylor University Medical Center, (214) 820-0111; Methodist Medical Center, (214) 947-8181; St. Paul Medical Center, (214) 879-1000.

WHERE TO LOOK

Newspapers

Dallas has one daily newspaper, the *Dallas Morning News*.

Radio

Dallas radio station WBAP (820 AM) is an all-news/weather station; KERA (90.1 FM) is a member of National Public Radio.

Visitor Information

The Dallas Visitor Center in the Old Red Courthouse at 100 S. Houston, Dallas, TX 75202, is open Mon.-Fri. 8-5. Phone (214) 746-6679 for events information.

TRANSPORTATION

Air Travel

Dallas/Fort Worth International Airport, 18 miles northwest of downtown between SRs 183 and 114, is served by domestic and foreign passenger carriers. Transportation to surrounding cities is provided by several shuttle services including SuperShuttle, a door-to-door ride-share system. Taxis are available at curbside. Seven miles northwest of downtown, Love Field offers commuter air transit throughout the region.

Rental Cars

Hertz, (972) 453-0370 or (800) 654-3080, at Dallas/Fort Worth International Airport, offers discounts to AAA members. For listings of other agencies check the telephone directory.

Rail Service

Amtrak's Union Station is at 400 S. Houston; for train schedule and ticket information phone (214) 653-1101 or (800) 872-7245.

Buses

The Greyhound Lines Inc. bus station, (800) 231-2222, is at 205 S. Lamar St.; five other bus lines depart from this address.

Taxis

Taxis are metered. The initial charge is $3.60 for the first mile; rates are then 40c for each additional quarter-mile, and $2 for each additional passenger. Yellow Cab, (214) 426-6262, is the main company serving the area; other companies are listed in the telephone directory.

Public Transport

The Dallas Area Rapid Transit System (DART) provides light-rail and bus service in the area. Fares are $1 for local routes and $2 for premium routes. Exact change is required. Phone (214) 979-1111.

The McKinney Avenue Trolley connects the historic West End district with downtown. Beginning near the Dallas Museum of Art, the trolley runs up McKinney Avenue to Blackburn Street and the DART Cityplace Station, and then back downtown. The free trolley runs Mon.-Fri. 7 a.m.-10 p.m., Sat. 10-10, Sun. noon-10. Phone (214) 855-0006.

Destination Dallas

*T*exas longhorn. Big business. Oil. A sophisticated metropolis where Southwestern hospitality blends with a touch of the Old West.

*S*top by Pioneer Plaza and visit with 70 bovine friends made of bronze. Or view the city's architecture atop Reunion Tower, a signature landmark. Museums, zoos, parks, sports and culture—the Big D has it all.

Morton H. Meyerson Symphony Center, Dallas. Italian marble and African cherrywood adorn this acoustically-superior hall, designed by I.M. Pei. (See mention page 84)

The Sixth Floor Museum at Dealey Plaza, Dallas. Photographs and artifacts document the assassination of John F. Kennedy—at the site from which the fatal shots were fired. (See listing page 83)

The Science Place, Dallas. Honeybees buzz and dinosaurs roar at this hands-on museum for kids of all ages. (See listing page 82)

See Vicinity map page 85

*P*laces included in this AAA Destination City:

Dallas Zoo. Endangered tigers are part of this zoo's worldwide conservation program. (See listing page 81)

Getting Around

Street System

Because the streets of Dallas are not designed in the traditional grid pattern, it is wise to refer to a map when driving downtown. Major thoroughfares run from northwest to southeast and northeast to southwest. The principal street is Main Street, which runs southwest to northeast; other key streets include Elm Street, which is one way southwest, and Commerce Street, one way northeast.

The speed limit on most streets is 30 mph or as posted. Freeway limits range from 40 to 65 mph as posted. Rush hours are generally from 7:30 to 9 a.m. and from 4 to 6:30 p.m. Most signal lights are on the corners, but be alert for signals hanging in the center of intersections. Right turns are permitted on red; exceptions are marked.

Parking

Numerous garages and parking lots compensate for the virtual absence of on-street parking downtown. Rates range from 50c to $3 each half-hour or $3-$6 a day.

What To See

BIBLICAL ARTS CENTER is off US 75 Park Ln. exit, then 2 mi. w. to 7500 Park Ln. at Boedeker. Nondenominational religious art is featured from around the world, including paintings, sculptures, icons and clerical artifacts displayed in a building reminiscent of early Christian-era architecture. The "Miracle at Pentecost" mural, two stories high and one-third the length of a football field, has a 30-minute sound and light presentation.

The center also includes the Miracle at Pentecost Museum, the Founder's Gallery and the Atrium Gallery, with a replica of the tomb of Christ. Exhibits in the East Gallery are changed every 6 to 8 weeks. Allow 1 hour minimum. Tues.-Sat. 10-5, Sun. 1-4; closed Jan. 1, Thanksgiving and Dec. 24-25. Art galleries free. Presentation $7; over 65 and ages 6-18, $6. MC, VI. Phone (214) 691-4661.

DALLAS ARBORETUM AND BOTANICAL GARDEN is at 8525 Garland Rd. The arboretum embraces 66 acres of trees, flowers and display gardens beside White Rock Lake. Perennials are the focus of Lay Ornamental Garden; the Jonsson Color Garden features azaleas. A Woman's Garden

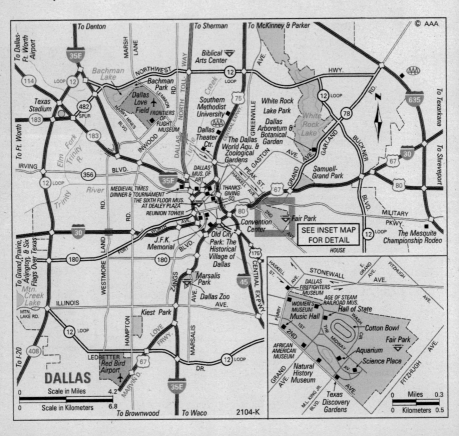

offers an enclosed sanctuary, wind-activated harps and a reflective basin. The arboretum has a self-guiding walks and a wildflower trail. Tours of the 1930s DeGolyer House and Gardens are available. Picnicking is permitted.

Mon.-Thurs. 10-9, Fri.-Sun. 10-5, June-Aug.; daily 10-5, rest of year. Tours of DeGolyer House are given every half-hour. Admission $6; over 65, $5; ages 3-12, $3. Parking $3. Phone (214) 327-8263.

DALLAS MUSEUM OF ART is at 1717 N. Harwood. Displays range from pre-Columbian and African artifacts to Impressionistic and contemporary works. Exhibited are works by Henri Matisse, Claude Monet and John Singer Sargent, sculpture by Henry Moore and Auguste Rodin as well as traveling displays. Thematic tours about sculpture, landscapes, textiles and crafts as well as varied programs are available. Sculpture and fountains adorn the grounds. Food is available.

Allow 2 hours minimum. Tues.-Sun. 11-5 (also Thurs. 5-9); closed Jan. 1, Thanksgiving and Dec. 25. Admission $6; over 65 and ages 12-18, $4; free to all Thurs. 5-9 and first Tues. of the month. Phone (214) 922-1200.

The Wendy and Emery Reves Collection is on the third floor of the Dallas Museum of Art. The collection includes Impressionist and post-Impressionist works by such masters as Paul Cézanne, Paul Gauguin, Claude Monet, Pierre Auguste Renoir and Vincent van Gogh. Also displayed are antique furniture, Chinese porcelain and Winston Churchill memorabilia. The wing re-creates rooms of the Reves' Mediterranean villa. Free guided tours are available. Allow 1 hour minimum. Phone (214) 922-1200.

DALLAS MUSEUM OF NATURAL HISTORY— *see Fair Park p. 82.*

THE DALLAS WORLD AQUARIUM & ZOOLOGICAL GARDEN is 1 blk. n. of Ross Ave. at 1801 N. Griffin St. in the West End District. Ocean exhibits include a walk-through tunnel from which stingrays, sharks and sea turtles can be seen. Jaguars, red howler monkeys, endangered Orinoco crocodiles, anacondas, piranhas and vampire bats live in the Venezuelan rain forest habitat. Manatees swim in a 22,000-gallon tank. The Cape of Good Hope exhibit is home to a penguin colony.

Food is available. Allow 1 hour minimum. Daily 10-5; closed Thanksgiving and Dec. 25. Admission $10.95; over 60, $8; ages 3-12, $6. Parking $3. AX, DC, DS, MC, VI. Phone (214) 720-2224.

DALLAS ZOO is in Marsalis Park, 3 mi. s. on I-35E (Marsalis Ave. exit) at 650 S. R.L. Thornton Frwy. A 67-foot giraffe statue, said to be the tallest in Texas, greets visitors at the entrance. The 85-acre zoo features rare and endangered species and includes a gorilla conservation center. The 25-acre Wilds of Africa wilderness reserve re-creates six habitats: bush, desert, forest, mountain, river and woodland. Visitors can take a monorail ride through the African exhibit or walk a 1,500-foot nature trail.

The Endangered Tiger Habitat is home to Sumatran and Indochinese tigers, part of the zoo's conservation program. The naturalistic, open-air environment of the chimpanzee forest encourages the primates to climb, fish and interact. Noteworthy in the reptile house is the collection of rattlesnakes. A walk-through tropical rain forest features exotic birds. The LaCerte Family Children's Zoo features exhibits and activities related to wildlife conservation.

Zoo daily 9-5. Monorail tours are given daily 10-4 (weather permitting). Closed Dec. 25. Admission $7; over 65 and ages 3-11, $4. Monorail $2. Parking $4. Phone (214) 670-5656.

FAIR PARK is 2 mi. e. on US 67/80, 3 blks. e. of I-30. This 277-acre complex was the site of the 1936 Texas Centennial Exhibition. Many *moderne* buildings—a type of Art Deco architecture popularized by movie theaters in the 1930s—now house museums and provide exposition space for the State Fair of Texas in October. Murals and sculptures of mermaids and winged horses adorn the park, which plays host to more than 100 events each year. Visitors also can view the Texas Vietnam Veterans Memorial. Food is available.

Grounds open daily 24 hours; closed 1 week in early Oct. prior to the state fair. When visiting the park at night, it is advisable to park in an attended lot and travel with a companion. Free. Phone (214) 670-8400, or (214) 421-9600 for event information.

African American Museum is at 3536 Grand Ave. Art, culture and history are preserved at this museum, which houses an extensive collection of African American folk art. Tues.-Fri. noon-5, Sat. 10-5, Sun. 1-5; closed major holidays. Donations. Phone (214) 565-9026.

The Age of Steam Railroad Museum is at 1105 Washington St. Housed in a 1905 depot that was relocated to the site, this museum displays an impressive collection of steam and early diesel-era trains. Visitors can board a complete passenger train that includes a 1926 Pullman first-class sleeping car, a 1937 dining car and a 1914 parlor-club car. Steam locomotives include the 1942 Union Pacific "Big Boy." Wed.-Sun. 10-5; closed major holidays. Admission $5; ages 3-12, $2.50. AX, DS, MC, VI. Phone (214) 428-0101.

Cotton Bowl is at 3750 Midway Plaza Blvd. The site of the New Year's Day football classic seats 72,000 for sports events.

Dallas Aquarium is at 1462 First Ave. Upside-down jellyfish and walking batfish are among the unusual creatures at the aquarium, which is home to more than 420 exotic and native aquatic species. Allow 1 hour minimum. Daily 9-4:30. Shark and piranha feedings are held Tues.-Sun. at 2:30. Closed

Thanksgiving and Dec. 25. Admission $3; ages 3-11, $1.50. Phone (214) 670-8443.

Dallas Firefighters Museum is at 3801 Parry Ave. This museum commemorates the history and service of the Dallas Fire Department from 1872 to the present. Horse-drawn and motorized fire engines, fire-fighting equipment and memorabilia are displayed in the Old No. 5 Hook & Ladder Station, erected in 1907. Wed.-Sat. 9-4; closed major holidays. Admission $2; ages 3-18, $1; over 65 free. Phone (214) 821-1500.

Dallas Museum of Natural History is at 3535 Grand Ave. Native animals, birds, minerals and plants are exhibited in their natural habitats. City Safari is a bilingual hands-on center for ages 3-10. Life-size skeleton casts, bones found in Big Bend National Park, real eggs and a simulated dig site are among the museum's dinosaur artifacts. National and international traveling exhibits also are featured. Allow 1 hour minimum. Daily 10-5; closed Thanksgiving and Dec. 25. Admission $6.50; over 55, $5.50; ages 13-18, $5; ages 3-12, $4. Phone (214) 421-3466.

Hall of State is at 3939 Grand Ave. Built in 1936, the centennial year of Texas independence, the state building contains the Museum of Texas History, statuary and two of the world's largest oil murals. A gold medallion symbolizing the six nations to which Texas has paid allegiance dominates the Hall of Six Flags. In the Sharp Gallery, the American Museum of Miniature Arts features permanent and traveling collections of doll houses, miniatures and militaria. Open Tues.-Sat. 9-5, Sun. 1-5; closed Thanksgiving and Dec. 25. Hall free. Admission to American Museum of Miniature Arts by donation. Phone (214) 421-4500.

Music Hall At Fair Park is at 909 First Ave. Home of the Dallas Opera, the hall also presents the Dallas Summer Musicals and a variety of special performances.

The Science Place is at 1318 Second Ave. Visitors can lift a ton using one hand, bend light, stargaze in the planetarium or watch films projected onto a 70-foot-high dome in the TI Founders IMAX Theater.

Tues.-Fri. 9:30-4:30, Sat. 9:30-5:30, Sun. 11:30-5:30. IMAX times and shows vary; phone ahead. Closed Dec. 25. Science Place $6; over 60 and ages 3-12, $3. IMAX Theater $6; over 60 and ages 3-12, $5. Planetarium $3. AX, DS, MC, VI. Phone (214) 428-5555.

Texas Discovery Gardens is at 3601 Martin Luther King Jr. Blvd. The 7-acre site features native Texas plants, roses and a conservatory for African flora. Allow 1 hour minimum. Tues.-Sat. 10-5, Sun. 1-5; closed Jan. 1, Thanksgiving and Dec. 25. Free. Phone (214) 428-7476.

The Women's Museum: An Institute for the Future is at 3800 Parry Ave. This museum celebrates the accomplishments and contributions of American women throughout history. Leaders, innovators, authors, artists, athletes and women of wit are highlighted in interactive exhibits that include an electronic quilt and a 30-foot-high media wall. Tues.-Sat., 10-5, Sun. noon-5; closed major holidays. Admission $5; over 65 and ages 12-18, $4; ages 5-11, $3. Phone (214) 915-0860.

FRONTIERS OF FLIGHT MUSEUM is at Love Field Terminal, 8008 Cedar Springs Rd. Maps, photographs, documents, model airplanes, artifacts and vintage airplane parts chronicle the history of aviation. Displays include Adm. Richard E. Byrd's fur parka and items recovered from the Hindenberg crash. Allow 1 hour minimum. Mon.-Sat. and holidays 10-5, Sun. 1-5; closed Jan. 1, Thanksgiving and Dec. 25. Admission $3; ages 2-12, $1.50. AX, MC, VI. Phone (214) 350-1651.

HALL OF STATE—*see Fair Park p. 82.*

INTERNATIONAL MUSEUM OF CULTURES is at 7500 W. Camp Wisdom Rd. This museum represents the work of an organization that creates written language for peoples who have none. Cultures and lifestyles are reflected through pottery, habitat displays and depictions of the life of an Indian from birth to adulthood. Allow 1 hour minimum. Tues.-Fri. 10-5, Sat.-Sun. 1:30-5. Donations. Guided tours $2, students with ID $1. Phone (972) 708-7406.

JOHN FITZGERALD KENNEDY MEMORIAL is at Main and Market sts. This monument to the 35th president, who was assassinated nearby in 1963, is designed as a place of meditation. It has walls to shut out noise and is open to the sky for spiritual communication. Free.

MEDIEVAL TIMES DINNER AND TOURNAMENT is off I-35 exit Market Center Blvd. (430B), then 1.5 mi. n.w. to 2021 N. Stemmons Frwy. Visitors are guests in a replica of an 11th-century castle, where, as in medieval days, a four-course dinner is served with no silverware. During dinner, knights on horseback compete in jousting matches and events of skill and accuracy. Allow 3 hours minimum. Shows Wed.-Thurs. at 7:30, Fri.-Sat. at 8, Sun. at 5. Admission $44; over 54, $39.60; under 13, $30.75. Reservations are required. AX, DS, MC, VI. Phone (214) 761-1800 or (800) 229-9900.

OLD CITY PARK: THE HISTORICAL VILLAGE OF DALLAS is downtown at 1717 Gano St. The village is a collection of 38 relocated and restored 1840-1910 structures. On the 13-acre site are a train depot, doctor's office, a Victorian bandstand on the village green, furnished log cabins, a general store, Southern Colonial mansions and a working farm, where costumed interpreters recreate the lives of 1861 homesteaders. Guided 1-hour tours are offered, and rides are available aboard 10-passenger donkey wagons.

Tues.-Sat. 10-4, Sun. noon-4; closed Jan. 1, Thanksgiving and Dec. 24-25 and 31. Tours depart Tues.-Sat. at 10:15, 11:30, 1:15 and 2:30; Sun. at 12:15, 1:45 and 3. Admission $7; over 65, $5; ages 3-12, $4. AX, MC, VI. Phone (214) 421-5141.

REUNION TOWER OF DALLAS is at 300 Reunion Blvd. The 50-story tower is the focal point of the Reunion area, a settlement of French emigrants in the 19th century. Topped by a three-level geodesic sphere that houses a restaurant, observation deck and revolving lounge, the tower is illuminated at night. Observation deck Sun.-Thurs. 10-10, Fri.-Sat. 9 a.m.-midnight. Admission $2; under 12, $1. Phone (214) 651-1234.

THE SCIENCE PLACE—*see Fair Park p. 82.*

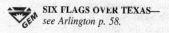 **SIX FLAGS OVER TEXAS—** *see Arlington p. 58.*

THE SIXTH FLOOR MUSEUM AT DEALEY PLAZA is at 411 Elm St. President John F. Kennedy's life, death and legacy are chronicled at the site of his assassination. More than 400 photographs, artifacts and models are displayed on the sixth floor of the former Texas School Book Depository. A 10-minute film narrated by Walter Cronkite reviews the long-term impact of Kennedy's death. Audio tours are available in seven languages. Children's audio tours for ages 6-12 are available in English.

Allow 1 hour, 30 minutes minimum. Daily 9-6; closed Thanksgiving and Dec. 25. Admission $10;

over 65 and ages 6-18, $9. Audio Tour $3. Phone (214) 747-6660 or (214) 653-6659.

TEXAS STADIUM—*see Irving p. 86.*

THANKS-GIVING SQUARE is bounded by Pacific Ave. and Bryan and Ervay sts. Dedicated to the principle of gratitude for life in all its manifestations, the square provides an oasis of calm in downtown Dallas with waterfalls, reflecting pools, a chapel, bell tower and meditation garden. The Hall of World Thanksgiving presents the detailed story of the American Thanksgiving tradition. Mon.-Fri. 9-5. Donations. Phone (214) 969-1977.

What To Do

Sightseeing

Boat Tours

The *Texas Queen,* an oldtime stern-wheeler docked at Robertson Park east off I-30, offers dinner cruises on Lake Ray Hubbard. Phone (972) 771-0039 for fare and schedule.

Bus Tours

The best way to familiarize yourself with Dallas is to take a tour of the city. Texas Trail Tours, (972) 222-5838, offers tours emphasizing the cultural, historical and economic aspects of Dallas, including Fair Park, the John Fitzgerald Kennedy Memorial and the World Trade Center. Longhorn Tours offers several tours that include Dallas' major attractions; phone (972) 228-4571.

Sports and Recreation

Athletes can enjoy many sports offered in and near Dallas. The list ranges from **golf** to **horseback riding** to **ice skating.** Many city parks have public golf courses, **tennis** courts and **swimming** pools. For **fishing, boating** and **water-skiing** enthusiasts, there are a number of lakes within an hour's drive.

A variety of professional sports is played in Dallas and nearby cities. The National **Football** League's Dallas Cowboys can be seen in action at Texas Stadium *(see Irving p. 85).* The Cotton Bowl in Fair Park *(see attraction listing p. 81)* sponsors Southern Methodist University college football and is packed with activities for football fans during Cotton Bowl Week, which runs from Dec. 26 to Jan. 1. The stadium also is home to the Dallas Burn of Major League **Soccer.** The Indoor Soccer League's Dallas Sidekicks compete at Reunion Arena.

The National **Basketball** Association's Dallas Mavericks and the National **Hockey** League's Dallas Stars play at American Airlines Center. The American League's Texas Rangers play **baseball** at The Ball Park in Arlington. Also popular are amateur basketball and tennis tournaments. During fair weather, **sailing** buffs can enjoy the amateur races on Sunday at White Rock Lake. Professional **rodeos** are held weekends April through September in suburban Mesquite *(see place listing p. 86).*

Shopping

For the shopper Dallas is utopia, offering everything from a midget submarine to Mexican imports. Without question, the legend in Dallas shopping is Neiman-Marcus, with its main store at Main and Ervay streets. This internationally known store has sold such frivolities as polar-bear rugs and "his and hers" camels. The store also has a supply of general merchandise.

Dallas is reputed to have more retail space per capita than any other American city and has some 630 shopping centers. One of the best known is The Dallas Galleria, at the intersection of Dallas Parkway and LBJ Freeway. Within this high-tech complex are more than 160 stores—including Macy's, Nordstrom and Saks Fifth Avenue—and an ice skating rink. An even larger collection of stores, including Dillard's, Foleys, JCPenney and Sears, is in the nearby Valley View Center.

The West End Marketplace is a former cracker factory transformed into a collection of specialty shops and eateries in downtown's historic West End. Just north of the Marketplace is the Quadrangle, between Cedar Springs and McKinney, where shops and galleries cluster around quiet courtyards.

Other areas noted for specialty shops include Old Town in the Village, Greenville Avenue and Lovers Lane. At the Farmers Market, 1010 S. Pearl Expwy., seasonal fresh fruits and vegetables are available daily.

Suburban shopping matches the downtown area for style with its complexes and malls. Among the largest of these facilities are North Park, corner of N.W. Highway and US 75; Southwest Center, Camp Wisdom and US 67; and Town East, at the intersection of Town East Boulevard and I-635. Eighteen miles north in Plano, Collin Creek Mall is one of the bigger malls in the state.

DID YOU KNOW

Famous
Texans include
Lyndon B. Johnson,
Willie Nelson and
Janis Joplin.

For more down-to-earth tastes, Traders Village covers 106 acres off SR 360 in Grand Prairie and offers a Texas-size flea market that includes rides, an arcade, a carousel and many events.

For outdoor adventurers, Bass Pro Shops Outdoor World, at the intersection of SR 121 and I-635 in Grapevine, features a 30,000-gallon aquarium and waterfall, archery and driving ranges, wildlife exhibits and sporting demonstrations.

Theater and Concerts

Throughout the year Dallas echoes with the sound of music. The celebrated Dallas Symphony Orchestra performs at Morton H. Meyerson Hall across from the Dallas Museum of Art. Each April the symphony heralds the arrival of spring with free park concerts; phone (214) 871-4000 for the symphony or (214) 443-1043 for the opera.

Summer brings the Dallas Summer Musicals to the Music Hall at Fair Park (see attraction listing p. 82) and varied performers to Smirnoff Music Center. The Black Dance Theatre troupe can be seen during the year at Majestic Theater, 1925 Elm St. Reunion Arena, 777 Sports St., is the scene of concerts and sporting events.

Stage plays are presented at Dallas Theatre Center, 3636 Turtle Creek Blvd., and at Theatre Three, 2800 Routh St. in Quadrangle Shopping Center. Southern Methodist University's Margo Jones Experimental Theatre and Bob Hope Theatre feature student productions during the academic year.

Special Events

On New Year's Eve afternoon, floats and marching bands kick off Dallas' year with the Southwestern Bell Cotton Bowl Parade and the college football classic, held at its Fair Park namesake. Fair Park also is home, during October, to Dallas' other major event, the State Fair of Texas, which many Texans consider the biggest and best state fair in the country.

Spring is ushered in with Dallas Blooms, a festival of flowers held during March and early April at the Dallas Arboretum and Botanical Garden. In early May the city honors one of its historic districts with the Swiss Avenue Tour of Homes. Closing out spring is the Artfest, over Memorial Day weekend; more than 300 artisans display their works amid a variety of entertainment.

During the summer entertainers perform at Fair Park's outdoor Smirnoff Music Center and the bandshell. Another theatrical highlight is the Shakespeare Festival of Dallas, which presents two plays during July and August in Samuel Grand Park.

In early August nearby Mesquite plays host to the Mesquite BalloonFest, a hot-air balloon rally.

Taking up the month of October is Cityfest, which includes exhibits, entertainment and sports events. Autumn at the Arboretum, which salutes fall with seasonal flowers, provides a splash of color.

The Dallas Vicinity

ATHENS (D-9) pop. 11,297, elev. 492′

Chosen as the seat of Henderson County in 1850, Athens was so named because it was expected to become the cultural center of the state, as was its namesake in Greece. A century later it was discovered that Athens, like its namesake, had been established on seven major hills.

Athens Visitor Center: 124 N. Palestine St., Athens, TX 75751; phone (903) 677-0775 or (888) 294-2847.

SAVE **TEXAS FRESHWATER FISHERIES CENTER** is 4 mi. e. of SR 31 on FM 2495. More than 300,000 gallons of aquarium exhibits display nearly every major species of freshwater fish found in Texas. The center includes a dive show auditorium, a fishing museum and hall of fame, an angler's pavilion and a 1.2-acre casting pond stocked with catfish and rainbow trout. Equipment is provided for catch-and-release fishing; no fishing license is required.

A 20-minute tram tour takes visitors to an outdoor hatchery and a wetlands environment, home to young American alligators. Interpretive stations along a 1.5-mile wetlands trail provide information about the region's plants, birds and wildlife. Tues.-Sat. 9-4, Sun. 1-4; closed Jan. 1, Easter, Thanksgiving and Dec. 24-25. Dive show and tram tour offered Tues.-Sat. at 11, Sat.-Sun. at 11 and 2. Admission (includes fishing) $5.50; over 64, $4.50; ages 4-12, $3.50. MC, VI. Phone (903) 676-2277.

RECREATIONAL ACTIVITIES
Scuba Diving

• **Athens Scuba Park** is 6 blks. e. on SR 31, then 1 blk. n. to 500 N. Murchison St., Athens, TX. Fri. noon-6, Sat. 8-6, Sun. 8-5, Apr.-Nov. Phone (903) 675-5762.

FARMERS BRANCH (C-9)
pop. 27,508, elev. 465′

Originating as part of a land grant in 1841, Farmers Branch came into being as Mustang Branch for the wild grapes that grew in the region. Although the tributaries of the Trinity River bring about the fertile land that gives the town its present name, industry plays a stronger role in the town's economy today.

City of Farmers Branch Office of Economic Development and Tourism: 13000 William Dodson Pkwy., P.O. Box 819010, Farmers Branch, TX 75381-9010; phone (972) 919-2634 or (800) 272-6249.

FARMERS BRANCH HISTORICAL PARK is e. of I-35E on Valley View Ln., .7 mi. s. on Rossford Rd., then e. to 2540 Farmers Branch Ln. Brick walkways link varied historic structures such as houses, a depot, a church and a school. Allow 2 hours minimum. Mon.-Thurs. 9:30-8, Sat.-Sun. noon-8, Apr.-Oct.; Mon.-Thurs. 9:30-6, Sat.-Sun. noon-6, rest of year. Closed major holidays. Free. Phone (972) 406-0184.

GRAND PRAIRIE (D-9) pop. 127,427

Originally named Dechman at the close of the Civil War, Grand Prairie has long been a thoroughfare between Dallas and Fort Worth. A historical marker denotes the Cross Timbers region, a meeting place of commerce between settlers and American Indians.

Lone Star Park, 1000 Lone Star Pkwy., holds Thoroughbred and quarter horse racing; phone (972) 263-7223 for schedule.

Note: Policies concerning admittance of children to pari-mutuel betting facilities vary. Phone for information.

Grand Prairie Convention and Visitors Bureau: 2170 N. Belt Line Rd., Grand Prairie, TX 75050; phone (972) 263-9588 or (800) 288-8386.

THE PALACE OF WAX AND RIPLEY'S BELIEVE IT OR NOT! is 1.5 mi. w. of I-30 (Belt Line Rd. exit) at 601 E. Safari Pkwy. The Palace of Wax showcases realistic wax figures portraying personalities from history, religion, childhood stories, Hollywood and horror. Ripley's offers a collection of curiosities, oddities and illusions gathered by cartoonist and world traveler Robert Ripley. Simulations allow visitors to experience an earthquake, survive a Texas tornado and walk across a bed of hot coals.

Allow 1 hour minimum. Daily 10-9, Memorial Day weekend-Labor Day; Mon.-Fri. 10-5, Sat.-Sun. 10-6, rest of year. Closed Jan. 1, Thanksgiving and Dec. 25. Last admission 1 hour before closing. Ripley's or Palace admission $11.95; over 65, $10.95; ages 4-12, $6.95. Combination ticket $15.95; ages 4-12, $9.95. AX, DS, MC, VI. Phone (972) 263-2391.

IRVING (D-9) pop. 191,615

Irving's proximity to the Dallas/Fort Worth International Airport fuels its prosperous service economy.

The city's centerpiece is the 12,000-acre development known as the Las Colinas Urban Center. Irving is home to hundreds of corporations and the Las Colinas Equestrian Center, a water ski course and The Mustangs of Las Colinas (see attraction listing).

Irving Convention and Visitors Bureau: 1231 Greenway Dr., Suite 1060, Irving, TX 75038; phone (972) 252-7476 or (800) 247-8464.

SAVE **THE MOVIE STUDIOS AT LAS COLINAS** is off SR 114 exit O'Connor Blvd., then 1.7 mi. n. to 6301 O'Connor Blvd. Guided tours offer a behind-the-scenes look at a working movie production facility that includes the state's largest soundstage. Visitors can participate in a green screen visual effects show and a Foley art demonstration. A costume museum features memorabilia from popular motion pictures. Allow 1 hour, 30 minutes minimum. Daily 9-5; closed Thanksgiving and Dec. 25. Hours may vary; phone ahead. Admission $12.95; over 65, $10.95; ages 4-12, $8.95. MC, VI. Phone (972) 869-7767.

THE MUSTANGS OF LAS COLINAS are in Williams Square of Las Colinas Urban Center at 5205 N. O'Connor Blvd. In the pink-granite plaza, nine larger-than-life bronze statues of wildly rushing mustangs appear to be splashing through a stream of water. This memorial to the heritage of Texas is believed to be the largest equestrian sculpture in the world.

The Mustangs Sculpture Exhibit is in the lobby of the West Tower at Williams Square. Photographs and a multimedia presentation explain the creation of the sculpture by renowned wildlife artist Robert Glen. Other works by Glen are displayed. Allow 30 minutes minimum. Wed.-Sat. 11-5. Closed major holidays. Last film begins 30 minutes before closing. Donations. Phone (972) 869-9047.

TEXAS STADIUM is at jct. SRs 114 and 183, Loop 12 and Carpenter Frwy., following signs to 2401 E. Airport Frwy., Gate 8. The home of the Dallas Cowboys, Texas Stadium seats 63,855. Guided tours take visitors to the Stadium Club, a luxury suite, the locker room, the players' tunnel and onto the field. Allow 1 hour minimum. Tours depart on the hour Mon.-Sat. 10-3, Sun. 11-3, except on game days and during special events. Fee $10; over 59 and ages 5-12, $6. Phone (972) 785-4787.

McKINNEY (C-9) pop. 54,369, elev. 592'

McKinney was named for Collin McKinney, a signer of the Texas Declaration of Independence. Diversified industry bolsters the city's economy.

McKinney Chamber of Commerce: 1801 W. Louisiana, McKinney, TX 75069; phone (972) 542-0163.

BOLIN WILDLIFE EXHIBIT is 1 blk. s. of US 380 at 1028 N. McDonald St. The museum features mounted wildlife from around the world. A 27-minute audiotape presentation describes the wildlife trophies; a shorter presentation covers antique automobiles. Another exhibit chronicles pioneer life in Texas. Allow 1 hour minimum. Mon.-Fri. 9-noon and 1-4; closed holidays. Free. Phone (972) 562-2639.

HEARD NATURAL SCIENCE MUSEUM AND WILDLIFE SANCTUARY is off US 75 exit 38A, then e. following signs to 1 Nature Pl. The 289-acre sanctuary is devoted to the natural history of north Texas. Displays include fossils, minerals, seashells and wildlife art. The area's native birds of prey, reptiles and amphibians also are exhibited. Four miles of nature trails lead through bottomland, woodland, prairie and wetland habitats. Picnicking is permitted. Allow 1 hour, 30 minutes minimum. Mon.-Sat. 9-5, Sun. 1-5; closed holidays. Last admission to nature trails 1 hour before closing. Admission $5; senior citizens and ages 3-12, $3. Phone (972) 562-5566.

MESQUITE (D-9) pop. 124,523, elev. 491'

Mesquite, an eastern suburb of Dallas, is the home of the Mesquite Championship Rodeo (see attraction listing). Probably the best known of the nation's rodeos, the event has elevated to fame such riders and ropers as Don Gay, Larry Mahan, Charles Sampson and Jim Shoulders. Joe Kool, considered by many to have been the toughest bull to ride, often appeared in Mesquite.

Mesquite Tourism, Convention and Promotion Division: 617 N. Ebrite, P.O. Box 850115, Mesquite, TX 75185-0115; phone (972) 285-0211.

THE MESQUITE CHAMPIONSHIP RODEO is 6.5 mi. e. off I-30 to I-635, s. 2.2 mi. to Military Pkwy. exit 4, then s. to 1818 Rodeo Dr. Held in the 5,500-seat Resistol Arena, the rodeo competition includes bull and bronco riding, steer and calf roping, barrel racing and specialty events. A grand entry parade, rodeo clowns, cowboy poker and a calf scramble are part of the entertainment, and pony rides and a petting zoo are offered before the show. Food is available. Allow 2 hours minimum. Shows are given Fri.-Sat. at 8 p.m., first weekend in Apr.-first weekend in Oct. Gates open at 6:30 p.m. Grandstand admission $10-$12; over 59 and ages 3-12, $5-$8. Pony rides $3. Parking $3. AX, DS, MC, VI. Phone (972) 285-8777.

PARKER (C-9) pop. 1,379

SAVE **SOUTHFORK RANCH** is off US 75 exit 30, 5.5 mi. e. on Parker Rd. then .2 mi. s. on FM 2551 to 3700 Hogge St. This working ranch was the setting for the television series "Dallas." A guided tour of the renowned mansion is available. Memorabilia of the show's characters are displayed, and Texas longhorns and American paint horses can be seen along the tour. Allow 1 hour minimum. Daily 9-5; closed Thanksgiving and Dec. 25. Last tour departs 30 minutes before closing. Admission $7.95; over 55, $6.95; ages 4-12, $5.95. AX, DS, MC, VI. Phone (972) 442-7800.

PLANO (C-9) pop. 222,030, elev. 655'

Originally known as Fillmore, Plano was renamed in 1851 when the post office was granted. Fires took a devastating toll on the city twice in the late 1800s. Proclaimed as the balloon capital of Texas, the city is host to hot-air balloon races on the last weekend in September.

Plano Convention and Visitors Bureau: 2000 E. Spring Creek Pkwy., Plano, TX 75074; phone (972) 422-0296.

HERITAGE FARMSTEAD is 1.2 mi. w. off US 75 exit 29 (FM 544) to 1900 W. 15th St. On the grounds of this 4-acre microcosm of early Texas farm life are a furnished late Victorian farmhouse and 12 outbuildings including a smokehouse, a country store and a windmill. The farmstead is furnished with period artifacts, including tools and vehicles. Costumed guides conduct tours.

Guided tours depart Thurs.-Fri. at 10 and noon, Sat.-Sun. at 1 and 2:45 (also Tues.-Wed. at 10, Dec.-July); closed holidays. Admission $3.50; over 62 and ages 5-17, $2.50. Phone (972) 424-7874 or (972) 881-0140.

UNIVERSITY PARK (C-9)
pop. 23,324, elev. 548'

When Southern Methodist University opened in 1915, a small community sprang up around it to house faculty members. University Park was incorporated in 1924; the university remains its largest employer.

MEADOWS MUSEUM is on the campus of Southern Methodist University at 5900 Bishop Blvd. The museum houses an extensive Spanish collection spanning the millennium from the 10th century to the end of the 20th century. These sculptures, paintings and works on paper include medieval objects from Islamic and Christian Spain; Renaissance and Baroque polychrome sculptures; and major works by such Golden Age and modern artists as El Greco, Francisco José de Goya, Bartolomé Esteban Murillo, Pablo Picasso, José Ribera and Diego Velázquez. Allow 30 minutes minimum. Mon.-Tues. and Thurs.-Sat. 10-5, (also Thurs. 5-8), Sun. 1-5; closed university holidays. Guided tours are offered Sun. at 2. Free. Phone (214) 768-2516.

WAXAHACHIE (D-9) pop. 21,426, elev. 585'

Only 30 minutes from high-tech Dallas, Waxahachie is nearly a century distant, for it is a town where the gingerbread of Victorian-era buildings sates even the most jaded architectural palate. Twenty percent of the Texas buildings listed on the National Register of Historic Places are in Waxahachie. The 1895 Ellis County Courthouse, one of the most photographed structures in the state, is a red sandstone and granite edifice decorated with ornate capitals, carved by expert Italian artisans.

Waxahachie Convention and Visitors Bureau: 102 YMCA Dr., Waxahachie, TX 75165; phone (972) 937-2390 or (972) 938-9617 in the Metroplex area.

This ends listings for the Dallas Vicinity.
The following page resumes the alphabetical listings
of cities in Texas.

DAVY CROCKETT NATIONAL FOREST (E-10)

Elevations in the forest range from 100 ft. at Cochino Bayou to 460 ft. at Neches Bluff. Refer to AAA maps for additional elevation information.

Davy Crockett National Forest borders the Neches River in east Texas. Since logging ended in the 1920s, this pine and hardwood forest has made a dramatic comeback. One of the best ways to see the 161,500-acre area is via the 20-mile-long Four C National Hiking Trail. The trail passes through a variety of terrains—sloughs, upland forests and pine woods—as it follows an old tramway from Ratcliff Lake to the Neches Overlook.

Near the forest is the Mission Tejas State Historic Park *(see Recreation Chart)*, which contains a replica of the first Spanish mission in east Texas and the Rice Stagecoach Inn.

For information contact the district ranger station at Route 1, Box 55 FS, Kennard, TX 75847, or write the Forest Supervisor, 701 N. First St., Lufkin, TX 75901. Phone (936) 655-2299, or (936) 831-2246 in Apple Springs. *See Recreation Chart and the AAA South Central CampBook.*

DEL RIO (G-6) pop. 33,867, elev. 948'

San Felipe Springs, flowing at a rate of 90 million gallons daily, provides water for domestic use and for irrigation in the Del Rio area. The city is a major inland shipping point for wool and mohair and also is an international entry point. Directly across the Rio Grande is Ciudad Acuña, Mexico.

Amistad National Recreation Area, northwest of town, offers a variety of activities *(see place listing p. 57 and Recreation Chart).*

Del Rio Chamber of Commerce: 1915 Ave. F, Del Rio, TX 78840; phone (830) 775-3551.

Self-guiding tours: The chamber of commerce offers a brochure that outlines a walking tour past historic downtown structures.

WHITEHEAD MEMORIAL MUSEUM is at 1308 S. Main St. This 2.5-acre frontier village includes 14 buildings and 21 exhibit sites. Buildings include the 1871 Perry Mercantile, a chapel, a log cabin and a blacksmith shop. A barn houses early farming and transportation equipment, including a Southern Pacific caboose and exhibits relating to the region's prehistoric inhabitants. The Jersey Lily, a replica of Judge Roy Bean's saloon and court, contains his memorabilia. The graves of the judge and his son are on the grounds. Tues.-Sat. 9-4:30, Sun. 1-5. Admission $4; senior citizens $3; ages 13-18, $2; ages 6-12, $1. Phone (830) 774-7568.

WINERIES

- **Val Verde Winery** is at 100 Qualia Dr. Open Mon.-Sat. 10-5; closed Jan. 1, Thanksgiving and Dec. 25. Phone (830) 775-9714.

DENISON (C-9) pop. 22,773, elev. 742'

Before the Civil War, Denison was the home of buffalo hunters, traders and ranchers but not of lawmen. Following the war, former Confederate soldiers forced an end to the rowdiness that had earned the settlement a reputation as a tough town. The establishment of a railroad division point and permanent industry also helped tame the town.

The city, credited with being the first to use ice in meat storage, is a center for meatpacking and transportation. Also a base for recreational opportunities, Denison is within a five-minute drive of Eisenhower State Recreation Area and Lake Texoma Recreation Area *(see attraction listing).*

Denison Area Chamber of Commerce: 313 W. Woodard, Denison, TX 75020; phone (903) 465-1551.

Self-guiding tours: Details about historical driving tours are available from the chamber of commerce.

Shopping areas: Katy Depot, 101 E. Main St., houses shops and restaurants in a restored train station.

EISENHOWER BIRTHPLACE STATE HISTORIC SITE is at Lamar Ave. and Day St. The two-story frame house in which Gen. Dwight D. Eisenhower was born has been restored to its 1890 appearance. Displays in the visitor center depict local history and Eisenhower's legacy. A 9-foot-tall bronze statue of the former President stands in the wooded 10-acre park, which includes hiking trails and picnic facilities. Tues.-Sat. 10-4, Sun. 1-5; closed Jan. 1 and Dec. 25. Admission $2; ages 6-12, $1. DS, MC, VI. Phone (903) 465-8908.

HAGERMAN NATIONAL WILDLIFE REFUGE is 6 mi. w. on FM 120, 2 mi. s. on FM 1417, then 6 mi. w. to 6465 Refuge Rd. This 11,320-acre area on the southern end of the Big Mineral Arm of Lake Texoma is a resting and feeding place for migratory birds and a winter home for geese and ducks. Shore bird migrations peak in the summer. Follow signs from FM 1417 to the refuge office.

Fishing, hiking and picnicking are permitted all year; boating is permitted April through September. The visitor center has interpretive displays and bird lists. Refuge open daily dawn-dusk. Visitor center Mon.-Fri. 7:30-4. Free. Phone (903) 786-2826.

LAKE TEXOMA RECREATION AREA lies along the Texas-Oklahoma border. The 89,000-acre Lake Texoma was created in 1944 with the construction of Denison Dam for flood control along the Red River. The 195,326-acre recreation area offers boating, camping, golf, hiking and swimming. For information contact the Texoma Project Office, U.S. Army Corps of Engineers, 351 Corps Rd., Denison, TX 75020. Daily 6 a.m.-10 p.m., Apr.-Oct. Boat ramp fee $2. Beach fee $3 per private vehicle or $1 per person. Phone (903) 465-4990. *See Recreation Chart.*

EAGLE PASS (G-6) pop. 22,413, elev. 726'

The first known settlement at this river crossing on the Mexican border was Camp Eagle Pass, a temporary observation post during the Mexican War. Fort Duncan was established by the First United States Infantry in 1849. The village that grew up around the fort earned the nickname "Camp California" when Forty-niners used it as a staging area on their way through Mazatlán to the gold fields. After the Civil War, an exiled Confederate force crossed the Rio Grande into Mexico at Eagle Pass, and the last flag to fly over Confederate troops was buried in the river by General Joseph Orville Shelby. The site came to be known as the "Grave of the Confederacy."

A major port of entry into Mexico, Eagle Pass serves as a tourism center and a retail/shipping hub for the 40,000-acre irrigated winter-garden region.

Eagle Pass Chamber of Commerce: 400 Garrison St., P.O. Box 1188, Eagle Pass, TX 78853-1188; phone (830) 773-3224 or (888) 355-3224.

Piedras Negras, Mexico

Piedras Negras (pee-EH-drahs NEH-grahs) faces Eagle Pass across a toll bridge over the Rio Grande. This typical border town is notable chiefly as the beginning of Mex. 57, the Constitution Highway *(Carretera de la Constitución),* which runs south to Mexico City. Piedras Negras offers the tourist Mexican wares and occasional summer bullfights. Stockraising and agriculture are the economic mainstays.

The U.S. Customs office is open 24 hours daily; the Mexican customs office is open Mon.-Fri. 8-8, Sat. 10-2. U.S. and Canadian visitors must carry proof of citizenship; a valid U.S. or Canadian passport is the most convenient, since it serves as a photo ID and facilitates many transactions, such as cashing traveler's checks. The U.S., Canadian and Mexican governments also recognize a birth certificate, which must be a certified copy from the government agency that issued it. A driver's license, voter registration card or baptismal certificate is **not** proof of citizenship.

All who plan to visit the interior or stay in the border area more than 72 hours also must obtain a Mexican government tourist card. Tourist cards are available, with proof of citizenship, from Mexican government tourism offices, Mexican consulates in the U.S. and Canada or immigration offices at official points of entry.

For a more detailed explanation of border crossing procedures and the requirements for temporary importation of vehicles, *see the Arriving in Mexico section in the AAA Mexico TravelBook.*

Mexico collects a visitor entry fee of 185 pesos (at press time, about $19) from each person entering the country. The fee must be paid in order to have your tourist card validated if you plan to remain anywhere in Mexico for more than 72 hours, or stay less than 72 hours and travel beyond the 16-mile (26-kilometer) border zone. If arriving by land, the fee is paid at a branch of any bank operating in Mexico. Upon payment your tourist card is stamped with an official "Fee paid" designation. All visitors are required to produce verification of payment by showing the "Fee paid" stamp on their tourist card upon departing Mexico. If arriving by air, the fee is included in the price of the ticket charged by the airline.

Visitors who limit their travel to destinations within the border zone, regardless of length of stay, are exempt. An exemption also applies to visitors staying more than 72 hours but limiting their visit to the following destinations/tourist routes: Ciudad Juárez to Paquime, Chihuahua; Piedras Negras to Santa Rosa, Coahuila; or Reynosa to China, Nuevo Leon, and Reynosa to Presa Cuchillo, Tamaulipas.

EDINBURG (I-8) pop. 48,465, elev. 91'

Originally named Chapin for the townsite promoter, Edinburg was renamed in 1911. The city's soil is hospitable to vegetables and citrus. Among area industries are food processing, furniture and dairying.

Edinburg Chamber of Commerce: 602 W. University, Edinburg, TX 78539; phone (956) 383-4974 or (800) 800-7214.

HIDALGO COUNTY HISTORICAL MUSEUM is at 121 E. McIntyre St. The museum is housed in the 1910 former county jail. Chronologically arranged displays start with the early American Indians, then focus on Spanish exploration and colonization through the Mexican War, the Rio Grande steamboat era, the Civil War, early ranching and farming, the border-bandit wars, early law enforcement and modern ranching and farming practices.

Allow 1 hour minimum. Tues.-Fri. 9-5, Sat. 10-5, Sun. 1-5; closed major holidays. Admission $2; over 62, $1.50; students with ID $1; under 12, 50c. Phone (956) 383-6911.

EL CAMPO (F-9) pop. 10,945, elev. 110'

Painted on the sides of businesses, 26 giant murals detail the history of El Campo. Among scenes are a war memorial, a blacksmith, a pasture of longhorns, a rice and cotton harvest and a horse and buggy. A map is available from the chamber of commerce.

El Campo Chamber of Commerce: 201 E. Jackson St., El Campo, TX 77437-4413; phone (979) 543-2713.

EL CAMPO MUSEUM is in the Civic Center Bldg. at 2350 N. Mechanic St. More than 100 big-game trophies from five continents are displayed. The Texas exhibit features animals indigenous to the area. Also presented are changing displays of art, natural science and history. A holiday presentation incorporating the animals with Christmas displays is offered late November to early January. Allow 30 minutes minimum. Mon.-Fri. 9-noon and 1-5, Sat. 1-5; closed holidays. Free. Phone (979) 543-6885.

EL PASO (D-2) pop. 563,662, elev. 3,710'

See map page 91.

El Paso, on the Mexican border, is a popular winter tourist destination because of its internationality, warm dry climate and proximity to the Rio Grande. The name El Paso is a shortened version of El Paso del Rio del Norte (the pass through the river of the north), given to the river valley by conquistador Don Juan de Oñate. Through this juncture, Spanish explorers found their way into what is now America.

Agriculture adds to the city's financial wellbeing. The region is one of the few in the nation where long-staple Egyptian cotton is grown. Other contributors to the economy are manufacturers and the military. Fort Bliss, in northeast El Paso, is the home of the U.S. Army Air Defense Center.

Founded in 1682 with the establishment of the Mission Nuestra Señora del Carmen, the eastern suburb of Ysleta, is the oldest settlement in Texas. Some of Ysleta's residents are among the last members of the Pueblo tribe in Texas. Ysleta Mission, built by Tigua Indians, Spanish refugees and Franciscan padres almost a century before the first California mission, adjoins the Tigua Indian Reservation.

Nearby is the *Camino Real*, the "Royal Highway." Once used by Spanish settlers and *conquistadores*, it is now a quiet farm road connecting Ysleta with two other Rio Grande Valley missions. These missions, which blend Spanish and American Indian styles of architecture, still operate.

The Socorro Mission, 3 miles east of Ysleta, was built in 1681 by Piro Indians, members of the Pueblo Nation, who incorporated ancient Piro symbols in the construction. The mission was originally in Mexico, but the river shifted course, leaving the site on the Texas side. It contains a hand-carved statue of San Miguel and an ox-cart. It is said that when the ox-cart was used to bring the statue to the site, it mysteriously lodged itself into the mire in front of the church. All efforts to move the cart failed, convincing the parishioners that destiny dictated that the statue remain at Socorro.

San Elizario Presidio was established in 1789 to protect the river settlements of Ysleta and Socorro. The military garrison, which included barracks, corrals, storerooms and an adobe chapel, was abandoned during the Mexican War. The restored chapel stands on the site of the original that was washed away by the Rio Grande.

San Jacinto Plaza in downtown El Paso is bordered by Oregon, Main, Mesa and Mills streets. The plaza dates from the early 1800s, when El Paso's park and street commissioner built the tree-shaded square at his own expense and stocked it with alligators, which lived in the plaza until the 1960s.

North between US 80 and N. Piedras St., a paved road leads to an overlook on the south side of the Franklin Mountains (*see attraction listing*).

The 15-minute scenic drive affords a spectacular view of El Paso and Ciudad Juárez, Mexico.

As an alternative to driving into Juárez, El Paso-Juárez Trolley Co. allows unlimited stops at Mexican shopping centers, arts and craft shops, and restaurants. The trolleys depart from El Paso's convention center, where pay parking is available on the lower level; phone (915) 544-0062.

Bus tours of El Paso and Ciudad Juárez operate daily. Arrangements can be made through the El Paso office of AAA Texas; phone (915) 778-9521 Mon.-Fri. 9-6, Sat. 9-1.

El Paso Convention and Visitors Bureau: 1 Civic Center Plaza, El Paso, TX 79901; phone (915) 534-0600, or (800) 351-6024 out of Texas.

Self-guiding tours: A walking tour of downtown El Paso features 22 historic sites; a brochure is available from the convention and visitors bureau. The El Paso Public Library offers brochures and maps detailing walking tours of some of the buildings designed by Henry C. Trost, the prominent Southwestern architect who was greatly responsible for El Paso's present appearance. Phone (915) 543-5400.

A 2-hour automobile tour of the missions begins at Ysleta Mission, 14 miles east on I-10 at exit Zaragoza. Maps, which denote communities and buildings dating from the early 1680s, can be picked up at the convention and visitors bureau.

Shopping areas: Cielo Vista Mall, I-10 and Hawkins, offers Dillard's, JCPenney and Sears. Sunland Park Mall, I-10 and Sunland Park Dr., includes Dillard's, JCPenney, Mervyn's and Sears.

CHAMIZAL NATIONAL MEMORIAL is at 800 S. San Marcial St. The 55-acre site commemorates the peaceful settlement of a century-old dispute between Mexico and the United States over the international boundary. A museum and visitor center are on the grounds. Allow 1 hour minimum. Daily 8-5; closed Jan. 1, Thanksgiving and Dec. 25. Free. Phone (915) 532-7273.

EL PASO CENTENNIAL MUSEUM is on the campus of the University of Texas at University Ave. and Wiggins Rd. This museum of natural and cultural history features exhibits dealing with the archeology, botany, ethnology, geology, mammalogy, ornithology and paleontology of the American Southwest and northern Mexico. The Chihuahuan Desert Gardens feature a series of native desert landscapes. Tues.-Sat. 10-5; closed Jan. 1, July 4, Thanksgiving, Dec. 25 and university holidays. Donations. Phone (915) 747-5565.

EL PASO MUSEUM OF ART is at 1 Arts Festival Plaza. The Kress Collection features 13th- to 18th-century European paintings, including Spanish and Italian masters. The American collection of painting and sculpture spans more than 200 years and includes a Gilbert Stuart painting of George Washington. In addition the museum offers frequent showings of Mexican and Southwestern art, as well as changing exhibits, films, lectures and workshops. Allow 1 hour minimum. Tues.-Sat. 9-5, Sun. noon-5; closed holidays. Free. Phone (915) 532-1707.

EL PASO MUSEUM OF HISTORY is 15 mi. s.e. on US 80 or I-10 at Loop 375, Americas Ave. exit to 12901 Gateway West. Exhibits relate the early history of El Paso with emphasis on the role horsemen played in its founding. Dioramas, artworks, riding gear, apparel and other articles of the settlement period are exhibited. Allow 1 hour minimum. Tues.-Sat. 9-4:50, Sun. 1-4:50; closed major holidays. Donations. Phone (915) 858-1928.

EL PASO ZOO is at 4001 E. Paisano. The 18-acre zoo, known for its exotic reptiles and colorful primates, features some 600 birds, mammals, amphibians, reptiles, fish and invertebrates in natural settings. The Asian complex is home to elephants, tigers and orangutans. The Americas Aviary contains a walkway for visitors as well as a waterfall, flowers and plants. Also featured is a historical Paraje reservation.

Allow 1 hour, 30 minutes minimum. Daily 9:30-6, Memorial Day-Labor Day; 9:30-4, rest of year. Closed Jan. 1, Thanksgiving and Dec. 25. Admission $4; over 61, $3; ages 3-12, $2. Phone (915) 521-1850.

FORT BLISS MUSEUM AND STUDY CENTER is off I-10 exit 23-B (Paisano), n.w. to Trowbridge to US 54, following signs to Bldg. 1735 off Marshall Rd. Museum exhibits chronicle the histories of the U.S. Army and the Air Defense Artillery branch in El Paso. An adjacent park contains anti-aircraft weapons and vehicles. Facing the main parade ground on Pleasonton Road is Old Fort Bliss, a replica of the 1854 fort. Four adobe buildings contain exhibits depicting the lives and daily routines of 1850s soldiers and civilians. Daily 9-4:30; closed Jan. 1, Easter, Thanksgiving and Dec. 25. Donations. Phone (915) 568-5412 or (915) 568-4518.

U.S. Army Air Defense Artillery Museum is in Bldg. 1735. Films, a slide show, photographs, dioramas and weapons trace the history of air defense. Daily 9-4:30; closed Jan. 1, Easter, Thanksgiving and Dec. 25. Donations. Phone (915) 568-5412.

FRANKLIN MOUNTAINS STATE PARK is off I-10 exit 6 (Canutillo), then 3.1 mi. e. on Transmountain Rd. (Loop 375). This park within El Paso city limits protects 24,248 acres of the Franklin Mountains

2160-K   © AAA

range and is home to mule deer, cougars, golden eagles and Chihuahuan Desert plants. Multi-use trails are open to hikers and mountain bikers. Picnicking is permitted. Daily 8-5. Admission $3; senior citizens $1.50; under 12 free. MC, VI. Phone (915) 566-6441 or (800) 792-1112.

Wyler Aerial Tramway is off I-10 exit US 54 (Patriot Frwy.), n. to Fred Wilson Blvd. exit, 1 mi. w. to Alabama St., then 1.5 mi. s. to 1700 McKinley Ave. Gondolas take passengers on a 4-minute narrated ride up the Franklin Mountains to the top of 5,632-foot Ranger Peak. The panoramic view from Wyler Observatory spans 7,000 square miles, encompassing three states and two countries. Allow 30 minutes minimum. Mon. and Thurs. noon-6, Fri.-Sun. and holidays noon-9, Memorial Day-Labor Day; Mon. and Thurs. noon-6, Fri.-Sun. noon-8, rest of year. Last tram departs 1 hour before closing. Fare $7; ages 4-12, $4. DS, MC, VI. Phone (915) 566-6622 or (800) 792-1112.

HUECO TANKS STATE HISTORIC SITE is 30 mi. e. on US 62/180, then 8 mi. n. on FM 2775 to 6900 Hueco Tanks Rd. #1. Used for almost 10,000 years, these rock basins, or *huecos,* collected rainwater. Some 2,000 pictographs serve as a legacy of the successive cultures that lived in the area. Ruins of a 19th-century stagecoach station and abandoned ranch buildings remain. Other highlights include caves and rock shelters, distinctive oak and juniper trees—rare for this desert environment—and the shrimp that appear seasonally in the water basins.

There are no roads within the park. Only 70 people are permitted in the self-guided areas at one time; access is granted on a first-come, first-served basis. Visitors must walk to view the park's features and are required to view an orientation videotape before entering the site. Mon.-Thurs. 8-6, Fri.-Sun. 7-7, May-Sept.; daily 8-6, rest of year. Admission $4, under 13 free. Reservations may be made up to 6 months in advance. DS, MC, VI. Phone (915) 857-1135. *See Recreation Chart and the AAA South Central CampBook.*

INSIGHTS—EL PASO SCIENCE CENTER is at 505 N. Santa Fe St. More than 300 participatory exhibits about science and technology are offered. Allow 1 hour minimum. Tues.-Fri. 9-3, Sat. 10-5 (also 5-9 first Sat. of the month), Sun. noon-5; closed holidays. Admission $5; over 62, students and military with ID $4; ages 3-5, $3. MC, VI. Phone (915) 534-0000.

MAGOFFIN HOME STATE HISTORIC SITE is at 1120 Magoffin Ave. This adobe home was built in 1875 by pioneer Joseph Magoffin, founder of Magoffinsville, which later became El Paso. An example of Territorial style architecture, the 20-room house combines Mexican and Victorian influences. Original family furnishings and decorative arts are displayed. Tours are given daily 9-4; closed Jan. 1, Thanksgiving and Dec. 25. Admission $2, students with ID $1. DS, MC, VI. Phone (915) 533-5147.

TIGUA INDIAN RESERVATION AND PUEBLO are in the suburb of Ysleta, 14 mi. e. via I-10 to exit 32 (Zaragoza Rd.), then 2.5 mi. s. to Alameda, then 1 blk. e. to 122 S. Old Pueblo Rd. The Tiguas (TEE-wahs), a Pueblo tribe, were relocated from New Mexico during the Pueblo revolt in 1680. The tribe completed the Ysleta mission, one of the oldest in North America, under Spanish direction in 1682.

The present structure incorporates the original foundations and some of the original adobe walls. Adjacent is the pueblo, with an arts and crafts center, a *kiva* or council chamber, bread ovens and a dance area. Food is available. Phone (915) 859-7913 or (915) 859-3916.

"VIVA! EL PASO!" is 2.5 mi. n. on Alabama St. in McKelligon Canyon Amphitheater. The 2-hour musical gives the history of El Paso and its four cultures—American Indian, Spanish, Mexican and Anglo. Shows are given Thurs.-Sat. at 8:30 p.m., June-Aug. Two hours prior to the show, dinner is offered at an additional cost. Show tickets $8-$17; ages 5-11, $6-$11. AX, DS, MC, VI. Phone (915) 565-6900.

WILDERNESS PARK MUSEUM is 8.5 mi. n. on Gateway North, then .5 mi. w. to 4301 Transmountain Dr. (Loop 375). The adobe museum presents dioramas and artifacts of the American Indians of the Southwest. A 1-mile nature trail includes a Pueblo ruin, a kiva and a pit house. Allow 1 hour minimum. Tues.-Sun. 9-4:45; closed holidays. Free. Phone (915) 755-4332.

Ciudad Juárez, Mexico

On the Rio Grande opposite El Paso, Ciudad Juárez (HWAH-res) once served as a stop on the Santa Fe Trail. Linked to El Paso first by mule-drawn trolley and later by electric trolleys, Juárez can be reached by several bridges. South on US 54 from I-10, the Bridge of the Americas (the Cordova or "free bridge") enters the suburb of San Lorenzo. The Santa Fe Street Bridge (toll) in downtown El Paso is actually two separate bridges: southbound vehicles enter Mexico via Stanton Street to Avenida Lerdo; northbound traffic returns on Avenida Juárez to Santa Fe Street. The Ysleta-Zaragoza Bridge (toll) on Zaragoza Avenue enters Mexico east of Ciudad Juárez. Toll fees are $2 per vehicle; pedestrians 50c.

A tourist information center at the Bridge of the Americas in Ciudad Juárez offers travel guides and bilingual assistance to those visiting the state of Chihuahua, as well as information about Mexico as a whole. The center is open daily 9-9; phone (888) 654-0394 in the U.S., or (800) 849-5200 in Mexico. A newer border crossing at Santa Teresa in New Mexico, just west of the El Paso/Ciudad Juárez area, can be used to bypass the cities. This port of entry also can process the paperwork necessary for travel into the interior.

Motorists returning to the United States from downtown Juárez must use the northbound-only Paseo del Norte Bridge (toll) via Avenida Juárez or the free Cordova Bridge via Avenida Lincoln. Toll fees are $2 per vehicle; pedestrians 70c. Dollars or pesos are accepted when entering or departing Mexico or the United States. Baggage must be inspected at the customs offices. Both Mexican and U.S. customs and immigration offices are open 24 hours daily.

U.S. and Canadian visitors must carry proof of citizenship. A valid U.S. or Canadian passport is the most convenient, since it serves as a photo ID and facilitates many transactions, such as cashing traveler's checks. The U.S., Canadian and Mexican governments also recognize a birth certificate, which must be a certified copy from the government agency that issued it. A driver's license, voter registration card or baptismal certificate is **not** proof of citizenship.

All who plan to visit the interior or stay in the border area more than 72 hours also must obtain a Mexican government tourist card. Tourist cards are available, with proof of citizenship, from Mexican government tourism offices, Mexican consulates in the U.S. and Canada or immigration offices at official points of entry. Before driving into Mexico, check with the El Paso AAA office for documentation and insurance requirements; phone (915) 778-9521.

For a more detailed explanation of border crossing procedures and the requirements for temporary importation of vehicles, *see the Arriving in Mexico section in the AAA Mexico TravelBook.*

Mexico collects a visitor entry fee of 185 pesos (at press time, about $19) from each person entering the country. The fee must be paid in order to have your tourist card validated if you plan to remain anywhere in Mexico for more than 72 hours, or stay less than 72 hours and travel beyond the 16-mile (26-kilometer) border zone. If arriving by land, the fee is paid at a branch of any bank operating in Mexico. Upon payment your tourist card is stamped with an official "Fee paid" designation. All visitors are required to produce verification of payment by showing the "Fee paid" stamp on their tourist card upon departing Mexico. If arriving by air, the fee is included in the price of the ticket charged by the airline.

Visitors who limit their travel to destinations within the border zone, regardless of length of stay, are exempt. An exemption also applies to visitors staying more than 72 hours but limiting their visit to the following destinations/tourist routes: Ciudad Juárez to Paquime, Chihuahua; Piedras Negras to Santa Rosa, Coahuila; or Reynosa to China, Nuevo Leon, and Reynosa to Presa Cuchillo, Tamaulipas.

Juárez is an interesting blend of both countries where markets offer local products ranging from pottery to fruit. English is as widely spoken as Spanish. AAA/CAA members can obtain Mexican automobile insurance and make arrangements for bus tours of the city through the El Paso office of AAA Texas.

Just across the Bridge of the Americas on Avenida de las Américas is El Chamizal National Park. Mexico claimed El Chamizal after the Mexican-American War established the Río Grande as the international border in 1848. However, the park fell into U.S. possession when the river changed its course 16 years later. In 1964 President Lyndon Johnson returned approximately 640 acres to Mexico, a goodwill gesture initiated by President John F. Kennedy. The land, reduced in size since then, now is used in reforestation efforts. The park offers several recreational facilities, including a wave pool and another pool with a toboggan run.

Bullfights are staged in the Plaza de Toros Monumental, Avenida 16 de Septiembre near the junction of Boulevard López Mateos and Mex. 45. Traditionally, the first *corrida de toros* of the season begins in spring, often on or near Easter Sunday. Thereafter, *corridas* are held on occasional Sundays (often in conjunction with long U.S. holiday weekends) through Labor Day, although scheduling decisions are often made on short notice.

From April through October *charreadas,* Mexican-style rodeos, take place on Sundays at the Lienzo Charro Adolfo López Mateos, on the Pan American Highway at Avenida del Charro. Horse racing is offered on some Sundays from mid-May to late September. During the rest of the year, greyhounds race at the dog track *(galgódromo)* north of the country club in Colonia Manuel Doblado.

Note: In recent years Ciudad Juárez has become a center of narcotics smuggling along the border. Exercise caution if visiting the nightspots in the entertainment districts west of Avenida Juárez.

Shopping areas: The traditional shopping area is close to the border, along Avenida Juárez.

CENTRO ARTESANAL (ARTS AND CRAFTS CENTER) is at Avenida Lincoln and Ignacio Mejia. The center displays and sells handicrafts from throughout Mexico. Glass, jewelry, pottery, textiles and leather goods range in style from pre-Columbian to contemporary. Daily 10-7. Free.

MUSEO DE ARTE (MUSEUM OF ART) is in the Plaza de las Americas at Avenida Lincoln and Ignacio Mejia. Regional arts and crafts are displayed at the museum, which is operated by the National Institute of Fine Arts. Tues.-Sun. 11-7; closed Mexican holidays. Admission 75c.

FALCON (I-7)

The village of Falcon was built by the federal government in 1949 during the construction of Falcon Dam. Residence is restricted to federal employees, including agents of the Drug Enforcement Administration, the Immigration and Naturalization Service and the International Boundary and Water Commission.

FALCON DAM is 4 mi. s. on US 83, then about 5 mi. w. on FM 2098 to Park Rd. 46. Part of the Falcon State Park *(see Recreation Chart),* the 5-mile-long earth and rock-fill dam on the Rio Grande is a combined effort of the United States and Mexico.

Simple metal shafts bearing the seals of both countries mark the international boundary. The spillway offers a good view of the Rio Grande Valley.

FARMERS BRANCH—*see Dallas p. 85.*

FORT DAVIS (E-4) pop. 1,050, elev. 4,927'

In the heart of the Davis Mountains, Fort Davis grew as a strategic point on the San Antonio-El Paso Road. Established in 1854, the fort was named in honor of Jefferson Davis, then Secretary of War. Fort Davis was first manned by troops of the Eighth U.S. Infantry who, mounted on mules, fought the Comanches.

The canyon formed by Limpia Creek, which flows through the Davis Mountains, is a centuries-old oasis for travelers. Davis Mountains State Park *(see Recreation Chart and the AAA South Central CampBook)* embraces a part of the creek and 1,869 acres of the rolling grasslands and intermittent trees that cover these mountains. A 74-mile scenic highway, SR 166/118, makes a loop through the Davis Mountains and includes Madera Canyon and McDonald Observatory.

Fort Davis Chamber of Commerce: P.O. Box 378, Fort Davis, TX 79734; phone (432) 426-3015.

FORT DAVIS NATIONAL HISTORIC SITE is n. of town near Limpia Creek off SRs 17 and 118. Occupying 474 acres, this well-preserved example of a frontier military post was a key defense post against American Indian attacks. Interpreters in period dress staff the commissary, commanding officer's quarters, enlisted men's barracks, kitchen and servants' quarters June through August. The post hospital features interpretive exhibits. Sounds of an 1875 dress retreat parade and bugle calls are presented daily on the parade grounds.

Visitors may view a 14-minute videotape about the fort's history at the museum, which also displays photographs, weapons, equipment, American Indian artifacts and paintings. Daily 8-5, Memorial Day-Labor Day; 8-6, rest of year. Closed Dec. 25. Admission $3, under 16 free. Phone (432) 426-3224.

McDONALD OBSERVATORY is 17 mi. n.w. on SR 118. Operated by the University of Texas, the observatory on 6,791-foot Mount Locke has several optical telescopes ranging in diameter from 30 to 432 inches. The visitor center at the base of the mountain offers astronomical exhibits, a multimedia theater, solar viewing programs and a self-guiding walking tour map of the observatory.

Guided tours of the Harlan J. Smith and Hobby-Eberly telescopes are offered. Star Parties offer a 2-hour glimpse of the moon, planets, constellations and galaxies. Food is available.

Allow 1 hour, 30 minutes minimum. Visitor center daily 9-5. Solar viewings daily at 11 and 3:30. Guided tours daily at 11:30 and 2. Star parties Tues. and Fri.-Sat. at 9:30 p.m., Apr.-Aug.; 9 p.m., Sept.-Oct.; 7:30 p.m., rest of year. Closed Jan. 1,

Thanksgiving and Dec. 25. Visitor center admission $5; ages 6-12, $4. Guided tours (includes visitor center) $7; ages 6-12, $6. Star parties (includes visitor center) $8; ages 6-12, $7. Combination ticket (includes visitor center, guided tour and star party) $9; ages 6-12, $8. Walking tour map $1. Phone (432) 426-3640 or (877) 984-7827.

FORT GRIFFIN (C-7) elev. 1,217'

Frequented by cavalry troopers, cowboys, buffalo hunters and outlaws during its settlement days, Fort Griffin counted 34 gunfight killings in one 12-year period. Once the fort was abandoned, the town declined. Only scattered rural homes remain on the farmlands. Fort Griffin is one of eight surviving frontier posts on the 650-mile Texas Forts Trail in west central Texas.

FORT GRIFFIN STATE HISTORIC SITE is on US 283. Built in 1867, Fort Griffin was a major base of operations for raids against the Comanches. The town that grew around the fort became one of the more notorious places on the frontier. Ruins of the fort, including barracks, a hospital, a mess hall and living quarters, are visible. A herd of Texas longhorn cattle grazes in the 506-acre park. Camping is available. Daily 8 a.m.-10 p.m. Admission $2, under 13 free. DS, MC, VI. Phone (325) 762-3592. *See Recreation Chart and the AAA South Central CampBook.*

FORT McKAVETT (E-7) elev. 2,171'

FORT McKAVETT STATE HISTORIC SITE is 17 mi. w. on US 190, then 6 mi. s. on FM 864. The 80-acre park preserves the remains of Camp San Saba, established in 1852 to protect frontier settlers and travelers on the Upper El Paso Road. Later renamed for Capt. Henry McKavett, the fort was once described by Gen. William T. Sherman as "the prettiest post in Texas." Abandoned after seven years, the fort was reactivated in 1869 by African-American "Buffalo Soldiers." The post finally closed in 1883. Over 25 limestone buildings have been restored, including the post headquarters, officers' quarters, a barracks, a school house and a bakery.

The 1870 hospital houses an interpretive center with historic photographs, dioramas and more than 200 artifacts. The half-mile Government Springs nature trail leads to an old lime kiln and rock quarry. Picnicking is permitted. Allow 1 hour minimum. Daily 8-5; closed Dec. 25. Admission $2, ages 6-17 and college students with ID $1. DS, MC, VI. Phone (325) 396-2358.

FORT STOCKTON (E-5)
pop. 7,846, elev. 3,000'

The town of Fort Stockton dates from 1858, when the U.S. Army established a cavalry post on the site. The first stores opened in 1870, and the community prospered as a trade center for a large ranching empire. The Yates oil field was discovered around 1925 in eastern Pecos County. Giant drilling rigs are part of the landscape, and the oil and gas industries are the mainstays of the local economy. A town landmark, the statue affectionately called Paisano Pete, 20 feet long, 11 feet tall and 860 pounds, is said to be the world's largest roadrunner.

The Overland-Butterfield Stage Stop, 20 miles east on US 290 and I-10, is a reconstructed stage remount stand from the San Antonio-San Francisco route. Originally 1.5 miles southwest, the stand was dismantled and rebuilt on the present site, using the original stones.

Fort Stockton Chamber of Commerce: P.O. Box 1000, Fort Stockton, TX 79735; phone (432) 336-8525.

Self-guiding tours: Brochures and a cassette tape about historic downtown, including old Fort Stockton, are available from the chamber of commerce.

ANNIE RIGGS MEMORIAL MUSEUM is at 301 S. Main St. This 1900 adobe brick and wood hotel once catered to early travelers on the Overland-Butterfield route. The museum has original furnishings, clothing, guns, saddles and documents. Guided tours are available. Allow 1 hour minimum. Mon.-Sat. 10-6, June-Aug.; Mon.-Sat. 10-5, rest of year. Admission $2; over 65, $1.50; ages 6-12, $1. Phone (432) 336-2167.

FORT WORTH (D-8) pop. 534,694, elev. 610'
See map page 96.

Fort Worth began in 1849 as a military post to protect a few struggling ranchers from American Indian attacks. When the camp dissolved, the settlement became a trading post. After the Civil War the dusty trails were filled with longhorns as Texas cowboys came to town. On their heels came adventure-seekers, trailhands who lived it up for a night, dreamers who rode on, and the American Indians, outlaws and settlers who stayed to make Fort Worth their home.

The bubble of high hopes burst in 1873 when the first railroad, left stranded in nearby Dallas by a financial panic, failed to come to town. Unlike settlers in many Texas boomtowns, some Fort Worth citizens stayed and convinced the Texas and Pacific Railroad they could finish the 26 miles of roadbed before the land grant expired in 1876. Every person who could swing a pick or drive a mule helped lay the rails.

Once the railroad was finished, Fort Worth regained its prominence as the capital of the Southwestern cattle empire. By the end of the 19th century stockyards ringed the city, and the great meatpacking houses moved in.

More fuel was added to Fort Worth's boomtown frenzy when the north Texas oil fields began producing in 1912, sparking a tripling of the town's population in the next 2 decades. During the 1930s oil eclipsed the cattle industry and remained the city's leading industry for 30 years.

Fort Worth has blended frontier heritage with such industries as defense, high technology and aviation into a cosmopolitan mix of skyscrapers and historic buildings. The Stockyards District consists of cobbled gaslit streets lined with shops and restaurants.

Visitors will find an innovative tribute to water at Water Garden, which features rushing and sprinkling water as well as water falling over stone slabs or lying quietly in pools. The garden now covers part of Hell's Half Acre, once a roaring, lawless area of saloons and brothels.

The Longhorn Trolley offers daily service between Sundance Square, the Stockyards, the Cultural District, the Fort Worth Zoo and the Convention Center; for schedules and fares, phone the Fort Worth Transportation Authority at (817) 215-8600.

Forest Park, off Colonial Parkway, offers outdoor recreation and one of the longest miniature railroads in the United States. Two streamlined trains and an old-fashioned steam engine operate in the park. Log Cabin Village, within the park, has eight restored frontier cabins furnished with pioneer articles that depict the life of early settlers. The village has a working gristmill. Spinning and candle-dipping demonstrations are given mornings and weekends.

Leading educational institutions—Southwestern Baptist Theological Seminary, Texas Christian University, Texas College of Osteopathic Medicine and Texas Wesleyan College—add further refinement to the city's cultural offerings. Among the institutional highlights is Southwestern's Baptist Theological Seminary's Tandy Archeological Museum, which features Holy Land artifacts and biblical history.

Another departure from the past are the lakes that now dot the once-empty prairie. Lake Worth lies within the city limits and was the first of several lakes built to meet the growing city's water needs. This lake is currently popular for its scenic vistas and water sports. Other nearby lakes include Eagle Mountain to the northwest and Benbrook to the southwest.

The Fort Worth Stock Show and Rodeo, held annually since 1896, attracts more than 850,000 people to the Will Rogers Center from mid-January to early February. Cattle drives of the past are reenacted twice daily as the Fort Worth longhorn herd makes its way down Exchange Avenue in the Stockyards. Minor-league baseball is played at LaGrave Field, home of the Fort Worth Cats. For race fans, Texas Motor Speedway is north at I-35W exit 70.

Fort Worth Convention & Visitors Bureau: 415 Throckmorton, Fort Worth, TX 76102; phone (817) 336-8791 or (800) 433-5747.

Self-guiding tours: Walking tours of the historic stockyards at Stockyard Station *(see attraction listing p. 98)* are available at 130 E. Exchange Ave.; phone (817) 625-9715.

Shopping areas: Stockyards Station, on East Exchange Avenue, has been restored and now accommodates restaurants, studios and crafts shops. Sundance Square is a 20-block area on Main Street where late 19th- and early 20th-century buildings have been restored.

The Fort Worth Public Market, in the old Santa Fe Warehouse downtown at 1401 Jones St., offers fresh seafood, produce, plants, flowers, wine and other local specialties.

THE AMERICAN AIRLINES C. R. SMITH MUSEUM is s. of Dallas/Fort Worth International Airport at 4601 US 360 and FAA Rd. American Airlines memorabilia from the 1930s to the present is housed at the museum. Displays illustrate the responsibilities of the cabin and cockpit crews, the effect of wind tunnels and how a plane is flown and maintained. Other exhibits include computer simulations, a jet engine and a restored DC3, American's flagship passenger plane, which accommodated 21 passengers.

Allow 1 hour minimum. Tues.-Sat. 10-6, Sun. noon-5; closed Jan. 1, Thanksgiving and Dec. 25. Free. Phone (817) 967-1560.

AMON CARTER MUSEUM is 2.5 mi. w. at 3501 Camp Bowie Blvd. One of the foremost collections of American art in the country includes some 250,000 works by such Western artists as Georgia O'Keeffe, Frederic Remington and Charles Russell. The museum also houses major paintings, sculpture, photographs and graphic art from the 19th century to the present. Allow 1 hour, 30 minutes minimum. Tues.-Sat. 10-5 (also Thurs. 5-8), Sun. noon-5; closed major holidays. Guided tours are offered Tues.-Sun. at 2. Free. Phone (817) 738-1933.

SAVE **CATTLE RAISERS MUSEUM** is at 1301 W. Seventh St. Computer and videotape presentations, movies, talking displays and cowboy memorabilia relate the development of the cattle industry. Allow 1 hour minimum. Mon.-Sat. 10-5, Sun. 1-5; closed major holidays. Admission $3; over 60 and ages 13-18, $2; ages 4-12, $1. AX, MC, VI. Phone (817) 332-8551.

FORT WORTH BOTANIC GARDEN is n. of I-30 off University Dr. at 3220 Botanic Garden Blvd., across from Trinity Park. This 109-acre garden has varied annuals and perennials; trees and shrubs line the stream winding through the park. It features 21 specialty gardens and a historic rose garden dating from 1933. The Conservatory has more than 2,500 plants native to Central and South America and the

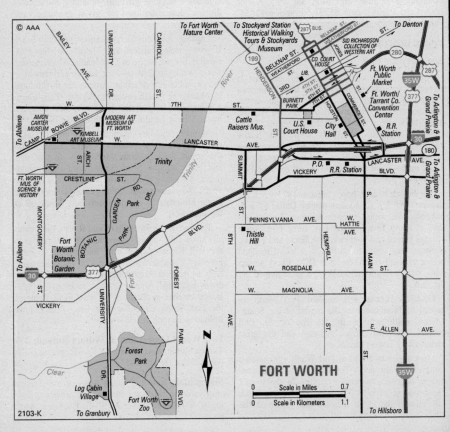

Far and Middle East, in addition to small ponds and waterfalls. The drive through Trinity Park and the gardens continues through Forest Park. Food is available.

Allow 4 hours minimum. Conservatory Mon.-Fri. 10-9, Sat. 10-6, Sun. 1-6, Apr.-Oct.; Mon.-Fri. 10-9, Sat. 10-4, Sun. 1-4, rest of year. Grounds daily 8-dusk. Conservatory $1; over 65 and ages 4-12, 50c. Grounds free. Phone (817) 871-7686.

Japanese Garden is in Fort Worth Botanic Garden. This blend of trees, shrubs, stones and water is arranged to emphasize the beauty of seasonal changes and to foster tranquillity. On the 7.5-acre grounds are a pagoda, a teahouse and a moon-viewing deck. Daily 10-5, Mar.-Nov.; Tues.-Sun. 11-2:30, rest of year. Admission Mon.-Fri. $2; over 65, $1.50; ages 4-12, $1. Admission Sat.-Sun. and holiday $2.50; over 65, $2; ages 4-12, $1. Phone (817) 871-7685.

 FORT WORTH MUSEUM OF SCIENCE AND HISTORY is 2.5 mi. w. at 1501 Montgomery St. Permanent exhibits include [SAVE] Lone Star Dinosaurs, Comin' Through Cowtown, Hands On Science and interactive traveling exhibits. Noble Planetarium presents regular showings. Omni Theater uses an 80-foot dome screen and 72 speakers to present 45-minute IMAX films. Programs change about every 4 months.

A children's area features interactive exhibits such as the Kidsfish dock, a market and a build-a-house display. Amateur paleontologists can dig for dinosaur bones and fossils in an outdoor discovery area.

Allow 1 hour minimum. Museum Mon.-Thurs. 9-5:30, Fri.-Sat. 9-8, Sun. noon-5:30; closed Thanksgiving and Dec. 24-25. Planetarium shows are given every 30 minutes daily during museum hours June-Aug.; Thurs.-Sun., rest of year. Omni Theater shows are given every hour and 10 min. beginning Mon.-Sat. at 10:10, Sun. at 12:30, June-Aug.; Mon.-Fri. at 1:40, Sat. at 10:10, Sun. at 12:30, rest of year. Hours may vary; phone ahead. Museum admission $7; over 60, $6; ages 3-12, $5. Planetarium admission $3.50. Theater admission $7; over 60, $6; ages 3-12, $5. The theater often sells out on weekends, spring break and summer; arrive early. AX, DS, MC, VI. Phone (817) 255-9300 or (888) 255-9300.

FORT WORTH NATURE CENTER AND REFUGE is 9 mi. n.w. on SR 199/Jacksboro Hwy., 2 mi. w. of Lake Worth Bridge. Hiking and nature trails make the interior of this 3,500-acre preserve accessible. Animals frequently seen include buffaloes, white-tailed deer, coyotes, turkeys, egrets and herons. A prairie dog town and bison range offer opportunities to see these animals in their natural habitat. Allow 2 hours, 30 minutes minimum. Refuge open daily 9-5 (also Sat. 7 9 a.m., Memorial Day-Labor Day). Center open Tues.-Sat. 9:30-4:30, Sun. 12:30-4:30. Closed major holidays. Free. Phone (817) 237-1111.

FORT WORTH ZOO is off I-30 exit University Dr., then s. to 1989 Colonial Pkwy. Ranked as one of the nation's top zoos, the 64-acre complex is home to more than 5,000 animals from around the world. Natural-habitat exhibits include Raptor Canyon, home to such birds of prey as bald eagles, hawks, vultures and Andean condors. Visitors can stroll along a boardwalk in the Asian Rhino Ridge, where one-horned Asian rhinos wallow in mud pools. Tigers, bears and elephants at Asian Falls live in natural settings complete with waterfalls and grassy hills.

Koala Outback is home to koalas, red kangaroos and yellow-footed rock wallabies. The 2.5-acre World of Primates contains a climate-controlled tropical rain forest where endangered lowland gorillas and other primates roam. The Herpetarium contains rare snakes, lizards and other reptiles and amphibians.

The cheetah exhibit places cheetahs, African warthogs and bongos in a natural African habitat. The Komodo dragon exhibit is home to two Komodo dragons, the largest lizard in the world, as well as gharial crocodiles. The African Savannah exhibit houses giraffes and black and white rhinoceroses. Flamingo Bay contains more than 50 flamingos representing three species. Penguin Island is an indoor-outdoor exhibit where two dozen South African black-footed penguins live.

More than 300 indigenous animals are featured at Texas Wild!, an 8-acre exhibit that re-creates an 1890s pioneer town and six geographic regions of the Lone Star State. A miniature train, the Yellow Rose Express, takes visitors on a zoo tour.

Allow 2 hours, 30 minutes minimum. Mon.-Fri. 10-5, Sat.-Sun. 10-6, Mar.-Oct.; daily 10-4, rest of year. Open noon-4 Jan. 1, Thanksgiving and Dec. 25. Admission $9; ages 3-12, $6.50; over 64, $5.50; half-price to all Wed. Parking $5; auxiliary lot $3. Phone (817) 871-7050.

KIMBELL ART MUSEUM is 2.5 mi. w. on Will Rogers Rd. W. to 3333 Camp Bowie Blvd. The vaulted building is the last completed work of architect Louis Kahn and is considered by many to be his masterpiece. The museum's holdings range in period from antiquity to the 20th century, including works by Fra Angelico, Michelangelo Caravaggio, Paul Cézanne, El Greco, Henri Matisse, Pieter Mondrian, Claude Monet, Pablo Picasso, Peter Paul Rubens and Diego Velázquez.

The Kimbell also houses collections of Egyptian, Greek and Roman antiquities, as well as Asian, African and pre-Columbian art. The museum provides an ongoing program of interpretive exhibitions and retrospectives, as well as traveling exhibitions. Food is available. Allow 2 hours, 30 minutes minimum. Tues.-Thurs. and Sat. 10-5, Fri. noon-8; closed Jan. 1, July 4, Thanksgiving and Dec. 25. Museum free. Admission may be charged for special exhibits. Phone (817) 332-8451.

MODERN ART MUSEUM OF FORT WORTH is at Camp Bowie Blvd. and University Dr. Designed by

Japanese architect Tadao Ando, this striking pavilion of concrete and glass hovers over a reflecting pool. The museum houses more than 2,400 works of modern and contemporary art, including pieces by Morris Louis, Pablo Picasso, Jackson Pollock, Mark Rothko, Frank Stella, Clyfford Still and Andy Warhol. Tues.-Fri. 10-5, Sat. 11-5, Sun. noon-5; closed holidays. Free. Phone (817) 738-9215.

SID RICHARDSON COLLECTION OF WESTERN ART is at 309 Main St. in Sundance Sq. Frederic Remington and Charles Russell are among the artists represented in the 60-work collection. Allow 30 minutes minimum. Tues.-Fri. 10-5 (also Thurs.-Fri. 5-8), Sat. 11-8, Sun. 1-5; closed holidays. Free. Phone (817) 332-6554.

 **SIX FLAGS OVER TEXAS—**
see Arlington p. 58.

STOCKYARDS MUSEUM is n. of downtown in the Stockyards Livestock Exchange Building. Exhibits illustrate the livestock industry of Fort Worth and the history of the Stockyards Company. Western saddles, antiques from the 1800s and photographs portraying life in Fort Worth also are displayed. Allow 30 minutes minimum. Mon.-Sat. 10-5; closed Jan. 1, July 4, Thanksgiving and Dec. 24-25. Donations. Phone (817) 625-5087.

SAVE **STOCKYARDS STATION HISTORICAL WALKING TOURS** depart from 130 E. Exchange Ave. Tours of the historic stockyard area include Cowtown Coliseum, the stockyards, the Livestock Exchange Building, the cattlemen's catwalk, Mule Alley and a local saloon that is said to be the largest honky-tonk in the country. In addition, a videotape presentation chronicles area history. A reduced-price tour excludes the saloon and visitor options. Carriage and horseback rides are available.

Allow 1 hour minimum. Tours depart Mon.-Sat. at 10, noon, 2 and 4, Sun. at noon, 2 and 4; closed Dec. 25. Fee $6; over 65, $5; ages 3-12, $4.25. AX, MC, VI. Phone (817) 625-9715.

THISTLE HILL is at 1509 Pennsylvania Ave. This Georgian Revival mansion was built in 1903 and remodeled in 1910. The restored house is furnished in period. Tours are given on the hour Mon.-Fri. 11-2, Sun. 1-3; closed major holidays. Schedule may vary; phone ahead. Admission $5; over 65 and ages 7-12, $3. Phone (817) 336-1212.

FREDERICKSBURG (E-7)
pop. 8,911, elev. 1,742'

This fertile area first was settled by German farmers who arrived in 1846. To quiet her children one evening, a pioneer mother composed the tale of the Fredericksburg Easter fires—a story of the Easter Rabbit who lit fires on the town's hillside to boil the children's Easter eggs. In reality the fires were those of American Indians watching the new

settlement. Now a cherished tradition, hillside fires glow each year on Easter eve.

Restoration and preservation are evident in Fredericksburg, considered one of the most attractive small towns in Texas. Several 19th-century Sunday Houses, one-room-and-loft structures used by ranchers and farmers when they traveled to town for shopping and Sunday church services, remain as originally constructed. Many of the town's stone houses have been restored by the present occupants.

A reproduction of the town's first church, the eight-sided Vereins Kirche, houses a local history collection. Enchanted Rock State Natural Area, 18 miles north on RR 965, centers around a pink granite exfoliation dome that rises 425 feet and covers 640 acres *(see Recreation Chart)*.

Fredericksburg Convention and Visitors Bureau: 302 E. Austin St., Fredericksburg, TX 78624; phone (830) 997-6523 or (888) 997-3600.

Self-guiding tours: A free brochure describing a walking tour of the historic district is available from the convention and visitors bureau.

NATIONAL MUSEUM OF THE PACIFIC WAR is at 340 E. Main St. The men and women who served in the Pacific and on the home front during World War II are honored here. The museum features artifacts from Pearl Harbor, Midway, Guadalcanal, the Mariana Islands and the Philippines. Visitors can step into history in the George Bush Gallery, which includes life-size exhibits such as the deck of the USS *Hornet* and a fortified Japanese cave.

The Admiral Nimitz Museum chronicles the career of Chester W. Nimitz, commander-in-chief of the Pacific Theater, born in Fredericksburg in 1885. The museum is housed in the restored steamboat-shaped hotel built by Nimitz's German grandfather in the 1850s. Also on the 9-acre grounds are the Veterans Walk of Honor and Memorial Walls, the Japanese Garden of Peace and the Plaza of the Presidents. The Pacific Combat Zone is an outdoor battlefield re-creation with tanks, vehicles, artillery and aircraft.

Allow 2 hours, 30 minutes minimum. Daily 10-5; closed Dec. 25. Admission $5, students with ID $3, under 6 free. Phone (830) 997-4379 or (830) 997-7269.

PIONEER MUSEUM COMPLEX is at 309 W. Main St. The 1849 stone house with eight furnished rooms and a wine cellar served as a house and store through the 1920s. Other buildings include the Fassel-Roeder house, Walton-Smith log cabin, a one-room schoolhouse, a barn and smokehouse and the Weber Sunday House. Self-guiding walking tour brochures are available. Mon.-Sat. 10-5, Sun. 1-5; closed major holidays. Admission $3, under 12 free. Phone (830) 997-2835.

WINERIES

• **Fredericksburg Winery** is at 247 W. Main. Open Mon.-Thurs. 10-6, Fri.-Sat. 10-8, Sun. noon-6. Phone (830) 990-8747.

FRITCH (A-6) pop. 2,235

Fritch was named for an agent of the Rock Island Railroad who plotted the region's first rail line in 1924. The town was incorporated in 1959 during construction of Sanford Dam, which created Lake Meredith *(see place listing p. 121)*.

ALIBATES FLINT QUARRIES NATIONAL MONUMENT—*see place listing p. 55.*

LAKE MEREDITH AQUATIC AND WILDLIFE MUSEUM is at 101 N. Roby. Dioramas show the habitats of animals and birds native to the Panhandle. Five aquariums display fish indigenous to the lake. Mon.-Sat. 10-5 (also Sun. 2-5, May-Aug.); closed Thanksgiving and Dec. 25. Donations. Phone (806) 857-2458.

GALVESTON (F-11) pop. 57,247, elev. 17'

Gaslights, stately Victorian buildings and the clip-clop of carriages along the Strand have revived Galveston's late 19th-century urbanity. Yet during its first incarnation, this barrier island city 2 miles offshore in the Gulf of Mexico was anything but refined. In 1817 Jean Lafitte and his pirates took over the abandoned base of a Mexican revolutionary and renamed it Campeachy. The town was abandoned and burned when the United States forced Lafitte to leave in 1821.

During the battle for Texan independence, the provincial government set up temporary headquarters. Galveston became the Republic's base of naval operations against Mexico and the temporary Texas capital in 1836. By the Civil War, Galveston was Texas' principal seaport and leading commercial center, and by 1890 it was Texas' largest and wealthiest city.

Galveston lost everything to the hurricane of 1900, in which some 6,000 people died. The island was lashed by winds in excess of 100 miles per hour and flooded by tides up to 15 feet high. Survivors woke to a city where whole sections along the Gulf had vanished or were piled high with the debris of thousands of buildings.

During Prohibition, Galveston reverted to its baser beginnings by offering illegal drinks and gambling in its saloons. This, combined with earlier acts of prostitution, earned Galveston the infamous nickname "the sin city of the Gulf."

Despite a massive engineering feat that in some places raised the city 17 feet behind a 10-mile-long, 17-foot-high seawall, Galveston lost its former status to its expanding neighbor, Houston. Galveston remained in Houston's shadow until the 1970s, when the Galveston Historical Foundation began restoring some of the city's Victorian buildings. These efforts and such natural assets as the island's 32 miles of sandy beaches have made Galveston Island *(see Recreation Chart)* a leading Gulf Coast resort.

The centerpiece of the island's resurgence is the city's Victorian neighborhoods that have been restored to their original splendor. The most prominent of these is the Strand district, once known as

"The Wall Street of the Southwest." The area between 20th and 25th streets is noted for its iron-fronted buildings, one of the country's best-known collections of such architecture.

Two other interesting sections are the East End Historic District—a 40-block residential neighborhood roughly bordered by 19th and 11th streets and Broadway and Market, near the downtown business district—and the Silk Stocking Historic Precinct District, a small area along 24th Street between avenues K and N. Oleanders—ranging from deep red to pure white—line many of these streets and add an exotic subtropical accent to the city's Victoriana.

Beaches are the city's major recreational refuge. One popular area is Stewart Beach Park, on the city's eastern edge at Seawall and Broadway boulevards. A scenic drive along the seawall and a ride on the harbor ferry are popular diversions.

A fleet of trolleys runs between the seawall, the Strand, downtown and Pier 19. Passengers can get on and off at various stops or take the entire 1-hour narrated tour. Tickets are available at Strand Visitors Center.

Mardi Gras Galveston is celebrated with parades, costume balls and musical entertainment on the two weekends preceding "Fat Tuesday." From early June through late August, Galveston Island Outdoor Musicals presents its summer series of plays at 14528 Stewart Rd.; phone (409) 737-1744.

Galveston Convention and Visitors Bureau: 2428 Seawall Blvd., Galveston, TX 77550; phone (409) 763-4311 or (888) 425-4753.

Self-guiding tours: A free walking-tour map of historic districts is available from the Heritage Visitor Center at Ashton Villa, 2328 Broadway, Galveston, TX 77550; phone (409) 762-3933.

ASHTON VILLA is at 23rd and Broadway. Built in 1859 by Texas entrepreneur James Moreau Brown, this restored three-story Italianate brick mansion is filled with antiques, art and family heirlooms. The opulence of the era is reflected in carved moldings, elaborate mantel-work and lavish furnishings. Guided tours leave from the carriage house visitor center. Allow 1 hour minimum. Tours depart on the hour Mon.-Sat. 10-4, Sun. noon-4, Memorial Day-Labor Day; daily noon-4, rest of year. Closed Thanksgiving and Dec. 24-25. Admission $6; ages 7-18, $5; family rate $18. AX, DS, MC, VI. Phone (409) 762-3933.

BISHOP'S PALACE is at 1402 Broadway. Galveston architect Nicholas Clayton designed this house for attorney Walter Gresham in 1887. The three-story residence took 7 years to build. The exterior is red sandstone, white limestone and rough granite. The interior, furnished in period, features a hand-carved grand staircase, jeweled glass windows and a mantel that won first prize at the 1876 Philadelphia World Fair. The Catholic Diocese purchased the house to be the seat of the local bishop in 1923.

Allow 1 hour minimum. Guided 30-minute tours are given Mon.-Sat. 10-4:30, Sun. noon-4:30, Memorial Day-Labor Day; daily noon-4, rest of year. Closed Jan. 1, Dec. 25 and church holidays. Admission $6; over 65, $5; ages 13-18, $3; ages 2-12, $1. Phone (409) 762-2475.

GALVESTON COUNTY HISTORICAL MUSEUM is at 2219 Market St. Housed in the 1921 City National Bank Building, the museum features exhibits about the county's history, architecture and lighthouses. An exhibit about the 1900 hurricane features film footage taken shortly after the storm. Allow 30 minutes minimum. Daily 10-5, Memorial Day weekend-Sept. 1; Mon.-Sat. 10-4, Sun. noon-4, rest of year. Closed Jan. 1, Thanksgiving and Dec. 25. Metered parking is available. Donations. Phone (409) 766-2340.

GALVESTON ISLAND RAILROAD MUSEUM is at 123 Rosenberg St. Restored railroad cars, model trains and a 1932 Santa Fe depot are preserved at the center. A sound-and-light show tells the story of Galveston from 1528 to the present. Allow 1 hour minimum. Daily 10-4, Apr.-Dec.; Wed.-Sun. 10-4, rest of year. Closed Mardi Gras, Thanksgiving and Dec. 24-25. Admission $5; over 65, $4.50; ages 4-12, $2.50. AX, MC, VI. Phone (409) 765-5700.

THE GRAND 1894 OPERA HOUSE is at 2020 Post Office St. Built in 1894, the theater survived the 1900 hurricane and has been restored to its Victorian-era grandeur. Al Jolson, John Philip Sousa and the Marx Brothers are among the celebrities who entertained on its stage. A performing-arts series continues to attract nationally known talent. Guided tours are offered by appointment. Open Mon.-Sat. 9-5, Sun. noon-5. Guided tour $3, under 12 free. Self-guiding tour $2, under 12 free. AX, DS, MC, VI. Phone (409) 765-1894 or (800) 821-1894.

[SAVE] **LONE STAR FLIGHT MUSEUM** is .8 mi. n. of Seawall Blvd. on 83rd St. to entrance of Galveston International Airport, following signs to 2002 Terminal Dr. Home of the Texas Aviation Hall of Fame, this museum details the history of aviation through exhibits of more than 40 restored aircraft as well as aviation artifacts and memorabilia. The collection includes World War II fighter planes and bombers such as the B-17 Thunderbird, many still in flying condition. Allow 1 hour minimum. Daily 9-5; closed Dec. 25. Admission $6; ages 13-17, $5; over 65, $4.50; ages 5-12, $4. DS, MC, VI. Phone (409) 740-7722 or (888) 354-4488.

[GEM] **MOODY GARDENS** is off I-45 exit 1A, 2 mi. s. to Seawall Blvd., 1.5 mi. w. to 81st St., then 10 mi. n. to 1 Hope Blvd. Three glass pyramids are the centerpiece of this 242-acre resort complex, which features beaches, paddle-wheel boat rides, IMAX theaters and a convention center.

The 12-story Aquarium Pyramid showcases 8,000 specimens of marine life from the oceans of the South Atlantic, North and South Pacific and the Caribbean. Inside the Rainforest Pyramid are streams, waterfalls, a Mayan colonnade, thousands of exotic plants, tropical fish and birds of the rain forests of Africa, Asia and South America, plus exhibits featuring bats, bugs, butterflies and frogs. The Discovery Pyramid offers traveling exhibits that explore the world of science.

The IMAX 3D Theater shows three-dimensional movies on a six-story screen. The Ridefilm Theater features a wraparound screen and seats that move with movie action. During the summer, Palm Beach offers swimming at a white sand beach, freshwater lagoons, waterfalls, sand volleyball courts and a yellow submarine that children can explore. Food is available.

Allow 4 hours minimum. Daily 10-9, late Apr.-early Oct.; Sun.-Thurs. 10-6, Fri.-Sat. 10-9, rest of year. Closed Dec. 25. Last admission 1 hour before closing. Hours may vary; phone ahead. Aquarium Pyramid $13; over 65, $9.95; ages 4-12, $6.95. Rainforest Pyramid $8.95; over 65, $6.95; ages 4-12, $5.95. Discovery Pyramid $4.95. IMAX Theater $8.95; over 65, $6.95; ages 4-12, $5.95. Ridefilm $7.95; over 65, $6.95; ages 4-12, $5.95. Palm Beach $7.95. One-day pass $29.95. An additional fee may be charged for special events. AX, DC, DS, MC, VI. Phone (409) 744-4673 or (800) 582-4673.

The *Colonel* departs from Palm Beach Pier in Moody Gardens. The three-deck paddlewheel boat accommodates up to 750 passengers for narrated sightseeing cruises of Offats Bayou. A dinner/dance cruise also is available. Sightseeing cruises depart daily at noon, 2 and 4, Apr. 1-Labor Day; at 2, rest of year (weather permitting). Hours and availability may vary; phone ahead. Sightseeing cruise $8; over 65, $6.95; ages 4-12, $5.95. Sightseeing cruise requires a minimum of 25 passengers. AX, DS, MC, VI. Phone (409) 740-7797 or (888) 740-7797. *See color ad.*

THE MOODY MANSION is at 2618 Broadway. Built about 1895 in the Richardsonian Romanesque style, the 28,000-square-foot mansion was purchased by entrepreneur William L. Moody Jr. after the great hurricane of 1900. The 32-room interior includes stained glass, carved wood, tile work, fancy plaster work and stencils. Visitors can tour three floors where rooms are furnished in the opulence of a wealthy family in the early 1900s. An introductory film is featured. Mon.-Sat. 10-4, Sun. noon-4; closed Easter, Thanksgiving and Dec. 24-25. Admission $6; over 65, $5; ages 6-18, $3. MC, VI. Phone (409) 762-7668.

TEXAS SEAPORT MUSEUM is at Pier 21 and Harborside Dr. Home of the tall ship *Elissa*, this museum brings to life Texas' history of sea commerce and immigration. A database containing the names of more than 133,000 immigrants who entered the U.S. through Galveston, "The Ellis Island of the West," is open to visitors. Allow 1 hour minimum. Daily 10-5; closed Thanksgiving and Dec. 25. Admission $6; ages 7-18, $4; family rate (4 people) $16. AX, DS, MC, VI. Phone (409) 763-1877.

The *Elissa* is docked at Pier 21 at the foot of 22nd St. This 1877 iron barque was built in Scotland and once carried Texas cotton to the mills of Europe. The 400-ton square-rigger's masts tower 103 feet above the water. Visitors may walk the decks and view the sailors' living and working quarters. A theater presentation details the ship's rescue from the scrapyard and the 5-year restoration process.

TREASURE ISLE TOUR TRAIN INC. departs from Seawall Blvd. at 21st St. A 1.5-hour open-car tour

covers 17 miles and passes the major points of interest in Galveston. Train departs daily at 9, 11, 1:30 and 3:30, May-Aug. (weather permitting); reduced schedule, rest of year. Fare $5.50; ages 3-12, $3. Phone (409) 765-9564.

GEORGETOWN (E-8) pop. 28,339

Established in 1848 as a trade center for the agricultural region, Georgetown features black, fertile farmland and ranch lands. Downtown is noteworthy for its Victorian architecture.

Georgetown Convention and Visitors Bureau: 103 W. 7th St., P.O. Box 409, Georgetown, TX 78627; phone (512) 930-3545 or (800) 436-8696.

INNER SPACE CAVERN is 1 mi. s. off I-35 exit 259. The cave was discovered in 1963 during construction of I-35. Entrance is by cable car, and sound and light effects enhance the cave's atmosphere. Prehistoric relics also are displayed during the 1 hour, 15 minute guided tour. Daily 9-6, Memorial Day-Labor Day; Mon.-Fri. 9-4, Sat.-Sun 10-5, rest of year. Closed Thanksgiving and Dec. 13-25. Admission $12; over 65 and military with ID $11; ages 4-12, $7. MC, VI. Phone (512) 931-2283.

GLEN ROSE (D-8) pop. 2,122, elev. 680′

Millions of years ago this region of central Texas was a coastal swampland where 60-foot dinosaurs dined on lush vegetation. The huge tracks of these prehistoric monsters can be seen in Dinosaur Valley State Park *(see Recreation Chart and the AAA South Central CampBook)*. Five miles west, the park now supports part of the official state herd of longhorns.

Glen Rose/Somervell County Chamber of Commerce: 611B Big Bend Trail, P.O. Box 605, Glen Rose, TX 76043; phone (254) 897-2286.

FOSSIL RIM WILDLIFE CENTER is 3 mi. s.w. via US 67, then 1 mi. s. following signs on CR 2008. The 1,500-acre haven replicates an African environment in which creatures roam freely. Among the 1,000 exotic and endangered animals along the 9.5-mile, self-guiding scenic wildlife drive are rhinoceroses, cheetahs, zebras and giraffes.

Allow 2 hours minimum. Daily 9-5; closed Jan. 1, Thanksgiving and Dec. 25. Admission $16.95; over 62, $12.95; ages 3-11, $10.95. Behind-the-scenes tour $35; ages 3-11, $25. Tour reservations are required. Phone (254) 897-2960.

"THE PROMISE" is at 5000 Texas Dr. Presented in the open-air Texas Amphitheatre, the epic musical drama portrays the life of Jesus. Allow 2 hours, 30 minutes minimum. Shows Fri.-Sat. at 8:30, June-Aug.; Fri.-Sat. at 8, Sept.-Oct. Admission $13-$24; over 62, $11-$22; ages 13-18, $10-$21; ages 4-12, $9-$20. AX, DS, MC, VI. Phone (254) 897-3926 or (800) 687-2661.

GOLIAD (G-8) pop. 1,975, elev. 167′

One of the oldest towns in Texas, Goliad began in 1749 when the Presidio La Bahia and the Espíritu Santo Mission were established. From its inception and well into the early 19th century the military post was the site of many bitter contests between various contending armies. The most infamous was the massacre in 1836 of Col. James Fannin Jr.'s 350 men by Mexican forces, a week after they had surrendered to Gen. Antonio López de Santa Anna.

News of the execution and the earlier defeat at the Alamo gave rise to the blood-curdling cry "Remember Goliad!" that was shouted as Sam Houston's forces swept to victory at San Jacinto. Fannin Battleground State Historic Site, 9 miles east on US 59, commemorates the Battle of Coleto Creek in March 1836, just 3 weeks after the fall of the Alamo.

Goliad County Chamber of Commerce: 131 S. Courthouse Sq., P.O. Box 606, Goliad, TX 77963; phone (361) 645-3563.

Self-guiding tours: A brochure detailing a walking tour of Courthouse Square is available from the chamber of commerce.

FANNIN'S GRAVE is 2 mi. s. on US 77A/183. The burial place of Colonel James Fannin and his men is a few hundred yards from the Presidio La Bahia. Daily dawn-dusk. Free.

GOLIAD STATE HISTORICAL PARK is .2 mi. s. on US 77A/183. The Texans slain during the Battle of Goliad are commemorated at the site. The 178-acre park features nature trails, quarry ruins, old brick and tile kilns and displays of American Indian and Spanish colonial items. Picnicking is permitted. Daily 8-5; closed Dec. 25. Admission $2, under 12 free. DS, MC, VI. Phone (361) 645-3405. *See Recreation Chart and the AAA South Central CampBook.*

Mission Espíritu Santo de Zuniga is in Goliad State Historical Park. The reconstructed 1749 church is furnished in period; the workshop displays period craft materials. Guided tours are available. A museum recounts mission history. Mission and museum daily 8-noon and 1-5; closed Dec. 25. Phone (361) 645-3405.

PRESIDIO LA BAHIA is 2 mi. s. on US 77A/183. The fortification was established in 1749 to protect Mission Espíritu Santo de Zuniga. Its chapel still is used for services. A museum shows articles found during restoration efforts that indicate nine previous levels of civilization at this site. Daily 9-4:45; closed Jan. 1, Easter, Thanksgiving and Dec. 25. Admission $3; over 59, $2.50; ages 6-11, $1. Phone (361) 645-3752.

GONZALES (F-9) pop. 7,202, elev. 309′

During the Texas Revolution, Gonzales citizens were the first to challenge the Mexicans. Rather than return a small brass cannon the Mexicans had left as protection against American Indians, the community unfurled the first Lone Star battle flag—with the words "Come and Take It"—and used the cannon to fire the first shots of the revolution Oct. 2, 1835. The First Shot Monument is 7 miles south on SR 97.

Gonzales Chamber of Commerce: 414 St. Lawrence St., P.O. Box 134, Gonzales, TX 78629; phone (830) 672-6532.

Self-guiding tours: Maps of historic points in Gonzales County can be obtained at the chamber of commerce office in the Old Jail Museum, 414 St. Lawrence St.

GONZALES PIONEER VILLAGE LIVING HISTORY CENTER is .1 mi. n. of SR 90A on US 183. Houses, a church, a smithy and a smokehouse are among the 19th-century buildings that have been moved to this 12-acre site and restored. Allow 1 hour minimum. Fri. 10-4, Sat. 10-5, Sun. 1-5 (weather permitting), June-Aug.; Sat. 10-5, Sun. 1-5, Feb.-May and Sept.-Dec. Admission $2.50; over 60, $2; ages 6-11, $1. Phone (830) 672-2157.

GRANBURY (D-8) pop. 5,718, elev. 725'

Contemporary commerce takes on a 19th-century flavor in Granbury's historic town square. The 1891 courthouse, 1886 opera house, 1885 county jail, bank building and several other structures have been restored. Live stage productions are offered in the Granbury Opera House on weekends most of the year.

Sightseeing trips and dinner cruises aboard the SAVE *Granbury Rose* Paddlewheeler depart from the landing on Lake Granbury; phone (817) 279-0204. Granbury Visitors Center offers guided walking and bus tours. Visitors can view Jesse James' grave at Granbury Cemetery, N. Crockett and Moore streets.

Granbury Visitors Center: 122 N. Crockett, Granbury, TX 76048; phone (817) 573-5548 or (800) 950-2212.

Shopping areas: Antique lovers will find more than 50 galleries and shops in Granbury. Antique Mall of Granbury, on E. Hwy. 377, offers more than 75 vendors. Artisans Craft Mall, also on E. Hwy. 377, features more than 150 vendors.

GRAND PRAIRIE—*see Dallas p. 85.*

GROOM (B-6) pop. 587, elev. 3,214'

Groom was named for B.B. Groom, an English cattle breeder who worked as a land agent for the Francklyn Land and Cattle Company. Groom's ranch on White Deer Creek was noted for its Hereford cattle. The town of Groom was incorporated in 1911.

CROSS OF OUR LORD JESUS CHRIST is at I-40 exit 112. The 190-foot-high cross is visible up to 20 miles away. Also on the grounds are 14 bronze stations of the cross. Daily 24 hours. Donations. Phone (806) 248-9006.

GUADALUPE MOUNTAINS NATIONAL PARK (D-3)

Elevations in the park range from 3,689 ft. at Lewis Well to 8,749 ft. at Guadalupe Peak. Refer to AAA maps for additional elevation information.

Guadalupe Mountains National Park is 110 miles east of El Paso on US 62/180. The park's 86,416

Look For Savings

When you pick up a AAA TourBook® guide, look for establishments that display a bright red AAA logo, SAVE icon, and Diamond rating in their listing. These Official Appointment establishments place a high value on the patronage they receive from AAA members. And, by offering members great room rates*, they are willing to go the extra mile to get your business.

So, when you turn to the AAA TourBook guide to make your travel plans, look for the establishments that will give you the special treatment you deserve.

* See TourBook Navigator section, page 14, for complete details.

acres occupy a rugged scenic section of the Guadalupe Mountains and include 8,749-foot Guadalupe Peak, the highest elevation in Texas.

The mountains are uplifted remains of the Capitan Reef that originated some 250 million years ago during the Permian era when an inland sea covered part of what is now Texas and New Mexico. The 400-mile-long, horseshoe-shaped reef lies exposed in three places—the Apache, Glass and Guadalupe mountains. The Guadalupe range forms a massive wedge towering above the west Texas desert; at the apex is the 2,000-foot sheer cliff, El Capitan.

Despite their barren appearance, the Guadalupes encompass stands of pine, fir and hardwoods that harbor elks and mule deer as well as wild turkeys, raccoons and an occasional cougar.

By the end of the 19th century the Mescalero Apaches, who had hunted and camped in the Guadalupes, had been expelled by the U.S. Army to make way for westward-bound settlers who wanted the mountains' water and shelter. Relics of this period can be seen in the park, including buildings from the Williams and Frijole ranches as well as the remains of a Butterfield Stage Station. *See Recreation Chart and the AAA South Central CampBook.*

General Information and Activities

Guadalupe Mountains National Park and its facilities are open all year. Information about ranger-guided hikes, amphitheater programs and other park activities can be obtained at the Headquarters Visitor Center, McKittrick Canyon Visitor Center and Dog Canyon Ranger Station.

There are no roads within the park. The only major route to the park is US 62/180. This road briefly crosses the southeast corner of the park and offers views of El Capitan, Guadalupe Peak and the eastern and western escarpment. Along the route are the ruins of the The Pinery, a Butterfield Stage Station, just east of the Headquarters Visitor Center.

Three short spurs off US 62/180 lead to McKittrick Canyon, the Pine Springs/Headquarters Visitor Center campground complex and Frijole Ranch. Frijole Ranch House contains The Cultural Museum, which traces the human history of the area from more than 10,000 years ago through the present.

While the park lacks roads, it does offer 85 miles of trails for hikers, ranging from .5 to 18 miles. One of the more popular routes begins at McKittrick Canyon Visitor Center and climbs steadily through the lush and twisting McKittrick Canyon. This trail, a relatively short round trip of 7 miles, is limited to day use.

An even shorter hike is the 2-mile loop from the Frijole historic site to Smith and Manzanita Springs and back. Longer hikes include travel to Guadalupe Peak, The Bowl and the base of El Capitan. Hikers should always carry water—at least one gallon per person per day.

Campgrounds at Pine Springs and Upper Dog Canyon are open all year on a first-come, first-served basis. Pine Springs is off US 62/180, and Upper Dog Canyon is at the end of New Mexico SR 137. Tent and RV camping are permitted at a cost of $8 per space per night; no hookups are available.

The closest gasoline stations are 35 miles northeast in White's City, 30 miles west in Dell City and 65 miles south in Van Horn.

The brilliant foliage of McKittrick Canyon makes fall the most popular season, but the spring also is beautiful and not as crowded. In general, the summers are warm and winters mild, with temperatures varying with the altitude. Be aware that sudden changes in the weather are common and often are accompanied by strong winds, electrical storms and occasional heavy downpours.

VISITOR CENTERS are in two locations. They provide maps, brochures and information to enhance visits to the park. Hours vary; see individual schedules. Both are closed Dec. 25.

Headquarters Visitor Center is off US 62/180 at the top of Guadalupe Pass. The Museum of Natural and Geologic Histories is housed at the center, which also offers a 13-minute orientation film, schedules of interpretive activities and posted information. Daily 8-6 (Mountain Time), Memorial Day-Labor Day; 8-4:30, rest of year. Closed Dec. 25. Phone (915) 828-3251.

McKittrick Canyon Visitor Center is at the end of the McKittrick Canyon access road off US 62/180. General park information and exhibits about the canyon are offered. Daily 8-6 (Mountain Time), late Apr.-Oct.; 8-4:30, rest of year. Closed Dec. 25. Access to the canyon varies with weather conditions. Phone (915) 828-3251.

ADMISSION to the park is free.

PETS must be on a leash or otherwise physically restricted; they are not permitted in public buildings or on trails.

ADDRESS inquiries to the Superintendent, Guadalupe Mountains National Park, HC 60, Box 400, Salt Flat, TX 79847; phone (915) 828-3251.

Points of Interest

McKITTRICK CANYON is at the end of an access road off US 62/180. The canyon is a mixture of desert, canyon woodland and highland forest. In late October the reds, yellows and oranges of the leaves resemble northern woods. Near the mouth of the canyon grow prickly pear and agaves; farther along big-tooth maples, ferns and wildflowers emerge beside a spring-fed stream. At the far end of the canyon the pine and Douglas fir of the mountain highlands appear.

Due to the fragility of the canyon, hiking is restricted to the designated trail. Brochures are available at the visitor centers. Access is limited to daylight hours. Phone (915) 828-3251.

HARLINGEN (I-8) pop. 57,564, elev. 40'

Named for a city in Holland, Harlingen earned a different moniker in its early days. Texas Rangers and U.S. Immigration and Customs officials patrolled the streets and railroad station in an attempt to maintain order in the border town, then known as "Six-shooter Junction."

Harlingen is the home of the Marine Military Academy. The academy, a private school, offers a training program designed to help its graduates gain admission to top colleges and universities. Another educational landmark is the 1928 Bowie Elementary School, a striking example of Aztec Revival architecture.

Harlingen Area Chamber of Commerce: 311 E. Tyler, Harlingen, TX 78550; phone (956) 423-5440 or (800) 531-7346.

THE IWO JIMA WAR MEMORIAL is on the south campus parade deck of the Marine Military Academy next to Harlingen International Airport. The original sculpture of World War II's Iwo Jima flag-raising was donated by its creator, Felix de Weldon, to the academy. This full-scale statue was the model used to cast the Marine Corps War Memorial for Arlington National Cemetery in Virginia.

Museum displays include items from the battle, brief biographies of the people portrayed in the sculpture, and the Hall of Fame of Iwo Jima Veterans, a series of books that contain information and "then and now" pictures of Iwo Jima veterans. A videotape documentary of the battle for Iwo Jima is shown daily. Allow 1 hour minimum. Mon.-Sat. 10-4, Sun. noon-4. Donations. Phone (956) 412-2207 or (800) 365-6006.

RIO GRANDE VALLEY MUSEUM AND HOSPITAL MUSEUM is 3 mi. n. in Harlingen Industrial Air Park at Boxwood and Raintree sts. This five-building complex features displays about the history of the lower Rio Grande Valley, especially its bicultural heritage. The 19th-century Paso Real Stagecoach Inn is restored and furnished in period. The hospital, which was the area's first, operated 1923-25 and now displays medical equipment of that era. The complex also includes the home of Lon C. Hill, founder of Harlingen. A videotape presentation is offered.

Allow 1 hour minimum. Wed.-Sat. 10-4, Sun. 1-4; closed Thanksgiving and Dec. 25. Admission $2; senior citizens and under 18, $1. Phone (956) 430-8500.

HENDERSON (D-10) pop. 11,273

Henderson experienced two decades of rapid growth before a devastating fire wiped out most of its business houses in 1860. The discovery of oil in 1930 fueled a rebirth.

Henderson Tourist Development and Chamber of Commerce: 201 N. Main, Henderson, TX 75652; phone (903) 657-5528.

Self-guiding tours: Information about walking tours of the historic downtown district is available from Henderson Tourist Development.

DEPOT MUSEUM AND CHILDREN'S DISCOVERY CENTER is at 514 N. High St. This living history museum features eight historic buildings and a visitor center. On the 5-acre grounds are an ornate Victorian outhouse, a syrup mill, an 1880 dogtrot house, a caboose, a print shop and an 1841 cabin. A museum in the former Missouri-Pacific Railroad Depot traces the history of Rusk County and features more than 100 hands-on activities that encourage children to solve problems. Mon.-Fri. 9-5, Sat. 9-1; closed state holidays. Admission $2; ages 4-12, $1. Phone (903) 657-4303.

HEREFORD (B-5) pop. 14,597, elev. 3,806'

Known as the "town without a toothache," Hereford has a water supply high in natural fluoride, resulting in a low rate of dental decay. Originally called Blue Water, the city is now named for the white-faced cattle first bred in Hereford County, England. The area leads the state in cattle and agricultural production.

Deaf Smith County Chamber of Commerce: 701 N. Main St., P.O. Box 192, Hereford, TX 79045; phone (806) 364-3333.

DEAF SMITH COUNTY HISTORICAL MUSEUM is at 400 Sampson St. The museum preserves the county's history with re-creations of a storefront and a one-room school, an original jail and wagon barn, a circus display and various tools, wagons and artifacts. The county was named for Erastus "Deaf" Smith, a Texas Revolution hero who lost his hearing in childhood. Mon.-Sat. 10-5; closed holidays. Donations. Phone (806) 363-7070.

HILLSBORO (D-8) pop. 8,232, elev. 617'

Hillsboro was established in the frontier tradition in the early 1800s. In fact, its first courthouse was a log cabin. Once a major cotton producer, the town is still rich in agriculture and is a gateway to Lake Whitney, a popular recreational spot.

Hillsboro Convention and Visitors Bureau: 115 N. Covington St., P.O. Box 358, Hillsboro, TX 76645; phone (254) 582-2481 or (800) 445-5726.

Shopping areas: Prime Outlets of Hillsboro, off I-35, features nearly 100 factory outlet stores, including Duck Head, J. Crew and Nike. With some 200 antique dealers in the Downtown Square District, Hillsboro is known as the "antique capital of I-35."

TEXAS HERITAGE MUSEUM is on the Hill College campus at 112 Lamar Dr. Dedicated to interpreting the experiences of Texans at war, the museum focuses on the Civil War and World War II. Galleries exhibit wartime artifacts with a special section dedicated to Texan Audie Murphy, World War II's most decorated U.S. combat soldier. Weapons from the Civil War to the present are displayed. The Confederate Research Center is open to visitors; phone ext. 242 for reservations. Museum Mon.-Sat. 9-4. Research facilities Mon.-Fri. 9-3. Admission $6; students through 12th grade, $4; under 6 free. Phone (254) 582-2555, ext. 295.

Houston

Although 50 miles inland from the Gulf of Mexico, Houston is one of the major seaports in the United States. Before there was a Houston there was a Harrisburg, a maritime trading post founded in 1824 by John Harris. In 1829 Harris died, leaving his brothers to resolve the inheritance of the town.

In 1836, the inheritance still unresolved, Augustus and John Allen attempted to purchase the town but found the price too high. They found a suitable plot of land farther up the bayou and established Houston, named for Gen. Sam Houston, who had just defeated the Mexicans at nearby San Jacinto.

The conversion of winding, marshy Buffalo Bayou into the Houston Ship Channel precipitated rapid industrial growth. With cotton reigning as king in Houston at the turn of the 20th century, textile mills the world over received and processed this commodity. The timber-, cotton- and cattle-shipping town evolved into not only a major port but also one of the energy capitals of the world.

The 20th century brought the discovery of oil, unleashing the potential of the refining and petrochemical industries. Steel, synthetic rubber and chemicals also are facets of the industrial market. Because of the city's proximity to NASA's Johnson Space Center, the first word uttered by a man on the moon in July 1969 was "Houston."

With petroleum, Houston became a boomtown, ever growing, ever changing. In 1940 it ranked as the country's 27th most populous city; 20 years later it had soared to 4th. Because there are no zoning ordinances, Houston has experienced unrestricted development. This has resulted in the city having more than one skyline and being a proving ground for innovative architecture. The Astrodome, billed as the "eighth wonder of the world" when it opened in 1965, set a futuristic standard for stadium construction. Minute Maid Park and Reliant Stadium have ushered in a new generation of sports complexes.

The influence of the arts is evident in the opera, symphony and jazz concerts, ballet, musical comedy and theater that enrich the city. Rapidly becoming a focal point of medical teaching, research and treatment, Houston's medical facilities are among the finest in the world. The city boasts about 25 institutions of higher learning, including Houston Baptist University, Rice University, Texas Southern University, the University of Houston and the research facilities of the University of Texas.

Approaches

By Car

Entering Houston from the north, I-45 continues through town, exits southeast toward Space Center Houston at Clear Lake City and continues to Galveston. Hardy

Toll Road parallels I-45 from north of Spring to I-610, which circles the city. I-10 enters the city from Louisiana, points east via Beaumont and picks up again as I-10 going to San Antonio.

From the northwest, US 290 connects Houston with Austin. From the northeast, US 59 runs from Texarkana through Houston to Victoria and the Mexican border.

Getting Around

Street System

Before tackling the freeway system, it is wise to study a city map. Freeways encircle and crisscross the city; names often change with the direction. The major city access routes spiral out from central downtown, not adhering to a north-south or east-west format.

The speed limit downtown is 35 mph or as posted. Rush hours generally occur Monday through Friday from 7 to 9 a.m. and from 4 to 6 p.m. Right turns on red are permitted unless otherwise posted.

Parking

Although metered parking is scarce, there are many commercial lots and garages downtown. The usual fee is $2 for the first 20 minutes, $5 per hour, $10 per day. Some places of business compensate for parking fees by stamping your parking ticket.

What To See

BAYOU BEND COLLECTION AND GARDENS is 4.5 mi. w. via Memorial Dr., then .5 mi. s. at 1 Westcott St. The American decorative arts collection of the Museum of Fine Arts, Houston *(see attraction listing p. 112)*, is housed in the former home of philanthropist Miss Ima Hogg. Displayed in 28 room settings, the collection traces the evolution in American style from the Colonial period to the mid-19th century. More than 5,000 works include ceramics, furniture, glass, paintings, paper, silver and textiles. The house is surrounded by 14 acres of woodlands and formal gardens with imported and native plants. Guided 90-minute tours of the house and gardens are offered; reservations are required.

Guided house tours depart every 15 minutes Tues.-Fri. 10-11:30 and 1-2:45, Sat. 10-11:15, Sept.-July. Self-guiding audio house tours Sat.-Sun. 1-4 (also Tues.-Sat. 10-4, Sun. 1-4 in Aug.). Guided garden tours Tues. and Fri. at 10 and 11. Self-guiding garden tours Tues.-Sat. 10-4:30, Sun. 1-4:30. Closed Jan. 1, July 4, Thanksgiving and Dec. 25. House tours (including gardens) $10; over 65 and students with ID $8.50; ages 10-18, $5. Gardens $3, under 11 free. Guided garden tours $7; over 65 and students with ID $6; ages 10-18, $4. Under 16 must be accompanied by an adult; under 10 not permitted on guided house tours. Gardens and first floor of house free to all third Sun. of month, Sept.-Mar. and in May. Phone (713) 639-7750.

(continued on p. 110)

The Informed Traveler

City Population: 1,953,631

Elevation: 38 ft.

Sales Tax: Municipalities may impose additional rates of up to 2 percent on the statewide 6.25 percent sales tax. Sales tax in the city of Houston is 8.25 percent; rates vary in the suburbs.

WHOM TO CALL

Emergencies: 911

Police (non-emergency): (713) 222-3131

Fire: (713) 222-7643

Time and Weather: (713) 529-4444

Hospitals: Columbia West Houston Medical Center, (281) 558-3444; Memorial Hermann Hospital, (713) 704-4000; Houston Northwest Medical Center, (281) 440-1000; Methodist Hospital, (713) 790-3311; St. Luke's Episcopal Hospital, (713) 785-8537.

WHERE TO LOOK

Newspapers

The city's major daily paper is the *Houston Chronicle.*

Radio

Houston radio station KTRH (740 AM) is an all-news/weather station; KUHF (88.7 FM) is a member of National Public Radio.

Visitor Information

The Greater Houston Convention and Visitors Bureau provides information about the area's many events, activities and attractions; phone (713) 437-5200 or (800) 446-8786, or write to 901 Bagby St., Suite 100, Houston, TX 77002-9396.

TRANSPORTATION

Air Travel

Houston has two airports. George Bush Intercontinental Airport, 15 miles north of downtown on US 59, is served by major domestic and international lines. William P. Hobby Airport to the south is served by domestic lines.

Rental Cars

Hertz, 2120 Louisiana Ave., offers discounts to AAA members; phone (713) 652-0436 or (800) 654-3080. Other companies are listed in the telephone books.

Rail Service

The Amtrak rail station is at 902 Washington Ave.; for train schedule and ticket information phone (713) 224-1577 or (800) 872-7245.

Buses

The Greyhound Lines Inc. bus station, (713) 759-6509 or (800) 231-2222, is at 2121 Main St.

Taxis

You can hire a taxi at cab stands near the major hotels in the downtown area or phone for one. One of the larger companies is Yellow, (713) 236-1111. The standard fare is $3 for the first mile and $1.65 for each additional mile; the rate is good for up to four people, the usual maximum capacity. Other companies are listed in the telephone books.

Public Transport

Air-conditioned buses crisscross the city and suburbs. Limited and local fares are $1. The Express costs $1 during regular hours and $1.50 during peak hours. Passengers must have correct change. Park-and-ride buses vary in location and fares. For details phone Metro Transit Authorities, (713) 635-4000.

Boats

Houston is a leading world seaport, and the Port of Houston accommodates passenger ships.

Destination Houston

With its innovative architecture, stellar museums and commitment to the arts, Houston is a city of great discovery.

Walk among butterflies in a tropical rain forest, view a cluster of historic buildings, or get lost in a collection of impressionist paintings. And if that's not enough, try the city's other museums of printing, health and firefighting.

Houston Zoo.
Koalas, pygmy hippos and Indochinese tigers are popular residents of Hermann Park, where some 5,000 animals live amidst tropical forests and Asian jungles. (See listing page 111)

Six Flags AstroWorld, Houston. Waterslides, raft rides and roller coasters are all part of the fun at this 100-acre theme park. (See listing page 113)

The Children's Museum of Houston. Blow bubbles, host a puppet show or go to Mexico—it's all in your hands! (See listing page 110)

See Vicinity map page 110

Houston

Bayou Bend Collection and Gardens, Houston. Decorative arts and formal gardens adorn the former home of philanthropist Ima Hogg. (See listing page 107)

*P*laces included in this AAA Destination City:

BLAFFER GALLERY, UNIVERSITY OF HOUSTON is off I-45 s. exit Scott/Cullen Blvd., then entrance 16 to the central campus. Housed in Room 120 of the Fine Arts Building, the university's art museum features changing exhibits of contemporary art. Tues.-Fri. 10-5. Sat.-Sun. 1-5; closed holidays. Free. Phone (713) 743-9530.

THE CHILDREN'S MUSEUM OF HOUSTON is at 1500 Binz St. Hands-on exhibits in 14 galleries represent such subjects as science, history, culture and the arts. Highlights include KID-TV studio, Farm to Market, a Mexican village, a science station, Kaleidoscope Gallery and a Bubble Lab. Allow 2 hours minimum. Mon.-Sat. 9-5 (also Thurs. 5-8), Sun. noon-5, Memorial Day-Labor Day; Tues.-Sat. 9-5 (also Thurs. 5-8), Sun. noon-5, rest of year. Closed Jan. 1, Thanksgiving and Dec. 25. Admission $5; over 64, $4; free to all Thurs. 5-8. After 3 p.m. $3, under 2 free. Parking $3 maximum. Phone (713) 522-1138.

CONTEMPORARY ARTS MUSEUM is at 5216 Montrose Blvd. Changing exhibits focus on recent themes in art as well as international, national and Texas artists. A Perspectives Gallery and an area for lectures and school activities are available. Along the east side of the museum is a small park. Tues.-Sat. 10-5 (also Thurs. 5-9), Sun. noon-5; closed Jan. 1, Thanksgiving and Dec. 25. Donations. Phone (713) 284-8250.

THE HERITAGE SOCIETY is at 1100 Bagby St. in Sam Houston Park. This outdoor museum contains seven historic homes and a small wooden church. Exhibits are housed in Duncan General Store and Heritage Gallery; a third gallery has changing exhibits. Houses include the 1847 Kellum-Noble House, believed to be Houston's oldest brick house; the San Felipe Cottage, a typical Texas German cottage of the 1870s; and the 1823 Old Place, a rough-hewn log structure said to be the oldest surviving building in Harris County.

Tues.-Sat. 10-4, Sun. 1-4; closed selected federal holidays. Guided tours are given at 10, 11:30, 1 and 2:30. Admission to galleries free. Guided tours $6; over 65 and ages 13-17, $4; ages 6-12, $2. Phone (713) 655-1912.

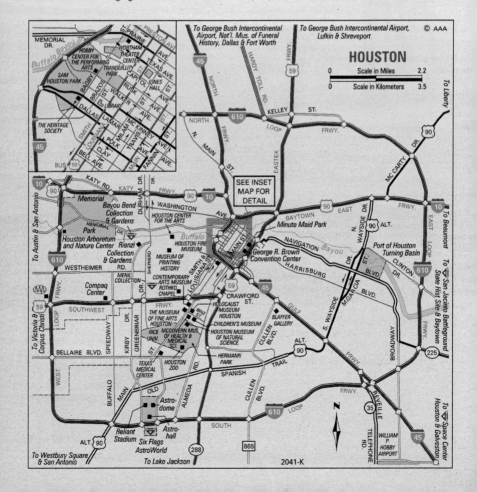

HERMANN PARK is off North MacGregor Way at 6001 Fannin, opposite Rice University. An equestrian statue of Gen. Sam Houston stands at the entrance to this 445-acre oasis in the heart of Houston's museum district. The wooded park contains a zoo, a natural science museum, a miniature train, a water playground, a nature education area and trails for jogging, bicycling and hiking.

McGovern Lake offers paddleboats, nature walks and a haven for migratory birds. The Japanese Garden features a tea house, waterfall and reflecting pond. Free entertainment is offered at Miller Outdoor Theatre March through October; phone (713) 284-8350. Golf and picnic facilities also are available. Park open daily 6 a.m.-11 p.m. Japanese Garden daily 10-6, Apr.-Sept.; 10-5, rest of year. Park admission free. Fee for train, paddleboats and golf. Phone (713) 845-1000 for park information.

Houston Museum of Natural Science is at 1 Hermann Circle Dr. Exhibits focus on astronomy, anthropology, geology, paleontology and natural history. Displays containing American Indian artifacts and a hall of gems and minerals are featured. The museum also hosts traveling exhibitions throughout the year. The Cockrell Butterfly Center, a three-story glass structure, is a rain forest home to thousands of exotic live butterflies, insects and plants.

Wortham IMAX Theatre shows natural-science films on a six-story, 80-foot-wide screen. Burke Baker Planetarium offers daily presentations, including constellation identification and children's features.

Museum exhibits Mon.-Sat. 9-6 (also Tues. 6-8, Mar.-Oct.), Sun. 11-6. IMAX shows are given on the hour Mon.-Thurs. 10-6, Fri.-Sat. 10-8, Sun. 11-6. Planetarium Mon.-Fri. noon-3, Sat.-Sun. noon-5. Closed Thanksgiving and Dec. 25. Museum $6; over 62 and ages 3-11, $3.50; free to all Tues. 2-6. An additional fee is charged for special exhibitions. IMAX shows $7; over 62 and ages 3-11, $4.50. Planetarium $5; over 62 and ages 3-11, $3.50. Butterfly Center $5; over 62 and ages 3-11, $3.50. Reservations are recommended for the IMAX theater. Phone (713) 639-4629.

Houston Zoo is at 1513 N. MacGregor Way. Home to more than 5,000 animals, the 50-acre zoo includes a rain forest aviary; gorilla, giraffe and Asian elephant habitats; a large cat facility; rare albino reptiles; vampire bats; and an aquarium. Pygmy hippopotamuses, koalas and Indochinese tigers are perennial favorites. Other highlights include the McGovern Children's Zoo and the Brown Education Center, where visitors can interact with animals in seasonally changing exhibits.

Allow 1 hour minimum. Daily 10-6. Last admission 45 minutes before closing. Admission $2.50; over 65, $2; ages 3-12, 50¢; free to all on city holidays. Phone (713) 523-5888.

HOLOCAUST MUSEUM HOUSTON is s. on SR 288 to Southmore/Calumet St., then .8 mi. w. on Calumet to 5401 Caroline St. The museum offers a historical and educational view of the Holocaust through photographs, a videotape, survivors' oral histories and labeled artifacts. The Holocaust is used as an example to teach the dangers of prejudice in today's society. A Memorial Room is available for contemplation. Changing exhibits also are featured in the Josef and Edith Mincberg Gallery. Mon.-Fri. 9-5, Sat.-Sun noon-5; closed Jan. 1, Rosh Hashana, Yom Kippur, Thanksgiving and Dec. 25. Free. Phone (713) 942-8000.

HOUSTON ARBORETUM & NATURE CENTER is just e. of I-610W at 4501 Woodway Dr. near Memorial Park. This 155-acre nature sanctuary supports many species of native plants and wildlife. Hiking trails wind through 5.5 miles of forest, pond and prairie habitats. The Discovery Room offers interactive exhibits. Allow 1 hour minimum. Grounds daily 8:30-6. Discovery Room Tues.-Sun. 10-4; closed holidays. Nature program Sun. at 2. Free guided tours are given Sat.-Sun. at 2 and 3. Donations. Phone (713) 681-8433.

HOUSTON FIRE MUSEUM is at 2403 Milam. An old firehouse contains fire equipment, exhibits about the history of fire fighting and videotapes about safety and fires. An interactive junior firehouse area is offered for children. Tues.-Sat. 10-4. Admission $2; over 65, students with ID and ages 3-17, $1. Phone (713) 524-2526.

McGOVERN MUSEUM OF HEALTH & MEDICAL SCIENCE is off SR 288 exit Calumet St., following service road to Binz St., then .5 mi. w. to La Branch St. at 1515 Hermann Dr. Visitors can walk through a giant brain at the Amazing Body Pavilion, which offers a three-dimensional look at larger-than-life anatomy models. Throughout the museum, computer simulators, video touch screens and interactive exhibits provide hands-on learning about health and the workings of the human body.

Allow 30 minutes minimum. Mon.-Sat. 9-5 (also Thurs. 5-7), Sun. noon-5, Memorial Day-Labor Day; Tues.-Sat. 9-5 (also Mon. federal holidays and Thurs. 5-7), Sun. noon-5, rest of year. Closed Thanksgiving and Dec. 25. Admission $5; ages 4-12, $3; over 65, $2; free to all Thurs. 4-7. Phone (713) 521-1515.

THE MENIL COLLECTION is at 1515 Sul Ross. Housed in a structure designed by Renzo Piano, this gallery features changing exhibits that draw from more than 15,000 pieces of Byzantine and medieval art, antiquities, Pacific and African tribal arts, 16th-century to present-day European paintings, as well as surrealistic and contemporary works.

The Cy Twombly Gallery contains work by the American artist. Other highlights include the nearby Rothko Chapel (see attraction listing p. 113), with murals by the abstract expressionist, and the Barnett Newman sculpture "Broken Obelisk," dedicated to Martin Luther King Jr. The Flavin Pavilion displays fluorescent work by the minimalist sculptor Dan

Flavin. Allow 1 hour, 30 minutes minimum. Wed.-Sun. 11-7; closed major holidays. Free. Phone (713) 525-9400.

MINUTE MAID PARK is downtown at Crawford and Texas sts. Home of the Houston Astros, the baseball stadium seats 42,000 and features a retractable roof that can close in 13 minutes. Adjacent to the natural-grass field is Union Station, a renovated train terminal built in 1911. A vintage locomotive runs on 840 feet of track on the left-field wall of the stadium. Guided 1-hour tours cover more than a mile of the facilities; comfortable walking shoes are recommended.

Tours depart Mon.-Sat. at 10, noon, and 2. No tours on afternoon or Saturday game days, holidays or during special events. Schedule may vary; phone ahead. Tours $7; over 65, $5; ages 3-14, $3. Phone (713) 259-8687.

THE MUSEUM OF FINE ARTS, HOUSTON is at 1001 Bissonnet between S. Main and Montrose Blvd. Two gallery buildings contain more than 45,000 American, European, African and Far Eastern art objects. The Caroline Wiess Law Building houses an African gold collection, pre-Columbian and Asian art, and modern and contemporary works.

The Audrey Jones Beck Building at 5601 Main St. features European art from antiquity to 1920; American art through 1945; prints, drawings and photographs; and the Beck Collection, which represents the avant-garde movements of Paris from Impressionism in the 1860s to Cubism and Expressionism in the early 20th century. Works by Pierre Bonnard, André Derain, Claude Monet, and Vincent van Gogh are among the masterpieces on display. The Cullen Sculpture Garden includes works by Henri Matisse, Auguste Rodin and Frank Stella. The museum's collection of American decorative arts is housed at Bayou Bend; European decorative arts are displayed at Rienzi *(see attraction listings p. 107 and 113, respectively).*

Guided tours are available, including special tours in English and Spanish. Food is available. Allow 2 hours minimum. Tues.-Wed. and Mon. holidays 10-5, Thurs. 10-9, Fri.-Sat. 10-7, Sun. 12:15-7; closed Thanksgiving and Dec. 25. Sculpture garden daily 9 a.m.-10 p.m. Admission $5; over 65 and ages 6-18, $2.50; free to all Thurs. Sculpture garden free. Parking $3. AX, DS, MC, VI. Phone (713) 639-7300 for English, (713) 639-7379 for Spanish, or TTY (713) 639-7390.

MUSEUM OF PRINTING HISTORY is at 1324 W. Clay between Montrose and Waugh. Antique printing equipment and fine art prints are displayed, including one of the oldest printed works in the world, the Dharani Scroll, dating from A.D. 764. Allow 1 hour minimum. Tues.-Sat. 10-5, Sun.

12:30-5; closed Jan. 1, Easter, Thanksgiving and Dec. 25. Admission $4, senior citizens and students $2; free to all Thurs. Phone (713) 522-4652.

NATIONAL MUSEUM OF FUNERAL HISTORY is off I-45 Richey Rd. exit w. over the interstate and w. to Ella Blvd., then s. to 415 Barren Springs Dr. The museum houses a collection of hearses, coffins, caskets and other exhibits tracing the history of funerals from the early Egyptians to the present. Replicas of King Tut's sarcophagus and Abraham Lincoln's coffin also are featured. Allow 30 minutes minimum. Mon.-Fri. 10-4, Sat.-Sun. noon-4; closed Jan. 1, Thanksgiving and Dec. 25. Admission $6; over 54, $5; ages 3-12, $3. AX, DS, MC, VI. Phone (281) 876-3063.

PORT OF HOUSTON TURNING BASIN is n.w. off the I-610 Clinton Dr. exit, in the 7300 block of Clinton Dr.; a security guard will direct visitors to Gate 8. The basin is the navigational head of the 50-mile Houston Ship Channel. Narrated 90-minute boat tours of the Port of Houston aboard the MV *Sam Houston* are given Tues.-Wed. and Fri.-Sat. at 10 and 2:30, Thurs. and Sun. at 2:30, Jan.-Aug. and Oct.-Dec. Free. Reservations are required and should be made at least 2 months in advance during the summer. Phone (713) 670-2416.

RIENZI COLLECTION AND GARDENS is off US 59 exit Kirby, then n. to 1406 Kirby Dr. The European decorative arts collection of the Museum of Fine Arts, Houston *(see attraction listing p. 112)* is displayed in the former home of philanthropists Carol Sterling Masterson and Harris Masterson III. The villa is a showcase for 18th- and 19th-century European art and antiques, including nearly 800 pieces of Worcester porcelain.

Guided 1-hour tours depart every 30 minutes Mon. and Thurs.-Sat. 10-3, Sept.-July. Self-guiding tours are offered Sun. 1-5. Closed Dec. 25. Reservations for tours and parking are required. Children over 11 are permitted on guided tours when accompanied by an adult. Admission $6; over 64 and ages 12-17, $4. AX, DS, MC, VI. Phone (713) 639-7800.

ROTHKO CHAPEL is at 1409 Sul Ross. American abstract expressionist Mark Rothko collaborated with architects Philip Johnson, Howard Barnstone and Eugene Aubrey to design this octagonal sanctuary, which contains 14 large Rothko paintings. The adjoining courtyard features a Barnett Newman sculpture dedicated to Rev. Martin Luther King Jr. Daily 10-6. Free. Phone (713) 524-9839.

SIX FLAGS ASTROWORLD is 5 mi. s.w. off I-610 Loop Fannin exit at 9001 Kirby Dr., across from Reliant Stadium. This 100-acre theme park features WaterWorld water park, rides, attractions, shops and shows. Ten roller coasters include Ultra Twister, a rare "loop-to-loop" ride; the Texas Cyclone; the Serial Thriller, with loops and spirals; and a stand-up coaster with a Batman theme. Greezed Lightnin' sends riders spinning around a 360-degree loop—both forward and backward.

Thematic areas are Americana Square, Nottingham Village, European Village, Oriental Village, Mexicana, Western Junction and U.S.A. Looney Tunes Town offers a cartoon city for kids complete with nine rides and shows. WaterWorld offers many ways to get wet, including raft rides, waterslides, a lazy river, pools, speed slides, a wave pool and interactive children's areas. Food is available.

Allow 6 hours minimum. Park open daily at 11, mid-May to mid-Aug. and for 1 week during spring break; Sat.-Sun. at 11, late Mar. to mid-May and mid-Aug. through Oct. 31. Closing time varies. Water park daily 11-6, May 1-late Aug.; Sat.-Sun. and holidays 11-6, late Aug.-Labor Day. Admission (including water park) $37.99, over 54 and the physically impaired $26.99, under 49 inches tall $22.99, under age 3 free. For the safety of all passengers, loose articles such as cameras are prohibited on most rides. Parking $7. AAA members save 10 percent on select in-park dining and merchandise. Check at the park's Guest Relations window for details. AX, DS, MC, VI. Phone (713) 799-1234.

SPACE CENTER HOUSTON is 25 mi. s.e. via I-45, then 3 mi. e. to 1601 NASA Rd. 1. The official visitor center of NASA's Johnson Space Center tells the story of America's manned space flight program through historic artifacts, hands-on exhibits, live presentations and behind-the-scenes tours.

Visitors can try on space helmets, touch a moon rock and climb aboard computer simulators to retrieve a satellite, land the space shuttle and walk on the moon. Spacecraft on display include Mercury, Gemini and Apollo capsules, Skylab and Lunar Module Trainers and a full-size replica of the space shuttle. The Astronaut Gallery features spacesuits from every era of space exploration.

Guided 90-minute tram tours to Johnson Space Center stop at Mission Control, the Space Shuttle Training Facility and other NASA laboratories. Films are shown daily in the Destiny Theater and the five-story IMAX theater. Food is available.

Allow 5 hours minimum. Daily 9-7, Memorial Day weekend-Labor Day weekend; Mon.-Fri. 10-5, Sat.-Sun. and holidays 10-7, rest of year. Closed Dec. 25. Admission $15.95; over 65, $14.95; ages 4-11, $11.95. Parking $4. AX, CB, DC, DS, MC, VI. Phone (281) 244-2100.

TRANQUILLITY PARK is downtown, bounded by Smith, Walker, Bagby and Rusk sts. The park commemorates the Apollo flights and is named for the *Apollo XI* moon landing on the Sea of Tranquillity. Five towers resembling rockets rise from a 32-level fountain and reflecting pool. Bronze plaques recount the Apollo story in 15 languages. Daily 6 a.m.-11 p.m. Free. Phone (713) 845-1000.

What To Do

Sightseeing

Bus Tours

HOUSTON TOURS picks up passengers at all major hotels inside Loop 610. Guided 3-hour tours of the city include the Astrodome, city center, Chase Tower, the Galleria, the museum district, Rice University, River Oaks and Texas Medical Center. Extended tours of area attractions, including Space Center Houston, are available. Tour times vary; phone for schedule. City tour $35; ages 4-11, $15. Reservations are required. AX, MC, VI. Phone (713) 988-5900 or (877) 440-8888.

Walking Tours

An area suited to walking tours is the original business district. Allen's Landing Park, at the corner of Main and Commerce, marks the site where Houston's founders, two brothers by the name of Allen, came ashore in 1836. Nearby Old Market Square is all that remains of Houston's original business section, bounded by Congress, Preston, Milam and Travis streets.

The 1845 Kennedy Trading Post, on the square at 813 Congress St., is Houston's oldest commercial building on its original site. The old Cotton Exchange Building is a four-story, Victorian-Italianate structure on the southwest corner of Travis and Franklin streets. Built in 1884, it served as a cotton exchange until 1923. The Old Sixth Ward is a residential-commercial area of Victorian gingerbread frame houses just northwest of downtown.

Driving Tours

Scenic drives wind through Memorial Park and residential River Oaks, with its large live oak trees and beautiful houses.

Sports and Recreation

Sports thrive in Houston. **Baseball's** National League Houston Astros, (713) 259-8500, play at Minute Maid Park. Houston's new NFL **football** team, the Houston Texans, (713) 336-7700, hits the turf at Reliant Stadium. The University of Houston's Cougars, (713) 743-9444, play football at Robertson Stadium and Texas Southern University's Tigers, (713) 313-7245, play in the Astrodome at the junction of I-610 and Kirby Drive.

The NBA's Rockets, (713) 627-3865, and the WNBA's Comets play **basketball** in Compaq Center at 10 Greenway Plaza. The AHL's Aeros, (713) 974-7825, also play **hockey** in this 17,000-seat arena, which features professional and amateur **boxing** and nonsporting events as well; phone (713) 627-9470. The various Rice University teams, (713) 348-4068, draw large crowds to their 72,000-seat facility. The indigenous Texas **rodeos** always are sellouts.

Houston has many public **tennis** courts. **Golf** is available at many public courses in the city: Bear Creek, (281) 859-8188, at 16001 Clay Rd.; Clear Lake, (281) 488-0252, at 1202 Reseda Dr.; Memorial Park, (713) 862-4033, at 6501 Memorial Dr.; and Woodlands Resort and Conference Center, (281) 367-1100, at 2301 N. Millbend.

Polo is played near Memorial Park, 8552 Memorial Drive at I-610; phone (713) 681-8571. There is professional **wrestling** at Compaq Center. Check the newspapers for a complete schedule of sporting events.

Challenger Seven Memorial Park, at 2301 W. NASA Blvd. and Mercer Arboretum and Botanical Gardens, 22306 Aldine-Westfield, contain **hiking** trails as well as picnic areas. Memorial Park, 6501 Memorial Dr., features the Lieberman jogging trail, a lighted, 2.9-mile course, as well as paths for **bicycling** and **skating**. **Track cycling** can be found at the Alkek Velodrome in Cullen Park, 19008 Saums Road; phone (281) 578-0693.

Tom Bass Park Section II is at 5050 Cullen Blvd. and contains jogging and nature trails as well as a

20-acre spring-fed **fishing** lake. As well as **canoeing,** visitors can enjoy a view of Houston's skyline from the Buffalo Bayou Park. **Boating** is popular at Clear Lake Park, 5001 NASA Road One.

Horse racing, both Thoroughbred and quarter horse, takes place at the Sam Houston Race Park, 7575 N. Sam Houston Pkwy. W. Simulcast racing is available daily. Phone (281) 807-8000.

Note: Policies concerning admittance of children to pari-mutuel betting facilities vary. Phone for information.

Shopping

Whether you seek a 12-carat emerald or a $12 scarf, you are sure to find what you seek in one of the large department stores. Neiman-Marcus, in the Post Oak Galleria on Houston's west side, is equipped to handle the wants of millionaires and eccentrics as well as those of browsers. The Galleria's 300 other stores include Lord & Taylor, Macy's and Saks Fifth Avenue, along with restaurants and an ice-skating rink.

Other malls offering restaurants, small shops, department stores and entertainment areas include Baybrook Mall, Bay Area Boulevard and I-45; Greenspoint Mall, North Belt and I-45; Memorial City Mall, Gessner and I-10; the Park Shops in Houston Center, on the east side of downtown; Sharpstown Center, Bellaire Boulevard at I-59; Town & Country Shopping Village, I-10 at West Belt; and Willowbrook Mall, SR 249 and FM 1960.

There also are shops at Rice Village near Rice University. Old Town Spring Shopping Village, north on I-45 at exit 70A, has antique and specialty shops, galleries and restaurants in 180 restored Victorian cottages along tree-lined streets.

Urban cowboys and cowgirls will find boots, hats and other Western garb at various locations of Cavender's Boot City and Stelzig's of Texas. Antique lovers are invited to forage for vintage treasures in Lower Westheimer.

Most stores are open Mon.-Sat. 9:30-6, and Mon. and Thurs. nights until 9. Most shopping centers are open Mon.-Sat. 10-9 and Sun. noon-6.

Kemah Boardwalk, 20 miles south of Houston off US 45 at exit 25, is a waterfront complex of shops, restaurants and amusements, including a Ferris wheel. For outdoor enthusiasts, Bass Pro Shops Outdoor World, in Katy at 5000 Katy Mills Circle, features a 20,000-gallon aquarium, wildlife exhibits and sporting demonstrations.

Theater and Concerts

Houston has been musically inclined from its earliest days. As a result, a wide variety of musical entertainment, ranging from classical to modern, is currently available in the city.

The stage of Jones Hall, 615 Louisiana St., is used throughout the year for productions by the Houston Symphony Orchestra and the Society for the Performing Arts; phone (713) 227-2787. Wortham Theater Center, at Texas Avenue and Smith Street, is the home of the Houston Grand Opera and the Houston Ballet.

The dramatic arts have flourished in the city. The centerpiece of the downtown theater district is Hobby Center for the Performing Arts, 800 Bagby St., home of Theatre Under the Stars and the Houston Broadway Series; phone (713) 227-2001. The city's professional repertory company can be found downtown at Alley Theatre, 615 Texas Ave., (713) 228-8421. Houston Center for the Arts, 3201 Allen Pkwy., is the venue for Stages Repertory Theatre and the Houston Children's Chorus. The Verizon Wireless Theater at 520 Texas Ave. in Bayou Place attracts big name performers and touring productions. In addition to various performances, two art galleries can be found at DiverseWorks Artspace, 1117 E. Freeway.

In summer the Miller Outdoor Theatre in Hermann Park presents free musicals and dramas as well as ballets and the Houston Symphony. Rock concerts are held at Compaq Center.

Special Events

The Go Texan Parade opens the 17-day Houston Livestock Show and Rodeo at Reliant Park in February. The River Oaks Garden Club sponsors the Azalea Trail through River Oaks in March, when many houses and gardens are open to the public.

The city's cultural institutions, as well as those from other regions and countries, are presented during the Houston International Festival. This 10-day event, held from late April to early May, features music, dance and theater on eight different stages. For golf lovers, the Shell Houston Open is played in April at the Redstone Golf Club in northeast Houston.

A 16th-century English village is re-created 45 miles northwest of Houston, between Plantersville and Magnolia, for the Texas Renaissance Festival. Food, merchants, craft booths, entertainers, street characters, royalty, jousting, games and skills of the period are presented weekends from early October to early November. Also in early November is the 4-day International Quilt Festival, which features new and antique quilts, classes, lectures and special events at the George R. Brown Convention Center.

The Thanksgiving Day Parade, a tradition since 1950, marches through downtown on Thanksgiving Day. During the second week in December the Harris County Heritage Society conducts three candlelight tours through seven historic structures in Sam Houston Park.

The Houston Vicinity

ANAHUAC (F-11) pop. 2,210, elev. 21'

Atakapan Indians were among the first inhabitants of the Anahuac region. By the 19th century, the bluff above the Trinity River was known as Perry's Point. A fort was built there in 1830 by a Mexican garrison under the command of Col. John Davis Bradburn, who named the installation after the ancient capital of the Aztecs. The first armed confrontation between Anglo-American and Mexican troops occurred at Anahuac in 1832, and the fort was left in ruins.

ANAHUAC NATIONAL WILDLIFE REFUGE is e. on Belton Lane to FM 562, s. to FM 1985, then 4 mi. e. The 34,000 acres of this coastal marsh refuge are the first landfall for birds flying north across the Gulf of Mexico. The refuge also is a nesting place for 40 bird species. Daily 24 hours. Free. Phone (409) 267-3337.

KATY (F-10) pop. 11,775, elev. 145'

Katy is thought to have been named for the Missouri-Kansas-Texas (M-K-T) railroad, which laid track through town in 1893. Prosperity came with the 1934 discovery of the Katy gas field, which remains one of the largest natural gas sources in the state.

SAVE **FORBIDDEN GARDENS** is 1.3 mi. n. of I-10 exit 743, then w. to 23500 Franz Rd. The 40-acre outdoor museum traces Chinese history through such displays as models of the Forbidden City and of Emperor Qin's terra-cotta army. A videotape about the city and soldiers is shown. Allow 1 hour, 30 minutes minimum. Fri.-Sun. 10-5

(weather permitting); closed major holidays. Admission $10; over 59 and ages 6-18, $5; one child under 5 free with adult (each additional child $3). MC, VI. Phone (281) 347-8000.

LA PORTE (F-10) pop. 31,880

When La Porte was founded in 1892, speculators advertised the area as a prime location for orange growers and farmers. Unfortunately, the land wasn't suited to many crops, but the town's location on Galveston Bay eventually made it a summer resort for Houston families.

SAN JACINTO BATTLEGROUND STATE HISTORIC SITE is 3 mi. n. of SR 225 on SR 134. The battle that resulted in Texas' independence from Mexico was fought on this 1,200-acre site April 21, 1836. Daily 8-9, Mar.-Oct.; 8-7, rest of year. Phone (281) 479-2431.

Battleship *Texas* is moored off San Jacinto Battleground. This vessel is the veteran of many campaigns of both World Wars. Daily 10-5; closed Dec. 24-25. Admission $5; over 65, $4; ages 6-18, $3. DS, MC, VI. Phone (281) 479-2431.

San Jacinto Monument and Museum of History is at One Monument Cir. Completed in 1939, the 50-story limestone obelisk is said to be the world's tallest monument column. The view from the observation deck, 489 feet above the battlefield, is spectacular. In the base of the monument, a museum depicts the region's history, from the American Indian civilization found by Hernando Cortez through the Civil War period. A 42-projector, multi-image slide show depicting

the Battle of San Jacinto and the Texas revolution is offered.

Daily 9-6; closed Thanksgiving and Dec. 24-25. Elevator $3; over 64, $2.50; under 12, $2. Slide show $3.50; over 64, $3; under 12, $2.50. Combination ticket $6; over 64, $5; under 12, $4. AX, DS, MC, VI. Phone (281) 479-2421.

PASADENA (G-10) pop. 141,674, elev. 32′

Pasadena's verdant landscape reminded early settlers of a similar city in California, from which the town took its name. The community became a major strawberry producer after Clara Barton of the American Red Cross donated 1.5 million plants to area farms damaged by the 1900 Galveston hurricane. Shipping and industry later replaced agriculture as mainstays in the local economy.

ARMAND BAYOU NATURE CENTER is 7 mi. e. of I-45 at 8500 Bay Area Blvd. A 2,500-acre preserve includes tall-grass prairie, estuarine bayou and coastal woods. On the preserve is a farm exhibit. Hiking trails are available; guided hikes and demonstrations are held Saturdays and Sundays. Adjacent is Bay Area Park, which has picnic facilities. Allow 2 hours minimum. Tues.-Sat. 9-5, Sun. noon-5; closed Jan. 1, July 4, Thanksgiving and Dec. 25. Admission $3; over 60 and ages 5-17, $1. DS, MC, VI. Phone (281) 474-2551.

RICHMOND (F-9) pop. 11,081, elev. 104′

In 1822 Stephen Austin's colonists built a blockhouse at the foot of the great bend in the Brazos River, making Richmond one of Texas' oldest settlements. At that time the Brazos River was a major transportation corridor, and the crossing had strategic significance. Deaf Smith and Mirabeau Lamar, two important figures in Texas' fight for independence, are buried in local cemeteries. The 1908 Fort Bend County Courthouse is still in use.

Richmond, a southwest suburb of Houston, offers a variety of outdoor recreation. Twenty miles southwest of town is Brazos Bend State Park (see Recreation Chart and the AAA South Central CampBook), one of the state's largest parks. Almost 5,000 acres of aquatic wetlands, hardwood forests and coastal prairies make up the park, which attracts a diversity of birds and migratory waterfowl.

Rosenberg/Richmond Area Chamber of Commerce: 4120 Ave. H, Rosenberg, TX 77471; phone (281) 342-5464.

FORT BEND MUSEUM is at 500 Houston St. The museum traces the history of the county from its original 300 families. On the grounds, the John M. Moore house is an example of Greek Revival architecture. The Long-Smith cottage, also on the grounds, offers tours. Tues.-Fri. 9-5, Sat. 10-5, Sun. 1-5; closed major holidays. Admission $3; over 50, $2.50; ages 3-12, $2. Phone (281) 342-6478.

THE GEORGE RANCH HISTORICAL PARK is 8 mi. s. on US 59 to Crabb River Rd. exit, then 5 mi. e. to 10215 FM 762. This 500-acre living-history site is located on a 23,000-acre working ranch. Trams take visitors to three areas representing 100 years of Texas history, including an 1830s stock farm with costumed interpreters; an 1890s Victorian mansion, cowboy camp, blacksmith shop and family cemetery; and a 1930s ranch house, live-oak treehouse and cowboy area with cattle-working demonstrations.

Juneteenth, commemorating the end of slavery in Texas, is celebrated the third Saturday of June with festivities and a rodeo. Picnicking is permitted. Daily 9-5; closed Jan. 1, Thanksgiving and Dec. 24-25 and 31. Admission $9; over 55, $8; ages 5-15, $5. Phone (281) 545-9212 or (281) 343-0218.

SPRING (F-10) pop. 36,385

Orcoquiza Indians were the first inhabitants of the region along Spring Creek, which was settled by a number of Stephen F. Austin's colonists in the 1820s. German farmers arrived in the mid-19th century, followed by immigrants from Louisiana and other southern states. Spring experienced a decline after the International-Great Northern Railroad moved its switchyard to Houston in 1923, but with the metropolitan area's northward expansion, Spring has become a thriving suburb.

Old Town Spring is a collection of Victorian cottages that now house antique stores, art galleries, specialty shops and restaurants.

[SAVE] SPLASHTOWN WATERPARK is off I-45 Louetta Rd. exit. This wooded 50-acre park features more than 40 rides, slides, chutes and lagoons. Highlights include Thunder Run, a five-story aqua speedway, and Crocodile Isle, a children's play area. Picnic facilities and food are available. Allow 4 hours minimum. Daily 10-8, late May-early Aug.; Sat.-Sun. 11-6, early May-late May and early Aug.-late Sept. Admission $24.99, over age 54 and under 49 inches tall $17.99, under 3 free. Parking $6. AX, MC, VI. Phone (281) 355-3300.

> The previous listings were for the Houston Vicinity.
> This page resumes the alphabetical listings of cities in Texas.

HUNTSVILLE (E-10) pop. 35,078, elev. 400′

Once known as a center of culture, the "Athens of Texas" was founded as an American Indian trading post in 1836, the year of Texas independence. Sam Houston was among the prominent early Texans who resided in Huntsville. Although Huntsville functions as a hub for agriculture and lumbering, its history is reflected in the many turn-of-the-20th-century houses that sprinkle the city's landscape.

Huntsville Visitor and Convention Bureau: 1327 11th St., P.O. Box 538, Huntsville, TX 77342-0538; phone (936) 295-8113 or (800) 289-0389.

SAM HOUSTON MEMORIAL MUSEUM COMPLEX is .5 mi. s. on the w. side of SR 75 business route at 1836 Sam Houston Ave. Two of Gen. Sam Houston's houses—Woodland, built in 1848, and the 1856 Steamboat House where he died—are preserved. On the grounds are his law office and the Sam Houston Memorial Museum containing his belongings and Texas Revolution artifacts. Tues.-Fri. 9-4:30, Sat.-Sun. 10-6, June 1 to mid-Sept.; Tues.-Sun. 9-4:30 rest of year. Closed Jan. 1, Thanksgiving and Dec. 24-25. Donations. Phone (936) 294-1832.

SAM HOUSTON'S GRAVE is in Oakwood Cemetery at Avenue I and 9th St. A large stone monument marks the burial ground. Daily dawn-dusk.

TEXAS PRISON MUSEUM is at 491 SR 75N. The museum chronicles the Texas prison system from its beginning in 1848 to the current system, which incarcerates 150,000 prisoners. Allow 30 minutes minimum. Tues.-Fri. and Sun. noon-5, Sat. 9-5. Admission $2; over 60, $1.50; ages 13-18, $1. Phone (936) 295-2155.

INDEPENDENCE (E-9)

Originally settled by and named for John Coles, a member of one of Stephen F. Austin's 300 colonizing families, Independence was renamed in 1836 to commemorate Texas' break from Mexico. Independence was the home of Baylor University until 1886, when the school was moved to Waco.

ANTIQUE ROSE EMPORIUM is 8.5 mi. n. of SR 105 on FM 50. More than 300 antique varieties of roses are represented. Herb, butterfly, perennial and water gardens also are on the grounds. Restored buildings include an 1855 stone kitchen; an 1840s log corn crib; an 1850s salt box house; and an early 1900s Victorian home. Allow 1 hour minimum. Mon.-Sat. 9-6, Sun. 11-5:30; closed holidays. Free. Phone (979) 836-5548.

TEXAS BAPTIST HISTORICAL CENTER-MUSEUM is at jct. FM 50 and 390. The state's oldest continuously active Baptist church was established in the Republic of Texas in 1839. Exhibits in the adjacent museum relate to the church, the community, the founding of Baylor University and Baylor Female College, and many of the area's notable residents, including Gen. Sam Houston. A nearby cemetery contains the graves of Mrs. Sam Houston and her mother, Nancy Lea. Tues.-Sat. 8-4; closed holidays. Donations. Phone (979) 836-5117.

IRVING—see Dallas p. 85.

JACKSBORO (C-8) pop. 4,533, elev. 1,084′

Jacksboro endured early existences as Lost Creek and Mesquiteville before it assumed its present identity. Some downtown buildings feature native limestone. Petroleum refining and related oil field services contribute to the economy.

FORT RICHARDSON STATE HISTORIC SITE is 1 mi. s. off US 281. Built in 1867, the fort was the northernmost in a chain of U.S. Cavalry posts used to halt American Indian raids and to guard the Overland-Butterfield mail route. The fort was abandoned in 1878. Present-day Fort Richardson Historic Site's 396 acres contain seven original and two replica buildings as well as picnic and camping facilities.

Grounds daily 8 a.m.-10 p.m. Museum Wed.-Sun. 8-5. Admission $2, under 12 free. DS, MC, VI. Phone (940) 567-3506. *See Recreation Chart and the AAA South Central CampBook.*

JEFFERSON (C-11) pop. 2,024, elev. 189′

Jefferson once was the state's largest city and inland port. Many families on their way west after the Civil War remained in the area, and sternwheelers traveling the Cypress River to St. Louis and New Orleans made stops in town. The city's rapid growth and development ended, however, with the decline of river transportation in the 1870s.

Jefferson's past is evident in a number of historical buildings reminiscent of the Old South. An example is House of the Seasons at 409 S. Alley St., built in 1872 in transitional style between Greek Revival and Victorian, with Italianate details. The house's name comes from its unusual cupola, which has stained-glass windows representing the seasons of the year. Guided tours are given by appointment; phone (903) 665-1218.

Jefferson-Marion County Chamber of Commerce: 118 N. Vale St., Jefferson, TX 75657; phone (903) 665-2672.

Self-guiding tours: Historic district maps are available from the chamber of commerce.

"ATALANTA" is at 211 W. Austin St. Named for a beautiful huntress of Greek mythology, the private railroad car of financier Jay Gould was built in 1890. The car has been restored to reflect the luxury of that era and contains four staterooms, a dining room, a lounge, a kitchen, a butler's pantry and a bathroom. Allow 30 minutes minimum. Daily 9:30-noon and 2:30-4:30; closed Dec. 24-25. Admission $2. AX, DS, VI. Phone (903) 665-2513.

EXCELSIOR HOUSE is at 211 W. Austin St. Built by Capt. William Perry in 1850, the hotel welcomed such notable guests as Jay Gould, Ulysses S. Grant, Rutherford B. Hayes and Oscar Wilde. In addition to the guest registers on view in the lobby, displays feature original documents and furniture. Tours are given daily at 1 and 2; closed Dec. 24-25. Schedule may change; phone ahead. Admission $4; under 8, $2. AX, DS, VI. Phone (903) 665-2513.

JEFFERSON HISTORICAL MUSEUM is at 223 W. Austin St. in the 1890 Federal Building. The museum depicts the life, industry and transportation of early east Texas. A collection of antique dolls from more than 20 countries is displayed. Daily 9:30-5; closed Easter, Thanksgiving and Dec. 24-25. Admission $3; ages 6-12, $1. Phone (903) 665-2775.

TEXAS HISTORY MUSEUM is at 202 Market St. Housed in the 1865 Haywood House, the museum features rare maps of Texas dating from 1513 as well as Texas banknotes and currency and other historical exhibits. A research library is available. Allow 1 hour minimum. Mon.-Sat. 9:30-5:30, Sun. noon-5. Free. Phone (903) 665-1101.

JOHNSON CITY (F-8)
pop. 1,191, elev. 1,193'

Named for the pioneer Johnson Family, ancestors of President Lyndon B. Johnson, the city is a retail center for a farm and ranch area. It also is the site of the Johnson City District of Lyndon B. Johnson National Historical Park (see place listing p. 124), which includes the Lyndon B. Johnson Boyhood Home and the Johnson Settlement. Lyndon B. Johnson Ranch, 15 miles west, is reached by a bus tour from nearby Lyndon B. Johnson State Park and Historic Site (see Stonewall p. 152).

A scenic overlook at Pedernales Falls State Park, 9 miles east on FM 2766, provides a view of the 3,000-foot limestone canyon through which the Pedernales River has carved steps, cascades and pools. See Recreation Chart and the AAA South Central CampBook.

Johnson City Chamber of Commerce: P.O. Box 485, Johnson City, TX 78636; phone (830) 868-7684.

JUSTIN (C-8) pop. 1,891, elev. 644'

French settlers established a colony at Justin in 1848 but abandoned the site a year later. It wasn't until 1883 that the community would be reestablished, bearing the name of a Santa Fe railroad engineer.

TEXAS LIL'S DUDE RANCH is off I-35W exit FM 407, 3 mi. w., then 1 mi. s. on Mulkey Ln. A day at this 200-acre ranch includes a 1-hour horseback ride, an all-you-can-eat barbecue lunch, swimming, hiking, fishing, a golfer's driving range, miniature golf and a hayride. Allow 5 hours, 30 minutes minimum. Daily 9-9, May-Aug.; 9-6, Mar.-Apr. and Sept.-Oct.; 10-5, rest of year. Closed Jan. 1, Thanksgiving and Dec. 24-31. Admission $40; ages 4-11, $35. Reservations are required. AX, DS, MC, VI. Phone (940) 242-3202 or (800) 545-8455.

KATY—see Houston p. 116.

KERRVILLE (F-7) pop. 20,425, elev. 1,654'

Kerrville, in a rugged hill region along the Guadalupe River, is a popular summer and winter resort. Camp Verde, 11 miles south on FM 689, was the eastern terminus of a camel route to Fort Yuma, Calif., during the late 1850s.

Kerrville Convention and Visitors Bureau: 2108 Sidney Baker St., Kerrville, TX 78028; phone (830) 792-3535 or (800) 221-7958.

[SAVE] **NATIONAL CENTER FOR AMERICAN WESTERN ART** is 1 mi. s.e. on SR 173 to 1550 Bandera Hwy. Home of the Cowboy Artists of America Museum, the center displays works by living Western American artists. Allow 2 hours minimum. Mon.-Sat. 9-5, Sun. 1-5, Memorial Day-Labor Day; Tues.-Sat. 9-5, Sun. 1-5, rest of year. Closed Jan. 1, Easter, Thanksgiving and Dec. 25. Admission $5; over 65, $3.50; ages 6-18, $1. AX, DS, MC, VI. Phone (830) 896-2553.

KILGORE (D-10) pop. 11,301, elev. 371'

Kilgore is known for its collection of Art Deco buildings, many of which are being restored. Also prominent are the oil derricks being reconstructed around town. At one time, more than 1,200 such derricks operated within Kilgore.

Kilgore Chamber of Commerce: 813 N. Kilgore St., P.O. Box 1582, Kilgore, TX 75663; phone (903) 984-5022.

[GEM] **EAST TEXAS OIL MUSEUM** is off US 259 exit Ross St. on the Kilgore College campus. A tribute to the pioneers of the Texas oil industry, this museum traces the history and development of the vast East Texas Oil Field through exhibits, audiovisual presentations, photographs and a re-created 1930s boomtown. Geological tools and equipment also are displayed.

Allow 1 hour, 30 minutes minimum. Tues.-Sat. 9-5, Sun. 2-5, Apr.-Sept.; Tues.-Sat. 9-4, Sun. 2-5, rest of year. Special holiday hours Dec. 20-Jan. 1. Closed Jan. 1, Easter, Thanksgiving and Dec. 25. Admission $5; ages 3-11, $3. DS, MC, VI. Phone (903) 983-8295 or (903) 983-8296.

RANGERETTE SHOWCASE MUSEUM is 1 blk. w. of US 259 at Broadway and Ross sts. Housed in the Physical Education Complex of Kilgore College, the museum traces the history and travels of the internationally known Kilgore College Rangerette Dance-Drill Team. Allow 30 minutes minimum. Mon.-Fri. 9-4, Sat. 10-4; closed Jan. 1, spring break, Thanksgiving and Dec. 25. Free. Phone (903) 983-8265.

KILLEEN (E-8) pop. 86,911, elev. 833'

More than 41,000 soldiers and their families are stationed in the Killeen area, home of Fort Hood. The 217,000-acre installation is the only U.S. Army post large enough to station and train two heavy-armored divisions.

Killeen Convention & Visitors Bureau: P.O. Box 1329, Killeen, TX 76540-1329; phone (254) 501-3888.

1ST CAVALRY DIVISION MUSEUM is at Fort Hood in Bldg. 2218 on Headquarters Ave. The museum traces the history of the Cav trooper from the 1850s through activation of the Division in 1921 and onto the Division's involvement in World War II, the Korean Conflict and Operation Desert Storm. Highlights include uniforms, weapons, vehicles and aircraft. Allow 1 hour minimum. Mon.-Fri. 9-4, Sat. 10-4, Sun. and federal holidays noon-4; closed Jan. 1, Easter, Thanksgiving and Dec. 25. Free. Phone (254) 287-3626.

4TH INFANTRY DIVISION MUSEUM is at Fort Hood in Bldg. 418, 27th and 761st Tank Battalion Ave. The Division's history is highlighted, starting with its inception in 1917 when its members were known as the "Ivy Men" due to their distinctive insignia. Visitors can view exhibits, photographs, artifacts and documents in addition to armored vehicles and helicopters. Allow 1 hour minimum. Mon.-Fri. 9-4, Sat. 10-4, Sun. and federal holidays noon-4; closed Jan. 1, Easter, Thanksgiving and Dec. 25. Free. Phone (254) 287-8811.

KINGSVILLE (H-8) pop. 25,575

When Capt. Richard King, a Rio Grande riverboat pilot, camped along a creek in the south Texas region called the Wild Horse Desert, he failed to see a parched flatland—rather, he saw its potential as a cattle range. The King Ranch, which covers about 825,000 acres, is purported to be the world's largest privately owned ranch.

Kingsville, the home of the King Ranch Headquarters, was founded in 1904 following development of a well-drilling system that could tap deeply buried water. The town has prospered from its association with the ranch and is now an agricultural, plastics and pharmaceuticals center. Texas A&M University-Kingsville and the Kingsville Naval Air Station also are in town.

Kingsville Visitor Center: 1501 N. Hwy. 77, Kingsville, TX 78363; phone (361) 592-8516 or (800) 333-5032.

JOHN E. CONNER MUSEUM is on the Texas A&M University-Kingsville campus at 905 W. Santa Gertrudis St. The museum focuses on the multicultural heritage of south Texas. Displays, ranging from prehistoric natural science to current economic development, include 19th-century ranch memorabilia, American Indian and early Spanish artifacts and game trophies. Allow 1 hour minimum. Mon.-Sat. 9-5; closed school holidays. Donations. Phone (361) 593-2819.

KING RANCH HEADQUARTERS is w. off SR 141. In 1853 Capt. Richard King purchased the 15,500-acre Santa Gertrudis Land Grant and stocked his ranch with longhorn cattle. Climate conditions and a demand for more flavorful and tender beef resulted in the creation of the Santa Gertrudis—the first cattle breed developed in the Western Hemisphere. A videotape about ranch history is followed by a 90-minute narrated tour focusing on daily life on a contemporary working ranch.

Tours depart Mon.-Sat. at 10, noon and 2; Sun. at 1 and 3. Admission $7; ages 5-12, $2.50. AX, DS, MC, VI. Phone (361) 592-8055.

LA GRANGE (F-9) pop. 4,478, elev. 324'

Famed for its brave fighters during the revolt against Mexico, La Grange took its name from the country home of the Marquis de Lafayette. The town was founded in 1831 near the crossing of the Colorado River and an old American Indian trail known as La Bahia Road.

La Grange Area Chamber of Commerce: 171 S. Main St., La Grange, TX 78945-2610; phone (979) 968-5756 or (800) 524-7264.

MONUMENT HILL AND KREISCHE BREWERY STATE HISTORIC SITE is 1.5 mi. s. on US 77, then .2 mi. w. on Spur 92. A tomb, marked by a memorial shaft, contains the bodies of men murdered by Mexicans in the 1842 Dawson Massacre and the bodies of members of the ill-fated Mier Expedition of 1843. Displays depict early methods of brewing beer at this former brewery, one of the first in Texas. A self-guiding interpretive trail winds through both historic sites, passing a scenic bluff that overlooks the Colorado River. Picnic facilities are available.

Daily 8-5. Guided brewery tours are given Sat.-Sun. at 2 and 3:30. Guided tours of the Kreische House are given first and second Sun. of the month

1:30-4. Park admission $2, under 12 free. Brewery tour $2, students with ID $1. DS, MC, VI. Phone (979) 968-5658.

LA PORTE—*see Houston p. 116.*

LAJITAS (G-4) elev. 2,342′

Lajitas (la-HEE-tas) is the Spanish word for "flagstones," which are noticeable in the area. The village was first established in 1915 when an Army post was stationed to protect the Big Bend area from the Mexican bandit Pancho Villa.

Known as the home of the beer-drinking goat Clay Henry, Lajitas also serves as a base from which to explore Big Bend National Park *(see place listing p. 64),* 20 miles east. Westbound travel on FM 170, also called The River Road, affords spectacular scenery as the paved highway climbs mountains and plunges into canyons along the Rio Grande.

Twelve miles east, Terlingua is a departure point for river-rafting expeditions. Once a prime source of quicksilver, Terlingua became a ghost town after the collapse of the Chisos Mining Company in 1942. In recent years, tourism and an annual chili cook-off have put the village back on the map.

BARTON WARNOCK ENVIRONMENTAL EDUCATION CENTER is 1 mi. e. on FM 170. Exhibits portray the natural history, geology, archeology and cultural history of the Big Bend region. A courtyard showcases a yucca forest, and 2.5 acres of gardens are planted with local cactuses, desert shrubs and trees. The center is the eastern entry point to Big Bend Ranch State Park *(see attraction listing p. 131).* Picnicking is permitted. Allow 1 hour minimum. Daily 8-4:30. Admission $3; ages 6-12, $1.50. DS, MC, VI. Phone (432) 424-3327.

BIG BEND RIVER TOURS departs from jct. SR 118 and FM 170, 5 mi. e. of Terlingua. Float trips range from a half-day to 21 days through the Rio Grande River canyons of Big Bend National Park and Big Bend Ranch State Park. Also available are canoe, kayak, hiking and combination float and horseback trips. For reservations write P.O. Box 317, Terlingua, TX 79852.

Trips are available all year. Half-day river trips $62, full-day $110-$155, overnight $250-$350 per person. Prices exclude park admission and river use fees. Minimum age varies from 2 to 6, depending on trip. Pets are not permitted. AX, DS, MC, VI. Phone (432) 371-3033 or (800) 545-4240.

RIO GRANDE ADVENTURES departs from jct. SR 118 and FM 170, 5 mi. e. of Terlingua. Guided half-day and full-day scenic float trips travel through the Big Bend area of the Rio Grande. A stop on the river's Mexican bank allows time for hiking and exploring. White-water rafting trips and jeep tours also are available. For reservations write P.O. Box 229, Terlingua, TX 79852. Trips are available all year. Half-day Colorado Canyon trip $60, full-day $100. Prices include park admission and

river use fees. Reservations are required 2 months in advance for March. AX, DS, MC, VI. Phone (800) 343-1640.

TEXAS RIVER EXPEDITIONS & FAR FLUNG ADVENTURES departs from jct. SR 118 and FM 170, 5 mi. e. of Terlingua. A variety of float trips range from a half-day to 10 days through the Rio Grande River canyons of Big Bend National Park. Full-day trips include excursions through Santa Elena, Colorado and Mariscal canyons. Half- and full-day jeep tours also are available. For reservations write P.O. Box 377, Terlingua, TX 79852.

Trips are available all year. Half-day river trips $50-70, full-day $100-$150, overnight $275-$300 per person. Under 15 discounted rate. Prices exclude park admission; river use fees are included. DS, MC, VI. Phone (432) 371-2489 or (800) 359-4138.

LAKE JACKSON (G-10)
pop. 26,386, elev. 15′

Lake Jackson, named for the small oxbow lake on Maj. Abner Jackson's plantation, was founded as a model community by Dow Chemical Company. The town is known for curiously named streets such as Any Way, This Way and That Way.

SEA CENTER TEXAS is off SR 288 exit Plantation Rd., then .7 mi. s. to 300 Medical Dr. Aquariums feature marine life found in the Texas Gulf Coast region, such as redfish, groupers and sharks. The center also includes a touch tank containing blue and hermit crabs, anemones, urchins and clams; a stocked fishing pond; and a fish hatchery. Tues.-Fri. 9-4, Sat. 10-5, Sun. 1-4; closed Jan. 1, Easter, Thanksgiving and Dec. 24-25. Donations. Phone (979) 292-0100.

LAKE MEREDITH NATIONAL RECREATION AREA (A-6)

Lake Meredith is about 45 miles northeast of Amarillo and 9 miles west of Borger via SR 136. Impounded by Sanford Dam on the Canadian River, the 16,504-acre lake offers recreational facilities at Blue West, Cedar Canyon, Fritch Fortress, Harbor Bay, Plum Creek and Sanford-Yake. Additional facilities are available at McBride and Bugbee Canyon. Boat rentals are available at the lake marina; phone (806) 865-3391 or (800) 255-5561. For more information about the recreation area, phone (806) 857-3151. *See Recreation Chart.*

LANGTRY (F-6) elev. 1,315′

Langtry, on the Rio Grande, was the home of Judge Roy Bean. Though he never met actress Lillie Langtry, Judge Bean claimed he had named the town in her honor. Langtry actually was named for a railroad engineer.

JUDGE ROY BEAN VISITOR CENTER is on US 90 at Loop 25. The frontier judge dispensed beer and the "law west of the Pecos" from a saloon named the Jersey Lily, preserved at the center. Dioramas portray the judge's life. The center also contains an extensive botanical garden with native desert plants. Allow 30 minutes minimum. Daily 8-5; closed Jan. 1, Easter, Thanksgiving and Dec. 24-25. Free. Phone (432) 291-3340.

LAREDO (H-7) pop. 176,576, elev. 438'

A chief port of entry into Mexico, Laredo is joined to Nuevo Laredo, Mexico, by four bridges across the Rio Grande. Laredo has been under seven flags since 1755, when it was founded by Don Tomás Sánchez, an officer of the Royal Army of Spain. At one time, Laredo was the capital of a separate republic known as "The Republic of the Rio Grande," which included south Texas and the area that is now the three northernmost states of Mexico.

The capitol of the republic stands in San Agustín Plaza, the site of the original town. An important commercial center, Laredo retains much of its colonial Spanish heritage and atmosphere.

Laredo Convention and Visitors Bureau: 501 San Agustín, Laredo, TX 78040; phone (956) 795-2200 or (800) 361-3360.

REPUBLIC OF THE RIO GRANDE MUSEUM is at 1005 Zaragoza St. During the Republic of the Rio Grande period (1839-41), this adobe building was used by neighboring communities in Texas and Mexico as the capitol of the proposed independent nation. The house is furnished with frontier antiques. Tues.-Sat. 9-4, Sun. 1-4; closed major holidays. Admission $1. Phone (956) 727-3480.

Nuevo Laredo, Mexico

Nuevo Laredo (noo-EH-voh lah-REH-doh) is a major point of entry to the Mexican mainland from the United States. It is connected to Laredo by four toll bridges across the Rio Grande. International Bridge 1 is open to vehicular and pedestrian traffic; International Bridge 2 is open to vehicular traffic only. Both are used for vehicles entering the interior. Bridges 3 and 4 are reserved for commercial traffic. For day trips to shop or dine, consider leaving your car in Laredo and walking across the border, which eliminates time-consuming crossing procedures.

The Mexican customs and immigration office is open daily 24 hours. U.S. customs offices at Bridges 1 and 2 are open daily 24 hours; the office at Columbia is open daily 8 a.m.-midnight.

U.S. and Canadian visitors must carry proof of citizenship; a valid U.S. or Canadian passport is the most convenient, since it serves as a photo ID and facilitates many transactions, such as cashing traveler's checks. The U.S., Canadian and Mexican governments also recognize a birth certificate (must be a certified copy from the government agency that issued it). A driver's license, voter registration card or baptismal certificate is **not** proof of citizenship.

All who plan to visit the interior or stay in the border area more than 72 hours also must obtain a Mexican government tourist card. Tourist cards are available, with proof of citizenship, from Mexican government tourism offices, Mexican consulates in the U.S. and Canada or immigration offices at official points of entry.

For a more detailed explanation of border crossing procedures and the requirements for temporary importation of vehicles, *see the Arriving in Mexico section in the AAA Mexico TravelBook.*

Mexico collects a visitor entry fee of 185 pesos (at press time, about $19) from each person entering the country. The fee must be paid in order to have your tourist card validated if you plan to remain anywhere in Mexico for more than 72 hours, or stay less than 72 hours and travel beyond the 16-mile (26-kilometer) border zone. If arriving by land, the fee is paid at a branch of any bank operating in Mexico. Upon payment your tourist card is stamped with an official "Fee paid" designation. All visitors are required to produce verification of payment by showing the "Fee paid" stamp on their tourist card upon departing Mexico. If arriving by air, the fee is included in the price of the ticket charged by the airline.

Visitors who limit their travel to destinations within the border zone, regardless of length of stay, are exempt. An exemption also applies to visitors staying more than 72 hours but limiting their visit to the following destinations/tourist routes: Ciudad Juárez to Paquime, Chihuahua; Piedras Negras to Santa Rosa, Coahuila; or Reynosa to China, Nuevo Leon, and Reynosa to Presa Cuchillo, Tamaulipas.

Nuevo Laredo is a center for *maquiladora* (foreign-owned) manufacturing plants utilizing inexpensive Mexican labor, and as a result the atmosphere is more industrial than picturesque. It does, however, offer an enormous variety of shops and souvenir stalls for those seeking bargains on Mexican crafts, and there are several good restaurants. While occasional Sunday bullfights are held, the city's racetrack, formerly a big attraction, is long gone.

The Falcon Dam, a joint Mexico/United States project on the Rio Grande River, can be reached on the Mexican side by taking Mex. 85 south to Mex. 2, then Mex. 2 about 63 miles (101 km) southeast to the town of Nueva Ciudad Guerrero. Local outfits offer boat rentals for fishing, water skiing and cruising the dam's lake.

LONGVIEW (D-10) pop. 73,344, elev. 339'

Longview was founded in 1870 as a rail center for the region's timber mills and farms. In the 1930s, the discovery of oil tripled Longview's population of 6,000 and transformed the quiet east Texas agricultural community into an industrial center.

Within an hour's drive of Longview there are more than a dozen lakes, which range from 2,500 to 25,000 acres, including Caddo Lake, Lake O' the Pines and Martin Creek. These lakes, as well as the surrounding pine and hardwood forests, make

Longview a popular recreational center. Anglers and canoeists also enjoy the Sabine River, on the city's doorstep.

Longview Convention and Visitors Bureau: 410 N. Center St., P.O. Box 472, Longview, TX 75606; phone (903) 753-3281.

GREGG COUNTY HISTORICAL MUSEUM is at 214 N. Fredonia St. Room reproductions include an early bank president's office, a dentist's office, a print shop, a parlor, a log cabin interior and a general store. Audiovisual shows concern the histories of Texas, Gregg County and printing. There is a display and videotape about the 1894 Longview bank robbery by Bill Dalton and his gang. The museum also is a Texas Heritage Resource center. Allow 1 hour minimum. Tues.-Sat. 10-4; closed holidays. Admission $2; over 60 and ages 3-18, $1. Phone (903) 753-5840.

LUBBOCK (C-5) pop. 199,564, elev. 3,195′

Lubbock was named for Col. Thomas S. Lubbock, a Confederate officer and brother of a Texas governor. The city's history as a commercial center dates back to the mid-1800s. Singer's Store, now in the Lubbock City Park, once was one of only two stores in the South Plains region. One of the major agricultural centers of Texas, Lubbock ships livestock, grain and cotton and is one of America's largest cotton producers.

The Buddy Holly Walk of Fame at Eighth Street and Avenue Q pays tribute to west Texas natives who have contributed to the fields of art, music and entertainment. Inductees include such celebrities as Dan Blocker, Mac Davis, Waylon Jennings, Roy Orbison and Tanya Tucker.

Lubbock Convention and Visitors Bureau: 1301 Broadway, Suite 200, Lubbock, TX 79401; phone (806) 747-5232 or (800) 692-4035.

BUDDY HOLLY CENTER is in the Ft. Worth & Denver Depot at 1801 Avenue G. A guitar-shaped gallery chronicles the life and music of Lubbock native Buddy Holly. The depot also houses the Texas Musicians' Hall of Fame and a Fine Arts Gallery, which offers changing exhibits by local, regional and national artists Allow 30 minutes minimum. Tues.-Fri. 10-6, Sat. 11-6; closed Jan. 1, Easter, Thanksgiving and Dec. 25. Buddy Holly gallery admission $3, senior citizens $2, under 12 free. Phone (806) 767-2686.

LUBBOCK LAKE LANDMARK is n. on Ave. Q to Loop 289, then w. to 2401 Landmark Dr. This 336-acre archeological and natural history preserve was once a prehistoric lake. Excavations have revealed a complete sequence of human habitation for the past 11,500 years. An interpretive center features archeological artifacts, dioramas and interactive exhibits; site excavations are conducted June through August. On the grounds are 4 miles of nature trails and life-size bronze statues of some of the extinct animals excavated at the site, including bison, giant armadillos, giant short-faced bears and mammoths. Picnicking is permitted.

Allow 1 hour minimum. Tues.-Sat. 9-5, Sun. 1-5; closed Jan. 1, Thanksgiving and Dec. 24-25 and 31. Guided tours are offered Sat. at 10 and 1, Sun. at 2. Donations. Phone (806) 742-1115.

MacKENZIE PARK adjoins Lubbock on the northeast. Prairie Dog Town, a community of several hundred of the rodents, was established in the early 1940s. Park facilities include picnic areas, ballfields, a golf course, disc golf and an amusement park. Phone the Parks Department at (806) 775-2687.

MUSEUM OF TEXAS TECH UNIVERSITY is at Fourth St. and Indiana Ave. Exhibits emphasize the environment, history and cultures of Texas, the Southwest and arid and semiarid lands around the world. An art collection includes sculpture, bronzes, ceramics, jades, ivories and Southwestern landscapes. There also are displays about Lubbock history, ethnohistory, natural history, and pre-Columbian and African art. The Moody Planetarium also is featured.

Allow 1 hour minimum. Museum Tues.-Sat. 10-5 (also Thurs. 5-8:30), Sun. 1-5. Planetarium shows are given Tues.-Fri. at 3:30 (also Thurs. at 7:30 p.m.), Sat.-Sun. at 2 and 3:30. Closed major holidays. Museum free. Planetarium admission $1; ages 5-18, 50c; over 65 free. Phone (806) 742-2490 or (806) 742-2456 to schedule a tour.

National Ranching Heritage Center is at 3121 Fourth St. This 16-acre exhibit includes more than 35 relocated, restored structures from the early days of ranching. A self-guiding trail leads from the museum to the historical park, which encompasses a ranch office, stone and log cabins, a Queen Anne house, a cattle barn, a bunkhouse, a schoolhouse, windmills and a train depot. Allow 1 hour minimum. Mon.-Sat. 10-5, Sun. 1-5; closed Jan. 1, Thanksgiving and Dec. 24-25. Free. Phone (806) 742-0498.

SCIENCE SPECTRUM OMNIMAX is at 2579 S. Loop 289. This hands-on science and technology museum offers 200 interactive exhibits, an aquarium and rotating displays. Documentary and educational films are shown on a 58-foot dome screen in the Omnimax Theater. Allow 2 hours minimum. Mon.-Fri. 10-5, Sat. 10-6, Sun. 1-5. Phone for theater show times. Admission $5.50; over 60 and ages 3-16, $4.50. Omnimax $6.75; over 60 and ages 3-16, $5.75. Combination ticket $9.75; over 60 and ages 3-16, $7.75. AX, MC, VI. Phone (806) 745-2525, or (806) 745-6299 for the theater.

LUFKIN (E-10) pop. 32,709, elev. 324′

Settled in 1882, Lufkin boasts the South's first paper mill. Currently the city's industries produce lumber, paper, metal castings, truck trailers, commercial gears and oil-drilling equipment.

Lufkin Convention and Visitors Bureau: 1615 S. Chestnut, P.O. Box 1606, Lufkin, TX 75902; phone (936) 634-6305.

Self-guiding tours: A walking-tour map of historic downtown is available at the chamber of commerce.

ELLEN TROUT ZOO is at 402 Zoo Cir. Home to more than 500 mammals, birds and reptiles from around the world, the zoo features Maasai giraffe and white rhinoceros exhibits, as well as a hippopotamus enclosure with an underwater viewing area. During the summer, a train takes visitors on a ride through the park. Food is available. Allow 1 hour minimum. Daily 9-6, Apr.-Oct.; 9-5, rest of year. Admission $2; ages 4-11, $1. Train fare $1. Phone (936) 633-0399.

MUSEUM OF EAST TEXAS is at 503 N. Second St. This art collection represents the character, history and heritage of East Texas. Changing exhibits highlight the works of regionally, nationally and internationally known artists. Allow 30 minutes minimum. Tues.-Fri. 10-5, Sat.-Sun. 1-5; closed holidays. Free. Phone (936) 639-4434.

TEXAS FORESTRY MUSEUM is w. of Loop 287 on SR 103 at 1905 Atkinson Dr. The museum explores the impact of lumbering and forest-products industries on eastern Texas. Outdoor exhibits, a hiking trail, a fire lookout tower, a logging train and a moonshiner's still are on the grounds. Allow 1 hour minimum. Mon.-Sat. 10-5, Sun. 1-5; closed Jan. 1, Easter, Thanksgiving and Dec. 24-25 and 31. Donations. Phone (936) 632-9535.

LYNDON B. JOHNSON NATIONAL HISTORICAL PARK (F-8)

Lyndon B. Johnson National Historical Park is 2 blks. s. of US 290 in Johnson City *(see place listing p. 119)*. Covering 675 acres, some of which the Johnson family had owned since the late 1860s, the park consists of two districts, each once home to President Johnson. The home where he was born has been reconstructed on the site where the original once stood. His boyhood home remains in its original location. The visitor center, in the former Pedernales Hospital, chronicles LBJ's life and accomplishments and features a tribute to Lady Bird Johnson. The visitor center is open daily 8:45-5; closed Jan. 1, Thanksgiving and Dec. 25.

JOHNSON CITY DISTRICT is 2 blks. s. of US 290 on Lady Bird Ln. Lyndon Johnson's boyhood home is furnished in period, reflecting rural Texas life in the 1920s. Tours are given daily every half-hour 9-4:30. Johnson Settlement open daily 9-dusk. Visitor Center daily 8:45-5. Closed Jan. 1, Thanksgiving and Dec. 25. Donations. Phone (830) 868-7128, ext. 244.

LBJ RANCH DISTRICT is 15 mi. w. of Johnson City on US 290 and can be reached only via a bus tour from the visitor center at Lyndon B. Johnson State Park and Historic Site near Stonewall *(see place listing p. 152)*. The 90-minute tour, which departs throughout the day, includes the ranch, a reconstruction of the farmhouse where LBJ was born, a one-room Junction School, a show barn, the "Texas White House" and the grave of former President Lyndon B. Johnson in the Johnson family cemetery.

Allow 2 hours minimum. Daily 10-4; closed Jan. 1, Thanksgiving and Dec. 25. Bus tour $3, under 6 free. Pets are not permitted on tours. Phone (830) 844-2420 or (830) 868-7128, ext. 244.

MARLIN (E-9) pop. 6,628, elev. 383′

The thermomineral wells under Marlin, reputed to be the deepest in the world, expel more than 380,000 gallons of 147-degree-Fahrenheit water daily. The water is used in geothermal heating projects. The chamber of commerce and the Falls Community Memorial Hospital are heated by geothermal energy.

Agribusiness, primarily cattle and grain production, maintains Marlin's economy. When not at work, residents enjoy sports and recreation at Falls on the Brazos Park *(see Recreation Chart)*.

Marlin Chamber of Commerce: 245 Coleman St., Marlin, TX 76661; phone (254) 803-3301.

MARSHALL (D-11) pop. 23,935, elev. 375′

During the Civil War Marshall was the capital of Missouri. It seemed strange that such a quiet town would be chosen by executives of Missouri and the Trans-Mississippi Department of the Confederacy as their administrative center. At that time Marshall was one of the biggest and wealthiest cities in the state, producing gun powder and ammunition for the Confederacy as well as saddles, harnesses and clothing.

On a major stagecoach route, Marshall became a stop on the Texas and Pacific Railroad in the 1870s. An original section of the old Stagecoach Road begins at the end of Poplar Street off US 59. The arrival of the railroad restored the town's fortunes—a prosperity expressed by the elegant Ginocchio Hotel built near the depot in 1896. This restored Victorian hostelry is the centerpiece of Marshall's three-block Ginocchio Historic District. At Christmas, millions of white lights decorate the downtown area in the Wonderland of Lights.

An abundance of red and white clay has made Marshall a center for pottery making. Stoneware is produced by more than a dozen companies in the area. Marshall Pottery, one of the country's largest manufacturers of terra-cotta flower pots, was established in 1895.

Marshall Visitor Development Division: 213 W. Austin St., P.O. Box 520, Marshall, TX 75671; phone (903) 935-7868.

Self-guiding tours: Maps outlining tours of historic Marshall and Harrison County are available from the chamber of commerce.

MICHELSON MUSEUM OF ART is at 216 N. Bolivar. The museum features more than 1,000 paintings, drawings and prints by Russian-born artist Leo Michelson, as well as African masks and works by American artists. The Dr. David Weisman Hirsch Discovery Room contains hands-on displays. Allow 1 hour minimum. Guided tours are available Tues.-Fri. noon-5, Sat.-Sun. 1-4; closed holidays. Donations. Phone (903) 935-9480.

STARR FAMILY STATE HISTORIC SITE is at 407 W. Travis St. This two-story, wood-sided house was built in 1870 by Dr. James Franklin Starr, the son of former Republic of Texas treasurer, Dr. James Harper Starr. Expanded and altered during the 115 years the family occupied it, the house and its furnishings reflect the development of Texas. Allow 1 hour minimum. Tours are given Mon. and Thurs.-Sat. 10-4, Sun. 1-4 and by appointment. Admission $3; ages 6-11, $1. Phone (903) 935-3044.

McALLEN (I-8) pop. 106,414, elev. 122′

McAllen was named in honor of its Scottish founder, John McAllen, who donated land for the establishment of a rail line in 1904. He also built the depot close to his hotel, thus increasing his occupancy rate. Construction of the McAllen-Hidalgo-Reynosa International Bridge in 1941 made the town a major port of entry into Mexico and a center for tourism. McAllen's culture reflects a strong Mexican influence.

Nicknamed the City of Palms for the 40 varieties of trees that line its streets, McAllen is a winter resort that lies on the same latitude as Fort Lauderdale and enjoys the same subtropical climate. The town bills itself as the "square dance capital of the world," attracting some 10,000 people each winter for daily promenades.

McAllen Convention and Visitors Bureau: 1200 Ash St., P.O. Box 790, McAllen, TX 78501; phone (956) 682-2871 or (877) 622-5536.

INTERNATIONAL MUSEUM OF ART AND SCIENCE is 3.2 mi. n.w. at jct. Nolana Loop and Bicentennial Blvd. Galleries present changing exhibits of paintings, sculpture, photographs, graphics and crafts. RioScape Science Discovery Park is an interactive science playground with waterfalls, climbing walls and mazes. Tues.-Wed. and Fri.-Sat. 9-5, Thurs. noon-8, Sun. 1-5; closed Jan. 1, Easter, Memorial Day, July 4, Thanksgiving and Dec. 25. Admission $3; senior citizens, students with ID and under 13, $2; free to all Thurs. 4-8. Phone (956) 682-1564.

Reynosa, Mexico

On the Rio Grande just south of McAllen, Reynosa (reh-NOH-sah) is reached by the McAllen International Toll Bridge. A major gas-processing and oil-refining center, Reynosa is decidedly short on charm but does have a small tourist district. The toll to enter Mexico is $1.50 per vehicle; the return toll is $1.95 per vehicle (U.S. dollars accepted).

Both Mexican and U.S. customs and immigration offices are open 24 hours daily.

U.S. and Canadian visitors must carry proof of citizenship. A valid U.S. or Canadian passport is the most convenient, since it serves as a photo ID and facilitates many transactions, such as cashing traveler's checks. The U.S., Canadian and Mexican governments also recognize a birth certificate (must be a certified copy from the government agency that issued it). A driver's license, voter registration card or baptismal certificate is **not** proof of citizenship.

All who plan to visit the interior or stay in the border area more than 72 hours also must obtain a Mexican government tourist card. Tourist cards are available, with proof of citizenship, from Mexican government tourism offices, Mexican consulates in the U.S. and Canada or immigration offices at official points of entry.

For a more detailed explanation of border crossing procedures and the requirements for temporary importation of vehicles, *see the Arriving in Mexico section in the AAA Mexico TravelBook.*

Mexico collects a visitor entry fee of 185 pesos (at press time, about $19) from each person entering the country. The fee must be paid in order to have your tourist card validated if you plan to remain anywhere in Mexico for more than 72 hours, or stay less than 72 hours and travel beyond the 16-mile (26-kilometer) border zone. If arriving by land, the fee is paid at a branch of any bank operating in Mexico. Upon payment your tourist card is stamped with an official "Fee paid" designation. All visitors are required to produce verification of payment by showing the "Fee paid" stamp on their tourist card upon departing Mexico. If arriving by air, the fee is included in the price of the ticket charged by the airline.

Visitors who limit their travel to destinations within the border zone, regardless of length of stay, are exempt. An exemption also applies to visitors staying more than 72 hours but limiting their visit to the following destinations/tourist routes: Ciudad Juárez to Paquime, Chihuahua; Piedras Negras to Santa Rosa, Coahuila; or Reynosa to China, Nuevo Leon, and Reynosa to Presa Cuchillo, Tamaulipas.

Shopping areas: Plaza Principal, the main plaza (some 20 blocks in from the toll bridge), is a typical Mexican square with shops and a Colonial-style cathedral upon which has been grafted an ultramodern addition. The Zona Rosa is a small area that contains a few shops and restaurants.

McKINNEY—see Dallas p. 86.

McLEAN (B-6) pop. 830, elev. 2,812′

McLean began with a water well and a railroad switch built by the Choctaw, Oklahoma and Texas Railroad Company in 1901. The town became a shipping point for area farmers, who sent several hundred carloads of hogs and watermelons to market annually. McLean profited from the oil boom of the 1920s and the construction of Route 66. Efforts have been made to preserve buildings along the historic route, which was bypassed in the early 1980s. A vintage Phillips 66 gas station and an antique pumper can be seen at First and Gray streets.

DEVIL'S ROPE MUSEUM is at jct. Old Route 66 and Kingsley St. Housed in a former brassier factory, the museum traces the history of barbed wire, the "devil's rope." Exhibits include tools for fence construction and entanglement wire used in warfare. Route 66 relics also are displayed. Allow 1 hour minimum. Mon.-Sat. 9-5, Sun. 1-4, Mar. 1-Dec. 15. Donations. Phone (806) 779-2225.

MESQUITE—see Dallas p. 86.

MIDLAND (D-5) pop. 94,996, elev. 2,769'

Midland is a west Texas oil center that lies on the former Chihuahua Trail, the Emigrant Road to California and the Comanche War Trail. The settlement, named in 1880 for its location halfway between Fort Worth and El Paso, was a quiet farming town until its economy changed in 1923 with the tapping of the huge Permian Basin petroleum supply.

President George W. Bush spent his formative years in Midland; the Bush family lived in the area 1948-1959. While working in Houston, George W. was introduced to Laura Welch, a young librarian from his home town. The couple married in 1977 and made their home in Midland.

Midland Convention and Visitors Bureau: 109 N. Main St., Midland, TX 79701; phone (432) 683-3381 or (800) 624-6435.

COMMEMORATIVE AIR FORCE AND AMERICAN AIRPOWER HERITAGE MUSEUM is next to Midland Airport at 9600 Wright Dr. The facility features one of the world's foremost collections of World War II aircraft in flying condition; 10-15 of the planes are displayed on a rotating basis. Interpretive exhibits detail airpower 1939-45. An annual air show is held the first full weekend in October.

Mon.-Sat. 9-5, Sun. and holidays noon-5; closed Thanksgiving and Dec. 25. Admission $9; over 64 and ages 13-18, $8; ages 6-12, $6. DS, MC, VI. Phone (432) 563-1000.

MUSEUM OF THE SOUTHWEST is 1 blk. s. of US 80 business route at 1705 W. Missouri Ave. The museum houses art and archeological artifacts in a 1934 mansion designed by Anton F. Korn. The permanent collection includes the Hogan Collection of works by founding members of the Taos Society of Artists, as well as graphics and sculpture. The museum also features a wing displaying traveling exhibitions and Fredda Turner Durham Children's Museum, with hands-on exhibits.

Allow 1 hour minimum. Tues.-Sat. 10-5, Sun. 2-5; closed Jan. 1, President's Day, Easter, July 4, Labor Day, Thanksgiving and Dec. 24-25. Donations. Phone (432) 683-2882.

Marian Blakemore Planetarium is 1 blk. s. at Indiana and K sts. A model of the Apollo Command Module is featured. Astronomy shows are given Fri. at 8 p.m. Phone to verify schedule. Admission $3; ages 3-11, $2. Phone (432) 683-2882.

THE PETROLEUM MUSEUM is at 1500 I-20 West exit 136, .7 mi. w. of jct. SR 349 and I-20. Located in the heart of the Permian Basin, this museum chronicles the origin and discovery of fossil fuel and its associated industries. Highlights include the Marine Diorama of the Ancient Permian Seas, the Boomtown Room, a well-fire display and antique drilling rigs. On permanent exhibit is a collection of Tom Lovell paintings. Pioneers of the oil and gas industry are honored in the Petroleum Hall of Fame, and a research library is open to visitors.

Allow 1 hour minimum. Mon.-Sat. 9-5, Sun. 2-5; closed Jan. 1, Thanksgiving and Dec. 24-25. Admission $5; over 65 and ages 12-17, $4; ages 6-11, $3. MC, VI. Phone (432) 683-4403.

MISSION (I-8) pop. 45,408, elev. 134'

Mission, in the Rio Grande Valley, was founded by Oblate Fathers in 1824. They are credited with being the first to plant citrus in this region, which is now known for Texas Ruby Red grapefruit. Situated on the migratory flyway between Central and South American and Canada, the Rio Grande Valley is a prime birdwatching destination; nearly 500 species have been sighted in the region.

Los Ebanos Ferry, 17 miles southwest on FM 886, is thought to be the last remaining hand-drawn ferry in the country. It transports three cars and several passengers across the Rio Grande at a time.

Mission Chamber of Commerce: 220 E. Ninth St., Mission, TX 78572; phone (956) 585-2727 or (800) 580-2700.

LA LOMITA CHAPEL is 3 mi. s. on FM 1016. The "Little Hill" Chapel is one of the oldest Texas missions still in use. Measuring 12 feet by 25 feet, the sandstone structure was built by the Oblate Fathers in 1865 and relocated to its present site in 1899. Picnicking along nature trails in the surrounding 7-acre park is permitted. Allow 30 minutes minimum. Daily dawn-dusk. Free. Phone (956) 580-8760.

MONAHANS (D-4) pop. 6,821, elev. 2,613'

Although the Spanish explored the area more than 400 years ago, it remained an undisturbed American Indian habitat until the mid-1800s. Monahans was established about 1881 as a railroad city.

MONAHANS SANDHILLS STATE PARK is 5 mi. e. off I-20 to Park Rd. 41. The park includes 3,840 acres of sand dunes, part of a vast area that stretches into New Mexico. Many dunes are active, growing and changing shape, unlike most of the surrounding area, which has been stabilized by shinoak and other vegetation. Exhibits in the visitor center depict the history of the dunes as well as that of the area's former inhabitants. A nature trail lets visitors explore the park.

Park daily 8 a.m.-10 p.m. Visitor center daily 8-5. Admission $2, under 13 free. DS, MC, VI. Phone (432) 943-2092. *See Recreation Chart and the AAA South Central CampBook.*

MULESHOE (B-5) pop. 4,530, elev. 3,769'

Muleshoe derived its name from a ranch of the same name. Ranches such as the Muleshoe, the Matador and the XIT represented large cattle syndicates that covered millions of acres on the High Plains in the late 19th century. The blizzard of 1888 spurred the demise of these ranches, which were eventually replaced by farms.

Muleshoe Chamber of Commerce: 115 E. American Blvd., P.O. Box 356, Muleshoe, TX 79347; phone (806) 272-4248.

MULESHOE NATIONAL WILDLIFE REFUGE is 20 mi. s. on SR 214 to CR 1248. The refuge encompasses 5,809 acres of rolling, largely treeless grasslands surrounding three lakes. From October to March the area has one of the country's largest concentrations of sandhill cranes. A favorite roosting area of these birds is Paul's Lake, which has water even during droughts. During a wet year when the other lakes are full, waterfowl descend on the refuge, joining the cranes and resident prairie dogs. Picnicking and camping are permitted. Free. Phone (806) 946-3341.

NACOGDOCHES (D-11)
pop. 29,914, elev. 283'

Texas' oldest town, Nacogdoches (Nak-a-DOE-chez) was named for the region's earliest inhabitants, a Caddoan Indian tribe. Hernando de Soto's lieutenant probably visited the area en route to Mexico 1541-42, after de Soto's death. The expedition of René Robert Cavelier, Sieur de La Salle, documented the settlement in 1687.

A Spanish mission was built among the Nacogdoche Indians in 1716 by Father Margil, who founded the Mission of Our Lady of the Guadalupe of Nacogdoches. Finding the upkeep of the mission too costly, Spain recalled its subjects to San Antonio in 1772, removing many settlers by force. A group led by Antonio Gil Y'Barbo returned to the abandoned mission in 1779, and Nacogdoches was granted the official designation of *pueblo*, or town.

Serving as Spanish lieutenant governor, Y'Barbo built a stone house that served as the local seat of government and business until its demolition in 1902. A replica of the Stone Fort, as it came to be known, was built for the Texas Centennial Celebration in 1936 *(see attraction listing).* During the early 1800s, the Stone Fort was the site of three failed attempts to establish a Republic of Texas, giving Nacogdoches the distinction of having nine national flags in its history, as opposed to the six that have flown over Texas.

Nacogdoches Convention and Visitors Bureau: 200 E. Main St., Nacogdoches, TX 75961; phone (936) 564-7351 or (888) 653-3788.

MILLARD'S CROSSING HISTORIC VILLAGE is at 6020 North St., .5 mi. n. off Loop 224 on US 59 Bus. Rte. A tour of this re-created east Texas village features live demonstrations, a schoolhouse lesson and hands-on activities for children. The 37-acre complex features structures built 1830-1905, including houses, a school, a chapel and a country store. Allow 1 hour, 30 minutes minimum. Mon.-Sat. 9-4, Sun. 1-4. Admission $4; ages 12-18, $3; ages 5-11, $2. Phone (936) 564-6631.

OAK GROVE CEMETERY is at the e. end of Hospital St. at N. Lanana St. Four signers of the Texas Declaration of Independence are buried here. Open daily dawn-dusk. Free.

OLD NACOGDOCHES UNIVERSITY BUILDING is on Washington Sq. Built in 1858, this is the only surviving structure of an institution of higher learning chartered by the Republic of Texas. The university building now is a museum of antique furniture and silver. Allow 30 minutes minimum. Tues.-Sun. 1-4 (also Sat. 10-1). Donations. Phone (936) 569-7292.

STERNE-HOYA HOME is at Pilar and Lanana sts. Restored sections of the 1828 house, which was built before the Texas Revolution, feature old tools, glassware, antiques and books. Allow 30 minutes minimum. Mon.-Sat. 9-11:30 and 2-5. Donations. Phone (936) 560-5426.

STONE FORT MUSEUM is on the campus of Stephen F. Austin State University at Alumni and Griffith blvds. Original stones were used in this reproduction of the 1779 Spanish Colonial stone house of Antonio Gil Y'Barbo, founder of Nacogdoches. Changing exhibits interpret the history of East Texas through 1900. Guided tours are offered by appointment. Allow 1 hour minimum. Tues.-Sat. 9-5, Sun. 1-5; closed holidays. Donations. Phone (936) 468-2408.

NEW BRAUNFELS—*see San Antonio p. 149.*

NEWCASTLE (C-8) pop. 575, elev. 1,126'

Petroleum production and agriculture have replaced coal mining in Newcastle, a town named after the English coal-mining city.

FORT BELKNAP is 3 mi. s. on FM 61. Once on the Overland-Butterfield Stage route, this 1851 outpost played an important part in defending the frontier. Seven original buildings are restored; two are small museums, and a third houses the county archives. Picnicking is permitted. Mon.-Tues. and Thurs.-Sat. 9-5, Sun. 1:30-5. Free. Phone (940) 846-3222.

ODESSA (D-5) pop. 90,943, elev. 2,891'

In 1881 Russian railroad laborers named Odessa after their homeland, which the wide, flat prairie resembled. By Texas standards, Odessa was a tame cowtown, primarily because local Methodists out-lawed saloons until 1898; the first bar was opened by the sheriff. The discovery of oil in 1926 brought prosperity and a population boom; by World War II, Odessa was one of the world's largest inland petro-leum complexes.

After his graduation from Yale, George Herbert Walker Bush moved to Odessa in 1948 to work in the oil fields, bringing his wife and 2-year-old son George W. with him. The family lived in the Odessa-Midland area for 11 years.

The second largest known meteor crater in the United States is 8 miles west of the city, between I-20 and US 80. The world's largest known hare, the 8-foot Odessa Jackrabbit statue, is downtown on Lincoln Street.

The Globe of the Great Southwest, 2308 Shake-speare Rd. on the Odessa College campus, is a rep-lica of Shakespeare's original playhouse. A re-creation of the Anne Hathaway Cottage contains a Shakespearean library. College and professional productions are staged in the theater; tours are of-fered by appointment. Phone (432) 332-1586 or (432) 580-3177 Mon.-Fri. 10-noon and 1-5.

The Parker House Museum, 1118 Maple Ave., features photographs, documents and other memo-rabilia; phone (432) 335-9918.

Odessa Convention and Visitors Bureau: 700 N. Grant St., Suite 200, P.O. Box 3626, Odessa, TX 79760; phone (432) 333-7871 or (800) 780-4678.

ELLEN NOËL ART MUSEUM is off I-20 exit 121, then 1.3 mi. n. to 4909 E. University on the U.T. Permian Basin campus. Three galleries feature per-manent and changing exhibits of European and American paintings, prints, photography and sculp-ture. The Permian Collection highlights American art from 1850 to the present. An outdoor sensory garden features bronze sculptures and fragrant herb beds for the visually impaired. Allow 30 minutes minimum. Tues.-Sat. 10-5, Sun. 2-5; closed major holidays. Donations. Phone (432) 550-9696.

HERO'S WATER WORLD is 10 mi. e. on US 80 at 12300 E. Bus. Loop 20. The 20-acre park features water slides, a water toboggan, a wave pool, a tube ride and a children's play area. Picnic facilities are available. Tues.-Sun. noon-7, Memorial Day-Labor Day. Admission $11; over 55 and ages 6-8, $6. AX, DS, MC, VI. Phone (432) 563-1933.

THE PRESIDENTIAL MUSEUM is off I-20 exit 121 (Loop 338), then n. 1.3 mi. to 4919 E. Univer-sity on the U.T. Permian Basin campus. Exhibits and educational programs are designed to provide a better understanding of the American presidency, presidential campaigns and election procedures. Permanent displays include campaign memorabilia, presidential medals and first ladies' inaugural gowns in miniature. Traveling exhibits also are pre-sented. Adjacent to the museum is the first Odessa home in which George H.W. Bush and his family lived; the 2-bedroom frame house is being restored.

Allow 30 minutes minimum. Tues.-Sat. 10-5; closed major holidays. Donations. Phone (432) 363-7737.

ORANGE (F-11) pop. 18,643, elev. 10'

Established in 1836, Orange's inland harbor, con-nected to the Gulf of Mexico by the Sabine-Neches waterway, was once frequented by Jean Lafitte's pi-rates. Now the port is the berth of the Navy's Texas Group, Atlantic Reserve Fleet.

Orange Convention & Visitors Bureau: 803 Green Ave., P.O. Box 520, Orange, TX 77631-0520; phone (409) 883-1011 or (800) 528-4906.

STARK MUSEUM OF ART is at 712 Green Ave. Five main viewing areas include the Western col-lection which chronicles the land, wildlife and people of the West. Among the exhibits are Audubon prints, works by members of the Taos So-ciety of Artists and bronzes by Frederic Remington and Charles Russell. The American Indian Collec-tion consists mostly of items crafted by tribes of the Great Plains and the Southwest. Also displayed are Steuben crystal and porcelains by Dorothy Doughty. Allow 1 hour, 30 minutes minimum. Tues.-Sat. 10-5; closed holidays. Free. Phone (409) 883-6661.

THE W.H. STARK HOUSE is at 610 W. Main St. This restored three-story Victorian mansion was built in 1894. The 15 rooms, nine of which have fireplaces, are furnished with original Stark family pieces, including furniture, rugs, lamps, cut glass, statues and paintings. Manicured grounds surround the building. Allow 1 hour minimum. Guided tours Tues.-Sat. 10-3. Admission $2. The tour includes stair climbing. Under 14 are not permitted; ages 14-18 must be with an adult. Reservations are rec-ommended. Phone (409) 883-0871.

PADRE ISLAND NATIONAL SEASHORE (H-9)

Parallel to the Gulf coast between Corpus Christi and Port Isabel, Padre Island National Seashore covers almost 66 miles of 113-mile Padre Island, considered the longest undeveloped barrier island in the world. Some 600 species of plants and wild-flowers can be found on the sand-duned strip of land, which is only .13 miles to 3 miles wide. To the east lies the Gulf and to the west Laguna Ma-dre, including a portion of the Intracoastal Water-way.

In 1519, when the first Spanish fleet sailed along the shore, the island was peopled by the Karankawa Indians. Padre Island became infamous as a grave-yard for ships blown onto the island during storms. In about 1800, Padre Nicholas Balli, for whom the island was named, used it for his ranching opera-tion. The ranch, and many subsequent settlements, were destroyed by tropical storms.

Causeways at Corpus Christi and Port Isabel connect both ends of the island to the mainland, but there is no through road; a paved road extends for only 6 miles within the national seashore. Picnicking, camping and driving are allowed on the seashore, except for a 4.5-mile stretch at Malaquite Beach reserved for pedestrian traffic. The Malaquite Beach Visitor Center presents interpretive naturalist programs daily in the summer. Food is available.

Seashore open daily 24 hours; closed Jan. 1 and Dec. 25. Visitor center open daily 8:30-5:30, Memorial Day-Labor Day; 9-4, rest of year. Admission $5 per person, $10 per vehicle. DS, MC, VI. Phone (361) 949-8068. *See Recreation Chart and the AAA South Central CampBook.*

PAINT ROCK (E-7) pop. 320, elev. 1,631'

Paint Rock, founded in 1879, is named for the historic pictographs found on limestone cliffs bordering the nearby Concho River. These pictures are the remnants of once prosperous American Indian settlements and nomads; archeologists surmise that some date from the prehistoric era.

PAINT ROCK EXCURSIONS departs .5 mi. n.w. on US 83. Guided 90-minute tours explore pictographs found along a nearby rock bluff. Most of the early paintings were made by nomadic tribes such as Comanches and Jumanos, while others may have been created by more permanent settlers such as Apaches. Mon.-Sat. 9-5, Sun. 1-5. Reservations are recommended. Admission $6; ages 5-18, $3. Phone (325) 732-4376.

PALESTINE (E-10) pop. 17,598, elev. 510'

In the 1840s it was discovered that the seat of Anderson County, Houston (not the major city of Harris County), was 2 miles off center. Literally obeying the legislature's guidelines that a county seat be at the center of the county, local residents constructed Palestine.

The town has old-fashioned charm, with Victorian and pioneer houses dating from 1849. The business area has preserved many of its original buildings. The Texas State Railroad offers 50-mile round-trip rides on steam-powered, late 19th- and early 20th-century trains, with departures from Palestine as well as from the Texas State Railroad Historic Site in Rusk, 3 miles east on US 84 *(see attraction listing p. 133).*

Palestine Convention and Visitors Bureau: 1819 Spring St., P.O. Box 2828, Palestine, TX 75802; phone (903) 723-3014 or (800) 659-3484.

PAMPA (A-6) pop. 17,887, elev. 3,234'

Founded in 1888 on the Santa Fe Railroad, Pampa was derived from the Spanish word *pampas,* meaning "plains." Recreational activities abound in the city's municipal parks.

WHITE DEER LAND MUSEUM is 3 blks. n. of US 60 at 116 S. Cuyler St. The building dates from 1916, when it was headquarters for the White Deer Land Co. Displays include rooms and offices furnished in period, American Indian artifacts, antiques

and the Time-Line History Wall. Of interest is the David F. Barry photograph collection begun in the 1870s. Barry is believed to be the first man allowed to photograph American Indian chiefs and leaders. Allow 1 hour minimum. Guided tours are given Tues.-Sun. 1-4; closed holidays. Donations. Phone (806) 669-8041.

PANHANDLE (B-6) pop. 2,589, elev. 3,451'

Aptly named for its location in the state, Panhandle counts wheat, cattle and petroleum products among its commodities.

CARSON COUNTY SQUARE HOUSE MUSEUM is 1 mi. n. of jct. US 60 and SR 207 at 501 Elsie St. Thirteen structures at the complex include a 24-foot-square structure built in the 1880s with lumber hauled by ox cart from Dodge City, Kansas. More than 10,000 artifacts are displayed at the museum, which relates the story of 12,000 years of human adaptation to the flat, treeless, windswept plains of north Texas. Wildlife dioramas feature mammals, birds and reptiles native to the Panhandle. On the grounds are two art galleries, a restored 24-foot windmill, a vintage caboose with railroad exhibits, a reconstructed dugout shelter as well as a church, a barn, buckboards and hardware. Picnicking is permitted.

Allow 1 hour minimum. Mon.-Sat. 9-5, Sun. 1-5; closed Jan. 1, Easter, Thanksgiving and Dec. 25. Donations. Phone (806) 537-3524.

PARIS (C-9) pop. 25,898, elev. 565'

Early settlement was rapid and constant in Lamar County, where Paris is situated. Between 1824, when John Emberson built the first house along the banks of the Red River, and 1837, when Claiborne Chisum purchased land west of the present city, many families moved to the area from Kentucky, Tennessee, Alabama and Georgia.

The county straddles the ridge of the Red and Sulphur rivers, with their many creeks and tributaries. Furs as well as goods from New Orleans and Shreveport, La., were shipped up the Red River in flatboats and paddlewheelers and then transported overland by wagon and oxcart.

In 1844 the Central National Road of the Republic of Texas was cut through the county, intersecting the city. Markers on US 82 and CR 195 denote the historic route. With the coming of such railroads as the Texas and Pacific in 1876, the Gulf Colorado, the Santa Fe and the Paris and Great Northern in 1888, the Texas Midland in 1895 and the Paris and Mount Pleasant in 1910, the town emerged as a rail center.

John Chisum, a local cattle baron expanded into New Mexico, pioneering cattle trails from Fort Sumner to Las Animas and Tascosa. These routes are known as "Chisum Trails." A monument marks his gravesite at the railroad tracks southeast of town. Twelve miles north is the 8,000-acre Pat Mayse Lake recreation area *(see Recreation Chart).*

Paris Visitors and Convention Council: 1651 Clarksville St., Paris, TX 75460; phone (903) 784-2501 or (800) 727-4789.

Self-guiding tours: Maps and brochures for driving tours of Paris and the surrounding countryside are available from the visitors and convention council.

MAXEY HOUSE STATE HISTORICAL STRUCTURE is at 812 S. Church St. The 1868 High Italianate Victorian house was the residence of Sam Bell Maxey, Confederate general and U.S. senator. The house remained in the family for almost a century. Surrounded by landscaped grounds, Maxey House contains family heirlooms and Civil War items. Fri.-Sun. 1-5 (also Sat. 8-noon); closed Jan. 1, Thanksgiving and Dec. 25. Admission $2; ages 6-12, $1. Phone (903) 785-5716.

PARKER—*see Dallas p. 86.*

PASADENA—*see Houston p. 117.*

PECOS (E-4) pop. 9,501, elev. 2,580′

Tales of the Wild West are incomplete without a mention of Pecos. Prompted by a June 1883 dispute in front of Red Newell's saloon, cowhands from the Hashknife, W, Lazy Y and NA ranches competed the following Fourth of July to determine which spread had the best ropers and riders.

Saddle-bronc riding and steer-riding contests were held next to the courthouse, and nearly 1,000 spectators watched the cowboys compete for the $40 prize in this first rodeo—an event that did not earn its name until some 40 years later.

Pecos Area Convention and Visitors Bureau: P.O. Box 27, Pecos, TX 79772; phone (432) 445-2406.

WEST OF THE PECOS MUSEUM is at US 285 and First St. Occupying more than 50 rooms of the restored 1896 Orient Hotel and Saloon, the museum depicts the frontier history of Pecos. Allow 1 hour minimum. Mon.-Sat. 9-5, Sun. 1-4, Memorial Day-Labor Day; Tues.-Sat. 9-5, rest of year. Closed Thanksgiving and Dec. 18-26. Admission $4; over 65, $3; ages 6-18, $1. AX, DS, MC, VI. Phone (432) 445-5076.

PERRYTON (A-6) pop. 7,774, elev. 2,943′

In 1919, the Santa Fe Railway built a new line through the Texas Panhandle, bypassing the towns of Ochiltree, Texas, and Gray, Oklahoma, eight miles to the north and south. Knowing their fortunes were tied to the railroad, residents of both towns loaded their belongings—and their buildings—onto wagons and relocated to Perryton. Called the "Wheatheart of the Nation" for its grain production, Perryton also is a major supplier of oil and natural gas.

Perryton-Ochiltree Chamber of Commerce: 2000 S. Main St., P.O. Box 789, Perryton, TX 79070; phone (806) 435-6575.

MUSEUM OF THE PLAINS is on US 83 at 1200 N. Main St. More than 10,000 artifacts trace the regional history, paleontology and archeology of the High Plains. Exhibits include photographs, fossils, arrowheads, antique vehicles, an oil field display, a pioneer settlement and a Kiowa Indian village. Findings from the "Buried City," a settlement along Wolf Creek dating from A.D. 1100, also are displayed. Allow 30 minutes minimum. Mon.-Fri. 9-5, Sat. 10-5, Sun. 1-5; closed Jan. 1, Thanksgiving and Dec. 25. Donations. Phone (806) 435-6400.

PHARR (I-8) pop. 46,660, elev. 107′

Named after a Louisiana sugar farmer, Pharr is a center for winter vegetables, citrus and cotton. The Old Clock Museum at 929 E. Preston St. houses 1,500 antique clocks dating from as early as 1790; phone (956) 787-1481.

Pharr Chamber of Commerce: 308 W. Park St., Pharr, TX 78577; phone (956) 787-1481.

PLAINVIEW (B-6) pop. 22,336

Named for the magnificent view of the plains, Plainview has an abundant water supply as a result of a huge, shallow underground water belt. Grain and cotton production as well as oil and gas contribute to the economy.

Plainview Chamber of Commerce: 710 W. Fifth St., Plainview, TX 79072-6234; phone (806) 296-7431.

MUSEUM OF THE LLANO ESTACADO is at 1900 W. Eighth St. on the campus of Wayland Baptist University. Exhibits show the geological formation and historical development of the High Plains region known as Llano Estacado—the Staked Plain. Among the displays are American Indian artifacts, replicas of pioneer rooms and cavalry and blacksmith equipment. Mon.-Fri. 9-5, Sat.-Sun. 1-5, Mar.-Nov.; Mon.-Fri. 9-5, rest of year. Donations. Phone (806) 291-3660.

PLANO—*see Dallas p. 86.*

PORT ARANSAS (H-9) pop. 3,370, elev. 6′

Port Aransas is at the northern tip of Mustang Island on the channel into Corpus Christi and Aransas bays. The barrier island, which took its name from the wild horses brought by Spanish explorers, was inhabited by the Karankawa Indians until the 19th century. First known as Sand Point, the town of Port Aransas was leveled by a hurricane in 1919.

Mustang Island State Park, 14 miles south, preserves nearly 4,000 acres of coastal dunes and 5 miles of gulf beach (*see Recreation Chart and the AAA South Central CampBook*). The island is connected to the mainland by the John F. Kennedy causeway and a free car ferry.

PORT ARANSAS BIRDING CENTER is s. on Cut-Off Rd. to Ross Ave. Home to hundreds of resident and visiting birds, such as roseate spoonbills, least grebes, crested caracara and rails, this center includes four designated sites on the Great Texas

Coastal Birding Trail. Boardwalks at two birding centers allow visitors to see more than 100 native Texas plant species, as well as wildlife including turtles, nutria and alligators. Allow 1 hour minimum. Daily 24 hours. Free. Phone (361) 749-4158.

PORT ARTHUR (F-11) pop. 57,755, elev. 8'

On Lake Sabine, 11 miles from the Gulf of Mexico, Port Arthur is connected with the Gulf by a ship channel 36 feet deep and 400 feet wide at the bottom. SR 87, between Port Arthur and Sabine Pass, skirts the canal much of the way. Just north of the city, the 1.5-mile-long Port Arthur-Orange Rainbow Bridge spans the Neches River 176 feet above the water.

Port Arthur Convention and Visitors Bureau: 3401 Cultural Center Dr., Port Arthur, TX 77642; phone (409) 985-7822 or (800) 235-7822.

MUSEUM OF THE GULF COAST is at 701 Fourth St. Artifacts, documents, photographs, fossils and memorabilia recount the area's history. The Southeast Musical Heritage Exhibit features mementos and recordings by such Port Arthur natives as Janis Joplin and Tex Ritter. The Sports Legends Gallery features interactive audiovisual exhibits. Works by artist Robert Rauschenberg also are featured. The John and Grace Snell Room houses a collection of decorative arts.

Allow 30 minutes minimum. Mon.-Sat. 9-5, Sun. 1-5; closed holidays. Admission $3; ages 6-18, $1.50; under 6, 50c. Children must be with an adult. Phone (409) 982-7000.

POMPEIIAN VILLA is at 1953 Lakeshore Dr. Built in 1900 by barbed-wire tycoon Isaac Ellwood, the pink stucco house is patterned after an A.D. 79 Pompeiian villa. The residence is furnished with pieces dating from the 18th century to the present. Allow 1 hour minimum. Guided tours are given Mon.-Fri. 10-2, Sat.-Sun. by appointment; closed holidays. Donations. Phone (409) 983-5977.

PORT ISABEL (I-9) pop. 4,865, elev. 15'

The Queen Isabella Causeway crosses the Laguna Madre from Port Isabel to the town of South Padre Island (see place listing p. 152), linking the mainland with the southern portion of Padre Island. Fishing-boat schedules and other information are available from the chamber of commerce.

Port Isabel Chamber of Commerce: 421 E. Queen Isabella Blvd., Port Isabel, TX 78578; phone (956) 943-2262 or (800) 527-6102.

PORT ISABEL HISTORICAL MUSEUM is opposite the lighthouse at 317 Railroad Ave. in the Champion Bldg. The museum commemorates the history of the Port Isabel area, highlighting American, Mexican and Texas history. Exhibits depict American Indian culture, Spanish exploration, the Mexican War, the Civil War, fishing and maritime history and border folklore. The Treasures of the Gulf Museum explores three Spanish ships that wrecked off South Padre Island in 1554. Exhibits include artifacts, murals and hands-on activities.

Allow 2 hours minimum. Tues.-Sat. 10-4; closed holidays. Admission to each museum $3; over 55, $2; students $1; under 5 free. Combination ticket (includes Port Isabel Lighthouse and both museums) $7; over 55, $5; students $2; under 5 free. DS, MC, VI. Phone (956) 943-7602.

PORT ISABEL LIGHTHOUSE STATE HISTORIC SITE is at Maxan and Tarnava sts. Visitors may climb to the top of the lighthouse, which guided ships along the Gulf Coast 1852-1905. Rubber-soled shoes are recommended. Daily 9-5. Admission $3, over 55, $2; students $1; under 5 free. DS, MC, VI. Phone (800) 527-6102.

PRESIDIO (F-4) pop. 4,167, elev. 2,594'

A sun-baked town of adobe houses along the Rio Grande, Presidio was settled in the 16th century by a handful of Spanish missionaries. By 1684 a series of missions had been constructed, and 2 centuries later the town became the Rio Grande crossing point of the Chihuahua Trail.

Presidio Chamber of Commerce: P.O. Box 2497, Presidio, TX 79845; phone (432) 229-3199.

BIG BEND RANCH STATE PARK is 4 mi. s.e. on FM 170 to Casa Piedra Rd. The park protects 287,000 acres of Chihuahuan Desert wilderness. A 60-mile scenic drive follows the Rio Grande from the park's western entrance at Fort Leaton State Historic Site to the Barton Warnock Environmental Education Center in Lajitas (see attraction listing p. 121). Park information is available at both facilities.

A 35-mile gravel road into the park interior leads to the overlook of a rare geologic formation, the Solitario. The mile-wide caldera was formed 35 million years ago by the eruption of a lava dome. Picnicking is permitted. Daily 8-5. Admission $3; ages 65-73, $2; over 73 and under 12 free. DS, MC, VI. Phone (432) 229-3416 or (800) 792-1112.

FORT LEATON STATE HISTORIC SITE is 4 mi. s.e. on FM 170. Former bounty-hunter Benjamin Leaton established the border trading post in 1848. Twenty-four of the 45 rooms around the patio of the adobe fortress have been restored. Exhibits depict the area's American Indian, Spanish, Mexican and American cultures, and a slide show describes desert ecology. Picnicking is permitted. Allow 30 minutes minimum. Daily 8-4:30; closed Dec. 25. Admission $2; ages 6-12, $1. DS, MC, VI. Phone (432) 229-3613.

RICHMOND—see Houston p. 117.

RIO HONDO (I-8) pop. 1,942, elev. 29'

On the eastern bank of Arroyo Colorado, Rio Hondo means "deep river." Cotton and grain are the principal crops of the town's fertile farmland.

LAGUNA ATASCOSA NATIONAL WILDLIFE REFUGE is 17 mi. e. on FM 106, then 3 mi. n. on Buena Vista Rd. Encompassing 45,187 acres of the former delta of the Rio Grande River, Laguna Atascosa is the central flyway's southern terminus and provides resting and feeding grounds for some 370 species of birds, including falcons, grebes, storks, sandhill cranes and wintering waterfowl. The redheaded duck is a prominent visitor—80 percent of the continent's population winters here.

The refuge is home to coyotes, bobcats, ocelots, white-tailed deer and several endangered species. Picnic facilities are available. Refuge and tour road daily dawn-dusk. Visitor center daily 10-4, Oct.-Apr.; Sat.-Sun. 10-4, in May. Closed Thanksgiving and Dec. 25. Admission $3 per private vehicle. Phone (956) 748-3607.

TEXAS AIR MUSEUM is 1 mi. e. on FM 106 at the Stinson Municipal Airport. Rare aircraft are collected and restored at the facility, which focuses on unusual and lesser-known aspects of aviation history, particularly in Texas and Mexico. Visitors may tour workshop areas and view restorations in progress. Exhibits include more than 50 historic aircraft as well as tanks, vehicles, uniforms, artifacts and the superstructure of the USS *Iwo Jima*. A memorial to the USS *Cabot* includes displays and artifacts from the aircraft carrier known as the "Iron Woman."

Allow 1 hour minimum. Daily 9-4, Sept.-May; Mon.-Sat. 9-4, rest of year. Closed Dec. 25. Admission $5; over 60, $4; ages 12-16, $3; under 12, $2. Phone (956) 748-2112.

ROCKPORT (H-9) pop. 7,385, elev. 6'

Rockport is a picturesque resort noted as an artists' colony and as one of the major birding areas in the country. Twice a year thousands of migratory waterfowl and other birds arrive to nest and breed on the nearby islands. A local wildlife refuge in Little Bay, Connie Hagar Wildlife Sanctuary was named for a legendary Rockport birder, whose efforts helped establish Rockport's birding reputation.

Birds are often the subject of Rockport's other major interest: art. By remodeling rundown buildings on Broadway for use as galleries and studios, the Rockport Art Association sparked a restoration of neighboring buildings that now house shops and restaurants.

Twelve miles northeast is Goose Island State Recreation Area. *See Recreation Chart and the AAA South Central CampBook.*

Rockport and Fulton Area Chamber of Commerce: 404 Broadway, Rockport, TX 78382; phone (361) 729-6445.

FULTON MANSION STATE HISTORIC SITE is 3.5 mi. n. on Fulton Beach Rd. at Henderson Dr. This restored 1876 house was built in the French Second Empire style. The elaborate house incorporated such innovations as gas lighting, forced-air heating and hot and cold running water. Allow 1 hour minimum. Tours are given on the hour Wed.-Sun. and holidays 9-11 and 1-3; closed Jan. 1, Thanksgiving and Dec. 25. Tour times may vary; phone ahead.

Admission $4; students with ID and ages 6-12, $2. DS, MC, VI. Phone (361) 729-0386.

TEXAS MARITIME MUSEUM is off SR 35 Bus. Rte. at the Rockport Harbor. This museum explores the maritime history of Texas, including Spanish and French exploration, seaport communities, maritime commerce and the search for offshore oil and gas. Nautical artifacts related to shipbuilding, the oil industry, commercial and recreational fishing and the U.S. Coast Guard are displayed. Highlights include an extensive collection of ship models and an outdoor display of Texas coastal workboats. A lighthouse observation deck provides a fine view of Aransas Bay. Allow 1 hour, 30 minutes minimum. Tues.-Sat. 10-4, Sun. 1-4. Admission $5; over 60, $4; ages 4-12, $2. Phone (361) 729-1271 or (361) 729-6644.

ROUND TOP (F-9) pop. 77, elev. 390'

In the late 1840s Alwin Soergel's octagonal building, or "the house with the round top," was a widely visible landmark in this open, rolling prairie and gave the town its name. Although some of Stephen Austin's colonists settled in the area, it was the German immigrants who gave the community its distinctive character and insularity.

This German heritage is preserved in such historic structures as the local Lutheran church, with its cedar pipe organ, and several of the buildings on the International Festival-Institute campus *(see attraction listing).*

Another of the town's cultural institutions is the University of Texas' Winedale Historical Center on FM 2714. Devoted to the study of the ethnic cultures of central Texas, the 225-acre farmstead includes a visitor center, two historic structures, a nature trail and a picnic area.

Round Top Chamber of Commerce: P.O. Box 216, Round Top, TX 78954; phone (979) 249-4042.

HENKEL SQUARE is in the town center. The square includes 14 restored buildings built 1820-70. Locally handcrafted antique furnishings are reminiscent of the everyday life of Anglo-American and German settlers. Allow 1 hour minimum. Thurs.-Sun. noon-5; closed Jan. 1, Easter, Thanksgiving and Dec. 25. Self-guiding tour $3, students with ID $1, under 8 free. Phone (979) 249-3308.

INTERNATIONAL FESTIVAL-INSTITUTE AT ROUND TOP is 8 mi. s. of jct. US 290 and SR 237 at Jaster Rd. Established in 1971, Festival Hill features historic buildings that were moved from other sites and restored, including the Edythe Bates Old Chapel, the 1885 Clayton House and the 1902 Menke House. A full schedule of summer festival concerts, ranging from intimate chamber music to major symphonic works, is held in the 1,100-seat Festival Concert Hall.

Gardens, herb collections, stone grottoes and fountains adorn the 200-acre campus; a self-guiding tour brochure is available from the concert hall office. Guided tours may be arranged by appointment.

Allow 1 hour minimum. Concert hall office open daily 9-5; closed Jan. 1 and Dec. 24-25. Free. Guided tour $5. Phone (979) 249-3129.

RUSK (D-10) pop. 5,085, elev. 489'

In 1846 Rusk was selected as the seat of Cherokee County even though only one family lived in the town. The settlement was named after Thomas Jefferson Rusk, a signer of the Texas Declaration of Independence. The town was the birthplace of James S. Hogg and Thomas M. Campbell, the state's first two native-born governors. Rusk and Palestine State Parks are 3 miles west on US 84 *(see Recreation Chart and the AAA South Central CampBook).*

Rusk Chamber of Commerce: 415 Main St., P.O. Box 67, Rusk, TX 75785; phone (903) 683-4242 or (800) 933-2381.

TEXAS STATE RAILROAD HISTORIC SITE is 2.7 mi. w. on US 84 at Park Rd. 76. The Texas state prison system began construction on the railroad in 1881. The line was built to transport iron ore to smelting furnaces at the East Texas State Penitentiary in Rusk. Today, passengers may travel the pineywoods line on 50-mile round-trip rides aboard steam-powered, late 19th- and early 20th-century trains.

Allow 4 hours minimum. Train departs Sat.-Sun. 11-3, late Mar.-late Oct.; additional departures Thurs.-Sun., Memorial Day-late July. Round-trip fare $15; ages 3-12, $9. One-way fare $10; ages 3-12, $6. Departures are from Rusk and Palestine. Reservations are recommended. DS, MC, VI. Phone (903) 683-2561.

SABINE NATIONAL FOREST (E-11)

Elevations in the forest range from 178 ft. in the Toledo Bend Reservoir to 550 ft. on a hilltop. Refer to AAA maps for additional elevation information.

Sabine National Forest stands in east Texas along the shores of the Toledo Bend Reservoir, which borders Louisiana. The forest encompasses 160,609 acres of Southern pine and hardwoods. Toledo Bend Reservoir, a 65-mile-long impoundment of the Sabine River, yields bass, bluegill, catfish and crappie; a number of recreation sites are along the shoreline.

Other areas of interest in the forest are Beech Ravines Scenic Area, Mill Cove Scenic Area, Red Hills Lake and Colorow Scenic Area. Recreation areas include Ragtown, Willow Oak, Lakeview and Indian Mounds Wilderness Area.

For information contact the district ranger station at 201 S. Palm, P.O. Box 227, Hemphill, TX 75948, or write the Forest Supervisor, 701 N. First St., Lufkin, TX 75901. Phone (409) 787-3870 in Hemphill. *See Recreation Chart and the AAA South Central CampBook.*

SAM HOUSTON NATIONAL FOREST (E-10)

Elevations in the forest range from 100 ft. along the Neches River to 300 ft. in San Augustine County. Refer to AAA maps for additional elevation information.

Sam Houston National Forest is approximately 40 miles north of Houston on Lake Conroe. Offering hiking, camping, fishing, boating, hunting and other recreational activities, the 161,654-acre forest includes Double Lake and Cagle recreation areas, Big Creek Scenic Area and Little Lake Creek Wilderness Area.

The 128-mile Lone Star Hiking Trail transects the forest, running from Richards in the west to near Cleveland in the east. A separate 67-mile system of marked trails is open for mountain biking and horseback riding; the Stubblefield Lake Interpretive Trail is a 1.1-mile loop with markers identifying features of the forest ecosystem.

For information contact the District Ranger, 394 FM 1375, New Waverly, TX 77358. Phone (936) 344-6205 or (888) 361-6908. *See Recreation Chart and the AAA South Central CampBook.*

SAN ANGELO (E-6) pop. 88,439, elev. 1,847'

The establishment of an army post, Fort Concho, precipitated the settlement of San Angelo. Several trails used by drovers, stage lines and pioneers intersected at the townsite, providing a setting for such historical figures as Smoky Joe, Mystic Maud, Miss Goldie and the Fighting Parson. The latter used gaming halls as his church and the faro table as his pulpit. Only once did someone protest, and the Fighting Parson replied with a rap on the head from the butt of his six-shooter.

San Angelo Convention and Visitors Bureau: 500 Rio Concho Dr., San Angelo, TX 76903; phone (325) 653-1206 or (800) 375-1206.

[SAVE] **FORT CONCHO MUSEUM** is at 630 S. Oakes St. The fort's early days and the development of the San Angelo area are depicted. Among the remaining 20 original buildings are the headquarters building, officers' quarters, enlisted men's barracks and chapel. Tues.-Sat. 10-5, Sun. 1-5; closed Jan. 1, Thanksgiving and Dec. 25. Admission $2; over 60 and military with ID $1.50; ages 6-18, $1.25. MC, VI. Phone (325) 481-2646 or (325) 657-4444.

SAN ANGELO MUSEUM OF FINE ARTS is adjacent to the El Paseo de Santa Angela Heritage Trail at 1 Love St. This museum features permanent and changing exhibits of ceramics, sculpture and paintings, as well as an education wing with working studios and an outdoor kiln yard for university students. Allow 30 minutes minimum. Tues.-Sat. 10-4, Sunday 1-4; closed major holidays. Admission $2; over 65, $1; students and military with ID free. MC, VI. Phone (325) 653-3333.

San Antonio

San Antonio's old-Spanish flavor, multicultural heritage and numerous parks and plazas make it one of America's more picturesque cities. Modern skyscrapers coexist harmoniously with 18th-century restorations. Since most of downtown was built before 1930, the architectural mix is as varied as periods and materials allowed.

The site that was to become San Antonio was a Coahuiltecan Indian village when a Franciscan mission, San Antonio de Valero, and its protecting fort were built in 1718. When Spanish cavalry occupied the mission in 1803, the name was changed to Pueblo del Alamo. It is thought the soldiers named the mission after their hometown; however it is possible it was named for the many cottonwood, or *alamo*, trees that line the nearby San Antonio River.

To populate and preserve Spain's hold on the region, the Spanish government sent several dozen colonists from the Canary Islands to the mission in 1731. Four other missions subsequently were built along the river south of town. The missions flourished at first but eventually were weakened by increased hostility from Apache and Comanche tribes. Inadequate military support made matters worse. By 1794, the mission era had come to an end, and the Alamo was secularized, becoming a military post.

The first American attempt to colonize the frontier was made by Moses Austin, a Missouri pioneer who obtained a land grant from the Spanish. Moses died before his plan came to fruition, but his son, Stephen, brought 300 American families to settle in Texas in 1821. The colony became the foundation of the Anglo-American presence in Texas, and in only 14 years, U.S. settlers came to outnumber the Mexicans four to one. Disgruntled with Mexican rule, the Anglo-American and Mexican colonists established a provisional government with Sam Houston as the head of the army in 1835.

Thus began a constant struggle between the Texans and Mexico for control of San Antonio, which became the site of many battles. Mexico's dictator, Gen. Antonio López de Santa Anna, sent Gen. Martín Perfecto de Cós to subdue the rebellious Texians, but Cós was unsuccessful. Infuriated by the defeat, Santa Anna and nearly 4,000 troops attacked the Alamo, where its 189 defenders fought valiantly to their deaths. Among the fallen were James Bowie and the legendary Davy Crockett.

The heroic stand of the Alamo defenders was not in vain, however, for the Battle of the Alamo gave Gen. Sam Houston time to organize his troops. Forty-six days after the fall of the Alamo, Houston and his men, inspired by the cry "Remember the Alamo!" launched a furious attack on Santa Anna's troops in the battle of San Jacinto.

After only 18 minutes of fighting, the Texians emerged victorious, and the Republic of Texas was born.

Texas' entry into the union in 1845 as the 28th state opened San Antonio to immigration from Europe, predominantly German. So prevailing was the Germans' influence, for a time street signs appeared in English, German and Spanish. Visitors to the Alamo City can view some of the German-style houses in The King William Historic District, Texas' first historic district.

San Antonio escaped the Civil War unscathed, but the economy suffered. The city soon found its niche in the beef industry. Local cattle barons blazed the legendary Chisholm Trail from San Antonio to the railheads in Abilene, Kan., to drive cattle to northern markets. With the arrival of the railroad in 1877 the city was directly linked to new northern markets; thus San Antonio's economy steadily improved.

In 1876, San Antonio's military tradition continued with the founding of Fort Sam Houston. The city was the birthplace of the Rough Riders, formed shortly after the U.S. battleship *Maine* exploded in Havana harbor in 1898. World War I brought the opening of two aviation training centers—Brooks Air Force Base and Kelly Air Force Base. Randolph Air Force Base opened in 1930, followed by Lackland Air Force Base in 1942. The military continues to be a vital economic factor in the city.

Education, a legacy of the Franciscans, thrives in San Antonio. Among the many institutions of higher learning are Incarnate Word University, Our Lady of the Lake University, St. Mary's University, San Antonio College, Trinity University and the University of Texas at San Antonio.

One of the city's premiere assets is the 2.5 mile tree-lined Riverwalk, or Paseo del Río *(see attraction listing p. 143)*. Today the San Antonio River symbolizes the beauty and romance of the city. There was a time, however, when the river continually overflowed—in 1921 a flood caused 50 deaths and millions of dollars in damage. After much deliberation, a bypass channel and two dams were constructed to control flooding, the river area was cleaned up and a footpath and parks bordering the river were created.

Approaches

By Car

Several of the country's more important transcontinental highways crisscross San Antonio.

The principal north-south route is I-35, heavy with traffic to and from the Mexican border and funneling an assortment of travelers from as far north as Lake Superior, near the Canadian border. US 281, similar in length and termini, carries a lighter flow of traffic. Sharing a frequently identical path with I-35 through much of Texas is US 81.

US 87 angles on a northwest-southeast course, bringing traffic from the ranches, the Great Plains and points

(continued on p. 138)

The Informed Traveler

City Population: 1,144,646

Elevation: 650 ft.

Sales Tax: Municipalities may impose additional rates of up to 2 percent on the statewide 6.25 percent sales tax. Sales tax in the city of San Antonio is 7.75 percent; rates vary in the suburbs.

WHOM TO CALL

Emergencies: 911

Police (non-emergency): (210) 207-7273

Fire (non-emergency): (210) 207-7744

Time: (210) 226-3232

Weather: (830) 609-2029

Hospitals: Baptist Medical Center, (210) 297-7000; Northeast Methodist Hospital, (210) 650-4949; San Antonio Community Hospital, (210) 575-8110; Southwest Texas Methodist, (210) 575-4000; University Health System, (210) 358-4000.

WHERE TO LOOK

Newspapers

San Antonio prints one daily newspaper, the *San Antonio Express-News*.

Radio

San Antonio radio station WOAI (1200 AM) is an all-news/weather station; KST (89.1 FM) is a member of National Public Radio.

Visitor Information

The San Antonio Visitors Information Center, 317 Alamo Plaza, San Antonio, TX 78205, offers brochures, maps and information about events; phone (210) 207-6748 or (800) 447-3372.

TRANSPORTATION

Air Travel

San Antonio International Airport, 5 miles north of downtown via Broadway Avenue, I-410 and SR 281, is served by U.S. and Mexican airlines. Taxis into the city charge $14-$16, depending on the departure point.

Rental Cars

Hertz, (210) 841-8800 or (800) 654-3080, 10219 John Saunders, offers discounts to AAA members. See the telephone book for other companies.

Rail Service

The Amtrak station is at 350 Hoefgen Ave.; for train schedule and ticket information phone (210) 223-3226 or (800) 872-7245.

Buses

The Greyhound Lines Inc. bus terminal is at 500 N. St. Mary's St.; phone (800) 231-2222. Via Metropolitan Transit also serves the city; phone (210) 362-2020.

Taxis

San Antonio taxis are metered. Fare is $1.60 when you enter the cab plus $1.50 for each mile. Four passengers can ride for a single fare. The major company is Yellow Checker, (210) 226-4242. The average fare is $3.10 for the first mile and $1.50 for each additional mile. Boat taxis travel the river's downtown loop daily 10-9 (weather permitting). One-way fare $3.50; all-day fare $10; three-day fare $25. Phone (210) 244-5700 or (800) 417-4139.

Public Transport

Metropolitan Transit routes buses through all sections. Express buses run daily 6:30-9:30 a.m. For shoppers, a bus runs mall to mall on I-410. Basic fare 75c; express bus service $1.50; transfers 5c each. Exact change is required. Phone (210) 362-2020. Streetcars travel main city routes daily from shortly before 7 a.m. to 9 p.m. or later. Tokens can be purchased at the VIA Information Center; phone (210) 362-2020.

Destination San Antonio

Welcome to Alamo Country. The Cradle of Texas Liberty. Where the legacy of rich history comes alive in various sites.

Hop aboard a trolley and tour the historic missions. Watch a folk dance at the Institute of Texan Cultures. Tour the adobe-walled Spanish Governor's Palace. Or just relax aboard a riverboat and enjoy the sights and sounds of the Paseo del Río.

San Antonio Zoo.
Reach out and touch a wild friend in Brackenridge Park. (See listing page 140)

Witte Museum, San Antonio.
Texas dinosaurs, a mummy and a treehouse bring science and natural history to life. (See listing page 140)

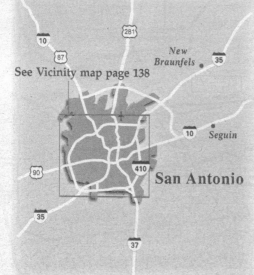

See Vicinity map page 138

Places included in this AAA Destination City:

Yanaguana Cruise, San Antonio.
First named Yanaguana, or "clear water," by the Payaya Indians, the San Antonio River now carries riverboats offering scenic tours of its historic banks. (See listing page 146)

Natural Bridge Caverns, San Antonio.
The state's largest cavern is a subterranean land of grandeur. (See listing page 143)

along the Gulf of Mexico. US 181 also channels travelers from the Gulf area, but neither this nor US 87 is any match for I-37, a fast, wide link between San Antonio and Corpus Christi.

The major east-west route, I-10, connects San Antonio with the Atlantic and Pacific oceans. US 90 parallels and frequently merges with I-10 east of the city but maintains a separate course through much of western Texas.

These routes converge in San Antonio's center, enclosing the heart of downtown, part of the river and HemisFair Park, and providing easy access to major streets within the area. Farther out, I-410 is a completely circumferential highway that defines the outer limits of the city, interchanging not only with major highways but also with local streets.

Note: There are no service stations in downtown San Antonio.

Getting Around
Street System
The street system of downtown San Antonio was laid out more than 150 years ago, and in many instances follows old cattle trails. Because the system

has been described as being roughly similar to a skillet of snakes, you should study a city map before starting out.

The speed limit on most streets is 30 mph or as posted. Freeway limits range from 40 to 55 mph. Rush hours generally are from 7 to 9 a.m. and 4 to 6 p.m. Right turns on red are permitted unless otherwise posted.

Use the circumferential loops to reach the different parts of the city. San Antonio is surrounded by two loops—Loop 1604 surrounds the outskirts, whereas I-410 encompasses the city's midsection. Interstates 10, 35 and 37 converge in the heart of San Antonio, forming another unofficial loop.

The proximity of most downtown attractions and accommodations to the San Antonio River prompts many visitors to use the Riverwalk or the boat taxis instead of driving. The outskirts of San Antonio tend to conform more closely to a grid pattern.

Parking
Although some metered parking is available in certain downtown areas, public parking lots and garages are more plentiful throughout the city. Rates

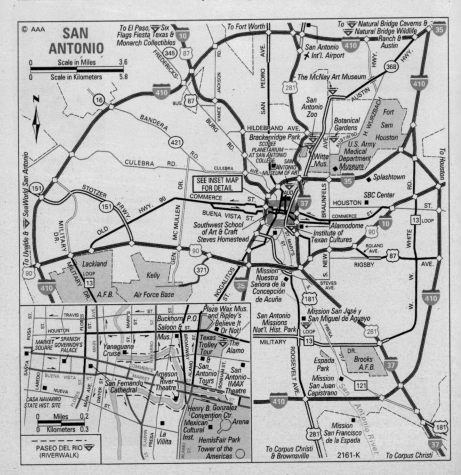

are usually 75c per half-hour, with a maximum charge of $3.

What To See

THE ALAMO is downtown near the river at 300 Alamo Plaza. Established in 1718 by Father Antonio Olivares, the site originally was a Spanish outpost called the Mission San Antonio de Valero. In 1803 Spanish cavalry from Alamo de Parras, Mexico, moved into the mission, and it became known as Pueblo del Alamo.

In 1835, Mexican general Martín Perfecto de Cós fortified the former mission in a failed attempt to subdue the revolting Texans. Several months later, learning of Cós' defeat, Mexican dictator general Antonio López de Santa Anna and his army of 4,000 headed toward San Antonio to launch an attack on the Alamo.

Upon hearing of the impending incursion, Texas general Sam Houston ordered Col. James Bowie to destroy the fortification in San Antonio and retire. However, Bowie, determined to fight for Texas' independence, disobeyed Houston's orders. In February 1836, Col. William Travis and David Crockett joined Bowie in San Antonio; estimates of the Alamo garrison range from 200 to 600 men.

The siege began on Feb. 23 and in the ensuing 13 days Bowie fell ill with pneumonia, Travis took full command and no reinforcements were sent. The Texans, committed to the freedom of Texas, held their ground until the pre-dawn hours of March 6 when Santa Anna's troops stormed the north wall, killing Travis. The patriots valiantly fought, but by 6:30 a.m. the battle was over—189 Texans had been killed.

The Alamo remains a symbol of Texas' pride and independent spirit. Visitors to the site can view the church, a reminder of the fort's original function as a mission. Exhibits in the church and the Long Barracks feature artifacts from the era of the Texas Revolution as well as personal items that belonged to the Alamo heroes. Scheduled history talks are offered in the Alamo Shrine, and a 17-minute documentary is shown continuously in the Long Barracks Museum. A research library also is available.

Allow 2 hours minimum. Mon.-Sat. 9-5:30, Sun. 10-5:30; closed Dec. 24-25. Donations. Phone (210) 225-1391.

ARNESON RIVER THEATRE is on the San Antonio River adjacent to La Villita. Unequaled among the city's theaters, this outdoor amphitheater features tiers of grass seats on one side of the river and a patio-type stage on the other side. Occasional passing boats enhance audience enjoyment of the Mexican folk dances, opera, flamenco and other musical events presented nightly June-Aug. Hours may vary; phone ahead. Phone (210) 207-8610.

BRACKENRIDGE PARK is 2 mi. n. at 3910 N. St. Mary's St. The San Antonio River flows through this 343-acre park, which features Japanese tea gardens, an outdoor theater, walking and bicycling trails and picnic facilities. Park open daily 5:30 a.m.-11 p.m. Free. Phone (210) 207-8000.

San Antonio Zoo is at 3903 N. St. Mary's St. Quarried limestone cliffs provide natural habitats for approximately 3,400 animals representing 750 species. The 50-acre zoo is noteworthy for its endangered animals, including snow leopards, Sumatran tigers, white rhinos, whooping cranes and Komodo Dragons.

Elephants, hippopotamuses, hyenas and lions inhabit African Hill, where a water hole brings ostriches, zebras, giraffes, gazelles and antelopes together. Marmosets, sloths, giant anteaters, armadillos, toucans, monkeys and jaguars are among the inhabitants of tropical Amazonia. Such unusual bird species as the red-billed leiothrix, quetzal, lesser green broadbill and Egyptian plover interact in a glass-domed aviary. A wide range of amphibians inhabit The Pad.

A miniature train offers daily trips through Brackenridge Park, and a children's petting zoo offers boat rides on weekends. Daily 9-6, Memorial Day-Labor Day; 9-5, rest of year. Admission $7; over 62 and ages 3-11, $5. AX, DS, MC, VI. Phone (210) 734-7183.

Witte Museum is at 3801 Broadway St. Hands-on exhibits explore Texas history, natural science and anthropology. One display focuses on the ecological diversity of the state's seven natural areas and features a walk-through diorama re-creating the south Texas thornbrush landscape and its wildlife. A dinosaur exhibit displays a life-size reproduction of a triceratops.

Another display gives insight to the culture and cave paintings of a prehistoric society that flourished in the area more than 8,000 years ago. The museum also includes an EcoLab of live Texas animals, a four-story science treehouse, an outdoor butterfly and hummingbird garden, log cabins and three restored houses.

Allow 3 hours minimum. Mon.-Sat. 10-5 (also Tues. 5-9), Sun. noon-5; closed Thanksgiving and Dec. 24-25. Admission $5.95; over 65, $4.95; ages 4-11, $3.95; free to all Tues. 3-9. AX, MC, VI. Phone (210) 357-1900.

SAVE **BUCKHORN SALOON & MUSEUM** is at 318 E. Houston St. The 1881 saloon and museum offers a step back to the Old West with artifacts from Texas history. Wildlife exhibits reflect African, Asian, Alaskan and North American themes. More than 520 mounted species are displayed, including fish from the seven seas. The Hall of Texas History presents life-size dioramas and wax figures depicting milestones in the state's past.

Allow 1 hour minimum. Sun.-Thurs. 10-5, Fri.-Sat. 10-6. Closed Jan. 1, Thanksgiving and Dec. 25. Admission $8.99; over 65, $8; ages 4-11, $6.50. Phone (210) 247-4000. *See color ad.*

CASA NAVARRO STATE HISTORIC SITE is at 228 S. Laredo St. This .7-acre complex in downtown San Antonio was the home of statesman José Antonio Navarro, a central figure in the formation of Texas. A signer of the Texas Declaration of Independence, Navarro served in the legislatures of both Mexico and Texas. The site consists of three 1850s adobe and limestone structures: a store and two separate residences, all furnished in period. Allow 1 hour minimum. Wed.-Sun. 10-4. Admission $2; ages 6-12, $1. DS, MC, VI. Phone (210) 226-4801.

FORT SAM HOUSTON is 2 mi. n. between I-35 and Harry Wurzbach Hwy. Founded in 1845, the 3,300-acre establishment houses the U.S. Army Medical Command, the Fifth Army Headquarters and Brooke Army Medical Center, one of the largest military medical facilities in the world.

In Building 123 is Fort Sam Houston Museum, which chronicles the history of the fort through exhibits of uniforms and equipment from 1845 to the present. Maps and self-guiding tour information are available in the museum. Allow 1 hour minimum. Wed.-Sun. 10-4; closed holidays. Free. Phone (210) 221-1886.

The U.S. Army Medical Department Museum is in Bldg. 1046 at the corner of Harry Wurzbach Hwy. and Stanley rds. Beginning with the Revolutionary War, exhibits trace the history of the U.S. Army medical department through uniforms, U.S. Army and enemy medical equipment, POW memorabilia, photographs and scale models. Allow 1 hour minimum. Tues.-Sat. 10-4; closed federal holidays. Free. Phone (210) 221-6358.

HANGAR 9—MUSEUM OF FLIGHT MEDICINE is on Brooks Air Force Base, at jct. I-37 and Military Dr. This 1918 hangar, the only remaining World War I aircraft hangar in the U.S. Air Force, contains exhibits about the history of the base, the development of manned flight and the evolution of aviation medicine. Allow 30 minutes minimum. Mon.-Fri. 9-2; closed holidays. Free. Phone (210) 536-2203.

HEMISFAIR PARK is bounded by I-37 and Commerce, Market, Durango and Alamo sts. The 92-acre area was the site of San Antonio's World's Fair in 1968, which marked the city's 250th anniversary. It now is the center of downtown recreation and entertainment. Daily 24 hours. Donations. Phone (210) 207-8611.

Henry B. Gonzalez Convention Center is on the northwestern quadrant of HemisFair Park. An extension of the San Antonio River flows through the heart of the complex, which houses an international conference center and a theater for the performing arts. Boat taxis provide an interesting way to travel to meetings from riverside hotels. "The Confluence of Civilizations" mural on the facade of the theater is by Juan O'Gorman of Mexico, and one of the exhibit halls features a mural by Carlos Merida. Phone (210) 207-8500.

Institute of Texan Cultures is in Hemis-Fair Park at 801 S. Bowie St. The contributions of the 26 ethnic groups that helped settle Texas are featured. Temporary and permanent exhibits illustrate the customs, dress and job skills of early Texas residents. The exhibits are supplemented by demonstrations and a 12-minute multiscreen audiovisual presentation. Allow 3 hours minimum. Tues.-Sun. 9-5; closed Jan. 1, Easter, Thanksgiving and Dec. 24-25. Admission $5; over 64 and military with ID $3; ages 3-12, $2. DS, MC, VI. Phone (210) 458-2300.

Mexican Cultural Institute is at 600 HemisFair Park behind the Convention Center. The center offers changing exhibits of works by contemporary Mexican artists as well as lectures, concerts, workshops and films. Allow 1 hour, 30 minutes minimum. Tues.-Fri. 10-5:30, Sat-Sun. 11-5:30; closed holidays, including day after Thanksgiving and Dec. 25-Jan. 5. Free. Phone (210) 227-0123.

Tower of the Americas is adjacent to the Convention Center. The concrete spire rises 750 feet, symbolizing the desire for achievement. A water park around the tower features calm water, fountains and waterfalls. Glass-fronted elevators speed passengers up the outside of the tower to an observation deck and revolving restaurant for views of the city and 100 miles of south Texas hill country. Observation deck elevator runs Sun.-Thurs. 9 a.m.-10 p.m., Fri.-Sat. 9 a.m.-11 p.m.; closed Dec. 25. Admission $4; over 55, $2.50; ages 4-11, $1.50. Phone (210) 207-8615.

LA VILLITA is at Villita St. between S. Presa and S. Alamo sts. La Villita (vee-YEE-tah) is a restoration of San Antonio's earliest residential settlement. Buildings along the cobblestone walkways house shops where crafts are demonstrated. The village contains adobe houses, art galleries and a museum complex of early American culture. In Cós House, Gen. Martín Perfecto de Cós signed articles of capitulation when Texans captured San Antonio prior to the siege of the Alamo. Allow 2 hours minimum. Daily 10-6; closed Jan. 1, Thanksgiving and Dec. 25. Free. Phone (210) 207-8610.

MARKET SQUARE is bounded by Dolorosa, Santa Rosa, W. Commerce St. and I-35. Now renovated, the market has operated on this site for more than a century. The Farmers Market Plaza and El Mercado both feature many specialty shops. Visitors can watch artists at work in the outdoor plaza on weekends. Food is available. Allow 1 hour minimum. Daily 10-8, June-Aug.; 10-6, rest of year. Closed Jan. 1, Thanksgiving and Dec. 24-25. Free. Paid parking is available on the roof of the Farmers Market and under the freeway. Phone (210) 207-8600.

THE McNAY ART MUSEUM is one-half blk. n. of Austin Hwy. at 6000 N. New Braunfels Ave. Housed in the 24-room mansion of philanthropist Marion Koogler McNay, the museum showcases 19th- and 20th-century

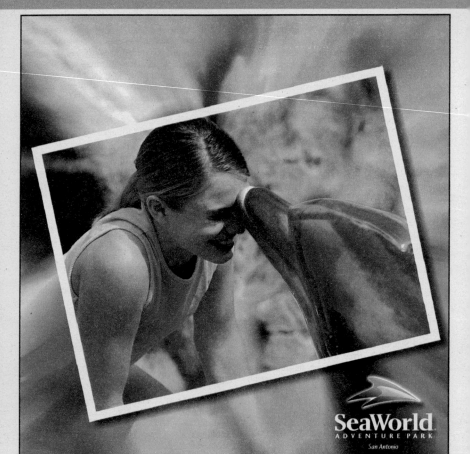

**Where moments
become memories.**

SeaWorld
ADVENTURE PARK
San Antonio

paintings, prints, drawings and sculpture. The European collection features works by Paul Cézanne, Paul Gauguin, El Greco, Henri Toulouse-Lautrec and Vincent van Gogh. Among the American artists represented are Winslow Homer, John Marin and Georgia O'Keeffe.

Other permanent exhibits include American Indian art and crafts from the Southwest, and Mexican graphics by artists such as José Clemente Orosco and Diego Rivera. The Tobin Collection of Theatre Arts includes rare books, stage design drawings and prints. Allow 2 hours minimum. Tues.-Sat. 10-5, Sun. noon-5; closed Jan. 1, July 4, Thanksgiving and Dec. 25. Donations. Admission charged for special events. Phone (210) 824-5368.

MONARCH COLLECTIBLES is .7 mi. n. of Loop 410 at 2012 N.W. Military Hwy. Some 3,000 dolls from around the world are displayed. Other exhibits include limited-edition plates featuring sports figures, movie stars, wildlife scenes and other subjects. Mon.-Sat. and holidays 10-5; closed Jan. 1, July 4 and Dec. 24-25. Free. Phone (210) 341-3655 or (800) 648-3655.

NATURAL BRIDGE CAVERNS is off I-35 exit 175, then 8 mi. w. on Natural Bridge Caverns Rd. (FM 3009). A guided 75-minute tour of the North Cavern takes visitors 180 feet below the surface through a half-mile of underground rooms and passages. Highlights range from the 40-foot King's Throne and Watchtower to tiny, delicate soda straw formations. Adventurers can climb, crawl and rappel through the South Cavern's undeveloped passages; special reservations are required.

Comfortable walking shoes are recommended. Picnic facilities and food are available. Allow 1 hour, 30 minutes minimum. Daily 9-6, June 1-Labor Day; 9-4, rest of year. Closed Jan. 1, Thanksgiving and Dec. 25. North Cavern admission $12; over 65, $10; ages 4-12, $7. MC, VI. Phone (210) 651-6101.

NATURAL BRIDGE WILDLIFE RANCH is off I-35 exit 175, then 17 mi. n.w. on Natural Bridge Caverns Rd. (FM 3009). This 400-acre, drive-through safari features more than 50 species of exotic animals that roam in open habitats, enticed to visitors' vehicles by a complimentary bag of food provided at the gate. The park also features enclosures for exotic birds and primates. Food is available.

Allow 1 hour, 30 minutes minimum. Daily 9-6:30, Memorial Day-Labor Day; 9-5, rest of year. Closed Jan. 1, Thanksgiving and Dec. 25. Admission $11; over 65, $10; ages 3-11, $6. Phone (830) 438-7400.

PASEO DEL RÍO (RIVERWALK) runs through the heart of the business district. A few steps below the city streets, the Riverwalk provides a pleasant stroll during the day, when craft shops and galleries are open and sidewalk terraces teem with diners. The tree-lined footpaths, romantically lighted at night, follow landscaped riverbanks bordered by nightspots, restaurants and handicraft shops.

Boat tours and dining cruises of the river are available; many ticket outlets exist along the water. The river is drained for cleaning during the first week in January; most shops remain open. To confirm the exact cleaning dates contact the San Antonio Convention and Visitors Bureau; phone (210) 207-6700.

THE PLAZA WAX MUSEUM AND RIPLEY'S BELIEVE IT OR NOT! is across from the Alamo at 301 Alamo Plaza. The Plaza Wax Museum features more than 250 lifelike wax figures from the annals of Hollywood, horror, history, religion and fairy tales. The Freedom's Journey exhibit includes a 66-foot mural depicting a century of American heroes, inventions and milestones. In the same building are more than 500 exhibits from Robert Ripley's Believe It or Not! collection, showcasing oddities and curiosities from around the world. Food is available.

Allow 1 hour minimum per attraction. Open daily at 9; closing times vary. Closed Dec. 25. Admission (includes both museums) $15.95; ages 4-12, $7.95. AX, DS, MC, VI. Phone (210) 224-9299.

SAN ANTONIO BOTANICAL GARDENS is 5 mi. n.e. at 555 Funston Pl. Covering 33 acres near Fort Sam Houston (see attraction listing p. 141), this botanical center balances formal gardens with several sections planted with native wildflowers to reflect the rural areas of east and southwest Texas and the Hill Country. Adobe houses, a log cabin and an east Texas lake reinforce this rural illusion.

In the more formally cultivated areas are a rose garden, an old-fashioned garden, a Japanese meditation garden, a touch and smell garden for the visually impaired, a children's vegetable garden and an herb garden. Occupying some of the highest ground in the city, the garden's gazebo observatory offers a panorama of the city.

Daily 9-6, Mar.-Oct.; 8-5, rest of year. Closed Jan. 1 and Dec. 25. Admission (including Lucile Halsell Conservatory) $4; over 55, $2; ages 3-13, $1. Phone (210) 207-3250, or TTY (210) 207-3255.

Lucile Halsell Conservatory is at San Antonio Botanical Gardens. Visitors enter this complex of exhibition greenhouses at ground level and take a tunnel 16 feet below the surface into a central courtyard with glass houses. These buildings include a tropical house, a desert house, a palm house, fern room and exhibit hall. Daily 9-6, Mar.-Oct.; 8-5, rest of year. Closed Jan. 1 and Dec. 25.

SAN ANTONIO IMAX THEATRE is in RiverCenter Mall downtown at 849 E. Commerce St. The docudrama "The Price of Freedom" is presented on a screen six stories tall. The film recounts the battle of the Alamo. Other films also are shown. Daily 9-9; phone ahead for show times. Admission $8.95; over 65, $7.95; ages 3-11, $5.50. AX, DS, MC, VI. Phone (210) 247-4629.

SAN ANTONIO MISSIONS NATIONAL HISTORICAL PARK includes four missions throughout the city. These 18th-century missions, in addition to Mission San Antonio de Valero (The Alamo), were Spain's outposts along its northern frontier. Together they were the heart of Spain's effort to colonize its possessions in North America. Each has an active parish church.

To see all five missions, visitors may drive, bicycle or walk the 10-mile Mission Trail, which begins at the Alamo and runs south to Mission Espada. Ancient waterworks of the Espada Dam and Aqueduct flow along parts of the route.

The park visitor center at Mission San José, 6701 San Jose Dr., offers an orientation film, exhibits and maps. Guided tours are available at each mission. A map of the Mission Trail is available at the park or the San Antonio Visitors Information Center, 317 Alamo Plaza. Park open daily 9-5; closed Jan. 1, Thanksgiving and Dec. 25. Donations. Phone (210) 932-1001, or TTY (210) 922-7152.

Espada Dam and Aqueduct is in Espada Park on Military Dr., just w. of the San Antonio River. Built by Franciscans in 1745, the dam controlled the river and filled a network of *acequias,* or irrigation ditches, that furnished water to the Spanish Colonial missions. Remnants of sluice gate foundations are visible near Mission Espada; the aqueduct still carries water over Piedras creek to nearby farms.

Mission Nuestra Señora de la Concepción de Acuña is at 807 Mission Rd. near Mitchell St. Relocated to its present location in 1731, the massive church with twin towers and dome was built by Franciscans and American Indians. Reputedly the oldest unrestored stone church in the country, it is known for its great acoustics. The chapel and convento contain frescoes that date from the colonial period. Phone (210) 534-1540.

Mission San Francisco de la Espada is 6.5 mi. s. on US 281 to Bergs Mill, w. on Mission Rd., then s. to 10040 Espada Rd. Founded in 1690 in East Texas, this mission was moved to its present site in 1731. The chapel doorway reflects Moorish influence. Phone (210) 627-2021.

Mission San José y San Miguel de Aguayo is next to the visitor center at 6701 San Jose Dr. Founded in 1720, it is called the "Queen of Missions." Most of the compound—including outer walls containing American Indian dwellings—has been restored. A 1794 Spanish Colonial gristmill, rebuilt outside the north wall, still is in operation. The domed church has a rich facade, and on its south side is one of the finest examples of stone carving in American, known as the Rose Window. Allow 1 hour, 30 minutes minimum. Phone (210) 932-1001.

Mission San Juan Capistrano is 6.5 mi. s. on US 181, w. on Bergs Mill, then .2 mi. s. to 9101 Graf Rd. The small chapel was relocated to the San Antonio River from East Texas in 1731 and restored in 1909; there are ruins of a larger church that was never completed. Phone (210) 534-0749.

SAN ANTONIO MUSEUM OF ART is 2 mi. n.e. on US 81 Bus. Rte. to 200 W. Jones Ave. The complex occupies 10 buildings of the 1884 Lone Star Brewing Co. off Broadway. The historic brewhouse, with its modified Romanesque towers and turrets, is now the art museum. The West and East towers contain four levels of galleries. Glass elevators operate in each of the towers. The complex along the San Antonio River includes a 2.5-acre sculpture garden.

Permanent collections emphasize regional materials and art of the Americas. Exhibits include Asian art, European and American paintings, decorative and contemporary arts, and Egyptian, Greek and Roman antiquities. The Nelson A. Rockefeller Center for Latin American Art features an extensive permanent collection of Spanish and Colonial art, modern and contemporary art, folk art and pre-Columbian art.

Allow 2 hours minimum. Tues.-Sat. 10-5 (also Tues. 5-9), Sun. noon-5; closed Thanksgiving and Dec. 25. Admission $6; over 65 and students with ID, $5; ages 4-11, $1.75; free to all Tues. 3-9. Phone (210) 978-8100.

SAN FERNANDO CATHEDRAL is at 115 Main Plaza. Colonists sent by King Philip of Spain arrived in San Antonio in 1731 and began work on the cathedral, the oldest parish in Texas. A French Gothic addition was completed in 1873; a modern restoration is in progress. Weekly services are held in the sanctuary, where a marble coffin is said to hold the remains of defenders of the Alamo. Allow 1 hour minimum. Daily 6:15 a.m.-7 p.m. Free. Phone (210) 227-1297.

SCOBEE PLANETARIUM AT SAN ANTONIO COLLEGE is 1 blk. e. of San Pedro Ave. on Park St. Demonstrations and lectures are offered. Shows are given Fri. at 6, 7:15 and 8:30 p.m., second week in Sept. to late July; closed holidays. Hours may vary; phone ahead. Admission $3, students with ID $1. Under 4 are not permitted. Phone (210) 733-2910.

SEAWORLD SAN ANTONIO is 16 mi. n.w. off SR 151 between loops 410 and 1604 at jct. Westover Hills Blvd. and Ellison Dr. This 250-acre marine life adventure park features more than 25 shows, rides and animal attractions that are designed to inform as well as entertain.

"Viva" is a show featuring not only graceful beluga whales and Pacific white-sided dolphins but also high divers, synchronized swimmers, acrobats and water effects. Daredevil feats on water skis are the focus of the Rockin' Ski Party show.

Shamu Visions, in Shamu Stadium, combines live action and close-ups projected on a two-story-high video screen. Cameras above and below water level capture images during the show and replay them, along with audience reactions, on the big screen. Sea lions, otters and walruses cavort with their human trainers in "Fools with Tools."

Highlights of Hollywood Night Magic include the figure skaters and singers of Hollywood Live on Ice, Clyde and Seamore's Movie Madness show and Shamu's Hollywood Night Magic.

Sharks/The Coral Reef brings visitors face to face with tropical fish, hammerhead sharks and eels. Other highlights include a penguin habitat featuring more than 200 polar birds and a feed-and-touch dolphin pool.

The park's thrill rides include The Steel Eel roller coaster, which races at speeds reaching 65 mph and features a 15-story drop; Rio Loco, a river ride that whisks passengers under a waterfall; Texas Splashdown, a half-mile flume ride; and The Great White, an inverted coaster that takes riders heels-over-head five times.

Shamu's Happy Harbor is a children's play area. Lost Lagoon is a 5-acre water park featuring a tropical-theme wave pool, waterslides, a play area for children and Splash Attack water funhouse. Swimsuits are recommended; lockers, changing facilities and showers are available.

Park open daily at 10, late May to mid-Aug.; Sat.-Sun. and some weekdays at 10, mid-Mar. to late May; Sat.-Sun. at 10, mid-Aug. through Thanksgiving weekend. Closing times vary; phone ahead. Water park open mid-Mar. to mid-Sept.; phone ahead for schedule. Admission $37.99; ages 3-11, $27.99. Phone to confirm hours and admission. AX, DS, MC, VI. Phone (210) 523-3611 or (800) 722-2762. *See color ad p. 142.*

SIX FLAGS FIESTA TEXAS is n.w. at 17000 I-10W. This 200-acre musical, theme and water park celebrates Texas and the Southwest. Set in a former rock quarry that has 100-foot cliff walls, the park has a number of thematic areas. Los Festivales is a Hispanic village with a continuous fiesta, while the village of Spassburg is German. Crackaxle Canyon, an old-time town of the Texas West, celebrates the 4th of July every day. Fiesta Bay Boardwalk and 1950s Rockville are thematic as well.

Armadillo Beach features waterslides, cannons and toboggans; a changing area is provided. Shows are performed in seven theaters, and performances by well-known musicians are scheduled periodically.

Join Scooby-Doo and friends in their own interactive family ride, Scooby-Doo Ghostblasters...The Mystery of the Haunted Mansion. Twists, turns, spiral loops and corkscrews, all at 70 miles per hour, await riders of the floorless Superman Krypton Coaster. Coaster thrills also abound on Poltergeist. Bug's White Water Rapids is a log flume ride, guaranteed to cool riders off. A five-story, interactive water treehouse, with more than 75 slides and mazes, is the focal point of Armadillo Beach. A Texas-shaped wave pool also is available.

Other rides include The Wagon Wheel, a ride that spins and lifts; the Road Runner Express, a fast-paced ride in an Acme rocket; and The Rattler—reputed to be one of the world's tallest and fastest wooden roller coasters. Also featured are a high-tech laser game, a free-fall and hang-gliding ride, a steam train and an old-fashioned carousel. In summer, the day ends with fireworks and a laser show is projected onto the canyon walls. Food is available.

Allow 4 hours minimum. Park opens daily at 10, Memorial Day weekend to mid-Aug.; Sat.-Sun. at 10, early Mar. to day before Memorial Day weekend and mid-Aug. to late Oct. Closing times vary. Phone ahead to confirm schedule. Admission $36.99; over age 54, $24.99; under 49 inches tall $22.99; under age 3 free. Rates may vary; phone ahead. Parking $7. AAA members save 10 percent on select in-park dining and merchandise. Check at the park's Guest Relations window for details. AX, DS, MC, VI. Phone (210) 697-5050.

SOUTHWEST SCHOOL OF ART AND CRAFT is n. on Soledad St. to Giraud, then 1 blk. e. to 300 Augusta St. Two adjacent campuses—Navarro and Ursuline—comprise the school. The former Ursuline Convent was established in 1851 and features elegant limestone architecture, gardens and courtyards; a visitor center museum is dedicated to the city's first school for girls. On the Navarro campus, the Russell Hill Rogers Galleries display the work of emerging and prominent artists. Guided tours of the Ursuline historic site are available.

Allow 2 hours minimum. Visitor center museum open Mon.-Sat. 10-5, Sun. 11-4. Galleries Mon.-Sat. 9-5. Guided tours Mon.-Fri. 10-3. Free. Phone (210) 224-1848.

SPANISH GOVERNOR'S PALACE faces the back of City Hall at 105 Military Plaza. The 10-room, adobe-walled structure was the original seat of government in the early 1700s. Commandants of Presidio de Bexar and many Spanish governors lived and ruled in the building, which features hand-carved doors, low-beam ceilings, a grape arbor and a mosaic-tiled patio typical of Colonial Spain. The entryway displays a keystone engraved with a double-headed eagle. Several rooms are furnished in period.

Allow 1 hour minimum. Mon.-Sat. 9-5, Sun. 10-5; closed Jan. 1, Thanksgiving and Dec. 24-25. Admission $1.50; ages 7-13, 75c. Phone (210) 224-0601.

SPLASHTOWN is 3 mi. n. off I-35 exit 160 at 3600 N. Pan Am Expwy. A variety of aquatic amusements are offered, including waterslides and a wave pool. Lockers and showers are available. Allow 3 hours minimum. Sun.-Thurs. 11-9, Fri.-Sat. 11-10, late May to mid-Sept. Admission $21.99, under 48 inches tall $16.99, over 65 and under age 4 free. Reduced prices after 5. MC, VI. Phone (210) 227-1100.

STEVES HOMESTEAD is at 509 King William St. The site includes a lavish Second Empire mansion built by Edward Steves in 1876 and River Haus, a carriage house originally intended to hold a swimming pool. The mansion, with its slate-covered mansard roof and 13-inch-thick limestone walls, displays Victorian antiques. Tours depart daily 10-3:30; closed major holidays. Admission $3, under 12 free. Phone (210) 225-5924.

TEXAS TRANSPORTATION MUSEUM is 3.5 mi. n. of jct. Loop 410 at 11731 Wetmore Rd. Vintage railcars, railroad exhibits, antique vehicles, antique fire equipment and horse-drawn carriages are housed at the museum. Picnic facilities are available. Allow 1 hour minimum. Thurs. and Sat.-Sun. 9-4; half-mile train rides are available on the hour Sat. noon-3; every 45 min. Sun. 12:30-3:30; closed Jan. 1 and Dec. 25. Admission (including train) $4; under 13, $2. Phone (210) 490-3554.

What To Do
Sightseeing
Boat Tours

YANAGUANA CRUISE departs from the Rivercenter at 315 E. Commerce St. Narrated 1-hour tours follow the San Antonio River. Guides point out the sites along the Paseo del Río/Riverwalk *(see attraction listing p. 143)* and relay the river's history. Barge tours also are available. Allow 1 hour minimum. Daily 9 a.m.-10 p.m., Apr.-Sept.; 10-8, rest of year. Fare $5.25; over 65 and military with ID $3.65; under 5, $1. AX, MC, VI. Phone (210) 244-5700 or (800) 417-4139.

Bus and Trolley Tours

SAN ANTONIO CITY TOURS departs from the Alamo Visitor Center at 217 Alamo Plaza. Guided bus tours of the city include the Alamo, Riverwalk and Mission San José. Tours of the Hill Country and Nuevo Laredo, Mexico, also are available. Full-day city tour departs daily at 9. Half-day city tours depart daily at 9 and 1:45. Closed holidays. Full-day city fare $45; ages 5-10, $22.50. Half-day city fare $28; ages 5-10, $14. AX, MC, VI. Phone (210) 228-9776.

TEXAS TROLLEY TOUR departs from the Alamo Visitor Center. The 60-minute narrated historic tour stops at seven points of interest: the Alamo, Hemis-Fair Park, La Villita, Mission Concepción, Mission San José, El Mercado Farmer's Market and the San Fernando Cathedral. An uptown tour visits various museums, the Botanical Gardens, the zoo, Brackenridge Park and Fort Sam Houston.

With an all-day pass, passengers may disembark and reboard the trolley. Historic and uptown tours daily 10-5. Closed Dec. 25. Sixty-minute excursion $10.95; ages 3-11, $4.95. All-day pass $12.95; ages 3-11, $5.95. AX, DS, MC, VI. Phone (210) 225-8587.

Walking Tours

The downtown loop of the San Antonio River provides unusual ways to see a portion of the city.

The Paseo del Río (Riverwalk), which follows the riverbanks, affords walkers a leisurely view of this downtown renewal project.

The San Antonio Conservation Society offers two self-guiding walking-tour brochures—Texas Star Trail and King William Street Historic District. Beginning at the Alamo, the 2.5-mile Texas Star Trail follows a signed route through the downtown area. The tour of the King William district spotlights many elegant Victorian houses built by prosperous German merchants during the mid-19th century.

For more information contact the Conservation Society at the Wulff House, 107 King William St., San Antonio, TX 78204; phone (210) 224-6163.

Beginning downtown, signs designate the Mission Trail, a 10-mile route linking the Alamo with the four sites of the San Antonio Missions National Historical Park *(see attraction listing p. 144).*

Sports and Recreation

Mild winters and summers filled with sunshine provide outdoor recreational opportunities all year in San Antonio. In addition to the 3,000 acres set aside for sports and recreation, three lakes within the city offer **sailboating** and **fishing.** Three 1-mile **jogging** trails pass through the downtown area; information is available at the Plaza San Antonio Hotel, (210) 229-1000, 555 S. Alamo. For those who enjoy **swimming,** 22 municipal pools are open daily noon-7, Memorial Day-Labor Day.

More than 80 municipal **tennis** courts can be found within the metropolitan area. Consult the telephone directories. **Golf** is available at four 18-hole courses in the city: Brackenridge Park, (210) 226-5612, at 2315 Ave. B; Olmos Basin, (210) 826-4041, at 7022 McCullough; Riverside Golf Course, (210) 533-8371, at 203 McDonald; and Willow Springs, (210) 226-6721, at 202 Coliseum Rd.

The surrounding Texas hill country has many lakes and dude ranches. **Horseback riding** along the wooded bridle trails of Brackenridge Park is popular; riding academies and stables are listed in the telephone directories.

Spectator sports include the **basketball** games of the San Antonio Spurs, who play at the SBC Center, 211 Coliseum Rd.; phone (210) 224-9600 for schedule and tickets. The San Antonio Missions of the Texas Baseball League play **baseball** April through August at Nelson Wolff Stadium at 5757 SR 90W; phone (210) 675-7275 for schedule and ticket information.

The San Antonio Iguanas play minor league **hockey** at the Freeman Coliseum; phone (210) 227-4449 for ticket information.

College teams add excitement to the sports seasons. The athletic program at Trinity University, 715 Stadium Dr., includes **volleyball, soccer,** tennis, **football** and basketball; phone (210) 999-8222 or (210) 999-8406. St. Mary's University offers soccer, volleyball, basketball and baseball; phone

(210) 436-3528. The University of Texas at San Antonio also presents basketball games; phone (210) 458-8872.

Automobile racing takes place at Alamo Drag-way, on SR 16 south of Loop 410; Pan American Speedway, on Toepperwein Road; and San Antonio Drag Race Track. The newspaper carries the schedules.

Horse racing, both Thoroughbred and quarter horse, occurs Wednesday through Saturday from early June through November at nearby Retama Park; phone (210) 651-7000. In addition, there are daily simulcasts.

Note: Policies concerning admittance of children to pari-mutuel betting facilities vary. Phone for information.

Shopping

Downtown shopping presents as varied a picture as does San Antonio itself. At the 10-acre River-Center Mall, the San Antonio River and the River-walk have been extended into this complex of 135 stores and restaurants, anchored by Dillard's and Foley's department stores.

The city also offers shopping on a smaller scale. Wolfman's is best known for women's fashions. A number of stores serve men's clothing needs, including Holland Ltd., in Alamo Heights at 5007 Broadway; Joseph's Inc., 233 E. Houston St. and in several area malls; and Todd's, 722 North Star Mall.

Specialty shops are scattered throughout the city. The Boardwalk, Cambridge Center and Oliver Square are in Alamo Heights; Loehmann's Village at The Summit is in northwest San Antonio; and Sheplers Western Stores adjoins Ingram Park Mall.

Lucchese Boots, 4039 Broadway, specializes in custom-made Western footwear. The SAS Factory Shoe Store, on New Laredo Highway and in several shopping centers, produces leather shoes for women. Handicrafts and Mexican imports are available along the Riverwalk and in La Villita.

Other shopping centers include Alamo Quarry Market, 255 E. Basse Rd.; Brookhollow Shopping Center in San Pedro; Central Park Shopping Center, 243 Central Park; Crossroads Mall, Fredericksburg Road and I-410 in northwest San Antonio; Huebner Oaks Center, 11745 I-10; Ingram Park Mall, 6301 N.W. Loop 410; McCreless Mall, in the southeast section of the city; North Star Mall, in the north-central part of town at San Pedro Avenue and I-410; Rolling Oaks Mall, Nacogdoches and SR 1604 in northeast San Antonio; and Windsor Park Mall, 7900 I-35 N.

Outlet shoppers will appreciate the offerings at Mill Store Plaza, off I-35 in New Braunfels, and Tanger Outlet Center, at I-35 exit 200 in San Marcos.

LOOK FOR THE RED

*N*ext time you pore over a AAA TourBook® guide in search of a lodging establishment, take note of the vibrant red AAA logo, icon, and [SAVE] Diamond rating just under a select group of property names! These Official Appointment properties place a high value on the business they receive from dedicated AAA travelers and offer members great room rates*.

* See TourBook Navigator section, page 14, for complete details.

Since 1830, San Antonio has had an open-air marketplace for vegetables, fruit and eggs, featuring lower prices and the possibility of bargaining. Market Square *(see attraction listing p. 141)* is in an area bounded by Pecos and Santa Rosa streets on the west and east and by Buena Vista and Commerce streets to the south and north. In addition to fresh garden produce, shoppers can find American Indian and Mexican goods as well as and arts and crafts in an array of specialty shops.

Theater and Concerts

One of the few remaining movie and vaudeville theaters in the country, the Majestic, has been restored and revived as the Majestic Theatre, 212 E. Houston St. Touring Broadway productions and concerts are presented throughout the year; phone (210) 226-3333. The theater also is home to the San Antonio Symphony, which performs September through June. Phone (210) 554-1010 for schedule and ticket information. In addition to classical performances, the symphony supplies the city with a pops series, chamber music and an opera season.

Convention Center Arena, Alamo and Market streets, is the scene of concerts, including pop, rock and jazz; phone (210) 224-9600 for schedule and tickets. The forum for instrumental soloists is Laurie Auditorium, 715 Stadium Dr.; phone (210) 999-8117.

Freeman Coliseum, 3201 E. Houston, is the locale of country performances; phone (210) 226-1177 for schedules. Strolling mariachi bands can be heard along the Riverwalk and in the Mexican Market area.

Beethoven Hall, (210) 222-1521, and Lila Cockerell Theatre, (210) 207-8500, both in HemisFair Park, feature traveling dancers, including ballet troupes.

Trinity University's drama department presents more than a dozen productions a year in its Ruth Taylor Theater. Ticket information can be obtained by phoning (210) 999-8515. Other colleges and the military bases occasionally produce theatrical shows.

Community theater also has a role in San Antonio's cultural environment. The San Antonio Little Theater's presentations are held at San Pedro Playhouse, in San Pedro Park at Ashby Street and San Pedro Avenue; phone (210) 733-7258. Harlequin Dinner Theater, at Fort Sam Houston in Building 2652 on Harney Road, also offers performances; phone (210) 222-9694.

The most unusual of the city's theaters is Arneson River Theatre *(see attraction listing p. 139)*, where performers are separated from the audience by the San Antonio River. Open-air concerts are held at the Verizon Wireless Amphitheatre, a 109-acre facility in Selma. The San Antonio IMAX Theatre *(see attraction listing p. 143)* in RiverCenter Mall presents "The Price of Freedom."

Special Events

Each January when the river is drained the Riverwalk holds its Riverwalk Mud Festival. The festival features parades, entertainment and the crowning of the Mud King and Queen. In mid-February, the San Antonio Livestock Show takes place, complete with a rodeo. In honor of St. Patrick, the San Antonio River is dyed green in March. The Starving Artists Show displays art at La Villita and along the Riverwalk at Easter.

The most widely celebrated event held in the city is the 10-day Fiesta San Antonio. Honoring the heroes of Texas and fostering Pan-American friendship, the fiesta takes place the week of San Jacinto Day, April 21. More than 150 events are scheduled during the celebration. Highlights include concerts, a pilgrimage to the Alamo, fireworks, street dances and carnivals as well as vividly costumed participants and torchlit floats on the street and decorated barges parading down the San Antonio River.

Possibly the most distinctive features of the celebration are the *cascarones*, decorated confetti-filled eggshells sold for the express purpose of being crushed on any heads that happen to be within reach.

Market Square is the locale for a number of celebrations throughout the spring and summer, including Cinco de Mayo. The May festival, which commemorates Mexican independence from the French, features food and music from noon to midnight. Music fans from around the world gather in Rosedale Park for the 6-day Tejano Conjunto Festival, sponsored in May by the Guadalupe Cultural Arts Center.

The Texas Folklife Festival in early June celebrates Texas' ethnic diversity and pioneer heritage. During this festival at the Institute of Texan Cultures, more than 30 ethnic groups share their traditions, crafts, music and foods.

The Diez y Seis celebration in mid-September focuses on the city's Mexican heritage. At the end of September the Great Country River Festival combines well-known Texas bands with Nashville sounds in a 3-day jamboree at six staging areas along the Riverwalk, from La Mansion del Río to the Arneson River Theatre and up the river to the Marriott Hotel. In October, the Greek community celebrates its heritage during the Greek Funstival.

The Christmas season is celebrated in colorful Mexican style during Fiestas Navideñas, complete with piñata parties and a blessing of children's pets by a priest. Fiesta de las Luminarias features thousands of candles lining the River Walk, symbolically showing the way for the holy family. Las Posadas is an ancient Spanish religious pageant.

The San Antonio Vicinity

NEW BRAUNFELS (F-8)
pop. 36,494, elev. 637'

New Braunfels was one of several towns north of San Antonio settled by Germans, one of the largest groups to immigrate to the new Republic of Texas. Settled in 1845, the town prospered from the region's plentiful water and rich soil, which soon produced a healthy agricultural economy. The city's German heritage and the region's natural beauty currently fuel a thriving tourism industry.

At the heart of the city is the spring-fed Comal River, a playground for inner tube riders and swimmers. The scenic Guadalupe River Road traverses the hill country through New Braunfels.

River Road, off SR 46, leads to Sattler and Canyon Dam before returning to the city via Sattler Road, Startzville and SR 46. The centerpiece of this scenic loop is the Guadalupe River Scenic Area, a popular river reserve for canoeing, inner tubing and fishing.

Another highlight is the restored late 19th-century community of Gruene and its historic district, which includes Texas' oldest dance hall as well as several general stores, antique stores, an art gallery and ethnic restaurants.

New Braunfels Convention and Visitors Bureau: 390 S. Seguin St., P.O. Box 311417, New Braunfels, TX 78131-1417; phone (830) 625-2385 or (800) 572-2626.

THE CHILDREN'S MUSEUM IN NEW BRAUNFELS is downtown at 386 W. San Antonio St. Interactive exhibits focus on science, history, geography and art. Mon.-Sat. 9-5, Sun. noon-5. Admission $3, senior citizens $2, under 1 free. Phone (830) 620-0939 or (888) 928-8326.

LANDA PARK is in the northwest section of town at 110 Golf Course Rd. Covering 196 acres, the recreation spot is unusual for Texas because of its tropical greenery. Tubing on the Comal River is a popular pastime, and paddleboats are available on 25-acre Landa Lake. There are two spring-fed swimming pools, an 18-hole golf course, a miniature golf course, a miniature train ride and facilities for fishing. Daily 6 a.m.-midnight. Park office open Mon.-Fri. 8-5, Sat.-Sun. 9-5, Easter-Labor Day; Mon.-Fri. 8-5, rest of year. Phone (830) 608-2160.

MUSEUM OF TEXAS HANDMADE FURNITURE AT HERITAGE VILLAGE is at 1370 Church Hill Dr. The 1858 Breustedt-Dillen house contains a large collection of furniture handmade by German immigrants during the 1800s. Among the items displayed are wardrobes, tables and sofas. In addition, collections of pewter, English ironstone and steins also are featured. Simpler furniture and cabinetmaker's tools used by early settlers are displayed in a log cabin on the grounds.

Tues.-Sun. 1-4, Feb.-Nov.; closed major holidays. Last tour begins one hour before closing. Admission $5; over 61, $4; ages 6-12, $1. Phone (830) 629-6504.

NEW BRAUNFELS CONSERVATION SOCIETY is .5 mi. w. jct. I-35 and SR 46 at 1300 Church Hill Dr. Guided tours of the area's restored historic buildings are offered. Tours begin at Conservation Plaza and include a rose conservatory, one-room school, general store, music studio, saloon, two-story pioneer house, cabinetmaker's shop and house, and log cabins. Tues.-Fri. 10-2:30, Sat.-Sun. 2-5. Admission $2.50; ages 6-18, 50c. Phone (830) 629-2943.

NEW BRAUNFELS MUSEUM OF ART & MUSIC is at 1257 Gruene Rd. This Smithsonian-affiliated museum focuses on the rich talent of Texan artists and musicians. Changing exhibits include folk art, crafts, music and the decorative arts. Allow 1 hour minimum. Mon.-Sat. 10-5, Sun. noon-5; closed Jan. 1, Easter, Thanksgiving, Dec. 24-25 and 31. Admission $3; over 65 and ages 13-18, $2.50. AX, MC, VI. Phone (830) 625-5636.

SCHLITTERBAHN WATERPARK RESORT is at 305 W. Austin St. The 65-acre water park features 17 waterslides, seven inner tube chutes and hot tubs. The Blastenhoff adventure area includes a hyperaction river, a six-story uphill water coaster, black tunnel slides, a family tubing area and a beach. A pirate-themed funhouse contains some 50 water features. The park includes volleyball and picnic facilities. Food is available.

Open daily at 10, mid-May to mid-Aug.; Sat.-Sun., late Apr. to mid-May and late Aug. to mid-Sept. (including Labor Day). Closing times vary between 6 and 8. Admission $27.70; ages 3-11, $22.99. After 3:30 p.m. for 8 closing or 2 p.m. for earlier closing $19.60; ages 3-11, $16.10. Prices may vary; phone ahead. Glass containers and alcohol are prohibited. AX, DC, DS, MC, VI. Phone (830) 625-2351.

SOPHIENBURG MUSEUM AND ARCHIVES is at 401 W. Coll St. Prince Carl of Solms-Braunfels built a log fortress on this hilltop site. Displays include many of the nobleman's personal effects, American Indian artifacts and household items of the pioneer era. Among the museum's highlights are the re-created bakery, pharmacy and barber shop. Allow 30 minutes minimum. Museum Mon.-Sat. 10-5, Sun. 1-5. Archives Mon.-Fri. 10-4. Closed holidays. Museum and archives $5, under 17 free. Phone (830) 629-1572 for the museum, or (830) 629-1900 for the archives.

SEGUIN (F-8) pop. 22,011

Home of the world's largest pecan, Seguin (sa-geen) was founded as Walnut Springs in 1838. The name was changed to honor Col. Juan N. Seguin, a distinguished Tejano patriot who served under Sam Houston in the fight for Texas independence.

The giant pecan—a sculpture on the courthouse lawn—marks Seguin as a major cultivator of the nut. Guided tours of the area include sites from Janice Woods Windle's historical novel "True Women." The town's first church, built for a Methodist conference in 1849, is among the oldest surviving protestant churches in the state. Seguin also is the home of Texas Lutheran University.

Seguin Convention and Visitors Bureau: 427 N. Austin, P.O. Box 710, Seguin, TX 78156; phone (830) 379-6382 or (800) 580-7322.

Self-guiding tours: Brochures for a walking tour of historic downtown Seguin and a driving tour of sites from "True Women" are available from the convention and visitors bureau.

SEGUIN WAVE POOL is 3 mi. s. off I-10 exit 609, following SR 123 to Max Starcke Park. Aquatic amusements include a 15,000-square-foot wave pool and a splash pool. Dressing rooms and grass volleyball are available. Daily 1-7, early June to mid-Aug. Admission $4; over 60 and ages 4-11, $3. Phone (830) 401-2480.

This ends listings for the San Antonio Vicinity.
The following page resumes the alphabetical listings
of cities in Texas.

SAN MARCOS (F-8) pop. 34,733, elev. 581'

One mile northwest of San Marcos are the headwaters of the San Marcos River at Aquarena Springs. Created by the Balcones Fault, the San Marcos Springs, from which the river flows, produce 150 million gallons of ice-cold water daily. San Marcos is the input point for the Texas Water Safari, a 240-mile, nonstop canoe race to the Gulf town of Seadrift. The record for this grueling race is 35 hours, 17 minutes.

San Marcos Convention and Visitors Bureau: 202 N. C.M. Allen Pkwy., P.O. Box 2310, San Marcos, TX 78667-2310; phone (512) 393-5900 or (888) 200-5620.

Shopping areas: Bargain shopping is popular at Prime Outlets and SAVE Tanger Outlet Center, both at I-35 exit 200.

AQUARENA CENTER is off I-35 exit 206, then w. to 921 Aquarena Springs Dr. Glass-bottom boats take visitors over the San Marcos Springs, which produce 150 million gallons of artesian water a day. The park focuses on natural science, research and education and features the Natural Aquarium, which displays endangered species. A 5,400-gallon tank is home to native fish. A wetlands walkway, nature trails and historic sites are on the grounds. Food is available, and picnicking is permitted. Allow 3 hours minimum. Daily 9:30-6. Aquarium and grounds free. Glass-bottom boat fare $6; over 54, $5; ages 4-14, $4. AX, MC, VI. Phone (512) 245-7570.

SAVE **WONDER WORLD** is off I-35 exit 202 via Wonder World Dr., following signs. One of the largest earthquake-formed caves in the United States, this underground labyrinth was discovered in 1893. A 90-minute guided tour includes the Balcones Fault Line Cave, the Tejas Observation Tower, the Anti-Gravity House and a train ride through the Wildlife Park, where visitors can feed native and exotic deer and other animals.

Daily 8-8, June-Aug.; Mon.-Fri. 9-5, Sat.-Sun. 9-6, rest of year. Closed Dec. 24-25. Tours depart every 15 minutes. Last admission 1 hour, 30 minutes before closing. All-inclusive admission $15.95; ages 4-11, $11.95. DS, MC, VI. Phone (512) 392-3760.

SEGUIN—see San Antonio p. 150.

SHAMROCK (B-6) pop. 2,029, elev. 2,342'

Incorporated in 1911, Shamrock originally was established as a post office 21 years prior at the home of an Irish sheep rancher. Cattle and farming sustain the economy of the Texas panhandle town. The 1936 Tower Station and U-Drop-Inn are Art Deco landmarks at the crossroads of Historic Route 66 and US 83.

Shamrock Chamber of Commerce: 207 N. Main St., Shamrock, TX 79079; phone (806) 256-2501.

PIONEER WEST MUSEUM is at 204 N. Madden St. More than 20 rooms contain artifacts, American Indian arrowheads, articles on loan from Houston Space Center, doctors' and dentists' office equipment and military items. Mon.-Fri. 10-noon and 1-3, Sat.-Sun. by appointment. Donations. Phone (806) 256-3941.

SHEFFIELD (F-5) elev. 2,168'

The San Antonio-El Paso Road was forged in 1851 to carry U.S. mail and passengers west. Despite Indian attacks, the stage line transported thousands of travelers as far as San Diego. By 1900, a small community had formed at a ford in the Pecos River where the stage line crossed, and the town eventually took the name of a local rancher, Will Sheffield. Oil was discovered in 1920, and natural gas became the town's second major commodity in the 1970s.

FORT LANCASTER STATE HISTORIC SITE is off I-10 exit 343, then 8 mi. e. on US 290. Established in 1855 as Camp Lancaster, the fort was a defense post against American Indian attacks along the San Antonio-El Paso Road. Troops stationed at the fort escorted settlers moving west. The installation grew to 25 buildings before it was abandoned at the onset of the Civil War. An interpretive center features fort artifacts, maps and exhibits about the site's history, natural history and archeology. The 82-acre park includes a nature trail and picnic facilities.

Allow 1 hour minimum. Daily 8-5; closed Dec. 25. Admission $2; ages 13-17, $1. DS, MC, VI. Phone (432) 836-4391.

SHERMAN (C-9) pop. 35,082, elev. 728'

Laid out in 1846 as the seat of Grayson County, Sherman gained early prominence when the Butterfield Stage was routed through town. The town is named for Sidney Sherman, who coined the phrase "Remember the Alamo!" during the Battle of San Jacinto. West of Sherman is the Hagerman National Wildlife Refuge (see Denison p. 88), which straddles part of the huge Lake Texoma reservoir.

Sherman Convention and Visitors Bureau: 307 W. Washington St., Suite 100, Sherman, TX 75090; phone (903) 893-1184 or (888) 893-1188.

Self-guiding tours: A brochure that outlines a driving tour of historic Sherman is available from the convention and visitors bureau.

SONORA (E-6) pop. 2,924, elev. 2,120'

Settled on the western slope of the Edwards Plateau in 1889, Sonora produces wool and mohair. The world's longest fenced cattle trail once ran from Brady to Sonora.

Sonora Chamber of Commerce: P.O. Box 1172, Sonora, TX 76950; phone (325) 387-2880.

CAVERNS OF SONORA is 8 mi. n.w. off I-10 exit 392 and 7 mi. s. on Cavern Rd. (Ranch Rd. 1989). A 2-mile trail winds through the cave, where the temperature is a constant 70 degrees F. Stalagmites, stalactites and helictites cover the walls, ceiling and floor of the cave. These translucent and phosphorescent formations exhibit a wide range of colors. Picnic facilities and food are available.

The guided 2-hour Crystal Palace Tour takes visitors through the original entrance, covering the 2-mile interior and all of the cave's major features, including Horseshoe Lake, the Corinthian Room and the Crystal Palace Room. A shorter 75-minute trip to Horseshoe Lake also is offered. Tours involve climbing stairs; comfortable walking shoes are recommended. Picnic facilities and food are available.

Guided tours depart every 10-30 minutes daily 8-6, Mar. 1-Labor Day; 9-5, rest of year. Closed Dec. 25. Crystal Palace Tour $20; ages 4-11, $16. Horseshoe Lake Tour $15; ages 4-11, $12. Prices may vary; phone ahead. AX, DS, MC, VI. Phone (325) 387-3105.

SOUTH PADRE ISLAND (I-9) pop. 2,422

The southernmost 5 miles of Padre Island, the resort town of South Padre Island, are connected by a causeway to Port Isabel on the mainland. The area is a haven for artists, photographers and ecologists. Gulls, herons and rare brown pelicans are found among the island's tropical foliage, waterways, dunes and long white beaches.

There is a seemingly limitless supply of seashells, and rumors allude to buried treasure beneath the sand—pirate plunder and debris from 5 centuries of shipwrecks.

Laguna Madre, the bay that separates the island from the mainland, has excellent fishing all year. Charter boats leave daily in search of red snapper, king mackerel, marlin, tarpon and sailfish in the Gulf. There also is fishing from the lighted 5,000-foot Queen Isabella Fishing Pier.

South Padre Island offers swimming, diving, windsurfing, sailing and parasailing. Boat ramps, slips and marinas accommodate all sizes of craft.

South Padre Island Convention and Visitors Bureau: 600 Padre Blvd., South Padre Island, TX 78597; phone (956) 761-6433 or (800) 767-2373.

SCHLITTERBAHN BEACH WATERPARK is .5 mi. s. of Queen Isabella Cswy. to 90 Park Rd. Hwy. 100. This 15-acre water park features a Brazilian beach theme. A half-mile river system carries visitors to rides throughout the park, including four Master Blaster uphill water coasters, the 245-foot Agua Blanca Tube Chute, the Rio Beach wave lagoon, and Boogie Bahn[2], one of the world's largest bodyboarding rides. The five-story Sandcastle features four water slides and more than 200 computerized water features. Volleyball and picnic facilities and food are available.

Allow 3 hours minimum. Opens daily at 10, mid-May to mid-Aug.; Sat.-Sun at 10, late Apr. to mid-May and late Aug. to mid-Sept. Closing times vary from 6 to 8 p.m. Admission $26.50; ages 3-11, $21.95. After 3:30 p.m. for 8 closing or 2 p.m. for earlier closing $18.75; ages 3-11, $15.40. Prices may vary; phone ahead. Glass containers and alcohol prohibited. AX, DC, DS, MC, VI. Phone (956) 772-7873.

THE UNIVERSITY OF TEXAS-PAN AMERICAN COASTAL STUDIES LABORATORY is at the southern tip of the island in Isla Blanca Park. This marine-biology research and education center offers self-guiding afternoon tours. Displays identify local flora and fauna; an aquarium holds colorful vertebrate and invertebrate species. Sun.-Fri. 1:30-4:30; closed holidays. Donations; admission to park $4 per private vehicle. Phone (956) 761-2644.

SPRING—see Houston p. 117.

STONEWALL (F-8) pop. 469, elev. 1,449'

Established in 1870, Stonewall was named for Gen. Stonewall Jackson and is known for its Gillespie County peaches. Lyndon B. Johnson, 36th president, was born near here Aug. 27, 1908.

LYNDON B. JOHNSON STATE PARK AND HISTORIC SITE is 2 mi. e. on US 290 on Park Rd. 52. The park is the boarding point for tours of the LBJ Ranch District of Lyndon B. Johnson National Historical Park *(see place listing p. 124),* across the Pedernales River.

Photographs and memorabilia at the visitor center chronicle Johnson's life and Hill Country history. The 732-acre site includes two restored dog-run cabins and the Sauer-Beckmann Living History Farm, where costumed interpreters perform the daily chores of a 1918 Texas-German family. Buffalo, longhorn cattle and white-tail deer graze in the park, which is best visited in the spring when wildflowers bloom. Nature trails and picnic facilities are on the grounds.

Park daily 8-5. Farm daily 8-4:30. Closed Jan. 1, Thanksgiving and Dec. 25. Johnson Ranch bus tours depart from the visitor center daily 10-4. Park and farm free. Ranch bus tour $3, under 7 free. DS, MC, VI. Phone (830) 644-2252. *See Recreation Chart.*

SULPHUR SPRINGS (C-10) pop. 14,551, elev. 494'

With nearly 500 dairies, the Sulphur Springs/Hopkins County area is a leading dairy producer in Texas. The town is named for its abundant underground springs; a source under the town square once heated a swimming pool.

Hopkins County Chamber of Commerce: 1200 Houston St., P.O. Box 347, Sulphur Springs, TX 75483; phone (903) 885-6515 or (888) 300-6623.

MUSIC BOX EXHIBIT is in the city library at 611 N. Davis St. More than 150 unusual and antique music boxes collected during a 50-year period are displayed. Allow 30 minutes minimum. Mon.-Fri. 9-6, Sat. 9-noon; closed holidays. Free. Phone (903) 885-4926.

SOUTHWEST DAIRY MUSEUM is off I-30 exit 122, n. 1.4 mi., then e. to 1210 Houston St. The center traces the history of the dairy industry from rural farm life before electricity to modern milking methods, bottling and transportation. Exhibits include a re-created 1930s kitchen and dairy barn. Guided tours are offered. Food is available. Allow 30 minutes minimum. Mon.-Sat. 9-4; closed holidays. Donations. Phone (903) 439-6455.

SWEETWATER (D-6)
pop. 11,415, elev. 2,164′

Many streams around Sweetwater are tainted by gypsum deposits, which are good for the local wallboard industry but not for drinking. Sweetwater Creek offered early settlers the only potable water in the area.

During World War II an experiment in military aviation took place outside Sweetwater at Avenger Field. More than 1,000 women were trained 1943-44 as military pilots in a program almost identical to that given their male counterparts. As part of the Women's Airforce Service Pilots (WASP), they flew every aircraft the Army Air Force had. Now Avenger Field is the municipal airport.

Displayed in the Nolan County Courthouse is the Walt Disney statue "Fifinella," the mascot of the women pilots who trained at Avenger Field.

Sweetwater Chamber of Commerce: 810 E. Broadway, P.O. Box 1148, Sweetwater, TX 79556; phone (325) 235-5488 or (800) 658-6757.

PIONEER CITY COUNTY MUSEUM is at 610 E. Third St. This 1906 house, partly decorated in period, displays American Indian artifacts, pioneer farming and ranching equipment, photographs and paintings of pioneer families, late 19th-century fashions, toys and dolls. One room is dedicated to the Women's Air Force Service Pilots (WASP) who trained at Avenger Field to ferry aircraft during World War II. Allow 30 minutes minimum. Tues.-Sat. 1-5; closed holidays. Donations. Phone (325) 235-8547.

TEMPLE (E-8) pop. 54,514, elev. 736′

Temple began as a rail and retail center serving the cattle trade. Currently, the city is best known for its concentration of hospitals and the proximity of one of the country's largest military bases, Fort Hood.

Temple Department of Tourism: Mayborn Civic and Convention Center, 3303 N. 3rd St., 2 N. Main, Temple, TX 75601; phone (254) 298-5720.

SAVE **RAILROAD AND HERITAGE MUSEUM** is off I-35 exit 301, .9 mi. on Central Ave. to 7th St., then s. to 315 W. Avenue B. Housed in a restored 1910 Santa Fe depot and working Amtrak station, the museum depicts railroad history and local heritage. Exhibits include railroad equipment, model trains, a telegraph room and listening stations for train communications. Locomotives, cabooses and passenger cars are displayed outside. Allow 1 hour minimum. Tues.-Sat. 10-4, Sun. 1-4; closed major holidays. Admission $4; over 62, $3; ages 5-12, $2. MC, VI. Phone (254) 298-5172.

TEXARKANA (C-11) pop. 34,782, elev. 290′

The Arkansas-Texas state line runs approximately through the center of the dual municipality of Texarkana, which has a combined population of about 61,000.

For hundreds of years before European settlement in the area, the Great Southwest Trail, the major route between the American Indian villages of the Mississippi Valley and the West and Southwest, crossed the area around what is now Texarkana. The Grand Caddoes, hospitable to explorers and settlers, farmed in the vicinity and maintained six villages along the banks of the Red River.

Shortly after 1840 a permanent settlement was established at Lost Prairie, 15 miles east of Texarkana. A number of mounds and other traces of former American Indian civilizations remain within a 30-mile radius of the town.

During the 1850s the Cairo and Fulton Railroad served portions of Arkansas and by 1874 had crossed the Red River into Texas, establishing direct rail service to St. Louis. The Texas and Pacific Railroad had laid track to the Arkansas boundary, and the place where the two lines met became a town—Texarkana.

The state line runs through the middle of the Texarkana Post Office and Courthouse, said to be the only federal building situated in two states. Built in 1932 of pink granite from Texas and limestone from Arkansas, the post office has two separate zip codes. Residents on both sides of the border enjoy the Perot Theater, 221 Main St., a restored 1924 facility that presents a variety of Broadway-type shows.

Texarkana Chamber of Commerce: 819 State Line Ave., P.O. Box 1468, Texarkana, TX 75504; phone (903) 792-7191.

SAVE **ACE OF CLUBS HOUSE AND MUSEUM** is at 420 Pine St. This 22-sided house was built in 1885 from the winnings of a poker game. The Italianate-Victorian style building has three octagonal wings and one rectangular wing and is furnished in period. A 30-minute videotape presentation is followed by a 45-minute guided tour that is offered as needed. High heels and photography are not permitted. Allow 1 hour, 30 minutes minimum. Tues.-Sat. 10-4. Last tour begins 1 hour before closing. Fee $5; over 54, $4.50; students with ID $3.50. MC, VI. Phone (903) 793-4831.

SAVE **DISCOVERY PLACE CHILDREN'S MUSEUM** is at the corner of Pine St. and State Line Ave. at 215 Pine St. Educational and entertaining hands-on exhibits focus on science and history.

A theater, lab demonstrations and a videotape presentation enhance the learning environment. Allow 1 hour minimum. Tues.-Sat. 10-4; closed major holidays. Admission $4, under 4 free. MC, VI. Phone (903) 793-4831.

SAVE **MUSEUM OF REGIONAL HISTORY** is 4 blks. s. of US 59/67/71/82 at 219 State Line Ave. Housed in an 1879 brick building, this museum traces the region's history from the early Caddo Indians through 20th-century citizens, including early industry, post World War II and the civil rights movement. In addition to the Native American Gallery, the Scott Joplin Gallery is dedicated to the composer's early life and career in Texarkana. Tues.-Sat. 10-4; closed holidays. Admission $4; over 64, $3.50; ages 4-12, $3. MC, VI. Phone (903) 793-4831.

TYLER (D-10) pop. 83,650, elev. 558′

Incorporated in 1846, Tyler was named for President John Tyler, who was instrumental in bringing Texas into the Union. The area is well known for its field-grown rosebushes, which are sold internationally.

The Goodman Museum, housed in an 1859 house, displays 18th-century medical paraphernalia, antebellum artifacts and period furniture; phone (903) 592-5993.

Tyler Area Chamber of Commerce: P.O. Box 390, Tyler, TX 75710; phone (903) 592-1661 or (800) 235-5712.

BROOKSHIRE'S WORLD OF WILDLIFE MUSEUM AND COUNTRY STORE is on FM 2493, .5 mi. s. of jct. W.S.W. Loop 323. Mammals, reptiles and fish from Africa and North America are displayed. A full-size replica of a 1920s grocery store portrays the grocery industry's development during the early 1900s; exhibits include an old-time gasoline pump and a 1926 Model T Ford delivery truck. Picnic facilities are available. Tues.-Sat. 9-noon and 1-5; closed holidays. Free. Phone (903) 534-2169.

GEM **CALDWELL ZOO** is 1 blk. e. of US 69 at 2203 Martin Luther King Jr. Blvd. The 85-acre zoo provides natural habitats for more than 2,000 animals from North and South America and Africa, including lions, leopards, elephants, giraffes, otters, flamingos, and a collection of ducks from around the world. Highlights include an aquarium and a native Texas exhibit. Tropical foliage, ponds and wooden walkways enhance the setting. Food is available. Allow 1 hour, 30 minutes minimum. Daily 9:30-6, Apr.-Sept.; 9:30-4:30, rest of year. Closed Jan. 1, Thanksgiving and Dec. 25. Free. Phone (903) 593-0121.

TYLER MUSEUM OF ART is at 1300 S. Mahon Ave. Contemporary art of the 19th and 20th century is featured. Allow 30 minutes minimum. Tues.-Sat. 10-5, Sun. 1-5; closed holidays. Free. Phone (903) 595-1001.

TYLER ROSE GARDEN CENTER is at 420 Rose Park Dr. Some 38,000 rosebushes representing 400 varieties blossom among 14 acres of tall pines, fountains, ponds, gazebos and archways. Blooms peak in early May and continue through October. The Rose Museum features historical exhibits about the Texas Rose Festival and the state's rose industry. Garden open Mon.-Fri. 8-5, Sat. 9-5, Sun. 1-5. Museum Tues.-Fri. 9-4:30, Sat. 10-4:30, Sun. 1:30-4:30. Garden free. Museum $3.50. Phone (903) 531-1212 for the garden, or (903) 597-3130 for the museum.

UNIVERSITY PARK—see Dallas p. 87.

UVALDE (G-7) pop. 14,929, elev. 920′

Known as Encina 1855-56, Uvalde once was the domain of notorious frontier sheriff and outlaw, J. King Fisher. A more respectable resident was John Nance Garner, President Franklin Delano Roosevelt's first- and second-term vice president. After serving two terms in office, Garner returned to Uvalde, where he died at age 98.

Uvalde Convention and Visitors Bureau: 300 E. Main, Uvalde, TX 78801; phone (830) 278-4115 or (800) 588-2533.

GARNER MEMORIAL MUSEUM is .2 mi. w. at 333 N. Park St. This museum contains memorabilia of John Nance Garner, a speaker of the House of Representatives and two-term vice president to Franklin Delano Roosevelt. His nickname, "Cactus Jack," came from his attempts to make the cactus the state flower of Texas. Allow 1 hour minimum. Mon.-Sat. 9-5; closed holidays. Free. Phone (830) 278-5018.

GRAND OPERA HOUSE is at 104 W. North St. Built in 1891, the performing arts center accommodates community performances, professional troupes and a concert series throughout the year. A visitor center features a pictorial history of Uvalde County. Allow 30 minutes minimum. Mon.-Fri. 9-noon and 1-5; closed city holidays. Donations. Phone (830) 278-4184.

VERNON (C-7) pop. 11,660, elev. 1,205′

Originally named Eagle Flats for the birds nesting nearby, Vernon is a commercial center for farming, ranching and oil.

RED RIVER VALLEY MUSEUM is at 4600 College Dr. (US 70W). The history of Texas ranching is presented through artifacts and the sculpture of Texas artist Electra Waggonner Biggs. Also displayed are 135 big-game trophies, collections of American Indian and pioneer items, gems, rocks and minerals. A Jack Teagarden exhibit contains memorabilia of the jazz trombonist, who was born in Vernon. Allow 1 hour minimum. Tues.-Sun. 1-5. Free. Phone (940) 553-1848.

VICTORIA (G-9) pop. 60,603, elev. 140′

Victoria, in an area originally settled in 1685 by French explorer René-Robert Cavelier, Sieur de La Salle, was organized by the Spanish and in 1824 named for a Mexican president, Guadalupe Victoria. The first military capital of the new republic was established here after the Battle of San Jacinto. The city is now a leading cattle market and the home of several petrochemical plants.

The influence of yet another nationality is present in Victoria; an old Dutch gristmill stands in Memorial Square, the city's oldest cemetery.

Victoria Convention and Visitors Bureau: 700 Main Center, Suite 101, P.O. Box 2465, Victoria, TX 77902; phone (361) 573-5277.

McNAMARA HOUSE is at 502 N. Liberty St. A historic house museum focusing on the Victorian era, the 1876 structure has period rooms. Tues.-Sun. 1-5; closed major holidays. Admission $2; under 13, $1. Phone (361) 575-8227.

NAVE MUSEUM is in the Royston Nave Memorial at 306 W. Commercial. Works by Royston Nave and other contemporary North American artists are exhibited. Nave, who painted extensively in and around Victoria, achieved distinction in New York art circles during the 1920s. Exhibits in the Greco-Roman hall change every 8 weeks, with a 1-week interval for installation. Wed.-Sun. 1-5 (also Fri.-Sat. 5-8); closed holidays. Admission $2; under 13, $1. Phone (361) 575-8227.

RIVERSIDE PARK is at the end of W. Stayton Ave. The park encompasses 400 acres of woodland and gardens bordered by the Guadalupe River. Recreational activities include fishing, picnicking and golf. Phone (361) 572-2767.

Texas Zoo is at 110 Memorial Dr. Native animals reside in environments similar to their natural habitats. Daily 9-5; closed Jan. 1, Thanksgiving and Dec. 25. Admission $3.50; over 64, $3; ages 3-12, $2.50. Phone (361) 573-7681.

WACO (E-9) pop. 113,726, elev. 427′

Waco probably derives its name from the Hueco (WAY-co) Indians. Bisected by the Brazos River, the city has long been at the crossroads of trade and travel in central Texas. Cattle drives northward along the Chisholm Trail traversed the area. One of the city's original settlers began ferry service across the Brazos shortly after Waco was settled in 1849.

The construction of a suspension bridge in 1870 increased business and trade, and Waco joined the ranks of the rough-and-tumble cowtowns. The railroad came to Waco the following year, thereby securing the town's commercial progress. Modern Waco is the largest marketing center between Dallas and Austin; its economy focuses on diversified industry, agriculture and education.

Waco Tourist Information Center: 106 Texas Ranger Trail, Waco, TX 76706; phone (254) 750-8696 or (800) 922-6386.

ARMSTRONG BROWNING LIBRARY OF BAYLOR UNIVERSITY is at Eighth and Speight sts. On the campus of Baylor University, the elegant, Italian Renaissance-style building features 58 stained-glass windows. The library holds one of the world's largest collections of books, manuscripts and artifacts relating to Robert and Elizabeth Barrett Browning. Mon.-Fri. 9-5, Sat. 9-noon; closed Jan. 1, Good Friday, July 4, mid- to late Aug., Thanksgiving, day after Thanksgiving and Dec. 24-25. Donations. Phone (254) 710-3566.

CAMERON PARK ZOO is off I-35 exit 335A, then 2 mi. w. to 1701 N. Fourth St. The zoo features 50 acres of natural habitats. The African savannah is home to giraffes, lions, white rhinoceroses and elephants; the herpetarium's inhabitants include king cobras, chameleons and alligators. Among other zoo residents are gibbons, Texas longhorn cattle, Galapagos tortoises, antelopes and an endangered Sumatran tiger. A children's play area features a tree house and splash water pond.

Mon.-Sat. 9-5, Sun. 11-5; closed Jan. 1, Thanksgiving and Dec. 25. Admission $5; over 60, $4.50; ages 4-12, $3. MC, VI. Phone (254) 750-8400.

STRECKER MUSEUM OF BAYLOR UNIVERSITY is at S. Fourth St. in the Sid Richardson Science Bldg. Biological science, fossil, mineral, archeological and anthropological exhibits are offered. Several displays, including a reconstructed 1835 log cabin, chronicle the history of central Texas. Mon.-Fri. 9-5, Sat. 10-4; closed major holidays. Free. Phone (254) 710-1110.

TEXAS RANGER HALL OF FAME AND MUSEUM is off I-35 exit 335B at 1108 University Parks Dr. in Fort Fisher Park. The Rangers date from 1823, when Stephen F. Austin selected the original ten men. The complex comprises the Hall of Fame, which pays tribute to 26 Texas Rangers; a library that contains books, photographs and oral histories about the Rangers; and Homer Garrison Museum, which contains artifacts such as badges, firearms and outlaw possessions.

A 45-minute slide show is presented every 90 minutes. Daily 9-5; closed Jan. 1, Thanksgiving and Dec. 25. Admission $5; ages 6-12, $2.50. Phone (254) 750-8631.

(SAVE) **TEXAS SPORTS HALL OF FAME** is .2 mi. e. of I-35 exit 335B at 1108 S. University Parks Dr. Notable Texas athletes, coaches and teams are lauded in exhibits that are grouped by sport—with emphasis on baseball, tennis, football and basketball—and span from high school to the professional leagues. Films of sports highlights are shown in the Tom Landry Theater. Mon.-Sat. 10-5, Sun. noon-5; closed Jan. 1, Easter, Thanksgiving and Dec. 25. Admission $5; over 56, $4; ages 6-18, $2. MC, VI. Phone (254) 756-1633 or (800) 567-9561.

WASHINGTON (F-9) elev. 245′

Also known as Washington-on-the-Brazos or Old Washington, Washington was established in 1834. The town was the site of the signing of the Texas Declaration of Independence.

WASHINGTON-ON-THE-BRAZOS STATE HISTORIC SITE is on FM 1155 just 1 mi. s. of jct. SR 105. The 293-acre park on the site of the first capital of the Republic of Texas includes a living history farm, a museum and Independence Hall, a replica of the building where the Texas Declaration of Independence was signed. Also on the grounds are an amphitheater, walking trails and a picnic area. Daily 8-dusk. Guided tours of Independence Hall are available Mon.-Fri. at 10, 11, 1 and 3. Park admission free. Independence Hall $4, students with ID $2, family rate (includes admission to farm and museum) $17. DS, MC, VI. Phone (936) 878-2214.

Barrington Living History Museum is at 23200 Park Rd. 12. This living history farm depicts Washington County life in the 1850s and features costumed interpreters carrying out everyday farm chores. The antebellum house of Anson Jones, last president of the Republic of Texas, has been restored on the grounds. Several outbuildings from the Jones cotton plantation have been reconstructed, including a kitchen, a barn and slave quarters. Allow 1 hour minimum. Wed.-Sat. 10-5, Sun. 11-5; closed Thanksgiving and Dec. 25-Jan. 2. Admission $4, students with ID $2. DS, MC, VI. Phone (936) 878-2461.

Star of the Republic Museum is at 23200 Park Rd. 12. The story of Texas' 1821-46 struggle for independence from Mexico is told in exhibits that include army uniforms and weaponry as well as artifacts from the Republic of Texas. A Lone Star flag, thought to be the oldest in existence, is displayed. A 20-minute film describes the founding of the republic. The Showers-Brown Discovery Center is a multi-sensory area that offers hands-on displays exploring Texas history.

Allow 2 hours minimum. Daily 10-5; closed Thanksgiving and Dec. 25-Jan. 2. Admission $2, students with ID $1. DS, MC, VI. Phone (936) 878-2461.

WAXAHACHIE—see Dallas p. 87.

WEST COLUMBIA (G-10)
pop. 4,255, elev. 40′

In 1836, Sam Houston was inaugurated the first president of the Republic of Texas, and Stephen F. Austin was named its secretary of state in West Columbia, Texas' first capital. The government moved to Houston after a few months because West Columbia lacked adequate accommodations. A replica of the first capitol is in the center of town.

West Columbia Chamber of Commerce: 247 E. Brazos Ave., P.O. Box 837, West Columbia, TX 77486; phone (979) 345-3921.

VARNER-HOGG PLANTATION STATE HISTORIC SITE is 1 mi. n.e. off SR 35 at 1702 N. 13th St. (FM 2852). Guides at the site draw upon its multicultural heritage to offer visitors a glimpse of the early days of Texas. The property's first owner was Martin Varner, who received one of Stephen F. Austin's original land grants in 1824. Later a sugar plantation, the land was purchased by Gov. James S. Hogg in 1901. The 66-acre site includes the 1836 plantation manor, outbuildings, a large pecan orchard and picnic facilities.

Allow 1 hour minimum. Grounds daily dawn-dusk. Guided tours are given Wed.-Sat. 9-11 and 1-4, Sun. 1-4. Grounds free. Tours $4, students with ID $2, under 6 free. DS, MC, VI. Phone (979) 345-4656.

WHARTON (F-9) pop. 9,237, elev. 111'

Rice, corn, cotton and grain make Wharton a major agricultural producer. The town was established along the banks of the Colorado River.

WHARTON COUNTY HISTORICAL MUSEUM is at 3615 N. Richmond Rd. (SR 60). The museum displays wildlife trophies as well as county artifacts and photographs dealing with ranching, agriculture, archeology, medicine, local sulfur mines and Wharton County's Congressional Medal of Honor recipients Roy Benavidez and Johnnie Hutchins. On the grounds is the original home of Dan Rather, TV news anchor. Mon.-Fri. 9:30-4:30, Sat.-Sun. 1-5. Free. Phone (979) 532-2600.

WICHITA FALLS (C-8)
pop. 104,197, elev. 946'

It is hard to believe that the waterfall that gave Wichita Falls its name could exist in this flat country. Although no Niagara, the 5-foot cascade was such a rare sight that early settlers and surveyors felt it no exaggeration to christen it "Wichita Falls." Four years after the railroad brought the town's first settlers in 1882, the falls were washed away by a flood.

The loss of the falls did not affect the new community, which grew into a marketplace for north Texas agriculture. The city restored a piece of its past when it re-established the falls; in 1987 a 54-foot-high, terraced cascade was built downstream from the original waterfall.

The oil boom in the early part of the 20th century changed the small community's fortunes dramatically. By 1920 a local business almanac listed 500 oil companies, and living space was so scarce that cots were rented on a sleeping-time rate. Modern Wichita Falls is a diversified industrial center based on its agricultural and petroleum past.

For lovers of the outdoors, nearby Lake Arrowhead, with its distinctive oil derricks, offers a variety of recreational opportunities (see Recreation Chart and the AAA South Central CampBook).

Wichita Falls' residents are ardent supporters of the arts. The city boasts a symphony orchestra, a ballet and theater companies.

Wichita Falls Convention and Visitors Bureau: 1000 Fifth St., P.O. Box 630, Wichita Falls, TX 76307-0630; phone (940) 716-5500 or (800) 799-6732.

WICHITA FALLS MUSEUM AND ART CENTER is off I-281 S. and SR 79, then 3 mi. w. on Midwestern Pkwy. to 2 Eureka Cir., adjoining Midwestern State University. In addition to permanent displays about art, history and science, there are changing art exhibits and a planetarium. Allow 30 minutes minimum. Museum Tues.-Fri. 9:30-4:30 (also Thurs. 4:30-7:30), Sat. 10:30-4:30; closed holidays. Planetarium shows Thurs. at 7 and Sat. at 1:30. Laser shows Sat. at 3. Museum admission $4; over 60 and military with ID $3.50; ages 4-11, $3. An additional fee is charged for special events. Planetarium shows $2. Laser show $3. Phone (940) 692-0923.

WOODVILLE (E-11) pop. 2,415, elev. 281'

Named for George T. Wood, the second governor of Texas, Woodville is a major commercial center for lumbering and forest products.

Tyler County Chamber of Commerce: 717 W. Bluff, Woodville, TX 75979; phone (409) 283-2632.

ALLAN SHIVERS MUSEUM is 1 blk. w. of US 69 and 2 blks. n. of US 190, at 302 N. Charlton St. The museum, in a restored Victorian house, displays mementos of the family of Allan Shivers, governor of Texas 1949-57. Allow 30 minutes minimum. Mon.-Fri. 9-5, Sat. 10-2; closed holidays. Last tour departs 30 minutes before closing. Admission $1; ages 5-17, 50c. Phone (409) 283-3709.

HERITAGE VILLAGE MUSEUM is 1.5 mi. w. on US 190. A living-history museum, the village offers a glimpse of life in a rural Texas farm community. Buildings on the property include a saloon, a railroad depot, blacksmith and apothecary shops, physician's and lawyer's offices, an old-fashioned water pump and a schoolhouse. An East Texas model railroad and a nature trail also are on the grounds. Guided tours are available by reservation. Picnicking is permitted. Food is available.

Allow 30 minutes minimum. Mon.-Sat. 9-5, Sun. 10-5; closed Jan. 1, Easter, Thanksgiving and Dec. 25 and 31. Admission $4; over 55, $3; under 12, $2. DS, MC, VI. Phone (409) 283-2272.

Fairytale Destinations.

Trust AAA to take you there.

Storybook lands. Magical worlds.

Enchanted voyages to paradise.

Whatever your dream,

there's a Disney vacation for you.

And when you book select vacation

packages through AAA Travel, you

can enjoy exclusive benefits

and great values.

Your fairytale is just a phone call away.

Call or visit your local AAA Travel office today.

WALT DISNEY World®

Disneyland®
RESORT
IN CALIFORNIA

Ships' Registry: the Bahamas
As to Disney artwork, logos and properties: ©Disney K7888194

CST# 1022229-50

Save with Howard Johnson and AAA and have more fun with the kids!

SAVE 10-20%*

When you're looking for a vacation value that doesn't skimp on the fun, look to Howard Johnson.®

A better quality of life on the road.℠

1-800-I-GO-HOJO® or visit **howardjohnson.com,** and request **"SA3"** for your **AAA rate.**

Texas

AREA CODE CHANGE - Several cities in Texas will change their area code from 915 to 325 or 432. Permissive dialing begins April 5, 2003; mandatory dialing begins October 4, 2003. The individual listings in this publication reflect the new area code.

ABILENE pop. 115,930

------ WHERE TO STAY ------

ANTILLEY INN
Phone: (325)695-3330
▼▼ ◆◆
Motel
All Year   1P: $50-$53   2P: $55-$57   XP: $5   F12
Location: US 83/84, exit Antilley Rd. Located next to Abilene Medical Center. 6550 S Hwy 83 79606.
Fax: 325/695-9872. **Facility:** 52 one-bedroom standard units. 2 stories (no elevator), exterior corridors.
Parking: on-site. **Terms:** [CP] meal plan available, pets ($5-$10 extra charge). **Amenities:** hair dryers.
Pool(s): outdoor. **Guest Services:** coin laundry. **Business Services:** fax (fee). **Cards:** AX, DS, MC, VI.

SOME UNITS

BEST WESTERN ABILENE INN & SUITES
Phone: (325)672-5501
SAVE
▼◆◆◆▼
Motel
All Year [ECP]   1P: $79-$89   2P: $89-$99   XP: $10   F14
Location: I-20, exit 286C, just n. 350 I-20 W 79601. Fax: 325/672-5125. **Facility:** 60 one-bedroom standard units. 2 stories, interior corridors. *Bath:* combo or shower only. **Parking:** on-site. **Terms:** pets ($15 fee).
Amenities: voice mail, irons, hair dryers. **Pool(s):** outdoor. **Leisure Activities:** exercise room. **Guest Services:** coin laundry. **Business Services:** meeting rooms, business center. **Cards:** AX, DC, DS, MC, VI.

SOME UNITS

BEST WESTERN MALL SOUTH
Phone: (325)695-1262
◆◆◆ SAVE
▼◆ ◆▼
Motel
All Year [CP]   1P: $75-$81   2P: $75-$86   XP: $5   F12
Location: Just s of US 83/84, exit Ridgemont Dr. Located adjacent to Abilene Mall. 3950 Ridgemont Dr 79606. Fax: 325/695-2593. **Facility:** 61 one-bedroom standard units. 2 stories (no elevator), exterior corridors. *Bath:* combo or shower only. **Parking:** on-site. **Terms:** 14 day cancellation notice, [ECP] meal plan available, small pets only. **Amenities:** irons, hair dryers. **Pool(s):** outdoor. **Leisure Activities:** whirlpool. **Guest Services:** valet laundry, airport transportation-Abilene Airport, area transportation-within 5 mi. **Business Services:** meeting rooms, fax (fee). **Cards:** AX, CB, DC, DS, MC, VI. **Special Amenities:** free continental breakfast and free newspaper.

SOME UNITS

BUDGET HOST COLONIAL INN
Phone: (325)677-2683
◆◆◆ SAVE
▼◆ ◆▼
Motel
All Year   1P: $32-$39   2P: $35-$40   XP: $5   F11
Location: Jct I-20 and US 83 business route, exit 286A. 3210 Pine St 79601. Fax: 325/677-8211. **Facility:** 98 one-bedroom standard units. 1 story, interior/exterior corridors. **Parking:** on-site. **Terms:** pets ($5 extra charge). **Amenities:** *Some:* hair dryers. **Pool(s):** outdoor, wading. **Guest Services:** airport transportation-Abilene Airport, area transportation-within 5 mi. **Business Services:** meeting rooms, fax (fee). **Cards:** AX, DC, DS, MC, VI. **Special Amenities:** free continental breakfast and free local telephone calls.
(See color ad below)

SOME UNITS

COMFORT SUITES
Phone: (325)795-8500
◆◆◆ SAVE
▼◆◆◆▼
Small-scale Hotel
All Year [ECP]   1P: $79-$124   2P: $84-$129   XP: $5   F16
Location: I-20, exit 279, s on US 83/84/277 to Southwest Dr, then just e. 3165 S Danville Dr 79606. Fax: 325/795-8507. **Facility:** 50 one-bedroom standard units. 3 stories, interior corridors. *Bath:* combo or shower only. **Parking:** on-site. **Terms:** small pets only ($30 fee). **Amenities:** high-speed Internet, dual phone lines, voice mail, irons, hair dryers. **Pool(s):** small heated outdoor. **Leisure Activities:** whirlpool, limited exercise equipment. **Guest Services:** valet and coin laundry. **Business Services:** meeting rooms, business center. **Cards:** AX, CB, DC, DS, MC, VI. **Special Amenities:** free local telephone calls and free newspaper.

SOME UNITS

COURTYARD BY MARRIOTT

AAA **SAVE**
▼▼▼▼

Small-scale Hotel

Phone: (325)695-9600

All Year   1P: $79-$125   2P: $79-$125
Location: I-20, exit 283A, 4.5 mi s on US 83/84. 4350 Ridgemont Dr 79606. Fax: 325/695-0250. **Facility:** 99 units. 97 one-bedroom standard units, some with whirlpools. 2 one-bedroom suites. 3 stories, interior corridors. *Bath:* combo or shower only. **Parking:** on-site. **Terms:** [BP] meal plan available. **Amenities:** video games (fee), voice mail, irons, hair dryers. **Dining:** 6:30-10 am, Sat & Sun 7-11 am. **Pool(s):** heated indoor. **Leisure Activities:** whirlpool, exercise room. **Business Services:** meeting rooms, fax (fee). **Cards:** AX, CB, DC, DS, MC, VI.

SOME UNITS

DAYS INN

SAVE
▼▼
Motel

Phone: (325)672-6433

All Year [CP]   1P: $48-$55   2P: $55-$60   XP: $5   F15
Location: I-20, exit 288. 1702 E Hwy 80 79601. Fax: 325/676-9312. **Facility:** 99 one-bedroom standard units. 2 stories (no elevator), exterior corridors. **Parking:** on-site. **Terms:** small pets only ($10 extra charge). **Amenities:** voice mail, hair dryers. **Pool(s):** small outdoor. **Guest Services:** valet and coin laundry. **Business Services:** fax (fee). **Cards:** AX, DC, DS, MC, VI.

SOME UNITS

ECONO LODGE

AAA **SAVE**
▼▼
Motel

Phone: (325)673-5424

All Year   1P: $40-$45   2P: $45-$55   XP: $5   F12
Location: S Frontage Rd off I-20 and US 80, exit 285 eastbound; exit 286A westbound. 1633 W Stamford 79601. Fax: 325/673-0412. **Facility:** 34 one-bedroom standard units. 1 story, exterior corridors. **Parking:** on-site. **Terms:** [CP] meal plan available, small pets only ($10 deposit). **Amenities:** hair dryers. **Business Services:** fax (fee). **Cards:** AX, CB, DC, MC, VI. **Special Amenities:** early check-in/late check-out and free local telephone calls.

SOME UNITS

EMBASSY SUITES HOTEL

SAVE
▼▼▼▼
Small-scale Hotel

Phone: (325)698-1234

All Year [BP]   1P: $99-$104   2P: $104-$109   XP: $5   F18
Location: 0.3 mi s of US 83/84, exit Ridgemont Dr. Located adjacent to Abilene Mall. 4250 Ridgemont Dr 79606. Fax: 325/698-2771. **Facility:** 176 one-bedroom suites, some with whirlpools. 3 stories, interior/exterior corridors. **Parking:** on-site. **Terms:** [AP] meal plan available, package plans, 16% service charge, small pets only ($25 fee). **Amenities:** video games (fee), voice mail, irons, hair dryers. **Pool(s):** heated indoor. **Leisure Activities:** sauna, whirlpool, steamroom. **Guest Services:** complimentary evening beverages, valet and coin laundry. **Business Services:** conference facilities, fax (fee). **Cards:** AX, CB, DC, DS, JC, MC, VI.

SOME UNITS

EXECUTIVE INN

▼▼
Motel

Phone: 325/677-2200

All Year   1P: $35-$225   2P: $60-$270   XP: $5   F12
Location: I-20, exit 288. 1650 I-20 E 79601. Fax: 325/677-0472. **Facility:** 41 one-bedroom standard units. 2 stories (no elevator), exterior corridors. **Parking:** on-site. **Terms:** weekly rates available, [CP] meal plan available. **Amenities:** *Some:* irons. **Pool(s):** outdoor. **Business Services:** fax (fee). **Cards:** AX, DS, MC, VI.

SOME UNITS

FAIRFIELD INN

SAVE
▼▼▼▼
Small-scale Hotel

Phone: (325)695-2448

All Year [ECP]   1P: $65-$85   2P: $65-$95   XP: $6   F18
Location: Just s of US 83/84, exit Ridgemont Dr. 3902 Turner Plaza 79606. Fax: 325/695-2448. **Facility:** 73 one-bedroom standard units. 4 stories, interior corridors. *Bath:* combo or shower only. **Parking:** on-site. **Terms:** 14 day cancellation notice. **Amenities:** irons. **Pool(s):** small heated indoor. **Leisure Activities:** whirlpool. **Guest Services:** valet laundry. **Business Services:** meeting rooms, fax (fee). **Cards:** AX, CB, DC, DS, MC, VI.

SOME UNITS

HAMPTON INN

SAVE
▼▼▼▼
Small-scale Hotel

Phone: (325)695-0044

All Year [ECP]   1P: $59-$79   2P: $59-$89   XP: $6   F18
Location: I-20, exit 283A, 5 mi s to exit Curry Ln. 3917 Ridgemont Dr 79606. Fax: 325/695-4192. **Facility:** 64 one-bedroom standard units. 4 stories, interior corridors. *Bath:* combo or shower only. **Parking:** on-site. **Terms:** 14 day cancellation notice. **Amenities:** voice mail, irons. **Pool(s):** heated indoor. **Leisure Activities:** whirlpool. **Guest Services:** valet laundry. **Business Services:** fax (fee). **Cards:** AX, CB, DC, DS, MC, VI.

SOME UNITS

HOLIDAY INN EXPRESS AND SUITES

▼▼▼▼
Small-scale Hotel

Phone: (325)675-9800

2/15-9/30 [ECP]   1P: $89-$99   2P: $94-$104   XP: $5   F19
2/1-2/14 & 10/1-1/31 [ECP]   1P: $79-$89   2P: $84-$94   XP: $5   F19
Location: I-20, exit 288, on westbound frontage road. 1802 E I-20 79601. Fax: 325/675-9810. **Facility:** 65 one-bedroom standard units. 3 stories, interior corridors. *Bath:* combo or shower only. **Parking:** on-site. **Amenities:** high-speed Internet, voice mail, irons, hair dryers. **Pool(s):** small outdoor. **Leisure Activities:** exercise room. **Guest Services:** valet and coin laundry. **Business Services:** meeting rooms, business center. **Cards:** AX, CB, DC, DS, JC, MC, VI.

SOME UNITS

LA QUINTA INN-ABILENE

SAVE
▼▼▼▼
Small-scale Hotel

Phone: (325)676-1676

All Year   1P: $69-$84   2P: $79-$94   XP: $10   F18
Location: I-20, exit 286C. 3501 W Lake Rd 79601-1909. Fax: 325/672-8323. **Facility:** 106 units. 104 one-bedroom standard units. 2 one-bedroom suites. 2 stories (no elevator), exterior corridors. **Parking:** on-site. **Terms:** [ECP] meal plan available, small pets only. **Amenities:** video games (fee), voice mail, irons, hair dryers. **Pool(s):** outdoor. **Business Services:** fax. **Cards:** AX, CB, DC, DS, JC, MC, VI.

SOME UNITS

QUALITY INN CIVIC CENTER
Phone: (325)676-0222

(AAA) [SAVE] All Year [BP]   1P: $49-$69   2P: $59-$79   XP: $10   F15
Location: Downtown. 505 Pine St 79601. Fax: 325/676-0513. **Facility:** 116 units. 115 one-bedroom standard units. 1 one-bedroom suite ($110-$135). 2 stories (no elevator), exterior corridors. **Parking:** on-site. **Terms:** pets ($10 fee). **Amenities:** *Some:* irons, hair dryers. **Dining:** 6 am-2 pm, cocktails. **Pool(s):** outdoor.
Small-scale Hotel **Guest Services:** valet and coin laundry, airport transportation-Abilene Airport. **Business Services:** meeting rooms, fax (fee). **Cards:** AX, CB, DC, DS, MC, VI.

SOME UNITS

RAMADA INN
Phone: (325)695-7700

All Year   1P: $52-$61   2P: $57-$66   XP: $5   F17
Location: 5 mi sw on US 83/84, exit Southwest Dr. 3450 S Clack St 79606. Fax: 325/698-0546. **Facility:** 145 one-
Small-scale Hotel bedroom standard units. 2 stories (no elevator), interior corridors. **Terms:** [ECP] meal plan available, pets ($15 fee). **Amenities:** voice mail, hair dryers. *Some:* irons. **Pool(s):** outdoor. **Leisure Activi-**ties: whirlpool. **Guest Services:** valet and coin laundry, area transportation. **Business Services:** meeting rooms, fax (fee). **Cards:** AX, CB, DC, DS, MC, VI.

SOME UNITS

SUPER 8 MOTEL
Phone: (325)673-5251

All Year [ECP]   1P: $45-$55   2P: $55-$65   XP: $6   F16
Location: I-20, exit 288. 1525 E I-20 79601. Fax: 325/673-5314. **Facility:** 97 one-bedroom standard units. 2 sto-ries (no elevator), exterior corridors. **Parking:** on-site. **Terms:** 7 day cancellation notice, pets ($5 extra
Motel charge). **Amenities:** hair dryers. **Pool(s):** outdoor. **Guest Services:** coin laundry. **Business Services:** meeting rooms, fax (fee). **Cards:** AX, CB, DC, DS, JC, MC, VI.

SOME UNITS

WHITTEN INN UNIVERSITY
Phone: 325/673-5271

Property failed to provide current rates
Location: I-20, exit 288. 1625 SR 351 79601. Fax: 325/673-8240. **Facility:** 163 one-bedroom standard units, some with whirlpools. 2 stories (no elevator), exterior corridors. *Bath:* combo or shower only. **Parking:** on-
Small-scale Hotel site. **Terms:** pets ($10 fee). **Amenities:** voice mail, irons, hair dryers. **Pool(s):** outdoor. **Guest Services:** valet and coin laundry, area transportation. **Business Services:** meeting rooms, fax (fee). **Cards:** AX, CB, DC, DS, MC, VI.

SOME UNITS

——— WHERE TO DINE ———

OXFORD STREET RESTAURANT   **Lunch:** $6-$17   **Dinner:** $9-$17   **Phone:** 325/695-1770
Location: West frontage road off US 83/84/277 S, exit S 14th St. 1882 S Clack St 79605. **Hours:** 11 am-9 pm,
Fri-10 pm, Sat 5 pm-10 pm. Closed: 12/25. **Reservations:** suggested. **Features:** Prime rib is the specialty at the dimly lit English pub, which also serves American fare, including chicken and fish. Wooden tables
American and chairs fill the small dining rooms. The salad bar offers such items as pickled carrots. Casual dress;
cocktails. **Parking:** on-site. **Cards:** AX, DC, DS, MC, VI.

ADDISON —See Dallas p. 285.

ALLEN —See Dallas p. 288.

ALPINE pop. 5,786

——— WHERE TO STAY ———

OAK TREE INN
Phone: (432)837-5711

(AAA) [SAVE] 2/1-4/30   1P: $69-$74   2P: $72-$79   XP: $5   F13
   5/1-11/30   1P: $72   2P: $72   XP: $5   F13
   12/1-1/31   1P: $69   2P: $69   XP: $5   F13
Location: US 90, 2 mi e. 2407 E Holland (Hwy 90/67) 79830 (8110 E 32nd St N, Suite 100, WICHITA, KS, 67226).
Small-scale Hotel Fax: 432/837-0017. **Facility:** 40 one-bedroom standard units. 2 stories (no elevator), interior corridors. *Bath:* combo or shower only. **Parking:** on-site. **Terms:** cancellation fee imposed, pets ($5 extra charge). **Leisure Activities:** whirlpool, exercise room. **Guest Services:** coin laundry. **Business Services:** meeting rooms, fax (fee). **Cards:** AX, DC, DS, JC, MC, VI. **Special Amenities:** early check-in/late check-out and free local telephone calls.

SOME UNITS

RAMADA LIMITED
Phone: 432/837-1100

(AAA) [SAVE] All Year [ECP]   1P: $80-$90   2P: $85-$95   XP: $5   F17
Location: US 90, 2 mi n. 2800 W Hwy 90 79830 (PO Box 907, 79831). Fax: 432/837-7032. **Facility:** 61 one-bedroom standard units. 2 stories (no elevator), interior corridors. *Bath:* combo or shower only. **Parking:** on-site. **Terms:** cancellation fee imposed, pets ($20 deposit). **Amenities:** voice mail, irons, hair dryers. **Leisure**
Small-scale Hotel **Activities:** whirlpool. **Guest Services:** coin laundry. **Business Services:** meeting rooms, fax (fee). **Cards:** AX, CB, DC, DS, MC, VI. **Special Amenities:** free continental breakfast and free local telephone
calls.

SOME UNITS

——— WHERE TO DINE ———

ORIENTAL EXPRESS   **Lunch:** $6   **Dinner:** $4-$10   **Phone:** 432/837-1159
Location: US 90, 2 mi w. 3000 A W Hwy 90 79830. **Hours:** 11 am-9 pm. Closed: 11/27, 12/25; also Sun.
Reservations: accepted. **Features:** Patrons can choose from either spicy or sweet-and-sour traditional
Chinese dinners. Casual dress; beer & wine only. **Parking:** on-site. **Cards:** AX, DC, DS, MC, VI.

REATA

Tex-Mex

Lunch: $5-$7   **Dinner:** $10-$28   **Phone:** 432/837-9232
Location: US 290, just n. 203 N 5th St 79830. **Hours:** 11:30 am-2 & 5-10 pm. Closed: 11/27, 12/25; also Sun.
Features: The menu lists such choices as beef, seafood and Mexican entrees. Food is moderately priced and prepared with fresh ingredients. Casual dress. **Parking:** street. **Cards:** AX, MC, VI.   🍽 ✕

ALVIN pop. 21,413

―――――― WHERE TO STAY ――――――

COUNTRY HEARTH INN
▼▼▼
Motel

All Year [CP]   1P: $52   2P: $59   XP: $4   F17   **Phone:** (281)331-0335
Location: CR 35 Bypass, 0.5 mi sw of SR 6. Located in a commercial area. 1588 S Hwy 35 Bypass 77511.
Fax: 281/585-3352. **Facility:** 40 one-bedroom standard units. 2 stories, exterior corridors. **Parking:** on-site.
Terms: small pets only. **Pool(s):** outdoor. **Guest Services:** complimentary evening beverages, coin laundry.
Business Services: fax (fee). **Cards:** AX, DC, DS, MC, VI.

SOME UNITS
(ASK) 🛏 🐾 💻 / ✕ 📱 🖥 /

―――――― WHERE TO DINE ――――――

JOE'S BARBEQUE COMPANY
▼
Barbecue

Lunch: $4-$9   **Dinner:** $4-$13   **Phone:** 281/331-9626
Location: Just e of jct SR 35 and 6. 1400 E Hwy 6 77511. **Hours:** 11 am-10 pm, Fri & Sat-11 pm. Closed: 4/20,
11/27, 12/25. **Features:** On the edge of town, this restaurant accommodates crowds of people with large,
shade trees and a huge parking lot. Texas barbecue is at the heart of a menu that also includes
hamburgers and po'boys. While someone may be available to fill tea glasses before they go dry, service is
mostly of the fast-paced counter variety. Smoke free premises. Casual dress; beer only. **Parking:** on-site. **Cards:** AX, DC, DS,
MC, VI.
✕

AMARILLO pop. 173,627

―――――― WHERE TO STAY ――――――

AMBASSADOR HOTEL
(AAA) (SAVE)
▼▼▼▼
Small-scale Hotel

All Year   1P: $109-$179   2P: $109-$179   **Phone:** (806)358-6161
Location: I-40, exit 68, just w on north frontage road. 3100 I-40 W 79102. Fax: 806/358-9869. **Facility:** 265 units.
263 one-bedroom standard units. 2 two-bedroom suites ($329-$479). 10 stories, interior corridors. **Parking:**
on-site. **Terms:** pets ($15 extra charge). **Amenities:** video games, voice mail, irons, hair dryers. *Some:* honor
bars. **Dining:** 2 restaurants, 6:30 am-midnight, cocktails. **Pool(s):** heated indoor. **Leisure Activities:** whirlpool, exercise room. **Fee:** massage. **Guest Services:** gift shop, valet laundry, airport transportation-Amarillo
Airport, area transportation-within 6 mi. **Business Services:** meeting rooms, fax (fee). **Cards:** AX, CB, DC, DS, JC, MC, VI.
Special Amenities: early check-in/late check-out and free local telephone calls.

SOME UNITS
🛏 🍴 24 🍽 🐾 ✕ 💻 / ✕ VCR 📱
FEE FEE

BEST WESTERN AMARILLO INN
(AAA) (SAVE)
▼▼▼
Motel

6/1-8/31	1P: $72-$82	2P: $72-$82
9/1-12/31	1P: $62-$72	2P: $62-$72
2/1-5/31 & 1/1-1/31	1P: $62	2P: $62

Phone: (806)358-7861
Location: I-40, exit 65 (Coulter Dr), 0.6 mi n. Located adjacent to Amarillo Medical Center. 1610 Coulter Dr 79106.
Fax: 806/352-7287. **Facility:** 103 units. 98 one-bedroom standard units. 5 one-bedroom suites ($89-$99). 2
stories (no elevator), interior/exterior corridors. **Bath:** combo or shower only. **Parking:** on-site. **Terms:** 30 day
cancellation notice-fee imposed, [BP] meal plan available, package plans, small pets only ($10 extra charge). **Amenities:** voice
mail, hair dryers. **Dining:** 6:30 am-10 & 5-9 pm. **Pool(s):** heated indoor. **Leisure Activities:** whirlpool. **Guest Services:** coin
laundry. **Business Services:** meeting rooms, fax (fee). **Cards:** AX, DC, DS, MC, VI. **Special Amenities:** free newspaper.
(See color ad below)

SOME UNITS
🛏 🍴 ⚙ 🐾 🦽 ✕ 💻 / ✕ 📱 🖥 /

BEST WESTERN SANTA FE INN
Phone: (806)372-1885

AAA SAVE

5/1-8/31	1P: $75-$85	2P: $95-$105	XP: $7 F15
2/1-4/30 & 9/1-1/31	1P: $70-$76	2P: $76-$82	XP: $7 F15

Motel

Location: I-40, exit 73 (Eastern St) eastbound; exit 73 (Bolton St) westbound, U-turn on south frontage road. 4600 I-40 E 79103. Fax: 806/372-5384. **Facility:** 57 one-bedroom standard units. 2 stories (no elevator), interior corridors. **Parking:** on-site. **Terms:** [ECP] meal plan available, small pets only ($35 deposit). **Amenities:** voice mail, irons, hair dryers. **Pool(s):** heated outdoor. **Business Services:** fax (fee). **Cards:** AX, CB, DC, DS, MC, VI. **Special Amenities:** free continental breakfast and free newspaper.

SOME UNITS

CLARION HOTEL
Phone: (806)373-3303

SAVE

All Year	1P: $75-$225

Motel

Location: I-40, exit 75 (Lakeside Dr), just nw. 7909 I-40 E 79118-6912. Fax: 806/373-3353. **Facility:** 206 units. 204 one-bedroom standard units. 2 one- and 1 two-bedroom suites ($150-$225), some with whirlpools. 2 stories, interior corridors. **Parking:** on-site. **Terms:** pets ($100 deposit). **Amenities:** dual phone lines, voice mail, irons, hair dryers. **Pool(s):** heated indoor. **Leisure Activities:** exercise room. *Fee:* game room. **Guest Services:** valet laundry, area transportation. **Business Services:** conference facilities, fax (fee). **Cards:** AX, CB, DC, DS, MC, VI.

SOME UNITS

COMFORT INN & SUITES-AMARILLO
Phone: 806/457-9100

SAVE

All Year [ECP]	1P: $79-$149	2P: $89-$179

Motel

Location: I-40, exit 64, just w. 2300 Soncy Rd 79121. Fax: 806/457-9101. **Facility:** 71 one-bedroom standard units, some with whirlpools. 3 stories, interior corridors. **Parking:** on-site. **Amenities:** high-speed Internet, dual phone lines, voice mail, irons, hair dryers. **Pool(s):** heated indoor. **Leisure Activities:** whirlpool, limited exercise equipment. **Guest Services:** coin laundry. **Business Services:** meeting rooms, business center. **Cards:** AX, DS, MC, VI.

SOME UNITS
VCR FEE

COMFORT INN-EAST
Phone: (806)376-9993

AAA SAVE

All Year [CP]	1P: $59-$99	2P: $59-$99	XP: $5 F18

Motel

Location: I-40, exit 71 (Ross-Osage), just w on north frontage road. 1515 I-40 E 79102. Fax: 806/373-5343. **Facility:** 112 one-bedroom standard units. 2 stories (no elevator), exterior corridors. **Parking:** on-site. **Terms:** small pets only ($10 fee). **Amenities:** hair dryers. *Some:* irons. **Pool(s):** outdoor. **Leisure Activities:** whirlpool. **Guest Services:** valet laundry. **Business Services:** fax (fee). **Cards:** AX, CB, DC, DS, MC, VI. **Special Amenities:** early check-in/late check-out and free continental breakfast.

SOME UNITS

COMFORT SUITES
Phone: (806)352-8300

AAA SAVE

6/1-8/31	1P: $129	2P: $129	XP: $10 F17
2/1-5/31 & 9/1-1/31	1P: $79-$89	2P: $89-$99	XP: $10 F17

Motel

Location: I-40, exit 68A (Paramount St), just s. 2103 Lakeview Dr 79109. Fax: 806/359-3616. **Facility:** 50 one-bedroom standard units, some with whirlpools. 2 stories (no elevator), interior corridors. *Bath:* combo or shower only. **Parking:** on-site. **Amenities:** irons, hair dryers. **Pool(s):** heated indoor. **Guest Services:** valet and coin laundry. **Business Services:** meeting rooms, fax (fee). **Cards:** AX, CB, DC, DS, JC, MC, VI. **Special Amenities:** free continental breakfast and free local telephone calls.

SOME UNITS

DAYS INN
Phone: (806)359-9393

AAA SAVE

6/1-8/31	1P: $79-$99	2P: $89-$119	XP: $10 F12
9/1-1/31	1P: $59-$79	2P: $69-$89	XP: $10 F12
3/1-5/31	1P: $59-$69	2P: $69-$79	XP: $10 F12
2/1-2/28	1P: $49-$59	2P: $59-$69	XP: $10 F12

Motel

Location: I-40, exit 65 (Coulter Dr), just n. 2102 S Coulter Dr 79106. Fax: 806/359-9450. **Facility:** 50 one-bedroom standard units. 2 stories (no elevator), exterior corridors. *Bath:* combo or shower only. **Parking:** on-site, winter plug-ins. **Terms:** cancellation fee imposed, [ECP] meal plan available. **Amenities:** safes (fee), hair dryers. *Some:* irons. **Pool(s):** heated indoor. **Leisure Activities:** whirlpool, limited exercise equipment. **Guest Services:** coin laundry. **Business Services:** fax (fee). **Cards:** AX, DC, DS, MC, VI. **Special Amenities:** free continental breakfast and free newspaper.

SOME UNITS

DAYS INN
Phone: (806)379-6255

AAA SAVE

All Year	1P: $49-$99	2P: $49-$99	XP: $5 F17

Small-scale Hotel

Location: I-40, exit 71 (Ross-Osage), just w on north frontage road. 1701 I-40 E 79102. Fax: 806/379-8204. **Facility:** 119 one-bedroom standard units. 5 stories, interior corridors. **Parking:** on-site. **Terms:** 14 day cancellation notice, [ECP] meal plan available, small pets only ($10 fee). **Amenities:** irons, hair dryers. **Pool(s):** heated outdoor. **Guest Services:** valet laundry, area transportation-within 5 mi. **Business Services:** meeting rooms, fax (fee). **Cards:** AX, CB, DC, DS, JC, MC, VI. **Special Amenities:** free continental breakfast and free newspaper.

SOME UNITS

DAYS INN SOUTH
Phone: (806)468-7100

SAVE

5/1-8/31 [CP]	1P: $59-$69	2P: $79-$89	XP: $5 F13
2/1-4/30 & 9/1-1/31 [CP]	1P: $50-$60	2P: $65-$75	XP: $5 F13

Motel

Location: I-27, exit 116, just n on east service road. 8601 Canyon Dr 79110. Fax: 806/468-7365. **Facility:** 63 one-bedroom standard units. 2 stories (no elevator), interior corridors. *Bath:* combo or shower only. **Parking:** on-site. **Terms:** small pets only ($20 fee). **Amenities:** dual phone lines, hair dryers. **Pool(s):** small heated indoor. **Leisure Activities:** whirlpool, exercise room. **Guest Services:** coin laundry. **Business Services:** meeting rooms, fax (fee). **Cards:** AX, CB, DC, DS, MC, VI.

SOME UNITS

FAIRFIELD INN-AMARILLO

SAVE

▽▽◇▽▽
Motel

Phone: (806)351-0172

6/1-8/31 [ECP]	1P: $85-$105	2P: $85-$115 · XP: $6 F18
2/1-5/31 & 9/1-1/31 [ECP]	1P: $69-$89	2P: $69-$99 XP: $6 F18

Location: I-40, exit 66 (Bell St), 0.5 mi w on north service road. 6600 I-40 W 79106. **Fax:** 806/351-0172. **Facility:** 76 one-bedroom standard units. 3 stories, interior corridors. *Bath:* combo or shower only. **Parking:** on-site. **Terms:** 14 day cancellation notice. **Amenities:** voice mail, irons. **Pool(s):** small heated indoor. **Leisure Activities:** whirlpool. **Guest Services:** valet laundry. **Business Services:** fax (fee). **Cards:** AX, CB, DC, DS, MC, VI.

SOME UNITS

(S̲D̲) (🍴) (⌖M) (🔲) (📶) (🛒) (📞) (📷) (DATA PORT) / (✕) (🔒) (🖥) (📺) /

HAMPTON INN

(AAA) SAVE

▽▽◇▽▽
Motel

Phone: (806)372-1425

5/30-8/9 [ECP]	1P: $69-$109	2P: $69-$109
2/1-5/29 & 8/10-1/31 [ECP]	1P: $49-$89	2P: $49-$89

Location: I-40, exit 71 (Ross-Osage), just e on south frontage road. 1700 I-40 E 79103. **Fax:** 806/379-8807. **Facility:** 116 one-bedroom standard units. 2 stories (no elevator), interior corridors. **Parking:** on-site. **Terms:** cancellation fee imposed. **Amenities:** video games (fee), irons. **Pool(s):** outdoor. **Guest Services:** valet laundry. **Business Services:** meeting rooms, fax (fee). **Cards:** AX, CB, DC, DS, MC, VI. **Special Amenities:** free continental breakfast and free newspaper.

SOME UNITS

(S̲D̲) (🛏) (🍴) (📶) (🛒) (📞) (📷) (DATA PORT) (🖥) / (✕) (🔒) (🖥) /

HOLIDAY INN EXPRESS

▽▽◇▽▽
Motel

Phone: (806)356-6800

All Year [CP]	1P: $79-$129	XP: $5

Location: I-40, exit 67, 0.3 mi e on south frontage road. 3411 I-40 W 79109. **Fax:** 806/356-0401. **Facility:** 97 units. 95 one-bedroom standard units. 2 one-bedroom suites with whirlpools. 2 stories (no elevator), interior corridors. **Parking:** on-site. **Amenities:** voice mail, irons, hair dryers. **Pool(s):** heated outdoor. **Leisure Activities:** exercise room. **Guest Services:** valet laundry. **Business Services:** meeting rooms, fax (fee). **Cards:** AX, CB, DC, DS, JC, MC, VI.

SOME UNITS

(ASK) (S̲D̲) (🍴) (📶) (🛒) (📷) (DATA PORT) (🖥) / (✕) (🔒) (🖥) /

HOLIDAY INN-I-40

▽▽◇▽▽
Motel

Phone: (806)372-8741

All Year	1P: $89-$129	2P: $89-$129

Location: I-40, exit 71 (Ross-Osage), on north frontage road. 1911 I-40 at Ross-Osage 79102. **Fax:** 806/372-2913. **Facility:** 248 one-bedroom standard units. 4 stories, interior corridors. *Bath:* combo or shower only. **Parking:** on-site. **Amenities:** voice mail, irons, hair dryers. **Pool(s):** heated indoor, wading. **Leisure Activities:** whirlpool, limited exercise equipment. **Guest Services:** valet and coin laundry. **Business Services:** meeting rooms, fax (fee). **Cards:** AX, CB, DC, DS, JC, MC, VI. *(See color ad below)*

SOME UNITS

(ASK) (S̲D̲) (✈) (🍴) (🍸) (⌖) (📶) (🛒) (📷) (DATA PORT) (🖥) / (✕) (🔒) /
FEE

LA QUINTA INN-AMARILLO-MEDICAL CENTER

(AAA) SAVE

▽▽◇▽▽
Motel

Phone: (806)352-6311

All Year	1P: $65-$85	2P: $71-$91

Location: I-40, exit 65 (Coulter Dr), just n. 2108 S Coulter St 79106. **Fax:** 806/359-3179. **Facility:** 129 one-bedroom standard units. 3 stories, exterior corridors. **Parking:** on-site. **Terms:** [ECP] meal plan available, small pets only. **Amenities:** voice mail, irons, hair dryers. **Pool(s):** heated outdoor. **Guest Services:** valet and coin laundry. **Business Services:** fax (fee). **Cards:** AX, CB, DC, DS, JC, MC, VI. **Special Amenities:** free continental breakfast and free local telephone calls.

SOME UNITS

(🛏) (🍴) (⌖M) (📶) (🛒) (📷) (DATA PORT) (🖥) / (✕) (🔒) (🖥) /

LA QUINTA INN EAST-AMARILLO
Phone: (806)373-7486
All Year   1P: $69-$89   2P: $75-$95
AAA SAVE **Location:** I-40, exit 71 (Ross-Osage), just e on south frontage road. 1708 I-40 E 79103-2114. Fax: 806/372-4100. **Facility:** 130 units. 128 one-bedroom standard units. 2 one-bedroom suites. 2 stories (no elevator), exterior corridors. **Parking:** on-site. **Terms:** [ECP] meal plan available, small pets only. **Amenities:** video games (fee), voice mail, irons, hair dryers. **Pool(s):** heated outdoor. **Guest Services:** valet and coin laundry. **Business Services:** fax (fee). **Cards:** AX, CB, DC, DS, JC, MC, VI. **Special Amenities:** free continental breakfast and free local telephone calls.
Motel
SOME UNITS

MICROTEL INN & SUITES
Phone: (806)372-8373
AAA SAVE   5/19-9/8 [ECP]   1P: $88-$110   2P: $88-$110   XP: $6   F12
2/1-5/18 & 9/9-1/31 [ECP]   1P: $58-$88   2P: $58-$88   XP: $6   F12
Location: I-40, exit 71 (Ross-Osage), just n. 1501 S Ross St 79102. Fax: 806/379-8834. **Facility:** 46 one-bedroom standard units. 2 stories, interior corridors. *Bath:* combo or shower only. **Parking:** on-site. **Amenities:** irons, hair dryers. **Pool(s):** small heated indoor. **Leisure Activities:** whirlpool, limited exercise equipment. **Guest Services:** coin laundry. **Business Services:** meeting rooms, fax (fee). **Cards:** AX, CB, DC, DS, JC, MC, VI. **Special Amenities:** free continental breakfast and free local telephone calls.
Small-scale Hotel
SOME UNITS

MOTEL 6 CENTRAL #72
Phone: 806/355-6554
All Year   1P: $31-$41   2P: $37-$47   XP: $3   F17
Location: I-40, exit 68A (Paramount Blvd), just nw. 2032 Paramount Blvd 79109. Fax: 806/355-5317. **Facility:** 116 one-bedroom standard units. 2 stories (no elevator), exterior corridors. *Bath:* combo or shower only. **Parking:** on-site. **Terms:** small pets only. **Pool(s):** heated outdoor. **Guest Services:** coin laundry. **Business Services:** fax (fee). **Cards:** AX, CB, DC, DS, MC, VI.
Motel
SOME UNITS

QUALITY INN & SUITES
Phone: (806)335-1561
AAA SAVE   All Year [ECP]   1P: $89-$149   2P: $89-$149   XP: $10   F17
Location: I-40, exit 75 (Lakeside Dr/Loop 335), just n. 1803 Lakeside Dr 79120 (PO Box 30338). Fax: 806/335-1808. **Facility:** 102 units. 77 one-bedroom standard units. 25 one-bedroom suites ($99-$149) with kitchens. 3 stories (no elevator), interior/exterior corridors. *Bath:* combo or shower only. **Parking:** on-site. **Terms:** 7 day cancellation notice-fee imposed, pets ($10 extra charge). **Amenities:** voice mail, irons, hair dryers. *Some:* dual phone lines. **Pool(s):** outdoor. **Leisure Activities:** exercise room, sports court. **Guest Services:** valet and coin laundry. **Business Services:** business center. **Cards:** AX, CB, DC, DS, MC, VI. **Special Amenities:** free continental breakfast and free newspaper.
Motel
SOME UNITS

RAMADA LIMITED
Phone: (806)374-2020
AAA SAVE   All Year [CP]   1P: $46-$53   2P: $66-$73   XP: $7   F18
Location: I-40, exit 71 (Ross-Osage), e on south frontage road. 1620 I-40 E 79103. Fax: 806/374-7140. **Facility:** 114 one-bedroom standard units. 2 stories (no elevator), exterior corridors. **Parking:** on-site, winter plug-in. **Pool(s):** small heated outdoor. **Guest Services:** coin laundry. **Business Services:** fax (fee). **Cards:** AX, CB, DC, DS, MC, VI. **Special Amenities:** free local telephone calls and free newspaper.
(See color ad below)
Motel
SOME UNITS

RESIDENCE INN-AMARILLO
Phone: (806)354-2978
AAA SAVE   All Year [ECP]   1P: $134   2P: $134
Location: I-40, exit 66 (Bell St), 0.5 mi w on north frontage road. 6700 I-40 W 79106. Fax: 806/354-2978. **Facility:** 78 units. 66 one- and 12 two-bedroom standard units with efficiencies. 3 stories, interior corridors. *Bath:* combo or shower only. **Parking:** on-site. **Terms:** pets ($50-$100 fee). **Amenities:** voice mail, irons, hair dryers. **Pool(s):** heated indoor. **Leisure Activities:** whirlpool, exercise room, sports court. **Guest Services:** valet and coin laundry. **Business Services:** meeting rooms, fax (fee). **Cards:** AX, DC, DS, MC, VI.
Motel
SOME UNITS

SLEEP INN AMARILLO

AAA **SAVE**

Motel

Phone: (806)372-6200

5/16-8/31	1P: $65-$99	2P: $75-$125	XP: $10	F18
2/1-5/15	1P: $55-$79	2P: $65-$89	XP: $5	F18
9/1-1/31	1P: $51-$75	2P: $59-$85	XP: $5	F18

Location: I-40, exit 72A (Nelson), 0.3 mi w on north frontage road. 2401 I-40 E 79104. **Fax:** 806/372-6242. **Facility:** 55 one-bedroom standard units. 2 stories (no elevator), interior corridors. *Bath:* combo or shower only. **Parking:** on-site. **Terms:** [CP] meal plan available, small pets only ($10 extra charge). **Amenities:** irons, hair dryers. **Pool(s):** small heated indoor. **Leisure Activities:** whirlpool. **Guest Services:** valet laundry. **Business Services:** fax (fee). **Cards:** AX, CB, DC, DS, MC, VI. **Special Amenities:** free continental breakfast and free local telephone calls.

SOME UNITS

🅂🄳 🐾 🍴 ♿🛍 ⬛ 🌀 🏊 📷 📠 🔌 / ✕ 🖥 /

The following lodging was either not evaluated or did not meet AAA rating requirements but is listed for your information only.

BIG TEXAN MOTEL

AAA **SAVE**

fyi

Motel

Phone: 806/372-5000

5/16-8/31	1P: $50-$55	2P: $60-$65	XP: $5	F10
2/1-5/15 & 9/1-1/31	1P: $45	2P: $45	XP: $5	F10

Under major renovation, scheduled to be completed June 2002. **Last rated:** ▼▼ **Location:** I-40, exit 75 (Lakeside Dr), 0.3 mi w on north frontage road. 7701 I-40 E 79118 (PO Box 37000, 79120). **Fax:** 806/371-0099. **Facility:** 55 one-bedroom standard units. 2 stories (no elevator), exterior corridors. **Parking:** on-site. **Terms:** small pets only ($30 deposit). **Amenities:** video library (fee). **Dining:** Big Texan Steak Ranch, see separate listing. **Pool(s):** heated outdoor. **Guest Services:** coin laundry. **Cards:** AX, DC, DS, MC, VI. **Special Amenities:** free continental breakfast and free local telephone calls.

SOME UNITS

🅂🄳 🐾 🍴 🏊 📷 📠 / ✕ 🆅🅲🆁 🔌 /

FEE

——— WHERE TO DINE ———

BIG TEXAN STEAK RANCH

▼▼▼

Steak House

Lunch: $5-$13   **Dinner:** $7-$28   **Phone:** 806/372-6000

Location: I-40, exit 75 (Lakeside Dr), 0.3 mi w on north frontage road; next to Big Texan Motel. 7701 I-40 E 79104. **Hours:** 10:30 am-10:30 pm. **Features:** Saturated with Western style, the restaurant features servers dressed in cowboy hats and boots who deliver hearty beef, chicken and seafood entrees. Diners who can polish off the enormous, 72-ounce steak in an hour receive it free. Casual dress; cocktails. **Parking:** on-site. **Cards:** AX, CB, DC, DS, MC, VI.

♿ ✕

CACTUS GRILL & BAR

▼▼▼

American

Lunch: $6-$20   **Dinner:** $6-$20   **Phone:** 806/352-4190

Location: I-40, exit 68A (Paramount Blvd), just e on south frontage road. 2915 I-40 W 79109. **Hours:** 11 am-10 pm, Fri & Sat-11 pm. Closed: 11/27, 12/25. **Features:** Diners at the rustic restaurant get a true taste of Western-style dining. Many hamburger varieties are offered alongside selections of steak, baby back ribs and chicken, as well as some Mexican dishes. Casual dress; cocktails. **Parking:** on-site. **Cards:** AX, DC, DS, MC, VI.

♿ 🍸 ✕

CALICO COUNTY

▼▼

American

Lunch: $6-$8   **Dinner:** $8-$11   **Phone:** 806/358-7664

Location: I-40, exit 68A (Paramount Blvd), just s. 2410 Paramount Blvd 79109. **Hours:** 7 am-10 pm. Closed: 11/27, 12/25. **Features:** Known for its great customer service, the family restaurant makes everything from scratch. Piping-hot chicken pot pie has a flaky, savory crust. Sweet cinnamon rolls are a perfect accent. Smoke free premises. Casual dress; cocktails. **Parking:** on-site. **Cards:** AX, DS, MC, VI.

✕

CHINA STAR

▼▼▼

Chinese

Lunch: $6-$8   **Dinner:** $7-$10   **Phone:** 806/359-4300

Location: I-40, exit 65, 0.4 mi e on south frontage road. 6721 I-40 W 79106. **Hours:** 11 am-9:30 pm, Fri & Sat-10 pm. Closed: 11/27. **Features:** Etched-glass and cherry-wood decor, as well as detailed carved-wood edging around the doorways, highlights the buffet restaurant. Lunch crowds gather for the variety of soups, salads and meat offerings. Soft-serve ice cream is a light, sweet meal ender. Casual dress. **Parking:** on-site. **Cards:** AX, DS, MC, VI.

♿ ✕

DYER'S BAR-B-QUE

▼▼▼

Barbecue

Lunch: $5-$13   **Dinner:** $5-$13   **Phone:** 806/358-7104

Location: I-40, exit 68 (Georgia St), just nw; in Wellington Square. 1619 Kentucky St, Bldg E #526 79102. **Hours:** 11 am-10 pm, Sun-9 pm. Closed: 4/20, 11/27, 12/25. **Reservations:** accepted. **Features:** The eatery serves delicious barbecue dishes in a rustic, Western-style atmosphere. Finger foods are favorites, as are preparations of Delta Dyer's Mississippi farm-raised catfish. Casual dress; cocktails. **Parking:** on-site. **Cards:** AX, DS, MC, VI.

♿ 🍸 ✕

GARDSKI'S RESTAURANT AND BAR

▼▼▼

American

Lunch: $6-$13   **Dinner:** $6-$13   **Phone:** 806/353-6626

Location: I-40, exit 68A (Paramount Blvd), just w on north frontage road. 1619 Kentucky St 79102. **Hours:** 11 am-11 pm, Fri & Sat-midnight, Sun-10 pm. Closed: 11/27, 12/25. **Reservations:** accepted. **Features:** High-quality food and service come together with a modern decor to create a pleasant, casual atmosphere. Contemporary artwork and '80s and '90s pop music energize the mood for patrons who long for such classics as USDA choice steaks, spicy chipotle chicken and a nice variety of fresh salads. Casual dress; cocktails. **Parking:** on-site. **Cards:** AX, CB, DC, DS, MC, VI.

♿ 🍸 ✕

HOFFBRAU STEAKS

▼▼▼

Steak & Seafood

Lunch: $5-$21   **Dinner:** $5-$21   **Phone:** 806/358-6595

Location: I-40, exit 65, just e on south frontage road. 7203 I-40 W 79106. **Hours:** 11 am-10 pm. Closed: 11/27, 12/24, 12/25. **Reservations:** accepted. **Features:** The varied menu incorporates many steak choices. In the dining room, the feel is comfortable and relaxed. Don't miss tasty pecan cobbler for dessert. Casual dress; cocktails. **Parking:** on-site. **Cards:** AX, CB, DC, DS, MC, VI.

♿ ✕

LEGEND'S BAR & GRILL   **Lunch:** $4-$10   **Dinner:** $8-$20   **Phone:** 806/358-4442
Location: I-40, exit 67, just w on north frontage road. 4000 I-40 W 79102. **Hours:** 11 am-10 pm, Fri & Sat-11 pm, Sun-9 pm. **Closed:** 11/27; 12/25. **Reservations:** accepted. **Features:** Prime rib, seven different steaks, pork, baby back ribs and chicken make up the core of the upscale restaurant's menu. Casual dress; cocktails. **Parking:** on-site. **Cards:** AX, DC, DS, MC, VI.
Steak House

PEKING RESTAURANT   **Lunch:** $4-$5   **Dinner:** $5-$12   **Phone:** 806/353-9179
Location: I-40, exit 68A (Paramount Blvd), just s. 2061 Paramount Blvd 79109. **Hours:** 11 am-3 & 5-9:30 pm, Sun-3 pm. Closed major holidays. **Reservations:** accepted. **Features:** Modern Chinese artwork decorates the dining room. Hot and crispy egg rolls at the buffet are scrumptious. The sweet flavor of General Chow's chicken and beef makes it a popular choice. A soft-serve ice cream cone is a fitting dessert. Casual dress; beer & wine only. **Parking:** on-site. **Cards:** AX, DC, DS, MC, VI.
Chinese

RUBY TEQUILA'S MEXICAN KITCHEN   **Lunch:** $5-$13   **Dinner:** $8-$13   **Phone:** 806/358-7829
Location: I-40, exit 68A (Paramount Blvd), just s. 2108 Paramount Blvd 79109. **Hours:** 11 am-10 pm, Fri & Sat-11 pm. **Closed:** 11/27, 12/25. **Features:** Close to downtown, the Mexican eatery serves sizzling fajitas and homemade tacos. Sweet margaritas wash down a spicy meal. Colorful murals cover the walls, and items from south of the border hang from the ceiling. Casual dress; cocktails. **Parking:** on-site. **Cards:** AX, DC, DS, MC, VI.
Mexican

SANTA FE   **Lunch:** $6-$12   **Dinner:** $6-$15   **Phone:** 806/358-8333
Location: I-40, exit 65 (Coulter Dr), just s. 3333 Coulter Dr 79106. **Hours:** 11 am-10 pm, Fri & Sat-10:30 pm. Closed 11/27, 12/25. **Features:** Festive and fun, the Tex-Mex restaurant serves such entrees as colorful vegetable tacos stuffed with diced tomatoes, lettuce, purple cabbage and white cheese. Guests can munch on chips and salsa before the meal. Attractive ceramic tile adds to the Southwestern decor. Casual dress; cocktails. **Parking:** on-site. **Cards:** AX, CB, DC, DS, MC, VI.
Mexican

ANGLETON pop. 18,130

——— WHERE TO STAY ———

BEST WESTERN ANGELTON INN   **Phone:** (979)849-5822
All Year   1P: $60-$70   2P: $70-$110   XP: $5   F12
Location: 1.5 mi n of jct SR 35 and Business 288, e of SR 288. 1809 N Velasco 77515. Fax: 979/849-2173. **Facility:** 45 one-bedroom standard units, some with whirlpools. 2 stories (no elevator), exterior corridors. **Parking:** on-site. **Terms:** [ECP] meal plan available, pets ($25 extra charge). **Amenities:** irons, hair dryers.
Motel **Pool(s):** outdoor. **Leisure Activities:** whirlpool. **Business Services:** meeting rooms, fax (fee). **Cards:** AX, CB, DC, DS, MC, VI. **Special Amenities:** free continental breakfast and free newspaper.

SOME UNITS

ANTHONY pop. 3,850

——— WHERE TO STAY ———

HOLIDAY INN EXPRESS   **Phone:** (915)886-3333
All Year [ECP]   1P: $79-$89   2P: $79-$89   XP: $8   F18
Location: I-10, exit 0. 9401 S Desert Blvd 79821. Fax: 915/886-2521. **Facility:** 62 one-bedroom standard units, some with whirlpools. 2 stories, exterior corridors. *Bath:* combo or shower only. **Parking:** on-site. **Terms:** 7 day cancellation notice-fee imposed. **Amenities:** irons, hair dryers. **Pool(s):** outdoor. **Leisure Activities:** sauna, whirlpool, exercise room. **Guest Services:** coin laundry. **Business Services:** meeting rooms, fax (fee). **Cards:** AX, CB, DC, DS, JC, MC, VI. **Special Amenities:** free continental breakfast and free newspaper. *(See color ad p 334)*
Small-scale Hotel

SOME UNITS

ARANSAS PASS pop. 8,138

——— WHERE TO STAY ———

——— *The following lodging was either not evaluated or did not* ———
meet AAA rating requirements but is listed for your information only.

HAWTHORN SUITES   **Phone:** 361/758-1774
[fyi] Not evaluated. **Location:** Just s of SR 361. 501 E Goodnight 78336. Facilities, services, and decor characterize a mid-range property.

ARLINGTON pop. 332,969   (See map p. 343; index p. 345)

——— WHERE TO STAY ———

AMERISUITES (DALLAS/ARLINGTON)   **Phone:** (817)649-7676   59
5/29-8/15   1P: $129   2P: $129
2/1-5/28 & 8/16-1/31   1P: $109   2P: $109
Location: I-30, exit 30 (SR 360), 0.5 mi sw. 2380 East Rd to Six Flags St 76011-5144. Fax: 817/649-7753. **Facility:** 128 one-bedroom standard units. 6 stories, interior corridors. *Bath:* combo or shower only. **Parking:** on-site. **Terms:** [ECP] meal plan available. **Amenities:** voice mail, irons, hair dryers. *Some:* dual phone lines. **Pool(s):** heated outdoor. **Leisure Activities:** walking trail, exercise room. **Guest Services:** valet and coin laundry, area transportation-within 5 mi. **Business Services:** meeting rooms, fax (fee). **Cards:** AX, DS, JC, MC, VI. **Special Amenities:** free continental breakfast and free newspaper. *(See color ad p 347)*
Small-scale Hotel

SOME UNITS

(See map p. 343)

ARLINGTON TOWNEPLACE SUITES BY MARRIOTT

Phone: (817)861-8728　65

	2/1-9/6 [ECP]	1P: $85	2P: $85
	9/7-1/31 [ECP]	1P: $56	2P: $56

Location: 2 mi w of SR 360. Located opposite entrance to Six Flags Hurricane Harbor Waterpark. 1709 E Lamar Ave 76006. Fax: 817/861-8752. **Facility:** 94 units. 68 one-bedroom standard units with kitchens. 4 one- and 22 two-bedroom suites with kitchens. 2-3 stories, interior corridors. *Bath:* combo or shower only. **Parking:** on-site. **Terms:** cancellation fee imposed, pets ($150 fee). **Amenities:** dual phone lines, voice mail, irons, hair dryers. **Pool(s):** small heated outdoor. **Leisure Activities:** barbecue grill, exercise room. **Guest Services:** valet and coin laundry, area transportation-Six Flags, Ball Park. **Business Services:** fax (fee). **Cards:** AX, DC, DS, JC, MC, VI. **Special Amenities: free continental breakfast and free local telephone calls.**

Small-scale Hotel

SOME UNITS

BAYMONT INN & SUITES-ARLINGTON

Phone: (817)633-2400　71

	5/1-8/31 [ECP]	1P: $69-$79	2P: $69-$79
	2/1-4/30 & 9/1-1/31 [ECP]	1P: $59-$69	2P: $59-$69

Location: I-30, exit 30 (SR 360), 0.5 mi s; off SR 360, exit Six Flags Dr northbound; exit Ave H/Lamar Blvd southbound, on southbound service road. 2401 Diplomacy Dr 76011. Fax: 817/633-3500. **Facility:** 102 one-bedroom standard units. 4 stories, interior corridors. *Bath:* combo or shower only. **Terms:** 15 day cancellation notice, small pets only ($50 deposit). **Amenities:** video games (fee), voice mail, irons, hair dryers. **Pool(s):** outdoor. **Guest Services:** coin laundry, area transportation-major attractions. **Business Services:** fax (fee). **Cards:** AX, CB, DC, DS, MC, VI. **Special Amenities: free continental breakfast and free newspaper.** *(See color ad below)*

Small-scale Hotel

SOME UNITS

The One For All

*Y*ou know how AAA can simplify your life. Now make the lives of those you love the most a little easier–give them AAA associate memberships.

Associate members are eligible for the same security, services, and savings as primary members–emergency road service, valuable savings, access to travel services, and more. And all this protection is available for a reduced enrollment fee.

Help your family members simplify their lives with AAA associate memberships. Call or stop by your nearest AAA office today. And make AAA the one for you.

(See map p. 343)

BEST WESTERN COOPER INN & SUITES   Phone: (817)784-9490   🅱🅾
All Year   1P: $69-$74   2P: $69-$74   XP: $5   F18
Location: I-20, exit 449 (Cooper St) westbound; exit 449A eastbound, 0.3 mi n. 4024 Melear Rd 76015.
Fax: 817/557-4450. **Facility:** 66 one-bedroom standard units, some with whirlpools. 2 stories, exterior corridors. *Bath:* combo or shower only. **Parking:** on-site. **Terms:** [ECP] meal plan available. **Amenities:** high-
Small-scale Hotel   speed Internet, voice mail, irons, hair dryers. **Pool(s):** outdoor. **Guest Services:** valet laundry. **Business Services:** meeting rooms, fax (fee). **Cards:** AX, CB, DC, DS, MC, VI. **Special Amenities:** free continental breakfast and free newspaper. *(See color ad below)*

SOME UNITS

BEST WESTERN-GREAT SOUTHWEST INN   Phone: (817)640-7722   🅱🅾
5/1-9/15   1P: $62-$85   2P: $62-$85   XP: $7   F16
2/1-4/30 & 9/16-1/31   1P: $50-$70   2P: $50-$70   XP: $7   F16
Location: SR 360, exit Division St, 0.8 mi e. Located next to a mall and railroad tracks. 3501 E Division St 76011.
Fax: 817/640-9043. **Facility:** 117 one-bedroom standard units. 2 stories, exterior corridors. **Parking:** on-site.
Motel   **Terms:** 1-2 night minimum stay - seasonal, [CP] meal plan available, package plans - seasonal. **Amenities:** irons, hair dryers. **Dining:** 6:30 am-11 pm, Fri & Sat-3 am. **Pool(s):** outdoor. **Leisure Activities:** whirlpool, playground. **Guest Services:** area transportation-major attractions. **Business Services:** meeting rooms, fax (fee). **Cards:** AX, DC, DS, MC, VI. **Special Amenities:** early check-in/late check-out and free room upgrade (subject to availability with advanced reservations).

SOME UNITS

COMFORT INN ARLINGTON   Phone: (817)467-3535   🅱🅾
4/1-8/15   1P: $59-$79   2P: $69-$89   XP: $10   F17
8/16-1/31   1P: $59-$69   2P: $69-$79   XP: $10   F17
2/1-3/31   1P: $49-$69   2P: $59-$79   XP: $10   F17
Location: I-20, exit 450 (Matlock Rd), just nw. 121 I-20 E 76018. Fax: 817/467-5570. **Facility:** 141 one-bedroom
Small-scale Hotel   standard units. 2 stories, exterior corridors. *Bath:* combo or shower only. **Parking:** on-site. **Terms:** weekly rates available, [ECP] meal plan available. **Amenities:** video games (fee), voice mail, irons. **Pool(s):** outdoor.
Guest Services: valet and coin laundry. **Business Services:** meeting rooms, fax (fee). **Cards:** AX, CB, DC, DS, JC, MC, VI.

SOME UNITS
FEE   FEE

COUNTRY INN & SUITES BY CARLSON   Phone: (817)261-8900   🅱🅾
4/1-7/31   1P: $98-$107   2P: $98-$107
2/1-3/31 & 8/1-1/31   1P: $80-$99   2P: $80-$99
Location: I-30, exit 28 (Collins St/SR 157), just ne. 1075 Wet 'N Wild Way 76011. Fax: 817/274-0343. **Facility:** 132
units. 9 one-bedroom standard units. 93 one- and 30 two-bedroom suites, some with kitchens. 3 stories, ex-
Small-scale Hotel   terior corridors. *Bath:* combo or shower only. **Parking:** on-site. **Terms:** [ECP] meal plan available, small pets only ($35 fee). **Amenities:** video games (fee), voice mail, irons, hair dryers. **Pool(s):** heated outdoor.
Leisure Activities: whirlpool. **Guest Services:** complimentary evening beverages: Mon-Thurs, valet and coin laundry, airport transportation-Dallas-Fort Worth International Airport, area transportation-within 5 mi. **Business Services:** meeting rooms, fax (fee). **Cards:** AX, DC, DS, MC, VI. **Special Amenities:** free continental breakfast and free local telephone calls. *(See color ad p 260)*

SOME UNITS

COURTYARD BY MARRIOTT   Phone: (817)277-2774   🅱🅾
4/1-9/30   1P: $119
2/1-3/31 & 10/1-1/31   1P: $109
Location: I-30, exit 28 (Collins St/SR 157) westbound, just s to Copeland, 0.4 mi e, then just s; exit 28B eastbound. 1500
Nolan Ryan Expwy 76011. Fax: 817/277-3103. **Facility:** 147 units. 132 one-bedroom standard units. 15 one-
Small-scale Hotel   bedroom suites ($129-$139). 3 stories, interior corridors. *Bath:* combo or shower only. **Parking:** on-site. **Amenities:** voice mail, irons, hair dryers. **Pool(s):** heated indoor/outdoor. **Leisure Activities:** whirlpool, exercise room. **Guest Services:** valet and coin laundry. **Business Services:** meeting rooms, fax (fee). **Cards:** AX, CB, DC, DS, MC, VI.

SOME UNITS

(See map p. 343)

DAYS INN BALLPARK AT ARLINGTON/SIX FLAGS   Phone: (817)261-8444 ⑤⓪

AAA SAVE

5/1-9/15 [CP]	1P: $59-$77	2P: $59-$95	XP: $6 F
9/16-1/31 [CP]	1P: $34-$44	2P: $39-$50	XP: $6 F
2/1-4/30 [CP]	1P: $33-$43	2P: $39-$49	XP: $6 F

Small-scale Hotel

Location: I-30, exit 28 (Collins St/SR 157), 1 mi s. 910 N Collins St 76011. Fax: 817/860-8326. **Facility:** 92 one-bedroom standard units. 4 stories, interior corridors. **Parking:** on-site. **Terms:** 3 day cancellation notice-fee imposed, pets ($10 extra charge). **Amenities:** hair dryers. **Pool(s):** outdoor. **Business Services:** fax (fee). **Cards:** AX, CB, DC, DS, MC, VI. **Special Amenities:** free continental breakfast and free newspaper.

SOME UNITS

⬛🛏️🍴🎣🏊/✕🅱️/
FEE FEE

FAIRFIELD INN BY MARRIOTT   Phone: (817)649-5800 ⑥④

SAVE

5/16-9/30	1P: $79-$99	2P: $79-$99
2/1-5/15 & 10/1-1/31	1P: $59-$79	2P: $59-$79

Small-scale Hotel

Location: Just w of SR 360, exit Ave H/ Lamar Blvd. 2500 E Lamar Blvd 76006. Fax: 817/649-5800. **Facility:** 109 one-bedroom standard units. 3 stories, interior corridors. **Parking:** on-site. **Terms:** [CP] meal plan available. **Amenities:** irons, hair dryers. **Pool(s):** heated outdoor. **Guest Services:** valet laundry. **Business Services:** fax (fee). **Cards:** AX, CB, DC, DS, JC, MC, VI.

SOME UNITS

⬛🍴🏋️🏊🎥📠/✕/

HAWTHORN SUITES HOTEL   Phone: (817)640-1188 ⑥③

All Year [BP]   1P: $59-$199   2P: $59-$199

Small-scale Hotel

Location: I-30, exit 30 (SR 360), just w of SR 360, exit Ave H/Lamar Blvd. 2401 Brookhollow Plaza Dr 76006. Fax: 817/649-4720. **Facility:** 129 units. 26 one-bedroom standard units. 95 one- and 8 two-bedroom suites ($89-$199) with kitchens, some with whirlpools. 3 stories, exterior corridors. **Parking:** on-site. **Terms:** small pets only ($50 fee). **Amenities:** video library (fee), dual phone lines, voice mail, irons, hair dryers. **Pool(s):** outdoor. **Leisure Activities:** whirlpool, exercise room, sports court. **Guest Services:** complimentary evening beverages: Mon-Thurs, valet and coin laundry, area transportation. **Business Services:** meeting rooms, fax (fee). **Cards:** AX, CB, DC, DS, MC, VI.

SOME UNITS

ASK ⬛🛏️🌀🏊✕🎥📠🅱️🖥️💻/✕🆅🅲🆁/
FEE

HILTON ARLINGTON   Phone: (817)640-3322 ⑥⑥

AAA SAVE

5/23-8/16	1P: $85-$109	2P: $85-$109	XP: $10 F18
2/1-5/22 & 8/17-1/31	1P: $79-$99	2P: $79-$99	XP: $10 F18

Small-scale Hotel

Location: Just w of SR 360, exit Ave H/Lamar Blvd; exit 30 (SR 360), 0.3 mi nw. 2401 E Lamar Blvd 76006. Fax: 817/633-1430. **Facility:** 309 units. 308 one-bedroom standard units. 1 two-bedroom suite. 16 stories, interior corridors. **Bath:** combo or shower only. **Parking:** on-site. **Terms:** cancellation fee imposed. **Amenities:** dual phone lines, voice mail, irons, hair dryers. **Fee:** video games, high-speed Internet. **Dining:** 6:30 am-11 pm, cocktails. **Pool(s):** indoor/outdoor. **Leisure Activities:** saunas, whirlpool, exercise room. **Guest Services:** gift shop, valet and coin laundry, airport transportation-Dallas-Fort Worth International Airport, area transportation-within 3 mi. **Business Services:** meeting rooms, business center. **Cards:** AX, CB, DC, DS, MC, VI. **Special Amenities:** free newspaper. *(See ad below)*

SOME UNITS

✈️🍴🍴🏋️🚗🌀🏊✕🎥📠💻/✕🅱️/

HOLIDAY INN-ARLINGTON   Phone: (817)640-7712 ⑥②

All Year   1P: $89   2P: $99   XP: $10 F18

Small-scale Hotel

Location: I-30, exit 30 (SR 360), 1 mi n on SR 360, exit Ave K/Brown Blvd. 1507 N Watson Rd 76006. Fax: 817/640-3174. **Facility:** 237 one-bedroom standard units. 5 stories, interior corridors. **Parking:** on-site. **Terms:** 3 day cancellation notice, [AP] meal plan available, 15% service charge. **Amenities:** voice mail, irons, hair dryers. **Some:** high-speed Internet. **Pool(s):** heated indoor/outdoor. **Leisure Activities:** whirlpool, exercise room. **Guest Services:** valet and coin laundry, area transportation. **Business Services:** meeting rooms, fax (fee). **Cards:** AX, CB, DC, DS, JC, MC, VI.

SOME UNITS

ASK ⬛✈️🍴🏋️🌀🏊🎥📠💻/✕🅱️/

(See map p. 343)

HOLIDAY INN EXPRESS
Phone: 817/784-8750   **48**

AAA **SAVE**

Small-scale Hotel

All Year   1P: $79   2P: $89   XP: $5   F18
Location: I-20, exit 449 (Cooper St) westbound; exit 449A eastbound, just nw. 1721 Pleasant Pl 76015. Fax: 817/465-0110. **Facility:** 66 one-bedroom standard units, some with whirlpools. 3 stories, interior corridors. *Bath:* combo or shower only. **Parking:** on-site. **Terms:** [ECP] meal plan available. **Amenities:** high-speed Internet, dual phone lines, voice mail, irons, hair dryers. **Pool(s):** outdoor. **Leisure Activities:** whirlpool. **Guest Services:** valet and coin laundry. **Business Services:** fax (fee). **Cards:** AX, CB, DC, DS, JC, MC, VI. **Special Amenities:** free continental breakfast and free newspaper. *(See color ad below)*

SOME UNITS

HOLIDAY INN EXPRESS HOTEL & SUITES ARLINGTON-SIX FLAGS
Phone: (817)640-5454   **61**

Small-scale Hotel

All Year   2P: $89
Location: I-30, exit 30 (SR 360), 0.4 mi s on SR 360. 2451 E Randol Mill Rd 76011. Fax: 817/652-0763. **Facility:** 103 units. 68 one-bedroom standard units. 35 one-bedroom suites ($109-$139), some with whirlpools. 3 stories, interior corridors. **Parking:** on-site. **Terms:** [ECP] meal plan available. **Amenities:** dual phone lines, voice mail, irons, hair dryers. **Pool(s):** outdoor. **Leisure Activities:** whirlpool, exercise room. **Guest Services:** valet and coin laundry, area transportation. **Business Services:** meeting rooms, fax (fee). **Cards:** AX, DC, DS, MC, VI.

SOME UNITS

HOMESTEAD STUDIO SUITES HOTEL-ARLINGTON
Phone: (817)633-7588   **54**

Small-scale Hotel

All Year   1P: $55-$65   2P: $60-$70   F17
Location: Jct SR 360, exit Ave K/Brown Blvd. 1221 N Watson Rd 76006. Fax: 817/633-2778. **Facility:** 137 one-bedroom standard units with efficiencies. 2 stories, exterior corridors. *Bath:* combo or shower only. **Parking:** on-site. **Terms:** pets ($75 extra charge). **Amenities:** voice mail, irons. **Guest Services:** valet and coin laundry. **Business Services:** fax (fee). **Cards:** AX, CB, DC, DS, JC, MC, VI.

SOME UNITS

HOMEWOOD SUITES-ARLINGTON
Phone: (817)633-1594   **69**

SAVE

Small-scale Hotel

5/2-8/20 [ECP]   1P: $129   2P: $129
2/1-5/1 & 8/21-1/31 [ECP]   1P: $109   2P: $109
Location: I-30, exit 30 (SR 360), 0.5 mi sw. 2401 East Rd to Six Flags St 76011. Fax: 817/649-7296. **Facility:** 89 units. 82 one- and 7 two-bedroom suites with efficiencies. 4 stories, interior corridors. *Bath:* combo or shower only. **Parking:** on-site. **Terms:** [BP] meal plan available, pets ($75 fee). **Amenities:** voice mail, irons, hair dryers. **Pool(s):** heated indoor. **Leisure Activities:** whirlpool, exercise room. **Guest Services:** sundries, complimentary evening beverages: Mon-Thurs, valet and coin laundry. **Business Services:** business center. **Cards:** AX, DC, DS, MC, VI.

SOME UNITS

HOWARD JOHNSON EXPRESS INN
Phone: (817)461-1122   **56**

AAA **SAVE**

Small-scale Hotel

4/16-8/15 [ECP]   1P: $60-$80   2P: $70-$90   XP: $10   F13
2/1-4/15 & 8/16-1/31 [ECP]   1P: $45-$65   2P: $55-$75   XP: $5   F13
Location: I-30, exit 30 (SR 360) westbound, just s to Six Flags Dr, then just w to Copeland Dr, 0.9 mi w; exit 29 (Ball Pkwy) eastbound. 2001 E Copeland Rd 76011. Fax: 817/860-5832. **Facility:** 96 one-bedroom standard units. 5 stories, interior corridors. **Parking:** on-site. **Terms:** small pets only ($5 fee). **Pool(s):** outdoor. **Business Services:** meeting rooms, fax (fee). **Cards:** AX, DS, MC, VI. **Special Amenities:** free continental breakfast and preferred room (subject to availability with advanced reservations).

SOME UNITS
FEE   FEE

LA QUINTA INN & SUITES SOUTH ARLINGTON
Phone: (817)467-7756   **72**

SAVE

Small-scale Hotel

All Year   1P: $99-$119   2P: $109-$129   XP: $10   F18
Location: I-20, exit 450 (Matlock Rd), on southbound service road. 4001 Scott's Legacy 76015. Fax: 817/467-5255. **Facility:** 128 units. 123 one-bedroom standard units. 5 one-bedroom suites ($129-$169). 5 stories, interior corridors. *Bath:* combo or shower only. **Parking:** on-site. **Terms:** [ECP] meal plan available, small pets only. **Amenities:** voice mail, irons, hair dryers. *Fee:* video games, high-speed Internet. *Some:* dual phone lines. **Pool(s):** heated outdoor. **Leisure Activities:** whirlpool, exercise room. **Guest Services:** valet and coin laundry. **Business Services:** meeting rooms, fax (fee). **Cards:** AX, CB, DC, DS, JC, MC, VI. *(See color ad p 272)*

SOME UNITS

(See map p. 343)

LA QUINTA INN-ARLINGTON-CONFERENCE CENTER

Phone: (817)640-4142   60

SAVE

Small-scale Hotel

All Year   1P: $69-$109   2P: $79-$119   XP: $10   F18
Location: I-30, exit 30 (SR 360), exit Six Flags Dr northbound; exit Ave H/Lamar Blvd southbound. 825 N Watson Rd 76011. Fax: 817/649-7864. **Facility:** 340 units. 300 one-bedroom standard units. 40 one-bedroom suites ($89-$149). 2 stories, exterior corridors. *Bath:* combo or shower only. **Parking:** on-site. **Terms:** [ECP] meal plan available, small pets only. **Amenities:** video games (fee), voice mail, irons, hair dryers. **Pool(s):** outdoor, heated outdoor, wading. **Leisure Activities:** whirlpool, jogging, exercise room. **Guest Services:** gift shop, valet and coin laundry, area transportation. **Business Services:** conference facilities, business center. **Cards:** AX, CB, DC, DS, JC, MC, VI. *(See color ad p 272)*

SOME UNITS

MOTEL 6 - 122

Phone: 817/649-0147   68

5/22-8/31   1P: $39-$49   2P: $45-$55   XP: $3   F17
9/1-1/31   1P: $37-$47   2P: $43-$53   XP: $3   F17
2/1-5/21   1P: $36-$46   2P: $42-$52   XP: $3   F17
Small-scale Hotel   **Location:** Jct SR 360 and Randol Mill Rd. 2626 E Randol Mill Rd 76011. Fax: 817/649-7130. **Facility:** 121 one-bedroom standard units. 2 stories, exterior corridors. *Bath:* shower only. **Parking:** on-site. **Terms:** small pets only. **Pool(s):** outdoor. **Guest Services:** coin laundry. **Business Services:** fax (fee). **Cards:** AX, CB, DC, DS, MC, VI.

SOME UNITS

RESIDENCE INN BY MARRIOTT

Phone: (817)649-7300   74

SAVE

5/18-9/8   1P: $85-$145   2P: $130-$179
2/1-5/17   1P: $79-$139   2P: $130-$179
9/9-1/31   1P: $69-$139   2P: $89-$179
Small-scale Hotel   **Location:** I-30, exit 30 (SR 360), just n on SR 360 to Lamar Blvd, then just w. 1050 Brookhollow Plaza Dr 76006. Fax: 817/649-7600. **Facility:** 114 units. 36 one-bedroom standard units with kitchens. 54 one- and 24 two-bedroom suites, some with efficiencies or kitchens. 3 stories, interior corridors. *Bath:* combo or shower only. **Parking:** on-site. **Terms:** cancellation fee imposed, pets ($100 fee, $5 extra charge). **Amenities:** voice mail, irons, hair dryers. **Pool(s):** heated outdoor. **Leisure Activities:** whirlpool, exercise room, sports court. **Guest Services:** complimentary evening beverages: Mon-Thurs, valet and coin laundry, area transportation. **Business Services:** meeting rooms, fax (fee). **Cards:** AX, CB, DC, DS, JC, MC, VI.

SOME UNITS

SLEEP INN MAIN GATE-SIX FLAGS

Phone: (817)649-1010   49

AAA SAVE

5/24-9/1 [ECP]   1P: $86-$90   2P: $90-$96   XP: $6   F18
3/2-5/23 [ECP]   1P: $66-$70   2P: $70-$76   XP: $6   F18
2/1-3/1 & 9/2-1/31 [ECP]   1P: $56-$60   2P: $60-$66   XP: $6   F18
Small-scale Hotel   **Location:** I-30, exit 30 (SR 360), 0.5 mi s. 750 Six Flags Dr 76011. Fax: 817/649-8811. **Facility:** 127 one-bedroom standard units. 4 stories, interior corridors. *Bath:* combo or shower only. **Parking:** on-site. **Terms:** $1 service charge, small pets only ($40 extra charge). **Amenities:** high-speed Internet, voice mail, irons, hair dryers. *Fee:* video games, safes. **Pool(s):** heated outdoor. **Guest Services:** coin laundry. **Business Services:** fax (fee). **Cards:** AX, CB, DC, DS, MC, VI. **Special Amenities:** early check-in/late check-out.

SOME UNITS

SPRINGHILL SUITES ARLINGTON

Phone: (817)860-2737   73

SAVE

Small-scale Hotel

All Year [ECP]   1P: $89-$109
Location: I-30, exit 29 (Ballpark Way), 0.4 mi n to Lamar Blvd, just w. 1975 E Lamar Blvd 76006. Fax: 817/860-4011. **Facility:** 122 one-bedroom standard units. 3 stories, interior corridors. *Bath:* combo or shower only. **Parking:** on-site. **Amenities:** dual phone lines, voice mail, irons, hair dryers. **Pool(s):** heated outdoor. **Leisure Activities:** whirlpool, exercise room. **Guest Services:** valet and coin laundry. **Business Services:** meeting rooms, fax (fee). **Cards:** AX, DC, DS, JC, MC, VI.

SOME UNITS

(See map p. 343)

STUDIO 6 #6036   Phone: 817/465-8500   **51**
♦♦♦ ♦♦♦   All Year   1P: $47-$57   2P: $51-$61   XP: $4   F17
           Location: I-20, exit 449 (Cooper St), 0.3 mi n, then w. 1980 W Pleasant Ridge Rd 76015. Fax: 817/465-8552.
Small-scale Hotel **Facility:** 141 one-bedroom standard units with efficiencies. 2 stories, exterior corridors. *Bath:* combo or
           shower only. **Parking:** on-site. **Terms:** weekly rates available, pets ($50 fee). **Amenities:** voice mail, irons.
Guest Services: valet and coin laundry. **Business Services:** fax (fee). **Cards:** AX, CB, DC, DS, MC, VI.

SOME UNITS
[icons] /⊠/

SUPER 8 IN ARLINGTON   Phone: (817)652-0917   **75**
(AAA) (SAVE) All Year [CP]   1P: $59-$69   2P: $64-$74   XP: $5   F12
♦♦♦   **Location:** SR 360, exit Abram St, just w. 2712 E Abrams St 76010. Fax: 817/652-3980. **Facility:** 50 one-bedroom
             standard units, some with whirlpools. 2 stories, exterior corridors. *Bath:* combo or shower only. **Parking:** on-
             site. **Amenities:** hair dryers. **Pool(s):** small outdoor. **Business Services:** fax (fee). **Cards:** AX, CB, DC, DS,
Small-scale Hotel MC, VI. **Special Amenities:** free continental breakfast and free newspaper. *(See color ad below)*

SOME UNITS
[icons] /⊠/

(See map p. 343)

WINGATE INN
Small-scale Hotel

4/1-8/17 [ECP]	1P: $89-$99	2P: $89-$99	XP: $10	F18
2/1-3/31 & 8/18-1/31 [ECP]	1P: $79-$89	2P: $79-$89	XP: $10	F18

Phone: (817)640-8686   **47**

Location: SR 360, exit Ave H/Lamar Blvd, 0.3 mi w to Brookhollow Plaza Dr, then 0.3 mi n. 1024 Brookhollow Plaza Dr 76006. Fax: 817/640-9922. **Facility:** 92 one-bedroom standard units, some with whirlpools. 4 stories, interior corridors. *Bath:* combo or shower only. **Parking:** on-site. **Amenities:** high-speed Internet, dual phone lines, voice mail, safes, irons, hair dryers. **Pool(s):** outdoor. **Leisure Activities:** whirlpool, exercise room. **Guest Services:** complimentary evening beverages: Tues & Wed, valet laundry, area transportation. **Business Services:** meeting rooms, business center. **Cards:** AX, CB, DC, DS, JC, MC, VI. *(See color ad p 176)*

SOME UNITS

WYNDHAM ARLINGTON-DFW AIRPORT SOUTH
Large-scale Hotel

All Year	1P: $94-$129	2P: $104-$139	XP: $10

Phone: (817)261-8200   **57**   F17

Location: I-30, exit 28B (Nolan Ryan Expwy), just s to Copeland, then just e; exit 29 (Ballpark Way), just s. Located adjacent to Arlington Convention Center and Station. 1500 Convention Center Dr 76011. Fax: 817/548-2873. **Facility:** 310 one-bedroom standard units. 19 stories, interior corridors. *Bath:* combo or shower only. **Parking:** on-site. **Terms:** cancellation fee imposed. **Amenities:** voice mail, irons, hair dryers. *Fee:* video games, high-speed Internet. **Dining:** 2 restaurants, 6:30 am-11 pm, cocktails. **Pool(s):** outdoor. **Leisure Activities:** whirlpool, exercise room. **Guest Services:** gift shop, valet and coin laundry, airport transportation-Dallas-Fort Worth International Airport, area transportation-within 3 mi. **Business Services:** conference facilities, business center. **Cards:** AX, CB, DC, DS, JC, MC, VI.

SOME UNITS

------ **WHERE TO DINE** ------

ARLINGTON STEAKHOUSE
American

Lunch: $6-$13	Dinner: $6-$13	Phone: 817/275-7881 **44**

Location: I-30, exit 26 (Fielder Rd), 3 mi s, then just w. 1724 W Division St 76012. **Hours:** 11 am-9:30 pm, Fri & Sat-10 pm. Closed: 11/27, 12/25. **Features:** Serving Arlington area residents since 1931, this friendly, folksy restaurant dishes up steaks, prime rib, pork chops, chicken fried steak and huge yeast rolls in a nostalgic Western atmosphere. A local favorite, it is sure to become your favorite, too. Casual dress; beer & wine only. **Parking:** on-site. **Cards:** AX, DC, DS, MC, VI.

BOBBY VALENTINE'S
American

Lunch: $7-$14	Dinner: $7-$14	Phone: 817/467-9922 **43**

Location: I-20, exit 448 (Bowen Rd), just n. 4301 S Bowen Rd 76016. **Hours:** 11 am-2 am. Closed: 11/27, 12/25. **Features:** Sports memorabilia, TVs for catching the big game and even a boxing ring are all part of the fun sports bar atmosphere. Munch on tasty burgers and sandwiches and test your game savvy with live sports trivia every Sunday night. A must for sports fans. Casual dress; cocktails; entertainment. **Parking:** on-site. **Cards:** AX, DC, DS, MC, VI.

CACHAREL
French

Lunch: $6-$20	Dinner: $21-$50	Phone: 817/640-9981 **46**

Location: I-30, exit 30 (SR 360), just n to Ave H/Lamar Blvd, then just w. 2221 E Lamar Blvd, Suite 910 76006. **Hours:** 11:30 am-2 & 6-10 pm, Fri-11 pm, Sat 5 pm-11 pm. Closed major holidays; also Sun. **Reservations:** suggested. **Features:** In addition to panoramic, ninth-floor views of the city, guests can enjoy beautiful paintings on the dining room walls of this elegant eatery. Representative of French-inspired cuisine are choices such as roasted breast of duck, filet mignon and grilled ostrich steak. Creme brulee is a perfect finish to any meal. Smoke free premises. Semi-formal attire; cocktails. **Parking:** on-site. **Cards:** AX, DC, DS, MC, VI.

MARSALA RISTORANTE
Continental

Lunch: $9-$10	Dinner: $10-$25	Phone: 972/988-1101 **45**

Location: I-30, exit 30 (SR 360), 1 mi n to exit Ave K/Brown Blvd. 1618 N Hwy 360 & Ave K 75050. **Hours:** 11:30 am-2 & 5:30-10:30 pm, Fri-11 pm, Sat 5:30 pm-11 pm. Closed major holidays; also Sun. **Reservations:** suggested. **Features:** Imagine quiet, intimate surroundings lit by chandeliers, accented by fresh roses, and staffed by tuxedo-clad waiters. Soft strains of classical guitar music are heard as you sample French and Italian cuisine including pasta, coq au vin and smoked salmon. Casual dress; cocktails. **Parking:** on-site. **Cards:** AX, CB, DC, DS, MC, VI.

DOWNTOWN
AUSTIN
ACCOMMODATIONS

Scale in Miles   0   0.4
Scale in Kilometers   0   0.7

© AAA

1989-K

Downtown Austin

This index helps you "spot" where approved accommodations and restaurants are located on the corresponding detailed maps. Lodging rate ranges are for comparison only and show the property's high season; rates are per night, unless only weekly (W) rates are available. Restaurant rate range is for dinner, unless only lunch (L) is served. Turn to the listing page for more detailed rate information and consult display ads for special promotions.

Spotter/Map Page Number	OA	DOWNTOWN AUSTIN - Lodgings	Diamond Rating	Rate Range High Season	Listing Page
1 / p. 178	AAA	Rodeway Inn-University/Downtown	◆◆	$59-$90 SAVE	188
2 / p. 178		Doubletree Guest Suites-Austin	◆◆◆	$129-$269	186
3 / p. 178	AAA	La Quinta Capitol - see color ad p 187	◆◆◆	$89-$129 SAVE	187
4 / p. 178		Austin Marriott at the Capitol	◆◆◆	$129-$204	184
5 / p. 178	AAA	Omni Austin Hotel & Suites	◆◆◆◆	$149-$369 SAVE	187
6 / p. 178		The Driskill	◆◆◆◆	$270-$340	186
7 / p. 178		Crowne Plaza Austin Hotel	◆◆◆	$129-$159	184
8 / p. 178	AAA	Radisson Hotel & Suites-Austin - see color ad p 178	◆◆◆	$99 SAVE	187
9 / p. 178	AAA	Hyatt Regency Austin - see color ad inside front cover	◆◆◆◆	$105-$245 SAVE	187
10 / p. 178		Embassy Suites Hotel-Downtown	◆◆◆	$109-$309	186
11 / p. 178		Four Seasons Hotel	◆◆◆◆	$280-$350	186
12 / p. 178		Holiday Inn-Town Lake - see color ad p 184	◆◆◆	$79-$149	186
13 / p. 178	AAA	Super 8 Central	◆	$55-$85 SAVE	188
14 / p. 178		Doubletree Club Hotel	◆◆◆	$139	186
15 / p. 178		Homestead Studio Suites Hotel-Austin/Downtown/Town Lake	◆◆◆	$89-$119	186
17 / p. 178		Austins Inn at Pearl Street	◆◆◆	$90-$175	184
		DOWNTOWN AUSTIN - Restaurants			
1 / p. 178		Cafe Serranos	◆◆	$8-$15	188
2 / p. 178		Louie's 106	◆◆◆	$10-$18	189
3 / p. 178		Carmelo's	◆◆◆	$17-$34	188
4 / p. 178		Dan McKlusky's Restaurant	◆◆	$15-$38	188
5 / p. 178		The Cafe	◆◆◆	$18-$33	188
6 / p. 178		Sullivan's Steakhouse	◆◆◆	$17-$29	189
7 / p. 178		Castle Hill Cafe	◆◆	$18-$21	188
8 / p. 178		Eastside Cafe	◆◆◆	$8-$20	189
9 / p. 178		El Sol y La Luna	◆◆	$5-$10	189
10 / p. 178		The Driskill Grill	◆◆◆◆	$20-$38	189
11 / p. 178		Ironworks Barbeque	◆	$7-$15	189
12 / p. 178		Malaga Tapas & Bar	◆◆	$9-$23	189
13 / p. 178		Clay Pit	◆◆◆	$9-$16	188
14 / p. 178		Manuel's Downtown	◆◆	$10-$16	189
15 / p. 178		Mars Restaurant & Bar	◆◆	$12-$22	189
16 / p. 178		Fleming's Prime Steakhouse & Wine Bar	◆◆◆	$18-$28	189

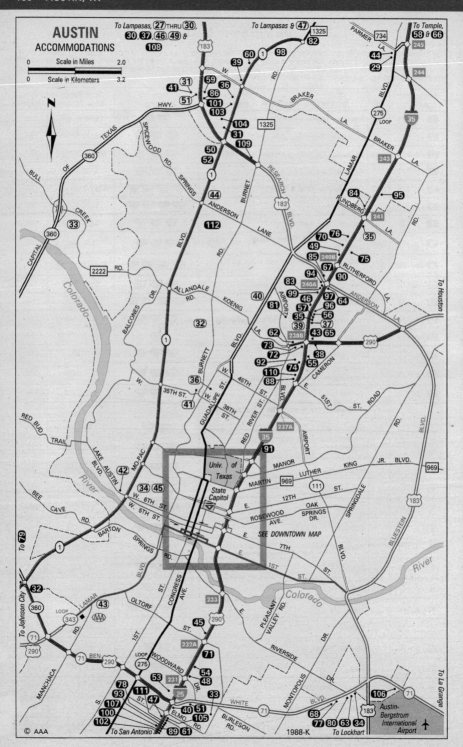

Austin

This index helps you "spot" where approved accommodations and restaurants are located on the corresponding detailed maps. Lodging rate ranges are for comparison only and show the property's high season; rates are per night, unless only weekly (W) rates are available. Restaurant rate range is for dinner, unless only lunch (L) is served. Turn to the listing page for more detailed rate information and consult display ads for special promotions.

Spotter/Map Page Number	OA	AUSTIN - Lodgings	Diamond Rating	Rate Range High Season	Listing Page
29 / p. 180		SpringHill Suites By Marriott-Austin North	◆◆◆	$79-$109	203
30 / p. 180		Comfort Suites	◆◆◆	$80-$90	192
31 / p. 180	AAA	**AmeriSuites (Austin/Arboretum)** - see color ad p 185	◆◆◆	$69-$159 (SAVE)	190
32 / p. 180	AAA	**La Quinta SW** - see color ad p 187	◆◆◆	$109-$149 (SAVE)	199
33 / p. 180		Homewood Suites-Austin South	◆◆◆	$125-$152	198
34 / p. 180	AAA	**Hawthorn Suites Ltd-Austin Airport**	◆◆◆	$99-$139 (SAVE)	196
35 / p. 180		Studio 6-Austin Midtown #6033	◆◆	$45-$59	203
36 / p. 180		Staybridge Suites Hotel	◆◆◆	$109-$139	203
37 / p. 180	AAA	**Wellesley Inn & Suites (Austin/NW)** - see color ad p 185	◆◆◆	$65-$95	204
38 / p. 180		Econo Lodge	◆◆	$50-$100	194
39 / p. 180		Hampton Inn Northwest	◆◆◆	$79-$109	196
40 / p. 180	AAA	**Omni Austin Hotel Southpark**	◆◆◆	$169 (SAVE)	200
41 / p. 180	AAA	**Renaissance Austin Hotel**	◆◆◆	$189-$239 (SAVE)	202
43 / p. 180		Red Lion Hotel Austin - see color ad p 201	◆◆◆	$89-$109	201
44 / p. 180		Residence Inn by Marriott-Austin North	◆◆◆	$119-$169	202
45 / p. 180		Clarion Inn & Suites Conference Center	◆◆◆	$60-$139	191
46 / p. 180	AAA	**La Quinta Inn-North** - see color ad p 187	◆◆◆	$69-$94 (SAVE)	199
47 / p. 180	AAA	**La Quinta Inn IH35 at Ben White** - see color ad p 187	◆◆◆	$69-$94 (SAVE)	199
48 / p. 180	AAA	**Holiday Inn Airport South** - see color ad p 184	◆◆	$109-$119 (SAVE)	197
49 / p. 180	AAA	**Super 8 Austin North**	◆◆	$39-$69 (SAVE)	203
50 / p. 180		Holiday Inn Northwest/Arboretum - see color ad p 184	◆◆◆	$79-$119	198
51 / p. 180		Hampton Inn Austin-South	◆◆◆	$84-$94	196
52 / p. 180		Hawthorn Suites Northwest	◆◆◆	$69-$199	196
53 / p. 180		Hawthorn Suites South	◆◆◆	$59-$159	197
54 / p. 180	AAA	**Exel Inn Of Austin**	◆	$40-$78 (SAVE)	105
55 / p. 180	AAA	**Embassy Suites Austin North**	◆◆◆	$99-$179 (SAVE)	195
56 / p. 180	AAA	**Drury Inn & Suites-North**	◆◆◆	$73-$103 (SAVE)	194
57 / p. 180	AAA	**Doubletree Hotel Austin** - see color ad p 194	◆◆◆	$79-$209 (SAVE)	194
58 / p. 180	AAA	**Baymont Inn & Suites Austin-Round Rock** - see color ad p 191	◆◆◆	$59-$89 (SAVE)	190
59 / p. 180		Embassy Suites Austin Arboretum	◆◆◆	$129-$229	194
60 / p. 180		SpringHill Suites by Marriott Austin NW	◆◆◆	$79-$89	203
61 / p. 180		Best Western Seville Plaza Inn	◆◆	$59-$09	190
62 / p. 180	AAA	**Hilton Austin North & Towers** - see color ad p 194, p 197	◆◆◆	$189-$229 (SAVE)	197
63 / p. 180	AAA	**La Quinta Inn & Suites at Austin-Airport** - see color ad p 187	◆◆◆	$79-$119 (SAVE)	199

Spotter/Map Page Number	OA	AUSTIN - Lodgings (continued)	Diamond Rating	Rate Range High Season	Listing Page
64 / p. 180		Hampton Inn Austin-North - see color ad p 196	◇◇◇	$74-$99	195
65 / p. 180		Hawthorn Suites Austin Central	◇◇◇	$69-$159	196
66 / p. 180		Quality Suites Austin North	◇◇◇	$80-$150	200
67 / p. 180		Four Points Hotel by Sheraton	◇◇◇	$112-$128	195
68 / p. 180		Comfort Suites Airport	◇◇◇	$89-$99	192
70 / p. 180	AAA	**Red Roof Inn Austin North**	◇◇	$39-$59 SAVE	202
71 / p. 180	AAA	**La Quinta Inn Oltorf** - see color ad p 187	◇◇◇	$69-$99 SAVE	199
72 / p. 180	AAA	**La Quinta Inn-Highland Mall** - see color ad p 187	◇◇◇	$69-$94 SAVE	199
73 / p. 180	AAA	**Drury Inn Austin-Highland Mall**	◇◇◇	$68-$98 SAVE	194
74 / p. 180		Courtyard by Marriott Austin Central	◇◇◇	$89-$109	192
75 / p. 180	AAA	**Wellesley Inn & Suites (Austin/North)** - see color ad p 185	◇◇◇	$85-$105 SAVE	203
76 / p. 180	AAA	**Wingate Inn North**	◇◇◇	$79-$109 SAVE	204
77 / p. 180	AAA	**AmeriSuites (Austin/Airport)** - see color ad p 185	◇◇◇	$85 SAVE	190
78 / p. 180		SpringHill Suites by Marriott-Austin South/Airport	◇◇◇	$109-$119	203
79 / p. 180		Barton Creek Resort	◇◇◇◇	$290-$1650	190
80 / p. 180		Hampton Inn & Suites	◇◇◇	$84-$89	195
81 / p. 180		Habitat Suites Hotel	◇◇◇	$127-$137	195
82 / p. 180	AAA	**Wellesley Inn & Suites (Austin/N Mopac)** - see color ad p 185	◇◇◇	$65-$89 SAVE	203
83 / p. 180		Comfort Inn	◇◇◇	$65-$89	191
84 / p. 180		Motel 6 Austin North - 360	◇	$41-$57	200
85 / p. 180	AAA	**Best Western Atrium North**	◇◇◇	$69-$99 SAVE	190
86 / p. 180		Courtyard by Marriott-Austin Northwest	◇◇◇	$139-$159	192
88 / p. 180		Motel 6 Central #1118	◇◇	$43-$59	200
89 / p. 180		Courtyard By Marriott Austin South	◇◇◇	$79-$109	192
90 / p. 180	AAA	**Days Inn Austin North**	◇◇	$56-$84 SAVE	193
91 / p. 180	AAA	**Days Inn University-Downtown** - see color ad p 193	◇◇	$64-$99 SAVE	193
92 / p. 180		Fairfield Inn-Austin Central	◇◇◇	$69-$119	195
93 / p. 180		Fairfield Inn South	◇◇◇	$79-$89	195
94 / p. 180	AAA	**AmeriSuites Austin N Central** - see color ad p 185	◇◇◇	$99-$129 SAVE	190
95 / p. 180	AAA	**Ramada Limited Austin North** - see color ad p 201	◇◇	$45-$82 SAVE	201
96 / p. 180		Holiday Inn-Austin North (Highland Mall) - see color ad p 184	◇◇◇	$110	198
97 / p. 180	AAA	**Holiday Inn Express** - see color ad p 198	◇◇◇	$72-$86 SAVE	198
98 / p. 180	AAA	**La Quinta Inn & Suites-Austin North Mopac** - see color ad p 187	◇◇◇	$79-$119 SAVE	199
99 / p. 180	AAA	**Country Inn & Suites By Carlson-Austin North** - see color ad p 260	◇◇◇	$90-$116 SAVE	192
100 / p. 180		Residence Inn Austin South	◇◇◇	$89-$179	202
101 / p. 180	AAA	**Residence Inn by Marriott-Austin Northwest/Arboretum**	◇◇◇	$89-$169 SAVE	202

Spotter/Map Page Number	OA	AUSTIN - Lodgings (continued)	Diamond Rating	Rate Range High Season	Listing Page
102 / p. 180	AAA	**Red Roof Inn-Austin South**	◆◆	$39-$59 SAVE	202
103 / p. 180		Bradford Homesuites	◆◆◆	$79-$109	191
104 / p. 180		Candlewood Suites Austin Northwest	◆◆◆	$75-$119	191
105 / p. 180		Comfort Suites-South	◆◆◆	$79-$99	192
106 / p. 180		Hilton Austin Airport	◆◆◆	$99-$189	197
107 / p. 180		Candlewood Suites-South	◆◆◆	$107-$134	191
108 / p. 180		Hilton Garden Inn	◆◆◆	$89	197
109 / p. 180		Homestead Studio Suites Hotel-Austin/Arboretum	◆◆	$55-$70	198
110 / p. 180	AAA	**Rodeway Inn-North**	◆◆	$38-$76 SAVE	202
111 / p. 180		Marriott Hotel-Austin South/Airport	◆◆◆	$99-$149	200
112 / p. 180		Northpark Executive Suite Hotel - see color ad p 200	◆◆◆	$129-$159	200
		AUSTIN - Restaurants			
27 / p. 180		Tony Roma's	◆◆	$6-$20	206
28 / p. 180		Texas Land & Cattle Steakhouse	◆◆◆	$11-$22	205
29 / p. 180		Shades Cafe	◆◆	$6-$22	205
30 / p. 180		Razzoo's Cajun Cafe	◆◆	$6-$17	205
31 / p. 180		Trattoria Grande	◆◆◆	$16-$25	206
32 / p. 180		Fonda San Miguel	◆◆◆	$13-$22	204
33 / p. 180		County Line On The Lake	◆◆	$8-$16	204
34 / p. 180		Jeffrey's	◆◆◆	$21-$36	205
35 / p. 180		Old San Francisco Steak House	◆◆◆	$15-$31	205
36 / p. 180		Central Market Cafe	◆	$6-$14	204
37 / p. 180		Pappadeaux Seafood Kitchen	◆◆	$12-$25	205
39 / p. 180		Taj Palace Indian Restaurant & Bar	◆◆	$8-$17	205
40 / p. 180		Threadgill's Restaurant	◆	$6-$18	206
41 / p. 180		Kerbey Lane Cafe-Central	◆◆	$5-$10	205
42 / p. 180		Zoot American Bistro & Wine Bar	◆◆◆	$19-$36	206
43 / p. 180		Matt's El Rancho	◆◆	$9-$15	205
44 / p. 180		Satay Restaurant	◆◆	$7-$15	205
45 / p. 180		West Lynn Cafe	◆◆	$8-$13	206
46 / p. 180		Bone Daddy's	◆◆	$6-$20	204
47 / p. 180		Cool River Cafe	◆◆◆	$0-$30	204
49 / p. 180		Ray's Steakhouse	◆◆◆	$17-$37	205
51 / p. 180		Dan McKlusky's Restaurant	◆◆	$13-$36	204

DOWNTOWN AUSTIN　(See map p. 178; index p. 179)

──────── WHERE TO STAY ────────

AUSTIN MARRIOTT AT THE CAPITOL

Phone: (512)478-1111　❹

SAVE

All Year　　1P: $129-$204　　2P: $129-$204

Location: I-35, exit 234B, 0.3 mi e. 701 E 11th St 78701. Fax: 512/478-3700. **Facility:** 365 one-bedroom standard units. 16 stories, interior corridors. *Bath:* combo or shower only. **Parking:** on-site (fee) and valet.

Large-scale Hotel

Terms: check-in 4 pm, package plans, small pets only. **Amenities:** dual phone lines, voice mail, irons, hair dryers. **Pool(s):** heated indoor/outdoor. **Leisure Activities:** saunas, whirlpool, exercise room. *Fee:* massage. **Guest Services:** gift shop, valet and coin laundry. **Business Services:** conference facilities, business center. **Cards:** AX, CB, DC, DS, JC, MC, VI.

SOME UNITS

🛏 🍴 🍸 ⚒ 🕸 🏊 ✕ 🐕 [DATA PORT] 🖥 / ✕ 🛗 /

AUSTINS INN AT PEARL STREET

Phone: (512)478-0051　❿

All Year [ECP]　　1P: $90-$175　　2P: $90-$175　　XP: $25

Location: Just w to Pearl St. 809 W Martin Luther King Blvd 78701. Fax: 512/478-0033. **Facility:** This property offers spacious accommodations in a convenient downtown location that also offers a quiet and shaded retreat.

Bed & Breakfast

Designated smoking area. 9 units. 7 one-bedroom standard units, some with whirlpools. 2 one-bedroom suites ($115-$200), some with efficiencies and/or whirlpools. 2 stories (no elevator), interior corridors. *Bath:* combo or shower only. **Parking:** on-site. **Terms:** 1-2 night minimum stay - weekends, 10 day cancellation notice-fee imposed, [BP] meal plan available. **Amenities:** video library, voice mail, irons, hair dryers. **Business Services:** meeting rooms. **Cards:** AX, DC, DS, MC, VI.

SOME UNITS

[A$K] ✕ [VCR] 🐕 / 🛗 🖥 /

CROWNE PLAZA AUSTIN HOTEL

Phone: (512)480-8181　❼

2/1-5/31 & 9/8-1/31	1P: $129-$159	2P: $129-$159	XP: $10　F18
6/1-9/7	1P: $109-$125	2P: $109-$125	XP: $10　F18

Large-scale Hotel

Location: I-35, exit 234B southbound; exit 234C northbound, on southbound frontage road. 500 N I-35 78701. Fax: 512/457-7990. **Facility:** 254 units. 247 one-bedroom standard units. 7 one-bedroom suites with whirlpools. 18 stories, interior corridors. *Bath:* combo or shower only. **Parking:** on-site (fee) and valet. **Terms:** cancellation fee imposed, pets ($50 extra charge). **Amenities:** dual phone lines, voice mail, irons, hair dryers. *Some:* fax. **Pool(s):** outdoor. **Leisure Activities:** exercise room. **Guest Services:** gift shop, valet laundry, area transportation. **Business Services:** conference facilities, business center. **Cards:** AX, CB, DC, DS, JC, MC, VI.

SOME UNITS

[A$K] [S FEE] 🔌 🛏 🍴 🍸 ⚒ 🕸 🏊 🐕 [DATA PORT] 🖥 / ✕ 🛗 🖥 /

(See map p. 178)

DOUBLETREE CLUB HOTEL

Phone: (512)479-4000 **14**

All Year   1P: $139   2P: $139   XP: $5   F18

SAVE

Location: I-35, exit Martin Luther King Jr Blvd, just n on northbound frontage road. 1617 I-35 N 78702. Fax: 512/479-6400. **Facility:** 152 one-bedroom standard units. 6 stories, interior corridors. *Bath:* combo or shower only. **Parking:** on-site. **Terms:** 21 day cancellation notice, [MAP] meal plan available, package plans.

Small-scale Hotel **Amenities:** high-speed Internet, dual phone lines, voice mail, irons, hair dryers. **Pool(s):** outdoor. **Leisure Activities:** exercise room. **Guest Services:** valet and coin laundry. **Business Services:** meeting rooms, business center. **Cards:** AX, DC, DS, MC, VI.

SOME UNITS

DOUBLETREE GUEST SUITES-AUSTIN

Phone: (512)478-7000 **2**

2/1-5/31   1P: $129-$269   2P: $129-$269
9/1-1/31   1P: $109-$269   2P: $109-$269
6/1-8/31   1P: $109-$229   2P: $109-$229

SAVE

Large-scale Hotel **Location:** Just nw of Capitol; center. 303 W 15th St 78701. Fax: 512/478-3562. **Facility:** 189 units. 175 one- and 14 two-bedroom suites ($109-$269) with kitchens. 15 stories, interior corridors. **Parking:** on-site (fee) and valet. **Terms:** small pets only ($25 extra charge). **Amenities:** dual phone lines, voice mail, irons, hair dryers. **Pool(s):** heated outdoor. **Leisure Activities:** saunas, whirlpool, exercise room. **Guest Services:** valet and coin laundry, area transportation. **Business Services:** meeting rooms, business center. **Cards:** AX, CB, DC, DS, JC, MC, VI.

SOME UNITS
FEE

THE DRISKILL

Phone: (512)474-5911 **6**

All Year   1P: $270-$340

Classic Historic Large-scale Hotel **Location:** 6th at Brazos. 604 Brazos St 78701. Fax: 512/474-2214. **Facility:** Named after the colonel said to have opened the property on December 20, 1886, The Driskill features displays of historic artwork and artifacts. 188 units. 178 one-bedroom standard units, some with whirlpools. 9 one- and 1 two-bedroom suites ($400-$2500), some with whirlpools. 5-12 stories, interior corridors. *Bath:* combo or shower only. **Parking:** valet. **Terms:** cancellation fee imposed, package plans, small pets only ($50 fee). **Amenities:** dual phone lines, voice mail, safes, honor bars, irons, hair dryers. *Fee:* video games, high-speed Internet. *Some:* CD players. **Dining:** The Driskill Grill, see separate listing. **Guest Services:** valet laundry. **Business Services:** meeting rooms, business center. **Cards:** AX, DC, DS, JC, MC, VI.

SOME UNITS
FEE

EMBASSY SUITES HOTEL-DOWNTOWN

Phone: (512)469-9000 **10**

All Year [BP]   1P: $109-$299   2P: $109-$309   XP: $10   F12

SAVE

Large-scale Hotel **Location:** Just s of Congress Ave Bridge. 300 S Congress Ave 78704. Fax: 512/480-9164. **Facility:** 262 units. 16 one-bedroom standard units. 246 one-bedroom suites. 9 stories, interior corridors. *Bath:* combo or shower only. **Parking:** on-site. **Terms:** small pets only ($25 fee). **Amenities:** video games (fee), dual phone lines, voice mail, irons, hair dryers. *Some:* fax. **Pool(s):** heated indoor. **Leisure Activities:** sauna, whirlpool, exercise room. **Guest Services:** gift shop, complimentary evening beverages, valet and coin laundry, area transportation. **Business Services:** meeting rooms, PC, fax (fee). **Cards:** AX, CB, DC, DS, JC, MC, VI.

SOME UNITS
FEE

FOUR SEASONS HOTEL

Phone: (512)478-4500 **11**

All Year   1P: $280-$350   2P: $280-$350

Large-scale Hotel **Location:** Bordering Town Lake. 98 San Jacinto Blvd 78701. Fax: 512/478-3117. **Facility:** This luxury hotel features a scenic lakeside setting; guest rooms are decorated in a sophisticated Southwestern style. 291 units. 264 one-bedroom standard units. 24 one- and 3 two-bedroom suites ($350-$1400). 9 stories, interior corridors. *Bath:* combo or shower only. **Parking:** on-site (fee) and valet. **Terms:** cancellation fee imposed, small pets only. **Amenities:** CD players, dual phone lines, voice mail, safes, honor bars, irons, hair dryers. *Fee:* video games, high-speed Internet. **Dining:** The Cafe, see separate listing. **Pool(s):** heated outdoor. **Leisure Activities:** saunas, whirlpool, jogging. *Fee:* bicycles, massage. **Guest Services:** gift shop, valet laundry, area transportation. **Business Services:** conference facilities, business center. **Cards:** AX, CB, DC, DS, JC, MC, VI.

SOME UNITS
FEE

HOLIDAY INN-TOWN LAKE

Phone: (512)472-8211 **12**

All Year   1P: $79-$139   2P: $89-$149   XP: $10   F19

Large-scale Hotel **Location:** I-35, exit 233. 20 N I-35 78701. Fax: 512/472-4636. **Facility:** 320 one-bedroom standard units. 11-14 stories, interior corridors. *Bath:* combo or shower only. **Parking:** on-site. **Terms:** 7% service charge, pets ($25 fee, $100 deposit). **Amenities:** voice mail, irons, hair dryers. **Pool(s):** heated outdoor. **Leisure Activities:** saunas, whirlpool, limited exercise equipment. **Guest Services:** gift shop, valet and coin laundry, area transportation. **Business Services:** meeting rooms, fax (fee). **Cards:** AX, CB, DC, DS, JC, MC, VI. *(See color ad p 184)*

SOME UNITS

HOMESTEAD STUDIO SUITES HOTEL-AUSTIN/DOWNTOWN/TOWN LAKE

Phone: (512)476-1818 **15**

All Year   1P: $89-$109   2P: $99-$119   XP: $10   F17

Small-scale Hotel **Location:** I-35, exit 234B southbound; exit 234A northbound, 1.8 mi w on Caesar Chavez/E First St, then 0.5 mi s. 507 S First St 78704. Fax: 512/476-0451. **Facility:** 130 one-bedroom standard units. 3 stories, interior corridors. *Bath:* combo or shower only. **Parking:** on-site. **Terms:** pets ($75 fee). **Amenities:** dual phone lines, voice mail, irons, hair dryers. **Guest Services:** valet and coin laundry. **Business Services:** meeting rooms. **Cards:** AX, CB, DC, DS, JC, MC, VI.

SOME UNITS
FEE   FEE   FEE

(See map p. 178)

HYATT REGENCY AUSTIN

Phone: (512)477-1234 **9**

(AAA) (SAVE) All Year   1P: $105-$245   2P: $105-$245   XP: $25   F18
Location: At south end of Congress Bridge; on south bank of Town Lake. 208 Barton Springs Rd 78704. Fax: 512/480-2069. **Facility:** Well-appointed accomodations await the traveller at this hotel located on the Colorado River with excellent views of downtown. 446 units. 428 one-bedroom standard units. 18 one-bedroom suites. 17 stories, interior corridors. *Bath:* combo or shower only. **Parking:** on-site (fee) and valet.
Large-scale Hotel
Terms: cancellation fee imposed. **Amenities:** high-speed Internet, dual phone lines, voice mail, safes, irons, hair dryers. *Some:* fax. **Dining:** 6:30 am-11 pm, Fri & Sat-midnight, cocktails. **Pool(s):** outdoor. **Leisure Activities:** whirlpool, jogging, exercise room. *Fee:* bicycles. **Guest Services:** gift shop, valet and coin laundry. **Business Services:** conference facilities, business center. **Cards:** AX, CB, DC, DS, JC, MC, VI. *(See color ad inside front cover)*

SOME UNITS

LA QUINTA CAPITOL

Phone: (512)476-1166 **3**

(AAA) (SAVE) All Year   1P: $89-$119   2P: $99-$129   XP: $10   F18
Location: Just e of State Capitol Building. 300 E 11 St 78701. Fax: 512/476-6044. **Facility:** 150 units. 147 one-bedroom standard units. 3 one-bedroom suites ($119-$169). 4 stories, interior/exterior corridors. *Bath:* combo or shower only. **Parking:** valet. **Terms:** [ECP] meal plan available, small pets only. **Amenities:** *Some:* video games (fee), dual phone lines, voice mail, irons, hair dryers. *Some:* fax. **Pool(s):** outdoor. **Leisure Activities:** exercise
Small-scale Hotel
room. **Guest Services:** valet laundry, airport transportation (fee)-Austin Airport. **Business Services:** meeting rooms, fax (fee). **Cards:** AX, CB, DC, DS, JC, MC, VI. **Special Amenities:** free continental breakfast and free local telephone calls. *(See color ad below)*

SOME UNITS

FEE

OMNI AUSTIN HOTEL & SUITES

Phone: (512)476-3700 **5**

(AAA) (SAVE) 2/1-5/17 & 9/7-1/31   1P: $149-$369   2P: $149-$369   XP: $20   F18
5/18-9/6   1P: $129-$369   2P: $129-$369   XP: $20   F18
Location: 8th St and San Jacinto. 700 San Jacinto 78701. Fax: 512/397-4885. **Facility:** In a convenient downtown location, this hotel offers large accomodations to its guests and is within walking distance to many of Austin's attractions. 375 units. 338 one-bedroom standard units. 18 one- and 19 two-bedroom suites with kitchens,
Large-scale Hotel
some with whirlpools. 20 stories, interior corridors. *Bath:* combo or shower only. **Parking:** on-site (fee) and valet. **Terms:** cancellation fee imposed. **Amenities:** video games (fee), dual phone lines, voice mail, irons, hair dryers. **Dining:** 6:30 am-10 pm, cocktails. **Pool(s):** small heated outdoor. **Leisure Activities:** sauna, whirlpool, exercise room. *Fee:* massage. **Guest Services:** gift shop, valet laundry. **Business Services:** conference facilities, business center. **Cards:** AX, CB, DC, DS, MC, VI. **Special Amenities:** free newspaper.

SOME UNITS

FEE

RADISSON HOTEL & SUITES-AUSTIN

Phone: (512)478-9611 **8**

(AAA) (SAVE) All Year   1P: $99   2P: $99   XP: $10   F16
Location: First St and Congress Ave. 111 E Cesar Chavez 78701. Fax: 512/473-8399. **Facility:** 413 units. 314 one-bedroom standard units. 99 one-bedroom suites. 12 stories, interior corridors. *Bath:* combo or shower only. **Parking:** on-site (fee) and valet. **Amenities:** dual phone lines, voice mail, irons, hair dryers. *Some:* honor
Large-scale Hotel
bars. **Dining:** 6:30 am-11 pm, Fri-midnight, Sat & Sun 7 am-11 pm, cocktails. **Pool(s):** outdoor. **Leisure Activities:** access to jogging trail, bicycles, hiking trails, exercise room. **Guest Services:** gift shop, valet laundry, airport transportation (fee)-Austin Airport. **Business Services:** conference facilities, business center. **Cards:** AX, CB, DC, DS, JC, MC, VI. *(See color ad p 178)*

SOME UNITS

FEE

(See map p. 178)

RODEWAY INN-UNIVERSITY/DOWNTOWN
Phone: (512)477-6395 ❶

AAA (SAVE) All Year   1P: $59-$90   2P: $59-$90   XP: $5   F17
Motel
Location: I-35, exit 235B (University of Texas/LBJ Library) southbound; exit 236A (26th and 32nd sts) northbound; north-east off lower level I-35, US 79 and SR 290. 2900 I-35 N 78705. Fax: 512/477-1830. **Facility:** 50 one-bedroom standard units. 2-3 stories (no elevator), exterior corridors. *Bath:* combo or shower only. **Parking:** on-site. **Amenities:** voice mail. **Pool(s):** small outdoor. **Guest Services:** airport transportation (fee)-Austin Airport. **Business Services:** fax (fee). **Cards:** AX, CB, DC, DS, JC, MC, VI. **Special Amenities:** free continental breakfast and free local telephone calls.

SOME UNITS

🆂ᴰ 🚼 🛏 👫 🐕 ➿ 🎥 [DATA PORT] 🛢 🖥 💻 / 🗙 /
FEE

SUPER 8 CENTRAL
Phone: (512)472-8331 ❶❸

AAA (SAVE) All Year   1P: $55-$75   2P: $62-$85   XP: $5   F12
Motel
Location: I-35, exit 234, at 12th St. 1201 N I-35 78702. Fax: 512/476-6610. **Facility:** 64 units. 59 one- and 5 two-bedroom standard units. 2 stories (no elevator), exterior corridors. *Bath:* combo or shower only. **Parking:** on-site. **Terms:** 3 day cancellation notice, [CP] meal plan available, package plans, pets ($20 deposit). **Amenities:** voice mail. **Pool(s):** small outdoor. **Guest Services:** coin laundry, airport transportation (fee)-Austin Airport. **Business Services:** fax (fee). **Cards:** AX, CB, DC, DS, MC, VI. **Special Amenities:** free continental breakfast and free room upgrade (subject to availability with advanced reservations).

SOME UNITS

🆂ᴰ 🚼 🛏 👫 🍴 🐕 ➿ 🎥 [DATA PORT] 🛢 🖥 / 🗙 💻 /
FEE

───── *The following lodging was either not evaluated or did not* ─────
meet AAA rating requirements but is listed for your information only.

LAKEWAY INN AND RESORT
Phone: 512/261-6600

(fyi) Not evaluated. **Location:** Jct FM 620 and Lakeway Blvd W to Lakeway Dr, then n. 101 Lakeway Dr 78734. Facilities, services, and decor characterize a mid-range property.

───── **WHERE TO DINE** ─────

THE CAFE   **Lunch:** $9-$16   **Dinner:** $18-$33   **Phone:** 512/685-8300 ⑤
American
Location: Bordering Town Lake; in Four Seasons Hotel. 98 San Jacinto Blvd 78701. **Hours:** 6:30 am-10 pm, Fri & Sat 7 am-11 pm, Sun 7 am-10 pm. **Reservations:** suggested. **Features:** The peaceful terrace overlooks a lake and beautifully landscaped grounds. An excellent choice is focaccia-encrusted pork medallions with mashed potatoes and grilled asparagus. The star over Texas dessert layers chocolate mousse and sponge cake. Dressy casual; cocktails. **Parking:** on-site. **Cards:** AX, CB, DC, DS, MC, VI.

🗙

CAFE SERRANOS Historic   **Lunch:** $6-$7   **Dinner:** $8-$15   **Phone:** 512/322-9922 ①
Tex-Mex
Location: Corner of 11th and Red River sts. 1111 Red River St 78701. **Hours:** 11 am-10 pm, Fri & Sat-11 pm. Closed: 11/27, 12/25. **Reservations:** suggested. **Features:** Minutes from the state capitol, the Tex-Mex cafe occupies a 120-year-old stone building. Stuffed jalapenos tempt those with a nearby water glass and a taste for something spicy. Among good choices are crunchy flautas and sizzling fajitas. Casual dress; cocktails. **Parking:** street. **Cards:** AX, CB, DC, DS, MC, VI.

🗙

CARMELO'S Historic   **Lunch:** $10-$17   **Dinner:** $17-$34   **Phone:** 512/477-7497 ③
Northern Italian
Location: I-35, exit 3rd and 8th sts, just w. 504 E 5th St 78701. **Hours:** 11 am-2:30 & 5-10:30 pm, Fri-11 pm, Sat 5 pm-11 pm, Sun 5 pm-10:30 pm. Closed major holidays. **Reservations:** suggested; weekends. **Features:** Built in 1872, the oldest standing train depot in Texas has become home to one of the area's most romantic eateries. An Italian patio with a garden and fountain makes a lovely scene in which to enjoy pasta, seafood, beef and chicken dishes. Smoke free premises. Dressy casual; cocktails. **Parking:** valet. **Cards:** AX, DC, DS, MC, VI.

🔼ᴹ 🗙

CASTLE HILL CAFE   **Lunch:** $7-$10   **Dinner:** $18-$21   **Phone:** 512/476-7218 ⑦
Continental
Location: Corner of W 5th and Baylor sts, just w of Lamar Blvd. 1101 W 5th St 78703. **Hours:** 11 am-2:30 & 6-10 pm, Sat from 6 pm. Closed major holidays; also Sun, week of 7/4 & 12/25. **Reservations:** accepted. **Features:** Nestled among tall trees and bushes, the two-story, split-level home was converted into a cafe. A melange of mouthwatering herbs and spices flavors every dish. A good starter is spicy duck and sausage gumbo or Lucinda's basil cheese torta. Wood-plank floors, wall-mounted plaster geckos and lush, potted greenery enhance the garden cafe appeal. Smoke free premises. Casual dress; beer & wine only. **Parking:** on-site. **Cards:** AX, DS, MC, VI.

🗙

CLAY PIT   **Lunch:** $7-$16   **Dinner:** $9-$16   **Phone:** 512/322-5131 ⑬
Indian
Location: I-35, exit 15th St, w to Guadalupe St, 1 blk n on the southbound lanes. 1601 Guadalupe St 78701. **Hours:** 11 am-2 & 5-10 pm, Fri & Sat-11 pm, Sun from 5. Closed: 1/1, 11/27, 12/25. **Reservations:** accepted. **Features:** Contemporary Indian fusion dishes highlight the dining experience in this establishment located in a late 1800s mercantile store. Enjoy the chicken, steak, lamb, prawns or mixed grill entrees. Smoke free premises. Casual dress; cocktails. **Parking:** on-site. **Cards:** AX, DC, DS, MC, VI.

🍸 🗙

DAN MCKLUSKY'S RESTAURANT   **Dinner:** $15-$38   **Phone:** 512/473-8924 ④
Steak House
Location: I-35, exit 3rd and 8th sts, just w. 301 E 6th St 78701. **Hours:** 5 pm-10 pm, Sat-11 pm, Sun-9 pm. Closed major holidays. **Reservations:** suggested. **Features:** A rustic, relaxing atmosphere is achieved through a combination of lovely artwork, jazz and contemporary music and subdued lighting from gas lamps. Choice cuts of steak, such as rib eye and strip, are cooked to order and served by a charming, casual staff. Casual dress; cocktails. **Parking:** street. **Cards:** AX, DC, DS, MC, VI.

🍸 🗙

(See map p. 178)

THE DRISKILL GRILL Classic Historic **Lunch:** $10-$14 **Dinner:** $20-$38 **Phone:** 512/474-5911 ⑩
American
DC, DS, MC, VI.
Location: 6th at Brazos; in The Driskill. 604 Brazos St 78701. **Hours:** 6:30 am-2 & 5:30-10 pm. **Reservations:** suggested. **Features:** Attentive, discreet service accents the experience at the intimate, elegant restaurant. Innovative preparations of seafood, steak, lamb and specialty items are pleasingly presented. Smoke free premises. Dressy casual; cocktails; entertainment. **Parking:** valet. **Cards:** AX, CB, DC, DS, MC, VI.

EASTSIDE CAFE **Lunch:** $8-$20 **Dinner:** $8-$20 **Phone:** 512/476-5858 ⑧
Continental
desserts. Smoke free premises. Casual dress; beer & wine only. **Parking:** on-site. **Cards:** AX, DC, DS, MC, VI.
Location: Just e of I-35 and University of Texas campus, exit Manor Rd. 2113 Manor Rd 78722. **Hours:** 11 am-10 pm, Fri-11 pm, Sat 10 am-11 pm, Sun 10 am-10 pm; Saturday & Sunday brunch. Closed: 11/27, 12/25. **Reservations:** suggested. **Features:** In a 1928 bungalow, the cafe is adorned with pictures and lush foliage. Diners can opt for patio seating. The menu centers on sophisticated fare, including tempting

EL SOL Y LA LUNA **Lunch:** $5-$8 **Dinner:** $5-$10 **Phone:** 512/444-7770 ⑨
Tex-Mex
Casual dress; beer & wine only. **Parking:** on-site. **Cards:** AX, DS, MC, VI.
Location: Between Riverside and Oltorf Blvd. 1224 S Congress 78704. **Hours:** 7 am-10 pm, Sun-Tues to 3 pm. Closed: 1/1, 11/27, 12/25. **Features:** The cafe walls are decorated with celestial artwork, while the patio's wrought-iron gate and greenery complete the decor. Representative of Tex-Mex cuisine are tasty enchiladas, the popular mole entree and mouthwatering chocolate flan. The staff is outgoing and prompt.

FLEMING'S PRIME STEAKHOUSE & WINE BAR **Dinner:** $18-$28 **Phone:** 512/457-1500 ⑯
Steak House
MC, VI.
Location: I-35, exit Cesar Chavez, w to Trinity, 1 blk n; across from the convention center. 320 E Second St 78701. **Hours:** 5 pm-10 pm, Fri & Sat-11 pm. Closed: 11/27, 12/25. **Reservations:** accepted. **Features:** Patrons can choose from more than 100 by-the-glass wines to accompany the upscale restaurant's fine steaks and chops. Smoke free premises. Dressy casual; cocktails. **Parking:** valet and street. **Cards:** AX, DC, DS,

IRONWORKS BARBEQUE **Lunch:** $7-$15 **Dinner:** $7-$15 **Phone:** 512/478-4855 ⑪
Barbecue
daily. Casual dress; beer only. **Parking:** on-site. **Cards:** AX, DC, MC, VI.
Location: Just w of I-35, at corner of E 1st and Red River sts; next to Convention Center. 100 Red River 78701. **Hours:** 11 am-9 pm. Closed major holidays; also Sun. **Features:** Overlooking Waller Creek from a converted ironworks building, the eatery features a fine range of beef, pork and chicken barbecue dishes generously served with fresh sides of beans and potato salad. Luscious desserts are prepared in house

LOUIE'S 106 **Lunch:** $7-$12 **Dinner:** $10-$18 **Phone:** 512/476-2010 ②
Mediterranean
appetizers. Smoke free premises. Casual dress; cocktails. **Parking:** street. **Cards:** AX, CB, DC, DS, MC, VI.
Location: I-35, exit 3rd and 8th sts, 0.8 mi w; in Littlefield Bldg. 106 E 6th St 78701. **Hours:** 11:30 am-10:30 pm, Fri-11 pm, Sat 5:30 pm-11 pm, Sun 5:30 pm-9:30 pm. Closed major holidays. **Reservations:** suggested. **Features:** The Mediterranean bistro projects casual elegance in an upscale, split-level dining room. A small loaf of hot, fresh bread begins the parade of hearty and healthy options, including Spanish tapas

MALAGA TAPAS & BAR **Dinner:** $9-$23 **Phone:** 512/236-8020 ⑫
Spanish
MC, VI.
Location: I-35, exit 3rd & 8th sts. 208 W Fourth St 78701. **Hours:** 5 pm-midnight, Thurs-Sat to 2 am. Closed: 5/26, 9/1, 12/25; also Sun. **Reservations:** suggested. **Features:** More than 350 wine selections await the patrons of this Spanish restaurant while sampling more than 20 different appetizer choices. Located in the historic Warehouse District of town. Casual dress; cocktails. **Parking:** street. **Cards:** AX, CB, DC, DS,

MANUEL'S DOWNTOWN **Lunch:** $9-$13 **Dinner:** $10-$16 **Phone:** 512/472-7555 ⑭
Mexican
jazz brunch adds spice to Sunday. Casual dress; cocktails. **Parking:** on-site. **Cards:** AX, CB, DC, DS, MC, VI.
Location: 3rd St and Congress Ave. 310 Congress 78701. **Hours:** 11 am-10 pm, Fri & Sat-11 pm, Sun-9 pm. Closed: 11/27, 12/24, 12/25. **Reservations:** accepted. **Features:** Designed in shades of black with columns and well-spaced tables, the dining room doesn't adopt the decor of a typical Mexican kitchen. An extensive tequila list complements such menu highlights as grilled fajitas and vegetarian chiles rellenos. A

MARS RESTAURANT & BAR **Dinner:** $12-$22 **Phone:** 512/472-3901 ⑮
International
MC, VI.
Location: Downtown; just nw of the Capitol. 1610 San Antonio St 78701. **Hours:** 5:30 pm-10:30 pm, Fri & Sat-11 pm. Closed major holidays. **Reservations:** accepted. **Features:** Asian-influenced Mediterranean fusion cooking also draws on Middle Eastern, Indian and Caribbean flavors. The friendly staff helps energize the upbeat atmosphere. Smoke free premises. Dressy casual; cocktails. **Parking:** on-site. **Cards:** AX, DS,

SULLIVAN'S STEAKHOUSE **Dinner:** $17-$29 **Phone:** 512/495-6504 ⑥
Steak House
Location: Corner of 3rd St and Colorado. 300 Colorado 78701. **Hours:** 5:30 pm-11 pm, Sat from 5 pm, Sun 5 pm-10 pm. Closed: 11/27, 12/25. **Features:** The specialty at the 1940s-style steakhouse is the thick, juicy, 20-ounce Kansas City strip. The signature salad of quartered iceberg lettuce is drizzled with homemade Roquefort dressing. Side dishes—including creamed spinach and garlic mashed, au gratin or baked potatoes—are ordered separately. Chocolate lovers shouldn't miss the bottomless brownie cake or souffle. Fresh stone crab is another good choice. The atmosphere blends traditional, slick and stylish. Smoke free premises. Dressy casual; cocktails; entertainment. **Parking:** valet. **Cards:** AX, CB, DC, DS, JC, MC, VI.

(See map p. 178)

AUSTIN pop. 656,562 (See map p. 180; index p. 181)

──────── WHERE TO STAY ────────

AMERISUITES (AUSTIN/AIRPORT)
AAA SAVE All Year | 1P: $85 | 2P: $85 | XP: $10

Phone: (512)386-7600 **77** F17

Location: I-35, exit 230B (Ben White Blvd), 3.2 mi e. 7601 Ben White Blvd 78741. Fax: 512/386-7601. **Facility:** 80 one-bedroom standard units. 4 stories, interior corridors. **Bath:** combo or shower only. **Parking:** on-site. **Terms:** [ECP] meal plan available. **Amenities:** video games (fee), voice mail, irons, hair dryers. **Leisure Activities:** whirlpool, putting green, limited exercise equipment. **Guest Services:** valet and coin laundry, airport transportation-Bergstrom International Airport, area transportation-within 10 mi. **Business Services:** meeting rooms, business center. **Cards:** AX, DS, JC, MC, VI. *(See color ad p 185)*

Small-scale Hotel

SOME UNITS

AMERISUITES (AUSTIN/ARBORETUM)
AAA SAVE All Year | 1P: $69-$159 | 2P: $69-$159

Phone: 512/231-8491 **31** F18

Location: Jct of US 183 and SR 360, e to Stonelake Blvd, s to Tudor Blvd, then just e. 3612 Tudor Blvd 78759. Fax: 512/231-9437. **Facility:** 128 one-bedroom standard units. 6 stories, interior corridors. **Bath:** combo or shower only. **Parking:** on-site. **Terms:** [ECP] meal plan available, small pets only. **Amenities:** video games (fee), voice mail, irons, hair dryers. *Some:* dual phone lines. **Pool(s):** heated outdoor. **Leisure Activities:** exercise room. **Guest Services:** complimentary evening beverages: Mon-Thurs, valet and coin laundry, airport transportation (fee)-Austin Airport, area transportation-within 5 mi. **Business Services:** meeting rooms. **Cards:** AX, CB, DC, DS, JC, MC, VI. **Special Amenities:** free continental breakfast and free newspaper. *(See color ad p 185)*

Small-scale Hotel

SOME UNITS

AMERISUITES AUSTIN N CENTRAL
AAA SAVE All Year [ECP] | 1P: $99-$129 | 2P: $99-$129 | XP: $10

Phone: (512)323-2121 **94** F18

Location: I-35, exit 240A, on west frontage road. 7522 N I-35 78752. Fax: 512/323-5118. **Facility:** 122 one-bedroom standard units. 5 stories, interior corridors. **Bath:** combo or shower only. **Parking:** on-site. **Amenities:** dual phone lines, voice mail, irons, hair dryers. *Fee:* video games, high-speed Internet. **Pool(s):** heated outdoor. **Leisure Activities:** limited exercise equipment. **Guest Services:** complimentary evening beverages, valet and coin laundry, airport transportation (fee)-Austin Airport, area transportation-within 5 mi. **Business Services:** meeting rooms, fax (fee). **Cards:** AX, DC, DS, JC, MC, VI. **Special Amenities:** free continental breakfast and free newspaper. *(See color ad p 185)*

Small-scale Hotel

SOME UNITS

BARTON CREEK RESORT
All Year | 1P: $290-$1650 | 2P: $290-$1650

Phone: (512)329-4000 **79**

Location: Jct Loop 360 and SR 2244 (Bee Caves Rd), 1 mi w to Barton Creek Blvd, 1.7 mi s to Barton Club Dr. 8212 Barton Club Dr 78735. Fax: 512/329-4597. **Facility:** A full service resort with 72 holes of championship golf, tennis, and a spa. Upscale accomodations and spectacular views of the Texas Hill Country. 295 units. 279 one-bedroom standard units. 12 one- and 4 two-bedroom suites ($495-$1650), some with whirlpools. 9 stories, interior corridors. **Bath:** combo or shower only. **Parking:** on-site and valet. **Terms:** check-in 4 pm, 14 day cancellation notice-fee imposed, [BP] meal plan available, package plans. **Amenities:** dual phone lines, voice mail, honor bars, irons, hair dryers. *Fee:* video games, high-speed Internet. *Some:* CD players. **Pool(s):** heated outdoor, heated indoor. **Leisure Activities:** whirlpools, steamrooms, 11 lighted tennis courts, recreation programs, hiking trails, jogging, playground, spa, sports court, basketball. *Fee:* golf-72 holes. **Guest Services:** gift shop, valet laundry, area transportation (fee). **Business Services:** conference facilities, business center. **Cards:** AX, DC, MC, VI.

Large-scale Hotel

SOME UNITS

BAYMONT INN & SUITES AUSTIN-ROUND ROCK
AAA SAVE All Year [ECP] | 1P: $59-$89 | 2P: $59-$89

Phone: (512)246-2800 **58**

Location: I-35, exit 250, on west frontage road. 150 Parker Dr 78728. Fax: 512/246-2824. **Facility:** 85 units. 81 one-bedroom standard units. 4 one-bedroom suites ($79-$129). 4 stories, interior corridors. **Bath:** combo or shower only. **Parking:** on-site. **Terms:** pets ($50 deposit). **Amenities:** video games (fee), voice mail, irons, hair dryers. **Pool(s):** outdoor. **Leisure Activities:** limited exercise equipment. **Guest Services:** valet and coin laundry, airport transportation (fee)-Austin Airport. **Business Services:** meeting rooms, fax (fee). **Cards:** AX, CB, DC, DS, MC, VI. **Special Amenities:** free continental breakfast and free newspaper. *(See color ad p 191)*

Small-scale Hotel

SOME UNITS

BEST WESTERN ATRIUM NORTH
AAA SAVE All Year [ECP] | 1P: $69-$99 | 2P: $69-$99 | XP: $5

Phone: (512)339-7311 **85** F13

Location: I-35, exit 240A, 0.4 mi w on Anderson Ln. 7928 Gessner Dr 78753. Fax: 512/339-3687. **Facility:** 122 one-bedroom standard units, some with whirlpools. 4 stories, interior corridors. **Parking:** on-site. **Terms:** small pets only ($25 deposit). **Amenities:** voice mail, irons, hair dryers. **Pool(s):** small heated indoor. **Leisure Activities:** sauna. **Guest Services:** valet laundry, airport transportation (fee)-Austin Airport. **Business Services:** meeting rooms, business center. **Cards:** AX, CB, DC, DS, JC, MC, VI. **Special Amenities:** free continental breakfast and free newspaper.

Small-scale Hotel

SOME UNITS

BEST WESTERN SEVILLE PLAZA INN
SAVE All Year | 1P: $59-$69 | 2P: $59-$89 | XP: $5

Phone: (512)447-5511 **61** F14

Location: I-35, exit 230A (Stassney Rd) southbound; exit 230 (Ben White Blvd) northbound. 4323 I-35 S 78744. Fax: 512/443-8055. **Facility:** 96 one-bedroom standard units. 4 stories, interior corridors. **Parking:** on-site. **Terms:** [ECP] meal plan available. **Amenities:** irons, hair dryers. **Pool(s):** outdoor. **Guest Services:** coin laundry. **Business Services:** meeting rooms, fax. **Cards:** AX, CB, DC, DS, JC, MC, VI.

Motel

SOME UNITS

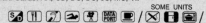

(See map p. 180)

BRADFORD HOMESUITES
Phone: (512)342-8080 `103`

All Year [CP] 1P: $79-$109 2P: $79-$109
Location: US 183 N to Capital of Texas Hwy, then just e. 10001 N Capital of Texas Hwy 78759. Fax: 512/342-0228.
Small-scale Hotel **Facility:** 135 units. 102 one-bedroom standard units with efficiencies. 33 one-bedroom suites with efficiencies. 3 stories, interior corridors. *Bath:* combo or shower only. **Parking:** on-site. **Terms:** cancellation fee imposed. **Amenities:** video games (fee), dual phone lines, voice mail, irons, hair dryers. **Pool(s):** outdoor. **Leisure Activities:** whirlpool. **Guest Services:** valet and coin laundry. **Business Services:** meeting rooms, business center. **Cards:** AX, CB, DC, DS, JC, MC, VI.

SOME UNITS
(ASK) (S/D) (X) (T+) (&) (~~) (+) (VCR) (K) (DATA PORT) (🛏) (🖥) (🖥) / (X) /
FEE

CANDLEWOOD SUITES AUSTIN NORTHWEST
Phone: (512)338-1611 `104`

All Year 1P: $75-$119 2P: $75-$119
Location: Jct of US 183 and SR 360, on northwest corner. 9701 Stonelake Blvd 78759. Fax: 512/338-9115.
Small-scale Hotel **Facility:** 125 units. 93 one-bedroom standard units with efficiencies. 32 one-bedroom suites with efficiencies. 4 stories, interior corridors. *Bath:* combo or shower only. **Parking:** on-site. **Terms:** cancellation fee imposed, weekly rates available. **Amenities:** video library, CD players, dual phone lines, voice mail, irons, hair dryers. **Leisure Activities:** exercise room. **Guest Services:** sundries, valet and coin laundry. **Business Services:** fax. **Cards:** AX, CB, DC, DS, JC, MC.

SOME UNITS
(ASK) (S/D) (T+) (&M) (🐕) (🍴) (VCR) (K) (DATA PORT) (🛏) (🖥) (🖥) / (X) /

CANDLEWOOD SUITES-SOUTH
Phone: (512)444-8882 `107`

All Year 1P: $107 2P: $134
Location: I-35, exit 230 northbound, exit 230B southbound; on southbound frontage road. 4320 I-35 Service Rd S 78745.
Small-scale Hotel Fax: 512/444-5514. **Facility:** 122 units. 98 one-bedroom standard units with efficiencies. 24 one-bedroom suites with efficiencies. 3 stories, interior corridors. *Bath:* combo or shower only. **Parking:** on-site. **Terms:** cancellation fee imposed, weekly rates available, pets ($100 fee). **Amenities:** video library, CD players, dual phone lines, voice mail, irons, hair dryers. **Leisure Activities:** exercise room. **Guest Services:** valet and coin laundry. **Business Services:** fax (fee). **Cards:** AX, CB, DC, DS, JC, MC, VI.

SOME UNITS
(ASK) (S/D) (🐄) (T+) (&M) (🐕) (🍴) (VCR) (K) (DATA PORT) (🛏) (🖥) (🖥) / (X) /

CLARION INN & SUITES CONFERENCE CENTER
Phone: (512)444-0561 `45`
SAVE All Year [ECP] 1P: $60-$129 2P: $65-$139 XP: $10 F18
Location: I-35, exit 232A (Oltorf Blvd), on westside access road. 2200 S I-35 78704. Fax: 512/444-7254.
Facility: 154 units. 142 one-bedroom standard units, some with whirlpools. 12 one-bedroom suites ($99-$149). 3 stories, interior/exterior corridors. *Bath:* combo or shower only. **Parking:** on-site. **Terms:** pets ($50 fee, in smoking units). **Amenities:** voice mail, irons, hair dryers. **Pool(s):** outdoor, wading. **Leisure Activities:** whirlpool, limited exercise equipment. **Guest Services:** coin laundry. **Business Services:** conference facilities, business center. **Cards:** AX, CB, DC, DS, MC, VI.

SOME UNITS
(S/D) (X) (🐄) (T) (🍴) (🐕) (🍴) (~~) (K) (DATA PORT) (🖥) / (X) (🛏) (🖥) /
FEE

COMFORT INN
Phone: (512)302-5576 `83`
SAVE All Year [ECP] 1P: $65-$89 2P: $65-$89 XP: $6 F18
Location: I-35, exit 240A, on west frontage road. 700 Delmar Ave 78752. Fax: 512/302-5576. **Facility:** 73 one-bedroom standard units. 4 stories, interior corridors. **Parking:** on-site. **Terms:** 14 day cancellation notice. **Amenities:** voice mail. *Some:* irons, hair dryers. **Pool(s):** small heated indoor. **Leisure Activities:** whirlpool.
Small-scale Hotel **Guest Services:** valet laundry. **Business Services:** meeting rooms, fax. **Cards:** AX, CB, DC, DS, MC, VI.

SOME UNITS
(S/D) (T+) (🐕) (~~) (K) (DATA PORT) / (X) (🛏) (🖥) (🖥) /

(See map p. 180)

COMFORT SUITES

SAVE

Small-scale Hotel

Phone: (512)219-1800   **30**

All Year [ECP]   1P: $80-$90   2P: $80-$90   XP: $5   F
Location: Just s of jct US 183 and CR 620. 13681 N Hwy 183 78750. **Fax:** 512/219-1500. **Facility:** 65 units. 63 one-bedroom standard units, some with whirlpools. 2 one-bedroom suites, some with whirlpools. 3 stories, interior corridors. *Bath:* combo or shower only. **Parking:** on-site. **Amenities:** dual phone lines, voice mail, irons, hair dryers. **Pool(s):** small heated outdoor. **Leisure Activities:** whirlpool, exercise room. **Guest Services:** coin laundry. **Business Services:** meeting rooms, business center. **Cards:** AX, CB, DC, DS, MC, VI.

SOME UNITS

COMFORT SUITES AIRPORT

SAVE

Motel

Phone: (512)386-6000   **68**

All Year   1P: $89-$99   2P: $89-$99   XP: $10   F14
Location: I-35, exit 230B (Ben White Blvd/SR 71), 3.6 mi e. 7501 E Ben White Blvd 78741. **Fax:** 512/386-6001. **Facility:** 84 units. 76 one-bedroom standard units. 8 one-bedroom suites. 4 stories, interior corridors. *Bath:* combo or shower only. **Parking:** on-site. **Terms:** [BP] meal plan available. **Amenities:** dual phone lines, voice mail, irons, hair dryers. **Leisure Activities:** limited exercise equipment. **Guest Services:** valet and coin laundry. **Business Services:** meeting rooms, business center. **Cards:** AX, CB, DC, DS, JC, MC, VI.

SOME UNITS

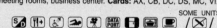

COMFORT SUITES-SOUTH

SAVE

Small-scale Hotel

Phone: (512)444-6630   **105**

All Year [ECP]   1P: $79-$89   2P: $89-$99   XP: $10   F17
Location: I-35 N, exit 228, on northbound frontage road. 1701 E St Elmo Rd 78744. **Fax:** 512/444-4122. **Facility:** 50 one-bedroom standard units. 3 stories, interior corridors. *Bath:* combo or shower only. **Parking:** on-site. **Amenities:** dual phone lines, voice mail, irons, hair dryers. **Pool(s):** small heated indoor/outdoor. **Leisure Activities:** whirlpool, exercise room. **Guest Services:** valet and coin laundry. **Business Services:** fax (fee). **Cards:** AX, CB, DC, DS, MC, VI.

SOME UNITS

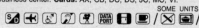

COUNTRY INN & SUITES BY CARLSON-AUSTIN NORTH

AAA   SAVE

Small-scale Hotel

Phone: (512)380-0008   **99**

3/1-9/30 [ECP]   1P: $90-$116   2P: $90-$116   XP: $6   F17
2/1-2/28 & 10/1-1/31 [ECP]   1P: $80-$106   2P: $80-$106   XP: $6   F17
Location: I-35, exit 240A. 7400 I-35 N 78752 (9313 Silk Oak Cove, 78748). **Fax:** 512/380-0046. **Facility:** 75 units. 56 one-bedroom standard units. 19 one-bedroom suites. 3 stories, interior corridors. *Bath:* combo or shower only. **Parking:** on-site. **Amenities:** dual phone lines, voice mail, irons, hair dryers. *Some:* high-speed Internet. **Pool(s):** small heated outdoor. **Leisure Activities:** whirlpool, limited exercise equipment. **Guest Services:** valet and coin laundry, airport transportation (fee)-Austin Airport. **Business Services:** meeting rooms, business center. **Cards:** AX, DC, DS, MC, VI. **Special Amenities:** free continental breakfast and free newspaper. *(See color ad p 260)*

SOME UNITS

FEE

COURTYARD BY MARRIOTT AUSTIN CENTRAL

SAVE

Large-scale Hotel

Phone: (512)458-2340   **74**

All Year   1P: $89-$109   2P: $89-$109
Location: I-35, exit 238B northbound; exit 238A southbound; on west frontage road. 5660 N I-35 78751. **Fax:** 512/458-8525. **Facility:** 198 one-bedroom standard units. 9 stories, interior corridors. *Bath:* combo or shower only. **Parking:** on-site. **Terms:** 15% service charge. **Amenities:** video games (fee), dual phone lines, voice mail, irons, hair dryers. **Pool(s):** heated outdoor. **Leisure Activities:** whirlpool, exercise room. **Guest Services:** valet and coin laundry. **Business Services:** meeting rooms, business center. **Cards:** AX, CB, DC, DS, JC, MC, VI.

SOME UNITS

FEE

COURTYARD BY MARRIOTT-AUSTIN NORTHWEST

SAVE

Small-scale Hotel

Phone: 512/502-8100   **86**

All Year   1P: $139-$159
Location: Jct of US 183 and SR 360, on northwest corner. 9409 Stonelake Blvd 78759. **Fax:** 512/502-2398. **Facility:** 102 one-bedroom standard units, some with whirlpools. 4 stories, interior corridors. *Bath:* combo or shower only. **Parking:** on-site. **Terms:** [BP] meal plan available. **Amenities:** video games (fee), dual phone lines, voice mail, irons, hair dryers. **Pool(s):** small heated indoor. **Leisure Activities:** whirlpool, exercise room. **Guest Services:** valet and coin laundry. **Business Services:** meeting rooms, business center. **Cards:** AX, DC, DS, JC, MC, VI.

SOME UNITS

FEE

COURTYARD BY MARRIOTT AUSTIN SOUTH

SAVE

Small-scale Hotel

Phone: (512)912-1122   **89**

All Year   1P: $79-$109   2P: $79-$109
Location: I-35, exit 229 (Stassney Rd) southbound; exit 230B (Ben White Blvd/SR 71) northbound. 4533 S I-35 78744. **Fax:** 512/912-8134. **Facility:** 110 units. 106 one-bedroom standard units, some with whirlpools. 4 one-bedroom suites ($89-$129). 4 stories, interior corridors. *Bath:* combo or shower only. **Parking:** on-site. **Terms:** weekly rates available, [BP] meal plan available, $8 service charge. **Amenities:** dual phone lines, voice mail, irons, hair dryers. **Pool(s):** heated indoor. **Leisure Activities:** whirlpool, exercise room. **Guest Services:** valet and coin laundry. **Business Services:** meeting rooms, fax (fee). **Cards:** AX, CB, DC, DS, JC, MC, VI.

SOME UNITS

(See map p. 180)

DAYS INN AUSTIN NORTH

[AAA] [SAVE]

♦♦♦♦ ♦♦♦♦

Small-scale Hotel

All Year

Phone: (512)835-4311   [90]
F17

1P: $56-$74   2P: $66-$84   XP: $5

Location: I-35, exit 240A, on east frontage road. 820 E Anderson Ln 78752. **Fax:** 512/835-1740. **Facility:** 146 units. 145 one-bedroom standard units. 1 one-bedroom suite ($85-$99). 3 stories, interior corridors. *Bath:* combo or shower only. **Parking:** on-site. **Terms:** weekly rates available, [ECP] meal plan available, pets ($10 extra charge). **Amenities:** voice mail, safes, hair dryers. *Some:* irons. **Pool(s):** outdoor. **Guest Services:** coin laundry. **Business Services:** meeting rooms, fax (fee). **Special Amenities:** free continental breakfast and free local telephone calls.

SOME UNITS

[icons] 🅂🄳 🛏 🔧 🕸 🏊 🍳 📶 DATA PORT 💻 / ✕ 🛗 📠 /

DAYS INN UNIVERSITY-DOWNTOWN

[AAA] [SAVE]

♦♦♦♦ ♦♦♦♦

Motel

All Year [CP]

Phone: (512)478-1631   [91]
F12

1P: $64-$95   2P: $64-$99   XP: $8

Location: I-35, exit 236A at 32nd St (from lower level). 3105 N I-35 78722. **Fax:** 512/236-0058. **Facility:** 61 one-bedroom standard units. 2 stories (no elevator), exterior corridors. **Parking:** on-site. **Terms:** cancellation fee imposed, small pets only ($7 fee). **Amenities:** voice mail, safes, hair dryers. *Some:* irons. **Pool(s):** outdoor. **Guest Services:** valet laundry. **Business Services:** fax (fee). **Cards:** AX, CB, DC, DS, MC, VI. **Special Amenities:** free continental breakfast and free newspaper. *(See color ad below)*

SOME UNITS

[icons] 🅂🄳 🛏 🍳 📶 DATA PORT 🛗 📠 💻 / ✕ /

DAYS INN

At University

Within Walking Distance From UT

3105 N. IH35
Austin, Texas 78722
Take lower level IH35
Exit 32nd St. (236A)
For reservations
call (512) 478-1631 or

1-800-725-ROOM

Updated Rooms

HBO • Pool

King Size Suites

24 Hr. Restaurant

$49⁹⁵

1-2 Persons
Subject to Availability
Valid Sunday - Thursday

St David's Hospital — DAYS INN
UT Campus — 32nd Street
Frank Erwin Center — 15th Street
6th Street
N ↑
IH-35
Austin
[AAA]

When You Really Need to Speak Their Language... Let the IDP Speak for You

When traveling overseas, carry an **International Driving Permit**... even if you're not planning to drive. Should you need to communicate with foreign authorities, this recognizable form of identification can help you get on your way more quickly. Valid in over 150 countries, the permit contains information translated into ten languages.

Before you travel the world, travel to any AAA office for your International Driving Permit. Bring your valid U.S. driver's license, $10, and two passport-size photos (also available at AAA offices).

Travel With Someone You Trust®

(See map p. 180)

DOUBLETREE HOTEL AUSTIN
(AAA) (SAVE) — All Year — 1P: $79-$209 — 2P: $79-$209 — **Phone:** (512)454-3737 — 57
▼▼▼▼ — XP: $20 — F18
Location: I-35, exit 238 southbound; exit 239 northbound. 6505 I-35 N 78752. **Fax:** 512/454-6915. **Facility:** 350 one-bedroom standard units. 6 stories, interior corridors. **Parking:** on-site (fee) and valet. **Terms:** check-in 4 pm, small pets only ($25 extra charge). **Amenities:** voice mail, irons, hair dryers. *Fee:* video games, high-speed
Large-scale Hotel Internet. *Some:* CD players. **Dining:** 6:30 am-3 & 5-10 pm, Fri & Sat-11 pm, cocktails. **Pool(s):** outdoor.
Leisure Activities: sauna, whirlpool, exercise room. **Guest Services:** gift shop, valet laundry, airport transportation (fee)-Austin Airport, area transportation-within 2 mi. **Business Services:** conference facilities, business center. **Cards:** AX, CB, DC, DS, MC, VI. **Special Amenities: early check-in/late check-out and free newspaper.**
(See color ad below)

SOME UNITS
(icons) FEE /

DRURY INN & SUITES-NORTH
(AAA) (SAVE) — 9/1-1/31 [ECP] — 1P: $73-$93 — 2P: $83-$103 — **Phone:** (512)467-9500 · — 56
▼▼▼▼ — 2/1-8/31 [ECP] — 1P: $70-$90 — 2P: $80-$100 — XP: $10 — F18
XP: $10 — F18
Location: I-35, exit 238 southbound; exit 239 northbound, on east frontage road. 6711 I-35 N 78752.
Small-scale Hotel — 4 stories, interior corridors. *Bath:* combo or shower only. **Parking:** on-site. **Terms:** small pets only.
Fax: 512/323-6198. **Facility:** 224 units. 159 one-bedroom standard units. 65 one-bedroom suites ($90-$113).
Amenities: voice mail, irons, hair dryers. **Pool(s):** outdoor. **Leisure Activities:** limited exercise equipment.
Guest Services: complimentary evening beverages: Mon-Thurs, valet and coin laundry, airport transportation (fee)-Austin Airport. **Business Services:** meeting rooms, business center. **Cards:** AX, CB, DC, DS, MC, VI. **Special Amenities: free continental breakfast and free local telephone calls.**

SOME UNITS
(icons) FEE /

DRURY INN AUSTIN-HIGHLAND MALL
(AAA) (SAVE) — 9/1-1/31 [ECP] — 1P: $68-$88 — 2P: $78-$98 — **Phone:** (512)454-1144 — 73
▼▼▼▼ — 2/1-8/31 [ECP] — 1P: $65-$85 — 2P: $75-$95 — XP: $10 — F18
XP: $10 — F18
Location: I-35, exit 238B southbound; exit 238A northbound, on west frontage road. 919 E Koenig Ln 78751.
Fax: 512/454-1144. **Facility:** 137 one-bedroom standard units. 5 stories, interior corridors. **Parking:** on-site.
Small-scale Hotel — **Terms:** small pets only. **Amenities:** dual phone lines, voice mail, irons, hair dryers. **Pool(s):** outdoor. **Leisure Activities:** limited exercise equipment. **Guest Services:** complimentary evening beverages: Mon-Thurs, valet and coin laundry, airport transportation (fee)-Austin Airport. **Business Services:** meeting rooms, fax (fee). **Cards:** AX, CB, DC, DS, MC, VI. **Special Amenities: free continental breakfast and free local telephone calls.**

SOME UNITS
(icons) FEE /

ECONO LODGE
(SAVE) — 2/1-7/31 [CP] — 1P: $50-$100 — 2P: $56-$100 — **Phone:** (512)458-4759 — 38
▼▼▼ — 8/1-1/31 [CP] — 1P: $40-$100 — 2P: $45-$100 — XP: $5 — F17
XP: $5 — F17
Location: I-35, exit 238, 0.3 mi e of jct I-35 and US 290 E. 6201 Hwy 290 E 78723. **Fax:** 512/458-4759. **Facility:** 48 one-bedroom standard units. 2 stories (no elevator), exterior corridors. **Parking:** on-site. **Terms:** small pets
Small-scale Hotel — only. **Amenities:** *Some:* hair dryers. **Pool(s):** outdoor, wading. **Business Services:** fax (fee). **Cards:** AX, CB, DC, DS, JC, MC, VI.

SOME UNITS
(icons) FEE /

EMBASSY SUITES AUSTIN ARBORETUM
(SAVE) — All Year — 1P: $129-$229 — 2P: $129-$229 — **Phone:** (512)372-8771 — 59
▼▼▼▼ — XP: $10 — F10
Location: Nw on US 183 to exit Loop 360. 9505 Stonelake Blvd 78759. **Fax:** 512/372-8710. **Facility:** 150 one-bedroom suites. 6 stories, interior corridors. *Bath:* combo or shower only. **Parking:** on-site. **Terms:** cancellation fee imposed, weekly rates available, [BP] meal plan available. **Amenities:** high-speed Internet (fee),
Small-scale Hotel — dual phone lines, voice mail, irons, hair dryers. **Pool(s):** heated indoor. **Leisure Activities:** whirlpool, exercise room. **Guest Services:** gift shop, complimentary evening beverages, valet laundry, area transportation.
Business Services: meeting rooms, fax (fee). **Cards:** AX, CB, DC, DS, JC, MC, VI.

SOME UNITS
(icons) FEE /

(See map p. 180)

EMBASSY SUITES AUSTIN NORTH   Phone: (512)454-8004   [55]
(AAA) (SAVE)   All Year [BP]   1P: $99-$179   2P: $99-$179   XP: $10   F18
▼▼▼   **Location:** I-35, exit 238A southbound; exit 238B northbound, on east frontage road. 5901 I-35 N 78723.
          Fax: 512/454-9047. **Facility:** 260 one-bedroom suites. 10 stories, interior corridors. **Parking:** on-site.
Large-scale Hotel   **Terms:** [CP] & [ECP] meal plans available. **Amenities:** video games (fee), voice mail, irons, hair dryers.
          Dining: 11 am-1:30 & 4-10 pm, cocktails. **Pool(s):** heated indoor. **Leisure Activities:** sauna, whirlpool, lim-
          ited exercise equipment. **Guest Services:** gift shop, complimentary evening beverages, valet and coin
          laundry, area transportation-within 5 mi. **Business Services:** meeting rooms, business center. **Cards:** AX, DC, DS, MC, VI.

SOME UNITS
[S⊘] [✈] [🍴] [Y] [⌖] [⇌] [✕] [🎥] [DATA PORT] [▤] [◻] [▯] / [✕] [◻] [VCR]
FEE   FEE

EXEL INN OF AUSTIN   Phone: (512)462-9201   [54]
(AAA) (SAVE)   All Year [CP]   1P: $40-$78   2P: $49-$78   XP: $6   F18
▼▼   **Location:** I-35, exit 231 (Woodward Ave) southbound; exit 232A (Oltorf St) northbound, on the northbound frontage road;
          just n of jct I-35 and US 290/SR 71. 2711 I-35 S 78741. Fax: 512/462-9371. **Facility:** 89 one-bedroom standard
Motel   units, some with whirlpools. 3 stories, interior corridors. **Parking:** on-site. **Terms:** weekly rates available,
          small pets only (in smoking units). **Amenities:** irons, hair dryers. **Pool(s):** small outdoor. **Leisure Activi-
          ties:** limited exercise equipment. **Guest Services:** valet and coin laundry. **Business Services:** fax (fee).
          Cards: AX, CB, DC, DS, MC, VI. **Special Amenities:** early check-in/late check-out and free continental breakfast.

SOME UNITS
[S⊘] [↻] [🍴↑] [⌖] [⇌] [🎥] [DATA PORT] [◻] / [✕] [◻] [◻] /

FAIRFIELD INN-AUSTIN CENTRAL   Phone: (512)302-5550   [92]
(SAVE)   All Year [ECP]   1P: $69-$119   2P: $69-$119
▼▼▼   **Location:** I-35, exit 238B northbound; exit 238A southbound on west frontage road. 959 Reinli St 78751.
          Fax: 512/454-8270. **Facility:** 63 one-bedroom standard units. 3 stories, interior corridors. *Bath:* combo or
Small-scale Hotel   shower only. **Parking:** on-site. **Amenities:** video games (fee), irons, hair dryers. **Pool(s):** small heated in-
          door. **Leisure Activities:** whirlpool, limited exercise equipment. **Guest Services:** valet and coin laundry.
          Business Services: fax (fee). **Cards:** AX, CB, DC, DS, JC, MC, VI.

SOME UNITS
[S⊘] [✈] [🍴↑] [&M] [⌖] [⇌] [🎥] [DATA PORT] / [✕] [◻] [◻] /
FEE

FAIRFIELD INN SOUTH   Phone: 512/707-8899   [93]
(SAVE)   All Year [ECP]   1P: $79-$89   2P: $79-$89
▼▼▼   **Location:** I-35, exit 230 (Ben White Blvd/SR 71) northbound; exit 229 (Stassney Rd) southbound. 4525 S I-35 78744.
          Fax: 512/441-5704. **Facility:** 63 one-bedroom standard units, some with whirlpools. 3 stories, interior corri-
Small-scale Hotel   dors. *Bath:* combo or shower only. **Parking:** on-site. **Amenities:** video games (fee), irons, hair dryers.
          Pool(s): small heated indoor. **Leisure Activities:** whirlpool, exercise room. **Guest Services:** valet and coin
          laundry. **Business Services:** fax (fee). **Cards:** AX, DC, DS, MC, VI.

[✈] [🍴↑] [&] [⌖] [⇌] [🎥] [DATA PORT] / [✕] [◻] [◻] /

FOUR POINTS HOTEL BY SHERATON   Phone: (512)836-8520   [67]
▼▼▼   All Year [BP]   1P: $112-$120   2P: $120-$128   XP: $8   F17
          Location: I-35, exit 240A, on west frontage road. 7800 I-35 N 78753. Fax: 512/837-0897. **Facility:** 188 one-
Small-scale Hotel   bedroom standard units. 2 stories (no elevator), interior corridors. *Bath:* combo or shower only. **Parking:** on-
          site. **Terms:** 15% service charge, small pets only ($50 deposit). **Amenities:** video games (fee), voice mail,
          irons, hair dryers. *Some:* dual phone lines. **Pool(s):** outdoor, wading. **Leisure Activities:** whirlpool, exercise room. **Guest Serv-
          ices:** valet and coin laundry, area transportation. **Business Services:** meeting rooms, fax (fee). **Cards:** AX, CB, DC, DS, JC,
          MC, VI.

SOME UNITS
(ASK) [S⊘] [✈] [↻] [🍴] [Y] [&] [⇌] [🎥] [DATA PORT] [▤] [◻] / [✕] [◻] [◻] /

HABITAT SUITES HOTEL   Phone: (512)467-6000   [81]
▼▼▼   All Year   1P: $127   2P: $137   XP: $10   F12
          Location: I-35, exit 238B, just w on SR 2222 to Airport Blvd, 0.6 mi n to Highland Mall Blvd, then 0.4 mi e. 500 E High-
Small-scale Hotel   land Mall Blvd 78752. Fax: 512/452-6712. **Facility:** 96 units. 72 one- and 24 two-bedroom standard units with
          kitchens. 2 stories, exterior corridors. **Parking:** on-site. **Terms:** cancellation fee imposed, [BP] meal plan
          available, small pets only ($50 fee). **Amenities:** dual phone lines, voice mail, irons, hair dryers. **Pool(s):** outdoor. **Leisure Ac-
          tivities:** whirlpool. **Guest Services:** complimentary evening beverages: Mon-Sat, valet and coin laundry. **Business Services:**
          meeting rooms, fax (fee). **Cards:** AX, CB, DC, DS, MC, VI.

SOME UNITS
(ASK) [S⊘] [✈] [↻] [🍴] [⌖] [⇌] [✕↑] [✕] [🎥] [DATA PORT] [▤] [◻] / [🖨] /
FEE   FEE

HAMPTON INN & SUITES   Phone: 512/389-1616   [80]
(SAVE)   All Year   1P: $84   2P: $89
▼▼▼   **Location:** I-35, exit 230B (Ben White Blvd/SR 71), 3.2 mi e on SR 71. 7712 E Riverside Dr 78744. Fax: 512/389-2201.
          Facility: 102 one-bedroom standard units. 5 stories, interior corridors. *Bath:* combo or shower only. **Parking:**
Small-scale Hotel   on-site. **Terms:** cancellation fee imposed, [ECP] meal plan available. **Amenities:** dual phone lines, voice
          mail, irons, hair dryers. *Fee:* video games, high-speed Internet. **Pool(s):** outdoor. **Leisure Activities:** lighted
          tennis court, exercise room, basketball. **Guest Services:** complimentary evening beverages, valet laundry.
          Business Services: meeting rooms, business center. **Cards:** AX, DC, DS, MC, VI.

SOME UNITS
[S⊘] [✈] [🍴↑] [&] [⌖] [⇌] [✕] [🎥] [DATA PORT] [◻] / [✕] [VCR] [◻] [◻] /

HAMPTON INN AUSTIN-NORTH   Phone: (512)452-3300   [64]
(SAVE)   All Year [ECP]   1P: $74-$89   2P: $84-$99
▼▼▼   **Location:** I-35, exit 240A, on east frontage road. 7619 I-35 N 78752. Fax: 512/452-3124. **Facility:** 121 one-
          bedroom standard units. 4 stories, interior corridors. **Parking:** on-site. **Terms:** cancellation fee imposed, 15%
Small-scale Hotel   service charge. **Amenities:** voice mail, irons, hair dryers. **Pool(s):** heated outdoor. **Leisure Activities:** exer-
          cise room. **Guest Services:** valet laundry. **Business Services:** meeting rooms, fax (fee). **Cards:** AX, CB,
          DC, DS, JC, MC, VI. *(See color ad p 196)*

SOME UNITS
[S⊘] [✈] [🍴↑] [&M] [⌖] [⇌] [🎥] [DATA PORT] [◻] / [✕] /
FEE

(See map p. 180)

HAMPTON INN AUSTIN-SOUTH

Motel

Phone: (512)442-4040 **51**

All Year   1P: $84-$89   2P: $89-$94

Location: I-35, exit 230 (Ben White Blvd/SR 71), just e. 4141 Governor's Row 78744. Fax: 512/442-7122. **Facility:** 123 one-bedroom standard units. 6 stories, interior corridors. *Bath:* combo or shower only. **Parking:** on-site. **Terms:** [ECP] meal plan available. **Amenities:** video games (fee), voice mail, irons, hair dryers. **Pool(s):** small outdoor. **Leisure Activities:** limited exercise equipment. **Guest Services:** valet laundry. **Business Services:** meeting rooms, fax (fee). **Cards:** AX, CB, DC, DS, JC, MC, VI.

SOME UNITS

HAMPTON INN NORTHWEST

Small-scale Hotel

Phone: (512)349-9898 **39** F18

All Year   1P: $79-$109   2P: $79-$109   XP: $10

Location: 1 mi n of US 183 on Loop 1 (Mopac Blvd) to Braker Ln exit. 3908 W Braker Ln 78759. Fax: 512/349-9494. **Facility:** 124 one-bedroom standard units. 6 stories, interior corridors. *Bath:* combo or shower only. **Parking:** on-site. **Terms:** [ECP] meal plan available. **Amenities:** dual phone lines, voice mail, irons, hair dryers. **Pool(s):** outdoor. **Leisure Activities:** limited exercise equipment. **Guest Services:** valet laundry. **Business Services:** fax. **Cards:** AX, CB, DC, DS, JC, MC, VI.

SOME UNITS

HAWTHORN SUITES AUSTIN CENTRAL

Small-scale Hotel

Phone: (512)459-3335 **65**

All Year [BP]   1P: $69-$159   2P: $69-$159

Location: I-35, exit 238B southbound; exit 239 northbound, just off east frontage road. 935 La Posada Dr 78752. Fax: 512/467-9736. **Facility:** 71 units. 44 one- and 27 two-bedroom standard units with kitchens. 2 stories (no elevator), exterior corridors. **Parking:** on-site. **Terms:** small pets only ($50 fee). **Amenities:** video library, dual phone lines, voice mail, irons, hair dryers. **Pool(s):** heated outdoor. **Leisure Activities:** whirlpool, sports court. **Guest Services:** complimentary evening beverages: Mon-Thurs, valet and coin laundry. **Business Services:** meeting rooms, fax (fee). **Cards:** AX, CB, DC, DS, MC, VI.

SOME UNITS

HAWTHORN SUITES LTD-AUSTIN AIRPORT

Small-scale Hotel

Phone: (512)247-6166 **34**

All Year [BP]   1P: $99-$139   2P: $99-$139

Location: I-35, exit 230B (Ben White Blvd), 3.2 mi e. 7800 E Riverside Dr 78744. Fax: 512/247-6866. **Facility:** 70 one-bedroom suites, some with efficiencies and/or whirlpools. 3 stories, interior corridors. *Bath:* combo or shower only. **Parking:** on-site. **Terms:** weekly rates available. **Amenities:** high-speed Internet, dual phone lines, voice mail, irons, hair dryers. **Pool(s):** small heated outdoor. **Leisure Activities:** lighted tennis court, exercise room, basketball. **Guest Services:** complimentary evening beverages, valet and coin laundry, airport transportation-Bergstrom International Airport, area transportation-within 7 mi. **Business Services:** meeting rooms, business center. **Cards:** AX, CB, DC, DS, JC, MC, VI. **Special Amenities:** free continental breakfast and free local telephone calls.

SOME UNITS

HAWTHORN SUITES NORTHWEST

Small-scale Hotel

Phone: (512)343-0008 **52**

All Year [BP]   1P: $69-$199   2P: $69-$199

Location: Just sw of jct US 183 and Loop 1 (Mopac Blvd). 8888 Tallwood Dr 78759. Fax: 512/343-6532. **Facility:** 105 units. 96 one- and 9 two-bedroom standard units, some with kitchens. 3 stories, exterior corridors. **Parking:** on-site. **Terms:** small pets only ($50 fee, $5 extra charge). **Amenities:** video games (fee), dual phone lines, voice mail, irons, hair dryers. **Pool(s):** outdoor. **Leisure Activities:** whirlpool, sports court. **Guest Services:** complimentary evening beverages: Mon-Thurs, valet and coin laundry. **Business Services:** meeting rooms, fax (fee). **Cards:** AX, CB, DC, DS, MC, VI.

SOME UNITS

(See map p. 180)

HAWTHORN SUITES SOUTH
Motel

Phone: (512)440-7722   53

All Year [BP]   1P: $59-$159   2P: $59-$159
Location: I-35, exit 230B (Ben White Blvd/SR 71) southbound; exit 231 (Woodward Dr) northbound, just n of jct SR 71, US 290 and I-35, on southbound frontage road. 4020 I-35 S 78704. **Fax:** 512/440-4815. **Facility:** 120 one-bedroom standard units with kitchens. 2 stories (no elevator), exterior corridors. **Parking:** on-site. **Terms:** pets ($50 fee, $10 extra charge). **Amenities:** dual phone lines, voice mail, irons, hair dryers. **Pool(s):** small heated outdoor. **Leisure Activities:** whirlpools, sports court, basketball, volleyball. **Guest Services:** complimentary evening beverages: Mon-Thurs, valet and coin laundry, area transportation. **Business Services:** meeting rooms, fax (fee). **Cards:** AX, CB, DC, DS, MC, VI.

SOME UNITS

HILTON AUSTIN AIRPORT
SAVE · Small-scale Hotel

Phone: (512)385-6767   106
  F18

All Year   1P: $99-$189   2P: $99-$189   XP: $10
Location: SR 71, service road exit at airport. 9515 New Airport Dr 78719. **Fax:** 512/385-6763. **Facility:** 262 units. 250 one-bedroom standard units. 11 one- and 1 two-bedroom suites ($169-$259). 5 stories, interior corridors. *Bath:* combo or shower only. **Parking:** valet. **Terms:** cancellation fee imposed. **Amenities:** video games (fee), high-speed Internet, dual phone lines, voice mail, irons, hair dryers. **Pool(s):** heated outdoor. **Leisure Activities:** whirlpool, jogging, exercise room. *Fee:* game room. **Guest Services:** gift shop, valet and coin laundry. **Business Services:** meeting rooms, business center. **Cards:** AX, CB, DC, DS, MC, VI.

SOME UNITS

FEE

HILTON AUSTIN NORTH & TOWERS
AAA · SAVE · Large-scale Hotel

Phone: (512)451-5757   62
  F18

All Year   1P: $189-$209   2P: $209-$229   XP: $20
Location: I-35, exit 238B, just off west frontage road. 6000 Middle Fiskville Rd 78752. **Fax:** 512/467-7644. **Facility:** 189 one-bedroom standard units. 9 stories, interior corridors. *Bath:* combo or shower only. **Parking:** on-site. **Terms:** cancellation fee imposed, small pets only ($50 fee). **Amenities:** high-speed Internet (fee), dual phone lines, voice mail, irons, hair dryers. *Some:* CD players. **Dining:** 6:30 am-11 pm, Sat & Sun from 7 am, cocktails. **Pool(s):** outdoor. **Leisure Activities:** exercise room. **Guest Services:** gift shop, valet laundry, airport transportation (fee)-Austin Airport, area transportation-within 2 mi. **Business Services:** meeting rooms, business center. **Cards:** AX, CB, DC, DS, JC, MC, VI. **Special Amenities:** early check-in/late check-out and free newspaper.
(See color ad p 194 & below)

SOME UNITS

FEE

HILTON GARDEN INN
SAVE · Small-scale Hotel

Phone: (512)241-1600   108
  F14

All Year   1P: $89   2P: $89   XP: $10
Location: US 183 N, exit Duval, just n on eastside access road. 11617 Research Blvd 78759. **Fax:** 512/241-1606. **Facility:** 138 units. 130 one-bedroom standard units. 8 one-bedroom suites ($109). 5 stories, interior corridors. *Bath:* combo or shower only. **Parking:** on-site. **Terms:** package plans - weekends. **Amenities:** video games (fee), high-speed Internet, dual phone lines, voice mail, irons, hair dryers. **Pool(s):** heated indoor. **Leisure Activities:** whirlpool, limited exercise equipment. **Guest Services:** valet and coin laundry. **Business Services:** meeting rooms, business center. **Cards:** AX, CB, DC, DS, JC, MC, VI.

SOME UNITS

FEE

HOLIDAY INN AIRPORT SOUTH
AAA · SAVE · Motel

Phone: (512)448-2444   48
  F18

All Year   1P: $109   2P: $119   XP: $10
Location: I-35, exit 231 (Woodward St) southbound; exit 230 (Ben White Blvd/SR 71) northbound, on northbound frontage road. 3401 I-35 S 78741. **Fax:** 512/448-4999. **Facility:** 210 units. 190 one-bedroom standard units. 20 one-bedroom suites. 5 stories, interior/exterior corridors. **Parking:** on-site. **Terms:** pets ($25 fee). **Amenities:** video games (fee), voice mail, irons, hair dryers. **Dining:** 6:30 am-2 & 5-10:30 pm, cocktails. **Pool(s):** outdoor. **Leisure Activities:** whirlpool, limited exercise equipment. **Guest Services:** gift shop, valet and coin laundry, airport transportation-Austin Airport, area transportation-within 5 mi. **Business Services:** meeting rooms, fax (fee). **Cards:** AX, CB, DC, DS, MC, VI. *(See color ad p 184)*

SOME UNITS

(See map p. 180)

HOLIDAY INN-AUSTIN NORTH (HIGHLAND MALL)   **Phone:** (512)459-4251   96
All Year   1P: $110
Location: I-35, exit 239 northbound; exit 238B southbound, on east frontage road. 6911 I-35 N 78752.
Small-scale Hotel   Fax: 512/459-9274. **Facility:** 291 one-bedroom standard units. 2 stories (no elevator), exterior corridors.
Bath: combo or shower only. **Parking:** on-site. **Terms:** pets ($15 fee). **Amenities:** video games (fee), voice
mail, irons, hair dryers. **Pool(s):** outdoor, wading. **Leisure Activities:** limited exercise equipment. **Guest Services:** valet and
coin laundry, area transportation. **Business Services:** meeting rooms, fax (fee). **Cards:** AX, CB, DC, DS, JC, MC, VI.
(See color ad p 184)

SOME UNITS

ASK SD 🚭 🛏 🍴 🐕 📷 🏊 🐾 🎬 DATAPORT 💻 / ✕ 🔒 🖼 /

HOLIDAY INN EXPRESS   **Phone:** (512)467-1701   97
All Year [ECP]   1P: $72-$79   2P: $76-$86   XP: $6   F12
Location: I-35, exit 240A, on west frontage road. 7622 N I-35 & 183 78752. Fax: 512/451-0966. **Facility:** 125 one-
bedroom standard units. 4 stories, interior corridors. *Bath:* combo or shower only. **Parking:** on-site.
Amenities: video games (fee), voice mail, irons, hair dryers. **Pool(s):** indoor. **Leisure Activities:** whirlpool.
Small-scale Hotel   **Guest Services:** valet laundry, airport transportation (fee)-Austin Airport. **Business Services:** meeting
rooms, fax (fee). **Cards:** AX, CB, DC, DS, MC, VI. **Special Amenities: free continental breakfast and free
local telephone calls.** *(See color ad below)*

SOME UNITS

SD 🚭 🍴 🐕 📷 🏊 🎬 DATAPORT 💻 / ✕ 🔒 🖼 /
FEE

HOLIDAY INN NORTHWEST/ARBORETUM   **Phone:** (512)343-0888   50
All Year   1P: $79-$119   2P: $79-$119
Location: Jct US 183 and Loop 1 (Mopac Blvd), on southwest corner. 8901 Business Park Dr 78759.
Small-scale Hotel   Fax: 512/343-6891. **Facility:** 194 one-bedroom standard units. 4 stories, interior corridors. *Bath:* combo or
shower only. **Parking:** on-site. **Terms:** small pets only ($25 fee). **Amenities:** *Some:* dual phone lines, voice
mail, irons, hair dryers. **Fee:** video games, high-speed Internet. **Pool(s):** heated indoor. **Leisure Activities:** whirlpool, exercise
room. **Guest Services:** gift shop, valet and coin laundry. **Business Services:** meeting rooms, business center. **Cards:** AX, CB,
DC, DS, JC, MC, VI. *(See color ad p 184)*

SOME UNITS

ASK SD 🚭 🛏 🍴 🍸 🐕 📷 🏊 🎬 / ✕ 🐕 📺 DATAPORT 🔒 🖼 💻 /
FEE

HOMESTEAD STUDIO SUITES HOTEL-AUSTIN/ARBORETUM   **Phone:** (512)837-6677   109
All Year   1P: $55-$65   2P: $60-$70   XP: $5   F17
Location: US 183, exit Burnet Rd; on westbound frontage road. 9100 Waterford Centre Blvd 78758.
Small-scale Hotel   Fax: 512/837-6696. **Facility:** 123 units. 114 one-bedroom standard units with efficiencies. 9 one-bedroom
suites with efficiencies. 2 stories (no elevator), exterior corridors. *Bath:* combo or shower only. **Parking:** on-
site. **Terms:** small pets only ($75 fee). **Amenities:** high-speed Internet, voice mail, irons. **Guest Services:** valet and coin laundry.
Business Services: fax (fee). **Cards:** AX, CB, DC, DS, JC, MC, VI.

SOME UNITS

ASK SD 🐕 🍴 📷 🏊 🎬 DATAPORT 🔒 🖼 💻 / ✕ /

HOMEWOOD SUITES-AUSTIN SOUTH   **Phone:** (512)445-5050   33
All Year [MAP]   1P: $125-$152
Location: I-35, exit 230B (Ben White Blvd/SR 71) southbound; exit 230 northbound. 4143 Governor's Row 78744.
Fax: 512/445-6744. **Facility:** 96 units. 87 one- and 9 two-bedroom suites with efficiencies. 5 stories, interior
corridors. *Bath:* combo or shower only. **Parking:** on-site. **Terms:** 15% service charge. **Amenities:** video
Motel   games (fee), dual phone lines, voice mail, irons, hair dryers. **Pool(s):** small outdoor. **Leisure Activities:** exercise room. **Guest Services:** complimentary evening beverages: Mon-Thurs, valet and coin laundry, area
transportation. **Business Services:** meeting rooms, fax (fee). **Cards:** AX, CB, DC, DS, MC, VI.

SOME UNITS

SD 🚭 🍴 🛁M 📷 🏊 🐾 VCR 🎬 DATAPORT 🔒 🖼 💻 / ✕ /

(See map p. 180)

LA QUINTA INN & SUITES AT AUSTIN-AIRPORT
Phone: (512)386-6800 [63]
(AAA) (SAVE)   All Year   1P: $79-$109   2P: $89-$119   XP: $10   F18
▼▼▼▼   **Location:** I-35, exit 230B (Ben White Blvd/SR 71), 3.8 mi e. 7625 E Ben White Blvd 78741. **Fax:** 512/386-8785. **Facility:** 142 units. 129 one-bedroom standard units. 13 one-bedroom suites ($109-$169). 5 stories, interior corridors. *Bath:* combo or shower only. **Parking:** on-site. **Terms:** [ECP] meal plan available, small pets only.
Motel   **Amenities:** video games (fee), voice mail, irons, hair dryers. *Some:* dual phone lines. **Pool(s):** heated outdoor. **Leisure Activities:** whirlpool, exercise room. **Guest Services:** valet and coin laundry, airport transportation-Bergstrom International Airport. **Business Services:** meeting rooms, fax (fee). **Cards:** AX, CB, DC, DS, JC, MC, VI. **Special Amenities:** free continental breakfast and free local telephone calls. *(See color ad p 187)*

SOME UNITS

LA QUINTA INN & SUITES-AUSTIN NORTH MOPAC
Phone: (512)832-2121 [98]
(AAA) (SAVE)   All Year   1P: $79-$109   2P: $89-$119   XP: $10   F18
▼▼▼   **Location:** US 183, 1 mi n on Loop 1 (Mopac Blvd) to exit Duval. 11901 N Mopac Expwy 78759. **Fax:** 512/832-5277. **Facility:** 149 units. 141 one-bedroom standard units. 8 one-bedroom suites ($119-$149). 3 stories, interior corridors. *Bath:* combo or shower only. **Parking:** on-site. **Terms:** [ECP] meal plan available, small pets only.
Small-scale Hotel   **Amenities:** video games (fee), dual phone lines, voice mail, irons, hair dryers. **Pool(s):** heated outdoor. **Leisure Activities:** whirlpool, exercise room. **Guest Services:** valet and coin laundry, airport transportation (fee)-Austin Airport. **Business Services:** meeting rooms, fax (fee). **Cards:** AX, CB, DC, DS, JC, MC, VI. **Special Amenities:** free continental breakfast and free local telephone calls. *(See color ad p 187)*

SOME UNITS
FEE

LA QUINTA INN-HIGHLAND MALL
Phone: (512)459-4381 [72]
(AAA) (SAVE)   All Year   1P: $69-$84   2P: $79-$94   XP: $10   F18
▼▼▼   **Location:** I-35, exit 238B, on west frontage road. 5812 I-35 N 78751. **Fax:** 512/452-3917. **Facility:** 122 units. 120 one-bedroom standard units. 2 one-bedroom suites. 2 stories (no elevator), exterior corridors. **Parking:** on-site. **Terms:** [ECP] meal plan available, small pets only. **Amenities:** video games (fee), voice mail, irons, hair dryers. **Pool(s):** outdoor. **Guest Services:** valet laundry, airport transportation (fee)-Austin Airport. **Business Services:** fax. **Cards:** AX, CB, DC, DS, JC, MC, VI. **Special Amenities:** free continental breakfast and free local telephone calls. *(See color ad p 187)*

SOME UNITS
FEE

LA QUINTA INN IH35 AT BEN WHITE
Phone: (512)443-1774 [47]
(AAA) (SAVE)   All Year   1P: $69-$84   2P: $79-$94   XP: $10   F18
▼▼▼   **Location:** I-35, exit 230B (Ben White Blvd/SR 71) southbound; exit 230 northbound, just s of jct I-35, SR 71 and 290, on frontage road. 4200 I-35 S 78745-1202. **Fax:** 512/447-1555. **Facility:** 130 units. 129 one-bedroom standard units. 1 one-bedroom suite. 2 stories (no elevator), exterior corridors. **Parking:** on-site. **Terms:** [ECP] meal plan available, small pets only. **Amenities:** video games (fee), voice mail, irons, hair dryers. **Pool(s):** outdoor. **Guest Services:** valet laundry. **Business Services:** fax (fee). **Cards:** AX, CB, DC, DS, JC, MC, VI. **Special Amenities:** free continental breakfast and free local telephone calls. *(See color ad p 187)*

SOME UNITS

LA QUINTA INN-NORTH
Phone: (512)452-9401 [46]
(AAA) (SAVE)   All Year   1P: $69-$84   2P: $79-$94   XP: $10   F18
▼▼▼   **Location:** I-35, exit 239, on west frontage road. 7100 I-35 N 78752. **Fax:** 512/452-0856. **Facility:** 115 units. 113 one-bedroom standard units. 2 one-bedroom suites. 2 stories (no elevator), exterior corridors. **Parking:** on-site. **Terms:** small pets only. **Amenities:** video games (fee), voice mail, irons, hair dryers. **Pool(s):** outdoor.
Small-scale Hotel   **Guest Services:** valet laundry, airport transportation (fee)-Austin Airport. **Business Services:** fax (fee). **Cards:** AX, CB, DC, DS, JC, MC, VI. **Special Amenities:** free continental breakfast and free local telephone calls. *(See color ad p 187)*

SOME UNITS
FEE

LA QUINTA INN OLTORF
Phone: (512)447-6661 [71]
(AAA) (SAVE)   All Year   1P: $69-$99   2P: $79-$99   XP: $10   F18
▼▼▼   **Location:** I-35, exit 232A (Oltorf Blvd), just s. 1603 E Oltorf Blvd 78741. **Fax:** 512/447-1744. **Facility:** 132 units. 130 one-bedroom standard units. 2 one-bedroom suites. 2 stories, interior/exterior corridors. **Parking:** on-site. **Terms:** [ECP] meal plan available, small pets only. **Amenities:** video games (fee), voice mail, irons, hair dryers. **Pool(s):** outdoor. **Guest Services:** valet laundry. **Business Services:** fax (fee). **Cards:** AX, CB, DC, DS, JC, MC, VI. **Special Amenities:** free continental breakfast and free local telephone calls.
(See color ad p 187)

SOME UNITS

LA QUINTA SW
Phone: (512)899-3000 [32]
(AAA) (SAVE)   All Year   1P: $109-$139   2P: $119-$149   XP: $10   F18
▼▼▼   **Location:** At jct Loop 1 (Mopac Blvd), US 290 and SR 71 E, on southbound frontage road. 4424 S Loop 1 (Mopac Blvd) 70735. **Fax:** 512/899-3885. **Facility:** 128 one-bedroom standard units. 5 stories, interior corridors. *Bath:* combo or shower only. **Parking:** on-site. **Terms:** small pets only. **Amenities:** video games (fee), voice mail, irons, hair dryers. **Pool(s):** heated outdoor. **Leisure Activities:** whirlpool, exercise room. **Guest Services:** valet and coin laundry. **Business Services:** meeting rooms, fax. **Cards:** AX, CB, DC, DS, JC, MC, VI. **Special Amenities:** free continental breakfast and free local telephone calls. *(See color ad p 187)*

SOME UNITS

(See map p. 180)

MARRIOTT HOTEL-AUSTIN SOUTH/AIRPORT   **Phone:** (512)441-7900   111

[SAVE] All Year   1P: $99-$149

Small-scale Hotel   **Location:** I-35 N, exit 228, on northbound frontage road. 4415 S I-35 78744. **Fax:** 512/441-7899. **Facility:** 199 units. 192 one-bedroom standard units. 7 one-bedroom suites ($199-$249). 5 stories, interior corridors. *Bath:* combo or shower only. **Parking:** on-site. **Amenities:** video games (fee), dual phone lines, voice mail, safes, irons, hair dryers. **Pool(s):** small heated indoor. **Leisure Activities:** whirlpool, exercise room. **Business Services:** meeting rooms, business center. **Cards:** AX, DC, DS, JC, MC, VI.

SOME UNITS

MOTEL 6 AUSTIN NORTH - 360   **Phone:** 512/339-6161   84

3/6-1/31	1P: $41-$51	2P: $47-$57	XP: $3	F17
2/1-3/5	1P: $39-$49	2P: $45-$55	XP: $3	F17

Motel   **Location:** I-35, exit 241 (Rundberg St), just w. 9420 N I-35 78753. Fax: 512/339-7852. **Facility:** 157 one-bedroom standard units. 2 stories (no elevator), exterior corridors. *Bath:* shower only. **Parking:** on-site. **Terms:** small pets only. **Pool(s):** outdoor. **Guest Services:** coin laundry. **Business Services:** fax (fee). **Cards:** AX, CB, DC, DS, MC, VI.

SOME UNITS

MOTEL 6 CENTRAL #1118   **Phone:** 512/467-9111   88

5/22-1/31	1P: $43-$53	2P: $49-$59	XP: $3	F17
2/1-5/21	1P: $41-$51	2P: $47-$57	XP: $3	F17

Motel   **Location:** I-35, exit 238B northbound; exit 238A southbound; on west frontage road. 5330 I-35 N 78751. Fax: 512/206-0573. **Facility:** 118 one-bedroom standard units. 2 stories (no elevator), exterior corridors. **Parking:** on-site. **Terms:** small pets only. **Pool(s):** outdoor. **Guest Services:** coin laundry. **Business Services:** fax (fee). **Cards:** AX, CB, DC, DS, MC, VI.

SOME UNITS

NORTHPARK EXECUTIVE SUITE HOTEL   **Phone:** (512)452-9391   112

All Year [BP]   1P: $129-$159   2P: $129-$159

Small-scale Hotel   **Location:** Loop 1 (Mopac Blvd), exit Anderson Rd, just e to Northcross Dr, then just s; behind Northcross Mall. 7685 Northcross Dr 78757. Fax: 512/459-4433. **Facility:** 198 units. 19 one-bedroom standard units. 159 one- and 20 two-bedroom suites with kitchens. 2 stories (no elevator), exterior corridors. **Parking:** on-site. **Terms:** small pets only ($50 fee, in smoking units). **Amenities:** video library, high-speed Internet (fee), voice mail, safes, irons, hair dryers. **Pool(s):** heated outdoor. **Leisure Activities:** whirlpool, limited exercise equipment. **Guest Services:** complimentary evening beverages: Mon-Thurs, valet and coin laundry, area transportation. **Business Services:** meeting rooms, business center. **Cards:** AX, CB, DC, DS, JC, MC, VI. *(See color ad below)*

SOME UNITS

[ASK] FEE

OMNI AUSTIN HOTEL SOUTHPARK   **Phone:** (512)448-2222   40

[AAA] [SAVE] All Year   1P: $169   2P: $169   XP: $20   F17

Small-scale Hotel   **Location:** I-35, exit 230B southbound; exit 230 northbound, on east frontage road. 4140 Governor's Row 78744. Fax: 512/442-8028. **Facility:** 313 units. 311 one-bedroom standard units. 2 two-bedroom suites. 14 stories, interior corridors. **Parking:** on-site. **Terms:** small pets only ($50 fee). **Amenities:** video games (fee), dual phone lines, voice mail, honor bars, irons, hair dryers. **Dining:** 6:30 am-2 & 5-10 pm, cocktails. **Pool(s):** heated indoor/outdoor. **Leisure Activities:** sauna, whirlpool, exercise room. **Guest Services:** gift shop, valet laundry, area transportation-within 4 mi. **Business Services:** conference facilities, business center. **Cards:** AX, CB, DC, DS, MC, VI.

SOME UNITS

FEE   FEE

QUALITY SUITES AUSTIN NORTH   **Phone:** (512)251-9110   66

[SAVE] All Year   1P: $80-$140   2P: $90-$150   XP: $6   F18

Small-scale Hotel   **Location:** I-35, exit 247, on west frontage road. 14620 N I-35 78728. Fax: 512/251-9112. **Facility:** 84 one-bedroom suites, some with whirlpools. 3 stories, interior corridors. *Bath:* combo or shower only. **Parking:** on-site. **Terms:** [BP] meal plan available. **Amenities:** voice mail, irons, hair dryers. *Fee:* video games, high-speed Internet. **Pool(s):** outdoor. **Leisure Activities:** exercise room. **Guest Services:** valet and coin laundry. **Business Services:** meeting rooms, fax (fee). **Cards:** AX, DC, DS, MC, VI.

SOME UNITS

FEE

(See map p. 180)

RAMADA LIMITED AUSTIN NORTH

			Phone: (512)836-0079	**95**
3/1-6/30 [ECP]	1P: $45-$75	2P: $52-$82	XP: $10	F13
7/1-1/31 [ECP]	1P: $42-$72	2P: $49-$79	XP: $5	F13
2/1-2/28 [ECP]	1P: $42-$72	2P: $49-$79	XP: $10	F13

Location: I-35, exit 241 northbound; exit 240 A southbound, on east frontage road. 9121 N I-35 78753. **Small-scale Hotel** Fax: 512/836-0681. **Facility:** 156 one-bedroom standard units. 3 stories, interior corridors. **Parking:** on-site. **Terms:** [BP] meal plan available, pets ($10 extra charge). **Amenities:** voice mail, irons, hair dryers. **Pool(s):** outdoor. **Guest Services:** airport transportation (fee)-Austin Airport. **Business Services:** meeting rooms, fax (fee). **Cards:** AX, DS, MC, VI. **Special Amenities:** free continental breakfast and free local telephone calls. *(See color ad below)*

SOME UNITS

RED LION HOTEL AUSTIN

		Phone: 512/323-5466	**43**
2/1-5/31 & 1/1-1/31	1P: $89-$109	XP: $10	F18
9/7-12/31	1P: $79-$99	XP: $10	F18
6/1-9/6	1P: $69-$99	XP: $10	F18

Large-scale Hotel **Location:** I-35, exit 238A northbound; exit 238B southbound, on east frontage road. 6121 I-35 N 78752. Fax: 512/453-1945. **Facility:** 300 one-bedroom standard units. 7 stories, interior corridors. **Parking:** on-site. **Amenities:** dual phone lines, voice mail, irons, hair dryers. **Pool(s):** outdoor. **Leisure Activities:** whirlpool, exercise room. **Guest Services:** gift shop, valet and coin laundry, area transportation. **Business Services:** conference facilities, business center. **Cards:** AX, CB, DC, DS, JC, MC, VI. *(See color ad below)*

SOME UNITS

(See map p. 180)

RED ROOF INN AUSTIN NORTH
Phone: (512)835-2200   **70**

(AAA) [SAVE]

Motel

All Year   1P: $39-$54   2P: $44-$59   XP: $5   F18
Location: I-35, exit 241, on west frontage road. 8210 I-35 N 78753. Fax: 512/339-9043. **Facility:** 143 one-bedroom standard units. 4 stories, exterior corridors. *Bath:* combo or shower only. **Parking:** on-site. **Amenities:** video games (fee), voice mail. **Dining:** 6 am-10 pm, wine/beer only. **Pool(s):** outdoor. **Business Services:** fax (fee). **Cards:** AX, CB, DC, DS, MC, VI. **Special Amenities: free local telephone calls and free newspaper.**

SOME UNITS
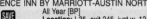
FEE

RED ROOF INN-AUSTIN SOUTH
Phone: (512)448-0091   **102**

(AAA) [SAVE]
Motel

All Year   1P: $39-$54   2P: $54-$59   XP: $5   F18
Location: I-35, exit 230B (Ben White Blvd) southbound; exit 229 (Stassney Rd) northbound, on northbound frontage road. 4701 I-35 S 78744. Fax: 512/448-0272. **Facility:** 137 units. 133 one-bedroom standard units. 4 one-bedroom suites ($60-$75). 4 stories, interior corridors. *Bath:* combo or shower only. **Parking:** on-site. **Amenities:** video games (fee), voice mail. **Pool(s):** heated outdoor. **Business Services:** fax (fee). **Cards:** AX, CB, DC, DS, MC, VI. **Special Amenities: free local telephone calls and free newspaper.**

SOME UNITS
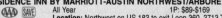

RENAISSANCE AUSTIN HOTEL
Phone: (512)343-2626   **41**

(AAA) [SAVE]
Large-scale Hotel

All Year   1P: $189-$219   2P: $209-$239   XP: $20   F18
Location: Jct of US 183 and SR 360; southwest corner. 9721 Arboretum Blvd 78759. Fax: 512/346-7953. **Facility:** 478 units. 460 one-bedroom standard units. 18 one-bedroom suites ($260-$350). 10 stories, interior corridors. **Parking:** on-site and valet. **Terms:** [AP] meal plan available, package plans, small pets only. **Amenities:** dual phone lines, voice mail, irons, hair dryers. *Fee:* video games, high-speed Internet. **Dining:** 2 restaurants, 24 hours, cocktails, also, Trattoria Grande, see separate listing, nightclub, entertainment. **Pool(s):** outdoor, heated indoor. **Leisure Activities:** sauna, whirlpool, exercise room. **Guest Services:** gift shop, valet laundry, airport transportation (fee)-Austin Airport. **Business Services:** conference facilities, business center. **Cards:** AX, CB, DC, DS, JC, MC, VI. **Special Amenities: free newspaper and free room upgrade (subject to availability with advanced reservations).**

SOME UNITS

FEE

RESIDENCE INN AUSTIN SOUTH
Phone: (512)912-1100   **100**

[SAVE]
Small-scale Hotel

All Year   1P: $89-$119   2P: $139-$179
Location: I-35, exit 229 (Stassney Rd) southbound; exit 230 (Ben White Blvd/SR 71) northbound, on northbound frontage road. 4537 S I-35 78744. Fax: 512/912-0119. **Facility:** 66 units. 18 one-bedroom standard units with efficiencies. 36 one- and 12 two-bedroom suites, some with efficiencies or kitchens. 3 stories, interior corridors. *Bath:* combo or shower only. **Parking:** on-site. **Terms:** cancellation fee imposed, [BP] meal plan available, pets ($125-$150 fee). **Amenities:** video games (fee), dual phone lines, voice mail, irons, hair dryers. **Pool(s):** small heated outdoor. **Leisure Activities:** whirlpool, exercise room, sports court, basketball. **Guest Services:** complimentary evening beverages: Mon-Thurs, valet and coin laundry. **Business Services:** meeting rooms, fax (fee). **Cards:** AX, CB, DC, DS, JC, MC, VI.

SOME UNITS

RESIDENCE INN BY MARRIOTT-AUSTIN NORTH
Phone: (512)977-0544   **44**

[SAVE]
Small-scale Hotel

All Year [BP]   1P: $119-$169   2P: $119-$169
Location: I-35, exit 245, just w. 12401 N Lamar Blvd 78753. Fax: 512/977-0545. **Facility:** 88 units. 76 one- and 12 two-bedroom standard units with kitchens. 4 stories, interior corridors. *Bath:* combo or shower only. **Parking:** on-site. **Terms:** pets ($75 fee). **Amenities:** video games (fee), dual phone lines, voice mail, irons, hair dryers. **Pool(s):** heated outdoor. **Leisure Activities:** whirlpool, limited exercise equipment, sports court. **Guest Services:** complimentary evening beverages: Mon-Thurs, valet and coin laundry. **Business Services:** meeting rooms, fax. **Cards:** AX, DC, DS, MC, VI.

SOME UNITS
FEE

RESIDENCE INN BY MARRIOTT-AUSTIN NORTHWEST/ARBORETUM
Phone: 512/502-8200   **101**

(AAA) [SAVE]
Small-scale Hotel

All Year   1P: $89-$169
Location: Northwest on US 183 to exit Loop 360. 3713 Tudor Blvd 78759. Fax: 512/502-0747. **Facility:** 84 units. 72 one- and 12 two-bedroom standard units, some with efficiencies or kitchens. 3 stories, interior corridors. *Bath:* combo or shower only. **Parking:** on-site. **Terms:** check-in 4 pm, [BP] & [ECP] meal plans available, pets ($50 fee, $5 extra charge). **Amenities:** video games (fee), voice mail, irons, hair dryers. **Pool(s):** small outdoor. **Leisure Activities:** whirlpool, exercise room, sports court. **Guest Services:** complimentary evening beverages: Mon-Thurs, valet and coin laundry. **Business Services:** administrative services, fax. **Cards:** AX, DC, DS, MC, VI.

SOME UNITS

RODEWAY INN-NORTH
Phone: (512)452-1177   **110**

(AAA) [SAVE]
Motel

All Year   1P: $38-$72   2P: $44-$76   XP: $6   F17
Location: I-35, 238B northbound; 238A southbound on frontage road. 5656 I-35 N 78751. Fax: 512/452-1638. **Facility:** 80 one-bedroom standard units. 2 stories (no elevator), exterior corridors. **Parking:** on-site. **Terms:** [CP] meal plan available, pets ($25 deposit). **Pool(s):** outdoor. **Business Services:** fax (fee). **Cards:** AX, CB, DC, DS, MC, VI.

SOME UNITS

(See map p. 180)

SPRINGHILL SUITES BY MARRIOTT-AUSTIN NORTH
Phone: (512)833-8100 **29**
SAVE
All Year [ECP] 1P: $79-$109
Small-scale Hotel
Location: I-35, exit 245, just w. 12520 N I-35 78753. Fax: 512/833-8115. **Facility:** 132 one-bedroom standard units, some with whirlpools. 5 stories, interior corridors. *Bath:* combo or shower only. **Parking:** on-site. **Terms:** cancellation fee imposed. **Amenities:** video games (fee), dual phone lines, voice mail, irons, hair dryers. **Pool(s):** heated indoor. **Leisure Activities:** whirlpool, jogging, exercise room. **Guest Services:** gift shop, valet and coin laundry. **Business Services:** meeting rooms, business center. **Cards:** AX, CB, DC, DS, MC, VI.
SOME UNITS

SPRINGHILL SUITES BY MARRIOTT AUSTIN NW
Phone: (512)349-0444 **60**
SAVE
All Year 1P: $79-$89 2P: $79-$89
Small-scale Hotel
Location: 1 mi n of US 183 on Loop 1 (Mopac Blvd). 10936 Stonelake Blvd 78759. Fax: 512/349-0475. **Facility:** 99 one-bedroom standard units. 5 stories, interior corridors. *Bath:* combo or shower only. **Parking:** on-site. **Terms:** cancellation fee imposed, weekly rates available, [ECP] meal plan available. **Amenities:** dual phone lines, voice mail, irons, hair dryers. **Pool(s):** small heated indoor. **Leisure Activities:** whirlpool, limited exercise equipment. **Guest Services:** valet and coin laundry. **Business Services:** meeting rooms, business center. **Cards:** AX, CB, DC, DS, MC, VI.
SOME UNITS

SPRINGHILL SUITES BY MARRIOTT-AUSTIN SOUTH/AIRPORT
Phone: (512)441-8270 **78**
SAVE
All Year 1P: $109-$119 2P: $109-$119
Motel
Location: I-35, exit 228, on northbound frontage road. 4501 S I-35 78744. Fax: 512/441-8416. **Facility:** 152 one-bedroom standard units, some with whirlpools. 6 stories, interior corridors. *Bath:* combo or shower only. **Parking:** on-site. **Terms:** [CP] meal plan available. **Amenities:** video games (fee), dual phone lines, voice mail, irons, hair dryers. **Pool(s):** small heated indoor. **Leisure Activities:** whirlpool, exercise room. **Guest Services:** valet and coin laundry. **Business Services:** business center. **Cards:** AX, CB, DC, DS, MC, VI.
SOME UNITS

STAYBRIDGE SUITES HOTEL
Phone: (512)349-0888 **36**
All Year [CP] 1P: $109-$139
Small-scale Hotel
Location: Jct of US 183 and SR 360; northwest corner. 10201 Stonelake Blvd 78759. Fax: 512/349-0809. **Facility:** 121 units. 106 one- and 15 two-bedroom standard units with efficiencies. 4 stories, interior corridors. *Bath:* combo or shower only. **Parking:** on-site. **Terms:** pets ($12-$75 extra charge). **Amenities:** dual phone lines, voice mail, irons, hair dryers. *Fee:* video library, high-speed Internet. **Pool(s):** heated outdoor. **Leisure Activities:** exercise room, sports court, basketball. **Guest Services:** sundries, complimentary evening beverages: Mon-Thurs. **Business Services:** meeting rooms, business center. **Cards:** AX, DC, DS, MC, VI.
SOME UNITS

STUDIO 6-AUSTIN MIDTOWN #6033
Phone: 512/458-5453 **35**
All Year 1P: $45-$55 2P: $49-$59 XP: $4 F17
Small-scale Hotel
Location: I-35, exit 239 northbound; exit 238B southbound, on east frontage road. 937 Camino La Costa 78752. Fax: 512/458-8265. **Facility:** 145 one-bedroom standard units with efficiencies. 2 stories (no elevator), exterior corridors. *Bath:* combo or shower only. **Parking:** on-site, winter plug-ins. **Terms:** weekly rates available, small pets only ($10-$50 extra charge). **Amenities:** voice mail, irons. **Guest Services:** coin laundry. **Business Services:** fax (fee). **Cards:** AX, DC, DS, MC, VI.
SOME UNITS

SUPER 8 AUSTIN NORTH
Phone: (512)339-1300 **49**
AAA SAVE
All Year [ECP] 1P: $39-$62 2P: $46-$69 XP: $4 F18
Small-scale Hotel
Location: I-35, exit 241, on west frontage road. 8128 N I-35 78753. Fax: 512/339-0820. **Facility:** 123 units. 117 one-bedroom standard units. 6 one-bedroom suites ($69-$99). 4 stories, interior corridors. **Parking:** on-site. **Terms:** small pets only. **Amenities:** *Some:* hair dryers. **Pool(s):** outdoor. **Leisure Activities:** whirlpool, limited exercise equipment. **Guest Services:** coin laundry. **Business Services:** meeting rooms, fax. **Cards:** AX, CB, DC, DS, MC, VI. **Special Amenities:** early check-in/late check-out and free local telephone calls.
SOME UNITS

WELLESLEY INN & SUITES (AUSTIN/N MOPAC)
Phone: (512)833-0898 **82**
AAA SAVE
All Year [ECP] 1P: $65-$89 2P: $65-$89 XP: $10 F18
Small-scale Hotel
Location: 2 mi n of US 183 on Loop 1 (Mopac Blvd), exit Burnet Rd (FM 1325). 2700 Gracy Farms Ln 78758. Fax: 512/833-0878. **Facility:** 113 units. 105 one-bedroom standard units with efficiencies. 8 one-bedroom suites with efficiencies. 2 stories (no elevator), interior corridors. *Bath:* combo or shower only. **Parking:** on-site. **Terms:** small pets only. **Amenities:** dual phone lines, voice mail, irons, hair dryers. *Fee:* video games, high-speed Internet. **Leisure Activities:** limited exercise equipment. **Guest Services:** valet and coin laundry, airport transportation (fee)-Austin Airport. **Business Services:** meeting rooms, fax. **Cards:** AX, CB, DC, DS, JC, MC, VI. **Special Amenities:** free continental breakfast and free newspaper. *(See color ad p 185)*
SOME UNITS

WELLESLEY INN & SUITES (AUSTIN/NORTH)
Phone: (512)339-6005 **75**
AAA SAVE
All Year 1P: $85-$105 2P: $85-$105 XP: $10 F17
Small-scale Hotel
Location: I-35, exit 241, on east frontage road. 8221 N I-35 78753. Fax: 512/339-6099. **Facility:** 119 units. 114 one- and 5 two-bedroom standard units with efficiencies. 3 stories, interior corridors. **Parking:** on-site. **Terms:** [ECP] meal plan available, small pets only. **Amenities:** voice mail, irons, hair dryers. *Fee:* video games, high-speed Internet. **Pool(s):** heated outdoor. **Leisure Activities:** limited exercise equipment. **Guest Services:** valet and coin laundry. **Business Services:** meeting rooms, fax (fee). **Cards:** AX, DS, JC, MC, VI. **Special Amenities:** free continental breakfast and free newspaper. *(See color ad p 185)*
SOME UNITS

(See map p. 180)

WELLESLEY INN & SUITES (AUSTIN/NW)
(AAA) (SAVE)   All Year [CP]   1P: $65-$95   2P: $65-$95   **Phone:** (512)219-6500   [37]
                                                     XP: $10   F18
▽▽▽   **Location:** US 183, exit Oak Knoll, on eastbound frontage road. 12424 Research Blvd 78759. **Fax:** 512/219-6468.
      Facility: 121 units. 116 one- and 5 two-bedroom standard units with efficiencies. 3 stories, interior corridors.
Small-scale Hotel   *Bath:* combo or shower only. **Parking:** on-site. **Terms:** pets ($100 deposit). **Amenities:** video games (fee),
      voice mail, irons, hair dryers. **Pool(s):** heated outdoor. **Leisure Activities:** exercise room. **Guest Services:**
      valet and coin laundry, airport transportation (fee)-Austin Airport. **Business Services:** meeting rooms, fax
(fee). **Cards:** AX, CB, DC, DS, JC, MC, VI. **Special Amenities: free continental breakfast and free newspaper.**
(See color ad p 185)

SOME UNITS

[S D] [✈] [🐾] [⚙M] [♿] [🎧] [🏊] [🎥] [DATA PORT] [📶] [🍽] [💻] / [✕] /
    FEE

WINGATE INN NORTH
(AAA) (SAVE)   All Year [ECP]   1P: $79-$89   2P: $99-$109   **Phone:** (512)821-0707   [76]
                                                     XP: $10   F17
▽▽▽   **Location:** I-35, exit 241, on west frontage road. 8500 N I-35 78753. **Fax:** 512/821-2230. **Facility:** 101 one-bedroom
      standard units. 4 stories, interior corridors. *Bath:* combo or shower only. **Parking:** on-site. **Terms:** cancella-
      tion fee imposed, package plans. **Amenities:** video games (fee), dual phone lines, voice mail, safes, irons,
Small-scale Hotel   hair dryers. **Pool(s):** outdoor. **Leisure Activities:** whirlpool, exercise room. **Guest Services:** valet laundry.
      Business Services: meeting rooms, business center. **Cards:** AX, CB, DC, DS, MC, VI. **Special Amenities:**
free continental breakfast and free newspaper.

SOME UNITS

[S D] [✈] [⚙M] [♿] [🎧] [🏊] [🎥] [DATA PORT] [📶] [🍽] [💻] / [✕] /
    FEE

────── *The following lodging was either not evaluated or did not* ──────
meet AAA rating requirements but is listed for your information only.

HOLIDAY INN EXPRESS HOTEL & SUITES
(fyi)   All Year [ECP]   1P: $89-$125   2P: $89-$125   **Phone:** 512/249-8166
                                                     XP: $5   F17
      Too new to rate. **Location:** US 183, 0.5 mi s on SR 620. 12703 N Hwy 620 78750. **Fax:** 512/249-7157.
      Amenities: coffeemakers, microwaves, refrigerators, pool. **Cards:** AX, CB, DC, DS, JC, MC, VI.

────── **WHERE TO DINE** ──────

BONE DADDY'S
▽▽▽   **Lunch:** $6-$20   **Dinner:** $6-$20   **Phone:** 512/346-3025   [46]
      Location: Jct I-35 and US 183, US 183 N to exit Duval, just n. 11617 Research Blvd 78759. **Hours:** 10:30 am-11
      pm, Fri-midnight, Sun 11 am-midnight, Sun 11 am-11 pm. Closed: 11/27, 12/25. **Features:** Guests
Barbecue   appreciate the relaxed atmosphere and diverse menu of smokehouse favorites. Also available is lighter
      fare, including sandwiches and salads. Cocktails. **Parking:** on-site. **Cards:** AX, DC, DS, MC, VI.

[⚙M] [Y] [✕]

CENTRAL MARKET CAFE
▽▽   **Lunch:** $6-$14   **Dinner:** $6-$14   **Phone:** 512/206-1020   [36]
      Location: Jct Lamar Blvd and 38th St, just n. 4001 N Lamar Blvd 78756. **Hours:** 7 am-10 pm. Closed: 4/20,
      11/27, 12/25. **Features:** The fun, energetic bistro offers large portions of such imaginative dishes as
American   pecan-crusted trout, which is deep-fried and served with potatoes and seasonal vegetables, and steak or
      chicken fajita salad with pico de gallo, sour cream and margarita dressing. Smoke free premises. Casual
dress; beer & wine only; entertainment. **Parking:** on-site. **Cards:** AX, DS, MC, VI.

[✕]

COOL RIVER CAFE
▽▽▽   **Lunch:** $9-$15   **Dinner:** $9-$30   **Phone:** 512/835-0010   [47]
      Location: Loop 1 (Mopac Blvd), exit Parmer Ln, 0.5 mi w. 4001 W Parmer Ln 78727. **Hours:** 11 am-11 pm.
      Closed: 11/27, 12/25; also Sun. **Reservations:** accepted. **Features:** The busy establishment presents a
American   menu of steaks, prime rib and such specialty dishes as lobster and Southwest-grilled food. On the
      premises are a large lounge and a cigar room. Dressy casual; cocktails; entertainment. **Parking:** on-site
and valet. **Cards:** AX, CB, DC, DS, MC, VI.

[Y] [✕]

COUNTY LINE ON THE LAKE
▽▽▽ ▽▽▽   **Lunch:** $5-$11   **Dinner:** $8-$16   **Phone:** 512/346-3664   [33]
      Location: 9.5 mi nw on FM 2222; 0.3 mi e of jct Loop 360. 5204 FM 2222 78731. **Hours:** 11:30 am-2 & 5-9 pm,
      Tues-Thurs to 9:30 pm, Fri-10 pm, Sat noon-10 pm, Sun 11:30 am-9 pm. Closed: 1/1, 11/27, 12/24-12/26.
Regional American   **Features:** With a view overlooking Mount Bonnell, the 1940s-style restaurant near the river serves
      barbecue specialties. Diners can feast on all-you-can-eat ribs, potato salad and veggies. A jukebox fills the
dining room with old standards. Casual dress; cocktails. **Parking:** on-site. **Cards:** AX, DC, DS, MC, VI.

[⚙M] [Y] [✕]

DAN MCKLUSKY'S RESTAURANT
▽▽▽   **Lunch:** $8-$16   **Dinner:** $13-$36   **Phone:** 512/346-0780   [51]
      Location: US 183 N, exit Great Hills, on west frontage road; in Arboretum Shopping Center. 10000 Research Blvd,
      Suite A 78759. **Hours:** 11:15 am-2 & 5-10 pm, Fri-11 pm, Sat 5 pm-11 pm, Sun 5 pm-9 pm. Closed major
Steak House   holidays. **Reservations:** accepted. **Features:** Diners can relax in a modern, cozy atmosphere and sample
      interesting combination dinners from a varied menu of steak, lamb and chicken dishes. The mixed grill is a
favorite. Casual dress; cocktails; entertainment. **Parking:** on-site. **Cards:** AX, CB, DC, DS, MC, VI.

[Y] [✕]

FONDA SAN MIGUEL
▽▽▽   **Dinner:** $13-$22   **Phone:** 512/459-4121   [32]
      Location: Just w of Burnet Rd. 2330 W North Loop Blvd 78756. **Hours:** 5:30 pm-9:30 pm, Fri & Sat-10:30 pm,
      Sun 11 am-2 pm. Closed: Sun for dinner & 12/24. **Reservations:** suggested. **Features:** The charming,
Mexican   Mexican inn decor comes complete with colorful paintings, pottery and other wares. Tex-Mex entrees, plus
      culinary delights from various regions in Mexico, fill an excellent menu that includes chicken, seafood and
beef dishes. Smoke free premises. Dressy casual; cocktails. **Parking:** on-site. **Cards:** AX, DC, DS, MC, VI.

[✕]

(See map p. 180)

JEFFREY'S
▽▽▽
American

Dinner: $21-$36   Phone: 512/477-5584   **34**
Location: Corner of 1500 blk and W 12th St. 1204 W Lynn 78703. **Hours:** 6 pm-10 pm, Fri & Sat 5:30 pm-10:30 pm, Sun 6 pm-9:30 pm. Closed major holidays. **Reservations:** suggested. **Features:** The ever-changing menu features imaginative, New Texas, Southwestern cuisine, including dishes along the lines of duck and shrimp with sweet potato gnocchi. Also notable are decadent desserts, such as chocolate intemperance and raspberry vanilla brulee. Casual dress; cocktails. **Parking:** valet and street. **Cards:** AX, DC, DS, MC, VI.

KERBEY LANE CAFE-CENTRAL
▽▽▽
American

Lunch: $5-$10   Dinner: $5-$10   Phone: 512/451-1436   **41**
Location: W of Lamar St off W 38th St and Kerbey Ln. 3704 Kerbey Ln 78731. **Hours:** 24 hours. Closed: 12/25.
Features: Gingerbread pancakes and eggs with tortillas are served all day. Separate dining rooms are built in the sleeping quarters of the renovated home. Wooden floors and floral-patterned walls add a pleasant touch. Casual dress; cocktails. **Parking:** on-site. **Cards:** AX, DC, DS, MC, VI.

MATT'S EL RANCHO
▽▽▽ ▽▽▽
Tex-Mex

Lunch: $7-$9   Dinner: $9-$15   Phone: 512/462-9333   **43**
Location: 0.5 mi s of jct Oltorf St and Lamar Blvd. 2613 S Lamar Blvd 78704. **Hours:** 11 am-10 pm, Fri & Sat-11 pm. Closed: 1/1, 12/25; also Tues. **Reservations:** accepted; weekdays. **Features:** Surrounded by beautiful oak trees, the family restaurant has a quaint patio for alfresco dining. All food, including the delicious desserts, is prepared from scratch. Try shrimp or steak, or for something a little different, the savory frog legs. Casual dress; cocktails. **Parking:** on-site. **Cards:** AX, DC, DS, MC, VI.

OLD SAN FRANCISCO STEAK HOUSE
▽▽▽
Steak & Seafood

Dinner: $15-$31   Phone: 512/835-9200   **35**
Location: I-35, exit 240A (Rutherford), on northbound access road. 8709 I-35 N 78753. **Hours:** 5 pm-10 pm, Fri & Sat-11 pm. **Reservations:** suggested. **Features:** Perched on a red, velvet seat, a woman swings over two baby grand pianos at the colorful restaurant. The rich textures and colors of the Gay '90s provide a lovely setting in which to savor specialty steaks, chicken and seafood. Dressy casual; cocktails; entertainment. **Parking:** on-site. **Cards:** AX, CB, DC, DS, MC, VI.

PAPPADEAUX SEAFOOD KITCHEN
▽▽▽
Cajun

Lunch: $7-$15   Dinner: $12-$25   Phone: 512/452-9363   **37**
Location: I-35, exit 239 northbound; exit 238B southbound, on east frontage road. 6319 I-35 N 78752. **Hours:** 11 am-10 pm, Fri & Sat-11 pm. Closed: 11/27, 12/25. **Features:** While Dixieland music plays in the background, patrons can dig into dirty rice at the New Orleans-style seafood warehouse. Gumbo is spicy and loaded with seafood. Well-seasoned shrimp and fish are prepared in varied ways. Smoke free premises. Casual dress; cocktails. **Parking:** on-site. **Cards:** AX, DC, DS, MC, VI.

RAY'S STEAKHOUSE
▽▽▽
Steak House

Lunch: $7-$15   Dinner: $17-$37   Phone: 512/219-9990   **49**
Location: US 183 and Anderson Hill Rd, just w; in Galleria Oaks Shopping Center. 13376 Hwy 183 N 78750. **Hours:** 11:30 am-2:30 & 5-10 pm, Fri-11 pm, Sat 5 pm-11 pm, Sun 5 pm-10 pm. Closed major holidays; also 1/2. **Reservations:** suggested. **Features:** Signature steaks, seafood, prime rib, lamb, pork chops and veal are among savory choices, which match well with a fine selection of appetizers and salads. A limited children's menu is available. Casual dress; cocktails. **Parking:** on-site. **Cards:** AX, MC, VI.

RAZZOO'S CAJUN CAFE
▽▽▽
Cajun

Lunch: $6-$17   Dinner: $6-$17   Phone: 522/241-0444   **30**
Location: US 183 N, exit Duval Rd, on northbound access road. 11617 Research Blvd, Bldg 3 78759. **Hours:** 11 am-11 pm, Fri & Sat-2 am. Closed: 11/27, 12/25. **Reservations:** accepted. **Features:** Catfish, shrimp, chicken, crawfish, pasta and ribs, all prepared Cajun style, are the laid-back restaurant's forte. Casual dress; cocktails. **Parking:** on-site. **Cards:** AX, DC, DS, MC, VI.

SATAY RESTAURANT
▽▽▽ ▽▽▽
Thai

Lunch: $5-$7   Dinner: $7-$15   Phone: 512/467-6731   **44**
Location: Northwest corner of Shoal Creek and Anderson Ln, just e of Loop 1 (Mopac Blvd). 3202 W Anderson Ln 78757. **Hours:** 11 am-2:30 & 5-10 pm, Fri-11 pm, Sat 5 pm-11 pm. Closed: 11/27, 12/25; also 1/1 for lunch. **Reservations:** suggested. **Features:** Specialties include coconut-based soup and skewer meats with steamed rice and peanut sauce. Yam cakes and fried egg rolls are particularly tasty. Natural lighting fills the large, open dining room, which features attractive Asian decor. Smoke free premises. Casual dress; cocktails. **Parking:** on-site. **Cards:** AX, CB, DC, DS, MC, VI.

SHADES CAFE
▽▽▽
Regional Steak & Seafood

Lunch: $6-$14   Dinner: $6-$22   Phone: 512/335-5772   **29**
Location: Jct of US 183 and FM 620, just n; in Lakeline Plaza. 11066 Pecan Park Blvd 78750. **Hours:** 11 am-10 pm, Fri & Sat-11 pm. Closed: 4/20, 11/27, 12/25. **Reservations:** accepted. **Features:** Guests can sit indoors or out to experience a Florida Keys atmosphere in the heart of Texas. South Florida cuisine consists of salads, seafood, steaks, chicken and rib entrees. Save room for homemade Key lime pie. Casual dress; cocktails. **Parking:** on-site. **Cards:** AX, DS, MC, VI.

TAJ PALACE INDIAN RESTAURANT & BAR
▽▽ ▽▽
Indian

Lunch: $6-$8   Dinner: $8-$17   Phone: 512/452-9959   **39**
Location: I-35, exit 239/240 southbound; exit 239 northbound, just off west frontage road. 6700 Middle Fiskville Rd 78752. **Hours:** 11 am-2 & 5:30-10 pm, Fri-10:30 pm, Sat & Sun 11:30 am-2:30 & 5:30-10:30 pm. Closed: 12/24 for dinner. **Reservations:** accepted. **Features:** The exotic scene is filled with Indian trinkets, wall hangings, brass, Taj Mahal marble, silk and beads. From curries to tandoori chicken, traditional entrees are well-prepared. Many choices line the Monday buffet and the Tuesday vegetarian buffet. Smoke free premises. Casual dress; beer & wine only. **Parking:** on-site. **Cards:** AX, DC, DS, MC, VI

TEXAS LAND & CATTLE STEAKHOUSE
▽▽▽
Steak House

Lunch: $6-$11   Dinner: $11-$22   Phone: 512/258-3733   **28**
Location: US 183 and FM 620, just n. 14010 N Hwy 183 78717. **Hours:** 11 am-10 pm, Fri & Sat-11 pm. Closed: 11/27, 12/25. **Reservations:** accepted. **Features:** The Texas-style ranch house treats patrons to appetizers, salads, chicken, ribs and specialty steaks, including the house favorite, slow-smoked sirloin. Smoke free premises. Casual dress; cocktails. **Parking:** on-site. **Cards:** AX, CB, DC, DS, MC, VI.

(See map p. 180)

THREADGILL'S RESTAURANT   **Lunch:** $6-$18   **Dinner:** $6-$18   **Phone:** 512/451-5440   ㊵

American

Location: I-35, exit 239 (St John's Ave), 1 mi w to Lamar Blvd, 0.5 mi s. 6416 N Lamar Blvd 78752. **Hours:** 11 am-10 pm, Sun-9 pm. **Features:** The historic 1930s restaurant serves Southern home-style cooking in the rustic setting of a converted gas station. After a hearty meal of fried Mississippi catfish or chicken-fried steak, guests can partake in luscious pecan pie. Smoke free premises. Casual dress; cocktails. **Parking:** on-site. **Cards:** DS, MC, VI.

ⓎⓍ

TONY ROMA'S   **Lunch:** $6-$20   **Dinner:** $6-$20   **Phone:** 512/258-3441   ㉗

American

Location: Jct US 183 and FM 620, just n. 11100 Pecan Park Blvd 78717. **Hours:** 11 am-midnight. Closed: 11/27, 12/25. **Reservations:** accepted. **Features:** Specializing in St. Louis-style ribs prepared in four flavors, the restaurant also offers chicken, steak, sausage and shrimp. Save room for the yummy desserts. Smoke free premises. Casual dress; cocktails. **Parking:** on-site. **Cards:** AX, DC, DS, MC, VI.

ⓎⓍ

TRATTORIA GRANDE   **Dinner:** $16-$25   **Phone:** 512/795-6100   ㉛

Northern
Italian

Location: Jct of US 183 and SR 360; southwest corner; in Renaissance Austin Hotel. 9721 Arboretum Blvd 78759. **Hours:** 5 pm-10 pm, Fri & Sat-11 pm. Closed: Sun & Mon. **Reservations:** suggested. **Features:** Well-prepared Italian dishes are served in a soothing, elegant atmosphere. Filetto alla Gorgonzola, an 8-ounce grilled beef tenderloin with portobello mushrooms and blue cheese, is excellent, as is olive-crusted snapper. Smoke free premises. Casual dress; cocktails. **Parking:** on-site. **Cards:** AX, CB, DC, DS, JC, MC, VI.

ⓂⓍ

WEST LYNN CAFE   **Lunch:** $6-$11   **Dinner:** $8-$13   **Phone:** 512/482-0950   ㊺

Vegetarian

Location: 1 mi e of Mopac Blvd, exit Enfield Rd; W Lynn and 12th St. 1110 W Lynn St 78703. **Hours:** 11:30 am-10 pm, Fri-10:30 pm, Sat 11 am-10:30 pm, Sun 11 am-9:30 pm. Closed major holidays; also Mon & 12/24 for dinner. **Features:** Stars decorate the high ceilings, and tables are draped in white linen. Delicious Southwestern food, such as poblano enchiladas, goes will with the specialty Energizer, a whipped drink with an assortment of fresh fruits. Smoke free premises. Dressy casual; beer & wine only. **Parking:** on-site. **Cards:** AX, DC, DS, MC, VI.

Ⓧ

ZOOT AMERICAN BISTRO & WINE BAR   **Dinner:** $19-$36   **Phone:** 512/477-6535   ㊷

American

Location: Loop 1 (Mopac Blvd) exit Lake Travis, 0.3 mi w to Hearn St, then just n. 509 Hearn St 78703. **Hours:** 5:30 pm-10 pm. Closed major holidays; also 12/24. **Reservations:** suggested. **Features:** A French flavor infuses sauces drizzled over freshly prepared entrees. Seasonings from the on-site herb garden add just the right flavor to such inventive dishes as seared Atlantic salmon with cinnamon-scented Israeli couscous served in a phyllo pastry basket. Smoke free premises. Dressy casual; beer & wine only. **Parking:** on-site. **Cards:** AX, CB, DC, DS, MC, VI.

Ⓧ

BANDERA pop. 957

——— WHERE TO STAY ———

BANDERA LODGE MOTEL   **Phone:** 830/796-3093

Ⓐ SAVE

Small-scale Hotel

All Year   1P: $55-$75   2P: $60-$80   XP: $5   F16
Location: 1 mi s on SR 16; 7 mi s of jct SR 173. 700 Hwy 16 S 78003 (PO Box 2609). Fax: 830/796-3191. **Facility:** 43 one-bedroom standard units. 2 stories (no elevator), exterior corridors. **Parking:** on-site. **Terms:** cancellation fee imposed, pets ($10 extra charge). **Amenities:** irons, hair dryers. **Dining:** 7 am-9:30 pm, Sun-2 pm. **Pool(s):** outdoor. **Leisure Activities:** volleyball. **Guest Services:** coin laundry. **Business Services:** meeting rooms, fax (fee). **Cards:** AX, CB, DC, DS, MC, VI. **Special Amenities:** free local telephone calls.

SOME UNITS

🐾 🍽 Ⓨ ⊇ 🛄 🗄 🖳 /Ⓧ/

BASTROP pop. 5,340

——— WHERE TO STAY ———

BASTROP INN MOTEL   **Phone:** (512)321-3949

Motel

All Year   1P: $45-$52   2P: $50-$60   XP: $5   F10
Location: Just e at jct SR 71/SR 21 and Loop 150. 102 Childers Dr 78602. Fax: 512/321-3108. **Facility:** 32 one-bedroom standard units. 2 stories (no elevator), exterior corridors. **Parking:** on-site. **Terms:** weekly rates available. **Pool(s):** small outdoor. **Guest Services:** coin laundry. **Business Services:** fax (fee). **Cards:** AX, CB, DC, DS, JC, MC, VI.

SOME UNITS

🛄⁺ ⊇ 🛄 🗄 🖳 /Ⓧ/

BAY CITY pop. 18,667

——— WHERE TO STAY ———

BEST WESTERN MATAGORDA HOTEL & CONFERENCE CENTER   **Phone:** (979)244-5400

SAVE

Small-scale Hotel

All Year   1P: $69-$89   2P: $75-$95   XP: $6   F12
Location: SR 35 (7th St), 1 mi s of jct SR 35 and 60. 407 7th St 77414 (PO Box 1949, 77404). Fax: 979/244-2706. **Facility:** 120 one-bedroom standard units, some with whirlpools. 2 stories, exterior corridors. *Bath:* combo or shower only. **Parking:** on-site. **Terms:** pets ($100 fee). **Amenities:** irons, hair dryers. **Pool(s):** outdoor, wading. **Guest Services:** valet laundry. **Business Services:** conference facilities, fax (fee).

SOME UNITS

🆂ⓓ 🐾 🍽 Ⓨ 🚹 ⊇ 🛄 🗄 🖳 /Ⓧ🛄/

FEE

BAYTOWN —See Houston p. 434.

BEAUMONT pop. 113,866

——— WHERE TO STAY ———

BEST WESTERN BEAUMONT INN

Motel

All Year [ECP]   1P: $59-$66   2P: $66-$76   XP: $7   F12
Phone: (409)898-8150
Location: I-10, exit 853B (11th St), just n. 2155 N 11th St 77703. Fax: 409/898-0078. **Facility:** 152 one-bedroom standard units. 2 stories (no elevator), exterior corridors. **Parking:** on-site. **Terms:** small pets only. **Amenities:** irons, hair dryers. **Pool(s):** outdoor. **Guest Services:** valet and coin laundry. **Business Services:** meeting rooms, fax (fee). **Cards:** AX, CB, DC, DS, JC, MC, VI. **Special Amenities:** free continental breakfast and free newspaper.

SOME UNITS

BEST WESTERN JEFFERSON INN

Motel

All Year [ECP]   1P: $59-$65   2P: $65-$71   XP: $6   F18
Phone: (409)842-0037
Location: I-10, exit 851 (College St), westbound service road, 0.5 mi s of jct US 90. 1610 I-10 S 77707. Fax: 409/842-0057. **Facility:** 120 one-bedroom standard units, some with kitchens. 2 stories, exterior corridors. **Parking:** on-site. **Terms:** weekly rates available, small pets only. **Amenities:** irons, hair dryers. **Pool(s):** outdoor. **Guest Services:** complimentary evening beverages: Mon-Fri, valet and coin laundry. **Business Services:** meeting rooms, fax (fee). **Cards:** AX, CB, DC, DS, MC, VI. **Special Amenities:** free continental breakfast and free newspaper.

SOME UNITS

HILTON BEAUMONT

Small-scale Hotel

All Year   1P: $79   2P: $79   XP: $10   F18
Phone: (409)842-3600
Location: I-10, exit 850 (Washington Blvd), on eastbound service road. 2355 I-10 S 77705. Fax: 409/842-1355. **Facility:** 281 one-bedroom standard units, some with whirlpools. 3-9 stories, interior corridors. *Bath:* combo or shower only. **Parking:** on-site. **Terms:** 20% service charge, small pets only ($50 deposit). **Amenities:** voice mail, irons, hair dryers. **Pool(s):** outdoor. **Leisure Activities:** exercise room. **Guest Services:** gift shop, valet and coin laundry, area transportation. **Business Services:** conference facilities, fax. **Cards:** AX, DC, DS, MC, VI. *(See color ad below)*

SOME UNITS

HOLIDAY INN ATRIUM PLAZA

Large-scale Hotel

All Year   1P: $117-$129   2P: $127-$139   XP: $10   F
Phone: (409)842-5995
Location: I-10, exit 848 (Walden Rd), just n. 3950 I-10 S 77705. Fax: 409/842-0315. **Facility:** 253 units. 202 one-bedroom standard units. 48 one- and 3 two-bedroom suites, some with whirlpools. 8 stories, interior corridors. *Bath:* combo or shower only. **Parking:** on-site. **Terms:** check-in 4 pm, pets ($10 deposit). **Amenities:** video games (fee), voice mail, irons, hair dryers. **Dining:** 2 restaurants, 6 am-11 pm, cocktails. **Pool(s):** heated indoor. **Leisure Activities:** saunas, whirlpool, exercise room. **Guest Services:** valet and coin laundry, area transportation-within 5 mi. **Business Services:** conference facilities, business center. **Cards:** AX, CB, DC, DS, MC, VI. **Special Amenities:** free newspaper.

SOME UNITS

HOLIDAY INN BEAUMONT MIDTOWN

Small-scale Hotel

All Year   1P: $59-$69   2P: $59-$69   XP: $10   F18
Phone: (409)892-2222
Location: I-10, exit 853B (11th St), just n. 2095 N 11th St 77703. Fax: 409/892-2231. **Facility:** 190 one-bedroom standard units. 6 stories, interior corridors. *Bath:* combo or shower only. **Parking:** on-site. **Terms:** pets ($100 deposit). **Amenities:** voice mail, irons, hair dryers. **Dining:** 6-10 am, 11-2 & 5-9:30 pm, cocktails, nightclub. **Pool(s):** outdoor. **Leisure Activities:** exercise room. **Guest Services:** valet and coin laundry, area transportation-within 15 mi. **Business Services:** meeting rooms, fax (fee). **Cards:** AX, CB, DC, DS, MC, VI. **Special Amenities:** early check-in/late check-out.

SOME UNITS

LA QUINTA INN-BEAUMONT

Phone: (409)838-9991

(AAA) (SAVE)

Motel

All Year   1P: $60-$70   2P: $66-$76   XP: $6   F18
Location: I-10, exit 852B (Calder Ave) eastbound; eastbound service road, exit 852A (Laurel Ave) westbound. 220 I-10 N 77702-2112. Fax: 409/832-1266. **Facility:** 122 one-bedroom standard units. 2 stories, exterior corridors. *Bath:* combo or shower only. **Parking:** on-site. **Terms:** [ECP] meal plan available, small pets only. **Amenities:** video games (fee), voice mail, irons, hair dryers. **Pool(s):** outdoor. **Guest Services:** valet laundry. **Business Services:** meeting rooms, fax (fee). **Cards:** AX, CB, DC, DS, JC, MC, VI.
Special Amenities: free continental breakfast and free local telephone calls.

SOME UNITS

🐾 🍴 ⚬ 🐕 🐎 🎿 DATA PORT 💻 / ✕ 🔌 🖨 /
                                                              FEE FEE

SUPER 8 BEAUMONT

Phone: (409)899-3040

(AAA) (SAVE)

Small-scale Hotel

All Year   1P: $40-$47   2P: $45-$47   XP: $4   F12
Location: I-10, exit 853B (11th St), on westbound service road. 2850 I-10 E 77703. Fax: 409/899-3040. **Facility:** 80 one-bedroom standard units. 3 stories, interior corridors. **Parking:** on-site. **Terms:** pets ($10.83 fee). **Amenities:** hair dryers. **Pool(s):** outdoor. **Business Services:** fax (fee). **Cards:** AX, DC, MC, VI.
Special Amenities: free continental breakfast and free local telephone calls.

SOME UNITS

SD 🐾 🍴 🐎 🎿 DATA PORT / ✕ 🔌 🖨 /

---

*The following lodging was either not evaluated or did not
meet AAA rating requirements but is listed for your information only.*

ECONO LODGE

(fyi)

Small-scale Hotel

Phone: 409/835-8800

All Year [CP]   1P: $55-$85   2P: $55-$85   XP: $5
Too new to rate. **Location:** I-10, exit 852. 50 I-10 N 77702. Fax: 409/835-8802. **Amenities:** microwaves, refrigerators. **Terms:** cancellation fee imposed. **Cards:** AX, DS, MC, VI.

--- **WHERE TO DINE** ---

HOFFBRAU STEAKS

Steak & Seafood

Lunch: $7-$10   **Dinner:** $12-$19   **Phone:** 409/892-6911
Location: I-10, exit 853B (11th St), just n. 2310 N 11th St 77703. **Hours:** 11 am-10 pm, Fri-11 pm, Sat 4 pm-11 pm, Sun 11 am-9 pm. Closed major holidays. **Features:** Kick back and enjoy a delicious steak dinner in a rustic saloon setting complete with mounted animals and neon beer signs. Covered outdoor dining is available year-round, with a large stone fireplace for those who enjoy eating al fresco even in winter. Casual dress; cocktails; entertainment. **Parking:** on-site. **Cards:** AX, DC, DS, MC, VI.

🍸 ✕

THE TAMALE CO

Mexican

Lunch: $4-$6   **Dinner:** $7-$13   **Phone:** 409/866-8033
Location: I-10, exit 852A (Laurel Ave) westbound; exit 852B (Calder Ave) eastbound; under I-10, 1.8 mi w on Phelan Blvd, southwestern corner of Phelan Blvd and Payton Dr. 6025 Phelan Blvd 77706. **Hours:** 11 am-10 pm, Sun-9 pm. Closed: 7/4, 11/27, 12/25. **Features:** Family owned and operated, this restaurant features the added spice of some Cajun specialties thrown in for good measure. An eclectic decor includes mounted animals, bottles and neon signs. Chicken and beef tacos with refried beans makes a tasty meal. Casual dress; cocktails. **Parking:** on-site. **Cards:** AX, DS, MC, VI.

✕

BEDFORD pop. 47,152   (See map p. 343; index p. 346)

--- **WHERE TO STAY** ---

COURTYARD BY MARRIOTT

(SAVE)

Small-scale Hotel

Phone: (817)545-2202   81
All Year   1P: $99   2P: $109   XP: $10   F18
Location: SR 121/183, exit Central Dr, just n to Plaza Dr. 2201 W Airport Frwy 76021. Fax: 817/545-2319. **Facility:** 145 units. 132 one-bedroom standard units. 13 one-bedroom suites. 3 stories, interior corridors. *Bath:* combo or shower only. **Parking:** on-site. **Amenities:** high-speed Internet (fee), dual phone lines, voice mail, irons, hair dryers. **Pool(s):** heated outdoor. **Leisure Activities:** whirlpool, exercise room. **Guest Services:** valet and coin laundry. **Business Services:** meeting rooms, fax (fee). **Cards:** AX, CB, DC, DS, JC, MC, VI.

SOME UNITS

SD 🍴 🍸 ⚬M ⚬ 🐎 🎿 DATA PORT 💻 / ✕ 🔌 🖨 /

(See map p. 343)

HOLIDAY INN-DFW-WEST
AAA SAVE
▽▽▽
Small-scale Hotel

Phone: (817)267-3181 76

All Year 1P: $79-$95 2P: $79-$95 XP: $10 F18
Location: SR 183, just e of jct SR 121, exit Murphy Dr N. 3005 W Airport Frwy 76021. Fax: 817/267-8091. **Facility:** 243 one-bedroom standard units. 5 stories, interior corridors. **Parking:** on-site. **Terms:** cancellation fee imposed, small pets only ($25 fee). **Amenities:** voice mail, irons, hair dryers. *Fee:* video games, high-speed Internet. **Dining:** 6 am-2 & 5-10 pm, cocktails. **Pool(s):** outdoor. **Leisure Activities:** sauna, exercise room. **Guest Services:** valet and coin laundry, airport transportation-Dallas-Fort Worth International Airport, area transportation-within 5 mi. **Business Services:** meeting rooms, fax (fee). **Cards:** AX, DC, DS, MC, VI. **Special Amenities:** free newspaper. *(See ad p 208)*

SOME UNITS
🆂 ➡️ 🛏️ 🍴 🍸 🛗 📷 🏊 🐕 DATA PORT 💻 / ✖️ 🔌 🖨️
FEE FEE

HOMEWOOD SUITES BY HILTON
SAVE
▽▽▽
Small-scale Hotel

Phone: (817)283-5006 80

All Year 1P: $106 2P: $106
Location: SR 183, just nw, exit Central/Murphy Dr. 2401 Airport Frwy 76021. Fax: 817/283-8370. **Facility:** 83 units. 75 one- and 8 two-bedroom suites with efficiencies, some with whirlpools. 3 stories, interior corridors. *Bath:* combo or shower only. **Parking:** on-site. **Terms:** [ECP] meal plan available. **Amenities:** video library (fee), dual phone lines, voice mail, irons, hair dryers. **Pool(s):** heated outdoor. **Leisure Activities:** whirlpool, exercise room, sports court. **Guest Services:** sundries, complimentary evening beverages: Mon-Thurs, valet and coin laundry, area transportation. **Business Services:** meeting rooms, business center. **Cards:** AX, CB, DC, DS, JC, MC, VI.

SOME UNITS
🆂 🛗 🛗 📷 🐕 ✖️ VCR 🏊 DATA PORT 🔌 🖨️ 💻 / ✖️ /

LA QUINTA INN-BEDFORD
AAA SAVE
▽▽▽
Small-scale Hotel

Phone: (817)267-5200 79

All Year 1P: $59-$79 2P: $69-$89 XP: $10 F18
Location: SR 121/183, 0.3 mi e of jct Bedford Rd/Forest Ridge Dr exit. 1450 Airport Frwy 76022. Fax: 817/283-1682. **Facility:** 116 one-bedroom standard units. 2 stories, exterior corridors. **Parking:** on-site. **Terms:** [ECP] meal plan available, small pets only. **Amenities:** voice mail, irons, hair dryers. *Fee:* video games, high-speed Internet. **Pool(s):** outdoor. **Guest Services:** valet and coin laundry, airport transportation-Dallas-Fort Worth International Airport, area transportation-within 5 mi. **Business Services:** fax (fee). **Cards:** AX, CB, DC, DS, JC, MC, VI. **Special Amenities:** free continental breakfast and free local telephone calls. *(See color ad p 354)*

SOME UNITS
🆂 ➡️ 🐕 📷 🏊 🐕 DATA PORT 💻 / ✖️ 🔌
FEE

SUPER 8 MOTEL-BEDFORD
▽▽▽
Small-scale Hotel

Phone: (817)545-8108 77

All Year 1P: $45 2P: $50 XP: $5 F12
Location: SR 183 at Bedford Rd, exit Forest Ridge Dr. 1800 Airport Frwy 76022. Fax: 817/545-8845. **Facility:** 113 one-bedroom standard units. 3 stories, interior corridors. *Bath:* combo or shower only. **Parking:** on-site. **Terms:** pets ($10 extra charge). **Amenities:** safes (fee). **Guest Services:** coin laundry. **Business Services:** meeting rooms, fax (fee). **Cards:** AX, DC, DS, MC, VI.

SOME UNITS
A$K 🆂 ➡️ 🛏️ 🛗 ✖️ 📷 / ✖️ /

—————— WHERE TO DINE ——————

HOFFBRAU STEAKS
▽
Steak House

Lunch: $7-$9 **Dinner: $10-$21** **Phone: 817/267-9303** 49
Location: SR 121/183, exit Forest Ridge Dr, on westbound access road. 1833 W Airport Frwy 76021. **Hours:** 11 am-10 pm, Fri & Sat-11 pm. Closed: 11/27, 12/25. **Features:** The traditional Texas steakhouse has none of the frills. It caters to diners who want a rustic atmosphere and simple home cooking. Although steaks are the specialty, the menu includes plenty of other choices. Casual dress; cocktails. **Parking:** on-site.
Cards: AX, DC, DS, MC, VI.

🍸 ✖️

BEEVILLE pop. 13,129

—————— WHERE TO STAY ——————

BEEVILLE DAYS INN
SAVE
▽▽▽
Small-scale Hotel

Phone: (361)358-4000

All Year 1P: $49 2P: $54 XP: $5 F12
Location: 0.3 mi s of jct US 59 and 181. 400 A S US 181 Bypass 78102. Fax: 361/358-7851. **Facility:** 60 one-bedroom standard units. 2 stories, exterior corridors. **Parking:** on-site. **Terms:** small pets only. **Amenities:** irons, hair dryers. **Pool(s):** outdoor. **Guest Services:** valet laundry. **Business Services:** fax (fee). **Cards:** AX, CB, DC, DS, JC, MC, VI.

SOME UNITS
🆂 🛏️ 🏊 📷 DATA PORT 🔌 🖨️ / ✖️ /

BELTON pop. 14,623

—————— WHERE TO STAY ——————

BUDGET HOST INN
AAA SAVE
▽▽
Small-scale Hotel

Phone: (254)939-0744

4/1-9/30 1P: $42-$50 2P: $50-$60 XP: $5 F12
2/1-3/31 & 10/1-1/31 1P: $36-$43 2P: $42-$50 XP: $5 F12
Location: I-35, exit 292 southbound; exit 293A northbound. 1520 S I-35 76513. Fax: 254/939-9238. **Facility:** 50 one-bedroom standard units, some with efficiencies. 2 stories, exterior corridors. **Parking:** on-site. **Terms:** [CP] meal plan available. **Pool(s):** outdoor. **Business Services:** fax (fee). **Cards:** AX, DC, MC, VI. **Special Amenities:** free continental breakfast and free local telephone calls. *(See color ad p 162)*

SOME UNITS
🆂 🛏️ 🏊 📷 DATA PORT 🔌 🖨️ 💻 / ✖️ VCR /
FEE

RIVER FOREST INN
▼▼   All Year [CP]   1P: $50-$70   2P: $55-$75   XP: $5   F12
                        Location: Jct of FM 93 and I-35, US 81 and 190, exit 294B (6th St). 1414 E 6th Ave 76513 (PO Box 504).
Small-scale Hotel   Fax: 254/939-5711. **Facility:** 49 one-bedroom standard units. 2 stories, exterior corridors. *Bath:* combo or
                        shower only. **Parking:** on-site. **Amenities:** hair dryers. **Pool(s):** outdoor. **Business Services:** fax (fee).
Cards: AX, CB, DC, DS, MC, VI.
                                                                                                              SOME UNITS

BENBROOK pop. 20,208   (See map p. 343; index p. 346)

—————— WHERE TO STAY ——————

MOTEL 6 - 4051   **Phone:** 817/249-8885
▼▼   All Year   1P: $43-$48   2P: $49-$55   XP: $6   F17
                        Location: I-20, exit 429A, 0.7 mi s. 8601 Hwy 377 S (Benbrook Blvd) 76126. Fax: 817/249-2564. **Facility:** 63 one-
Small-scale Hotel   bedroom standard units. 3 stories, interior corridors. *Bath:* combo or shower only. **Parking:** on-site.
                        Terms: small pets only. **Amenities:** voice mail. **Pool(s):** small outdoor. **Guest Services:** coin laundry. **Busi-**
ness Services: fax (fee). **Cards:** AX, CB, DC, DS, MC, VI.
                                                                                                              SOME UNITS

BIG SPRING pop. 25,233

—————— WHERE TO STAY ——————

GREAT WESTERN INN   **Phone:** (432)267-4553
AAA [SAVE]   All Year   1P: $45   2P: $60
                        Location: I-20, exit 179. 2900 E I-20 79720. Fax: 432/267-4553. **Facility:** 64 one-bedroom standard units. 2 sto-
▼▼ ▼▼   ries (no elevator), exterior corridors. **Parking:** on-site. **Terms:** pets ($50 deposit, in smoking units.)
Motel   **Amenities:** hair dryers. *Some:* irons. **Pool(s):** outdoor. **Business Services:** meeting rooms, fax (fee).
                        Cards: AX, DC, DS, MC, VI.
                                                                                                              SOME UNITS

SUPER 8 MOTEL   **Phone:** (432)267-1601
AAA [SAVE]   All Year   1P: $49   2P: $79   XP: $6   F12
                        Location: I-20, exit 177, just n. 700 W I-20 79720. Fax: 432/267-6916. **Facility:** 150 units. 148 one-bedroom stan-
▼▼ ▼▼   dard units. 2 one-bedroom suites. 2 stories (no elevator), exterior corridors. **Parking:** on-site. **Terms:** can-
Motel   cellation fee imposed. **Amenities:** voice mail, irons, hair dryers. **Pool(s):** outdoor. **Guest Services:** valet
                        laundry. **Business Services:** meeting rooms, fax (fee). **Cards:** AX, CB, DC, MC.
                                                                                                              SOME UNITS

—————— WHERE TO DINE ——————

K-C STEAK & SEAFOOD   **Dinner:** $8-$21   **Phone:** 432/263-1651
▼▼   **Location:** N Service Rd to I-20, exit 176; 0.5 mi w jct SR 176. N Service Rd, I-20 W 79720. **Hours:** 5 pm-10 pm.
                        Closed major holidays; also Sun. **Reservations:** accepted. **Features:** The restaurant has served simply
Steak & Seafood   good food throughout its 40 years in operation. Everything, from the bread to the salad dressing, is made
                        from scratch. An elegant supper-club atmosphere remains the setting for delicious prime rib, steak, Alaskan
crab and lobster. Casual dress; beer & wine only. **Parking:** on-site. **Cards:** AX, CB, DC, DS, MC, VI.

BISHOP pop. 3,305

—————— WHERE TO STAY ——————

DAYS INN SUITES   **Phone:** (361)584-4444
[SAVE]   All Year   1P: $53-$59   2P: $59-$69   XP: $6   F12
                        Location: At northern city limits. Located in a rural area. 715 S Hwy 77 78343. Fax: 361/584-5555. **Facility:** 40 units.
▼▼ ▼▼   37 one-bedroom standard units. 3 one-bedroom suites ($75-$89). 2 stories, exterior corridors. *Bath:* combo
Small-scale Hotel   or shower only. **Parking:** on-site. **Terms:** [CP] meal plan available. **Amenities:** hair dryers. **Pool(s):** outdoor.
                        Leisure Activities: whirlpool, exercise room. **Guest Services:** coin laundry. **Business Services:** meeting
                        rooms, fax (fee). **Cards:** AX, DC, DS, MC, VI.
                                                                                                              SOME UNITS

BOERNE pop. 6,178

—————— WHERE TO STAY ——————

BEST WESTERN TEXAS COUNTRY INN   **Phone:** (830)249-9791
AAA [SAVE]   All Year   1P: $59-$65   2P: $65-$73   XP: $6   F12
                        Location: I-10, exit 540 (US 46). 35150 I-10 W 78006. Fax: 830/249-9791. **Facility:** 82 units. 81 one- and 1 two-
▼▼ ▼▼   bedroom standard units, some with kitchens. 2 stories (no elevator), exterior corridors. **Parking:** on-site.
Small-scale Hotel   **Terms:** pets ($10 extra charge). **Amenities:** irons, hair dryers. **Pool(s):** outdoor. **Guest Services:** coin
                        laundry. **Business Services:** meeting rooms, fax. **Cards:** AX, DC, DS, MC, VI. **Special Amenities:** free
                        continental breakfast and free newspaper.
                                                                                                              SOME UNITS

BOERNE COUNTRY INN

Country Inn

Phone: (830)249-9563

All Year 1P: $60 2P: $70 XP: $5 F12
Location: I-10, exit US 87 (Main St), 1.5 mi n. 911 S Main 78006. Fax: 830/249-9563. **Facility:** 14 one-bedroom standard units. 1 story, exterior corridors. *Bath:* combo or shower only. **Parking:** on-site. **Terms:** 7 day cancellation notice. **Business Services:** fax. **Cards:** AX, DC, DS, MC.

HOLIDAY INN EXPRESS HOTEL & SUITES-SIX FLAGS WEST

Small-scale Hotel

Phone: (830)249-6800

All Year [ECP] 1P: $79-$129 2P: $79-$129
Location: I-10, exit 46. 35000 I-10 W 78006. Fax: 830/249-6900. **Facility:** 62 one-bedroom standard units. **Parking:** on-site. **Amenities:** voice mail, irons, hair dryers. **Pool(s):** outdoor. **Leisure Activities:** whirlpool, exercise room. **Guest Services:** coin laundry. **Business Services:** meeting rooms, business center.
Cards: AX, DC, DS, JC, MC, VI.

SOME UNITS

TAPATIO SPRINGS RESORT AND CONFERENCE CENTER

Resort
Large-scale Hotel

Phone: (830)537-4611

All Year 1P: $205-$235 2P: $205-$235 XP: $15 F12
Location: I-10, exit 639 (Johns Rd), 3.5 mi w. 314 Blue Heron Blvd 78006 (PO Box 550). Fax: 830/537-4420. **Facility:** 154 units. 112 one-bedroom standard units, some with kitchens. 33 one- and 9 two-bedroom suites ($225-$250) with kitchens. 2 stories (no elevator), exterior corridors. *Bath:* combo or shower only. **Parking:** on-site. **Terms:** 3 day cancellation notice-fee imposed, package plans - weekends, 18% service charge. **Amenities:** voice mail. *Some:* irons, hair dryers. **Pool(s):** 2 heated outdoor. **Leisure Activities:** sauna, whirlpools, steamroom, fishing, golf-27 holes, 2 lighted tennis courts. *Fee:* horseback riding, massage. **Guest Services:** valet and coin laundry. **Business Services:** conference facilities, fax (fee). **Cards:** AX, CB, DC, DS, MC, VI.

SOME UNITS

YE KENDALL INN

Historic Bed
& Breakfast

Phone: (830)249-2138

All Year [BP] 1P: $99-$190 2P: $109-$190 XP: $10 F7
Location: 2 blks w of Main St; in front of town square. 128 W Blanco 78006. Fax: 830/249-7371. **Facility:** Smoke free premises. 17 one-bedroom standard units. 2 stories (no elevator), interior/exterior corridors. *Bath:* combo or shower only. **Parking:** on-site. **Terms:** 5 day cancellation notice-fee imposed. **Amenities:** voice mail. **Business Services:** meeting rooms, fax (fee).

BONHAM pop. 9,990

────── WHERE TO STAY ──────

DAYS INN

Motel

Phone: (903)583-3121

All Year [CP] 1P: $46-$55 2P: $46-$55 XP: $5 F18
Location: US 82 (SR 56) at west jct of SR 121. 1515 Old Ector Rd 75418. Fax: 903/583-1912. **Facility:** 53 one-bedroom standard units. **Parking:** on-site. **Terms:** cancellation fee imposed, small pets only ($10 deposit, in smoking units). **Amenities:** hair dryers. **Pool(s):** outdoor. **Business Services:** fax (fee). **Cards:** AX, DC, DS, MC, VI. **Special Amenities:** early check-in/late check-out and free local telephone calls.

SOME UNITS

BORGER pop. 14,302

────── WHERE TO STAY ──────

BEST WESTERN BORGER INN

Small-scale Hotel

Phone: (806)274-7050

All Year [ECP] 1P: $69-$120 2P: $69-$120 XP: $10 F16
Location: Jct SR 136 and 207, just n. 206 S Cedar 79007. Fax: 806/274-7377. **Facility:** 60 one-bedroom standard units. 2 stories (no elevator), interior corridors. *Bath:* combo or shower only. **Parking:** on-site. **Terms:** small pets only ($10 extra charge). **Amenities:** irons, hair dryers. *Some:* dual phone lines. **Pool(s):** heated indoor. **Leisure Activities:** whirlpool, limited exercise equipment. **Guest Services:** valet and coin laundry. **Business Services:** meeting rooms, fax (fee). **Cards:** AX, DC, DS, MC, VI. **Special Amenities:** early check-in/late check-out and free continental breakfast.

SOME UNITS

SELECT INN

Motel

Phone: 806/273-9556

Property failed to provide current rates
Location: Jct SR 136 and 207. 100 Bulldog Blvd 79007. Fax: 806/274-2014. **Facility:** 89 units. 88 one-bedroom standard units, some with efficiencies. 1 one-bedroom suite. 2 stories (no elevator), exterior corridors. **Parking:** on-site. **Terms:** small pets only. **Amenities:** safes. **Pool(s):** small heated outdoor. **Guest Services:** valet and coin laundry. **Business Services:** meeting rooms. **Cards:** AX, CB, DC, DS, MC, VI.

SOME UNITS

BOWIE pop. 5,219

────── WHERE TO STAY ──────

DAYS INN

Small-scale Hotel

Phone: (940)872-5426

All Year [CP] 1P: $50-$55 2P: $60-$70 XP: $5 F10
Location: On US 287 at jct SR 59. SR 59 & US 287 76230 (RR 5, Box 138). Fax: 940/872-6970. **Facility:** 60 one-bedroom standard units. 2 stories, exterior corridors. **Parking:** on-site. **Terms:** weekly rates available, pets ($5 extra charge). **Amenities:** hair dryers. **Pool(s):** outdoor. **Guest Services:** coin laundry. **Business Services:** fax (fee). **Cards:** AX, CB, DC, DS, JC, MC, VI. **Special Amenities:** free continental breakfast and free newspaper.

SOME UNITS

PARK'S INN

Motel

Phone: (940)872-1111

All Year   1P: $30-$45   2P: $41-$55   XP: $5   F11
Location: 0.5 mi n of jct SR 59; downtown. 708 W Wise St 76230. Fax: 940/872-1111. **Facility:** 40 one-bedroom standard units, some with kitchens (no utensils). 1 story, exterior corridors. **Parking:** on-site. **Terms:** small pets only ($5 extra charge). **Pool(s):** outdoor. **Guest Services:** coin laundry. **Business Services:** fax (fee). **Cards:** AX, DS, MC, VI.

SOME UNITS

BRADY pop. 5,523

-------- WHERE TO STAY --------

BEST WESTERN BRADY INN

Motel

Phone: 325/597-3997

All Year [CP]   1P: $45-$75   2P: $55-$75   XP: $5   D12
Location: 1.1 mi s on US 87/377. 2200 S Bridge St 76825. Fax: 325/597-1894. **Facility:** 40 one-bedroom standard units, some with whirlpools. 2 stories (no elevator), exterior corridors. **Parking:** on-site. **Terms:** small pets only. **Amenities:** irons, hair dryers. **Pool(s):** outdoor. **Guest Services:** coin laundry. **Business Services:** meeting rooms, business center. **Cards:** AX, CB, DC, DS, JC, MC, VI. **Special Amenities: free continental breakfast.**

SOME UNITS

DAYS INN

Motel

Phone: (325)597-0789

All Year [ECP]   1P: $39-$55   2P: $49-$79   XP: $10   F18
Location: 1 mi s on US 87/377 at jct US 190. 2108 S Bridge St 76825. Fax: 325/597-9099. **Facility:** 44 one-bedroom standard units, some with whirlpools. 1 story, exterior corridors. **Parking:** on-site. **Terms:** small pets only ($10 fee). **Amenities:** hair dryers. **Pool(s):** outdoor. **Guest Services:** coin laundry. **Business Services:** fax (fee). **Cards:** AX, CB, DC, DS, JC, MC, VI.

SOME UNITS

BRENHAM pop. 13,507

-------- WHERE TO STAY --------

ANT STREET INN

Classic Historic Bed & Breakfast

Phone: (979)836-7393

All Year   1P: $105-$235   2P: $105-$235   XP: $30   F
Location: US 290, exit Business SR 36, 1.6 mi n to W Commerce St, just e. Located in the historic district. 107 W Commerce 77833. Fax: 979/836-7595. **Facility:** All 14 guest rooms are furnished with antiques at this property housed in a renovated historic mercantile building; common areas are spacious. Designated smoking area. 14 one-bedroom standard units, some with whirlpools. 2 stories (no elevator), interior corridors. *Bath:* combo or shower only. **Parking:** on-site. **Terms:** age restrictions may apply, 10 day cancellation notice, [BP] meal plan available. **Amenities:** irons, hair dryers. **Guest Services:** gift shop, complimentary evening beverages: Fri & Sat, valet laundry. **Business Services:** meeting rooms, fax (fee). **Cards:** AX, DC, DS, MC, VI.

SOME UNITS

BEST WESTERN INN OF BRENHAM

Small-scale Hotel

Phone: (979)251-7791

All Year   1P: $64   2P: $109   F17
Location: 0.7 mi w of jct US 290 E and SR 577 eastbound; westbound 1.3 mi e of jct SR 36 and US 290. 1503 Hwy 290 E 77833. Fax: 979/251-7792. **Facility:** 59 one-bedroom standard units, some with kitchens. 2 stories (no elevator), exterior corridors. **Parking:** on-site. **Terms:** small pets only ($10 fee). **Amenities:** irons, hair dryers. *Some:* high-speed Internet, dual phone lines. **Dining:** 6 am-9 pm. **Pool(s):** outdoor. **Leisure Activities:** whirlpool. **Guest Services:** coin laundry. **Business Services:** meeting rooms, fax (fee). **Cards:** AX, DC, MC, VI. **Special Amenities: free newspaper and free room upgrade (subject to availability with advanced reservations).**

SOME UNITS

FAR VIEW BED & BREAKFAST

Classic Historic Bed & Breakfast

Phone: 979/836-1672

All Year [BP]   2P: $85-$195   XP: $20   F4
Location: US 290, exit Business SR 36, 0.6 mi n to Lubbock St, just e; on Lubbock St between Park and Church sts. 1804 S Park St 77833. Fax: 979/836-5893. **Facility:** Extensive manicured grounds and 70-year-old live oaks contribute Gatsbylike elegance to this historic 1925 home. Designated smoking area. 7 one-bedroom standard units. 2 stories (no elevator), interior/exterior corridors. *Bath:* combo or shower only. **Parking:** on-site. **Terms:** 2 night minimum stay - weekends, 6 day cancellation notice-fee imposed. **Amenities:** hair dryers. **Pool(s):** outdoor. **Leisure Activities:** putting green, horseshoes. **Guest Services:** complimentary evening beverages. **Business Services:** fax. **Cards:** AX, DS, MC, VI.

SOME UNITS

-------- WHERE TO DINE --------

MANUEL'S MEXICAN RESTAURANT

Mexican

Lunch: $7-$15   **Dinner:** $7-$15   **Phone:** 979/277-9620
Location: Just w of jct SR 36 and Main St. 409 W Main St 77833. **Hours:** 7 am-9 pm, Mon from 11 am, Fri & Sat-10 pm. Closed major holidays. **Features:** A fiesta-like atmosphere punctuates the colorful dining room, where patrons nosh on tasty shrimp fajitas, Spanish rice and bean soup. Lovely murals depicting Mexican scenes adorn the walls, and bright ribbons and streamers add festive touches. Casual dress; cocktails. **Parking:** on-site. **Cards:** AX, CB, DC, DS, MC, VI.

BROWNSVILLE pop. 139,722

——— WHERE TO STAY ———

BEST WESTERN ROSE GARDEN INN
Phone: (956)546-5501

(AAA) (SAVE)
◆◆◆/◆◆◆

Motel

| All Year [BP] | 1P: $50-$80 | 2P: $50-$100 | XP: $8 | F18 |

Location: US 77 and 83 Expwy, exit Price Rd, 0.3 mi s on access road. 845 N Expressway 78520. Fax: 956/546-6474. **Facility:** 121 units. 118 one-bedroom standard units. 3 two-bedroom suites. 2 stories (no elevator), exterior corridors. *Bath:* combo or shower only. **Parking:** on-site. **Amenities:** irons, hair dryers. **Pool(s):** outdoor. **Guest Services:** valet and coin laundry. **Cards:** AX, CB, DC, DS, MC, VI.

SOME UNITS

DAYS INN
Phone: (956)541-2201

(AAA) (SAVE)
◆◆◆◆

Small-scale Hotel

| 3/1-3/31 [CP] | 1P: $75-$95 | 2P: $95-$105 | XP: $10 | F13 |
| 2/1-2/28 & 4/1-1/31 [CP] | 1P: $45-$65 | 2P: $45-$65 | XP: $6 | F13 |

Location: US 83, exit Price Rd, 0.5 mi on southbound access road. Located in a quiet area. 715 N Frontage Rd 78520. Fax: 956/541-6011. **Facility:** 124 one-bedroom standard units. 2 stories (no elevator), interior/exterior corridors. **Parking:** on-site. **Terms:** 3 day cancellation notice. **Amenities:** hair dryers. *Some:* irons. **Dining:** 6 am-10 pm. **Pool(s):** outdoor. **Guest Services:** valet and coin laundry. **Business Services:** meeting rooms. **Cards:** AX, CB, DC, DS, JC, MC, VI. **Special Amenities:** free continental breakfast and free newspaper.

SOME UNITS

FOUR POINTS BY SHERATON
Phone: (956)547-1500

◆◆◆◆

Small-scale Hotel

| All Year | 1P: $79-$129 | | XP: $10 | F12 |

Location: US 77 and 83, exit McAllen Rd, 0.5 mi s on west frontage road. 3777 N Expressway 78520. Fax: 956/547-1550. **Facility:** 141 units. 140 one-bedroom standard units, some with whirlpools. 1 one-bedroom suite ($175-$275) with whirlpool. 2 stories (no elevator), interior corridors. **Parking:** on-site. **Terms:** small pets only ($125 deposit). **Amenities:** video games, dual phone lines, voice mail, irons, hair dryers. **Pool(s):** outdoor, heated outdoor. **Leisure Activities:** whirlpool, exercise room. **Guest Services:** valet laundry, area transportation. **Business Services:** meeting rooms, administrative services. **Cards:** AX, DS, MC, VI.

SOME UNITS

HOLIDAY INN FORT BROWN
Phone: 956/546-2201

◆◆◆

Motel

Property failed to provide current rates

Location: Just e of International Bridge. Located adjacent to the Mexican border. 1900 E Elizabeth St 78520. Fax: 956/546-0756. **Facility:** 168 one-bedroom standard units, some with whirlpools. 2 stories (no elevator), interior/exterior corridors. *Bath:* combo or shower only. **Parking:** on-site. **Amenities:** voice mail, irons, hair dryers. **Pool(s):** 2 outdoor. **Leisure Activities:** exercise room. **Guest Services:** valet and coin laundry. **Business Services:** meeting rooms. **Cards:** AX, CB, DC, DS, MC, VI.

SOME UNITS
FEE

RAMADA LIMITED FORT BROWN
Phone: 956/541-2921

◆◆◆

Motel

Property failed to provide current rates

Location: Just e of International Bridge. 1900 E Elizabeth St 78520. Fax: 956/541-2695. **Facility:** 103 one-bedroom standard units. 3 stories, exterior corridors. *Bath:* combo or shower only. **Parking:** on-site. **Amenities:** voice mail. **Guest Services:** valet and coin laundry. **Business Services:** meeting rooms. **Cards:** AX, CB, DC, DS, MC, VI.

SOME UNITS

RED ROOF INN
Phone: (956)504-2300

(AAA) (SAVE)
◆◆

Motel

| All Year [CP] | 1P: $39-$69 | 2P: $46-$76 | XP: $5 | F18 |

Location: US 83, exit FM 802, just s. 2377 N Expressway 78520. Fax: 956/504-2303. **Facility:** 123 units. 120 one-bedroom standard units. 3 one-bedroom suites ($68-$79). 3 stories, exterior corridors. *Bath:* combo or shower only. **Parking:** on-site. **Amenities:** video games (fee). **Pool(s):** heated outdoor. **Leisure Activities:** whirlpool, exercise room. **Guest Services:** valet and coin laundry. **Business Services:** meeting rooms. **Cards:** AX, CB, DC, DS, MC, VI. **Special Amenities:** free local telephone calls and free newspaper.

SOME UNITS
FEE

RESIDENCE INN BY MARRIOTT
Phone: 956/350-8100

(SAVE)
◆◆◆

Condominium

| All Year [BP] | 1P: $74-$154 | 2P: $74-$154 |

Location: US 83 and 77 Expwy, exit McAllen Rd. 3975 N Expressway 78520. Fax: 956/350-8101. **Facility:** 102 units. 34 one-bedroom standard units with kitchens. 47 one- and 21 two-bedroom suites ($84-$154) with kitchens. 3 stories, interior corridors. *Bath:* combo or shower only. **Parking:** on-site. **Terms:** weekly rates available, pets ($50 fee, $5 extra charge). **Amenities:** high-speed Internet, dual phone lines, voice mail, irons, hair dryers. **Pool(s):** heated outdoor. **Leisure Activities:** whirlpool, exercise room, sports court. **Guest Services:** complimentary evening beverages, valet and coin laundry. **Business Services:** meeting rooms, administrative services, PC. **Cards:** AX, CB, DC, DS, JC, MC, VI.

SOME UNITS

SUPER 8 MOTEL
Phone: 956/546-0381

◆◆◆

Motel

Property failed to provide current rates

Location: US 77 and 83, exit 12th St, 1 mi w on 12th St. 55 Sam Perl Blvd 78520-5050. Fax: 956/541-5313. **Facility:** 100 one-bedroom standard units, some with kitchens. 2 stories (no elevator), exterior corridors. **Parking:** on-site. **Amenities:** video games (fee). **Pool(s):** outdoor. **Guest Services:** valet and coin laundry. **Business Services:** meeting rooms. **Cards:** AX, CB, DC, DS, MC, VI.

SOME UNITS

BROWNWOOD pop. 18,813

──────── WHERE TO STAY ────────

BEST WESTERN
Phone: 325/646-3511

SAVE

♦♦♦ ♦♦♦
Motel

2/1-4/15	1P: $49-$59	2P: $55-$69	XP: $5	F17
4/16-9/30	1P: $59-$69	2P: $69	XP: $5	F17
10/1-1/31	1P: $49-$59	2P: $49-$59	XP: $5	F17

Location: On US 67/84/377; just n of jct Main Ave. 410 E Commerce 76801. **Fax:** 325/646-3517. **Facility:** 81 one-bedroom standard units. 1 story, exterior corridors. **Parking:** on-site. **Terms:** pets ($15 fee). **Amenities:** voice mail, irons, hair dryers. **Pool(s):** outdoor. **Guest Services:** valet laundry. **Business Services:** meeting rooms, fax. **Cards:** AX, DC, MC, VI.

SOME UNITS
🐕 📶 🅰 🏊 🎬 📠 🔌 📺 🖥 / ⊗ /

DAYS INN-BROWNWOOD
Phone: (325)646-2551

SAVE

♦♦♦ ♦♦♦
Small-scale Hotel

4/1-10/31 [CP]	1P: $49-$59	2P: $55-$69	XP: $5	F14
2/1-3/31 & 11/1-1/31 [CP]	1P: $45-$55	2P: $49-$59	XP: $5	F14

Location: On US 67/84/377, 0.4 mi n of jct Main Ave. 515 E Commerce St 76801. **Fax:** 325/643-6064. **Facility:** 139 one-bedroom standard units. 2 stories (no elevator), exterior corridors. **Parking:** on-site. **Terms:** small pets only ($15 fee). **Amenities:** *Some:* irons, hair dryers. **Pool(s):** heated outdoor. **Leisure Activities:** whirlpool. **Guest Services:** coin laundry. **Business Services:** meeting rooms, fax (fee). **Cards:** AX, DC, DS, MC, VI.

SOME UNITS
🅢 🐕 🏊 🎬 🖥 / ⊗ 🔌 🖥 /

HOLIDAY INN EXPRESS HOTEL & SUITES
Phone: (325)641-8085

♦♦♦ ♦♦♦
Small-scale Hotel

All Year [ECP]   1P: $78   2P: $78

Location: On US 67/84/377; just s of jct Main Ave. 504 W Commerce 76801. **Fax:** 325/641-1047. **Facility:** 58 one-bedroom standard units. 3 stories, interior corridors. *Bath:* combo or shower only. **Parking:** on-site. **Amenities:** dual phone lines, voice mail, irons, hair dryers. **Pool(s):** outdoor. **Leisure Activities:** whirlpool, limited exercise equipment. **Guest Services:** valet and coin laundry. **Business Services:** meeting rooms, business center. **Cards:** AX, CB, DC, DS, JC, MC, VI.

SOME UNITS
ASK 🅢 📶 🔧 🏊 🎬 🔌 📺 🖥 / ⊗ /

BRYAN pop. 65,660

──────── WHERE TO STAY ────────

FAIRFIELD INN BY MARRIOTT-BRYAN
Phone: (979)268-1552

SAVE

♦♦♦ ♦♦♦
Motel

All Year [ECP]   1P: $69-$89   2P: $69-$99   XP: $6   F18

Location: Just n of jct SR 60 on SR 6 business route (Texas Ave). 4613 S Texas Ave 77802. **Fax:** 979/268-1552. **Facility:** 62 one-bedroom standard units. 3 stories, interior corridors. *Bath:* combo or shower only. **Parking:** on-site. **Terms:** 14 day cancellation notice. **Amenities:** irons. **Pool(s):** heated indoor. **Leisure Activities:** whirlpool. **Guest Services:** valet laundry. **Business Services:** fax (fee). **Cards:** AX, CB, DC, DS, MC, VI.

SOME UNITS
🅢 📶 🔧 🅰 🏊 🎬 🔌 / ⊗ 🔌 🖥 /

REVEILLE INN
Phone: 979/846-0858

♦♦♦♦
Bed & Breakfast

All Year [BP]   1P: $95-$120   2P: $120   XP: $15   F10

Location: 1 mi n of jct SR 60 (University Dr) and College Main St to jct Old College Rd and College Main St. 4400 Old College Rd 77801. **Fax:** 979/846-0859. **Facility:** This Southern Colonial-style 1941 home, once a fraternity house, sits on a shaded acre a mile from the university. Smoke free premises. 4 one-bedroom standard units. 2 stories (no elevator), interior corridors. *Bath:* combo or shower only. **Parking:** on-site. **Terms:** check-in 4 pm, 14 day cancellation notice. **Amenities:** hair dryers. *Some:* fax. **Business Services:** fax. **Cards:** AX, DS, MC, VI.

ASK 🅢 🔧 🔧 ⊗ 🔌

──────── WHERE TO DINE ────────

OXFORD STREET RESTAURANT   **Lunch:** $6-$19   **Dinner:** $10-$19   **Phone:** 979/268-0792

♦♦♦ ♦♦♦
American

Location: 1 mi e of jct SR 6 business route (Texas Ave) and CR 1179; 1 mi w of jct US 190 and SR 6. 1710 Briarcrest Dr 77802. **Hours:** 11 am-9 pm, Fri-10 pm, Sat 4 pm-10 pm. **Closed:** 12/25. **Reservations:** suggested. **Features:** An Old English tavern is the setting, with subdued lighting and lots of wood. Featuring beef, chicken and seafood, the menu lists a good variety of choices. Try filet mignon and a loaded baked potato, with a slice of chocolate cheesecake for dessert. Casual dress; cocktails. **Parking:** on-site. **Cards:** AX, DC, DS, MC, VI.

🍸 ⊗

BUDA pop. 2,404

──────── WHERE TO STAY ────────

BEST WESTERN SOUTHGATE INN & SUITES
Phone: (512)295-4559

SAVE

♦♦♦ ♦♦♦
Small-scale Hotel

6/1-9/1 [ECP]	1P: $69-$119	2P: $69-$119
2/1-5/31 & 9/2-1/31 [ECP]	1P: $49-$89	2P: $49-$89

Location: I-35, exit 217, just s on southbound frontage road. 18658 S I-35 78610. **Fax:** 512/295-2679. **Facility:** 50 one-bedroom standard units. 3 stories, interior corridors. **Parking:** on-site. **Amenities:** dual phone lines, voice mail, irons, hair dryers. **Pool(s):** small outdoor. **Leisure Activities:** whirlpool, exercise room. **Guest Services:** coin laundry. **Business Services:** meeting rooms, fax (fee). **Cards:** AX, CB, DC, DS, MC, VI.

SOME UNITS
🅢 🆓 📶 🏊 🎬 🔌 📺 🖥 / ⊗ /
FEE

BURLESON pop. 20,976

——— WHERE TO STAY ———

COMFORT SUITES
AAA SAVE
◆◆◆◆ Small-scale Hotel

Phone: (817)426-6666
All Year 1P: $79 2P: $89 XP: $5 F18
Location: I-35 W, exit 36 (Renfro St), just e. 321 S Burleson Blvd 76028. Fax: 817/426-1400. **Facility:** 69 one-bedroom standard units, some with kitchens and/or whirlpools. 3 stories, interior corridors. *Bath:* combo or shower only. **Parking:** on-site. **Terms:** 7 day cancellation notice-fee imposed, [CP] meal plan available, pets ($10 fee, $25 deposit). **Amenities:** dual phone lines, voice mail, irons, hair dryers. **Pool(s):** heated indoor. **Leisure Activities:** whirlpool, limited exercise equipment. **Guest Services:** coin laundry. **Business Services:** meeting rooms, fax (fee). **Cards:** AX, DC, DS, JC, MC, VI. **Special Amenities:** free continental breakfast and free local telephone calls.

SOME UNITS

DAYS INN
AAA SAVE
◆◆◆ Motel

Phone: 817/447-1111
All Year [ECP] 1P: $55-$65 2P: $65-$75 XP: $6 F17
Location: I-35, exit 36 (Renfro St), just w to east frontage road, 0.5 mi s. Located in a rural area. 329 S Burleson Blvd 76028. Fax: 817/447-1111. **Facility:** 43 one-bedroom standard units. 2 stories, exterior corridors. **Parking:** on-site. **Terms:** weekly rates available, pets ($10 fee). **Amenities:** hair dryers. **Pool(s):** outdoor. **Guest Services:** coin laundry. **Business Services:** fax (fee). **Cards:** AX, DC, DS, MC, VI. **Special Amenities:** free continental breakfast and free newspaper.

SOME UNITS

BURNET pop. 4,735

——— WHERE TO STAY ———

HOLIDAY INN EXPRESS CONFERENCE CENTER
◆◆◆ Small-scale Hotel

Phone: (512)756-1789
4/1-9/15 [ECP] 1P: $89-$129 2P: $89-$189 XP: $10 F19
9/16-1/31 [ECP] 1P: $89 2P: $99 XP: $10 F19
2/1-3/31 [ECP] 1P: $89 2P: $89 XP: $10 F19
Location: Jct US 281 and FM 29, just s. 810 S Water St (US 281) 78611. Fax: 512/756-6459. **Facility:** 75 one-bedroom standard units, some with kitchens (no utensils) and/or whirlpools. 3 stories, interior corridors. *Bath:* combo or shower only. **Parking:** on-site. **Terms:** 2 night minimum stay - weekends/seasonal. **Amenities:** high-speed Internet, dual phone lines, voice mail, irons, hair dryers. **Pool(s):** outdoor. **Leisure Activities:** limited exercise equipment. **Guest Services:** coin laundry. **Business Services:** meeting rooms, fax (fee). **Cards:** AX, DC, DS, MC, VI.

SOME UNITS

TRAVEL INN
AAA SAVE
◆◆ Motel

Phone:(512)756-4747
4/1-9/7 [ECP] 1P: $55-$90 2P: $60-$90 XP: $6 F18
2/1-3/31 [ECP] 1P: $45-$60 2P: $50-$70 XP: $6 F18
9/8-1/31 [ECP] 1P: $45-$60 2P: $45-$70 XP: $6 F18
Location: Jct US 281 and FM 29, 1 mi w. Hwy 29 W 78611. Fax: 512/756-7839. **Facility:**46 one-bedroom standard units. 1 story, exterior corridors. **Parking:** on-site. **Amenities:**irons, hair dryers. **Pool(s):** outdoor. **Business Services:** meeting rooms, fax (fee). **Cards:**AX, CB, DC, DS, MC, VI. **Special Amenities:**free continental breakfast and free local telephone calls.

SOME UNITS

CANTON pop. 3,292

——— WHERE TO STAY ———

BEST WESTERN CANTON INN
AAA SAVE
◆◆ Motel

Phone: (903)567-6591
All Year [CP] 1P: $59-$159 2P: $59-$159 XP: $10 F12
Location: Jct I-20 and SR 19, exit 527. Located in a semi-rural area. 2251 N Trade Days Blvd 75103. Fax: 903/567-4703. **Facility:** 82 one-bedroom standard units. 2 stories, exterior corridors. *Bath:* combo or shower only. **Parking:** on-site. **Terms:** cancellation fee imposed, small pets only ($5 fee). **Amenities:** voice mail, irons, hair dryers. **Pool(s):** outdoor. **Guest Services:** coin laundry. **Business Services:** fax (fee). **Cards:** AX, DC, DS, MC, VI. **Special Amenities:** free continental breakfast.

SOME UNITS
FEE

HOLIDAY INN EXPRESS
◆◆◆ Small-scale Hotel

Phone: (903)567-0909
All Year [ECP] 1P: $69-$75 2P: $69-$75 XP: $6 F17
Location: I-20, exit 527. 2406 N Trade Days Blvd 75103. Fax: 903/567-1601. **Facility:** 58 one-bedroom standard units, some with whirlpools. 2 stories, exterior corridors. *Bath:* combo or shower only. **Parking:** on-site. **Amenities:** irons, hair dryers. **Pool(s):** heated outdoor. **Leisure Activities:** whirlpool. **Guest Services:** coin laundry. **Business Services:** meeting rooms, business center. **Cards:** AX, DC, DS, JC, MC, VI.

SOME UNITS
FEE

SUPER 8 MOTEL
◆◆◆ Motel

Phone: 903/567-6567
All Year 1P: $45-$150 2P: $48-$150 XP: $5 F10
Location: I-20, exit 527. 17350 Interstate 20 75103. Fax: 903/567-6435. **Facility:** 40 one-bedroom standard units. 2 stories, exterior corridors. **Parking:** on-site. **Terms:** [CP] meal plan available. **Pool(s):** outdoor. **Business Services:** fax (fee). **Cards:** AX, DC, DS, MC, VI.

SOME UNITS

CANYON pop. 12,875

——— WHERE TO STAY ———

BUFFALO INN
Phone: (806)655-2124

(AAA) [SAVE]

| 6/1-8/31 | 1P: $50-$55 | 2P: $55-$60 | XP: $5 | F12 |
| 2/1-5/31 & 9/1-1/31 | 1P: $34-$36 | 2P: $36-$40 | XP: $5 | F12 |

Motel

Location: US 87. 300 23rd St 79015. Fax: 806/655-5844. **Facility:** 21 one-bedroom standard units. 1 story, exterior corridors. *Bath:* combo or shower only. **Parking:** on-site, winter plug-ins. **Business Services:** fax (fee).

SOME UNITS

🆂🅳 🍴 🐾 / ⊠ 🛢 🖥 /

HOLIDAY INN EXPRESS HOTEL & SUITES
Phone: (806)655-4445

(AAA) [SAVE]

| 5/2-8/31 | 1P: $76-$90 | 2P: $76-$90. |
| 2/1-5/1 & 9/1-1/31 | 1P: $64-$80 | 2P: $64-$80 |

Motel

Location: I-27, exit 106, 2 mi w. 2901 4th Ave 79015. Fax: 806/655-4445. **Facility:** 66 units. 60 one-bedroom standard units. 4 one- and 2 two-bedroom suites ($75-$130), some with whirlpools. 3 stories, interior corridors. *Bath:* combo or shower only. **Parking:** on-site, winter plug-ins. **Terms:** [ECP] meal plan available, small pets only ($10 fee). **Amenities:** irons, hair dryers. *Some:* dual phone lines. **Pool(s):** small heated indoor. **Leisure Activities:** whirlpool, exercise room. **Guest Services:** valet and coin laundry. **Business Services:** meeting rooms, fax (fee). **Cards:** AX, DC, DS, JC, MC, VI. **Special Amenities: free continental breakfast and free newspaper.**

SOME UNITS

🆂🅳 🐕 🅼 🛢 🐾 🎥 DATA PORT / ⊠ 🛢 🖥 🖥 /

CARROLLTON —See Dallas p. 289.

CARTHAGE pop. 6,664

——— WHERE TO STAY ———

BEST WESTERN INN OF CARTHAGE
Phone: 903/694-2809

(AAA) [SAVE]

All Year   1P: $62-$65   2P: $62-$65

Small-scale Hotel

Location: Southwest corner jct E US 59 Loop and SR 699. 2332 Southeast Loop 75633. Fax: 903/694-2809. **Facility:** 40 one-bedroom standard units, some with whirlpools. 2 stories, exterior corridors. **Parking:** on-site. **Terms:** [CP] meal plan available. **Amenities:** irons, hair dryers. **Pool(s):** outdoor. **Leisure Activities:** exercise room. **Guest Services:** coin laundry. **Business Services:** meeting rooms, fax (fee). **Cards:** AX, DC, DS, MC, VI.

SOME UNITS

🆂🅳 🐾 🎥 DATA PORT 🛢 🖥 🖥 / ⊠ /

CASTROVILLE pop. 2,664

——— WHERE TO STAY ———

THE LANDMARK INN
Phone: 830/931-2133

| 12/2-1/1 [ECP] | 1P: $66-$75 | 2P: $66-$75 |
| 2/1-12/1 & 1/2-1/31 [ECP] | 1P: $62-$70 | 2P: $62-$70 |

Historic Bed
& Breakfast

Location: 0.3 mi e on US 90 at Fiorella St. 402 Florence St. 78009. Fax: 830/538-3858. **Facility:** Designated smoking area. 8 one-bedroom standard units. 1 story, interior/exterior corridors. *Bath:* shared or private, shower only. **Parking:** on-site. **Terms:** cancellation fee imposed. **Leisure Activities:** recreation programs. **Guest Services:** gift shop. **Business Services:** meeting rooms, fax (fee). **Cards:** DS, MC, VI.

🍴 🅲 ⊠ 🕖 📠

CEDAR HILL —See Dallas p. 289.

CEDAR PARK pop. 26,049

——— WHERE TO STAY ———

BEST WESTERN CEDAR INN
Phone: (512)259-7300

(AAA) [SAVE]

All Year [CP]   1P: $59-$79   2P: $64-$84   XP: $5   F12

Small-scale Hotel

Location: Jct US 183 and FM 1431, just e. 425 E Whitestone Blvd 78613. Fax: 512/260-8200. **Facility:** 40 one-bedroom standard units, some with whirlpools. 2 stories (no elevator), exterior corridors. **Parking:** on-site. **Amenities:** voice mail, irons, hair dryers. **Pool(s):** outdoor. **Leisure Activities:** limited exercise equipment. **Business Services:** fax (fee). **Cards:** AX, CB, DC, DS, JC, MC, VI. **Special Amenities: free continental breakfast.**

SOME UNITS

🆂🅳 🍴 🐾 🎥 DATA PORT 🛢 🖥 🖥 / ⊠ /

COMFORT INN
Phone: 512/259-1810

[SAVE]

| 5/24-9/3 | 1P: $80 | 2P: $85 | XP: $5 | F18 |
| 2/1-5/23 & 9/4-1/31 | 1P: $65 | 2P: $70 | XP: $5 | F18 |

Small-scale Hotel

Location: I-35, exit 256, 8 mi w on FM 1431. 300 E Whitestone Blvd 78613. Fax: 512/259-9155. **Facility:** 58 one-bedroom standard units. 2 stories, interior corridors. *Bath:* combo or shower only. **Parking:** on-site. **Terms:** small pets only ($10 extra charge). **Amenities:** irons, hair dryers. **Pool(s):** small outdoor. **Business Services:** fax (fee). **Cards:** AX, DC, DS, MC, VI.

SOME UNITS

FEE

HOLIDAY INN EXPRESS HOTEL & SUITES
Phone: (512)259-8200
All Year [ECP]   1P: $69-$99   2P: $69-$109   XP: $10   F18
Small-scale Hotel   Location: US 183 and FM 1431, 1.3 mi e. 1605 E Whitestone Blvd 78613. Fax: 512/259-8204. Facility: 62 one-bedroom standard units. 3 stories, interior corridors. Bath: combo or shower only. Parking: on-site. Terms: 3 day cancellation notice. Amenities: dual phone lines, voice mail, irons, hair dryers. Pool(s): outdoor. Leisure
Activities: whirlpool, limited exercise equipment. Guest Services: coin laundry. Business Services: meeting rooms, business center. Cards: AX, CB, DC, DS, JC, MC, VI.

SOME UNITS
(ASK) (S/D) [✈] [⟶M] [⟨⟩] [∅] [⟿] [🎥] [DATA PORT] [🛏] [📶] [📺] / [✕] /
FEE

CENTER pop. 5,678

―――― WHERE TO STAY ――――

BEST WESTERN CENTER INN
Phone: (936)598-3384
[SAVE]
All Year   1P: $52   2P: $89   XP: $5   F12
Location: On US 96, at jct SR 87. 1005 Hurst St 75935. Fax: 936/598-3384. Facility: 72 one-bedroom standard units, some with efficiencies (no utensils). 2 stories, exterior corridors. Terms: [CP] meal plan available, small pets only ($10 fee). Amenities: irons, hair dryers. Pool(s): outdoor. Business Services: fax (fee). Cards: AX, DC, DS, MC, VI.
Motel

SOME UNITS
(S/D) [✈] [⟶] [⟿] [🎥] [DATA PORT] [📺] / [✕] [🛏] [📶] /

CHANNELVIEW —See Houston p. 435.

CHILDRESS pop. 6,778

―――― WHERE TO STAY ――――

BEST WESTERN CHILDRESS
Phone: 940/937-6353
(AAA) [SAVE]
All Year [ECP]   1P: $60-$70   2P: $65-$80   XP: $5   F12
Location: On US 287, just s of jct US 62/83. 1801 Ave F NW (Hwy 287) 79201. Fax: 940/937-3478. Facility: 65 one-bedroom standard units. 1-2 stories (no elevator), exterior corridors. Bath: combo or shower only. Parking: on-site, winter plug-ins. Terms: small pets only ($5 extra charge). Amenities: irons, hair dryers. Pool(s): small outdoor. Cards: AX, DC, DS, MC, VI. Special Amenities: free continental breakfast.
Motel

SOME UNITS
(S/D) [✈] [⟶] [🐾] [¶↑] [⟿] [🎥] [DATA PORT] [🛏] [📺] / [✕] [📶] /

COMFORT INN
Phone: 940/937-6363
(AAA) [SAVE]
All Year [ECP]   1P: $74   2P: $79   XP: $5   F16
Location: US 287, just s of jct US 62/83. 1804 Ave F NW (Hwy 287) 79201. Fax: 940/937-6724. Facility: 46 one-bedroom standard units. 2 stories (no elevator), exterior corridors. Parking: on-site. Terms: pets ($5 extra charge). Amenities: irons, hair dryers. Pool(s): small heated indoor. Leisure Activities: sauna, whirlpool. Guest Services: coin laundry. Business Services: meeting rooms. Cards: AX, CB, DC, DS, MC, VI. Special Amenities: free continental breakfast and free local telephone calls.
Motel

SOME UNITS
[🐾] [¶↑] [⟶M] [∅] [⟿] [🎥] [DATA PORT] [📺] / [✕] [🛏] [📶] /

DAYS INN
Phone: 940/937-0622
(AAA) [SAVE]
5/1-9/30   1P: $69-$79   2P: $74-$84   XP: $5   F10
10/1-12/31   1P: $62-$72   2P: $67-$77   XP: $5   F10
2/1-4/30 & 1/1-1/31   1P: $59-$69   2P: $64-$74   XP: $5   F10
Location: 1.8 mi w on US 287, from jct US 62/83. 2220 Ave F (Hwy 287) 79201. Fax: 940/937-0833. Facility: 42 one-bedroom standard units. 2 stories (no elevator), interior corridors. Bath: combo or shower only. Parking: on-site. Amenities: dual phone lines, hair dryers. Pool(s): small heated indoor. Leisure Activities: whirlpool, limited exercise equipment. Guest Services: coin laundry. Business Services: fax (fee). Cards: AX, DC, DS, MC, VI. Special Amenities: free continental breakfast and free local telephone calls.
Motel

SOME UNITS
(S/D) [¶↑] [∅] [⟿] [🎥] [DATA PORT] / [✕] [🛏] [📶] /

ECONO LODGE
Phone: (940)937-3695
(AAA) [SAVE]
All Year [CP]   1P: $38-$48   2P: $48-$65   XP: $4   F12
Location: On US 287, just s of jct US 62/83. 1612 Ave F NW Hwy 287 79201. Fax: 940/937-6956. Facility: 28 one-bedroom standard units. 2 stories (no elevator), exterior corridors. Parking: on-site. Terms: pets ($5 extra charge). Amenities: hair dryers. Some: dual phone lines. Pool(s): outdoor. Cards: AX, DS, MC, VI.
Small-scale Hotel   Special Amenities: free continental breakfast and free local telephone calls.

SOME UNITS
(S/D) [🐾] [⟿] [🎥] / [✕] [DATA PORT] [📺] /

HOLIDAY INN EXPRESS
Phone: 940/937-3434
All Year   1P: $69-$79   2P: $79-$99   XP: $6   F18
Location: US 287, just n of jct US 62/83. 2008 Ave F NW (Hwy 287) 79201. Fax: 940/937-2270. Facility: 52 one-bedroom standard units. 2 stories (no elevator), interior corridors. Bath: combo or shower only. Parking: on-site. Terms: [ECP] meal plan available. Amenities: irons, hair dryers. Pool(s): small heated indoor. Leisure
Motel
Activities: sauna, whirlpool, exercise room. Guest Services: coin laundry. Cards: AX, CB, DC, DS, MC, VI.

SOME UNITS
(ASK) (S/D) [¶↑] [⟶M] [∅] [⟿] [✕] [🎥] [DATA PORT] [📺] / [✕] [🛏] [📶] /

CISCO pop. 3,851

———— WHERE TO STAY ————

BEST WESTERN INN CISCO
Phone: 254/442-3735

SAVE
Motel

5/16-10/1 [ECP]	1P: $54-$64	2P: $59-$69	XP: $5	F12
2/1-5/15 & 10/2-1/31 [ECP]	1P: $49-$59	2P: $54-$64	XP: $5	F12

Location: I-20, exit 330. 1898 Hwy 206 W 76437. Fax: 254/442-1340. **Facility:** 31 one-bedroom standard units. 1 story, exterior corridors. *Bath:* combo or shower only. **Parking:** on-site. **Terms:** small pets only ($10 fee, $25 deposit). **Amenities:** irons, hair dryers. **Pool(s):** outdoor. **Business Services:** meeting rooms, fax (fee). **Cards:** AX, CB, DC, DS, JC, MC, VI.

SOME UNITS

CLARENDON pop. 1,974

———— WHERE TO STAY ————

WESTERN SKIES MOTEL
Phone: 806/874-3501

AAA SAVE
Motel

All Year	1P: $35-$45	2P: $45-$50	XP: $5	F10

Location: 0.5 mi nw on US 287 and SR 70. 800 W 2nd St 79226 (PO Box 850). Fax: 806/874-5303. **Facility:** 23 one-bedroom standard units. 1 story, exterior corridors. *Bath:* combo or shower only. **Parking:** on-site. **Terms:** 7 day cancellation notice-fee imposed, small pets only (in limited units, no cats). **Amenities:** hair dryers. **Pool(s):** outdoor. **Leisure Activities:** playground. **Business Services:** fax (fee). **Cards:** AX, DS, MC, VI. **Special Amenities:** early check-in/late check-out and free local telephone calls.

SOME UNITS

CLAUDE pop. 1,313

———— WHERE TO STAY ————

L A MOTEL
Phone: 806/226-4981

AAA SAVE
Motel

All Year	1P: $35-$45	2P: $45-$50	XP: $5	F10

Location: 0.3 mi s. Hwy 287/200 E 1st St 79019. Fax: 806/226-2127. **Facility:** 15 one-bedroom standard units. 1 story, exterior corridors. **Parking:** on-site, winter plug-ins. **Terms:** 7 day cancellation notice, small pets only. **Dining:** 6 am-9 pm. **Business Services:** fax (fee). **Cards:** AX, DS, MC, VI. **Special Amenities:** early check-in/late check-out and free local telephone calls.

SOME UNITS

CLEBURNE pop. 26,005

———— WHERE TO STAY ————

AMERICAN INN
Phone: (817)641-3451

AAA SAVE
Motel

All Year	1P: $45-$50	2P: $50-$60	XP: $7	F6

Location: On SR 174 (Main St), just e of jct US 67. 1836 N Main St 76031. Fax: 817/641-6001. **Facility:** 39 one-bedroom standard units. 1 story, exterior corridors. **Parking:** on-site. **Terms:** [CP] meal plan available, pets ($30 deposit). **Amenities:** voice mail, hair dryers. **Pool(s):** outdoor. **Business Services:** fax (fee). **Cards:** AX, DC, MC, VI. **Special Amenities:** free continental breakfast and free local telephone calls.

SOME UNITS

COMFORT INN
Phone: (817)641-4702

AAA SAVE
Small-scale Hotel

All Year [ECP]	1P: $69-$125	2P: $69-$125

Location: On SR 174, just s of jct US 67. 2117 N Main St 76033. Fax: 817/641-4336. **Facility:** 54 units. 51 one-bedroom standard units. 3 one-bedroom suites ($89-$125), some with whirlpools. 3 stories, interior corridors. *Bath:* combo or shower only. **Parking:** on-site. **Terms:** package plans, pets ($10 fee). **Amenities:** dual phone lines, voice mail, irons, hair dryers. **Pool(s):** outdoor. **Leisure Activities:** exercise room. **Guest Services:** valet and coin laundry. **Business Services:** meeting rooms, business center. **Cards:** AX, CB, DC, DS, JC, MC, VI. **Special Amenities:** free continental breakfast and free local telephone calls.

SOME UNITS
FEE

SAGAMAR INN
Phone: 817/556-3631

AAA SAVE
Motel

All Year [CP]	1P: $56	2P: $60	XP: $5	D7

Location: US 67, exit SR 174 (Main St), just e. 2107 N Main St 76033. Fax: 817/556-2829. **Facility:** 28 one-bedroom standard units. 1 story, exterior corridors. **Parking:** on-site. **Terms:** small pets only ($5 extra charge). **Amenities:** hair dryers. **Pool(s):** outdoor. **Business Services:** fax (fee). **Cards:** AX, DS, MC, VI. **Special Amenities:** free continental breakfast and free local telephone calls.

SOME UNITS

CLUTE pop. 10,424

———— WHERE TO STAY ————

DAYS INN
Phone: (979)265-3301

AAA SAVE
Motel

All Year [CP]	1P: $52	2P: $52	XP: $6	F18

Location: Just w of jct SR 288. Located in a commercial area. 805 W Hwy 332 77531. Fax: 979/265-0831. **Facility:** 98 one-bedroom standard units. 2 stories, exterior corridors. **Parking:** on-site. **Amenities:** hair dryers. **Pool(s):** small outdoor. **Guest Services:** coin laundry. **Business Services:** fax (fee). **Cards:** AX, CB, DC, DS, MC, VI. **Special Amenities:** free continental breakfast and free local telephone calls.

SOME UNITS

FEE

LA QUINTA INN

AAA SAVE

Small-scale Hotel

Phone: (979)265-7461

All Year 1P: $63-$70 2P: $70-$77 XP: $7 F18
Location: 3.5 mi e on jct SR 288 and 332. Located in a commercial area. 1126 Hwy 332 W 77531-5399. Fax: 979/265-3804. **Facility:** 135 units. 134 one-bedroom standard units. 1 one-bedroom suite ($99-$149). 2 stories, exterior corridors. **Parking:** on-site. **Terms:** [ECP] meal plan available, small pets only. **Amenities:** video games (fee), voice mail, irons, hair dryers. **Pool(s):** outdoor. **Guest Services:** valet laundry. **Business Services:** meeting rooms, fax (fee). **Cards:** AX, CB, DC, DS, JC, MC, VI.
Special Amenities: free continental breakfast and free local telephone calls.

SOME UNITS
[icons] FEE / FEE FEE

MAINSTAY SUITES CLUTE/LAKE JACKSON

AAA SAVE

Small-scale Hotel

Phone: (979)388-9300

All Year 1P: $100 2P: $139
Location: Just w of jct SR 288. Located in a commercial area. 1003 W Hwy 332 77531. Fax: 979/388-9393. **Facility:** 52 units. 46 one- and 6 two-bedroom suites with efficiencies. 2 stories, interior corridors. *Bath:* combo or shower only. **Parking:** on-site. **Terms:** weekly rates available, [ECP] meal plan available, small pets only. **Amenities:** dual phone lines, voice mail, irons, hair dryers. **Pool(s):** outdoor. **Leisure Activities:** whirlpool, barbecue grill, exercise room. **Guest Services:** complimentary evening beverages: Mon-Wed, valet and coin laundry. **Business Services:** meeting rooms, fax (fee). **Cards:** AX, CB, DC, DS, JC, MC, VI.
Special Amenities: free continental breakfast and free local telephone calls.

SOME UNITS
[icons] / [icons]

COLLEGE STATION pop. 67,890

—— WHERE TO STAY ——

COURTYARD BY MARRIOTT

SAVE

Small-scale Hotel

Phone: (979)695-8111

All Year 1P: $89-$145
Location: SR 6 S, exit Rock Prairie, just e. 3939 SH 6 S 77845. Fax: 979/695-8228. **Facility:** 125 one-bedroom standard units, some with whirlpools. 3 stories, interior corridors. *Bath:* combo or shower only. **Parking:** on-site. **Terms:** cancellation fee imposed, [BP] meal plan available. **Amenities:** high-speed Internet, voice mail, irons, hair dryers. **Pool(s):** outdoor. **Leisure Activities:** whirlpool, exercise room. **Guest Services:** valet and coin laundry. **Business Services:** meeting rooms, business center. **Cards:** AX, DC, DS, JC, MC, VI.

SOME UNITS
[icons] / [icons]

DAYS INN

AAA SAVE

Motel

Phone: (979)696-6988

All Year 1P: $50-$90 2P: $50-$90
Location: 2.4 mi s of jct of 60; on SR 6 business route (Texas Ave). 2514 Texas Ave S 77840. Fax: 979/693-1174. **Facility:** 98 one-bedroom standard units. 2 stories (no elevator), exterior corridors. **Parking:** on-site. **Amenities:** voice mail, hair dryers. **Pool(s):** outdoor. **Leisure Activities:** whirlpool, playground, basketball, horseshoes, volleyball. **Guest Services:** valet laundry, airport transportation-Easterwood Airport, area transportation-within 4 mi. **Business Services:** meeting rooms, fax (fee). **Cards:** AX, CB, DC, DS, JC, MC, VI. **Special Amenities:** free continental breakfast and free local telephone calls.

SOME UNITS
[icons] / [icons]

HAMPTON INN

SAVE

Small-scale Hotel

Phone: (979)846-0184

All Year 1P: $74 2P: $84 XP: $10 F18
Location: Just n of jct SR 60; on SR 6 business route (Texas Ave). 320 S Texas Ave 77840. Fax: 979/268-5807. **Facility:** 134 one-bedroom standard units. 4 stories, interior corridors. **Parking:** on-site. **Terms:** 3 day cancellation notice, weekly rates available. **Amenities:** video games (fee), voice mail, irons. **Pool(s):** outdoor. **Guest Services:** valet laundry, area transportation. **Business Services:** meeting rooms, fax (fee). **Cards:** AX, CB, DC, DS, MC, VI.

SOME UNITS
[icons] / [icons]

HOLIDAY INN-COLLEGE STATION

Small-scale Hotel

Phone: (979)693-1736

All Year [CP] 1P: $65-$79 2P: $65-$79
Location: 1.3 mi s of jct SR 60; on SR 6 business route (Texas Ave). 1503 S Texas Ave 77840. Fax: 979/693-1736. **Facility:** 125 one-bedroom standard units. 6 stories, interior corridors. **Parking:** on-site. **Terms:** weekly rates available, [BP], [ECP] & [MAP] meal plans available, small pets only ($15 fee). **Amenities:** voice mail, irons, hair dryers. **Pool(s):** outdoor. **Leisure Activities:** exercise room. **Guest Services:** valet laundry. **Business Services:** meeting rooms, fax (fee). **Cards:** AX, CB, DC, DS, JC, MC, VI.

SOME UNITS
ASK [icons] / [icons]

HOLIDAY INN EXPRESS HOTEL & SUITES

Small-scale Hotel

Phone: (979)846-8700

All Year [ECP] 1P: $71-$149 2P: $71-$149 XP: $10 F18
Location: SR 6, exit University Dr, 1 mi w. 1203 University Dr E 77840. Fax: 979/260-8709. **Facility:** 77 one-bedroom standard units. 3 stories, interior corridors. *Bath:* combo or shower only. **Parking:** on-site. **Terms:** 7 day cancellation notice. **Amenities:** dual phone lines, irons, hair dryers. **Pool(s):** small outdoor. **Leisure Activities:** limited exercise equipment. **Guest Services:** valet and coin laundry. **Business Services:** meeting rooms, business center. **Cards:** AX, CB, DC, DS, JC, MC, VI.

SOME UNITS
ASK [icons] / [icons]

LA QUINTA INN

AAA SAVE

Motel

Phone: (979)696-7777

All Year 1P: $69-$89 2P: $79-$99 XP: $10 F18
Location: Just s on jct SR 60/6 business route to Live Oak St, just e. Located across from Texas A & M University. 607 Texas Ave 77840. Fax: 979/696-0531. **Facility:** 176 units. 174 one-bedroom standard units. 2 one-bedroom suites. 2 stories (no elevator), exterior corridors. **Parking:** on-site. **Terms:** [ECP] meal plan available, small pets only. **Amenities:** video games (fee), voice mail, irons, hair dryers. **Pool(s):** outdoor. **Guest Services:** valet laundry, airport transportation-Easterwood Airport, area transportation-university campus. **Business Services:** fax (fee). **Cards:** AX, CB, DC, DS, JC, MC, VI. **Special Amenities:** free continental breakfast and free local telephone calls.

SOME UNITS
[icons] / [icons] FEE FEE

MANOR HOUSE INN
Phone: (979)764-9540

Motel

All Year [ECP]   1P: $65-$70   2P: $70-$76   XP: $6   F12
Location: 2.4 mi s of jct SR 60; on SR 6 business route (Texas Ave). 2504 Texas Ave S 77840. Fax: 979/693-2430. **Facility:** 116 one-bedroom standard units. 2 stories (no elevator), exterior corridors. **Parking:** on-site. **Terms:** weekly rates available, package plans - seasonal & weekends, small pets only ($40 extra charge). **Amenities:** voice mail. **Pool(s):** outdoor. **Guest Services:** valet laundry, area transportation. **Business Services:** meeting rooms, fax (fee). **Cards:** AX, CB, DC, DS, JC, MC, VI.

SOME UNITS

QUALITY SUITES HOTEL
Phone: (979)695-9500

Motel

All Year [ECP]   1P: $79-$135   2P: $89-$135
Location: E Bypass (SR 6), exit University Dr, 0.5 mi w. 1010 University Dr E 77840. Fax: 979/695-9501. **Facility:** 81 one-bedroom suites. 3 stories, interior corridors. **Parking:** on-site. **Amenities:** high-speed Internet (fee), dual phone lines, voice mail, irons, hair dryers. **Pool(s):** outdoor. **Leisure Activities:** limited exercise equipment. **Guest Services:** valet and coin laundry, area transportation. **Business Services:** meeting rooms, fax (fee). **Cards:** AX, CB, DC, DS, JC, MC, VI.

SOME UNITS

RAMADA INN
Phone: (979)693-9891

Small-scale Hotel

All Year   1P: $65-$125   2P: $69-$125   XP: $9   F18
Location: 1.3 mi s of jct SR 60; on SR 6 business route (Texas Ave). 1502 Texas Ave S 77840. Fax: 979/696-1334. **Facility:** 167 one-bedroom standard units. 5 stories, interior corridors. **Parking:** on-site. **Terms:** 3 day cancellation notice, [MAP] meal plan available, small pets only ($10 fee). **Amenities:** voice mail, irons, hair dryers. **Dining:** 6:30 am-1:30 & 6-9 pm, Sun from 7 am, cocktails. **Pool(s):** outdoor. **Leisure Activities:** whirlpool. **Guest Services:** valet laundry, airport transportation-Easterwood Airport, area transportation-within 5 mi. **Business Services:** meeting rooms, fax (fee). **Cards:** AX, DC, DS, MC, VI. **Special Amenities:** free local telephone calls and free newspaper.

SOME UNITS

SUPER 8 MOTEL-COLLEGE STATION
Phone: (979)846-8800

Motel

All Year [CP]   1P: $49-$69   2P: $49-$69   XP: $5   F12
Location: Just n of jct SR 60; on SR 6 (Texas Ave). 301 Texas Ave 77840. Fax: 979/260-9801. **Facility:** 89 one-bedroom standard units. 3 stories, interior corridors. *Bath:* combo or shower only. **Parking:** on-site. **Amenities:** safes (fee). **Business Services:** fax (fee). **Cards:** AX, CB, DC, DS, MC, VI.

SOME UNITS

TOWNEPLACE SUITES BY MARRIOTT
Phone: 979/260-8500

Small-scale Hotel

All Year   1P: $89-$150
Location: SR 6, exit University Dr, 1 mi w. 1300 E University Dr 77840. Fax: 979/260-0907. **Facility:** 94 one-bedroom standard units with kitchens. 3 stories, exterior corridors. *Bath:* combo or shower only. **Parking:** on-site. **Terms:** check-in 4 pm, pets ($60 fee). **Amenities:** voice mail, irons, hair dryers. **Pool(s):** outdoor. **Leisure Activities:** limited exercise equipment. **Business Services:** business center. **Cards:** AX, CB, DC, DS, JC, MC, VI.

SOME UNITS

———— WHERE TO DINE ————

CENARE
Phone: 979/696-7311

Italian

Lunch: $7-$13   **Dinner:** $9-$17
Location: SR 60, 0.3 mi e jct SR 6 business route (Texas Ave). 404 University Dr E 77840. **Hours:** 11 am-2 & 5-10 pm, Sat from 5 pm. Closed: 1/1, 12/25; also Sun. **Reservations:** suggested. **Features:** Contributing to the inviting, romantic atmosphere are candlelight, white linens, Italian paintings and tuxedo-clad waiters. Among mouthwatering entrees are lasagna, salmon and shrimp Vesuvio and veal Marsala. Casual dress. **Parking:** on-site. **Cards:** AX, DC, DS, MC, VI.

JOHNNY CARINO'S COUNTRY ITALIAN
Phone: 979/764-7374

Italian

Lunch: $6-$8   **Dinner:** $8-$14
Location: Jct Business 6 and SR 60, s to SR 30, 0.5 mi e. 620 Harvey Rd 77840. **Hours:** 11 am-10 pm, Fri & Sat 11 pm. Closed: 12/25. **Features:** Representative of the fare are homemade lasagna, manicotti, meatballs, freshly baked bread, pizzas cooked in a wood-fired oven and Northern Italian preparations of chicken, shrimp, veal, pork or rib eye entrees. Tiramisu is prepared from an old family recipe. Smoke free premises. Casual dress; cocktails. **Parking:** on-site. **Cards:** AX, CB, DC, DS, MC, VI.

KONA RANCH HAWAIIAN GRILL
Phone: 979/694-4618

American

Lunch: $4-$9   **Dinner:** $9-$19
Location: Jct Business 6 and SR 60, s to SR 30, 0.5 mi e. 520 Harvey Rd 77840. **Hours:** 11 am-10 pm, Fri-11 pm, Sat 9 am-11 pm, Sun 9 am-9 pm. Closed: 12/25. **Reservations:** accepted. **Features:** Guests can experience the ambience of the islands in a Hawaiian ranch house setting. Steaks, chicken, St. Louis-style ribs, pork loin and seafood selections make up the menu. Smoke free premises. Casual dress; cocktails. **Parking:** on-site. **Cards:** AX, DS, MC, VI.

COLLEYVILLE pop. 19,636   (See map p. 343; index p. 346)

———— WHERE TO DINE ————

MAC'S STEAKS & SEAFOOD
Phone: 817/318-6227   (60)

Steak & Seafood

Lunch: $10-$16   **Dinner:** $10-$21
Location: SR 121, exit Hall Johnson on southbound access road. 5120 Hwy 121 76034. **Hours:** 11 am-10 pm, Fri & Sat-midnight, Sun 10 am-10 pm. Closed: 11/27, 12/25. **Features:** This small chain in the greater Dallas Fort Worth area specializes in steaks and seafood with a Southwestern flair. Casual dress; cocktails. **Parking:** on-site. **Cards:** AX, DC, DS, MC, VI.

(See map p. 343)

THE COLONY —See Dallas p. 289.

COLUMBUS pop. 3,916

———— WHERE TO STAY ————

COUNTRY HEARTH INN
Motel
All Year [ECP]   1P: $50-$54   2P: $58-$62   XP: $8   F18
Phone: (979)732-6293
Location: I-10, exit 696 (SR 71). 2436 Hwy 71 S 78934. Fax: 979/732-6211. **Facility:** 40 one-bedroom standard units. 2 stories (no elevator), exterior corridors. **Parking:** on-site. **Terms:** weekly rates available, small pets only ($25 deposit, in smoking units). **Pool(s):** outdoor. **Guest Services:** complimentary evening beverages, coin laundry. **Business Services:** fax (fee). **Cards:** AX, DC, DS, MC, VI.
SOME UNITS
ASK SD 🐾 🍴 ➿ 🎥 💻 / ✕ 🛢 📠 /

HOLIDAY INN EXPRESS HOTEL & SUITES
Motel
All Year   2P: $69-$89   XP: $10   F18
Phone: (979)733-9300
Location: I-10, exit 696 (SR 71), just w on westbound service road. 4321 I-10 78934. Fax: 979/732-2364. **Facility:** 67 one-bedroom standard units, some with whirlpools. 3 stories, interior corridors. *Bath:* combo or shower only. **Parking:** on-site. **Terms:** pets ($15 fee, $50 deposit). **Amenities:** dual phone lines, voice mail, irons, hair dryers. **Pool(s):** outdoor. **Guest Services:** valet and coin laundry. **Business Services:** meeting rooms, fax (fee). **Cards:** AX, DC, DS, JC, MC, VI.
SOME UNITS
ASK SD 🐾 🍴 🚪 ➿ 🎥 DATA PORT / ✕ 🛢 📠 💻 /

———— WHERE TO DINE ————

SCHOBEL'S RESTAURANT
American
Lunch: $6-$19   **Dinner:** $6-$19   **Phone:** 979/732-2385
Location: I-10, exit 696 (SR 71), just n. 2020 Milam St 78934. **Hours:** 6 am-9 pm, Fri & Sat-9:30 pm. Closed: 1/1, 12/25. **Features:** In a convenient location near the interstate, the popular restaurant serves a widely varied noon buffet at a price that's easy on the budget. Simple dishes such as fried chicken offer a taste of home. Casual dress; cocktails. **Parking:** on-site. **Cards:** AX, CB, DC, DS, MC, VI.
✕

CONROE —See Houston p. 435.

CONWAY

———— WHERE TO STAY ————

BUDGET HOST S & S MOTEL
Motel
All Year   1P: $35-$45   2P: $44-$50   XP: $5   F12
Phone: (806)537-5111
Location: I-40, exit 96 (SR 207), 0.3 mi w on southbound access road. I-40 & SR 207 79068 (Rt 2, Box 58, PAN-HANDLE). Fax: 806/537-5539. **Facility:** 24 one-bedroom standard units. 1 story, exterior corridors. **Parking:** on-site. **Terms:** small pets only. **Dining:** 6 am-10 pm. **Business Services:** fax (fee). **Cards:** AX, DC, MC, VI. **Special Amenities:** early check-in/late check-out and free local telephone calls. *(See color ad p 162)*
SOME UNITS
SD 🐾 🍴 🎥 / ✕ /

COPPERAS COVE pop. 29,592

———— WHERE TO STAY ————

BEST WESTERN INN & SUITES
Small-scale Hotel
All Year [ECP]   1P: $79   2P: $79   XP: $7   F17
Phone: (254)518-3363
Location: Just s of jct US 190. 321 Constitution Dr 76522. Fax: 254/518-4405. **Facility:** 60 one-bedroom standard units. 2 stories, interior corridors. *Bath:* combo or shower only. **Parking:** on-site. **Terms:** [CP] meal plan available. **Amenities:** voice mail, irons, hair dryers. **Pool(s):** outdoor. **Leisure Activities:** exercise room. **Guest Services:** valet and coin laundry. **Business Services:** meeting rooms, fax (fee). **Cards:** AX, DC, DS, MC, VI. **Special Amenities:** free continental breakfast and free newspaper.
SOME UNITS
SD 🍴 🚪 ➿ 🎥 DATA PORT 🛢 📠 💻 / ✕ /

HOWARD JOHNSON EXPRESS INN
Small-scale Hotel
All Year   1P: $54   2P: $59   XP: $5   F17
Phone: (254)547-2345
Location: On US 190 at jct Georgetown Rd, 0.4 mi w of jct US 190 and SR 116. 302 W US 190 76522. Fax: 254/547-5124. **Facility:** 49 one-bedroom standard units, some with whirlpools. 2 stories, exterior corridors. **Parking:** on-site. **Terms:** cancellation fee imposed, [ECP] meal plan available, pets ($10 fee). **Amenities:** safes (fee), hair dryers. **Pool(s):** small outdoor. **Business Services:** fax (fee). **Cards:** AX, CB, DC, MC, VI.
SOME UNITS
ASK SD 🐾 🍴 ➿ 🚿 🎥 DATA PORT 🛢 📠 💻 / ✕ VCR /
FEE   FEE

CORPUS CHRISTI pop. 277,454

———— WHERE TO STAY ————

BEST WESTERN GARDEN INN
Phone: (361)241-6675

	6/1-8/20 [CP]	1P: $69-$129	2P: $74-$129	XP: $5	F12
AAA SAVE	3/1-5/31 [CP]	1P: $69-$89	2P: $74-$94	XP: $5	F12
▽▽▽▽	2/1-2/28 & 8/21-1/31 [CP]	1P: $64-$74	2P: $69-$79	XP: $5	F12

Motel

Location: I-37, exit 11B (Violet Rd), on southbound access road. 11217 I-37 78410. Fax: 361/241-4532. **Facility:** 39 units. 38 one-bedroom standard units. 1 one-bedroom suite. 2 stories (no elevator), exterior corridors. **Parking:** on-site. **Terms:** small pets only ($5 extra charge). **Amenities:** safes, irons, hair dryers. **Pool(s):** outdoor. **Leisure Activities:** sauna, whirlpools, playground. **Guest Services:** complimentary evening beverages: Mon-Thurs, coin laundry. **Cards:** AX, DC, DS, MC, VI. **Special Amenities: early check-in/late check-out and free continental breakfast.**

SOME UNITS

BEST WESTERN MARINA GRAND HOTEL
Phone: (361)883-5111

| AAA SAVE | 5/1-8/31 | 1P: $79-$195 | 2P: $89-$195 | XP: $10 | F17 |
| ▽▽ ▽▽ | 2/1-4/30 & 9/1-1/31 | 1P: $59-$109 | 2P: $69-$109 | XP: $10 | F17 |

Small-scale Hotel

Location: Downtown. 300 N Shoreline Dr 78401. Fax: 361/883-7702. **Facility:** 172 one-bedroom standard units. 7 stories, interior corridors. **Parking:** on-site. **Terms:** [BP] meal plan available. **Amenities:** voice mail, irons, hair dryers. **Pool(s):** outdoor. **Leisure Activities:** exercise room. **Guest Services:** coin laundry. **Business Services:** meeting rooms, fax (fee). **Cards:** AX, DC, DS, MC, VI. **Special Amenities: free continental breakfast.** *(See color ad below)*

SOME UNITS

BEST WESTERN ON THE ISLAND
Phone: (361)949-2300

	3/1-9/17 [ECP]	1P: $79-$129	2P: $84-$134	XP: $5	F
SAVE	2/1-2/28 & 9/18-1/31 [ECP]	1P: $69-$109	2P: $74-$114	XP: $5	F
▽▽▽▽					

Small-scale Hotel

Location: On Park Rd 22. 14050 S Padre Island Dr 78418. Fax: 361/949-1883. **Facility:** 40 one-bedroom standard units. 2 stories (no elevator), exterior corridors. *Bath:* combo or shower only. **Parking:** on-site. **Terms:** weekly rates available. **Amenities:** irons, hair dryers. **Pool(s):** outdoor, wading. **Guest Services:** coin laundry. **Business Services:** fax (fee). **Cards:** AX, CB, DC, DS, MC, VI.

SOME UNITS

BEST WESTERN PARADISE INN
Phone: (361)992-3100

| AAA SAVE | All Year [ECP] | 1P: $69-$140 | 2P: $74-$150 | XP: $6 | F12 |
| ▽▽▽▽ | | | | | |

Motel

Location: SR 358, just e of Airline Dr. 6301 S Padre Island Dr 78412. Fax: 361/992-3100. **Facility:** 50 one-bedroom standard units. 2 stories, exterior corridors. **Parking:** on-site. **Terms:** 7 day cancellation notice. **Amenities:** irons, hair dryers. **Pool(s):** outdoor. **Leisure Activities:** whirlpool. **Guest Services:** coin laundry. **Business Services:** fax (fee). **Cards:** AX, CB, DC, DS, MC, VI. **Special Amenities: free continental breakfast and free newspaper.**

SOME UNITS

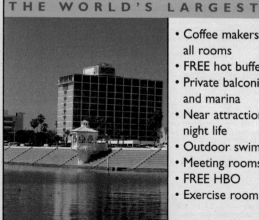

CHRISTY ESTATE SUITES   **Phone:** (361)854-1091

AAA SAVE   5/26-9/5   1P: $129-$189   2P: $129-$189
                2/1-5/25 & 9/6-1/31   1P: $109-$169   2P: $109-$169
◆◆◆◆◆◆   **Location:** SR 358, exit Weber Rd, 0.5 mi s. Located in a residential area. 3942 Holly Rd 78415. **Fax:** 361/854-4766.
Condominium   **Facility:** 150 units. 102 one- and 48 two-bedroom suites ($149-$229) with kitchens, some with whirlpools. 2
                stories, interior/exterior corridors. **Parking:** on-site. **Terms:** weekly rates available, small pets only ($300 de-
posit). **Amenities:** voice mail, hair dryers. **Pool(s):** 2 outdoor. **Leisure Activities:** whirlpool. **Guest Services:**
coin laundry. **Cards:** AX, CB, DC, DS, MC, VI. **Special Amenities:** early check-in/late check-out and free local telephone
calls. *(See color ad below)*

SOME UNITS

(📶) (🛏️) (📶) (🏊) (🐕) (DATA PORT) (🖥️) (📺) (💻) / (🚭) /

Savings at Your Fingertips

When you have a AAA TourBook® guide in your hand, you have a world of savings right at your fingertips. Official Appointment lodgings that display the bright-red AAA logo, SAVE icon and Diamond rating in their listing want AAA member business, and many offer discounts and special amenities to members*.

So, when planning your next vacation, be sure to consult your AAA TourBook for the familiar red SAVE icon.

SAVE

*See TourBook Navigator, page 14, for details.

CLARION HOTEL

Phone: (361)883-6161

4/15-9/15 [ECP]	1P: $69-$129	2P: $69-$129	XP: $5	F18
2/1-4/14 & 9/16-1/31 [ECP]	1P: $59-$99	2P: $59-$99	XP: $5	F18

Location: I-37, exit 3A (Navigation Blvd), on northbound access lane. 5224 I-37 (Navigation Blvd) 78407. Fax: 361/888-5802. **Facility:** 90 one-bedroom standard units. 2 stories (no elevator), exterior corridors. *Bath:* Small-scale Hotel combo or shower only. **Parking:** on-site. **Terms:** 14 day cancellation notice, pets (with prior approval). **Amenities:** irons. **Business Services:** fax (fee). **Cards:** AX, CB, DC, DS, MC, VI. **Special Amenities:** free continental breakfast and free local telephone calls. *(See color ad below)*

SOME UNITS

COMFORT INN

Phone: (361)888-8333

5/1-9/5	1P: $59-$119	2P: $64-$129	XP: $6	F18
3/1-4/30	1P: $59-$99	2P: $59-$99	XP: $6	F18
2/1-2/28	1P: $49-$89	2P: $49-$89	XP: $6	F18
9/6-1/31	1P: $49-$79	2P: $49-$79	XP: $6	F18

Small-scale Hotel **Location:** I-37 S, exit 3A (Navigation Blvd), on southbound access road. 902 N Navigation Blvd 78408. Fax: 361/887-7457. **Facility:** 49 one-bedroom standard units. 2 stories (no elevator), exterior corridors. **Parking:** on-site. **Terms:** 7 day cancellation notice-fee imposed, [ECP] meal plan available. **Amenities:** irons, hair dryers. **Pool(s):** outdoor. **Leisure Activities:** whirlpools, exercise room. **Guest Services:** complimentary evening beverages: Mon-Thurs, coin laundry. **Business Services:** fax (fee). **Cards:** AX, CB, DC, DS, MC, VI. **Special Amenities:** free continental breakfast and free newspaper.

SOME UNITS

COMFORT INN & SUITES

Phone: (361)241-6363

All Year [ECP]	1P: $69-$104	2P: $74-$109	XP: $35	F12

Location: I-35, exit 14, 0.3 mi s on northbound access road. 3838 Hwy 77 N 78410. Fax: 361/241-6365. **Facility:** 61 units. 41 one-bedroom standard units. 20 one-bedroom suites ($84-$129). 2 stories, interior corridors. *Bath:* combo or shower only. **Parking:** on-site. **Amenities:** voice mail, irons, hair dryers. **Pool(s):** outdoor. **Leisure** Small-scale Hotel **Activities:** exercise room. **Guest Services:** coin laundry. **Business Services:** meeting rooms, fax (fee). **Cards:** AX, CB, DC, DS, MC, VI.

SOME UNITS

COMFORT SUITES

Phone: (361)225-2500

5/21-8/15 [ECP]	1P: $79-$129	2P: $89-$149	XP: $10	F17
1/1-1/31 [ECP]	1P: $75-$95	2P: $85-$135	XP: $10	F17
2/1-5/20 & 8/16-12/31 [ECP]	1P: $69-$89	2P: $79-$129	XP: $10	F17

Location: SR 358, exit Weber St. 3925 S Padre Island Dr 78415. Fax: 361/225-3000. **Facility:** 68 units. 51 one-Small-scale Hotel and 3 two-bedroom standard units. 14 one-bedroom suites. 2 stories, interior/exterior corridors. *Bath:* combo or shower only. **Parking:** on-site. **Amenities:** voice mail, irons, hair dryers. **Pool(s):** outdoor. **Leisure Activities:** whirlpool, exercise room. **Guest Services:** complimentary evening beverages: Mon-Thurs, valet and coin laundry. **Business Services:** meeting rooms, business center. **Cards:** AX, CB, DC, DS, JC, MC, VI. **Special Amenities:** free continental breakfast and free newspaper.

SOME UNITS

DAYS INN

Phone: (361)888-8599

All Year	1P: $35-$80	2P: $40-$90	XP: $5	F18

Location: I-37, exit 3A (Navigation Blvd). 901 Navigation Blvd 78408. Fax: 361/888-5746. **Facility:** 121 one-bedroom standard units. 2 stories (no elevator), exterior corridors. **Parking:** on-site. **Terms:** weekly rates available, small pets only ($10 extra charge). **Amenities:** voice mail, safes, hair dryers. *Some:* irons. **Pool(s):** Small-scale Hotel outdoor. **Leisure Activities:** playground. **Guest Services:** coin laundry. **Business Services:** meeting rooms. **Cards:** AX, CB, DC, DS, JC, MC, VI.

SOME UNITS

FEE FEE

DAYS INN-CORPUS CHRISTI BEACH

AAA **SAVE**

Phone: (361)882-3297

3/1-9/30	1P: $45-$125	2P: $55-$145	XP: $10	F18
2/1-2/28	1P: $45-$60	2P: $45-$75	XP: $10	F18
10/1-1/31	1P: $45-$60	2P: $45-$60	XP: $10	F18

Location: 1 mi n off US 181, at north end of Harbor Bridge, exit Beach St. 4302 Surfside Blvd 78402.

Small-scale Hotel Fax: 361/882-6865. **Facility:** 55 one-bedroom standard units. 2 stories, exterior corridors. **Parking:** on-site. **Terms:** cancellation fee imposed, [CP] meal plan available. **Amenities:** safes (fee), hair dryers. **Business Services:** fax (fee). **Cards:** AX, DC, DS, MC, VI. **Special Amenities:** free continental breakfast and free newspaper.

SOME UNITS

VCR / ⊠ ⬚ ⬚ /
FEE

DAYS INN CORPUS CHRISTI SOUTH

SAVE

Phone: (361)854-0005

5/16-9/10	1P: $79-$169	2P: $79-$169	XP: $10
2/15-5/15	1P: $69-$169	2P: $79-$169	XP: $10
2/1-2/14 & 9/11-1/31	1P: $59-$99	2P: $59-$99	XP: $10

Location: On SR 358 westbound access road, 0.4 mi w, exit Kostoryz Rd. 2838 S Padre Island Dr 78415.

Small-scale Hotel Fax: 361/854-2642. **Facility:** 138 one-bedroom standard units, some with whirlpools. 4 stories, exterior corridors. **Parking:** on-site. **Terms:** cancellation fee imposed, [ECP] meal plan available, pets ($25 deposit). **Amenities:** voice mail, safes (fee). **Pool(s):** outdoor. **Leisure Activities:** whirlpool. **Guest Services:** complimentary evening beverages: Mon-Thurs, valet and coin laundry. **Business Services:** meeting rooms, fax. **Cards:** AX, CB, DC, DS, MC, VI.

SOME UNITS

SD ⬚ ⬚ ⬚ ⬚ DATA PORT / ⊠ ⬚ ⬚ /

DRURY INN-CORPUS CHRISTI

AAA **SAVE**

Motel

Phone: (361)289-8200

9/1-1/31 [BP]	1P: $64-$84	2P: $74-$94	XP: $10	F18
2/1-8/31 [BP]	1P: $62-$82	2P: $72-$92	XP: $10	F18

Location: Just se of jct I-37; on SR 358 at Leopard St. 2021 N Padre Island Dr 78408. Fax: 361/289-8200. **Facility:** 105 one-bedroom standard units. 4 stories, interior corridors. **Parking:** on-site. **Terms:** small pets only. **Amenities:** voice mail, irons, hair dryers. **Pool(s):** outdoor. **Leisure Activities:** exercise room. **Guest Services:** complimentary evening beverages: Mon-Thurs, valet and coin laundry. **Business Services:** meeting rooms, fax (fee). **Cards:** AX, CB, DC, DS, MC, VI. **Special Amenities:** free continental breakfast and free local telephone calls.

SOME UNITS

⬚ ⬚ ⬚ ⬚ ⬚ DATA PORT ⬚ / ⊠ ⬚ ⬚ /

EMBASSY SUITES HOTEL

Phone: 361/853-7899

Property failed to provide current rates

Location: SR 358, exit Weber St. 4337 S Padre Island Dr 78411. Fax: 361/851-1310. **Facility:** 150 units. 148 one- and 2 two-bedroom suites. 3 stories, interior corridors. **Parking:** on-site. **Terms:** check-in 4 pm.

Small-scale Hotel **Amenities:** video games, voice mail, irons, hair dryers. **Pool(s):** heated indoor. **Leisure Activities:** sauna, whirlpool, exercise room. **Guest Services:** gift shop, complimentary evening beverages, valet and coin laundry, area transportation. **Business Services:** meeting rooms, fax (fee). **Cards:** AX, CB, DC, DS, JC, MC, VI.

SOME UNITS

⬚ ⬚ ⬚ ⬚ ⬚ ⬚ DATA PORT ⬚ ⬚ ⬚ /⊠ /

THE GULFSTREAM CONDOMINIUMS

Condominium

Phone: 361/949-8061

3/9-9/6	2P: $150-$200	XP: $5
2/1-3/8 & 9/7-10/16	2P: $115-$160	XP: $5
10/17-1/31	2P: $115-$145	XP: $5

Location: Park Rd 22 on N Padre Island Dr, jct of Whitecap Blvd, 1.2 mi ne. 14810 Windward Dr 78418. Fax: 361/949-1497. **Facility:** 92 one-bedroom suites with kitchens. 6 stories (no elevator), exterior corridors. **Parking:** on-site. **Terms:** check-in 4 pm, 3 day cancellation notice. **Pool(s):** heated outdoor, wading. **Leisure Activities:** fishing, shuffleboard. *Fee:* game room. **Guest Services:** coin laundry. **Business Services:** fax (fee). **Cards:** AX, DS, MC, VI.

SOME UNITS

ASK ⬚ ⊠ ⬚ ⬚ ⬚ ⬚ /⊠ /

HAMPTON INN-CORPUS CHRISTI

SAVE

Small-scale Hotel

Phone: (361)985-8395

All Year [ECP]	1P: $75-$95	2P: $75-$105	XP: $6	F18

Location: SR 358 E, exit Everhart Rd, 0.3 mi e. 5209 Blanch Moore Dr 78411. Fax: 361/985-1199. **Facility:** 64 one-bedroom standard units. 3 stories, interior corridors. *Bath:* combo or shower only. **Parking:** on-site. **Terms:** 14 day cancellation notice. **Amenities:** voice mail, irons, hair dryers. **Pool(s):** heated indoor. **Leisure Activities:** whirlpool. **Guest Services:** valet laundry. **Business Services:** meeting rooms, fax (fee). **Cards:** AX, CB, DC, DS, MC, VI.

SOME UNITS

SD ⬚ ⬚ ⬚ ⬚ ⬚ ⬚ DATA PORT ⬚ /⊠ ⬚ ⬚ /

HAWTHORN SUITES

Small-scale Hotel

Phone: (361)854-3400

3/1-8/31	1P: $89-$159	2P: $99-$159	XP: $10	F17
2/1-2/28 & 9/1-1/31	1P: $69-$89	2P: $79-$89	XP: $10	F17

Location: SR 358 (S Padre Island Dr) jct Greenwood Ave. 1442 S Padre Island Dr 78416. Fax: 361/854-2100. **Facility:** 62 units. 46 one- and 16 two-bedroom suites, some with kitchens. 4 stories, interior corridors. *Bath:* combo or shower only. **Parking:** on-site. **Amenities:** video games, dual phone lines, voice mail, irons, hair dryers. **Pool(s):** outdoor. **Leisure Activities:** sauna, whirlpools, exercise room. **Guest Services:** complimentary evening beverages: Mon-Thurs, coin laundry. **Business Services:** meeting rooms, business center.

SOME UNITS

ASK SD ⬚ ⬚ ⬚ ⊠ VCR ⬚ DATA PORT ⬚ ⬚ ⬚ /⊠ /

HOLIDAY INN-EMERALD BEACH

AAA **SAVE** **▼▼▼▼**

Phone: (361)883-5731

	5/16-9/5	1P: $149-$179	2P: $149-$179	XP: $10	F18
	2/24-5/15	1P: $105-$159	2P: $105-$159	XP: $10	F18
	9/6-1/31	1P: $105-$149	2P: $105-$149	XP: $10	F18
	2/1-2/23	1P: $99-$139	2P: $99-$139	XP: $10	F18

Large-scale Hotel **Location:** 1.5 mi s on bay from downtown marina. 1102 S Shoreline Blvd 78401. Fax: 361/883-9079. **Facility:** 368 one-bedroom standard units, some with whirlpools. 2-7 stories, interior/exterior corridors. **Parking:** on-site. **Terms:** check-in 4 pm. **Amenities:** voice mail, irons, hair dryers. **Dining:** 6 am-2 & 5-10 pm, Sat & Sun from 7 am, cocktails. **Pool(s):** heated indoor. **Leisure Activities:** sauna, whirlpool, fishing, indoor playground, ping pong, pool table, bicycles, playground, exercise room, shuffleboard. *Fee:* waverunner, game room. **Guest Services:** gift shop, valet laundry. **Business Services:** meeting rooms, fax. **Cards:** AX, CB, DC, DS, MC, VI. **Special Amenities:** free newspaper. *(See color ad below)*

SOME UNITS

[icons] / FEE

HOLIDAY INN-PADRE ISLAND DRIVE

AAA **SAVE** **▼▼▼▼**

Phone: (361)289-5100

| | All Year | 1P: $89-$129 | 2P: $89-$129 | XP: $5 | F19 |

Location: 5.5 mi w at jct SR 358 and Leopard St. 5549 Leopard St 78408. Fax: 361/289-6209. **Facility:** 247 units. 241 one-bedroom standard units. 6 one-bedroom suites ($159-$199) with whirlpools. 6 stories, interior corridors. **Parking:** on-site. **Terms:** [BP] meal plan available, package plans, small pets only. **Amenities:** voice **Large-scale Hotel** mail, irons, hair dryers. **Dining:** 6 am-2 & 5-11 pm, Sat & Sun from 6:30 am, cocktails. **Pool(s):** heated indoor. **Leisure Activities:** whirlpool, sun deck, exercise room. **Guest Services:** valet laundry. **Business Services:** meeting rooms, business center. **Cards:** AX, CB, DC, DS, JC, MC, VI. **Special Amenities:** free newspaper.

SOME UNITS

[icons] / [icons] /

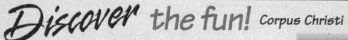

HOLIDAY INN SUNSPREE CORPUS CHRISTI GULF BEACH RESORT

Phone: (361)949-8041

2/1-3/31 & 5/15-9/15	1P: $109-$209	2P: $109-$209	XP: $10 F12
4/1-5/14	1P: $89-$169	2P: $89-$169	XP: $10 F12
9/16-1/31	1P: $89-$159	2P: $89-$159	XP: $10 F12

Location: Park Rd 22, jct Whitecap Blvd, just e. 15202 Windward Dr 78418. Fax: 361/949-9139. **Facility:** The property offers many guest rooms with balconies overlooking the Gulf of Mexico. 152 units. 136 one-bedroom standard units. 16 one-bedroom suites. 6 stories, interior corridors. **Parking:** on-site. **Terms:** check-in 4 pm.

Resort
Small-scale Hotel

Amenities: video games, voice mail, safes, irons, hair dryers. **Dining:** 7 am-10 pm; off-season hours may vary, cocktails. **Pool(s):** 2 outdoor. **Leisure Activities:** sauna, whirlpool, rental boats, fishing, recreation programs, children's activities center, ping pong, exercise room. *Fee:* skates, bicycles, game room. **Guest Services:** gift shop, valet and coin laundry. **Business Services:** meeting rooms, fax. **Cards:** AX, DC, DS, MC, VI. *(See color ad p 226)*

SOME UNITS

HOWARD JOHNSON EXPRESS INN & SUITES

Phone: 361/883-7400

3/16-8/15	1P: $69-$99	2P: $79-$109	XP: $10 F18
2/1-3/15 & 8/16-1/31	1P: $59-$69	2P: $69-$79	XP: $10 F18

Location: I-37, exit 1D (Port Ave), on southbound access road. 722 N Port Ave 78408. Fax: 361/883-0333. **Facility:** 44 units. 36 one-bedroom standard units. 8 one-bedroom suites (\$120-\$145), some with kitchens.

Small-scale Hotel

2 stories (no elevator), exterior corridors. **Parking:** on-site. **Terms:** 3 day cancellation notice, [CP] meal plan available. **Amenities:** irons, hair dryers. **Pool(s):** outdoor. **Leisure Activities:** exercise room. **Guest Services:** coin laundry. **Business Services:** fax (fee). **Cards:** AX, CB, DC, DS, MC, VI. **Special Amenities:** free continental breakfast and free local telephone calls. *(See color ad below)*

SOME UNITS

ISLAND HOUSE CONDOMINIUMS

Phone: (361)949-8166

All Year	1P: $76-$250	2P: $76-$250

Location: Park Rd 22 on N Padre Island; jct Whitecap Blvd, 0.6 mi ne. 15340 Leeward Dr 78418. Fax: 361/949-8904. **Facility:** 68 units. 2 one-, 63 two- and 3 three-bedroom suites with kitchens. 3 stories, exterior corridors.

Condominium

Parking: on-site. **Terms:** check-in 4 pm, 2-30 night minimum stay, 3 day cancellation notice, weekly rates available. **Pool(s):** heated outdoor, wading. **Leisure Activities:** fishing. **Guest Services:** coin laundry. **Business Services:** fax. **Cards:** AX, DC, MC, VI.

SOME UNITS

KNIGHTS INN

Phone: (361)883-4411

5/16-9/16 [BP]	1P: $65	2P: $99	XP: $8 F12
2/1-5/15 & 9/17-1/31 [BP]	1P: $48	2P: $79	XP: $8 F12

Location: 1 mi n on US 181 at north end of Harbor Bridge, exit Beach St. 3615 Timon Blvd 78402. Fax: 361/654-4411. **Facility:** 40 units. 39 one-bedroom standard units, some with kitchens (no utensils). 1 one-bedroom suite. 3 stories (no elevator), exterior corridors. **Parking:** on-site. **Terms:** 7 day cancellation notice. **Pool(s):** outdoor. **Leisure Activities:** shuffleboard, volleyball. **Guest Services:** coin laundry. **Business Services:** fax (fee). **Cards:** AX, DS, MC, VI.

Motel

SOME UNITS

LA QUINTA INN-CORPUS CHRISTI-NORTH

Phone: (361)888-5721

5/26-9/7	1P: $79-$99	2P: $85-$105
2/1-5/25 & 9/8-1/31	1P: $69-$89	2P: $75-$95

Location: I-37, exit 3A (Navigation Blvd), on southbound access road. 5155 I-37 N 78408-2614. Fax: 361/888-5401. **Facility:** 121 one-bedroom standard units. 2 stories (no elevator), exterior corridors. **Parking:** on-site.

Small-scale Hotel

Terms: [ECP] meal plan available, small pets only. **Amenities:** video games, voice mail, irons, hair dryers. **Pool(s):** outdoor. **Guest Services:** coin laundry. **Business Services:** meeting rooms, fax (fee). **Cards:** AX, CB, DC, DS, JC, MC, VI. **Special Amenities:** free continental breakfast and free local telephone calls.

SOME UNITS

LA QUINTA INN-SOUTH

SAVE

Small-scale Hotel

| | 5/26-9/7 | 1P: $79-$99 | 2P: $85-$105 |
| | 2/1-5/25 & 9/8-1/31 | 1P: $69-$89 | 2P: $75-$95 |

Phone: (361)991-5730

Location: SR 358 Expwy, exit Airline Rd. 6225 S Padre Island Dr 78412-4011. Fax: 361/993-1578. **Facility:** 129 one-bedroom standard units. 3 stories, exterior corridors. **Parking:** on-site. **Terms:** [ECP] meal plan available, small pets only. **Amenities:** video games, voice mail, irons, hair dryers. **Pool(s):** outdoor. **Guest Services:** coin laundry. **Business Services:** meeting rooms, fax (fee). **Cards:** AX, CB, DC, DS, JC, MC, VI.

SOME UNITS

MOTEL 6 LANTANA - 231

Motel

	6/12-9/20	1P: $35-$45	2P: $41-$51	XP: $3	F17
	9/21-1/31	1P: $33-$43	2P: $39-$49	XP: $3	F17
	2/1-6/11	1P: $32-$42	2P: $38-$48	XP: $3	F17

Phone: 361/289-9397

Location: I-37, exit 4B (Lantana St), on southbound access road. 845 Lantana St 78408. Fax: 361/289-0280. **Facility:** 124 one-bedroom standard units. 2 stories (no elevator), exterior corridors. *Bath:* shower only. **Parking:** on-site. **Terms:** pets (with prior approval). **Pool(s):** outdoor. **Guest Services:** coin laundry. **Business Services:** fax (fee). **Cards:** AX, CB, DC, DS, MC, VI.

SOME UNITS

MOTEL 6 SPI DRIVE - 413

Small-scale Hotel

	6/26-8/9	1P: $47-$57	2P: $53-$63	XP: $3	F17
	5/22-6/25	1P: $41-$51	2P: $47-$57	XP: $3	F17
	8/10-1/31	1P: $37-$47	2P: $43-$53	XP: $3	F17
	2/1-5/21	1P: $35-$45	2P: $41-$51	XP: $3	F17

Phone: 361/991-8858

Location: S Padre Island Ave at Paul Jones St. 8202 S Padre Island Dr 78412. Fax: 361/991-1698. **Facility:** 126 one-bedroom standard units. 2 stories (no elevator), exterior corridors. *Bath:* shower only. **Parking:** on-site. **Terms:** pets (with prior approval). **Pool(s):** outdoor. **Guest Services:** coin laundry. **Business Services:** fax (fee). **Cards:** AX, CB, DC, DS, MC, VI.

SOME UNITS

OMNI CORPUS CHRISTI HOTEL-BAYFRONT TOWER

Large-scale Hotel

| | 5/4-8/16 | 1P: $130-$134 | 2P: $130-$143 | XP: $10 | F18 |
| | 2/1-5/3 & 8/17-1/31 | 1P: $89-$125 | 2P: $89-$134 | XP: $10 | F18 |

Phone: (361)887-1600

Location: In town across from bay; downtown. Located in the marina district. 900 N Shoreline 78401. Fax: 361/887-6715. **Facility:** Overlooking the harbor, this hotel features on-site shops and restaurants; guest rooms include private, water-view balconies. 475 units. 462 one-bedroom standard units. 13 one-bedroom suites ($225-$1200). 20 stories, interior corridors. **Parking:** on-site (fee) and valet. **Terms:** cancellation fee imposed. **Amenities:** video games, voice mail, irons, hair dryers. *Some:* safes. **Dining:** Republic of Texas Bar & Grill, see separate listing. **Pool(s):** heated indoor/outdoor, wading. **Leisure Activities:** saunas, whirlpool, steamroom, racquetball courts. *Fee:* massage. **Guest Services:** gift shop, valet laundry. **Business Services:** conference facilities, business center. **Cards:** AX, CB, DC, DS, JC, MC, VI.
(See color ad below)

SOME UNITS

OMNI CORPUS CHRISTI HOTEL-MARINA TOWER

Large-scale Hotel

| | 5/4-8/16 | 1P: $130-$134 | 2P: $130-$143 | XP: $10 | F18 |
| | 2/1-5/3 & 8/17-1/31 | 1P: $89-$125 | 2P: $89-$134 | XP: $10 | F18 |

Phone: (361)887-1600

Location: Just n across from bay. 707 N Shoreline Blvd 78401. Fax: 361/882-3113. **Facility:** 346 units. 327 one-bedroom standard units. 19 one-bedroom suites ($225-$1200). 20 stories, interior corridors. **Parking:** on-site. **Terms:** cancellation fee imposed. **Amenities:** video games, voice mail, irons, hair dryers. **Pool(s):** heated indoor/outdoor. **Leisure Activities:** sauna, whirlpool, exercise room. *Fee:* massage. **Guest Services:** gift shop, valet laundry. **Business Services:** meeting rooms, fax (fee). **Cards:** AX, CB, DC, DS, JC, MC, VI.

SOME UNITS

FEE

QUALITY INN & SUITES

AAA SAVE

Phone: (361)289-2500

5/27-9/7 [ECP]	1P: $59-$119	2P: $59-$119	XP: $10 F18
3/2-5/26 [ECP]	1P: $59-$89	2P: $59-$89	XP: $10 F18
2/1-3/1 & 9/8-1/31 [ECP]	1P: $49-$69	2P: $49-$69	XP: $10 F18

Small-scale Hotel **Location:** Just s of jct I-37 on SR 358 at Leopard St. 1901 N Parde Island Dr 78408. Fax: 361/289-6100. **Facility:** 47 units. 40 one-bedroom standard units. 7 one-bedroom suites. 2 stories (no elevator), exterior corridors. **Parking:** on-site. **Terms:** cancellation fee imposed. **Amenities:** irons, hair dryers. **Business Services:** fax (fee). **Cards:** AX, CB, DC, DS, JC, MC, VI. **Special Amenities:** free continental breakfast and free local telephone calls.

SOME UNITS

QUALITY INN SANDY SHORES

AAA SAVE

Phone: (361)883-7456

5/15-9/15	1P: $99-$159	2P: $99-$159	XP: $10
2/1-3/31	1P: $89-$159	2P: $99-$159	XP: $10
9/16-1/31	1P: $89-$159	2P: $89-$159	XP: $10
4/1-5/14	1P: $69-$109	2P: $69-$109	XP: $10

Small-scale Hotel **Location:** 1 mi n on US 181 at north end of Harbor Bridge, exit Bridge St. 3250 Surfside Blvd 78403. Fax: 361/883-1437. **Facility:** 112 units. 104 one-bedroom standard units, some with whirlpools. 8 one-bedroom suites. 2 stories (no elevator), interior/exterior corridors. *Bath:* combo or shower only. **Parking:** on-site. **Terms:** cancellation fee imposed. **Amenities:** voice mail, irons, hair dryers. **Pool(s):** outdoor. **Leisure Activities:** whirlpool. **Guest Services:** valet and coin laundry. **Business Services:** fax (fee). **Cards:** AX, CB, DC, MC, VI. **Special Amenities:** free continental breakfast and free local telephone calls.

SOME UNITS

RADISSON BEACH HOTEL

AAA SAVE

Phone: (361)883-9700

5/15-9/15	1P: $109-$209	2P: $109-$209	XP: $10 F12
2/1-3/31	1P: $99-$169	2P: $99-$169	XP: $10 F12
4/1-5/14	1P: $89-$169	2P: $89-$169	XP: $10 F12
9/16-1/31	1P: $89-$159	2P: $89-$159	XP: $10 F12

Large-scale Hotel **Location:** 1 mi n on US 181, at north end of Harbor Bridge, exit Beach St. 3200 Surfside Blvd 78403 (PO Box 839). Fax: 361/883-1437. **Facility:** 139 one-bedroom standard units. 7 stories, interior corridors. **Parking:** on-site. **Terms:** check-in 4 pm, cancellation fee imposed. **Amenities:** voice mail, irons, hair dryers. **Dining:** 7 am-10 pm. **Pool(s):** heated outdoor, wading. **Leisure Activities:** whirlpool, exercise room. **Guest Services:** gift shop, valet laundry. **Business Services:** meeting rooms, business center. **Cards:** AX, CB, DC, DS, MC, VI. **Special Amenities:** free local telephone calls and free newspaper.

SOME UNITS

RAMADA INN BAYFRONT

AAA SAVE

Phone: (361)882-8100

5/23-8/31	1P: $98-$119	2P: $107-$129	XP: $10 F17
3/1-5/22	1P: $89-$109	2P: $98-$119	XP: $10 F17
2/1-2/28 & 9/1-1/31	1P: $71-$90	2P: $80-$100	XP: $10 F17

Large-scale Hotel **Location:** Just n. 601 N Water St 78401. Fax: 361/888-6540. **Facility:** 200 units. 185 one-bedroom standard units. 15 one-bedroom suites ($110-$149). 10 stories, interior corridors. **Parking:** on-site. **Terms:** 2 night minimum stay - weekends. **Amenities:** voice mail, irons, hair dryers. **Dining:** 2 restaurants, 6:30 am-1:30 & 6-10 pm, cocktails. **Pool(s):** outdoor. **Leisure Activities:** exercise room. **Guest Services:** gift shop, valet and coin laundry. **Business Services:** meeting rooms, fax (fee). **Cards:** AX, CB, DC, DS, MC, VI. **Special Amenities:** free local telephone calls and free newspaper.

SOME UNITS

RAMADA LIMITED

Phone: (361)289-5861

6/1-9/4 [CP]	1P: $89-$109	2P: $89-$109	XP: $10 F13
2/1-5/31 & 9/5-1/31 [CP]	1P: $59-$69	2P: $59-$69	XP: $10 F13

Small-scale Hotel **Location:** I-37, exit 3A (Navigation St), take loop around to McBride, then left. 5501 I-37 at McBride Ln 78408. Fax: 361/299-1718. **Facility:** 157 one-bedroom standard units. 2 stories (no elevator), interior corridors. **Parking:** on-site. **Terms:** 4 day cancellation notice, pets ($100 deposit). **Amenities:** high-speed Internet, irons, hair dryers. **Pool(s):** outdoor. **Leisure Activities:** whirlpool, exercise room. **Guest Services:** valet laundry. **Business Services:** meeting rooms, business center. **Cards:** AX, DC, DS, MC, VI.

SOME UNITS

RED ROOF INN

AAA SAVE

Phone: (361)992-9222

All Year [CP]	1P: $35-$59	2P: $42-$66	XP: $7 F18

Motel **Location:** SR 358, exit Nile Dr. 6805 S Padre Island Dr 78412. Fax: 361/992-7008. **Facility:** 121 units. 118 one-bedroom standard units. 3 one-bedroom suites. 3 stories, exterior corridors. **Parking:** on-site. **Amenities:** video games. *Some:* irons, hair dryers. **Pool(s):** heated outdoor. **Leisure Activities:** whirlpool. **Guest Services:** coin laundry. **Business Services:** fax (fee). **Cards:** AX, CB, DC, DS, MC, VI. **Special Amenities:** free local telephone calls and free newspaper.

SOME UNITS
FEE FEE

RED ROOF INN CORPUS CHRISTI AIRPORT

AAA SAVE

Phone: 361/289-6925

5/22-7/31	1P: $39-$69	2P: $44-$74	XP: $5
2/1-5/21	1P: $35-$41	2P: $41-$47	XP: $5
8/1-1/31	1P: $36-$42	2P: $41-$340	XP: $5

Motel **Location:** I-37, exit 5 (Corn Products Rd), southbound access road. Located in a semi-rural area. 6301 I-37 78409. Fax: 361/289-2239. **Facility:** 142 one-bedroom standard units. 3 stories (no elevator), exterior corridors. **Parking:** on-site. **Terms:** weekly rates available, small pets only. **Amenities:** video games, voice mail. **Pool(s):** outdoor. **Leisure Activities:** whirlpool. **Guest Services:** coin laundry. **Business Services:** fax (fee). **Cards:** AX, DC, MC, VI. **Special Amenities:** free local telephone calls and free newspaper.

SOME UNITS

SEA SHELL INN BEACH HOTEL

Phone: (361)888-5391

AAA SAVE

| | 5/16-9/15 | 1P: $50-$125 | 2P: $50-$125 | XP: $10 | F12 |
| | 2/1-5/15 & 9/16-1/31 | 1P: $40-$75 | 2P: $40-$75 | XP: $10 | F12 |

Motel

Location: 1 mi n on US 181, at north end of Harbor Bridge, exit Beach St; on the beach. 202 Kleberg Pl 78402. Fax: 361/888-5391. **Facility:** 26 units. 24 one- and 2 two-bedroom standard units, some with efficiencies. 2 stories, exterior corridors. **Parking:** on-site. **Terms:** cancellation fee imposed, weekly rates available. **Pool(s):** heated outdoor. **Leisure Activities:** shuffleboard. **Guest Services:** coin laundry. **Business Services:** fax (fee). **Cards:** AX, DC, DS, MC, VI.

SOME UNITS

SURFSIDE CONDOMINIUM APARTMENTS

Phone: 361/949-8128

	5/24-9/7	1P: $125-$135	2P: $125-$135
	3/2-5/23	1P: $110-$135	2P: $110-$135
	2/1-3/1 & 9/8-1/31	1P: $100	2P: $100

Condominium

Location: Park Rd 22 on N Padre Island Dr, jct Whitecap Blvd, just e. 15005 Windward Dr 78418. Fax: 361/949-8024. **Facility:** 31 two-bedroom suites with kitchens. 2 stories, exterior corridors. **Parking:** on-site. **Terms:** check-in 4 pm, 3 day cancellation notice, weekly rates available, pets (with prior approval). **Amenities:** voice mail. **Pool(s):** outdoor. **Guest Services:** coin laundry. **Cards:** AX, DS, MC, VI.

ASK

TRAVELODGE AIRPORT

Phone: (361)289-5666

| | All Year [BP] | 1P: $49-$89 | 2P: $49-$89 | F17 |

Small-scale Hotel

Location: I-37, exit 5 (Corn Products Rd), 0.3 mi w. 910 Corn Products Rd 78409. Fax: 361/289-0932. **Facility:** 170 one-bedroom standard units, some with whirlpools. 2 stories, interior corridors. **Parking:** on-site. **Terms:** 7 day cancellation notice, weekly rates available. **Amenities:** Some: irons. **Pool(s):** heated indoor/outdoor. **Leisure Activities:** tennis court, exercise room. **Guest Services:** gift shop, complimentary evening beverages, coin laundry. **Business Services:** meeting rooms, business center. **Cards:** AX, CB, DC, DS, MC, VI.

SOME UNITS

ASK

VILLA DEL SOL

Phone: (361)883-9748

AAA SAVE

	5/24-9/1	2P: $119-$129
	2/1-3/31	2P: $98-$128
	4/1-5/23	2P: $93-$123
	9/2-1/31	2P: $93-$102

Cottage

Location: 1 mi n off US 181, 0.5 mi n of north end of Harbor Bridge. 3938 Surfside Blvd 78402. Fax: 361/883-7537. **Facility:** 234 one-bedroom standard units with efficiencies. 3 stories, exterior corridors. **Parking:** on-site. **Terms:** check-in 4 pm, 2 night minimum stay - weekends 5/3-9/3, 3 day cancellation notice, weekly rates available, package plans. **Pool(s):** outdoor, heated outdoor. **Leisure Activities:** whirlpools, recreation programs in winter, playground. *Fee:* jet skis in season. **Guest Services:** coin laundry. **Business Services:** meeting rooms, fax (fee). **Cards:** AX, CB, DC, DS, MC, VI. **Special Amenities:** free local telephone calls.

SOME UNITS

The following lodging was either not evaluated or did not meet AAA rating requirements but is listed for your information only.

FAIRWAY VILLAS

Phone: 361/949-7021

[fyi]

Not evaluated. Location: CR 358 to Park Rd 22. 14401 Commodores 78418. Facilities, services, and decor characterize a mid-range property.

WHERE TO DINE

ANCIENT MARINER SEAFOOD RESTAURANT

Lunch: $4-$6   **Dinner:** $6-$11   **Phone:** 361/992-7371

Seafood

Location: 0.8 mi ne of jct I-358 and Everhart Rd, then just e. 4366 S Alameda St 78412. **Hours:** 11 am-9 pm, Fri & Sat-10 pm. Closed major holidays; also Sun. **Reservations:** accepted. **Features:** Seafood brought in fresh from the Gulf of Mexico and steaks that are cooked to order have been served at this location for the past 26 years. Casual dress; cocktails. **Parking:** on-site. **Cards:** AX, CB, DC, DS, MC, VI.

CATFISH CHARLIES

Lunch: $4-$8   **Dinner:** $6-$10   **Phone:** 361/993-0363

Seafood

Location: SR 358 Expwy, exit Airline Rd, 0.5 mi n; in Crossroads Shopping Village. 5830 McArdle Rd #12 at Airline 78412. **Hours:** 11 am-9:30 pm, Thurs-10 pm, Fri & Sat-11 pm. Closed: 1/1, 11/27, 12/25. **Features:** Family owned for 21 years, this casual eatery serves up scrumptious, made-from-scratch, Southern comfort food in a wharf-style setting. From the complimentary hushpuppies to the crispy fried catfish fillets, every bite will make you feel right at home. Casual dress; beer & wine only. **Parking:** on-site. **Cards:** AX, DS, MC, VI.

CITY DINER & OYSTER BAR

Lunch: $7-$12   **Dinner:** $10-$16   **Phone:** 361/883-1609

Seafood

Location: Downtown. 622 N Water St 78401. **Hours:** 11 am-9 pm, Fri & Sat-11 pm. Closed major holidays. **Features:** Located in downtown Corpus Christi, this seafood diner features such '60s-era touches as black and white domino tiles. Cordial servers deliver tender and moist fish filets served with warm rolls and butter. Casual dress; cocktails. **Parking:** on-site. **Cards:** AX, DC, DS, MC, VI.

LA BAHIA

Lunch: $4-$7   **Dinner:** $8-$10   **Phone:** 361/888-6555

Mexican

Location: Downtown. 224 N Mesquite St 78401. **Hours:** 7 am-2 pm, Fri & Sat also 5 pm-10 pm, Sun 8 am-2 pm. **Features:** A cantina-style decor features clay tile floors and many Mexican arts and crafts on display. Authentic dishes include picadillo, gorditas and carne quisado, all very tasty and well-seasoned. On Friday nights, request your favorite song from the live band. Casual dress; beer & wine only. **Parking:** on-site. **Cards:** AX, DS, MC, VI.

LANDRY'S SEAFOOD HOUSE   **Lunch:** $10   **Dinner:** $18   Phone: 361/882-6666
Seafood
Location: On the waterfront. 600 N Shoreline Dr 78401. **Hours:** 11 am-10:15 pm, Fri & Sat-11 pm. **Features:** In the downtown marina, the distinctive, two-story, floating restaurant serves fresh seafood in a fun atmosphere. Casual dress; cocktails. **Parking:** on-site. **Cards:** AX, MC, VI.

REPUBLIC OF TEXAS BAR & GRILL   **Dinner:** $13-$32   Phone: 361/887-1600
Steak House
Location: In town across from bay; downtown; in Omni Corpus Christi Hotel-Bayfront Tower. 900 N Shoreline 78401. **Hours:** 5:30 pm-10:30 pm. Closed: Sun. **Reservations:** suggested. **Features:** Enjoy heavenly dining 20 stories above the dramatic panorama of the Corpus Christi bayfront. Elegant yet cozy dining is enhanced by a well-trained staff, a comprehensive wine list, and intriguing regional fare including steak, seafood, chicken and salad. Casual dress; cocktails. **Parking:** valet. **Cards:** AX, CB, DC, DS, JC, MC, VI.

WATER STREET OYSTER BAR   **Lunch:** $8-$10   **Dinner:** $11-$16   Phone: 361/881-9448
Seafood
Location: Just e. 309 N Water St 78401. **Hours:** 11 am-11 pm, Fri & Sat-midnight. Closed: 11/27, 12/25. **Features:** Located one block from where the actual Nina, Pinta and Santa Maria are docked, you will find meals hand-prepared from only the highest quality ingredients. Several-catch-of-the day specials are offered including mahi-mahi, amberjack and red snapper. Casual dress; cocktails. **Parking:** valet.
Cards: AX, DS, MC, VI.

THE YARDARM RESTAURANT   **Dinner:** $11-$15   Phone: 361/855-8157
Seafood
Location: I-37 or US 181, exit Shoreline Dr, 5.3 mi s. 4310 Ocean Dr 78412. **Hours:** Open 2/14-12/1; 5:30 pm-10 pm. Closed major holidays; also Sun & Mon. **Reservations:** accepted. **Features:** Inside this old wooden house overlooking picturesque Corpus Christi Bay, is an intimate restaurant with an outdoor deck boasting the best view. The oysters Rockefeller and snapper papillote are fresh and delicious. Casual dress; cocktails. **Parking:** on-site. **Cards:** AX, CB, DC, DS, MC, VI.

CORSICANA pop. 24,485

——— WHERE TO STAY ———

COMFORT INN   Phone: (903)875-0616
Small-scale Hotel

All Year [ECP]	1P: $69-$114	2P: $74-$114	XP: $5 F17

Location: I-45, exit 231. 1946 E Hwy 31 75110. Fax: 903/875-1279. **Facility:** 59 units. 57 one-bedroom standard units, some with whirlpools. 2 one-bedroom suites with whirlpools. 3 stories, interior corridors. *Bath:* combo or shower only. **Parking:** on-site. **Amenities:** voice mail, safes, irons, hair dryers. **Pool(s):** outdoor. **Leisure Activities:** exercise room. **Guest Services:** coin laundry. **Business Services:** meeting rooms, fax (fee). **Cards:** AX, CB, DC, DS, MC, VI.

SOME UNITS

Do you know the facts?

AAA publishes the Digest of Motor Laws to assist traveling motorists. Filled with facts and information, this one-of-a-kind compilation includes a comprehensive description of the laws that govern motor vehicle registration and operation in the United States and Canada. This sixty-eighth edition guide has a new, easy-to-read format with graphics, state-by-state tax summary tables and detailed information on occupant protection laws, driver licensing laws, automated enforcement laws and motor vehicle fees and taxes.

You can easily locate various licensing and motor laws governing the states in which you are traveling. In addition to vehicle registration and operation laws, the Digest contains information and facts about alcohol laws, traffic safety laws and more.

Call your local club or 1-877-AAA-BOOK to obtain a copy of the Digest.

The book retails for $13.95.

DALHART pop. 7,237

———— WHERE TO STAY ————

BEST WESTERN NURSANICKEL MOTEL　　　　　　　　　　　　　　**Phone:** (806)244-5637

AAA SAVE
▼▼▼ ▼▼▼
Motel

5/21-9/30 [ECP]	1P: $56-$66	2P: $66-$76
2/1-5/20 & 10/1-1/31 [ECP]	1P: $46-$56	2P: $56-$66

Location: Just s of jct US 54 and 87. Located near railroad tracks. 102 Scott Ave (Hwy 87 S) 79022. Fax: 806/244-5803. **Facility:** 55 one-bedroom standard units. 2 stories (no elevator), exterior corridors. **Parking:** on-site. **Terms:** small pets only (no cats). **Amenities:** hair dryers. **Pool(s):** heated outdoor. **Guest Services:** coin laundry. **Business Services:** meeting rooms, fax (fee). **Cards:** AX, CB, DC, DS, MC, VI. **Special Amenities:** free continental breakfast.

SOME UNITS

⬛ 🛏 🍴 🌊 📺 📠 / ✕ 🖥 /

BUDGET INN　　　　　　　　　　　　　　　　　　　　　　　　**Phone:** (806)244-4557

AAA SAVE
▼▼▼
Motel

11/15-1/31	1P: $39-$59	2P: $49-$69	XP: $5	F14
5/1-8/31	1P: $39-$59	2P: $45-$69	XP: $5	F14
9/1-11/14	1P: $29-$36	2P: $39-$54	XP: $5	F14
2/1-4/30	1P: $29-$39	2P: $36-$54	XP: $5	F14

Location: US 54, just e of US 87 and 385. 415 Liberal St (Hwy 54) 79022. Fax: 806/244-4557. **Facility:** 23 one-bedroom standard units. 1 story, exterior corridors. **Parking:** on-site, winter plug-ins. **Terms:** small pets only ($20 deposit). **Business Services:** fax (fee). **Cards:** AX, DS, MC, VI. **Special Amenities:** free continental breakfast and free newspaper.

SOME UNITS

⬛ 🛏 🍴 📺 📠 / ✕ 🖥 /

COMFORT INN　　　　　　　　　　　　　　　　　　　　　　　**Phone:** (806)249-8585

AAA SAVE
▼▼▼ ▼▼▼
Motel

All Year	1P: $60	2P: $80	XP: $6	F18

Location: 0.5 mi e of jct US 54 and 87. 1110 Hwy 54 E 79022 (HC 2, Box 22). Fax: 806/249-2827. **Facility:** 36 one-bedroom standard units. 1 story, exterior corridors. **Parking:** on-site. **Terms:** [CP] meal plan available, small pets only. **Amenities:** irons, hair dryers. **Pool(s):** small outdoor. **Leisure Activities:** whirlpool. **Business Services:** fax. **Cards:** AX, CB, DC, DS, MC, VI. **Special Amenities:** free continental breakfast and free local telephone calls.

SOME UNITS

⬛ 🛏 🍴 🌊 📺 📠 🖥 / ✕ 🖥 /

DAYS INN　　　　　　　　　　　　　　　　　　　　　　　　　**Phone:** (806)244-5246

AAA SAVE
▼▼▼ ▼▼▼
Motel

All Year	1P: $69-$129	2P: $79-$169	XP: $20	F12

Location: 0.5 mi e on US 54. 701 Liberal St (Hwy 54) 79022. Fax: 806/244-0805. **Facility:** 43 one-bedroom standard units. 2 stories (no elevator), interior corridors. *Bath:* combo or shower only. **Parking:** on-site, winter plug-ins. **Terms:** cancellation fee imposed, [ECP] meal plan available, small pets only ($5-$20 fee). **Amenities:** irons, hair dryers. **Pool(s):** small heated indoor. **Leisure Activities:** limited exercise equipment. **Guest Services:** coin laundry. **Business Services:** fax (fee). **Cards:** AX, CB, DC, DS, JC, MC, VI. **Special Amenities:** free continental breakfast and free local telephone calls.

SOME UNITS

⬛ 🛏 🍴 ♿ 🌊 VCR 📺 📠 🖥 / ✕ /

HOLIDAY INN EXPRESS　　　　　　　　　　　　　　　　　　　**Phone:** (806)249-1145

▼▼▼ ▼▼▼
Small-scale Hotel

All Year	1P: $79-$139	2P: $89-$169

Location: 1 mi e of jct US 54 and 87. 801 Liberal St (Hwy 54) 79022. Fax: 806/244-3787. **Facility:** 52 one-bedroom standard units, some with whirlpools. 2 stories, interior corridors. *Bath:* combo or shower only. **Parking:** on-site. **Terms:** cancellation fee imposed, [ECP] meal plan available. **Amenities:** voice mail, irons, hair dryers. **Pool(s):** heated indoor. **Leisure Activities:** limited exercise equipment. **Guest Services:** coin laundry. **Business Services:** meeting rooms, fax (fee). **Cards:** AX, CB, DC, DS, JC, MC, VI.

SOME UNITS

ASK ⬛ 🛏 🍴 ♿ 🌊 VCR 📺 📠 🖥 🖨 / ✕ /

SANDS MOTEL　　　　　　　　　　　　　　　　　　　　　　　**Phone:** (806)244-4568

AAA SAVE
▼
Motel

All Year	1P: $25-$65	2P: $30-$70	XP: $10	F

Location: US 54, just e of US 87 and 385. 301 Liberal St (Hwy 54) 79022. **Facility:** 36 one-bedroom standard units. 1 story, exterior corridors. **Parking:** on-site. **Terms:** cancellation fee imposed, small pets only. **Pool(s):** heated outdoor. **Cards:** AX, DC, DS, MC, VI.

SOME UNITS

⬛ 🛏 🍴 🌊 📺 / ✕ 🖥 /

SUPER 8 MOTEL　　　　　　　　　　　　　　　　　　　　　　**Phone:** (806)249-8526

▼▼▼ ▼▼▼
Motel
DS, MC, VI.

All Year	1P: $49-$59	2P: $54-$64	XP: $5	F12

Location: Jct US 87/54, 0.5 mi e. 403 Tanglewood Rd 79022 (PO Box 1325). Fax: 806/249-5119. **Facility:** 45 one-bedroom standard units. 2 stories (no elevator), interior corridors. **Parking:** on-site, winter plug-ins. **Terms:** small pets only ($25 deposit, in smoking units). **Business Services:** fax (fee). **Cards:** AX, CB, DC, DS, MC, VI.

SOME UNITS

ASK ⬛ 🛏 🍴 📺 📠 / ✕ /

———— WHERE TO DINE ————

BAR-H STEAK HOUSE　　　　**Lunch:** $5-$17　　　　**Dinner:** $5-$17　　　　**Phone:** 806/244-3813

▼▼▼
▼
American

Location: 0.5 mi e on US 54. 1010 US 54 E 79022. **Hours:** 11 am-9 pm. Closed major holidays; also Sun. **Features:** Thick steaks cut on the premises are the specialty at the rustic, Western-themed cafe. The salad bar is set up on an old-time frontier wagon, and wagon-wheel chandeliers hang from the ceiling of the dimly lit dining room. Casual dress. **Parking:** on-site. **Cards:** AX, DS, MC, VI.

✕

Destination Dallas
pop. 1,188,580

Dallas—what started with one little log cabin blossomed into one of our largest cities.

Her buildings are as famous as her "Cowboys." Visit I.M. Pei's City Hall and Frank Lloyd Wright's Dallas Theatre Center. Or, for an inkling of how it all began, that lone log cabin is preserved in Historic Square—huddled beneath its towering neighbors.

Skyline, Dallas.
The geodesic sphere of Reunion Tower is a shining example of the city's modern architecture. (See listing page 83)

Dallas Cowboys. This NFL team is best known for its championship wins—and its cheerleaders. (See listing page 86)

Lone Star Park, Grand Prairie. And they're off... to the races, that is. Thoroughbred racing is prime in this nearby suburb. (See mention page 85)

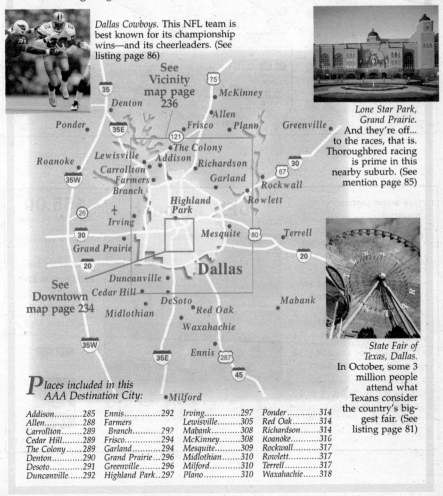

State Fair of Texas, Dallas. In October, some 3 million people attend what Texans consider the country's biggest fair. (See listing page 81)

See Vicinity map page 236

See Downtown map page 234

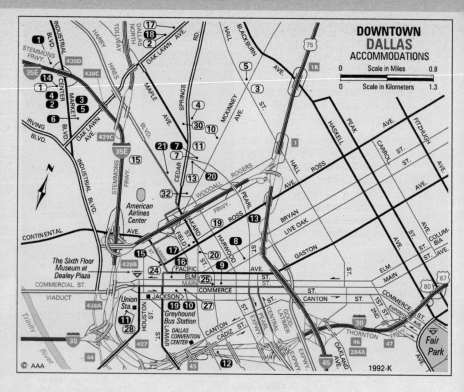

DOWNTOWN DALLAS ACCOMMODATIONS

1992-K

© AAA

Downtown Dallas

This index helps you "spot" where approved accommodations and restaurants are located on the corresponding detailed maps. Lodging rate ranges are for comparison only and show the property's high season; rates are per night, unless only weekly (W) rates are available. Restaurant rate range is for dinner, unless only lunch (L) is served. Turn to the listing page for more detailed rate information and consult display ads for special promotions.

Spotter/Map Page Number	OA	DOWNTOWN DALLAS - Lodgings	Diamond Rating	Rate Range High Season	Listing Page
❶ / p. 234	🆀	Renaissance Dallas Hotel	▽▽▽	$79-$199 SAVE	256
❷ / p. 234		Best Western Market Center	▽▽	$59-$110	252
❸ / p. 234		Sheraton Suites Market Center-Dallas	▽▽▽	$115	257
❹ / p. 234	🆀	Wyndham Dallas Market Center	▽▽▽	$89-$149 SAVE	257
❺ / p. 234	🆀	Courtyard by Marriott-Market Center	▽▽▽	$119-$169 SAVE	253
❻ / p. 234		Fairfield Inn Market Center	▽▽▽	$49-$124	253
❼ / p. 234	🆀	Hotel St. Germain	▽▽▽▽	$290-$650 SAVE	254
❽ / p. 234	🆀	Adam's Mark Hotel	▽▽▽	$197-$249 SAVE	250
❾ / p. 234		Holiday Inn-Aristocrat Hotel - see ad p 254	▽▽▽	$119-$199	253
❿ / p. 234		The Adolphus	▽▽▽▽	$149-$340	250
⓫ / p. 234	🆀	Hyatt Regency Dallas at Reunion - see color ad inside front cover	▽▽▽▽	$109-$245 SAVE	254
⓬ / p. 234	🆀	Ramada Plaza Hotel	▽▽▽	$99-$109 SAVE	256
⓭ / p. 234		Le Meridien Dallas	▽▽▽	$119-$169	254
⓮ / p. 234	🆀	Wyndham Anatole	▽▽▽	$139-$219 SAVE	257
⓯ / p. 234	🆀	AmeriSuites (Dallas/West End) - see color ad p 251	▽▽▽	$149-$169 SAVE	250
⓰ / p. 234		Hampton Inn West End	▽▽▽	$69-$159	253
⓱ / p. 234		The Fairmont Dallas	▽▽▽▽	$129-$309	253
⓲ / p. 234		The Melrose Hotel	▽▽▽	$144-$196	256
⓳ / p. 234		Magnolia Hotel Dallas	▽▽▽	$239-$399	254
⓴ / p. 234		Hotel Crescent Court	▽▽▽▽	$370-$2500	254
㉑ / p. 234		Bradford Homesuites Downtown	▽▽▽	$89-$129	252
		DOWNTOWN DALLAS - Restaurants			
① / p. 234		Nana Grill	▽▽▽▽	$30-$46	258
② / p. 234		The Landmark Restaurant	▽▽▽	$19-$35	258
③ / p. 234		La Trattoria Lombardi	▽▽▽	$11-$29	258
④ / p. 234		Dream Cafe	▽▽	$10-$16	258
⑤ / p. 234		Bread Winners Cafe	▽▽	$13-$22	257
⑦ / p. 234		Hotel St. Germain	▽▽▽▽	$85	258
⑩ / p. 234		S & D Oyster Company	▽▽	$6-$14	259
⑪ / p. 234		Old Warsaw	▽▽▽▽	$21-$32	258
⑬ / p. 234		Beau Nash	▽▽▽	$12-$28	257
⑮ / p. 234		Baby Doe's Matchless Mine Restaurant	▽▽	$17-$26	257
⑰ / p. 234		Green Papaya	▽▽	$7-$13	258
⑲ / p. 234		The Pyramid Grill	▽▽▽▽	$17-$39	259
⑳ / p. 234		Dakota's	▽▽▽	$13-$26	258
㉔ / p. 234		Palm Restaurant	▽▽▽	$16-$35	259
㉕ / p. 234		Zodiac Restaurant	▽▽	$10-$16(L)	259
㉗ / p. 234		The French Room	▽▽▽▽▽	$60-$90	258
㉘ / p. 234		Antares	▽▽▽	$18-$30	257
㉚ / p. 234		Lola The Restaurant	▽▽▽	$32-$47	258
㉜ / p. 234		Palomino Euro Bistro	▽▽▽	$8-$17	259

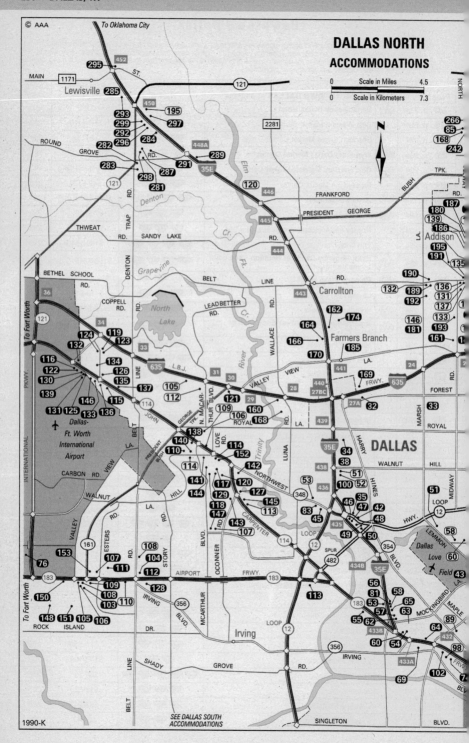

© AAA

To Oklahoma City

DALLAS NORTH
ACCOMMODATIONS

Scale in Miles 0 — 4.5
Scale in Kilometers 0 — 7.3

SEE DALLAS SOUTH
ACCOMMODATIONS

1990-K

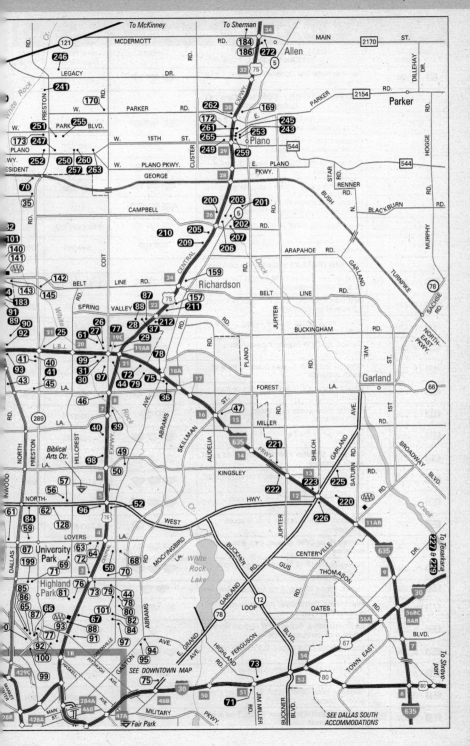

✈ Airport Accommodations

Spotter/Map Page Number	OA	DALLAS-FORT WORTH INTERNATIONAL	Diamond Rating	Rate Range High Season	Listing Page
76 / p. 236		Terraces Hotel and Conference Center, 2 mi s of terminal	◆◆◆	$125-$135	277
		GRAPEVINE (FORT WORTH VICINITY) - Lodgings			
N/A	AAA	**AmeriSuites (Dallas/DFW Airport N), 2 mi n of north entrance**	◆◆◆	$119-$129 SAVE	367
N/A	AAA	**Baymont Inn-Dallas-Ft Worth/Airport North, 2.5 mi w of north entrance**	◆◆	$89 SAVE	367
N/A	AAA	**Embassy Suites Outdoor World, 1.5 mi n from terminal**	◆◆◆	$119-$269 SAVE	367
N/A		Hilton DFW Lakes, 2.5 mi n of north entrance	◆◆◆	$69-$249	368
N/A		Holiday Inn Express Hotel & Suites DFW/Grapevine, 3.2 mi w of terminal	◆◆◆	$119	368
N/A	AAA	**Hyatt Regency DFW, at the terminal**	◆◆◆	$79-$199 SAVE	368
N/A		Super 8 Motel-Grapevine, 2.5 mi w of north entrance	◆◆	$49-$69	368
		IRVING (DALLAS VICINITY) - Lodgings			
107 / p. 236	AAA	**AmeriSuites (Dallas/DFW Airport South), 3.5 mi e of south entrance**	◆◆◆	$79-$109 SAVE	297
109 / p. 236		Best Western Irving Inn & Suites DFW Airport, 3.5 mi e of south entrance	◆◆◆	$70-$78	297
116 / p. 236		Clarion Inn & Suites at DFW Airport, 1 mi e of north entrance	◆◆◆	$69-$159	298
124 / p. 236		Comfort Inn DFW Airport, 1 mi e of north entrance	◆◆	$59-$75	298
148 / p. 236	AAA	**Comfort Inn DFW Airport South, 3 mi e of south entrance**	◆◆◆	$69-$99 SAVE	298
146 / p. 236		Comfort Suites DFW Airport, 1 mi e of north entrance	◆◆◆	$60	298
115 / p. 236		Country Inn & Suites By Carlson, 1.5 mi e of north entrance	◆◆	$85-$119	298
137 / p. 236		Days Inn DFW North, 1.5 mi e of north entrance	◆◆◆	$59-$70	299
108 / p. 236	AAA	**Drury Inn & Suites - DFW Airport, 2 mi se of south entrance**	◆◆◆	$73-$103 SAVE	299
150 / p. 236		Embassy Suites-DFW South, 3 mi se of south entrance	◆◆◆	$109-$219	299
130 / p. 236		Fairfield Inn by Marriott, 1 mi e of north entrance	◆◆◆	$51-$75	300
106 / p. 236		Hampton Inn-DFW Airport, 2 mi to south entrance	◆◆◆	$93-$119	300
134 / p. 236	AAA	**Harvey Hotel-DFW Airport, 1 mi e of north entrance**	◆◆◆	$130-$170 SAVE	300
133 / p. 236		Harvey Suites-DFW Airport, 1 mi e of north entrance	◆◆◆	$110-$152	300
125 / p. 236		Hearthside by Villager, 1 mi e of north entrance	◆◆	$39-$109	300
135 / p. 236	AAA	**Holiday Inn Select-DFW Airport-North, 1 mi e of north entrance**	◆◆◆	$155-$165 SAVE	301
122 / p. 236	AAA	**La Quinta Inn & Suites DFW Airport North, 1.5 mi e of north entrance**	◆◆◆	$69-$129 SAVE	301
132 / p. 236		Marriott Hotel-DFW Airport, 0.3 mi e of north entrance	◆◆◆	$89-$189	302
131 / p. 236		Motel 6 #1274 DFW North, 1 mi e of north entrance	◆◆	$39-$55	302
151 / p. 236		Radisson Hotel-DFW Airport South, 3 mi e of south entrance	fyi	$89-$99	304
123 / p. 236	AAA	**Red Roof Inn/DFW Airport North, 1 mi e of north entrance**	◆◆	$39-$63 SAVE	302

Enjoy Texas.

We'll take care of the rest.

We have nearly 100 convenient locations.

How may I help you?

Did you enjoy your swim?

How about free breakfast?

Need a ride to the airport?

Don't forget to book us online.

We hope you enjoy your stay.

www.LQ.com • 1-800-221-4731

Relax. We'll take care of the rest.

Nearly 100 locations in Texas

First-run movies

25" TV

Children stay free

In-room coffeemaker

Swimming pool

Free local calls

Free breakfast

Airport shuttle service*

Ironing board

Hair dryer

100% satisfaction guarantee

Guaranteed lowest rates

Show Your Card & Save

AAA. Every Day.®
16-yr partner

www.LQ.com • 1-800-221-4731

*Select locations

Spotter/Map Page Number	OA	IRVING (DALLAS VICINITY) - Lodgings (continued)	Diamond Rating	Rate Range High Season	Listing Page
126 / p. 236		Residence Inn by Marriott-DFW/Irving, 1.9 mi e of north entrance	◈◈◈	$139-$179	303
136 / p. 236		Sheraton Grand Hotel, 1.5 mi e of north entrance	◈◈◈	$112	303
139 / p. 236		Shoney's Inn & Suites, 1 mi e of north entrance	◈◈	$45-$60	303
153 / p. 236		Super 8 Motel-Irving, 3.5 mi e of south entrance	◈◈	$49-$64	303
119 / p. 236	◬	Wingate Inn DFW, 1 mi e of north entrance	◈◈◈	$59-$109 SAVE	303

✈ Airport Accommodations

Spotter/Map Page Number	OA	DALLAS LOVE FIELD	Diamond Rating	Rate Range High Season	Listing Page
43 / p. 236		Holiday Inn Select Love Field, just e	◈◈◈	$82-$115	270

Dallas North and Vicinity

This index helps you "spot" where approved accommodations and restaurants are located on the corresponding detailed maps. Lodging rate ranges are for comparison only and show the property's high season; rates are per night, unless only weekly (W) rates are available. Restaurant rate range is for dinner, unless only lunch (L) is served. Turn to the listing page for more detailed rate information and consult display ads for special promotions.

Spotter/Map Page Number	OA	DALLAS NORTH - Lodgings	Diamond Rating	Rate Range High Season	Listing Page
25 / p. 236		Terra Cotta Inn	◈◈	$63-$83	277
26 / p. 236		Crowne Plaza Suites Hotel and Resort Dallas Park Central	◈◈◈	$159	265
27 / p. 236		The Harvey Hotel-Dallas	◈◈	$59	269
28 / p. 236		Goldmark Suites	◈◈◈	$99-$129	267
29 / p. 236		Embassy Suites Hotel-Dallas/Park Central - see color ad p 267	◈◈◈	$89-$159	267
30 / p. 236		The Westin Park Central Dallas	◈◈◈◈	$148-$168	277
31 / p. 236	◬	AmeriSuites (Dallas/Park Central) - see color ad p 251	◈◈◈	$94 SAVE	260
32 / p. 236		Motel 6 Forest Lane-South #1119	◈	$35-$51	273
33 / p. 236		Courtyard by Marriott-LBJ at Josey	◈◈◈	$99-$109	265
34 / p. 236	◬	Hampton Inn-Dallas North I-35 at Walnut Hill - see color ad p 268	◈◈◈	$76-$89 SAVE	268
35 / p. 236		Comfort Suites	◈◈◈	$69-$109	263
36 / p. 236		Fairfield Inn-Park Central	◈◈◈	$59-$89	267
37 / p. 236		Holiday Inn Express Park Central	◈◈◈	$55-$85	269
38 / p. 236	◬	Drury Inn & Suites-Dallas North	◈◈◈	$66-$96 SAVE	266
39 / p. 236	◬	Holiday Inn Select Dallas North Park - see color ad p 270	◈◈◈	$119-$189 SAVE	270
40 / p. 236		Residence Inn by Marriott at Central-Northpark	◈◈◈	$89-$135	276
41 / p. 236		The Guest Lodge Hotel at the Cooper Aerobics Center	◈◈◈	$155-$205	268
42 / p. 236	◬	Best Western Millennium Inn	◈◈◈	$59-$89 SAVE	260
43 / p. 236		Holiday Inn Select Love Field	◈◈◈	$82-$115	270
44 / p. 236		Doubletree Club Hotel Dallas Park Central	◈◈◈	$53-$99	265
45 / p. 236	◬	Red Roof Inn-Northwest	◈◈	$36-$54 SAVE	276
46 / p. 236		Radisson Hotel & Suites Dallas - see ad p 274	◈◈◈	$149	274
47 / p. 236		Clarion Suites	◈◈◈	$79-$159	263

Spotter/Map Page Number	OA	DALLAS NORTH - Lodgings (continued)	Diamond Rating	Rate Range High Season	Listing Page
48 / p. 236	◆◆◆	Courtyard by Marriott	◆◆◆	$69-$129 SAVE	264
49 / p. 236		Holiday Inn Express-Love Field	◆◆◆	$69-$79	269
50 / p. 236		Quality Suites	◆◆◆	$69-$99	273
51 / p. 236	◆◆◆	Embassy Suites Hotel-Dallas/Love Field - see ad p 268 & color ad p 266	◆◆◆	$109-$269 SAVE	266
52 / p. 236		Doubletree Hotel at Campbell Centre	◆◆◆	$79-$169	265
53 / p. 236		Fairfield Inn-Regal Row - see ad p 253	◆◆◆	$49-$67	267
54 / p. 236		Clarion Inn Market Center	◆◆◆	$69-$99	262
55 / p. 236	◆◆◆	Super 8 Motel	◆◆	$49-$64 SAVE	277
56 / p. 236	◆◆◆	La Quinta Inn Love Field - see color ad p 272	◆◆◆	$64-$89 SAVE	272
57 / p. 236	◆◆◆	Sheraton Dallas Brookhollow Hotel - see color ad p 275	◆◆◆	$79-$89 SAVE	276
58 / p. 236	◆◆◆	Red Roof Inn-Market Center	◆◆	$39-$54 SAVE	276
59 / p. 236	◆◆◆	Radisson Hotel Central/Dallas - see ad p 274	◆◆◆	$139 SAVE	274
60 / p. 236		Crowne Plaza Hotel and Resort Dallas Market Center	◆◆◆	$79-$139	265
61 / p. 236		Staybridge Suites Dallas-Park Central	◆◆◆	$114-$129	276
62 / p. 236		Candlewood Dallas Market Center	◆◆◆	$70-$94	261
63 / p. 236	◆◆◆	Radisson Hotel Dallas - see color ad p 275	◆◆◆	$59-$69 SAVE	274
64 / p. 236		Residence Inn by Marriott-Dallas Market Center	◆◆◆	$94	276
65 / p. 236		Hawthorn Suites Hotel-Dallas- Market Center	◆◆	$59-$199	269
66 / p. 236	◆◆◆	The Mansion On Turtle Creek	◆◆◆◆◆	$405-$2400 SAVE	273
67 / p. 236	◆◆◆	La Quinta Inn-Dallas-City Place - see color ad p 272	◆◆◆	$69-$109 SAVE	272
69 / p. 236		Embassy Suites Dallas-Market Center - see color ad p 267	◆◆◆	$99-$219	266
70 / p. 236		Microtel Inn & Suites Dallas/Plano	◆◆	$40-$69	273
71 / p. 236		Motel 6 #1479	◆◆	$37-$57	273
72 / p. 236	◆◆◆	Wellesley Inn & Suites (Dallas/Park Central) - see color ad p 250	◆◆	$70-$80 SAVE	277
73 / p. 236	◆◆◆	La Quinta Inn-Dallas-East - see color ad p 272	◆◆◆	$59-$89 SAVE	272
74 / p. 236	◆◆◆	Dallas Marriott Suites Market Center	◆◆◆	$149 SAVE	265
75 / p. 236		Homewood Suites by Hilton	◆◆◆	$99-$159	271
76 / p. 236		Terraces Hotel and Conference Center	◆◆◆	$125-$135	277
77 / p. 236	◆◆◆	Wyndham Garden Hotel-Dallas Park Central	◆◆◆	$79-$109 SAVE	278
78 / p. 236		Candlewood Suites Dallas North/Richardson	◆◆◆	$89-$109	262
79 / p. 236		Hawthorn Suites Ltd Dallas Park Central	◆◆◆	$99-$129	269
80 / p. 236		Hawthorn Suites North Dallas	◆◆◆	$79-$129	269
81 / p. 236		Wingate Inn	◆◆◆	$79-$89	277
83 / p. 236		Delux Inn Express & Suites	◆◆	$40	265
84 / p. 236		Hilton Dallas Park Cities	◆◆◆	$89-$199	269
85 / p. 236	◆◆◆	Holiday Inn Express & Suites Plano	◆◆◆	$74-$84 SAVE	269
86 / p. 236		Homestead Studio Suites Hotel-Dallas/North Addison/Tollway	◆◆	$55-$70	270

Spotter/Map Page Number	OA	**DALLAS NORTH** - Lodgings (continued)	Diamond Rating	Rate Range High Season	Listing Page
87 / p. 236	AAA	**La Quinta Inn-Richardson** - see color ad p 272	◇◇◇	$59-$89 [SAVE]	273
88 / p. 236		Quality Suites-Park Central (now known as Comfort Suites)	◇◇◇	$74	273
89 / p. 236		Embassy Suites Hotel Dallas Near the Galleria - see color ad p 267	◇◇◇	$129-$229	267
90 / p. 236		Candlewood Suites-Dallas Galleria	◇◇◇	$79-$99	261
91 / p. 236	AAA	**AmeriSuites (Dallas/Near the Galleria)** - see color ad p 251	◇◇◇	$99 [SAVE]	260
92 / p. 236		The Westin Galleria, Dallas	◇◇◇◇	$209-$299	277
93 / p. 236	AAA	**Doubletree Hotel, Lincoln Centre near the Galleria**	◇◇◇◇	$90-$170 [SAVE]	266
94 / p. 236		Comfort Inn Hotel by the Galleria	◇◇◇	$75-$89	263
95 / p. 236	AAA	**La Quinta Inn & Suites-Dallas Addison** - see color ad p 272	◇◇◇	$69-$119 [SAVE]	271
96 / p. 236		Bradford Suites at Lincoln Park	◇◇◇	$99-$139	261
97 / p. 236		Homestead Studio Suites Hotel-Dallas/North/Park Central	◇◇	$65-$80	270
98 / p. 236	AAA	**La Quinta Inn & Suites** - see color ad p 272	◇◇◇	$79-$119 [SAVE]	271
99 / p. 236		Residence Inn by Marriott-Dallas Park Central	◇◇◇	$79-$139	276
100 / p. 236		Country Inn & Suites-Dallas NW - see color ad p 260	◇◇◇	$69-$89	263
102 / p. 236		Homewood Suites by Hilton	◇◇◇	$59-$139	270
		DALLAS NORTH - Restaurants			
35 / p. 236		Mediterraneo	◇◇◇◇	$17-$34	282
40 / p. 236		Mario & Alberto's	◇◇	$8-$14	282
41 / p. 236		India Palace Restaurant & Bar	◇◇	$9-$13	281
43 / p. 236		Tupinamba	◇◇	$8-$12	284
44 / p. 236		Gloria's Restaurant	◇◇	$9-$13	280
45 / p. 236		Popolos	◇◇◇	$19-$21	283
46 / p. 236		Dickey's	◇	$7-$13	280
47 / p. 236		Yoli's Seafood & Grill	◇	$10-$15	284
49 / p. 236	AAA	**Royal Tokyo Japanese Restaurant**	◇◇	$16-$25	283
50 / p. 236		Gershwin's	◇◇◇	$17-$31	280
51 / p. 236		Old San Francisco Steak House	◇◇◇	$10-$28	282
52 / p. 236		Trail Dust Steak House	◇	$9-$22	284
53 / p. 236		Mercado Juarez	◇	$9-$20	282
56 / p. 236		Il Sorrento	◇◇◇	$12-$25	281
57 / p. 236		El Fenix	◇◇	$8-$12	280
58 / p. 236		Celebration	◇◇	$9-$17	279
59 / p. 236		Hofstetter's Spargel Cafe	◇◇	$14-$22	281
60 / p. 236		Dunston's Steak House	◇	$10-$25	280
61 / p. 236		City Cafe	◇◇◇	$14-$21	279
62 / p. 236		Mo Mo's Italian Specialties	◇◇	$13-$16	282
63 / p. 236		Kuby's Sausage House	◇	$10-$12	281
64 / p. 236		Peggy Sue Barbeque	◇◇	$5-$7	283

Spotter/Map Page Number	OA	**DALLAS NORTH** - Restaurants (continued)	Diamond Rating	Rate Range High Season	Listing Page
65 / p. 236		Bob's Steak & Chop House	◆◆◆	$23-$40	279
67 / p. 236		The Riviera	◆◆◆◆	$25-$38	283
68 / p. 236		Kostas Cafe	◆◆	$11-$20	281
69 / p. 236		Zu Zu	◆	$6-$8	284
70 / p. 236		Campisi's Egyptian	◆	$10-$21	279
71 / p. 236		Patrizio	◆◆◆	$13-$18	283
72 / p. 236		La Madeleine French Bakery & Cafe-SMU	◆	$7-$11	282
73 / p. 236		Jason's Deli	◆	$5-$8	281
75 / p. 236		Kalachandji's Garden Restaurant	◆	$7-$11	281
76 / p. 236		Aw Shucks	◆	$6-$10	279
77 / p. 236		Ciudad	◆◆◆◆	$16-$29	280
78 / p. 236		Snuffer's	◆	$7-$9	283
79 / p. 236		Javier's Restaurante	◆◆	$13-$19	281
80 / p. 236		St Martin's	◆◆◆	$14-$23	283
81 / p. 236		Sipango	◆◆◆	$10-$21	283
82 / p. 236		Blue Goose Cantina	◆◆	$9-$20	279
84 / p. 236		Terilli's	◆◆	$11-$23	284
85 / p. 236		La Madeleine French Bakery & Cafe-Lemmon	◆	$9-$13	282
86 / p. 236		Mia's Tex-Mex Restaurant	◆◆	$8-$12	282
87 / p. 236	AAA	**The Mansion On Turtle Creek Restaurant**	◆◆◆◆◆	$26-$56	282
88 / p. 236		Chip's	◆	$6-$8	279
89 / p. 236		Sonny Bryan's	◆	$6-$10(L)	283
90 / p. 236		Uncle Julio's	◆◆	$9-$20	284
91 / p. 236		Cuba Libre	◆◆	$9-$18	280
92 / p. 236		Good Eats	◆◆	$9-$16	280
93 / p. 236		Chez Gerard	◆◆◆	$16-$20	279
94 / p. 236		Dixie House	◆	$8-$13	280
95 / p. 236		La Dolce Vita	◆◆	$8-$21	281
97 / p. 236		The Grape	◆◆◆	$11-$28	280
98 / p. 236		Ninfa's	◆◆	$7-$15	282
99 / p. 236		Star Canyon	◆◆◆◆	$20-$29	283
100 / p. 236		Abacus	◆◆◆◆	$20-$45	279
101 / p. 236		Kirby's Steakhouse	◆◆◆	$22-$39	281
		IRVING - Lodgings			
103 / p. 236	AAA	**Country Inn & Suites-DFW Airport South -** see color ad p 260	◆◆◆	$59 [SAVE]	299
104 / p. 236		MainStay Suites Hotel DFW Airport South	◆◆◆	$79-$109	301
105 / p. 236	AAA	**Holiday Inn Select DFW Airport South -** see ad p 268	◆◆◆	$79-$109 [SAVE]	301
106 / p. 236		Hampton Inn-DFW Airport	◆◆◆	$93-$119	300
107 / p. 236	AAA	**AmeriSuites (Dallas/DFW Airport South) -** see color ad p 251	◆◆◆	$79-$109 [SAVE]	297

Spotter/Map Page Number	OA	IRVING - Lodgings (continued)	Diamond Rating	Rate Range High Season	Listing Page
108 / p. 236	AAA	**Drury Inn & Suites - DFW Airport**	◆◆◆	$73-$103 SAVE	299
109 / p. 236		Best Western Irving Inn & Suites DFW Airport	◆◆◆	$70-$78	297
110 / p. 236		Staybridge Suites Dallas-Las Colinas	◆◆◆	$119-$149	303
111 / p. 236	AAA	La Quinta Inn-DFW-South - see color ad p 272	◆◆◆	$69-$99 SAVE	301
112 / p. 236		Motel 6/DFW Airport South #1476	◆◆	$39-$55	302
113 / p. 236		Microtel Inn & Suites-Texas Stadium	◆◆	$50-$89	302
114 / p. 236		Dallas Las Colinas TownePlace Suites	◆◆◆	$80	299
115 / p. 236		Country Inn & Suites By Carlson - see color ad p 260	◆◆	$85-$119	298
116 / p. 236		Clarion Inn & Suites at DFW Airport	◆◆◆	$69-$159	298
117 / p. 236	AAA	AmeriSuites (Dallas Las Colinas/Walnut Hill) - see color ad p 251	◆◆◆	$115-$119 SAVE	297
118 / p. 236	AAA	Wellesley Inn & Suites (Dallas/Las Colinas) - see color ad p 250	◆◆◆	$79 SAVE	303
119 / p. 236	AAA	**Wingate Inn DFW**	◆◆◆	$59-$109 SAVE	303
120 / p. 236		Candlewood Las Colinas	◆◆◆	$95-$114	298
121 / p. 236		Hilton Garden Inn Las Colinas	◆◆◆	$159-$169	301
122 / p. 236	AAA	La Quinta Inn & Suites DFW Airport North - see color ad p 272	◆◆◆	$69-$129 SAVE	301
123 / p. 236	AAA	**Red Roof Inn/DFW Airport North**	◆◆	$39-$63 SAVE	302
124 / p. 236		Comfort Inn DFW Airport - see color ad p 234	◆◆	$59-$75	298
125 / p. 236		Hearthside by Villager	◆◆	$39-$109	300
126 / p. 236		Residence Inn by Marriott-DFW/Irving	◆◆◆	$139-$179	303
127 / p. 236	AAA	**Dallas Marriott Las Colinas**	◆◆◆	$79-$229 SAVE	299
128 / p. 236		Microtel Inn & Suites	◆◆	$46-$55	302
129 / p. 236	AAA	**Fairfield Inn by Marriott-Las Colinas**	◆◆◆	$79-$84 SAVE	300
130 / p. 236		Fairfield Inn by Marriott	◆◆◆	$51-$75	300
131 / p. 236		Motel 6 #1274 DFW North	◆◆	$39-$55	302
132 / p. 236		Marriott Hotel-DFW Airport	◆◆◆	$89-$189	302
133 / p. 236		Harvey Suites-DFW Airport	◆◆◆	$110-$152	300
134 / p. 236	AAA	**Harvey Hotel-DFW Airport**	◆◆◆	$130-$170 SAVE	300
135 / p. 236	AAA	**Holiday Inn Select-DFW Airport-North**	◆◆◆	$155-$165 SAVE	301
136 / p. 236		Sheraton Grand Hotel	◆◆◆	$112	303
137 / p. 236		Days Inn DFW North	◆◆◆	$59-$70	299
138 / p. 236	AAA	**Comfort Suites in Las Colinas**	◆◆◆	$119 SAVE	298
139 / p. 236		Shoney's Inn & Suites	◆◆	$45-$60	303
140 / p. 236		Courtyard by Marriott-Las Colinas	◆◆	$99-$150	299
141 / p. 236		Residence Inn by Marriott at Las Colinas	◆◆◆	$139-$149	302
142 / p. 236	AAA	AmeriSuites (Dallas Las Colinas/Hidden Ridge) - see color ad p 251	◆◆◆	$115-$120 SAVE	297
143 / p. 236	AAA	**Wyndham Garden Hotel-Las Colinas**	◆◆◆	$79-$139 SAVE	304
144 / p. 236		Homestead Studio Suites Hotel-Las Colinas	◆◆	$60-$79	301
145 / p. 236	AAA	**Omni Mandalay Hotel at Las Colinas**	◆◆◆◆	$87-$219 SAVE	302

Spotter/Map Page Number	OA	IRVING - Lodgings (continued)	Diamond Rating	Rate Range High Season	Listing Page
146 / p. 236		Comfort Suites DFW Airport	◆◆◆	$60	298
147 / p. 236		Four Seasons Resort & Club	◆◆◆◆	$335-$435	300
148 / p. 236	AAA	Comfort Inn DFW Airport South - see color ad p 263	◆◆◆	$69-$99 [SAVE]	298
150 / p. 236		Embassy Suites-DFW South - see color ad p 267	◆◆◆	$109-$219	299
151 / p. 236		Radisson Hotel-DFW Airport South - see color ad p 275	[fyi]	$89-$99	304
152 / p. 236		Wingate Inn-Las Colinas	◆◆◆	$69-$119	303
153 / p. 236		Super 8 Motel-Irving	◆◆	$49-$64	303
		IRVING - Restaurants			
105 / p. 236		I Fratelli Italian Restaurant	◆◆	$8-$13	304
106 / p. 236		BD's Mongolian Barbeque at Los Colinas	◆◆	$9-$13	304
107 / p. 236		Via Real	◆◆◆	$10-$35	305
108 / p. 236		LaMargarita	◆	$6-$12	304
109 / p. 236		Rockfish Seafood Grill	◆◆	$11-$15	304
110 / p. 236		Spring Creek Barbeque	◆	$9-$11	304
112 / p. 236		Texadelphia	◆	$5-$8	305
113 / p. 236		Thai Chili	◆◆	$10-$20	305
114 / p. 236		Veranda Greek Cafe	◆◆	$12-$17	305
		FARMERS BRANCH - Lodgings			
160 / p. 236	AAA	Omni Dallas Hotel Parkwest	◆◆◆◆	$89-$199 [SAVE]	294
161 / p. 236	AAA	Renaissance Dallas North Hotel - see color ad p 275	◆◆◆	$69-$170 [SAVE]	294
162 / p. 236	AAA	Comfort Inn of North Dallas	◆◆	$55-$120 [SAVE]	292
164 / p. 236	AAA	Days Inn - North Dallas	◆◆	$49-$59 [SAVE]	292
165 / p. 236		Hilton Dallas Parkway	◆◆◆	$125-$155	293
166 / p. 236		Best Western Dallas North	◆◆	$50-$69	292
168 / p. 236		Doubletree Club Dallas-Farmers Branch	◆◆◆	$59-$129	293
169 / p. 236		Holiday Inn Select North Dallas - see ad p 293	◆◆◆	$89-$159	293
170 / p. 236	AAA	La Quinta Inn-Dallas-Northwest-Farmers Branch - see color ad p 272	◆◆◆	$59-$89 [SAVE]	294
		CARROLLTON - Lodgings			
174 / p. 236	AAA	Red Roof Inn-Carrollton	◆◆	$33-$49 [SAVE]	289
		CARROLLTON - Restaurant			
120 / p. 236		Tia's Tex & Mex	◆	$7-$15	289
		ADDISON - Lodgings			
180 / p. 236		Addison Quorum Courtyard By Marriott	◆◆◆	$56-$134	285
181 / p. 236		Crowne Plaza North Dallas/Addison Near the Galleria	◆◆◆	$69-$119	285
182 / p. 236		Inter-Continental Hotel Dallas	◆◆◆	$109-$235	286
183 / p. 236		Dallas Addison Marriott Quorum	◆◆◆	$159-$189	285
185 / p. 236		Country Inn & Suites By Carlson - see color ad p 260	◆◆◆	$89-$109	285
186 / p. 236		MainStay Suites Addison	◆◆◆	$54-$89	286
187 / p. 236		Wingate Inn-Addison/North Dallas	◆◆◆	$119	286

Spotter/Map Page Number	OA	ADDISON - Lodgings (continued)	Diamond Rating	Rate Range High Season	Listing Page
189 / p. 236		Hilton Garden Inn-Addison	◆◆◆	$59-$89	286
190 / p. 236		Holiday Inn Express	◆◆◆	$105-$115	286
191 / p. 236		Homewood Suites by Hilton	◆◆◆	$119-$149	286
192 / p. 236		Hampton Inn	◆◆◆	$71-$81	285
193 / p. 236		Courtyard by Marriott-Addison/Midway	◆◆◆	$59-$99	285
195 / p. 236		Quality Suites-Addison (now known as Comfort Suites)	◆◆◆	$89-$129	286
		ADDISON - Restaurants			
128 / p. 236		Lombardi Mare	◆◆◆	$16-$25	287
129 / p. 236		Thai Orchid Restaurant	◆◆	$12-$20	288
130 / p. 236		Lawry's The Prime Rib	◆◆◆	$22-$31	287
131 / p. 236		Tokyo One	◆◆	$22	288
132 / p. 236		Jasmine Restaurant	◆◆◆	$9-$24	287
133 / p. 236		Cantina Laredo-Addison	◆◆	$7-$14	287
135 / p. 236		Remington's Seafood Grill	◆◆	$9-$16	288
136 / p. 236		Fogo de Chao	◆◆◆	$39	287
137 / p. 236		Snuffer's	◆	$6-$8	288
139 / p. 236		Magic Time Machine	◆◆	$11-$26	287
140 / p. 236		Blue Mesa Grill	◆◆	$9-$15	287
141 / p. 236		Copeland's	◆◆◆	$10-$21	287
142 / p. 236		August Moon	◆◆	$9-$20	287
143 / p. 236		Addison Cafe	◆◆◆	$13-$20	286
145 / p. 236		Mi Piaci	◆◆◆	$11-$35	288
146 / p. 236		Dovie's	◆◆◆	$13-$21	287
		RICHARDSON - Lodgings			
200 / p. 236		Bradford Homesuites	◆◆◆	$79-$119	314
201 / p. 236	AAA	Renaissance Dallas-Richardson Hotel - see color ad p 256	◆◆◆◆	$135-$259 SAVE	316
202 / p. 236		Residence Inn by Marriott Richardson	◆◆◆	$99-$159	316
203 / p. 236		Sleep Inn	◆◆	$55-$59	316
205 / p. 236	AAA	The Radisson Hotel Dallas North At Richardson	◆◆◆	$62-$92 SAVE	315
206 / p. 236		Omni Richardson Hotel	◆◆◆	$62-$117	315
207 / p. 236		ClubHouse Inn & Suites Richardson	◆◆◆	$79-$119	314
209 / p. 236		Holiday Inn Select	◆◆◆	$89-$129	315
210 / p. 236		Hampton Inn	◆◆◆	$59-$69	315
211 / p. 236	AAA	Comfort Inn	◆◆◆	$65 SAVE	315
212 / p. 236		Courtyard By Marriott-Richardson at Spring Valley	◆◆◆	$99-$119	315
		RICHARDSON - Restaurants			
157 / p. 236		Hong Kong Royale Seafood Restaurant	◆	$7-$17	316
159 / p. 236		Spring Creek Barbeque	◆	$7-$10	316
		GARLAND - Lodgings			
220 / p. 236	AAA	Microtel Inn & Suites	◆◆	$40-$85 SAVE	295

Spotter/Map Page Number	OA	GARLAND - Lodgings (continued)	Diamond Rating	Rate Range High Season	Listing Page
221 / p. 236		Super 8 Motel	◆◆	$53-$63	295
222 / p. 236	AAA	Holiday Inn Select LBJ NE (Garland) - see color ad p 295	◆◆◆	$89-$99 SAVE	295
223 / p. 236	AAA	La Quinta Inn-Dallas-LBJ Northeast-Garland - see color ad p 272	◆◆◆	$64-$89 SAVE	295
225 / p. 236		Days Inn-Dallas Garland	◆◆◆	$45-$60	294
226 / p. 236	AAA	Comfort Inn	◆◆◆	$55-$59 SAVE	294
227 / p. 236		Days Inn-Dallas/Garland	◆◆	$47-$49	295
229 / p. 236	AAA	Best Western Lakeview Inn	◆◆◆	$59-$79 SAVE	294
		PLANO - Lodgings			
240 / p. 236		Courtyard by Marriott	◆◆◆	$129-$189	311
241 / p. 236		Residence Inn by Marriott Dallas/Plano	◆◆◆	$129-$199	313
242 / p. 236	AAA	AmeriSuites (Dallas/Plano) - see color ad p 251	◆◆◆	$109-$134 SAVE	310
243 / p. 236		Best Western Park Suites Hotel	◆◆◆	$69-$89	310
245 / p. 236		Ramada Limited	◆◆	$39-$59	313
246 / p. 236		Candlewood Suites-Plano	◆◆◆	$89-$122	310
247 / p. 236		Courtyard by Marriott-Plano	◆◆◆	Failed to provide	311
249 / p. 236	AAA	Days Inn & Suites	◆◆◆	$55-$70 SAVE	311
250 / p. 236		Fairfield Inn	◆◆◆	$65-$95	311
251 / p. 236		Hampton Inn Plano	◆◆◆	$89	311
252 / p. 236		Holiday Inn Express	◆◆◆	$55-$75	311
253 / p. 236		Holiday Inn-Plano	◆◆◆	$70-$119	311
255 / p. 236		Homewood Suites by Hilton	◆◆◆	$129	311
257 / p. 236	AAA	La Quinta Inn & Suites-West Plano - see color ad p 272	◆◆◆	$69-$109 SAVE	312
259 / p. 236	AAA	La Quinta Inn-Plano - see color ad p 272	◆◆◆	$59-$89 SAVE	312
260 / p. 236	AAA	MainStay Suites - see color ad p 312	◆◆◆	$69-$89 SAVE	312
261 / p. 236		Motel 6 - 1121	◆◆	$41-$57	313
262 / p. 236	AAA	Red Roof Inn Dallas-Plano	◆◆	$38-$55 SAVE	313
263 / p. 236	AAA	Sleep Inn Plano - see ad p 312	◆◆	$50-$70 SAVE	313
265 / p. 236		Super 8 Motel-Plano	◆◆	$45-$59	313
266 / p. 236	AAA	Wellesley Inn & Suites (Dallas/Plano) - see color ad p 250	◆◆◆	$80-$89 SAVE	313
		PLANO - Restaurants			
168 / p. 236		Abuelo's Mexican Food Embassy	◆◆	$10-$20	313
169 / p. 236		Abuelo's Mexican Food Embassy	◆◆	$11-$20	313
170 / p. 236		Martinez Cafe	◆	$7-$19	314
172 / p. 236		Fishmongers Seafood Market & Cafe	◆	$9-$20	314
173 / p. 236		Osaka Sushi	◆◆	$24	314

Spotter/Map Page Number	OA	ALLEN - Lodgings	Diamond Rating	Rate Range High Season	Listing Page
272 / p. 236	AAA	AmeriHost Inn-Allen	▽▽▽	$74-$84 SAVE	288
		ALLEN - Restaurants			
184 / p. 236		Samui Thai Cuisine	▽▽	$10-$14	289
186 / p. 236		Brazos Cattle Company	▽▽	$9-$21	289
		LEWISVILLE - Lodgings			
281 / p. 236	AAA	Baymont Inn & Suites - see color ad p 305	▽▽▽	$89-$119 SAVE	305
282 / p. 236		Fairfield Inn-Lewisville	▽▽▽	$74-$94	306
283 / p. 236		Courtyard by Marriott-Lewisville	▽▽▽	$99-$114	306
284 / p. 236		Best Western Inn & Suites - see ad p 306	▽▽▽	$90	306
285 / p. 236	AAA	Microtel Inn & Suites	▽▽	$45-$60 SAVE	307
287 / p. 236	AAA	Comfort Suites	▽▽▽	$69-$99 SAVE	306
289 / p. 236		Homewood Suites by Hilton	▽▽▽	$119-$169	307
291 / p. 236		Country Inn & Suites By Carlson - see color ad p 260	▽▽▽	$69-$99	306
292 / p. 236		Days Inn	▽▽	$40-$46	306
293 / p. 236	AAA	Hampton Inn	▽▽▽	$79-$85 SAVE	307
295 / p. 236		Howard Johnson	▽▽▽	$68	307
296 / p. 236	AAA	La Quinta Inn-Dallas-Lewisville - see color ad p 272	▽▽▽	$69-$94 SAVE	307
297 / p. 236		Motel 6	▽▽	$35-$49	307
298 / p. 236		Residence Inn	▽▽▽	$120	307
299 / p. 236		Super 8-Lewisville/Dallas North/Airport	▽▽	$45-$75	307
		LEWISVILLE - Restaurant			
195 / p. 236		China Dragon Super Buffet	▽	$6-$16	308
		HIGHLAND PARK - Restaurant			
199 / p. 236		Cafe Pacific	▽▽▽	$14-$26	297

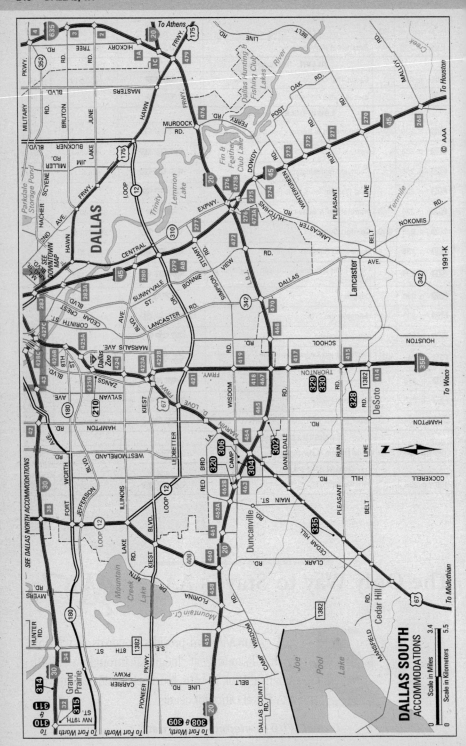

DALLAS SOUTH
ACCOMMODATIONS

Dallas South and Vicinity

This index helps you "spot" where approved accommodations and restaurants are located on the corresponding detailed maps. Lodging rate ranges are for comparison only and show the property's high season; rates are per night, unless only weekly (W) rates are available. Restaurant rate range is for dinner, unless only lunch (L) is served. Turn to the listing page for more detailed rate information and consult display ads for special promotions.

Spotter/Map Page Number	OA	DALLAS SOUTH - Lodgings	Diamond Rating	Rate Range High Season	Listing Page
302 / p. 248		Comfort Inn South	◈◈◈	$66-$86	284
304 / p. 248		Lexington Hotel Suites	◈◈	$80-$160	284
306 / p. 248		Best Western Inn	◈◈	$50-$65	284
		DALLAS SOUTH - Restaurant			
210 / p. 248		La Calle Doce	◈◈	$6-$13	285
		GRAND PRAIRIE - Lodgings			
308 / p. 248	◬	**Quality Inn & Suites**	◈◈◈	$75-$90 SAVE	296
309 / p. 248		Comfort Inn	◈◈	$65-$89	296
310 / p. 248	◬	**Comfort Suites DFW Airport South**	◈◈◈	$79-$119 SAVE	296
311 / p. 248		Hampton Inn Arlington/DFW Airport Area	◈◈◈	$79-$99	296
314 / p. 248		Motel 6 - 446	◈◈	$39-$55	296
315 / p. 248	◬	**La Quinta Inn-Dallas-Grand Prairie (Six Flags) - see color ad p 272**	◈◈◈	$59-$95 SAVE	296
		DUNCANVILLE - Lodgings			
320 / p. 248		Ramada Inn-Dallas Southwest	◈◈	$55-$59	292
		DESOTO - Lodgings			
328 / p. 248	◬	**Best Western of Desoto**	◈◈◈	$70-$96 SAVE	291
329 / p. 248		Holiday Inn	◈◈◈	$71-$84	291
330 / p. 248	◬	**Red Roof Inn Dallas/DeSoto**	◈◈	$39-$54 SAVE	292
		CEDAR HILL - Lodgings			
335 / p. 248	◬	**Ramada Limited**	◈◈	$59-$79 SAVE	289

DOWNTOWN DALLAS   (See map p. 234; index p. 235)

―――――― WHERE TO STAY ――――――

ADAM'S MARK HOTEL
Phone: 214/922-8000 [8]

2/1-3/22	1P: $197-$249	2P: $197-$249	XP: $20	F17
9/7-1/31	1P: $182-$249	2P: $182-$249	XP: $20	F17
3/23-6/14	1P: $182-$239	2P: $182-$239	XP: $20	F17
6/15-9/6	1P: $153-$219	2P: $153-$219	XP: $20	F17

Large-scale Hotel Location: Live Oak and Olive sts, just w off Central Expwy. 400 N Olive St 75201. Fax: 214/777-6532. **Facility:** 1841 units. 1598 one-bedroom standard units. 220 one- and 23 two-bedroom suites, some with whirlpools. 26-36 stories, interior corridors. *Bath:* combo or shower only. **Parking:** on-site (fee) and valet. **Terms:** cancellation fee imposed, package plans. **Amenities:** dual phone lines, voice mail, irons, hair dryers. *Fee:* video games, high-speed Internet. **Dining:** 4 restaurants, 6:30 am-10:30 pm, cocktails, entertainment. **Pool(s):** heated outdoor, heated indoor. **Leisure Activities:** saunas, whirlpools. **Guest Services:** gift shop, valet and coin laundry. **Business Services:** conference facilities, business center. **Cards:** AX, CB, DC, JC, MC, VI. **Special Amenities:** early check-in/late check-out and preferred room (subject to availability with advanced reservations).

SOME UNITS

🆂🅳 🍽 24 🍸 🄰 🏊 📠 📺 📠 💻 / ⊠ ☎ /
FEE

THE ADOLPHUS
Phone: (214)742-8200 [10]

All Year   1P: $149-$325   2P: $164-$340   XP: $15   F12

Location: Corner of Commerce and Aband sts. 1321 Commerce St 75202. Fax: 214/651-3588. **Facility:** Built in 1912, this ornate hotel founded by the famous beer baron Adolphus Busch is a city landmark. 428 units. 404 one-bedroom standard units. 23 one- and 1 two-bedroom suites ($750-$2750), some with kitchens. 22 stories, interior corridors. *Bath:* combo or shower only. **Parking:** valet. **Terms:** 7 day cancellation notice, pets ($250 deposit). **Amenities:** dual phone lines, voice mail, honor bars, irons, hair dryers. **Dining:** The French Room, see separate listing. **Leisure Activities:** exercise room. *Fee:* massage. **Guest Services:** gift shop, valet laundry, area transportation. **Business Services:** conference facilities, business center. **Cards:** AX, CB, DC, DS, JC, MC, VI.

SOME UNITS

(ASK) 🆂🅳 🐾 🍽 24 🚗 🍸 🄼 🖐 🄰 📺 📠 📶 💻 / ⊠ ☎ /

AMERISUITES (DALLAS/WEST END)
Phone: (214)999-0500 [15]

All Year   1P: $149-$169   2P: $149-$169   XP: $10   F18

Location: I-35, exit Commerce St, just e, then just n. Located in the historic district. 1907 N Lamar St 75202. Fax: 214/999-0501. **Facility:** 149 one-bedroom standard units. 10 stories, interior corridors. **Parking:** valet. **Terms:** [ECP] meal plan available, small pets only. **Amenities:** video games (fee), voice mail, irons, hair dryers. *Some:* dual phone lines. **Pool(s):** small heated outdoor. **Leisure Activities:** exercise room. **Guest Services:** valet and coin laundry. **Business Services:** meeting rooms, fax (fee). **Cards:** AX, CB, DC, DS, MC, VI. **Special Amenities:** free continental breakfast and free newspaper. (See color ad p 251)

SOME UNITS

🆂🅳 🐾 🍽 🚗 🄰 📠 📶 📠 💻 / ⊠ /

(See map p. 234)

BEST WESTERN MARKET CENTER
SAVE
♦♦♦♦
Small-scale Hotel

All Year [ECP]   1P: $59-$105   2P: $64-$110   XP: $10
Phone: (214)741-9000   **2**
F17
Location: I-35 E, exit 430D (Market Center Blvd), 0.3 mi w. 2023 Market Center Blvd 75207. Fax: 214/741-6100.
Facility: 98 one-bedroom standard units. 3 stories, interior/exterior corridors. **Parking:** on-site. **Terms:** cancellation fee imposed. **Amenities:** high-speed Internet, voice mail, safes, irons, hair dryers. **Pool(s):** outdoor. **Leisure Activities:** whirlpool. **Guest Services:** valet and coin laundry. **Business Services:** meeting rooms, fax (fee). **Cards:** AX, CB, DC, DS, JC, MC, VI.

SOME UNITS

BRADFORD HOMESUITES
♦♦♦♦
Small-scale Hotel

All Year [CP]   1P: $79-$109   2P: $79-$109
Phone: (972)726-9990
Location: North Dallas Tollway, exit Keller Springs, just s on north access road. 16060 North Dallas Tollway 75248. Fax: 972/726-0165. **Facility:** 131 units. 109 one-bedroom standard units with efficiencies. 22 one-bedroom suites with efficiencies. 3 stories, interior corridors. *Bath:* combo or shower only. **Parking:** on-site. **Terms:** cancellation fee imposed. **Amenities:** video games (fee), dual phone lines, voice mail, irons, hair dryers. **Pool(s):** outdoor. **Leisure Activities:** whirlpool, exercise room. **Guest Services:** sundries, complimentary evening beverages: Wed, valet and coin laundry. **Business Services:** fax (fee). **Cards:** AX, CB, DC, DS, JC, MC, VI.

SOME UNITS

BRADFORD HOMESUITES DOWNTOWN
♦♦♦
Small-scale Hotel

All Year [CP]   1P: $89-$129   2P: $89-$129
Phone: (214)965-9990   **21**
Location: I-35, exit 430A (Oaklawn), just n to Harry Hines Blvd, 0.6 mi s. 2914 Harry Hines Blvd 75201. Fax: 214/965-9996. **Facility:** 146 units. 95 one-bedroom standard units with efficiencies. 51 one-bedroom suites with efficiencies. 4 stories, interior corridors. *Bath:* combo or shower only. **Parking:** on-site. **Terms:** cancellation fee imposed. **Amenities:** video games (fee), dual phone lines, voice mail, irons, hair dryers. **Pool(s):** outdoor. **Leisure Activities:** whirlpool, exercise room. **Guest Services:** sundries, complimentary evening beverages: Wed, valet and coin laundry, area transportation. **Business Services:** meeting rooms, business center. **Cards:** AX, DC, DS, MC, VI.

SOME UNITS

(See map p. 234)

COURTYARD BY MARRIOTT-MARKET CENTER
AAA SAVE
▼▼▼▼
Small-scale Hotel

Phone: (214)653-1166   **5**

All Year   1P: $119-$169   2P: $119-$169
Location: Se off I-35 E and US 77, exit 430B (Market Center Blvd). 2150 Market Center Blvd 75207. Fax: 214/653-1892. **Facility:** Designated smoking area. 184 units. 171 one-bedroom standard units. 13 one-bedroom suites ($179-$189). 5 stories, interior corridors. **Parking:** on-site. **Terms:** 19% service charge. **Amenities:** high-speed Internet (fee), voice mail, irons, hair dryers. **Dining:** 6:30 am-10:30 & 5-10 pm, cocktails. **Pool(s):** heated outdoor. **Leisure Activities:** whirlpool, exercise room. **Guest Services:** valet and coin laundry. **Business Services:** meeting rooms, fax (fee). **Cards:** AX, CB, DC, DS, MC, VI. **Special Amenities:** free newspaper.

SOME UNITS
🍴 ⊘ 🏊 📷 📠 💻 / ✕ 🖥 /

FAIRFIELD INN MARKET CENTER
SAVE
▼▼▼
Small-scale Hotel

Phone: 214/760-8800   **6**

All Year [ECP]   1P: $49-$119   2P: $54-$124
Location: I-35, exit 438 (Market Center Blvd), 1 mi ne. 2110 Market Center Blvd 75207. Fax: 214/760-1659. **Facility:** 117 one-bedroom standard units. 3 stories, interior corridors. *Bath:* combo or shower only. **Parking:** on-site. **Terms:** cancellation fee imposed, weekly rates available. **Amenities:** high-speed Internet (fee), irons, hair dryers. **Pool(s):** small heated indoor. **Guest Services:** valet and coin laundry. **Business Services:** meeting rooms, fax (fee). **Cards:** AX, CB, DC, DS, JC, MC, VI.

SOME UNITS
🍴 ♿ ⊘ 🏊 📠 📶 / ✕ 🖥 /

THE FAIRMONT DALLAS
▼▼▼ ◆◆◆◆
Large-scale Hotel

Phone: (214)720-2020   **17**
XP: $30   F

All Year   1P: $129-$279   2P: $159-$309
Location: Corner of Ross Ave and N Akard St. 1717 N Akard St 75201. Fax: 214/720-5269. **Facility:** Central to the arts, finance and entertainment districts, this hotel offers 77,000 square feet of meeting space. 550 units. 500 one-bedroom standard units. 50 one-bedroom suites. 24 stories, interior corridors. *Bath:* combo or shower only. **Parking:** valet. **Terms:** small pets only ($25 fee). **Amenities:** video games (fee), dual phone lines, voice mail, safes, honor bars, irons, hair dryers. *Some:* fax. **Dining:** The Pyramid Grill, see separate listing. **Pool(s):** outdoor. **Leisure Activities:** exercise room. **Guest Services:** gift shop, valet laundry, area transportation. **Business Services:** conference facilities, business center. **Cards:** AX, CB, DC, DS, JC, MC, VI.

SOME UNITS
A$K S🔒 ✚ 🐾 🍴 24🕐 Ⓨ 🍷M 🔌 ⊘ 🏊 📠 📶 / ✕ 🖥 💻 /
FEE

HAMPTON INN WEST END
SAVE
▼▼▼
Small-scale Hotel

Phone: (214)742-5678   **16**

All Year [ECP]   1P: $69-$149   2P: $79-$159
Location: Near Historic West End District. 1015 Elm St 75202. Fax: 214/744-6167. **Facility:** 311 one-bedroom standard units. 19 stories, interior corridors. *Bath:* combo or shower only. **Parking:** on-site (fee). **Terms:** cancellation fee imposed. **Amenities:** video games (fee), voice mail, irons, hair dryers. **Pool(s):** outdoor. **Leisure Activities:** exercise room. **Guest Services:** valet and coin laundry. **Business Services:** meeting rooms, fax (fee). **Cards:** AX, DC, DS, MC, VI.

SOME UNITS
S🔒 🍴 ♿ 🏊 📷 📶 💻 / ✕ 🖥 💻 /

HOLIDAY INN-ARISTOCRAT HOTEL
▼▼▼▼
Historic
Small-scale Hotel

Phone: (214)741-7700   **9**
XP: $10   F16

All Year   1P: $119-$189   2P: $129-$199
Location: Corner of Main and Harwood sts. 1933 Main St 75201. Fax: 214/939-3639. **Facility:** 172 units. 99 one-bedroom standard units. 73 one-bedroom suites ($189-$209). 14 stories, interior corridors. **Parking:** on-site (fee). **Terms:** 3 day cancellation notice-fee imposed, 20% service charge. **Amenities:** dual phone lines, voice mail, honor bars, irons, hair dryers. *Fee:* video games, high-speed Internet. **Leisure Activities:** exercise room. **Guest Services:** valet laundry, area transportation. **Business Services:** meeting rooms, fax (fee). **Cards:** AX, CB, DC, DS, JC, MC, VI. *(See ad p 254)*

SOME UNITS
A$K S🔒 🍴 Ⓨ ⊘ 📷 📶 💻 / ✕ /

(See map p. 234)

HOTEL CRESCENT COURT　　　　　　　　　　　　　　　　**Phone: (214)871-3200**　[20]
▼▼▼▼ ▼▼▼▼　All Year　　　　1P: $370-$2500　　2P: $370-$2500　　XP: $40　　　F18
　　　　　　　Location: Corner of Crescent Ct and McKinney Ave; uptown. 400 Crescent Ct 75201. **Fax:** 214/871-3272. **Facility:** A
Large-scale Hotel　stately gray limestone building houses this full-service hotel; notable are the health club and elegant common
　　　　　　　areas. 220 units. 191 one-bedroom standard units. 26 one- and 3 two-bedroom suites ($700-$2500), some
with kitchens. 8 stories, interior corridors. **Parking:** on-site (fee) and valet. **Terms:** cancellation fee imposed, package plans.
Amenities: video library, video games, CD players, dual phone lines, voice mail, fax, safes, irons, hair dryers. *Some:* DVD
players. **Dining:** Beau Nash, see separate listing. **Pool(s):** heated outdoor. **Leisure Activities:** saunas, whirlpools, steamrooms,
spa. **Guest Services:** gift shop, valet laundry, area transportation. **Business Services:** conference facilities, business center.
Cards: AX, CB, DC, DS, JC, MC, VI.

SOME UNITS
[icons]

HOTEL ST. GERMAIN　　　　　　　　　　　　　　　　　**Phone: (214)871-2516**　[7]
(AAA) [SAVE]　All Year [ECP]　　　1P: $290-$650　　2P: $290-$650
▼▼▼▼ ▼▼▼▼　**Location:** Woodall Rogers Pkwy, exit Pearl St, 0.3 mi n. 2516 Maple Ave 75201. **Fax:** r14/871-0740. **Facility:** This
　　　　　　　Victorian home features two guest rooms with balconies and fireplaces; phone for seasonal closures. 7 one-
Historic　　　bedroom standard units, some with whirlpools. 3 stories (no elevator), interior corridors. *Bath:* combo or
Country Inn　shower only. **Parking:** valet. **Terms:** check-in 4 pm, 7 day cancellation notice-fee imposed, package plans,
　　　　　　　20% service charge, pets ($50 extra charge). **Amenities:** video library (fee), CD players, honor bars, hair
dryers. *Some:* fax. **Dining:** dining room, see separate listing. **Guest Services:** valet laundry. **Business Services:** meeting rooms. **Cards:** AX, MC, VI. **Special Amenities:** free continental breakfast and free newspaper.

[icons]

HYATT REGENCY DALLAS AT REUNION　　　　　　　　**Phone: (214)651-1234**　[11]
(AAA) [SAVE]　2/1-5/14 & 9/16-1/31　　1P: $109-$245　　2P: $109-$245　　XP: $25　　F18
　　　　　　　5/15-9/15　　　　　　1P: $95-$199　　　2P: $95-$199　　　XP: $25　　F18
▼▼▼▼ ▼▼▼▼　**Location:** Just e of I-35 E and US 77, exit Reunion Blvd; just n of I-30, exit Commerce St eastbound. 300 Reunion Blvd
Large-scale Hotel　75207. **Fax:** 214/742-8126. **Facility:** Convention facility. 1122 units. 1081 one-bedroom standard units. 15
　　　　　　　one- and 26 two-bedroom suites. 28 stories, interior corridors. *Bath:* combo or shower only. **Parking:** on-site
(fee) and valet. **Terms:** cancellation fee imposed. **Amenities:** video games (fee), voice mail, irons, hair
dryers. *Some:* CD players, dual phone lines, fax. **Dining:** 4 restaurants, 6:30 am-midnight, cocktails, also, Antares, see separate
listing. **Pool(s):** small outdoor. **Leisure Activities:** whirlpool, exercise room. **Guest Services:** gift shop, valet laundry, airport
transportation (fee)-Dallas-Fort Worth International & Dallas Love Field airports, area transportation-downtown. **Business Services:** conference facilities, business center. **Cards:** AX, CB, DC, DS, JC, MC, VI. *(See color ad inside front cover)*

SOME UNITS
[icons]
FEE

LE MERIDIEN DALLAS　　　　　　　　　　　　　　　　**Phone: (214)979-9000**　[13]
　▼▼▼▼　All Year　　　　1P: $119-$169　　2P: $119-$169　　XP: $10
　　　　　　　Location: Between San Jacinto and Bryan St, 0.3 mi w of US 75 Central Expwy. Located in Plaza of The Americans
Large-scale Hotel　Complex. 650 N Pearl St 75201. **Fax:** 214/953-1931. **Facility:** 407 units. 404 one-bedroom standard units. 3
　　　　　　　one-bedroom suites, some with kitchens. 14 stories, interior corridors. *Bath:* combo or shower only. **Parking:**
valet. **Terms:** small pets only ($25 deposit). **Amenities:** video games (fee), dual phone lines, voice mail, fax, irons, hair dryers.
Leisure Activities: Fee: massage. **Guest Services:** gift shop, valet laundry, area transportation. **Business Services:** conference facilities, business center. **Cards:** AX, DC, DS, JC, MC, VI.

SOME UNITS
[icons]
FEE　　　FEE

MAGNOLIA HOTEL DALLAS　　　　　　　　　　　　　**Phone: (214)915-6500**　[19]
　▼▼▼▼　All Year [ECP]　　　1P: $239-$389　　2P: $249-$399
　　　　　　　Location: Corner of Commerce and Akard sts. 1401 Commerce St 75201. **Fax:** 214/888-0053. **Facility:** 330 units.
Large-scale Hotel　200 one-bedroom standard units. 130 one-bedroom suites ($289-$499) with kitchens. 28 stories, interior cor-
　　　　　　　ridors. **Parking:** on-site (fee) and valet. **Terms:** 3 day cancellation notice-fee imposed. **Amenities:** video
games, high-speed Internet (fee), dual phone lines, irons, hair dryers. *Some:* CD players. **Leisure Activities:** saunas,
whirlpool, exercise room. **Guest Services:** complimentary evening beverages, valet and coin laundry, area transportation. **Business Services:** meeting rooms. **Cards:** AX, CB, DC, MC, VI.

SOME UNITS
[icons]

Look For Savings

When you pick up a AAA TourBook® guide, look for establishments that display a bright red AAA logo, SAVE icon, and Diamond rating in their listing. These Official Appointment establishments place a high value on the patronage they receive from AAA members. And, by offering members great room rates*, they are willing to go the extra mile to get your business.

So, when you turn to the AAA TourBook guide to make your travel plans, look for the establishments that will give you the special treatment you deserve.

See TourBook Navigator section, page 14, for complete details

(See map p. 234)

THE MELROSE HOTEL   **Phone:** (214)521-5151   **18**

All Year   1P: $144-$196

Small-scale Hotel

Location: I-35 E, exit 430, 0.8 mi n, entrance off Cedar Springs, just n. Located in a quiet area. 3015 Oak Lawn Ave 75219. Fax: 214/521-2470. **Facility:** 184 units. 163 one-bedroom standard units. 21 one-bedroom suites, some with kitchens. 8 stories, interior corridors. **Parking:** on-site (fee). **Terms:** 15% service charge. **Amenities:** dual phone lines, voice mail. safes, honor bars, irons, hair dryers. *Fee:* video games, high-speed Internet. **Dining:** The Landmark Restaurant, see separate listing. **Leisure Activities:** limited exercise equipment. **Guest Services:** gift shop, valet laundry, area transportation. **Business Services:** meeting rooms, fax. **Cards:** AX, CB, DC, DS, JC, MC, VI.

SOME UNITS

(ASK) (SD) 🛏 🍽 24📶 🍸 🏋 🎦 (DATA PORT) 💻 / ⊗ 🔒 /

RAMADA PLAZA HOTEL   **Phone:** (214)421-1083   **12**

AAA SAVE

All Year   1P: $99   2P: $109

Small-scale Hotel

Location: I-30 E, exit 45 (Ervay St); I-30 W, exit 45 to Cadiz-Griffin ramp. 1011 S Akard St 75215. Fax: 214/428-3973. **Facility:** 236 one-bedroom standard units. 12 stories, interior corridors. *Bath:* combo or shower only. **Parking:** on-site. **Terms:** 3 day cancellation notice-fee imposed, [AP] meal plan available. **Amenities:** high-speed Internet, voice mail, irons, hair dryers. **Pool(s):** heated indoor. **Leisure Activities:** whirlpool, exercise room. **Guest Services:** gift shop, valet laundry, airport transportation-Dallas Love Field Airport, area transportation-within 5 mi. **Business Services:** meeting rooms, fax (fee). **Cards:** AX, CB, DC, DS, MC, VI. **Special Amenities: free room upgrade (subject to availability with advanced reservations).**

SOME UNITS

(SD) ✈ 🍽 🍸 ♿ 🗣 🌊 🎣 🎦 (DATA PORT) 💻 / ⊗ (VCR) 🔒 🍴 /
                                                                  FEE FEE FEE

RENAISSANCE DALLAS HOTEL   **Phone:** (214)631-2222   **1**

AAA SAVE

All Year   1P: $79-$189   2P: $79-$199

Large-scale Hotel

Location: Nw off I-35 E and US 77, 0.3 mi nw of exit 430D (Market Center Blvd). 2222 Stemmons Frwy 75207. Fax: 214/905-3814. **Facility:** 518 units. 488 one-bedroom standard units. 30 one-bedroom suites, some with whirlpools. 30 stories, interior corridors. *Bath:* some combo or shower only. **Parking:** on-site. **Terms:** pets (with prior approval). **Amenities:** video games (fee), dual phone lines, voice mail, honor bars, irons, hair dryers. **Dining:** 2 restaurants, 6:30 am-10 pm, cocktails. **Pool(s):** heated outdoor. **Leisure Activities:** sauna, whirlpool. **Guest Services:** gift shop, valet laundry. **Business Services:** conference facilities, business center. **Cards:** AX, CB, DC, DS, JC, MC, VI. **Special Amenities: free newspaper.**

SOME UNITS

(SD) 🛏 🍽 24📶 🍸 🗣 🎣 👥 🎦 (DATA PORT) 💻 / ⊗ (VCR) /
                                                                  FEE

(See map p. 234)

SHERATON SUITES MARKET CENTER-DALLAS
All Year   1P: $115   XP: $10   F17
Phone: (214)747-3000   **3**
▼▼▼▼
Location: Nw off I-35 E and US 77, exit 430D (Market Center Blvd). 2101 Stemmons Frwy 75207. **Fax:** 214/742-5713.
Large-scale Hotel   **Facility:** 251 one-bedroom suites. 11 stories, interior corridors. **Parking:** on-site. **Terms:** pets ($50 deposit).
Amenities: video games (fee), voice mail, irons, hair dryers. *Some:* dual phone lines, fax. **Pool(s):** heated
indoor/outdoor. **Leisure Activities:** whirlpool, exercise room. **Guest Services:** gift shop, valet laundry, area transportation. **Business Services:** meeting rooms, business center. **Cards:** AX, CB, DC, DS, JC, MC, VI.

SOME UNITS
(ASK) (SD) 🐾 🍴 ▽ ⊘ 🏊 📶 (DATA PORT) 🔒 💻 / ✕ (VCR) 🍽 / FEE

WYNDHAM ANATOLE
Phone: (214)748-1200   **14**
(AAA) (SAVE)
2/1-5/22 & 9/7-11/20	1P: $139-$199	2P: $139-$219	XP: $20	F18
11/21-1/31	1P: $139-$199	2P: $129-$219	XP: $20	F18
5/23-9/6	1P: $129-$189	2P: $129-$209	XP: $20	F18

▼▼▼▼   **Location:** I-35 E, exit 430D (Market Center Blvd), just nw. 2201 Stemmons Frwy 75207. **Fax:** 214/761-7520.
Large-scale Hotel **Facility:** 1620 units. 1614 one-bedroom standard units, some with whirlpools. 6 one-bedroom suites. 27 stories, interior corridors. *Bath:* combo or shower only. **Parking:** on-site (fee) and valet. **Terms:** check-in 4 pm, cancellation fee imposed. **Amenities:** video games (fee), dual phone lines, voice mail, safes, honor bars, irons, hair dryers. **Dining:** 5 restaurants, 24 hours, cocktails, also, Nana Grill, see separate listing, nightclub, entertainment. **Pool(s):** outdoor, 2 heated indoor. **Leisure Activities:** whirlpool, steamroom, jogging, spa. *Fee:* sauna, 6 lighted tennis courts, racquetball courts. **Guest Services:** gift shop, valet laundry. **Business Services:** conference facilities, business center. **Cards:** AX, CB, DC, DS, JC, MC, VI.

SOME UNITS
(SD) 🍴 (24) ▽ (⊖M) (⚿) ⊘ 🏊 📶 ✕ 📶 (DATA PORT) 💻 / ✕ 🍽 / FEE

WYNDHAM DALLAS MARKET CENTER
Phone: (214)741-7481   **4**
(AAA) (SAVE)
9/8-1/31	1P: $89-$139	2P: $89-$149	XP: $10	F18
2/1-6/23	1P: $89-$135	2P: $89-$145	XP: $10	F18
6/24-9/7	1P: $79-$119	2P: $79-$129	XP: $10	F18

▼▼▼▼   **Location:** 0.3 mi s off I-35 E and US 77, exit 430D (Market Center Blvd). 2015 Market Center Blvd 75207.
Small-scale Hotel **Fax:** 214/747-6191. **Facility:** 228 units. 217 one-bedroom standard units. 11 one-bedroom suites ($220-$230). 11 stories, interior corridors. *Bath:* combo or shower only. **Parking:** on-site. **Terms:** cancellation fee imposed. **Amenities:** dual phone lines, irons, hair dryers. *Fee:* video games, high-speed Internet. *Some:* CD players. **Dining:** 6:30 am-10 pm, cocktails. **Pool(s):** outdoor. **Leisure Activities:** exercise room. **Guest Services:** valet and coin laundry. **Business Services:** meeting rooms, fax (fee). **Cards:** AX, DC, DS, MC, VI.

SOME UNITS
(SD) 🍴 ▽ ⊘ 🏊 📶 (DATA PORT) 💻 / ✕ 🔒 / FEE

The following lodging was either not evaluated or did not
meet AAA rating requirements but is listed for your information only.

HOTEL LAWRENCE
Phone: 214/761-9090
(fyi)   Not evaluated. **Location:** I-35, e on Commerce 0.8 mi to Griffin, s 1 blk to Jackson, just w. 302 S Houston St 75202.
Facilities, services, and decor characterize a mid-range property.

WHERE TO DINE

ANTARES
Lunch: $8-$16   **Dinner:** $18-$30   **Phone:** 214/712-7145   **28**
▼▼▼▼
Location: Just e of I-35 E and US 77, exit Reunion Blvd; just n of I-30, exit Commerce St eastbound; in Hyatt Regency Dallas at Reunion. 300 Reunion Blvd 75207. **Hours:** 11:30 am-2 & 6-11 pm, Sun 10:30 am-2:30 pm.
Northern American **Reservations:** suggested. **Features:** Located on the top floor of the Renaissance Tower, this restaurant takes one hour to revolve completely, affording guests a 360-degree panoramic view of the Dallas area. A creative cuisine is offered, featuring meals like prime rib with garlic potatoes. Dressy casual; cocktails. **Parking:** valet and street. **Cards:** AX, DC, DS, MC, VI.

🍷 ✕

BABY DOE'S MATCHLESS MINE RESTAURANT
Dinner: $17-$26   **Phone:** 214/871-7310   **15**
▼▼ ▼▼
Location: I-35 E, exit 230A (Oakland Ave), just e to Harry Hines Blvd, then 0.3 mi s. 3305 Harry Hines Blvd 75201.
Hours: 4 pm-10 pm, Fri & Sat-11 pm, Sun 10 am-2 & 4-10 pm. **Reservations:** accepted. **Features:** Inside
Steak House this replica of a 19th-century Colorado silver mine is a fun, family restaurant with solid wood walls and floors. The smooth beer-cheese soup is their specialty. Entrees range from prime rib to shrimp dishes like scampi to chicken picatta. Casual dress; cocktails. **Parking:** on-site and valet. **Cards:** AX, DS, MC, VI.

🍷 ✕

BEAU NASH
Lunch: $8-$16   **Dinner:** $12-$28   **Phone:** 214/871-3240   **13**
▼▼▼▼
Location: Corner of Crescent Ct and McKinney Ave; uptown; in Hotel Crescent Court. 400 Crescent Ct 75201.
Hours: 6:30-11 am, 11:30-2:30 & 6-10:30 pm, Fri & Sat-midnight, Sun-10:30 pm.
Continental **Reservations:** suggested. **Features:** Entry to the full-service restaurant is through the hotel's marble-clad lobby. The conservatory provides a serene setting. Representative of American and Continental cuisine are grilled salmon with couscous and herb-crusted Chilean sea bass with sun-dried tomato risotto and morel vin blanc. The international staff delivers crisp service. An expanded wine list with a varied price range is available. Dressy casual; cocktails; entertainment. **Parking:** valet. **Cards:** AX, CB, DC, DS, JC, MC, VI.

🍷 ✕

BREAD WINNERS CAFE
Lunch: $7-$8   **Dinner:** $13-$22   **Phone:** 214/754-4940   **5**
▼▼ ▼▼
Location: Corner with Hall St; uptown. 3301 McKinney Ave 75204. **Hours:** 7 am-4 & 5-10 pm, Fri & Sat-11 pm;
Sunday brunch. Closed: 1/1, 9/1, 12/25; also Mon & Tues for dinner. **Reservations:** suggested.
American **Features:** A small plate stacked with delicious breads welcomes guests to the neighborhood eatery. Menus vary, but lunches normally comprise sandwiches, burgers and daily specials. More ambitious dinner entrees might include such selections as stuffed Chilean sea bass or honey-pecan-glazed pork tenderloin. Desserts and breads are sold in the storefront bakery. Cocktails. **Parking:** on-site. **Cards:** AX, DC, DS, MC, VI.

🍷 ✕

(See map p. 234)

DAKOTA'S   Lunch: $9-$15   Dinner: $13-$26   Phone: 214/740-4001   (20)
American
Location: Lower level of Lincoln Plaza. 600 N Akard St 75201. **Hours:** 11 am-2:30 & 5-10 pm, Fri-10:30 pm, Sat 5 pm-10:30 pm, Sun 5:30 pm-9 pm. Closed major holidays. **Reservations:** suggested. **Features:** An upscale American grill, it has the distinction of being located below street level with access from either a free-standing elevator or from the office tower across the street. A glass wall overlooks an exterior patio showing the street above. Dressy casual; cocktails. **Parking:** on-site. **Cards:** AX, DC, DS, MC, VI.

DREAM CAFE   Lunch: $6-$9   Dinner: $10-$16   Phone: 214/954-0486   (4)
Southwest American
Location: Just w of jct McKinney Ave and Routh St to Laclede St, just n; at the corner of the Quadrangle area. 2800 Routh St 75201. **Hours:** 7 am-10 pm. Closed: 11/27, 12/24, 12/25. **Reservations:** accepted. **Features:** The dark ceiling with a paper moon gives this eatery a mysterious feel. Start with the crunchy coconut shrimp appetizer and work your way into the savory Southwestern fare. For dessert, try the sweet fruit crisp with ice cream. Smoke free premises. Casual dress; beer & wine only. **Parking:** on-site. **Cards:** AX, CB, DC, DS, MC, VI.

THE FRENCH ROOM   Dinner: $60-$90   Phone: 214/742-8200   (27)
Nouvelle French
Location: Corner of Commerce and Aband sts; in The Adolphus. 1321 Commerce St 75202. **Hours:** 6 pm-10:30 pm, last seating 9:45 pm. Closed: Sun & Mon. **Reservations:** required. **Features:** The classic formal dining room occupies the grand, old Adolphus Hotel, a magnificently preserved Edwardian hotel. Entry into the French Room takes diners a step back into the court of Louis XV in Versailles. Contributing to the opulent feel is a vaulted ceiling supported by pink, marble Corinthian columns and decorated in gold and powder-blue plaster friezes and adorned with cherubim. Flawlessly trained servers present elegant preparations of game, seafood, beef and veal. Smoke free premises. Semi-formal attire; cocktails. **Parking:** valet. **Cards:** AX, CB, DC, DS, JC, MC, VI.

GREEN PAPAYA   Lunch: $6-$8   Dinner: $7-$13   Phone: 214/521-4811   (17)
Vietnamese
Location: I-35, exit 430A (Oak Lawn Ave). 0.9 mi e. 3211 Oak Lawn Ave, Suite B 75219. **Hours:** 11 am-3 & 5-10 pm, Sat & Sun from noon. Closed major holidays. **Features:** The neighborhood restaurant serves such dishes as fresh spring rolls, noodle plates and sauteed beef with lemon grass, vermicelli, lettuce and cucumbers. Patrons can sit in the small dining room, which offers closely set tables, or on the patio. Casual dress; beer & wine only. **Parking:** on-site. **Cards:** AX, DC, DS, MC, VI.

HOTEL ST. GERMAIN   Country Inn   Dinner: $85   Phone: 214/871-2516   (7)
Continental
Location: Woodall Rodgers Pkwy, exit Pearl St, 0.3 mi n; in Hotel St. Germain. 2516 Maple Ave 75201. **Hours:** 7 pm-11 pm. Closed: 12/25; also Sun, Mon & 1st week of Aug. **Reservations:** required. **Features:** In the dining room of a country inn, the intimate restaurant presents diners a choice of two international types of cuisine. Seven courses unfold as a gastronomical adventure. The atmosphere is formal but friendly, and attentive servers entertain with light-hearted comments and savoir-faire. Skillful, experienced chefs prepare memorable dishes. Smoke free premises. Formal attire; cocktails. **Parking:** valet. **Cards:** AX, MC, VI.

THE LANDMARK RESTAURANT   Lunch: $9-$16   Dinner: $19-$35   Phone: 214/522-1453   (2)
American
Location: I-35 E, exit 430, 0.8 mi n, entrance off Cedar Springs, just n; in The Melrose Hotel. 3015 Oak Lawn Ave 75219. **Hours:** 6:30 am-2 & 5-10 pm, Fri-11 pm, Sat 7 am-11 & 5-11 pm, Sun 7 am-10:30 & 11-2 pm. **Reservations:** suggested. **Features:** Windows are on all sides of the light, airy dining room, which is decorated in shades of yellow and mirrored walls. Eclectic music plays in the background. The progressive American menu lists creative preparations of venison, sea bass and lamb. Innovative desserts are tempting. Smoke free premises. Dressy casual; cocktails. **Parking:** valet. **Cards:** AX, DC, DS, MC, VI.

LA TRATTORIA LOMBARDI   Lunch: $10-$18   Dinner: $11-$29   Phone: 214/954-0803   (3)
Northern Italian
Location: Woodall Rodgers Pkwy, exit Pearl St, n to McKinney Ave, 0.7 mi e to Hall St, then just s. 2916 N Hall St 75204. **Hours:** 11 am-2 & 5-11 pm, Sun 5 pm-10 pm. Closed major holidays. **Reservations:** accepted. **Features:** Its romantic ambience is achieved through a tasteful combination of brick walls, columns, paintings and checked tablecloths. A bottle of wine is waiting at your table as you sit down to any of several traditional favorites from veal marsala to osso buco. Casual dress; cocktails. **Parking:** on-site. **Cards:** AX, CB, DC, MC, VI.

LOLA THE RESTAURANT   Dinner: $32-$47   Phone: 214/855-0700   (30)
American
Location: 0.3 mi n of Woodall Rogers Pkwy, exit Pearl St, just w of McKinney Ave. 2917 Fairmont 75201. **Hours:** 5:30 pm-11 pm. Closed: Sun & Mon. **Reservations:** suggested. **Features:** New American cuisine is the focus with a menu that offers two- to four-course dinners. Excellent choices include beef tenderloin, grilled loin of lamb and grilled sika venison. Smoke free premises. Casual dress; cocktails. **Parking:** valet. **Cards:** AX, DC, DS, MC, VI.

NANA GRILL   Dinner: $30-$46   Phone: 214/761-7479   (1)
American
Location: I-35 E, exit 430D (Market Center Blvd), just nw; in Wyndham Anatole. 2201 Stemmons Frwy 75207. **Hours:** 6 pm-10 pm, Fri & Sat-10:30 pm. **Reservations:** required. **Features:** From this Victorian dining room on the 27th floor, you will have a spectacular view of Dallas. A menu of New American cuisine offers surprising varieties, from appetizers such as pan-seared abalone, to entrees such as crab-crusted Chilean sea bass, or the signature dish of prime grilled filet with wheat berry-shiitake "risotto", raspberries, roquefort, pinenuts and cabernet sauce. A roving string trio provides the background music. You'll find delicious food in a romantic setting. Dressy casual; cocktails; entertainment. **Parking:** on-site and valet. **Cards:** AX, CB, DC, DS, MC, VI.

OLD WARSAW   Dinner: $21-$32   Phone: 214/528-0032   (11)
Continental
Location: 1 mi n. 2610 Maple Ave 75201. **Hours:** 5:30 pm-10:30 pm. **Reservations:** required. **Features:** The well-established restaurant invites guests to unwind in the richly decorated dining room to sample preparations of seafood, meat and fowl, as well as tempting appetizers. Dim lighting and low-key entertainment add to the romantic ambience. Jackets are required. Semi-formal attire; cocktails; entertainment. **Parking:** valet. **Cards:** AX, CB, DC, DS, MC, VI.

(See map p. 234)

PALM RESTAURANT **Lunch:** $11-$20 **Dinner:** $16-$35 **Phone:** 214/698-0470 ㉔
Steak House **Location:** In West End; corner of Market St and Ross Ave. 701 Ross Ave 75202. **Hours:** 11:30 am-10:30 pm, Sat from 5 pm, Sun 5 pm-9:30 pm. Closed major holidays. **Reservations:** suggested. **Features:** With walls adorned by hundreds of drawings of celebrities, the bustling restaurant is noted for prime, dry-aged steaks and Nova Scotia lobsters. At the end of the meal, servers present tempting pastries tableside. Dressy casual; cocktails. **Parking:** valet. **Cards:** AX, CB, DC, DS, MC, VI.

PALOMINO EURO BISTRO **Lunch:** $7-$13 **Dinner:** $8-$17 **Phone:** 214/999-1222 ㉜
Ethnic **Location:** 0.3 mi n of Woodall Rogers Pkwy, exit Penn St; corner of Maple and Cedar Springs. 500 Crescent Ct, Suite 165 75201. **Hours:** 11:30 am-2:30 & 5:30-10 pm, Fri & Sat-11 pm, Sun 5:30 pm-9 pm. Closed: 7/4, 12/25. **Reservations:** suggested. **Features:** This bistro, located in the Crescent Court, features upscale, casual dining and oak-fired ovens. A combination of French, Italian, North African and Spanish fare, selections include spit-roasted chicken, pasta, pizza and the popular tiramisu for dessert. Smoke free premises. Casual dress; cocktails. **Parking:** on-site and valet. **Cards:** AX, DC, DS, MC, VI.

THE PYRAMID GRILL **Lunch:** $12-$19 **Dinner:** $17-$39 **Phone:** 214/720-2020 ⑲
Nouvelle American **Location:** Corner of Ross Ave and N Akard St; in The Fairmont Dallas. 1717 N Akard St 75201. **Hours:** 6:30-11 am, 11:30-2:30 & 6-10 pm. **Reservations:** suggested. **Features:** A pianist entertains as expert servers bring elegant cuisine from a varied menu. Begin with a warm lobster cocktail and fresh Caesar salad; then savor the perfectly cooked filet mignon; and finish with a souffle with Grand Marnier. Smoke free premises. Dressy casual; cocktails. **Parking:** valet. **Cards:** AX, DC, DS, MC, VI.

S & D OYSTER COMPANY **Lunch:** $6-$14 **Dinner:** $6-$14 **Phone:** 214/880-0111 ⑩
South Seafood **Location:** N of downtown; between Routh and Allen sts. 2701 McKinney Ave 75204. **Hours:** 11 am-10 pm, Fri & Sat-11 pm. Closed major holidays; also Sun. **Features:** Fresh Southern Gulf coast seafood is served New Orleans style in a 100-year-old building which was once a neighborhood grocery store. Oysters on the half-shell is the house specialty, along with royal red snapper and a homemade icebox lemon meringue pie. Smoke free premises. Casual dress; beer & wine only. **Parking:** on-site. **Cards:** MC, VI.

ZODIAC RESTAURANT **Lunch:** $10-$16 **Phone:** 214/573-5800 ㉕
American **Location:** 6th floor of Neiman-Marcus Department Store. 1618 Main St 75201. Closed major holidays; also Sun. **Reservations:** suggested. **Features:** Inside Neiman Marcus, the classic downtown cafe serves heritage cuisine. Talented chefs prepare upscale dishes, including ruby trout and grilled sea bass. Smoke free premises. Casual dress; beer & wine only. **Parking:** on-site and valet. **Cards:** AX, DC.

DALLAS NORTH   (See map p. 236; index p. 239)

———— WHERE TO STAY ————

AMERISUITES (DALLAS/NEAR THE GALLERIA)
Phone: (972)716-2001   **91**

All Year [ECP]   1P: $99   2P: $99   XP: $10   F18

Location: I-635, exit Dallas Pkwy/Inwood Rd, 0.5 mi n to Spring Valley, just e. 5229 Spring Valley Rd 75240. Fax: 972/716-4054. **Facility:** 125 one-bedroom standard units. 6 stories, interior corridors. *Bath:* combo or shower only. **Parking:** on-site. **Terms:** small pets only. **Amenities:** video games (fee), dual phone lines, voice mail, irons, hair dryers. **Pool(s):** heated outdoor. **Leisure Activities:** exercise room. **Guest Services:** valet and coin laundry, area transportation-within 5 mi. **Business Services:** meeting rooms, fax (fee).

Small-scale Hotel

Cards: AX, CB, DC, DS, JC, MC, VI. **Special Amenities:** free continental breakfast and free newspaper.
(See color ad p 251)

SOME UNITS

AMERISUITES (DALLAS/PARK CENTRAL)
Phone: (972)458-1224   **31**

All Year   1P: $94   2P: $94   XP: $10   F17

Location: US 75, exit 8B (Coit Rd) northbound; exit 8 (Coit Rd), on southbound access road. 12411 N Central Expwy 75243. Fax: 972/458-2887. **Facility:** 128 one-bedroom standard units. 6 stories, interior corridors. *Bath:* combo or shower only. **Parking:** on-site. **Terms:** [ECP] meal plan available, small pets only. **Amenities:** dual phone lines, voice mail, irons, hair dryers. *Some:* high-speed Internet (fee). **Pool(s):** outdoor. **Leisure Activities:** exercise room. **Guest Services:** valet and coin laundry. **Business Services:** meeting rooms, business

Small-scale Hotel

center. **Cards:** AX, DS, JC, MC, VI. **Special Amenities:** free continental breakfast and free newspaper.
(See color ad p 251)

SOME UNITS

BEST WESTERN MILLENNIUM INN
Phone: (214)353-8774   **42**

All Year   1P: $59-$89   2P: $59-$89   XP: $5   F12

Location: I-35 E, exit 436, 0.4 mi e. 2361 W Northwest Hwy 75220. Fax: 214/353-8775. **Facility:** 65 one-bedroom standard units, some with whirlpools. 3 stories, interior corridors. *Bath:* combo or shower only. **Parking:** on-site. **Amenities:** dual phone lines, voice mail, irons, hair dryers. **Pool(s):** small outdoor. **Leisure Activi-

Small-scale Hotel

ties: whirlpool, exercise room. **Guest Services:** coin laundry. **Business Services:** meeting rooms, fax (fee). **Cards:** AX, CB, DC, DS, MC, VI. **Special Amenities:** free continental breakfast and free newspaper.

SOME UNITS

In Texas:

Addison	DFW-Airport North	Houston at Sugarland
Arlington	DFW-Airport South	Houston Hobby Airport
Austin-North	Fort Worth	Houston-Intercontinental Airport East
Dallas-Northwest	Harlingen	Houston-Intercontinental Airport South

(See map p. 236)

BRADFORD SUITES AT LINCOLN PARK **Phone:** (214)696-1555 96
▼▼▼ All Year [ECP] 1P: $99-$139 2P: $99-$139
Location: US 75, exit 5A southbound; exit 4B northbound, just w on Caruth Haven to Lincoln Pl, just n. 8221 N Central
Small-scale Hotel Expwy 75225. Fax: 214/696-1550. **Facility:** 155 units. 78 one-bedroom standard units with efficiencies. 77
one-bedroom suites with efficiencies. 4 stories, interior corridors. *Bath:* combo or shower only. **Parking:** on-
site. **Terms:** cancellation fee imposed. **Amenities:** video games (fee), dual phone lines, voice mail, irons, hair dryers. **Pool(s):**
outdoor. **Leisure Activities:** whirlpool, exercise room. **Guest Services:** sundries, complimentary evening beverages: Wed, valet
and coin laundry. **Business Services:** meeting rooms, fax (fee). **Cards:** AX, CB, DC, DS, JC, MC, VI.

SOME UNITS
(A$K) (S🌅) (🍴+) (🔊M) (👥*) (🐾) (VCR) (🎥) (DATA PORT) (🖥) (📷) (💻) / (✕) /

CANDLEWOOD DALLAS MARKET CENTER **Phone:** 214/631-3333 62
▼▼▼ All Year 1P: $70-$94 XP: $10 F12
Location: I-35, exit 433B (Mockingbird Ln), just w. 7930 N Stemmons Frwy 75247. Fax: 214/631-7474. **Facility:** 150
Small-scale Hotel units. 40 one-bedroom standard units with efficiencies. 101 one- and 9 two-bedroom suites ($87-$144) with
efficiencies. 3 stories, interior corridors. *Bath:* combo or shower only. **Parking:** on-site. **Terms:** [CP] meal
plan available, small pets only ($75 fee, $100 deposit). **Amenities:** video library, CD players, high-speed Internet, dual phone
lines, voice mail, irons, hair dryers. **Pool(s):** outdoor. **Leisure Activities:** exercise room. **Guest Services:** complimentary
evening beverages: Wed, valet and coin laundry, area transportation. **Business Services:** business center. **Cards:** AX, CB, DC,
DS, JC, MC, VI.

SOME UNITS
(A$K) (S🌅) (✈) (🐾) (🐾) (VCR) (🎥) (DATA PORT) (🖥) (📷) (💻) / (✕) /

CANDLEWOOD SUITES-DALLAS GALLERIA **Phone:** (972)233-6888 90
▼▼▼ All Year 1P: $79-$99 2P: $79-$99
Location: Jct Dallas Pkwy and Spring Valley, just e to Noel Rd, then just s. 13939 Noel Rd 75240. Fax: 972/233-1449.
Small-scale Hotel **Facility:** 134 units. 98 one-bedroom standard units with efficiencies. 36 one-bedroom suites with efficiencies.
3 stories, interior corridors. *Bath:* combo or shower only. **Parking:** on-site. **Terms:** weekly rates available,
[AP] meal plan available, small pets only ($25 extra charge). **Amenities:** video library, CD players, dual phone lines, voice mail,
irons, hair dryers. **Leisure Activities:** exercise room. **Guest Services:** sundries. **Business Services:** business center.
Cards: AX, CB, DC, DS, JC, MC, VI.

SOME UNITS
(A$K) (S🌅) (🐾) (🔊M) (VCR) (🎥) (DATA PORT) (🖥) (📷) (💻) / (✕) /

(See map p. 236)

CANDLEWOOD SUITES DALLAS NORTH/RICHARDSON   **Phone:** (972)669-9606   78
All Year   1P: $89-$109   2P: $89-$109
Location: I-635, exit 18A (Greenville Ave), just n. 12525 Greenville Ave 75243. Fax: 972/669-9560. **Facility:** 122
Small-scale Hotel   units. 98 one-bedroom standard units with efficiencies. 24 one-bedroom suites with efficiencies. 3 stories. interior corridors. *Bath:* combo or shower only. **Parking:** on-site. **Amenities:** video library, CD players, dual phone lines, voice mail, irons, hair dryers. **Leisure Activities:** exercise room. **Guest Services:** complimentary laundry. **Business Services:** fax. **Cards:** AX, DC, DS, MC, VI.

SOME UNITS
(ASK) (SD) (&M) (&') (VCR) (☎) (DATA PORT) ◨ ▣ ▣ / (✕) /

CLARION INN MARKET CENTER   **Phone:** (214)461-2677   54
SAVE   All Year [ECP]   1P: $69-$99   2P: $69-$99   XP: $5   F16
Location: I-35 E, exit 433C (Mockingbird Ln) northbound; exit 433A southbound. 7138 N Stemmons Frwy 75247. Fax: 214/461-2678. **Facility:** 62 one-bedroom standard units, some with whirlpools. 3 stories, interior corridors. *Bath:* combo or shower only. **Parking:** on-site. **Terms:** cancellation fee imposed, 15% service charge.
Small-scale Hotel   **Amenities:** dual phone lines, voice mail, irons, hair dryers. **Leisure Activities:** exercise room. **Guest Services:** complimentary evening beverages: Mon-Wed, valet laundry. **Business Services:** meeting rooms, business center. **Cards:** AX, DC, DS, JC, MC, VI.

SOME UNITS
(SD) (&') (♨) (☎) (DATA PORT) ◨ ▣ / (✕) ▣ /

(See map p. 236)

CLARION SUITES

[SAVE]

[diamond diamond diamond]

Small-scale Hotel

Phone: (214)350-2300 **47**

All Year   1P: $79-$159   2P: $79-$159
Location: Nw off I-35 E and US 77; 0.3 mi se of jct Loop 12 and SR 348, exit 436. 2363 Stemmons Tr 75220. Fax: 214/350-5144. **Facility:** 96 units. 94 one- and 2 two-bedroom suites, some with kitchens and/or whirlpools. 3 stories, interior corridors. *Bath:* combo or shower only. **Parking:** on-site. **Terms:** 14 day cancellation notice, [ECP] meal plan available. **Amenities:** voice mail, irons, hair dryers. *Fee:* video games, safes. **Pool(s):** outdoor. **Leisure Activities:** whirlpool, exercise room. **Guest Services:** valet and coin laundry, area transportation. **Business Services:** meeting rooms, PC, fax (fee). **Cards:** AX, DC, DS, JC, MC, VI.

SOME UNITS

[icons] 🆂 🕆 🛬 🎿 🐬 🎥 DATA PORT 📞 🖥 📺 /✕/

COMFORT INN HOTEL BY THE GALLERIA

[SAVE]

[diamond diamond diamond]

Small-scale Hotel

Phone: (972)701-0881 **94**

All Year [ECP]   1P: $75-$89   2P: $75-$89
Location: Jct of Beltway Rd and Landmark Blvd, just s. 14975 Landmark Blvd 75254. Fax: 972/701-0815. **Facility:** 86 one-bedroom standard units, some with whirlpools. 2 stories, interior corridors. *Bath:* combo or shower only. **Parking:** on-site. **Amenities:** dual phone lines, voice mail, irons, hair dryers. **Pool(s):** outdoor. **Leisure Activities:** whirlpool, exercise room. **Guest Services:** valet and coin laundry, area transportation. **Business Services:** meeting rooms, fax (fee). **Cards:** AX, CB, DC, DS, JC, MC, VI.

SOME UNITS

[icons] 🆂 🅼 🎿 🐬 🎥 DATA PORT 📺 /✕/ 📞 🖥 /

COMFORT SUITES

[SAVE]

[diamond diamond diamond]

Small-scale Hotel

Phone: (214)350-4011 **35**
                                                          F18

All Year [CP]   1P: $69-$109   2P: $69-$109   XP: $10
Location: I-35 E, exit 436 (Northwest Hwy); I-35 E and US 77 at jct Loop 12 (Northwest Hwy). 2287 W Northwest Hwy 75220. Fax: 214/350-4408. **Facility:** 103 units. 102 one-bedroom standard units. 1 two-bedroom suite. 3 stories, interior corridors. *Bath:* combo or shower only. **Parking:** on-site. **Terms:** 3 day cancellation notice. **Amenities:** dual phone lines, voice mail, irons, hair dryers. *Fee:* video games, safes. **Pool(s):** outdoor. **Leisure Activities:** whirlpool, exercise room. **Guest Services:** complimentary evening beverages: Mon-Thurs, valet and coin laundry, area transportation. **Business Services:** meeting rooms, fax (fee). **Cards:** AX, CB, DC, DS, MC, VI.

SOME UNITS

[icons] 🆂 🛬 🎿 🐬 🎥 DATA PORT 📞 🖥 📺 /✕/

COUNTRY INN & SUITES-DALLAS NW

[diamond diamond diamond]

Small-scale Hotel

Phone: (214)358-4300 **100**

All Year   1P: $69-$89   2P: $69-$89
Location: I-35, exit 438 (Walnut Hill Ln), just e to Composite Dr, then just s. 10835 Composite Dr 75220. Fax: 214/358-1505. **Facility:** 85 units. 54 one-bedroom standard units, some with whirlpools. 31 one-bedroom suites ($89-$105). 4 stories, interior corridors. *Bath:* combo or shower only. **Parking:** on-site. **Terms:** [CP] meal plan available. **Amenities:** dual phone lines, voice mail, irons, hair dryers. **Pool(s):** small heated outdoor. **Leisure Activities:** whirlpool, exercise room. **Guest Services:** complimentary evening beverages: Mon-Thurs, valet and coin laundry. **Business Services:** meeting rooms, business center. **Cards:** AX, CB, DC, DS, MC, VI. *(See color ad p 260)*

SOME UNITS

[icons] (ASK) 🆂 🅼 🎿 🐬 🎥 DATA PORT 📞 🖥 📺 /✕/

(See map p. 236)

COURTYARD BY MARRIOTT
(AAA) (SAVE)   All Year   1P: $69-$129   XP: $10
Phone: (214)352-7676 [48]
F12
▽▽▽▽   **Location:** I-35 E, exit 436, 0.3 mi se jct Loop 12 and SR 348. 2383 Stemmons Tr 75220. **Fax:** 214/352-4914.
Small-scale Hotel   **Facility:** 146 units. 134 one-bedroom standard units. 12 one-bedroom suites ($119-$139). 3 stories, interior
corridors. *Bath:* combo or shower only. **Parking:** on-site. **Terms:** package plans. **Amenities:** high-speed In-
ternet (fee), dual phone lines. voice mail, irons, hair dryers. **Dining:** 6:30-10 am, Sat & Sun 7-11 am. **Pool(s):**
outdoor. **Leisure Activities:** whirlpool, exercise room. **Guest Services:** valet and coin laundry. **Business
Services:** meeting rooms, fax (fee). **Cards:** AX, CB, DC, DS, JC, MC, VI. **Special Amenities:** free newspaper and preferred
room (subject to availability with advanced reservations).   SOME UNITS

🍽 🍷 🐕 📶 🐾 📹 [DATA PORT] 📺 / ✕ 🛏 🖥 /

(See map p. 236)

COURTYARD BY MARRIOTT-LBJ AT JOSEY

SAVE

Small-scale Hotel

All Year — 1P: $99 — 2P: $109 — XP: $10 — F18 — **Phone:** (972)620-8000 — 33

Location: I-635, exit 25 (Josey Ln) westbound; exit 26 (Josey Ln) eastbound. 2930 Forest Ln 75234. Fax: 972/620-9267. **Facility:** 146 units. 134 one-bedroom standard units. 12 one-bedroom suites ($129). 3 stories, interior corridors. *Bath:* combo or shower only. **Parking:** on-site. **Amenities:** high-speed Internet (fee), dual phone lines, voice mail, irons, hair dryers. **Pool(s):** heated outdoor. **Leisure Activities:** whirlpool, exercise room. **Guest Services:** valet and coin laundry. **Business Services:** meeting rooms, fax (fee).
Cards: AX, CB, DC, DS, MC, VI.

SOME UNITS

CROWNE PLAZA HOTEL AND RESORT DALLAS MARKET CENTER

Large-scale Hotel

2/1-6/30 & 9/9-11/30 — 1P: $79-$129 — 2P: $89-$139 — XP: $10 — F18 — **Phone:** (214)630-8500 — 60
7/1-9/8 & 12/1-1/31 — 1P: $69-$119 — 2P: $79-$129 — XP: $10 — F18

Location: I-35 E, exit 433B northbound; exit 432B southbound. 7050 Stemmons Frwy 75247. Fax: 214/630-9486. **Facility:** 354 units. 352 one-bedroom standard units. 2 one-bedroom suites. 21 stories, interior corridors. *Bath:* combo or shower only. **Parking:** on-site. **Terms:** cancellation fee imposed, small pets only ($125 deposit, $25 extra charge). **Amenities:** video games (fee), voice mail, irons, hair dryers. **Pool(s):** heated indoor. **Leisure Activities:** sauna, whirlpool, exercise room. **Guest Services:** gift shop, valet and coin laundry, area transportation. **Business Services:** meeting rooms, business center. **Cards:** AX, CB, DC, DS, JC, MC, VI.

SOME UNITS
FEE FEE

CROWNE PLAZA SUITES HOTEL AND RESORT DALLAS PARK CENTRAL

Large-scale Hotel

All Year — 1P: $159 — **Phone:** (972)233-7600 — 26

Location: Just n of I-635, 0.3 mi nw of jct I-635 and US 75, exit 19C (Coit Rd) eastbound; exit 19B (Coit Rd) westbound. 7800 Alpha Rd 75240. Fax: 972/701-8618. **Facility:** 295 units. 4 one-bedroom standard units. 291 one-bedroom suites. 10 stories, interior corridors. *Bath:* combo or shower only. **Parking:** on-site. **Terms:** pets ($25 fee, $125 deposit). **Amenities:** voice mail, irons, hair dryers. *Some:* fax. **Pool(s):** heated indoor/outdoor. **Leisure Activities:** whirlpool, exercise room. **Guest Services:** gift shop, valet and coin laundry, area transportation. **Business Services:** meeting rooms, business center. **Cards:** AX, CB, DC, DS, JC, MC, VI.

SOME UNITS

DALLAS MARRIOTT SUITES MARKET CENTER

AAA SAVE

Small-scale Hotel

All Year — 1P: $149 — 2P: $149 — **Phone:** (214)905-0050 — 74

Location: I-35, exit 431 (Motor St). 2493 N Stemmons Frwy 75207. Fax: 214/905-0060. **Facility:** 266 units. 60 one-bedroom standard units. 206 one-bedroom suites. 12 stories, interior corridors. *Bath:* combo or shower only. **Parking:** on-site. **Terms:** cancellation fee imposed, small pets only ($50 fee). **Amenities:** high-speed Internet (fee), dual phone lines, voice mail, irons, hair dryers. **Dining:** 6:30 am-10 pm, cocktails. **Pool(s):** outdoor. **Leisure Activities:** whirlpool, exercise room. **Guest Services:** sundries, valet and coin laundry, airport transportation-Dallas Love Field Airport, area transportation-within 5 mi. **Business Services:** conference facilities, business center. **Cards:** AX, CB, DC, DS, MC, VI. **Special Amenities:** free newspaper.

SOME UNITS

DELUX INN EXPRESS & SUITES

Small-scale Hotel

All Year — 1P: $40 — 2P: $40 — XP: $5 — F10 — **Phone:** (972)373-9555 — 83

Location: From SR 12, 0.4 mi w on Northwest Hwy to Newkirk Rd, just s. 2144 California Crossing 75220. Fax: 972/373-9555. **Facility:** 38 one-bedroom standard units, some with efficiencies (no utensils) and/or whirlpools. 2 stories, interior corridors. *Bath:* combo or shower only. **Parking:** on-site. **Terms:** weekly rates available, [CP] meal plan available. **Guest Services:** coin laundry. **Business Services:** fax (fee). **Cards:** AX, DC, DS, MC, VI.

SOME UNITS

DOUBLETREE CLUB HOTEL DALLAS PARK CENTRAL

SAVE

Small-scale Hotel

All Year — 1P: $53-$99 — 2P: $53-$99 — XP: $10 — F18 — **Phone:** (972)960-6555 — 44

Location: I-635, exit 19C (Coit Rd) eastbound; exit 19B (US 75/Coit Rd) westbound. Located in a commercial area. 8102 LBJ Frwy 75251. Fax: 972/960-6553. **Facility:** 202 one-bedroom standard units. 4 stories, interior corridors. *Bath:* combo or shower only. **Parking:** on-site. **Amenities:** *Some:* high-speed Internet. **Pool(s):** outdoor, wading. **Leisure Activities:** exercise room. **Guest Services:** valet and coin laundry, area transportation. **Business Services:** meeting rooms, business center. **Cards:** AX, CB, DC, DS, MC, VI.

SOME UNITS
FEE FEE

DOUBLETREE HOTEL AT CAMPBELL CENTRE

SAVE

Large-scale Hotel

All Year — 1P: $79-$169 — **Phone:** (214)691-8700 — 52

Location: N off US 75, exit 4B (Caruth-Haven). 8250 N Central Expwy 75206. Fax: 214/706-0186. **Facility:** 300 units. 299 one-bedroom standard units. 1 one-bedroom suite. 21 stories, interior corridors. **Parking:** on-site. **Amenities:** video games (fee), voice mail, irons, hair dryers. **Leisure Activities:** whirlpools, limited exercise equipment. **Guest Services:** gift shop, valet laundry, area transportation. **Business Services:** meeting rooms, fax (fee). **Cards:** AX, CB, DC, DS, JC, MC, VI.

SOME UNITS
FEE

(See map p. 236)

DOUBLETREE HOTEL, LINCOLN CENTRE NEAR THE GALLERIA   Phone: (972)934-8400   93
(AAA) [SAVE]   All Year   1P: $90-$160   2P: $100-$170   XP: $10   F18
▼▼▼ ▼▼▼   **Location:** N at jct I-635 and North Dallas Tollway/Dallas Pkwy, exit 22C (Montford Dr) eastbound; exit 22B (Dallas Pkwy/Inwood Rd) westbound. Located across from Galleria Mall. 5410 LBJ Frwy 75240. Fax: 972/701-5244.
                Facility: Elegant public areas. 500 units. 482 one-bedroom standard units. 13 one- and 5 two-bedroom
Large-scale Hotel suites, some with whirlpools. 18 stories, interior corridors. *Bath:* combo or shower only. **Parking:** on-site (fee)
                and valet. **Terms:** cancellation fee imposed. **Amenities:** dual phone lines, voice mail, irons, hair dryers.
Dining: 3 restaurants, 6:30 am-midnight, cocktails. **Pool(s):** outdoor, wading. **Leisure Activities:** whirlpool, exercise room.
Guest Services: gift shop, valet laundry, area transportation-within 3 mi & Galleria. **Business Services:** conference facilities,
business center. **Cards:** AX, DC, DS, MC, VI. **Special Amenities:** free newspaper.

SOME UNITS

[icons]

DRURY INN & SUITES-DALLAS NORTH   Phone: (972)484-3330   38
(AAA) [SAVE]   9/1-1/31 [ECP]   1P: $66-$86   2P: $76-$96   XP: $10   F18
            2/1-8/31 [ECP]   1P: $64-$84   2P: $74-$94   XP: $10   F18
▼▼▼▼   **Location:** I-35E, exit 438 (Walnut Hill Ln). 2421 Walnut Hill Ln 75229. Fax: 972/484-3330. **Facility:** 123 units. 111
            one-bedroom standard units. 12 one-bedroom suites. 4 stories, interior corridors. **Parking:** on-
Small-scale Hotel site. **Terms:** small pets only. **Amenities:** voice mail, irons, hair dryers. **Pool(s):** outdoor. **Leisure Activi-
            ties:** exercise room. **Guest Services:** complimentary evening beverages: Mon-Thurs, coin laundry.
Business Services: meeting rooms, fax (fee). **Cards:** AX, CB, DC, DS, MC, VI. **Special Amenities: free continental break-
fast and free local telephone calls.**

SOME UNITS

[icons]

EMBASSY SUITES DALLAS-MARKET CENTER   Phone: (214)630-5332   69
[SAVE]   All Year [BP]   1P: $99-$209   2P: $109-$219   XP: $10   F17
        Location: I-35 E, exit 432 (Inwood Rd). 2727 Stemmons Frwy 75207. Fax: 214/631-3025. **Facility:** 244 units. 236
▼▼▼▼   one- and 8 two-bedroom suites. 9 stories, interior corridors. *Bath:* combo or shower only. **Parking:** on-site.
        Terms: pets ($25 fee). **Amenities:** video games (fee), dual phone lines, voice mail, irons, hair dryers.
Large-scale Hotel **Pool(s):** heated indoor. **Leisure Activities:** sauna, whirlpool, steamroom, exercise room. **Guest Services:**
        gift shop, complimentary evening beverages, valet and coin laundry, area transportation. **Business Serv-
ices:** meeting rooms, fax (fee). **Cards:** AX, CB, DC, DS, MC, VI. *(See color ad p 267)*

SOME UNITS

[icons]

EMBASSY SUITES HOTEL-DALLAS/LOVE FIELD   Phone: (214)357-4500   51
(AAA) [SAVE]   All Year [BP]   1P: $109   2P: $269   XP: $10   F18
▼▼▼▼   **Location:** Just se of jct Northwest Hwy/Loop 12 and Marsh Ln. 3880 W Northwest Hwy 75220. Fax: 214/357-0683.
        Facility: 248 units. 16 one-bedroom standard units. 232 one-bedroom suites. 8 stories, interior corridors.
        Parking: on-site. **Amenities:** video games (fee), voice mail, irons, hair dryers. *Some:* dual phone lines.
Small-scale Hotel **Dining:** 11 am-2 & 5-10 pm, cocktails. **Pool(s):** heated indoor, wading. **Leisure Activities:** sauna, whirlpool,
        steamroom, pool table, jogging, exercise room. **Guest Services:** gift shop, complimentary evening bever-
ages, valet and coin laundry, airport transportation-Dallas Love Field Airport, area transportation-North Park Mall, within 5 mi.
Business Services: meeting rooms, fax (fee). **Cards:** AX, CB, DC, DS, JC, MC, VI. **Special Amenities: early check-in/late
check-out and free newspaper.** *(See ad p 268 & color ad below)*

SOME UNITS

[icons]

(See map p. 236)

EMBASSY SUITES HOTEL DALLAS NEAR THE GALLERIA
SAVE

Small-scale Hotel

All Year [BP]   1P: $129-$229   2P: $129-$229   **Phone: (972)364-3640**   **89**
Location: North Dallas Tollway, 0.5 mi e on Spring Valley Rd, then just s. 14021 Noel Rd 75240. Fax: 972/364-3641. **Facility:** 150 one-bedroom suites. 6 stories, interior corridors. *Bath:* combo or shower only. **Parking:** on-site. **Terms:** cancellation fee imposed. **Amenities:** dual phone lines, voice mail, irons, hair dryers. *Some:* high-speed Internet (fee). **Pool(s):** small heated indoor. **Leisure Activities:** whirlpool, exercise room. **Guest Services:** sundries, complimentary evening beverages, valet laundry, area transportation. **Business Services:** meeting rooms, fax (fee). **Cards:** AX, CB, DC, DS, MC, VI. *(See color ad below)*

SOME UNITS

EMBASSY SUITES HOTEL-DALLAS/PARK CENTRAL
SAVE

Small-scale Hotel

All Year   1P: $89-$159   2P: $89-$159   **Phone: 972/234-3300**   **29**
Location: N off US 75, just n of jct Midpark Rd; exit 22 (Midpark Rd) northbound; exit 21 (service road) southbound. 13131 N Central Expwy 75243. Fax: 972/437-9863. **Facility:** 279 units. 278 one- and 1 two-bedroom suites. 9 stories, interior corridors. *Bath:* combo or shower only. **Parking:** on-site. **Terms:** [BP] meal plan available, package plans, small pets only ($25 extra charge). **Amenities:** dual phone lines, voice mail, irons, hair dryers. **Pool(s):** heated indoor. **Leisure Activities:** sauna, whirlpool, steamroom, racquetball courts, exercise room. **Guest Services:** gift shop, complimentary evening beverages, coin laundry, area transportation. **Business Services:** meeting rooms, fax (fee). **Cards:** AX, CB, DC, DS, MC, VI. *(See color ad below)*

SOME UNITS

FAIRFIELD INN-PARK CENTRAL
SAVE

Small-scale Hotel

All Year [ECP]   1P: $59-$79   2P: $59-$89   XP: $6   **Phone: (972)437-9905**   **36**
F18
Location: I-635, exit 18A (Greenville Ave S), just s, then just e. 9230 LBJ Frwy 75243. Fax: 972/437-9905. **Facility:** 95 one-bedroom standard units. 3 stories, interior corridors. *Bath:* combo or shower only. **Parking:** on-site. **Terms:** 14 day cancellation notice. **Amenities:** voice mail, irons, hair dryers. **Pool(s):** heated indoor. **Leisure Activities:** whirlpool. **Guest Services:** valet laundry. **Business Services:** meeting rooms, fax (fee). **Cards:** AX, CB, DC, DS, MC, VI.

SOME UNITS

FAIRFIELD INN-REGAL ROW
SAVE

Small-scale Hotel

All Year   1P: $49-$67   2P: $49-$67   XP: $10   **Phone: (214)638-6100**   **53**
F12
Location: I-35 E, exit 434B (Regal Row), just sw. 1575 Regal Row 75247. Fax: 214/905-1963. **Facility:** 204 one-bedroom standard units. 4 stories, interior corridors. *Bath:* combo or shower only. **Parking:** on-site. **Terms:** 7 day cancellation notice-fee imposed, [ECP] meal plan available. **Amenities:** video games (fee), irons. **Pool(s):** outdoor. **Leisure Activities:** exercise room. **Guest Services:** valet and coin laundry, area transportation. **Business Services:** meeting rooms, fax (fee). **Cards:** AX, CB, DC, DS, JC, MC, VI. *(See ad p 253)*

SOME UNITS

GOLDMARK SUITES

Small-scale Hotel

All Year [ECP]   1P: $99-$129   2P: $99-$129   XP: $10   **Phone: (972)669-0478**   **28**
F18
Location: US 75, exit 22 (Midpark Rd). 13636 Goldmark Dr 75240. Fax: 972/644-2632. **Facility:** 70 units. 60 one- and 10 two-bedroom suites ($169-$189) with kitchens. 2 stories, interior/exterior corridors. **Parking:** on-site. **Terms:** cancellation fee imposed, small pets only ($60 extra charge). **Amenities:** voice mail, irons, hair dryers. **Pool(s):** outdoor. **Leisure Activities:** whirlpool. **Guest Services:** complimentary evening beverages: Mon-Thurs, valet and coin laundry. **Business Services:** fax (fee). **Cards:** AX, CB, DC, DS, MC, VI.

SOME UNITS

(See map p. 236)

THE GUEST LODGE HOTEL AT THE COOPER AEROBICS CENTER   **Phone:** (972)386-0306   41
▼▼▼▼   All Year [ECP]   1P: $155-$195   2P: $165-$205   XP: $10
Resort   **Location:** I-635, exit Preston Rd, 0.5 mi s. 12230 Preston Rd 75230. **Fax:** 972/386-5415. **Facility:** On 30 manicured
Large-scale Hotel   acres, this European-style hotel features mahogany furniture and marble floors. Designated smoking area.
62 units. 50 one-bedroom standard units. 12 one-bedroom suites ($250-$415). 2 stories, interior corridors.
Bath: combo or shower only. **Parking:** on-site. **Terms:** cancellation fee imposed, package plans.
Amenities: voice mail, irons, hair dryers. *Some:* CD players, safes. **Pool(s):** 2 heated outdoor. **Leisure Activities:** saunas, whirlpools, steamrooms, 4 lighted tennis courts, recreation programs, jogging, spa, sports court, basketball. **Guest Services:** gift
shop, valet laundry. **Business Services:** meeting rooms. *Fee:* administrative services, fax. **Cards:** AX, CB, DC, DS, MC, VI.

SOME UNITS

HAMPTON INN-DALLAS NORTH I-35 AT WALNUT HILL   **Phone:** (972)484-6557   34
AAA (SAVE)   All Year [ECP]   1P: $76-$79   2P: $86-$89
▼▼▼▼   **Location:** I-35 E, exit 438 (Walnut Hill Ln). 11069 Composite Dr 75229. **Fax:** 972/243-6486. **Facility:** 116 one-
bedroom standard units. 4 stories, interior corridors. **Parking:** on-site. **Amenities:** dual phone lines, voice
mail, irons, hair dryers. **Pool(s):** outdoor. **Leisure Activities:** exercise room. **Guest Services:** complimen-
Small-scale Hotel   tary evening beverages: Mon-Thurs, valet laundry. **Business Services:** meeting rooms, fax (fee). **Cards:** AX,
CB, DC, DS, MC, VI. **Special Amenities:** free continental breakfast and free local telephone calls.
(See color ad below)

SOME UNITS

(See map p. 236)

THE HARVEY HOTEL-DALLAS
Phone: (972)960-7000 27
All Year 1P: $59 2P: $59
Location: I-635, exit 19C (Coit Rd) eastbound; exit 19B westbound. 7815 LBJ Frwy at Coit Rd 75251.
Small-scale Hotel   Fax: 972/788-4227. **Facility:** 313 units. 310 one-bedroom standard units. 3 two-bedroom suites. 3 stories, interior corridors. **Parking:** on-site. **Terms:** pets ($25 fee, $100 deposit). **Amenities:** video games (fee), voice mail, irons. **Pool(s):** outdoor. **Leisure Activities:** sauna, whirlpool. **Guest Services:** gift shop, valet and coin laundry, area transportation. **Business Services:** conference facilities, fax (fee). **Cards:** AX, CB, DC, DS, JC, MC, VI.

SOME UNITS
FEE   FEE

HAWTHORN SUITES HOTEL-DALLAS- MARKET CENTER
Phone: (214)688-1010 65
All Year [BP] 1P: $59-$199 2P: $59-$199
Location: I-35 E, exit 433B (Mockingbird Ln), just se. 7900 Brookriver Dr 75247. Fax: 214/638-5215. **Facility:** 98
Small-scale Hotel   units. 63 one-bedroom standard units with kitchens. 35 two-bedroom suites ($69-$199) with kitchens. 3 stories (no elevator), exterior corridors. **Parking:** on-site. **Terms:** small pets only ($50 fee, $100 deposit).
Amenities: video games (fee), dual phone lines, voice mail, irons, hair dryers. **Pool(s):** outdoor. **Leisure Activities:** sports court.
Guest Services: sundries, complimentary evening beverages: Mon-Thurs, valet and coin laundry, area transportation. **Business Services:** meeting rooms, fax (fee). **Cards:** AX, CB, DC, DS, MC, VI.

SOME UNITS

HAWTHORN SUITES LTD DALLAS PARK CENTRAL
Phone: (972)889-9972 79
All Year [BP] 1P: $99-$129 2P: $99-$129
Location: I-635, exit 18A, just sw. 9089 Vantage Point Dr 75243. Fax: 972/235-6129. **Facility:** 78 units. 41 one-
Small-scale Hotel   bedroom standard units. 37 one-bedroom suites, some with kitchens and/or whirlpools. 4 stories, interior corridors. **Bath:** combo or shower only. **Parking:** on-site. **Amenities:** dual phone lines, voice mail, irons, hair dryers. **Leisure Activities:** exercise room. **Guest Services:** complimentary evening beverages: Mon-Wed, valet and coin laundry. **Business Services:** meeting rooms, fax. **Cards:** AX, CB, DC, DS, MC, VI.

SOME UNITS

HAWTHORN SUITES NORTH DALLAS
Phone: (972)248-2233 80
All Year [BP] 1P: $79-$129 2P: $79-$129
Location: North Dallas Tollway, exit Frankford, just ne. 18470 North Dallas Pkwy 75287. Fax: 972/248-4747.
Small-scale Hotel   **Facility:** 112 units. 61 one-bedroom standard units with efficiencies. 34 one- and 17 two-bedroom suites with efficiencies. 3 stories, interior corridors. **Bath:** combo or shower only. **Parking:** on-site. **Terms:** 3 day cancellation notice-fee imposed, pets ($50 fee, small dogs only). **Amenities:** dual phone lines, voice mail, irons, hair dryers. **Fee:** video library, high-speed Internet. **Pool(s):** outdoor. **Leisure Activities:** whirlpool, exercise room. **Guest Services:** sundries, complimentary evening beverages: Mon-Thurs, valet and coin laundry, area transportation. **Business Services:** meeting rooms, PC, fax (fee). **Cards:** AX, DC, DS, MC, VI.

SOME UNITS

HILTON DALLAS PARK CITIES
Phone: (214)368-0400 84
SAVE
All Year 1P: $89-$199 2P: $89-$199 XP: $10   F18
Location: North Dallas Tollway, exit Northwest Hwy (Loop 12), n to Douglas Ave, then just s. 5954 Luther Ln 75225.
Small-scale Hotel   Fax: 214/369-9571. **Facility:** 224 one-bedroom standard units. 11 stories, interior corridors. **Bath:** combo or shower only. **Parking:** on-site. **Amenities:** video games (fee), dual phone lines, voice mail, irons, hair dryers. **Some:** CD players. **Pool(s):** small heated outdoor. **Leisure Activities:** whirlpool, exercise room. **Guest Services:** gift shop, valet laundry. **Business Services:** meeting rooms, business center. **Cards:** AX, CB, DC, DS, JC, MC, VI.

SOME UNITS

HOLIDAY INN EXPRESS & SUITES PLANO
Phone: (972)403-1112 85
SAVE
All Year [BP] 1P: $74-$84 2P: $74-$84
Location: Communications Pkwy and Parker Rd. 3101 North Dallas Pkwy 75093. Fax: 972/403-7330. **Facility:** 80 one-bedroom standard units. 3 stories, interior corridors. **Bath:** combo or shower only. **Parking:** on-site.
Amenities: high-speed Internet (fee), dual phone lines, voice mail, irons, hair dryers. **Pool(s):** outdoor.
Small-scale Hotel   **Leisure Activities:** limited exercise equipment. **Guest Services:** valet and coin laundry, area transportation-within 5 mi. **Business Services:** meeting rooms, business center. **Cards:** AX, CB, DC, DS, JC, MC, VI.
Special Amenities: free local telephone calls and free newspaper.

SOME UNITS

HOLIDAY INN EXPRESS-LOVE FIELD
Phone: (214)350-5577 49
All Year [ECP] 1P: $69-$79 2P: $69-$79
Location: I-35 E, exit 436 (W Northwest Hwy), 0.8 mi e. 2370 W Northwest Hwy 75220. Fax: 214/350-5577.
Small-scale Hotel   **Facility:** 92 one-bedroom standard units. 3 stories, interior corridors. **Bath:** combo or shower only. **Parking:** on-site. **Terms:** small pets only ($25 fee, $50 deposit). **Amenities:** dual phone lines, voice mail, irons, hair dryers. **Pool(s):** small heated indoor. **Leisure Activities:** whirlpool. **Guest Services:** valet laundry. **Business Services:** fax (fee). **Cards:** AX, CB, DC, DS, MC, VI.

SOME UNITS

HOLIDAY INN EXPRESS PARK CENTRAL
Phone: (972)907-9500 37
All Year [ECP] 1P: $55-$75 2P: $55-$85 XP: $6   F18
Location: US 75 N, exit 22 (Midpart Rd). 13185 Central Expwy 75243. Fax: 972/907-1875. **Facility:** 62 one-
Small-scale Hotel   bedroom standard units. 3 stories, interior corridors. **Bath:** combo or shower only. **Parking:** on-site.
Terms: 14 day cancellation notice, small pets only ($25 fee). **Amenities:** dual phone lines, voice mail, irons, hair dryers. **Pool(s):** heated indoor. **Guest Services:** valet laundry. **Business Services:** meeting rooms, fax (fee). **Cards:** AX, CB, DC, DS, MC, VI.

SOME UNITS

(See map p. 236)

HOLIDAY INN SELECT DALLAS NORTH PARK
Phone: (214)373-6000 **39**
AAA SAVE All Year 1P: $119-$179 2P: $129-$189 XP: $10 F18
Location: N US 75, exit 6 (Walnut Hill Ln/Meadow Rd). 10650 N Central Expwy 75231. Fax: 214/373-1037. **Facility:** 284 units. 281 one-bedroom standard units. 3 one-bedroom suites, some with whirlpools. 9 stories, interior corridors. *Bath:* combo or shower only. **Parking:** on-site. **Terms:** [AP] meal plan available.
Large-scale Hotel **Amenities:** video games (fee), voice mail, irons, hair dryers. **Dining:** 6 am-11 pm, Fri & Sat-midnight, cocktails. **Pool(s):** heated indoor. **Leisure Activities:** whirlpool, exercise room. **Guest Services:** gift shop, valet and coin laundry, area transportation-within 5 mi. **Business Services:** meeting rooms, PC, fax (fee). **Cards:** AX, CB, DC, DS, JC, MC, VI. **Special Amenities:** free local telephone calls and free newspaper. *(See color ad below)*

SOME UNITS
(icons)

HOLIDAY INN SELECT LOVE FIELD
Phone: (214)357-8500 **43**
All Year 1P: $82-$115 XP: $10 F18
Location: I-35, exit 433B (Mockingbird Ln), 2.3 mi e. 3300 W Mockingbird Ln 75235. Fax: 214/366-2670.
Large-scale Hotel **Facility:** 244 units. 230 one-bedroom standard units. 14 one-bedroom suites. 8 stories, interior corridors. *Bath:* combo or shower only. **Parking:** on-site. **Terms:** cancellation fee imposed. **Amenities:** dual phone lines, voice mail, irons, hair dryers. *Fee:* video games, high-speed Internet. **Pool(s):** outdoor. **Leisure Activities:** exercise room. **Guest Services:** gift shop, complimentary evening beverages: Mon-Fri, valet laundry, area transportation. **Business Services:** meeting rooms, business center. **Cards:** AX, CB, DC, DS, JC, MC, VI.

SOME UNITS
(icons)

HOMESTEAD STUDIO SUITES HOTEL-DALLAS/NORTH ADDISON/TOLLWAY
Phone: 972/447-1800 **86**
All Year 1P: $55-$65 2P: $60-$70 XP: $5
Location: On North Dallas Tollway, exit Trinity Mills, just s on southbound access road. 17425 North Dallas Tollway
Small-scale Hotel 75287. Fax: 972/497-1900. **Facility:** 119 one-bedroom standard units with efficiencies. 2 stories, exterior corridors. *Bath:* combo or shower only. **Parking:** on-site. **Terms:** pets ($75 fee). **Amenities:** voice mail, irons.
Guest Services: coin laundry. **Business Services:** fax. **Cards:** AX, CB, DC, DS, JC, MC, VI.

SOME UNITS
(icons)

HOMESTEAD STUDIO SUITES HOTEL-DALLAS/NORTH/PARK CENTRAL
Phone: (972)663-1800 **97**
All Year 1P: $65-$75 2P: $70-$80 XP: $5 F17
Location: I-635, exit 19C (Coit Rd), 0.7 mi s. 12121 Coit Rd 75251. Fax: 972/663-1900. **Facility:** 133 one-bedroom
Small-scale Hotel standard units with efficiencies. 2 stories, exterior corridors. *Bath:* combo or shower only. **Parking:** on-site.
Terms: pets ($75 fee). **Amenities:** voice mail, irons. **Guest Services:** valet and coin laundry. **Business Services:** fax (fee). **Cards:** AX, CB, DC, DS, JC, MC, VI.

SOME UNITS
(icons)
FEE

HOMEWOOD SUITES BY HILTON
Phone: 214/819-9700 **102**
SAVE All Year [ECP] 1P: $59-$139 2P: $59-$139
Location: I-35, exit 432 (Inwood Rd). 2747 N Stemmons Frwy 75207. Fax: 214/819-9701. **Facility:** 137 units. 132 one- and 5 two-bedroom suites with efficiencies. 7 stories, interior corridors. *Bath:* combo or shower only.
Small-scale Hotel **Parking:** on-site. **Terms:** small pets only ($75 fee). **Amenities:** video library, video games (fee), dual phone lines, voice mail, irons, hair dryers. **Pool(s):** small heated outdoor. **Leisure Activities:** exercise room. **Guest Services:** sundries, complimentary evening beverages: Mon-Thurs, valet and coin laundry, area transportation. **Business Services:** meeting rooms, business center. **Cards:** AX, CB, DC, DS, MC, VI.

SOME UNITS
(icons)

(See map p. 236)

HOMEWOOD SUITES BY HILTON   Phone: (972)437-6966   **75**
[SAVE]   All Year   1P: $99-$159
                    Location: I-635, exit 18A (Greenville Ave S), just s, then just e. 9169 Markville Dr 75243. Fax: 972/671-8088.
▽▽▽▽▽   **Facility:** 78 units. 70 one- and 8 two-bedroom suites, some with efficiencies or kitchens. 3 stories, interior
Motel   corridors. *Bath:* combo or shower only. **Parking:** on-site. **Terms:** 7 day cancellation notice, [BP] meal plan
available, small pets only ($50 extra charge). **Amenities:** video library (fee), dual phone lines, voice mail,
irons, hair dryers. **Pool(s):** heated indoor. **Leisure Activities:** whirlpool, sports court. **Guest Services:** complimentary evening beverages: Mon-Thurs, valet and coin laundry. **Business Services:** meeting rooms, business center.
Cards: AX, DC, DS, MC, VI.

SOME UNITS

LA QUINTA INN & SUITES   Phone: (214)361-8200   **98**
(AAA) [SAVE]   All Year   1P: $79-$109   2P: $89-$119   XP: $10   F18
                    Location: I-75, exit 6 (Walnut Hill Ln/Meadow Rd) northbound, 0.5 mi n to Meadow Rd, U-turn under highway; exit 7
▽▽▽▽▽   (Royal Meadow Rd) southbound, 1 mi s on feeder. 10001 N Central Expwy 75231-4193. Fax: 214/691-0482.
                    Facility: 127 units. 120 one-bedroom standard units. 7 one-bedroom suites ($109-$169). 7 stories, interior
Small-scale Hotel   corridors. *Bath:* combo or shower only. **Parking:** on-site. **Terms:** 7 day cancellation notice, [BP] meal plan available. **Amenities:** dual
phone lines, voice mail, irons, hair dryers. **Fee:** video games, high-speed Internet. **Pool(s):** heated outdoor.
Leisure Activities: whirlpool, exercise room. **Guest Services:** valet and coin laundry, airport transportation-Dallas Love Field
Airport, area transportation-within 3 mi. **Business Services:** meeting rooms, business center. **Cards:** AX, CB, DC, DS, JC,
MC, VI. **Special Amenities:** free continental breakfast and free local telephone calls. *(See color ad p 272)*

SOME UNITS

LA QUINTA INN & SUITES-DALLAS ADDISON   Phone: (972)404-0004   **95**
(AAA) [SAVE]   All Year   1P: $69-$109   2P: $79-$119   XP: $10   F18
                    Location: Jct of Belt Line Rd and Landmark Blvd, just s. 14925 Landmark Blvd 75254. Fax: 972/960-6439.
▽▽▽▽▽   **Facility:** 152 units. 144 one-bedroom standard units. 8 one-bedroom suites ($109-$169). 3 stories, interior
                    corridors. *Bath:* combo or shower only. **Parking:** on-site. **Terms:** [ECP] meal plan available, small pets only.
Small-scale Hotel   **Amenities:** video games (fee), voice mail, irons, hair dryers. **Pool(s):** heated outdoor. **Leisure Activities:** whirlpool, limited exercise equipment. **Guest Services:** valet and coin laundry, area transportation-
within 5 mi. **Business Services:** meeting rooms, fax (fee). **Cards:** AX, CB, DC, DS, JC, MC, VI. **Special Amenities:** free
continental breakfast and free local telephone calls. *(See color ad p 272)*

SOME UNITS

(See map p. 236)

LA QUINTA INN-DALLAS-CITY PLACE

(AAA) (SAVE)   **Phone:** (214)821-4220   **67**
All Year   1P: $69-$99   2P: $79-$109   XP: $10   F18
Location: N off US 75, exit 2 (Henderson-Knox) northbound; exit 1B (Haskell/Blackburn) southbound. 4440 N Central Expwy 75206-6525. **Fax:** 214/821-7685. **Facility:** 101 one-bedroom standard units. 2 stories, exterior corridors. *Bath:* combo or shower only. **Parking:** on-site. **Terms:** [ECP] meal plan available, small pets only.
Small-scale Hotel **Amenities:** video games (fee), voice mail, irons, hair dryers. **Pool(s):** outdoor. **Business Services:** fax (fee).
Cards: AX, CB, DC, DS, JC, MC, VI. **Special Amenities:** free continental breakfast and free local telephone calls. *(See color ad below)*

SOME UNITS

LA QUINTA INN-DALLAS-EAST

(AAA) (SAVE)   **Phone:** (214)324-3731   **73**
All Year   1P: $59-$79   2P: $69-$89   XP: $10   F18
Location: E off I-30, US 67 and 80, exit 52A (Jim Miller), 0.8 mi w of jct Loop 12. 8303 E R L Thornton Frwy 75228-7105. **Fax:** 214/324-1652. **Facility:** 102 units, 99 one-bedroom standard units. 2 one- and 1 two-bedroom suites. 2 stories, exterior corridors. *Bath:* combo or shower only. **Parking:** on-site. **Terms:** [ECP] meal plan available,
Small-scale Hotel small pets only. **Amenities:** video games (fee), voice mail, irons, hair dryers. **Pool(s):** outdoor. **Business Services:** fax (fee). **Cards:** AX, CB, DC, DS, JC, MC, VI. **Special Amenities:** free continental breakfast and free local telephone calls. *(See color ad below)*

SOME UNITS

LA QUINTA INN LOVE FIELD

(AAA) (SAVE)   **Phone:** (214)630-5701   **56**
All Year   1P: $64-$79   2P: $74-$89   XP: $10   F18
Location: I-35 E, exit 434B (Regal Row). 1625 Regal Row 75247-3621. **Fax:** 214/634-2315. **Facility:** 133 one-bedroom standard units. 2 stories, exterior corridors. *Bath:* combo or shower only. **Parking:** on-site. **Terms:** [ECP] meal plan available, small pets only. **Amenities:** video games (fee), voice mail, irons, hair
Small-scale Hotel dryers. **Pool(s):** small outdoor. **Guest Services:** valet and coin laundry, airport transportation-Dallas Love Field Airport, area transportation-within 5 mi. **Business Services:** meeting rooms, fax (fee). **Cards:** AX, CB, DC, DS, JC, MC, VI. **Special Amenities:** free continental breakfast and free local telephone calls. *(See color ad below)*

SOME UNITS

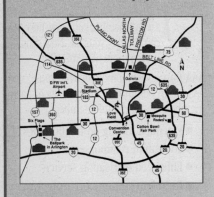

(See map p. 236)

LA QUINTA INN-RICHARDSON

Phone: (972)234-1016 [87]
All Year   1P: $59-$79   2P: $68-$89   XP: $10   F18
Location: US 75 N, exit 22 (Midpark Rd). 13685 N Central Expwy 75243-1001. Fax: 972/234-0682. **Facility:** 120 one-bedroom standard units. 2 stories, interior/exterior corridors. *Bath:* combo or shower only. **Parking:** on-site. **Terms:** [ECP] meal plan available, small pets only. **Amenities:** video games, voice mail, irons, hair dryers. **Pool(s):** outdoor. **Guest Services:** valet laundry, area transportation-within 5 mi. **Business Services:** meeting rooms, fax (fee). **Cards:** AX, CB, DC, DS, JC, MC, VI. **Special Amenities:** free continental breakfast and free local telephone calls. *(See color ad p 272)*
Small-scale Hotel

SOME UNITS

THE MANSION ON TURTLE CREEK

Phone: (214)559-2100 [66]
All Year   1P: $405-$2400   2P: $405-$2400   XP: $40   F18
Location: 2 mi nw, entrance on Gillespie St. Located in a residential area. 2821 Turtle Creek Blvd 75219. Fax: 214/528-4187. **Facility:** In a manicured hilltop setting, this restored 1925 mansion offers spacious guest units with traditional appointments. 143 units. 127 one-bedroom standard units, some with whirlpools. 16 one-bedroom suites, some with kitchens and/or whirlpools. 9 stories, interior corridors. *Bath:* combo or shower only. **Parking:** valet. **Terms:** cancellation fee imposed, package plans, small pets only. **Amenities:** video library, video games, CD players, high-speed Internet, dual phone lines, voice mail, fax, safes, honor bars, hair dryers. **Dining:** 7 am-3 & 6-10:30 pm, Fri & Sat-11 pm, cocktails, dining room, see separate listing, entertainment. **Pool(s):** heated outdoor. **Leisure Activities:** saunas, whirlpool, steamrooms. *Fee:* massage. **Guest Services:** sundries, valet laundry, area transportation-within 5 mi. **Business Services:** meeting rooms, business center. **Cards:** AX, CB, DC, DS, JC, MC, VI. **Special Amenities:** early check-in/late check-out and free newspaper. Affiliated with A Preferred Hotel.
Large-scale Hotel

SOME UNITS

MICROTEL INN & SUITES DALLAS/PLANO

Phone: (972)248-7045 [70]
All Year [CP]   1P: $40-$45   2P: $50-$69   XP: $5   F16
Location: George Bush Toll Rd, exit Preston Rd, on southwest corner. 19373 Preston Rd 75252. Fax: 972/248-7039. **Facility:** 81 one-bedroom standard units, some with whirlpools. 3 stories, interior corridors. *Bath:* combo or shower only. **Parking:** on-site. **Terms:** check-in 4 pm, weekly rates available. **Amenities:** high-speed Internet (fee), voice mail. *Some:* dual phone lines, hair dryers. **Pool(s):** small outdoor. **Leisure Activities:** exercise room. **Guest Services:** valet and coin laundry. **Business Services:** meeting rooms, business center. **Cards:** AX, CB, DC, DS, JC, MC, VI.
Small-scale Hotel

SOME UNITS

MOTEL 6 #1479

Phone: 214/388-8741 [71]
All Year   1P: $37-$51   2P: $43-$57   XP: $3   F17
Location: I-30, US 67 and 80, exit 52A (Jim Miller Rd). 0.8 mi w of jct Loop 12. 8108 E R L Thornton Frwy 75228. Fax: 214/388-3185. **Facility:** 106 one-bedroom standard units. 2 stories, exterior corridors. **Parking:** on-site. **Terms:** small pets only. **Amenities:** voice mail. **Guest Services:** coin laundry. **Business Services:** fax (fee). **Cards:** AX, CB, DC, DS, MC, VI.
Motel

SOME UNITS

MOTEL 6 FOREST LANE-SOUTH #1119

Phone: 972/484-9111 [32]
2/1-5/21   1P: $35-$45   2P: $41-$51   XP: $3   F17
5/22-1/31   1P: $37-$47   XP: $3   F17
Location: I-635, exit 26 (Josey Ln) eastbound, 0.5 mi s to Forest Ln, just w; exit 25 (Josey Ln) westbound, just s to Forest Ln, just w. 2660 Forest Ln 75234. Fax: 972/484-0214. **Facility:** 117 one-bedroom standard units. 3 stories, exterior corridors. *Bath:* combo or shower only. **Parking:** on-site. **Terms:** small pets only. **Pool(s):** outdoor. **Guest Services:** coin laundry. **Business Services:** fax (fee). **Cards:** AX, CB, DC, DS, MC, VI.
Motel

SOME UNITS

QUALITY SUITES

Phone: (214)904-9955 [50]
All Year [ECP]   1P: $69-$99   XP: $10   F17
Location: I-35, exit 436 (W Northwest Hwy), 0.8 mi e. 2380 W Northwest Hwy 75220. Fax: 214/904-9955. **Facility:** 78 units. 31 one-bedroom standard units. 47 one-bedroom suites ($104-$149), some with whirlpools. 3 stories, interior corridors. *Bath:* combo or shower only. **Parking:** on-site. **Terms:** pets ($25 fee). **Amenities:** voice mail, irons, hair dryers. **Pool(s):** heated indoor. **Leisure Activities:** whirlpool, exercise room. **Guest Services:** complimentary evening beverages: Mon-Thurs, valet and coin laundry. **Business Services:** meeting rooms, PC, fax (fee). **Cards:** AX, DC, DS, MC, VI.
Small-scale Hotel

SOME UNITS

QUALITY SUITES-PARK CENTRAL (NOW KNOWN AS COMFORT SUITES)

Phone: (972)699-7400 [88]
All Year [ECP]   1P: $74   2P: $74   F17
Location: US 75, exit 22 (Midpark Rd). Located in a commercial area. 13165 Central Expwy 75243. Fax: 972/231-8174. **Facility:** 78 units. 32 one-bedroom standard units, 46 one-bedroom suites, some with whirlpools. 3 stories, interior corridors. *Bath:* combo or shower only. **Parking:** on-site. **Terms:** [CP] meal plan available. **Amenities:** voice mail, irons, hair dryers. **Pool(s):** small heated indoor. **Leisure Activities:** whirlpool, limited exercise equipment. **Guest Services:** complimentary evening beverages: Mon-Thurs, valet and coin laundry. **Business Services:** meeting rooms, business center. **Cards:** AX, DC, DS, MC, VI.
Small-scale Hotel

SOME UNITS

(See map p. 236)

RADISSON HOTEL & SUITES DALLAS Phone: (214)351-4477 **46**
All Year 1P: $149 2P: $149 XP: $10 F18
Location: Nw off I-35 E and US 77 at jct Loop 12, exit 436. 2330 W Northwest Hwy 75220. Fax: 214/351-4499.
Large-scale Hotel Facility: 199 units. 193 one-bedroom standard units. 6 one-bedroom suites ($159). 8 stories, interior/exterior corridors. Bath: combo or shower only. Parking: on-site. Terms: cancellation fee imposed. Amenities: voice mail, irons, hair dryers. Fee: video games, high-speed Internet. Pool(s): outdoor. Leisure Activities: whirlpool, exercise room. Guest Services: gift shop, valet and coin laundry, area transportation. Business Services: meeting rooms, fax (fee). Cards: AX, CB, DC, DS, JC, MC, VI. *(See ad below)*

SOME UNITS

RADISSON HOTEL CENTRAL/DALLAS Phone: (214)750-6060 **59**
All Year 1P: $139 2P: $139 XP: $10 F18
Location: US 75, exit 3 (Mockingbird Ln). 6060 N Central Expwy 75206. Fax: 214/750-5959. Facility: 293 units. 290 one-bedroom standard units. 3 one-bedroom suites. 9 stories, interior corridors. Bath: combo or shower only. Parking: on-site. Terms: 3 day cancellation notice-fee imposed. Amenities: voice mail, irons, hair dryers. Some: dual phone lines. Dining: 6:30 am-2 & 5-10 pm, cocktails. Pool(s): heated indoor/outdoor. Leisure
Large-scale Hotel Activities: sauna, whirlpool. Guest Services: gift shop, valet laundry, airport transportation-Dallas Love Field Airport, area transportation-within 5 mi. Business Services: meeting rooms, fax (fee). Cards: AX, CB, DC, DS, MC, VI. Special Amenities: early check-in/late check-out and free newspaper. *(See ad below)*

SOME UNITS

FEE

RADISSON HOTEL DALLAS Phone: (214)634-8850 **63**
All Year 1P: $59-$69 2P: $59-$69 XP: $10 F18
Location: I-35 E, exit 433C (Mockingbird Ln), 0.8 mi e. 1893 W Mockingbird Ln 75235. Fax: 214/630-8134.
Facility: 307 units. 301 one-bedroom standard units. 6 one-bedroom suites. 8 stories, interior corridors. Bath: combo or shower only. Parking: on-site. Terms: small pets only ($25 fee, $50 deposit). Amenities: video
Small-scale Hotel games (fee), voice mail, irons, hair dryers. Some: dual phone lines. Dining: 6 am-11 pm, cocktails. Pool(s): outdoor, wading. Leisure Activities: sauna, whirlpool, racquetball courts, exercise room, basketball, volleyball. Guest Services: gift shop, valet and coin laundry, airport transportation-Dallas Love Field Airport, area transportation-within 5 mi. Business Services: meeting rooms, business center. Cards: AX, CB, DC, DS, JC, MC, VI. Special Amenities: early check-in/late check-out and free newspaper. *(See color ad p 275)*

SOME UNITS

(See map p. 236)

RED ROOF INN-MARKET CENTER
AAA SAVE
Motel

Phone: (214)638-5151 58

All Year   1P: $39-$49   2P: $44-$54   XP: $5   F18
Location: I-35 E, exit 434A (Empire Central Dr), 0.3 mi e. 1550 Empire Central Dr 75235. **Fax:** 214/638-3920. **Facility:** 111 one-bedroom standard units. 2 stories, exterior corridors. **Parking:** on-site. **Terms:** small pets only. **Amenities:** video games (fee), voice mail. **Guest Services:** coin laundry. **Business Services:** fax (fee). **Cards:** AX, CB, DC, DS, MC, VI. **Special Amenities:** free local telephone calls and free newspaper.

SOME UNITS

RED ROOF INN-NORTHWEST
AAA SAVE
Small-scale Hotel

Phone: (972)506-8100 45

All Year   1P: $36-$49   2P: $41-$54   XP: $5   F18
Location: Just sw of jct Loop 12 (Northwest Hwy) and Spur 348, 0.8 mi w of I-35 E and US 77, exit 436. 10335 Gardner Rd 75220. **Fax:** 972/556-0072. **Facility:** 112 one-bedroom standard units. 2 stories, exterior corridors. **Parking:** on-site. **Terms:** small pets only. **Amenities:** video games (fee), voice mail. **Business Services:** fax (fee). **Cards:** AX, CB, DC, DS, MC, VI. **Special Amenities:** free local telephone calls and free newspaper.

SOME UNITS

RESIDENCE INN BY MARRIOTT AT CENTRAL-NORTHPARK
SAVE
Condominium

Phone: (214)750-8220 40

All Year   1P: $89-$135
Location: I-75 N, exit 6 (Meadow Rd) northbound; exit 7 (Royal Ln) southbound. 10333 N Central Expwy 75231. **Fax:** 214/750-8244. **Facility:** 103 units. 85 one- and 18 two-bedroom suites ($89-$184) with efficiencies. 3 stories, exterior corridors. **Parking:** on-site. **Terms:** [BP] meal plan available, pets ($100 fee). **Amenities:** voice mail, irons, hair dryers. **Pool(s):** heated outdoor. **Leisure Activities:** whirlpool, exercise room, sports court. **Guest Services:** complimentary evening beverages: Mon-Thurs, valet and coin laundry, area transportation. **Business Services:** meeting rooms, fax (fee). **Cards:** AX, DC, DS, MC, VI.

SOME UNITS

RESIDENCE INN BY MARRIOTT-DALLAS MARKET CENTER
SAVE
Small-scale Hotel

Phone: 214/631-2472 64

All Year   1P: $94   2P: $94
Location: I-35 E, exit 432B (Commonwealth), on northbound frontage road. 6950 N Stemmons Frwy 75247. **Fax:** 214/634-9645. **Facility:** 142 units. 107 one- and 35 two-bedroom suites with efficiencies. 3 stories, interior/exterior corridors. *Bath:* combo or shower only. **Parking:** on-site. **Terms:** [ECP] meal plan available, pets ($50 deposit). **Amenities:** voice mail, irons, hair dryers. **Pool(s):** heated outdoor. **Leisure Activities:** whirlpool, exercise room, sports court. **Guest Services:** complimentary evening beverages: Mon-Thurs, valet and coin laundry, area transportation. **Business Services:** meeting rooms, fax (fee). **Cards:** AX, CB, DC, DS, JC, MC, VI.

SOME UNITS

RESIDENCE INN BY MARRIOTT-DALLAS PARK CENTRAL
SAVE
Small-scale Hotel

Phone: (972)503-1333 99

All Year   1P: $79-$109   2P: $104-$139
Location: I-635, exit 20 (Hillcrest), just e, on eastbound access road. 7642 LBJ Frwy 75251. **Fax:** 972/503-8333. **Facility:** 139 units. 60 one-bedroom standard units, some with efficiencies or kitchens. 56 one- and 23 two-bedroom suites, some with efficiencies or kitchens. 3 stories, interior corridors. *Bath:* combo or shower only. **Parking:** on-site. **Terms:** cancellation fee imposed, [BP] meal plan available, small pets only ($75-$100 fee). **Amenities:** video games (fee), dual phone lines, voice mail, irons, hair dryers. **Pool(s):** heated outdoor. **Leisure Activities:** whirlpool, exercise room, sports court. **Guest Services:** sundries, complimentary evening beverages: Mon-Thurs, valet and coin laundry, area transportation. **Business Services:** meeting rooms, fax (fee). **Cards:** AX, CB, DC, DS, JC, MC, VI.

SOME UNITS

SHERATON DALLAS BROOKHOLLOW HOTEL
AAA SAVE
Large-scale Hotel

Phone: (214)630-7000 57

All Year   1P: $79-$89   2P: $79-$89   XP: $10   F18
Location: I-35 E, exit 433B, just nw of jct I-35 E and W Mockingbird Ln. 1241 W Mockingbird Ln 75247. **Fax:** 214/638-6943. **Facility:** 348 units. 341 one-bedroom standard units. 7 one-bedroom suites. 13 stories, interior corridors. *Bath:* combo or shower only. **Parking:** on-site. **Terms:** cancellation fee imposed, small pets only ($50 deposit). **Amenities:** dual phone lines, voice mail, irons, hair dryers. **Fee:** video games, high-speed Internet. *Some:* fax. **Dining:** 6 am-2 & 5-11 pm, Sat & Sun 6:30 am-2 pm, cocktails. **Pool(s):** outdoor, wading. **Leisure Activities:** exercise room. **Guest Services:** gift shop, valet and coin laundry, airport transportation-Dallas Love Field Airport, area transportation-within 5 mi. **Business Services:** conference facilities, business center. **Cards:** AX, CB, DC, DS, MC, VI. **Special Amenities:** early check-in/late check-out and free newspaper. *(See color ad p 275)*

SOME UNITS

STAYBRIDGE SUITES DALLAS-PARK CENTRAL
Small-scale Hotel

Phone: (972)391-0000 61

All Year [BP]   1P: $114-$129   2P: $114-$129   XP: $10   F16
Location: I-635, exit 19B (Coit Rd), 0.3 mi n, then just w. 7880 Alpha Rd 75240. **Fax:** 972/391-0008. **Facility:** 114 units. 101 one- and 13 two-bedroom suites with efficiencies. 3 stories, interior corridors. *Bath:* combo or shower only. **Parking:** on-site. **Terms:** pets ($25 fee, $100 deposit). **Amenities:** video games, dual phone lines, voice mail, fax, irons, hair dryers. **Pool(s):** outdoor. **Leisure Activities:** whirlpool, limited exercise equipment. **Guest Services:** complimentary evening beverages: Tues & Wed, valet and coin laundry, area transportation. **Business Services:** meeting rooms. **Cards:** AX, CB, DC, DS, JC, MC, VI.

SOME UNITS

(See map p. 236)

SUPER 8 MOTEL

(AAA) [SAVE]
▼▼▼ ▼▼▼
Motel

All Year   1P: $49-$59   2P: $54-$64   Phone: (214)631-6633 🟥55
          XP: $5   F
Location: Nw off SR 183, 1 mi nw jct I-35 E and US 77, exit Regal Row. 9229 John Carpenter Frwy 75247.
Fax: 214/631-6616. **Facility:** 134 one-bedroom standard units. 2 stories, exterior corridors. *Bath:* combo or shower only. **Parking:** on-site. **Terms:** 7 day cancellation notice, [BP] & [ECP] meal plans available. **Amenities:** video library. **Pool(s):** small outdoor. **Leisure Activities:** sauna, exercise room. **Guest Services:** coin laundry, airport transportation-Dallas Love Field Airport. **Business Services:** meeting rooms, fax (fee). **Cards:** AX, DC, DS, MC, VI. **Special Amenities: free continental breakfast and free local telephone calls.**

SOME UNITS
[S][D] ✈ 🍴 ⚙ ➡ 🐾 🎬 [DATA PORT] / [✕] [VCR] 🛡 📠 /
                    FEE   FEE

TERRACES HOTEL AND CONFERENCE CENTER

▼▼▼ ▼▼▼
Small-scale Hotel

All Year   1P: $125   2P: $135   Phone: (972)453-0600 🟥76
Location: SR 183, exit Dallas-Forth Worth Airport, 0.5 mi n to Airfield Dr S, then 2.5 mi w. Located within the airport. 2200 W Airfield Dr 75261 (PO Box 612427, DALLAS). Fax: 972/453-0292. **Facility:** 109 units. 107 one-bedroom standard units. 2 one-bedroom suites ($159-$169). 3 stories, interior corridors. **Parking:** on-site. **Terms:** cancellation fee imposed. **Amenities:** dual phone lines, voice mail, irons, hair dryers. **Pool(s):** outdoor. **Leisure Activities:** saunas, 2 lighted tennis courts, racquetball courts, jogging, sports court. **Guest Services:** gift shop, valet and coin laundry, area transportation. **Business Services:** meeting rooms, business center. **Cards:** AX, DC, DS, MC, VI.

SOME UNITS
[ASK][S][D] ✈ 🍴 ⚙ ➡ 🎬 🏋 ✕ [DATA PORT] 🛡 💻 / ✕ /

TERRA COTTA INN

▼▼▼ ▼▼▼
Small-scale Hotel

All Year [ECP]   1P: $63-$83   2P: $63-$83   Phone: (972)387-2525 🟥25
          XP: $4   F12
Location: I-635, exit 21 (Preston Rd). 6101 Lyndon B Johnson Frwy 75240. Fax: 972/387-3784. **Facility:** 97 units. 96 one-bedroom standard units. 1 one-bedroom suite ($125-$129). 3 stories, exterior corridors. **Parking:** on-site. **Amenities:** irons, hair dryers. **Pool(s):** outdoor. **Business Services:** meeting rooms, fax (fee). **Cards:** AX, DC, DS, MC, VI.

SOME UNITS
[ASK][S][D] 🍴 🎬 ➡ 🎬 [DATA PORT] 💻 / ✕ /

WELLESLEY INN & SUITES (DALLAS/PARK CENTRAL)

(AAA) [SAVE]
▼▼▼ ▼▼▼
Small-scale Hotel

All Year   1P: $70-$80   2P: $70-$80   Phone: (972)671-7722 🟥72
          XP: $10   F17
Location: I-635, exit 18A (Greenville Ave), just sw. 9019 Vantage Point Rd 75243. Fax: 972/671-7723. **Facility:** 134 units. 130 one-bedroom standard units with efficiencies. 4 one-bedroom suites ($99-$149) with efficiencies. 3 stories (no elevator), exterior corridors. *Bath:* combo or shower only. **Parking:** on-site. **Terms:** weekly rates available, [ECP] meal plan available, small pets only. **Amenities:** high-speed Internet, dual phone lines, voice mail, irons, hair dryers. **Leisure Activities:** limited exercise equipment. **Guest Services:** valet and coin laundry. **Business Services:** meeting rooms, fax (fee). **Cards:** AX, DS, JC, MC, VI. **Special Amenities: free continental breakfast and free newspaper.** *(See color ad p 250)*

SOME UNITS
[S][D] 🛏 🍴 ⚙ 🎬 🎬 [DATA PORT] 🛡 📠 💻 / ✕ /

THE WESTIN GALLERIA, DALLAS

▼▼▼ ▼▼▼ ▼▼▼
Large-scale Hotel

All Year   1P: $209-$299   2P: $209-$299   Phone: (972)934-9494 🟥92
Location: Just n of jct I-635 and N Dallas Pkwy. Located in the Galleria Center. 13340 Dallas Pkwy 75240. Fax: 972/851-2869. **Facility:** The hotel is within walking distance from stores and restaurants. 432 units. 428 one-bedroom standard units. 4 one-bedroom suites, some with whirlpools. 21 stories, interior corridors. *Bath:* combo or shower only. **Parking:** on-site and valet. **Terms:** small pets only. **Amenities:** dual phone lines, voice mail, safes, honor bars, irons, hair dryers. *Some:* fax. **Pool(s):** heated outdoor. **Leisure Activities:** jogging. **Guest Services:** gift shop, valet laundry. **Business Services:** meeting rooms, business center. **Cards:** AX, CB, DC, DS, JC, MC, VI.

SOME UNITS
[ASK][S][D] 🛏 🍴 24🍴 ⚙ 🐾 🎬 ➡ 🏋 ✕ [DATA PORT] 💻 / ✕ /
                    FEE

(See map p. 236)

THE WESTIN PARK CENTRAL DALLAS   **Phone:** (972)385-3000   🔟
🔻🔻🔻🔻🔻🔻 All Year   1P: $148-$168   2P: $148-$168   XP: $10   F12
Location: N off I-635, 0.3 mi w of jct US 75, exit 19C (Coit Rd) eastbound; exit 19B (US 75/Coit Rd) westbound. 12720
Large-scale Hotel Merit Dr 75251. Fax: 972/991-4557. **Facility:** The hotel offers large, tastefully appointed rooms conveniently
located near two major shopping malls. 536 units. 524 one-bedroom standard units. 12 one-bedroom suites
($325-$925), some with whirlpools. 20 stories, interior corridors. *Bath:* combo or shower only. **Parking:** on-site and valet.
Terms: cancellation fee imposed. **Amenities:** video games (fee), dual phone lines, voice mail, honor bars, irons, hair dryers.
Some: fax, safes. **Pool(s):** heated outdoor. **Leisure Activities:** whirlpool. **Guest Services:** gift shop, valet laundry, area transportation. **Business Services:** conference facilities, business center. **Cards:** AX, CB, DC, DS, MC, VI.

SOME UNITS

(ASK) (S☐) (🍽) (&M) (🐕) (🖉) (🛏) (➕) (🎦) (DATA PORT) (🖥) / (✕) (🔋) (🖥)
                                                                          FEE   FEE FEE

WINGATE INN   **Phone:** (214)267-8400   🔢
🔻🔻🔻 All Year [ECP]   1P: $79-$89
Location: I-35, exit 434A (Empire Central), just n. 8650 N Stemmons 75247. Fax: 214/267-1122. **Facility:** 89 one-
Small-scale Hotel bedroom standard units. 3 stories, interior corridors. *Bath:* combo or shower only. **Parking:** on-site.
Amenities: video games (fee), high-speed Internet, dual phone lines, voice mail, safes, irons, hair dryers.
Pool(s): heated indoor. **Leisure Activities:** exercise room. **Guest Services:** valet and coin laundry, area transportation. **Busi-
ness Services:** meeting rooms, business center. **Cards:** AX, CB, DC, DS, JC, MC, VI.
                                                                          SOME UNITS

(ASK) (S☐) (✈) (&M) (🐕) (🛏) (🎦) (DATA PORT) (🔋) (🖥) (🖥) / (✕) /

WYNDHAM GARDEN HOTEL-DALLAS PARK CENTRAL   **Phone:** (972)680-3000   🔢
(AAA) (SAVE) 2/1-4/19 & 9/8-1/31   1P: $79-$99   2P: $79-$109   XP: $10   F18
              4/20-9/7   1P: $79-$89   2P: $79-$99   XP: $10   F18
🔻🔻🔻🔻 **Location:** I-635, exit 19C (Coit Rd), just ne. 8051 Lyndon B Johnson Frwy 75251. Fax: 972/680-3200. **Facility:** 197
Small-scale Hotel units. 191 one-bedroom standard units. 6 one-bedroom suites ($175-$185). 6 stories, interior corridors.
Parking: on-site. **Terms:** cancellation fee imposed. **Amenities:** video games, high-speed Internet (fee), dual
phone lines, voice mail, irons, hair dryers. **Dining:** 6:30 am-10 pm, cocktails. **Pool(s):** outdoor. **Leisure Activities:** limited exercise equipment. **Guest Services:** valet laundry, area transportation-within 5 mi. **Business Services:** meeting
rooms, fax (fee). **Cards:** AX, DC, DS, MC, VI.
                                                                          SOME UNITS

(S☐) (🍽) (Y) (&M) (🖉) (🛏) (🎦) (DATA PORT) (🖥) / (✕) (🔋) /

────── *The following lodging was either not evaluated or did not* ──────
meet AAA rating requirements but is listed for your information only.

HILTON SUITES DALLAS NORTH   **Phone:** 972/503-8700
(fyi) All Year   1P: $99-$269   2P: $99-$269   XP: $10   F18
Motel Too new to rate, opening scheduled for November 2002. **Location:** From Dallas Pkwy, exit e on Alpha Tonoel Rd,
then s on Noel. 13402 Noel Rd 75240. **Amenities:** restaurant, coffeemakers, microwaves, refrigerators, pool.
Cards: AX, CB, DC, DS, JC, MC, VI. *(See color ad p 277)*

See Red for Savings

*L*ook for the red (SAVE) icon next to
lodging listings in this book, and as
a AAA member you'll enjoy great room
rates from that establishment!*

Remember, if you see the red (SAVE) icon,
you'll save some green!

See TourBook Navigator section, page 14, for complete details.

(See map p. 236)

──────── WHERE TO DINE ────────

ABACUS
▼▼▼▼ ▼▼▼▼
Continental

Dinner: $20-$45   **Phone:** 214/559-3111   100
Location: Corner of McKinney Ave and Armstrong; between Knox and Fitzhugh. 4511 McKinney Ave 75205. **Hours:** 6 pm-10 pm, Fri & Sat-11 pm. Closed major holidays; also Sun. **Reservations:** suggested. **Features:** You may see some of the elite of Dallas in the Abacus if you look closely. This is definitely one of the restaurants the "in-crowd" hangs out at. The upscale dining and Art Deco decor make for an enjoyable evening. Smoke free premises. Dressy casual; cocktails. **Parking:** valet. **Cards:** AX, CB, DC, DS, MC, VI.

AW SHUCKS
▼▼
Steak & Seafood

Lunch: $6-$10   **Dinner:** $6-$10   **Phone:** 214/821-9449   76
Location: N on US 75, exit 3 (Mockingbird Ln), 0.5 mi e to Greenville Ave, then 0.4 mi s. 3601 Greenville Ave 75206. **Hours:** 11 am-11 pm, Fri & Sat-11:45 pm, Sun 11:30 am-10 pm. Closed: 11/27, 12/25. **Features:** A popular eatery with a modest nautical theme, it offers a sidewalk patio with either covered or open al fresco dining. Oysters, shrimp and gumbo are a few of the tasty items served in what is truly a "make-yourself-at-home" dining experience. Casual dress; beer & wine only. **Parking:** on-site. **Cards:** AX, CB, DC, DS, MC, VI.

BLUE GOOSE CANTINA
▼▼ ▼▼
Mexican

Lunch: $6-$10   **Dinner:** $9-$20   **Phone:** 214/823-8339   82
Location: N from US 75, exit 3 (Mockingbird Ln), 0.5 mi e to Greenville Ave, then 0.9 mi s. 2905 Greeenville Ave 75206. **Hours:** 11 am-11 pm, Fri & Sat-midnight. Closed: 11/27, 12/25. **Features:** Guests can sample a best-selling margarita—Grandma's favorite recipe—as they relax in a Mexican cantina setting. Sour cream enchiladas—a mixture of rice, beans and chicken in sour cream sauce rolled in a fresh tortilla—are a favorite selection. Casual dress; cocktails. **Parking:** on-site. **Cards:** AX, CB, DC, DS, MC, VI.

BOB'S STEAK & CHOP HOUSE
▼▼▼
Steak House

Dinner: $23-$40   **Phone:** 214/528-9446   65
Location: Between US 75/Central Expwy and North Dallas Tollway. 4300 Lemmon Ave 75219. **Hours:** 5 pm-10 pm, Fri & Sat-11 pm. Closed major holidays; also Sun. **Reservations:** suggested. **Features:** Popular award-winning steakhouse dining in a refined dining room setting is enhanced by mahogany booths and white table cloths. Beef dominates the menu with all entrees served with the signature colossal glazed carrot and choice of potato. The cogenial service is crisp. The eatery is cigar friendly. Dressy casual; cocktails. **Parking:** on-site (fee) and valet. **Cards:** AX, DC, DS, MC, VI.

CAMPISI'S EQYPTIAN
▼▼
Italian

Lunch: $8   **Dinner:** $10-$21   **Phone:** 214/827-0355   70
Location: US 75, exit 3 (Mockingbird Ln), just e. 5610 E Mockingbird Ln 75206. **Hours:** 11 am-10 pm, Fri & Sat-11 pm. Closed major holidays; also evening of 12/24. **Features:** This Dallas landmark serves traditional favorites like pan pizza, spaghetti, minestrone soup, salad, pasta and desserts. A fun and energetic atmosphere is enhanced by an ever-smiling staff and upbeat jukebox music. This is a great place to bring the kids. Casual dress; cocktails. **Parking:** on-site. **Cards:** AX, DS, MC, VI.

CELEBRATION
▼▼ ▼▼
American

Lunch: $7-$11   **Dinner:** $9-$17   **Phone:** 214/351-5681   58
Location: Between Inwood Rd and Lemon Ave; near Dallas Love Field Airport. 4503 W Lovers Ln 75209. **Hours:** 11 am-2:30 & 5:30-9:30 pm, Fri-10:30 pm, Sat 11:30 am-3 & 5-10:30 pm, Sun 11 am-9:30 pm. Closed: 11/27, 12/24, 12/25. **Reservations:** accepted. **Features:** Made-from-scratch cooking and family-style service make diners feel right at home. Dinner entrees are served with a choice of three side dishes, such as glazed carrots, mashed potatoes and beans. Be sure to save room for a homemade dessert. Casual dress; cocktails. **Parking:** on-site. **Cards:** AX, CB, DC, DS, MC, VI.

CHEZ GERARD
▼▼ ▼▼
Provincial French

Lunch: $5-$10   **Dinner:** $16-$20   **Phone:** 214/522-6865   93
Location: Corner of McKinney Ave and Armstrong; between Knox St and Fitzhugh Ave. 4444 McKinney Ave 75205. **Hours:** 11:30 am-2 & 6-10 pm, Fri & Sat-11 pm. Closed major holidays; also Sun. **Reservations:** suggested. **Features:** Classic French cuisine is offered including selections of fish, beef, chicken, pork, veal, lamb and rabbit dishes. Elaborate desserts include an assortment of souffles, oromo brulee and iced cream puffs. All dishes are skillfully prepared and decorated to be both flavorful and eye- catching. The restaurant depicts a small French country house with its wood floors, petite wall lamp sconces, lace curtains and colorful floral walls. Outside dining is also available. Smoke free premises. Dressy casual; cocktails. **Parking:** on-site. **Cards:** AX, CB, DC, DS, MC, VI.

CHIP'S
▼▼
American

Lunch: $6-$8   **Dinner:** $6-$8   **Phone:** 214/526-1092   88
Location: US 75, exit 2, 0.3 mi w on Knox St, then just s. 4501 N Cole Ave 75205. **Hours:** 11 am-10 pm, Fri & Sat-11 pm. Closed: 11/27, 12/25. **Features:** Located inside a bright, yellow and green two-story house, this self-serve eatery offers up traditional fast food. The large hamburgers with crispy fries and onion rings are yummy. Wash down your meal with one of Chip's creamy milkshakes. Outdoor patio seating is available. Casual dress; beer & wine only. **Parking:** on-site. **Cards:** AX, MC, VI.

CITY CAFE
▼▼▼
American

Lunch: $8-$13   **Dinner:** $14-$21   **Phone:** 214/351-2233   61
Location: Jct of W Lovers Ln and North Dallas Tollway. 5757 W Lovers Ln 75209. **Hours:** 11:30 am-2:30 & 5:30-10 pm, Sun from 11 am. Closed: 1/1, 11/27, 12/25. **Reservations:** accepted. **Features:** Great food, such as warm cabbage salad appetizers to special crabcake entrees, is the hallmark of the trendy bistro. The monthly changing menu offers a fresh variety of chicken, steak and seafood dishes. Casual dress; cocktails. **Parking:** on-site. **Cards:** AX, CB, DC, DS, MC, VI.

(See map p. 236)

CIUDAD
Lunch: $8-$12   **Dinner:** $16-$29   **Phone:** 214/219-3141   (77)
Location: Just n of jct Lemmon and Oak Lawn aves; in Turtle Creek Village. 3888 Oak Lawn Ave 75219. **Hours:** 6 pm-10 pm, Fri & Sat-11 pm, Sun 11 am-2 & 6-10 pm. Closed major holidays. **Reservations:** suggested.
Mexican
Features: The Ciudad is a different type of Mexican cuisine. They specialize in the more sophisticated and complex cuisine of Mexico City. They offer a wide variety of dishes from the city. Be sure to sample the ceviche or raw fish through the "bocadillos" (small bites) on a tostada. The restaurant has been listed in such magazines as: Bon Apetit, Esquire, Dallas Guide, & Metropolitan Home. Smoke free premises. Casual dress; cocktails. **Parking:** on-site.
Cards: AX, DC, DS, MC, VI.

CUBA LIBRE
Lunch: $9-$18   **Dinner:** $9-$18   **Phone:** 214/827-2820   (91)
Location: US 75, exit 2 (Knox St/Henderson Ave), just e. 2822 N Henderson Ave 75206. **Hours:** 11 am-2 am, Sun & Mon-midnight. Closed: 12/25. **Reservations:** suggested. **Features:** The restaurant presents of menu of
Nouvelle
Caribbean
what it calls new Caribbean cuisine. In addition to tacos, the menu lists some exotic dishes prepared blackened, grilled, sauteed or fried. Caribbean seasonings match the bright decor. A large lounge is upstairs, and the patio appeals to diners willing to brave the elements. Casual dress; cocktails;
entertainment. **Parking:** on-site. **Cards:** AX, DC, DS, MC, VI.

DICKEY'S
Lunch: $7-$13   **Dinner:** $7-$13   **Phone:** 972/691-1494   (46)
Location: Just w of US 75. 7770 Forest Ln 75230. **Hours:** 11 am-8 pm, Fri & Sat-9 pm. Closed major holidays.
Features: Go back for seconds at this self-serve cafeteria where a Western flair characterizes the decor.
Regional American
The buffet is filled with barbecue beef, chicken and ribs. Side dishes include beans, coleslaw and homemade potato salad. Casual dress. **Parking:** on-site. **Cards:** AX, CB, DC, DS, MC, VI.

DIXIE HOUSE
Lunch: $8-$13   **Dinner:** $8-$13   **Phone:** 214/826-2412   (94)
Location: Lakewood section, near Abrams Rd. 6400 Gaston Ave 75214. **Hours:** 11 am-10 pm. Closed: 12/25.
Features: The chicken-fried steak is seasoned and deep fried. The juicy pot roast is filled with carrots and
Regional American
onions. An open dining room resembles a warehouse. Hand-crafted memorabilia like quilts and old kitchen utensils hang from the walls. Casual dress; cocktails. **Parking:** on-site. **Cards:** AX, CB, DC, DS, MC, VI.

DUNSTON'S STEAK HOUSE
Lunch: $6-$9   **Dinner:** $10-$25   **Phone:** 214/352-8320   (60)
Location: Between North Dallas Tollway and Inwood Rd on north side of road. 5423 W Lover's Ln 75209. **Hours:** 11 am-11 pm, Sat from 5 pm, Sun 5 pm-10 pm. Closed: 1/1, 12/25. **Reservations:** accepted.
Steak House
Features: Family owned and operated, this neighborhood restaurant is a casually familiar place to dine. Steaks are cooked over an open-fire in the main dining room using mesquite wood. Such desserts as Key lime pie and bread pudding are made daily. Casual dress; cocktails. **Parking:** on-site. **Cards:** AX, DC, DS, MC, VI.

EL FENIX
Lunch: $7-$9   **Dinner:** $8-$12   **Phone:** 214/363-5279   (57)
Location: Just w of jct Hillcrest Ave. 6811 W Northwest Hwy 75225. **Hours:** 11 am-10 pm. Closed: 11/27, 12/25.
Features: Since 1918, this Tex-Mex cafe has been serving a spicy variety of food. Salsa and chips are a
Regional Mexican
great way to start your meal. Fajitas are delivered to your table sizzling. The Mexican-style chandeliers add to the colorful dining area. Casual dress; cocktails. **Parking:** on-site. **Cards:** AX, DC, DS, MC, VI.

GERSHWIN'S
Lunch: $10-$18   **Dinner:** $17-$31   **Phone:** 214/373-7171   (50)
Location: N, 0.5 mi e of US 75, exit 6 (Walnut Hill Ln); southeast corner of Walnut Hill Ln and Greenville Ave. 8442 Walnut Hill Ln 75231. **Hours:** 11:30 am-10 pm, Fri & Sat-11 pm. Closed major holidays.
Continental
Reservations: suggested. **Features:** Brass, polished wood and soft lighting create a chic New York-style ambience. Enjoy popular starters like duck confit enchiladas and spicy rabbit spring rolls, plus an assortment of seafood and beef dishes while a pianist performs Gershwin classics. Dressy casual; cocktails; entertainment.
Parking: on-site. **Cards:** AX, DC, DS, MC, VI.

GLORIA'S RESTAURANT
Lunch: $6-$7   **Dinner:** $9-$13   **Phone:** 214/874-0088   (44)
Location: US 75, exit Mockingbird Ln, 0.5 mi e to Greenville Ave, 0.4 mi s. 3715 Greenville Ave 75206. **Hours:** 11 am-10:30 pm, Fri & Sat-11:30 pm, Sun-11 pm. Closed: 11/27, 12/25. **Features:** Authentic Salvadoran
English
recipes with eye-catching presentation are served in a relaxing, colorful atmosphere, and include regional specialty dishes such as plantain pupusa, tamales wrapped in banana leaves, fajitas, pollo asado and black beans with rice. Casual dress; cocktails. **Parking:** on-site and valet. **Cards:** AX, DC, DS, MC, VI.

GOOD EATS
Lunch: $7-$10   **Dinner:** $9-$16   **Phone:** 214/522-3287   (92)
Location: Just n of Lemmon Ave and Oak Lawn Ave; in Turtle Creek Village. 3888 Oak Lawn Ave 75219. **Hours:** 11 am-10 pm, Fri & Sat-11 pm. Closed: 11/27, 12/25. **Features:** An efficient wait staff delivers hearty portions
American
of traditional Texas-style home cooking. Start out with the crispy onion dipsticks. The mesquite-grilled chicken is brushed with seasoned juices. The dining room has a familiar, relaxed ambience. Casual dress;
cocktails. **Parking:** on-site. **Cards:** AX, CB, DC, DS, MC, VI.

THE GRAPE
Lunch: $8-$13   **Dinner:** $11-$28   **Phone:** 214/828-1981   (97)
Location: N on US 75, exit 3 (Mockingbird Ln), 0.5 mi e to Greenville Ave then 0.9 mi s. 2808 Greenville Ave 75206.
Hours: 11:30 am-2:30 & 5:30-11 pm. Closed major holidays. **Features:** Candlelight and soft music fill this
Continental
small bistro with cozy romance. An ever-changing menu features regional specialties from France, Italy, and Asia, served in either the dining room with its grapevine motif, or in the very European sidewalk cafe.
Smoke free premises. Casual dress; cocktails. **Parking:** on-site. **Cards:** AX, CB, DC, DS, MC, VI.

(See map p. 236)

HOFSTETTER'S SPARGEL CAFE

German

Lunch: $7-$11   **Dinner:** $14-$22   **Phone:** 214/368-3002   59

Location: Between North Dallas Tollway and Preston Rd on the north side of Lovers Ln. 4326 Lovers Ln 75209. **Hours:** 11:30 am-2 & 5:30-10 pm, Sat from 5:30, Sun 11 am-2 pm. Closed major holidays. **Reservations:** suggested. **Features:** Very popular eatery serving contemporary Euro-Continental cuisine in addition to more traditional German fare in a fashionable, vogue style. Some of the popular entress are the perch fillet served and ringed with an orange tarragon sauce or the veal cordon bleu stuffed with Black Forest ham and munster cheese. Dressy casual; cocktails. **Parking:** on-site. **Cards:** AX, DC, MC, VI.

IL SORRENTO

Italian

Dinner: $12-$25   **Phone:** 214/352-8759   56

Location: Just n; w of jct Northwest Hwy and Hillcrest Ave. 8616 Turtle Creek Blvd 75225. **Hours:** 5:30 pm-10 pm, Fri & Sat-11:30 pm. Closed: 11/27, 12/25. **Reservations:** accepted. **Features:** Strolling musicians and a romantic Italian village decor have generated Old World charm at this popular eatery for the past 50 years. An extensive menu features pasta, seafood, beef and poultry dishes, plus several appealing desserts including tiramisu. Casual dress; cocktails; entertainment. **Parking:** on-site. **Cards:** AX, CB, DC, MC, VI.

INDIA PALACE RESTAURANT & BAR

Indian

Lunch: $7-$9   **Dinner:** $9-$13   **Phone:** 972/392-0190   41

Location: I-635, exit 21 (Preston Rd), just sw. 12817 Preston Rd, Suite 105 75230. **Hours:** 11:30 am-2:30 & 5:30-10 pm, Fri-11 pm, Sat noon-3 & 5:30-11 pm, Sun noon-3 & 5:30-10 pm. **Reservations:** suggested; weekends. **Features:** Traditional Indian adornments mix with chandeliers, flowers and candles to create a cozy and relaxing atmosphere. Tandoori specialties are the focus, along with Indian-style barbecue with chicken, lamb and seafood. Fresh baked bread adds a nice touch. Semi-formal attire; cocktails. **Parking:** on-site. **Cards:** AX, DC, DS, MC, VI.

JASON'S DELI

American

Lunch: $5-$8   **Dinner:** $5-$8   **Phone:** 214/821-7021   73

Location: US 75, exit 3 (Mockingbird Ln), just e. 5400 E Mockingbird Ln 75206. **Hours:** 10 am-10 pm. Closed: 4/20, 11/27, 12/25. **Features:** Chrome accents and black tones line the dining room tables at this sandwich shop. Enjoy large varieties of deli meat piled high on freshly baked bread. Finish your meal with a slice of smooth strawberry cheesecake. Smoke free premises. Casual dress; beer & wine only. **Parking:** on-site. **Cards:** AX, CB, DC, DS, MC, VI.

JAVIER'S RESTAURANTE

Mexican

Dinner: $13-$19   **Phone:** 214/521-4211   79

Location: US 75, exit Knox St/Henderson Ave, just w to McKinney Ave, then 0.4 mi n to Harvard. 4912 Cole Ave 75205. **Hours:** 5:30 pm-10 pm, Fri & Sat-11 pm. Closed major holidays. **Reservations:** suggested. **Features:** Continental Mexico City cuisine is served amid a delightful Mexican colonial decor. Appetizers like smoked chicken nachos, and entrees like snapper with mushrooms and garlic, attract guests from all over Texas. After dinner, relax in the trendy cigar bar. Casual dress; cocktails. **Parking:** valet. **Cards:** AX, DC, DS, MC, VI.

KALACHANDJI'S GARDEN RESTAURANT

Vegetarian

Lunch: $6-$8   **Dinner:** $7-$11   **Phone:** 214/821-1048   75

Location: I-30, exit 49A (E Grand), just w to Phillip St, just ne to Fairview St, just n to Gurley Ave, then just e. 5430 Gurley Ave 75223. **Hours:** 11:30 am-2 & 5:30-9 pm, Sat noon-3 & 5:30-9 pm, Sun 5:30 pm-9 pm. Closed: 1/1, 12/25; also Mon. **Features:** The restaurant offers a menu of moderately priced vegetarian dishes. Smoke free premises. Casual dress. **Parking:** street. **Cards:** AX, DS, MC, VI.

KIRBY'S STEAKHOUSE

Steak House

Dinner: $22-$39   **Phone:** 214/821-2122   101

Location: US 75, exit 3 (Mockingbird Ln), 0.5 mi e to Greenville Ave, then 0.6 mi s. 3525 Greenville Ave 75206. **Hours:** 5:30 pm-10 pm, Fri & Sat-11 pm. Closed major holidays. **Reservations:** suggested. **Features:** Established in 1954, the restaurant is a local favorite for reasonably priced steaks. Dressy casual; cocktails. **Parking:** valet. **Cards:** AX, CB, DC, DS, MC, VI.

KOSTAS CAFE

Greek

Lunch: $11-$20   **Dinner:** $11-$20   **Phone:** 214/987-3225   68

Location: US 75, exit Lovers Ln, just e to Greenville Ave, then just s. 4914 Greenville Ave 75602. **Hours:** 11 am-2:30 & 5-10 pm, Sat noon-11 pm, Sun 5 pm-10 pm. Closed major holidays. **Reservations:** accepted. **Features:** Greek specialties include gyros, souvlaki, and lemon soup with rice. Each dish is accented with tomatoes and onions. The pita bread is light and tasty. The dining room is decorated with blue and white tones and Greek posters. Casual dress; beer & wine only. **Parking:** on-site. **Cards:** AX, DC, DS, MC, VI.

KUBY'S SAUSAGE HOUSE

Traditional German

Lunch: $5-$8   **Dinner:** $10-$12   **Phone:** 214/363-2231   63

Location: Just w of jct Daniel and Hilcrest aves; in Snyder Plaza across from Southern Methodist University. 6601 Snider Plaza 75205. **Hours:** 6 am-5 pm, Fri & Sat-9 pm, Sun 9 am-2 pm. Closed major holidays. **Features:** Decorated with family crests, this eatery is located within a German food store. Homemade sausage is made from an old family recipe. Old World butcher-shop fare like knockwurst and bratwurst make up the tasty sausage plate. Smoke free premises. Casual dress; beer & wine only. **Parking:** street. **Cards:** AX, DS, MC, VI.

LA DOLCE VITA

Italian

Lunch: $7-$10   **Dinner:** $8-$21   **Phone:** 214/821-2608   95

Location: Just w of jct Abrams Pkwy and Gaston Rd; in the Lakewood section. 1924 Abrams Pkwy 75214. **Hours:** 11 am-2:30 & 5:30-10 pm, Fri & Sat-11 pm, Sun noon-10 pm. Closed: 1/1, 12/25. **Features:** A covered walkway through one side of a small shopping center with worn brick paving, high ceiling and murals on the wall is half of the seating area, creates an interesting and casual dining environment. Homemade pastas and a selection of sauces are central to the menu, which includes pizza and a few printed entrees. Most of the patrons you'll see here are from surrounding Lakewood, and one of their favorites is the lasagna; the tiramisu is excellent. Casual dress; cocktails. **Parking:** on-site. **Cards:** AX, DC, DS, MC, VI.

(See map p. 236)

LA MADELEINE FRENCH BAKERY & CAFE-LEMMON   Lunch: $6-$13   Dinner: $9-$13   Phone: 214/521-0183   (85)
Location: Just w of Oak Lawn Ave. 3906 Lemmon Ave, Suite 110 75219. **Hours:** 6:30 am-10 pm. Closed: 12/25; also 12/24 from 6 pm. **Features:** The aroma of fresh breads and pastries fills the dining room, which has a cafe atmosphere. Topped with sun-dried tomatoes and mozzarella, the pizza rivera is a mouthwatering treat rivaled only by the pastries on display at the entrance. The infusion of flowers here are always delightful. Casual dress; beer & wine only. **Parking:** on-site. **Cards:** AX, DS, MC, VI.
Traditional French

LA MADELEINE FRENCH BAKERY & CAFE-SMU   Lunch: $7-$11   Dinner: $7-$11   Phone: 214/696-0800   (72)
Location: Just w off US 75 (North Central Expwy), exit 3 (Mockingbird Ln); in Park City Plaza. 3072 Mockingbird Ln 75205. **Hours:** 6:30 am-11 pm. Closed: 12/25. **Features:** A glass case imported from France shows off fresh pastries. The savory chicken in wine sauce with broccoli, tomatoes and mushrooms should not be missed. Homemade pizzas are baked in the wood-burning oven. Smoke free premises. Casual dress.
Traditional French
Parking: on-site. **Cards:** AX, DS, MC, VI.

THE MANSION ON TURTLE CREEK RESTAURANT   Lunch: $16-$25   Dinner: $26-$56   Phone: 214/559-2100   (87)
Location: 2 mi nw, entrance on Gillespie St, just e of jct Gillespie and Lawn sts; in The Mansion On Turtle Creek. 2821 Turtle Creek Blvd 75219. **Hours:** 11:30 am-2:30 & 6-10:30 pm, Fri & Sat-11 pm, Sun 11 am-2 & 6-10:30 pm. **Reservations:** suggested. **Features:** Guests pass through a courtyard entrance that leads to a richly appointed rotunda with marble floors and walls. From there, they are seated in one of several elegant dining rooms, where an attentive and intuitive staff serves outstanding selections from imaginative seasonal menus that draw on the rich culinary heritage of Texas and the American Southwest. Smoke free premises. Dressy casual; cocktails; entertainment. **Parking:** valet. **Cards:** AX, CB, DC, DS, JC, MC, VI.
Southwest American

MARIO & ALBERTO'S   Lunch: $6-$7   Dinner: $8-$14   Phone: 972/980-7297   (40)
Location: I-635, exit 21 (Preston Rd), just sw; in Preston Valley Shopping Center. 12817 Preston Rd, Suite 425 75230. **Hours:** 11 am-9 pm, Fri-10 pm, Sat 11:30 am-10 pm. Closed major holidays; also Sun. **Features:** Mexico City-style cuisine is served in an attractive dining room with white linen-covered tables. Classy Mexican scenes cover the walls, and candles illuminate the room. The variety of entrees include tamales, enchiladas, fajitas, and authentic chicken or pork mole. The flan is a popular dessert item. Casual dress; cocktails. **Parking:** on-site. **Cards:** AX, DC, DS, MC, VI.
Mexican

MEDITERRANEO   Lunch: $9-$14   Dinner: $17-$34   Phone: 972/447-0066   (35)
Location: I-635, exit 21 (Preston Rd), northwest corner of Preston Rd and Frankford Dr. 18111 Preston Rd, Suite 120 75252. **Hours:** 11:30 am-2 & 6-10 pm, Fri & Sat-11 pm, Sun-9 pm. Closed major holidays. **Reservations:** suggested. **Features:** Mediterranean cuisine superbly prepared and presented—colorful, inviting and sophisticated. Enjoy tempting appetizers, an array of seafood dishes, steaks and an excellent selection of desserts. Smoke free premises. Dressy casual; cocktails. **Parking:** on-site. **Cards:** AX, DC, DS, MC, VI.
Mediterranean

MERCADO JUAREZ   Lunch: $6-$9   Dinner: $9-$20   Phone: 972/556-0796   (53)
Location: Northwest Hwy, 0.5 mi w of Loop 12. 1901 W Northwest Hwy 75220. **Hours:** 11 am-10 pm, Fri & Sat-11 pm. Closed: 11/27, 12/25. **Features:** Brightly-painted walls, window frames and doors liven up this Mexican cafe. The Tex-Mex fare includes fajitas, tacos al carbon and plenty of crunchy nachos. A mariachi band adds to the festive atmosphere. Casual dress; cocktails; entertainment. **Parking:** on-site. **Cards:** AX, CB, DC, DS, MC, VI.
Regional Tex-Mex

MIA'S TEX-MEX RESTAURANT   Lunch: $6-$12   Dinner: $8-$12   Phone: 214/526-1020   (86)
Location: Just e of Dallas, between Wycliff and Herschel St. 4322 Lemmon Ave 75219. **Hours:** 11 am-10 pm. Closed major holidays; also Sun. **Features:** You may think enchiladas are just normal fare. Try the chicken enchiladas with sour cream sauce - you'll see they can be special. And, if there is such a thing as, "Mexican cantina art deco" this is the place. It's very popular with folks around Dallas for good reasons. Casual dress; beer & wine only. **Parking:** on-site. **Cards:** AX, CB, DC, DS, JC, MC, VI.
Mexican

MO MO'S ITALIAN SPECIALTIES   Lunch: $7-$9   Dinner: $13-$16   Phone: 214/987-2082   (62)
Location: Southwest corner of Preston Rd and Northwest Hwy. 8300 Preston Ctr Plaza 75225. **Hours:** 11 am-9:30 pm, Fri & Sat-10:30 pm, Sun-9 pm. Closed major holidays. **Reservations:** suggested. **Features:** Thirty different pastas fill the menu at this fine Italian cafe. The split-level dining room has brass railings and a small fireplace. Each table has a small vase filled with flowers. Savor one of the homemade desserts. Smoke free premises. Casual dress; cocktails. **Parking:** on-site. **Cards:** AX, MC, VI.
Traditional Italian

NINFA'S   Lunch: $4-$9   Dinner: $7-$15   Phone: 214/638-6865   (98)
Location: Northwest corner of I-35 (Stemmons Frwy) and Inwood Rd. 2701 N Stemmons Frwy 75207. **Hours:** 11 am-10 pm. Closed: 11/27, 12/25. **Reservations:** accepted. **Features:** Airy and festive, the decor features high ceilings, white stucco walls and wrought-iron chandeliers. Fresh tortillas, fajitas, taco salad and many other tasty, traditional favorites are served in large helpings. On Friday nights, try your hand at karaoke. Casual dress; cocktails. **Parking:** on-site. **Cards:** AX, DC, DS, MC, VI.
Traditional Mexican

OLD SAN FRANCISCO STEAK HOUSE   Lunch: $6-$14   Dinner: $10-$28   Phone: 214/357-0484   (51)
Location: Northwest off I-35 E and US 77, exit 438 (Walnut Hill Ln). 10965 Composite Dr 75220. **Hours:** 11 am-2 & 5-10 pm, Fri-10:30 pm, Sat 4:30 pm-10:30 pm, Sun 4:30 pm-10 pm. **Reservations:** suggested. **Features:** Accented in velvet, the dining room features a woman on a red velvet swing who flies back and forth above two baby grand pianos. Servers wear tuxedos and Gay 90s period uniforms. Feast on specialty steaks, chicken and seafood entrees. Casual dress; cocktails; entertainment. **Parking:** on-site and valet. **Cards:** AX, CB, DC, DS, MC, VI.
Steak House

(See map p. 236)

PATRIZIO
▼▼▼
Northern
Italian

Lunch: $9-$12   **Dinner:** $13-$18   **Phone:** 214/522-7878   [71]
Location: Mockingbird Ln and Preston Rd. 25 Highland Park Village 75205. **Hours:** 11 am-11 pm, Fri & Sat-midnight, Sun & Mon-10 pm. Closed major holidays. **Reservations:** accepted; weekends. **Features:** Large, hand-tossed pizzas are made-to-order. Fresh seafood like the award-winning crab claws are delicious. Rustic Italian oil paintings hang on the walls. Enjoy dessert on the romantic patio. Casual dress; cocktails. **Parking:** valet. **Cards:** AX, CB, DC, DS, MC, VI.

PEGGY SUE BARBEQUE
▼
Regional American

Lunch: $5-$7   **Dinner:** $5-$7   **Phone:** 214/987-9188   [64]
Location: Just w of jct Daniel and Hilcrest aves; in Snyder Plaza across from Southern Methodist University Campus. 6600 Snider Plaza 75205. **Hours:** 11 am-9 pm, Fri & Sat-10 pm. Closed major holidays. **Features:** Clad with old photographs of Western movie stars, this 1950s diner serves homemade barbecue and Mexican cuisine. Decorative hanging lamps give the two dining rooms a friendly glow. Start with the chicken quesadilla appetizer. Smoke free premises. Casual dress; cocktails. **Parking:** street. **Cards:** MC, VI.

POPOLOS
▼▼▼
Italian

Lunch: $10-$12   **Dinner:** $19-$21   **Phone:** 214/692-5497   [45]
Location: I-635, exit 21 (Preston Rd), 2.5 mi s. 707 Preston-Royal Shopping Ctr 75230. **Hours:** 11 am-2 & 5-10 pm, Fri-11 pm, Sat 5 pm-11 pm. Closed: 11/27, 12/25. **Reservations:** suggested. **Features:** Fresh flowers grace the tables at this busy bistro. Interesting paintings hang in the bright, split-level dining room, dominated by the cocktail bar in the middle of one side. The cuisine menu offers a good variety of "new American." Located on the corner of two busy streets, the eatery has plenty of parking in the shopping center lot. Smoke free premises. Casual dress; cocktails. **Parking:** on-site. **Cards:** AX, DC, DS, MC, VI.

THE RIVIERA
▼▼▼ ▼▼▼
Continental

Dinner: $25-$38   **Phone:** 214/351-0094   [67]
Location: Just s of Lovers Ln. 7709 Inwood Rd 75209. **Hours:** 6:30 pm-10 pm, Fri & Sat 6 pm-11 pm. Closed major holidays. **Reservations:** suggested. **Features:** Superb, seasonal French and Italian fare, such as the spinach-escargot torte, is stylishly presented at the popular dining spot. Country French decor shows no hint of pretense. Jackets are preferred. Cocktails. **Parking:** valet. **Cards:** AX, CB, DC, DS, MC, VI.

ROYAL TOKYO JAPANESE RESTAURANT   **Lunch:** $6-$15   **Dinner:** $16-$25   **Phone:** 214/368-3304   [49]
ⒶⒶⒶ
▼▼ ▼▼
Japanese

Location: I-75, exit 6 (Walnut Hill Ln), 0.8 mi e. 7525 Greenville Ave 75231. **Hours:** 11:30 am-2 & 5:30-11 pm, Mon-10:30 pm, Fri-11:30 pm, Sat noon-2:30 & 5:30-11:30 pm, Sun 5 pm-10:30 pm. Closed: 11/27, 12/25. **Reservations:** suggested; Fri-Sat. **Features:** One of Dallas's largest and oldest Japanese restaurants featuring a sushi bar, hibachi cooking and tatami rooms. Moderately priced. Dressy casual; cocktails. **Parking:** on-site. **Cards:** AX, CB, DC, DS, JC, MC, VI.

ST MARTIN'S
▼▼▼
French

Dinner: $14-$23   **Phone:** 214/826-0940   [80]
Location: US 75, exit 3 (Mockingbird Ln/University), 0.5 mi e to Greenville Ave, then 1.2 mi s. 3020 Greenville Ave 75206. **Hours:** 5 pm-10 pm, Fri & Sat-midnight, Sun 10:30 am-10 pm. **Reservations:** suggested. **Features:** Intimate and attractive, the dining area of this French-American bistro has a gorgeous 14 foot ceiling and fabric wall coverings. The smoked salmon appetizer is almost a meal in itself. A talented pianist plays soothing music throughout the evening. Casual dress; cocktails; entertainment. **Parking:** valet. **Cards:** AX, DC, DS, MC, VI.

SIPANGO
▼▼▼
American

Dinner: $10-$21   **Phone:** 214/522-2411   [81]
Location: US 75, exit 3 (Mockingbird Ln), 0.5 mi w to Travis St, then just s. 4513 Travis St 75205. **Hours:** 5:30 pm-10:30 pm, Thurs-Sat to 11:30 pm. Closed: 1/1, 11/27, 12/25; also Sun. **Reservations:** suggested. **Features:** In a very attractive warehouse setting, chefs prepare California-Italian cuisine in an oak-fired oven and grill. The aroma of fresh-baked pizza fills the dining room from high ceiling to wooden floor, and whets your appetite for many delicious selections. Dressy casual; cocktails; entertainment. **Parking:** valet. **Cards:** AX, DC, MC, VI.

SNUFFER'S
▼▼
American

Lunch: $7-$9   **Dinner:** $7-$9   **Phone:** 214/826-6850   [78]
Location: S on Greenville Ave from Mockingbird Ln. 3526 Greenville Ave 75206. **Hours:** 11 am-2 am. **Features:** For more than 20 years this restaurant has been a great spot for juicy hamburgers, margaritas and people watching. Ask your server about the legend of the ghost. Period pictures and dark wooden booths distinguish the bustling dining room. Casual dress; cocktails. **Parking:** on-site. **Cards:** AX, DC, DS, MC, VI.

SONNY BRYAN'S
▼▼
Southwest
American

Lunch: $6-$10   **Phone:** 214/357-7120   [89]
Location: I-35, n on Inwood Rd, near jct Harry Hines Blvd. 2202 Inwood Rd 75235. **Hours:** 10 am-4 pm, Sat-3 pm, Sun 11 am-2 pm. Closed major holidays. **Features:** This 1958 Texas barbecue stand, known for huge portions of hickory smoked beef and ribs, has served a wide variety of patrons from U.S. presidents to the cast of Saving Private Ryan. When the barbecue's gone, it's gone, so come and get it before it goes! Casual dress; beer only. **Parking:** on-site. **Cards:** AX, DS, MC, VI.

STAR CANYON
▼▼▼ ▼▼▼
Southwest
American

Lunch: $8-$15   **Dinner:** $20-$29   **Phone:** 214/520-7827   [99]
Location: N of jct Oak Lawn Ave and Cedar Springs. 3102 Oak Lawn Ave, Suite 144 75219. **Hours:** 11:30 am-2 & 5:30-10 pm, Fri-10:30 pm, Sat 5:30 pm-10:30 pm, Sun-9:30 pm. Closed major holidays. **Reservations:** suggested. **Features:** Chef Matthew Dunn has created an extraordinary menu of beautifully presented Lone Star dishes, such as shrimp taquitos with mango barbecue salsa. Star-shaped blue corn muffins and heaven-and-hell cake are signature dishes. Dressy casual; cocktails. **Parking:** valet and street. **Cards:** AX, CB, DC, DS, MC, VI.

(See map p. 236)

TERILLI'S
♦♦ ♦♦
Northern
Italian

Lunch: $11-$23   Dinner: $11-$23   Phone: 214/827-3993   84
Location: US 75, exit 3 (Mockingbird Ln), 0.5 mi e to Greenville Ave, 1 mi s. 2815 Greenville Ave 75206.
Hours: 11:30 am-2 am, Sun & Mon-midnight. Closed: 12/25. Reservations: accepted. Features: An
energetic nightclub atmosphere is fueled by live music six nights a week by various local jazz bands.
Featuring seafood, pasta and pizza, the menu lists a great selection of appetizers and signature dishes like
cappolini d'angelo and chicken terilli. Casual dress; cocktails; entertainment. Parking: on-site. Cards: AX,
DC, DS, MC, VI.   ⓨ Ⓧ

TRAIL DUST STEAK HOUSE
♦♦
Steak House

Lunch: $7-$17   Dinner: $9-$22   Phone: 214/357-3862   52
Location: Nw off I-35 E and US 77, exit 438 Walnut Hill Ln. 10841 Composite Dr 75220. Hours: 11 am-2 & 5-10
pm, Fri-11 pm, Sat 4 pm-11 pm, Sun noon-10 pm. Closed: 11/27, 12/25. Features: Country music videos
play on big screen TVs, and a large slide extends from the second floor, adding an air of fun and frivolity.
Dine at picnic tables that seat multiple parties, and enjoy such fare as barbecue ribs, chicken-fried steak
and sandwiches. Casual dress; cocktails; entertainment. Parking: on-site. Cards: AX, DC, DS, MC, VI.   Ⓧ

TUPINAMBA
♦♦ ♦♦
Mexican

Lunch: $7-$9   Dinner: $8-$12   Phone: 972/991-8148   43
Location: I-635, between North Dallas Tollway and Willow Ln; in the Summertree shopping center. 12270 Inwood Rd
75244. Hours: 11 am-9:30 pm, Fri & Sat-10 pm, Sun noon-9 pm. Closed major holidays.
Reservations: accepted. Features: Covered with ivy and paintings of trees and water, this attractive cafe
is characterized by the aroma of Tex-Mex cuisine. Start off with chips and salsa, crunchy nachos or fajita
salad. The shrimp fajitas are delivered to your table sizzling. Casual dress. Parking: on-site. Cards: AX, DC, DS, MC, VI.   ⓨ Ⓧ

UNCLE JULIO'S
♦♦ ♦♦
Mexican

Lunch: $8-$11   Dinner: $9-$20   Phone: 214/520-6620   90
Location: Between North Dallas Tollway and Oak Lawn Blvd. 4125 Lemmon Ave 75219. Hours: 11 am-10:30 pm,
Fri & Sat-11 pm. Closed: 11/27, 12/24, 12/25. Features: Open and airy dining rooms are filled with
Mexican decor. Start your meal with homemade tortilla soup and salsa with chips. The sizzle of the
specialty fajitas can be heard throughout the dining rooms. The flan is praised for its sweet, caramel
coating. Brunch is served on Sundays. Casual dress; cocktails. Parking: on-site. Cards: AX, CB, DC, DS, MC, VI.   Ⓧ

YOLI'S SEAFOOD & GRILL
♦
Steak & Seafood

Lunch: $6-$10   Dinner: $10-$15   Phone: 214/341-3533   47
Location: Ne from I-635, exit 16 Skillman St, 0.3 mi n. Hours: 11 am-10 pm, Fri & Sat-11 pm, Sun 11:30 am-9
pm. Closed: 11/27, 12/25. Reservations: accepted. Features: Cajun seafood with an Italian touch is the
main attraction in this casual dining experience, but a nice selection of sandwiches are also served for
those patrons looking for a more basic meal. Shrimp scampi with salmon over linguine makes a tasty
choice. Casual dress; cocktails. Parking: on-site. Cards: AX, CB, DC, DS, MC, VI.   ⓨ Ⓧ

ZU ZU
♦♦
Mexican

Lunch: $6-$8   Dinner: $6-$8   Phone: 214/521-4456   69
Location: Between Mockingbird and Lovers lns; across from Southern Methodist University's west side of campus.
6423 Hillcrest Ave 75205. Hours: 10 am-9 pm. Closed: 1/1, 12/25. Features: California-style Mexican cuisine
is served in quiet, modest surroundings across from Southern Methodist University. A reasonably priced
menu features such signature items as chicken salad tacos made with chicken marinated for 24 hours in a
secret sauce. Smoke free premises. Casual dress. Parking: on-site. Cards: AX, DC, DS, MC, VI.   Ⓧ

DALLAS SOUTH   (See map p. 248; index p. 249)

──────── WHERE TO STAY ────────

BEST WESTERN INN
SAVE
♦♦ ♦♦
Small-scale Hotel

Phone: (972)298-4747   306
All Year [CP]   1P: $50-$55   2P: $60-$65   XP: $10   F17
Location: I-20, exit 463 (Cockrell Hill Rd), just e to Independence Dr, then just s. 4154 Preferred Pl 75237.
Fax: 972/283-1305. Facility: 119 one-bedroom standard units. 2 stories, exterior corridors. Parking: on-site.
Amenities: irons, hair dryers. Pool(s): outdoor. Guest Services: valet and coin laundry. Business Serv-
ices: meeting rooms, fax (fee). Cards: AX, CB, DC, DS, MC, VI.   SOME UNITS
Ⓢ⌂ 🏊 🏃 DATA PORT ▭ / Ⓧ /

COMFORT INN SOUTH
SAVE
♦♦ ♦♦
Small-scale Hotel

Phone: (972)572-1030   302
All Year   1P: $66-$81   2P: $71-$86
Location: I-20, exit 465, 0.3 mi e to S Hampton Rd, then just s. 8541 S Hampton Rd 75232. Fax: 972/572-1036.
Facility: 50 one-bedroom standard units, some with whirlpools. 2 stories, exterior corridors. Bath: combo or
shower only. Parking: on-site. Terms: 15 day cancellation notice. Amenities: hair dryers. Pool(s): small
outdoor. Guest Services: coin laundry. Business Services: meeting rooms, fax (fee). Cards: AX, CB, DC,
DS, JC, MC, VI.   SOME UNITS
Ⓢ⌂ 🍴 🏊 🏃 DATA PORT 🔌 ▭ ▭ / Ⓧ /

LEXINGTON HOTEL SUITES
♦♦ ♦♦
Small-scale Hotel

Phone: (972)298-7014   304
All Year   1P: $80-$150   2P: $90-$160   XP: $10   F18
Location: I-20, exit 463 (Cockrell Hill Rd), just e to Independence Dr, then just s. 4150 Independence Dr 75237.
Fax: 972/709-1680. Facility: 108 units. 63 one-bedroom standard units with kitchens. 39 one- and 6 two-
bedroom suites with kitchens. 3 stories, exterior corridors. Bath: combo or shower only. Parking: on-site.
Amenities: voice mail. Some: irons, hair dryers. Pool(s): heated outdoor. Leisure Activities: whirlpool. Guest Services: valet
and coin laundry, area transportation. Business Services: meeting rooms, fax (fee). Cards: AX, DC, DS, MC, VI.
SOME UNITS
ASK Ⓢ⌂ 🏊 🛁 DATA PORT 🔌 ▭ ▭ / Ⓧ /

(See map p. 248)

──────── **WHERE TO DINE** ────────

LA CALLE DOCE

♦♦♦ ♦♦♦

Mexican

Lunch: $5-$12   **Dinner:** $6-$13   **Phone:** 214/941-4304   (210)
Location: I-35, exit 425A (Beckley and Zang Blvd), 0.5 mi w. 415 W 12th St 75208. **Hours:** 11 am-9:30 pm, Fri & Sat-10:30 pm, Sun-9 pm. **Closed:** 11/27, 12/25. **Reservations:** accepted. **Features:** Lakewood, and one of their favorites is the lasagna. Start with sopa de pescado - cod stew with tomatoes, onions, potatoes and cilantro, Tampico Bay style. Move on to a Spanish favorite like paella, or try a Mexican dish like chile relleno de mariscos - poblano pepper stuffed with shrimp, scallops, octopus and fish. Dine in the simple ambience of the house or in the outside covered front patio. Casual dress; cocktails. **Parking:** on-site. **Cards:** AX, CB, DC, DS, MC, VI.

[Y] [X]

The Dallas Vicinity

ADDISON pop. 14,166   (See map p. 236; index p. 244)

──────── **WHERE TO STAY** ────────

ADDISON QUORUM COURTYARD BY MARRIOTT   **Phone:** (972)404-1555   (180)

SAVE

♦♦♦♦♦♦

Small-scale Hotel

9/2-1/31	1P: $56-$124	2P: $56-$134
2/1-9/1	1P: $56-$119	2P: $56-$129

Location: Just n of jct Belt Line Rd and Quorum Dr. 15160 Quorum Dr. Fax: 972/404-1553. **Facility:** 176 units. 174 one-bedroom standard units. 2 one-bedroom suites ($99-$154). 7 stories, interior corridors. *Bath:* combo or shower only. **Parking:** on-site. **Amenities:** high-speed Internet (fee), dual phone lines, voice mail, irons, hair dryers. **Pool(s):** outdoor. **Leisure Activities:** whirlpool, exercise room. **Guest Services:** valet and coin laundry, area transportation. **Business Services:** meeting rooms, fax (fee). **Cards:** AX, DC, DS, JC, MC, VI.

SOME UNITS
[icons] / [X] [H] [☐] /

COUNTRY INN & SUITES BY CARLSON   **Phone:** (972)503-7800   (185)

♦♦♦♦

Small-scale Hotel

All Year   1P: $89-$109

Location: Jct of Beltway Dr and Midway Rd, just s, then just e. 4355 Beltway Dr 75001. Fax: 972/503-2300. **Facility:** 102 units. 84 one-bedroom standard units. 18 one-bedroom suites, some with whirlpools. 4 stories, interior corridors. *Bath:* combo or shower only. **Parking:** on-site. **Amenities:** video games (fee), high-speed Internet, dual phone lines, voice mail, irons, hair dryers. **Pool(s):** small outdoor. **Leisure Activities:** whirlpool, exercise room. **Guest Services:** complimentary evening beverages: Mon-Thurs, valet and coin laundry, area transportation. **Business Services:** meeting rooms, business center. **Cards:** AX, DC, DS, MC, VI. *(See color ad p 260)*

SOME UNITS
(ASK) [icons] [H] [☐] [☐] /[X]/

COURTYARD BY MARRIOTT-ADDISON/MIDWAY   **Phone:** 972/490-7390   (193)

SAVE

♦♦♦♦

Small-scale Hotel

MC, VI.

All Year   1P: $59-$99   2P: $59-$99

Location: 0.8 mi s of jct Belt Line and Midway rds, then just w. 4165 Proton Dr 75001. Fax: 972/490-0002. **Facility:** 145 units. 134 one-bedroom standard units. 11 one-bedroom suites. 2 stories, interior corridors. *Bath:* combo or shower only. **Parking:** on-site. **Terms:** [BP] meal plan available. **Amenities:** voice mail, irons, hair dryers. **Pool(s):** outdoor. **Leisure Activities:** whirlpool, exercise room. **Guest Services:** valet and coin laundry, area transportation. **Business Services:** meeting rooms, fax (fee). **Cards:** AX, CB, DC, DS,

SOME UNITS
[icons] / [X] [H] [☐] /

CROWNE PLAZA NORTH DALLAS/ADDISON NEAR THE GALLERIA   **Phone:** (972)980-8877   (181)

♦♦♦♦

Large-scale Hotel

All Year   1P: $69-$119   XP: $10   F18

Location: 0.8 mi s of jct Belt Line and Midway rds. 14315 Midway Rd 75001. Fax: 972/991-2740. **Facility:** 429 units. 411 one-bedroom standard units. 18 one-bedroom suites. 4 stories, interior corridors. *Bath:* combo or shower only. **Parking:** on-site. **Terms:** pets ($25 fee, $100 deposit). **Amenities:** voice mail, irons, hair dryers. **Pool(s):** heated outdoor. **Leisure Activities:** whirlpool. **Guest Services:** gift shop, valet and coin laundry, area transportation. **Business Services:** conference facilities, business center. **Cards:** AX, CB, DC, DS, JC, MC, VI.

SOME UNITS
(ASK) [icons]   [icons]   [icons] / [X] [H] [☐] /
FEE   FEE FEE

DALLAS ADDISON MARRIOTT QUORUM   **Phone:** (972)661-2800   (183)

SAVE

♦♦♦♦♦

Large-scale Hotel

All Year   1P: $159-$189   2P: $159-$189   XP: $10   F16

Location: I-635, exit 22D, 2 mi n of jct I-635 and North Dallas Tollway west side. 14901 Dallas Pkwy 75254. Fax: 972/934-1731. **Facility:** 548 units. 538 one-bedroom standard units. 10 one-bedroom suites ($250-$500). 12 stories, interior corridors. *Bath:* combo or shower only. **Parking:** on-site and valet. **Terms:** package plans. **Amenities:** high-speed Internet (fee), dual phone lines, voice mail, irons, hair dryers. **Pool(s):** heated indoor/outdoor. **Leisure Activities:** sauna, whirlpool, lighted tennis court, exercise room, basketball. **Guest Services:** gift shop, valet and coin laundry, area transportation. **Business Services:** conference facilities, business center. **Cards:** AX, CB, DC, DS, JC, MC, VI.

SOME UNITS
[icons] / [X] [VCR] [H] /

HAMPTON INN   **Phone:** (972)991-2800   (192)

SAVE

♦♦♦♦

Small-scale Hotel

All Year [ECP]   1P: $71   2P: $81   XP: $10   F18

Location: Jct of Beltway Dr and Midway Rd, just s, then just e. Located in a business park. 4505 Beltway Dr 75001. Fax: 972/991-7691. **Facility:** 159 one-bedroom standard units. 4 stories, interior corridors. **Parking:** on-site. **Amenities:** video games (fee), voice mail, irons, hair dryers. **Pool(s):** outdoor. **Leisure Activities:** exercise room. **Guest Services:** valet laundry, area transportation. **Business Services:** meeting rooms, fax (fee). **Cards:** AX, DC, DS, MC, VI.

SOME UNITS
[icons] /[X]/

(See map p. 236)

HILTON GARDEN INN-ADDISON
Phone: (972)233-8000 [189]

All Year   1P: $59-$89   2P: $59-$89
[SAVE]
Location: Just e of jct Belt Line Rd and Marsh Ln, set back on south side of road. Located in a quiet area. 4090 Belt Line Rd 75001. Fax: 972/239-8777. **Facility:** 96 units. 86 one-bedroom standard units, some with whirlpools. 10 one-bedroom suites ($145-$165). 3 stories, interior corridors. *Bath:* combo or shower only. **Parking:** on-
Small-scale Hotel site. **Amenities:** video games (fee), high-speed Internet, dual phone lines, voice mail, irons, hair dryers. **Pool(s):** heated outdoor. **Leisure Activities:** whirlpool, exercise room. **Guest Services:** sundries, valet and coin laundry, area transportation. **Business Services:** meeting rooms, business center. **Cards:** AX, CB, DC, DS, JC, MC, VI.

SOME UNITS

HOLIDAY INN EXPRESS
Phone: (972)991-8888 [190]

All Year [ECP]   1P: $105   2P: $115
Location: Between Midway Rd and Marsh Ln. 4103 E Belt Line Rd 75001. Fax: 972/991-3609. **Facility:** 115 one-
Small-scale Hotel bedroom standard units. 2 stories, exterior corridors. *Bath:* combo or shower only. **Parking:** on-site. **Amenities:** dual phone lines, voice mail, irons, hair dryers. **Pool(s):** outdoor. **Leisure Activities:** whirlpool.
Guest Services: complimentary evening beverages: Mon & Thurs, valet and coin laundry, area transportation. **Business Services:** meeting rooms, fax (fee). **Cards:** AX, CB, DC, DS, MC, VI.

SOME UNITS

HOMEWOOD SUITES BY HILTON
Phone: (972)788-1342 [191]

All Year [ECP]   1P: $119-$149   2P: $119-$149
[SAVE]
Location: Just e of jct Belt Line and Midway rds. 4451 Belt Line Rd 75001. Fax: 972/788-1373. **Facility:** 120 units. 112 one- and 8 two-bedroom suites with efficiencies. 3 stories, interior/exterior corridors. *Bath:* combo or shower only. **Parking:** on-site. **Terms:** cancellation fee imposed, [CP] meal plan available, pets ($75 fee).
Small-scale Hotel **Amenities:** video library (fee), voice mail, irons, hair dryers. **Pool(s):** heated outdoor. **Leisure Activities:** whirlpool, exercise room, basketball. **Guest Services:** sundries, complimentary evening beverages: Mon-Thurs, valet and coin laundry, area transportation. **Business Services:** meeting rooms, PC, fax (fee). **Cards:** AX, CB, DC, DS, JC, MC, VI.

SOME UNITS

INTER-CONTINENTAL HOTEL DALLAS
Phone: (972)386-6000 [182]

All Year   1P: $109-$235   2P: $109-$235
Location: 2.8 mi n of jct I-635 (LBJ Frwy) and Dallas Pkwy. 15201 Dallas Pkwy 75001. Fax: 972/404-1848.
Large-scale Hotel **Facility:** 529 units. 498 one-bedroom standard units. 29 one- and 2 two-bedroom suites, some with whirlpools. 15 stories, interior corridors. **Parking:** on-site and valet. **Amenities:** video games (fee), dual phone lines, voice mail, irons, hair dryers. *Some:* high-speed Internet (fee), honor bars. **Pool(s):** heated outdoor, heated indoor. **Leisure Activities:** saunas, whirlpools, steamroom, sports court. *Fee:* 4 lighted tennis courts, racquetball courts, massage. **Guest Services:** gift shop, valet laundry, area transportation. **Business Services:** conference facilities, business center. **Cards:** AX, CB, DC, DS, JC, MC, VI.

SOME UNITS

FEE

MAINSTAY SUITES ADDISON
Phone: (972)340-3001 [186]

All Year [ECP]   1P: $54-$89
Location: Just n of Belt Line Rd. 15200 Addison Rd 75001. Fax: 972/340-2700. **Facility:** 70 units. 39 one-bedroom
Small-scale Hotel standard units with efficiencies. 31 one-bedroom suites with efficiencies. 3 stories, interior corridors. *Bath:* combo or shower only. **Parking:** on-site. **Amenities:** high-speed Internet, dual phone lines, voice mail, irons, hair dryers. **Pool(s):** small heated outdoor. **Leisure Activities:** whirlpool, exercise room. **Guest Services:** complimentary evening beverages: Mon-Wed, valet and coin laundry, area transportation. **Business Services:** meeting rooms, PC, fax (fee). **Cards:** AX, CB, DC, DS, JC, MC, VI.

SOME UNITS

QUALITY SUITES-ADDISON (NOW KNOWN AS COMFORT SUITES)
Phone: (972)503-6500 [195]

All Year [BP]   1P: $89-$129   2P: $89-$129   XP: $5   F18
[SAVE]
Location: Just ne of jct Midway and Belt Line rds. 4555 Belt Line Rd 75001. Fax: 972/503-6500. **Facility:** 78 units. 29 one-bedroom standard units. 49 one-bedroom suites, some with whirlpools. 3 stories, interior corridors. *Bath:* combo or shower only. **Parking:** on-site. **Terms:** small pets only ($50 deposit). **Amenities:** voice mail,
Small-scale Hotel irons, hair dryers. **Pool(s):** heated indoor. **Leisure Activities:** whirlpool, limited exercise equipment. **Guest Services:** complimentary evening beverages: Mon-Thurs, valet and coin laundry. **Business Services:** meeting rooms, business center. **Cards:** AX, CB, DC, DS, JC, MC, VI.

SOME UNITS

WINGATE INN-ADDISON/NORTH DALLAS
Phone: (972)490-1212 [187]

All Year [ECP]   1P: $119   2P: $119
Location: Just n of jct Belt Line and Inwood rds, on Addison Rd, then just e. 4960 Arapaho Rd 75001.
Small-scale Hotel Fax: 972/233-4283. **Facility:** 101 one-bedroom standard units, some with whirlpools. 4 stories, interior corridors. *Bath:* combo or shower only. **Parking:** on-site. **Amenities:** video games (fee), high-speed Internet, dual phone lines, voice mail, safes, irons, hair dryers. **Leisure Activities:** whirlpool, exercise room. **Guest Services:** valet laundry, area transportation. **Business Services:** meeting rooms, business center. **Cards:** AX, DC, DS, MC, VI.

SOME UNITS

——— WHERE TO DINE ———

ADDISON CAFE
Lunch: $9-$13   Dinner: $13-$20   Phone: 972/991-8824 [143]

Location: Just e of North Dallas Tollway; corner of Monfort Dr and Belt Line Rd. 5290 Belt Line Rd 75254.
Hours: 11:30 am-2 & 5:30-10 pm, Sun 5:30 pm-9:30 pm. Closed: 1/1, 12/25. **Reservations:** suggested.
Northern French **Features:** Glass walls and sleek black and white tones are contrasted by colorful artwork and lush greenery in this romantic bistro setting. Upscale Northern French fare features entrees like veal and smoked salmon, all pleasingly presented and very well-prepared. Semi-casual attire; cocktails. **Parking:** on-site. **Cards:** AX, CB, DC, DS, MC, VI.

(See map p. 236)

AUGUST MOON **Lunch:** $7-$10 **Dinner:** $9-$20 **Phone:** 972/385-7227 (142)
Chinese
Location: Just s of jct Belt Line and Preston rds. 15030 Preston Rd 75240. **Hours:** 11 am-10:30 pm, Fri & Sat-11 pm. Closed: 11/27. **Reservations:** accepted. **Features:** The three dining rooms are decorated in a Chinese motif. Choose from a large selection of appetizers such as the seafood cakes made with scallops, shrimp and king crab or the yummy pot stickers. The chef gourmet specialties range from five flavored shrimp served with candied walnuts or the perennial Peking duck. Complete family dinners are available with multiple course selections. Casual dress; cocktails. **Parking:** on-site. **Cards:** AX, CB, DC, DS, MC, VI.

BLUE MESA GRILL **Lunch:** $7-$11 **Dinner:** $9-$15 **Phone:** 972/934-0165 (140)
Mexican
Location: Jct of Dallas Tollway and Belt Line Rd; in Village on the Parkway Shopping Center. 5100 Belt Line Rd, Suite 500 75240. **Hours:** 11 am-10 pm, Fri & Sat-10:30 pm, Sun 10 am-9 pm. Closed: 11/27, 12/25. **Reservations:** accepted. **Features:** Decorated in a rustic Southwestern motif, this cafe offers spicy entrees with a New Mexican flair. Crunch on blue corn and sweet potato chips in the airy dining room before diving into one of the sampler plates that include an original tamale pie and mesquite-grilled skewers of meat. For dessert, try the honey-caramel-coated flan topped with a raspberry sauce. Casual dress; cocktails. **Parking:** on-site. **Cards:** AX, CB, DC, DS, MC, VI.

CANTINA LAREDO-ADDISON **Lunch:** $6-$11 **Dinner:** $7-$14 **Phone:** 972/458-0962 (133)
Mexican
Location: 0.3 mi e of jct Midway and Belt Line rds. 4546 Belt Line Rd 75001. **Hours:** 11 am-10 pm, Fri & Sat-11 pm. Closed: 11/27, 12/25. **Features:** Fun, fresh and festive are the words for this colorful eatery offering a nice variety of Tex-Mex fare. Alongside traditional favorites like tacos, enchiladas and nachos are more unusual dishes like caberito, which is roasted baby goat in a special sauce. Casual dress; cocktails. **Parking:** on-site. **Cards:** AX, DC, DS, MC, VI.

COPELAND'S **Lunch:** $7-$10 **Dinner:** $10-$21 **Phone:** 972/661-1883 (141)
Ethnic
Location: 0.4 mi e of jct North Dallas Tollway. 5353 Belt Line Rd 75240. **Hours:** 11 am-11 pm, Fri & Sat-midnight. Closed: 11/27, 12/25. **Reservations:** accepted. **Features:** Step into Victorian New Orleans with all its charming brass and dark wood trimmings. Authentic Cajun and Creole cooking features shrimp and redfish Creole, blackened chicken, spicy gumbo and bananas Foster, all cordially presented in a relaxed atmosphere. Casual dress; cocktails. **Parking:** on-site. **Cards:** AX, CB, DC, DS, MC, VI.

DOVIE'S **Lunch:** $8-$14 **Dinner:** $13-$21 **Phone:** 972/233-9846 (146)
American
Location: I-63 S, exit Midway Rd, 1.5 mi n; behind office building. 14671 Midway Rd 75001. **Hours:** 11 am-2 & 5:30-9 pm, Sat 5:30 pm-9:30 pm, Sun 10:30 am-2 pm. Closed: 1/1, 12/25. **Reservations:** accepted. **Features:** Built in 1930, this restored home offers several candlelit dining rooms, each with a different theme. Quaint, cozy surroundings, sure to inspire even the most hopeless of romantics, feature fresh flowers, three fireplaces and hardwood floors. Casual dress; cocktails. **Parking:** on-site. **Cards:** AX, CB, DC, MC, VI.

FOGO DE CHAO **Lunch:** $25 **Dinner:** $39 **Phone:** 972/503-7300 (136)
Brazilian
Location: Just e of jct Midway Rd. 4300 Belt Line Rd 75001. **Hours:** 11 am-2 & 5-10 pm, Fri & Sat-10:30 pm. Closed: 11/27, 12/25. **Reservations:** suggested. **Features:** A smokehouse ambience taken from the styles of southern Brazil features a large pit at the entrance and a staff in gaucho dress. No menu, simply one price for all you care to enjoy of 12 slow-roasted cuts of meat, salad, fried bananas and mashed potatoes. Smoke free premises. Casual dress; cocktails. **Parking:** on-site. **Cards:** AX, DC, DS, MC, VI.

JASMINE RESTAURANT **Lunch:** $5-$9 **Dinner:** $9-$24 **Phone:** 972/991-6867 (132)
Chinese
Location: I-635, exit Midway Rd, 2 mi n to Belt Line Rd, 0.3 mi w. 4002 Belt Line Rd 75001. **Hours:** 11 am- 3 & 4:30-10 pm, Sat 4:30 pm-11 pm, Sun 11:30 am-10 pm. **Reservations:** suggested. **Features:** Dark wood set off by bright colors envelopes you in a casual supper club atmosphere as you enjoy delicious, traditional favorites. Egg and shrimp rolls, soups and many reliable choices like the tasty lemon chicken combine to create a satisfying meal. Casual dress; cocktails; entertainment. **Parking:** on-site. **Cards:** AX, CB, DC, MC, VI.

LAWRY'S THE PRIME RIB **Lunch:** $22-$31 **Dinner:** $22-$31 **Phone:** 972/503-6688 (130)
Steak House
Location: 0.5 mi e of jct Dallas Pkwy and Belt Line Rd; on west side service road. 14655 Dallas Pkwy 75240. **Hours:** 11 am-2 & 5:30-10 pm, Sat from 5 pm, Sun 11 am-2 & 5-9 pm. Closed: 7/4, 12/25. **Reservations:** suggested. **Features:** Frosted glass chandeliers hang from the ceiling of this upscale dining room. The airy room contains several theme paintings and Edwardian decor. Tender prime rib is the specialty and is served table-side from stainless steel carts. Yorkshire pudding or creamed spinach can accompany most meals. Try the lofty banana cream pie for dessert. Formalized service performed by well-trained staff. Smoke free premises. Dressy casual; cocktails. **Parking:** on-site. **Cards:** AX, DC, DS, MC, VI.

LOMBARDI MARE **Lunch:** $9-$15 **Dinner:** $16-$25 **Phone:** 972/503-1233 (128)
Italian
Location: Jct of North Dallas Tollway and Belt Line Rd; in The Village on the Parkway Shopping Center. 5100 Belt Line Rd, Suite 410 75254. **Hours:** 11 am-4 & 5-11 pm, Sat & Sun from 5 pm. Closed: 7/4, 9/1, 12/25. **Reservations:** suggested. **Features:** The restaurant was featured in the 2001 edition of Bon Appetit magazine. Although the menu centers on Italian cuisine, other selections are offered. Oven-baked focaccia and daily specials are sure-fire day brighteners. Cheesecake is almost too good to eat. Casual dress; cocktails. **Parking:** on-site. **Cards:** AX, DC, MC, VI.

MAGIC TIME MACHINE **Lunch:** $7-$16 **Dinner:** $11-$26 **Phone:** 972/980-1903 (139)
American
Location: Just w of North Dallas Tollway. 5003 Belt Line Rd 75240. **Hours:** 5:30 pm-9:30 pm, Sat 11 am-10:30 pm, Sun-9 pm m. Closed: 11/27, 12/25. **Reservations:** suggested; dinner/weekdays. **Features:** Ever have Little Bo Peep serve you a steak in a house built of crayons? Or has Elvis ever visited your teepee to take the family's drink orders? These fanciful events are commonplace at this fun restaurant filled with themed seating and costumed servers. Casual dress; cocktails. **Parking:** on-site. **Cards:** AX, CB, DC, DS, MC, VI.

(See map p. 236)

MI PIACI Lunch: $11-$18 Dinner: $11-$35 Phone: 972/934-8424 (145)
▼▼▼ **Location:** From jct North Dallas Tollway and Belt Line Rd, just e to Monfort Dr, then just s. 14854 Monfort Dr 75240.
Italian **Hours:** 11 am-10 pm, Fri-11 pm, Sat 5 pm-11 pm, Sun 5 pm-10 pm. Closed: 1/1, 11/27, 12/25.
Reservations: suggested. **Features:** The open and airy dining rooms are decorated in a charming Italian
style. The fresh ingredients used for each entree are displayed near the foyer. Delicious scallops are
served with a mix of creamy risotto and sugared yams. Smoke free premises. Dressy casual; cocktails. **Parking:** valet.
Cards: AX, DC, DS, MC, VI. Ⓨ Ⓧ

REMINGTON'S SEAFOOD GRILL Lunch: $7-$13 Dinner: $9-$16 Phone: 972/386-0122 (135)
▼▼ ▼▼ **Location:** I-635, exit Midway Rd, 1.5 mi n to Belt Line Rd, then just e. 4580 Belt Line Rd 75244. **Hours:** 11:30 am-10
Steak & Seafood pm, Fri-11 pm, Sat 5 pm-11 pm, Sun 5 pm-10 pm. Closed major holidays. **Reservations:** accepted.
Features: Fresh New England-style seafood has been consistently served for the past 20 years in an
artsy, nautical decor. Enjoy grilled, blackened or sauteed red snapper, oysters on the half-shell and hearty
chowder, all served in a casual split-level dining area. Casual dress; cocktails. **Cards:** AX, DC, DS, MC, VI. Ⓜ Ⓨ Ⓧ

SNUFFER'S Lunch: $6-$8 Dinner: $6-$8 Phone: 972/991-8811 (137)
▼▼ **Location:** I-635, exit Midway Rd, 1.5 mi n. 14910 Midway Rd 75244. **Hours:** 11 am-midnight, Fri & Sat-2 am,
Southwest Sun-11 pm. **Features:** This popular "burger joint" is perfect for getting together with friends, sipping
American margaritas and munching on some of the tastiest burgers in Dallas. Kick back with the classic sounds of
Motown and chow down! Casual dress; cocktails. **Parking:** on-site. **Cards:** AX, DC, DS, MC, VI. Ⓨ Ⓧ

THAI ORCHID RESTAURANT Lunch: $12-$20 Dinner: $12-$20 Phone: 972/720-8424 (129)
▼▼▼ ▼▼▼ **Location:** Jct of Belt Line Rd and Landmark Blvd, just s. 4930 Belt Line Rd 75254. **Hours:** 11 am-3 & 5-10 pm,
Thai Fri-11 pm, Sat noon-11 pm, Sun 5 pm-10 pm. Closed: 11/27, 12/25. **Reservations:** suggested.
Features: In a small strip center, the small, family-owned restaurant serves traditional Thai cuisine that is
as exotic and subtle as it is healthy and delicious. Dishes are prepared with beef, poultry, seafood and
vegetables. Casual dress; cocktails. **Parking:** on-site. **Cards:** AX, DC, DS, MC, VI. Ⓨ Ⓧ

TOKYO ONE Lunch: $12 Dinner: $22 Phone: 972/386-8899 (131)
▼▼ ▼▼ **Location:** I-635, exit Midway Rd, 0.3 mi e of jct of Midway and Belt Line rds. 4350 Belt Line Rd 75244. **Hours:** 11
Japanese am-2:30 & 5:30-9:30 pm, Fri & Sat 11:30 am-3 & 5:30-10:30 pm. **Reservations:** suggested. **Features:** For
lunch and dinner, the restaurant lays out an extensive buffet of Japanese food. Chefs eagerly grill teriyaki
MC, VI. bowls and prepare selections of fresh sushi. Casual dress; cocktails. **Parking:** on-site. **Cards:** AX, DC, DS,
Ⓧ

ALLEN pop. 43,554 (See map p. 236; index p. 247)

——— WHERE TO STAY ———

AMERIHOST INN-ALLEN Phone: (972)396-9494 (272)
ⒶⒶⒶ ⑤ⒶⓥⒺ All Year 1P: $74-$79 2P: $79-$84
▼▼▼▼ **Location:** US 75, exit 34 (McDermott Rd). 407 Central Expwy S 75013. Fax: 972/396-9595. **Facility:** 60 one-
bedroom standard units, some with whirlpools. 2 stories, interior corridors. *Bath:* combo or shower only.
Parking: on-site. **Terms:** cancellation fee imposed, [ECP] meal plan available. **Amenities:** voice mail, safes,
Small-scale Hotel irons, hair dryers. **Pool(s):** heated indoor. **Leisure Activities:** sauna, whirlpool, exercise room. **Guest Serv-
ices:** valet laundry. **Business Services:** meeting rooms, fax (fee). **Cards:** AX, DC, DS, MC, VI.
Special Amenities: early check-in/late check-out and free continental breakfast.
SOME UNITS
Ⓢ🄳 🄳 ➳ Ⓧ 🄫 DATA PORT 🄻 / Ⓧ 🄷 🄳 /

(See map p. 236)

———— *The following lodging was either not evaluated or did not* ————
meet AAA rating requirements but is listed for your information only.

HILTON GARDEN INN DALLAS/ALLEN   **Phone:** 214/547-1700
   [fyi]   All Year   1P: $99   2P: $99
                 Too new to rate. **Location:** 705 Central Expwy S 75013. **Fax:** 214/547-1705. **Amenities:** coffeemakers, micro-
Small-scale Hotel   waves, refrigerators, pool. **Terms:** cancellation fee imposed. **Cards:** AX, CB, DC, DS, JC, MC, VI.
                 (See ad p 288)

———— **WHERE TO DINE** ————

BRAZOS CATTLE COMPANY   **Lunch:** $7-$21   **Dinner:** $9-$21   **Phone:** 972/727-1614   [186]
   ▽▽ ▽▽   **Location:** I-75, exit 34 (McDermott Rd). 401 Central Expwy S 75013. **Hours:** 11 am-10 pm, Fri & Sat-11 pm.
             Closed: 12/25. **Features:** Southwestern cuisine and decor characterize the gritty restaurant, which has a
    Southwest   facade resembling an Old West building. Western furnishings and a fireplace give the dining room the
    American   feeling of a bunkhouse. Menu choices include steak, chicken and some seafood dishes. Casual dress;
             cocktails. **Parking:** on-site. **Cards:** AX, DC, DS, MC, VI.

SAMUI THAI CUISINE   **Lunch:** $10-$14   **Dinner:** $10-$14   **Phone:** 972/747-7452   [184]
   ▽▽ ▽▽   **Location:** US 75, exit 34 (McDermott Rd), just w. 906 W McDermott Rd, Suite 104 75013. **Hours:** 11 am-2:30 &
             5-10 pm, Fri-10:30 pm, Sat & Sun 11 am-10 pm. Closed: 1/1, 11/27, 12/25. **Reservations:** suggested;
     Thai   weekends. **Features:** Thai cuisine is at the heart of the family-owned restaurant's menu. Flavor-filled
premises. Casual dress; cocktails. **Parking:** on-site. **Cards:** AX, DC, DS, MC, VI.

CARROLLTON pop. 109,576 (See map p. 236; index p. 244)

———— **WHERE TO STAY** ————

RED ROOF INN-CARROLLTON   **Phone:** (972)245-1700   [174]
   AAA [SAVE]   All Year   1P: $33-$44   2P: $38-$49   XP: $5   F18
  ▽▽▽ ▽▽▽   **Location:** I-35 E, exit 442 (Valwood Pkwy), just ne. 1720 S Broadway 75006. **Fax:** 972/245-4402. **Facility:** 137 one-
             bedroom standard units. 3 stories, exterior corridors. **Parking:** on-site. **Terms:** small pets only.
    Motel   **Amenities:** video games (fee), voice mail. **Business Services:** meeting rooms, fax (fee). **Cards:** AX, CB,
             DC, DS, MC, VI. **Special Amenities:** free local telephone calls and free newspaper.

SOME UNITS
FEE   FEE

———— **WHERE TO DINE** ————

TIA'S TEX & MEX   **Lunch:** $6-$9   **Dinner:** $7-$15   **Phone:** 972/245-2997   [120]
   ▽▽   **Location:** I-35, exit 445 (Trinty Mills Rd), 0.9 mi e to jct Old Denton Rd. 2625 Old Denton Rd, Suite 800 75007.
            Hours: 11 am-10 pm, Fri & Sat-11 pm. Closed: 11/27, 12/25. **Features:** Friendly service and large, tasty
Regional Mexican   portions of Tex-Mex cuisine make this a very nice choice. Select from a good variety of appetizers
            including excellent salsa and homemade tortillas; then savor pleasing favorites like tacos, enchiladas, and
fajitas. Smoke free premises. Casual dress; cocktails. **Parking:** on-site. **Cards:** AX, DC, DS, MC, VI.

CEDAR HILL pop. 32,093 (See map p. 248; index p. 249)

———— **WHERE TO STAY** ————

RAMADA LIMITED   **Phone:** 972/299-0100   [335]
   AAA [SAVE]   2/1-12/31   1P: $59-$69   2P: $69-$79   XP: $5   F16
             1/1-1/31   1P: $69   2P: $79   XP: $5   F16
  ▽▽ ▽▽   **Location:** US 67, exit Wintergreen. 1439 N Hwy 67 75104. **Fax:** 972/291-1009. **Facility:** 68 ono-bedroom standard
             units. 2 stories, interior corridors. **Parking:** on-site. **Terms:** [ECP] meal plan available. **Amenities:** voice mail,
Small-scale Hotel   irons, hair dryers. **Pool(s):** outdoor. **Leisure Activities:** whirlpool. **Guest Services:** coin laundry. **Business
Services:** meeting rooms, fax (fee). **Cards:** AX, DC, DS, MC, VI. **Special Amenities:** free continental
breakfast and free local telephone calls.

SOME UNITS

THE COLONY pop. 26,531

———— **WHERE TO STAY** ————

COMFORT SUITES   **Phone:** (972)668-5555
   AAA [SAVE]   All Year   1P: $79   2P: $89   XP: $5   F18
  ▽▽ ▽▽   **Location:** Just n of jct SR 121. 4796 Memorial Dr 75056. **Fax:** 972/370-2950. **Facility:** 71 units. 70 one-bedroom
             standard units, some with whirlpools. 1 one-bedroom suite with kitchen (no utensils). 3 stories, interior corri-
Small-scale Hotel   dors. **Bath:** combo or shower only. **Parking:** on-site. **Terms:** 7 day cancellation notice-fee imposed, [CP]
meal plan available, small pets only ($25 fee, $10 extra charge). **Amenities:** dual phone lines, voice mail,
irons, hair dryers. **Pool(s):** heated indoor. **Leisure Activities:** whirlpool, exercise room. **Guest Services:**
coin laundry. **Business Services:** meeting rooms, fax (fee). **Cards:** AX, DC, DS, JC, MC, VI. **Special Amenities:** free continental breakfast and free local telephone calls.

SOME UNITS

DENTON pop. 66,300

———— **WHERE TO STAY** ————

BEST WESTERN DENTON INN & SUITES   Phone: (940)591-7726

SAVE

Small-scale Hotel

2/1-8/31 & 1/1-1/31 [CP]   1P: $82-$91   2P: $82-$91
9/1-12/31 [CP]   1P: $74-$82   2P: $74-$82
Location: I-35 E, exit 469, just e. 2910 W University Dr 76201. **Fax:** 940/591-7736. **Facility:** 65 one-bedroom standard units, some with whirlpools. 3 stories, interior corridors. *Bath:* combo or shower only. **Parking:** on-site. **Terms:** 13% service charge. **Amenities:** dual phone lines, voice mail, irons, hair dryers. **Pool(s):** heated outdoor. **Leisure Activities:** whirlpool, exercise room. **Guest Services:** valet and coin laundry. **Business Services:** meeting rooms, fax. **Cards:** AX, DC, DS, MC, VI. *(See color ad below)*

SOME UNITS

🅂📢 🚻 🐾 🏊 🎥 📡 🔌 🛏 🍽 ☕ /✕/

COMFORT SUITES   Phone: (940)898-8510

AAA SAVE

Small-scale Hotel

All Year [ECP]   1P: $90-$179   2P: $100-$189   XP: $10   F17
Location: I-35, exit 465B southbound; exit 466A northbound, on northbound service road. 1100 I-35 E 76205. **Fax:** 940/898-8235. **Facility:** 69 one-bedroom standard units, some with whirlpools. 3 stories, interior corridors. *Bath:* combo or shower only. **Parking:** on-site. **Amenities:** dual phone lines, voice mail, irons, hair dryers. **Pool(s):** heated indoor. **Leisure Activities:** whirlpool, exercise room. **Guest Services:** coin laundry. **Business Services:** meeting rooms, business center. **Cards:** AX, DC, DS, MC, VI. **Special Amenities:** free continental breakfast and free local telephone calls. *(See color ad below)*

SOME UNITS

🅂📢 ♿ⓂⒶ 🐾 🏊 🎥 📡 🔌 🛏 🍽 ☕ /✕/

EXEL INN OF DENTON

AAA SAVE
◇◇◇ ◇◇
Small-scale Hotel

All Year [CP]   1P: $36-$54   2P: $42-$65   XP: $6   F18
Location: Jct US 380 and I-35, exit 469, just n. 4211 I-35 E N 76207. Fax: 940/898-0329. **Facility:** 112 one-bedroom standard units, some with whirlpools. 3 stories, interior corridors. **Parking:** on-site. **Terms:** weekly rates available, small pets only (in smoking units). **Amenities:** irons. **Pool(s):** small outdoor. **Leisure Activities:** exercise room. **Guest Services:** coin laundry. **Business Services:** fax (fee). **Cards:** AX, CB, DC, DS, MC, VI. **Special Amenities:** early check-in/late check-out and free continental breakfast.

Phone: (940)383-1471

SOME UNITS

THE HERITAGE INNS

◇◇ ◇◇
Bed & Breakfast

All Year [BP]   1P: $85-$95   2P: $85-$95   XP: $15   F10
Location: Jct of Ferguson and Locust sts (Court House Square), 0.5 mi e of Court House Square. 815 N Locust 76201. Fax: 940/565-6515. **Facility:** 11 units. 8 one- and two-bedroom standard units, some with whirlpools. 2 one-bedroom suites ($105-$135), some with whirlpools. 2 stories (no elevator), interior corridors. *Bath:* combo, shower or tub only. **Parking:** on-site. **Terms:** check-in 4 pm, 3 day cancellation notice-fee imposed. **Amenities:** hair dryers. **Leisure Activities:** whirlpool. **Cards:** AX, DS, MC, VI.

Phone: 940/565-6414

SOME UNITS

HOLIDAY INN

◇◇◇◇
Small-scale Hotel

All Year   Property failed to provide current rates
Location: 2 mi se of jct I-35 E and US 77 business route, exit 464 westbound; exit 465A (Teasley Ln) eastbound. 1500 Dallas Dr 76205. Fax: 940/387-7917. **Facility:** 143 units. 140 one-bedroom standard units. 3 one-bedroom suites. 2 stories, exterior corridors. **Parking:** on-site. **Amenities:** voice mail, irons, hair dryers. **Pool(s):** outdoor. **Leisure Activities:** exercise room. **Guest Services:** valet and coin laundry. **Business Services:** meeting rooms, fax (fee). **Cards:** AX, CB, DC, DS, JC, MC, VI.

Phone: 940/387-3511

SOME UNITS

LA QUINTA INN-DENTON

AAA SAVE
◇◇◇ ◇◇
Small-scale Hotel

All Year   1P: $65-$79   2P: $75-$89   XP: $10   F18
Location: I-35 E, exit 465B (Fort Worth Dr), just n. 700 Fort Worth Dr 76201. Fax: 940/387-2493. **Facility:** 99 units. 98 one-bedroom standard units. 1 one-bedroom suite. 2 stories, exterior corridors. *Bath:* combo or shower only. **Parking:** on-site. **Terms:** [ECP] meal plan available, small pets only. **Amenities:** video games (fee), voice mail, irons, hair dryers. **Pool(s):** outdoor. **Guest Services:** valet and coin laundry. **Business Services:** meeting rooms, fax (fee). **Cards:** AX, CB, DC, DS, JC, MC, VI. **Special Amenities:** free continental breakfast and free local telephone calls.

Phone: (940)387-5840

SOME UNITS

RADISSON HOTEL DENTON & EAGLE POINT GOLF CLUB

◇◇◇◇
Small-scale Hotel

All Year   1P: $109-$139   2P: $109-$139   XP: $10   F18
Location: Off I-35 E and US 77, exit 466B (Ave D), 2.5 mi sw. 2211 I-35 E N 76205. Fax: 940/384-2244. **Facility:** 150 units. 146 one-bedroom standard units. 4 one-bedroom suites ($150-$360). 8 stories, interior corridors. **Parking:** on-site. **Terms:** 7 night minimum stay - seasonal, small pets only ($100 deposit). **Amenities:** video games (fee), dual phone lines, voice mail, irons, hair dryers. **Pool(s):** outdoor. **Leisure Activities:** exercise room. *Fee:* golf-18 holes. **Guest Services:** valet laundry. **Business Services:** conference facilities, fax (fee). **Cards:** AX, CB, DC, DS, JC, MC, VI.

Phone: (940)565-8499

SOME UNITS

SUPER 8 MOTEL-DENTON

◇◇◇ ◇◇
Small-scale Hotel

All Year [CP]   1P: $49-$69   2P: $49-$69   XP: $5   F12
Location: I-35, exit 465A (Teasley Ln). 620 South I-35 E 76205. Fax: 940/380-8880. **Facility:** 80 one-bedroom standard units. 3 stories, interior corridors. *Bath:* combo or shower only. **Parking:** on-site. **Terms:** small pets only ($25 fee). **Amenities:** safes (fee). *Some:* irons, hair dryers. **Guest Services:** valet laundry. **Business Services:** meeting rooms, fax (fee). **Cards:** AX, CB, DC, DS, MC, VI.

Phone: (940)380-8888

SOME UNITS

DESOTO pop. 37,646 (See map p. 248; index p. 249)

──────── **WHERE TO STAY** ────────

BEST WESTERN OF DESOTO

AAA SAVE
◇◇◇◇
Small-scale Hotel

4/1-10/31   1P: $70-$90   2P: $76-$96   XP: $6   F16
2/1-3/31 & 11/1-1/31   1P: $60-$80   2P: $66-$86   XP: $6   F16
Location: I-35, exit 416 (Wintergreen Rd). 1135 N Beckley Dr 75115. Fax: 972/224-5569. **Facility:** 47 one-bedroom standard units. 2 stories, exterior corridors. **Parking:** on-site. **Amenities:** hair dryers. *Some:* irons. **Pool(s):** outdoor. **Guest Services:** coin laundry. **Business Services:** fax (fee). **Cards:** AX, CB, DC, DS, JC, MC. **Special Amenities:** free continental breakfast.

Phone: (972)224-8575   [328]

SOME UNITS

HOLIDAY INN

◇◇◇◇
Small-scale Hotel

All Year   1P: $71-$84   2P: $71-$84
Location: I-35 E, exit 416. 1515 N Beckley Dr 75115. Fax: 972/228-8238. **Facility:** 149 one-bedroom standard units. 4 stories, interior corridors. **Parking:** on-site. **Amenities:** video games (fee), voice mail, irons, hair dryers. **Pool(s):** heated indoor. **Leisure Activities:** sauna, whirlpool, exercise room. **Guest Services:** valet and coin laundry, area transportation. **Business Services:** meeting rooms, fax (fee). **Cards:** AX, CB, DC, DS, MC, VI.

Phone: (972)224-9100   [329]

SOME UNITS

(See map p. 248)

RED ROOF INN DALLAS/DESOTO
Phone: (972)224-7100   330

(AAA) (SAVE)

All Year   1P: $39-$49   2P: $44-$54   XP: $5   F18
Location: I-35, exit 416. 1401 N Beckley 75115. Fax: 972/224-7260. **Facility:** 108 one-bedroom standard units. 3 stories, interior/exterior corridors. **Parking:** on-site. **Amenities:** video games (fee), voice mail. **Business Services:** fax (fee). **Cards:** AX, CB, DC, DS, MC, VI. **Special Amenities:** free local telephone calls and free newspaper.

Motel

SOME UNITS

DUNCANVILLE pop. 36,081   (See map p. 248; index p. 249)

——— WHERE TO STAY ———

RAMADA INN-DALLAS SOUTHWEST
Phone: (972)298-8911   320

All Year   1P: $55   2P: $59
Location: I-20, exit 463, 0.3 mi w of jct I-20 and Cockrell Hill Rd; 2 mi w of US 67. 711 E Camp Wisdom Rd 75116. Small-scale Hotel Fax: 972/298-8983. **Facility:** 123 one-bedroom standard units. 2 stories, interior/exterior corridors. **Parking:** on-site. **Terms:** [BP] meal plan available, small pets only ($25 fee). **Amenities:** voice mail, irons, hair dryers. **Pool(s):** outdoor. **Leisure Activities:** exercise room. **Guest Services:** coin laundry. **Business Services:** meeting rooms, fax (fee). **Cards:** AX, DC, DS, MC, VI.

SOME UNITS

ENNIS pop. 16,045

——— WHERE TO STAY ———

BEST WESTERN ENNIS
Phone: (972)875-3390

(AAA) (SAVE)

All Year   1P: $65-$69   2P: $65-$69   XP: $5   F17
Location: I-45, exit 251B. 100 S I-45 75119. Fax: 972/875-6066. **Facility:** 52 one-bedroom standard units. 2 stories, interior/exterior corridors. *Bath:* combo or shower only. **Parking:** on-site. **Terms:** [ECP] meal plan available. **Amenities:** voice mail, irons, hair dryers. **Pool(s):** outdoor. **Leisure Activities:** whirlpool. **Guest** Small-scale Hotel **Services:** valet and coin laundry. **Business Services:** meeting rooms, fax (fee). **Cards:** AX, CB, DC, DS, MC, VI. **Special Amenities:** free continental breakfast and free newspaper.

SOME UNITS

QUALITY INN
Phone: (972)875-9641

(AAA) (SAVE)

All Year [ECP]   1P: $64-$79   2P: $64-$79   XP: $5   F18
Location: Jct I-45 and SR 34, exit 251B. Located in a semi-rural area. 107 Chamber of Commerce Dr 75119. Fax: 972/875-4026. **Facility:** 68 one-bedroom standard units. 2 stories, exterior corridors. **Parking:** on-site. **Amenities:** video games (fee), dual phone lines, voice mail, irons, hair dryers. **Pool(s):** outdoor. **Leisure Ac-** Small-scale Hotel **tivities:** whirlpool. **Guest Services:** valet laundry. **Business Services:** meeting rooms, fax (fee). **Cards:** AX, CB, DC, DS, JC, MC, VI. **Special Amenities:** free continental breakfast and free newspaper.

SOME UNITS

FEE

FARMERS BRANCH pop. 27,508   (See map p. 236; index p. 244)

——— WHERE TO STAY ———

BEST WESTERN DALLAS NORTH
Phone: 972-241-8521   166

(SAVE)

All Year [BP]   1P: $50-$60   2P: $59-$69   XP: $5   F12
Location: I-35 E, exit 441 (Valley View Ln), on west side of frontage road. 13333 N Stemmons Frwy 75234. Fax: 972/243-4103. **Facility:** 181 units. 177 one-bedroom standard units. 4 one-bedroom suites. 2 stories, interior/exterior corridors. **Parking:** on-site. **Terms:** cancellation fee imposed, 13% service charge, small pets Small-scale Hotel only ($25 deposit). **Amenities:** video games (fee), voice mail, irons, hair dryers. *Some:* high-speed Internet. **Pool(s):** outdoor. **Leisure Activities:** sauna, whirlpool. **Guest Services:** valet and coin laundry. **Business Services:** meeting rooms, fax (fee). **Cards:** AX, CB, DC, DS, MC, VI.

SOME UNITS

FEE FEE

COMFORT INN OF NORTH DALLAS
Phone: (972)406-3030   162

(AAA) (SAVE)

All Year [ECP]   1P: $55-$85   2P: $60-$120   XP: $5   F
Location: I-35 E, exit 442 (Valwood Pkwy). 14040 Stemmons Frwy 75234. Fax: 972/406-2929. **Facility:** 49 one-bedroom standard units, some with whirlpools. 2 stories, interior corridors. *Bath:* combo or shower only. **Parking:** on-site. **Terms:** weekly rates available, package plans. **Amenities:** dual phone lines, irons, hair dryers. **Pool(s):** outdoor. **Leisure Activities:** whirlpool, exercise room. **Guest Services:** valet and coin laundry. **Business Services:** fax. **Cards:** AX, CB, DC, DS, JC, MC, VI.

SOME UNITS

DAYS INN - NORTH DALLAS
Phone: (972)488-0800   164

(AAA) (SAVE)

7/1-9/30   1P: $49-$55   2P: $54-$59   XP: $2   F12
4/1-6/30   1P: $45-$50   2P: $49-$54   XP: $2   F12
2/1-3/31 & 10/1-1/31   1P: $40-$45   2P: $45-$49   XP: $2   F12
Location: I-35 E, exit 441 (Valley View Ln), on west side of frontage road. 13313 Stemmons Frwy 75234. Small-scale Hotel Fax: 972/488-0757. **Facility:** 73 one-bedroom standard units, some with whirlpools. 2 stories, interior corridors. *Bath:* combo or shower only. **Parking:** on-site. **Terms:** 7 day cancellation notice-fee imposed, weekly rates available, [CP] meal plan available, package plans - weekends, pets ($20 deposit, $10 extra charge). **Amenities:** safes (fee), irons, hair dryers. **Pool(s):** outdoor. **Guest Services:** valet and coin laundry, airport transportation-Dallas-Fort Worth International & Dallas Love Field airports. **Business Services:** meeting rooms, fax (fee). **Cards:** AX, CB, DC, DS, JC, MC, VI. **Special Amenities:** free continental breakfast and free newspaper.

SOME UNITS

(See map p. 236)

DOUBLETREE CLUB DALLAS-FARMERS BRANCH   **Phone:** (972)506-0055 [168]
SAVE All Year   1P: $59-$129   2P: $59-$129   XP: $10   F18
Location: I-635, exit 28, just s. Located in a business park area. 11611 Luna Rd 75234. Fax: 972/506-0030.
Facility: 160 one-bedroom standard units. 6 stories, interior corridors. *Bath:* combo or shower only. **Parking:** on-site. **Terms:** cancellation fee imposed, small pets only ($25 deposit). **Amenities:** video games (fee), dual phone lines, voice mail, irons, hair dryers. **Pool(s):** heated outdoor. **Leisure Activities:** jogging, exercise room. **Guest Services:** valet laundry, area transportation. **Business Services:** meeting rooms, fax (fee).
Small-scale Hotel
Cards: AX, DC, DS, MC, VI.

SOME UNITS
🛏️ 🍽️ 🍸 👤 📷 🏊 🎥 📶 ⬛ / ✖️ /

HILTON DALLAS PARKWAY   **Phone:** (972)661-3600 [165]
SAVE All Year   1P: $125-$155   XP: $10   F18
Location: I-635 eastbound, exit 22C (Inwood Rd), then n; exit 22B (Dallas Pkwy) westbound. 4801 LBJ Frwy 75244.
Fax: 972/385-3156. **Facility:** 310 units. 308 one-bedroom standard units. 2 two-bedroom suites ($175-$200). 14 stories, interior corridors. *Bath:* combo or shower only. **Parking:** on-site. **Terms:** cancellation fee imposed, [BP] & [CP] meal plans available, package plans. **Amenities:** video games (fee), voice mail, irons, hair dryers. **Pool(s):** heated indoor/outdoor. **Leisure Activities:** sauna, whirlpool, exercise room. **Guest Serv-**
Large-scale Hotel
ices: gift shop, valet laundry, area transportation. **Business Services:** meeting rooms, business center. **Cards:** AX, CB, DC, DS, MC, VI.

SOME UNITS
🛏️ 🍽️ 🏋️ 📷 🏊 ✖️ 🎥 📶 ⬛ / ✖️ 📱

HOLIDAY INN SELECT NORTH DALLAS   **Phone:** (972)243-3363 [169]
All Year   1P: $89-$159   2P: $89-$159
Location: I-635, exit 26 (Josey Ln) eastbound, just n; exit 25 westbound, 0.4 mi w. 2645 LBJ Frwy 75234.
Fax: 972/243-1153. **Facility:** 377 one-bedroom standard units, some with whirlpools. 6 stories, interior corri-
Small-scale Hotel
dors. *Bath:* combo or shower only. **Parking:** on-site. **Amenities:** voice mail, irons, hair dryers. **Fee:** video games, high-speed Internet. **Pool(s):** heated indoor/outdoor. **Leisure Activities:** whirlpool, exercise room. **Fee:** game room. **Guest Services:** gift shop, valet and coin laundry, area transportation. **Business Services:** meeting rooms, business center.
Cards: AX, CB, DC, DS, MC, VI. *(See ad below)*

SOME UNITS
(ASK) 🛏️ ➕ 🍽️ 📷 🏊 ✖️ 🎥 📶 ⬛ / ✖️ 📱 /
FEE FEE

Look For Savings

When you pick up a AAA TourBook® guide, look for establishments that display a bright red AAA logo, SAVE icon, and Diamond rating in their listing. These Official Appointment establishments place a high value on the patronage they receive from AAA members. And, by offering members great room rates*, they are willing to go the extra mile to get your business.

So, when you turn to the AAA TourBook guide to make your travel plans, look for the establishments that will give you the special treatment you deserve.

See TourBook Navigator section, page 14, for complete details.

(See map p. 236)

LA QUINTA INN-DALLAS-NORTHWEST-FARMERS BRANCH
Phone: (972)620-7333 **170**
All Year 1P: $59-$79 2P: $69-$89 XP: $10 F18
Location: I-35 E, exit 441 (Valley View Ln), on west side of frontage road. 13235 Stemmons Frwy N 75234-5757.
Fax: 972/484-6533. **Facility:** 121 one-bedroom standard units. 2 stories, exterior corridors. *Bath:* combo or shower only. **Parking:** on-site. **Terms:** [ECP] meal plan available, small pets only. **Amenities:** video games (fee), voice mail, irons, hair dryers. *Some:* dual phone lines. **Pool(s):** outdoor. **Guest Services:** valet laundry.
Small-scale Hotel
Business Services: meeting rooms, fax (fee). **Cards:** AX, CB, DC, DS, JC, MC, VI. **Special Amenities:** free continental breakfast and free local telephone calls. *(See color ad p 272)*

SOME UNITS
FEE FEE

OMNI DALLAS HOTEL PARKWEST
Phone: (972)869-4300 **160**
All Year 1P: $89-$199 2P: $89-$199 XP: $20 F18
Location: Northwest off I-635 (LBJ Frwy), 1.5 mi w of jct I-35 E, exit 29 (Luna Rd). 1590 LBJ Frwy 75234.
Fax: 972/869-3295. **Facility:** 337 units. 335 one-bedroom standard units. 2 one-bedroom suites with whirlpools. 12 stories, interior corridors. *Bath:* combo or shower only. **Parking:** on-site and valet. **Terms:** cancellation fee imposed, small pets only ($50 fee). **Amenities:** video games (fee), dual phone lines, voice mail, honor bars, irons, hair dryers. **Dining:** 6 am-10 pm, Fri & Sat-11 pm, Sun 11 am-2:30 pm, cocktails. **Pool(s):** heated outdoor. **Leisure Activities:** saunas, whirlpool, exercise room. **Guest Services:** gift shop, valet laundry, area transportation-within 5 mi. **Business Services:** conference facilities, business center. **Cards:** AX, CB, DC, DS, MC, VI.

SOME UNITS

RENAISSANCE DALLAS NORTH HOTEL
Phone: (972)385-9000 **161**
All Year 1P: $69-$170 2P: $69-$170
Location: I-635, exit 23 (Midway Rd), just w on service road. 4099 Valley View Ln 75244. **Fax:** 972/788-1174.
Facility: 289 units. 282 one-bedroom standard units. 7 one-bedroom suites, some with whirlpools. 10 stories, interior corridors. *Bath:* combo or shower only. **Parking:** on-site. **Terms:** cancellation fee imposed, small pets only. **Amenities:** high-speed Internet (fee), voice mail, irons, hair dryers. **Dining:** 6:30 am-2 & 5-10 pm, cocktails. **Pool(s):** outdoor. **Leisure Activities:** exercise room. **Guest Services:** gift shop, valet laundry, area transportation-within 5 mi. **Business Services:** meeting rooms, business center. **Cards:** AX, DC, DS, MC, VI.
(See color ad p 275)

SOME UNITS

FRISCO pop. 33,714

——— WHERE TO STAY ———

THE WESTIN STONEBRIAR RESORT, NORTH DALLAS
Phone: (972)668-8000
All Year 1P: $109-$319 2P: $109-$319 XP: $20 F17
Location: 0.3 mi n of jct SR 121. 1549 Legacy Dr 75034. **Fax:** 976/668-8100. **Facility:** 301 units. 288 one-bedroom standard units. 13 one-bedroom suites. 5 stories, interior corridors. *Bath:* combo or shower only.
Large-scale Hotel
Parking: on-site and valet. **Terms:** cancellation fee imposed, package plans. **Amenities:** dual phone lines, voice mail, safes, honor bars, irons, hair dryers. **Fee:** video games, high-speed Internet. **Pool(s):** heated outdoor. **Leisure Activities:** sauna, whirlpools, steamroom, exercise room, spa. **Guest Services:** gift shop, valet laundry, area transportation. **Business Services:** conference facilities, business center. **Cards:** AX, CB, DC, DS, JC, MC, VI.

SOME UNITS

GARLAND pop. 215,768   (See map p. 236; index p. 245)

——— WHERE TO STAY ———

BEST WESTERN LAKEVIEW INN
Phone: (972)303-1601 **229**
All Year [ECP] 1P: $59-$69 2P: $59-$79 XP: $4 F15
Location: I-30, exit 62 (Chaha Rd). 1635 E I-30 at Chaha Rd 75043. **Fax:** 972/303-1466. **Facility:** 49 one-bedroom standard units, some with whirlpools. 2 stories, exterior corridors. *Bath:* combo or shower only. **Parking:** on-site. **Terms:** small pets only ($10 fee, $20 deposit). **Amenities:** video library (fee), safes, irons, hair dryers.
Motel
Pool(s): outdoor. **Leisure Activities:** whirlpool, exercise room. **Guest Services:** valet and coin laundry. **Business Services:** meeting rooms, fax (fee). **Cards:** AX, CB, DC, DS, MC, VI. **Special Amenities:** early check-in/late check-out and free continental breakfast.

SOME UNITS
FEE

COMFORT INN
Phone: (972)613-5000 **226**
All Year 1P: $55-$59 2P: $55-$59 XP: $5 F18
Location: I-635, exit 11B, just s. 12670 E Northwest Hwy 75228. **Fax:** 972/613-4535. **Facility:** 125 one-bedroom standard units. 3 stories, exterior corridors. **Parking:** on-site. **Terms:** [CP] meal plan available, pets ($5 extra charge). **Amenities:** voice mail, irons. *Some:* hair dryers. **Pool(s):** outdoor. **Guest Services:** valet and coin
Motel
laundry. **Business Services:** meeting rooms, fax (fee). **Cards:** AX, DC, DS, MC, VI.

SOME UNITS

DAYS INN-DALLAS GARLAND
Phone: (972)840-0020 **225**
All Year [ECP] 1P: $45-$55 2P: $50-$60 XP: $10 F14
Location: I-635, exit 11B, 0.5 mi s on E Northwest Pkwy, 0.8 mi w on Garland Ave. 3645 Leon Rd 75041.
Fax: 972/840-1280. **Facility:** 45 one-bedroom standard units, some with whirlpools. 3 stories, interior corridors. *Bath:* combo or shower only. **Parking:** on-site. **Amenities:** irons, hair dryers. **Pool(s):** outdoor. **Leisure**
Small-scale Hotel
Activities: whirlpool. **Guest Services:** coin laundry. **Business Services:** meeting rooms, fax (fee). **Cards:** AX, CB, DC, DS, JC, MC, VI.

SOME UNITS

(See map p. 236)

DAYS INN-DALLAS/GARLAND   **Phone: (972)226-7621**   227

[SAVE]

Motel

All Year [CP]   1P: $47   2P: $49
Location: I-30, exit 59, just s. 6222 Broadway Blvd 75043. Fax: 972/226-3617. **Facility:** 120 one-bedroom standard units. 2 stories, exterior corridors. **Parking:** on-site. **Terms:** weekly rates available, small pets only ($10 extra charge). **Amenities:** hair dryers. *Some:* irons. **Pool(s):** outdoor. **Leisure Activities:** whirlpool. **Guest Services:** coin laundry. **Business Services:** meeting rooms, fax (fee). **Cards:** AX, CB, DC, DS, MC, VI.

SOME UNITS

HOLIDAY INN SELECT LBJ NE (GARLAND)   **Phone: (214)341-5400**   222

[AAA] [SAVE]

Small-scale Hotel

All Year   1P: $89-$99   2P: $89-$99
Location: I-635, exit 13 (Jupiter/Kingsley rds). 11350 LBJ Frwy 75238. Fax: 214/553-9349. **Facility:** 244 one-bedroom standard units. 5 stories, interior corridors. **Parking:** on-site. **Terms:** 30 day cancellation notice, package plans. **Amenities:** video games (fee), voice mail, irons, hair dryers. **Dining:** 6 am-2 & 5-11 pm, cocktails. **Pool(s):** outdoor. **Leisure Activities:** sauna, exercise room. **Guest Services:** gift shop, valet and coin laundry, area transportation-within 5 mi. **Business Services:** conference facilities, fax (fee). **Cards:** AX, DC, DS, MC, VI. **Special Amenities:** free local telephone calls and free newspaper. *(See color ad below)*

SOME UNITS

FEE FEE

LA QUINTA INN-DALLAS-LBJ NORTHEAST-GARLAND   **Phone: (972)271-7581**   223

[AAA] [SAVE]

Motel

(See color ad p 272)

All Year   1P: $64-$79   2P: $74-$89   XP: $10   F18
Location: I-635, exit 11B (Northwest Hwy), just nw. 12721 I-635 75041. Fax: 972/271-1388. **Facility:** 121 units. 120 one-bedroom standard units. 1 one-bedroom suite. 2 stories, exterior corridors. **Parking:** on-site. **Terms:** [ECP] meal plan available, small pets only. **Amenities:** video games, voice mail, irons, hair dryers. **Pool(s):** outdoor. **Guest Services:** valet laundry. **Business Services:** meeting rooms, fax (fee). **Cards:** AX, CB, DC, DS, JC, MC, VI. **Special Amenities:** free continental breakfast and free local telephone calls.

SOME UNITS

MICROTEL INN & SUITES   **Phone: (972)270-7200**   220

[AAA] [SAVE]

Small-scale Hotel

All Year   1P: $40-$85   2P: $40-$85   XP: $5   F16
Location: I-635, exit 11B, just n to Pendleton Dr, then just e. 1901 Pendleton Dr 75041. Fax: 972/279-6664. **Facility:** 53 one-bedroom standard units, some with whirlpools. 3 stories, interior corridors. *Bath:* combo or shower only. **Parking:** on-site. **Terms:** weekly rates available, [CP] meal plan available, pets ($5 fee). **Amenities:** hair dryers. *Some:* dual phone lines, irons. **Business Services:** fax (fee). **Cards:** AX, CB, DC, DS, MC, VI. **Special Amenities:** free continental breakfast and free local telephone calls.

SOME UNITS

SUPER 8 MOTEL   **Phone: (972)278-3300**   221

Small-scale Hotel

All Year   1P: $53-$63   2P: $53-$63   XP: $5   F12
Location: I-635, exit 13 (Jupiter Rd). 11421 LBJ Frwy 75041. Fax: 972/271-6578. **Facility:** 60 one-bedroom standard units, some with kitchens (no utensils) and/or whirlpools. 3 stories, interior corridors. *Bath:* combo or shower only. **Parking:** on-site. **Terms:** [CP] meal plan available. **Amenities:** dual phone lines, voice mail. **Pool(s):** heated indoor. **Leisure Activities:** whirlpool, exercise room. **Business Services:** meeting rooms, fax (fee). **Cards:** AX, DC, MC, VI.

SOME UNITS

GRAND PRAIRIE pop. 127,427 (See map p. 248; index p. 249)

──────── WHERE TO STAY ────────

COMFORT INN
SAVE

Small-scale Hotel

MC, VI.

			Phone: (972)606-2800	**309**
5/1-8/31 [ECP]	1P: $65-$79	2P: $79-$89	XP: $5	F
2/1-4/30 & 9/1-1/31 [ECP]	1P: $55-$65	2P: $59-$69	XP: $5	F

Location: I-20, exit 454, just s. 4020 Great SW Pkwy 75052. Fax: 972/606-4728. **Facility:** 61 one-bedroom standard units, some with whirlpools. 2 stories, exterior corridors. *Bath:* combo or shower only. **Parking:** on-site. **Terms:** 30 day cancellation notice. **Amenities:** irons, hair dryers. **Pool(s):** outdoor. **Leisure Activities:** whirlpool. **Guest Services:** coin laundry. **Business Services:** fax (fee). **Cards:** AX, DC, DS, JC,

SOME UNITS

COMFORT SUITES DFW AIRPORT SOUTH
AAA **SAVE**

Small-scale Hotel

			Phone: (817)633-6311	**310**
All Year	1P: $79-$119	2P: $79-$119	XP: $5	F17

Location: I-30, exit 30, 1.7 mi n on SR 360 to Carrier Pkwy. 2075 N Hwy 360 75050. Fax: 817/633-1082. **Facility:** 71 one-bedroom standard units, some with whirlpools. 4 stories, interior corridors. *Bath:* combo or shower only. **Terms:** cancellation fee imposed, [ECP] meal plan available. **Amenities:** high-speed Internet, dual phone lines, voice mail, safes, irons, hair dryers. **Pool(s):** outdoor. **Leisure Activities:** exercise room. **Guest Services:** complimentary evening beverages: Mon-Wed, valet and coin laundry, airport transportation-Dallas-Fort Worth International Airport, area transportation-within 5 mi. **Business Services:** meeting rooms, business center. **Cards:** AX, DC, DS, MC, VI. **Special Amenities:** free continental breakfast and free local telephone calls.

SOME UNITS

HAMPTON INN ARLINGTON/DFW AIRPORT AREA
SAVE

Small-scale Hotel

			Phone: (972)988-8989	**311**
4/1-9/30 [ECP]	1P: $79-$89	2P: $89-$99		
2/1-3/31 & 10/1-1/31 [ECP]	1P: $74-$84	2P: $84-$94		

Location: I-30, exit 30, 1.7 mi n on SR 360 (Watson Rd), exit Green Oaks Blvd/Carrier Pkwy. 2050 N Hwy 360 75050. Fax: 972/623-0004. **Facility:** 137 one-bedroom standard units. 4 stories, interior corridors. *Bath:* combo or shower only. **Parking:** on-site. **Terms:** 5 day cancellation notice, small pets only ($25 fee). **Amenities:** voice mail, irons, hair dryers. **Pool(s):** outdoor. **Leisure Activities:** exercise room. **Guest Services:** valet and coin laundry, area transportation. **Business Services:** meeting rooms, fax (fee). **Cards:** AX, CB, DC, DS, MC, VI.

SOME UNITS

FEE

LA QUINTA INN-DALLAS-GRAND PRAIRIE (SIX FLAGS)
AAA **SAVE**

Motel

			Phone: (972)641-3021	**315**
All Year	1P: $59-$85	2P: $69-$95	XP: $10	F18

Location: I-30, exit 32, just se. 1410 NW 19th St 75050-2802. Fax: 972/660-3041. **Facility:** 122 units. 121 one-bedroom standard units. 1 one-bedroom suite. 2 stories, exterior corridors. *Bath:* combo or shower only. **Parking:** on-site. **Terms:** [ECP] meal plan available, small pets only. **Amenities:** video games (fee), voice mail, irons, hair dryers. **Pool(s):** outdoor. **Guest Services:** coin laundry. **Business Services:** fax (fee). **Cards:** AX, CB, DC, DS, JC, MC, VI. **Special Amenities:** free continental breakfast and free local telephone calls. *(See color ad p 272)*

SOME UNITS

FEE

MOTEL 6 - 446

Small-scale Hotel

			Phone: 972/642-9424	**314**
5/22-8/16	1P: $39-$49	2P: $45-$55	XP: $3	F17
8/17-1/31	1P: $37-$47	2P: $43-$53	XP: $3	F17
2/1-5/21	1P: $35-$45	2P: $41-$51	XP: $3	F17

Location: I-30, exit 34 (Belt Line Rd), just n to Safari Pkwy, then 0.6 mi w. 406 E Safari Pkwy 75050. Fax: 972/262-3482. **Facility:** 119 one-bedroom standard units, some with efficiencies. 2 stories, exterior corridors. *Bath:* combo or shower only. **Parking:** on-site. **Terms:** small pets only ($25 fee, in efficiency units). **Amenities:** *Some:* irons. **Pool(s):** outdoor. **Guest Services:** coin laundry. **Business Services:** fax (fee). **Cards:** AX, CB, DC, DS, MC, VI.

SOME UNITS

QUALITY INN & SUITES
AAA **SAVE**

Small-scale Hotel

			Phone: 972/602-9400	**308**
5/1-8/31	1P: $75-$80	2P: $80-$90	XP: $5	F18
2/1-4/30 & 9/1-1/31	1P: $65-$70	2P: $70-$75	XP: $5	F18

Location: I-20, exit 454, just ne. 3891 Great SW Pkwy 75052. Fax: 972/602-7888. **Facility:** 50 one-bedroom standard units, some with whirlpools. 2 stories, interior corridors. **Parking:** on-site. **Terms:** 3 day cancellation notice, [CP] meal plan available. **Amenities:** dual phone lines, safes (fee), irons, hair dryers. **Pool(s):** small outdoor. **Guest Services:** coin laundry. **Business Services:** meeting rooms, fax (fee). **Cards:** AX, CB, DC, DS, MC, VI. **Special Amenities:** free continental breakfast and free local telephone calls.

SOME UNITS

GREENVILLE pop. 23,960

──────── WHERE TO STAY ────────

BEST WESTERN INN & SUITES
SAVE

Motel

			Phone: 903/454-1792	
All Year	1P: $53	2P: $53	XP: $5	F17

Location: I-30, exit 94B. 1216 I-30 W 75402. Fax: 903/454-1792. **Facility:** 99 units. 98 one-bedroom standard units. 1 one-bedroom suite. 2 stories, interior/exterior corridors. **Parking:** on-site. **Terms:** 30 day cancellation notice, [CP] meal plan available, small pets only ($100 deposit). **Amenities:** irons, hair dryers. **Pool(s):** outdoor. **Guest Services:** valet and coin laundry. **Business Services:** meeting rooms, fax (fee). **Cards:** AX, CB, DC, DS, JC, MC, VI.

SOME UNITS

COMFORT INN

SAVE ▽▼▽▼▽
Motel

All Year [CP]   1P: $55-$60   2P: $60-$65   **Phone:** (903)455-7700   XP: $5   F16
Location: I-30, exit 94B. 1209 E I-30 75401. Fax: 903/455-7700. **Facility:** 42 one-bedroom standard units, some with whirlpools. 2 stories, interior corridors. *Bath:* combo or shower only. **Parking:** on-site. **Terms:** package plans. **Amenities:** irons, hair dryers. **Pool(s):** outdoor. **Leisure Activities:** exercise room. **Guest Services:** coin laundry. **Business Services:** fax (fee). **Cards:** AX, DC, DS, MC, VI.

SOME UNITS

HOLIDAY INN EXPRESS HOTEL & SUITES

▽▼▽▼▽
Motel

All Year [ECP]   1P: $74-$125   2P: $74-$125   **Phone:** (903)454-8680   XP: $5   F18
Location: I-30, exit 93A. 2901 Mustang Crossing 75402. Fax: 903/454-8036. **Facility:** 80 units. 76 one-bedroom standard units, 4 one-bedroom suites, some with whirlpools. 3 stories, interior corridors. *Bath:* combo or shower only. **Parking:** on-site. **Terms:** small pets only ($100 deposit). **Amenities:** video games, dual phone lines, voice mail, safes, irons, hair dryers. **Pool(s):** outdoor. **Leisure Activities:** limited exercise equipment. **Guest Services:** valet and coin laundry. **Business Services:** meeting rooms, business center. **Cards:** AX, CB, DC, DS, JC, MC, VI.

SOME UNITS

HIGHLAND PARK pop. 8,842 (See map p. 236; index p. 247)

———— WHERE TO DINE ————

CAFE PACIFIC

▽▼▽▼▽
Continental

Lunch: $7-$13   **Dinner:** $14-$26   **Phone:** 214/526-1170   (199)
Location: Just sw of jct Mockingbird Ln and Preston Rd. 24 Highland Park Village 75205. **Hours:** 11:30 am-2:30 & 5:30-10 pm, Fri & Sat-11 pm. Closed major holidays; also Sun. **Reservations:** suggested. **Features:** For polished, professional service and appealing cuisine, this award-winning restaurant makes an impressive choice. Just a taste of dishes like short-smoked salmon and pepper steak with cognac sauce, and you are certain to agree. Dressy casual; cocktails. **Parking:** valet. **Cards:** AX, DC, DS, MC, VI.

IRVING pop. 191,615 (See map p. 236; index p. 242)

———— WHERE TO STAY ————

AMERISUITES (DALLAS/DFW AIRPORT SOUTH)

(AAA) **SAVE**
▽▼▽▼▽
Small-scale Hotel

All Year [ECP]   1P: $79-$109   2P: $79-$109   **Phone:** (972)659-1272   (107)
XP: $10   F18
Location: SR 183, exit Esters Rd on access road. 4235 W Airport Frwy 75062. Fax: 972/570-0676. **Facility:** 128 one-bedroom standard units. 6 stories, interior corridors. *Bath:* combo or shower only. **Parking:** on-site. **Amenities:** voice mail, irons, hair dryers. *Some:* dual phone lines. **Pool(s):** heated outdoor. **Leisure Activities:** exercise room. **Guest Services:** valet and coin laundry, airport transportation-Dallas-Fort Worth International Airport, area transportation-within 2 mi. **Business Services:** meeting rooms, business center. **Cards:** AX, CB, DC, DS, JC, MC, VI. **Special Amenities:** free continental breakfast and free newspaper. *(See color ad p 251)*

SOME UNITS

AMERISUITES (DALLAS LAS COLINAS/HIDDEN RIDGE)

(AAA) **SAVE**
▽▼▽▼▽
Small-scale Hotel

All Year   1P: $115-$120   **Phone:** (972)910-0302   (142)
Location: SR 114, exit Hidden Ridge. 393 W John Carpenter Frwy 75039-2102. Fax: 972/910-0299. **Facility:** 128 one-bedroom standard units. 6 stories, interior corridors. *Bath:* combo or shower only. **Parking:** on-site. **Terms:** small pets only. **Amenities:** voice mail, irons, hair dryers. *Fee:* video games, high-speed Internet. *Some:* dual phone lines. **Pool(s):** heated outdoor. **Leisure Activities:** exercise room. **Guest Services:** valet and coin laundry, area transportation-within 5 mi. **Business Services:** meeting rooms, business center. **Cards:** AX, DC, DS, MC, VI. **Special Amenities:** free continental breakfast and free newspaper. *(See color ad p 251)*

SOME UNITS

AMERISUITES (DALLAS LAS COLINAS/WALNUT HILL)

(AAA) **SAVE**
▽▼▽▼▽
Small-scale Hotel

All Year   1P: $115-$119   2P: $115-$119   **Phone:** (972)550-7400   (117)
Location: SR 114, exit Walnut Hill Ln. 5455 Green Park Dr 75038. Fax: 972/550-7252. **Facility:** 124 one-bedroom standard units. 6 stories, interior corridors. *Bath:* combo or shower only. **Parking:** on-site. **Terms:** [ECP] meal plan available, small pets only. **Amenities:** video games (fee), dual phone lines, voice mail, irons, hair dryers. **Pool(s):** heated outdoor. **Leisure Activities:** exercise room, sports court. **Guest Services:** valet and coin laundry, area transportation-within 5 mi. **Business Services:** meeting rooms, fax (fee). **Cards:** AX, CB, DC, DS, JC, MC, VI. **Special Amenities:** free continental breakfast and free newspaper. *(See color ad p 251)*

SOME UNITS

BEST WESTERN IRVING INN & SUITES DFW AIRPORT

SAVE
▽▼▽▼▽
Small-scale Hotel

All Year [ECP]   1P: $70-$78   2P: $70-$78   **Phone:** (972)790-2262   (109)
XP: $8   F18
Location: 3 mi nw of Irving off SR 183, exit Esters Rd; on south access road. 4110 W Airport Frwy 75062. Fax: 972/986-7620. **Facility:** 141 units. 125 one-bedroom standard units. 16 one-bedroom suites ($88-$98). 2 stories, exterior corridors. **Parking:** on-site. **Amenities:** voice mail, irons, hair dryers. **Pool(s):** outdoor. **Leisure Activities:** whirlpool, exercise room. **Guest Services:** valet and coin laundry, area transportation. **Business Services:** meeting rooms, fax (fee). **Cards:** AX, CB, DC, DS, JC, MC, VI.

SOME UNITS

(See map p. 236)

CANDLEWOOD LAS COLINAS
▼▼▼▼ (rating)
Small-scale Hotel
Phone: (972)714-9990 `120`
All Year   2P: $95-$114
Location: SR 114, exit Walnut Hill Ln, just s. Located within a business center area. 5300 Greenpark Dr 75038. Fax: 972/714-4242. **Facility:** 117 units. 85 one-bedroom standard units with efficiencies. 32 one-bedroom suites with efficiencies. 4 stories, interior corridors. *Bath:* combo or shower only. **Parking:** on-site. **Amenities:** video library, CD players, dual phone lines, voice mail, irons, hair dryers. **Leisure Activities:** exercise room. **Guest Services:** complimentary laundry. **Business Services:** fax. **Cards:** AX, CB, DC, DS, JC, MC, VI.

SOME UNITS
(ASK) (SD) (占M) (占) (今) (VCR) (⚡) (DATA PORT) 🍴 📶 🖥 / (⊠) /

CLARION INN & SUITES AT DFW AIRPORT
(SAVE)
▼▼▼▼
Small-scale Hotel
Phone: 972/929-5757 `116`
All Year   1P: $69-$149   2P: $79-$159   XP: $5   F12
Location: SR 114, exit Freeport Pkwy. 5000 W John Carpenter Hwy 75063. Fax: 972/870-9567. **Facility:** 101 units. 79 one-bedroom standard units. 22 one-bedroom suites. 3 stories, interior corridors. *Bath:* combo or shower only. **Parking:** on-site. **Terms:** [ECP] meal plan available. **Amenities:** dual phone lines, voice mail, irons, hair dryers. **Pool(s):** outdoor. **Leisure Activities:** whirlpool, exercise room. **Guest Services:** sundries. **Business Services:** meeting rooms, business center. **Cards:** AX, CB, DC, DS, JC, MC, VI.

SOME UNITS
(SD) (✈) (占M) (占) (今) (⚡) (DATA PORT) 🍴 📶 🖥 / (⊠) /

COMFORT INN DFW AIRPORT
(SAVE)
▼▼▼ ▼▼▼
Small-scale Hotel
Phone: (972)929-0066 `124`
All Year [ECP]   1P: $59-$69   2P: $65-$75   XP: $5   F18
Location: Nw off SR 114, exit Esters Blvd. 8205 Esters Blvd 75063. Fax: 972/929-5083. **Facility:** 150 one-bedroom standard units. 3 stories, interior corridors. **Parking:** on-site. **Terms:** weekly rates available, package plans. **Amenities:** video games (fee), voice mail, irons, hair dryers. **Pool(s):** small outdoor. **Leisure Activities:** exercise room. **Guest Services:** valet and coin laundry, area transportation. **Business Services:** business center. **Cards:** AX, CB, DC, DS, JC, MC, VI. *(See color ad p 234)*

SOME UNITS
(SD) (✈) (今) (今) (⚡) (DATA PORT) 🖥 / (⊠) 🍴 📶 /

COMFORT INN DFW AIRPORT SOUTH
(AAA) (SAVE)
▼▼▼▼
Small-scale Hotel
Phone: (972)790-7979 `148`
All Year [ECP]   1P: $69-$99   2P: $69-$99   XP: $5   F18
Location: US 183, exit Valley View. 4940 W Airport Frwy 75062. Fax: 972/790-0031. **Facility:** 94 one-bedroom standard units, some with whirlpools. 2 stories, interior corridors. *Bath:* combo or shower only. **Parking:** on-site. **Amenities:** high-speed Internet, dual phone lines, voice mail, safes, irons, hair dryers. **Pool(s):** small outdoor. **Leisure Activities:** whirlpool, exercise room. **Guest Services:** complimentary evening beverages: Wed, valet and coin laundry, airport transportation-Dallas-Fort Worth International Airport, area transportation-within 5 mi. **Business Services:** meeting rooms, fax (fee). **Cards:** AX, CB, DC, DS, MC, VI. **Special Amenities:** free continental breakfast and free local telephone calls. *(See color ad p 263)*

SOME UNITS
(SD) (✈) (🍴) (占M) (占) (今) (⚡) (DATA PORT) 🍴 📶 🖥 / (⊠) /

COMFORT SUITES DFW AIRPORT
(SAVE)
▼▼▼▼
Small-scale Hotel
Phone: (972)929-9097 `146`
All Year [BP]   1P: $60   2P: $60   XP: $5   F18
Location: SR 114, exit Freeport Pkwy on southbound service road. 4700 W John Carpenter Frwy 75063. Fax: 972/929-9247. **Facility:** 108 one-bedroom suites, some with whirlpools. 3 stories, interior corridors. *Bath:* combo or shower only. **Parking:** on-site. **Terms:** weekly rates available. **Amenities:** high-speed Internet, dual phone lines, voice mail, irons, hair dryers. **Pool(s):** heated outdoor. **Leisure Activities:** whirlpool, exercise room. **Guest Services:** sundries, complimentary evening beverages: Mon-Thurs, valet and coin laundry, area transportation. **Business Services:** meeting rooms, business center. **Cards:** AX, CB, DC, DS, MC, VI.

SOME UNITS
(SD) (✈) (占M) (占) (今) (⚡) (DATA PORT) 🍴 📶 🖥 / (⊠) (VCR) /

COMFORT SUITES IN LAS COLINAS
(AAA) (SAVE)
▼▼▼▼
Small-scale Hotel
Phone: (972)518-0606 `138`
All Year   1P: $119   2P: $119   XP: $10   F12
Location: Just sw of jct SR 114 and McArthur Blvd, just s to Corporate Dr, then 0.3 mi w on Executive Dr. 1223 Greenway Cir 75038. Fax: 972/518-0722. **Facility:** 54 one-bedroom standard units, some with whirlpools. 3 stories, interior corridors. *Bath:* combo or shower only. **Parking:** on-site. **Terms:** 2 night minimum stay, [ECP] meal plan available, package plans. **Amenities:** dual phone lines, voice mail, irons, hair dryers. **Leisure Activities:** exercise room. **Guest Services:** complimentary evening beverages: Tues & Wed, valet laundry. **Business Services:** meeting rooms, fax (fee). **Cards:** AX, CB, DC, DS, MC, VI. **Special Amenities:** free continental breakfast and free local telephone calls.

SOME UNITS
(SD) (占) (⚡) (DATA PORT) 🍴 📶 🖥 / (⊠) /

COUNTRY INN & SUITES BY CARLSON
▼▼▼ ▼▼▼
Small-scale Hotel
Phone: (972)929-4008 `115`
All Year   1P: $85-$119   XP: $10   F18
Location: Nw off SR 114, exit Esters Rd, just s to Reese St, just e. 4100 W John Carpenter Frwy 75063. Fax: 972/929-4224. **Facility:** 90 units. 18 one-bedroom standard units. 54 one- and 18 two-bedroom suites ($99-$119), some with kitchens. 3 stories, exterior corridors. *Bath:* combo or shower only. **Parking:** on-site. **Terms:** weekly rates available, [ECP] meal plan available, small pets only ($50 fee, $50 deposit). **Amenities:** video games (fee), voice mail, irons, hair dryers. *Some:* fax. **Pool(s):** heated outdoor. **Leisure Activities:** whirlpool, exercise room. **Guest Services:** complimentary evening beverages: Mon-Thurs, valet and coin laundry, area transportation. **Business Services:** meeting rooms, fax. **Cards:** AX, CB, DC, DS, MC, VI. *(See color ad p 260)*

SOME UNITS
(ASK) (SD) (✈) (🐾) (🍴) (占) (今) (今) (⚡) (DATA PORT) 🍴 📶 🖥 / (⊠) /

(See map p. 236)

COUNTRY INN & SUITES-DFW AIRPORT SOUTH

Phone: (972)399-9874   103

All Year   1P: $59   2P: $59

Location: SR 183 E, exit Esters Rd, just s. 2000 Hardrock Rd 75061. **Fax:** 972/313-1113. **Facility:** 81 units. 60 one-bedroom standard units, some with whirlpools. 21 one-bedroom suites ($69-$79). 4 stories, interior corridors. *Bath:* combo or shower only. **Parking:** on-site. **Terms:** [CP] meal plan available. **Amenities:** high-speed Internet, voice mail, irons, hair dryers. **Pool(s):** heated indoor. **Leisure Activities:** whirlpool, exercise room. **Guest Services:** valet and coin laundry, airport transportation-Dallas-Fort Worth International Airport, area transportation-within 5 mi. **Business Services:** meeting rooms, fax (fee). **Cards:** AX, DC, DS, MC, VI. **Special Amenities: free continental breakfast and free newspaper.** *(See color ad p 260)*

Small-scale Hotel

SOME UNITS

COURTYARD BY MARRIOTT-LAS COLINAS

Phone: (972)550-8100   140

1/1-1/31   1P: $99-$150

2/1-12/31   1P: $99-$140

Location: Nw off SR 114, 1.5 mi sw on Walnut Hill Ln, just w of jct exit MacArthur Blvd. 1151 W Walnut Hill Ln 75038. **Fax:** 972/550-0764. **Facility:** 147 units. 134 one-bedroom standard units. 13 one-bedroom suites ($150-$200). 3 stories, interior corridors. *Bath:* combo or shower only. **Parking:** on-site. **Amenities:** high-speed Internet (fee), dual phone lines, voice mail, irons, hair dryers. **Pool(s):** heated indoor/outdoor. **Leisure Activities:** whirlpool, exercise room. **Guest Services:** valet and coin laundry. **Business Services:** meeting rooms, fax (fee). **Cards:** AX, CB, DC, DS, JC, MC, VI.

Small-scale Hotel

SOME UNITS

DALLAS LAS COLINAS TOWNEPLACE SUITES

Phone: (972)550-7796   114

All Year [ECP]   1P: $80   2P: $80

Location: SR 114, exit Walnut Hill Ln, then w. 900 W Walnut Hill Ln 75038. **Fax:** 972/550-8562. **Facility:** 135 units. 95 one-bedroom standard units with kitchens. 6 one- and 34 two-bedroom suites with kitchens. 3 stories, interior corridors. *Bath:* combo or shower only. **Parking:** on-site. **Terms:** cancellation fee imposed, small pets only ($125 fee). **Amenities:** dual phone lines, voice mail, irons, hair dryers. **Pool(s):** small heated outdoor. **Leisure Activities:** exercise room. **Guest Services:** valet and coin laundry. **Business Services:** fax (fee). **Cards:** AX, CB, DC, DS, JC, MC, VI.

Small-scale Hotel

SOME UNITS

DALLAS MARRIOTT LAS COLINAS

Phone: (972)831-0000   127

All Year   1P: $79-$229   2P: $79-$229

Location: SR 114, exit O'Connor Rd, n to Las Colinas, then just e. Located in an up-scale office park. 223 Las Colinas Blvd 75039. **Fax:** 972/831-8861. **Facility:** 364 units. 361 one-bedroom standard units. 3 one-bedroom suites. 14 stories, interior corridors. *Bath:* combo or shower only. **Parking:** on-site. **Amenities:** video games (fee), dual phone lines, voice mail, irons, hair dryers. **Dining:** 6 am-11 pm, cocktails. **Pool(s):** small heated indoor. **Leisure Activities:** whirlpool, exercise room. *Fee:* golf privileges. **Guest Services:** gift shop, valet and coin laundry. **Business Services:** conference facilities, business center. **Cards:** AX, DC, DS, MC, VI. **Special Amenities: preferred room (subject to availability with advanced reservations).**

Large-scale Hotel

SOME UNITS

FEE

DAYS INN DFW NORTH

Phone: 972/621-8277   137

All Year   1P: $59-$70   XP: $5   F12

Location: SR 114, exit Belt Line Rd on westbound service road. 4325 W Hwy 114 75063. **Fax:** 972/929-4932. **Facility:** 128 one-bedroom standard units. 3 stories, exterior corridors. **Parking:** on-site. **Terms:** [BP] meal plan available. **Amenities:** voice mail, hair dryers. *Some:* irons. **Pool(s):** outdoor. **Leisure Activities:** exercise room. **Guest Services:** valet laundry, area transportation. **Business Services:** fax (fee). **Cards:** AX, DC, DS, JC, MC, VI.

Small-scale Hotel

SOME UNITS

DRURY INN & SUITES - DFW AIRPORT

Phone: (972)986-1200   100

9/1-1/31 [ECP]   1P: $73-$93   2P: $83-$103   XP: $10   F18

2/1-8/31 [ECP]   1P: $70-$90   2P: $80-$100   XP: $10   F18

Location: SR 183, exit Esters Rd, on southbound access road. 4210 W Airport Frwy 75062. **Fax:** 972/986-1200. **Facility:** 124 units. 112 one-bedroom standard units. 12 one-bedroom suites ($90-$113). 4 stories, interior corridors. **Parking:** on-site. **Terms:** small pets only. **Amenities:** dual phone lines, voice mail, irons, hair dryers. **Pool(s):** outdoor. **Leisure Activities:** exercise room. **Guest Services:** complimentary evening beverages: Mon-Thurs, coin laundry, airport transportation-Dallas-Fort Worth International Airport, area transportation-within 1 mi. **Business Services:** meeting rooms, fax (fee). **Cards:** AX, CB, DC, DS, MC, VI. **Special Amenities: free continental breakfast and free local telephone calls.**

Small-scale Hotel

SOME UNITS

EMBASSY SUITES-DFW SOUTH

Phone: (972)790-0093   150

All Year [BP]   1P: $109-$219   2P: $109-$219   XP: $10   F17

Location: SR 183, exit Valley View on southbound access road. 4650 W Airport Frwy 75062. **Fax:** 972/790-4768. **Facility:** 305 one-bedroom suites. 10 stories, interior corridors. *Bath:* combo or shower only. **Parking:** on-site. **Amenities:** video games, dual phone lines, voice mail, irons, hair dryers. **Pool(s):** heated indoor. **Leisure Activities:** sauna, whirlpool, exercise room. **Guest Services:** gift shop, complimentary evening beverages, valet and coin laundry, area transportation. **Business Services:** meeting rooms, business center. **Cards:** AX, DC, MC, VI. *(See color ad p 267)*

Large-scale Hotel

SOME UNITS

(See map p. 236)

FAIRFIELD INN BY MARRIOTT
Phone: (972)929-7257 [130]

SAVE

Small-scale Hotel

All Year [ECP]   1P: $51-$75
Location: SR 114, exit Freeport on eastbound service road. 4800 W John Carpenter Frwy 75063. Fax: 972/929-7257. **Facility:** 108 one-bedroom standard units. 3 stories, interior corridors. *Bath:* combo or shower only. **Parking:** on-site. **Amenities:** irons, hair dryers. **Pool(s):** heated outdoor. **Leisure Activities:** whirlpool. **Guest Services:** valet and coin laundry. **Business Services:** meeting rooms, fax (fee). **Cards:** AX, CB, DC, DS, JC, MC, VI.

SOME UNITS

FAIRFIELD INN BY MARRIOTT-LAS COLINAS
Phone: (972)550-8800 [129]

AAA SAVE

Small-scale Hotel

All Year [ECP]   1P: $79   2P: $84   XP: $5   F12
Location: SR 114 (John Carpenter Frwy), exit Walnut Hill Ln. 630 W John Carpenter Frwy 75039. Fax: 972/756-9175. **Facility:** 118 one-bedroom standard units, some with whirlpools. 3 stories, interior corridors. *Bath:* combo or shower only. **Parking:** on-site. **Amenities:** irons, hair dryers. **Pool(s):** heated indoor. **Leisure Activities:** whirlpool, exercise room. **Guest Services:** valet and coin laundry. **Business Services:** fax (fee). **Cards:** AX, CB, DC, DS, MC, VI. **Special Amenities:** free continental breakfast and free local telephone calls.

SOME UNITS

FOUR SEASONS RESORT & CLUB
Phone: (972)717-0700 [147]

Resort
Large-scale Hotel

9/1-1/31   1P: $335-$435   2P: $335-$435
2/1-8/31   1P: $320-$435   2P: $320-$415
Location: Se off SR 114, 1.5 mi s of exit MacArthur Blvd. 4150 N MacArthur Blvd 75038. Fax: 972/717-2428. **Facility:** A spa, a golf course and a high-end health club with tennis facilities give this resort a retreatlike ambience; the villas offer added seclusion. 357 units. 341 one-bedroom standard units. 12 one- and 4 two-bedroom suites ($600-$2000). 9 stories, interior corridors. *Bath:* combo or shower only. **Parking:** on-site. **Terms:** small pets only. **Amenities:** CD players, dual phone lines, voice mail, safes, honor bars, irons, hair dryers. *Fee:* video games, high-speed Internet. *Some:* DVD players. **Pool(s):** 3 heated outdoor, heated indoor. **Leisure Activities:** saunas, whirlpools, steamrooms, recreation programs, jogging, playground, spa, basketball, volleyball. *Fee:* golf-18 holes, 12 tennis courts (4 indoor, 12 lighted), racquetball courts. **Guest Services:** gift shop, valet laundry, area transportation, beauty salon. **Business Services:** conference facilities, business center. **Cards:** AX, MC, VI.

SOME UNITS

HAMPTON INN-DFW AIRPORT
Phone: (972)986-3606 [106]

SAVE

Small-scale Hotel

9/1-1/31 [ECP]   1P: $93-$109   2P: $103-$119   XP: $10   F18
2/1-8/31 [ECP]   1P: $91-$107   2P: $101-$117   XP: $10   F18
Location: SR 183, exit Valley View on southbound access road. 4340 W Airport Frwy 75062. Fax: 972/986-6852. **Facility:** 81 one-bedroom standard units. 4 stories, interior corridors. *Bath:* combo or shower only. **Parking:** on-site. **Terms:** small pets only. **Amenities:** voice mail, irons. **Pool(s):** outdoor. **Guest Services:** valet laundry, area transportation. **Business Services:** fax (fee). **Cards:** AX, CB, DC, DS, MC, VI.

SOME UNITS

HARVEY HOTEL-DFW AIRPORT
Phone: (972)929-4500 [134]

AAA SAVE

Large-scale Hotel

All Year   1P: $130-$170   2P: $130-$170   XP: $10   F12
Location: Nw off SR 114, exit Esters Rd. 4545 W John Carpenter Frwy 75063. Fax: 972/929-8451. **Facility:** 506 units. 504 one-bedroom standard units. 2 one-bedroom suites with whirlpools. 15 stories, interior corridors. **Parking:** on-site. **Terms:** cancellation fee imposed, 20% service charge, small pets only ($25 fee, $100 deposit). **Amenities:** voice mail, irons, hair dryers. **Dining:** 2 restaurants, 6 am-midnight, cocktails. **Pool(s):** heated indoor/outdoor. **Leisure Activities:** whirlpool, exercise room. **Guest Services:** gift shop, complimentary evening beverages: Tues, valet and coin laundry, airport transportation-Dallas-Fort Worth International Airport, area transportation (fee)-Grapevine Mills Mall. **Business Services:** conference facilities, business center. **Cards:** AX, CB, DC, DS, MC, VI. **Special Amenities:** early check-in/late check-out and free local telephone calls.

SOME UNITS

HARVEY SUITES-DFW AIRPORT
Phone: (972)929-4499 [133]

Small-scale Hotel

All Year [BP]   1P: $110-$152   2P: $110-$152   XP: $10   F12
Location: SR 114, exit Freeport Pkwy on southbound service road. 4550 W John Carpenter Frwy 75063. Fax: 972/929-0774. **Facility:** 164 units. 101 one-bedroom standard units. 63 one-bedroom suites. 3 stories, interior corridors. *Bath:* combo or shower only. **Parking:** on-site. **Terms:** cancellation fee imposed, 20% service charge, small pets only ($125 deposit, $25 extra charge). **Amenities:** voice mail, irons, hair dryers. **Pool(s):** heated outdoor. **Leisure Activities:** whirlpool, limited exercise equipment. **Guest Services:** sundries, complimentary evening beverages: Sun-Thurs, valet and coin laundry, area transportation (fee). **Business Services:** meeting rooms. **Cards:** AX, CB, DC, DS, MC, VI.

SOME UNITS

HEARTHSIDE BY VILLAGER
Phone: (972)929-3333 [125]

Small-scale Hotel

All Year   1P: $39-$99   2P: $49-$109
Location: SR 114, exit Esters Blvd, then s to Plaza Dr, then w. 7825 Heathrow Dr 75063. Fax: 972/929-4801. **Facility:** 146 units. 140 one-bedroom standard units with efficiencies. 6 one-bedroom units with kitchens. 3 stories, interior corridors. *Bath:* combo or shower only. **Parking:** on-site. **Terms:** weekly rates available, package plans, small pets only ($150 fee). **Amenities:** voice mail, hair dryers. *Some:* high-speed Internet (fee). **Leisure Activities:** exercise room. **Guest Services:** valet and coin laundry. **Business Services:** meeting rooms, fax (fee). **Cards:** AX, DS, MC, VI.

SOME UNITS

(See map p. 236)

HILTON GARDEN INN LAS COLINAS　　　　　　　**Phone: (972)444-8434**　**121**

[SAVE]

All Year　1P: $159　2P: $169　XP: $10　F18
Location: I-635, exit 31 (MacArthur Blvd), just s, then e. 7516 Las Colinas Blvd 75063. Fax: 972/910-9246.
Facility: 174 units. 130 one-bedroom standard units. 44 one-bedroom suites ($179-$249). 5 stories, interior
corridors. *Bath:* combo or shower only. **Parking:** on-site. **Terms:** package plans. **Amenities:** video games

Small-scale Hotel (fee), high-speed Internet, dual phone lines, voice mail, irons, hair dryers. **Pool(s):** heated outdoor. **Leisure Activities:** exercise room. **Guest Services:** sundries, valet and coin laundry, area transportation. **Business Services:** meeting rooms, business center. **Cards:** AX, CB, DC, DS, MC, VI.

SOME UNITS

[icons]

HOLIDAY INN SELECT-DFW AIRPORT-NORTH　　　　**Phone: (972)929-8181**　**135**

[AAA] [SAVE]

All Year　1P: $155　2P: $165　XP: $10　F18
Location: N off SR 114, exit Esters Rd. 4441 Hwy 114 75063. Fax: 972/929-8233. **Facility:** 282 one-bedroom standard units. 8 stories, interior corridors. *Bath:* combo or shower only. **Parking:** on-site. **Terms:** cancellation fee imposed, [AP] meal plan available. **Amenities:** dual phone lines, voice mail, irons, hair dryers. **Dining:** 6

Small-scale Hotel am-2 & 5-11 pm, cocktails. **Pool(s):** outdoor. **Leisure Activities:** sauna, exercise room. **Guest Services:** gift shop, valet and coin laundry, airport transportation-Dallas-Fort Worth International Airport, area transportation-Grapevine Mills Mall. **Business Services:** meeting rooms, business center. **Cards:** AX, DC, DS, MC, VI.

SOME UNITS

[icons]

HOLIDAY INN SELECT DFW AIRPORT SOUTH　　　　**Phone: (972)399-1010**　**105**

[AAA] [SAVE]

All Year　1P: $79-$109　2P: $79-$109　XP: $10　F18
Location: SR 183, exit Valley View on southbound access road. 4440 W Airport Frwy 75062. Fax: 972/790-8545.
Facility: 409 units. 402 one-bedroom standard units. 7 one-bedroom suites ($175-$350), some with whirlpools. 4 stories, interior corridors. *Bath:* combo or shower only. **Parking:** on-site. **Terms:** cancellation fee imposed. **Amenities:** voice mail, irons, hair dryers. *Fee:* video games, high-speed Internet. *Some:* fax.

Large-scale Hotel **Dining:** 2 restaurants, 6 am-2 & 5-10 pm, Sat & Sun 7 am-2 pm, cocktails. **Pool(s):** outdoor, heated indoor. **Leisure Activities:** sauna, whirlpool, putting green, exercise room. **Guest Services:** gift shop, valet and coin laundry, airport transportation-Dallas-Fort Worth International Airport, area transportation-within 5 mi. **Business Services:** conference facilities. *Fee:* PC, fax. **Cards:** AX, DC, DS, MC, VI. **Special Amenities:** free newspaper. *(See ad p 268)*

SOME UNITS

[icons]

HOMESTEAD STUDIO SUITES HOTEL-LAS COLINAS　　**Phone: (972)756-0458**　**144**

[icons]

All Year　1P: $60-$75　2P: $65-$79　XP: $5　F17
Location: SR 114, exit MacArthur Blvd, 0.5 mi s on MacArthur Blvd, then just e on Meadow Creek. 5315 Carnaby St

Motel 75038. Fax: 972/756-0553. **Facility:** 148 units. 146 one-bedroom standard units with efficiencies. 2 one-bedroom suites with efficiencies. 2 stories, exterior corridors. *Bath:* combo or shower only. **Parking:** on-site. **Terms:** pets ($75 fee). **Amenities:** voice mail, irons. **Guest Services:** coin laundry. **Cards:** AX, CB, DC, DS, JC, MC, VI.

SOME UNITS

[icons]

LA QUINTA INN & SUITES DFW AIRPORT NORTH　　**Phone: (972)915-4022**　**122**

[AAA] [SAVE]

All Year　1P: $69-$119　2P: $79-$129　XP: $10　F18
Location: SR 114, exit Freeport on eastbound service road. 4850 W John Carpenter Frwy 75063. Fax: 972/915-6960.
Facility: 140 units. 132 one-bedroom standard units. 8 one-bedroom suites ($109-$169). 3 stories, interior corridors. *Bath:* combo or shower only. **Parking:** on-site. **Terms:** [ECP] meal plan available, small pets only.

Small-scale Hotel **Amenities:** video games, dual phone lines, voice mail, irons, hair dryers. **Pool(s):** heated outdoor. **Leisure Activities:** whirlpool, exercise room. **Guest Services:** coin laundry, airport transportation-Dallas-Fort Worth International Airport, area transportation-within 10 mi. **Business Services:** meeting rooms, fax (fee). **Cards:** AX, CB, DC, DS, JC, MC, VI. **Special Amenities:** free continental breakfast and free local telephone calls. *(See color ad p 272)*

SOME UNITS

[icons]

LA QUINTA INN-DFW-SOUTH　　　　　　　　　**Phone: (972)252-6546**　**111**

[AAA] [SAVE]

All Year　1P: $69-$99　XP: $10　F18
Location: 3 mi nw of Irving off SR 183, exit Esters Rd; on northbound access road. 4105 W Airport Frwy 75062-5997.
Fax: 972/570-4225. **Facility:** 168 one-bedroom standard units. 5 stories, interior corridors. *Bath:* combo or shower only. **Parking:** on-site. **Terms:** [ECP] meal plan available. **Amenities:** dual phone lines, voice mail,

Small-scale Hotel irons, hair dryers. *Fee:* video games, high-speed Internet. **Pool(s):** outdoor. **Leisure Activities:** whirlpool, exercise room. **Guest Services:** valet and coin laundry, area transportation-within 10 mi. **Business Services:** meeting rooms. **Cards:** AX, CB, DC, DS, JC, MC, VI. **Special Amenities:** free continental breakfast and free local telephone calls. *(See color ad p 272)*

SOME UNITS

[icons]

MAINSTAY SUITES HOTEL DFW AIRPORT SOUTH　　**Phone: 972/257-5400**　**104**

[icons]

All Year [CP]　1P: $79-$99　2P: $99-$109　XP: $10　F10
Location: SR 183, exit Story Rd, 0.6 mi w on westbound access road. 2323 Imperial Dr 75062. Fax: 972/258 6173.
Facility: 55 units. 26 one-bedroom standard units with efficiencies. 28 one- and 1 two-bedroom suites ($99-$109), some with efficiencies. 2 stories, interior corridors. *Bath:* combo or shower only. **Parking:** on-site.

Small-scale Hotel **Terms:** cancellation fee imposed, weekly rates available, package plans, small pets only. **Amenities:** dual phone lines, voice mail, safes (fee), irons, hair dryers. **Leisure Activities:** exercise room. **Guest Services:** valet and coin laundry, area transportation. **Business Services:** meeting rooms, business center. **Cards:** AX, DC, DS, MC, VI.

SOME UNITS

[icons]

(See map p. 236)

MARRIOTT HOTEL-DFW AIRPORT

SAVE

Large-scale Hotel

Phone: **(972)929-8800**   **132**

All Year   1P: $89-$189   XP: $10   F17

Location: Nw off SR 114, exit Freeport Pkwy. 8440 Freeport Pkwy 75063. Fax: 972/929-6501. **Facility:** 491 units. 484 one-bedroom standard units. 7 one-bedroom suites. 20 stories, interior corridors. *Bath:* combo or shower only. **Parking:** on-site. **Amenities:** high-speed Internet (fee), dual phone lines, voice mail, irons, hair dryers. *Some:* CD players. **Pool(s):** heated indoor/outdoor. **Leisure Activities:** saunas, whirlpool, exercise room. **Guest Services:** gift shop, valet and coin laundry. **Business Services:** conference facilities, business center. **Cards:** AX, CB, DC, DS, JC, MC, VI.

SOME UNITS

MICROTEL INN & SUITES

Small-scale Hotel

Phone: **(972)986-7800**   **128**

All Year   1P: $46-$50   2P: $55   XP: $5   F12

Location: SR 183, exit S Belt Ln. 3232 W Irving Blvd 75061. Fax: 972/986-2118. **Facility:** 47 one-bedroom standard units, some with whirlpools. 3 stories, interior corridors. **Parking:** on-site. **Terms:** [CP] meal plan available. **Amenities:** irons, hair dryers. **Business Services:** fax (fee). **Cards:** AX, DC, DS, MC, VI.

SOME UNITS

MICROTEL INN & SUITES-TEXAS STADIUM

Small-scale Hotel

Phone: **(972)438-4022**   **113**

All Year [ECP]   1P: $50-$79   2P: $56-$89   XP: $8   F15

Location: SR 183 E Loop 12 but stay straight to SR 183 service road; SR 183 W, exit Carl Rd, U-turn, stay on service road. 2440 E Airport Frwy 75062. Fax: 972/554-0818. **Facility:** 44 one-bedroom standard units. 2 stories, interior corridors. *Bath:* combo or shower only. **Parking:** on-site. **Terms:** [AP], [CP] & [MAP] meal plans available. **Pool(s):** small outdoor. **Guest Services:** coin laundry. **Business Services:** fax (fee). **Cards:** AX, CB, DC, DS, JC, MC, VI.

SOME UNITS

MOTEL 6 #1274 DFW NORTH

Small-scale Hotel

Phone: **972/915-3993**   **131**

5/22-1/31   1P: $39-$49   2P: $45-$55   XP: $3   F17
2/1-5/21   1P: $37-$47   2P: $43-$53   XP: $3   F17

Location: Nw off SR 114, exit Freeport Pkwy. 7800 Heathrow Dr 75063. Fax: 972/915-6843. **Facility:** 121 one-bedroom standard units. 3 stories, interior corridors. *Bath:* combo or shower only. **Parking:** on-site. **Terms:** small pets only. **Amenities:** voice mail. **Pool(s):** outdoor. **Guest Services:** coin laundry. **Business Services:** fax (fee). **Cards:** AX, CB, DC, DS, MC, VI.

SOME UNITS

MOTEL 6/DFW AIRPORT SOUTH #1476

Small-scale Hotel

Phone: **972/570-7500**   **112**

5/22-1/31   1P: $39-$49   2P: $45-$55   XP: $3   F17
2/1-5/21   1P: $35-$45   2P: $41-$51   XP: $3   F17

Location: SR 183, exit Story Rd. 2611 W Airport Frwy 75062. Fax: 972/594-1693. **Facility:** 125 one-bedroom standard units. 3 stories, interior corridors. *Bath:* combo or shower only. **Parking:** on-site. **Terms:** small pets only. **Amenities:** voice mail. **Pool(s):** small outdoor. **Guest Services:** coin laundry. **Business Services:** meeting rooms, fax (fee). **Cards:** AX, CB, DC, DS, MC, VI.

SOME UNITS

OMNI MANDALAY HOTEL AT LAS COLINAS

AAA SAVE

Large-scale Hotel

Phone: **(972)556-0800**   **145**

2/1-5/24 & 9/7-11/22   1P: $87-$219   2P: $87-$219   XP: $10   F17
5/25-9/6 & 11/23-1/31   1P: $87-$209   2P: $87-$209   XP: $10   F17

Location: Nw off SR 114, exit O'Connor Rd. Located in a trendy office-park and residential area. 221 E Las Colinas Blvd 75039. Fax: 972/556-0729. **Facility:** The hotel fronts a man-made lake and canals and offers easy access to restaurants and Irving's center for business; guest rooms are spacious. 410 units. 401 one-bedroom standard units. 9 one-bedroom suites, some with whirlpools. 27 stories, interior corridors. **Parking:** on-site. **Terms:** cancellation fee imposed, 19% service charge, small pets only ($75 fee). **Amenities:** video games (fee), dual phone lines, voice mail, honor bars, irons, hair dryers. **Dining:** 2 restaurants, 6:30 am-11 pm, Sun 7 am-10:30 pm, cocktails, entertainment. **Pool(s):** heated outdoor. **Leisure Activities:** saunas, whirlpool, playground. *Fee:* massage. **Guest Services:** gift shop, valet laundry, area transportation-within 5 mi. **Business Services:** conference facilities, business center. **Cards:** AX, CB, DC, DS, JC, MC, VI.

SOME UNITS

FEE

RED ROOF INN/DFW AIRPORT NORTH

AAA SAVE

Motel

Phone: **(972)929-0020**   **123**

All Year   1P: $39-$57   2P: $45-$63   XP: $6   F18

Location: SR 114, exit Esters Blvd, just n. 8150 Esters Blvd 75063. Fax: 972/929-6664. **Facility:** 156 one-bedroom standard units. 3 stories, exterior corridors. **Parking:** on-site. **Terms:** small pets only. **Amenities:** video games, voice mail. **Guest Services:** coin laundry, airport transportation-Dallas-Fort Worth International Airport. **Business Services:** meeting rooms. **Cards:** AX, CB, DC, DS, MC, VI. **Special Amenities:** free local telephone calls and free newspaper.

SOME UNITS

RESIDENCE INN BY MARRIOTT AT LAS COLINAS

SAVE

Small-scale Hotel

Phone: **(972)580-7773**   **141**

All Year [ECP]   1P: $139   2P: $149

Location: SR 114, exit MacArthur Blvd, 0.5 mi s, then e. 950 W Walnut Hill Ln 75038. Fax: 972/550-8824. **Facility:** 120 units. 90 one-bedroom standard units with kitchens. 30 two-bedroom suites ($149) with kitchens. 2 stories, exterior corridors. *Bath:* combo or shower only. **Parking:** on-site. **Terms:** pets ($125 fee, $5 extra charge). **Amenities:** voice mail, irons, hair dryers. **Pool(s):** heated outdoor. **Leisure Activities:** whirlpool, limited exercise equipment, sports court. **Guest Services:** complimentary evening beverages-Mon-Thurs, valet and coin laundry, area transportation. **Business Services:** meeting rooms, fax (fee). **Cards:** AX, CB, DC, DS, MC, VI.

SOME UNITS

(See map p. 236)

RESIDENCE INN BY MARRIOTT-DFW/IRVING   **Phone:** (972)871-1331   126
SAVE   All Year [BP]   1P: $139   2P: $179
▼▼▼▼   **Location:** SR 114, exit Esters Blvd, 0.9 mi n. 8600 Esters Blvd 75063. Fax: 972/871-1332. **Facility:** 100 units. 49
Small-scale Hotel   one-bedroom standard units, some with efficiencies or kitchens. 36 one- and 15 two-bedroom suites, some
            with efficiencies or kitchens. 3 stories, interior corridors. **Bath:** combo or shower only. **Parking:** on-site.
Terms: small pets only ($75-$100 fee). **Amenities:** dual phone lines, voice mail, irons, hair dryers. **Pool(s):**
small heated outdoor. **Leisure Activities:** whirlpool, exercise room, sports court, basketball, volleyball.
Guest Services: sundries, complimentary evening beverages: Mon-Thurs, valet and coin laundry. **Business Services:** meeting
rooms, business center. **Cards:** AX, CB, DC, DS, JC, MC, VI.
                                                              SOME UNITS

[icons]

SHERATON GRAND HOTEL   **Phone:** (972)929-8400   136
▼▼▼▼   All Year   1P: $112   2P: $112   XP: $10   F18
            Location: SR 114, exit Esters Blvd, just s. 4440 W John Carpenter Frwy 75063. Fax: 972/929-3189. **Facility:** 300
Large-scale Hotel   units. 296 one-bedroom standard units. 4 one-bedroom suites ($250-$450). 12 stories, interior corridors.
Bath: combo or shower only. **Parking:** on-site. **Terms:** small pets only ($25 fee). **Amenities:** video games
(fee), voice mail, irons, hair dryers. *Some:* fax. **Pool(s):** heated indoor/outdoor. **Leisure Activities:** saunas, whirlpool, exercise
room. **Guest Services:** valet laundry. **Business Services:** meeting rooms, business center. **Cards:** AX, CB, DC, DS, JC,
MC, VI.
                                                              SOME UNITS

[icons]

SHONEY'S INN & SUITES   **Phone:** (214)441-9000   139
▼▼▼ ▼▼▼   All Year   2P: $45-$60   XP: $5   F12
            Location: SR 114, exit Freeport Pkwy. 4770 W John Carpenter Frwy (SR 114) 75063. Fax: 214/441-9022.
Small-scale Hotel   **Facility:** 59 one-bedroom standard units, some with whirlpools. 3 stories, interior corridors. **Bath:** combo or
shower only. **Parking:** on-site. **Terms:** small pets only ($25 deposit). **Amenities:** high-speed Internet, voice
mail, irons, hair dryers. **Guest Services:** valet and coin laundry, area transportation. **Business Services:** meeting rooms, fax
(fee). **Cards:** AX, CB, DC, MC, VI.
                                                              SOME UNITS

[icons]

STAYBRIDGE SUITES DALLAS-LAS COLINAS   **Phone:** (972)465-9400   110
▼▼▼▼   All Year   1P: $119-$149
            Location: SR 114, exit MacArthur Blvd, just s to W Walnut Hill Ln, then just w. 1201 Executive Cir 75038.
Small-scale Hotel   Fax: 972/465-9402. **Facility:** 118 units. 61 one-bedroom standard units with efficiencies. 34 one- and 23 two-
bedroom suites with efficiencies. 3 stories, interior corridors. **Bath:** combo or shower only. **Parking:** on-site.
Terms: [ECP] meal plan available, pets ($75 fee). **Amenities:** video library (fee), dual phone lines, voice mail, irons, hair dryers.
Pool(s): heated outdoor. **Leisure Activities:** exercise room, sports court. **Guest Services:** sundries, complimentary evening
beverages: Tues-Thurs, valet and coin laundry, area transportation. **Business Services:** meeting rooms, fax. **Cards:** AX, CB,
DC, DS, JC, MC, VI.
                                                              SOME UNITS

[icons]

SUPER 8 MOTEL-IRVING   **Phone:** (972)257-1810   153
▼▼▼▼ ▼▼   All Year   1P: $49-$59   2P: $54-$64   XP: $5   F18
            Location: SR 183, exit Esters Rd, 3 mi nw. 4245 W Airport Frwy 75062. Fax: 972/257-1932. **Facility:** 104 one-
Small-scale Hotel   bedroom standard units. 3 stories, interior corridors. **Parking:** on-site. **Terms:** [CP] meal plan available.
Amenities: safes. **Business Services:** meeting rooms. **Cards:** AX, DC, DS, MC, VI.
                                                              SOME UNITS

[icons]

WELLESLEY INN & SUITES (DALLAS/LAS COLINAS)   **Phone:** (972)751-0808   118
(AAA) **SAVE**   All Year [ECP]   1P: $79   2P: $79
▼▼▼▼   **Location:** SR 114, exit Walnut Hill Ln, just s. 5401 Green Park Dr 75038. Fax: 972/550-1434. **Facility:** 127 units.
            123 one-bedroom standard units with efficiencies. 4 one-bedroom suites with efficiencies. 3 stories, interior
Small-scale Hotel   corridors. **Bath:** combo or shower only. **Parking:** on-site. **Terms:** small pets only ($50 fee). **Amenities:** dual
phone lines, voice mail, irons, hair dryers. **Pool(s):** heated outdoor. **Leisure Activities:** gas barbecue grill,
exercise room. **Guest Services:** valet and coin laundry, area transportation-within 3 mi. **Business Services:**
fax (fee). **Cards:** AX, DC, DS, MC, VI. **Special Amenities:** free continental breakfast and free newspaper.
(See color ad p 250)
                                                              SOME UNITS

[icons]

WINGATE INN DFW   **Phone:** (972)929-4600   119
(AAA) **SAVE**   All Year [ECP]   1P: $59-$109   2P: $59-$109   XP: $10   F
▼▼▼▼   **Location:** Nw off SR 114. 8220 Esters Blvd 75063. Fax: 972/929-4602. **Facility:** 113 one-bedroom standard units,
            some with whirlpools. 3 stories, interior corridors. **Bath:** combo or shower only. **Parking:** on-site.
Small-scale Hotel   **Amenities:** video games (fee), high-speed Internet, dual phone lines, voice mail, safes, irons, hair dryers.
Pool(s): heated outdoor. **Leisure Activities:** whirlpool, exercise room. **Guest Services:** complimentary
evening beverages: Mon-Wed, valet and coin laundry, airport transportation-Dallas-Fort Worth International
Airport, area transportation-within 3 mi. **Business Services:** meeting rooms, business center. **Cards:** AX, CB, DC, DS, JC,
MC, VI. **Special Amenities:** free continental breakfast and free local telephone calls.
                                                              SOME UNITS

[icons]

WINGATE INN-LAS COLINAS   **Phone:** (972)751-1031   152
▼▼▼▼   All Year [ECP]   1P: $69-$109   2P: $79-$119   XP: $10   F17
            Location: SR 114, exit Walnut Hill Ln. 850 W Walnut Hill Ln 75038. Fax: 972/465-0111. **Facility:** 101 one-bedroom
Small-scale Hotel   standard units, some with whirlpools. 3 stories, interior corridors. **Bath:** combo or shower only. **Parking:** on-
site. **Amenities:** video games (fee), high-speed Internet, dual phone lines, voice mail, safes, irons, hair
dryers. **Leisure Activities:** whirlpool, exercise room. **Guest Services:** complimentary evening beverages: Mon-Thurs, valet
laundry, area transportation. **Business Services:** meeting rooms, business center. **Cards:** AX, CB, DC, DS, JC, MC, VI.
                                                              SOME UNITS

[icons]

(See map p. 236)

WYNDHAM GARDEN HOTEL-LAS COLINAS Phone: (972)650-1600 `143`

| (AAA) (SAVE) | 9/8-1/31 | 1P: $79-$129 | 2P: $79-$139 | XP: $10 | F18 |
| | 2/1-9/7 | 1P: $79-$125 | 2P: $79-$135 | XP: $10 | F18 |

Location: Nw off SR 114, exit O'Connor Rd. 110 W John Carpenter Frwy 75039. Fax: 972/541-0501. **Facility:** 168 units. 123 one-bedroom standard units. 45 one-bedroom suites ($196-$209). 3 stories, interior corridors.
Small-scale Hotel **Bath:** combo or shower only. **Parking:** on-site. **Terms:** cancellation fee imposed. **Amenities:** voice mail, irons, hair dryers. **Fee:** video games, high-speed Internet. **Dining:** 6:30 am-2:30 & 5-10 pm, Sat & Sun from 7 am, cocktails. **Pool(s):** heated indoor. **Leisure Activities:** sauna, whirlpool. **Guest Services:** valet laundry, area transportation-within 3 mi. **Business Services:** meeting rooms, fax (fee). **Cards:** AX, DC, DS, MC, VI.

SOME UNITS

The following lodgings were either not evaluated or did not meet AAA rating requirements but are listed for your information only.

COURTYARD BY MARRIOTT Phone: 972/790-8990

| (fyi) | 9/2-1/31 | 1P: $119 | 2P: $119 |
| | 2/1-9/1 | 1P: $109 | 2P: $109 |

Small-scale Hotel Too new to rate, opening scheduled for October 2002. **Location:** 2280 Valley View Ln 75062. **Amenities:** 154 units.

RADISSON HOTEL-DFW AIRPORT SOUTH Phone: (972)513-0800 `151`

| (fyi) | All Year | 1P: $89-$99 | 2P: $89-$99 | XP: $10 | F16 |

Under major renovation, scheduled to be completed November 2002. **Last rated:** ♦♦ **Location:** SR 183, exit
Small-scale Hotel Valley View Ln, 3.3 mi nw. 4600 W Airport Frwy 75062. Fax: 972/513-0106. **Facility:** 200 units. 112 one-bedroom standard units. 88 one-bedroom suites. 5 stories, interior corridors. **Parking:** on-site. **Terms:** 14 day cancellation notice, small pets only. **Amenities:** video games, dual phone lines, voice mail, irons, hair dryers. **Pool(s):** heated indoor. **Leisure Activities:** whirlpool, exercise room. **Guest Services:** gift shop, coin laundry. **Business Services:** meeting rooms, business center. **Cards:** AX, CB, DC, DS, JC, MC, VI. *(See color ad p 275)*

SOME UNITS

WHERE TO DINE

BD'S MONGOLIAN BARBEQUE AT LOS COLINAS **Lunch:** $9-$11 **Dinner:** $9-$13 **Phone:** 972/432-8881 `106`

Location: SR 114, exit MacArthur Blvd, just nw; in strip center. 5910 N MacArthur Blvd, Suite 121 75039. **Hours:** 10:30 am-10 pm, Fri & Sat-11 pm. Closed: 11/27, 12/25. A unique dining experience for the
Mongolian adventurous. Just stroll to the buffet and create your own entree from a selection of meats, poultry and fish. Add any number of the available fresh vegetables, top with a couple of dollops of sauce, add spices if you dare, then present your concoction to the grill chef. Now relax around the large round grill with other diners and watch as your own creation is prepared. If you're not feeling creative you can always use one of the restaurant's own recipes. Smoke free premises. Casual dress; cocktails. **Parking:** on-site. **Cards:** AX, DS, MC, VI.

I FRATELLI ITALIAN RESTAURANT **Lunch:** $6-$8 **Dinner:** $8-$13 **Phone:** 972/501-9700 `105`

Location: Southwest corner of I-635 and MacArthur Blvd, exit 31. 7750 N MacArthur Blvd, Suite 195 75063. **Hours:** 11 am-10 pm, Fri & Sat-11 pm. Closed major holidays. **Features:** This cozy eatery features such
Italian specialties as veal marsala and shrimp scampi. Wall fountains, candlelight and a hand-painted mural of the Italian countryside add a touch of romance. Casual dress; cocktails. **Parking:** on-site. **Cards:** AX, CB, DC,
DS, MC, VI.

LAMARGARITA **Lunch:** $5-$7 **Dinner:** $6-$12 **Phone:** 972/570-1137 `108`

Location: SR 183, exit Belt Line Rd, 0.5 mi n. 2922 N Belt Line Rd 75062. **Hours:** 11 am-10 pm, Fri & Sat-11 pm. Closed major holidays. **Features:** South of the border cuisine shows a focus on fresh ingredients and creative recipes. Count on generous portions of chiles rellenos, fajitas, enchiladas and house specialties
Mexican along the lines of charbroiled rib eye topped with chipotle sauce. Colorful murals, festive lights and Spanish music make for an enjoyable dining experience. Casual dress; cocktails. **Parking:** on-site. **Cards:** AX, DC, DS, MC, VI.

ROCKFISH SEAFOOD GRILL **Lunch:** $11-$15 **Dinner:** $11-$15 **Phone:** 214/574-4111 `109`

Location: SR 114, exit MacArthur Blvd, 1.3 mi n. 7400 N MacArthur Blvd 75063. **Hours:** 11 am-10 pm, Fri & Sat-11 pm, Sun-9 pm. Closed: 11/27, 12/25. **Features:** Watch your step as you navigate to your seat among the peanut shells on the floor because you'll be easily distracted by the numerous pieces of hunting
Seafood and fishing memorabilia adorning the walls and ceiling. The log cabin style interior gets you in the mood for a good piece of freshly caught fish, but don't expect something roasted over a campfire. The chef uses an array of sauces and cooking styles to please your palate, and the soups are hearty and fresh. Smoke free premises. Casual dress; cocktails. **Parking:** on-site. **Cards:** AX, DC, DS, MC, VI.

SPRING CREEK BARBEQUE **Lunch:** $9-$11 **Dinner:** $9-$11 **Phone:** 972/313-0987 `110`

Location: Southwest corner, jct SR 183 and Belt Line Rd. 3514 W Airport Frwy 75061. **Hours:** 11 am-9 pm, Fri & Sat-10 pm. Closed: 11/27, 12/25. Get in line and order up a hearty portion of Texas style barbecued ribs or hickory smoked slabs of beef, ham, chicken or sausage. Better yet, get a combination platter. Move further
Barbecue down the line in this cafeteria style restaurant and pile on the beans, potato salad, slaw, a baked potato "All the Way" and some corn on the cob. Now you're almost ready; just don't let that basket full of warm, fresh-baked rolls pass your table as it comes around or you'll miss an important part of this feast. Smoke free premises. Casual dress; beer only. **Parking:** on-site. **Cards:** AX, DS, MC, VI.

(See map p. 236)

TEXADELPHIA
Specialty

Lunch: $5-$8   Dinner: $5-$8   Phone: 972/432-0725 112
Location: I-635, exit 31 (MacArthur Blvd), just s. 7601 N MacArthur Blvd 75063. **Hours:** 11 am-9 pm, Sun from 11:30 am. Closed major holidays. **Features:** The Texas chain specializes in cheese steak, which patrons can customize with such items as jalapenos, hickory barbecue sauce or marinara sauce. Televised sporting events contribute to the casual atmosphere. Smoke free premises. Casual dress; beer & wine only.
Parking: on-site. **Cards:** AX, DS, MC, VI.
⊠

THAI CHILI
Thai

Lunch: $7-$10   Dinner: $10-$20   Phone: 972/831-0797 113
Location: SR 114, exit O'Connor Rd, just s to E Las Colinas Blvd, just e. 397 E Las Colinas Blvd, Suite 170 75039. **Hours:** 11 am-2:30 & 5:30-10 pm, Fri-11 pm, Sat 5:30 pm-11 pm, Sun 5:30 pm-10 pm. Closed: 11/27, 12/25. **Reservations:** accepted. **Features:** Within walking distance of Los Colinas Lake, the small Thai restaurant prepares traditional Thai cuisine. Mango and rice dessert is delicious. Reservations are recommended, as this place can be busy. The staff is friendly and accommodating. Smoke free premises. Casual dress; beer & wine only. **Parking:** on-site. **Cards:** AX, DC, DS, MC, VI.
⊠

VERANDA GREEK CAFE
Greek

Lunch: $6-$17   Dinner: $12-$17   Phone: 972/518-0939 114
Location: SR 114, exit MacArthur, just s. 5433 N MacArthur Blvd 75038. **Hours:** 11 am-2 & 5-10 pm, Sat from 5 pm. Closed major holidays; also Sun. **Reservations:** accepted. **Features:** The quiet restaurant presents a menu of traditional favorites, including spanakopita, souvlaki, moussaka and kebabs. Hummus is tasty with warm pita bread. The lunch buffet lines up interesting choices. Casual dress; cocktails. **Parking:** on-site.
Cards: AX, DC, MC, VI.
⊠

VIA REAL
Mexican

Lunch: $6-$18   Dinner: $10-$35   Phone: 972/650-9001 107
Location: US 183, exit MacArthur Blvd, 1.5 mi n. 4020 N MacArthur Blvd 75038. **Hours:** 11 am-10 pm, Fri-11 pm, Sat 5 pm-11 pm, Sun 11 am-9 pm. Closed major holidays. **Reservations:** suggested. **Features:** This restaurant—designed with open beams, fireplaces and water fountains—features authentic recipes with an upscale flair. Enjoy flavorful selections like spicy enchiladas and smoked mozzarella quesadillas. Casual dress; cocktails. **Parking:** on-site and valet. **Cards:** AX, CB, DC, DS, MC, VI.
Ⴤ ⊠

LEWISVILLE pop. 77,737 (See map p. 236; index p. 247)

——— WHERE TO STAY ———

BAYMONT INN & SUITES
AAA SAVE
Small-scale Hotel

Phone: 972/459-8000 281
All Year [CP]   1P: $89-$119   2P: $89-$119
Location: I-35 E, exit 448A, just w on Round Grove Rd, just n. 780 E Vista Ridge Mall Dr 75067. Fax: 972/221-8640. **Facility:** 90 one-bedroom standard units, some with whirlpools. 4 stories, interior corridors. *Bath:* combo or shower only. **Parking:** on-site. **Terms:** small pets only ($100 deposit). **Amenities:** video games (fee), dual phone lines, voice mail, irons, hair dryers. **Pool(s):** outdoor. **Leisure Activities:** exercise room. **Guest Services:** valet and coin laundry. **Business Services:** meeting rooms, fax (fee). **Cards:** AX, DC, DS, MC, VI.
Special Amenities: free continental breakfast and free newspaper. *(See color ad below)*

SOME UNITS
🆂🅳 🛏 🍽 🛗 ㄥᴍ 🛁 🚬 📷 DATA PORT 🖥 / ⊠ 🔌 🖨 /

(See map p. 236)

BEST WESTERN INN & SUITES
Phone: (972)459-5300   284
SAVE
All Year [ECP]　　1P: $90　　2P: $90
Location: I-35 E, exit 449, just w. 330 E Corporate Dr 75067. Fax: 972/459-0660. **Facility:** 64 one-bedroom standard units, some with whirlpools. 3 stories, interior corridors. *Bath:* combo or shower only. **Parking:** on-site.
Small-scale Hotel
Amenities: high-speed Internet, dual phone lines, voice mail, irons, hair dryers. **Pool(s):** outdoor. **Leisure Activities:** whirlpool, exercise room. **Guest Services:** valet and coin laundry. **Business Services:** meeting rooms, fax (fee). **Cards:** AX, CB, DC, DS, MC, VI. *(See ad below)*
SOME UNITS

COMFORT SUITES
Phone: (972)315-6464   287
AAA SAVE
All Year [ECP]　　1P: $69-$89　　2P: $69-$99　　XP: $6　　F18
Location: I-35 E, exit 448A (Round Grove Rd), 0.5 mi s of jct I-35 and Round Grove Rd on southbound service road to Vista Ridge Mall Dr, just w. 755A Vista Ridge Mall Dr 75067. Fax: 972/315-6464. **Facility:** 60 one-bedroom standard units. 3 stories, interior corridors. *Bath:* combo or shower only. **Parking:** on-site. **Terms:** 14 day cancel-
Small-scale Hotel lation notice, pets ($50 fee). **Amenities:** irons. *Some:* hair dryers. **Pool(s):** small heated indoor. **Leisure Activities:** whirlpool, exercise room. **Guest Services:** valet laundry. **Business Services:** fax (fee).
Cards: AX, CB, DC, DS, MC, VI. **Special Amenities: free continental breakfast and free local telephone calls.**
SOME UNITS

COUNTRY INN & SUITES BY CARLSON
Phone: (972)315-6565   291
All Year [ECP]　　1P: $69-$89　　2P: $69-$99　　XP: $6　　F18
Location: I-35 E, exit 448A (Round Grove Rd), 0.5 mi s; I-35, exit Round Grove Rd on southbound service road to Vista
Small-scale Hotel Ridge Rd, then just w. 755B Vista Ridge Mall Dr 75067. Fax: 972/315-6565. **Facility:** 64 units. 54 one-bedroom standard units. 10 one-bedroom suites. 3 stories, interior corridors. *Bath:* combo or shower only. **Parking:** on-site. **Terms:** 14 day cancellation notice, small pets only. **Amenities:** voice mail, irons, hair dryers. **Pool(s):** small heated indoor. **Leisure Activities:** whirlpool. **Guest Services:** valet laundry. **Business Services:** fax (fee). **Cards:** AX, CB, DC, DS, MC, VI. *(See color ad p 260)*
SOME UNITS

COURTYARD BY MARRIOTT-LEWISVILLE
Phone: (972)316-3100   283
SAVE
All Year　　1P: $99-$114　　2P: $99-$114
Location: I-35, exit 448A (Grapevine/McKinney), just w on SR 121. 2701 Lake Vista Dr 75067. Fax: 972/410-2979. **Facility:** 122 units. 118 one-bedroom standard units, some with whirlpools. 4 one-bedroom suites. 3 stories, interior corridors. *Bath:* combo or shower only. **Parking:** on-site. **Terms:** [BP] meal plan available, 15%
Small-scale Hotel service charge. **Amenities:** dual phone lines, voice mail, irons, hair dryers. **Pool(s):** heated outdoor. **Leisure Activities:** whirlpool, exercise room. **Guest Services:** valet and coin laundry. **Business Services:** meeting rooms, fax (fee). **Cards:** AX, DC, DS, MC, VI.
SOME UNITS

DAYS INN
Phone: (972)436-0080   292
SAVE
All Year　　1P: $40　　2P: $46　　XP: $10　　F12
Location: I-35 E, exit 450, just sw. 1401 S Stemmons Frwy 75067. Fax: 972/221-2282. **Facility:** 104 one-bedroom standard units, some with efficiencies, kitchens and/or whirlpools. 2 stories, exterior corridors. **Parking:** on-site. **Terms:** small pets only. **Amenities:** hair dryers. **Pool(s):** outdoor. **Guest Services:** coin laundry. **Business Services:** fax (fee).
Motel
SOME UNITS

FAIRFIELD INN-LEWISVILLE
Phone: 972/899-6900   282
SAVE
All Year　　1P: $74-$94
Location: I-35, exit 448A, just w on SR 121. 2697 Lake Vista Dr 75067. Fax: 972/899-6901. **Facility:** 71 one-bedroom standard units. 3 stories, interior corridors. *Bath:* combo or shower only. **Parking:** on-site.
Amenities: irons, hair dryers. **Pool(s):** small heated indoor. **Leisure Activities:** whirlpool, exercise room.
Small-scale Hotel **Guest Services:** valet laundry. **Business Services:** meeting rooms, fax (fee). **Cards:** AX, DC, DS, MC, VI.
SOME UNITS

(See map p. 236)

HAMPTON INN
(AAA) (SAVE)

Small-scale Hotel

Phone: (972)420-1318 [293]

All Year [CP] 1P: $79 2P: $85
Location: I-35 E, exit 451, just w. 885 S Stemmons Frwy 75067. Fax: 972/353-2600. **Facility:** 54 one-bedroom standard units, some with whirlpools. 2 stories, interior corridors. *Bath:* combo or shower only. **Parking:** on-site. **Amenities:** voice mail, irons, hair dryers. **Pool(s):** outdoor. **Leisure Activities:** exercise room. **Guest Services:** valet and coin laundry. **Business Services:** meeting rooms, fax (fee). **Cards:** AX, CB, DC, DS, JC, MC, VI. **Special Amenities:** free continental breakfast and free local telephone calls.

SOME UNITS

HOMEWOOD SUITES BY HILTON
(SAVE)

Small-scale Hotel

Phone: (972)315-6123 [289]

All Year [ECP] 1P: $119-$139 2P: $129-$169
Location: I-35 E, exit 448A, just e. 700 Hebron Pkwy 75057. Fax: 972/315-2943. **Facility:** 96 units. 89 one- and 7 two-bedroom suites, some with efficiencies and/or whirlpools. 3 stories, interior corridors. *Bath:* combo or shower only. **Parking:** on-site. **Terms:** cancellation fee imposed. **Amenities:** dual phone lines, voice mail, irons, hair dryers. **Pool(s):** outdoor. **Leisure Activities:** whirlpool, exercise room, sports court. **Guest Services:** sundries, complimentary evening beverages: Mon-Thurs, valet and coin laundry, area transportation. **Business Services:** meeting rooms, fax (fee). **Cards:** AX, CB, DC, DS, MC, VI.

SOME UNITS

HOWARD JOHNSON

Small-scale Hotel

Phone: (972)434-1000 [295]

All Year [CP] 1P: $68 2P: $68 XP: $6 F18
Location: I-35 E, exit 452 (Main St), just ne. 200 N Stemmons Frwy 75067. Fax: 972/221-1323. **Facility:** 116 one-bedroom standard units. 4 stories, interior corridors. **Parking:** on-site. **Terms:** small pets only ($20 fee). **Amenities:** irons, hair dryers. **Pool(s):** outdoor. **Guest Services:** valet and coin laundry. **Business Services:** meeting rooms, fax (fee). **Cards:** AX, DC, DS, MC, VI.

SOME UNITS

LA QUINTA INN-DALLAS-LEWISVILLE
(AAA) (SAVE)

Small-scale Hotel

Phone: (972)221-7525 [296]

All Year 1P: $69-$84 2P: $79-$94 XP: $10 F18
Location: I-35 E, exit 449, just w. 1657 S Stemmons Frwy 75067-6401. Fax: 972/221-8795. **Facility:** 129 one-bedroom standard units. 2 stories, exterior corridors. **Parking:** on-site. **Terms:** [ECP] meal plan available, small pets only. **Amenities:** video games (fee), voice mail, irons, hair dryers. **Pool(s):** outdoor. **Guest Services:** valet laundry, airport transportation-Dallas-Fort Worth International Airport, area transportation-within 10 mi. **Business Services:** meeting rooms, fax (fee). **Cards:** AX, CB, DC, DS, JC, MC, VI. **Special Amenities:** free continental breakfast and free local telephone calls. *(See color ad p 272)*

SOME UNITS

MICROTEL INN & SUITES
(AAA) (SAVE)

Small-scale Hotel

Phone: (972)434-0447 [285]

All Year 1P: $45-$50 2P: $55-$60 XP: $5 F10
Location: I-35 E, exit 451, just w. 881 S Stemmons Frwy 75067. Fax: 972/434-0700. **Facility:** 51 one-bedroom standard units. 2 stories, interior corridors. *Bath:* combo or shower only. **Parking:** on-site. **Terms:** 5 day cancellation notice, weekly rates available, pets ($10 fee). **Amenities:** safes (fee). **Guest Services:** coin laundry. **Business Services:** fax (fee). **Cards:** AX, CB, DC, DS, MC, VI. **Special Amenities:** free continental breakfast and free local telephone calls.

SOME UNITS

MOTEL 6

Small-scale Hotel

Phone: 972/436-5008 [297]

All Year 1P: $35-$43 2P: $41-$49 XP: $3 F17
Location: I-35 E, exit 449, just n on access road. 1705 Lakepointe Dr 75057. Fax: 972/436-4862. **Facility:** 119 one-bedroom standard units. 3 stories, interior corridors. *Bath:* combo or shower only. **Parking:** on-site. **Pool(s):** outdoor. **Guest Services:** coin laundry. **Business Services:** fax (fee). **Cards:** AX, CB, DC, DS, MC, VI.

SOME UNITS

RESIDENCE INN
(SAVE)

Small-scale Hotel

Phone: 972/315-3777 [298]

All Year [BP] 1P: $120 2P: $120
Location: I-33 E, exit 448A (Round Grove Rd), 0.5 mi s on service road; jct I-35 and Round Grove Rd to Vista Ridge Rd, just w. 755C Vista Ridge Mall Dr 75067. Fax: 972/315-3777. **Facility:** 72 units. 24 one-bedroom standard units with efficiencies. 36 one- and 12 two-bedroom suites, some with efficiencies or kitchens. 3 stories, interior corridors. *Bath:* combo or shower only. **Parking:** on-site. **Terms:** cancellation fee imposed, pets ($100 fee, $20 extra charge). **Amenities:** dual phone lines, voice mail, irons, hair dryers. **Pool(s):** heated indoor. **Leisure Activities:** whirlpool, exercise room, sports court. **Guest Services:** complimentary evening beverages: Mon-Thurs, valet and coin laundry. **Business Services:** meeting rooms, fax (fee). **Cards:** AX, DC, DS, MC, VI.

SOME UNITS

SUPER 8-LEWISVILLE/DALLAS NORTH/AIRPORT

Motel

Phone: (972)221-7511 [299]

All Year [CP] 1P: $45-$75 2P: $45-$75 XP: $5 F12
Location: I-35 E, exit 450, just sw. 1305 S Stemmons Frwy 75067. Fax: 972/221-2108. **Facility:** 86 one-bedroom standard units. 2 stories, exterior corridors. **Parking:** on-site. **Terms:** weekly rates available, pets ($20 deposit, $5 extra charge). **Amenities:** *Some:* irons, hair dryers. **Pool(s):** outdoor. **Leisure Activities:** exercise room. **Guest Services:** coin laundry. **Business Services:** meeting rooms, fax (fee). **Cards:** AX, CB, DC, DS, JC, MC, VI.

SOME UNITS

(See map p. 236)

——— WHERE TO DINE ———

CHINA DRAGON SUPER BUFFET   **Lunch:** $5-$7   **Dinner:** $6-$16   **Phone:** 972/353-8636   195
Chinese
Location: I-35, exit 449, just n on access road. 1630 S Stemmons Frwy 75067. **Hours:** 11 am-10 pm, Fri &
Sat-10:30 pm. **Closed:** 11/27, 12/25. **Features:** The all-you-can-eat buffet lines up favorite Chinese dishes
beside some Mexican and American choices. The restaurant offers a good value. Casual dress; beer &
wine only. **Parking:** on-site. **Cards:** AX, DC, DS, MC, VI.

MABANK pop. 2,151

——— WHERE TO STAY ———

THE BIRDHOUSE B & B
All Year [BP]   1P: $63-$79   2P: $63-$79   **Phone:** (903)887-1242
Bed & Breakfast
XP: $13   F13
Location: US 175 Bypass and 198, 0.3 mi s. 103 E Kaufman St 75147. **Fax:** 903/887-7698. **Facility:** Smoke free
premises. 4 one-bedroom standard units. 3 stories (no elevator), interior corridors. *Bath:* combo or shower
only. **Parking:** on-site. **Terms:** check-in 4 pm, 3 day cancellation notice. **Amenities:** video library, hair dryers.
Some: irons. **Business Services:** fax. **Cards:** AX, DS, MC, VI.
SOME UNITS
(A$K) (S⊘) (✕) (VCR) (DATA PORT) (▣) / (🛏) /

MCKINNEY pop. 54,369

——— WHERE TO STAY ———

AMERIHOST INN-MCKINNEY   **Phone:** (972)547-4500
(AAA) (SAVE)
All Year   1P: $72-$159   2P: $78-$159   XP: $6   F18
Small-scale Hotel
Location: US 75, exit 39, 1.3 mi n of jct US 75 and Eldorado Pkwy on northbound access road. 951 S Central Expwy
75070. **Fax:** 972/547-4340. **Facility:** 61 one-bedroom standard units, some with whirlpools. 2 stories, interior
corridors. *Bath:* combo or shower only. **Parking:** on-site. **Terms:** check-in 4 pm, 5 day cancellation notice,
[ECP] meal plan available. **Amenities:** voice mail, safes (fee), irons, hair dryers. **Pool(s):** heated indoor.
Leisure Activities: sauna, whirlpool, exercise room. **Guest Services:** valet laundry. **Business Services:**
meeting rooms, fax (fee). **Cards:** AX, CB, DC, DS, MC, VI. **Special Amenities: free continental breakfast and free news-
paper.**
SOME UNITS
(S⊘) (🐕) (🏊) (✕) (🎬) (DATA PORT) (▣) / (✕) (🛏) (🖥) /

BEST WESTERN MCKINNEY INN & SUITES   **Phone:** (972)548-3000
(SAVE)
3/29-8/31 [ECP]   1P: $79   2P: $79   XP: $10   F16
2/1-3/28 & 9/1-1/31 [ECP]   1P: $69   2P: $69   XP: $10   F16
Small-scale Hotel
Location: US 75, exit 40A. 480 Wilson Creek Blvd 75069. **Fax:** 972/548-4967. **Facility:** 68 units. 64 one-bedroom
standard units. 4 one-bedroom suites ($89-$119) with efficiencies. 3 stories, interior corridors. *Bath:* combo
or shower only. **Parking:** on-site. **Amenities:** high-speed Internet, dual phone lines, voice mail, irons, hair
dryers. **Pool(s):** outdoor. **Leisure Activities:** whirlpool, exercise room. **Guest Services:** valet and coin
laundry. **Business Services:** meeting rooms, business center. **Cards:** AX, CB, DC, DS, JC, MC, VI.
SOME UNITS
(S⊘) (🛗M) (🛗) (🏊) (🎬) (DATA PORT) (▣) / (✕) (🛏) (🖥) /

COMFORT SUITES OF MCKINNEY   **Phone:** (972)548-9595
(SAVE)
All Year [CP]   1P: $69-$109   2P: $69-$109   XP: $10   F18
Small-scale Hotel
Location: US 75, exit 40B, 0.4 mi n on north access road. 1590 N Central Expwy 75069. **Fax:** 972/548-2208.
Facility: 63 units. 62 one-bedroom standard units, some with whirlpools. 1 one-bedroom suite ($109-$175)
with kitchen (no utensils). 3 stories, interior corridors. *Bath:* combo or shower only. **Parking:** on-site.
Amenities: high-speed Internet, voice mail, irons, hair dryers. **Pool(s):** outdoor. **Leisure Activities:** exercise
room. **Guest Services:** valet and coin laundry. **Business Services:** meeting rooms, fax (fee). **Cards:** AX,
CB, DC, DS, MC, VI.
SOME UNITS
(S⊘) (🍴) (🛗M) (🛗) (🏊) (🎬) (DATA PORT) (🛏) (🖥) (▣) / (✕) /

DAYS INN MCKINNEY   **Phone:** (972)548-8888
(AAA) (SAVE)
All Year   1P: $55-$60   2P: $60-$75   XP: $5   F17
Motel
Location: US 75, 0.5 mi n of jct US 380, exit 41. 2104 N Central Expwy 75070. **Fax:** 972/548-2615. **Facility:** 78
one-bedroom standard units. 2 stories, exterior corridors. **Parking:** on-site. **Terms:** [CP] meal plan available,
small pets only ($5 extra charge). **Amenities:** safes, hair dryers. *Some:* irons. **Pool(s):** outdoor. **Guest Serv-
ices:** coin laundry. **Business Services:** fax (fee). **Cards:** AX, DC, DS, MC, VI. **Special Amenities: free con-
tinental breakfast and free local telephone calls.**
SOME UNITS
(S⊘) (🐕) (🏊) (🎬) (DATA PORT) / (✕) (🛏) (🖥) /
FEE   FEE

SUPER 8 MOTEL-MCKINNEY   **Phone:** 972/548-8880
All Year   1P: $51   2P: $55   XP: $5   F12
Small-scale Hotel
Location: US 75, exit 40A (Virginia/Louisiana Pkwy), 0.5 mi n on northbound service road. 910 N Central Expwy 75070.
Fax: 972/548-0486. **Facility:** 80 one-bedroom standard units. 3 stories, interior corridors. *Bath:* combo or
shower only. **Parking:** on-site. **Amenities:** safes. **Guest Services:** valet laundry. **Business Services:**
meeting rooms, fax. **Cards:** AX, CB, DC, DS, MC, VI.
SOME UNITS
(A$K) (S⊘) (🍴) (🛗) (🎬) / (✕) (🛏) (🖥) /

MESQUITE pop. 124,523

──────── WHERE TO STAY ────────

COMFORT INN

Small-scale Hotel

Phone: (972)285-6300

All Year | 1P: $65-$89 | 2P: $65-$89 | XP: $5 | F18

Location: I-635, exit 5, just e. 923 Windbell Cir 75149. Fax: 972/285-7677. **Facility:** 62 one-bedroom standard units, some with whirlpools. 2 stories, interior corridors. *Bath:* combo or shower only. **Parking:** on-site. **Terms:** [CP] meal plan available. **Amenities:** voice mail, irons, hair dryers. **Pool(s):** heated indoor. **Leisure Activities:** whirlpool, exercise room. **Guest Services:** coin laundry. **Business Services:** meeting rooms, fax (fee). **Cards:** AX, CB, DC, DS, MC, VI.

SOME UNITS

COUNTRY INN & SUITES BY CARLSON

Phone: (972)216-7460

All Year | 1P: $66 | 2P: $71 | XP: $5 | F18

Location: E US 80, exit Belt Line Rd. 118 E Hwy 80 75149. Fax: 972/288-4430. **Facility:** 60 units. 39 one-bedroom standard units. 21 one-bedroom suites ($80-$90), some with whirlpools. 3 stories, interior corridors. *Bath:* combo or shower only. **Parking:** on-site. **Terms:** [ECP] meal plan available, pets ($50 deposit). Small-scale Hotel **Amenities:** dual phone lines, voice mail, irons, hair dryers. **Pool(s):** small heated outdoor. **Leisure Activities:** whirlpool, exercise room. **Guest Services:** valet and coin laundry. **Business Services:** meeting rooms, fax (fee). **Cards:** AX, CB, DC, DS, MC, VI. **Special Amenities:** free continental breakfast and free newspaper. *(See color ad p 260)*

SOME UNITS

COURTYARD BY MARRIOTT MESQUITE

Small-scale Hotel

Phone: (972)681-3300

All Year | 1P: $71-$116 | 2P: $71-$116

Location: I-30, exit 56A (Gus Thomasson/Galloway). 2300 US Hwy 67 75150. Fax: 972/681-3324. **Facility:** 101 units. 97 one-bedroom standard units, some with whirlpools. 4 one-bedroom suites. 4 stories, interior corridors. *Bath:* combo or shower only. **Parking:** on-site. **Terms:** [BP] meal plan available. **Amenities:** dual phone lines, voice mail, irons, hair dryers. **Pool(s):** heated indoor. **Leisure Activities:** whirlpool, exercise room. **Guest Services:** valet and coin laundry. **Business Services:** meeting rooms, fax (fee). **Cards:** AX, DC, DS, JC, MC, VI.

SOME UNITS

FAIRFIELD INN-MESQUITE

Small-scale Hotel

Phone: (972)686-8286

All Year [ECP] | 1P: $65-$85 | 2P: $65-$95 | XP: $6 | F18

Location: I-635, exit 7 (Town East Blvd), just w to Towne Crossing Blvd, 0.5 mi n. 4020 Towne Crossing Blvd 75150. Fax: 972/686-8286. **Facility:** 82 one-bedroom standard units. 3 stories, interior corridors. *Bath:* combo or shower only. **Parking:** on-site. **Terms:** 14 day cancellation notice. **Amenities:** voice mail, irons. **Pool(s):** heated indoor. **Leisure Activities:** whirlpool. **Guest Services:** valet laundry. **Business Services:** fax (fee). **Cards:** AX, CB, DC, DS, MC, VI.

SOME UNITS

HAMPTON INN AND SUITES AT RODEO CENTER
Small-scale Hotel

Phone: 972/329-3100

All Year | 1P: $84 | 2P: $94 | XP: $10 | F18

Location: I-635, exit 4 (Military Pkwy), 0.5 mi s on Hickory Tree Rd. 1700 Rodeo Dr 75149. Fax: 972/329-3101. **Facility:** 160 units. 106 one-bedroom standard units. 54 one-bedroom suites ($119-$129) with efficiencies, some with whirlpools. 6 stories, interior corridors. *Bath:* combo or shower only. **Parking:** on-site. **Terms:** cancellation fee imposed, [CP] meal plan available. **Amenities:** dual phone lines, voice mail, irons, hair dryers. *Fee:* video games, high-speed Internet. **Pool(s):** heated outdoor. **Leisure Activities:** exercise room. **Guest Services:** sundries, valet and coin laundry. **Business Services:** conference facilities, fax (fee). **Cards:** AX, CB, DC, DS, MC, VI. **Special Amenities:** free continental breakfast and free newspaper. *(See color ad below)*

SOME UNITS

MICROTEL INN & SUITES
Small-scale Hotel

Phone: (972)216-4418

All Year | 1P: $40-$70 | 2P: $50-$80 | XP: $10 | F16

Location: US 80 E, exit Belt Line Rd. 317 Hwy 80 E 75150. Fax: 972/216-2171. **Facility:** 40 one-bedroom standard units, some with whirlpools. 2 stories, interior corridors. *Bath:* combo or shower only. **Parking:** on-site. **Terms:** [CP] meal plan available. **Leisure Activities:** limited exercise equipment. **Business Services:** meeting rooms, fax (fee). **Cards:** AX, DS, MC, VI.

SOME UNITS

QUALITY INN-MESQUITE
AAA SAVE

Small-scale Hotel

Phone: (972)285-1500
All Year 1P: $59-$74 2P: $59-$74 XP: $7 F12
Location: I-635, exit 4 (Military Pkwy), just w. 140 Commerce Way 75149. Fax: 972/285-6500. **Facility:** 51 one-bedroom standard units. 2 stories, interior corridors. *Bath:* combo or shower only. **Parking:** on-site. **Terms:** [ECP] meal plan available. **Amenities:** voice mail, irons, hair dryers. **Pool(s):** small heated indoor. **Leisure Activities:** whirlpool. **Guest Services:** coin laundry. **Business Services:** meeting rooms, fax (fee). **Cards:** AX, DC, DS, MC, VI. **Special Amenities: free continental breakfast and free newspaper.**

SOME UNITS

SUPER 8 MOTEL
AAA SAVE

Motel

Phone: (972)289-5481
All Year 1P: $39-$54 2P: $47-$61 XP: $4 F18
Location: I-635, exit 4 (Military Pkwy). 121 Grand Junction 75149. Fax: 972/289-1382. **Facility:** 118 one-bedroom standard units. 2 stories, exterior corridors. **Parking:** on-site. **Amenities:** *Some:* irons, hair dryers. **Pool(s):** heated outdoor. **Guest Services:** coin laundry. **Business Services:** fax. **Cards:** AX, CB, DC, DS, MC, VI. **Special Amenities: early check-in/late check-out and free local telephone calls.**

SOME UNITS

MIDLOTHIAN pop. 7,480

——— WHERE TO STAY ———

BEST WESTERN MIDLOTHIAN INN
AAA SAVE

Motel

Phone: (972)775-1891
All Year [CP] 1P: $64-$69 2P: $64-$69 XP: $8 F12
Location: 1 mi w on US 67, just n of jct US 287. Located in a semi-rural area. 220 N Hwy 67 76065. Fax: 972/723-1371. **Facility:** 40 one-bedroom standard units, some with whirlpools. 2 stories, exterior corridors. *Bath:* combo or shower only. **Parking:** on-site. **Terms:** 3 day cancellation notice-fee imposed, weekly rates available, small pets only ($20 deposit). **Amenities:** video library (fee), irons, hair dryers. **Pool(s):** outdoor. **Guest Services:** coin laundry. **Business Services:** fax (fee). **Cards:** AX, CB, DC, DS, JC, MC, VI. **Special Amenities: early check-in/late check-out and free continental breakfast.**

SOME UNITS
FEE

MILFORD pop. 685

——— WHERE TO STAY ———

BARONESS INN

Bed & Breakfast

Phone: (972)493-4924
All Year [BP] 1P: $80-$100 2P: $110-$150 XP: $20 F10
Location: I-35, exit 381, 0.8 mi e on SR 566 to US 77 (Main St), just s. 206 S Main St 76670. Fax: 972/493-3100. **Facility:** Once the Milford hotel, rooms here provide comfortable appointments with richly painted walls and flowery baths with pedestal sinks. Designated smoking area. 7 one-bedroom standard units, some with whirlpools. 2 stories (no elevator), exterior corridors. *Bath:* combo, shower or tub only. **Parking:** street. **Terms:** check-in 4 pm, 2 night minimum stay - weekends, cancellation fee imposed, package plans. **Amenities:** video library. **Business Services:** fax. **Cards:** AX, DS, MC, VI.

PLANO pop. 222,030 (See map p. 236; index p. 246)

——— WHERE TO STAY ———

AMERISUITES (DALLAS/PLANO)
AAA SAVE

Small-scale Hotel

Phone: (972)378-3997 242
All Year [ECP] 1P: $109-$124 2P: $119-$134 XP: $10 F18
Location: Dallas Pkwy, exit Park Blvd northbound; exit Parker Blvd southbound on northbound service road. 3100 Dallas Pkwy 75093. Fax: 972/378-3887. **Facility:** 128 one-bedroom standard units with efficiencies. 6 stories, interior corridors. *Bath:* combo or shower only. **Parking:** on-site. **Terms:** small pets only. **Amenities:** voice mail, irons, hair dryers. *Fee:* video games, high-speed Internet. *Some:* dual phone lines. **Pool(s):** heated outdoor. **Leisure Activities:** exercise room. **Guest Services:** valet and coin laundry, area transportation-within 5 mi. **Business Services:** meeting rooms, business center. **Cards:** AX, CB, DC, DS, JC, MC, VI. **Special Amenities: free continental breakfast and free newspaper.** *(See color ad p 251)*

SOME UNITS

BEST WESTERN PARK SUITES HOTEL
SAVE

Small-scale Hotel

Phone: (972)578-2243 243
All Year 1P: $69-$79 2P: $79-$89
Location: US 75, exit 29A northbound, just e; exit 29 southbound, 0.5 mi s on access road, just e on 15th St, 0.5 mi n on access road. 640 Park Blvd E 75074. Fax: 972/578-0563. **Facility:** 84 one-bedroom standard units. 3 stories, interior corridors. *Bath:* combo or shower only. **Parking:** on-site. **Terms:** weekly rates available, package plans, small pets only ($20 deposit). **Amenities:** dual phone lines, irons, hair dryers. **Pool(s):** heated outdoor. **Leisure Activities:** whirlpool, exercise room. **Guest Services:** complimentary evening beverages Mon-Thurs, valet and coin laundry. **Business Services:** meeting rooms, business center. **Cards:** AX, DC, MC, VI.

SOME UNITS

CANDLEWOOD SUITES-PLANO

Small-scale Hotel

Phone: 972/618-5446 246
All Year 1P: $89-$122 2P: $89-$122
Location: Jct SR 289 (Preston Rd) and Legacy Dr, just e. 4701 Legacy Dr 75024. Fax: 972/618-4581. **Facility:** 122 units. 98 one-bedroom standard units with efficiencies. 24 one-bedroom suites with efficiencies. 3 stories, interior corridors. *Bath:* combo or shower only. **Parking:** on-site. **Terms:** weekly rates available, small pets only ($5 extra charge). **Amenities:** video library, CD players, voice mail, irons, hair dryers. *Some:* dual phone lines. **Leisure Activities:** exercise room. **Guest Services:** sundries, complimentary laundry. **Business Services:** fax (fee). **Cards:** AX, CB, DC, DS, MC, VI.

SOME UNITS

(See map p. 236)

COURTYARD BY MARRIOTT
Phone: 972/403-0802 [240]

SAVE

Small-scale Hotel

All Year   1P: $129-$179   2P: $139-$189   XP: $10   F18
Location: North Dallas Tollway, exit Springcreek, on north service road. 6840 N Dallas Pkwy 75024. Fax: 972/378-9245. **Facility:** 153 units. 148 one-bedroom standard units. 5 one-bedroom suites. 3 stories, interior corridors. *Bath:* combo or shower only. **Parking:** on-site. **Terms:** 13% service charge. **Amenities:** high-speed Internet (fee), voice mail, irons, hair dryers. **Pool(s):** outdoor. **Leisure Activities:** whirlpool, exercise room. **Guest Services:** valet and coin laundry, area transportation. **Business Services:** meeting rooms, fax (fee). **Cards:** AX, CB, DC, DS, JC, MC, VI.

SOME UNITS

COURTYARD BY MARRIOTT-PLANO
Phone: 972/867-8000 [247]

Small-scale Hotel

Property failed to provide current rates
Location: Jct Plano Pkwy and SR 289 (Preston Rd). 4901 W Plano Pkwy 75093. Fax: 972/596-4009. **Facility:** 149 units. 137 one-bedroom standard units. 12 one-bedroom suites. 3 stories, interior corridors. *Bath:* combo or shower only. **Parking:** on-site. **Amenities:** high-speed Internet (fee), voice mail, irons, hair dryers. **Pool(s):** outdoor. **Leisure Activities:** whirlpool, exercise room. **Guest Services:** valet and coin laundry, area transportation. **Business Services:** meeting rooms, fax (fee). **Cards:** AX, CB, DC, DS, MC, VI.

SOME UNITS

DAYS INN & SUITES
Phone: (972)633-8200 [249]

AAA **SAVE**

Small-scale Hotel

All Year [ECP]   1P: $55-$65   2P: $60-$70   XP: $5   F17
Location: US 75, exit 30 southbound, 0.8 mi s on access road; exit 29A northbound, just n to Central Park E, 0.3 mi e to Park Blvd, 0.5 mi to Enterprise Rd, then just n. 2101 N Central Expwy 75075. Fax: 972/633-0410. **Facility:** 62 one-bedroom standard units, some with whirlpools. 2 stories, interior corridors. *Bath:* combo or shower only. **Parking:** on-site. **Amenities:** dual phone lines, voice mail, irons, hair dryers. **Pool(s):** outdoor. **Leisure Activities:** whirlpool, exercise room. **Guest Services:** valet and coin laundry. **Business Services:** meeting rooms, fax (fee). **Cards:** AX, CB, DC, DS, JC, MC, VI. **Special Amenities:** free continental breakfast and free local telephone calls.

SOME UNITS

FAIRFIELD INN
Phone: (972)519-0303 [250]

SAVE

Small-scale Hotel

All Year [ECP]   1P: $65-$85   2P: $65-$95   XP: $6   F18
Location: US 75, exit 28A, 4.5 mi w. 4712 W Plano Pkwy 75093. **Facility:** 100 one-bedroom standard units. 3 stories, interior corridors. *Bath:* combo or shower only. **Parking:** on-site. **Terms:** 14 day cancellation notice. **Amenities:** irons, hair dryers. **Pool(s):** heated indoor. **Leisure Activities:** whirlpool. **Guest Services:** valet laundry. **Business Services:** meeting rooms, fax (fee). **Cards:** AX, CB, DC, DS, MC, VI.

SOME UNITS

HAMPTON INN PLANO
Phone: (972)519-1000 [251]

SAVE

Small-scale Hotel

All Year [ECP]   1P: $89   2P: $89
Location: I-635, exit 21 (Preston Rd), 6 mi n, then just e. 4901 Old Shepherd Pl 75093. Fax: 972/519-1001. **Facility:** 131 one-bedroom standard units, some with whirlpools. 5 stories, interior corridors. *Bath:* some combo or shower only. **Parking:** on-site. **Terms:** 10% service charge, pets ($50 extra charge). **Amenities:** voice mail, irons, hair dryers. **Pool(s):** outdoor. **Guest Services:** complimentary evening beverages: Mon-Thurs, valet and coin laundry, area transportation. **Business Services:** meeting rooms, fax (fee). **Cards:** AX, CB, DC, DS, JC, MC, VI.

SOME UNITS

FEE

HOLIDAY INN EXPRESS
Phone: (972)733-4700 [252]

Small-scale Hotel

All Year   1P: $55-$75   2P: $55-$75   XP: $8   F16
Location: Jct Plano Pkwy and SR 289 (Preston Rd), just w on westbound service road. 5021 W Plano Pkwy 75093. Fax: 972/733-4558. **Facility:** 65 one-bedroom standard units, some with whirlpools. 2 stories, interior corridors. **Parking:** on-site. **Terms:** [CP] meal plan available. **Amenities:** voice mail, safes, irons, hair dryers. **Guest Services:** valet laundry. **Business Services:** meeting rooms, business center. **Cards:** AX, CB, DC, DS, JC, MC, VI.

SOME UNITS

HOLIDAY INN-PLANO
Phone: (972)881-1881 [253]

Small-scale Hotel

All Year   1P: $70-$119   2P: $70-$119   XP: $10   F18
Location: Just e of US 75; 0.3 mi ne of jct FM 544, exit 29A. 700 Central Pkwy E 75074. Fax: 972/422-2184. **Facility:** 160 one-bedroom standard units. 6 stories, interior corridors. *Bath:* combo or shower only. **Parking:** on-site. **Terms:** [BP] meal plan available, pets ($125 deposit, $25 extra charge). **Amenities:** voice mail, irons, hair dryers. **Pool(s):** outdoor. **Leisure Activities:** whirlpool, limited exercise room. **Guest Services:** valet and coin laundry, area transportation. **Business Services:** meeting rooms, fax (fee). **Cards:** AX, CB, DC, DS, JC, MC, VI.

SOME UNITS

FEE FEE

HOMEWOOD SUITES BY HILTON
Phone: (972)758-8800 [255]

SAVE

Small-scale Hotel

All Year   1P: $129   2P: $129
Location: US 75, exit 28A, 4.6 mi w, just n on Preston (SH 289), then just e. 4705 Old Shepherd Pl 75093. Fax: 972/758-8801. **Facility:** 99 units. 92 one- and 7 two-bedroom suites with efficiencies. 4 stories, interior corridors. *Bath:* combo or shower only. **Parking:** on-site. **Terms:** cancellation fee imposed, [CP] meal plan available, pets ($75 fee). **Amenities:** video games, dual phone lines, voice mail, irons, hair dryers. **Pool(s):** heated outdoor. **Leisure Activities:** whirlpool, exercise room, basketball. **Guest Services:** sundries, complimentary evening beverages: Mon-Thurs, valet and coin laundry, area transportation. **Business Services:** meeting rooms, business center. **Cards:** AX, DC, DS, MC, VI.

SOME UNITS

(See map p. 236)

LA QUINTA INN & SUITES-WEST PLANO　　　　　　　　　　　　　Phone: (972)599-0700　257
AAA SAVE
All Year　　　　1P: $69-$99　　　2P: $79-$109　　　XP: $10　　　F18
Location: US 75, exit 28A, 4.6 mi w at jct Preston (SR 289). 4800 W Plano Pkwy 75093. Fax: 972/599-1361.
Facility: 129 units. 121 one-bedroom standard units. 8 one-bedroom suites ($109-$169). 4 stories, interior corridors. *Bath:* combo or shower only. **Parking:** on-site. **Terms:** [ECP] meal plan available, small pets only.
Small-scale Hotel　**Amenities:** dual phone lines, voice mail, irons, hair dryers. *Fee:* video games, high-speed Internet. **Pool(s):** heated outdoor. **Leisure Activities:** whirlpool, exercise room. **Guest Services:** valet and coin laundry, area transportation-within 5 mi. **Business Services:** meeting rooms, fax. **Cards:** AX, CB, DC, DS, JC, MC, VI. **Special Amenities:** free continental breakfast and free local telephone calls. *(See color ad p 272)*

SOME UNITS

LA QUINTA INN-PLANO　　　　　　　　　　　　　　　　　　Phone: (972)423-1300　259
AAA SAVE
All Year　　　　1P: $59-$79　　　2P: $69-$89　　　XP: $10　　　F18
Location: US 75, exit 29A, just ne. 1820 N Central Expwy 75074-5606. Fax: 972/423-6593. **Facility:** 114 one-bedroom standard units. 2 stories, exterior corridors. *Bath:* combo or shower only. **Parking:** on-site.
Terms: [ECP] meal plan available, small pets only. **Amenities:** video games (fee), dual phone lines, voice
Motel　mail, irons, hair dryers. **Pool(s):** outdoor. **Leisure Activities:** limited exercise equipment. **Guest Services:** valet and coin laundry. **Business Services:** meeting rooms, fax. **Cards:** AX, CB, DC, DS, JC, MC, VI.
Special Amenities: free continental breakfast and free local telephone calls. *(See color ad p 272)*

SOME UNITS

FEE FEE

MAINSTAY SUITES　　　　　　　　　　　　　　　　　　　　Phone: (972)596-9966　260
AAA SAVE
All Year [CP]　　　　1P: $69-$79　　　2P: $79-$89
Location: US 75, exit 28A, 4.5 mi w. 4709 W Plano Pkwy 75093. Fax: 972/596-9967. **Facility:** 97 units. 70 one-bedroom standard units with efficiencies. 26 one- and 1 two-bedroom suites with efficiencies. 2 stories, interior corridors. *Bath:* combo or shower only. **Parking:** on-site. **Terms:** weekly rates available, pets ($100
Small-scale Hotel　deposit, $5 extra charge). **Amenities:** video library, video games, dual phone lines, voice mail, irons, hair dryers. **Pool(s):** heated outdoor. **Leisure Activities:** exercise room. **Guest Services:** complimentary evening beverages: Mon-Wed, valet and coin laundry. **Business Services:** fax (fee). **Cards:** AX, CB, DC, DS, MC, VI.
Special Amenities: early check-in/late check-out. *(See color ad below)*

SOME UNITS

(See map p. 236)

MOTEL 6 - 1121
◆◆ ◆◆
Motel

5/22-1/31	1P: $41-$51	2P: $47-$57	XP: $3
2/1-5/21	1P: $37-$47	2P: $43-$53	XP: $3

Phone: 972/578-1626   **261**
F17
F17

Location: US 75, exit 29A (Park Blvd). 2550 N Central Expwy 75074. Fax: 972/423-6994. **Facility:** 118 one-bedroom standard units. 2 stories, exterior corridors. *Bath:* combo or shower only. **Parking:** on-site. **Terms:** small pets only. **Pool(s):** outdoor. **Guest Services:** coin laundry. **Business Services:** fax (fee). **Cards:** AX, CB, DC, DS, MC, VI.

SOME UNITS

RAMADA LIMITED
◆◆ ◆◆
Small-scale Hotel

All Year [CP].
1P: $39-$49
2P: $49-$59

Phone: (972)424-5568   **245**

Location: Just e of US 75; exit 29A northbound; exit 29 southbound, 0.5 mi s on access road, just e on 15th St, 0.5 mi n on access road. 621 Central Pkwy E 75074. Fax: 972/881-7265. **Facility:** 103 one-bedroom standard units. 3 stories, interior corridors. **Parking:** on-site. **Terms:** small pets only ($20 fee). **Amenities:** *Some:* irons, hair dryers. **Pool(s):** outdoor. **Guest Services:** coin laundry. **Business Services:** meeting rooms. **Cards:** AX, DC, DS, MC, VI.

SOME UNITS

RED ROOF INN DALLAS-PLANO
AAA [SAVE]
◆◆ ◆◆
Small-scale Hotel

All Year
1P: $38-$50
2P: $43-$55

Phone: (972)881-8191   **262**
XP: $5   F18

Location: SR 75, exit 30 (Parker Rd), 0.5 mi w to Premier, then just n. 301 Ruisseau Dr 75023. Fax: 972/881-0722. **Facility:** 123 one-bedroom standard units. 3 stories, interior/exterior corridors. *Bath:* combo or shower only. **Parking:** on-site. **Terms:** weekly rates available, small pets only. **Amenities:** video games (fee), voice mail. *Some:* hair dryers. **Business Services:** fax (fee). **Cards:** AX, DC, MC, VI. **Special Amenities:** free local telephone calls and free newspaper.

SOME UNITS

RESIDENCE INN BY MARRIOTT DALLAS/PLANO
[SAVE]
◆◆ ◆◆
Small-scale Hotel

All Year [ECP]
1P: $129-$189
2P: $139-$199

Phone: (972)473-6761   **241**

Location: North Dallas Tollway, exit Spring Creek Pkwy, 1.9 mi e, then n on Preston Rd; between Spring Creek Pkwy and Tennyson. 5001 White Stone Ln 75024. Fax: 972/473-6628. **Facility:** 115 units. 84 one-bedroom standard units with efficiencies. 31 one-bedroom suites, some with kitchens. 3 stories, interior corridors. *Bath:* combo or shower only. **Parking:** on-site. **Terms:** pets ($150 fee). **Pool(s):** small heated outdoor. **Leisure Activities:** whirlpool, exercise room, sports court. **Guest Services:** complimentary evening beverages: Mon-Thurs, valet and coin laundry, area transportation. **Business Services:** meeting rooms, fax (fee). **Cards:** AX, CB, DC, DS, JC, MC, VI.

SOME UNITS

SLEEP INN PLANO
AAA [SAVE]
◆◆ ◆◆
Small-scale Hotel

All Year [ECP]
1P: $50-$60
2P: $50-$70

Phone: (972)867-1111   **263**
XP: $5   F16

Location: US 75, exit 28A, 4.6 mi w at jct Preston (SR 289). 4801 W Plano Pkwy 75093. Fax: 972/612-6753. **Facility:** 104 one-bedroom standard units. 2 stories, interior corridors. *Bath:* combo or shower only. **Parking:** on-site. **Terms:** small pets only ($25 fee, $10 extra charge). **Amenities:** video games, irons, hair dryers. **Pool(s):** heated outdoor. **Business Services:** fax (fee). **Cards:** AX, CB, DC, DS, JC, MC, VI. **Special Amenities:** free continental breakfast and free local telephone calls. *(See ad p 312)*

SOME UNITS

SUPER 8 MOTEL-PLANO
◆◆ ◆◆
Small-scale Hotel

All Year [CP]
1P: $45-$59
2P: $45-$59

Phone: (972)423-8300   **265**
XP: $5   F12

Location: US 75, exit 29A northbound, just e; exit 29 southbound, 0.5 mi s on access road, just e on 15th St, then just n on access road. 1704 N Central Expwy 75074. Fax: 972/881-7744. **Facility:** 123 units. 93 one-bedroom standard units. 3 stories, interior corridors. *Bath:* combo or shower only. **Parking:** on-site. **Terms:** pets ($20 deposit). **Amenities:** safes (fee). **Business Services:** meeting rooms, fax (fee). **Cards:** AX, CB, DC, DS, MC, VI.

SOME UNITS

WELLESLEY INN & SUITES (DALLAS/PLANO)
AAA [SAVE]
◆◆◆ ◆◆◆
Small-scale Hotel

All Year
1P: $80-$89

Phone: 972/378-9978   **266**

Location: Dallas Pkwy, exit Park Blvd northbound; exit Parker Blvd southbound, on northbound service road. 2900 Dallas Pkwy 75093. Fax: 972/378-9979. **Facility:** 123 units. 93 one-bedroom standard units with efficiencies. 30 one-bedroom suites with efficiencies. 4 stories, interior corridors. *Bath:* combo or shower only. **Parking:** on-site. **Terms:** 14 day cancellation notice, package plans, small pets only. **Amenities:** video games (fee), dual phone lines, voice mail, irons, hair dryers. **Pool(s):** heated outdoor. **Leisure Activities:** exercise room. **Guest Services:** valet and coin laundry, area transportation-within 5 mi. **Business Services:** meeting rooms, fax (fee). **Cards:** AX, CB, DC, DS, JC, MC, VI. **Special Amenities:** free continental breakfast and free newspaper. *(See color ad p 250)*

SOME UNITS

———— **WHERE TO DINE** ————

ABUELO'S MEXICAN FOOD EMBASSY
◆◆ ◆◆
Mexican

Lunch: $9-$12   **Dinner:** $11-$20   **Phone:** 972/423-9290   **169**

Location: US 75, exit 30 (Parker Rd), just e on Parker Rd, then just n on access road. 3420 N Central Expwy 75075. **Hours:** 11 am-10 pm, Fri & Sat-11 pm. Closed: 11/27, 12/24, 12/25. **Features:** Off the busy highway, this dining retreat is relaxed and inviting. Beautiful architectural enhancements make you feel as if you're dining in the courtyard of a Mexican villa. Plants, archways, pillars and a fountain add interest to the inside dining area, while the outdoor patio boasts a parklike feel. Service is welcoming and professional. Casual dress; cocktails. **Parking:** on-site. **Cards:** AX, DC, DS, MC, VI.

ABUELO'S MEXICAN FOOD EMBASSY
◆◆ ◆◆
Mexican

Lunch: $8-$12   **Dinner:** $10-$20   **Phone:** 972/781-1613   **168**

Location: N Dallas Pkwy, exit Park Blvd, on south access road. 3701 N Dallas Pkwy 75093. **Hours:** 11 am-10 pm, Fri & Sat-10:30 pm. Closed: 11/27, 12/25. **Features:** Beautiful architecture enhancements help diners feel as though they're dining in the courtyard of a Mexican villa. Plants, archways, pillars and a large fountain add interest to the inside dining area. Service is welcoming and professional. Casual dress; cocktails. **Parking:** on-site. **Cards:** AX, DC, DS, MC, VI.

(See map p. 236)

FISHMONGERS SEAFOOD MARKET & CAFE   **Lunch:** $7-$11   **Dinner:** $9-$20   **Phone:** 972/423-3699   172
◇◇◇
Location: US 75, exit 30 (Parker Rd), 0.8 mi s on west side access road; at Chisholm Rd in Chisholm Plaza. 1915 N
Central Expwy 75075. **Hours:** 11 am-10 pm, Fri & Sat-11 pm, Sun-9 pm. Closed: 1/1, 11/27, 12/25.
Seafood   **Features:** Cajun and Tex-Mex seafood dishes are the focus at this eatery. Baked scallops, a very popular
shrimp tortilla soup, fried butterfly shrimp, and what customers call the best homemade bread pudding in
the world, fill the menu with a variety of good tastes. Casual dress; cocktails. **Parking:** on-site. **Cards:** AX, DC, DS, MC, VI.

MARTINEZ CAFE   **Lunch:** $6-$7   **Dinner:** $7-$19   **Phone:** 972/964-7898   170
◇◇◇
Location: Northwest corner of Coit and Park Rd; (SR 544) in Park Pavilion Strip Center. 2001 Coit Rd, Suite 102
75075. **Hours:** 11 am-10 pm, Sun-9 pm. Closed: 1/1, 11/27, 12/25. **Features:** Although the music isn't live,
Mexican   it is lively at this festive restaurant, which also boasts colorful art. Shrimp adds an appealing twist to
traditional fajitas, and reliable favorites, such as tacos, enchiladas and quesadillas, are certain to satisfy.
Smoke free premises. Casual dress; cocktails. **Parking:** on-site. **Cards:** AX, DC, DS, MC, VI.

⊠

OSAKA SUSHI   **Lunch:** $14   **Dinner:** $24   **Phone:** 972/931-8898   173
◇◇◇ ◇◇◇
Location: Southwest corner of jct Preston Rd and W Park Blvd. 5012 W Park Blvd 75093. **Hours:** 11 am-2:30 &
5:30-9:30 pm, Fri-10 pm, Sat 11:30 am-3 & 5:30-10 pm, Sun 11:30 am-9 pm. **Reservations:** suggested.
Japanese   **Features:** A very popular restaurant specializing in Japanese cuisine. All you can eat buffet features all the
traditional Japanese specials such as sushi, tempura, teriyaki steak and chicken. Smoke free premises.
Casual dress; cocktails. **Parking:** on-site. **Cards:** AX, DC, DS, MC, VI.

☱ ⊠

PONDER pop. 507

─────── **WHERE TO DINE** ───────

RANCHMAN'S CAFE "THE PONDER STEAKHOUSE"   **Lunch:** $8-$26   **Dinner:** $10-$26   **Phone:** 940/479-2221
ⒶⒶⒶ
Location: Downtown. 110 Bailey St 76259. **Hours:** 11 am-10 pm. Closed: 1/1, 12/24, 12/25.
◇◇◇   **Reservations:** suggested. **Features:** Featuring a charming Western decor complete with longhorns and
cowboy hats adorning the walls, this cafe serves steaks, burgers, homemade pies and cobblers. Call
Steak House   ahead for baked potatoes as they are cooked slowly for one and a half hours. Casual dress. **Parking:**
on-site. **Cards:** AX, MC, VI.

RED OAK pop. 4,301

─────── **WHERE TO STAY** ───────

HOWARD JOHNSON   **Phone:** (972)617-7797
ⒶⒶⒶ ⓢⒶⓋⒺ   5/1-1/31 [ECP]   1P: $69-$109   2P: $79-$109   XP: $10   F12
2/1-4/30 [ECP]   1P: $59-$109   2P: $69-$109   XP: $10   F12
◇◇◇ ◇◇◇   **Location:** I-35 E, exit 410 northbound, 1 mi on feeder; exit 411 southbound, just e on Ovilla to Bride, then just s. 404
Small-scale Hotel   N I-35 E 75154. **Fax:** 972/617-7841. **Facility:** 65 one-bedroom standard units, some with whirlpools. 2 stories,
interior corridors. *Bath:* combo or shower only. **Parking:** on-site. **Amenities:** voice mail, safes (fee), hair
dryers. **Pool(s):** small outdoor. **Leisure Activities:** exercise room. **Business Services:** meeting rooms, fax
(fee). **Cards:** AX, DC, DS, MC, VI. **Special Amenities:** free continental breakfast and free local telephone calls.

SOME UNITS
ⓈⒹ ⑪ ⓰ ⓹ ⓦ ⓦ ⓓⓐⓣⓐⓟⓞⓡⓣ 🖵 / ⊠ 🖬 🖿 /
FEE   FEE

RICHARDSON pop. 91,802   (See map p. 236; index p. 245)

─────── **WHERE TO STAY** ───────

BRADFORD HOMESUITES   **Phone:** (972)671-8080   200
◇◇◇◇◇   All Year [CP]   1P: $79-$119   2P: $79-$119
Location: US 75, exit 26 (Campbell Rd), 0.5 mi w to Collins Blvd, 0.6 mi n. 2301 N Central Expressway 75080.
Small-scale Hotel   **Fax:** 972/671-1292. **Facility:** 132 units. 98 one-bedroom standard units with efficiencies. 34 one-bedroom
suites with efficiencies. 2-3 stories, interior corridors. *Bath:* combo or shower only. **Parking:** on-site.
Terms: cancellation fee imposed. **Amenities:** video games (fee), dual phone lines, voice mail, irons, hair dryers. **Pool(s):** outdoor. **Leisure Activities:** whirlpool, exercise room, sports court. **Guest Services:** complimentary evening beverages: Wed, valet
and coin laundry. **Business Services:** meeting rooms, fax. **Cards:** AX, CB, DC, DS, JC, MC, VI.

SOME UNITS
Ⓐ$Ⓚ ⓈⒹ Ⓛ Ⓜ ⓹ ⓦ ⊠ ⓋⒸⓇ ⓦ ⓓⓐⓣⓐⓟⓞⓡⓣ 🖬 🖿 🖵 / ⊠

CLUBHOUSE INN & SUITES RICHARDSON   **Phone:** (972)479-0500   207
◇◇◇ ◇◇◇   All Year [BP]   1P: $79-$119   2P: $79-$119   XP: $10   F18
Location: US 75, exit 26 (Campbell Rd), just e. 901 E Campbell Rd 75081. **Fax:** 972/231-5066. **Facility:** 137 units.
Small-scale Hotel   122 one-bedroom standard units. 15 one-bedroom suites. 2 stories, interior corridors. *Bath:* combo or shower
only. **Parking:** on-site. **Terms:** pets ($35 extra charge). **Amenities:** high-speed Internet (fee), voice mail,
irons, hair dryers. **Pool(s):** outdoor. **Leisure Activities:** whirlpool, exercise room. **Guest Services:** complimentary evening beverages: Mon-Sat, valet and coin laundry, area transportation. **Business Services:** meeting rooms, fax (fee). **Cards:** AX, CB, DC,
DS, JC, MC, VI.

SOME UNITS
Ⓐ$Ⓚ ⓈⒹ ⓰ Ⓛ Ⓜ ⓹ ⓓ ⓦ ⓦ ⓓⓐⓣⓐⓟⓞⓡⓣ 🖵 / ⊠ 🖬 🖿 /

(See map p. 236)

COMFORT INN
AAA SAVE
▼▼▼▼

Small-scale Hotel

MC, VI.

Phone: (972)680-8884 **211**
All Year — 1P: $65 — 2P: $65 — XP: $5 — F18
Location: US 75, exit 23 (Spring Valley Rd), 0.3 mi e. 220 W Spring Valley Rd 75081. Fax: 972/680-9096. **Facility:** 57 units. 56 one-bedroom standard units, some with whirlpools. 1 one-bedroom suite ($110) with kitchen. 2 stories, exterior corridors. *Bath:* combo or shower only. **Parking:** on-site. **Terms:** cancellation fee imposed. **Amenities:** voice mail, irons, hair dryers. **Pool(s):** outdoor. **Leisure Activities:** sauna, exercise room. **Guest Services:** valet and coin laundry. **Business Services:** fax (fee). **Cards:** AX, CB, DC, DS,

SOME UNITS

🛎️ 🍴 📶 🛏️ 🐾 🐕 📶 DATA PORT 🛗 💻 / ✕ 📷 /

COURTYARD BY MARRIOTT-RICHARDSON AT SPRING VALLEY
SAVE
▼▼▼▼

Small-scale Hotel

Phone: 972/235-5000 **212**
All Year — 1P: $99-$119 — 2P: $99-$119
Location: US 75, exit 23 (Spring Valley Rd), 0.6 mi s on access road, then just e. 1000 S Sherman St 75081. Fax: 972/235-3423. **Facility:** 149 units. 137 one-bedroom standard units. 12 one-bedroom suites ($129). 3 stories, interior corridors. *Bath:* combo or shower only. **Parking:** [BP] meal plan available, 15% service charge. **Amenities:** high-speed Internet (fee), voice mail, irons, hair dryers. **Pool(s):** heated outdoor. **Leisure Activities:** whirlpool, exercise room. **Guest Services:** valet and coin laundry. **Business Services:** meeting rooms, fax (fee). **Cards:** AX, DC, DS, MC, VI.

SOME UNITS

🍴 🛗 🐾 🐕 📶 DATA PORT 💻 / ✕ 🛗 📷 /

HAMPTON INN
SAVE
▼▼▼▼

Small-scale Hotel

Phone: (972)234-5400 **210**
All Year — 1P: $59 — 2P: $69
Location: US 75, exit 26 (Campbell Rd), 0.4 mi s on access road, just w, then 0.5 mi s. 1577 Gateway Blvd 75080. Fax: 972/234-8942. **Facility:** 130 one-bedroom standard units. 4 stories, interior corridors. *Bath:* combo or shower only. **Parking:** on-site. **Terms:** cancellation fee imposed. **Amenities:** video games (fee), voice mail, irons, hair dryers. **Pool(s):** outdoor. **Guest Services:** valet laundry, area transportation. **Business Services:** meeting rooms, fax (fee). **Cards:** AX, DC, DS, MC, VI.

SOME UNITS

🛎️ 🐕 🍴 🛗 🐾 🐾 📶 DATA PORT 💻 / ✕ /

HOLIDAY INN SELECT
▼▼▼

Small-scale Hotel

Leisure Activities: sauna, exercise room. Guest Services: valet and coin laundry. Business Services: meeting rooms, business center. Cards: AX, CB, DC, DS, JC, MC, VI.

Phone: (972)238-1900 **209**
All Year — 1P: $89-$129 — 2P: $89-$129
Location: 1.5 mi n on US 75; 0.3 mi s of jct SR 5 (Campbell Rd), exit 26. 1655 N Central Expwy 75080. Fax: 972/644-7728. **Facility:** 219 one-bedroom standard units. 6 stories, interior corridors. **Parking:** on-site. **Amenities:** high-speed Internet, dual phone lines, voice mail, irons, hair dryers. **Pool(s):** heated indoor.

SOME UNITS

(ASK) 🛎️ 🍴 🍸 📶 🐾 📶 DATA PORT 💻 / ✕ 🛗 /

OMNI RICHARDSON HOTEL
▼▼▼▼

Large-scale Hotel

voice mail, irons, hair dryers. Pool(s): heated outdoor. Leisure Activities: sauna, whirlpool, exercise room. Fee: massage. Guest Services: gift shop, valet laundry, area transportation. Business Services: meeting rooms, business center. Cards: AX, CB, DC, MC, VI.

Phone: (972)231-9600 **206**
All Year — 1P: $62-$107 — 2P: $72-$117 — XP: $10 — F18
Location: I-75, exit 26 (Campbell Rd) southbound; northbound, on access road. 701 E Campbell Rd 75081. Fax: 972/907-2578. **Facility:** 342 units. 340 one-bedroom standard units. 2 one-bedroom suites ($300-$500), some with whirlpools. 17 stories, interior corridors. **Parking:** on-site. **Amenities:** high-speed Internet (fee),

SOME UNITS

(ASK) 🛎️ 🍴 🍸 📶 🐾 ✕ 📶 DATA PORT 💻 / ✕ 🛗 📷 /

THE RADISSON HOTEL DALLAS NORTH AT RICHARDSON
AAA SAVE
▼▼▼▼

Large-scale Hotel

rooms, business center. Cards: AX, CB, DC, DS, JC, MC, VI. Special Amenities: early check-in/late check-out and free newspaper.

Phone: (972)644-4000 **205**
All Year — 1P: $62-$79 — 2P: $72-$92 — XP: $10 — F18
Location: 1.8 mi n on US 75, at jct SR 5, exit 26 (Campbell Rd). 1981 N Central Expwy 75080. Fax: 972/644-1079. **Facility:** 296 one-bedroom standard units. 12 stories, interior corridors. *Bath:* combo or shower only. **Parking:** on-site. **Amenities:** video games (fee), dual phone lines, voice mail, safes, irons, hair dryers. **Dining:** 6 am-11 pm, Sat & Sun from 7 am, cocktails. **Pool(s):** outdoor. **Leisure Activities:** saunas. **Guest Services:** complimentary evening beverages: Wed, valet and coin laundry. **Business Services:** meeting

SOME UNITS

🛎️ 🍴 🍸 🛗 🐕 📶 🐾 🐾 📶 DATA PORT 💻 / ✕ 🛗 📷 /

(See map p. 236)

RENAISSANCE DALLAS-RICHARDSON HOTEL
Phone: (972)367-2000 **201**

AAA SAVE

▼▼▼▼ ▼▼▼▼

Large-scale Hotel

All Year   1P: $135-$249   2P: $145-$259   XP: $10   F18
Location: US 75, exit 26 (Campbell Rd), e to Glenville Dr, 0.8 mi n to Lookout Dr, then just w. 900 E Lookout Dr 75082. Fax: 972/367-3333. **Facility:** Ultra contemporary, with an atrium-style design featuring jewel-tone colors and sculpted furnishings, this hotel is on the Dallas light-rail line. 336 units. 302 one-bedroom standard units. 34 one-bedroom suites, some with whirlpools. 12 stories, interior corridors. *Bath:* combo or shower only. **Parking:** on-site (fee). **Terms:** package plans, small pets only. **Amenities:** video games (fee), dual phone lines, voice mail, irons, hair dryers. *Some:* high-speed Internet. **Dining:** 2 restaurants, 6:30 am-2 & 5:30-10 pm, cocktails. **Pool(s):** heated indoor. **Leisure Activities:** sauna, whirlpool, jogging. *Fee:* massage. **Guest Services:** gift shop, valet and coin laundry, area transportation-within 5 mi. **Business Services:** conference facilities, business center. **Cards:** AX, CB, DC, DS, JC, MC, VI. **Special Amenities:** free newspaper. *(See color ad p 256)*

SOME UNITS

RESIDENCE INN BY MARRIOTT RICHARDSON
Phone: (972)669-5888 **202**

SAVE

▼▼▼▼

Condominium

All Year   1P: $99-$119   2P: $119-$159
Location: US 75, exit 26 (Campbell Rd), e to Greenville Ave, then just n. 1040 Waterwood Dr 75082. Fax: 972/669-2338. **Facility:** 120 units. 36 one-bedroom standard units with efficiencies. 60 one- and 24 two-bedroom suites with kitchens. 3 stories, interior corridors. *Bath:* combo or shower only. **Parking:** on-site. **Terms:** [BP] meal plan available, pets ($8 extra charge). **Amenities:** voice mail, irons, hair dryers. **Pool(s):** small heated outdoor. **Leisure Activities:** whirlpool, exercise room, sports court. **Guest Services:** complimentary evening beverages: Mon-Thurs, valet and coin laundry, area transportation. **Business Services:** meeting rooms, fax (fee). **Cards:** AX, DC, DS, JC, MC, VI.

SOME UNITS

SLEEP INN
Phone: (972)470-9440 **203**

SAVE

▼▼

Small-scale Hotel

All Year   1P: $55   2P: $59
Location: US 75, exit 27 northbound; exit 26 southbound, 0.8 mi n on access road. 2458 N Central Expwy 75080. Fax: 972/470-0996. **Facility:** 65 one-bedroom standard units. 2 stories, interior corridors. *Bath:* combo or shower only. **Parking:** on-site. **Terms:** weekly rates available, [CP] meal plan available. **Amenities:** voice mail, irons, hair dryers. **Leisure Activities:** limited exercise equipment. **Guest Services:** coin laundry. **Business Services:** fax (fee). **Cards:** AX, CB, DC, DS, JC, MC, VI.

SOME UNITS

------- **WHERE TO DINE** -------

HONG KONG ROYALE SEAFOOD RESTAURANT
Lunch: $7-$17   Dinner: $7-$17   Phone: 972/238-8888 **157**

▼▼▼

Chinese

Location: US 75, exit 23 (Spring Valley Rd), just e, 0.7 mi n on access road. 221 W Polk St 75081. **Hours:** 11 am-10 pm, Fri-11 pm, Sat 10 am-11 pm, Sun 10 am-10 pm. **Features:** Located off the busy highway on the second floor of a group of Oriental restaurants and oriental grocery area, you'll find this popular spot. The service is welcoming and gracious. Authentic Japanese cuisine is served with such choices as kung pao chicken, moo goo chicken, vermicelli cantonese, Szechuan cabbage and young chow fried rice. The sweet and sour chicken is definitely worth a try! Smoke free premises. Casual dress; beer & wine only. **Parking:** on-site. **Cards:** AX, DS, MC, VI.

SPRING CREEK BARBEQUE
Lunch: $5-$10   Dinner: $7-$10   Phone: 972/669-0505 **159**

▼▼

Regional American

Location: US 75, exit 24 southbound; exit 23 northbound on northbound access road; between Belt Line and Arapaho rds. 270 N Central Expwy 75201. **Hours:** 11 am-9 pm, Fri & Sat-10 pm. Closed: 11/27, 12/25. **Features:** Expect Texas-style barbecue at its simple, homey best. Hickory smoked ribs, beef, pork and turkey lace the air with a spicy aroma that mingles with the scent of freshly baked rolls and cold ice cream slowly melting over a dish of homemade peach cobbler. Casual dress. **Parking:** on-site. **Cards:** AX, DS, MC, VI.

ROANOKE pop. 2,810

------- **WHERE TO STAY** -------

COMFORT SUITES ROANOKE
Phone: (817)490-1455

SAVE

▼▼▼

Small-scale Hotel

All Year [CP]   1P: $60-$300   2P: $60-$300   XP: $10   F18
Location: I-35, exit 70 (SR 114), 3.4 mi e, exit Rufe/Snow, just se. 801 W Hwy 114 Business 76262. Fax: 817/490-1280. **Facility:** 88 one-bedroom standard units, some with whirlpools. 3 stories, interior corridors. *Bath:* combo or shower only. **Parking:** on-site. **Terms:** small pets only ($10 fee). **Amenities:** voice mail, irons, hair dryers. **Pool(s):** outdoor. **Leisure Activities:** whirlpool, exercise room. **Business Services:** meeting rooms, fax (fee). **Cards:** AX, DC, DS, MC, VI.

SOME UNITS

SPEEDWAY SLEEP INN & SUITES
Phone: (817)491-3120

AAA SAVE

▼▼▼

Small-scale Hotel

All Year [ECP]   1P: $64-$100   2P: $64-$100   XP: $10   F18
Location: I-35 W, exit 70, just e on SR 114, then just s. 13471 Raceway Dr 76262. Fax: 817/491-3124. **Facility:** 78 one-bedroom standard units, some with whirlpools. 3 stories, interior corridors. *Bath:* combo or shower only. **Parking:** on-site. **Terms:** 2 night minimum stay - summer, weekly rates available, package plans - seasonal, small pets only ($100 deposit). **Amenities:** voice mail, irons, hair dryers. *Some:* irons. **Pool(s):** outdoor. **Leisure Activities:** exercise room. **Guest Services:** coin laundry. **Business Services:** meeting rooms, fax (fee). **Cards:** AX, CB, DC, DS, JC, MC, VI. **Special Amenities:** free continental breakfast and free newspaper.

SOME UNITS

------- **WHERE TO DINE** -------

PRAIRIE HOUSE
Lunch: $6-$16   Dinner: $8-$23   Phone: 817/491-4855

▼▼

American

Location: Jct SR 114, 1 mi s. 304 S Hwy 377 76262. **Hours:** 11 am-9 pm, Fri & Sat-10 pm. Closed major holidays. **Features:** Frontier cooking best describes such dishes as chicken-fried chicken, steaks, barbecued meats and grilled catfish. Cobbler of the day is a tasty finish to any meal. Casual dress; cocktails. **Parking:** on-site. **Cards:** AX, DC, MC, VI.

ROCKWALL pop. 17,976

------ WHERE TO STAY ------

HOLIDAY INN EXPRESS HOTEL & SUITES   Phone: 972/722-3265

4/1-8/31	1P: $75-$130	2P: $75-$130	XP: $5	F18
2/1-3/31	1P: $74-$99	2P: $74-$99	XP: $5	F18
9/1-11/30	1P: $70-$99	2P: $70-$99	XP: $5	F18
12/1-1/31	1P: $69-$99	2P: $69-$99	XP: $5	F18

Small-scale Hotel

Location: I-30, exit 68, just w on westbound frontage road. 996 E I-30 75087. Fax: 972/722-3285. **Facility:** 60 units. 59 one-bedroom standard units, some with whirlpools. 1 one-bedroom suite ($80-$130) with whirlpool. 3 stories, interior corridors. *Bath:* combo or shower only. **Parking:** on-site. **Terms:** [ECP] meal plan available. **Amenities:** dual phone lines, voice mail, irons, hair dryers. **Pool(s):** small heated outdoor. **Leisure Activities:** whirlpool, exercise room. **Guest Services:** valet laundry. **Business Services:** meeting rooms, fax. **Cards:** AX, DC, DS, MC, VI. *(See color ad below)*

SOME UNITS

ASK SD TI+ (+) 2+ ** DATA PORT 8 @ @ /X/

------ WHERE TO DINE ------

CULPEPPER CATTLE CO   **Lunch:** $7-$11   **Dinner:** $14-$26   Phone: 972/771-1001

Steak House

Location: I-30, exit 67 (Ridge Rd) westbound, 1 mi to Horizon Rd, on access road south; exit 67A (Horizon Rd) eastbound. 309 E I-30 75087. **Hours:** 11 am-10 pm, Fri & Sat-11 pm. **Closed:** 11/27, 12/25. **Reservations:** suggested. **Features:** This popular steak house is located on the edge of the metro-plex. Features live jazz music on the weekends. Steaks and other grilled specialties are served in a rustic mountain-type lodge setting. Casual dress; cocktails. **Parking:** on-site. **Cards:** AX, CB, DC, DS, MC, VI.

Y X

ROWLETT pop. 44,503

------ WHERE TO STAY ------

COMFORT SUITES LAKE RAY HUBBARD   Phone: (972)463-9595

AAA SAVE   All Year   1P: $80   2P: $80   XP: $8   F

Location: I-30, exit 64 (Dalrock Rd). 8701 E I-30 75088. Fax: 972/463-9229. **Facility:** 62 units. 61 one-bedroom standard units, some with whirlpools. 1 one-bedroom suite ($80-$149) with whirlpool. 3 stories, interior corridors. *Bath:* combo or shower only. **Parking:** on-site. **Terms:** weekly rates available. **Amenities:** dual phone Small-scale Hotel lines, safes, irons, hair dryers. **Pool(s):** outdoor. **Leisure Activities:** exercise room. **Guest Services:** valet and coin laundry. **Business Services:** meeting rooms, business center. **Cards:** AX, DC, DS, JC, MC, VI. **Special Amenities:** free continental breakfast and free room upgrade (subject to availability with advanced reservations).

SOME UNITS

SD (+M) (+) 2+ ** DATA PORT 8 @ @ /X/

TERRELL pop. 13,606

------ WHERE TO STAY ------

BEST INN   Phone: (972)563-2676

AAA SAVE

5/1-10/31 [ECP]	1P: $45-$50	2P: $50-$55	XP: $5	F12
2/1-4/30 & 11/1-1/31 [ECP]	1P: $40-$45	2P: $45-$50	XP: $5	F12

Motel

Location: Jct I-20 and SR 34, exit 501. 309 I-20 E 75160. Fax: 972/563-7448. **Facility:** 60 one-bedroom standard units. 2 stories, exterior corridors. **Parking:** on-site. **Terms:** small pets only ($5 extra charge). **Pool(s):** outdoor. **Guest Services:** coin laundry. **Business Services:** fax (fee). **Cards:** AX, CB, DC, DS, JC, MC, VI. **Special Amenities:** free continental breakfast and free local telephone calls.

SOME UNITS

SD (+) TI+ 2+ ** DATA PORT @ /X 8 @/

COMFORT INN

AAA SAVE
◆◆◆◆

Small-scale Hotel

Phone: (972)524-5590

All Year [ECP]   1P: $69-$150   2P: $69-$150   XP: $6   F18
Location: I-20, exit 501, just nw of jct I-20 and SR 34. 103 Mira Pl 75160. Fax: 972/524-5591. **Facility:** 50 one-bedroom standard units, some with whirlpools. 2 stories, interior corridors. **Parking:** on-site.
Amenities: irons, hair dryers. **Pool(s):** outdoor. **Leisure Activities:** whirlpool, exercise room. **Guest Services:** coin laundry. **Business Services:** meeting rooms, fax (fee). **Cards:** AX, CB, DC, DS, JC, MC, VI.
Special Amenities: free continental breakfast and free local telephone calls.

SOME UNITS

[icons]

WAXAHACHIE pop. 21,426

———— **WHERE TO STAY** ————

BEST WESTERN GINGERBREAD INN

AAA SAVE
◆◆ ◆◆

Small-scale Hotel

Phone: (972)937-4202

All Year [ECP]   1P: $62   2P: $69   XP: $7   F18
Location: I-35 E and US 287 business route, 1.8 mi s of jct US 287, exit 401B. 200 N I-35 E 75165. Fax: 972/923-0611. **Facility:** 60 one-bedroom standard units. 2 stories, exterior corridors. **Parking:** on-site. **Terms:** small pets only. **Amenities:** irons, hair dryers. **Pool(s):** outdoor. **Guest Services:** coin laundry. **Business Services:** meeting rooms, fax (fee). **Cards:** AX, CB, DC, DS, MC, VI. **Special Amenities:** free continental breakfast and free newspaper.

SOME UNITS

[icons]

SUPER 8 MOTEL

◆◆◆ ◆◆◆

Small-scale Hotel

Phone: (972)938-9088

All Year   1P: $60   2P: $75   XP: $5   F17
Location: I-35 E, exit 401B. 400 I-35 E 75165. Fax: 972/923-9888. **Facility:** 38 one-bedroom standard units. 2 stories, interior corridors. **Parking:** on-site. **Terms:** weekly rates available, [CP] meal plan available. **Amenities:** *Some:* hair dryers. **Pool(s):** small outdoor. **Guest Services:** coin laundry. **Business Services:** fax (fee). **Cards:** AX, DC, DS, MC, VI.

SOME UNITS

[icons]   FEE   FEE

———— *The following lodging was either not evaluated or did not* ————
meet AAA rating requirements but is listed for your information only.

BEST VALUE CONVENTION CENTER INN & SUITES

fyi

Small-scale Hotel

Phone: 888/315-2378

Under construction, scheduled to open April 2003. **Location:** I-35 & 287. **Planned Amenities:** coffeemakers, microwaves, refrigerators, pool.

This ends listings for the Dallas Vicinity.
The following page resumes the alphabetical listings of
cities in Texas.

DALLAS NORTH —*See Dallas p. 260.*

DALLAS SOUTH —*See Dallas p. 284.*

DECATUR pop. 5,201

——— **WHERE TO STAY** ———

BEST WESTERN DECATUR INN

(AAA) [SAVE]

◆◆ (diamonds)

Motel

Phone: 940/627-5982

4/16-9/4 [ECP]	1P: $62-$90	2P: $62-$90	XP: $5 F12
2/1-4/15 & 9/5-1/31 [ECP]	1P: $57-$85	2P: $57-$85	XP: $5 F12

Location: On US 287, 0.6 mi s of jct Business SR 380. 1801 S Hwy 287 76234. Fax: 940/627-7133. **Facility:** 46 one-bedroom standard units, some with whirlpools. 1 story, exterior corridors. **Parking:** on-site. **Terms:** small pets only ($10-$20 extra charge). **Amenities:** irons, hair dryers. **Pool(s):** outdoor. **Leisure Activities:** whirlpool, playground. **Guest Services:** coin laundry. **Business Services:** meeting rooms, fax (fee). **Cards:** AX, DC, DS, MC, VI. **Special Amenities:** free continental breakfast.

SOME UNITS

(icons)

COMFORT INN

(AAA) [SAVE]

◆◆◆ (diamonds)

Small-scale Hotel

Phone: 940/627-6919

All Year	1P: $54-$90	2P: $59-$110	XP: $5 F15

Location: On US 287, 0.6 mi s of jct Business SR 380. 1709 S US 287 S 76234. **Facility:** 44 one-bedroom standard units, some with whirlpools. 2 stories, exterior corridors. **Parking:** on-site. **Terms:** [ECP] meal plan available, small pets only ($20 deposit). **Amenities:** *Some:* hair dryers. **Pool(s):** outdoor. **Leisure Activities:** whirlpool. **Guest Services:** coin laundry. **Business Services:** meeting rooms, fax (fee). **Cards:** AX, CB, DC, DS, MC, VI. **Special Amenities:** free continental breakfast and free local telephone calls.

SOME UNITS

(icons) FEE

DEER PARK —*See Houston p. 437.*

DEL RIO pop. 33,867

——— **WHERE TO STAY** ———

BEST WESTERN INN OF DEL RIO

(AAA) [SAVE]

◆◆◆ (diamonds)

Small-scale Hotel

Phone: (830)775-7511

All Year	1P: $45-$60	2P: $55-$70	XP: $10 F12

Location: 0.8 mi nw on US 90, 277 and 377. 810 Ave F 78840. Fax: 830/774-2194. **Facility:** 62 one-bedroom standard units. 2 stories (no elevator), exterior corridors. **Parking:** on-site. **Terms:** [CP] meal plan available, pets ($5 extra charge). **Amenities:** irons, hair dryers. **Pool(s):** outdoor. **Leisure Activities:** whirlpool. **Guest Services:** valet and coin laundry. **Business Services:** fax (fee). **Cards:** AX, CB, DC, DS, MC, VI. **Special Amenities:** free newspaper and free room upgrade (subject to availability with advanced reservations). *(See ad below)*

SOME UNITS

(icons)

DAYS INN AND SUITES

(AAA) [SAVE]

◆◆ (diamonds)

Small-scale Hotel

Phone: (830)775-0585

All Year [ECP]	1P: $49-$59	2P: $59-$69	XP: $10 F17

Location: 3.5 mi nw on US 90. 3808 Ave F 78840. Fax: 830/775-1981. **Facility:** 95 one-bedroom suites, some with kitchens (no utensils). 2 stories (no elevator), exterior corridors. **Parking:** on-site. **Terms:** weekly rates available, small pets only ($5 extra charge). **Amenities:** voice mail, hair dryers. **Pool(s):** heated outdoor. **Leisure Activities:** whirlpool, picnic area, barbecue pit. **Guest Services:** coin laundry. **Business Services:** fax (fee). **Cards:** AX, CB, DC, DS, MC, VI. **Special Amenities:** free continental breakfast and free local telephone calls.

SOME UNITS

(icons)

HOLIDAY INN EXPRESS & SUITES

Phone: (830)775-2933

All Year   1P: $59   2P: $69   XP: $5   F18
Location: 3.2 mi nw on US 90. 3616 Ave F 78840. **Fax:** 830/775-2466. **Facility:** 60 one-bedroom standard units. 2 stories (no elevator), interior/exterior corridors. *Bath:* combo or shower only. **Parking:** on-site. **Terms:** small pets only ($10 fee). **Amenities:** irons, hair dryers. **Pool(s):** small outdoor. **Guest Services:** coin laundry.
Small-scale Hotel
Business Services: fax (fee). **Cards:** AX, CB, DC, DS, MC, VI.

SOME UNITS

LA QUINTA INNS-DEL RIO

Phone: (830)775-7591

(AAA) SAVE   All Year   1P: $59-$79   2P: $65-$85
Location: 1.8 mi nw on US 90, 277 and 377. 2005 Ave F 78840. **Fax:** 830/774-0809. **Facility:** 101 one-bedroom standard units. 2 stories (no elevator), interior/exterior corridors. *Bath:* combo or shower only. **Parking:** on-site. **Terms:** [ECP] meal plan available, small pets only. **Amenities:** video games (fee), voice mail, irons, hair dryers. **Pool(s):** outdoor. **Guest Services:** valet and coin laundry. **Business Services:** meeting rooms, fax (fee). **Cards:** AX, CB, DC, DS, JC, MC, VI. **Special Amenities:** free continental breakfast and free local telephone calls.

SOME UNITS

RAMADA INN

Phone: (830)775-1511

(AAA) SAVE   All Year   1P: $74-$104   2P: $84-$114   XP: $10   F18
Location: 1.8 mi nw on US 90, 277 and 377. 2101 Veterans Blvd 78840. **Fax:** 830/775-1476. **Facility:** 155 one-bedroom standard units. 2 stories (no elevator), interior/exterior corridors. **Parking:** on-site. **Terms:** check-in 4 pm, package plans, small pets only. **Amenities:** voice mail, irons, hair dryers. *Some:* safes. **Dining:** 6 am-3 & 5-10 pm, cocktails. **Pool(s):** heated outdoor. **Leisure Activities:** saunas, whirlpools, jogging, exercise room. **Guest Services:** valet and coin laundry, airport transportation-Del Rio Airport, area transportation.
Business Services: meeting rooms, business center. **Cards:** AX, CB, DC, DS, JC, MC, VI. **Special Amenities:** free continental breakfast and free newspaper. *(See color ad below)*

SOME UNITS

VILLA DEL RIO

Classic Historic
Bed & Breakfast

Phone: (830)768-1100
All Year 1P: $85-$175 2P: $95-$195 XP: $25
Location: US 77 to Pecan St, w to Hudson Dr. Located adjacent to the oldest Texas winery. 123 Hudson Dr 78840 (PO Box 421002, 78842). Fax: 830/775-2691. **Facility:** Regional distinctions define this home, said to be the oldest and largest in West Texas and among the first to have indoor plumbing and electricity. 4 units. 3 one- and 1 two-bedroom standard units, some with kitchens. 2 stories, interior/exterior corridors. *Bath:* some shared or private. **Parking:** on-site. **Terms:** 8 day cancellation notice-fee imposed, weekly rates available, [BP] meal plan available. **Business Services:** fax. **Cards:** AX, CB, MC, VI.

ASK ✕ 🕦 ☎

----- **WHERE TO DINE** -----

AVANTI

Italian

Lunch: $5-$18 **Dinner:** $5-$18 **Phone:** 830/775-3363
Location: US 90 W to 12th St, 1 blk n. 600 E 12th St 78840. **Hours:** 11 am-9 pm, Fri & Sat-10 pm, Sun noon-8 pm. Closed: 1/1, 11/27, 12/25. **Reservations:** suggested. **Features:** Pasta, seafood, veal and beef entrees, as well as some lighter fare, are put together in original preparations. Delicious tiramisu is made from an old family recipe. Casual dress; beer & wine only. **Parking:** on-site. **Cards:** AX, DC, DS, MC, VI.

✕

CRIPPLE CREEK SALOON

Steak House

MC, VI.

Dinner: $6-$21 **Phone:** 830/775-0153
Location: 4.5 mi nw on US 90. Hwy 90 W 78840. **Hours:** 5 pm-10 pm, Sat-11 pm. Closed major holidays; also Sun. **Features:** On four acres near Big Lake Reservoir, the restaurant offers an experience right out of the Wild West. The on-site menagerie comprises llamas, chickens, ducks and rabbits. Log cabin decor provides a fun setting for a good family meal. Casual dress; cocktails. **Parking:** on-site. **Cards:** AX,

DENTON —*See Dallas p. 290.*

DESOTO —*See Dallas p. 291.*

D'HANIS

----- **WHERE TO STAY** -----

----- *The following lodging was either not evaluated or did not* -----
meet AAA rating requirements but is listed for your information only.

J.M. KOCH'S HOTEL
fyi
Classic Bed
& Breakfast

Phone: 830/363-7500
Did not meet all AAA rating requirements for locking devices in some guest rooms at time of last evaluation on 04/08/2002. **Location:** Center of town. Main St 78850. Facilities, services, and decor characterize a mid-range property.

DIBOLL pop. 5,470

----- **WHERE TO STAY** -----

BEST WESTERN DIBOLL INN
AAA SAVE

Motel

tions).

Phone: (936)829-2055
All Year 1P: $56-$89 2P: $56-$89 XP: $6 F12
Location: 0.8 mi n on US 59 and Loop 210 and SR 1818. 910 N Temple Dr 75641. Fax: 936/829-2063. **Facility:** 40 one-bedroom standard units, some with efficiencies and/or whirlpools. 2 stories, exterior corridors. **Parking:** on-site. **Terms:** [ECP] meal plan available, small pets only. **Amenities:** irons, hair dryers. *Some:* dual phone lines. **Pool(s):** outdoor. **Business Services:** fax (fee). **Cards:** AX, CB, DC, DS, MC, VI. **Special Amenities:** early check-in/late check-out and free room upgrade (subject to availability with advanced reserva-

SOME UNITS
S/D 🐾 🌊 🎥 DATA/PORT 💻 / ✕ 🛢 🖥 /

DONNA pop. 14,768

----- **WHERE TO STAY** -----

HOWARD JOHNSON EXPRESS INN-SUITES

Small-scale Hotel

Phone: 956/464-4656
2/1-4/30	1P: $95-$100	XP: $10	F17
12/1-1/31	1P: $67-$100	XP: $10	F17
9/1-11/30	1P: $67-$69	XP: $10	F17
5/1-8/31	1P: $65-$67	XP: $10	F17

Location: US 83, exit Victoria Rd. 602 N Victoria Rd 78537. Fax: 956/782-3218. **Facility:** 120 one-bedroom standard units, some with whirlpools. 1 story, exterior corridors. **Parking:** on-site. **Terms:** weekly rates available, [CP] meal plan available. **Amenities:** dual phone lines, voice mail, safes, hair dryers. *Some:* irons. **Pool(s):** heated outdoor. **Leisure Activities:** whirlpools, 4 lighted tennis courts, exercise room. **Guest Services:** coin laundry. **Business Services:** meeting rooms, fax (fee). **Cards:** AX, DC, DS, MC, VI.

SOME UNITS
ASK S/D 🍴 🌊 ✕ 🎥 DATA/PORT 💻 / ✕ VCR 🛢 🖥 /

SUPER 8 MOTEL
AAA SAVE

Motel

Phone: 956/461-2226
All Year [CP] 1P: $45-$55 2P: $55-$65
Location: US 83, exit CR 493. 2005 E Expwy 83 78537. Fax: 956/461-2226. **Facility:** 40 one-bedroom standard units. 2 stories, interior corridors. *Bath:* combo or shower only. **Parking:** on-site. **Terms:** 7 day cancellation notice. **Amenities:** dual phone lines, hair dryers. **Pool(s):** small outdoor. **Leisure Activities:** whirlpool. **Guest Services:** coin laundry. **Business Services:** fax (fee). **Cards:** AX, CB, DC, DS, JC, MC, VI. **Special Amenities:** free continental breakfast and free local telephone calls.

SOME UNITS

S/D 🌊 🎥 DATA/PORT 🛢 🖥 / ✕ VCR /
FEE

DUBLIN pop. 3,754

—— WHERE TO STAY ——

CENTRAL INN
🔺🔺🔺 [SAVE]
▽▽ ▽▽
Motel

All Year   1P: $35-$40   2P: $40-$45   **Phone:** (254)445-2138
                                                              XP: $5   F12
Location: 1 mi n on US 67/377. 723 N Patrick 76446 (PO Box 441). Fax: 254/445-0236. **Facility:** 21 one-bedroom standard units. 1 story, exterior corridors. **Parking:** on-site. **Pool(s):** small outdoor. **Business Services:** fax (fee). **Cards:** AX, CB, DC, DS, MC, VI. **Special Amenities: free local telephone calls.**

SOME UNITS
🍴 🚲 🎦 💾 / ⊠ 🖥 /

DUMAS pop. 13,747

—— WHERE TO STAY ——

BEST WESTERN WINDSOR INN
🔺🔺🔺 [SAVE]
▽▽▽▽▽
Motel

5/15-9/15 [ECP]   1P: $69-$89   2P: $79-$99   XP: $10   F18
2/1-5/14 & 9/16-1/31 [ECP]   1P: $59-$69   2P: $69-$79   XP: $10   F18
Location: US 287, 2 mi s of US 87 and SR 152. 1701 S Dumas Ave 79029. Fax: 806/935-9730. **Facility:** 57 one-bedroom standard units. 2 stories (no elevator), exterior corridors. **Parking:** on-site. **Terms:** 5 day cancellation notice, small pets only ($5 fee). **Amenities:** irons, hair dryers. **Pool(s):** heated indoor. **Leisure Activities:** sauna, whirlpool, limited exercise equipment. **Guest Services:** coin laundry. **Business Services:** fax (fee). **Cards:** AX, DC, DS, MC, VI. **Special Amenities: free continental breakfast and free newspaper.**
(See color ad below)

SOME UNITS
🆂 🐾 🍴 🚲 ⊠ 🎦 DATA PORT 🖥 / ⊠ 💾 /

COMFORT INN OF DUMAS
🔺🔺🔺 [SAVE]
▽▽▽▽▽
Motel

5/16-9/13   1P: $78-$99   2P: $98-$99   XP: $10   F18
2/1-5/15 & 9/14-1/31   1P: $68-$75   2P: $75-$80   XP: $10   F18
Location: US 287, 1 mi s of jct US 87 and SR 152. 1620 S Dumas Ave 79029. Fax: 806/935-6924. **Facility:** 51 one-bedroom standard units, some with whirlpools. 2 stories (no elevator), interior corridors. *Bath:* combo or shower only. **Parking:** on-site, winter plug-ins. **Terms:** 5 day cancellation notice, [CP] meal plan available. **Amenities:** voice mail, irons, hair dryers. **Pool(s):** heated indoor. **Leisure Activities:** whirlpool, limited exercise equipment. **Guest Services:** coin laundry. **Business Services:** meeting rooms, fax (fee). **Cards:** AX, CB, DC, DS, JC, MC, VI. **Special Amenities: free continental breakfast and free newspaper.**

SOME UNITS
🆂 🍴 📺 🎬 🚲 🎦 DATA PORT 🖥 / ⊠ 💾 🖥 /

ECONO LODGE
🔺🔺🔺 [SAVE]
▽▽ ▽▽
Motel

5/1-8/31   1P: $56   2P: $60   XP: $5   F15
2/1-4/30 & 9/1-1/31   1P: $50   2P: $56   XP: $5   F15
Location: US 287, 2 mi s of US 87/SR 152. 1719 S Dumas Ave 79029. Fax: 806/935-7483. **Facility:** 41 one-bedroom standard units. 2 stories (no elevator), interior corridors. **Parking:** on-site. **Terms:** pets ($5 extra charge). **Guest Services:** coin laundry. **Business Services:** fax. **Cards:** AX, DC, DS, MC, VI. **Special Amenities: free continental breakfast and free local telephone calls.**

SOME UNITS
🆂 🐾 🍴 🎦 / ⊠ 💾 🖥 /

HOLIDAY INN EXPRESS
Motel

5/26-9/20 [CP]   1P: $90-$120   2P: $90-$120   XP: $10   F17
2/1-5/25 & 9/21-1/31 [CP]   1P: $70-$110   2P: $70-$110   XP: $10   F17

Phone: (806)935-4000

Location: US 87, 1.1 mi s. 1525 S Dumas Ave 79029. Fax: 806/935-9585. **Facility:** 54 one-bedroom standard units. 2 stories (no elevator), interior corridors. **Parking:** on-site. **Terms:** small pets only. **Amenities:** voice mail, irons, hair dryers. **Pool(s):** heated outdoor. **Leisure Activities:** limited exercise equipment. **Guest Services:** coin laundry. **Business Services:** meeting rooms, fax (fee). **Cards:** AX, CB, DC, DS, JC, MC, VI.

SOME UNITS

[ASK] [S/D] [🛏] [🍽↑] [🏊] [VCR] [📷] [DATA PORT] [🔌] [📺] / [✕] /

KONA KAI DUMAS INN MOTEL
Motel

All Year   1P: $65-$95   2P: $75-$95   XP: $5   F12

Phone: (806)935-6441

Location: US 287, 1.5 mi s from jct US 87/SR 152. 1712 S Dumas Ave 79029. Fax: 806/935-9331. **Facility:** 100 one-bedroom standard units. 2 stories (no elevator), interior/exterior corridors. **Parking:** on-site. **Terms:** pets ($20 deposit). **Pool(s):** heated indoor. **Leisure Activities:** whirlpool. **Business Services:** meeting rooms.
Cards: AX, DC, DS, MC, VI.

SOME UNITS

[ASK] [S/D] [🛏] [Y] [🏊] [VCR] [📷] / [✕] [🔌] [📺] [📺] /
                                              FEE   FEE

SUPER 8 MOTEL
[AAA] [SAVE]
Motel

All Year [CP]   1P: $59-$79   2P: $69-$79   XP: $10   F12

Phone: (806)935-6222

Location: US 287, 2 mi s of jct US 87/SR 152. 119 W 17th St 79029. Fax: 806/935-6222. **Facility:** 26 one-bedroom standard units. 2 stories (no elevator), exterior corridors. **Parking:** on-site. **Terms:** small pets only ($10 fee). **Amenities:** irons, hair dryers. **Business Services:** fax (fee). **Cards:** AX, CB, DC, DS, MC, VI. **Special Amenities:** free continental breakfast and free local telephone calls. *(See color ad below)*

SOME UNITS

[S/D] [🛏] [🍽↑] [VCR] [📷] [DATA PORT] [🔌] [📺] / [✕] /

May I Take Your Order Please?

When you look through a AAA TourBook® guide in search of a place to dine while traveling, **look for restaurants that advertise**. These establishments are committed to increasing their AAA patronage, and are willing to go the extra mile to capture your attention ... and your appetite!

―――― **WHERE TO DINE** ――――

K-BOB'S

American

Lunch: $5-$15 **Dinner:** $5-$15 **Phone:** 806/935-6823
Location: 1.5 mi s from jct US 87/SR 152. 1800 S Dumas Ave 79029. **Hours:** 11 am-9 pm, Fri & Sat-9:30 pm. Closed major holidays; also Sun. **Features:** The steakhouse offers a great variety of plump, juicy filets. A fireplace opens up into both dining rooms, and antique clocks decorate the walls. Rustic wagon-wheel chandeliers illuminate the room. Casual dress. **Parking:** on-site. **Cards:** AX, DS, MC, VI.

DUNCANVILLE —See Dallas p. 292.

EAGLE PASS pop. 22,413

―――― **WHERE TO STAY** ――――

BEST WESTERN

Small-scale Hotel

Phone: (830)758-1234
All Year 1P: $70-$80 2P: $70-$80 XP: $6 F16
Location: US 57 and jct Loop 431 (US 277). 1923 Loop 431 78852. Fax: 830/758-1235. **Facility:** 40 one-bedroom standard units. 2 stories (no elevator), exterior corridors. **Parking:** on-site. **Terms:** [ECP] meal plan available, small pets only. **Amenities:** dual phone lines, irons, hair dryers. **Pool(s):** outdoor. **Guest Services:** valet and coin laundry. **Business Services:** meeting rooms, fax (fee). **Cards:** AX, CB, DC, DS, MC, VI.
Special Amenities: free continental breakfast and free room upgrade (subject to availability with advanced reservations).

SOME UNITS

HAMPTON INN EAGLE PASS

Small-scale Hotel

Phone: (830)757-5565
All Year [CP] 1P: $79 2P: $84 XP: $5 F18
Location: Just e of jct US 57 and 277. 3301 E Main St 78852. Fax: 830/757-5512. **Facility:** 65 one-bedroom standard units, some with whirlpools. 3 stories, interior corridors. *Bath:* combo or shower only. **Parking:** on-site. **Amenities:** video games (fee), dual phone lines, voice mail, irons, hair dryers. **Pool(s):** outdoor. **Leisure Activities:** limited exercise equipment. **Guest Services:** valet and coin laundry. **Business Services:** meeting rooms, business center. **Cards:** AX, CB, DC, DS, MC, VI.

SOME UNITS

HOLIDAY INN EXPRESS HOTEL & SUITES

Small-scale Hotel

Phone: (830)757-3050
All Year 1P: $80-$88 2P: $80-$88 XP: $6 F17
Location: 1.5 mi n on Loop 431 (US 277). 2007 Loop 431 78852. Fax: 830/757-3774. **Facility:** 66 one-bedroom standard units. 3 stories, interior corridors. *Bath:* combo or shower only. **Parking:** on-site. **Terms:** [ECP] meal plan available, small pets only. **Amenities:** dual phone lines, voice mail, irons, hair dryers. **Pool(s):** heated outdoor. **Leisure Activities:** whirlpool, exercise room. **Guest Services:** valet laundry. **Business Services:** meeting rooms, business center. **Cards:** AX, CB, DC, DS, MC, VI.

SOME UNITS

LA QUINTA INN-EAGLE PASS

Small-scale Hotel

Phone: (830)773-7000
All Year 1P: $69-$89 2P: $75-$95
Location: US 57 and 277 at jct Loop 431. 2525 E Main St 78852-4498. Fax: 830/773-8852. **Facility:** 129 one-bedroom standard units. 2 stories (no elevator), exterior corridors. **Parking:** on-site. **Terms:** [ECP] meal plan available, small pets only. **Amenities:** video games (fee), voice mail, irons, hair dryers. **Pool(s):** outdoor. **Guest Services:** valet and coin laundry. **Business Services:** meeting rooms, fax (fee). **Cards:** AX, CB, DC, DS, JC, MC, VI. **Special Amenities:** free continental breakfast and free local telephone calls.

SOME UNITS

SUPER 8 MOTEL

Small-scale Hotel

Phone: (830)773-9531
All Year 1P: $54-$60 2P: $54-$60 XP: $6 F16
Location: 4 mi n on US 277. 2150 N US Hwy 277 78852. Fax: 830/773-9535. **Facility:** 56 one-bedroom standard units. 2 stories (no elevator), exterior corridors. **Parking:** on-site. **Terms:** weekly rates available, small pets only. **Pool(s):** outdoor. **Business Services:** fax (fee). **Cards:** AX, CB, DC, DS, MC, VI.

SOME UNITS

EARLY pop. 2,588

―――― **WHERE TO STAY** ――――

POST OAK INN

Motel

Phone: 325/643-5621
All Year 1P: $55 2P: $65 XP: $5 F6
Location: On SR 377 at jct Northline. 606 Early Blvd 76802. Fax: 325/643-3409. **Facility:** 40 one-bedroom standard units. 1 story, exterior corridors. **Parking:** on-site. **Terms:** cancellation fee imposed, pets ($3 extra charge). **Amenities:** hair dryers. **Pool(s):** outdoor. **Business Services:** fax (fee). **Cards:** AX, DS, MC, VI. **Special Amenities:** free continental breakfast and free local telephone calls.

SOME UNITS

EASTLAND pop. 3,769

------ WHERE TO STAY ------

BUDGET HOST
AAA SAVE
Motel

Phone: 254/629-3324

All Year · 1P: $43-$47 · 2P: $55-$60 · XP: $5 · F12
Location: I-20, exit 343, on south service road. 2001 I-20 W 76448. Fax: 254/629-8601. **Facility:** 46 one-bedroom standard units. 1 story, exterior corridors. *Bath:* combo or shower only. **Parking:** on-site. **Terms:** weekly rates available, [CP] meal plan available, small pets only ($10 fee). **Pool(s):** outdoor. **Business Services:** fax (fee). **Cards:** AX, DC, DS, MC, VI. *(See color ad p 162)*

SOME UNITS

THE EASTLAND
Bed & Breakfast
MC, VI.

Phone: 254/629-8397

All Year · 1P: $70-$90 · 2P: $70-$90
Location: I-20, exit 343, 1.7 mi n to Lamar St, just e; downtown. 112 N Lamar St 76448. Fax: 254/629-8994. **Facility:** Charming 1918 brick building. Smoke free premises. 6 one-bedroom standard units. 3 stories (no elevator), interior corridors. **Parking:** street. **Business Services:** meeting rooms, fax. **Cards:** AX, DS, MC, VI.

SUPER 8 MOTEL & RV PARK
Motel
MC, VI.

Phone: (254)629-3336

All Year [CP] · 1P: $49-$54 · 2P: $59-$69 · XP: $5 · F10
Location: I-20, exit 343, on north service road. 3900 I-20 E 76448. Fax: 254/629-3338. **Facility:** 30 one-bedroom standard units, some with whirlpools. 1 story, exterior corridors. **Parking:** on-site. **Terms:** pets ($3 extra charge). **Amenities:** hair dryers. **Pool(s):** outdoor. **Business Services:** fax (fee). **Cards:** AX, CB, DC, DS,

SOME UNITS

EDINBURG pop. 48,465

------ WHERE TO STAY ------

------ *The following lodging was either not evaluated or did not* ------
meet AAA rating requirements but is listed for your information only.

COMFORT INN EDINBURG
fyi
Motel

Phone: 956/318-1117

All Year · 1P: $79-$89 · XP: $10 · F16
Too new to rate. **Location:** I-281, exit Trenton. 4001 Closner Blvd 78539. **Amenities:** coffeemakers, microwaves, refrigerators, pool. **Cards:** AX, DC, DS, JC, MC, VI.

EL CAMPO pop. 10,945

------ WHERE TO STAY ------

SHONEY'S INN & SUITES
Motel
MC, VI.

Phone: 979/543-1666

All Year [CP] · 1P: $59-$65 · 2P: $65-$70 · XP: $6 · F15
Location: US 59, exit SR 71 on southbound access road. 310 W Hwy 59 77437. Fax: 979/543-1183. **Facility:** 50 one-bedroom standard units, some with whirlpools. 2 stories (no elevator), exterior corridors. *Bath:* combo or shower only. **Parking:** on-site. **Amenities:** irons, hair dryers. **Pool(s):** outdoor. **Leisure Activities:** whirlpool, exercise room. **Guest Services:** valet and coin laundry. **Business Services:** meeting rooms, fax (fee). **Cards:** AX, DC, DS,

SOME UNITS

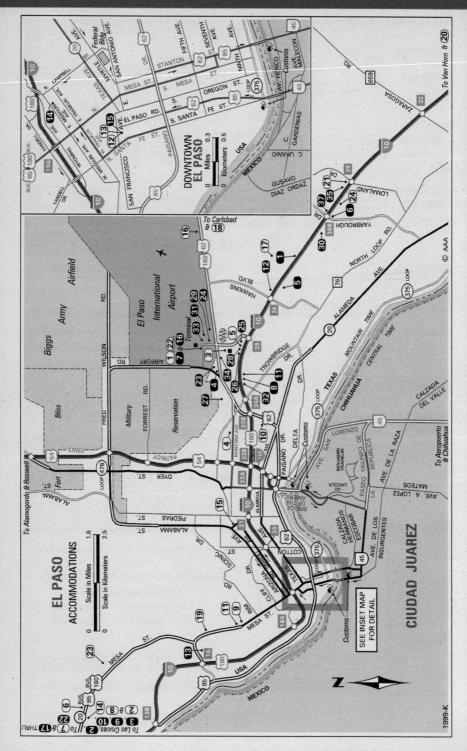

EL PASO
ACCOMMODATIONS

Scale in Miles
0   1.6
Scale in Kilometers
0   2.5

DOWNTOWN
EL PASO

Miles   0.3   0.5
0   Kilometers   0.5

CIUDAD JUAREZ

1999-K

© AAA

✈ Airport Accommodations

Spotter/Map Page Number	OA	EL PASO INTERNATIONAL	Diamond Rating	Rate Range High Season	Listing Page
24 / p. 326		Chase Suites by Woodfin, 0.8 mi s of terminal	▼▼▼	$79-$170	330
29 / p. 326		El Paso Marriott Hotel, 0.8 mi s of terminal	▼▼▼	$165	332
31 / p. 326		Hawthorn Inn & Suites, 0.5 mi s of terminal	▼▼▼	$79-$109	333
7 / p. 326		Hilton El Paso Airport, just s of terminal	▼▼▼	$114-$123	333
33 / p. 326		Radisson Suite Inn El Paso Airport, 0.5 mi s of terminal	▼▼▼	$139-$179	335

El Paso

This index helps you "spot" where approved accommodations and restaurants are located on the corresponding detailed maps. Lodging rate ranges are for comparison only and show the property's high season; rates are per night, unless only weekly (W) rates are available. Restaurant rate range is for dinner, unless only lunch (L) is served. Turn to the listing page for more detailed rate information and consult display ads for special promotions.

Spotter/Map Page Number	OA	EL PASO - Lodgings	Diamond Rating	Rate Range High Season	Listing Page
1 / p. 326	ⓐⓐⓐ	La Quinta Inn-El Paso-Cielo Vista - see color ad p 334	▼▼▼	$66-$75 [SAVE]	334
2 / p. 326	ⓐⓐⓐ	Holiday Inn Sunland Park - see color ad p 333	▼▼▼	$88-$102 [SAVE]	333
3 / p. 326	ⓐⓐⓐ	Best Western Sunland Park Inn - see color ad p 330	▼▼▼	$49-$99 [SAVE]	330
4 / p. 326	ⓐⓐⓐ	Econo Lodge	▼▼	$50-$65 [SAVE]	332
5 / p. 326	ⓐⓐⓐ	Best Western Airport Inn	▼▼▼	$59-$78 [SAVE]	330
6 / p. 326		Comfort Inn Airport East - see color ad p 331	▼▼▼	$59-$94	330
7 / p. 326		Hilton El Paso Airport	▼▼▼	$114-$123	333
8 / p. 326		Embassy Suites Hotel	▼▼▼	$89-$149	332
9 / p. 326		Comfort Suites	▼▼▼	$69-$99	331
10 / p. 326		Sleep Inn	▼▼	$55-$85	335
11 / p. 326	ⓐⓐⓐ	La Quinta Inn-El Paso-Airport - see color ad p 334	▼▼▼	$62-$85 [SAVE]	334
12 / p. 326		Howard Johnson Inn	▼▼	$57-$72	334
13 / p. 326	ⓐⓐⓐ	Executive Inn & Suites - see color ad p 332	▼▼	$40-$60 [SAVE]	332
14 / p. 326	ⓐⓐⓐ	Travelodge Hotel El Paso City Center	▼▼	$54-$84 [SAVE]	335
15 / p. 326		Camino Real Hotel, El Paso	▼▼▼	$99-$174	330
16 / p. 326		Microtel Inn & Suites	▼▼	$50-$77	335
17 / p. 326	ⓐⓐⓐ	La Quinta Inn-El Paso-West - see color ad p 334	▼▼▼	$63-$80 [SAVE]	335
18 / p. 326	ⓐⓐⓐ	Baymont Inn & Suites El Paso West	▼▼▼	$49-$64 [SAVE]	330
19 / p. 326	ⓐⓐⓐ	Travelodge	▼▼▼	$39-$83 [SAVE]	335
20 / p. 326		Comfort Inn West	▼▼	$58-$74	331
21 / p. 326		Days Inn	▼▼▼	$55-$70	331
22 / p. 326	ⓐⓐⓐ	Red Roof Inn West	▼▼	$36-$58 [SAVE]	335
23 / p. 326	ⓐⓐⓐ	Travelodge La Hacienda Airport	▼▼	$53-$67 [SAVE]	336
24 / p. 326		Chase Suites by Woodfin	▼▼▼	$79-$170	330
25 / p. 326		Holiday Inn-Airport	▼▼▼	Failed to provide	333
26 / p. 326		El Paso Airport Courtyard by Marriott	▼▼▼	$119-$159	332

Spotter/Map Page Number	OA	EL PASO - Lodgings (continued)	Diamond Rating	Rate Range High Season	Listing Page
27 / p. 326		Ramada Inn & Suites	◇◇◇	$55-$67	335
28 / p. 326		Hampton Inn & Suites	◇◇◇	$99-$134	333
29 / p. 326		El Paso Marriott Hotel	◇◇◇	$165	332
30 / p. 326	AAA	Baymont Inn & Suites El Paso East - see color ad p 329	◇◇◇	$54-$69 [SAVE]	329
31 / p. 326		Hawthorn Inn & Suites	◇◇◇	$79-$109	333
32 / p. 326	AAA	AmeriSuites (El Paso/Airport) - see color ad p 329	◇◇◇	$113 [SAVE]	329
33 / p. 326		Radisson Suite Inn El Paso Airport	◇◇◇	$139-$179	335
34 / p. 326	AAA	Coral Motel	◇	$36-$48 [SAVE]	331
35 / p. 326		La Quinta Inn-El Paso-Lomaland - see color ad p 334	◇◇◇	$55-$68	334
37 / p. 326	AAA	Days Inn	◇◇	$42-$72 [SAVE]	331
		EL PASO - Restaurants			
1 / p. 326		Canarozzo's	◇◇◇	$8-$22	336
2 / p. 326		Meili's Garden Restaurant & Lounge	◇◇	$7-$9	338
3 / p. 326		Dominguez Mexican Food	◇	$5-$11	337
4 / p. 326		Leo's Mexican Food	◇	$6-$9	337
5 / p. 326		Jaxon's Restaurant & Brewery	◇◇	$6-$15	337
6 / p. 326		Avila's Mexican Restaurant (West)	◇◇	$5-$10	336
7 / p. 326	AAA	Hudson's Grill	◇◇	$6-$9	337
8 / p. 326		State Line Steaks & Barbecue	◇◇	$9-$21	338
9 / p. 326		Casa Jurado	◇◇	$5-$14	336
10 / p. 326		Forti's Mexican Elder Restaurant	◇◇	$7-$15	337
11 / p. 326		Ardovino's	◇	$5-$15	336
12 / p. 326		The Dome Restaurant	◇◇◇	$17-$30	337
13 / p. 326		Azulejos Restaurant	◇◇◇	$10-$17	336
14 / p. 326		Bella Napoli	◇◇	$7-$14	336
15 / p. 326		Cappeto's Italian Restaurant	◇◇	$6-$14	336
16 / p. 326		Senor Juan's Griggs	◇◇	$5-$11	338
17 / p. 326		Smokey's Pit Stop & Saloon	◇	$5-$8	338
18 / p. 326		Avila's Mexican Food Restaurant (East)	◇◇	$6-$9	336
19 / p. 326		Como's Italian Restaurant	◇◇	$6-$13	337
20 / p. 326	AAA	Cattleman's Steak House	◇◇◇	$11-$38	337
21 / p. 326		Gunther's Edelweiss	◇◇	$5-$14	337
22 / p. 326		Magnim's	◇◇	$11-$24	338
23 / p. 326		Uncle Bao's	◇◇	$6-$15	339
24 / p. 326	AAA	Julio's Cafe Corona Restaurant	◇◇	$6-$16	337

EL PASO pop. 563,662 (See map p. 326; index p. 327)

———— **WHERE TO STAY** ————

AMERISUITES (EL PASO/AIRPORT)   Phone: (915)771-0022   **32**
(AAA) (SAVE)   All Year [ECP]   1P: $113   2P: $113   XP: $10   F18
▼▼▼▼   **Location:** I-10, exit 24B (Geronimo St) westbound, 0.6 mi to Trowbridge, U-turn under interstate, then just e. 6030 Gateway Blvd E 79905. Fax: 915/771-0599. **Facility:** 113 one-bedroom standard units. 6 stories, interior corridors. *Bath:* combo or shower only. **Parking:** on-site. **Terms:** 5 day cancellation notice, weekly rates available,
Small-scale Hotel   small pets only ($50 deposit). **Amenities:** voice mail, irons, hair dryers. **Pool(s):** outdoor. **Leisure Activities:** exercise room. **Guest Services:** coin laundry, area transportation-within 3 mi. **Business Services:** meeting rooms, fax (fee). **Cards:** AX, CB, DC, DS, JC, MC, VI. **Special Amenities:** free continental breakfast and free newspaper. *(See color ad below)*   SOME UNITS

(S/D) ✈ 🛏 🍴 (&M) (&) 📷 🏊 🎥 DATA-PORT 🔌 📺 📠 /✕/

BAYMONT INN & SUITES EL PASO EAST   Phone: (915)591-3300   **30**
(AAA) (SAVE)   All Year [ECP]   1P: $54-$69   2P: $54-$69
▼▼▼▼   **Location:** I-10, exit 28B. 7944 Gateway Blvd E 79915. Fax: 915/591-3700. **Facility:** 104 units. 101 one-bedroom standard units. 3 one-bedroom suites ($74-$84). 4 stories, interior corridors. *Bath:* combo or shower only.
   Parking: on-site. **Terms:** small pets only. **Amenities:** video games (fee), voice mail, irons, hair dryers.
Small-scale Hotel   **Pool(s):** heated outdoor. **Guest Services:** valet and coin laundry. **Business Services:** fax (fee). **Cards:** AX, CB, DC, DS, MC, VI. **Special Amenities:** free continental breakfast and free newspaper.
(See color ad below)   SOME UNITS

(S/D) 🛏 🍴 (&M) (&) 📷 🏊 📶 🎥 DATA-PORT 📺 /✕ 🔌 📠 /
       FEE

(See map p. 326)

BAYMONT INN & SUITES EL PASO WEST
    (AAA) SAVE   All Year [ECP]   1P: $49-$64   2P: $49-$64   Phone: (915)585-2999 **18**
    ▽▽▽▽   **Location:** I-10, exit 11 (Mesa St). 7620 N Mesa St 79912. **Fax:** 915/585-1667. **Facility:** 102 units. 99 one-bedroom standard units. 3 one-bedroom suites ($69-$79). 4 stories, interior corridors. **Parking:** on-site. **Terms:** pets ($50 deposit). **Amenities:** video games (fee), voice mail, irons, hair dryers. **Pool(s):** heated outdoor. **Guest Services:** coin laundry. **Business Services:** fax (fee). **Cards:** AX, CB, DC, DS, MC, VI. **Special Amenities: free continental breakfast and free newspaper.**
Small-scale Hotel

SOME UNITS

🆂🅳 🛏 🍴 📶 🛋 📷 [DATA PORT] 💻 / ✕ 📱 📠 /

BEST WESTERN AIRPORT INN
    (AAA) SAVE   All Year [ECP]   1P: $59-$78   2P: $59-$78   Phone: (915)779-7700 **5**
    ▽▽▽▽   XP: $5   F18
    Location: I-10, exit 26 (Hawkins Blvd). 7144 Gateway E 79915. **Fax:** 915/772-1920. **Facility:** 162 one-bedroom standard units. 2 stories, exterior corridors. *Bath:* combo or shower only. **Parking:** on-site. **Terms:** 10 day cancellation notice, small pets only. **Amenities:** irons, hair dryers. **Dining:** 24 hours. **Pool(s):** heated outdoor. **Leisure Activities:** exercise room. **Guest Services:** coin laundry, area transportation-within 2 mi.
Small-scale Hotel **Business Services:** meeting rooms, fax (fee). **Cards:** AX, CB, DC, DS, JC, MC, VI. **Special Amenities: early check-in/late check-out and free continental breakfast.**

SOME UNITS

🆂🅳 ✈ 🛏 🍴 🎿 📶 🛋 📷 [DATA PORT] 💻 / ✕ 📱 📠 /

BEST WESTERN SUNLAND PARK INN
    (AAA) SAVE   All Year [CP]   1P: $49-$69   2P: $59-$99   Phone: 915/587-4900 **3**
    ▽▽▽▽   XP: $10   F12
    Location: I-10, exit 13, just s. 1045 Sunland Park Dr 79922. **Fax:** 915/587-4950. **Facility:** 50 one-bedroom standard units. 2 stories, exterior corridors. **Parking:** on-site. **Terms:** 14 day cancellation notice, small pets only. **Amenities:** irons, hair dryers. **Pool(s):** heated outdoor. **Leisure Activities:** limited exercise equipment.
Motel   **Business Services:** PC, fax (fee). **Cards:** AX, CB, DC, DS, MC, VI. **Special Amenities: free continental breakfast and free newspaper.** *(See color ad below)*

SOME UNITS

🆂🅳 🛏 🍴 🛋 📷 [DATA PORT] 📱 📠 / ✕ /

CAMINO REAL HOTEL, EL PASO
    ▽▽▽   All Year   1P: $99-$159   2P: $99-$174   Phone: (915)534-3000 **15**
                                                              XP: $15   F12
    Location: Center. 101 S El Paso St 79901. **Fax:** 915/534-3024. **Facility:** 359 units. 347 one-bedroom standard units. 12 one-bedroom suites ($275-$1000). 17 stories, interior corridors. *Bath:* combo or shower only. **Parking:** on-site (fee). **Terms:** cancellation fee imposed, 14% service charge, small pets only.
Large-scale Hotel **Amenities:** voice mail, irons, hair dryers. **Dining:** The Dome Restaurant, Azulejos Restaurant, see separate listing. **Pool(s):** outdoor. **Leisure Activities:** sauna, exercise room. **Fee:** massage. **Guest Services:** gift shop, valet laundry. **Business Services:** meeting rooms, business center. **Cards:** AX, DC, DS, MC, VI.

SOME UNITS

✈ 🛏 🍴 24️ 🛋 ✕ 📷 [DATA PORT] 💻 / ✕ 📱 /

CHASE SUITES BY WOODFIN
    ▽▽▽   All Year [ECP]   1P: $79-$140   2P: $99-$170   Phone: (915)772-8000 **24**
                                                              XP: $10   F
    Location: I-10, exit 25 (Airway Blvd), 1 mi n, then just e. 6791 Montana Ave 79925. **Fax:** 915/772-7254. **Facility:** 200 units. 165 one-bedroom standard units with kitchens. 35 one-bedroom suites with kitchens. 2 stories, exterior
Small-scale Hotel corridors. *Bath:* combo or shower only. **Parking:** on-site. **Terms:** pets ($150 deposit, $5 extra charge). **Amenities:** voice mail, irons, hair dryers. **Pool(s):** 2 heated outdoor. **Leisure Activities:** whirlpools, sports court. **Guest Services:** complimentary evening beverages: Mon-Thurs, valet and coin laundry, area transportation. **Business Services:** meeting rooms, fax (fee). **Cards:** AX, CB, DC, DS, MC, VI.

SOME UNITS

ASK 🆂🅳 ✈ 🛏 🛋 📶 📷 [DATA PORT] 📱 📠 💻 / ✕ VCR /

COMFORT INN AIRPORT EAST
    SAVE   All Year [ECP]   1P: $59-$89   2P: $64-$94   Phone: (915)594-9111 **6**
    ▽▽▽▽   **Location:** I-10, exit 28B. 900 Yarbrough Dr 79915. **Fax:** 915/590-4364. **Facility:** 200 one-bedroom standard units. 3 stories, exterior corridors. **Parking:** on-site. **Terms:** small pets only ($25 deposit). **Amenities:** Some: irons, hair dryers. **Pool(s):** outdoor. **Leisure Activities:** whirlpool. **Guest Services:** coin laundry. **Business Serv-**
Small-scale Hotel **ices:** meeting rooms. **Cards:** AX, CB, DC, DS, MC, VI. *(See color ad p 331)*

SOME UNITS

🆂🅳 ✈ 🛏 🍴 🛋 📶 📷 [DATA PORT] / ✕ 📱 📠 💻 /

(See map p. 326)

COMFORT INN WEST

Small-scale Hotel

Phone: (915)845-1906 [20]

All Year [BP]   1P: $58-$64   2P: $64-$74   XP: $5   F18
Location: I-10, exit 11 (Mesa St). 7651 N Mesa St 79912. Fax: 915/585-1235. **Facility:** 53 one-bedroom standard units. 2 stories, interior corridors. *Bath:* combo or shower only. **Parking:** on-site. **Terms:** pets ($10 fee). **Amenities:** hair dryers. *Some:* irons. **Pool(s):** outdoor. **Leisure Activities:** whirlpool. **Guest Services:** coin laundry. **Business Services:** fax (fee). **Cards:** AX, DC, DS, MC, VI.

SOME UNITS

COMFORT SUITES

Small-scale Hotel

Phone: (915)587-5300 [9]

All Year [ECP]   1P: $69-$89   2P: $69-$99   XP: $6   F18
Location: I-10, exit 13. 949 Sunland Park Dr 79922. Fax: 915/587-6165. **Facility:** 61 one-bedroom standard units. 3 stories, interior corridors. *Bath:* combo or shower only. **Parking:** on-site. **Terms:** 14 day cancellation notice, small pets only ($15 fee). **Amenities:** hair dryers. *Some:* irons. **Pool(s):** small heated indoor. **Leisure Activities:** whirlpool, exercise room. **Guest Services:** valet and coin laundry. **Business Services:** meeting rooms, fax (fee). **Cards:** AX, CB, DC, DS, MC, VI.

SOME UNITS

CORAL MOTEL

Motel

Phone: (915)772-3263 [34]

All Year   1P: $36-$40   2P: $40-$48   XP: $5   D10
Location: I-10, exit 24 (Geronimo St) westbound; exit 24B (Geronimo St) eastbound, 0.5 mi n, then 0.5 mi e. Located in a commercial area. 6420 Montana Rd 79925. Fax: 915/779-6053. **Facility:** 32 one-bedroom standard units. 1 story, exterior corridors. *Bath:* combo or shower only. **Parking:** on-site. **Terms:** 7 day cancellation notice-fee imposed, weekly rates available. **Pool(s):** outdoor. **Cards:** AX, CB, DC, DS, JC, MC, VI. **Special Amenities:** free local telephone calls.

SOME UNITS

DAYS INN

Motel

Phone: 915/845-3500 [21]

All Year [CP]   1P: $55-$65   2P: $60-$70   XP: $8   F13
Location: I-10, exit 11 (Mesa) eastbound; exit 9 (Redd) northbound, 1.5 mi e on eastbound service road. 5035 S Desert Blvd 79932. Fax: 915/845-3501. **Facility:** 46 one-bedroom standard units, some with whirlpools. 2 stories, exterior corridors. **Parking:** on-site. **Terms:** 3 day cancellation notice-fee imposed, pets ($20 fee). **Amenities:** hair dryers. **Pool(s):** outdoor. **Leisure Activities:** whirlpool. **Guest Services:** coin laundry. **Business Services:** fax (fee). **Cards:** AX, DC, DS, MC, VI.

SOME UNITS

DAYS INN

Motel

Phone: (915)595-1913 [37]

All Year   1P: $42-$65   2P: $49-$72   XP: $4   F18
Location: I-10, exit 28B westbound; exit 29 (Lomaland) eastbound, U-turn under freeway, 1 mi w on frontage road. 10635 Gateway Blvd W 79935. Fax: 915/591-8307. **Facility:** 122 one-bedroom standard units. 3 stories, exterior corridors. **Parking:** on-site. **Terms:** small pets only. **Amenities:** *Some:* irons, hair dryers. **Pool(s):** heated outdoor. **Business Services:** meeting rooms, fax (fee). **Cards:** AX, CB, DC, DS, MC, VI. **Special Amenities:** early check-in/late check-out and free local telephone calls.

SOME UNITS

(See map p. 326)

ECONO LODGE

Motel

Phone: (915)778-3311 ④

All Year   1P: $50-$60   2P: $55-$65   XP: $5   F

Location: I-10, exit 24 (Geronimo St) westbound; exit 24B eastbound, 0.5 mi n on Geronimo St, then 0.5 mi e. 6363 Montana Ave 79925. Fax: 915/778-1097. **Facility:** 59 one-bedroom standard units. 2 stories, exterior corridors. **Parking:** on-site. **Terms:** small pets only ($10 fee). **Pool(s):** small outdoor. **Guest Services:** coin laundry. **Cards:** AX, CB, DC, DS, MC, VI. **Special Amenities:** free continental breakfast and free local telephone calls.

SOME UNITS

EL PASO AIRPORT COURTYARD BY MARRIOTT

Small-scale Hotel

Phone: (915)772-5000 ㉖

All Year   1P: $119-$159   2P: $119-$159

Location: I-10, exit 25 (Airway Blvd), on westound frontage road. 6610 International Dr 79925. Fax: 915/772-5009. **Facility:** 90 units. 87 one-bedroom standard units, some with whirlpools. 3 one-bedroom suites ($159-$169). 3 stories, interior corridors. *Bath:* combo or shower only. **Parking:** on-site. **Terms:** [AP] & [CP] meal plans available, 17% service charge. **Amenities:** video games (fee), dual phone lines, voice mail, irons, hair dryers. **Pool(s):** heated outdoor. **Leisure Activities:** whirlpool, exercise room. **Guest Services:** valet and coin laundry. **Business Services:** PC, fax (fee). **Cards:** AX, CB, DC, DS, JC, MC, VI.

SOME UNITS

EL PASO MARRIOTT HOTEL

Large-scale Hotel

Phone: (915)779-3300 ㉙

All Year   1P: $165   2P: $165

Location: I-10, exit 25 (Airway Blvd), 1 mi n. Located in a commercial area. 1600 Airway Blvd 79925. Fax: 915/772-0915. **Facility:** 296 units. 292 one-bedroom standard units. 3 two- and 1 three-bedroom suites. 6 stories, interior corridors. *Bath:* combo or shower only. **Parking:** on-site. **Terms:** check-in 4 pm, cancellation fee imposed, [AP], [BP], [CP] & [ECP] meal plans available, 17% service charge. **Amenities:** video games (fee), voice mail, irons, hair dryers. **Pool(s):** heated indoor/outdoor. **Leisure Activities:** sauna, whirlpool, exercise room. **Guest Services:** gift shop, valet laundry. **Business Services:** meeting rooms, business center. **Cards:** AX, CB, DC, DS, JC, MC, VI.

SOME UNITS

FEE

EMBASSY SUITES HOTEL

Small-scale Hotel

Phone: (915)779-6222 ⑧

All Year [BP]   1P: $89-$139   2P: $89-$149   XP: $18   F18

Location: I-10, exit 24B (Geronimo St), exit 24B (Geronimo St) westbound, 0.6 mi to Trowbridge, U-turn under interstate, 0.5 mi e; exit 24B (Geronimo St) eastbound. 6100 Gateway Blvd E 79905. Fax: 915/779-8846. **Facility:** 185 one-bedroom suites. 8 stories, interior corridors. *Bath:* combo or shower only. **Parking:** on-site. **Amenities:** video games (fee), voice mail, irons, hair dryers. **Pool(s):** heated indoor. **Leisure Activities:** sauna, whirlpool, exercise room. **Guest Services:** gift shop, complimentary evening beverages, valet and coin laundry, area transportation. **Business Services:** meeting rooms, PC, fax (fee). **Cards:** AX, CB, DC, DS, JC, MC, VI.

SOME UNITS

FEE

EXECUTIVE INN & SUITES

Small-scale Hotel

Phone: (915)532-8981 ⑬

2/1-3/1   1P: $40-$45   2P: $50-$60   XP: $5   F
3/2-8/1   1P: $45-$50   XP: $5   F
8/2-1/31   1P: $40-$45   XP: $5   F

Location: I-10, exit 16 (Executive Blvd), just n. 500 Executive Blvd 79902. Fax: 915/577-9997. **Facility:** 99 units. 98 one-bedroom standard units. 1 one-bedroom suite ($80-$120) with whirlpool. 2 stories, interior corridors. *Bath:* combo or shower only. **Parking:** on-site. **Terms:** [ECP] meal plan available, pets ($20 fee). **Amenities:** voice mail, safes (fee), irons, hair dryers. **Pool(s):** outdoor. **Leisure Activities:** whirlpool. **Guest Services:** valet and coin laundry. **Business Services:** fax. **Cards:** AX, CB, DC, DS, JC, MC, VI. **Special Amenities:** free continental breakfast and free room upgrade (subject to availability with advanced reservations). *(See color ad below)*

SOME UNITS

(See map p. 326)

HAMPTON INN & SUITES
Phone: (915)771-6644 [28]

SAVE

▼▼▼▲▲▲▼▼

Small-scale Hotel

All Year [ECP]   1P: $99-$124   2P: $109-$134
Location: I-10, exit 25 (Airway Blvd), on westbound frontage road. 6635 Gateway Blvd W 79925. Fax: 915/771-6368. **Facility:** 139 units. 94 one-bedroom standard units. 45 one-bedroom suites ($144-$154) with efficiencies. 4 stories, interior corridors. *Bath:* combo or shower only. **Parking:** on-site. **Amenities:** voice mail, irons, hair dryers. *Some:* dual phone lines. **Pool(s):** heated outdoor. **Leisure Activities:** whirlpool, exercise room. **Guest Services:** sundries, complimentary evening beverages: Mon-Thurs, valet and coin laundry, area transportation. **Business Services:** meeting rooms, fax. **Cards:** AX, CB, DC, DS, MC, VI.

SOME UNITS

[S/D] [✦] [🛗] [♿] [⊙] [🏊] [🎥] [DATA PORT] [🖥] / [✕] [🍴] [📷] /

HAWTHORN INN & SUITES
Phone: (915)778-6789 [31]

▼▼▼▲▲▲▼▼

Small-scale Hotel

All Year   1P: $79-$109   2P: $79-$109   XP: $10   F18
Location: 7 mi e on US 62 and 180 to Airway Blvd, then just n. 6789 Boeing 79925. Fax: 915/778-2288. **Facility:** 191 units. 173 one-bedroom standard units. 18 one-bedroom suites ($109-$129) with efficiencies. 3 stories, interior corridors. *Bath:* combo or shower only. **Parking:** on-site. **Terms:** age restrictions may apply, [BP] meal plan available, package plans. **Amenities:** video games (fee), high-speed Internet, voice mail, irons, hair dryers. **Pool(s):** heated outdoor. **Leisure Activities:** whirlpool, exercise room. **Guest Services:** complimentary evening beverages, valet and coin laundry, area transportation. **Business Services:** meeting rooms, PC. **Cards:** AX, CB, DC, DS, MC, VI.

SOME UNITS

[ASK] [S/D] [✦] [🐾] [🛗] [🍴] [♿] [⊙] [🏊] [🎥] [DATA PORT] [🖥] / [✕] [🍴] [📷] /

HILTON EL PASO AIRPORT
Phone: (915)778-4241 [7]

SAVE

▼▼▼▲▲▲▼▼

Large-scale Hotel

All Year   2P: $114-$123   XP: $10   F18
Location: I-10, exit 25 (Airway Blvd), 1.3 mi n. 2027 Airway Blvd 79925. Fax: 915/772-6871. **Facility:** 272 units. 121 one-bedroom standard units. 151 one-bedroom suites ($123-$133), some with whirlpools. 2-4 stories, interior corridors. *Bath:* combo or shower only. **Parking:** on-site. **Terms:** pets ($200 deposit). **Amenities:** high-speed Internet (fee), dual phone lines, voice mail, irons, hair dryers. *Some:* honor bars. **Dining:** Magnim's, Canarozzo's, see separate listing. **Pool(s):** heated outdoor, wading. **Leisure Activities:** whirlpool, waterslide, exercise room. **Guest Services:** gift shop, valet and coin laundry, area transportation. **Business Services:** meeting rooms, business center. **Cards:** AX, CB, DC, DS, MC, VI.

SOME UNITS

[✦] [🐾] [🍴] [24] [♿] [⊙] [🏊] [✕] [🎥] [DATA PORT] [🖥] / [✕] [VCR] [🍴] /
FEE

HOLIDAY INN-AIRPORT
Phone: 915/778-6411 [25]

▼▼▼▲▲▲▼▼

Small-scale Hotel

Property failed to provide current rates
Location: I-10, exit 25 (Airway Blvd). 6655 Gateway Blvd W 79925. Fax: 915/778-6517. **Facility:** 206 one-bedroom standard units, some with whirlpools. 2 stories, interior/exterior corridors. *Bath:* combo or shower only. **Parking:** on-site. **Amenities:** high-speed Internet (fee), dual phone lines, voice mail, irons, hair dryers. **Pool(s):** outdoor, heated indoor/outdoor. **Leisure Activities:** whirlpool, exercise room. **Guest Services:** valet and coin laundry. **Business Services:** meeting rooms, PC, fax (fee). **Cards:** AX, CB, DC, DS, JC, MC, VI.

SOME UNITS

[✦] [🍴] [⊙] [♿] [🏊] [🎥] [DATA PORT] [🖥] / [✕] [🍴] [📷] /

HOLIDAY INN SUNLAND PARK
Phone: (915)833-2900 [2]

[AAA] SAVE

▼▼▼▲▲▲▼▼

Small-scale Hotel

All Year   1P: $88-$102   2P: $88-$102
Location: I-10, exit 13. 900 Sunland Park Dr 79922. Fax: 915/833-6338. **Facility:** 178 units. 169 one-bedroom standard units. 9 one-bedroom suites ($125-$149). 2 stories, exterior corridors. **Parking:** on-site. **Terms:** pets ($50 deposit). **Amenities:** video games (fee), dual phone lines, voice mail, irons, hair dryers. **Dining:** 6 am-10 & 6-10 pm, Sat & Sun 7 am-11 & 6-10 pm, cocktails. **Pool(s):** outdoor, wading. **Leisure Activities:** whirlpool, exercise room. **Guest Services:** sundries, valet laundry, area transportation-within 5 mi. **Business Services:** meeting rooms, business center. **Cards:** AX, CB, DC, DS, MC, VI. **Special Amenities:** free local telephone calls. *(See color ad below)*

SOME UNITS

[S/D] [✦] [🐾] [🍴] [🏊] [🎥] [DATA PORT] [🖥] / [✕] [🍴] [📷] /

(See map p. 326)

HOWARD JOHNSON INN   **Phone:** (915)591-9471   🔲 12
   ▼▼▼ ▼▼▼   All Year   1P: $57-$67   2P: $62-$72   XP: $5   F17
        Location: I-10, exit 26 (Hawkins Blvd). 8887 Gateway Blvd W 79925. Fax: 915/591-5602. **Facility:** 140 one-
Small-scale Hotel   bedroom standard units. 2 stories, interior corridors. **Parking:** on-site. **Pool(s):** outdoor, wading. **Leisure Activities:** exercise room. **Guest Services:** valet and coin laundry. **Business Services:** meeting rooms, fax (fee). **Cards:** AX, CB, DC, DS, JC, MC, VI.

SOME UNITS
(ASK) 🆘 (✈) 🐕 (🍴) 🛄 (📞) 🖥 / (✕) 🔲 /

LA QUINTA INN-EL PASO-AIRPORT   **Phone:** (915)778-9321   🔲 11
  (AAA) (SAVE)   All Year   1P: $62-$79   2P: $68-$85   XP: $6   F18
   ▼▼▼ ▼▼▼   **Location:** I-10, exit 24B (Geronimo St) westbound, 0.6 mi to Trowbridge, U-turn under interstate, then 0.5 mi e. 6140
        Gateway Blvd E 79905-2004. Fax: 915/779-1505. **Facility:** 121 units. 119 one-bedroom standard units. 2 one-
        bedroom suites ($99-$149). 2 stories, exterior corridors. **Parking:** on-site. **Terms:** [ECP] meal plan available,
Motel   small pets only. **Amenities:** video games (fee), voice mail, irons, hair dryers. **Pool(s):** heated outdoor. **Guest Services:** valet and coin laundry. **Business Services:** meeting rooms, fax (fee). **Cards:** AX, CB, DC, DS, JC, MC, VI. **Special Amenities:** free continental breakfast and free local telephone calls. *(See color ad below)*

SOME UNITS
(✈) 🐕 (🍴) 🐾 (📞) 🖥 / (✕) 🔲 /

LA QUINTA INN-EL PASO-CIELO VISTA   **Phone:** (915)593-8400   🔲 1
  (AAA) (SAVE)   All Year   1P: $66-$69   2P: $72-$75   XP: $6   F18
   ▼▼▼ ▼▼▼   **Location:** I-10, exit 28B westbound; exit 27 eastbound. 9125 Gateway Blvd W 79925. Fax: 915/599-1268.
        Facility: 117 units. 116 one-bedroom standard units. 1 one-bedroom suite ($99-$149). 2 stories, exterior cor-
        ridors. **Parking:** on-site. **Terms:** [ECP] meal plan available, small pets only. **Amenities:** video games (fee),
Motel   voice mail, irons, hair dryers. **Pool(s):** outdoor. **Leisure Activities:** whirlpool. **Guest Services:** valet laundry. **Business Services:** fax (fee). **Cards:** AX, CB, DC, DS, JC, MC, VI. **Special Amenities:** free continental breakfast and free local telephone calls. *(See color ad below)*

SOME UNITS
🐕 (🍴) 🐾 (📞) 🖥 / (✕) 🔲 🛏 /

LA QUINTA INN-EL PASO-LOMALAND   **Phone:** (915)591-2244   🔲 35
  (SAVE)   All Year   1P: $55-$62   2P: $61-$68   XP: $6   F18
   ▼▼▼ ▼▼▼   **Location:** I-10, exit 29 eastbound; exit 30 westbound, 1 mi w. 11033 Gateway Blvd W 79935-5003. Fax: 915/592-9300.
        Facility: 138 units. 136 one-bedroom standard units. 2 one-bedroom suites ($99-$149). 2 stories, exterior
Motel   corridors. *Bath:* combo or shower only. **Parking:** on-site. **Terms:** [ECP] meal plan available, small pets only.
        Amenities: video games (fee), voice mail, irons, hair dryers. **Pool(s):** heated outdoor. **Guest Services:** valet
        laundry. **Business Services:** fax (fee). **Cards:** AX, CB, DC, DS, JC, MC, VI. *(See color ad below)*

SOME UNITS
🐕 (🍴) (♿M) 🛌 🐾 🛄 (📞) 🖥 / (✕) 🔲 🛏 /
FEE

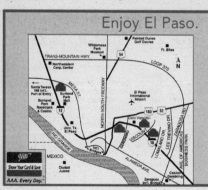

(See map p. 326)

LA QUINTA INN-EL PASO-WEST

🔺🔺🔺 (SAVE)
▽▽▽▽
Motel

Phone: (915)833-2522 🔢 **17**

All Year   1P: $63-$73   2P: $70-$80   XP: $7   F18
Location: I-10, exit 11 (Mesa St). 7550 Remcon Cir 79912-3513. Fax: 915/581-9303. **Facility:** 130 units. 128 one-bedroom standard units. 2 one-bedroom suites ($99-$149). 3 stories, exterior corridors. *Bath:* combo or shower only. **Parking:** on-site. **Terms:** [ECP] meal plan available, small pets only. **Amenities:** video games (fee), voice mail, irons, hair dryers. **Pool(s):** heated outdoor. **Business Services:** fax (fee). **Cards:** AX, CB, DC, DS, JC, MC, VI. **Special Amenities: free continental breakfast and free local telephone calls.**

(See color ad p 334)

SOME UNITS

🛏️ 🍴 ♿ 🍳 🏊 📶 📷 💻 / ✕ 🖥️ /
FEE

MICROTEL INN & SUITES

▽▽ ▽▽
Small-scale Hotel

Phone: (915)772-3650 🔢 **16**

1/1-1/31   1P: $50-$72   2P: $55-$77   XP: $5   F14
2/1-12/31   1P: $49-$71   2P: $54-$76   XP: $5   F14
Location: I-10, exit 25 (Airway Blvd), 1.3 mi n. 2001 Airway Blvd 79925. Fax: 915/298-3161. **Facility:** 77 one-bedroom standard units. 3 stories, interior corridors. *Bath:* combo or shower only. **Parking:** on-site. **Terms:** weekly rates available, [CP] meal plan available, pets ($100 deposit). **Amenities:** *Some:* irons, hair dryers. **Guest Services:** valet laundry, area transportation. **Business Services:** fax (fee). **Cards:** AX, DC, DS, JC, MC, VI.

SOME UNITS

📶 🛏️ 🍴 ♿M 🍳 📷 / ✕ 🖥️ 🖨️ 💻 /

RADISSON SUITE INN EL PASO AIRPORT

▽▽▽
Large-scale Hotel

Phone: (915)772-3333 🔢 **33**

All Year   1P: $139-$169   2P: $149-$179   XP: $10   F17
Location: I-10, exit 25 (Airway Blvd), 1.2 mi n. 1770 Airway Blvd 79925. Fax: 915/779-3323. **Facility:** 239 units. 218 one-bedroom standard units. 20 one- and 1 two-bedroom suites ($179-$199) with whirlpools. 3-4 stories, interior/exterior corridors. *Bath:* combo or shower only. **Parking:** on-site. **Terms:** [BP] meal plan available. **Amenities:** video library, dual phone lines, voice mail, irons, hair dryers. *Some:* high-speed Internet (fee). **Pool(s):** heated outdoor, heated indoor. **Leisure Activities:** whirlpools, exercise room, game room. **Guest Services:** complimentary evening beverages, valet and coin laundry, area transportation. **Business Services:** meeting rooms, business center. **Cards:** AX, CB, DC, DS, JC, MC, VI.

SOME UNITS

(ASK) (S/D) 📶 🍴 ♿ 🍳 🏊 ✕ (VCR) 📷 📶 🖥️ 🖨️ 💻 / ✕ /

RAMADA INN & SUITES

▽▽▽
Small-scale Hotel

Phone: (915)772-3300 🔢 **27**

All Year [CP]   1P: $55-$67   2P: $55-$67   XP: $5   F18
Location: I-10, exit 24 (Geronimo St) westbound; exit 24B (Geronimo St) eastbound, 0.5 mi n. 6099 Montana Ave 79925. Fax: 915/775-0808. **Facility:** 72 units. 52 one-bedroom standard units, some with whirlpools. 20 one-bedroom suites, some with efficiencies (no utensils) and/or whirlpools. 2 stories, exterior corridors. *Bath:* combo or shower only. **Parking:** on-site. **Terms:** cancellation fee imposed. **Amenities:** irons, hair dryers. **Pool(s):** outdoor. **Guest Services:** valet and coin laundry, area transportation. **Business Services:** meeting rooms, fax (fee). **Cards:** AX, DC, DS, MC, VI.

SOME UNITS

(ASK) (S/D) 📶 🍴 ⬜ ♿ 🍳 📶 📷 💻 / ✕ 🖥️ 🖨️ /
FEE

RED ROOF INN WEST

🔺🔺🔺 (SAVE)
▽▽▽
Small-scale Hotel

Phone: (915)587-9977 🔢 **22**

All Year   1P: $36-$53   2P: $41-$58   XP: $5   F18
Location: I-10, exit 11 (Mesa St). 7530 Remcon Cir 79912. Fax: 915/587-9965. **Facility:** 123 one-bedroom standard units. 3 stories, interior/exterior corridors. *Bath:* combo or shower only. **Parking:** on-site. **Terms:** small pets only. **Amenities:** video games (fee), voice mail. **Pool(s):** heated outdoor. **Business Services:** meeting rooms, fax (fee). **Cards:** AX, CB, DC, DS, MC, VI. **Special Amenities: free local telephone calls and free newspaper.**

SOME UNITS

🛏️ 🍴 ♿M 🍳 🍳 🏊 📷 📶 / ✕ 🖥️ /
FEE

SLEEP INN

(SAVE)
▽▽▽
Small-scale Hotel

Phone: (915)585-7577 🔢 **10**

All Year [ECP]   1P: $55-$75   2P: $55-$85   XP: $6   F18
Location: I-10, exit 13. 953 Sunland Park Dr 79922. Fax: 915/585-7579. **Facility:** 63 one-bedroom standard units. 3 stories, interior corridors. *Bath:* combo or shower only. **Parking:** on-site. **Terms:** 14 day cancellation notice, pets ($15 fee). **Amenities:** hair dryers. **Pool(s):** small heated indoor. **Leisure Activities:** whirlpool. **Guest Services:** valet laundry. **Business Services:** fax (fee). **Cards:** AX, CB, DC, DS, MC, VI.

SOME UNITS

(S/D) 🛏️ ♿ 🍴 📶 📷 📶 / ✕ 🖥️ 🖨️ /

TRAVELODGE

🔺🔺🔺 (SAVE)
▽▽▽▽
Motel

Phone: (915)833-2613 🔢 **19**

All Year   1P: $39-$79   2P: $43-$83   XP: $4   F18
Location: I-10, exit 11 (Mesa St). 7815 N Mesa St 79932. Fax: 915/833-1006. **Facility:** 126 one-bedroom standard units. 3 stories, exterior corridors. **Parking:** on-site. **Terms:** small pets only ($25 deposit). **Amenities:** *Some:* irons. **Pool(s):** heated outdoor. **Leisure Activities:** whirlpool. **Guest Services:** coin laundry. **Business Services:** fax (fee). **Cards:** AX, CB, DC, DS, MC, VI. **Special Amenities: early check-in/late check-out and free local telephone calls.**

SOME UNITS

(S/D) 🛏️ 🍴 🏊 📷 📶 💻 / ✕ 🖥️ 🖨️ /

TRAVELODGE HOTEL EL PASO CITY CENTER

🔺🔺🔺 (SAVE)
▽▽▽▽
Small-scale Hotel

Phone: (915)544-3333 🔢 **14**

All Year   1P: $54-$79   2P: $59-$84   XP: $5   F17
Location: I-10, exit 19A, just s. 409 E Missouri St 79901. Fax: 915/533-4109. **Facility:** 108 one-bedroom standard units. 9 stories, interior corridors. **Parking:** on-site. **Terms:** small pets only ($50 deposit). **Amenities:** safes, irons, hair dryers. **Dining:** 7 am-10 pm, cocktails. **Pool(s):** heated outdoor. **Guest Services:** valet and coin laundry, area transportation-bus station. **Business Services:** meeting rooms, fax. **Cards:** AX, CB, DC, DS, MC, VI. **Special Amenities: early check-in/late check-out and free newspaper.**

SOME UNITS

(S/D) 📶 🛏️ 🍴 ⬜ 🏊 📷 📶 💻 / ✕ /

(See map p. 326)

TRAVELODGE LA HACIENDA AIRPORT **Phone:** (915)772-4231   ⑳

 Motel

All Year 1P: $53-$58 2P: $62-$67 XP: $5 F17
Location: I-10, exit 24 (Geronimo St) westbound; exit 24B eastbound, 0.5 mi n on Geronimo St, then 0.5 mi e. 6400 Montana Ave 79925. Fax: 915/779-2918. **Facility:** 91 units. 85 one-bedroom standard units, some with whirlpools. 6 one-bedroom suites ($85). 2 stories, exterior corridors. *Bath:* combo or shower only. **Parking:** on-site. **Terms:** weekly rates available, [CP] meal plan available, small pets only ($10 extra charge). **Amenities:** voice mail, safes. **Dining:** 8 am-8 pm, entertainment. **Pool(s):** heated outdoor. **Leisure Activities:** exercise room. **Guest Services:** coin laundry. **Business Services:** meeting rooms, PC, fax. **Cards:** AX, CB, DC, DS, JC, MC, VI. **Special Amenities:** early check-in/late check-out and free room upgrade (subject to availability with advanced reservations).

SOME UNITS

ⓢ⒟ ➕ 🐾 🍴 🍸 ➿ 🏃 📠 ▣ / ✕ 🛢 🖥 /

──── WHERE TO DINE ────

ARDOVINO'S **Lunch:** $5-$15 **Dinner:** $5-$15 **Phone:** 915/532-9483 ⑪

Pizza

Location: I-10, exit 18A (Schuster), 0.7 mi ne to Mesa St, 0.6 mi n, then just e. 206 Cincinnati 79902. **Hours:** 11 am-9 pm, Fri & Sat-10 pm. Closed major holidays; also Sun. **Features:** Originally a market that specialized in Italian foods, Ardovino's has evolved from the foodmart of 1961 to a pizzeria and delicatessen. Diners will enjoy the thin, crispy pizzas, easily among the best in the area. Shop for wine, Italian specialties, and gourmet chocolates. Smoke free premises. Casual dress; beer & wine only. **Parking:** street. **Cards:** AX, DC, MC, VI. ✕

AVILA'S MEXICAN FOOD RESTAURANT (EAST) **Lunch:** $6-$9 **Dinner:** $6-$9 **Phone:** 915/598-3333 ⑱

Mexican

Location: 13 mi e on US 62 and 180. 10600 Montana Ave 79935. **Hours:** 11 am-8:30 pm, Fri & Sat-9 pm, Sun-8 pm. Closed: 11/27, 12/25. **Features:** In its third generation of family ownership, the original Avila's location is a favorite for casual dining. Menu choices range from tacos and burritos to enchiladas and fajitas. Also offered is a limited selection of American dishes. Smoke free premises. Casual dress; beer & wine only. **Parking:** on-site. **Cards:** AX, DS, MC, VI. ✕

AVILA'S MEXICAN RESTAURANT (WEST) **Lunch:** $5-$10 **Dinner:** $5-$10 **Phone:** 915/584-3621 ⑥

Mexican

Location: I-10, exit 13, 2 mi e to Mesa St, just n. 6232 N Mesa St 79912. **Hours:** 11 am-8:30 pm, Sun 11:30 am-8 pm. Closed major holidays; also 7/1-7/4. **Features:** Hearty, modestly presented dishes draw patrons to the second Avila's location. Menu choices range from tacos and burritos to enchiladas and fajitas. Smoke free premises. Casual dress; beer & wine only. **Parking:** on-site. **Cards:** AX, CB, DC, DS, MC, VI. ✕

AZULEJOS RESTAURANT **Lunch:** $8-$10 **Dinner:** $10-$17 **Phone:** 915/534-3020 ⑬

Continental

Location: Center; in Camino Real Hotel, El Paso. 101 S El Paso St 79901. **Hours:** 6 am-2:30 & 5-9 pm. **Reservations:** accepted. **Features:** A popular spot for downtown business lunches and shoppers respite, Azulejo means tile in Spanish and plenty of colorful talavera is on display at this central eatery. A creative menu offers items such as penne pasta with grilled chicken and cilantro pesto sauce, or a luncheon buffet for the person on the go. Smoke free premises. Casual dress; cocktails. **Parking:** on-site (fee). **Cards:** AX, DC, DS, MC, VI. ✕

BELLA NAPOLI **Dinner:** $7-$14 **Phone:** 915/584-3321 ⑭

Italian

Location: 6 mi nw on US 80 business route. 6331 N Mesa St 79912. **Hours:** 4 pm-10 pm, Sun from 11 am. Closed: 11/27, 12/25; also Mon & Tues. **Features:** What has become thought of as a traditional Italian decor finds expression here with checkered tablecloths and wine-bottle candle holders. Choose from a good variety of freshly made pizzas and pasta dishes with chicken, beef, veal and seafood options. Smoke free premises. Casual dress; beer & wine only. **Parking:** on-site. **Cards:** AX, MC, VI. ✕

CANAROZZO'S **Dinner:** $8-$22 **Phone:** 915/778-4241 ①

Italian

Location: I-10, exit 25 (Airway Blvd), 1.3 mi n; in Hilton El Paso Airport. 2027 Airway Blvd 79925. **Hours:** 5 pm-11 pm. **Reservations:** suggested; weekends. **Features:** Among Northern Italian selections served in the intimate, dimly lit dining room are fettuccine con frutti di mare, a seafood fettuccine Alfredo dish; and grilled bistecca al forno, an 8-ounce filet beef tenderloin in Marsala wine. Smoke free premises. Dressy casual; cocktails. **Parking:** on-site. **Cards:** AX, DC, DS, MC, VI. ✕

CAPPETO'S ITALIAN RESTAURANT **Lunch:** $6-$14 **Dinner:** $6-$14 **Phone:** 915/566-9357 ⑮

Italian

Location: I-10, exit 21 (Piedras), 0.4 mi n on Piedras, then just w. 2716 Montana Ave 79930. **Hours:** 11 am-11 pm, Sat & Sun from noon. Closed: 11/27, 12/25. **Features:** Operating since 1956, Capetto's has been an El Paso favorite for years. The menu is long with a multitude of items such as pasta dishes, veal, chicken, seafood, pizza, and panini sandwiches. Outdoor dining available. Smoke free premises. Casual dress; beer only. **Parking:** on-site. **Cards:** AX, CB, DC, DS, MC, VI. ✕

CASA JURADO **Lunch:** $5-$14 **Dinner:** $5-$14 **Phone:** 915/532-6429 ⑨

Mexican
DS, MC, VI.

Location: 2 mi n on Mesa St. 226 Cincinnati St 79902. **Hours:** 11 am-8 pm, Fri & Sat-8:30 pm. Closed: 1/1, 11/27, 12/25; also Sun. **Features:** Twinkling lights on the ceiling and Diego Riveraesque art on the walls gives this intimate dining room an eclectic look. Count on authentic favorites like Mexican meatball soup and stuffed gorditas. Smoke free premises. Casual dress; beer & wine only. **Parking:** on-site. **Cards:** AX,

(See map p. 326)

CATTLEMAN'S STEAK HOUSE   Dinner: $11-$38   Phone: 915/544-3200   20
Steak House
Location: I-10, exit 49, 4.5 mi n. 5 mi n of exit 49 on I-10. **Hours:** 5 pm-10 pm, Sat from 12:30 pm, Sun 12:30 pm-9 pm. **Features:** Some would say that a visit to El Paso is incomplete without a meal at Cattleman's. A drive out into the Fabens desert will take you to this oasis that is thought by many to serve the best steaks in El Paso. With a decidedly Western appeal, dining here is like visiting a friends' ranch. A short menu of steaks and sides are served up family style by gracious hosts. Casual dress; cocktails. **Parking:** on-site. **Cards:** AX, DC, DS, MC, VI.

COMO'S ITALIAN RESTAURANT   Lunch: $6-$13   Dinner: $6-$13   Phone: 915/533-0287   19
Italian
Location: I-10, exit 16 (Executive Blvd), 0.4 mi ne, then 0.4 mi s. 4030 N Mesa St. **Hours:** 11 am-10 pm, Sun noon-9 pm. **Closed:** 11/27, 12/25. **Features:** Traditional Old World decor and mood lighting sustain a casual setting. Patrons can design their own Italian dish from a list of pastas and sauces or choose from such classics as eggplant parmigiana and homemade lasagna. Pizza and sandwiches round out the menu. Smoke free premises. Casual dress; beer & wine only. **Parking:** on-site. **Cards:** AX, DS, MC, VI.

THE DOME RESTAURANT   Dinner: $17-$30   Phone: 915/534-3010   12
Continental
Location: Center; in Camino Real Hotel, El Paso. 101 S El Paso St 79901. **Hours:** 6 pm-10 pm, Fri & Sat 5:30 pm-11 pm. **Closed:** Sun. **Reservations:** suggested. **Features:** Fine dining with the opulent decor of the early 20th century, high ceilings, massive stained glass windows, beautiful crystal chandeliers, takes you back to a time of classical elegance. Smoke free premises. Semi-formal attire; cocktails. **Parking:** on-site (fee). **Cards:** AX, DC, DS, MC, VI.

DOMINGUEZ MEXICAN FOOD   Lunch: $5-$11   Dinner: $5-$11   Phone: 915/772-2160   3
Mexican
Location: I-10, exit 25 (Airway Blvd), 0.3 mi n; in Junction Center. 1201 Airway Blvd, Suite C-5 79925. **Hours:** 11 am-9:30 pm, Fri & Sat-10 pm. Closed major holidays; also Sun. **Features:** Home-style cooking is key at the laid-back establishment. Diners can sample hearty portions of burritos, enchiladas, fajitas and more. Tasty beef gorditas are served with refried beans and Spanish rice. Smoke free premises. Casual dress; beer & wine only. **Parking:** on-site. **Cards:** AX, DS, MC, VI.

FORTI'S MEXICAN ELDER RESTAURANT   Lunch: $6-$14   Dinner: $7-$15   Phone: 915/772-0066   10
Mexican
Location: I-10, exit 238 (Paisano St) westbound, just w, then just s; exit 23A (Reynolds) eastbound, 0.7 mi e on service road, then just s. 321 Chelsea St 79905. **Hours:** 11 am-10 pm, Fri & Sat-11 pm. **Closed:** 11/27, 12/25. **Reservations:** accepted. **Features:** Mariachis bring the nights to life at this authentic Mexican hacienda. An enclosed patio features a lovely fountain, and three levels of dining space are accented by 25-foot-high ceilings. A good selection of steak and seafood includes shrimp Mexicana. Smoke free premises. Casual dress; cocktails. **Parking:** on-site. **Cards:** AX, DC, DS, MC, VI.

GUNTHER'S EDELWEISS   Lunch: $3-$8   Dinner: $5-$14 '   Phone: 915/592-1084   21
German
Location: I-10, exit 29 (Lomaland). 11055 Gateway Blvd W 79935. **Hours:** 11 am-10 pm, Sun noon-9 pm. Closed major holidays; also Mon. **Features:** Bavarian decor punctuates the lively family restaurant. On the menu are such well-prepared dishes as schnitzels, bratwurst and Polish sausage. The staff is pleasant. Casual dress; cocktails. **Parking:** on-site. **Cards:** AX, DS, MC, VI.

HUDSON'S GRILL   Lunch: $6-$9   Dinner: $6-$9   Phone: 915/581-3990   7
American
Location: I-10, exit 11 (Mesa St), 0.4 mi s. 8041 N Mesa St 79932. **Hours:** 11 am-11 pm, Fri & Sat-midnight. Closed: 7/4, 11/27, 12/25. **Features:** Specializing in sandwiches, burgers, salads and appetizers, Hudson's Grill is a good bet for the budget-conscious diner. Smoke free premises. Casual dress; cocktails. **Parking:** on-site. **Cards:** AX, DC, DS, MC, VI.

JAXON'S RESTAURANT & BREWERY   Lunch: $6-$15   Dinner: $0-$15   Phone: 915/778-9696   5
American
Location: I-10, exit 25 (Airway Blvd), just n. 1135 Airway Blvd 79925. **Hours:** 11 am-10 pm, Fri & Sat-11 pm. Closed major holidays. **Features:** Sandwiches, salads, fajitas and steaks make for a well-rounded menu. Beer lovers will relish the opportunity to enjoy the many house specialties. Smoke free premises. Casual dress; cocktails. **Parking:** on-site. **Cards:** AX, DC, DS, MC, VI.

JULIO'S CAFE CORONA RESTAURANT   Lunch: $6-$12   Dinner: $6-$16   Phone: 915/591-7676   24
Mexican
Location: I-10, exit 28B, on east frontage road. 8050 Gateway Blvd E 79907. **Hours:** 11 am-9 pm, Thurs-Sat to 10 pm, Sun 8 am-8 pm. **Closed:** 11/27. **Reservations:** suggested. **Features:** Popular with local residents, this eatery provides a casual, family-oriented atmosphere in which to enjoy a wide variety of well-prepared dishes including tacos, enchiladas, fajitas and filet tampiquena. Some steak and seafood options add an even wider appeal. Smoke free premises. Casual dress; cocktails; entertainment. **Parking:** on-site. **Cards:** AX, DC, DS, MC, VI.

LEO'S MEXICAN FOOD   Lunch: $6-$9   Dinner: $6-$9   Phone: 915/566-4972   4
Mexican
Location: I-10, exit 23B (Paisano) westbound, just w on frontage road, 0.5 mi n on Chelsea Rd, then just w; exit 23A (Reynolds) eastbound, 0.7 mi e on service road to Chelsea Rd. 5103 Montana Ave 79903. **Hours:** 11 am-2 & 4:30-8:15 pm. Closed major holidays; also Sun. **Features:** In business since 1946, the restaurant prepares simple Mexican cuisine, including such standbys as enchiladas, tacos, gorditas and flautas. Portions are generous. Smoke free premises. Casual dress; beer & wine only. **Parking:** on-site. **Cards:** AX, DS, MC, VI.

(See map p. 326)

MAGNIM'S   Lunch: $7-$11   Dinner: $11-$24   Phone: 915/778-4241   ㉒
Continental   **Location:** I-10, exit 25 (Airway Blvd), 1.3 mi n; in Hilton El Paso Airport. 2027 Airway Blvd 79925. **Hours:** 6 am-11 pm. **Features:** A talented chef prepares Italian-style cuisine with a Southwestern flair. The fettuccine con frutti di mere is ladled with a creamy crab sauce. The ultimate fajitas are stuffed with chicken, beef and shrimp marinated in fine herbs and covered in salsa. Smoke free premises. Casual dress; cocktails.
Parking: on-site. **Cards:** AX, DC, DS, MC, VI.   Ⓨ Ⓧ

MEILI'S GARDEN RESTAURANT & LOUNGE   Lunch: $5-$9   Dinner: $7-$9   Phone: 915/833-1166   ②
Chinese   **Location:** I-10, exit 11 (Mesa St), just n. 7575 N Mesa St 79912. **Hours:** 11 am-9 pm, Fri & Sat-9:30 pm. Closed: 11/27. **Features:** The palatial restaurant offers simply prepared Chinese food, both on its menu and on the expansive buffet. Smoke free premises. Casual dress; beer & wine only. **Parking:** on-site. **Cards:** AX, DS, MC, VI.   Ⓧ

SENOR JUAN'S GRIGGS ‹   Lunch: $5-$11   Dinner: $5-$11   Phone: 915/598-3451   ⑯
Mexican   **Location:** 9 mi e on US 62 and 180. 9007 Montana Ave 79925. **Hours:** 11 am-9 pm, Sun-8 pm. Closed: 11/27, 12/25. **Features:** Simple dishes like the ever-popular tacos, burritos and enchiladas are served by a friendly staff in a casual, family environment. Savor the tamale entree with refried beans, coleslaw and enchilada sauce. A selection of American fare is also offered. Smoke free premises. Casual dress; cocktails. **Parking:** on-site. **Cards:** MC, VI.   Ⓨ Ⓧ

SMOKEY'S PIT STOP & SALOON   Lunch: $5-$8   Dinner: $5-$8   Phone: 915/592-3141   ⑰
Barbecue   **Location:** I-10, exit 26 (Hawkins), just n on Hawkins, then just e. 9100 Viscount 79925. **Hours:** 10:30 am-10 pm. Closed: 11/27, 12/25. **Features:** Brisket is the house specialty but chicken, sausage, and sandwiches can all enjoyed with sides like corn on the cob and coleslaw. Nothing fancy here, just some small tables and a TV to enjoy your lunch. Smoke free premises. Casual dress. **Parking:** on-site. **Cards:** AX, DS, MC, VI.   Ⓨ Ⓧ

STATE LINE STEAKS & BARBECUE   Lunch: $9-$21   Dinner: $9-$21   Phone: 915/581-3371   ⑧
Steak House   **Location:** I-10, exit 13 (Sunland Park Dr), 0.6 mi s. 1222 Sunland Park Dr 79922. **Hours:** 11:30 am-10 pm, Sun-9 pm. Closed: 1/1, 11/27, 12/24, 12/25. **Features:** On the far west side of town, just about any El Pasoan would agree the trip is well worth it. No nonsense barbecue and steaks are served up with the traditional sides of beans, baked potatoes and sausage. Many diners eagerly await the homemade bread. Expect a wait on weekends. Smoke free premises. Casual dress; cocktails. **Parking:** on-site. **Cards:** AX, DC, DS, MC, VI.   Ⓨ Ⓧ

(See map p. 326)

UNCLE BAO'S | **Lunch:** $5-$15 | **Dinner:** $6-$15 | **Phone:** 915/585-1818 | 23

Chinese

Location: I-10, exit 13 (Sunland Park Dr), 1.5 mi ne, then 0.6 mi sw. 5668 N Mesa St 79912. **Hours:** 11 am-10 pm, Fri-10:30 pm, Sat 11:30 am-10:30 pm, Sun 11:30 am-9 pm. Closed: 11/27. **Reservations:** accepted. **Features:** A classic chinese eatery with laquer tables, chinese art, and a classic menu. Enjoy favorites such as mongolian beef, general tsou's chicken, and szechwan shrimp. Count on ever friendly service. Smoke free premises. Casual dress; cocktails. **Parking:** on-site. **Cards:** AX, DS, MC, VI.

ENNIS *—See Dallas p. 292.*

EULESS pop. 46,005 (See map p. 343; index p. 346)

— WHERE TO STAY —

LA QUINTA INN-DFW AIRPORT WEST-EULESS | **Phone:** (817)540-0233 | 85

AAA SAVE

Small-scale Hotel

All Year | 1P: $59-$79 | 2P: $69-$89 | XP: $10 | F18

Location: SR 183, just e of FM 157, exit Industrial Blvd. 1001 W Airport Frwy 76040-4299. Fax: 817/283-8712. **Facility:** 129 units. 128 one-bedroom standard units. 1 one-bedroom suite. 2 stories, exterior corridors. **Parking:** on-site. **Terms:** [ECP] meal plan available, small pets only. **Amenities:** video games (fee), voice mail, irons, hair dryers. **Pool(s):** outdoor. **Guest Services:** valet laundry, airport transportation-Dallas-Fort Worth International Airport, area transportation-within 5 mi. **Business Services:** meeting rooms, fax (fee). **Cards:** AX, CB, DC, DS, JC, MC, VI. **Special Amenities: free continental breakfast and free local telephone calls.**
(See color ad p 272)

SOME UNITS
DATA PORT / FEE

MICROTEL INN AND SUITES | **Phone:** (817)545-1111 | 86

Small-scale Hotel

All Year | 1P: $49-$69 | 2P: $59-$79 | XP: $5 | F16

Location: SR 183, exit Industrial Blvd (FM 157), just e. 901 W Airport Frwy 76040. Fax: 817/545-1010. **Facility:** 56 one-bedroom standard units. 2 stories, interior corridors. *Bath:* combo or shower only. **Parking:** on-site. **Terms:** [ECP] meal plan available, small pets only ($30 deposit). **Amenities:** hair dryers. **Pool(s):** outdoor. **Leisure Activities:** exercise room. **Business Services:** fax (fee). **Cards:** AX, DC, DS, MC, VI.

SOME UNITS
ASK DATA PORT /

— WHERE TO DINE —

NORTH MAIN BBQ | **Lunch:** $4-$10 | **Dinner:** $4-$10 | **Phone:** 817/283-0884 | 51

American

Location: SR 183, exit Euless Main, just n. 406 N Main 76039. **Hours:** 11 am-9 pm, Sun 11 am-4 pm. Closed major holidays; also Mon-Thurs. **Features:** Bring the family and appetite to this all-you-can-eat buffet. Barbecued ribs, chicken, sausages and trimmings offered in a simple setting with long tables and folding chairs. Tea and water only. No credit cards. A lot of locals eat here. Casual dress. **Parking:** on-site. **Cards:** MC, VI.

FALFURRIAS pop. 5,297

— WHERE TO STAY —

DAYS INN | **Phone:** 361/325-2515

SAVE

Motel

All Year | 1P: $55-$60 | 2P: $60-$66 | XP: $8 | F18

Location: 1.8 mi s of SR 285. Hwy 281 S 78355 (Box 208D). Fax: 361/325-5504. **Facility:** 31 one-bedroom standard units. 1 story, exterior corridors. **Parking:** on-site. **Terms:** 3 day cancellation notice, [CP] meal plan available. **Amenities:** voice mail, irons, hair dryers. **Leisure Activities:** exercise room. **Business Services:** meeting rooms. **Cards:** AX, CB, DC, DS, MC, VI.

SOME UNITS
DATA PORT /

FARMERS BRANCH *—See Dallas p. 292.*

FLINT

— WHERE TO STAY —

— The following lodging was either not evaluated or did not meet AAA rating requirements but is listed for your information only. —

SILVERLEAF'S LAKE O' THE WOODS | **Phone:** 903/825-7755

fyi

Not evaluated. **Location:** 17446 Pintail Dr, Hwy 155 75762. Facilities, services, and decor characterize a mid-range property.

FLORESVILLE *—See San Antonio p. 545.*

FORT DAVIS pop. 1,050

―――――― WHERE TO STAY ――――――

HISTORICAL PRUDE GUEST RANCH   **Phone:** 432/426-3202
▼▼▼ ▼▼▼   All Year [ECP]   1P: $55-$65   2P: $65-$75   XP: $10   D6
Classic Ranch   **Location:** 4.5 mi n jct SR 118 and 17. 6 mi N Hwy 118 79734 (PO Box 1431). Fax: 432/426-4401. **Facility:** 41 units.
40 one-bedroom standard units. 1 one-bedroom suite ($125) with kitchen (no utensils). 1 story, exterior cor-
ridors. *Bath:* combo or shower only. **Parking:** on-site. **Terms:** 3 day cancellation notice-fee imposed. **Pool(s):**
heated indoor. **Leisure Activities:** 2 lighted tennis courts, bicycles, hiking trails, jogging, basketball, volleyball. *Fee:* horseback
riding. **Business Services:** meeting rooms, fax (fee). **Cards:** AX, DS, MC, VI.

SOME UNITS
(ASK) (S☐) (🍴) (🖥) (🗙) (🗙) (🕨) (📞) / (📠) /

FORT STOCKTON pop. 7,846

―――――― WHERE TO STAY ――――――

ATRIUM WEST INN   **Phone:** (432)336-6666
(AAA) (SAVE)   All Year [ECP]   1P: $60-$89   2P: $70-$99   XP: $8   F12
▼▼▼▼   **Location:** I-10, exit 257, just s. 1305 N Hwy 285 79735. Fax: 432/336-5777. **Facility:** 84 one-bedroom standard
Motel   units, some with whirlpools. 2 stories (no elevator), exterior corridors. **Parking:** on-site. **Terms:** [CP] meal
plan available, small pets only (in designated units). **Amenities:** *Some:* dual phone lines. **Pool(s):** heated indoor. **Leisure Activities:** sauna, whirlpool, exercise room. **Guest Services:** valet and coin laundry. **Business Services:** meeting rooms, fax (fee). **Cards:** AX, CB, DC, DS, MC, VI.

SOME UNITS
(S☐) (🛏) (🖥) (🗙) (🎞) (DATA PORT) (📞) (🖥) (💻) / (🗙) (VCR) /

BEST WESTERN SWISS CLOCK INN   **Phone:** (432)336-8521
(AAA) (SAVE)   All Year [BP]   1P: $58-$68   2P: $68-$78   XP: $10   F12
▼▼▼▼   **Location:** I-10, exit 256, 0.5 mi e. 3201 W Dickinson Blvd 79735. Fax: 432/336-6513. **Facility:** 112 one-bedroom
Motel   standard units. 2 stories (no elevator), exterior corridors. *Bath:* combo or shower only. **Parking:** on-site.
Terms: 5 day cancellation notice. **Amenities:** irons, hair dryers. **Dining:** 6 am-2 & 5-10 pm, cocktails.
Pool(s): outdoor. **Guest Services:** valet and coin laundry, area transportation-Fort Stockton. **Business
Services:** meeting rooms, fax (fee). **Cards:** AX, DC, DS, MC, VI. **Special Amenities:** early check-in/late
check-out and free continental breakfast.

SOME UNITS
(S☐) (✈) (🖥) (🍴) (🍸) (🐾) (🛏) (🎞) (DATA PORT) (💻) / (🗙) /

COMFORT INN OF FORT STOCKTON   **Phone:** (432)336-8531
(AAA) (SAVE)   All Year [ECP]   1P: $54-$59   2P: $59-$64   XP: $6   F18
▼▼▼▼   **Location:** I-10, exit 256, just s. 3200 W Dickinson Blvd 79735. Fax: 432/336-6789. **Facility:** 95 one-bedroom stan-
Motel   dard units, some with whirlpools. 2 stories (no elevator), interior corridors. *Bath:* combo or shower only.
Parking: on-site. **Terms:** cancellation fee imposed, pets ($5 fee). **Amenities:** irons, hair dryers. **Pool(s):** out-
door. **Guest Services:** valet and coin laundry, area transportation-Fort Stockton. **Business Services:**
meeting rooms, fax (fee). **Cards:** AX, DC, DS, MC, VI. **Special Amenities:** free continental breakfast and
free local telephone calls.

SOME UNITS
(S☐) (🛏) (🖥) (📺) (🐾) (🎞) (DATA PORT) (💻) / (🗙) (📞) (🖥) /

DAYS INN   **Phone:** (432)336-7500
(AAA) (SAVE)   All Year   1P: $46-$56   2P: $56-$76   XP: $6   F14
▼▼▼▼   **Location:** I-10, exit 257, just s. 1408 N US Hwy 285 79735. Fax: 432/336-7501. **Facility:** 50 one-bedroom stan-
Motel   dard units. 2 stories (no elevator), exterior corridors. **Parking:** on-site. **Amenities:** hair dryers. **Pool(s):** out-
door. **Leisure Activities:** whirlpool. **Business Services:** fax (fee). **Special Amenities:** free continental
breakfast and free local telephone calls.

SOME UNITS
(S☐) (🛏) (🖥) (📀) (🐾) (🎞) (DATA PORT) / (🗙) (📞) (🖥) /

ECONO LODGE   **Phone:** (432)336-9711
(SAVE)   All Year   1P: $39-$49   2P: $44-$54   XP: $5   F12
▼▼▼ ▼▼▼   **Location:** I-10, exit 261, 1.3 mi w on I-20 business route. 800 E Dickinson Blvd 79735. Fax: 432/336-5815.
Motel   **Facility:** 86 one-bedroom standard units. 2 stories (no elevator), exterior corridors. **Parking:** on-site.
Terms: weekly rates available, [CP] meal plan available, pets ($8 fee). **Amenities:** *Some:* safes. **Pool(s):**
outdoor. **Guest Services:** coin laundry. **Business Services:** meeting rooms, fax (fee). **Cards:** AX, DC, DS,
MC, VI.

SOME UNITS
(S☐) (🛏) (🐾) (🎞) (DATA PORT) / (🗙) (📞) (🖥) /

HOLIDAY INN EXPRESS   **Phone:** (432)336-5955
(AAA) (SAVE)   All Year [ECP]   1P: $57-$85   2P: $57-$90   XP: $6   F18
▼▼▼▼   **Location:** I-10, exit 257, just s. 1308 N US Hwy 285 79735. Fax: 432/336-3540. **Facility:** 41 one-bedroom stan-
Motel   dard units. 2 stories (no elevator), exterior corridors. **Parking:** on-site. **Terms:** small pets only ($25 fee, in
designated units). **Amenities:** irons, hair dryers. **Pool(s):** outdoor. **Leisure Activities:** whirlpool, exercise
room. **Guest Services:** valet and coin laundry. **Business Services:** meeting rooms, fax (fee). **Cards:** AX,
CB, DC, DS, JC, MC, VI. **Special Amenities:** free continental breakfast and free newspaper.

SOME UNITS
(S☐) (🛏) (🖥) (📀) (🐾) (🎞) (DATA PORT) (📞) (🖥) / (🗙) /

LA QUINTA INN-FORT STOCKTON   **Phone:** (432)336-9781
(AAA) (SAVE)   All Year   1P: $49-$69   2P: $55-$75
▼▼▼▼   **Location:** I-10, exit 257. 2601 I-10 W 79735. Fax: 432/336-3634. **Facility:** 95 one-bedroom standard units. 2 sto-
Motel   ries (no elevator), exterior corridors. *Bath:* combo or shower only. **Parking:** on-site. **Terms:** [ECP] meal plan
available, small pets only. **Amenities:** video games (fee), voice mail, irons, hair dryers. **Pool(s):** outdoor.
Guest Services: valet and coin laundry. **Business Services:** meeting rooms, fax (fee). **Cards:** AX, CB, DC,
DS, JC, MC, VI. **Special Amenities:** free continental breakfast and free local telephone calls.

SOME UNITS
(🛏) (📺) (📀) (🐾) (🎞) (DATA PORT) (💻) / (🗙) (📞) /

AAA's *The Disabled Driver's Mobility Guide* Now Available!

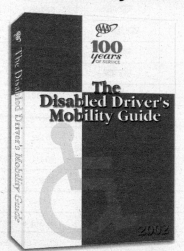

A well-known resource throughout the United States and Canada, this publication aids disabled drivers in the often difficult task of finding equipment and locating services to improve their mobility. *The Disabled Driver's Mobility Guide* includes traveling tips, information about adaptive equipment, driver evaluation and training services, publications and other related topics.

The Disabled Driver's Mobility Guide is available for just $8.95 from your local AAA club. For local club information, visit www.aaa.com or check your local white pages. For AAA membership information, call 1-800-JOIN-AAA.

Downtown Fort Worth

This index helps you "spot" where approved accommodations and restaurants are located on the corresponding detailed maps. Lodging rate ranges are for comparison only and show the property's high season; rates are per night, unless only weekly (W) rates are available. Restaurant rate range is for dinner, unless only lunch (L) is served. Turn to the listing page for more detailed rate information and consult display ads for special promotions.

Spotter/Map Page Number	OA	DOWNTOWN FORT WORTH - Lodgings	Diamond Rating	Rate Range High Season	Listing Page
1 / p. 341		The Texas White House B&B	◆◆◆	$105-$185	349
2 / p. 341	AAA	Best Western InnSuites - see color ad p 347	◆◆◆	$62-$129 (SAVE)	348
3 / p. 341		Ramada Plaza Hotel Fort Worth Convention Center	◆◆◆	$109-$139	348
4 / p. 341		Residence Inn By Marriott Fort Worth-River Plaza	◆◆◆	$135-$140	348
5 / p. 341	AAA	The Renaissance Worthington Hotel	◆◆◆◆	$142-$199 (SAVE)	348
6 / p. 341		Comfort Inn	◆◆	$59	348
7 / p. 341		Fort Worth Courtyard by Marriott	◆◆◆	$125-$135	348
8 / p. 341	AAA	Radisson Plaza Hotel Fort Worth	◆◆◆	$179-$189 (SAVE)	348
9 / p. 341		Fairfield Inn-University Drive	◆◆◆	$79-$109	348
10 / p. 341		The Ashton Hotel	◆◆◆◆	$230-$320	347
		DOWNTOWN FORT WORTH - Restaurants			
2 / p. 341		Angeluna	◆◆	$13-$30	349
3 / p. 341		Los Vaqueros	◆◆	$7-$15	349
5 / p. 341		Angelo's Bar-B-Que	◆	$5-$11	349
6 / p. 341		Mi Cocina Sundance Square	◆◆	$9-$18	349
7 / p. 341		Parthenon	◆◆	$9-$22	350
8 / p. 341		Saint-Emilion	◆◆◆	$22-$35	350
9 / p. 341		Sardine's Ristorante	◆◆	$12-$26	350
10 / p. 341		Byblos Lebanese Restaurant	◆◆	$10-$20	349
11 / p. 341		Riscky's Barbeque	◆	$8-$12	350
12 / p. 341		Riscky's Steakhouse	◆◆	$12-$26	350
13 / p. 341		The Star Cafe	◆	$6-$22	350
14 / p. 341		Costa Azul	◆	$6-$11	349
15 / p. 341		Grande	◆	$8-$20	349
16 / p. 341		Del Frisco's Double Eagle Steak House	◆◆◆	$20-$48	349
17 / p. 341		El Rancho Grande	◆◆	$6-$13	349

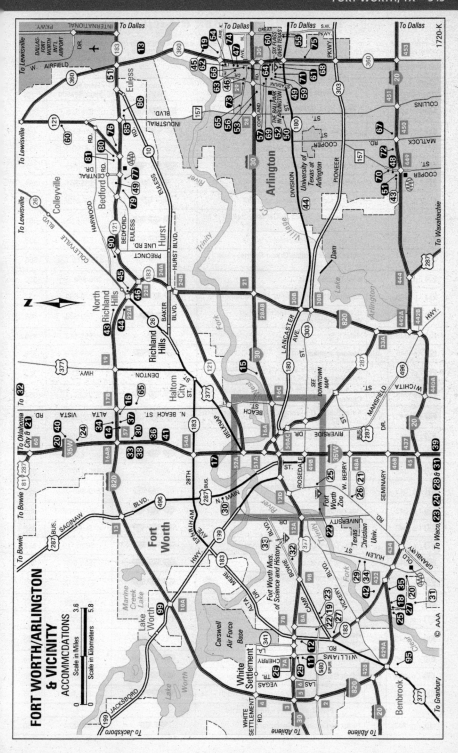

FORT WORTH/ARLINGTON & VICINITY

ACCOMMODATIONS

Fort Worth/Arlington & Vicinity

This index helps you "spot" where approved accommodations and restaurants are located on the corresponding detailed maps. Lodging rate ranges are for comparison only and show the property's high season; rates are per night, unless only weekly (W) rates are available. Restaurant rate range is for dinner, unless only lunch (L) is served. Turn to the listing page for more detailed rate information and consult display ads for special promotions.

Spotter/Map Page Number	OA	FORT WORTH - Lodgings	Diamond Rating	Rate Range High Season	Listing Page
11 / p. 343		Holiday Inn Express Hotel & Suites-Fort Worth West	◆◆◆	$79-$99	353
12 / p. 343		Hawthorn Suites Ltd	◆◆◆	$79-$129	352
13 / p. 343	AAA	**DFW Airport Marriott South**	◆◆◆	$99-$199 SAVE	352
14 / p. 343		Candlewood Suites	◆◆◆	$45-$95	351
15 / p. 343		Motel 6 East - 1341	◆◆	$35-$51	355
16 / p. 343		Super 8 Motel - see color ad p 354	◆◆	$53-$125	355
17 / p. 343		Country Inn & Suites by Carlson - see color ad p 260	◆◆◆	$79-$129	351
18 / p. 343		Holiday Inn Express Hotel & Suites	◆◆◆	$79-$94	353
19 / p. 343	AAA	**AmeriSuites (Dallas/Grand Prairie)** - see color ad p 251	◆◆◆	$79-$109 SAVE	350
20 / p. 343	AAA	**Best Western Inn**	◆◆◆	$59-$62 SAVE	350
21 / p. 343		Hampton Inn & Suites-FW Alliance Airport	◆◆◆	$79-$99	352
22 / p. 343		Homestead Studio Suites Hotel-Fort Worth/Medical Center	◆◆	$69-$85	353
23 / p. 343		Motel 6 South - 405	◆	$37-$53	355
24 / p. 343		Howard Johnson Inn	◆◆◆	$69-$79	353
25 / p. 343		La Quinta Inn & Suites Fort Worth Southwest - see color ad p 354	◆◆◆	$89-$119	353
26 / p. 343	AAA	**La Quinta Inn-Fort Worth West Medical Center** - see color ad p 354	◆◆◆	$59-$89 SAVE	354
27 / p. 343	AAA	**AmeriSuites (Ft Worth/City View)** - see color ad p 347	◆◆◆	$99-$109 SAVE	350
28 / p. 343		Microtel Inn & Suites	◆◆	$49-$69	354
29 / p. 343		Hampton Inn West Side/I30	◆◆◆	$72	352
30 / p. 343	AAA	**Comfort Inn-North**	◆◆	$55-$70 SAVE	351
31 / p. 343	AAA	**Best Western Inn & Suites** - see color ad p 351	◆◆◆	$79-$89 SAVE	351
32 / p. 343		Residence Inn-Alliance Airport	◆◆◆	$94-$139	355
33 / p. 343		Hampton Inn Meacham	◆◆◆	$69-$89	352
34 / p. 343		Fossil Creek Courtyard by Marriott	◆◆◆	$99-$119	352
35 / p. 343		Hampton Inn-Southwest	◆◆◆	$69-$99	352
36 / p. 343		La Quinta Inn & Suites-Fort Worth North - see color ad p 354	◆◆◆	$79-$109	353
37 / p. 343		Comfort Suites North-Fossil Creek	◆◆◆	$74-$89	351
38 / p. 343	AAA	**Holiday Inn North/Conference Center**	◆◆◆	$99 SAVE	353
39 / p. 343	AAA	**Holiday Inn Ft. Worth South & Conference Center**	◆◆◆	$105 SAVE	353
40 / p. 343		Residence Inn by Marriott-Fossil Creek	◆◆◆	$99	355
41 / p. 343		Hilton Garden Inn Fort Worth North	◆◆◆	$69-$119	352
42 / p. 343		TownePlace Suites by Marriott-Fort Worth	◆◆◆	$52-$82	355
		FORT WORTH - Restaurants			
19 / p. 343		Hedary's Lebanese Restaurant	◆◆	$10-$24	356

Spotter/Map Page Number	OA	FORT WORTH - Restaurants (continued)	Diamond Rating	Rate Range High Season	Listing Page
20 / p. 343		Maharaja Indian Restaurant & Bar	◆◆	$9-$13	356
21 / p. 343		Fiesta Mexican Restaurant	◆	$8-$12	356
22 / p. 343		Szechuan Restaurant	◆◆	$10-$17	357
23 / p. 343		The Balcony	◆◆◆	$15-$30	355
24 / p. 343		Zio's Italian Kitchens	◆◆	$6-$10	357
25 / p. 343		Massey's Restaurant	◆	$6-$11	356
26 / p. 343		Carshon's Deli	◆	$4-$7(L)	356
27 / p. 343		Edelweiss	◆◆	$10-$20	356
29 / p. 343		Bistro Louise	◆◆◆	$12-$37	355
30 / p. 343		Joe T Garcia's	◆◆	$11-$14	356
31 / p. 343		On Broadway Ristorante	◆◆	$9-$20	357
32 / p. 343		Kincaids	◆	$3-$5(L)	356
33 / p. 343		The Buffet Restaurant at the Kimbell	◆	$9-$13	356
34 / p. 343		Charleston's Restaurant	◆◆	$11-$20	356
		NORTH RICHLAND HILLS - Lodgings			
43 / p. 343		Country Inn & Suites by Carlson - see color ad p 260	◆◆◆	$68-$142	473
44 / p. 343		Studio 6 #6034	◆◆	$39-$53	474
45 / p. 343	AAA	**Ramada Limited**	◆◆◆	$40-$60 SAVE	474
46 / p. 343		Motel 6 - 1336	◆	$35-$51	473
		ARLINGTON - Lodgings			
47 / p. 343		Wingate Inn - see color ad p 176	◆◆◆	$89-$99	177
48 / p. 343	AAA	**Holiday Inn Express** - see color ad p 174	◆◆◆	$79-$89 SAVE	174
49 / p. 343	AAA	**Sleep Inn Main Gate-Six Flags**	◆◆	$86-$96 SAVE	175
50 / p. 343	AAA	**Days Inn Ballpark at Arlington/Six Flags**	◆◆	$59-$95 SAVE	173
51 / p. 343		Studio 6 #6036	◆◆	$47-$61	176
52 / p. 343		Courtyard by Marriott	◆◆◆	$119	172
53 / p. 343	AAA	**Country Inn & Suites By Carlson** - see color ad p 260	◆◆◆	$98-$107 SAVE	172
54 / p. 343		Homestead Studio Suites Hotel-Arlington	◆◆	$55-$70	174
55 / p. 343	AAA	**Best Western-Great Southwest Inn**	◆◆	$62-$85 SAVE	172
56 / p. 343	AAA	**Howard Johnson Express Inn**	◆◆	$60-$90 SAVE	174
57 / p. 343	AAA	**Wyndham Arlington-DFW Airport South**	◆◆◆	$94-$139 SAVE	177
59 / p. 343	AAA	**AmeriSuites (Dallas/Arlington)** - see color ad p 347	◆◆◆	$129 SAVE	170
60 / p. 343		La Quinta Inn-Arlington-Conference Center - see color ad p 272	◆◆◆	$69-$119	175
61 / p. 343		Holiday Inn Express Hotel & Suites Arlington-Six Flags	◆◆◆	$89	174
62 / p. 343		Holiday Inn-Arlington	◆◆	$89-$99	173
63 / p. 343		Hawthorn Suites Hotel	◆◆◆	$59-$199	173
64 / p. 343		Fairfield Inn by Marriott	◆◆◆	$79-$99	173
65 / p. 343	AAA	**Arlington TownePlace Suites by Marriott**	◆◆◆	$85 SAVE	171
66 / p. 343	AAA	**Hilton Arlington** - see ad p 173	◆◆◆	$85-$109 SAVE	173

Spotter/Map Page Number	OA	ARLINGTON - Lodgings (continued)	Diamond Rating	Rate Range High Season	Listing Page
67 / p. 343		Comfort Inn Arlington	◆◆◆	$59-$89	172
68 / p. 343		Motel 6 - 122	◆	$39-$55	175
69 / p. 343		Homewood Suites-Arlington	◆◆◆	$129	174
70 / p. 343	AAA	Best Western Cooper Inn & Suites - see color ad p 172	◆◆◆	$69-$74 SAVE	172
71 / p. 343	AAA	Baymont Inn & Suites-Arlington - see color ad p 171	◆◆◆	$69-$79 SAVE	171
72 / p. 343		La Quinta Inn & Suites South Arlington - see color ad p 272	◆◆◆	$99-$129	174
73 / p. 343		SpringHill Suites Arlington	◆◆◆	$89-$109	175
74 / p. 343		Residence Inn by Marriott	◆◆◆	$85-$179	175
75 / p. 343	AAA	Super 8 in Arlington - see color ad p 176	◆	$59-$74 SAVE	176
		ARLINGTON - Restaurants			
43 / p. 343		Bobby Valentine's	◆	$7-$14	177
44 / p. 343		Arlington Steakhouse	◆	$6-$13	177
45 / p. 343		Marsala Ristorante	◆◆◆	$10-$25	177
46 / p. 343		Cacharel	◆◆◆	$21-$50	177
		BEDFORD - Lodgings			
76 / p. 343	AAA	Holiday Inn-DFW-West - see ad p 208	◆◆◆	$79-$95 SAVE	209
77 / p. 343		Super 8 Motel-Bedford	◆◆	$45-$50	209
79 / p. 343	AAA	La Quinta Inn-Bedford - see color ad p 354	◆◆◆	$59-$89 SAVE	209
80 / p. 343		Homewood Suites by Hilton	◆◆◆	$106	209
81 / p. 343		Courtyard by Marriott	◆◆◆	$99-$109	208
		BEDFORD - Restaurant			
49 / p. 343		Hoffbrau Steaks	◆	$10-$21	209
		EULESS - Lodgings			
85 / p. 343	AAA	La Quinta Inn-DFW Airport West-Euless - see color ad p 272	◆◆◆	$59-$89 SAVE	339
86 / p. 343		Microtel Inn and Suites	◆◆	$49-$79	339
		EULESS - Restaurant			
51 / p. 343		North Main BBQ	◆	$4-$10	339
		HURST - Lodgings			
90 / p. 343	AAA	AmeriSuites (Ft Worth/Hurst) - see color ad p 347	◆◆◆	$99-$114 SAVE	448
		BENBROOK - Lodgings			
95 / p. 343		Motel 6 - 4051	◆◆	$43-$55	210
		LAKE WORTH - Lodgings			
99 / p. 343	AAA	Best Western Inn & Suites	◆◆◆	$79-$89 SAVE	454
		COLLEYVILLE - Restaurant			
60 / p. 343		Mac's Steaks & Seafood	◆◆	$10-$21	220
		HALTOM CITY - Restaurant			
65 / p. 343		Scotty's Deluxe Diners	◆	$7-$10	369

DOWNTOWN FORT WORTH   (See map p. 341; index p. 342)
—— WHERE TO STAY ——

THE ASHTON HOTEL **Phone:** (817)332-0100 🔟
〰〰〰〰〰 All Year 2P: $230-$320 XP: $50
Location: Jct of 6th and Main sts; center. 610 Main St 76102. Fax: 817/332-0110. **Facility:** As part of the Small
Small-scale Hotel Luxury Hotels of the World, this boutique hotel presents intimate hospitality in a nurturing environment, fea-
turing custom mahogany furniture and large baths with pedestal sinks. 39 units. 38 one-bedroom standard
units, some with whirlpools. 1 one-bedroom suite ($260-$750) with whirlpool. 6 stories, interior corridors. *Bath:* combo or shower
only. **Parking:** on-site (fee). **Terms:** cancellation fee imposed, [AP] meal plan available, package plans, 15% service charge.
Amenities: high-speed Internet (fee), dual phone lines, voice mail, safes, honor bars, hair dryers. *Some:* CD players. **Leisure
Activities:** exercise room. **Guest Services:** valet laundry. **Business Services:** meeting rooms, fax (fee). **Cards:** AX, DC, DS,
MC, VI.

(See map p. 341)

BEST WESTERN INNSUITES
Phone: (817)534-4801 **2**

AAA SAVE

Small-scale Hotel

All Year — 1P: $62-$129 — 2P: $62-$129
Location: I-30, exit 16C (Beach St), just e. 2000 Beach St 76103. Fax: 817/536-5384. **Facility:** 167 units. 135 one-bedroom standard units. 32 one-bedroom suites ($129), some with kitchens and/or whirlpools. 2-3 stories, interior/exterior corridors. *Bath:* combo or shower only. **Parking:** on-site. **Terms:** weekly rates available, pets ($25 fee). **Amenities:** video games (fee), irons, hair dryers. *Some:* voice mail. **Pool(s):** heated outdoor. **Leisure Activities:** lighted tennis court, exercise room. **Guest Services:** complimentary evening beverages, valet and coin laundry, airport transportation-Dallas-Fort Worth International Airport, area transportation-within 5 mi. **Business Services:** conference facilities, fax. **Cards:** AX, DC, DS, MC, VI. **Special Amenities:** early check-in/late check-out and free continental breakfast. *(See color ad p 347)*

SOME UNITS

COMFORT INN
Phone: (817)535-2591 **6**

SAVE

Small-scale Hotel

All Year — 1P: $59 — 2P: $59 — XP: $6 — F18
Location: I-30, exit 16C (Beach St). 2425 Scott Ave 76103. Fax: 817/531-1373. **Facility:** 99 one-bedroom standard units. 4 stories, interior corridors. **Parking:** on-site. **Amenities:** voice mail. *Some:* hair dryers. **Pool(s):** outdoor. **Guest Services:** coin laundry. **Business Services:** meeting rooms, fax (fee). **Cards:** AX, DC, DS, JC, MC, VI.

SOME UNITS

FAIRFIELD INN-UNIVERSITY DRIVE
Phone: (817)335-2000 **9**

SAVE

Small-scale Hotel

All Year [ECP] — 1P: $79-$99 — 2P: $79-$109 — XP: $6 — F18
Location: I-30, exit 12 (University Dr), just s. 1505 S University Dr 76107. Fax: 817/335-2000. **Facility:** 81 one-bedroom standard units. 4 stories, interior corridors. *Bath:* combo or shower only. **Parking:** on-site. **Terms:** 14 day cancellation notice. **Amenities:** voice mail, irons, hair dryers. **Pool(s):** heated indoor. **Leisure Activities:** whirlpool. **Guest Services:** valet and coin laundry. **Business Services:** meeting rooms, fax (fee). **Cards:** AX, CB, DC, DS, MC, VI.

SOME UNITS

FORT WORTH COURTYARD BY MARRIOTT
Phone: 817/335-1300 **7**

SAVE

Small-scale Hotel

All Year [ECP] — 1P: $125 — 2P: $135
Location: I-30, exit 12 (University Dr), 0.5 mi s. 3150 Riverfront Dr 76107. Fax: 817/336-6926. **Facility:** 130 units. 120 one-bedroom standard units. 10 one-bedroom suites ($135-$145). 2 stories, interior corridors. *Bath:* combo or shower only. **Parking:** on-site. **Amenities:** voice mail, irons, hair dryers. **Pool(s):** heated outdoor. **Leisure Activities:** whirlpool, exercise room. **Guest Services:** valet and coin laundry. **Business Services:** meeting rooms, fax (fee). **Cards:** AX, CB, DC, DS, JC, MC, VI.

SOME UNITS

RADISSON PLAZA HOTEL FORT WORTH
Phone: (817)870-2100 **8**

AAA SAVE

Historic
Large-scale Hotel

All Year — 1P: $179 — 2P: $189 — XP: $10 — F18
Location: Northeast corner of Main and Eighth sts; center. 815 Main St 76102. Fax: 817/335-3408. **Facility:** 517 units. 514 one-bedroom standard units. 3 two-bedroom suites, some with kitchens (no utensils) and/or whirlpools. 15 stories, interior corridors. *Bath:* combo or shower only. **Parking:** on-site (fee). **Amenities:** voice mail, irons, hair dryers. **Dining:** 2 restaurants, 6:30 am-11 pm, cocktails. **Pool(s):** heated outdoor. **Leisure Activities:** sauna, exercise room. **Guest Services:** gift shop, valet laundry. **Business Services:** meeting rooms, fax (fee). **Cards:** AX, CB, DC, DS, MC, VI. **Special Amenities:** free newspaper.

SOME UNITS
FEE

RAMADA PLAZA HOTEL FORT WORTH CONVENTION CENTER
Phone: (817)335-7000 **3**

Large-scale Hotel

All Year — 1P: $109-$129 — 2P: $119-$139 — XP: $10 — F18
Location: Center. 1701 Commerce St 76102. Fax: 817/335-3333. **Facility:** 430 units. 420 one-bedroom standard units. 9 one- and 1 two-bedroom suites ($275-$495), some with kitchens. 12 stories, interior corridors. **Parking:** on-site (fee). **Terms:** 3 day cancellation notice. **Amenities:** dual phone lines, voice mail, irons, hair dryers. **Pool(s):** heated indoor. **Leisure Activities:** whirlpool, exercise room. **Guest Services:** gift shop, valet laundry, area transportation. **Business Services:** conference facilities, business center. **Cards:** AX, DS, MC, VI.

SOME UNITS

THE RENAISSANCE WORTHINGTON HOTEL
Phone: (817)870-1000 **5**

AAA SAVE

Large-scale Hotel

All Year — 1P: $142-$199 — 2P: $142-$199
Location: Northwest corner of 2nd and Main sts. Located at Sundance Square. 200 Main St 76102. Fax: 817/338-9176. **Facility:** Within Sundance Square, the epicenter of Fort Worth's downtown social scene, the hotel is a few miles from the cultural and arts districts. 504 units. 477 one-bedroom standard units. 27 one-bedroom suites. 12 stories, interior corridors. *Bath:* combo or shower only. **Parking:** on-site (fee). **Terms:** cancellation fee imposed, small pets only. **Amenities:** video games (fee), voice mail, honor bars, irons, hair dryers. *Some:* fax. **Dining:** 2 restaurants, 6 am-11 pm, cocktails. **Pool(s):** heated indoor. **Leisure Activities:** sauna, whirlpool, lighted tennis court, basketball. *Fee:* massage. **Guest Services:** gift shop, valet laundry. **Business Services:** conference facilities, business center. **Cards:** AX, CB, DC, DS, JC, MC, VI.

SOME UNITS

RESIDENCE INN BY MARRIOTT FORT WORTH-RIVER PLAZA
Phone: (817)870-1011 **4**

SAVE

Small-scale Hotel

All Year [ECP] — 1P: $135-$140
Location: I-30, exit 12 (University Dr), 0.4 mi s. 1701 S University Dr 76107. Fax: 817/877-5500. **Facility:** 120 units. 90 one-bedroom standard units with kitchens. 30 one-bedroom suites with kitchens. 2 stories, exterior corridors. **Parking:** on-site. **Terms:** small pets only ($5 extra charge). **Amenities:** voice mail, irons, hair dryers. **Pool(s):** heated outdoor. **Leisure Activities:** whirlpool, jogging, exercise room, sports court. **Guest Services:** complimentary evening beverages: Mon-Thurs, valet and coin laundry, area transportation. **Business Services:** meeting rooms, fax (fee). **Cards:** AX, CB, DC, DS, JC, MC, VI.

SOME UNITS
FEE

(See map p. 341)

THE TEXAS WHITE HOUSE B&B   Phone: (817)923-3597   ❶
▽▽▽▽ All Year [BP]   1P: $105-$185   2P: $105-$185
         Location: I-30, exit 8th Ave, 1 mi s. Located in a residential area. 1417 8th Ave 76104. Fax: 817/923-0410.
Historic Bed **Facility:** Simple but elegant country-style decor gives this historic in-town landmark the ambience of a re-
& Breakfast   treat. Smoke free premises. 5 one-bedroom standard units, some with whirlpools. 2 stories (no elevator),
              interior/exterior corridors. **Parking:** on-site. **Terms:** 7 day cancellation notice-fee imposed. **Amenities:** irons,
hair dryers. **Cards:** AX, CB, DC, DS, MC, VI.

SOME UNITS

(ASK) (¶†) (♿) (✕) (DATA PORT) / (☐) /

------- **WHERE TO DINE** -------

ANGELO'S BAR-B-QUE   **Lunch:** $5-$11   **Dinner:** $5-$11   **Phone:** 817/332-0357   ⑤
▽   **Location:** 2 mi nw, cross Trinity River, n from Jacksboro Hwy (SR 199). 2533 White Settlement Rd 76107. **Hours:** 11
           am-10 pm. Closed major holidays; also Sun. **Features:** For lunch, have a fully-loaded deli sandwich with
Barbecue   salami, ham, turkey and homemade sauce. The barbecue beef and ribs are luscious. The simple dining
           room is decorated with wild game and hunting trophies. Casual dress; beer & wine only. **Parking:** on-site.

(✕)

ANGELUNA   **Lunch:** $8-$16   **Dinner:** $13-$30   **Phone:** 817/334-0080   ②
▽▽   **Location:** Between Calhoun and Commerce sts; center. 215 E 4th St 76102. **Hours:** 11:30 am-2 & 5:30-9:30 pm,
           Fri-11 pm, Sat 5 pm-11 pm. Closed: 11/27, 12/25. **Reservations:** suggested. **Features:** Attractive and
American   colorful with an Art Deco design, the dining room has very high ceilings with windows that afford a nice
           view of Bass Performance Hall. Good variety and imaginative presentations abound from appetizers to
chicken, beef and seafood entrees. Smoke free premises. Casual dress; cocktails. **Parking:** on-site. **Cards:** AX, DS, MC, VI.

(✕)

BYBLOS LEBANESE RESTAURANT   **Lunch:** $5-$10   **Dinner:** $10-$20   **Phone:** 817/625-9667   ⑩
▽▽   **Location:** Corner of N Main St and Central Ave; 1.5 mi n of downtown. 1406 N Main St 76106. **Hours:** 11 am-10
           pm, Fri-11 pm, Sat 5 pm-11 pm. Closed: 11/27, 12/25; also Sun. **Features:** The authentic Lebanese
Lebanese   artwork and musical instruments adorning the walls create a festive atmosphere. Your taste buds will be
           pleasantly surprised by the slowly roasted lamb shank with seasonal vegetables and light spices that
literally falls off the bone. Try the sambouseck bel-lahm appetizer of thinly rolled half moon shaped dough stuffed with ground
sirloin, onions and pine nuts then skillet fried; very pleasing to the palate. Casual dress; cocktails. **Parking:** on-site.
Cards: AX, CB, DC, DS, MC, VI.

(✕)

COSTA AZUL   **Lunch:** $6-$11   **Dinner:** $6-$11   **Phone:** 817/624-0506   ⑭
▽   **Location:** 1 mi s of jct US 287 and SR 183. 1521 N Main St 76106. **Hours:** 10 am-midnight, Fri & Sat-3 am, Sun
           9 am-midnight. **Features:** Costa Azul serves traditional Mexican fare and seafood. Try the seviche for an
Mexican   added treat. Smoke free premises. Casual dress; beer only. **Parking:** on-site. **Cards:** AX, DS, MC, VI. (✕)

DEL FRISCO'S DOUBLE EAGLE STEAK HOUSE   **Dinner:** $20-$48   **Phone:** 817/877-3999   ⑯
▽▽▽▽ **Location:** Northwest corner of 8th and Main sts; center. 812 Main St 76102. **Hours:** 5 pm-10 pm, Fri & Sat-11 pm.
           Closed major holidays; also Sun. **Reservations:** suggested. **Features:** This is the place to go in downtown
Steak House Fort Worth if you're looking for thick, juicy steaks. Dressy casual; cocktails. **Parking:** valet. **Cards:** AX, CB,
           DC, DS, MC, VI.

(¶) (✕)

EL RANCHO GRANDE   **Lunch:** $6-$13   **Dinner:** $6-$13   **Phone:** 817/624-9206   ⑰
▽▽   **Location:** Corner of N Main St and Central Ave; 1.5 mi n of downtown. 1400 N Main St 76106. **Hours:** 11 am-9 pm,
           Fri & Sat-10 pm. Closed major holidays; also Sun. **Features:** Mexican tile floors and wooden beams
Regional Mexican decorate this bustling cafe. Get warmed up with the stuffed jalapeno peppers. Hearty portions of tamales
           are loaded with meat and veggies. Finish with a sliver of the sweet margarita pie. Casual dress; cocktails.
Parking: on-site. **Cards:** AX, CB, DC, DS, MC, VI.

(¶) (✕)

GRANDE   **Lunch:** $3-$6   **Dinner:** $8-$20   **Phone:** 817/348-8226   ⑮
▽   **Location:** Between Main and Houston sts; center. 115 W 2nd St 76102. **Hours:** 11 am-10 pm, Fri & Sat-midnight.
           Closed major holidays. **Features:** Variations on a Tex-Mex theme include habanero shrimp tacos and
Mexican   yellowfin tuna enchiladas. Casual dress; cocktails. **Parking:** street. **Cards:** AX, CB, DC, DS, MC, VI. (✕)

LOS VAQUEROS   **Lunch:** $7-$15   **Dinner:** $7-$15   **Phone:** 817/624-1511   ③
▽▽ ▽▽ **Location:** Just s of jct SR 183 and US 287, just n of historic Stockyards. 2629 N Main St 76106. **Hours:** 11 am-9 pm,
           Fri & Sat-11 pm, Sun-4 pm. Closed major holidays. **Reservations:** suggested. **Features:** This longtime
Mexican   favorite serves traditional Tex-Mex in a sprawling converted warehouse which is located in historic
           Stockyards. An extensive menu features popular dishes like quesadillas and nachos along with seafood
selections such as snapper a la Veracruz. Casual dress; cocktails; entertainment. **Parking:** on-site. **Cards:** AX, DC, DS,
MC, VI.

(¶) (✕)

MI COCINA SUNDANCE SQUARE   **Lunch:** $8-$10   **Dinner:** $9-$18   **Phone:** 817/877-3600   ⑥
▽▽ ▽▽ **Location:** Just s of Sundance Square; center. 509 Main St 76102. **Hours:** 11 am-10 pm, Fri & Sat-11 pm.
           Closed: 4/20, 11/27, 12/25. **Features:** Latin music fills the air at this eatery. Mama's tacos are filled with
Tex-Mex   fajita meat, cheese and green onions. The Spanish rice is perfectly seasoned and colorful. For dessert, try
           the homemade flan coated with caramel. Smoke free premises. Casual dress; beer & wine only. **Parking:**
street. **Cards:** AX, DC, DS, MC, VI.

(✕)

PARTHENON

Greek

Lunch: $8-$22   **Dinner:** $9-$22   **Phone:** 817/810-0800   7

Location: Jct of Peace and N Henderson; just n of downtown. 401 N Henderson 76102. **Hours:** 11 am-2 & 5-9 pm, Fri & Sat-10 pm. Closed major holidays; also Sun. **Reservations:** suggested. **Features:** This recent addition to the Fort Worth restaurant scene is a welcome one. A combination of Greek and American fare makes for enjoyable choices at Parthenon. The atmosphere here is casual with the feel of a Mediterranean cafe. Also the service at Parthenon is warm, attentive and knowledgeable. Smoke free premises. Casual dress; beer & wine only. **Parking:** on-site. **Cards:** AX, DS, MC, VI.

RISCKY'S BARBEQUE

Barbecue

Lunch: $8-$12   **Dinner:** $8-$12   **Phone:** 817/626-7777   11

Location: 0.5 mi s of jct US 287 and SR 183, on N Main St to E Exchange Ave, just e. 140 E Exchange Ave 76106. **Hours:** 11 am-10 pm, Fri & Sat-midnight, Sun-9 pm. Closed major holidays. **Features:** The Texas barbecue house in the Stockyards has been in business since 1927. Casual dress; cocktails. **Parking:** on-site. **Cards:** AX, DC, DS, MC, VI.

RISCKY'S STEAKHOUSE

Steak House

Lunch: $7-$9   **Dinner:** $12-$26   **Phone:** 817/624-4800   12

Location: 0.5 mi s of jct US 287 and SR 183 to E Exchange Ave, just e. 120 E Exchange Ave 76106. **Hours:** 11 am-10 pm, Fri & Sat-11 pm, Sun-9 pm. Closed major holidays. **Reservations:** suggested; weekends. **Features:** This is a popular steak house located in the heart of the Stockyards near downtown Fort Worth. Casual dress; cocktails. **Parking:** on-site. **Cards:** AX, DC, DS, MC, VI.

SAINT-EMILION

French

Dinner: $22-$35   **Phone:** 817/737-2781   8

Location: 0.5 mi w of University Dr. 3617 W 7th St 76107. **Hours:** 6 pm-10 pm. Closed major holidays; also Sun & Mon. **Reservations:** suggested; weekends. **Features:** Country French cuisine is served in a delightful country inn atmosphere. Thoughtful touches like vases with fresh flowers at each table add to the graciousness of the experience. Bacon-wrapped shrimp makes a delicious appetizer, colorful and flavorful. Smoke free premises. Casual dress; cocktails. **Parking:** on-site. **Cards:** AX, DC, DS, MC, VI.

SARDINE'S RISTORANTE

Italian

Lunch: $8-$11   **Dinner:** $12-$26   **Phone:** 817/332-9937   9

Location: 0.3 mi w of University Dr. 509 University Dr 76107. **Hours:** 11 am-2 & 5-11:30 pm, Fri & Sat-12:30 am, Sun 3 pm-11:30 pm. Closed major holidays. **Reservations:** suggested; weekends. **Features:** This longtime area favorite enjoys a convenient location near museums and other cultural attractions. Featuring pasta, veal, chicken and seafood dishes, it offers outdoor seating, split-level dining rooms, and presents a jazz trio that plays nightly. Casual dress; cocktails. **Parking:** on-site. **Cards:** AX, DC, MC, VI.

THE STAR CAFE

Southwest
Southwestern

Lunch: $6-$22   **Dinner:** $6-$22   **Phone:** 817/624-8701   13

Location: 0.5 mi s of jct US 287 and SR 183 to W Exchange Ave, just w. 111 W Exchange Ave 76106. **Hours:** 11 am-3 pm, Tues-Thurs to 9 pm, Fri-10 pm, Sat 8 am-10 pm, Sun 8 am-noon. Closed major holidays. **Features:** The Star Cafe, in the heart of the historic Stockyards, serves home cooking in a Western-style decor. Casual dress; beer & wine only. **Parking:** street. **Cards:** AX, CB, DC, DS, MC, VI.

FORT WORTH pop. 534,694 (See map p. 343; index p. 344)

——— WHERE TO STAY ———

AMERISUITES (DALLAS/GRAND PRAIRIE)

(AAA) (SAVE)

Small-scale Hotel

Phone: (972)988-6800   19

All Year [ECP]   1P: $79-$109   2P: $79-$109   XP: $10   F17

Location: SR 360, exit J/K aves. 1542 N Hwy 360 75050 (1542 N Hwy 360, GRAND PRAIRIE). Fax: 972/988-6822. **Facility:** 135 one-bedroom standard units. 6 stories, interior corridors. *Bath:* combo or shower only. **Parking:** on-site. **Amenities:** video games (fee), high-speed Internet, dual phone lines, voice mail, irons, hair dryers. **Pool(s):** heated outdoor. **Leisure Activities:** exercise room. **Guest Services:** valet and coin laundry, airport transportation-Dallas-Fort Worth International Airport, area transportation-within 5 mi. **Business Services:** meeting rooms, fax (fee). **Cards:** AX, CB, DC, DS, JC, MC, VI. **Special Amenities:** free continental breakfast and free newspaper. *(See color ad p 251)*

SOME UNITS

AMERISUITES (FT WORTH/CITY VIEW)

(AAA) (SAVE)

Small-scale Hotel

Phone: (817)361-9797   27

All Year [CP]   1P: $99-$109   2P: $99-$109   XP: $10   F17

Location: I-20, exit 431 (Bryant Irvin Rd). 5900 City View Blvd 76132. Fax: 817/361-9444. **Facility:** 128 one-bedroom standard units. 6 stories, interior corridors. *Bath:* combo or shower only. **Parking:** on-site. **Terms:** small pets only. **Amenities:** video games (fee), voice mail, irons, hair dryers. *Some:* dual phone lines. **Pool(s):** heated outdoor. **Leisure Activities:** exercise room. **Guest Services:** valet and coin laundry. **Business Services:** meeting rooms, fax (fee). **Cards:** AX, CB, DC, DS, JC, MC, VI. **Special Amenities:** free continental breakfast and free newspaper. *(See color ad p 347)*

SOME UNITS

BEST WESTERN INN

(AAA) (SAVE)

Small-scale Hotel

Phone: (817)847-8484   20

All Year   1P: $59   2P: $62   XP: $5   F16

Location: I-35 W, exit 58 (Western Center Blvd), north on service road, then just e. 6700 Fossil Bluff Dr 76131. Fax: 817/847-9495. **Facility:** 63 one-bedroom standard units, some with whirlpools. 3 stories, interior corridors. *Bath:* combo or shower only. **Parking:** on-site. **Terms:** [ECP] meal plan available, small pets only ($10 extra charge). **Amenities:** dual phone lines, safes, irons, hair dryers. **Pool(s):** outdoor. **Leisure Activities:** whirlpool, exercise room. **Guest Services:** valet and coin laundry. **Business Services:** fax (fee). **Cards:** AX, CB, DC, DS, MC, VI. **Special Amenities:** early check-in/late check-out and free continental breakfast.

SOME UNITS

(See map p. 343)

BEST WESTERN INN & SUITES Phone: (817)551-6700 **31**
(AAA) (SAVE)
4/1-8/31 [ECP]	1P: $79-$84	2P: $84-$89
2/1-3/31 & 9/1-1/31 [ECP]	1P: $74-$79	2P: $79-$84

Location: I-35, exit 44. 6500 S Frwy 76134. Fax: 817/568-9378. Facility: 60 one-bedroom standard units. 2 stories, interior corridors. Bath: combo or shower only. Parking: on-site. Amenities: voice mail, irons, hair
Small-scale Hotel dryers. Pool(s): outdoor. Leisure Activities: whirlpool, exercise room. Guest Services: coin laundry. Business Services: meeting rooms, fax (fee). Cards: AX, CB, DC, DS, JC, MC, VI. Special Amenities: free continental breakfast and free newspaper. (See color ad below)

SOME UNITS

CANDLEWOOD SUITES Phone: (817)838-8229 **14**
All Year 1P: $45-$85 2P: $55-$95
Location: I-820, exit 17B, just s. 5201 Endicott Ave 76137. Fax: 817/838-8355. Facility: 98 units. 74 one-bedroom
Small-scale Hotel standard units with efficiencies. 24 one-bedroom suites with efficiencies. 3 stories, interior corridors. Bath: combo or shower only. Parking: on-site. Terms: office hours 7 am-8 pm, pets ($100 fee). Amenities: video library, CD players, dual phone lines, voice mail, irons, hair dryers. Leisure Activities: exercise room. Guest Services: sundries, valet and coin laundry. Business Services: fax. Cards: AX, CB, DC, DS, MC, VI.

SOME UNITS

COMFORT INN-NORTH Phone: 817/834-8001 **30**
(AAA) (SAVE)
5/16-8/15 [ECP]	1P: $55-$60	2P: $65-$70	XP: $5	F15
8/16-10/15 [ECP]	1P: $55-$60	2P: $60-$65	XP: $5	F15
2/1-5/15 & 10/16-1/31 [ECP]	1P: $50-$55	2P: $60-$65	XP: $5	F15

Location: I-35 W, exit 56A. 4850 North Frwy 76137. Fax: 817/834-3159. Facility: 60 one-bedroom standard units.
Small-scale Hotel 2 stories, interior corridors. Bath: combo or shower only. Parking: on-site. Amenities: irons, hair dryers. Pool(s): outdoor. Guest Services: valet and coin laundry. Business Services: fax (fee). Cards: AX, DC, DS, MC, VI.

SOME UNITS

COMFORT SUITES NORTH-FOSSIL CREEK Phone: (817)222-2333 **37**
(SAVE)
6/1-8/31 [ECP]	1P: $74-$89	2P: $74-$89	XP: $5	F18
9/1-1/31 [ECP]	1P: $69-$84	2P: $69-$84	XP: $5	F18
2/1-5/31 [ECP]	1P: $64-$79	2P: $64-$79	XP: $5	F18

Location: I-820, exit 17B. 3751 Tanacross Dr 76137. Fax: 817/222-9666. Facility: 75 one-bedroom standard
Small-scale Hotel units, some with whirlpools. 3 stories, interior corridors. Bath: combo or shower only. Parking: on-site. Amenities: voice mail, irons, hair dryers. Pool(s): outdoor. Leisure Activities: whirlpool, exercise room. Guest Services: complimentary evening beverages: Mon-Thurs, valet and coin laundry. Business Services: meeting rooms, fax. Cards: AX, CB, DC, DS, JC, MC, VI.

SOME UNITS

COUNTRY INN & SUITES BY CARLSON Phone: (817)831-9200 **17**
All Year [ECP] 1P: $79-$129 2P: $79-$129
Location: I-35 W, exit 53, just w. 2200 Mercado Dr 76106. Fax: 817/838-7567. Facility: 68 units. 26 one-bedroom
Small-scale Hotel standard units. 42 one-bedroom suites, some with whirlpools. 3 stories, interior corridors. Bath: combo or shower only. Parking: on-site. Amenities: high-speed Internet, dual phone lines, voice mail, irons, hair dryers. Pool(s): small outdoor. Leisure Activities: whirlpool, exercise room. Guest Services: coin laundry, area transportation. Business Services: meeting rooms, fax (fee). Cards: AX, CB, DC, DS, MC, VI. (See color ad p 260)

SOME UNITS

(See map p. 343)

DFW AIRPORT MARRIOTT SOUTH
Phone: (817)358-1700 — 13

(AAA) [SAVE]
▽▽▽▽ F

All Year   1P: $99-$199   2P: $99-$199   XP: $10   F
Location: SR 360, exit Trinity Blvd, 0.3 mi e, then just n. 4151 Centreport Blvd 76155. **Fax:** 817/359-4644.
Facility: 295 units. 291 one-bedroom standard units. 4 one-bedroom suites, some with whirlpools. 8 stories,
interior corridors. *Bath:* combo or shower only. **Parking:** on-site. **Amenities:** high-speed Internet (fee), voice
Small-scale Hotel   mail, irons, hair dryers. **Dining:** 6 am-11 pm, cocktails. **Pool(s):** heated indoor. **Leisure Activities:** exercise
room. **Guest Services:** sundries, valet and coin laundry, airport transportation-Dallas-Fort Worth International Airport. **Business Services:** conference facilities, business center. **Cards:** AX, CB, DC, DS, JC, MC, VI.
Special Amenities: free newspaper.

SOME UNITS

FOSSIL CREEK COURTYARD BY MARRIOTT
Phone: (817)847-0044 — 34

[SAVE]
▽▽▽▽ F18

All Year   1P: $99-$109   2P: $109-$119   XP: $10   F18
Location: I-820, exit 17B, just w on westbound service road. 3751 NE Loop 820 76137. **Fax:** 817/847-6188.
Facility: 154 units. 149 one-bedroom standard units, some with whirlpools. 5 one-bedroom suites. 3 stories,
interior corridors. *Bath:* combo or shower only. **Parking:** on-site. **Amenities:** high-speed Internet (fee), voice
Small-scale Hotel   mail, irons, hair dryers. **Pool(s):** heated outdoor. **Leisure Activities:** whirlpool, exercise room. **Guest Serv-
ices:** valet and coin laundry. **Business Services:** meeting rooms, fax. **Cards:** AX, CB, DC, DS, JC,
MC, VI.

SOME UNITS

HAMPTON INN & SUITES-FW ALLIANCE AIRPORT
Phone: (817)439-0400 — 21

[SAVE]
▽▽▽▽ F12

All Year [ECP]   1P: $79   2P: $99   XP: $10   F12
Location: I-35 W, exit 66 (Westport Pkwy). 13600 North Frwy 76178. **Fax:** 817/439-1158. **Facility:** 102 units. 78
one-bedroom standard units. 24 one-bedroom suites with efficiencies. 5 stories, interior corridors. *Bath:*
combo or shower only. **Parking:** on-site. **Terms:** small pets only ($50 fee). **Amenities:** voice mail, irons, hair
Small-scale Hotel   dryers. **Pool(s):** outdoor. **Leisure Activities:** limited exercise equipment. **Guest Services:** sundries, valet
and coin laundry, area transportation. **Business Services:** meeting rooms, fax (fee). **Cards:** AX, DC, DS,
MC, VI.

SOME UNITS

HAMPTON INN MEACHAM
Phone: (817)625-5327 — 33

[SAVE]
▽▽▽▽ F18

All Year   1P: $69-$79   2P: $79-$89   XP: $10   F18
Location: I-35 W, exit 56A. 4681 Gemini Pl 76106. **Fax:** 817/625-7727. **Facility:** 64 one-bedroom standard units.
3 stories, interior corridors. *Bath:* combo or shower only. **Parking:** on-site. **Terms:** [CP] meal plan available.
Amenities: dual phone lines, voice mail, irons, hair dryers. **Pool(s):** outdoor. **Leisure Activities:** exercise
Small-scale Hotel   room. **Guest Services:** valet and coin laundry, area transportation. **Business Services:** meeting rooms, fax
(fee). **Cards:** AX, CB, DC, DS, MC, VI.

SOME UNITS
FEE   FEE

HAMPTON INN-SOUTHWEST
Phone: (817)346-7845 — 35

[SAVE]
▽▽▽▽ F18

All Year [ECP]   1P: $69-$89   2P: $69-$99   XP: $6   F18
Location: I-20, exit 431. 4799 SW Loop 820 76132. **Fax:** 817/346-4901. **Facility:** 78 one-bedroom standard units.
4 stories, interior corridors. *Bath:* combo or shower only. **Parking:** on-site. **Terms:** 14 day cancellation no-
tice. **Amenities:** voice mail, irons, hair dryers. **Pool(s):** small heated indoor. **Leisure Activities:** whirlpool.
Small-scale Hotel   **Guest Services:** valet laundry. **Business Services:** meeting rooms, fax (fee). **Cards:** AX, CB, DC, DS,
MC, VI.

SOME UNITS
FEE

HAMPTON INN WEST SIDE/I30
Phone: (817)560-4180 — 29

[SAVE]
▽▽▽▽

All Year [ECP]   1P: $72   2P: $72
Location: I-30, exit 7A, just s. 2700 Cherry Ln 76116. **Fax:** 817/560-8032. **Facility:** 125 one-bedroom standard
units. 3 stories, exterior corridors. *Bath:* combo or shower only. **Parking:** on-site. **Terms:** small pets only ($25
deposit). **Amenities:** video games (fee), voice mail, irons. **Pool(s):** outdoor. **Guest Services:** valet laundry.
Small-scale Hotel   **Business Services:** meeting rooms, fax. **Cards:** AX, CB, DC, DS, MC, VI.

SOME UNITS

HAWTHORN SUITES LTD
Phone: 817/731-9600 — 12

▽▽▽▽

All Year   1P: $79-$129   2P: $79-$129
Location: I-30, exit 7B. 6851 West Frwy 76116. **Fax:** 817/731-9608. **Facility:** 70 units. 68 one-bedroom standard
Small-scale Hotel   units, some with kitchens and/or whirlpools. 2 one-bedroom suites with kitchens and whirlpools. 3 stories, interior corridors. *Bath:* combo or shower only. **Parking:** on-site. **Terms:** cancellation fee imposed, [BP] meal
plan available. **Amenities:** video games (fee), dual phone lines, voice mail, irons, hair dryers. **Pool(s):** small heated indoor.
Leisure Activities: whirlpool, exercise room. **Guest Services:** valet and coin laundry. **Business Services:** meeting rooms, fax
(fee). **Cards:** AX, DC, DS, MC, VI.

SOME UNITS

HILTON GARDEN INN FORT WORTH NORTH
Phone: (817)222-0222 — 41

[SAVE]
▽▽▽▽

All Year   1P: $69-$119   2P: $69-$119
Location: I-35 W, exit 56A, just e. 4400 North Frwy 76137. **Fax:** 817/222-0770. **Facility:** 98 units. 74 one-bedroom
standard units. 24 one-bedroom suites ($139-$189), some with whirlpools. 3 stories, interior corridors. *Bath:*
combo or shower only. **Parking:** on-site. **Amenities:** video games (fee), dual phone lines, voice mail, irons,
Small-scale Hotel   hair dryers. **Pool(s):** heated outdoor, heated indoor. **Leisure Activities:** whirlpool, exercise room. **Guest
Services:** sundries, valet and coin laundry, area transportation. **Business Services:** meeting rooms, business center. **Cards:** AX, CB, DC, DS, JC, MC, VI.

SOME UNITS

(See map p. 343)

HOLIDAY INN EXPRESS HOTEL & SUITES　　　　　　　　**Phone:** (817)292-4900　**18**
▽▽△△▽▽　All Year [ECP]　　　1P: $79-$94　　　2P: $79-$94
Small-scale Hotel　**Location:** I-20, exit 431. 4609 City Lake Blvd W 76132. **Fax:** 817/263-6731. **Facility:** 91 units. 86 one-bedroom standard units, some with whirlpools. 5 one-bedroom suites ($114). 4 stories, interior corridors. *Bath:* combo or shower only. **Parking:** on-site. **Terms:** small pets only ($25 fee). **Amenities:** video games (fee), dual phone lines, voice mail, irons, hair dryers. **Pool(s):** heated outdoor. **Leisure Activities:** whirlpool, exercise room. **Guest Services:** valet and coin laundry, area transportation. **Business Services:** meeting rooms, business center. **Cards:** AX, CB, DC, DS, JC, MC, VI.
SOME UNITS
(ASK) [SD] [🛏] [🍴] [📺] [🎱] [≈] [🎬] [DATA PORT] [💻] / [✕] [🔒] [🖨] /

HOLIDAY INN EXPRESS HOTEL & SUITES-FORT WORTH WEST　　　**Phone:** (817)560-4200　**11**
▽▽△△▽▽　All Year　　　1P: $79-$99　　　2P: $89-$99　　　XP: $10　F18
Small-scale Hotel　**Location:** I-30, exit 7A. 2730 Cherry Ln 76116. **Fax:** 817/560-9250. **Facility:** 60 units. 54 one-bedroom standard units. 6 one-bedroom suites ($89-$150), some with whirlpools. 3 stories, interior corridors. **Parking:** on-site. **Terms:** [CP] meal plan available, pets ($50 deposit). **Amenities:** dual phone lines, voice mail, irons, hair dryers. **Pool(s):** small outdoor. **Leisure Activities:** whirlpool, exercise room. **Guest Services:** valet and coin laundry, area transportation. **Business Services:** meeting rooms, fax (fee). **Cards:** AX, CB, DC, DS, JC, MC, VI.
SOME UNITS
(ASK) [SD] [🛬]FEE [🛏] [≈] [🎬] [DATA PORT] [🔒] [🖨] [💻] / [✕] /

HOLIDAY INN FT. WORTH SOUTH & CONFERENCE CENTER　　　**Phone:** 817/293-3088　**39**
(AAA) (SAVE)　All Year　　　1P: $105　　　2P: $105
▽▽△△▽▽
Small-scale Hotel　**Location:** I-35, exit 44. 100 Altamesa E Blvd 76134. **Fax:** 817/551-5877. **Facility:** 247 units. 241 one-bedroom standard units. 6 one-bedroom suites ($185) with whirlpools. 6 stories, interior corridors. **Parking:** on-site. **Terms:** 3 day cancellation notice, [BP] meal plan available, small pets only ($25 deposit). **Amenities:** dual phone lines, voice mail, irons, hair dryers. **Dining:** 6 am-2 & 5-10 pm, Sat & Sun from 7 am, cocktails. **Pool(s):** heated indoor. **Leisure Activities:** whirlpool, exercise room. **Guest Services:** gift shop, complimentary evening beverages: Tues, valet and coin laundry, area transportation-within 5 mi. **Business Services:** conference facilities, fax (fee). **Cards:** AX, CB, DC, DS, MC, VI. **Special Amenities:** free newspaper.
SOME UNITS
[SD] [🛏] [🍴] [📺] [🎱] [≈] [🎬] [DATA PORT] [💻] / [✕] [🔒] /

HOLIDAY INN NORTH/CONFERENCE CENTER　　　　　**Phone:** (817)625-9911　**38**
(AAA) (SAVE)　All Year　　　1P: $99　　　2P: $99　　　XP: $10　F18
▽▽△△▽▽
Small-scale Hotel　**Location:** I-35 W, exit 56A. 2540 Meacham Blvd 76106. **Fax:** 817/625-5132. **Facility:** 247 units. 241 one-bedroom standard units. 6 one-bedroom suites with whirlpools. 6 stories, interior corridors. **Parking:** on-site. **Terms:** [BP] meal plan available, small pets only ($20 deposit). **Amenities:** dual phone lines, voice mail, irons, hair dryers. **Dining:** 2 restaurants, 6 am-2 & 5-10 pm, Sat & Sun from 7 am, cocktails. **Pool(s):** heated indoor. **Leisure Activities:** whirlpool, exercise room. **Guest Services:** gift shop, valet and coin laundry. **Business Services:** meeting rooms, fax (fee). **Cards:** AX, DC, DS, MC, VI. **Special Amenities:** free newspaper.
SOME UNITS
[SD] [🛏] [🍴] [📺] [🎱] [≈] [🎬] [DATA PORT] [💻] / [✕] [🔒] [🖨] /

HOMESTEAD STUDIO SUITES HOTEL-FORT WORTH/MEDICAL CENTER　**Phone:** (817)338-4808　**22**
▽▽△△ ▽▽△△　All Year　　　1P: $69-$79　　　2P: $75-$85　　　XP: $5　F17
Small-scale Hotel　**Location:** I-30, exit 12 (University Dr), just s. 1601 River Run 76107. **Fax:** 817/338-4779. **Facility:** 97 one-bedroom standard units with efficiencies. 2 stories, exterior corridors. *Bath:* combo or shower only. **Parking:** on-site. **Terms:** office hours 6:30 am-7 pm, pets ($75 extra charge). **Amenities:** voice mail, irons. **Guest Services:** coin laundry. **Cards:** AX, CB, DC, DS, JC, MC, VI.
SOME UNITS
(ASK) [SD] [🛏] [🍴] [📺] [🛁] [🎬] [DATA PORT] [🔒] [🖨] [💻] / [✕] /

HOWARD JOHNSON INN　　　　　　　　　　**Phone:** (817)447-2000　**24**
▽▽△△▽▽　All Year　　　1P: $69　　　2P: $79　　　XP: $10　F18
Small-scale Hotel　**Location:** I-35 W, exit 39, just w. 12450 South Frwy 76028. **Fax:** 817/447-3028. **Facility:** 50 one-bedroom standard units, some with whirlpools. 2 stories, interior corridors. **Parking:** on-site. **Terms:** [ECP] meal plan available. **Amenities:** irons, hair dryers. **Pool(s):** outdoor. **Leisure Activities:** whirlpool. **Guest Services:** coin laundry. **Business Services:** meeting rooms, fax (fee). **Cards:** AX, DC, DS, JC, MC, VI.
SOME UNITS
(ASK) [SD] [🍴] [📺] [🛁M] [≈] [🎬] [DATA PORT] [🔒] [🖨] / [✕] /

LA QUINTA INN & SUITES-FORT WORTH NORTH　　　　**Phone:** (817)222-2888　**36**
(SAVE)　All Year　　　1P: $79-$99　　　2P: $89-$109　　　XP: $10　F18
▽▽△△▽▽　**Location:** I-35 W, exit 56A, just n. 4700 North Frwy 76137. **Fax:** 817/222-2229. **Facility:** 133 units. 125 one-bedroom standard units. 8 one-bedroom suites ($109-$159). 4 stories, interior corridors. *Bath:* combo or shower only.
Small-scale Hotel　**Parking:** on-site. **Terms:** [ECP] meal plan available, small pets only. **Amenities:** video games (fee), voice mail, irons, hair dryers. **Pool(s):** heated outdoor. **Leisure Activities:** whirlpool, exercise room. **Guest Services:** valet and coin laundry. **Business Services:** meeting rooms, fax (fee). **Cards:** AX, CB, DC, DS, JC, MC, VI. *(See color ad p 354)*
SOME UNITS
[SD] [🛏] [🎱] [≈] [🎬] [DATA PORT] [💻] / [✕] [🔒] [🖨] /

LA QUINTA INN & SUITES FORT WORTH SOUTHWEST　　　**Phone:** (817)370-2700　**25**
(SAVE)　All Year　　　1P: $89-$109　　　2P: $99-$110　　　XP: $10　F18
▽▽△△▽▽　**Location:** I-20, exit 431. 4900 Bryant Irving Rd 76132. **Fax:** 817/370-2733. **Facility:** 128 units. 120 one-bedroom standard units. 8 one-bedroom suites ($119-$159). 4 stories, interior corridors. *Bath:* combo or shower only.
Small-scale Hotel　**Parking:** on-site. **Terms:** [ECP] meal plan available, small pets only. **Amenities:** video games (fee), dual phone lines, voice mail, irons, hair dryers. **Pool(s):** heated outdoor. **Leisure Activities:** whirlpool, exercise room. **Guest Services:** valet and coin laundry. **Business Services:** meeting rooms, fax (fee). **Cards:** AX, CB, DC, DS, JC, MC, VI. *(See color ad p 354)*
SOME UNITS
[SD] [🛏] [🍴] [🛁M] [🎱] [≈] [🎬] [DATA PORT] [💻] / [✕] [🔒] [🖨] /

(See map p. 343)

LA QUINTA INN-FORT WORTH WEST MEDICAL CENTER   Phone: (817)246-5511   **26**

AAA SAVE   All Year   1P: $59-$79   2P: $69-$89   XP: $10   F18
▼▼▼▼   **Location:** I-30, exit 7A. 7888 I-30 W 76108. Fax: 817/246-8870. **Facility:** 106 one-bedroom standard units. 3 stories, interior/exterior corridors. *Bath:* combo or shower only. **Parking:** on-site. **Terms:** [ECP] meal plan available, small pets only. **Amenities:** video games (fee), voice mail, irons, hair dryers. **Pool(s):** outdoor.
Small-scale Hotel   **Guest Services:** valet laundry. **Business Services:** fax (fee). **Cards:** AX, CB, DC, DS, JC, MC, VI. **Special Amenities:** free continental breakfast and free local telephone calls. *(See color ad below)*

SOME UNITS

🔊 🛏 🛗 ♿ 🚭 🏊 🛗 🎥 📠 💻 / ✖ 🔲 📷 /

MICROTEL INN & SUITES   Phone: 817/551-7000   **28**
▼▼▼ ▼▼▼   All Year   1P: $49-$59   2P: $59-$69   XP: $5   F16
Location: I-35 W, exit 40. 10675 South Frwy 76140. Fax: 817/293-7662. **Facility:** 63 one-bedroom standard units.
Small-scale Hotel   3 stories, interior corridors. *Bath:* combo or shower only. **Parking:** on-site. **Terms:** cancellation fee imposed, weekly rates available, [CP] meal plan available. **Guest Services:** coin laundry. **Business Services:** fax (fee). **Cards:** AX, CB, DC, DS, MC, VI.

SOME UNITS

ASK 🔊 🛗 ♿ 🎥 / ✖ 📠 🔲 📷 💻 /

(See map p. 343)

MOTEL 6 EAST - 1341   **Phone:** 817/834-7361   **15**

5/22-1/31	1P: $35-$45	2P: $41-$51	XP: $3 F17
2/1-5/21	1P: $31-$41	2P: $37-$47	XP: $3 F17

Small-scale Hotel   **Location:** I-30, exit 18. 1236 Oakland Blvd 76103. **Fax:** 817/834-1573. **Facility:** 95 one-bedroom standard units. 2 stories, exterior corridors. *Bath:* combo or shower only. **Parking:** on-site. **Terms:** small pets only. **Pool(s):** outdoor. **Business Services:** fax (fee). **Cards:** AX, CB, DC, DS, MC, VI.

SOME UNITS

MOTEL 6 SOUTH - 405   **Phone:** 817/293-8595   **23**

5/22-1/31	1P: $37-$47	2P: $43-$53	XP: $3 F17
2/1-5/21	1P: $36-$46	2P: $42-$52	XP: $3 F17

Small-scale Hotel   **Location:** I-35, exit 44. 6600 South Frwy 76134. **Fax:** 817/293-8577. **Facility:** 147 one-bedroom standard units. 2 stories, exterior corridors. *Bath:* combo or shower only. **Parking:** on-site. **Terms:** small pets only. **Pool(s):** outdoor. **Guest Services:** coin laundry. **Business Services:** fax (fee). **Cards:** AX, CB, DC, DS, MC, VI.

SOME UNITS

RESIDENCE INN-ALLIANCE AIRPORT   **Phone:** 817/750-7000   **32**

SAVE

All Year	1P: $94-$139	2P: $94-$139

Small-scale Hotel   **Location:** I-35 W, exit 66. 13400 North Frwy 76177. **Fax:** 817/750-7500. **Facility:** 111 units. 60 one-bedroom standard units with efficiencies. 24 one- and 27 two-bedroom suites, some with efficiencies or kitchens. 5 stories, interior corridors. *Bath:* combo or shower only. **Parking:** on-site. **Terms:** [BP] meal plan available, pets ($175 deposit, $6 extra charge). **Amenities:** dual phone lines, voice mail, irons, hair dryers. **Pool(s):** outdoor. **Leisure Activities:** whirlpool, exercise room, sports court. **Guest Services:** sundries, complimentary evening beverages: Mon-Thurs, valet and coin laundry, area transportation. **Business Services:** meeting rooms, fax (fee). **Cards:** AX, DC, DS, JC, MC, VI.

SOME UNITS

RESIDENCE INN BY MARRIOTT-FOSSIL CREEK   **Phone:** (817)439-1300   **40**

SAVE

All Year [BP]	1P: $99	2P: $99

Small-scale Hotel   **Location:** I-35 W, exit 58 (Western Center Blvd) northbound to Sandshell, 0.7 mi s; southbound, take first road to the right through strip center, just s to Sandshell, 0.7 mi s. 5801 Sandshell 76137. **Fax:** 817/439-3329. **Facility:** 114 units. 32 one-bedroom standard units with efficiencies. 61 one- and 21 two-bedroom suites ($109-$175), some with efficiencies or kitchens. 3 stories, interior corridors. *Bath:* combo or shower only. **Parking:** on-site. **Terms:** pets ($125 fee). **Amenities:** voice mail, irons, hair dryers. **Pool(s):** heated outdoor. **Leisure Activities:** whirlpool, exercise room, sports court. **Guest Services:** complimentary evening beverages: Mon-Thurs, valet and coin laundry, area transportation. **Business Services:** meeting rooms, fax (fee). **Cards:** AX, CB, DC, DS, JC, MC, VI.

SOME UNITS

SUPER 8 MOTEL   **Phone:** 817/222-0892   **16**

All Year [ECP]	1P: $53-$125	2P: $58-$125	XP: $5 F12

Small-scale Hotel   **Location:** I-820, exit 17B. 5225 N Beach St 76137-2729. **Fax:** 817/222-1910. **Facility:** 71 units. 69 one-bedroom standard units, some with whirlpools. 2 one-bedroom suites ($100-$175), some with whirlpools. 3 stories, interior corridors. *Bath:* combo or shower only. **Parking:** on-site. **Terms:** cancellation fee imposed. **Amenities:** hair dryers. **Pool(s):** outdoor. **Leisure Activities:** whirlpool, exercise room. **Guest Services:** coin laundry. **Business Services:** meeting rooms, fax (fee). **Cards:** AX, CB, DC, DS, JC, MC, VI. *(See color ad p 354)*

SOME UNITS

TOWNEPLACE SUITES BY MARRIOTT-FORT WORTH   **Phone:** (817)732-2224   **42**

SAVE

All Year	1P: $52-$82	2P: $52-$82

Small-scale Hotel   **Location:** I-20, exit 433. 4200 International Plaza Dr 76109. **Fax:** 817/732-2114. **Facility:** 95 units. 71 one-bedroom standard units with kitchens. 4 one- and 20 two-bedroom suites ($72-$102) with kitchens. 3 stories, interior corridors. *Bath:* combo or shower only. **Parking:** on-site. **Terms:** cancellation fee imposed, pets ($10 extra charge). **Amenities:** voice mail, irons, hair dryers. **Pool(s):** heated outdoor. **Leisure Activities:** exercise room. **Guest Services:** valet and coin laundry. **Business Services:** business center. **Cards:** AX, CB, DC, DS, MC, VI.

SOME UNITS

─────── **WHERE TO DINE** ───────

THE BALCONY   **Dinner:** $15-$30   **Phone:** 817/731-3719   **23**

Continental   **Location:** I-30, exit Camp Bowie Blvd westbound; exit Horne St eastbound, 1 mi w. 6100 Camp Bowie Blvd 76116. **Hours:** 4:30 pm-10 pm, Sat-11 pm. Closed: 12/25. **Reservations:** suggested; weekends. **Features:** True to its name, The Balcony is perched atop a local business. The green awnings and decorative railings beckon you to make the trip up the stairs. Entrees are prepared in your choice of sauce and are accompanied by two vegetable choices as well. The simple, contemporary decor has pastel peach-colored walls adorned with local artists' paintings. The cozy dining room has live piano music playing softly in the background. Semi-formal attire; cocktails. **Parking:** on-site. **Cards:** AX, CB, DS, MC, VI.

BISTRO LOUISE   **Lunch:** $8-$15   **Dinner:** $12-$37   **Phone:** 817/922-9244   **29**

Mediterranean   **Location:** I-30, exit 10 (Hulen St), 1.5 mi s; at northwest corner of Oak Park and Hulen St. 2900 S Hulen St, Suite 40 76109. **Hours:** 11 am-2 & 5:30-9 pm, Fri & Sat-10 pm. Closed major holidays; also Sun. **Reservations:** suggested. **Features:** The bistro serves Mediterranean and New Mediterranean fare, ranging from traditional selections to seafood. Menu prices are moderate. Dressy casual; cocktails. **Parking:** on-site. **Cards:** AX, DC, DS, MC, VI.

(See map p. 343)

THE BUFFET RESTAURANT AT THE KIMBELL **Lunch:** $6-$9 **Dinner:** $9-$13 **Phone:** 817/332-8451 (33)
American
Location: 2.5 mi w on Will Rogers Rd, then w to Camp Bowie Blvd. 3333 Camp Bowie Blvd 76107. **Hours:** 11:30 am-2 pm, Fri noon-2 & 5:30-7:30 pm, Sun noon-2 pm. Closed major holidays; also Mon. **Features:** Soup, salad, sandwiches and great artwork are the highlights of this restaurant, which features New American cuisine served in a delightful setting. Smoke free premises. Casual dress; wine only. **Parking:** on-site. **Cards:** AX, DS, MC, VI.

CARSHON'S DELI **Lunch:** $4-$7 **Phone:** 817/923-1907 (26)
American
Location: Sw from I-35, exit Berry St, 2 mi w to Cleburne Rd, then just s. 3133 Cleburne Rd 76110. **Hours:** 9 am-3 pm. Closed major holidays; also Sun. **Features:** A popular kosher-style deli close to Texas Christian University, it offers a selection of big, old-fashioned sandwiches like Reubens and Rebeccas. All desserts are homemade including the famous chocolate pie. Choose from either dine-in or takeout options. Smoke free premises. Casual dress; beer & wine only. **Parking:** on-site.

CHARLESTON'S RESTAURANT **Lunch:** $11-$20 **Dinner:** $11-$20 **Phone:** 817/735-8900 (34)
American
Location: I-20/Loop 820, exit 433, 1.9 mi n. 3020 S Hulen St 76109. **Hours:** 11 am-10 pm, Fri & Sat-11 pm. Closed major holidays. **Reservations:** suggested; weekends. **Features:** The menu here offers standard American cuisine plus samplings of Southwestern, Cajun and Italian dishes. Casual dress; cocktails. **Parking:** on-site. **Cards:** AX, DC, DS, MC, VI.

EDELWEISS **Dinner:** $10-$20 **Phone:** 817/738-5934 (27)
Traditional German
Location: I-30, 1.3 mi s on US 183 (exit 7B) to Weatherford Traffic Circle. 3801-A Southwest Blvd 76116. **Hours:** 5 pm-11 pm. Closed major holidays; also Sun & Mon. **Reservations:** accepted. **Features:** Eat, drink and dance to live music in a friendly, authentic German atmosphere. Traditional German fare includes cheese soup, marinated herring, sauerbraten with red cabbage and potato pancakes, and a luscious German cheesecake. Casual dress; cocktails; entertainment. **Parking:** on-site. **Cards:** AX, CB, DC, DS, MC, VI.

FIESTA MEXICAN RESTAURANT **Lunch:** $6-$8 **Dinner:** $8-$12 **Phone:** 817/923-6941 (21)
Tex-Mex
Location: I-35 W, exit 48A, 0.7 mi w, just s. 3233 Hemphill St 76110. **Hours:** 11 am-9 pm, Fri & Sat-10 pm. Closed major holidays; also Sun. **Reservations:** accepted. **Features:** Terra cotta tile, brightly colored walls and wrought iron partitions add to the festive atmosphere at Fiesta Mexican Restaurant. Are the tortillas fresh? Stand by in the lobby and watch as they crank up the machine and make them. Typical Tex-Mex selections with straightforward presentation and adequate portions are the norm. Casual dress; beer & wine only. **Parking:** on-site. **Cards:** AX, CB, DC, DS, MC, VI.

HEDARY'S LEBANESE RESTAURANT **Dinner:** $10-$24 **Phone:** 817/731-6961 (19)
Lebanese
Location: I-30, exit 9B (Camp Bowie Blvd) westbound, 0.3 mi w. 3308 Fairfield Ave 76116. **Hours:** 5 pm-10 pm, Fri & Sat-11 pm. Closed major holidays; also Mon. **Features:** Serving Middle Eastern fare for nearly 25 years, this family-owned establishment offers a lively atmosphere with an open kitchen and Lebanese background music. Lamb, beef or chicken entrees like the tasty shish kebab are featured with warm pita bread. Casual dress; beer & wine only. **Parking:** on-site. **Cards:** AX, DC, DS, MC, VI.

JOE T GARCIA'S **Lunch:** $7-$9 **Dinner:** $11-$14 **Phone:** 817/429-5166 (30)
Tex-Mex
Location: Corner of 22nd and Commerce sts. 2201 N Commerce St 76106. **Hours:** 11 am-2:30 & 5-10 pm, Fri & Sat 11 am-11 pm, Sun 11 am-10 pm. Closed: 4/20, 11/27, 12/25. **Features:** Strolling cantors provide entertainment at this 60-year-old family-owned Mexican restaurant that is highly revered by the locals. The traditional Mexican motif with murals and paintings creates a festive atmosphere. The bi-level dining room is comfortable, but the patio area is endless and is reminiscent of a courtyard in Mexico with fountains, foliage and statues. Casual dress; cocktails. **Parking:** on-site.

KINCAIDS **Lunch:** $3-$5 **Phone:** 817/732-2881 (32)
American
Location: I-30, exit 9B (Camp Bowie Blvd/Horne St) westbound; exit 9B (Horne St) eastbound, 0.8 mi nw. 4901 Camp Bowie Blvd 76107. **Hours:** 11 am-6 pm. Closed major holidays; also Sun. **Features:** Kincaids' has been delighting locals for decades with their big and delicious hamburgers. Smoke free premises. Casual dress; beer & wine only. **Parking:** on-site.

MAHARAJA INDIAN RESTAURANT & BAR **Lunch:** $6-$8 **Dinner:** $9-$13 **Phone:** 817/263-7156 (20)
Indian
Location: I-20, exit 433 (Hulen St), 1.4 mi s. 6308 Hulen Bend Blvd 76132. **Hours:** 11 am-2 & 5:30-10 pm, Fri-10:30 pm, Sat 11 am-2:30 & 5:30-10:30 pm, Sun 11:30 am-2:30 & 5:30-10 pm. Closed major holidays. **Features:** This quiet northern Indian dining room, located in a small shopping center near a mall and theaters, is popular with both locals and tourists. A lunch buffet and a la carte dinners feature tandoori items plus the always popular curry dishes. Smoke free premises. Casual dress; cocktails. **Parking:** on-site. **Cards:** AX, DS, MC, VI.

MASSEY'S RESTAURANT **Lunch:** $6-$8 **Dinner:** $6-$11 **Phone:** 817/921-5582 (25)
American
Location: I-35, exit W Allen Ave, 1.5 mi w to 8th Ave, just s. 1805 8th Ave 76110. **Hours:** 11 am-9 pm, Fri-10 pm, Sun 11 am-3 pm. Closed major holidays. **Features:** Serving Fort Worth since 1947. Massey's offers inexpensive, American-style home cooking. Try the chicken fried steak. Smoke free premises. Casual dress; beer & wine only. **Parking:** on-site. **Cards:** AX, DC, DS, MC, VI.

(See map p. 343)

ON BROADWAY RISTORANTE   **Lunch:** $8-$9   **Dinner:** $9-$20   **Phone:** 817/346-8841   31

Northern Italian

Location: I-20, exit 433, 1.5 mi s, then just w. 6306 Hulen Bend Blvd 76132. **Hours:** 11:30 am-2:30 & 5:30-10 pm, Fri-10:30 pm, Sat 5:30 pm-10:30 pm, Sun 5:30 pm-10 pm. **Reservations:** accepted. **Features:** At the heart of a commercial strip mall just a short drive from the interstate, this quaint New York-style Italian restaurant's dim lighting softly accents the pink and pale green color scheme. The juicy pollo cordon bleu is stuffed with prosciutto and cheese in mornay sauce. For dessert, try the napoli (puffed pastry with three layers of cream and strawberries drizzled with chocolate icing). Smoke free premises. Casual dress; cocktails. **Parking:** on-site. **Cards:** AX, CB, DC, DS, MC, VI.

SZECHUAN RESTAURANT   **Lunch:** $7-$9   **Dinner:** $10-$17   **Phone:** 817/738-7300   22

Chinese

Location: I-30, exit 8A (Camp Bowie Blvd) westbound; exit Horne St eastbound to Locke Ave, just sw; northwest corner of Horne St and Camp Bowie Blvd. 5712 Locke Ave 76107. **Hours:** 11 am-10 pm, Fri & Sat-11 pm. Closed: 11/27. **Reservations:** accepted. **Features:** Szechuan-style cooking is the specialty at this restaurant, which features beef with mushrooms and bamboo shoots and such spicy favorites as tung ting chicken and pork with black bean sauce. Chinese music complements the cuisine and the decor. Smoke free premises. Casual dress; cocktails. **Parking:** on-site. **Cards:** AX, MC, VI.

ZIO'S ITALIAN KITCHENS   **Lunch:** $6-$10   **Dinner:** $6-$10   **Phone:** 817/232-3632   24

Italian

Location: I-35 W, exit 58 (Western Center Blvd), just e to Sandshell, then just n. 6631 Fossil Bluff Dr 76137. **Hours:** 11 am-10 pm, Fri & Sat-11 pm. Closed: 11/27, 12/25. **Reservations:** suggested. **Features:** The small chain of Italian restaurants specializes in in-house preparation. Fresh vegetables are chopped by hand, lasagna is hand-layered, and sauces are made from scratch. Pizzas are baked in aromatic brick ovens. Even many of the desserts are prepared on site, including Oreo mountain and bread pudding. Smoke free premises. Casual dress; cocktails. **Parking:** on-site. **Cards:** AX, DS, MC, VI.

FREDERICKSBURG pop. 8,911

——— WHERE TO STAY ———

BEST WESTERN FREDERICKSBURG   **Phone:** (830)992-2929

Small-scale Hotel

All Year   1P: $79-$135   2P: $79-$135

Location: Jct US 290 and 87, 6 blks s. 314 E Highway St 78624. **Fax:** 830/990-1479. **Facility:** 56 units. 55 one-bedroom standard units. 1 one-bedroom suite ($99-$135) with kitchen (no utensils). 2 stories, interior corridors. *Bath:* combo or shower only. **Parking:** on-site. **Terms:** [ECP] meal plan available, small pets only ($10 extra charge, in smoking units). **Amenities:** dual phone lines, irons, hair dryers. **Pool(s):** outdoor. **Guest Services:** airport transportation-Gillespie County Airport, area transportation-within 5 mi. **Business Services:** meeting rooms, fax (fee). **Cards:** AX, DS, MC, VI. **Special Amenities:** free continental breakfast.

SOME UNITS

BUDGET HOST DELUXE INN   **Phone:** 830/997-3344

Motel

(See color ad p 162)

All Year   1P: $38-$65   2P: $45-$75

Location: US 290, 0.5 mi e. 901 E Main St 78624-4818. **Fax:** 830/997-4381. **Facility:** 25 units. 22 one-bedroom standard units. 2 two- and 1 three-bedroom suites with kitchens (no utensils). 1-2 stories (no elevator), exterior corridors. *Bath:* combo or shower only. **Parking:** on-site. **Terms:** [CP] meal plan available. **Leisure Activities:** whirlpool. **Guest Services:** coin laundry. **Business Services:** fax (fee). **Cards:** AX, DC, DS, JC, MC, VI. **Special Amenities:** free continental breakfast and free local telephone calls.

SOME UNITS

COMFORT INN   **Phone:** (830)997-9811

Small-scale Hotel

2/28-1/31		1P: $75-$135	2P: $80-$155	XP: $6	F18
2/1-2/27		1P: $65-$125	2P: $70-$145	XP: $6	F18

Location: 0.8 mi sw on SR 16; 0.8 mi sw of jct US 87 and 290. 908 S Adams St 78624. **Fax:** 830/997-2068. **Facility:** 46 one-bedroom standard units. 2 stories (no elevator), exterior corridors. **Parking:** on-site. **Terms:** [CP] meal plan available. **Amenities:** irons. **Pool(s):** outdoor. **Leisure Activities:** tennis court. **Guest Services:** valet laundry. **Business Services:** fax (fee). **Cards:** AX, CB, DC, DS, JC, MC, VI. **Special Amenities:** free continental breakfast and free local telephone calls.

SOME UNITS

FEE

CREEKSIDE INN   **Phone:** 830/997-6316

Bed & Breakfast

All Year   1P: $100-$115   2P: $100-$115   XP: $20   D18

Location: Just s of jct Main St and US 87. 304 S Washington 78624. **Fax:** 830/997-9864. **Facility:** Designated smoking area. 7 one-bedroom standard units, some with whirlpools. 1 story, exterior corridors. *Bath:* combo or shower only. **Parking:** on-site. **Terms:** 2 night minimum stay - weekends, age restrictions may apply, [BP] meal plan available. **Amenities:** video library, irons, hair dryers. **Business Services:** fax. **Cards:** AX, DS, MC, VI.

DAS COLLEGE HAUS BED & BREAKFAST   **Phone:** (830)997-9047

Historic Bed & Breakfast

All Year   1P: $99-$115   2P: $115-$135   XP: $25

Location: 0.4 mi n of jct US 290 and SR 965 (Milam St), then 0.4 mi e. 106 W College St 78624. **Fax:** 830/990-5047. **Facility:** Designated smoking area. 4 one-bedroom standard units. 2 stories (no elevator), interior corridors. *Bath:* combo or shower only. **Parking:** on-site. **Terms:** 2 night minimum stay - weekends, 10 day cancellation notice-fee imposed, [BP] meal plan available. **Amenities:** hair dryers. **Leisure Activities:** Fee: massage. **Business Services:** fax. **Cards:** DS, MC, VI.

DAYS INN SUITES

Phone: (830)997-1086

All Year [CP]   1P: $70-$150   2P: $70-$150   XP: $10   F15

Small-scale Hotel

Location: 0.6 mi sw of jct US 290 and SR 16. 808 S Adams St 78624. Fax: 830/997-8342. **Facility:** 30 units. 29 one- and 1 two-bedroom standard units, some with whirlpools. 2 stories (no elevator), exterior corridors. **Parking:** on-site. **Amenities:** hair dryers. **Pool(s):** outdoor. **Guest Services:** coin laundry. **Business Services:** fax (fee). **Cards:** AX, DC, DS, MC, VI. **Special Amenities:** free continental breakfast and free local telephone calls. *(See color ad below)*

SOME UNITS

THE DELFORGE PLACE

Phone: 830/997-6212

Classic Bed
& Breakfast

All Year   2P: $110-$125   XP: $25

Location: Jct US 290 and SR 16, 0.7 mi s to Walnut, 3 blks e. 710 Ettie St 78624. Fax: 830/997-7190. **Facility:** Built in 1898, this historic home offers comfortable accomodations decorated in period pieces. Situated within blocks of downtown. Designated smoking area. 4 units. 3 one-bedroom standard units. 1 one-bedroom suite. 2 stories (no elevator), interior/exterior corridors. *Bath:* combo or shower only. **Parking:** on-site. **Terms:** 2 night minimum stay - weekends, 7 day cancellation notice-fee imposed, [ECP] meal plan available. **Business Services:** fax (fee). **Cards:** AX, DC, MC, VI.

SOME UNITS

DIETZEL MOTEL

Phone: 830/997-3330

Motel

All Year   1P: $45-$72   2P: $47-$72   XP: $7

Location: 1 mi w on US 290 at jct US 87. 1141 W US 290 78624 (PO Box 266). **Facility:** 20 one-bedroom standard units. 1 story, exterior corridors. *Bath:* shower only. **Parking:** on-site. **Terms:** pets ($5 extra charge, limit 2). **Cards:** AX, DS, MC, VI.

SOME UNITS

ECONO LODGE

Phone: (830)997-3437

Motel

All Year [CP]   1P: $74-$109   2P: $79-$114   XP: $5   F18

Location: 0.7 mi sw jct US 290 and SR 16. 810 S Adams St 78624. Fax: 830/997-4405. **Facility:** 36 one-bedroom standard units, some with whirlpools. 1 story, exterior corridors. **Parking:** on-site. **Pool(s):** outdoor. **Leisure Activities:** whirlpool. **Business Services:** fax (fee). **Cards:** AX, CB, DC, DS, MC, VI.

SOME UNITS

FREDERICKSBURG LODGE
AAA SAVE
Small-scale Hotel
Phone: 830/997-6568
All Year [CP] 1P: $54-$89 2P: $59-$89 XP: $5 F17
Location: US 290, just e of jct US 87. 514 E Main St 78624. **Fax:** 830/997-7897. **Facility:** 61 units. 60 one-bedroom standard units. 1 one-bedroom suite ($125-$225). 2 stories (no elevator), exterior corridors. **Parking:** on-site. **Terms:** small pets only ($10 fee, must be attended). **Amenities:** hair dryers. **Pool(s):** outdoor. **Leisure Activities:** whirlpool. **Guest Services:** coin laundry. **Business Services:** fax (fee). **Cards:** AX, CB, DC, DS, MC, VI.

SOME UNITS

HOLIDAY INN EXPRESS
Small-scale Hotel
Phone: (830)990-4200
3/1-8/15 [ECP] 1P: $84-$109 2P: $84-$109 XP: $10 F17
2/1-2/28 & 8/16-1/31 [ECP] 1P: $79-$99 2P: $79-$99 XP: $10 F17
Location: 1 mi w on US 290 at jct US 87. 1220 N Hwy 87 78624. **Fax:** 830/997-0349. **Facility:** 50 one-bedroom standard units. 2 stories, interior corridors. *Bath:* combo or shower only. **Parking:** on-site. **Terms:** check-in 4 pm, small pets only ($25 fee). **Amenities:** dual phone lines, voice mail, irons, hair dryers. **Pool(s):** small outdoor. **Guest Services:** valet laundry. **Business Services:** fax. **Cards:** AX, DC, DS, MC, VI.

SOME UNITS

THE MAGNOLIA HOUSE
Historic Bed & Breakfast
Phone: (830)997-0306
All Year 2P: $95-$115 XP: $25
Location: SR 16, 0.6 mi n of jct US 290, just w. 101 E Hackberry 78624. **Fax:** 830/997-0766. **Facility:** This restored 1923 home furnished with antiques includes a stone patio overlooking a tranquil fishpond. Smoke free premises. 5 one-bedroom standard units. 2 stories (no elevator), interior corridors. **Parking:** street. **Terms:** 2 night minimum stay - weekends, age restrictions may apply, 7 day cancellation notice-fee imposed, [BP] meal plan available. **Amenities:** hair dryers. **Business Services:** fax. **Cards:** AX, DS, MC, VI.

SOME UNITS

SUNSET INN
AAA SAVE
Motel
Phone: 830/997-9581
All Year 1P: $55-$65 2P: $55-$70 XP: $4 F12
Location: 0.8 mi sw of jct US 290 and SR 16. 900 S Adams St 78624. **Fax:** 830/990-8437. **Facility:** 24 one-bedroom standard units, some with efficiencies or kitchens. 1 story, exterior corridors. **Parking:** on-site. **Terms:** weekly rates available, small pets only. **Dining:** 11 am-8 pm, Fri-9 pm; closed Sun & Mon. **Guest Services:** coin laundry. **Business Services:** fax. **Cards:** AX, DC, DS, MC, VI. **Special Amenities:** early check-in/late check-out and free local telephone calls.

SOME UNITS

— WHERE TO DINE —

COTTON GIN SEAFOOD AND STEAK KITCHEN
Steak & Seafood
Dinner: $14-$23 **Phone:** 830/990-5734
Location: Jct US 290 and SR 16, 2.8 mi s; in Cotton Gin Cabins. 2805 S Hwy 16 78624. **Hours:** 5 pm-9 pm. **Closed:** 1/1, 12/24, 12/25. **Reservations:** suggested. **Features:** A variety of seafood and beef choices are available as well as daily specials with a Texas Hill Country flair. Smoke free premises. Casual dress; cocktails. **Parking:** on-site. **Cards:** AX, DS, MC, VI.

DER LINDENBAUM
German
Lunch: $6-$10 **Dinner:** $11-$30 **Phone:** 830/997-9126
Location: Downtown. 312 E Main St 78624. **Hours:** 11 am-10 pm. **Closed:** 4/20, 11/27, 12/25. **Features:** Lunches and dinners consist of schnitzels, steak, sausages, and chicken prepared in a traditional German manner. Guests also can savor excellent pastries, as well as German beer, wine and gourmet coffee. Smoke free premises. Casual dress; beer & wine only. **Parking:** street. **Cards:** AX, DS.

Savings at Your Fingertips

When you have a AAA TourBook® guide in your hand, you have a world of savings right at your fingertips. Official Appointment lodgings that display the bright-red AAA logo, SAVE icon and Diamond rating in their listing want AAA member business, and many offer discounts and special amenities to members*.

So, when planning your next vacation, be sure to consult your AAA TourBook for the familiar red SAVE icon.

*See TourBook Navigator, page 14, for details.

MAMACITA'S MEXICAN RESTAURANT   Lunch: $6-$10   Dinner: $7-$12   Phone: 830/997-9546
Mexican
Location: US 290, just e of jct US 87. 506 E Main 78624. **Hours:** 11 am-9:30 pm, Fri & Sat-10 pm. Closed: 11/27, 12/25. **Reservations:** accepted. **Features:** Colorful and fun, the Mexican eatery serves such traditional foods as fajitas and rice. Large stained-glass windows cover the walls, and a central fountain fills the room with the relaxing sound of splashing water. Casual dress; cocktails. **Parking:** on-site.
Cards: AX, CB, DC, DS, MC, VI.

FRISCO —See Dallas p. 294.

FULTON pop. 1,553

——— WHERE TO STAY ———

BEST WESTERN INN BY THE BAY   Phone: (361)729-8351
Motel
All Year [BP]   1P: $75-$80   2P: $85-$90   XP: $8   F12
Location: SR 35, 0.5 mi n of jct Business Rt 35 and FM 3063. 3902 N Hwy 35 78358 (PO Box 310). Fax: 361/729-0950. **Facility:** 73 one-bedroom standard units, some with kitchens. 2 stories, exterior corridors. **Parking:** on-site. **Terms:** small pets only ($5 extra charge). **Amenities:** voice mail, irons, hair dryers. **Pool(s):** outdoor. **Guest Services:** coin laundry, airport transportation-Aransas County Airport. **Business Services:** meeting rooms, fax (fee). **Cards:** AX, CB, DC, DS, MC, VI. *(See color ad p 483)*

SOME UNITS

——— WHERE TO DINE ———

CHARLOTTE PLUMMER'S SEAFARE RESTAURANT   Lunch: $7-$10   Dinner: $14-$18   Phone: 361/729-1185
Seafood
Location: Just e of SR 35. 202 N Fulton Beach Rd 78358. **Hours:** 11 am-10 pm; to 8:30 pm off season, hours may vary. Closed: 11/27, 12/24, 12/25. **Features:** Take in the outstanding bayside view as you sample fresh seafood that includes oysters on ice. Undulating floors and cracked, crooked walls are all part of the charm in this rambling dining room with tables tucked into corners and niches. A covered outside deck is also available for dining. Casual dress; cocktails. **Parking:** on-site. **Cards:** AX, DC, DS, MC, VI.

GAINESVILLE pop. 15,538

——— WHERE TO STAY ———

BEST WESTERN SOUTHWINDS   Phone: (940)665-7737
Motel
5/1-8/31 [CP]   1P: $63-$80   2P: $66-$80   XP: $5   F12
2/1-4/30 [CP]   1P: $60-$80   2P: $65-$80   XP: $5   F12
9/1-1/31 [CP]   1P: $60-$70   2P: $60-$80   XP: $5   F12
Location: I-35, exit 499 northbound, stay on access road 1.4 mi around to S Frontage Rd; exit 498B southbound. 2103 N I-35 76240. Fax: 940/668-2651. **Facility:** 35 one-bedroom standard units. 1 story, exterior corridors. **Parking:** on-site. **Terms:** 3 day cancellation notice, small pets only ($5 extra charge). **Amenities:** video library (fee), high-speed Internet, irons, hair dryers. **Pool(s):** heated outdoor. **Leisure Activities:** whirlpool. **Guest Services:** coin laundry. **Business Services:** fax (fee). **Cards:** AX, CB, DC, DS, JC, MC, VI. **Special Amenities:** early check-in/late check-out and free continental breakfast. *(See color ad below)*

SOME UNITS

FEE

BUDGET HOST INN   Phone: (940)665-2856
Motel
All Year   1P: $40   2P: $40   XP: $5   F12
Location: I-35, exit 499 northbound; exit 498B southbound. 1900 N I-35 76240. **Facility:** 24 one-bedroom standard units. 1 story, exterior corridors. **Parking:** on-site. **Cards:** AX, DS, MC, VI. **Special Amenities:** early check-in/late check-out and free local telephone calls. *(See color ad p 162)*

SOME UNITS

GALVESTON pop. 57,247

—— **WHERE TO STAY** ——

CASA DEL MAR BEACHFRONT SUITES

			Phone: (409)740-2431
(AAA) (SAVE)	6/1-8/15	1P: $99-$199	2P: $99-$199	XP: $5	F12
	8/16-10/1	1P: $79-$199	2P: $79-$199	XP: $5	F12
▼▼▼▼	2/1-5/31 & 10/2-1/31	1P: $69-$199	2P: $69-$199	XP: $5	F12

Condominium

Location: Seawall Blvd at 61st St. Located across from beach. 6102 Seawall Blvd 77551. **Fax:** 409/740-1303. **Facility:** 180 one-bedroom suites with kitchens. 4 stories, interior/exterior corridors. **Parking:** on-site. **Terms:** check-in 4 pm, 2 night minimum stay - summer weekends, weekly rates available, package plans. **Amenities:** video games (fee), voice mail. **Pool(s):** outdoor, heated outdoor. **Leisure Activities:** barbecue grills, horseshoes. **Guest Services:** valet and coin laundry. **Business Services:** meeting rooms, fax (fee). **Cards:** AX, DC, DS, MC, VI.
(See color ad below)

SOME UNITS

🅂🄳 🍴 🚗 ❄ 🖧 🔌 🛏 📺 / ⊠ /

COMMODORE ON THE BEACH

			Phone: (409)763-2375
▼▼▼	5/2-8/31	1P: $70-$159	2P: $70-$159	XP: $12	F15
	2/1-5/1	1P: $49-$159	2P: $49-$159	XP: $12	F15
Small-scale Hotel	9/1-1/31	1P: $59-$99	2P: $59-$99	XP: $12	F15

Location: Seawall Blvd at 37th St. Located across from beach. 3618 Seawall Blvd 77550 (PO Box 3830, 77552-3830). **Fax:** 409/763-2379. **Facility:** 92 one-bedroom standard units. 4 stories, exterior corridors. **Bath:** combo or shower only. **Parking:** on-site. **Terms:** 2 night minimum stay - summer weekends, [CP] meal plan available. **Amenities:** *Some:* hair dryers. **Pool(s):** outdoor. **Guest Services:** area transportation. **Business Services:** meeting rooms, fax (fee). **Cards:** AX, MC, VI.

SOME UNITS

(ASK) 🅂🄳 ✈ 🍴 ♿ 🅟 🚗 🔌 / ⊠ 🛏 /
FEE

Galveston Island

More Sand For Your Dollar

• Fully furnished suites • Gulfview balconies
• 2 swimming pools • Centrally located

800-392-1205
409-740-2431
61st & Seawall
www.casadelmartx.com

CASA del MAR
BEACHFRONT SUITES

HILTON GALVESTON ISLAND RESORT
Phone: (409)744-5000

[SAVE]

5/14-9/3	1P: $129-$249	2P: $129-$249	XP: $10	F18
2/1-5/13 & 9/4-1/31	1P: $99-$159	2P: $99-$159	XP: $10	F18

▼▼▼▼▼
Location: Seawall Blvd at 54th St. Located across from beach. 5400 Seawall Blvd 77551. Fax: 409/740-2209.
Large-scale Hotel **Facility:** 150 units. 148 one-bedroom standard units. 2 one-bedroom suites. 6 stories, interior corridors.
Parking: on-site. **Terms:** check-in 4 pm, cancellation fee imposed, [BP] meal plan available.
Amenities: voice mail, irons, hair dryers. **Pool(s):** heated outdoor. **Leisure Activities:** sauna, whirlpool, 2 lighted tennis courts, recreation programs, playground, exercise room. *Fee:* massage. **Guest Services:** gift shop, valet and coin laundry, area transportation. **Business Services:** conference facilities. *Fee:* PC, fax. **Cards:** AX, CB, DC, DS, MC, VI.

SOME UNITS

HOLIDAY INN ON THE BEACH
Phone: (409)740-3581

▼▼▼▼▼
All Year   1P: $89-$199   2P: $89-$199
Location: Just e of jct Seawall Blvd and 53rd St. Located across from beach. 5002 Seawall Blvd 77551.
Large-scale Hotel Fax: 409/744-6677. **Facility:** 181 units. 179 one-bedroom standard units. 2 one-bedroom suites ($399-$599). 8 stories, exterior corridors. **Parking:** on-site. **Terms:** check-in 4 pm, cancellation fee imposed.
Amenities: video games (fee), voice mail, irons, hair dryers. **Pool(s):** outdoor, wading. **Guest Services:** gift shop, valet and coin laundry. **Business Services:** meeting rooms, fax (fee). **Cards:** AX, DC, DS, MC, VI. *(See color ad p 390 & below)*

SOME UNITS

HOTEL GALVEZ-A WYNDHAM HISTORIC HOTEL
Phone: (409)765-7721

[AAA] [SAVE]

5/23-8/17	1P: $135-$199	2P: $135-$199	XP: $20	F17
2/1-5/22 & 8/18-1/31	1P: $119-$159	2P: $119-$159	XP: $20	F17

▼▼▼▼▼
Location: Seawall Blvd at 21st St. Located across from beach. 2024 Seawall Blvd 77550. Fax: 409/765-5623.
Facility: 231 units. 224 one-bedroom standard units. 7 one-bedroom suites, some with whirlpools. 8 stories,
Large-scale Hotel interior corridors. *Bath:* combo or shower only. **Parking:** on-site and valet. **Terms:** check-in 4 pm, cancellation fee imposed. **Amenities:** voice mail, irons, hair dryers. *Fee:* video games, high-speed Internet. *Some:* CD players, safes. **Dining:** 6 am-2:30 & 5-10 pm, Fri & Sat-11 pm, cocktails. **Pool(s):** heated outdoor, wading. **Leisure Activities:** whirlpool, exercise room. **Guest Services:** gift shop, valet laundry, area transportation-within 5 mi. **Business Services:** conference facilities, business center. **Cards:** AX, CB, DC, DS, MC, VI.

SOME UNITS

LA QUINTA INN
Phone: (409)763-1224

[AAA] [SAVE]

All Year   1P: $63-$170   2P: $70-$177   XP: $7   F18
▼▼▼▼▼
Location: Seawall Blvd at 14th St. Located across from beach. 1402 Seawall Blvd 77550. Fax: 409/765-8663.
Facility: 117 units. 114 one-bedroom standard units. 3 one-bedroom suites ($119-$209). 3 stories, exterior corridors. *Bath:* combo or shower only. **Parking:** on-site. **Terms:** [ECP] meal plan available, small pets only.
Small-scale Hotel **Amenities:** video games (fee), voice mail, irons, hair dryers. **Pool(s):** outdoor. **Guest Services:** valet laundry. **Business Services:** fax (fee). **Cards:** AX, CB, DC, DS, JC, MC, VI. **Special Amenities:** free continental breakfast and free local telephone calls.

SOME UNITS

MOODY GARDENS HOTEL & SPA
Phone: (409)741-8484

[AAA] [SAVE]

All Year   1P: $180-$190   2P: $190-$200   XP: $10   F17
▼▼▼▼▼
Location: I-45, exit 1A, 0.9 mi s on 61st St to Stewart Rd, then 1 mi w on Stewart/Jones Rd to entrance. Located adjacent to convention center. Seven Hope Blvd 77554. Fax: 409/683-4937. **Facility:** 303 units. 296 one-bedroom standard units. 1 one- and 6 two-bedroom suites ($295-$795) with whirlpools. 9 stories, interior corridors.
Large-scale Hotel *Bath:* combo or shower only. **Parking:** on-site and valet. **Terms:** check-in 4 pm, 2 night minimum stay - weekends, cancellation fee imposed, [BP] meal plan available, package plans. **Amenities:** video games (fee), dual phone lines, voice mail, safes, irons, hair dryers. *Some:* CD players, honor bars. **Dining:** 3 restaurants, 6 am-10 pm, cocktails. **Pool(s):** outdoor, heated indoor. **Leisure Activities:** saunas, whirlpool, yoga. *Fee:* boat dock, massage. **Guest Services:** gift shop, valet and coin laundry, airport transportation-Galveston Airport, area transportation-attractions. **Business Services:** conference facilities, business center. **Cards:** AX, CB, DC, DS, JC, MC, VI. *(See color ad p 101)*

SOME UNITS

THE SAN LUIS RESORT SPA & CONFERENCE CENTER   Phone: (409)744-1500
(AAA) SAVE   5/1-8/31   1P: $149-$329   2P: $149-$329   XP: $10   F
          2/1-4/30 & 9/1-1/31   1P: $129-$289   2P: $129-$289   XP: $10   F
▽▽▽▽ ▽▽▽▽ **Location:** I-45, exit Broadway Ave, 1.5 mi s on 53rd St (Mary Moody Northern Blvd), just e. Located in a commercial
          area. 5222 Seawall Blvd 77551. Fax: 409/744-8452. **Facility:** This property offers upscale appointments with full
Large-scale Hotel service spa, boutique shopping, pool bar and recreation for children. 246 units. 244 one-bedroom standard
          units. 2 one-bedroom suites. 16 stories, interior corridors. *Bath:* combo or shower only. **Parking:** on-site and
valet. **Terms:** check-in 4 pm, 3 day cancellation notice-fee imposed. **Amenities:** dual phone lines, voice mail, irons, hair dryers.
Some: fax. **Dining:** 2 restaurants, 6:30 am-10 pm, Fri & Sat-11 pm, cocktails. **Pool(s):** heated outdoor. **Leisure Activities:** saunas, whirlpool, 2 lighted tennis courts, recreation programs in summer, exercise room. *Fee:* massage. **Guest Services:**
gift shop, valet and coin laundry, area transportation-island. **Business Services:** conference facilities, business center.
Cards: AX, CB, DC, DS, MC, VI. **Special Amenities:** free newspaper and free room upgrade (subject to availability with
advanced reservations).** *(See color ad below)*
SOME UNITS

[icons] FEE   FEE

SUPER 8 MOTEL   Phone: 409/740-6640
▽▽▽▽ ▽▽▽▽ All Year   1P: $49-$250   2P: $49-$250
▽▽ ▽▽   **Location:** Just n of jct Seawall Blvd and 61st St. Located in a commercial area. 2825 1/2 B 61st St 77551.
          Fax: 409/740-1308. **Facility:** 57 one-bedroom standard units, some with whirlpools. 2 stories, exterior corri-
Small-scale Hotel dors. *Bath:* combo or shower only. **Parking:** on-site. **Terms:** [CP] meal plan available. **Amenities:** voice mail,
safes. **Pool(s):** small outdoor. **Business Services:** fax (fee). **Cards:** AX, DC, MC, VI.
SOME UNITS

[icons]

THE TREMONT HOUSE-A WYNDHAM HISTORIC HOTEL   Phone: (409)763-0300
(AAA) SAVE   5/23-8/17   1P: $135-$175   2P: $135-$175   XP: $20   F17
          2/1-5/22 & 8/18-1/31   1P: $119-$155   2P: $119-$155   XP: $20   F17
▽▽▽ ▽▽▽   **Location:** Broadway Ave, 0.4 mi n on 23rd St, hotel entrance just w; downtown. 2300 Ship's Mechanic Row 77550.
          Fax: 409/763-1539. **Facility:** 117 units. 100 one-bedroom standard units. 17 one-bedroom suites. 4 stories,
Large-scale Hotel interior corridors. *Bath:* combo or shower only. **Parking:** valet. **Terms:** check-in 4 pm, cancellation fee imposed. **Amenities:** voice mail, irons, hair dryers. *Fee:* video games, high-speed Internet. **Dining:** 6 am-2 &
5:30-10 pm, Fri & Sat-11 pm, cocktails, entertainment. **Leisure Activities:** exercise room. **Guest Services:** valet laundry. **Business Services:** meeting rooms, fax (fee). **Cards:** AX, CB, DC, DS, MC, VI.
SOME UNITS

[icons]

THE VICTORIAN CONDO HOTEL & CONFERENCE CENTER   Phone: (409)740-3555
(AAA) SAVE   5/1-8/31   1P: $99-$375   2P: $99-$375   XP: $5   F
          2/1-4/30 & 9/1-10/31   1P: $89-$315   2P: $89-$315   XP: $5   F
▽▽▽ ▽▽▽   11/1-1/31   1P: $79-$210   2P: $79-$210   XP: $5   F
          Location: 1.5 mi sw of I-45 and US 75, exit 1A, just w of 61st St. Located across from beach. 6300 Seawall Blvd 77551.
Condominium Fax: 409/744-3801. **Facility:** 239 units. 213 one- and 26 two-bedroom suites with efficiencies. 3 stories, ex-
          terior corridors. **Parking:** on-site. **Terms:** check-in 4 pm, 2 night minimum stay, cancellation fee imposed.
Amenities: video games (fee), voice mail, safes. **Dining:** 11 am-2 pm, Sat & Sun from 8 am, wine/beer only. **Pool(s):** outdoor,
heated outdoor. **Leisure Activities:** whirlpools, lighted tennis court, barbecue pits, playground, exercise room. **Guest Services:**
coin laundry. **Business Services:** conference facilities, fax (fee). **Cards:** AX, DS, MC, VI.

[icons]

─────── *The following lodgings were either not evaluated or did not* ───────
meet AAA rating requirements but are listed for your information only.

BEST VALUE INN & SUITES
[fyi]
Under construction, scheduled to open March 2003. **Location:** I-45, exit 61st St. 6311 Central City Blvd 77551.
Planned Amenities: coffeemakers, pool.
Phone: 409/744-3515

CASTAWAYS RESORT PROPERTIES
[fyi]
Not evaluated. **Location:** 16510 FM 3005 77554. Facilities, services, and decor characterize a mid-range property.
Phone: 409/737-5300

FOUR SEASONS ON THE GULF
[fyi]
Not evaluated. **Location:** 4000 Seawall Blvd 77550. Facilities, services, and decor characterize a mid-range property.
Phone: 409/763-7138

INVERNESS BY THE SEA
[fyi]
Not evaluated. **Location:** 7600 Seawall Blvd 77551. Facilities, services, and decor characterize a mid-range property.
Phone: 409/683-1006

SAND 'N SEA PIRATES BEACH
[fyi]
Not evaluated. **Location:** FM 3005 and 12 Mile Rd 77554. Facilities, services, and decor characterize a mid-range property.
Phone: 409/737-2556

─────── **WHERE TO DINE** ───────

GAIDO'S RESTAURANT
▼▼ ▼▼
Seafood
Lunch: $15-$25   **Dinner:** $11-$27   Phone: 409/762-9625
Location: Between 38th and 39th sts. 3828 Seawall Blvd 77552. **Hours:** 11:45 am-9:30 pm, Fri & Sat-10:30 pm.
Closed: 12/25. **Features:** Locally popular, this nautically themed restaurant specializes in a variety of freshly prepared seafood with some beef and poultry selections also available. For a delicious meal, start with a tasty cup of tortilla soup, then savor the blackened salmon. Casual dress; cocktails. **Parking:** on-site. **Cards:** AX, DC, DS, MC, VI.

ORIGINAL MEXICAN CAFE
▼▼ ▼▼
Mexican
Lunch: $6-$14   **Dinner:** $6-$13   Phone: 409/762-6001
Location: Jct W 14th St. 1401 Market St 77550. **Hours:** 11 am-9:30 pm, Fri-10 pm, Sat 8 am-10 pm, Sun-9:30 pm. **Features:** The decor is reminiscent of the Yucatan, but the menu of fresh, tasty Tex-Mex fare is closer to home. Flavorful slices of prickly pear cactus pads make an interesting treat. Casual dress; cocktails. **Parking:** on-site. **Cards:** AX, DC, MC, VI.

GARLAND —See Dallas p. 294.

GARLAND —See Dallas p. 294.

GATESVILLE pop. 15,591

─────── **WHERE TO STAY** ───────

REGENCY MOTOR INN
AAA [SAVE]
▼▼ ▼▼
Motel
Phone: 254/865-8405

5/16-9/16	1P: $65	2P: $80	XP: $8	F12
2/1-5/15 & 9/17-1/31	1P: $50	2P: $65	XP: $8	F12

Location: 1 mi e on US 84, jct of Business 36 and US 84. 2307 Main St 76528. Fax: 254/865-9241. **Facility:** 30 one-bedroom standard units. 1 story, exterior corridors. **Parking:** on-site. **Pool(s):** small outdoor. **Leisure Activities:** whirlpool. **Business Services:** fax (fee). **Cards:** AX, DS, MC, VI.
SOME UNITS

GEORGETOWN pop. 28,339

─────── **WHERE TO STAY** ───────

LA QUINTA-GEORGETOWN-SUN CITY
AAA [SAVE]
▼▼▼▼
Small-scale Hotel
Phone: (512)869-2541

All Year	1P: $59-$79	2P: $69-$89	XP: $10	F18

Location: I-35, exit 264 northbound; exit 262 southbound; on west frontage road. 333 I-35 N 78628. Fax: 512/863-7073. **Facility:** 99 units. 96 one-bedroom standard units. 2 one- and 1 two-bedroom suites, some with kitchens. 3 stories, exterior corridors. *Bath:* combo or shower only. **Parking:** on-site. **Terms:** [ECP] meal plan available. **Amenities:** video games (fee), voice mail, irons, hair dryers. **Pool(s):** small outdoor. **Leisure Activities:** whirlpool. **Guest Services:** valet laundry, airport transportation (fee)-Austin Airport. **Business Services:** meeting rooms, fax (fee). **Cards:** AX, CB, DC, DS, JC, MC, VI. **Special Amenities:** free continental breakfast and free local telephone calls.
SOME UNITS
FEE

GEORGE WEST pop. 2,524

─────── **WHERE TO STAY** ───────

BEST WESTERN EXECUTIVE INN
AAA [SAVE]
▼▼ ▼▼
Small-scale Hotel
Phone: (361)449-3300

All Year	1P: $60-$65	2P: $65-$70	XP: $5	F12

Location: Just n of US 59 on SR 281. Located in a quiet area. 208 N Nueces St 78022. Fax: 361/449-3446. **Facility:** 30 one-bedroom standard units, some with whirlpools. 2 stories, exterior corridors. *Bath:* combo or shower only. **Parking:** on-site. **Terms:** 2 night minimum stay - weekends, small pets only. **Amenities:** irons, hair dryers. **Pool(s):** outdoor. **Leisure Activities:** whirlpool. **Guest Services:** coin laundry. **Business Services:** meeting rooms, fax (fee). **Cards:** AX, CB, DC, DS, MC, VI. **Special Amenities:** free continental breakfast.
SOME UNITS

GIDDINGS pop. 5,105

------ WHERE TO STAY ------

RAMADA LIMITED
Phone: (979)542-9666
AAA SAVE
▼▼▼ ▼▼▼
Motel

All Year — 1P: $45-$54 — 2P: $50-$59 — XP: $5 — F
Location: 2.5 mi e on US 290. 4002 E Austin St 78942. Fax: 979/542-1245. **Facility:** 67 one-bedroom standard units. 2 stories (no elevator), exterior corridors. **Parking:** on-site. **Terms:** [ECP] meal plan available, small pets only (in designated units). **Amenities:** voice mail, safes, irons, hair dryers. **Pool(s):** outdoor. **Guest Services:** coin laundry. **Business Services:** meeting rooms, fax (fee). **Cards:** AX, DC, DS, MC, VI. **Special Amenities:** free continental breakfast and free local telephone calls.

SOME UNITS

SUPER 8 MOTEL
Phone: (979)542-5791
AAA SAVE
▼▼▼ ▼▼▼
Motel

All Year — 1P: $44-$54 — 2P: $49-$59 — XP: $5 — F12
Location: 2 mi e on US 290. 3556 E Austin Rd 78942. Fax: 979/542-5791. **Facility:** 60 one-bedroom standard units. 2 stories, exterior corridors. **Parking:** on-site. **Terms:** small pets only. **Pool(s):** outdoor. **Leisure Activities:** whirlpool. **Business Services:** fax (fee). **Cards:** AX, DC, DS, MC, VI. **Special Amenities:** free continental breakfast and free local telephone calls.

SOME UNITS

GLEN ROSE pop. 2,122

------ WHERE TO STAY ------

BEST WESTERN DINOSAUR VALLEY INN & SUITES
Phone: (254)897-4818
AAA SAVE
▼▼▼ ▼▼▼
Small-scale Hotel

All Year [ECP] — 1P: $73-$139 — 2P: $83-$150 — XP: $5 — F17
Location: On US 67. 1311 NE Big Ben Tr 76043 (PO Box 1460). Fax: 254/897-4828. **Facility:** 53 units. 46 one-bedroom standard units. 1 one- and 6 two-bedroom suites ($105-$150). 3 stories, interior corridors. *Bath:* combo or shower only. **Parking:** on-site. **Terms:** 2-3 night minimum stay - weekends, cancellation fee imposed, pets ($20 fee). **Amenities:** video library (fee), dual phone lines, voice mail, irons, hair dryers. *Some:* safes. **Pool(s):** heated outdoor, wading. **Leisure Activities:** whirlpool, jogging, exercise room, game room. **Guest Services:** sundries, coin laundry. **Business Services:** fax (fee). **Cards:** AX, CB, DC, DS, JC, MC, VI. **Special Amenities:** free continental breakfast.

HUMMINGBIRD LODGE
Phone: 254/897-2787
▼▼▼
Bed & Breakfast

All Year [BP] — 1P: $92-$105 — 2P: $92-$122 — XP: $18 — D16
Location: Jct US 67 and SR 56, 5.9 mi s to SR 203, 1.6 mi e on SR 203. Located in a rural area. 2674 CR 203 76690 (PO Box 128, 76043). Fax: 254/897-3459. **Facility:** In a country setting on some 140 acres, this property features waterfalls, a pond and a walking trail on the grounds. Designated smoking area. 6 one-bedroom standard units. 2 stories (no elevator), interior/exterior corridors. *Bath:* combo or shower only. **Parking:** on-site. **Terms:** 7 day cancellation notice, package plans. **Leisure Activities:** whirlpool, fishing, hiking trails. **Business Services:** fax. **Cards:** AX, DS, MC, VI.

SOME UNITS

------ WHERE TO DINE ------

HAMMOND'S BBQ
Lunch: $5-$10 — Dinner: $5-$10 — Phone: 254/897-3008
▼
Barbecue

Location: On US 67. 1106 NE Big Bend Tr 76043. **Hours:** 11 am-2, Fri & Sat-8 pm. Closed: 1/1, 11/27, 12/25; also Tues & Wed. **Features:** The no-frills restaurant features red picnic tables with rolls of paper towels—although finger licking is perfectly acceptable—and license plate adorning the walls. Service is just as can be expected in a small Texas town, familiar and friendly. Casual dress. **Parking:** on-site. **Cards:** AX, MC, VI.

GONZALES pop. 7,202

------ WHERE TO STAY ------

REGENCY INN & SUITES
Phone: 830/672-5555
▼▼ ▼▼
Motel

All Year — 1P: $60-$80 — 2P: $65-$85 — XP: $6 — F10
Location: 1.2 mi e of jct US 183 and Alternate SR 90. 1811 E Sarah Dewitt 78629. Fax: 830/672-4441. **Facility:** 27 one-bedroom standard units. 1 story, exterior corridors. **Parking:** on-site. **Terms:** 3 day cancellation notice, [CP] meal plan available. **Amenities:** hair dryers. **Pool(s):** outdoor. **Leisure Activities:** whirlpool. **Business Services:** meeting rooms, fax (fee). **Cards:** AX, CB, DC, DS, MC, VI.

SOME UNITS

ST JAMES INN BED & BREAKFAST
Phone: (830)672-7066
▼▼▼
Bed & Breakfast

All Year [BP] — 1P: $70-$80 — 2P: $95-$125 — XP: $20
Location: 2 blks w of US Business 183 on St Andrews. 723 St James St 78629. **Facility:** A 10,000-square-foot 1914 South Texas mansion situated in the historic district, this B&B offers nicely appointed, spacious rooms. Smoke free premises. 5 one-bedroom standard units. 3 stories (no elevator), interior corridors. **Parking:** on-site. **Terms:** 2-3 night minimum stay - weekends, 5 day cancellation notice, weekly rates available. **Amenities:** hair dryers. **Leisure Activities:** horseback riding. **Cards:** AX, MC, VI.

SOME UNITS

GRANBURY pop. 5,718

──── WHERE TO STAY ────

COMFORT INN
AAA SAVE
◥◢◥◢◥◢
Motel

Phone: (817)573-2611

All Year   1P: $65-$150   2P: $75-$180   XP: $5   F18
Location: 2 mi e on US 377 Bypass. 1201 Plaza Dr N 76048. **Fax:** 817/573-2695. **Facility:** 48 one-bedroom standard units, some with whirlpools. 2 stories, exterior corridors. *Bath:* combo or shower only. **Parking:** on-site. *Some:* irons. **Pool(s):** outdoor. **Guest Services:** coin laundry. **Business Services:** fax. **Cards:** AX, CB, DC, DS, JC, MC, VI. **Special Amenities:** free continental breakfast and free local telephone calls.

SOME UNITS
🅂🄳 🍴 🛗 ♿ 🏊 🎥 🛗 🖥 / ✕ 📠 💻 /

DAYS INN OF GRANBURY

Phone: (817)573-2691

(AAA) [SAVE]
▽▽ ▽▽
Motel

6/1-10/31 [ECP]　　　　　1P: $59-$84　　　　2P: $59-$84　　　　XP: $5　　　　F17
2/1-5/31 & 11/1-1/31 [ECP]　1P: $49-$75　　　　2P: $49-$75　　　　XP: $5　　　　F17
Location: 2 mi e on US 377 Bypass. 1339 N Plaza Dr 76048. Fax: 817/573-7662. **Facility:** 67 one-bedroom standard units, some with efficiencies. 2 stories, exterior corridors. *Bath:* combo or shower only. **Parking:** on-site.
Terms: cancellation fee imposed, small pets only ($20 fee). **Amenities:** *Some:* irons, hair dryers. **Pool(s):** outdoor. **Guest Services:** coin laundry. **Business Services:** fax (fee). **Cards:** AX, DC, DS, MC, VI.
Special Amenities: free continental breakfast and free local telephone calls.

SOME UNITS

HOLIDAY INN EXPRESS

Phone: (817)573-4411

(AAA) [SAVE]
▽▽▽▽▽
Small-scale Hotel

All Year　　　　　　　1P: $70-$180　　　　2P: $75-$195　　　　XP: $5　　　　F18
Location: 2 mi e on US 377 Bypass. 800 Plaza Dr 76048. Fax: 817/573-5010. **Facility:** 53 one-bedroom standard units, some with whirlpools. 2 stories, interior corridors. *Bath:* combo or shower only. **Parking:** on-site.
Terms: [CP] meal plan available. **Amenities:** dual phone lines, voice mail, safes (fee), irons, hair dryers. **Pool(s):** outdoor. **Guest Services:** valet and coin laundry. **Business Services:** fax. **Cards:** AX, CB, DC, DS, JC, MC, VI. **Special Amenities:** free continental breakfast and free local telephone calls.

SOME UNITS

PLANTATION INN ON THE LAKE

Phone: (817)573-8846

(AAA) [SAVE]
▽▽ ▽▽
Motel

All Year　　　　　　　1P: $60-$75　　　　2P: $65-$80　　　　XP: $5　　　　F6
Location: 0.3 mi w of Business Rt 377 at jct US 377 Bypass. 1451 E Pearl St 76048. Fax: 817/579-0917. **Facility:** 53 one-bedroom standard units, some with whirlpools. 2 stories, interior/exterior corridors. **Parking:** on-site.
Terms: 4-10 night minimum stay - weekends 6/1-10/31, [CP] meal plan available, small pets only ($10 extra charge). **Amenities:** voice mail. **Pool(s):** outdoor. **Guest Services:** airport transportation-Granbury Municipal Airport. **Business Services:** meeting rooms, fax (fee). **Cards:** AX, CB, DC, DS, MC, VI. **Special Amenities:** free continental breakfast and free local telephone calls.

────── *The following lodging was either not evaluated or did not* ──────
meet AAA rating requirements but is listed for your information only.

THE RIDGE ON LAKE GRANBURY

Phone: 817/279-7148

[fyi]　　Not evaluated. **Location:** 6450 Kelly Dr 76048. Facilities, services, and decor characterize a mid-range property.

GRAND PRAIRIE —*See Dallas p. 296.*

GRAPEVINE pop. 42,059

────── **WHERE TO STAY** ──────

AMERISUITES (DALLAS/DFW AIRPORT N)

Phone: (972)691-1199

(AAA) [SAVE]
▽▽▽▽▽
Small-scale Hotel

All Year [ECP]　　　　1P: $119-$129　　　2P: $119-$129　　　XP: $10　　　F17
Location: SR 121 N, exit Bass Pro Dr. 2220 Grapevine Mills Cir W 76051. Fax: 972/691-3596. **Facility:** 125 one-bedroom standard units. 6 stories, interior corridors. *Bath:* combo or shower only. **Parking:** on-site.
Terms: pets ($50 fee). **Amenities:** video games (fee), dual phone lines, voice mail, irons, hair dryers. **Pool(s):** heated outdoor. **Leisure Activities:** exercise room. **Guest Services:** complimentary evening beverages: Wed, valet and coin laundry, airport transportation-Dallas-Fort Worth International Airport, area transportation-within 5 mi. **Business Services:** meeting rooms, business center. **Cards:** AX, CB, DC, DS, JC, MC, VI.
Special Amenities: free continental breakfast and free newspaper. *(See color ad p 251)*

SOME UNITS

BAYMONT INN-DALLAS-FT WORTH/AIRPORT NORTH

Phone: (817)329-9300

(AAA) [SAVE]
▽▽ ▽▽
Small-scale Hotel

All Year　　　　　　1P: $89　　　　　　　　　XP: $6　　　　F16
Location: SR 114 at Main St exit. 301 Capital St 76051. Fax: 817/329-0892. **Facility:** 106 one-bedroom standard units. 4 stories, interior corridors. *Bath:* combo or shower only. **Parking:** on-site. **Terms:** [CP] meal plan available. **Amenities:** irons, hair dryers. *Fee:* video games, safes. *Some:* dual phone lines. **Pool(s):** outdoor. **Guest Services:** valet and coin laundry, airport transportation-Dallas-Fort Worth International Airport, area transportation-Grapevine Mills Mall. **Business Services:** meeting rooms, fax (fee). **Cards:** AX, DC, DS, MC, VI. **Special Amenities:** free continental breakfast and free newspaper.

SOME UNITS

EMBASSY SUITES OUTDOOR WORLD

Phone: (972)724-2600

(AAA) [SAVE]
▽▽▽▽▽
Large-scale Hotel

All Year [BP]　　　　1P: $119-$269　　　2P: $119-$269　　　XP: $10　　　F18
Location: US 121, exit Bass Pro Dr. 2401 Bass Pro Dr 76051. Fax: 972/724-5145. **Facility:** 329 units. 326 one- and 3 two-bedroom suites, some with whirlpools. 12 stories, interior corridors. *Bath:* combo or shower only. **Parking:** on-site and valet. **Terms:** 3 day cancellation notice-fee imposed, package plans, small pets only ($25 deposit). **Amenities:** dual phone lines, voice mail, irons, hair dryers. *Fee:* video games, high-speed Internet. **Dining:** 11 am-midnight, Fri & Sat 2 am, cocktails. **Pool(s):** heated indoor. **Leisure Activities:** sauna, whirlpool, local marina privileges for jet skis, water skiing, pontoon and fishing, exercise room. *Fee:* massage, game room. **Guest Services:** gift shop, complimentary evening beverages: Sun & Mon, valet and coin laundry, airport transportation-Dallas-Fort Worth International Airport, area transportation-within 2 mi. **Business Services:** conference facilities, business center. **Cards:** AX, CB, DC, DS, JC, MC, VI. **Special Amenities:** free continental breakfast and free newspaper.
(See color ad p 267 & p 252)

SOME UNITS

HILTON DFW LAKES

[SAVE]

[symbols]

Large-scale Hotel

All Year 1P: $69-$229   2P: $89-$249   **XP:** $20   F18
Location: SR 26A, 0.3 mi sw of jct SR 121; 0.5 mi nw of I-635, exit SR 121 N. 1800 Hwy 26 E 76051.
Fax: 817/481-3160. **Facility:** 395 units. 390 one-bedroom standard units. 5 one-bedroom suites, some with whirlpools. 10 stories, interior corridors. *Bath:* combo or shower only. **Parking:** on-site and valet. **Terms:** cancellation fee imposed. **Amenities:** video games (fee), dual phone lines, voice mail, honor bars, irons, hair dryers. *Some:* high-speed Internet (fee). **Pool(s):** outdoor, heated indoor. **Leisure Activities:** sauna, whirlpool, fishing, 8 tennis courts (2 indoor, 8 lighted), racquetball courts, jogging, exercise room, basketball, horseshoes, volleyball. **Guest Services:** gift shop, valet laundry, area transportation. **Business Services:** conference facilities, business center. **Cards:** AX, CB, DS, MC, VI. *(See color ad below)*

Phone: 817/481-8444

SOME UNITS

[symbols row]

HOLIDAY INN EXPRESS HOTEL & SUITES DFW/GRAPEVINE

[symbols]

Small-scale Hotel

All Year [ECP] 1P: $119   2P: $119
Location: Just sw of jct Main St. 309 State Hwy 114 W 76051. Fax: 817/442-5960. **Facility:** 95 units. 94 one-bedroom standard units, some with whirlpools. 1 one-bedroom suite ($129). 3 stories, interior corridors. *Bath:* combo or shower only. **Parking:** on-site. **Amenities:** dual phone lines, voice mail, irons, hair dryers. *Fee:* video games, high-speed Internet. **Pool(s):** heated outdoor. **Leisure Activities:** whirlpool, exercise room. **Business Services:** meeting rooms, business center. **Cards:** AX, CB, DC, DS, JC, MC, VI.

Phone: (817)442-5919

SOME UNITS

[symbols row]

HYATT REGENCY DFW

[AAA] [SAVE]

[symbols]

Large-scale Hotel

All Year 1P: $79-$199   2P: $79-$199   **XP:** $25   F18
Location: In Dallas/Fort Worth Airport Terminal C area. (2335 N International Pkwy, Grapevine, 76051). Fax: 972/456-8668. **Facility:** 811 units. 800 one-bedroom standard units. 11 one-bedroom suites, some with whirlpools. 12 stories, interior corridors. *Bath:* combo or shower only. **Parking:** on-site and valet. **Terms:** cancellation fee imposed. **Amenities:** dual phone lines, voice mail, irons, hair dryers. *Some:* fax. **Dining:** 2 restaurants, 6 am-midnight, cocktails. **Pool(s):** heated outdoor. **Leisure Activities:** exercise room. **Guest Services:** gift shop, valet laundry, airport transportation-Dallas-Forth Worth International Airport. **Business Services:** conference facilities, business center. **Cards:** AX, CB, DC, DS, JC, MC, VI. *(See color ad inside front cover)*

Phone: (972)453-1234

SOME UNITS

[symbols row]

FEE

SUPER 8 MOTEL-GRAPEVINE

[symbols]

Small-scale Hotel

All Year [CP] 1P: $49-$69   2P: $49-$69   **XP:** $5   F12
Location: SR 114, exit Main St. 250 E Hwy 114 76051. Fax: 817/421-2182. **Facility:** 102 one-bedroom standard units. 3 stories, interior corridors. *Bath:* combo or shower only. **Parking:** on-site. **Terms:** pets ($10 extra charge). **Amenities:** safes (fee). *Some:* hair dryers. **Pool(s):** small outdoor. **Guest Services:** valet laundry, area transportation. **Business Services:** meeting rooms, fax (fee). **Cards:** AX, CB, DC, DS, MC, VI.

Phone: (817)329-7222

SOME UNITS

[symbols row]

——— WHERE TO DINE ———

BIG BUCK BREWERY & STEAKHOUSE   **Lunch:** $9-$12   **Dinner:** $15-$22   **Phone:** 214/513-2337

▼▼ ▼▼   **Location:** US 121, exit Bass Pro Dr, just nw. 2501-1 Bass Pro Dr 76051. **Hours:** 11 am-10 pm, Sat-11 pm.
                Closed: 12/25. **Reservations:** accepted. **Features:** A state-of-the-art brewing facility, where hand-crafted
American   beers and sodas are made from the finest ingredients, encompasses one side of the restaurant. Everything
                on the menu is made from scratch, including the sauces and soups. High-quality beef is well-prepared.
Contributing to a Northwest feel are mounted animal trophies, rock columns and log woodwork. Casual dress; cocktails.
Parking: on-site. **Cards:** AX, DC, DS, MC, VI.   🍸 ✕

BOI NA BRAZA   **Lunch:** $25-$35   **Dinner:** $40-$60   **Phone:** 817/329-5514

▼▼▼ ▼▼   **Location:** SR 121, exit Hall-Johnson northbound; exit Glade St southbound, 0.6 mi n on north access road. 4025
                William D Tate (Hwy 121) 76051. **Hours:** 11 am-2 & 5-10 pm, Fri-10:30 pm, Sat 5 pm-10:30 pm. Closed: 1/1,
Brazilian   12/25. **Reservations:** suggested. **Features:** Experience a gaucho-inspired unique type of cooking called
churrasco. Large portions of prime meats are skewered and slowly roasted to prefection. Slices of
skewered meats are served to guests at their table. Dressy casual; cocktails. **Parking:** on-site. **Cards:** AX, CB, DC, DS,
MC, VI.   🍸 ✕

GREENVILLE —See Dallas p. 296.

GROOM pop. 587

——— WHERE TO STAY ———

CHALET INN   **Phone:** 806/248-7524

🅰🅰🅰 [SAVE]   All Year   1P: $44   2P: $59   XP: $6
                Location: I-40, exit 113, just s. I-40 FM 2300 79039 (PO Drawer 430). **Fax:** 806/248-7484. **Facility:** 26 one-
▼▼ ▼▼   bedroom standard units. 1 story, exterior corridors. **Parking:** on-site. **Business Services:** fax (fee).
                Cards: AX, DS, MC, VI. **Special Amenities:** free local telephone calls.
Motel   SOME UNITS
                                                                        [S🅳] [🅼] [🐾] / [✕] /

HALTOM CITY pop. 39,018   (See map p. 343; index p. 346)

——— WHERE TO DINE ———

SCOTTY'S DELUXE DINERS   **Lunch:** $7-$10   **Dinner:** $7-$10   **Phone:** 817/281-0057   [65]

▼▼▼   **Location:** I-820, exit 17B, just s. 5100 N Beach St 76137. **Hours:** 7 am-10 pm, Fri & Sat-11 pm. Closed: 12/25.
                Features: The replicated '50s diner takes guests back in time. Neon lights line the chrome exterior, while
American   rock 'n' roll music and automobile and movie posters set the mood inside. Representative of diner fare are
                sandwiches, soft drinks, malts and shakes, as well as such entrees as chicken-fried steak, pot roast and
pork chops. Casual dress. **Parking:** on-site. **Cards:** AX, DS, MC, VI.
                                                                                                           ✕

HARLINGEN pop. 57,564

——— WHERE TO STAY ———

COMFORT INN   **Phone:** (956)412-7771

[SAVE]   All Year   1P: $69   2P: $79   XP: $10   F18
                Location: On US 77, 0.5 mi n on US 83. 406 N Expressway 83 78550. **Fax:** 956/412-5751. **Facility:** 51 units. 33
▼▼▼ ▼▼   one-bedroom standard units. 18 one-bedroom suites. 2 stories, exterior corridors. *Bath:* combo or shower
                only. **Parking:** on-site. **Terms:** weekly rates available. **Amenities:** irons, hair dryers. **Pool(s):** outdoor.
Small-scale Hotel **Leisure Activities:** whirlpool. **Guest Services:** valet and coin laundry. **Business Services:** fax (fee).
                Cards: AX, DC, DS, MC, VI.
                                                                        [S🅳] [⛄] [🐾] [🎥] [DATA PORT] [▭]

COUNTRY INN & SUITES BY CARLSON
▼▼▼ ▼▼   All Year [ECP]   1P: $59-$105   2P: $64-$110   **Phone:** (956)428-0043
                Location: US 83/77 Expwy, exit Ed Carrey. 3825 S Expressway 83 78550. **Fax:** 956/428-0053. **Facility:** 65 units.   XP: $5   F17
Small-scale Hotel 30 one-bedroom standard units, some with whirlpools. 35 one-bedroom suites ($100-$125). 3 stories, inte-
                rior corridors. *Bath:* combo or shower only. **Parking:** on-site. **Terms:** small pets only. **Amenities:** dual phone
lines, voice mail, irons, hair dryers. **Pool(s):** heated outdoor. **Leisure Activities:** whirlpool, exercise room. **Guest Services:** valet,
and coin laundry, area transportation. **Business Services:** meeting rooms, fax (fee). **Cards:** AX, DC, DS, MC, VI.
(See color ad p 260)
                                                                                                SOME UNITS
                [A$K] [S🅳] [✈] [🐾] [🍸] [👶] [🐾] [🎥] [DATA PORT] [▭] / [✕] [🔒] [🖥] /

COURTYARD BY MARRIOTT   **Phone:** 956/412-7800

[SAVE]   All Year   1P: $69-$125   2P: $69-$125
                Location: US 83 and 77 Expwy, exit M St, 0.5 mi on Frontage Rd. 1725 W Filmore Ave 78550. **Fax:** 956/412-7889.
▼▼▼ ▼▼   **Facility:** 114 one-bedroom standard units, some with whirlpools. 3 stories, interior corridors. *Bath:* combo or
                shower only. **Parking:** on-site. **Terms:** package plans. **Amenities:** voice mail, irons, hair dryers. **Pool(s):**
Small-scale Hotel heated outdoor. **Leisure Activities:** whirlpool, exercise room. **Guest Services:** valet and coin laundry. **Busi-
                ness Services:** meeting rooms, fax (fee). **Cards:** AX, DS, MC, VI.
                                                                                                SOME UNITS
                [✈] [🍽] [🅼] [👶] [🐾] [🐾] [🎥] [DATA PORT] [▭] / [✕] [🔒] [🖥] /

ECONO LODGE

Phone: (956)425-1040

3/1-3/31 [CP]	1P: $60-$90	2P: $60-$90	XP: $10 F17
2/1-2/28 [CP]	1P: $46-$60	2P: $50-$70	XP: $6 F17
4/1-1/31 [CP]	1P: $42-$60	2P: $46-$70	XP: $6 F17

Location: 0.8 mi e of US 77, downtown exit. 1821 W Tyler 78550. Fax: 956/428-3309. **Facility:** 109 units. 108 one-
Small-scale Hotel and 1 two-bedroom standard units. 2 stories, exterior corridors. **Parking:** on-site. **Terms:** 7 day cancellation
notice, weekly rates available. **Pool(s):** outdoor. **Guest Services:** valet and coin laundry. **Business Services:** fax (fee). **Cards:** AX, CB, DC, DS, JC, MC, VI. **Special Amenities:** free continental breakfast and free local telephone
calls.

SOME UNITS

HOWARD JOHNSON INN

Phone: (956)425-7070

All Year [BP] 1P: $52-$57 2P: $57-$62 XP: $5 F17
Location: Jct US 77, 2.3 mi w on US 83, exit Stuart Place Rd. 6779 W Expwy 83 78552. Fax: 956/423-1114.
Facility: 91 one-bedroom standard units, some with efficiencies. 2 stories, exterior corridors. **Parking:** on-
site. **Terms:** small pets only ($25 deposit). **Amenities:** irons, hair dryers. **Dining:** 7 am-3 pm. **Pool(s):** out-
Small-scale Hotel door. **Guest Services:** valet and coin laundry. **Business Services:** meeting rooms, fax (fee). **Cards:** AX,
DC, DS, MC, VI. **Special Amenities:** free local telephone calls and free newspaper.

SOME UNITS

LA QUINTA INN-HARLINGEN

Phone: (956)428-6888

All Year 1P: $75-$95 2P: $81-$105
Location: US 83 and 77 Expwy, exit M St. Located across from shopping mall. 1002 US 83 S Expwy 78552.
Fax: 956/425-5840. **Facility:** 130 units. 129 one-bedroom standard units. 1 one-bedroom suite. 2 stories, ex-
terior corridors. **Parking:** on-site. **Terms:** [ECP] meal plan available, small pets only. **Amenities:** video
Small-scale Hotel games (fee), voice mail, irons, hair dryers. **Pool(s):** heated outdoor. **Guest Services:** valet and coin laundry,
area transportation. **Business Services:** meeting rooms, fax (fee). **Cards:** AX, CB, DC, DS, JC, MC, VI.

SOME UNITS

RAMADA LIMITED

Phone: (956)425-1333

All Year [CP] 1P: $77-$82 2P: $82-$86 XP: $8 F17
Location: US 83 and 77, exit Ed Carrey. 4401 S Expwy 83 78550. Fax: 956/425-1457. **Facility:** 45 units. 41 one-
bedroom standard units, some with whirlpools. 4 one-bedroom suites. 1 story, exterior corridors. *Bath:* combo
Small-scale Hotel or shower only. **Parking:** on-site. **Amenities:** voice mail, irons, hair dryers. **Pool(s):** outdoor. **Guest Services:** valet laundry. **Business Services:** meeting rooms, fax (fee). **Cards:** AX, CB, DC, DS, JC, MC, VI.

SOME UNITS

SUPER 8 MOTEL

Phone: (956)412-8873

All Year 1P: $40-$50 2P: $45-$55 XP: $5 F17
Location: US 83 and 77 Expwy, exit M St, just n. Located in a commercial area. 1115 S Expwy 77/83 78550.
Fax: 956/412-8873. **Facility:** 55 one-bedroom standard units. 3 stories, interior corridors. *Bath:* combo or
shower only. **Parking:** on-site. **Terms:** weekly rates available, pets ($5 extra charge). **Amenities:** video li-
Small-scale Hotel brary (fee), hair dryers. *Some:* irons. **Pool(s):** heated outdoor. **Guest Services:** valet and coin laundry. **Business Services:** fax (fee). **Cards:** AX, CB, DC, DS, JC, MC, VI. **Special Amenities:** free continental
breakfast and free local telephone calls.

SOME UNITS

HEARNE pop. 4,690

—— WHERE TO STAY ——

OAK TREE INN

Phone: (979)279-5599

All Year 1P: $62-$75 2P: $67-$80 XP: $5 F15
Location: 0.6 mi n of jct US 79 and SR 6. 1051 N Market St 77859 (PO Box 847). Fax: 979/279-3551. **Facility:** Des-
ignated smoking area. 116 one-bedroom standard units. 2 stories (no elevator), interior/exterior corridors.
Bath: combo or shower only. **Parking:** on-site. **Leisure Activities:** whirlpool, limited exercise equipment.
Motel **Guest Services:** coin laundry. **Business Services:** meeting rooms, fax (fee). **Cards:** AX, CB, DC, DS,
MC, VI. **Special Amenities:** early check-in/late check-out and free local telephone calls.

SOME UNITS

HENDERSON pop. 11,273

—— WHERE TO STAY ——

BEST WESTERN INN OF HENDERSON

Phone: (903)657-9561

All Year [ECP] 1P: $59 2P: $79 XP: $5 F15
Location: 2 mi s on US 259, 0.7 mi s of jct US 79 and 259 S. 1500 Hwy 259 S 75654. Fax: 903/657-9183.
Facility: 77 one-bedroom standard units, some with whirlpools. 2 stories, interior/exterior corridors. **Parking:**
on-site. **Terms:** cancellation fee imposed, weekly rates available, small pets only ($10 extra charge).
Small-scale Hotel **Amenities:** irons, hair dryers. **Pool(s):** outdoor. **Guest Services:** coin laundry. **Business Services:** meeting
rooms, fax (fee). **Cards:** AX, CB, DC, DS, MC, VI. **Special Amenities:** early check-in/late check-out and
free continental breakfast.

SOME UNITS

HEREFORD pop. 14,597

—— WHERE TO STAY ——

BEST WESTERN RED CARPET INN

Phone: (806)364-0540

All Year [ECP] 1P: $60-$75 2P: $62-$75
Location: Just w of jct US 385 and 60. 830 W 1st St 79045. Fax: 806/364-0818. **Facility:** 90 one-bedroom stan-
dard units. 2 stories (no elevator), exterior corridors. **Parking:** on-site, winter plug-ins. **Terms:** small pets
Motel only. **Amenities:** irons, hair dryers. **Pool(s):** outdoor. **Cards:** AX, DC, DS, MC, VI.

SOME UNITS

HIGHLAND PARK —*See Dallas p. 297.*

HILLSBORO pop. 8,232

──── **WHERE TO STAY** ────

BEST WESTERN HILLSBORO INN   Phone: (254)582-8465
🔷🔷 SAVE All Year [CP]   1P: $59-$65   2P: $65-$71   XP: $6   F12
🔷🔷   **Location:** I-35, exit 368A northbound; exit 368B southbound, just w. 307 I-35 76645 (PO Box 632). Fax: 254/582-5664.
Motel   **Facility:** 52 one-bedroom standard units. 2 stories, exterior corridors. **Parking:** on-site. **Terms:** small pets
         only. **Amenities:** irons, hair dryers. **Pool(s):** outdoor. **Guest Services:** coin laundry. **Business Services:** fax
         (fee). **Cards:** AX, CB, DC, DS, MC, VI. **Special Amenities: free continental breakfast and free room up-**
         grade (subject to availability with advanced reservations).
                                                                                SOME UNITS

COMFORT INN OF HILLSBORO   Phone: (254)582-3333
SAVE   All Year   1P: $50-$199   2P: $55-$199   XP: $10   F18
         Location: I-35, exit 368A northbound; exit 368B southbound, just w. 1515 Old Brandon Rd 76645. Fax: 254/582-3333.
🔷🔷🔷   **Facility:** 50 one-bedroom standard units, some with whirlpools. 2 stories, exterior corridors. *Bath:* combo or
Small-scale Hotel shower only. **Parking:** on-site. **Terms:** cancellation fee imposed, [ECP] meal plan available, package plans.
         Amenities: *Some:* irons, hair dryers. **Pool(s):** outdoor. **Guest Services:** coin laundry. **Business Services:**
         fax (fee). **Cards:** AX, CB, DC, DS, MC, VI.
                                                                                SOME UNITS

HOLIDAY INN EXPRESS   Phone: (254)582-0220
🔷🔷🔷   All Year [CP]   1P: $75-$85   2P: $75-$85
         Location: I-35, exit 368 southbound; exit 368A northbound, on northbound access road. 1505 Hillview Ave 76645.
Small-scale Hotel Fax: 254/582-1003. **Facility:** 50 one-bedroom standard units, some with whirlpools. 2 stories, interior corri-
dors. *Bath:* combo or shower only. **Parking:** on-site. **Amenities:** irons, hair dryers. **Pool(s):** outdoor. **Leisure**
Activities: whirlpool. **Guest Services:** coin laundry. **Business Services:** meeting rooms, fax (fee). **Cards:** AX, CB, DC, DS, JC,
MC, VI. *(See color ad below)*
                                                                                SOME UNITS

HONDO pop. 7,897

──── **WHERE TO STAY** ────

HONDO EXECUTIVE INN   Phone: (830)426-2535
🔷🔷   7/1-9/30   1P: $50-$65   2P: $55-$70
         4/1-6/30 & 10/1-1/31   1P: $45-$60   2P: $50-$65
Motel   2/1-3/31   1P: $45-$55   2P: $50-$60
         Location: On US 90 W. 102 E 19th St 78861. Fax: 830/426-8202. **Facility:** 26 one-bedroom standard units, some
with whirlpools. 1 story, exterior corridors. *Bath:* combo or shower only. **Parking:** on-site. **Terms:** pets ($10 fee). **Amenities:** hair
dryers. **Pool(s):** outdoor. **Business Services:** fax (fee). **Cards:** AX, DS, MC, VI.
                                                                                SOME UNITS

WHITETAIL LODGE   Phone: 830/426-3031
🔷🔷 SAVE All Year [CP]   1P: $45-$75   2P: $56-$86   XP: $5
🔷🔷   **Location:** US 90 at jct SR 173. 401 Hwy 90 E 78861 (PO Box 637). **Facility:** 52 one-bedroom standard units. 1
Motel   story, exterior corridors. *Bath:* combo or shower only. **Parking:** on-site. **Terms:** cancellation fee imposed,
         pets ($10 fee). **Pool(s):** outdoor. **Cards:** AX, DC, DS, MC, VI. **Special Amenities: free continental break-**
         fast and free local telephone calls.
                                                                                SOME UNITS

Destination Houston
pop. 1,953,631

H ouston, the largest city in Texas, is where things come in huge proportions.

I ts port is one of the largest and busiest in the nation. Its colleges and universities, including Baylor, Rice, Texas Southern and University of Houston, enroll some 230,000 students. Its Texas Medical Center is the largest in the world. And its residents are some of the country's wealthiest.

Houston Astros. This National League team rolls out the turf at Minute Maid Park, a state-of-the-art ballfield with old-fashioned appeal. (See listing page 112)

Skyline, Houston. Rising from the prairie, this haphazard blend of style, size and shape is the result of no zoning laws.

Space Center Houston. Spacesuits, rockets and moon rocks are out of this world at NASA's official visitor center. (See listing page 113)

See Downtown map page 373

See Vicinity map page 374

Houston

Golf, Houston. Houston's top-flight public and private golf courses are up to par with visitors year-round. (See mention page 114)

Downtown Houston

This index helps you "spot" where approved accommodations and restaurants are located on the corresponding detailed maps. Lodging rate ranges are for comparison only and show the property's high season; rates are per night, unless only weekly (W) rates are available. Restaurant rate range is for dinner, unless only lunch (L) is served. Turn to the listing page for more detailed rate information and consult display ads for special promotions.

Spotter/Map Page Number	OA	DOWNTOWN HOUSTON - Lodgings	Diamond Rating	Rate Range High Season	Listing Page
2 / above	AAA	Four Seasons Hotel Houston	◆◆◆◆	$290-$310 SAVE	393
3 / above	AAA	Doubletree Hotel at Allen Center - see color ad p 392	◆◆◆	$99-$305 SAVE	391
4 / above	AAA	Hyatt Regency Houston - see color ad inside front cover	◆◆◆	$105-$245 SAVE	393
		DOWNTOWN HOUSTON - Restaurants			
① / above		Clive's	◆◆◆	$18-$36	393
② / above		Quattro	◆◆◆◆	$9-$28	393
③ / above		Treebeards	◆	$5-$8(L)	393
④ / above		Sambuca Jazz Cafe	◆◆◆	$20-$30	393

© AAA

HOUSTON
LOOP FREEWAY
ACCOMMODATIONS

Scale in Miles   0 — 4.7
Scale in Kilometers   0 — 7.6

To Dallas
CROSS-
TIMBERS
To Livingston
To Beaumont

52B
15
51
17BC
50
49B
48B
768A

91
75
94

19B
20AB
21
22
23B
24A
24B
ALT. 90
90
773A
773B
775
26A
26B

KELLEY   ST.
CAVALCADE   ST.
LIBERTY
WALLISVILLE
MARKET   ST.

EASTEX   FRWY.
HOMESTEAD   RD.
E. HOUSTON   RD.
MESA   DR.
RD.
RD.
N.
LOOP   E.   FRWY.

90
IRVINGTON   BLVD.
QUITMAN   RD.
FRWY.
ST.

770A
771B
10
EAST   90
BAYTOWN
NAVIGATION
HARRISBURG
LOCKWOOD   DR.
N. WAYSIDE   DR.
GARCIA   ST.
CLINTON   DR.
BLVD.

SEE DOWNTOWN MAP
46AB
45
45A
44C
44B
5
43B
42
41B
41A
118
ELGIN   ST.
GULF
S. WAYSIDE   DR.
M.
GRIGGS   RD.
116
28
DR.
30D
30BC
31
32 40A

88
ALT.
90
SPANISH
TRAIL
FRWY.
610
34A
33
LONG
DR.
82 39
45
38B
81

SCOTT   ST.
8C
37
36
S.   LOOP   FRWY.
MYKAWA   ST.
BLVD.
TELEPHONE   RD.
HOWARD   RD.
ALLENDALE   RD.
BROADWAY
WINKLER   DR.

CULLEN   BLVD.
MOLOKO   ST.
BELLFORT
865
88
SOUTH   ACRES   DR.
AIRPORT   BLVD.
AIRPORT
William
P. Hobby
Airport
BLVD.

86
87
85   89
92
84   90
93   96
36
To Baytown
To Galveston

1996-K

✈ Airport Accommodations

Spotter/Map Page Number	OA	WILLIAM P HOBBY	Diamond Rating	Rate Range High Season	Listing Page
89 / p. 374		Courtyard by Marriott-Houston Hobby Airport, 2 mi ne of airport	◇◇◇	$59-$125	395
92 / p. 374	AAA	Drury Inn & Suites-Houston Hobby, 2 mi ne of airport	◇◇◇	$79-$109 SAVE	396
84 / p. 374	AAA	Hampton Inn Hobby Airport, 1.3 mi e	◇◇◇	$89-$110 SAVE	397
82 / p. 374		Hidden Oaks Bed and Breakfast, 2 mi ne of terminal	◇◇◇	$95-$159	397
85 / p. 374		Holiday Inn Hobby Airport, 1.3 mi e of terminal	◇◇◇	$89	398
87 / p. 374	AAA	Houston Hobby Airport Marriott, 2 mi se of airport	◇◇◇	$79-$209 SAVE	399
93 / p. 374	AAA	Red Roof Inn Hobby Airport, 1.8 mi e of terminal	◇◇	$41-$62 SAVE	404

Houston Loop Freeway

This index helps you "spot" where approved accommodations and restaurants are located on the corresponding detailed maps. Lodging rate ranges are for comparison only and show the property's high season; rates are per night, unless only weekly (W) rates are available. Restaurant rate range is for dinner, unless only lunch (L) is served. Turn to the listing page for more detailed rate information and consult display ads for special promotions.

Spotter/Map Page Number	OA	HOUSTON (LOOP FREEWAY) - Lodgings	Diamond Rating	Rate Range High Season	Listing Page
20 / p. 374	AAA	Comfort Inn-Brookhollow	◇◇◇	$60-$73 SAVE	394
21 / p. 374		Sara's Bed & Breakfast	◇◇◇	$70-$200	405
22 / p. 374	AAA	La Quinta Inn-BrookHollow - see color ad p 401	◇◇◇	$53-$72 SAVE	400
23 / p. 374	AAA	Baymont Inn & Suites Houston Northwest	◇◇◇	$59-$69 SAVE	394
24 / p. 374	AAA	Sheraton Houston Brook Hollow - see color ad p 405	◇◇◇	$58-$122 SAVE	405
25 / p. 374	AAA	Courtyard by Marriott-Brookhollow - see ad p 395	◇◇◇	$107-$127 SAVE	395
26 / p. 374	AAA	La Quinta Inn-Wirt Rd - see color ad p 401	◇◇◇	$50-$70 SAVE	401
27 / p. 374		Holiday Inn Hotel and Suites - see color ad p 390	◇◇◇	$99	398
28 / p. 374		Comfort Inn Memorial Park I-10 West	◇◇	$62	394
29 / p. 374		Ramada Plaza Hotel Houston Near Greenway	◇◇◇	$59-$179	403
30 / p. 374	AAA	Howard Johnson Express Inn	◇	$55-$60 SAVE	400
31 / p. 374		Angel Arbor Bed & Breakfast	◇◇◇	$85-$125	394
32 / p. 374		SpringHill Suites by Marriott-Houston	◇◇◇	$70-$110	405
33 / p. 374	AAA	Omni Houston Hotel	◇◇◇◇◇	$265-$315 SAVE	402
34 / p. 374	AAA	The Houstonian Hotel, Club & Spa	◇◇◇◇	$225-$295 SAVE	399
35 / p. 374	AAA	Marriott-West Loop-By The Galleria - see color ad p 398, p 402	◇◇◇	$89-$189 SAVE	402
36 / p. 374	AAA	Drury Inn & Suites-Near Galleria	◇◇◇	$108-$138 SAVE	396
37 / p. 374		La Quinta Inn & Suites Houston-Galleria Area - see color ad p 401	◇◇◇	$70-$131	400

Spotter/Map Page Number	OA	HOUSTON (LOOP FREEWAY) - Lodgings (continued)	Diamond Rating	Rate Range High Season	Listing Page
38 / p. 374		Hampton Inn By The Galleria	◆◆◆	$65-$139	397
39 / p. 374		Embassy Suites Near The Galleria	◆◆◆	$129-$289	396
40 / p. 374		Homestead Studio Suites Hotel-Houston/Galleria Area	◆◆◆	$89-$109	399
41 / p. 374	AAA	**The St. Regis Houston**	◆◆◆◆◆	$520 (SAVE)	404
42 / p. 374	AAA	**J. W. Marriott Houston by the Galleria**	◆◆◆	$89-$299 (SAVE)	400
43 / p. 374	AAA	**Doubletree Hotel Post Oak-Galleria Area -** see color ad p 392	◆◆◆	$169 (SAVE)	396
44 / p. 374		Inter-Continental Houston	[fyi]	$299-$369	406
45 / p. 374		Candlewood Suites Houston by the Galleria	◆◆◆	$109-$159	394
46 / p. 374		Patrician Bed & Breakfast Inn	◆◆	$85-$165	403
47 / p. 374		Bradford Homesuites Houston Galleria	◆◆◆	$99-$139	394
48 / p. 374	AAA	**Doubletree Guest Suites -** see color ad p 392	◆◆◆	$109-$219 (SAVE)	395
49 / p. 374		Courtyard by Marriott-Galleria - see color ad p 392	◆◆◆	$149	395
50 / p. 374		Fairfield Inn by Marriott Galleria - see color ad p 392	◆◆◆	$94	396
51 / p. 374	AAA	**Renaissance Houston Hotel**	◆◆◆◆	$79-$179 (SAVE)	404
52 / p. 374		Ramada Plaza Hotel Near the Galleria	◆◆◆	$55-$79	403
53 / p. 374		The Lovett Inn	◆◆	$85-$225	401
54 / p. 374	AAA	**La Quinta Inn-Greenway Plaza -** see color ad p 401	◆◆◆	$60-$93 (SAVE)	400
55 / p. 374		Rodeway Inn-Southwest Freeway	◆	$53-$69	404
56 / p. 374	AAA	**Wellesley Inn & Suites (Houston/Memorial)**	◆◆◆	$95-$140 (SAVE)	406
57 / p. 374		Holiday Inn Select-Greenway Plaza - see color ad p 390	◆◆◆	$60-$130	399
58 / p. 374		Robin's Nest Bed & Breakfast Inn	◆◆	$89-$150	404
60 / p. 374		The Warwick	◆◆◆	$179-$189	406
61 / p. 374	AAA	**Comfort Suites**	◆◆◆	$98 (SAVE)	394
62 / p. 374	AAA	**Hilton Houston Southwest -** see color ad p 398	◆◆◆	$119-$185 (SAVE)	397
63 / p. 374		Hilton Houston Plaza	◆◆◆	$105-$300	397
64 / p. 374	AAA	**Houston Marriott Medical Center Hotel**	◆◆◆	$89-$229 (SAVE)	400
65 / p. 374		Homestead Studio Suites Hotel-Houston/Medical Center/Reliant Park	◆◆	$109-$124	399
66 / p. 374		Holiday Inn Hotel & Suites-Houston Medical Center - see color ad p 390	◆◆◆	$80-$159	398
67 / p. 374		Crowne Plaza Hotel and Resort Houston Medical Center	◆◆◆	$100-$160	395

Spotter/Map Page Number	OA	HOUSTON (LOOP FREEWAY) - Lodgings (continued)	Diamond Rating	Rate Range High Season	Listing Page
68 / p. 374		Residence Inn by Marriott-Medical Center/Astrodome	◇◇◇	$139-$159	404
69 / p. 374	AAA	Grant's Palm Court Inn	◇	$44-$66 [SAVE]	396
70 / p. 374		Residence Inn by Marriott	◇◇◇	$179-$299	404
71 / p. 374	AAA	Sheraton Suites Houston Near The Galleria	◇◇◇	$189-$259 [SAVE]	405
72 / p. 374		Staybridge Suites by Holiday Inn Houston-Near The Galleria	◇◇◇	$149-$179	406
73 / p. 374	AAA	Park Place Suites Best Western - see color ad p 402	◇◇◇	$99-$159 [SAVE]	403
74 / p. 374		Holiday Inn Astrodome - see color ad p 390	◇◇◇	$170-$190	398
76 / p. 374	AAA	Wellesley Inn & Suites (Houston/Reliant Park Medical Ctr)	◇◇	$99-$144 [SAVE]	406
78 / p. 374	AAA	Radisson Hotel Astrodome Convention Center - see ad p 403	◇◇◇	$129-$179 [SAVE]	403
79 / p. 374	AAA	La Quinta Inn-Houston-Astrodome - see color ad p 401	◇◇◇	$70-$93 [SAVE]	400
81 / p. 374		Econo Lodge-Hobby Airport	◇◇	$49-$65	396
82 / p. 374		Hidden Oaks Bed and Breakfast	◇◇◇	$95-$159	397
84 / p. 374	AAA	Hampton Inn Hobby Airport - see color ad p 397	◇◇◇	$89-$110 [SAVE]	397
85 / p. 374		Holiday Inn Hobby Airport - see color ad p 390	◇◇◇	$89	398
86 / p. 374		Best Western Hobby Airport Inn	◇◇	$55-$65	394
87 / p. 374	AAA	Houston Hobby Airport Marriott - see color ad p 399	◇◇◇	$79-$209 [SAVE]	399
89 / p. 374		Courtyard by Marriott-Houston Hobby Airport	◇◇◇	$59-$125	395
90 / p. 374	AAA	AmeriSuites (Houston/Hobby Airport) - see color ad p 391	◇◇◇	$105 [SAVE]	393
92 / p. 374	AAA	Drury Inn & Suites-Houston Hobby	◇◇◇	$79-$109 [SAVE]	396
93 / p. 374	AAA	Red Roof Inn Hobby Airport	◇◇	$41-$62 [SAVE]	404
96 / p. 374	AAA	La Quinta Inn-Houston-Hobby Airport - see color ad p 401	◇◇◇	$63-$79 [SAVE]	401
		HOUSTON (LOOP FREEWAY) - Restaurants			
5 / p. 374		La Tour d'Argent Restaurant Francais	◇◇◇	$16-$39	411
6 / p. 374		Las Alamedas	◇◇	$13-$25	411
7 / p. 374		Prince's	◇	$5-$9	413
8 / p. 374		Tony Mandola's Blue Oyster Bar	◇◇	$10-$25	415
9 / p. 374		Shug's Cafe & Restaurant	◇◇	$8-$15(L)	414
10 / p. 374		Patisserie Descours	◇	$5-$7(L)	413
11 / p. 374		Cadillac Bar	◇◇	$8-$15	408
12 / p. 374		La Reserve	◇◇◇◇	$21-$100	411

Spotter/Map Page Number	OA	HOUSTON (LOOP FREEWAY) - Restaurants (continued)	Diamond Rating	Rate Range High Season	Listing Page
14 / p. 374	AAA	Rainbow Lodge	◆◆◆	$16-$32	413
15 / p. 374		Post Oak Grill	◆◆◆	$13-$26	413
16 / p. 374		Otto's Barbeque & Hamburgers	◆	$4-$10	412
17 / p. 374		Americas	◆◆◆	$16-$25	406
18 / p. 374		Backstreet Cafe	◆◆	$12-$23	407
19 / p. 374		Daily Review Cafe	◆◆	$8-$23	409
20 / p. 374		Golden Room	◆◆	$9-$18	409
21 / p. 374		Old Heidelberg	◆	$10-$19	412
22 / p. 374		Fountainview Cafe and Breakfast	◆	$4-$6(L)	409
23 / p. 374		Kenny & Ziggy's Delicatessen Restaurant	◆◆	$7-$15	410
24 / p. 374		The Remington	◆◆◆◆	$25-$31	413
25 / p. 374		Hunan Restaurant	◆◆	$15-$22	410
26 / p. 374		Cafe Annie	◆◆◆	$28-$42	408
27 / p. 374		Ouisie's Table	◆◆◆	$16-$30	412
28 / p. 374		Scott's Cellar	◆◆◆	$14-$30	414
29 / p. 374		Grotto	◆◆	$8-$24	410
30 / p. 374		Capital Grille	◆◆◆	$18-$35	408
31 / p. 374		Andre's Pastry Shop and Cafe	◆◆	$10(L)	407
32 / p. 374		Crostini	◆◆	$11-$25	409
33 / p. 374		La Griglia	◆◆◆	$9-$28	411
34 / p. 374		Mark's	◆◆◆	$18-$31	412
35 / p. 374		Mesa Grill	◆◆	$10-$17	412
37 / p. 374		Nino's	◆◆◆	$11-$28	412
38 / p. 374		Barnaby's Cafe	◆	$8-$18	407
39 / p. 374		Vincent's Restaurant	◆◆	$9-$26	415
40 / p. 374		Teppay	◆◆	$12-$40	414
41 / p. 374		Pino's Italian Restaurant	◆◆	$11-$21	413
42 / p. 374		Kim Son Restaurant	◆◆	$5-$12	410
43 / p. 374		Barbecue Inn	◆	$7-$11	407
44 / p. 374		The Palm Restaurant of Houston	◆◆◆	$15-$32	412
45 / p. 374		King Fish Market	◆◆	$14-$22	410
46 / p. 374		Truluck's Steak & Stone Crab	◆◆	$11-$27	415

Spotter/Map Page Number	OA	HOUSTON (LOOP FREEWAY) - Restaurants (continued)	Diamond Rating	Rate Range High Season	Listing Page
(47) / p. 374		Tony's	◆◆◆◆	$25-$39	414
(48) / p. 374		India's	◆◆	$8-$17	410
(49) / p. 374		Pappas Bros Steakhouse	◆◆◆	$30-$74	412
(50) / p. 374		Texadelphia	◆	$4-$6	414
(52) / p. 374		Mama's Cafe	◆	$6-$14	411
(53) / p. 374		James Coney Island	◆	$3-$6	410
(54) / p. 374		Canyon Cafe	◆◆	$9-$17	408
(55) / p. 374		Cheesecake Factory	◆◆	$8-$23	408
(56) / p. 374		Doneraki Mexican Restaurant	◆	$7-$16	409
(59) / p. 374		Anthony's	◆◆◆	$18-$35	407
(62) / p. 374		Palazzo's Italian Cafe	◆◆	$7-$16	412
(64) / p. 374		The Brownstone	◆◆◆	$25-$32	408
(65) / p. 374		River Oaks Grill	◆◆◆	$21-$30	413
(68) / p. 374		Berryhill Hot Tamales	◆	$6-$15	407
(69) / p. 374		Shanghai River	◆◆	$7-$17	414
(71) / p. 374		Churrascos	◆◆◆	$14-$24	408
(73) / p. 374		La Mora	◆◆◆	$12-$26	411
(74) / p. 374		Ruggles Grill	◆◆	$10-$19	414
(75) / p. 374		Damian's Cucina Italiana	◆◆◆	$12-$28	409
(76) / p. 374		Dave & Buster's	◆◆	$10-$14	409
(78) / p. 374		Magnolia Bar & Grill	◆◆	$13-$22	411
(80) / p. 374		Pappasito's Cantina	◆◆	$6-$19	412
(81) / p. 374		Cafe Express	◆	$5-$8	408
(82) / p. 374		Star Pizza	◆	$10-$18	414
(83) / p. 374		59 Diner	◆	$5-$9	406
(86) / p. 374		Lexington Grille	◆◆	$16-$28	411
(88) / p. 374		La Colombe D'or Restaurant	◆◆◆	$29-$38	411
(89) / p. 374		The Black Labrador	◆◆	$8-$13	407
(90) / p. 374		Dong Ting	◆◆◆	$9-$22	409
(91) / p. 374		Van Loc Restaurant	◆◆	$4-$10	415
(92) / p. 374		Brennan's of Houston	◆◆◆◆	$25-$32	408
(94) / p. 374		Kim Son	◆◆	$7-$20	410

Spotter/Map Page Number	OA	HOUSTON (LOOP FREEWAY) - Restaurants (continued)	Diamond Rating	Rate Range High Season	Listing Page
98 / p. 374		Pappas Seafood House and Oyster Bar	♦♦	$14-$31	413
99 / p. 374		Cleburne Cafeteria	♦	$7-$14	409
100 / p. 374		Magic Island	♦♦	$32-$40	411
101 / p. 374		Sierra Grill	♦♦♦	$12-$24	414
102 / p. 374		Boulevard Bistrot	♦♦♦	$12-$26	407
103 / p. 374		Redwood Gril	♦♦♦	$9-$26	413
104 / p. 374		Goode Co. Seafood	♦	$10-$24	410
105 / p. 374		Wings N Things	♦	$4-$8	415
106 / p. 374		Goode Company Hamburgers & Taqueria	♦	$5-$15	410
107 / p. 374		Benjy's	♦♦	$8-$24	407
108 / p. 374		Prego Restaurant	♦♦	$11-$23	413
109 / p. 374		Fusion Cafe	♦♦	$7-$13	409
116 / p. 374		Brady's Landing	♦♦	$16-$20	408
118 / p. 374		Bonnie's Beef & Seafood Co	♦♦♦	$15-$28	407

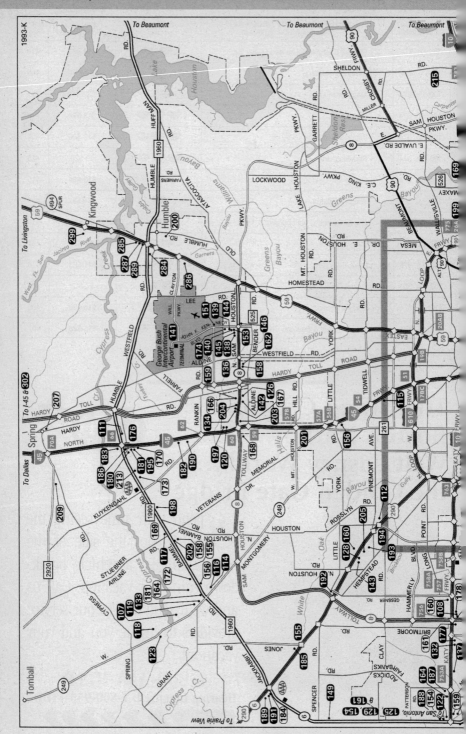

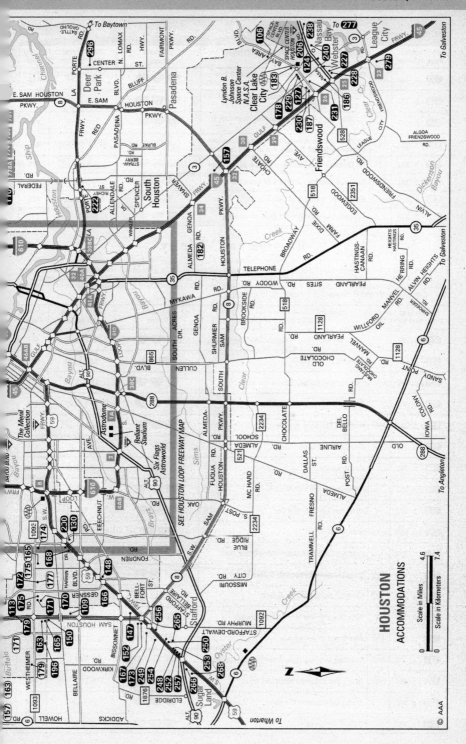

HOUSTON
ACCOMMODATIONS

Scale in Miles

Scale in Kilometers

© AAA

✈ Airport Accommodations

Spotter/Map Page Number	OA	GEORGE BUSH INTERCONTINENTAL AIRPORT	Diamond Rating	Rate Range High Season	Listing Page
153 / p. 382		Comfort Suites Intercontinental Plaza, 3.2 mi s of terminal	◆◆◆	$69-$194	418
146 / p. 382		Holiday Inn Houston Intercontinental Airport, 5.4 mi s of terminal	◆◆◆	$80-$150	423
141 / p. 382		Houston Airport Marriott, between terminals B & C	◆◆◆	$89-$210	424
139 / p. 382	AAA	Hyatt Regency Houston Airport at Houston Intercontinental Airport, 4.8 mi s of terminal	◆◆◆	$75-$195 (SAVE)	425
174 / p. 382	AAA	La Quinta Inn & Suites, 3.3 mi s of terminal	◆◆◆	$70-$115 (SAVE)	425
144 / p. 382	AAA	Ramada Limited, 3.5 mi s of terminal	◆◆	$59-$109 (SAVE)	427
138 / p. 382	AAA	Sleep Inn, 3.1 mi s of terminal	◆◆	$66-$79 (SAVE)	428
140 / p. 382		Wingate Inn-Houston, 3.1 mi s of terminal	◆◆◆	$87-$101	430

Houston and Vicinity

This index helps you "spot" where approved accommodations and restaurants are located on the corresponding detailed maps. Lodging rate ranges are for comparison only and show the property's high season; rates are per night, unless only weekly (W) rates are available. Restaurant rate range is for dinner, unless only lunch (L) is served. Turn to the listing page for more detailed rate information and consult display ads for special promotions.

Spotter/Map Page Number	OA	HOUSTON - Lodgings	Diamond Rating	Rate Range High Season	Listing Page
106 / p. 382		Candlewood Suites-Houston-Clear Lake	◆◆◆	$84-$129	417
107 / p. 382		Ramada Ltd/S.H. 249	◆◆	$80-$100	427
108 / p. 382		Candlewood Suites-Town & Country	◆◆◆	$109-$129	417
109 / p. 382		Candlewood Suites-Westchase	◆◆◆	$49-$129	417
110 / p. 382	AAA	Comfort Inn East Houston	◆◆◆	$61-$91 (SAVE)	418
111 / p. 382	AAA	Days Inn & Suites	◆◆◆	$59 (SAVE)	419
112 / p. 382		Econo Lodge	◆	$47-$55	419
113 / p. 382		Fairfield Inn Marriott-Westchase	◆◆◆	$69-$99	420
114 / p. 382		Hampton Inn-Willowbrook	◆◆◆	$99	421
115 / p. 382		Star Inn & Suites	◆◆	$49-$60	428
116 / p. 382		Homewood Suites Hotel-Willowbrook Mall	◆◆◆	$99-$169	424
117 / p. 382	AAA	Best Western Executive Suites Hotel	◆◆◆	$62-$69 (SAVE)	416
118 / p. 382	AAA	Comfort Suites-Willowbrook	◆◆◆	$89-$159 (SAVE)	418
119 / p. 382		Hilton Garden Inn Houston Northwest	◆◆◆	$69-$219	422
120 / p. 382	AAA	Wyndham Greenspoint	◆◆◆	$99-$179 (SAVE)	430
121 / p. 382	AAA	Comfort Inn Houston West/Energy Corridor	◆◆◆	$69-$84 (SAVE)	418
122 / p. 382	AAA	Drury Inn & Suites Houston West	◆◆◆	$75-$105 (SAVE)	419
123 / p. 382		Northwest Houston Courtyard By Marriott	◆◆◆	$129	426
124 / p. 382		Quality Inn-Nasa	◆◆◆	$59-$79	427

Spotter/Map Page Number	OA	HOUSTON - Lodgings (continued)	Diamond Rating	Rate Range High Season	Listing Page
125 / p. 382	AAA	La Quinta Inn & Suites Park 10 - see color ad p 401	◆◆◆	$80-$100 [SAVE]	425
126 / p. 382		Hampton Inn-Houston Bush Intercontinental Airport	◆◆◆	$69-$94	421
127 / p. 382		Homewood Suites by Hilton	◆◆◆	$139-$179	424
128 / p. 382	AAA	Red Roof Inns	◆◆	$39-$64 [SAVE]	428
129 / p. 382		Bradford Homesuites Park 10 West	◆◆◆	$89-$119	417
130 / p. 382	AAA	Baymont Inn & Suites Houston Southwest	◆◆◆	$54-$64 [SAVE]	416
131 / p. 382	AAA	Fairfield Inn by Marriott I-10 East	◆◆◆	$72 [SAVE]	420
132 / p. 382		Hampton Inn- Houston I-10 W	◆◆◆	$61-$101	421
133 / p. 382		Homestead Studio Suites Hotel-Houston/Willowbrook	◆◆	$75-$94	424
134 / p. 382		Houston Marriott North at Greenspoint	◆◆◆	$200	425
135 / p. 382	AAA	Radisson Suite Hotel Houston West - see ad p 427	◆◆◆	$119 [SAVE]	427
136 / p. 382		Quality Suites	◆◆◆	$85-$100	427
137 / p. 382	AAA	GuestHouse International Inn & Suites Houston West	◆◆	$59-$95 [SAVE]	421
138 / p. 382	AAA	Sleep Inn	◆◆	$66-$79 [SAVE]	428
139 / p. 382	AAA	Hyatt Regency Houston Airport at Houston Intercontinental Airport - see color ad inside front cover	◆◆◆	$75-$195 [SAVE]	425
140 / p. 382		Wingate Inn-Houston	◆◆◆	$87-$101	430
141 / p. 382		Houston Airport Marriott	◆◆◆	$89-$210	424
142 / p. 382		Clarion Inn Intercontinental Airport	◆◆	$79-$119	417
143 / p. 382	AAA	GuestHouse International Inn & Suites	◆◆	$59-$95 [SAVE]	420
144 / p. 382	AAA	Ramada Limited	◆◆	$59-$109 [SAVE]	427
145 / p. 382		Country Inn & Suites by Carlson - see color ad p 260	◆◆◆	$69-$194	419
146 / p. 382		Holiday Inn Houston Intercontinental Airport - see color ad p 390	◆◆◆	$80-$150	423
147 / p. 382		Travelodge Southwest Frwy	◆◆◆	$45-$49	430
148 / p. 382		Super 8-Houston-Gessner	◆◆◆	$45-$49	429
149 / p. 382		Studio 6	◆◆	$43-$57	428
150 / p. 382		Motel 6 - 1401	◆◆	$43-$59	426
151 / p. 382		Hilton Garden Inn Houston/Bush Airport	◆◆◆	$149-$169	422
152 / p. 382	AAA	Wingate Inn Southwest	◆◆◆	$89-$100 [SAVE]	430
153 / p. 382		Comfort Suites Intercontinental Plaza	◆◆◆	$69-$194	418
154 / p. 382		Fairfield Inn	◆◆◆	$65-$95	420

Spotter/Map Page Number	OA	HOUSTON - Lodgings (continued)	Diamond Rating	Rate Range High Season	Listing Page
155 / p. 382		Motel 6 - 1140	◆	$41-$57	426
156 / p. 382	AAA	**Econo Lodge**	◆◆	$55-$65 SAVE	419
157 / p. 382		Studio 6-Houston Hobby South #6039	◆◆	$46-$60	429
158 / p. 382		Holiday Inn Express Hotel & Suites-Intercontinental	◆◆◆	$89	423
159 / p. 382		Hotel Sofitel Houston	fyi	$199-$229	430
160 / p. 382		MainStay Suites-Houston (now known as TownePlace Suites Houston-Northwest Freeway)	◆◆◆	$49-$84	426
161 / p. 382		TownePlace Suites by Marriott-Westlake	◆◆	$90-$140	430
162 / p. 382		Hawthorn Suites	◆◆◆	$59-$155	421
163 / p. 382	AAA	**Best Western Westchase Mini Suites**	◆◆◆	$79-$89 SAVE	417
164 / p. 382	AAA	**Red Roof Inn Houston West**	◆◆	$39-$62 SAVE	428
165 / p. 382	AAA	**Red Roof Inns**	◆◆	$43-$64 SAVE	428
166 / p. 382		Embassy Suites Hotel	◆◆◆	$109-$139	420
167 / p. 382		Holiday Inn Houston Southwest/Sugar Land - see color ad p 390	◆◆◆	$76-$109	423
168 / p. 382		Ainsworth Suites	◆◆	$89-$189	415
169 / p. 382	AAA	**La Quinta Inn-Houston East** - see color ad p 401	◆◆◆	$70-$76 SAVE	425
170 / p. 382	AAA	**Adam's Mark Houston**	◆◆◆	$146-$251 SAVE	415
171 / p. 382	AAA	**The Hilton Houston Westchase & Towers** - see color ad p 422	◆◆◆	$89-$194 SAVE	422
172 / p. 382	AAA	**Comfort Inn**	◆◆	$69-$79 SAVE	418
173 / p. 382		Country Inn & Suites Houston at Sugarland - see color ad p 260	◆◆◆	$79-$89	419
174 / p. 382	AAA	**La Quinta Inn & Suites** - see color ad p 401	◆◆◆	$70-$115 SAVE	425
175 / p. 382		Residence Inn by Marriott Houston Westchase	◆◆◆	$94-$204	428
176 / p. 382		Holiday Inn Houston North - see color ad p 390	◆◆◆	$99-$109	423
177 / p. 382	AAA	**La Quinta Inn-Wilcrest** - see color ad p 401	◆◆◆	$50-$70 SAVE	426
178 / p. 382		Residence Inn-Houston Clear Lake	◆◆◆	$125-$175	428
179 / p. 382		Homewood Suites by Hilton-Westchase	◆◆◆	$112	424
180 / p. 382		Studio 6-Cypress Station #6037	◆◆	$41-$55	429
181 / p. 382	AAA	**Comfort Suites**	◆◆◆	$69-$89 SAVE	418
182 / p. 382	AAA	**GuestHouse Inn & Suites Intercontinental**	◆◆◆	$64-$89 SAVE	420
183 / p. 382		Fairfield Inn By Marriott	◆◆◆	$69-$99	420
185 / p. 382		Comfort Suites	◆◆◆	$79-$150	418
186 / p. 382		Super 8 Motel	◆◆	$60-$70	429

Spotter/Map Page Number	OA	HOUSTON - Lodgings (continued)	Diamond Rating	Rate Range High Season	Listing Page
187 / p. 382		Omni Houston Hotel Westside	♦♦♦	$209-$239	426
188 / p. 382		Holiday Inn Select I-10 - see color ad p 390	♦♦♦	$79-$122	423
189 / p. 382		Hampton Inn-Houston Northwest	♦♦♦	$81-$119	421
190 / p. 382	AAA	Best Western Greenspoint Inn & Suites	♦♦♦	$67-$115 [SAVE]	417
191 / p. 382	AAA	La Quinta Inn-Houston-Cy-Fair - see color ad p 401	♦♦♦	$73-$87 [SAVE]	425
192 / p. 382		Holiday Inn-Northwest Freeway - see color ad p 390 & ad p 424	♦♦♦	$69-$79	423
193 / p. 382	AAA	Crowne Plaza Hotel and Resort Brookhollow Hotel	♦♦♦	$149 [SAVE]	419
194 / p. 382		Holiday Inn Express Hotel & Suites	♦♦♦	$95	423
195 / p. 382	AAA	La Quinta Inn-Houston-I-45 North(Loop 1960) - see color ad p 401	♦♦♦	$60-$73 [SAVE]	426
196 / p. 382	AAA	Comfort Suites-Westchase	♦♦♦	$90-$100 [SAVE]	418
197 / p. 382	AAA	Baymont Inn & Suites Houston-Greenspoint	♦♦♦	$49-$69 [SAVE]	416
198 / p. 382		Holiday Inn Express-FM 1960	♦♦♦	$85-$119	423
199 / p. 382		Hampton Inn I-10 East	♦♦♦	$87	421
200 / p. 382	AAA	GuestHouse International Inn & Suites	♦♦	$59-$95 [SAVE]	420
201 / p. 382		Days Inn-Houston North	♦	$44-$61	419
202 / p. 382		Champions Lodge Motel	♦♦	$39-$65	417
206 / p. 382		Microtel Inn & Suites	♦♦	$50-$60	426
203 / p. 382		La Quinta Inn-Greenspoint - see color ad p 401	♦♦♦	$55-$63	425
204 / p. 382	AAA	AmeriSuites (Houston Intercontinental Airport/Greenspoint) - see color ad p 391	♦♦♦	$129-$139 [SAVE]	415
205 / p. 382		Hampton Inn-Brookhollow	♦♦♦	$81-$85	421
		HOUSTON - Restaurants			
154 / p. 382		Cattleguard Restaurant & Bar	♦♦	$12-$25	431
155 / p. 382		Empress	♦♦	$15-$70	432
156 / p. 382		Doneraki Mexican Restaurant	♦	$8-$19	431
157 / p. 382		El Yucatan Mexican Restaurant	♦♦	$9-$20	431
158 / p. 382		Matsu Japanese Restaurant	♦♦	$11-$18	432
159 / p. 382		Lupe Tortillas	♦	$6-$16	432
160 / p. 382		Luther's Bar-B-Q	♦	$5-$11	432
161 / p. 382		Brenner's Steakhouse	♦♦	$25-$33	431
162 / p. 382		Carmelo's Italian Restaurant	♦♦♦	$14-$32	431
163 / p. 382		Lynn's Steakhouse	♦♦	$19-$40	432

Spotter/Map Page Number	OA	HOUSTON - Restaurants (continued)	Diamond Rating	Rate Range High Season	Listing Page
(164) / p. 382		The County Line Barbeque	◆	$8-$20	431
(165) / p. 382		Elvia's Mexican Pub	◆	$8-$18	431
(166) / p. 382		Le Cafe Royal	◆◆◆	$18-$40	432
(167) / p. 382		Jimmy G's Seafood Cajun Restaurant	◆	$13-$20	432
(168) / p. 382		Pappas Seafood House And Oyster Bar	◆◆	$13-$23	433
(169) / p. 382		Resa's Prime Steakhouse	◆◆◆	$18-$36	433
(170) / p. 382		House of Creole	◆◆	$7-$15	432
(171) / p. 382		Rotisserie for Beef & Bird	◆◆◆	$19-$39	433
(172) / p. 382		Tubtim Siam Thai Restaurant	◆	$8-$13	433
(173) / p. 382		Woodlands House Chinese Restaurant	◆	$7-$10	433
(174) / p. 382		Old San Francisco Steak House	◆◆	$15-$37	432
(175) / p. 382		Vargo's	◆◆◆	$20-$30	433
(177) / p. 382		Churrasco's-West Chase	◆◆◆	$12-$26	431
(178) / p. 382		Taste of Texas	◆◆	$10-$37	433
(179) / p. 382		Bistro Provence	◆◆	$10-$22	431
(181) / p. 382		Pappasito's	◆◆	$9-$21	433
(182) / p. 382		Chris' Texas Cheesecake & Grill	◆	$5-$22	431
(183) / p. 382		Tommy's Patio Cafe	◆◆	$12-$24	433
(184) / p. 382		Harris Country Smokehouse	◆	$4-$15	432
		CHANNELVIEW - Lodgings			
(212) / p. 382		Travelodge Suites	◆◆	$60-$65	435
(213) / p. 382		Holiday Inn Houston East - see color ad p 390	◆◆◆	$95-$150	435
(215) / p. 382		Best Western Houston East	◆◆	$70-$74	435
		PASADENA - Lodgings			
(222) / p. 382		Econo Lodge	◆◆	$50-$70	441
		WEBSTER - Lodgings			
(227) / p. 382	AAA	**Howard Johnson Express Inn-NASA**	◆◆◆	$55-$75 [SAVE]	444
(228) / p. 382		Motel 6 Houston Nasa/Clear Lake #551	◆	$41-$57	444
(229) / p. 382		Hampton Inn & Suites Clear Lake/NASA	◆◆◆	$82-$132	444
(230) / p. 382	AAA	**Wellesley Inn & Suites (Houston/NASA Clear Lake)**	◆◆◆	$81-$101 [SAVE]	445
(231) / p. 382	AAA	**Best Western-NASA**	◆◆	$49-$109 [SAVE]	444
		WEBSTER - Restaurants			
(186) / p. 382		Lupe Tortilla	◆◆	$6-$10	445
(187) / p. 382		Zio's Italian Kitchen	◆	$6-$10	445
		NASSAU BAY - Lodgings			
(238) / p. 382		Holiday Inn Houston/Nasa - see color ad p 390	◆◆	$99-$109	440

Spotter/Map Page Number	OA	NASSAU BAY - Lodgings (continued)	Diamond Rating	Rate Range High Season	Listing Page
240 / p. 382		Hilton Houston NASA Clear Lake	◆◆◆	$189	440
		STAFFORD - Lodgings			
248 / p. 382		Hampton Inn-Stafford	◆◆◆	$65-$95	443
249 / p. 382	AAA	**Wellesley Inn & Suites (Houston/Stafford)**	◆◆	$85-$115 SAVE	443
250 / p. 382		Courtyard by Marriott-Houston/Sugarland	◆◆◆	$59-$119	443
252 / p. 382	AAA	**Comfort Suites**	◆◆◆	$95-$100 SAVE	443
253 / p. 382	AAA	**La Quinta Inn-Stafford** - see color ad p 401	◆◆◆	$60-$82 SAVE	443
254 / p. 382		Days inn	◆◆	$50-$60	443
256 / p. 382	AAA	**Best Western Fort Bend Inn & Suites**	◆◆◆	$49-$129 SAVE	442
257 / p. 382		Studio 6 #6044	◆◆	$46-$60	443
265 / p. 382		Residence Inn by Marriott Sugarland	◆◆◆	$129	443
		SUGAR LAND - Lodgings			
266 / p. 382	AAA	**Drury Inn & Suites-Houston/Sugar Land**	◆◆◆	$79-$109 SAVE	444
268 / p. 382		Shoney's Inn & Suites Houston-Sugar Land	◆◆	$52-$63	444
		LEAGUE CITY - Lodgings			
277 / p. 382		South Shore Harbour Resort & Conference Center	◆◆◆	$140-$210	457
279 / p. 382		Super 8 Motel	◆◆	$50-$60	457
		HUMBLE - Lodgings			
284 / p. 382	AAA	**Econo Lodge**	◆◆	$50-$64 SAVE	437
285 / p. 382	AAA	**Country Inn & Suites By Carlson-Houston Intercontinental Airport East** - see color ad p 260	◆◆◆	$74 SAVE	437
286 / p. 382	AAA	**Best Western Intercontinental Airport Inn** - see color ad p 437	◆◆◆	$70-$112 SAVE	437
287 / p. 382		Fairfield Inn By Marriott-Humble	◆◆◆	$69-$99	438
289 / p. 382		Hampton Inn Humble	◆◆◆	$78-$85	438
		HUMBLE - Restaurant			
200 / p. 382		Chez Nous	◆◆◆	$19-$31	439
		DEER PARK - Lodgings			
296 / p. 382		Best Western Deer Park Inn & Suites	◆◆◆	$72-$95	437
		KINGWOOD - Lodgings			
299 / p. 382		Comfort Suites Kingwood	◆◆◆	$90-$100	439
		TOMBALL - Lodgings			
302 / p. 382		Holiday Inn Express	◆◆◆	$85	444
		SPRING - Restaurants			
207 / p. 382		Wunsche Bros Cafe	◆	$7-$11	442
209 / p. 382		Amerigo's Seafood & Pasta	◆◆	$11-$23	442
213 / p. 382		Woodlands House Chinese Restaurant	◆	$7-$10	442

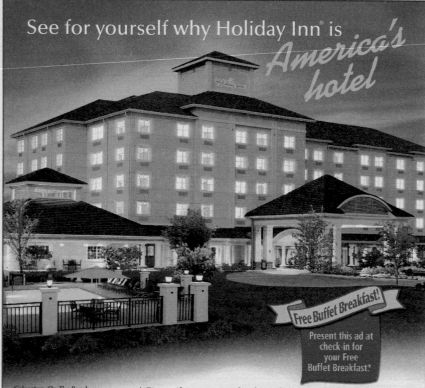

See for yourself why Holiday Inn® is *America's hotel*

Free Buffet Breakfast!

Present this ad at check-in for your Free Buffet Breakfast.*

Galveston–On The Beach
(409) 740-3581

HOUSTON AIRPORT AREA

Hobby Airport
(713) 947-0000

Intercontinental Airport (Airport Entrance)
(281) 449-2311

North Freeway (Richey Road & FM 1960)
(281) 821-2570

HOUSTON DOWNTOWN AREA

Astrodome
(713) 790-1900

Greenway Plaza Area ■
(713) 523-8448

Medical Center •
(713) 528-7744

Near The Galleria–
At I-10 West & Loop 610 •
(713) 681-5000

HOUSTON AREA

I-10 East (Channelview Area)
(281) 452-7304

I-10 West & Highway 6 (Park 10 Area) ■
(281) 558-5580

NASA/Clear Lake
(281) 333-2500

Northwest Freeway (US 290)
(713) 939-9955

Southwest/Sugar Land/Beltway 8 & 59 S.
(281) 530-1400

For good reasons, travelers have chosen Holiday Inn® hotels for over fifty years. Comfort, value, convenient locations throughout Houston...and a great place to create family memories.

Here's what you can expect at every Greater Houston Area Holiday Inn hotel:**

- Kids Eat & Stay Free
- Swimming pool
- Restaurant, lounge, room service, and fitness center
- In-room amenities, including: dataport, iron/ironing board, coffeemaker, and hair dryer.

Ask for the AAA rate when making your reservations in Houston.

For Reservations:
Call **1-800-HOLIDAY**,
your AAA Travel Professional
or visit **holiday-inn.com/aaa**

Holiday Inn
HOTELS · RESORTS

DOWNTOWN HOUSTON　(See map p. 373; index p. 373)

─── **WHERE TO STAY** ───

DOUBLETREE HOTEL AT ALLEN CENTER　　　　　　**Phone:** (713)759-0202　③
(AAA) (SAVE)　All Year　　　　　1P: $99-$295　　2P: $109-$305　　XP: $10　　　F18
▼▼▼▼　**Location:** At Dallas and Bagby sts. Adjoins a pedestrian tunnel and sky bridge. 400 Dallas St 77002.
　　　Fax: 713/752-2734. **Facility:** 350 units. 344 one-bedroom standard units. 6 one-bedroom suites. 20 stories,
Large-scale Hotel　interior corridors. *Bath:* combo or shower only. **Parking:** on-site (fee). **Terms:** cancellation fee imposed, 15%
　　　service charge, pets ($75 deposit, $25 extra charge). **Amenities:** video games (fee), dual phone lines, voice
　　　mail, irons, hair dryers. **Dining:** 6 am-10 pm, cocktails, entertainment. **Leisure Activities:** exercise room.
Guest Services: gift shop, valet and coin laundry, area transportation-within 3 mi. **Business Services:** conference facilities,
business center. **Cards:** AX, CB, DC, DS, JC, MC, VI. **Special Amenities:** early check-in/late check-out and free newspaper. *(See color ad p 392)*
　　　　　　　　　　　　　　　　　　　　　　　　　　　　　SOME UNITS
　　　　(S/D) (⌂) (⫟⫟) (Y) (&) (♫) (✇) (DATA PORT) (🖵) / (✕) (🔒) (▤) /

(See map p. 373)

FOUR SEASONS HOTEL HOUSTON

Phone: (713)650-1300   **2**

AAA **SAVE**

All Year   1P: $290-$310   2P: $290-$310
Location: Lamar St and Austin. Located across from a shopping center. 1300 Lamar St 77010-3098.
Fax: 713/650-1203. **Facility:** This lavish hotel offers extensive fitness facilities and a notable lobby bar. 404
units. 392 one-bedroom standard units. 12 one-bedroom suites ($330-$360). 19 stories, interior corridors.
Large-scale Hotel   **Parking:** valet. **Terms:** 17% service charge, small pets only. **Amenities:** CD players, dual phone lines, voice
mail, safes, honor bars, irons, hair dryers. *Fee:* video games, high-speed Internet. *Some:* DVD players, fax.
Dining: 6:30 am-11 pm, cocktails, also, Quattro, see separate listing, entertainment. **Pool(s):** heated outdoor. **Leisure Activities:** saunas, whirlpool, spa. **Guest Services:** gift shop, valet laundry, area transportation-within downtown. **Business Services:**
conference facilities, business center. **Cards:** AX, CB, DC, DS, JC, MC, VI.

SOME UNITS

HYATT REGENCY HOUSTON

Phone: (713)654-1234   **4**

AAA **SAVE**

All Year   1P: $105-$245   2P: $105-$245   XP: $25   F18
Location: Between Polk and Dallas St. 1200 E Louisiana St 77002. Fax: 713/951-0934. **Facility:** 984 units. 954
one-bedroom standard units. 30 one-bedroom suites. 30 stories, interior corridors. *Bath:* combo or shower
only. **Parking:** on-site (fee). **Terms:** cancellation fee imposed. **Amenities:** voice mail, irons, hair dryers.
Large-scale Hotel   *Some:* CD players, fax. **Dining:** 3 restaurants, 6 am-11 pm, cocktails. **Pool(s):** heated outdoor. **Leisure Ac-
tivities:** exercise room. **Guest Services:** gift shop, valet laundry, area transportation-within 7 mi & Galleria.
Business Services: conference facilities, business center. **Cards:** AX, CB, DC, DS, JC, MC, VI.
(See color ad inside front cover)

SOME UNITS
FEE

The following lodging was either not evaluated or did not meet AAA rating requirements but is listed for your information only.

THE LANCASTER HOTEL

Phone: 713/228-9500

fyi

Not evaluated. **Location:** 701 Texas Ave 77002. Facilities, services, and decor characterize a mid-range property.

--- WHERE TO DINE ---

CLIVE'S

Lunch: $9-$18   Dinner: $18-$36   Phone: 713/224-4438   **1**

Location: Downtown theater district; between Texas and Prairie sts. 517 Louisiana St 77002. **Hours:** 11:30 am-2 &
5:30-10 pm, Thurs-Sat to 11 pm. Closed major holidays; also Sun. **Reservations:** suggested.
American   **Features:** The oldest restaurant in downtown Houston has large murals depicting the city's history. This
low-ceilinged bistro with wall-and-mirror walls offers sophisticated elegance. Guests can choose their
favorite preparation including char-grilled, pan seared and oven roasted entrees. A medley of dry spice rubs and heavenly
condiments and enhancers give each entree a singular taste. Extensive wine list, emphasizing French and Californian
varieties. Dressy casual; cocktails. **Parking:** valet. **Cards:** AX, CB, DC, MC, VI.

QUATTRO

Lunch: $9-$24   Dinner: $9-$28   Phone: 713/650-1300   **2**

Location: Lamar St and Austin; in Four Seasons Hotel Houston. 1300 Lamar St 77010. **Hours:** 6:30 am-midnight.
Reservations: suggested. **Features:** A subtle, refined ambience is achieved through a mix of classic and
Italian   modern artwork and impeccable service. Diverse, artistically designed menu selections—ranging from foie
gras to double-grilled lamb chops to crabcakes—combine with the chef's seasonal specials to create a
distinct fusion of flavors. Dressy casual; cocktails; entertainment. **Parking:** valet. **Cards:** AX, CB, DC, DS, JC, MC, VI.

SAMBUCA JAZZ CAFE

Lunch: $10-$16   Dinner: $20-$30   Phone: 713/224-5299   **4**

Location: Between Travis and Main. 909 Texas Ave 77002. **Hours:** 11 am-11 pm, Thurs-midnight, Fri-1 am, Sat
5 pm-1 am. Closed: 1/1, 5/26; also Super Bowl Sun. **Reservations:** required; weekends.
Mediterranean   **Features:** Welcome to the jungle. Leopard and zebra prints abound in this chic eatery that serves up a
creative Mediterranean cuisine and offers live jazz nightly. On weekends, going without a reservation may
be an exercise in futility. Dressy casual; cocktails; entertainment. **Parking:** on-site and valet. **Cards:** AX, DC, DS, MC, VI.

TREEBEARDS

Lunch: $5-$8   Phone: 713/228-2622   **3**

Location: Corner of Travis and Preston; across from Market Square Park. 315 Travis 77002. **Hours:** 11 am-2 pm.
Closed major holidays; also Sat & Sun. **Features:** Earthy gumbos, chunky red beans and rice with
Regional American   sausage, savory chili, jambalaya, and daily specials with fresh vegetables come together to give a
cafeteria-style taste of Louisiana. Smoke free premises. Casual dress; cocktails. **Parking:** on-site (fee).
Cards: AX, CB, DC, MC, VI.

HOUSTON (LOOP FREEWAY)   (See map p. 374; index p. 376)

--- WHERE TO STAY ---

AMERISUITES (HOUSTON/HOBBY AIRPORT)

Phone: (713)943-1713   **90**

AAA **SAVE**

All Year   1P: $105   2P: $105   XP: $10   F16
Location: I-45, exit 36 (Airport Blvd/College Rd), off southbound service road. 7922 Mosley Rd 77061.
Fax: 713/943-1813. **Facility:** 122 one-bedroom standard units. 5 stories, interior corridors. *Bath:* combo or
shower only. **Parking:** on-site. **Terms:** [ECP] meal plan available, small pets only ($25 fee). **Amenities:** high-
Small-scale Hotel   speed Internet (fee), voice mail, irons, hair dryers. **Pool(s):** outdoor. **Leisure Activities:** exercise room.
Guest Services: coin laundry, airport transportation-William P Hobby Airport, area transportation-within 5 mi.
Business Services: meeting rooms, fax (fee). **Cards:** AX, CB, DC, DS, JC, MC, VI. **Special Amenities:** free continental
breakfast and free newspaper. *(See color ad p 391)*

SOME UNITS

(See map p. 374)

ANGEL ARBOR BED & BREAKFAST   Phone: 713/868-4654   31
▼▼▼▼
                All Year [BP]   1P: $85-$115   2P: $95-$125
Historic Bed   **Location:** 0.8 mi n of I-10, exit 766 (Heights Blvd) westbound; exit 767A (Studemont) eastbound, U-turn under I-10. Lo-
& Breakfast   cated in a historic neighborhood. 848 Heights Blvd 77007. Fax: 713/861-3189. **Facility:** Built in 1923, this
                Georgian-style B&B features an arbor and garden. Smoke free premises. 6 one-bedroom standard units,
some with whirlpools. 3 stories (no elevator), interior/exterior corridors. *Bath:* combo or shower only. **Parking:**
street. **Terms:** 2 night minimum stay, age restrictions may apply, 3 day cancellation notice, no pets allowed (owner's pet on
premises). **Amenities:** video library. *Some:* CD players, irons. **Leisure Activities:** jogging. **Cards:** AX, DC, MC, VI.

SOME UNITS
(ASK) (S/D) (T/+) (X) (VCR) / (◻) /

BAYMONT INN & SUITES HOUSTON NORTHWEST   Phone: (713)680-8282   23
(AAA) (SAVE)
                All Year [ECP]   1P: $59-$69   2P: $59-$69
▼▼▼▼   **Location:** US 290 W, exit W 34th St, just ne. 11130 Northwest Frwy 77092. Fax: 713/680-1887. **Facility:** 106 units.
                102 one-bedroom standard units. 4 one-bedroom suites ($79-$109). 4 stories, interior corridors. *Bath:* combo
Small-scale Hotel or shower only. **Parking:** on-site. **Terms:** small pets only ($25 deposit). **Amenities:** video games (fee), voice
                mail, irons, hair dryers. **Pool(s):** outdoor. **Guest Services:** valet and coin laundry. **Business Services:** fax
                (fee). **Cards:** AX, CB, DC, DS, MC, VI. **Special Amenities:** free continental breakfast and free news-
paper.

SOME UNITS
(S/D) (🐾) (T/+) (&) (≈) (🎥) (DATA PORT) (◻) / (X) (◻) (◻) /

BEST WESTERN HOBBY AIRPORT INN   Phone: (713)910-8600   86
(SAVE)
                All Year [ECP]   1P: $55   2P: $55-$65   XP: $7   F
▼▼ ▼▼   **Location:** I-45, exit 38 (Monroe St), just w. 8600 Gulf Frwy 77017. Fax: 713/910-8600. **Facility:** 50 one-bedroom
                standard units. 2 stories, exterior corridors. **Parking:** on-site. **Terms:** weekly rates available.
Motel   **Amenities:** safes, irons. *Some:* hair dryers. **Pool(s):** outdoor. **Leisure Activities:** whirlpool. **Guest Services:**
                valet and coin laundry. **Business Services:** meeting rooms, fax (fee). **Cards:** AX, CB, DC, DS, JC,
                MC, VI.

SOME UNITS
(S/D) (T/+) (≈) (🎥) (DATA PORT) / (X) (◻) (◻) /

BRADFORD HOMESUITES HOUSTON GALLERIA   Phone: (713)629-9711   47
▼▼▼▼
                All Year [CP]   1P: $99-$139   2P: $99-$139
Small-scale Hotel **Location:** I-610, exit 9A (San Felipe/Westheimer rds) southbound; exit 8C (Westheimer Rd) northbound, just w to Sage
                Rd, 0.8 mi s. 3440 Sage Rd 77056. Fax: 713/629-9092. **Facility:** 150 units. 92 one-bedroom standard units with
                efficiencies. 58 one-bedroom suites with efficiencies. 4 stories, interior corridors. *Bath:* combo or shower only.
Parking: on-site. **Terms:** cancellation fee imposed. **Amenities:** video games (fee), dual phone lines, voice mail, irons, hair
dryers. **Pool(s):** outdoor. **Leisure Activities:** whirlpool, exercise room. **Guest Services:** sundries, complimentary evening beverages: Wed, valet and coin laundry. **Business Services:** meeting rooms, business center. **Cards:** AX, CB, DC, DS, JC,
MC, VI.

SOME UNITS
(ASK) (S/D) (&) (≈) (VCR) (🎥) (DATA PORT) (◻) (◻) (◻) / (X) /

CANDLEWOOD SUITES HOUSTON BY THE GALLERIA   Phone: (713)839-9411   45
▼▼▼▼
                All Year   1P: $109-$159
Small-scale Hotel **Location:** I-610, exit 7 (Fournace Pl), northbound frontage road. 4900 Loop Central Dr 77081. Fax: 713/839-9622.
                Facility: 122 units. 98 one-bedroom standard units with efficiencies. 24 one-bedroom suites ($109-$159)
                with efficiencies. 3 stories, interior corridors. *Bath:* combo or shower only. **Parking:** on-site. **Terms:** cancel-
lation fee imposed. **Amenities:** video library, CD players, high-speed Internet, dual phone lines, voice mail, irons, hair dryers.
Leisure Activities: exercise room. **Guest Services:** valet and coin laundry. **Cards:** AX, CB, DC, DS, JC, MC, VI.

SOME UNITS
(ASK) (S/D) (VCR) (🎥) (DATA PORT) (◻) (◻) (◻) / (X) /

COMFORT INN-BROOKHOLLOW   Phone: (713)686-5525   20
(AAA) (SAVE)
                All Year [ECP]   1P: $60-$69   2P: $63-$73   XP: $6   F14
▼▼▼▼   **Location:** US 290, exit Magnum Rd, just n to Sherwood Ln, just w. 4760 Sherwood Ln 77092. Fax: 713/686-5365.
                Facility: 46 one-bedroom standard units, some with whirlpools. 2 stories, exterior corridors. *Bath:* combo or
Motel   shower only. **Parking:** on-site. **Terms:** 14 day cancellation notice-fee imposed, package plans.
                Amenities: dual phone lines, voice mail, irons. *Some:* hair dryers. **Pool(s):** outdoor. **Guest Services:** valet
                and coin laundry. **Business Services:** fax (fee). **Cards:** AX, DC, DS, MC, VI. **Special Amenities:** free con-
tinental breakfast and free local telephone calls.

SOME UNITS
(S/D) (T/+) (&) (≈) (🎥) (DATA PORT) (◻) (◻) / (X) (◻) /

COMFORT INN MEMORIAL PARK I-10 WEST   Phone: (713)869-9211   28
(SAVE)
                All Year [CP]   1P: $62   2P: $62   XP: $5   F18
▼▼ ▼▼   **Location:** I-10, exit 764 (Washington Ave). 5820 Katy Frwy 77007. Fax: 713/869-5677. **Facility:** 93 units. 88 one-
                bedroom standard units, some with efficiencies (no utensils). 5 one-bedroom suites ($75). 2 stories, exterior
·Motel   corridors. *Bath:* combo or shower only. **Parking:** on-site. **Terms:** 7 day cancellation notice. **Amenities:** hair
                dryers. **Pool(s):** outdoor. **Guest Services:** coin laundry. **Business Services:** meeting rooms, fax (fee).
                Cards: AX, CB, DC, DS, MC, VI.

SOME UNITS
(T/+) (&) (≈) (🎥) (DATA PORT) (◻) / (X) (◻) (◻) /

COMFORT SUITES   Phone: (713)787-0004   61
(AAA) (SAVE)
                All Year   1P: $98   2P: $98   XP: $10   F16
▼▼▼▼   **Location:** US 59, exit Hillcroft, 1 mi n to Richmond, 0.6 mi e. 6221 Richmond Ave 77057. Fax: 713/787-0004.
                Facility: 62 units. 61 one-bedroom standard units, some with whirlpools. 1 one-bedroom suite. 3 stories, in-
Motel   terior corridors. *Bath:* combo or shower only. **Parking:** on-site. **Terms:** check-in 4 pm, [ECP] meal plan avail-
                able, pets ($25 extra charge). **Amenities:** voice mail, irons, hair dryers. **Pool(s):** small outdoor. **Leisure
                Activities:** whirlpool, exercise room. **Guest Services:** coin laundry, area transportation-Galleria Mall. **Busi-
ness Services:** meeting rooms. **Cards:** AX, CB, DC, DS, JC, MC, VI. **Special Amenities:** free continental breakfast and free
local telephone calls.

SOME UNITS
(S/D) (🐾) (T/+) (&) (≈) (🎥) (DATA PORT) (◻) (◻) (◻) / (X) /

(See map p. 374)

COURTYARD BY MARRIOTT-BROOKHOLLOW
Phone: 713/688-7711   25
F

All Year   1P: $107-$117   2P: $117-$127   XP: $10
Location: I-610, exit 13C (TC Jester), just nw. 2504 N Loop W 77092. Fax: 713/688-3561. **Facility:** 198 one-bedroom standard units. 3 stories, interior corridors. *Bath:* combo or shower only. **Parking:** on-site.
Amenities: voice mail, irons, hair dryers. **Dining:** 6:30-10 am, Sat & Sun 7-11 am. **Pool(s):** outdoor. **Leisure**
Small-scale Hotel **Activities:** whirlpool, exercise room. **Guest Services:** coin laundry. **Business Services:** meeting rooms, fax (fee). **Cards:** AX, DC, DS, MC, VI. **Special Amenities:** free newspaper. *(See ad below)*

SOME UNITS / FEE

COURTYARD BY MARRIOTT-GALLERIA
Phone: (713)961-1640   49

All Year   1P: $149   2P: $149
Location: 610 Loop on Frontage Rd northbound, exit 8C (Westheimer Rd) northbound; exit 8B (Richmond St) south-bound on northbound access road. 3131 W Loop S 77027. Fax: 713/439-0989. **Facility:** 209 units. 202 one-bedroom standard units. 7 one-bedroom suites ($169). 6 stories, interior corridors. *Bath:* combo or shower
Large-scale Hotel only. **Parking:** on-site. **Terms:** cancellation fee imposed, [BP] meal plan available. **Amenities:** video games, voice mail, irons, hair dryers. **Pool(s):** outdoor, wading. **Leisure Activities:** whirlpool, exercise room. **Guest**
Services: valet and coin laundry. **Business Services:** meeting rooms, fax (fee). **Cards:** AX, CB, DC, DS, MC, VI.
(See color ad p 392)

SOME UNITS / FEE

COURTYARD BY MARRIOTT-HOUSTON HOBBY AIRPORT
Phone: (713)910-1700   89
F12

All Year   1P: $59-$119   2P: $59-$125   XP: $10
Location: I-45, exit 36 (Airport Blvd/College Rd) on southbound service road. 9190 Gulf Frwy 77017.
Fax: 713/910-1701. **Facility:** 153 units. 149 one-bedroom standard units. 4 one-bedroom suites ($138-$160).
3 stories, interior corridors. *Bath:* combo or shower only. **Parking:** on-site. **Terms:** weekly rates available.
Small-scale Hotel **Amenities:** high-speed Internet (fee), dual phone lines, voice mail, irons, hair dryers. **Pool(s):** outdoor.
Leisure Activities: whirlpool, exercise room. **Guest Services:** valet and coin laundry, area transportation.
Business Services: meeting rooms, PC, fax (fee). **Cards:** AX, CB, DC, DS, JC, MC, VI.

SOME UNITS

CROWNE PLAZA HOTEL AND RESORT HOUSTON MEDICAL CENTER
Phone: (713)797-1110   67

All Year   1P: $100-$160   2P: $100-$160
Location: I-610, exit 2 (Main St), 2.5 mi ne. Located adjacent to Texas Medical Center. 6701 S Main St 77030.
Fax: 713/797-1034. **Facility:** 293 units. 290 one-bedroom standard units. 3 one-bedroom suites. 12 stories,
Small-scale Hotel interior corridors. *Bath:* combo or shower only. **Parking:** on-site (fee) and valet. **Terms:** [AP] meal plan avail-able. **Amenities:** video games (fee), voice mail, irons, hair dryers. *Some:* dual phone lines. **Pool(s):** outdoor. **Leisure Activi-ties:** exercise room. **Fee:** massage. **Guest Services:** gift shop, valet and coin laundry, area transportation. **Business Services:**
conference facilities, business center. **Cards:** AX, CB, DC, DS, MC, VI.

SOME UNITS / FEE

DOUBLETREE GUEST SUITES
Phone: (713)961-9000   48

All Year   1P: $109-$209   2P: $109-$219
Location: 0.8 mi w off I-610, exit 8C (Westheimer Rd) northbound; exit 9A (San Felipe/Westheimer rds) southbound. Lo-cated next to Galleria Shopping Center. 5353 Westheimer Rd 77056. Fax: 713/877-8835. **Facility:** 334 units. 287
one- and 47 two-bedroom suites with kitchens. 26 stories, interior corridors. *Bath:* combo or shower only.
Large-scale Hotel **Parking:** on-site (fee). **Terms:** pets ($10 extra charge). **Amenities:** voice mail, safes, irons, hair dryers.
Some: dual phone lines. **Dining:** 6:30-9:30 am, 11-2 & 5-10 pm, Sat 7 am-11 & 5-10 pm, Sun 7 am-2 & 5-10
pm, cocktails. **Pool(s):** outdoor. **Leisure Activities:** whirlpool. **Guest Services:** valet and coin laundry, area transportation-within
3 mi. **Business Services:** conference facilities, business center. **Cards:** AX, CB, DC, DS, MC, VI. **Special Amenities:** free
newspaper. *(See color ad p 392)*

SOME UNITS
FEE   FEE   FEE

(See map p. 374)

DOUBLETREE HOTEL POST OAK-GALLERIA AREA

Phone: (713)961-9300   **43**

(AAA) (SAVE) All Year   1P: $169   XP: $20   F18

Location: I-610, exit 8C (Westheimer Rd) northbound, just w; exit 9A (San Felipe/Westheimer rds) southbound; between San Felipe and Westheimer rds. Located in middle of Galleria Shopping area/business district. 2001 Post Oak Blvd 77056. Fax: 713/623-6685. **Facility:** 449 units. 447 one-bedroom standard units. 2 two-bedroom suites

Large-scale Hotel ($250-$1500). 14 stories, interior corridors. **Parking:** on-site (fee) and valet. **Amenities:** video games, dual phone lines, voice mail, safes, honor bars, irons, hair dryers. **Dining:** 6:30 am-11 pm, Sun-10 pm, cocktails, entertainment. **Pool(s):** outdoor. **Leisure Activities:** saunas, exercise room. **Guest Services:** gift shop, valet laundry, area transportation-within 3 mi. **Business Services:** conference facilities, business center. **Cards:** AX, DC, DS, JC, MC, VI. **Special Amenities:** free room upgrade (subject to availability with advanced reservations). *(See color ad p 392)*

SOME UNITS

(icons) FEE · FEE

DRURY INN & SUITES-HOUSTON HOBBY

Phone: (713)941-4300   **92**

(AAA) (SAVE) 9/1-1/31 [ECP]   1P: $79-$99   2P: $89-$109   XP: $10   F18
2/1-8/31 [ECP]   1P: $76-$96   2P: $86-$106   XP: $10   F18

Location: I-45, exit 36 (Airport Blvd/College Rd) off southbound service road. 7902 Mosley Rd 77061. Fax: 713/941-4300. **Facility:** 134 units. 122 one-bedroom standard units. 12 one-bedroom suites ($96-$124).

Small-scale Hotel 5 stories, interior corridors. *Bath:* combo or shower only. **Parking:** on-site. **Terms:** small pets only. **Amenities:** voice mail, irons, hair dryers. **Pool(s):** heated indoor/outdoor. **Leisure Activities:** whirlpool, exercise room. **Guest Services:** complimentary evening beverages: Mon-Thurs, valet and coin laundry, airport transportation-William P Hobby Airport. **Business Services:** meeting rooms, fax (fee). **Cards:** AX, CB, DC, DS, MC, VI. **Special Amenities:** free continental breakfast and free local telephone calls.

SOME UNITS

(icons)

DRURY INN & SUITES-NEAR GALLERIA

Phone: (713)963-0700   **36**

(AAA) (SAVE) 9/1-1/31 [ECP]   1P: $108-$128   2P: $118-$138   XP: $10   F18
2/1-8/31 [ECP]   1P: $105-$125   2P: $115-$135   XP: $10   F18

Location: I-610, exit 9 (San Felipe Rd) northbound; exit 9A (San Felipe/Westheimer rds) southbound, on east service road. 1615 W Loop S 77027. Fax: 713/963-0700. **Facility:** 133 units. 119 one-bedroom standard units. 14 one-

Small-scale Hotel bedroom suites ($130-$148). 5 stories, interior corridors. *Bath:* combo or shower only. **Parking:** on-site. **Terms:** small pets only. **Amenities:** voice mail, irons, hair dryers. **Pool(s):** heated indoor/outdoor. **Leisure Activities:** whirlpool, exercise room. **Guest Services:** complimentary evening beverages, valet and coin laundry. **Business Services:** meeting rooms, fax (fee). **Cards:** AX, CB, DC, DS, MC, VI. **Special Amenities:** free continental breakfast and free local telephone calls.

SOME UNITS

(icons)

ECONO LODGE-HOBBY AIRPORT

Phone: 713/645-1333   **81**

(SAVE) All Year   1P: $49-$55   2P: $60-$65   XP: $10   F12

Location: I-45, exit Broadway, 1.2 mi s. 8381 Broadway 77061. Fax: 713/645-1649. **Facility:** 38 one-bedroom standard units. 2 stories, interior/exterior corridors. **Parking:** on-site. **Terms:** 1-5 night minimum stay, cancellation fee imposed, [CP] meal plan available, package plans. **Amenities:** hair dryers. **Business Services:** fax (fee). **Cards:** AX, DC, DS, MC, VI.

Motel

SOME UNITS

(icons)

EMBASSY SUITES NEAR THE GALLERIA

Phone: (713)626-5444   **39**

(SAVE) All Year [BP]   1P: $129-$289

Location: I-610, exit 9A (San Felipe/Westheimer rds) southbound; exit 8C (Westheimer Rd) northbound, 0.4 mi w on Westheimer Rd to Sage Rd, then just s. 2911 Sage Rd 77056. Fax: 713/843-4799. **Facility:** 150 one-bedroom suites. 6 stories, interior corridors. *Bath:* combo or shower only. **Parking:** on-site. **Terms:** cancellation fee

Large-scale Hotel imposed. **Amenities:** dual phone lines, voice mail, irons, hair dryers. **Pool(s):** heated indoor. **Leisure Activities:** whirlpool, exercise room. **Guest Services:** complimentary evening beverages, valet laundry, area transportation. **Business Services:** meeting rooms, fax (fee). **Cards:** AX, CB, DC, DS, MC, VI.

SOME UNITS

(icons)

FAIRFIELD INN BY MARRIOTT GALLERIA

Phone: 713/961-1690   **50**

(SAVE) All Year [CP]   1P: $94   2P: $94   XP: $10   F

Location: 610 Loop, exit 8C (Westheimer Rd) northbound, then U-turn under 610 Loop, s to Richmond, U-turn again; exit 8B (Richmond) southbound on northbound frontage road. 3131 W Loop S 77027. Fax: 713/627-8434. **Facility:** 107 one-bedroom standard units. 2 stories, exterior corridors. *Bath:* combo or shower only. **Parking:**

Motel on-site. **Terms:** [ECP] meal plan available. **Amenities:** video games, voice mail, irons. **Pool(s):** outdoor, wading. **Leisure Activities:** whirlpool, exercise room. **Guest Services:** valet and coin laundry. **Business Services:** PC, fax (fee). **Cards:** AX, CB, DC, DS, JC, MC, VI. *(See color ad p 392)*

SOME UNITS

(icons)

GRANT'S PALM COURT INN

Phone: 713/668-8000   **69**

(AAA) (SAVE) All Year [CP]   1P: $44-$55   2P: $44-$66

Location: I-610, exit 2 (Main St), 1.4 mi ne. Located within easy access to the medical center. 8200 S Main St 77025. Fax: 713/668-7777. **Facility:** 64 one-bedroom standard units. 1 story, exterior corridors. *Bath:* combo or shower only. **Parking:** on-site. **Terms:** 3 day cancellation notice, pets (in kennel). **Pool(s):** outdoor, wading.

Motel **Leisure Activities:** whirlpool, playground. **Guest Services:** coin laundry. **Business Services:** fax (fee). **Cards:** AX, CB, DC, DS, MC, VI.

SOME UNITS

(icons) FEE

(See map p. 374)

HAMPTON INN BY THE GALLERIA
Phone: (713)871-9911 **38**

All Year [CP] 1P: $65-$109 2P: $75-$139

SAVE

Location: I-610, exit 9 (San Felipe Rd) northbound; exit 9A (San Felipe/Westheimer rds), on east service road, just n of San Felipe Rd southbound. 4500 Post Oak Pkwy 77027. Fax: 713/871-9960. **Facility:** 176 units. 171 one-bedroom standard units. 5 one-bedroom suites ($139-$159). 6 stories, interior corridors. *Bath:* combo or shower only. Small-scale Hotel **Parking:** on-site. **Amenities:** video games (fee), dual phone lines, voice mail, irons, hair dryers. **Pool(s):** heated outdoor. **Leisure Activities:** exercise room. **Guest Services:** complimentary evening beverages: Wed, valet laundry. **Business Services:** meeting rooms, business center. **Cards:** AX, CB, DC, DS, MC, VI.

SOME UNITS

HAMPTON INN HOBBY AIRPORT
Phone: (713)641-6400 **84**

All Year [ECP] 1P: $89-$105 2P: $94-$110

AAA **SAVE**

Location: I-45, exit 36 (Airport Blvd/College Rd), 1.3 mi w. 8620 Airport Blvd 77061. Fax: 713/641-5888. **Facility:** 119 one-bedroom standard units, some with whirlpools. 5 stories, interior corridors. *Bath:* combo or shower only. Small-scale Hotel **Parking:** on-site. **Amenities:** voice mail, irons. **Pool(s):** outdoor. **Leisure Activities:** whirlpool. **Guest Serv**ices: complimentary evening beverages: Mon-Thurs, valet laundry, airport transportation-William P Hobby Airport, area transportation-within 5 mi. **Business Services:** meeting rooms, fax (fee). **Cards:** AX, CB, DC, DS, MC, VI. **Special Amenities:** free continental breakfast and free local telephone calls. *(See color ad below)*

SOME UNITS

HIDDEN OAKS BED AND BREAKFAST
Phone: (713)640-2457 **82**

All Year [BP] 1P: $95-$110 2P: $124-$159 XP: $15

Location: I-45, exit 39 (Broadway), just w, then 0.3 mi n. Located in a quiet area. 7808 Dixie Dr 77087-4614. Fax: 713/640-2505. **Facility:** This brick, plantation-style 1920s home has an expansive lawn shaded by large Bed & Breakfast live oaks; rooms include amenities geared toward business travelers. Smoke free premises. 4 units. 2 one-bedroom standard units, some with kitchens and/or whirlpools. 2 one-bedroom suites. 2 stories (no elevator), interior/exterior corridors. *Bath:* combo or shower only. **Parking:** on-site. **Terms:** age restrictions may apply, 3 day cancellation notice. **Amenities:** video library, CD players, hair dryers. *Some:* fax, irons. **Leisure Activities:** whirlpool. **Guest Services:** complimentary laundry. **Cards:** AX, DS, MC, VI.

SOME UNITS

HILTON HOUSTON PLAZA
Phone: (713)313-4000 **63**

All Year 1P: $105-$300 2P: $105-$300 XP: $20 F18

SAVE

Location: I-610, exit 2 (Main St), 2.6 mi ne to Dryden St, just w to Travis St, then just n. 6633 Travis St 77030. Fax: 713/313-4660. **Facility:** 181 units. 41 one-bedroom standard units. 140 one-bedroom suites. 19 stories, interior corridors. **Parking:** on-site (fee). **Terms:** 3 day cancellation notice-fee imposed, package plans - weekends. **Amenities:** dual phone lines, voice mail, honor bars, irons, hair dryers. *Some:* high-speed Internet (fee). **Pool(s):** heated outdoor. **Leisure Activities:** saunas, whirlpools, jogging, exercise room. *Fee:* massage. **Guest Services:** gift shop, valet laundry, area transportation. **Business Services:** meeting rooms, business center. **Cards:** AX, CB, DC, DS, JC, MC, VI.

SOME UNITS

HILTON HOUSTON SOUTHWEST
Phone: (713)977-7911 **62**

All Year 1P: $119-$175 2P: $129-$185 XP: $10 F18

AAA **SAVE**

Location: On service road of US 59, just sw of exit Hillcroft Rd. 6780 Southwest Frwy 77074. Fax: 713/974-5808. **Facility:** 292 units. 280 one-bedroom standard units. 12 one-bedroom suites. 12 stories, interior corridors. *Bath:* combo or shower only. **Parking:** on-site. **Amenities:** high-speed Internet (fee), voice mail, irons, hair dryers. **Dining:** 6 am-11 pm, cocktails. **Pool(s):** outdoor. **Leisure Activities:** playground, exercise room. **Guest Services:** gift shop, valet laundry, area transportation-within 5 mi. **Business Services:** conference facilities, fax (fee). **Cards:** AX, CB, DC, DS, JC, MC, VI. **Special Amenities:** free continental breakfast and free local telephone calls. *(See color ad p 398)*

SOME UNITS
FEE

(See map p. 374)

HOLIDAY INN ASTRODOME
Phone: 713/790-1900   **74**

2/19-3/16	1P: $170-$190	XP: $10	F20
5/4-1/31	1P: $130-$170	XP: $10	F20
2/1-2/18 & 3/17-5/3	1P: $130	XP: $10	F20

Large-scale Hotel   **Location:** I-610, exit 1C (Kirby Dr), 0.3 mi n. Located next to Astrodome. 8111 Kirby Dr 77054. **Fax:** 713/799-1378. **Facility:** 235 units. 229 one-bedroom standard units. 4 one- and 2 two-bedroom suites. 11 stories, interior corridors. *Bath:* combo or shower only. **Parking:** on-site. **Terms:** check-in 4 pm, 3 day cancellation notice-fee imposed, [AP], [BP], [CP], [ECP] & [MAP] meal plans available, 17% service charge. **Amenities:** video games (fee), voice mail, irons, hair dryers. **Pool(s):** outdoor. **Leisure Activities:** whirlpool, exercise room. **Guest Services:** gift shop, valet laundry, area transportation. **Business Services:** conference facilities, fax (fee). **Cards:** AX, CB, DC, DS, MC, VI. *(See color ad p 390)*

SOME UNITS

HOLIDAY INN HOBBY AIRPORT
Phone: (713)947-0000   **85**

All Year	1P: $89	2P: $89	XP: $10	F12

Small-scale Hotel   **Location:** I-45, exit 36 (Airport Blvd-College Rd), 1.3 mi w. 8611 Airport Blvd 77061. **Fax:** 713/947-9060. **Facility:** 187 one-bedroom standard units. 6 stories, interior corridors. *Bath:* combo or shower only. **Parking:** on-site. **Amenities:** dual phone lines, voice mail, irons, hair dryers. **Pool(s):** outdoor. **Leisure Activities:** whirlpool, exercise room. **Guest Services:** complimentary evening beverages, valet and coin laundry, area transportation. **Business Services:** meeting rooms, fax (fee). **Cards:** AX, DC, DS, MC, VI. *(See color ad p 390)*

SOME UNITS

HOLIDAY INN HOTEL AND SUITES
Phone: (713)681-5000   **27**

All Year	1P: $99	2P: $99	XP: $10	F

Small-scale Hotel   **Location:** I-10, exit 762 (Antoine Dr) westbound; exit 762 (Silber/Post Oak Rd) eastbound, on eastbound service road. 7787 Katy Frwy 77024. **Fax:** 713/682-8400. **Facility:** 260 units. 233 one-bedroom standard units, some with whirlpools. 27 one-bedroom suites ($119-$169). 2-11 stories, interior corridors. *Bath:* combo or shower only. **Parking:** on-site. **Terms:** 7 day cancellation notice, [AP] meal plan available, package plans, 18% service charge, pets ($25 fee). **Amenities:** video games, voice mail, irons, hair dryers. **Pool(s):** outdoor, wading. **Leisure Activities:** exercise room. **Guest Services:** gift shop, valet laundry, area transportation. **Business Services:** conference facilities, fax (fee). **Cards:** AX, CB, DC, DS, JC, MC, VI. *(See color ad p 390)*

SOME UNITS

HOLIDAY INN HOTEL & SUITES-HOUSTON MEDICAL CENTER
Phone: (713)528-7744   **66**

All Year	1P: $80-$159	2P: $80-$159

Small-scale Hotel   **Location:** I-610, exit 2 (Main St), 2.4 mi ne. 6800 Main St 77030. **Fax:** 713/528-6983. **Facility:** 284 units. 119 one-bedroom standard units. 142 one- and 23 two-bedroom suites, some with efficiencies or kitchens. 12 stories, interior corridors. *Bath:* combo or shower only. **Parking:** on-site. **Terms:** [AP] meal plan available. **Amenities:** voice mail, irons, hair dryers. *Some:* safes (fee). **Pool(s):** outdoor. **Leisure Activities:** exercise room. *Fee:* game room. **Guest Services:** gift shop, valet and coin laundry, area transportation. **Business Services:** meeting rooms, business center. **Cards:** AX, CB, DC, DS, MC, VI. *(See color ad p 390)*

SOME UNITS

(See map p. 374)

HOLIDAY INN SELECT-GREENWAY PLAZA
Phone: (713)523-8448   **57**

All Year   1P: $60-$130

Location: US 59, exit Kirby Dr. 2712 Southwest Frwy 77098. Fax: 713/526-7948. **Facility:** 355 units. 321 one-bedroom standard units. 34 one-bedroom suites. 18 stories, interior corridors. *Bath:* combo or shower only. **Parking:** on-site (fee). **Terms:** [BP] meal plan available, pets ($100 deposit, $25 extra charge). **Amenities:** voice mail, irons, hair dryers. **Pool(s):** outdoor. **Leisure Activities:** whirlpool, exercise room. **Guest Services:** gift shop, valet and coin laundry, area transportation. **Business Services:** conference facilities, business center. **Cards:** AX, CB, DC, DS, JC, MC, VI. *(See color ad p 390)*

Large-scale Hotel

SOME UNITS

HOMESTEAD STUDIO SUITES HOTEL-HOUSTON/GALLERIA AREA
Phone: (713)960-9660   **40**

All Year   1P: $89-$99   2P: $99-$109   XP: $5   F17

Location: I-10 W to 610 Loop S, exit San Felipe/Westheimer rds) southbound; exit 9 (San Felipe Rd) northbound. 2300 W Loop S 77027. Fax: 713/960-0991. **Facility:** 136 one-bedroom standard units with efficiencies. 3 stories, interior corridors. *Bath:* combo or shower only. **Parking:** on-site. **Terms:** small pets only ($75 fee). **Amenities:** dual phone lines, voice mail, irons, hair dryers. **Guest Services:** valet and coin laundry, area transportation. **Business Services:** fax. **Cards:** AX, CB, DC, DS, JC, MC, VI.

Small-scale Hotel

SOME UNITS

HOMESTEAD STUDIO SUITES HOTEL-HOUSTON/MEDICAL CENTER/RELIANT PARK
Phone: (713)797-0000   **65**

2/25-3/16   1P: $109-$119   2P: $114-$124   XP: $5   F17
2/1-2/24 & 3/17-1/31   1P: $60-$70   2P: $70-$80   XP: $5   F17

Location: I-610, exit 1B, 0.8 mi n. 7979 Fannin St 77054. Fax: 713/797-1907. **Facility:** 153 units. 141 one-bedroom standard units with efficiencies. 12 one-bedroom suites with efficiencies. 2 stories, exterior corridors. *Bath:* combo or shower only. **Parking:** on-site. **Terms:** pets ($75 fee). **Amenities:** voice mail, irons. **Guest Services:** coin laundry, area transportation. **Business Services:** fax (fee). **Cards:** AX, CB, DC, DS, JC, MC, VI.

Small-scale Hotel

SOME UNITS
FEE

HOUSTON HOBBY AIRPORT MARRIOTT
Phone: (713)943-7979   **87**

All Year   1P: $79-$209   2P: $79-$209

Location: I-45, exit 36 (Airport Blvd/College Rd), on west service road. 9100 Gulf Frwy 77017. Fax: 713/943-2160. **Facility:** 287 units. 231 one-bedroom standard units. 55 one- and 1 two-bedroom suites, some with whirlpools. 10 stories, interior corridors. *Bath:* combo or shower only. **Parking:** on-site. **Terms:** [AP] meal plan available, 15% service charge, small pets only ($50 deposit). **Amenities:** video games (fee), dual phone lines, voice mail, irons, hair dryers. **Dining:** 2 restaurants, 6 am-midnight, cocktails. **Pool(s):** heated indoor. **Leisure Activities:** sauna, whirlpool, exercise room. **Guest Services:** gift shop, valet laundry, airport transportation-William P Hobby Airport, area transportation-within 3 mi. **Business Services:** conference facilities, business center. **Cards:** AX, CB, DC, DS, JC, MC, VI. **Special Amenities:** free newspaper. *(See color ad below)*

Large-scale Hotel

SOME UNITS
FEE   FEE   FEE

THE HOUSTONIAN HOTEL, CLUB & SPA
Phone: (713)680-2626   **34**

All Year   1P: $225-$295   2P: $225-$295

Location: I-610, exit 10 (Woodway Dr), just w on Woodway Dr to N Post Oak Ln, 0.5 mi nw. Located in a quiet area. 111 N Post Oak Ln 77024. Fax: 713/680-2992. **Facility:** Amid wooded surroundings, this hotel has a retreat-like ambience. A world class health club and day spa make the hotel, not houston, the destination. 286 units. 277 one-bedroom standard units. 9 one-bedroom suites ($495-$1500). 4 stories, interior corridors. *Bath:* combo or shower only. **Parking:** on-site. **Terms:** check-in 4 pm. **Amenities:** video games (fee), dual phone lines, voice mail, safes, honor bars, irons, hair dryers. *Some:* CD players. **Dining:** 3 restaurants, 6:30 am-10 pm, Sat & Sun 7 am-10:30 pm, cocktails. **Pool(s):** 3 heated outdoor. **Leisure Activities:** saunas, whirlpool, 5 lighted tennis courts, racquetball courts, 3 squash court; 2 paddle courts, recreation programs, indoor & outdoor jogging tracks, indoor climbing wall, indoor basketball, jogging, playground. *Fee:* golf-18 holes, massage. **Guest Services:** gift shop, valet laundry, area transportation-Galleria Mall. **Business Services:** conference facilities, business center. **Cards:** AX, DC, DS, MC, VI. **Special Amenities:** free newspaper and preferred room (subject to availability with advanced reservations).

Resort
Large-scale Hotel

SOME UNITS
FEE

(See map p. 374)

HOUSTON MARRIOTT MEDICAL CENTER HOTEL
Phone: (713)796-0080 **64**

Ⓐ SAVE   All Year   1P: $89-$229
▽▽▽▽   **Location:** I-610, exit 2 (Main St), 2.5 mi ne to Holcombe St, 0.3 mi e. Connected to the medical center and shopping venues. 6580 Fannin St 77030. Fax: 713/770-8100. **Facility:** 386 units. 354 one-bedroom standard units. 10 one- and 22 two-bedroom suites, some with kitchens. 26 stories, interior corridors. *Bath:* combo or shower
Large-scale Hotel only. **Parking:** on-site (fee). **Terms:** check-in 4 pm, cancellation fee imposed, small pets only ($50 deposit). **Amenities:** voice mail, irons, hair dryers. **Dining:** 2 restaurants, 6:30 am-11 pm, cocktails. **Pool(s):** heated indoor. **Leisure Activities:** whirlpool, exercise room. **Guest Services:** gift shop, valet and coin laundry, area transportation-Medical Center. **Business Services:** conference facilities, business center. **Cards:** AX, CB, DC, DS, MC, VI. **Special Amenities:** free newspaper.

SOME UNITS

HOWARD JOHNSON EXPRESS INN
Phone: (713)861-9000 **30**

Ⓐ SAVE   All Year   1P: $55   2P: $60   XP: $7   F17
▽   **Location:** I-10, exit 765B (Shepherd Durham) eastbound; exit 765B (Patterson Rd) westbound, n on westbound service road. 4602 Katy Frwy 77007. Fax: 713/861-9000. **Facility:** 30 one-bedroom standard units, some with whirl-pools. 2 stories, exterior corridors. **Parking:** on-site. **Terms:** [CP] meal plan available. **Amenities:** hair
Motel   dryers. **Business Services:** fax (fee). **Cards:** AX, DC, DS, MC, VI. **Special Amenities: free continental breakfast and free newspaper.**

SOME UNITS

J. W. MARRIOTT HOUSTON BY THE GALLERIA
Phone: 713/961-1500 **42**

Ⓐ SAVE   All Year   1P: $89-$299   XP: $20   F
▽▽▽▽   **Location:** I-610, exit 8C (Westheimer Rd) northbound; exit 9A (San Felipe/Westheimer rds) southbound, just w. Located across from Galleria Mall. 5150 Westheimer Rd 77056. Fax: 713/961-5045. **Facility:** 514 units. 507 one-bedroom standard units. 7 one-bedroom suites, some with kitchens. 23 stories, interior corridors. **Parking:** on-site (fee)
Large-scale Hotel and valet. **Terms:** 3 day cancellation notice. **Amenities:** dual phone lines, voice mail, irons, hair dryers. *Fee:* video games, high-speed Internet. **Dining:** 6:30 am-2 & 5:30-11 pm, cocktails. **Pool(s):** heated indoor/outdoor. **Leisure Activities:** sauna, whirlpool, steamroom, sports court, basketball. *Fee:* racquetball courts, massage. **Guest Services:** gift shop, valet laundry, area transportation-within 2 mi. **Business Services:** conference facilities, business center. **Cards:** AX, CB, DC, DS, JC, MC, VI.

SOME UNITS

LA QUINTA INN & SUITES HOUSTON-GALLERIA AREA
Phone: (713)355-3440 **37**

SAVE   All Year   1P: $70-$121   2P: $80-$131   XP: $10   F18
▽▽▽   **Location:** I-610, exit 9 (San Felipe Rd) northbound; exit 9A (San Felipe/Westheimer rds) southbound, on northbound service road. 1625 W Loop S 77027. Fax: 713/355-2990. **Facility:** 173 units. 155 one-bedroom standard units. 18 one-bedroom suites ($119-$169). 6 stories, interior corridors. *Bath:* combo or shower only. **Parking:** on-
Small-scale Hotel site. **Terms:** [ECP] meal plan available, small pets only. **Amenities:** video games (fee), voice mail, irons, hair dryers. *Some:* dual phone lines. **Pool(s):** heated outdoor. **Leisure Activities:** whirlpool, exercise room. **Guest Services:** valet and coin laundry. **Business Services:** meeting rooms, fax (fee). **Cards:** AX, CB, DC, DS, JC, MC, VI.
(See color ad p 401)

SOME UNITS

LA QUINTA INN-BROOKHOLLOW
Phone: (713)688-2581 **22**

Ⓐ SAVE   All Year   1P: $53-$66   2P: $59-$72   XP: $6   F18
▽▽▽   **Location:** Nw on US 290, exit Magnum-Dacoma. 11002 Northwest Frwy 77092-7312. Fax: 713/686-2146. **Facility:** 122 units. 121 one-bedroom standard units. 1 one-bedroom suite ($99-$149). 2 stories, exterior corridors. *Bath:* combo or shower only. **Parking:** on-site. **Terms:** [ECP] meal plan available, small pets only.
Small-scale Hotel **Amenities:** video games (fee), voice mail, irons, hair dryers. **Pool(s):** outdoor. **Guest Services:** valet laundry. **Business Services:** meeting rooms, fax (fee). **Cards:** AX, CB, DC, DS, JC, MC, VI. **Special Amenities: free continental breakfast and free local telephone calls.** *(See color ad p 401)*

SOME UNITS

LA QUINTA INN-GREENWAY PLAZA
Phone: (713)623-4750 **54**

Ⓐ SAVE   All Year   1P: $60-$83   2P: $70-$93   XP: $10   F18
▽▽▽   **Location:** Sw off US 59 (Southwest Frwy), exit Weslayan. 4015 Southwest Frwy 77027-7499. Fax: 713/963-0599. **Facility:** 131 units. 114 one- and 16 two-bedroom standard units. 1 one-bedroom suite ($99-$149). 2-3 stories, interior/exterior corridors. *Bath:* combo or shower only. **Parking:** on-site. **Terms:** [ECP] meal plan avail-
Motel   able, small pets only. **Amenities:** video games (fee), voice mail, irons, hair dryers. **Pool(s):** outdoor. **Guest Services:** valet and coin laundry, area transportation-medical center. **Business Services:** meeting rooms, fax (fee). **Cards:** AX, CB, DC, DS, JC, MC, VI. **Special Amenities: free continental breakfast and free local telephone calls.** *(See color ad p 401)*

SOME UNITS
FEE FEE

LA QUINTA INN-HOUSTON-ASTRODOME
Phone: (713)668-8082 **79**

Ⓐ SAVE   All Year   1P: $70-$86   2P: $77-$93   XP: $7   F18
▽▽▽   **Location:** I-610, exit 2 (Buffalo Speedway/S Main St), just s. 9911 Buffalo Speedway 77054. Fax: 713/668-0821. **Facility:** 113 units. 112 one-bedroom standard units. 1 one-bedroom suite ($99-$149). 3 stories, exterior corridors. **Parking:** on-site. **Terms:** [ECP] meal plan available, small pets only. **Amenities:** video games (fee),
Small-scale Hotel voice mail, irons, hair dryers. **Pool(s):** outdoor. **Leisure Activities:** whirlpool. **Guest Services:** coin laundry, area transportation-medical center. **Business Services:** meeting rooms, fax (fee). **Cards:** AX, CB, DC, DS, JC, MC, VI. **Special Amenities: free continental breakfast and free local telephone calls.** *(See color ad p 401)*

SOME UNITS

(See map p. 374)

LA QUINTA INN-HOUSTON-HOBBY AIRPORT
Phone: (713)941-0900 🅰🅰🅰 ⑯
🅰🅰🅰 SAVE All Year 1P: $63-$73 2P: $69-$79 XP: $6 F18
▼▼▼ ▼▼▼ **Location:** I-45 S, exit 36 (Airport Blvd/College Rd), just s on southbound frontage road. 9902 Gulf Frwy 77034-1043.
Motel Fax: 713/946-1987. **Facility:** 127 units. 126 one-bedroom standard units. 1 one-bedroom suite ($99-$149). 3 stories, interior/exterior corridors. **Parking:** on-site. **Terms:** [ECP] meal plan available, small pets only. **Amenities:** video games (fee), voice mail, irons, hair dryers. **Pool(s):** outdoor. **Guest Services:** airport transportation-William P Hobby Airport, area transportation-within 5 mi. **Business Services:** meeting rooms, fax. **Cards:** AX, CB, DC, DS, JC, MC, VI. **Special Amenities:** free continental breakfast and free local telephone calls.
(See color ad below)

SOME UNITS
✈ 🛏 🍴 🛄M 📷 🍳 📷 DATA PORT 💻 / ⊠ 📵 📶 /

LA QUINTA INN-WIRT RD
Phone: (713)688-8941 ⑳
🅰🅰🅰 SAVE All Year 1P: $50-$66 2P: $54-$70 XP: $4 F18
▼▼▼ ▼▼▼ **Location:** I-10, exit 761A (Wirt Rd), just w. 8017 Katy Frwy 77024-1907. Fax: 713/683-8410. **Facility:** 100 one-
Motel bedroom standard units. 2 stories, exterior corridors. *Bath:* combo or shower only. **Parking:** on-site. **Terms:** [ECP] meal plan available, small pets only. **Amenities:** video games (fee), voice mail, irons, hair dryers. **Pool(s):** outdoor. **Guest Services:** valet laundry. **Business Services:** fax (fee). **Cards:** AX, CB, DC, DS, JC, MC, VI. **Special Amenities:** free continental breakfast and free local telephone calls.
(See color ad below)

SOME UNITS
🛏 🍴 📷 🍳 📷 DATA PORT 💻 / ⊠ 📵 📶 /

THE LOVETT INN
Phone: (713)522-5224 ⑬
▼▼ ▼▼ All Year [ECP] 1P: $85-$225 2P: $85-$225 XP: $35
Bed & Breakfast **Location:** I-610, exit Westheimer Rd, 4.5 mi e to Montrose Blvd, s to Lovett Blvd, just e. 501 Lovett Blvd 77006. Fax: 713/528-6708. **Facility:** Designated smoking area. 8 one-bedroom standard units, some with whirlpools. 2 stories (no elevator), interior/exterior corridors. *Bath:* combo or shower only. **Parking:** on-site. **Terms:** 2-5 night minimum stay - weekends, cancellation fee imposed, small pets only (in designated rooms). **Amenities:** irons, hair dryers. **Pool(s):** outdoor. **Guest Services:** valet and coin laundry. **Business Services:** meeting rooms, fax. **Cards:** AX, CB, DC, DS, MC, VI.

SOME UNITS
🛏 🍳 ⊠ 💻 / VCR 📵 📶 /

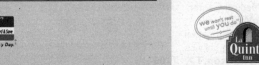

(See map p. 374)

MARRIOTT-WEST LOOP-BY THE GALLERIA   Phone: (713)960-0111 [35]

(AAA) (SAVE)   2/1-6/30 & 9/8-1/31   1P: $89-$179   2P: $89-$189   XP: $10   F18
▼▼▼▼▼   7/1-9/7   1P: $89-$159   2P: $89-$169   XP: $10   F18
              Location: Just w of I-610, exit 9 northbound; exit 9A (San Felipe/Westheimer rds) southbound, entrance from Fe-
              lipe Rd or service road. 1750 W Loop S 77027. Fax: 713/624-1560. **Facility:** Designated smoking area. 302 units.
Large-scale Hotel 298 one-bedroom standard units, some with whirlpools. 4 one-bedroom suites. 14 stories, interior corridors.
              Bath: combo or shower only. **Parking:** on-site (fee). **Terms:** cancellation fee imposed. **Amenities:** video
games (fee), high-speed Internet, voice mail, irons, hair dryers. **Dining:** 6 am-10:30 pm, cocktails. **Pool(s):** heated indoor.
Leisure Activities: sauna, whirlpool, exercise room. **Guest Services:** gift shop, valet and coin laundry, area transportation-within
1.5 mi. **Business Services:** conference facilities, business center. **Cards:** AX, DC, DS, JC, MC, VI. **Special Amenities:** free
newspaper. *(See color ad p 398 & below)*

SOME UNITS

[icons row] [$D] [†¶] [Y] [🛠] [🏷] [🏊] [✖] [🐾] [DATA PORT] [💻] / [✖] [VCR] [🔒] [🖨] /
FEE

OMNI HOUSTON HOTEL   Phone: (713)871-8181 [33]

(AAA) (SAVE)   All Year   1P: $265-$315   2P: $265-$315   XP: $10   F18
▼▼▼▼▼   **Location:** I-610, exit 10 (Woodway Dr), 0.5 mi w. Located in Memorial Park, a quiet area. Four Riverway 77056-1999.
              Fax: 713/871-0719. **Facility:** This service-oriented hotel surrounds itself with contemporary art sculptures.
              Shopping at the Galleria Mall is also convenient. 378 units. 340 one-bedroom standard units. 38 one-
Large-scale Hotel bedroom suites. 11 stories, interior corridors. *Bath:* combo or shower only. **Parking:** on-site and valet.
              Terms: small pets only ($50 extra charge). **Amenities:** CD players, dual phone lines, voice mail, honor bars,
irons, hair dryers. *Fee:* video library, video games. *Some:* DVD players. **Dining:** 2 restaurants, 6:30 am-10:30 pm, cocktails,
La Reserve, see separate listing, entertainment. **Pool(s):** outdoor, heated outdoor, lap. **Leisure Activities:** saunas, whirlpool,
pool equipped with underwater music, 4 tennis courts (2 lighted), equipment for tennis & basketball courts, jogging, exercise
room, spa, sports court, basketball. **Guest Services:** gift shop, valet laundry, area transportation-within 3 mi and Galleria. **Business Services:** meeting rooms, business center. **Cards:** AX, CB, DC, DS, MC, VI. **Special Amenities:** free newspaper.

SOME UNITS

[icons row] [$D] [🆓] [🛏] [†¶] [24†] [Y] [🏷] [🏊] [✖] [🐾] [DATA PORT] / [✖] [VCR] [🔒] [🖨] /
FEE

(See map p. 374)

PARK PLACE SUITES BEST WESTERN
Phone: (713)796-1000 🞵73

AAA SAVE
▼▼▼▼▼

Small-scale Hotel

All Year [ECP]   1P: $99-$149   2P: $109-$159   XP: $10   F17
Location: I-610, exit 1C (Kirby), 0.9 mi n, then just e. 1400 Old Spanish Tr 77054. Fax: 713/796-8055. **Facility:** 191 one-bedroom suites, some with whirlpools. 7 stories, interior corridors. *Bath:* combo or shower only. **Parking:** on-site. **Terms:** weekly rates available, [CP] meal plan available, pets ($75 fee). **Amenities:** dual phone lines, voice mail, irons, hair dryers. **Dining:** 6-9 am, 11-2 & 5-8 pm. **Pool(s):** outdoor. **Leisure Activities:** exercise room. **Guest Services:** sundries, valet and coin laundry, area transportation-within 2 mi. **Business Services:** meeting rooms. **Cards:** AX, CB, DC, DS, JC, MC, VI. **Special Amenities:** early check-in/late check-out and free continental breakfast. *(See color ad p 402)*

�🐾🍴🍸🦽🛥🎦 DATA PORT 🔌📠💻

PATRICIAN BED & BREAKFAST INN
Phone: (713)523-1114 🞵46

▼▼▼▼▼

Historic Bed
& Breakfast

All Year   1P: $85-$105   2P: $100-$165   XP: $15   D10
Location: Southbound on US 59, exit Fannin, s to Southmore Ave, just e of Main St. Located in the museum district. 1200 Southmore Ave 77004. Fax: 713/523-0790. **Facility:** Smoke free premises. 7 one-bedroom standard units, some with whirlpools. 3 stories (no elevator), interior corridors. *Bath:* combo or shower only. **Parking:** on-site. **Terms:** check-in 4 pm, 2 night minimum stay - weekends, age restrictions may apply, 7 day cancellation notice-fee imposed, [BP] meal plan available. **Amenities:** voice mail, irons, hair dryers. *Some:* CD players. **Cards:** AX, DC, DS, MC, VI.

SOME UNITS
ASK 🛱 🆇 DATA PORT / VCR /

RADISSON HOTEL ASTRODOME CONVENTION CENTER
Phone: (713)748-3221 🞵78

AAA SAVE
▼▼▼▼▼

Large-scale Hotel

All Year   1P: $129-$169   2P: $139-$179   XP: $10   F
Location: I-610, exit 1C (Kirby Dr). Located opposite the Astrodome. 8686 Kirby Dr 77054. Fax: 713/796-9371. **Facility:** 630 units. 604 one-bedroom standard units. 26 one-bedroom suites. 8 stories, interior corridors. *Bath:* combo or shower only. **Parking:** on-site. **Terms:** [AP] meal plan available, 15% service charge, small pets only ($75 fee). **Amenities:** video games (fee), voice mail, irons, hair dryers. **Dining:** 6:30 am-10 pm, cocktails. **Pool(s):** 2 outdoor, 2 wading. **Leisure Activities:** sauna, whirlpool, exercise room. *Fee:* game room. **Guest Services:** gift shop, valet laundry, area transportation-within 3 mi. **Business Services:** conference facilities, business center. **Cards:** AX, CB, DC, DS, MC, VI. **Special Amenities:** free room upgrade and preferred room (each subject to availability with advanced reservations). *(See ad below)*

SOME UNITS
🛱æ🍴🍸🦽🛋🛥🆇🎦 DATA PORT 💻 / 🆇🔌📠 /

RAMADA PLAZA HOTEL HOUSTON NEAR GREENWAY
Phone: (713)942-2111 🞵29

▼▼▼▼

Small-scale Hotel

All Year   1P: $59-$179   2P: $59-$179   XP: $10   F18
Location: US 59, exit Kirby Dr on southbound access road. 2828 Southwest Frwy 77098. Fax: 713/526-8709. **Facility:** 216 one-bedroom standard units. 9 stories, interior corridors. *Bath:* combo or shower only. **Parking:** on-site. **Terms:** weekly rates available. **Amenities:** video games (fee), dual phone lines, voice mail, irons, hair dryers. **Pool(s):** outdoor. **Leisure Activities:** exercise room. **Guest Services:** valet laundry. **Business Services:** meeting rooms, business center. **Cards:** AX, CB, DC, DS, JC, MC, VI.

SOME UNITS
ASK 🛱 🍴 🆖 🦽 🛋 🛥 🎦 DATA PORT 💻 / 🆇 /

RAMADA PLAZA HOTEL NEAR THE GALLERIA
Phone: 713/688-2222 🞵52

▼▼▼▼

Small-scale Hotel

All Year   1P: $55-$79   2P: $55-$79   XP: $10   F
Location: I-10, exit 762 (Silber Rd). 7611 Katy Frwy 77024. Fax: 713/680-0147. **Facility:** 197 units. 192 one-bedroom standard units, some with whirlpools. 5 one-bedroom suites, some with whirlpools. 6 stories, interior corridors. **Parking:** on-site. **Terms:** 30 day cancellation notice, small pets only ($10 extra charge). **Amenities:** video games (fee), voice mail, irons, hair dryers. **Pool(s):** outdoor. **Leisure Activities:** whirlpool, exercise room. **Guest Services:** gift shop, valet and coin laundry, area transportation. **Business Services:** conference facilities. **Cards:** AX, CB, DC, DS, JC, MC, VI.

SOME UNITS
🛱 🍴 🍸 🛥 🎦 DATA PORT 💻 / 🆇 🔌 📠 /

(See map p. 374)

RED ROOF INN HOBBY AIRPORT

Phone: (713)943-3300 **93**

AAA (SAVE)

Small-scale Hotel

All Year — 1P: $41-$56 — 2P: $46-$62 — XP: $5 — F18
Location: I-45, exit 36 (Airport Blvd/College Rd), just w. 9005 Airport Blvd 77061. Fax: 713/943-1370. **Facility:** 151 one-bedroom standard units. 2 stories, interior corridors. *Bath:* combo or shower only. **Parking:** on-site. **Terms:** small pets only. **Amenities:** video games, voice mail. **Pool(s):** heated outdoor. **Leisure Activities:** whirlpool. **Guest Services:** airport transportation-William P Hobby Airport. **Business Services:** meeting rooms, fax (fee). **Cards:** AX, CB, DC, DS, MC, VI. **Special Amenities:** free local telephone calls and free newspaper.

SOME UNITS

RENAISSANCE HOUSTON HOTEL

Phone: (713)629-1200 **51**

AAA (SAVE)

Large-scale Hotel

All Year — 1P: $79-$179 — 2P: $79-$179
Location: At US 59 (Southwest Frwy), exit Buffalo Speedway. Located in Greenway Plaza complex. 6 Greenway Plaza E 77046. Fax: 713/629-4706. **Facility:** With its attractively appointed rooms, this hotel is also self sufficient complete with on-site Kinkos, Starbucks, sports bar, and a theater next door. 388 units. 379 one-bedroom standard units. 9 one-bedroom suites ($350-$900), some with whirlpools. 20 stories, interior corridors. *Bath:* combo or shower only. **Parking:** on-site (fee). **Amenities:** dual phone lines, irons, hair dryers. *Fee:* video games, high-speed Internet. **Dining:** 2 restaurants, 6 am-11 pm, cocktails. **Pool(s):** heated outdoor. **Leisure Activities:** saunas, exercise room. **Guest Services:** gift shop, valet laundry, area transportation-within 3 mi. **Business Services:** conference facilities, PC (fee), fax. **Cards:** AX, CB, DC, DS, JC, MC, VI.

SOME UNITS

RESIDENCE INN BY MARRIOTT

Phone: (713)840-9757 **70**

(SAVE)

Motel

All Year [BP] — 1P: $179 — 2P: $299
Location: I-610, exit 8C (Westheimer Rd) northbound; exit 9A (San Felipe/Westheimer rds) southbound, just w to McCue, then just n. Located in a residential area. 2500 McCue 77056. Fax: 713/840-9759. **Facility:** 92 units. 12 one-bedroom standard units with kitchens. 80 one-bedroom suites with kitchens. 2-3 stories, interior/exterior corridors. *Bath:* combo or shower only. **Parking:** on-site. **Terms:** cancellation fee imposed, pets ($5 fee, $25 deposit). **Amenities:** dual phone lines, voice mail, irons, hair dryers. **Pool(s):** outdoor. **Leisure Activities:** whirlpool, exercise room. **Guest Services:** complimentary evening beverages: Mon-Thurs, valet and coin laundry. **Business Services:** meeting rooms. **Cards:** AX, DC, DS, MC, VI.

SOME UNITS

RESIDENCE INN BY MARRIOTT-MEDICAL CENTER/ASTRODOME

Phone: (713)660-7993 **68**

(SAVE)

Small-scale Hotel

All Year [BP] — 2P: $139-$159
Location: I-610, exit 2 (S Main St/Buffalo Speedway), 1.5 mi n. 7710 Main St 77030. Fax: 713/660-8019. **Facility:** 287 units. 214 one-bedroom standard units with kitchens. 73 one-bedroom suites with kitchens. 2 stories, exterior corridors. *Bath:* combo or shower only. **Parking:** on-site. **Terms:** small pets only ($50 fee, $7 extra charge). **Amenities:** video games (fee), voice mail, irons, hair dryers. **Pool(s):** heated outdoor. **Leisure Activities:** whirlpool, sports court. **Guest Services:** complimentary evening beverages, valet and coin laundry, area transportation. **Business Services:** meeting rooms, fax (fee). **Cards:** AX, CB, DC, DS, MC, VI.

SOME UNITS

ROBIN'S NEST BED & BREAKFAST INN

Phone: (713)528-5821 **58**

Bed & Breakfast

All Year [BP] — 1P: $89-$150 — 2P: $110-$150 — XP: $30
Location: US 59 (Southwest Frwy), exit Richmond Ave, just e on Richmond, then just n. 4104 Greeley St 77006. Fax: 713/529-4821. **Facility:** Smoke free premises. 4 one-bedroom standard units. 2 stories (no elevator), interior corridors. **Parking:** on-site. **Terms:** check-in 4 pm, 7 day cancellation notice, pets ($30 extra charge). **Business Services:** fax (fee). **Cards:** AX, DS, MC, VI.

SOME UNITS

RODEWAY INN-SOUTHWEST FREEWAY

Phone: (713)526-1071 **55**

(SAVE)

Motel

All Year — 1P: $53-$65 — 2P: $57-$69 — XP: $6 — F17
Location: Just se of US 59 (Southwest Frwy), exit Buffalo Speedway, on service road. 3135 Southwest Frwy 77098. Fax: 713/526-8668. **Facility:** 83 one-bedroom standard units. 2 stories, exterior corridors. **Parking:** on-site. **Terms:** small pets only ($20 deposit). **Pool(s):** outdoor. **Business Services:** meeting rooms, fax (fee). **Cards:** AX, CB, DC, DS, MC, VI.

SOME UNITS

THE ST. REGIS HOUSTON

Phone: (713)840-7600 **41**

AAA (SAVE)

Small-scale Hotel

1/1-1/31 — 1P: $520 — 2P: $520
9/8-12/31 — 1P: $495 — 2P: $495
2/1-9/7 — 1P: $480 — 2P: $480
Location: I-610, exit 9A (San Felipe/Westheimer rds), 0.3 mi e. 1919 Briar Oaks Ln 77027. Fax: 713/840-8036. **Facility:** Offering refined service and richly appointed rooms. 232 units. 180 one-bedroom standard units. 52 one-bedroom suites ($530-$2500), some with kitchens and/or whirlpools. 12 stories, interior corridors. **Parking:** valet. **Terms:** 1-6 night minimum stay - weekends, seasonal, cancellation fee imposed, package plans - weekends, seasonal. **Amenities:** video games (fee), CD players, dual phone lines, voice mail, safes, honor bars, hair dryers. *Some:* DVD players, fax, irons. **Dining:** 24 hours, cocktails, also, The Remington, see separate listing, entertainment. **Pool(s):** heated outdoor. **Leisure Activities:** exercise room, spa. **Guest Services:** gift shop, valet laundry, area transportation-within 5 mi. **Business Services:** meeting rooms, business center. **Cards:** AX, CB, DC, DS, JC, MC, VI.

SOME UNITS

(See map p. 374)

SARA'S BED & BREAKFAST

All Year [BP]   1P: $70-$200   2P: $70-$200   **Phone:** (713)868-1130   XP: $25   **21**

Bed & Breakfast   **Location:** I-10, exit 766 (Heights Blvd) westbound; exit 767A (Studemont) eastbound, 0.5 mi n. Located in the historic Houston Heights district; in a quiet area. 941 Heights Blvd 77008. Fax: 713/868-3284. **Facility:** Furnished with antiques and collectibles, this Queen Anne Victorian B&B is near downtown. 12 units. 8 one-bedroom standard units, some with whirlpools. 3 one- and 1 two-bedroom suites. 2 stories (no elevator), interior corridors. *Bath:* combo or shower only. **Parking:** on-site. **Terms:** age restrictions may apply. **Amenities:** video library, voice mail, irons, hair dryers. **Leisure Activities:** jogging. **Business Services:** meeting rooms, fax (fee). **Cards:** AX, CB, DC, DS, MC, VI.

SOME UNITS

(ASK) (SD) (X) (VCR) (DATA PORT) / (🛏) (🖨) (💻) /

SHERATON HOUSTON BROOK HOLLOW

(AAA) (SAVE)   All Year   1P: $58-$122   2P: $58-$122   **Phone:** (713)688-0100   XP: $10   **24**   F18

Large-scale Hotel   **Location:** Jct I-610 and US 290, exit 13C (TC Jester), just nw. 3000 N Loop W 77092. Fax: 713/688-9224. **Facility:** 382 units. 380 one-bedroom standard units. 2 one-bedroom suites. 10 stories, interior corridors. *Bath:* combo or shower only. **Parking:** on-site. **Terms:** cancellation fee imposed, pets ($50 deposit). **Amenities:** high-speed Internet (fee), dual phone lines, voice mail, irons, hair dryers. *Some:* fax. **Dining:** 6 am-10:30 pm, cocktails, nightclub. **Pool(s):** heated outdoor. **Leisure Activities:** sauna, whirlpool, exercise room. **Guest Services:** gift shop, valet laundry, area transportation-within 5 mi. **Business Services:** conference facilities, business center. **Cards:** AX, DC, DS, MC, VI. **Special Amenities:** early check-in/late check-out and free newspaper.
(See color ad below)

SOME UNITS

(SD) (🛏) (🍴) (Y) (&) (🐕) (🏊) (X) (🎿) (DATA PORT) (💻) / (X) (🛏) /

SHERATON SUITES HOUSTON NEAR THE GALLERIA

(AAA) (SAVE)   All Year   1P: $189-$259   2P: $189-$259   **Phone:** (713)586-2444   XP: $10   **71**   F18

Small-scale Hotel   **Location:** I-610, exit 9 (San Felipe Rd) northbound; exit 9A (San Filipe/Westheimer rds) southbound. 2400 W Loop S 77027. Fax: 713/586-2445. **Facility:** 281 one-bedroom suites. 12 stories, interior corridors. *Bath:* combo or shower only. **Parking:** on-site (fee). **Amenities:** dual phone lines, voice mail, irons, hair dryers. *Fee:* video games, high-speed Internet. *Some:* fax. **Dining:** 6:30 am-2 & 5-10 pm, cocktails. **Pool(s):** outdoor. **Leisure Activities:** whirlpool, exercise room. **Guest Services:** sundries, valet laundry, area transportation-within 3 mi. **Business Services:** conference facilities, PC, fax (fee). **Cards:** AX, CB, DC, DS, JC, MC, VI. **Special Amenities:** early check-in/late check-out and free newspaper.

SOME UNITS

(🍴) (Y) (&) (🏊) (🎿) (DATA PORT) (💻) / (X) (VCR) (🛏) /
FEE

SPRINGHILL SUITES BY MARRIOTT-HOUSTON

(SAVE)   All Year   1P: $70-$110   **Phone:** 713/290-9242   XP: $5   **32**   F18

Small-scale Hotel   **Location:** I-610, exit 13C (E and W TC Jester), 0.4 mi on westbound service road. 2750 N Loop W 610 77092. Fax: 713/290-9242. **Facility:** 79 one-bedroom standard units. 3 stories, interior corridors. *Bath:* combo or shower only. **Parking:** on-site. **Amenities:** dual phone lines, voice mail, irons, hair dryers. **Pool(s):** heated indoor. **Leisure Activities:** whirlpool, exercise room. **Guest Services:** valet laundry. **Business Services:** fax (fee). **Cards:** AX, CB, DC, DS, JC, MC, VI.

SOME UNITS

(SD) (🍴) (&) (🏊) (🎿) (DATA PORT) (🛏) (🖨) (💻) / (X) /

(See map p. 374)

STAYBRIDGE SUITES BY HOLIDAY INN HOUSTON-NEAR THE GALLERIA   Phone: (713)355-8888   72
▼▼〰〰▼   All Year [ECP]   1P: $149-$179   2P: $149-$179

Large-scale Hotel   **Location:** I-610, exit 9A (San Felipe/Westheimer rds) southbound; exit 8C (Westheimer Rd) northbound, 0.4 mi w on Westheimer Rd to Sage Rd, just s. Located 1 block from Galleria Shopping Center. 5190 Hidalgo St 77056. **Fax:** 713/355-4445. **Facility:** 93 units. 45 one-bedroom standard units with efficiencies. 42 one- and 6 two-bedroom suites with efficiencies. 4 stories, interior corridors. *Bath:* combo or shower only. **Parking:** on-site. **Terms:** pets ($75 fee). **Amenities:** video library (fee), high-speed Internet, dual phone lines, voice mail, irons, hair dryers. **Pool(s):** heated outdoor. **Leisure Activities:** exercise room. **Guest Services:** complimentary evening beverages: Tues-Thurs. **Business Services:** business center. **Cards:** AX, CB, DC, DS, MC, VI.

SOME UNITS
(ASK) (S◻) (⊕)(🛏)(¶¶+)(⌣M)(🌊)(VCR)(🐾)(DATA PORT)(📶)(🖥)(💻)/(✕)/
                FEE

THE WARWICK   Phone: (713)526-1991   60
▼▼〰〰▼   All Year   1P: $179-$189   2P: $179-$189   XP: $20   F18

Small-scale Hotel   **Location:** Jct of Main and Ewing sts, just n of Herman Park. 5701 Main St 77005. **Fax:** 713/526-0359. **Facility:** 308 units. 250 one-bedroom standard units. 58 one-bedroom suites. 12 stories, interior corridors. *Bath:* combo or shower only. **Parking:** on-site (fee). **Terms:** small pets only ($25 fee). **Amenities:** dual phone lines, voice mail, irons, hair dryers. *Some:* honor bars. **Pool(s):** heated outdoor. **Leisure Activities:** saunas, exercise room. *Fee:* massage. **Guest Services:** gift shop, valet laundry, area transportation. **Business Services:** conference facilities. *Fee:* PC, fax. **Cards:** AX, DC, DS, MC, VI.

SOME UNITS
(🐾)(¶¶)(24↑)(Y)(⌣M)(⌣)(⬚)(🌊)(✕)(🐾)(DATA PORT)(💻)/(✕)(VCR)(📶)(🖥)/
                                                        FEE FEE

WELLESLEY INN & SUITES (HOUSTON/MEMORIAL)   Phone: (713)263-9770   56
(AAA) (SAVE)   All Year   1P: $95-$135   2P: $100-$140   XP: $5
▼▼◆◆▼   **Location:** I-10, exit 762 (Antoine Dr) westbound; exit 762 (Sleber/Post Oak Rd) eastbound, on eastbound service road. 7855 Katy Frwy 77024. **Fax:** 713/263-9771. **Facility:** 134 units. 64 one-bedroom standard units with efficiencies. 70 one-bedroom suites with efficiencies. 3 stories, interior corridors. *Bath:* combo or shower only. Small-scale Hotel   **Parking:** on-site. **Terms:** [ECP] meal plan available, small pets only. **Amenities:** dual phone lines, voice mail, irons, hair dryers. **Pool(s):** outdoor. **Leisure Activities:** exercise room. **Guest Services:** valet and coin laundry. **Business Services:** meeting rooms, fax (fee). **Cards:** AX, DC, DS, MC, VI. **Special Amenities:** free continental breakfast and free newspaper.

SOME UNITS
(S◻)(🛏)(⌣)(🌊)(🐾)(DATA PORT)(📶)(🖥)(💻)/(✕)(VCR)

WELLESLEY INN & SUITES (HOUSTON/RELIANT PARK MEDICAL CTR)   Phone: (713)794-0800   76
(AAA) (SAVE)   All Year   1P: $99-$144   2P: $99-$144   XP: $10   F17
▼▼◆◆   **Location:** I-610, exit 1B, 1.5 mi n, then just e. 1301 S Braeswood Blvd 77030. **Fax:** 713/794-0925. **Facility:** 130 one-bedroom standard units with efficiencies. 3 stories, interior corridors. *Bath:* combo or shower only. Small-scale Hotel   **Parking:** on-site. **Terms:** [ECP] meal plan available, small pets only. **Amenities:** video games (fee), voice mail, irons, hair dryers. **Pool(s):** outdoor. **Leisure Activities:** picnic & barbecue area with grills, exercise room, sports court. **Guest Services:** valet and coin laundry, area transportation-medical center. **Business Services:** fax (fee). **Cards:** AX, CB, DC, DS, JC, MC, VI. **Special Amenities:** free continental breakfast and free newspaper.

SOME UNITS
(S◻)(🛏)(⌣)(🌊)(✕)(🐾)(DATA PORT)(📶)(⬚)(💻)/(✕)/

───── *The following lodging was either not evaluated or did not* ─────
meet AAA rating requirements but is listed for your information only.

INTER-CONTINENTAL HOUSTON   Phone: (713)627-7600   44
(fyi)   All Year   1P: $299-$349   2P: $319-$369   XP: $20

Large-scale Hotel   Under major renovation, scheduled to be completed April 2002. **Last rated:** ▼▼▼ **Location:** I-610, exit 9 (San Felipe Rd) northbound; exit 9A (San Felipe/Westheimer rds) southbound. Located in the Galleria Business and shopping district. 2222 W Loop S 77027. **Fax:** 713/961-3327. **Facility:** 485 units. 464 one-bedroom standard units. 19 one- and 2 two-bedroom suites ($399-$2500), some with whirlpools. 23 stories, interior corridors. **Parking:** on-site (fee) and valet. **Terms:** cancellation fee imposed. **Amenities:** CD players, high-speed Internet, dual phone lines, voice mail, safes, honor bars, irons, hair dryers. *Some:* video games, fax. **Pool(s):** heated outdoor. **Leisure Activities:** sauna, whirlpool, exercise room. *Fee:* massage. **Guest Services:** gift shop, valet and coin laundry, area transportation. **Business Services:** conference facilities, business center. **Cards:** AX, CB, DC, DS, JC, MC, VI.

SOME UNITS
(ASK)(S◻)(¶¶)(24↑)(Y)(⌣)(⬚)(🌊)(✕)(🐾)(DATA PORT)(💻)/(✕)(VCR)(📶)/
                                                        FEE

───── **WHERE TO DINE** ─────

59 DINER   Lunch: $5-$9   Dinner: $5-$9   Phone: 713/523-2333   83
▼▼▼   **Location:** US 59 Shepherd/Greenbriar Rd, just n on Shepherd to Farnham, just se. 3801 Farnham 77098. **Hours:** 6 am-11 pm, Fri-midnight, Sat 7 am-midnight, Sun 7 am-11 pm. **Closed:** 11/27, 12/25. **Features:** Guests can American   travel down memory lane, as nostalgia abounds in the rock 'n' roll diner. Typifying the style of '50s and '60s diners, the dining room features teal vinyl booths, a pink and black tile floor, counter dining with low, red, padded stools and period paraphernalia scattered throughout. True to its theme, the restaurant specializes in burgers, hot dogs and such fountain drinks as root beer floats and shakes. Casual dress; beer & wine only. **Parking:** on-site. **Cards:** AX, DC, DS, MC, VI.

(✕)

AMERICAS   Lunch: $10-$22   Dinner: $16-$25   Phone: 713/961-1492   17
▼▼▼   **Location:** I-610, exit 9 (San Felipe Rd) northbound; exit 9B (Post Oak Blvd) southbound, just s; in Pavillion Shopping Center. 1800 Post Oak Blvd, Suite 164 77056. **Hours:** 11 am-10 pm, Fri-11 pm, Sat 5 pm-11 pm. Closed major Latino   holidays; also Sun. **Reservations:** suggested. **Features:** Pseudo stone and black mosaic trees form a cave-like dining room. Guests can start with a plate of plantain chips and then fill up on delicious Latin American-inspired cuisine. Although churrasco (beef tenderloin) is the signature dish, the menu also lists chicken and fish selections, as well as creative appetizers. Tres leches cake is delicious. Dressy casual; cocktails. **Parking:** valet. **Cards:** AX, CB, DC, DS, MC, VI.

(Y)(✕)

(See map p. 374)

ANDRE'S PASTRY SHOP AND CAFE
Lunch: $10   Phone: 713/524-3863   [31]

▼▼▼▼   **Location:** Corner of Westheimer Rd and River Oaks Blvd; between Kirby and Buffalo Speedway. 2515 River Oaks Blvd 77019. **Hours:** 7 am-5:30 pm, Fri & Sat 6:30 am-5 & 6-10 pm. Closed: 1/1, 12/25; also Sun.
Continental   **Features:** The cozy cafe and bakery specializes in quiche, but the daily specials add good variety to the menu and move quickly. One delicious example of the temptations that await is the rich cafe au lait, which goes perfectly with sweet selections from the gleaming pastry case of Swiss treats. Smoke free premises. Casual dress. **Parking:** on-site. **Cards:** AX, DS, MC, VI.

ANTHONY'S
Lunch: $14-$17   Dinner: $18-$35   Phone: 713/961-0552   [59]

▼▼▼▼   **Location:** I-610, exit 8C (Westheimer Rd) northbound; exit 9A (San Felipe/Westheimer rds) southbound, 0.5 mi e. 4007 Westheimer Rd 77027. **Hours:** 11:30 am-2 & 5:30-11 pm, Mon-10 pm, Fri-11:30 pm, Sat 5:30 pm-11:30
American   pm. Closed major holidays; also Sun. **Reservations:** suggested. **Features:** Specializing in Italian cuisine, this restaurant is located near Herman Park. The smoked salmon is tender and served with asparagus. The freshly-baked bread is delivered warm to your table. Don't leave without indulging in the luscious creme brulee. Casual dress; cocktails. **Parking:** on-site and valet. **Cards:** AX, DC, DS, MC, VI.

BACKSTREET CAFE
Lunch: $12-$23   Dinner: $12-$23   Phone: 713/521-2239   [18]

▼▼   **Location:** Between Dallas and Clay sts. 1103 S Shepherd 77019. **Hours:** 11 am-10 pm, Fri & Sat-11 pm. Closed: 12/25; also 12/24 for dinner. **Features:** The rustic, outdoor patio has umbrellas over each table. The
American   red-corn enchiladas are stuffed with smoked chicken, diced potatoes, tomatoes and onions. A personable wait staff delivers a great selection of breads and desserts. Casual dress; cocktails. **Parking:** valet.
Cards: AX, MC, VI.

BARBECUE INN
Lunch: $7-$11   Dinner: $7-$11   Phone: 713/695-8112   [43]

▼▼▼   **Location:** I-610, exit 16A, 1.4 mi n; northwest corner of Crosstimbers and Yale sts. 116 W Crosstimbers 77018.
Hours: 10:30 am-10 pm. Closed major holidays; also Sun, Mon & 7/1-7/5. **Features:** The restaurant has
Barbecue   been in business for more than 50 years, and it's easy to see why. Flavorful food is offered at reasonable prices. Although the name is telling, the owner admits his bestsellers are chicken-fried steak and seafood.
Casual dress; beer only. **Parking:** on-site. **Cards:** AX, DC, DS, MC, VI.

BARNABY'S CAFE
Lunch: $8-$18   Dinner: $8-$18   Phone: 713/522-0106   [38]

▼   **Location:** Just e of jct Montrose and Fairview; between Stanford and Hopkins sts. 604 Fairview 77006. **Hours:** 11 am-10 pm, Fri & Sat-11 pm. **Features:** Nestled in a residential area, you will have to actively search for
American   this restaurant. Rest assured it will be worth the work. The menu features such american classics as cobb salad, hamburgers, and meatloaf but you will be pleasantly surprised with the diversity of the choices.
Casual dress; beer & wine only. **Parking:** on-site. **Cards:** AX, DC, DS, MC, VI.

BENJY'S
Lunch: $8-$16   Dinner: $8-$24   Phone: 713/522-7602   [107]

▼▼▼   **Location:** Jct US 59 and Kirby Dr, 0.8 mi s to Dunstan, just e. 2424 Dunstan 77005. **Hours:** 11 am-10 pm, Fri & Sat-11 pm, Sun & Mon-9 pm. Closed major holidays. **Reservations:** suggested. **Features:** The hip cafe
American   boasts great house specialties, such as pistachio-crusted chicken served over melted onions and potatoes au gratin or Asian marinated pork tenderloin stir-fry. High ceilings give the dining room the feel of an art gallery. Its location in the village makes it a popular meeting place, and tables in close proximity don't exactly allow for intimacy. Smoke free premises. Casual dress; cocktails. **Parking:** on-site. **Cards:** AX, DC, MC, VI.

BERRYHILL HOT TAMALES
Lunch: $6-$15   Dinner: $6-$15   Phone: 713/526-8080   [68]

▼▼   **Location:** Corner of Westheimer Rd and Revere; between Kirby and Shephard Dr. 2639 Revere 77098. **Hours:** 10 am-10 pm, Sun-9 pm. Closed major holidays. **Features:** Located on the far end of Houston's restaurant
Mexican   row, this restaurant's size may be misleading of what it can deliver. Tamales are the specialty but you will find many other Mexican favorites such as enchiladas, tacos, burritos, and as would be expected you can order margaritas and cervezas. Although the service at this restaurant is every man for himself, it reflects the character of the young crowd that frequents this eatery. Casual dress; cocktails. **Parking:** on-site. **Cards:** AX, DC, DS, MC, VI.

THE BLACK LABRADOR
Lunch: $8-$13   Dinner: $8-$13   Phone: 713/529-1199   [89]

▼▼   **Location:** I-45, exit 47A (Allen Pkwy), 1.5 mi w to Montrose Blvd, 3 mi s. 4100 Montrose Blvd at Richmond 77006.
Hours: 11 am-11 pm, Fri & Sat-midnight, Sun-10 pm. Closed major holidays. **Features:** Dig into British
Ethnic   and American cuisine at this pub-like restaurant. Try the kidney pie, fish and chips or sausage with garlic-mashed potatoes, and for dessert, the homemade bread pudding really hits the spot. Casual dress; cocktails. **Parking:** on-site. **Cards:** AX, DC, MC, VI.

BONNIE'S BEEF & SEAFOOD CO
Lunch: $15-$28   Dinner: $15-$28   Phone: 713/641-2397   [118]

▼▼▼   **Location:** I-45, exit 41A (Woodridge Dr), e on service road. 6867 Gulf Frwy/I-45 S 77087. **Hours:** 11 am-9 pm, Wed & Thurs-10 pm, Fri & Sat-11 pm. Closed major holidays; also Sun. **Reservations:** suggested.
Steak & Seafood   **Features:** Sharp enough for business, comfortable enough for families, this steakhouse is well known for prime rib, strip steak, fried shrimp and baked potatoes with all the trimmings. Crates of produce over the salad bar give the impression of a farmers' market. Casual dress; cocktails. **Parking:** on-site. **Cards:** AX, CB, DC, DS, MC, VI.

BOULEVARD BISTROT
Lunch: $8-$25   Dinner: $12-$26   Phone: 713/524-6922   [102]

▼▼▼▼   **Location:** Jct Westheimer Rd and Montrose Blvd S, 0.7 mi on Montrose Blvd; between Richmond Ave and Oakley St. 4319 Montrose Blvd 77006. **Hours:** 11:30 am-2 & 5:30-10 pm, Fri-11 pm, Sat 5:30-11 pm, Sun 10 am-2:30
American   pm. Closed: Mon. **Reservations:** suggested. **Features:** Once heralded as one of the top 10 new chefs by Food & Wine magazine, chef Monica Pope artfully fuses cuisines and offers true diversity in her creations. The seasonally changing menu might list such selections as orange chili noodles, Indonesian rice and spicy Moroccan halibut. Diners also have the option to eat light or vegetarian. Smokers are welcomed on the patio. Smoke free premises. Casual dress; cocktails. **Parking:** on-site. **Cards:** AX, DC, DS, MC, VI.

(See map p. 374)

BRADY'S LANDING
▼▼▼
American

Lunch: $12   **Dinner:** $16-$20   **Phone:** 713/928-9921   116
Location: I-610, exit 30C (Lawndale Ave) southbound; exit 30D (Lawndale Ave) northbound, w to Broadway St, 0.6 mi n to Cypress St, just e. 8505 Cypress St 77012. **Hours:** 11 am-2:30 & 5-10 pm, Sat from 5 pm, Sun from 10:30 am. **Closed:** Mon. **Reservations:** suggested. **Features:** This wooden former warehouse has a seaside, rustic interior with high ceilings. The relaxing lounge has recliners by the fireplace. Try the lunch buffet full of fish, chicken, roast beef, veggies, fruit, salad, soup and dessert. Casual dress; cocktails. **Parking:** on-site. **Cards:** AX, CB, DC, DS, MC, VI.

BRENNAN'S OF HOUSTON
▼▼▼ ▼▼▼
Creole

Lunch: $12-$25   **Dinner:** $25-$32   **Phone:** 713/522-9711   92
Location: Jct of US 59 (Smith St) and Stuart St; southwest corner of downtown. 3300 Smith St 77006. **Hours:** 11:30 am-1:30 & 5:45-9:30 pm, Sat from 11 am, Sun from 10 am. **Closed:** 5/26. **Reservations:** suggested. **Features:** Diners are in for a Creole treat in a quiet, sophisticated corner of downtown. The flavor of the signature turtle soup hints at a mildly spicy Creole finish. Although such entrees as lamb mint julep, crawfish, and maple leaf duck are outstanding, the sublime signature Louisiana pecan-crusted fish should be given special consideration. Finish with the superb Creole pudding souffle. Semi-formal attire; cocktails. **Parking:** valet. **Cards:** AX, CB, DC, DS, MC, VI.

THE BROWNSTONE
▼▼▼
Continental

Lunch: $9-$17   **Dinner:** $25-$32   **Phone:** 713/520-5666   64
Location: Just s of Westheimer Rd; from US 59 (Southwest Frwy), exit Kirby Dr, 0.8 mi n to Westheimer Rd, just w. 2736 Virginia St 77098. **Hours:** 11 am-2 & 6-10 pm, Fri & Sat-10:30 pm. Closed major holidays. **Reservations:** suggested. **Features:** Attractive gardens and an antique gallery enhance the artful feel of this innovative restaurant. Dining here is a bit like dining at a museum, with rooms filled with fine paintings and objets d'art. An ambitious wine list beautifully complements an abbreviated menu of steak, game, fish and chicken compositions. Semi-formal attire; cocktails. **Parking:** valet. **Cards:** AX, CB, DC, DS, MC, VI.

CADILLAC BAR
▼▼
Mexican

Lunch: $8-$15   **Dinner:** $8-$15   **Phone:** 713/862-2020   11
Location: I-10, exit 765B (N Durham Dr/N Shepherd Dr), just s. 1802 Shepherd Dr 77007. **Hours:** 11 am-10 pm, Fri-midnight, Sun 4 pm-midnight. **Reservations:** accepted. **Features:** This border-town cantina is funky to the extreme and great fun. Good mesquite-roasted cabrito (baby goat), buttery shrimp queso flameado and ceviche are among the flavorful choices. Add your own bons mots to the Magic Markerisms graffiti on the wall. Casual dress; cocktails. **Parking:** on-site. **Cards:** AX, CB, DC, DS, MC, VI.

CAFE ANNIE
▼▼▼
Regional American

Lunch: $17-$25   **Dinner:** $28-$42   **Phone:** 713/840-1111   26
Location: Just w of I-610 (W Loop Frwy); between Westheimer Rd and San Felipe Rd exits, exit 9A southbound. 1728 Post Oak Blvd 77056. **Hours:** 11:30 am-2 & 6:30-10 pm, Fri-10:30 pm. Closed major holidays; also Sun. **Reservations:** suggested. **Features:** In the trendy Galleria area, the restaurant is a favorite for locals and tourists alike. Imaginative preparation and creative presentation characterize outstanding dishes of New American cuisine with heavy Southwestern influences. Service is sophisticated and attentive. Semi-formal attire; cocktails. **Parking:** on-site and valet. **Cards:** AX, CB, DC, DS, MC, VI.

CAFE EXPRESS
▼
American

Lunch: $5-$8   **Dinner:** $5-$8   **Phone:** 713/522-3994   81
Location: Between W Alabama and Richmond Ave. 3200 Kirby Dr 77098. **Hours:** 11 am-11 pm. Closed: 11/27, 12/25; also 12/31 for dinner. **Features:** Offering a quick-serve experience with a more wholesome benefit, the eatery offers pasta, sandwiches and salads. It's a comfortable place for lone diners. Casual dress; cocktails. **Parking:** on-site. **Cards:** AX, CB, DC, DS, MC, VI.

CANYON CAFE
▼▼
Southwest American

Lunch: $7-$13   **Dinner:** $9-$17   **Phone:** 713/629-5565   54
Location: I-610, exit 9A (San Felipe/Westheimer rds) southbound; exit 8C (Westheimer Rd) northbound, just w to Post Oak Blvd, just n. 5000 Westheimer Rd, Suite 250 77056. **Hours:** 11 am-10 pm, Fri & Sat-11 pm, Sun-9 pm. Closed: 11/27, 12/25. **Reservations:** required; weekends. **Features:** A trendy concept restaurant with the look of a Santa Fe lodge, it projects a perfect blend of wit and kitsch. Many taco or quesadilla choices are offered, along with "king ranch" chicken casserole, chicken-fried steak, grilled tuna and several salads. Casual dress; cocktails. **Parking:** on-site. **Cards:** AX, DC, DS, MC, VI.

CAPITAL GRILLE
▼▼▼
Steak & Seafood

Dinner: $18-$35   **Phone:** 713/623-4600   30
Location: I-610, exit 9A (San Felipe/Westheimer rds) southbound; exit 8C (Westheimer Rd) northbound, 0.5 mi w. 5365 Westheimer Rd 77056. **Hours:** 5 pm-10 pm, Fri & Sat-11 pm. Closed: 12/25. **Reservations:** suggested. **Features:** In the Galleria area, the upscale steakhouse is perfect for a special night out. Selections on extensive wine list complement the superb selection of dry-aged beef. Also on the menu are well-prepared seafood dishes. Dressy casual; cocktails. **Parking:** on-site and valet. **Cards:** AX, CB, DC, DS, MC, VI.

CHEESECAKE FACTORY
▼▼
American

Lunch: $8-$23   **Dinner:** $8-$23   **Phone:** 713/840-0600   55
Location: In the Galleria Mall. 5015 Westheimer Rd 77056. **Hours:** 11 am-11 pm, Fri & Sat-midnight, Sun 10 am-10 pm. **Closed:** 11/27, 12/25. **Features:** Very popular with a lively, eye-catching Art Nouveau atmosphere, it features 60 types of cheesecake including peanut butter and cookie dough flavors. Also, the menu ranges from "roadside sliders" (bite-sized burgers on mini-buns) to Szechuan dumplings. Casual dress; cocktails. **Parking:** on-site. **Cards:** AX, CB, DC, DS, MC, VI.

CHURRASCOS
▼▼▼
Latino

Lunch: $7-$10   **Dinner:** $14-$24   **Phone:** 713/527-8300   71
Location: At Shepherd, in Shepherd Square Shopping Center. 2055 Westheimer Rd 77098. **Hours:** 11 am-10 pm, Fri-11 pm, Sat 5 pm-11 pm. Closed major holidays; also Sun. **Reservations:** suggested. **Features:** Authentic South American specialties include charcoal-grilled steak, seafood, and the delicious grilled tenderloin that shares the restaurant's name. Plantain chips are an addictive appetizer, and tres leches, or three-milk cake, sweetly ends your meal. Casual dress; cocktails. **Parking:** on-site. **Cards:** AX, CB, DC, DS, MC, VI.

(See map p. 374)

CLEBURNE CAFETERIA

American

Lunch: $7-$14   **Dinner:** $7-$14   **Phone:** 713/667-2386   [99]
Location: Between Buffalo Speedway and Weslayan St. 3606 Bissonnet 77005. **Hours:** 11 am-2:30 & 4-8:30 pm, Sun 11 am-8:30 pm. Closed major holidays; also Sat. **Features:** Established in 1941, the former speakeasy has a rich local history. Offerings of traditional American fare include broiled fish, roast beef and fried chicken, as well as an array of salads, breads, sides and desserts. Casual dress. **Parking:** on-site.

CROSTINI
Italian

Lunch: $11-$25   **Dinner:** $11-$25   **Phone:** 713/524-8558   [32]
Location: Between Westheimer Rd and Fairview. 2411 S Shepherd Dr 77019. **Hours:** 11 am-2 & 5-10 pm, Fri & Sat-11 pm, Sun 11 am-9 pm. Closed major holidays. **Reservations:** suggested. **Features:** Don't look for traditional Italian fare, as the selections here are wonderfully creative. Among original dishes is crostini jalapeno, which combines tasty jalapeno fettuccine with grilled chicken, cilantro, black beans and tomato. The artistically contemporary surroundings provide an adult dining experience. Casual dress; cocktails. **Parking:** valet. **Cards:** AX, DC, DS, MC, VI.

DAILY REVIEW CAFE
American

Lunch: $5-$13   **Dinner:** $8-$23   **Phone:** 713/520-9217   [19]
Location: Just s of Allen Pkwy; corner of W Lamar and Dunlavy sts. 3412 W Lamar St 77019. **Hours:** 11:30 am-2 & 6-10 pm, Fri & Sat-10:30 pm, Sun 11 am-2:30 & 6-9 pm. Closed major holidays; also Mon for dinner. **Reservations:** suggested. **Features:** Expect quaint, casual dining set in a candlelit bistro atmosphere. Only the freshest ingredients are selected for a variety of well-prepared dishes like the black bean vegetarian chili and the grilled beef tenderloin served with garlic mashed potatoes. Casual dress; cocktails. **Parking:** valet. **Cards:** AX, DC, MC, VI.

DAMIAN'S CUCINA ITALIANA
Italian

Lunch: $12-$28   **Dinner:** $12-$28   **Phone:** 713/522-0439   [75]
Location: 0.8 mi s, just n of Elgin, just w of Main St. 3011 Smith St 77006. **Hours:** 11 am-2 & 5:30-10 pm, Fri-11:30 pm, Sat 5 pm-11:30 pm. Closed major holidays; also Sun. **Reservations:** suggested. **Features:** Near the theater district, the attractive eatery features earth-colored walls and Italian countryside murals. Hanging copper pots and rich woods complete the look of a warm, rustic eatery. While the pasta menu is long, offerings also include many fish, veal, beef and chicken selections. Leave room for homemade tiramisu. Smoke free premises. Dressy casual; cocktails. **Parking:** valet. **Cards:** AX, CB, DC, MC, VI.

DAVE & BUSTER'S
American

Lunch: $6-$20   **Dinner:** $10-$14   **Phone:** 713/952-2233   [76]
Location: Just e of jct Fountainview Rd and Richmond Ave. 6010 Richmond Ave 77057. **Hours:** 11 am-midnight, Wed & Thurs-1 am, Fri 11 am-2 am, Sat 11:30 am-2 am, Sun 11:30 am-1 am. Closed: 12/24. **Features:** This outrageous combination of restaurant and adult playground allows guests to play pool, shoot baskets or play virtual reality video games. Choose from a variety of entrees including sandwiches and burgers, as well as chicken, beef and seafood dishes. Casual dress; cocktails. **Parking:** on-site. **Cards:** AX, MC, VI.

DONERAKI MEXICAN RESTAURANT
Mexican

Lunch: $7-$16   **Dinner:** $7-$16   **Phone:** 713/975-9815   [56]
Location: Between Hillcroft/Voss Rd and Stoney Brook Dr. 7705 Westheimer Rd 77063. **Hours:** 9 am-midnight, Fri-3 am, Sun 8 am-midnight. **Reservations:** accepted. **Features:** A mariachi band plays festive music as patrons nosh on Tex-Mex food. Murals of Mexico cover the walls, and pinatas and colored lights hang from the ceiling. Try the tortilla with fajita chicken, charro beans and Spanish rice. Casual dress; cocktails; entertainment. **Parking:** on-site. **Cards:** AX, DC, DS, MC, VI.

DONG TING
Chinese

Lunch: $9-$22   **Dinner:** $9-$22   **Phone:** 713/527-0005   [90]
Location: 1 mi s on Smith St, between Louisiana and Stuart sts. 611 Stuart St 77006. **Hours:** 11:30 am-10 pm, Fri-10:30 pm, Sat from 5:30 pm. Closed: 11/27, 12/25; also Sun. **Reservations:** suggested. **Features:** Bathed in soft music, the dining room exudes a quiet elegance. Adept, attentive servers offer suggestions from an extensive traditional menu with spicy selections. Dishes are tastefully presented in healthy portions. Dressy casual; cocktails. **Parking:** on-site. **Cards:** AX, DC, DS, MC, VI.

FOUNTAINVIEW CAFE AND BREAKFAST
American

Lunch: $4-$6   **Dinner:** ---   **Phone:** 713/785-9060   [22]
Location: Between Westheimer and San Felipe rds. 1842 Fountainview Dr 77057. **Hours:** 7 am-3 pm, Sat & Sun from 8 am. Closed: 11/27, 12/25. **Features:** Comfort cuisine is the specialty, featuring red beans and rice, fried catfish with coleslaw and smothered pork chops. These are only a sampling of the many homestyle dishes offered. Breakfast is served all day, every day. Casual dress. **Parking:** on-site. **Cards:** MC, VI.

FUSION CAFE
Soul Food

Lunch: $7-$13   **Dinner:** $7-$13   **Phone:** 713/522-1884   [109]
Location: US 59, exit Kirby, 1 mi s to Times, then just e. 2442 Times 77005. **Hours:** 11 am-9 pm, Fri & Sat-11 pm. Closed: Sun. **Reservations:** accepted. **Features:** The menu best describes the restaurant's food as "an amalgamation of flavors." Southern, island and Louisiana influences go into such dishes as chicken and waffles, crawfish etouffee and jerk chicken. The small, contemporary dining room provides a relaxing atmosphere. Casual dress; cocktails. **Parking:** on-site. **Cards:** AX, DC, DS, MC, VI.

GOLDEN ROOM
Thai

Lunch: $7-$14   **Dinner:** $9-$18   **Phone:** 713/524-9614   [20]
Location: Just s of jct W Dallas and Montrose Blvd. 1209 Montrose Blvd 77019. **Hours:** 11:30 am-2:30 & 5-9:30 pm, Fri-10:30 pm, Sat 5 pm-10:30 pm. Closed: 1/1, 11/27, 12/25; also Sun. **Reservations:** suggested; weekends. **Features:** This restaurant with a spirit house outside the front door offers delicious, authentic Thai food. Try pahd thai—stir-fried noodles with egg, chicken, ground peanuts and bean sprouts—or call ahead for the off-the-menu glass noodles baked with shrimp. Smoke free premises. Casual dress; beer & wine only. **Parking:** on-site. **Cards:** AX, CB, DC, DS, MC, VI.

(See map p. 374)

GOODE COMPANY HAMBURGERS & TAQUERIA   **Lunch:** $6-$15   **Dinner:** $5-$15   **Phone:** 713/520-9153   [106]
Location: Southwest Frwy (US 59), exit Kirby Dr, just s. 4902 Kirby Dr 77098. **Hours:** 11 am-10 pm, Fri from
10:30 am, Sat & Sun from 7:30 am. Closed: 1/1, 11/27, 12/25. **Features:** Diners whose pockets, wardrobe
and palate long for something less ambitious would be well-served to drop by the relaxed restaurant.
American

Friendly, efficient servers bring out reliably good food, including crispy tacos, enchiladas and
mesquite-grilled burgers. Patrons can pick their own beer out of the ice chest. Casual dress; beer & wine only. **Parking:**
on-site. **Cards:** AX, CB, DC, DS, MC, VI.

GOODE CO. SEAFOOD   **Lunch:** $10-$22   **Dinner:** $10-$24   **Phone:** 713/523-7154   [104]
Location: 0.4 mi s of jct Southwest Frwy (US 59), exit Kirby Dr. 2621 Westpark Dr 77098. **Hours:** 11 am-10 pm, Fri
& Sat-11 pm. Closed: 1/1, 11/27, 12/25. **Features:** Catering to a wide range of clientele, this spiffy railway
Regional Seafood   diner is the setting for lip-blistering gumbo, overstuffed, fried seafood po'boys, and boisterous fun. A special
delight is the sweet ceviche-like campeche with cubed avocado and chopped onion. Casual dress;
cocktails. **Parking:** on-site. **Cards:** AX, CB, DC, DS, MC, VI.

GROTTO   **Lunch:** $7-$15   **Dinner:** $8-$24   **Phone:** 713/622-3663   [29]
Location: Between Drexel Dr and Weslayan St. 3920 Westheimer Rd 77027. **Hours:** 11:30 am-11 pm, Fri &
Sat-midnight, Sun 11:30 am-10 pm. Closed major holidays. **Features:** Chic and energetic, the Italian cafe
Italian   serves homemade, but unpredictable, fare. A lavish assortment of antipasto is displayed at the entry
display kitchen. Lively murals cover the walls. Seating also is offered on the patio. Casual dress; cocktails.
Parking: on-site. **Cards:** AX, CB, DC, MC, VI.

HUNAN RESTAURANT   **Lunch:** $8-$15   **Dinner:** $15-$22   **Phone:** 713/965-0808   [25]
Location: I-610, exit 8C (Westheimer Rd) northbound, just w; exit 9A (San Felipe/Westheimer rds) southbound;
between San Felipe and Westheimer rds. 1800 Post Oak Blvd 77056. **Hours:** 11:30 am-10 pm, Fri-11 pm, Sat
Chinese   from noon, Sun noon-10 pm. Closed: 11/27. **Reservations:** suggested. **Features:** Chicken marinated with
ginger is one of the Hunan specialties prepared at this family restaurant. Smoked chicken is sauteed with
vegetables and served over steamed rice. Appropriately enough, the dining area is decorated in a Chinese motif. Casual
dress; cocktails. **Parking:** on-site and valet. **Cards:** AX, DC, DS, MC, VI.

INDIA'S   **Lunch:** $8-$17   **Dinner:** $8-$17   **Phone:** 713/266-0131   [48]
Location: Just n of US 59 (Southwest Frwy); between Chimney Rock and Fountainview Rd. 5704 Richmond Ave
77057. **Hours:** 11 am-2:30 & 5 pm-10 pm, Fri & Sat-10:30 pm. **Reservations:** suggested; weekends.
Indian   **Features:** Featuring seafood, lamb and chicken dishes, the cuisine emphasizes curried items as well as
selections prepared in the tandoori, or clay oven, tradition. A well-stocked lunch buffet makes a good
choice, with items like tandoori chicken and fried spinach. Casual dress; beer & wine only. **Parking:** on-site. **Cards:** AX, CB,
DC, DS, MC, VI.

JAMES CONEY ISLAND   **Lunch:** $3-$6   **Dinner:** $3-$6   **Phone:** 713/785-9333   [53]
Location: Between Hillcroft and Chimney Rock. 5745 Westheimer Rd 77057. **Hours:** 10:30 am-11 pm, Fri & Sat-3
am. Closed: 11/27, 12/25. **Features:** Claiming to have sold more than 35,000 miles of hot dogs, this busy
American   eatery offers a taste of the 50s with hamburgers, french fries, fountain drinks, and, of course, hot dogs
served any way you like. Try the James #1 with two chili-cheese dogs and fries. Casual dress; beer only.
Parking: on-site. **Cards:** AX, DS, MC, VI.

KENNY & ZIGGY'S DELICATESSEN RESTAURANT   **Lunch:** $7-$15   **Dinner:** $7-$15   **Phone:** 713/871-8883   [23]
Location: I-610, exit 8C (Westheimer Rd) northbound; exit 9A (San Felipe/Westheimer rds) southbound, just w on
Westheimer Rd, then just n. 2327 Post Oak Blvd 77056. **Hours:** 7 am-9 pm, Sat & Sun from 8 am. Closed:
Deli/Subs/Sandwiches   12/25; also major Jewish holidays. **Features:** The restaurant treats patrons to a New York
delicatessen-style experience. The menu is an encyclopedia of sandwich choices, franks, bagels and lox,
salads and such dinner plates as corned beef and cabbage. Although sandwich prices may seem high, the portions make
them worthwhile. Smoke free premises. Casual dress; beer & wine only. **Parking:** on-site. **Cards:** AX, DS, MC, VI.

KIM SON   **Lunch:** $6-$20   **Dinner:** $7-$20   **Phone:** 713/222-2461   [94]
Location: Corner of Chartres and Jefferson, between Pease and Jefferson on Chartres; downtown area; US 59, exit
Gray and Pierce sts. 2001 Jefferson 77003. **Hours:** 11 am-11 pm, Fri & Sat-midnight.
Chinese   **Reservations:** suggested. **Features:** American-Oriental decorations include a lovely entrance fountain.
Cordial servers deliver beef, chicken and seafood entrees with vegetables, noodles and rice. The curry
chicken with peanuts is served over white rice. Casual dress; cocktails. **Parking:** on-site and valet. **Cards:** AX, CB, DC, DS,
MC, VI.

KIM SON RESTAURANT   **Lunch:** $5-$12   **Dinner:** $5-$12   **Phone:** 713/783-0054   [42]
Location: Between Hillcroft/Voss Rd and Stoney Brook Dr. 7531 Westheimer Rd 77063. **Hours:** 11 am-11 pm, Fri &
Sat-midnight. **Features:** Inside a mall, this attractive Vietnamese restaurant is bathed in natural lighting
Ethnic   thanks to large windows. The egg roll and crab puff appetizers are luscious, and the Hunan chicken is
sauteed with vegetables and brown sauce. Casual dress; cocktails. **Parking:** on-site. **Cards:** AX, DC, DS,
MC, VI.

KING FISH MARKET   **Lunch:** $7-$11   **Dinner:** $14-$22   **Phone:** 713/974-3474   [45]
Location: Between W Greenridge and Unity Dr. 6356 Richmond Ave 77057. **Hours:** 11 am-10 pm, Fri-11 pm, Sat
noon-11 pm, Sun noon-10 pm. **Features:** Although there's a seafood market here, most of the floor space
Seafood   is dedicated to a handsome dining room that serves wonderful bisques, huge boiled crawfish, fine shrimp
tacos and grilled fish by the boatload. Also offered is delicious steak and prime rib. Casual dress; cocktails.
Parking: on-site. **Cards:** AX, CB, DC, DS, MC, VI.

(See map p. 374)

LA COLOMBE D'OR RESTAURANT   Lunch: $13-$18   Dinner: $29-$38   Phone: 713/524-7999   (88)
▼▼△△▼▼ **Location:** Just s in La Colombe D'or Hotel, jct Westheimer Rd and Montrose Blvd; between Hawthorne and Harold
Regional French sts. 3410 Montrose Blvd 77006. **Hours:** 11:30 am-2 & 6-9 pm, Sat & Sun from 6 pm. Closed: 7/4, 11/27, 12/25. **Reservations:** suggested. **Features:** All the charm and warmth of a bygone era may still be found in this restored mansion built in 1923 by the founder of Exxon. Try the flavorful red fish with spiced tomatoes and black olives in the main dining room, or in one of two private party rooms. Dressy casual; cocktails. **Parking:** on-site and valet. **Cards:** AX, CB, DC, DS, MC, VI.

LA GRIGLIA   Lunch: $8-$17   Dinner: $9-$28   Phone: 713/526-4700   (33)
▼▼△△▼▼ **Location:** US 59, exit Kirby Rd, 1.5 mi n, then 0.6 mi e on Inwood Dr and Gray St. 2002 W Gray St 77019.
Italian **Hours:** 11:30 am-2 & 5:30-11 pm, Fri-midnight, Sat 5:30 pm-midnight, Sun 5:30 pm-10 pm. Closed major holidays. **Features:** A whimsical and visually captivating decor is achieved with cartoon-like murals, hodgepodge mosaic pillars and commemorative floor tiles engraved with the names and dates of various visitors. A festive ambience is enhanced by creative entree presentation. Casual dress; cocktails. **Parking:** on-site. **Cards:** AX, CB, DC, DS, MC, VI.

LA MORA   Lunch: $12-$26   Dinner: $12-$26   Phone: 713/522-7412   (73)
▼▼△△▼▼ **Location:** Just s on Montrose Blvd, jct Montrose Blvd and Westheimer Rd; just e of Montrose Blvd. 912 Lovett Blvd
Italian 77006. **Hours:** 11 am-2 & 5:30-10 pm, Fri-11 pm, Sat 5:30 pm-11 pm, Mon from 5:30 pm. Closed major holidays; also Sun. **Reservations:** suggested; weekends. **Features:** A menu with a pure Tuscan accent offers hearty grilled meat and bean dishes that get as much emphasis as traditional pasta meals. Pleasures are quiet and basic with the casual charm of stenciled pastel walls, a skylit atrium and a rustic stone fireplace. Casual dress; cocktails. **Parking:** valet. **Cards:** AX, DC, DS, MC, VI.

LA RESERVE   Dinner: $21-$100   Phone: 713/871-8177   (12)
▼▼△△▼▼ **Location:** I-610, exit 10 (Woodway Dr), 0.5 mi w; in Memorial Park; in Omni Houston Hotel. Four Riverway 77056.
Continental **Hours:** 6:30 pm-10:30 pm, Fri & Sat-11 pm. Closed major holidays; also Sun. **Reservations:** suggested. **Features:** Superbly prepared regional dishes are offered on a focused Continental menu with some California infusion from the San Francisco-trained chef. Some notable delights include a zesty brie soup, and a chilled seafood sampler with shrimp and seasoned oysters. Smoke free premises. Semi-formal attire; cocktails. **Parking:** valet. **Cards:** AX, CB, DC, DS, JC, MC, VI.

LAS ALAMEDAS   Lunch: $10-$20   Dinner: $13-$25   Phone: 713/461-1503   (6)
△△▼▼ △△▼▼ **Location:** I-10, exit 759 (Campbell Rd), on south frontage road. 8615 Katy Frwy 77024. **Hours:** 11 am-3 & 6-10
Mexican pm, Fri-11 pm, Sat 6 pm-11 pm, Sun 11 am-9 pm. Closed major holidays. **Reservations:** suggested; Fri & Sat. **Features:** A tremendously romantic spot, it resembles a grand 19th-century hacienda. Excellent selections include the beef tenderloin smothered in chipotle sauce, caldo loco (chicken soup), and sauteed red snapper with mushrooms, shrimp and lump crab topping. Dressy casual; cocktails; entertainment. **Parking:** on-site. **Cards:** AX, DC, DS, MC, VI.

LA TOUR D'ARGENT RESTAURANT FRANCAIS   Lunch: $12-$18   Dinner: $16-$39   Phone: 713/864-9864   (5)
▼▼△△▼▼ **Location:** Ella Blvd at East TC Jester. 2011 Ella Blvd 77008. **Hours:** 11:30 am-2 & 6-10 pm, Fri & Sat 6 pm-11
French pm. Closed: 12/25; also Sun. **Reservations:** suggested. **Features:** The early-20th-century log cabin has been transformed into an elegant, stylish eatery. Accenting the dining area are mounted hunting trophies, masterpiece paintings and soothing fireplaces. The cuisine may be French and the dining upscale, but there is no sense of pretense. Graceful servers help explain why this place is one of the city's top spots for special-occasion dining. Semi-formal attire; cocktails. **Parking:** valet. **Cards:** AX, CB, DC, DS, MC, VI.

LEXINGTON GRILLE   Lunch: $10-$20   Dinner: $16-$28   Phone: 713/524-9877   (86)
△△▼▼ △△▼▼ **Location:** US 59, exit Shepherd/Greenbriar Rd, just n on Shepherd to Lexington, just e. 2005 Lexington 77098.
Continental **Hours:** 11 am-2 & 5-10 pm, Fri-11 pm, Sat 5 pm-11 pm. Closed major holidays; also Sun. **Reservations:** suggested; weekends. **Features:** Diners can bring their favorite recipe to the Continental eatery, and the cooks will do their best to please. The dining room has an elegant mahogany bar. Try chicken Marsala with mushrooms and grilled vegetables. Casual dress; cocktails. **Parking:** valet. **Cards:** AX, DC, DS, MC, VI.

MAGIC ISLAND   Dinner: $32-$40   Phone: 713/526-2442   (100)
△△▼▼ △△▼▼ **Location:** Just s of US 59 Southwest Frwy, at Kirby. 2215 Southwest Frwy 77098. **Hours:** 6:30 pm-midnight.
Continental Closed: 11/27, 12/25; also Sun & Mon. **Reservations:** required. **Features:** An Egyptian palace houses a dining experience that is as theatrical as it is culinary. Magic acts, comedy shows, psychics and games of chance and skill, thrill and delight as a friendly, professional staff serves up a variety of well-prepared meals. Dressy casual; cocktails; entertainment. **Parking:** valet. **Cards:** AX, CB, DC, DS, MC, VI.

MAGNOLIA BAR & GRILL   Lunch: $9-$20   Dinner: $13-$22   Phone: 713/781-6207   (78)
△△▼▼ △△▼▼ **Location:** Jct of Fountainview Rd and Richmond Ave. 6400 Richmond Ave, Suite 1 77057. **Hours:** 11 am-10 pm,
Seafood Fri & Sat-11 pm, Sun 10:30 am-10 pm. Closed: 12/25. **Features:** A Creole plantation, complete with shuttered windows and ceiling fans, provides the setting for sampling spicy etouffee and classic po'boy sandwiches. A stupendous Cajun brunch is offered on Sundays, and huge crawfish boils are hosted seasonally. Casual dress; cocktails. **Parking:** on-site. **Cards:** AX, CB, DC, DS, MC, VI.

MAMA'S CAFE   Lunch: $6-$14   Dinner: $6-$14   Phone: 713/266-8514   (52)
△△▼▼ **Location:** 6019 Westheimer Rd 77057. **Hours:** 6:30 am-1 am, Thurs & Fri-4 am, Sat 8 am-4 am, Sun 8 am-1
American am. Closed: 11/27. **Features:** Patrons can take a nostalgic trip to their mother's kitchen, where commemorative state plates line the dining room walls. Comfort foods—such as meatloaf, chicken-fried chicken, hamburgers and steaks—share menu space with a few Tex-Mex items. Breakfast is served until 11 a.m. Casual dress; cocktails. **Parking:** on-site. **Cards:** AX, CB, DC, DS, MC, VI.

(See map p. 374)

MARK'S
▼▼▼▼
American

Lunch: $12-$19   **Dinner:** $18-$31   **Phone:** 713/523-3800   **34**
Location: Northeast corner of Westheimer and Dunlavy. 1658 Westheimer 77006. **Hours:** 11 am-2 & 6-11 pm, Fri 11 am-2 & 5:30-midnight, Sat 5 pm-midnight, Sun 5 pm-10 pm. Closed major holidays. **Reservations:** suggested. **Features:** Located, very appropriately, in the arts district this eatery is housed in the shell of a 1920s church. The past of the interior resonates in the arched windows, high ceiling, loft, and modestly sized dining rooms. The theme here is American cuisine with such choices as lime grilled chicken, cobb salad, grilled lamb chops, and delightful desserts such as camp s'mores. All items are artistic and reflect the chef's creativity. Smoke free premises. Dressy casual; cocktails. **Parking:** on-site. **Cards:** AX, DC, DS, MC, VI.

MESA GRILL
▼▼
Mexican

Lunch: $7-$10   **Dinner:** $10-$17   **Phone:** 713/520-8900   **35**
Location: Between Shepherd and Woodhead sts. 1971 W Gray 77019. **Hours:** 11 am-10 pm, Fri & Sat-11 pm, Sun from 10 am. Closed: 11/27, 12/25. **Reservations:** suggested. **Features:** A colorful and contemporary Santa Fe style makes this eatery a romantic destination. Choose from a variety of steak and seafood dishes all in keeping with a Tex-Mex theme, and sample the famous chocolate mousse taco served in an almond shell. Casual dress; cocktails. **Parking:** valet. **Cards:** AX, DC, DS, MC, VI.

NINO'S
▼▼▼▼
Traditional Italian

Lunch: $11-$23   **Dinner:** $11-$28   **Phone:** 713/522-5120   **37**
Location: I-45, exit 47A (Allen Pkwy), 1.5 mi w to Montrose Blvd, s to W Dallas St, then just w. 2817 W Dallas St 77019. **Hours:** 11 am-2:30 & 5:30-10 pm, Fri-11 pm, Sat 5:30 pm-11 pm. Closed major holidays; also Sun. **Reservations:** suggested. **Features:** Featuring a variety of well-prepared dishes served in pleasant, convivial surroundings, this very popular restaurant specializes in excellent pasta, white beans with piquant homemade sausage, and tender roasted chicken served hot from the rotisserie. Casual dress; cocktails. **Parking:** on-site. **Cards:** AX, MC, VI.

OLD HEIDELBERG
▼
Ethnic

Lunch: $10-$19   **Dinner:** $10-$19   **Phone:** 713/781-3581   **21**
Location: Loop 610, exit 9 (San Felipe Rd) northbound; exit 9A (San Felipe/Westheimer rds) southbound, 2 mi w on San Felipe Rd. 1810 Fountainview Rd 77057. **Hours:** 11:30 am-2:30 & 5:30-2 am, Sat from 5:30 pm. Closed: Sun. **Reservations:** accepted. **Features:** Such tasty Teutonic treats as Wiener schnitzel and German potatoes are served in a Bavarian-themed atmosphere. While the dining room shares the ambience of the bar, a nice day is a good excuse to sit outside. Casual dress; cocktails; entertainment. **Parking:** on-site. **Cards:** AX, DC, DS, MC, VI.

OTTO'S BARBEQUE & HAMBURGERS
▼
American

Lunch: $4-$10   **Dinner:** $4-$10   **Phone:** 713/864-2573   **16**
Location: 0.6 mi w, jct Shepherd Rd and Memorial Blvd; between Reinke and Wescott sts. 5502 Memorial Dr 77007. **Hours:** 11 am-9 pm. Closed: 1/1, 7/4, 12/25; also Sun. **Features:** Otto's has been serving barbecue and burgers at two locations in Houston for almost 50 years. A popular barbecue restaurant where you may run into a celebrity. Pictures on the walls of ex-president George Bush, Warren Moon (quarterback) and Tommy Lee Jones (movie star). All have enjoyed the "Down-Home Texas BBQ". Casual dress; beer only. **Parking:** on-site. **Cards:** AX, CB, DC, DS, MC, VI.

OUISIE'S TABLE
▼▼▼
American

Lunch: $8-$23   **Dinner:** $16-$30   **Phone:** 713/528-2264   **27**
Location: Just w of Weslayan on southside of San Felipe Rd; between Weslayan and Drexel Dr. 3939 San Felipe Rd 77027. **Hours:** 11 am-10 pm, Fri-11 pm, Sat 10 am-2:30 & 5:30-11 pm. Closed major holidays. **Reservations:** suggested. **Features:** Enjoy selections like chicken-fried steak, grilled salmon and egg salad sandwiches in the main dining hall with its high ceilings and large fireplace; or choose a smaller room with French doors that open onto a small garden for more intimate gatherings. Smoke free premises. Casual dress; cocktails. **Parking:** on-site. **Cards:** AX, CB, DC, DS, MC, VI.

PALAZZO'S ITALIAN CAFE
▼▼
Italian

Lunch: $6-$16   **Dinner:** $7-$16   **Phone:** 713/529-6959   **62**
Location: W on Westheimer Rd; between Kirby Dr and River Oaks Blvd. 3215 Westheimer Rd 77098. **Hours:** 11 am-10 pm, Fri-11 pm, Sat 5 pm-11 pm. Closed: 12/25. **Features:** Mustard-colored walls and consigned art lend to the casually soothing mood of the dining room. Diners can sample personal pizzas, pasta entrees or a classic dish, such as chicken Marsala. Patio seating is an option. Casual dress; cocktails. **Parking:** on-site. **Cards:** AX, MC, VI.

THE PALM RESTAURANT OF HOUSTON
▼▼▼
Steak & Seafood

Lunch: $14-$17   **Dinner:** $15-$32   **Phone:** 713/977-2544   **44**
Location: Between Fountainview Rd and Voss. 6100 Westheimer Rd 77057. **Hours:** 11 am-11 pm, Sat from 5 pm, Sun 5 pm-10 pm. Closed major holidays. **Reservations:** suggested. **Features:** The original restaurant was born in New York City in the 1920s, but this eatery carries on the tradition of the white-tablecloth steakhouse. Although steaks are the claim to fame, the menu also lists veal and seafood choices. Drawings of famous and not-so-famous people line the walls. Servers are friendly and attentive. Casual dress; cocktails. **Parking:** valet. **Cards:** AX, CB, DC, DS, MC, VI.

PAPPAS BROS STEAKHOUSE
▼▼▼
Steak House

Dinner: $30-$74   **Phone:** 713/780-7352   **49**
Location: Between Chimney Rock St and Fountainview Rd. 5839 Westheimer Rd 77057. **Hours:** 5 pm-10 pm, Fri & Sat-11 pm. Closed major holidays; also Sun. **Reservations:** suggested. **Features:** The beef is prime; the wine list boasts more than 500 entries; cigars and expensive liquors are offered after dinner; and you can mix and match any number of side dishes you like with your steak. No wonder this popular restaurant recommends reservations! Dressy casual; cocktails; entertainment. **Parking:** valet. **Cards:** AX, MC, VI.

PAPPASITO'S CANTINA
▼▼
Mexican

Lunch: $6-$19   **Dinner:** $6-$19   **Phone:** 713/784-5253   **80**
Location: SR 59, exit Hillcroft St, 1 mi w, then just n. 6445 Richmond Ave 77057. **Hours:** 11 am-10 pm, Fri & Sat-11 pm. Closed: 11/27, 12/25. **Reservations:** accepted. **Features:** Mexican and Tex-Mex cuisines are served at this airy eatery which also features outdoor dining. The fajitas are delivered to your table sizzling. Don't pass up the ice cream with cinnamon on chocolate bread pudding for dessert. Casual dress; cocktails. **Parking:** on-site. **Cards:** AX, DC, DS, MC, VI.

(See map p. 374)

PAPPAS SEAFOOD HOUSE AND OYSTER BAR   **Lunch:** $14-$25   **Dinner:** $14-$31   **Phone:** 713/784-4729   (98)
▼▼ ▼▼
Seafood
MC, VI.
Location: Sw off US 59, exit Hillcroft St. 6894 Southwest Frwy 77074. **Hours:** 11 am-10 pm, Fri & Sat-11 pm. Closed: 11/27, 12/25. **Features:** This quaint, family-owned cafe lists a variety of Southcoast seafood on its menu. Fried shrimp is served with butter sauce. The dining room is done in soothing blue and maroon tones, and family photographs cover the walls. Casual dress; cocktails. **Parking:** on-site. **Cards:** AX, MC, VI.

PATISSERIE DÉSCOURS   **Lunch:** $5-$7   **Phone:** 713/681-8894   (10)
▼▼
Bakery/Desserts
Location: I-10, exit 761A (Wirt Rd), 0.6 mi n. 1330-D Wirt Rd 77055. **Hours:** 5:30 pm-9 pm, Fri & Sat-10 pm. Closed major holidays; also Sun & Mon. **Features:** Known city-wide for its desserts, the sandwiches and soups also are fantastic. Smoke free premises. Casual dress. **Parking:** on-site. **Cards:** DS, MC, VI.

PINO'S ITALIAN RESTAURANT   **Lunch:** $9-$12   **Dinner:** $11-$21   **Phone:** 713/783-2232   (41)
▼▼ ▼▼
Italian
Location: 1.5 mi n of jct US 59 (Southwest Frwy), exit Hillcroft St; 3 mi w of W Loop 610, exit Westheimer Rd; at Hillcroft St and Westheimer Rd. 2711 Hillcroft St 77057. **Hours:** 11 am-3 & 5-9:30 pm, Fri & Sat-10 pm. Closed major holidays; also Sun. **Reservations:** accepted. **Features:** Casual family dining features a variety of well-prepared dishes including homemade pasta with chicken, beef and seafood options. Having operated under the same ownership since 1960, it offers consistently good service and reliably tasty meals. Casual dress; cocktails. **Parking:** on-site. **Cards:** AX, CB, DC, DS, MC, VI.

POST OAK GRILL   **Lunch:** $8-$15   **Dinner:** $13-$26   **Phone:** 713/993-9966   (15)
▼▼▼▼▼
Traditional
American
DS, MC, VI.
Location: Between San Felipe Rd and Wood Way, just w. 1415 S Post Oak Ln 77056. **Hours:** 11 am-11 pm, Fri & Sat-1 am. Closed major holidays; also Sun. **Reservations:** suggested. **Features:** A cozy dining room tucked away near The Pavilion, it provides guests with a straightforward menu of pasta dishes, grilled entrees and fresh salads. Choose from a variety of daily bistro classics such as roasted lamb shanks or trout with lemon butter. Semi-formal attire; cocktails; entertainment. **Parking:** on-site. **Cards:** AX, CB, DC,

PREGO RESTAURANT   **Lunch:** $9-$23   **Dinner:** $11-$23   **Phone:** 713/529-2420   (108)
▼▼ ▼▼
Italian
Location: SR 59, exit Kirby Dr, 1 mi s to Amherst St, just e; in University Village. 2520 Amherst St 77005. **Hours:** 11 am-10 pm, Fri & Sat-11 pm. Closed major holidays. **Reservations:** suggested. **Features:** Boisterous and bustling, this casual dining room features a mouthwatering variety of fresh, well-prepared dishes served in ample portions. For a delicious Tex-Mex twist, try the jalapeno fettuccine with grilled chicken, tomatoes, onions and black beans. Casual dress; cocktails. **Parking:** on-site. **Cards:** AX, MC, VI.

PRINCE'S   **Lunch:** $5-$9   **Dinner:** $5-$9   **Phone:** 713/722-8822   (7)
▼▼
American
Location: I-10, exit 758A (Bunkerhill), on south serivce road. 9535 Katy Frwy, Suite A 77024. **Hours:** 11 am-10 pm, Fri & Sat-11 pm. Closed: 1/1, 11/27, 12/25. **Features:** A pioneer in the carhop business and a fun tribute to the early 'n' roll era, this diner features a nifty jukebox, milkshakes served right out of the metal blender cup, and a full slate of 1950s-style fast food, such as cheeseburgers and home fries. Casual dress; beer only. **Parking:** on-site. **Cards:** AX, DC, DS, MC, VI.

RAINBOW LODGE   **Lunch:** $8-$17   **Dinner:** $16-$32   **Phone:** 713/861-8666   (14)
ⒶⒶⒶ
▼▼▼▼▼
Regional
Continental
Location: Just e of jct Wescott St and Memorial Dr to Birdsall, just s. 1 Birdsall 77007. **Hours:** 11:30 am-10:30 pm, Sat from 6 pm, Sun from 10:30 am. Closed: 1/1, 12/25; also Mon. **Reservations:** suggested. **Features:** Built circa 1935, this rustic restaurant overlooks Buffalo Bayou. A romantic mixture of rich wood, antiques and hunting/fishing themes creates a cozy, "great outdoors" feel. Only the freshest ingredients are used in the wild game and seafood specialties. Cocktails. **Parking:** on-site. **Cards:** AX, CB, DC, DS, MC, VI.

REDWOOD GRIL   **Lunch:** $9-$22   **Dinner:** $9-$26   **Phone:** 713/523-4611   (103)
▼▼▼▼▼
American
Location: 0.9 mi s of jct Montrose Blvd and Westheimer Rd. 4611 Montrose Blvd 77006. **Hours:** 11 am-2 & 5:30-10 pm, Sat from 5:30 pm, Sun 5:30 pm-9 pm. Closed: 1/1, 12/25. **Reservations:** suggested. **Features:** Venison chops with a generous serving of mashed potatoes and salmon in a tasty pistachio crust are among the many innovative and creatively designed dishes served at this popular eatery. Whimsical wall murals provide a casual backdrop for the more serious power lunches that seem to occur regularly here. USA Today once branded the restaurant "one of Houston's top five lunch spots.". Smoke free premises. Semi-formal attire; cocktails. **Parking:** valet. **Cards:** AX, CB, DC, DS, MC, VI.

THE REMINGTON   **Lunch:** $15-$20   **Dinner:** $25-$31   **Phone:** 713/840-7600   (24)
▼▼▼ ▼▼▼
Continental
Location: I-610, exit 9A (San Felipe/Westheimer rds), 0.3 mi e; in The St. Regis Houston. 1919 Briar Oaks Ln 77027. **Hours:** 6:30 am-2:30 & 5:30-11:30 pm. **Reservations:** suggested. **Features:** Fine dining in elegant atmosphere. Smoke free premises. Dressy casual; cocktails; entertainment. **Parking:** valet. **Cards:** AX, CB, DC, DS, JC, MC, VI.

RIVER OAKS GRILL   **Dinner:** $21-$30   **Phone:** 713/520-1738   (65)
▼▼▼ ▼▼
American
Location: 0.5 mi n of jct US 59, exit Kirby Dr, just s. 2630 Westheimer Rd 77098. **Hours:** 5:30 pm-10 pm, Fri & Sat-11 pm. Closed major holidays; also Sun. **Reservations:** suggested. **Features:** In the affluent neighborhood that shares its name, the traditional grill serves progressive American preparations of steak, seafood and veal. The fine wood interior, sparkling tables and nostalgic murals provide the background for a decidedly adult dining experience. Portions are overwhelming, and live piano music is played nightly. Dressy casual; cocktails; entertainment. **Parking:** valet. **Cards:** AX, DC, DS, MC, VI.

(See map p. 374)

RUGGLES GRILL
♦♦♦ ♦♦♦

American

Lunch: $10-$19   **Dinner:** $10-$19   **Phone:** 713/524-3839   (74)
Location: Just e of Montrose Blvd. 903 Westheimer Rd 77006. **Hours:** 11 am-2 & 5:30-11 pm, Fri & Sat-midnight, Sun 11 am-4 pm & 5:30-10 pm. Closed: 11/27, 12/25; also Mon. **Reservations:** suggested. **Features:** Enjoy casual dining set in a bustling atmosphere and featuring a variety of well-prepared entrees including beef, chicken and seafood dishes. Only the freshest ingredients are used in such selections as grilled chicken in a flavorful tequila-butter sauce. Casual dress; cocktails. **Parking:** valet. **Cards:** AX, DC, MC, VI.

☒

SCOTT'S CELLAR
♦♦♦ ♦♦♦ ♦♦♦

Continental

Lunch: $8-$15   **Dinner:** $14-$30   **Phone:** 713/785-8889   (28)
Location: I-610, exit 9 (San Felipe Rd) northbound; exit 9A (San Felipe/Westheimer rds) southbound, 2.8 mi w on San Felipe Rd, northeast corner of Voss and San Felipe Rd. 6540 San Felipe Rd 77057. **Hours:** 11 am-2:30 & 5:30-10:30 pm, Fri-11 pm, Sat 5:30 pm-11 pm. Closed major holidays; also Sun. **Reservations:** suggested. **Features:** Don't expect Chinese here. Owner and chef Scott Chen artfully fuses French and Asian cuisines. Temptations include grilled foie gras, soft-shell crab, filet mignon and teriyaki chicken. The dessert menu is equally pleasing. If you decide to order wine, plan to stay awhile, as the wine list is a feat. Servers are formal and attentive, and a pianist entertains most evenings. Dressy casual; cocktails; entertainment. **Parking:** on-site and valet. **Cards:** AX, CB, DC, DS, JC, MC, VI.

⬛ ☒

SHANGHAI RIVER
♦♦♦ ♦♦♦

Traditional Chinese

Lunch: $7-$17   **Dinner:** $7-$17   **Phone:** 713/528-5528   (69)
Location: Between Kirby and Shepherd drs. 2407 Westheimer Rd 77098. **Hours:** 11 am-10 pm, Fri & Sat-11 pm. Closed: 12/25. **Reservations:** accepted. **Features:** This lovely restaurant offers traditional cuisine featuring chicken, beef, seafood and vegetarian dishes. Try a large helping of the delicious cashew chicken and shrimp with fried rice, an egg roll and dark, crispy walnuts with a wonderful sugary taste. Casual dress; cocktails. **Parking:** on-site. **Cards:** AX, CB, DC, MC, VI.

🍽 ☒

SHUG'S CAFE & RESTAURANT
♦♦♦ ♦♦♦

American

Lunch: $8-$15   **Phone:** 713/688-0068   (9)
Location: I-610, exit 11B (Katy Rd) southbound, 0.4 mi to Katy Rd, just w, then 0.6 mi s; exit 10 (Woodway and Memorial Dr) northbound, just w. 520 N Post Oak Rd 77024. **Hours:** 11 am-2 pm. Closed major holidays. **Features:** A casual spot, it offers a simple menu with most dishes being a comfortable mix of Italian and Gulf Coast sensibilities. Chicken parmesan, fresh garlic bread, homemade salad dressings and desserts, are all served in large, tasty portions. Casual dress; cocktails. **Parking:** on-site. **Cards:** AX, MC, VI.

☒

SIERRA GRILL
♦♦♦ ♦♦♦

American

Dinner: $12-$24   **Phone:** 713/942-7757   (101)
Location: 0.9 mi s of jct Montrose Blvd and Westheimer Rd. 4704 Montrose Blvd 77006. **Hours:** 5 pm-10 pm, Fri & Sat-11 pm. Closed: 11/27, 12/25. **Reservations:** suggested. **Features:** The restaurant invites guests to take a walk on the wild side with such unusual entrees as wild boar enchiladas, ostrich and venison. The pecan and chocolate torte with peanut butter ice cream is smooth and scrumptious. Dishes emphasize specially selected herbs. Live music is a nice touch Wednesday through Saturday from 10 p.m. to 1:30 a.m. Dressy casual; cocktails. **Parking:** on-site. **Cards:** AX, CB, DC, DS, MC, VI.

🍽 ☒

STAR PIZZA
♦

Pizza

Lunch: $7-$12   **Dinner:** $10-$18   **Phone:** 713/523-0800   (82)
Location: US 59 S; between Shepherd and Greenbriar Dr. 2111 Norfolk 77098. **Hours:** 11 am-10:30 pm, Fri & Sat-midnight. Closed: 4/20, 11/27, 12/25. **Reservations:** accepted. **Features:** Near the arts district, the eatery offers outside dining on a spacious wrap-around patio. Service here is casual, as if the waiters are used to waiting on their classmates. Pizza is sold by the pie or the slice, and even buffet-style at lunch. Other menu selections include pasta dishes, sandwiches and salads. Smoke free premises. Casual dress; beer & wine only. **Parking:** on-site. **Cards:** AX, DS, MC, VI.

☒

TEPPAY
♦♦♦ ♦♦♦

Ethnic

Dinner: $12-$40   **Phone:** 713/789-4506   (40)
Location: At Voss. 6516 A-2 Westheimer Rd 77057. **Hours:** 6 pm-11 pm. Closed major holidays; also Sun. **Reservations:** suggested; for dinner. **Features:** Sushi is the specialty at this Oriental cafe. Start your meal with the complimentary fried octopus and onion appetizer. The catfish is marinated and broiled. Japanese photographs and decor accent the attractive dining room. Casual dress; cocktails. **Parking:** on-site. **Cards:** AX, DS, MC, VI.

☒

TEXADELPHIA
♦

American

Lunch: $4-$6   **Dinner:** $4-$6   **Phone:** 713/785-6700   (50)
Location: Between Fountainview Rd and Voss. 6025 Westheimer Rd 77057. **Hours:** 11 am-10 pm, Fri & Sat-11 pm. Closed major holidays. **Features:** Texas cheese steak and beer are the name of the game at the laid-back eatery. While catching up on sports statistics, guests can wash down customized sandwiches and juicy burgers with a selection from an encyclopedia of beers. Casual dress; beer & wine only. **Parking:** on-site. **Cards:** AX, CB, DS, MC, VI.

🍽

TONY'S
♦♦♦ ♦♦♦ ♦♦♦

Continental

Dinner: $25-$39   **Phone:** 713/622-6778   (47)
Location: I-610, exit 8C (Westheimer Rd) northbound; exit 9A (San Felipe/Westheimer rds) southbound, just n of Westheimer Rd, then just s of San Felipe Rd. 1801 Post Oak Blvd 77056. **Hours:** 6 pm-11 pm, Fri & Sat-midnight. Closed major holidays; also Sun. **Reservations:** suggested. **Features:** In the Galleria area, the elegant Italian-Continental restaurant serves expertly prepared and artfully appealing dishes. The menu blends made-to-order seafood and meat offerings, from scaloppine of lobster Bristow to roasted Nimen Ranch boar chop. Pepper-crusted tuna with Asian risotto is superb. The wine list is extensive and generally expensive, with some more modest selections. Service is excellent. Semi-formal attire; cocktails; entertainment. **Parking:** on-site and valet. **Cards:** AX, CB, DC, DS, MC, VI.

🍽 ☒

(See map p. 374)

TONY MANDOLA'S BLUE OYSTER BAR **Lunch:** $9-$20 **Dinner:** $10-$25 **Phone:** 713/680-3333 (8)

Seafood

Location: I-10, exit 761A (Wirt Rd) westbound; exit 761B (Antoine Rd) eastbound, on south service road. 7947 Katy Frwy 77024. **Hours:** 11 am-9 pm, Fri-10 pm, Sat 5 pm-10 pm, Sun 11 am-9 pm. Closed major holidays. **Reservations:** suggested; weekends. **Features:** Resembling an old saloon, the comfortable dining room includes many nautical touches of mounted fish and oceanic art. The friendly staff provides homey service and delivers simple, tasty meals, such as charbroiled snapper and Mexican-inspired ceviche. Casual dress; cocktails. **Parking:** on-site. **Cards:** AX, DC, MC, VI.

TRULUCK'S STEAK & STONE CRAB **Lunch:** $10-$16 **Dinner:** $11-$27 **Phone:** 713/783-7270 (46)

Steak & Seafood

Location: Jct Fountainview Rd, just w. 5919 Westheimer Rd 77057. **Hours:** 11 am-10 pm, Fri-11 pm, Sat noon-11 pm. Closed: 1/1, 11/27, 12/25. **Reservations:** accepted. **Features:** Casual yet sophisticated, the decor is suggestive of a 1950s diner, but with an upscale sensibility. Steak and stone crab are house specialties, but don't miss the grilled sesame tuna with parmesan potatoes or the triple chocolate "malt" cake for dessert. Casual dress; cocktails. **Parking:** on-site and valet. **Cards:** AX, CB, DC, DS, MC, VI.

VAN LOC RESTAURANT **Lunch:** $4-$10 **Dinner:** $4-$10 **Phone:** 713/528-6441 (91)

Ethnic

Location: 0.8 mi s on Milam, just n of Elgin. 3010 Milam 77006. **Hours:** 9 am-11 pm, Fri & Sat-midnight. Closed: 11/27. **Features:** The spring rolls at this Vietnamese restaurant are handmade and filled with fresh shrimp and pork. The seasoned vegetables and rice are delicious. Green tones and statues of Buddha accent the bustling dining area. Casual dress; beer & wine only. **Parking:** on-site. **Cards:** AX, MC, VI.

VINCENT'S RESTAURANT **Lunch:** $9-$26 **Dinner:** $9-$26 **Phone:** 713/528-4313 (39)

Traditional Italian

Location: I-45, exit 47A (Allen Pkwy), 1.5 mi w to Montrose Blvd, s to W Dallas St, just w. 2701 W Dallas St 77019. **Hours:** 11 am-3 & 5-10 pm, Fri & Sat 5 pm-11 pm. Closed: Sun. **Reservations:** accepted. **Features:** Family owned and operated, this restaurant offers a nice view of the downtown skyline that's particularly stunning during the Fourth of July fireworks. While taking in the sights, enjoy the popular house specialty, pecan-wood-fired rotisserie chicken. Casual dress; cocktails. **Parking:** on-site. **Cards:** AX, CB, DC, MC, VI.

WINGS N THINGS **Lunch:** $4-$8 **Dinner:** $4-$8 **Phone:** 713/592-8579 (105)

American

Location: I-610, exit 1C (Kirby), 1.1 mi n. 2491 S Braeswood 77054. **Hours:** 11 am-10 pm, Fri & Sat-11 pm. Closed major holidays. **Features:** Although the name points to the obvious—delicious wings spiced to diners' liking—the eatery also serves sandwiches and salads. Casual dress; beer only. **Parking:** on-site. **Cards:** AX, DC, DS, MC, VI.

The following restaurant has not been evaluated by AAA but is listed for your information only.

ANTONE'S **Phone:** 713/667-3400

fyi

Not evaluated. **Location:** I-610, exit 1B (Kirby Dr), 0.3 mi n. 8110 Kirby Dr 77054. **Features:** Barrels of olives, bulk grains, crates of wine and imported meats fill this grocery and delicatessen with a pleasing array of sights, smells and tastes. Antone's po'boys are a Houston tradition, either made-to-order or pre-wrapped for the lunch crowd. Smoke free premises.

HOUSTON pop. 1,953,631 (See map p. 382; index p. 384)

WHERE TO STAY

ADAM'S MARK HOUSTON **Phone:** (713)978-7400 (170)

AAA SAVE

Large-scale Hotel

All Year 1P: $146-$236 2P: $161-$251 XP: $15 F18

Location: Just s of Westheimer Rd. 2900 Briarpark Dr 77042. Fax: 713/735-2726. **Facility:** 604 units. 556 one-bedroom standard units. 48 one-bedroom suites ($194-$394), some with whirlpools. 10 stories, interior corridors. *Bath:* combo or shower only. **Parking:** on-site. **Terms:** 2-3 night minimum stay - seasonal, package plans - weekends. **Amenities:** video games (fee), voice mail, irons, hair dryers. **Dining:** 6 am-10 pm, cocktails. **Pool(s):** heated indoor/outdoor, 2 wading. **Leisure Activities:** saunas, whirlpool, putting green. *Fee:* massage, game room. **Guest Services:** gift shop, valet and coin laundry, area transportation-the Galleria. **Business Services:** conference facilities, business center. **Cards:** AX, CB, DC, DS, JC, MC, VI. **Special Amenities: early check-in/late check-out and preferred room (subject to availability with advanced reservations).**

SOME UNITS

24 DATA PORT / VCR / FEE FEE

AINSWORTH SUITES **Phone:** 713/785-3415 (168)

Motel

All Year 1P: $89-$189 2P: $89-$189 XP: $10 F17

Location: US 59 (Southwest Frwy), exit Hillcroft St. 6910 Southwest Frwy 77074. Fax: 713/785-1130. **Facility:** 151 units. 113 one-bedroom standard units with kitchens. 38 one-bedroom suites with kitchens. 2 stories, exterior corridors. **Parking:** on-site. **Terms:** weekly rates available, [BP] meal plan available, 17% service charge, small pets only ($15 fee). **Amenities:** video games (fee), voice mail, irons. **Pool(s):** heated outdoor. **Leisure Activities:** whirlpools, sports court. **Guest Services:** complimentary evening beverages: Mon-Thurs, coin laundry, area transportation. **Business Services:** meeting rooms, fax (fee). **Cards:** AX, CB, DC, DS, JC, MC, VI.

SOME UNITS

ASK DATA PORT / VCR /

AMERISUITES (HOUSTON INTERCONTINENTAL AIRPORT/GREENSPOINT) **Phone:** (281)820-6060 (204)

AAA SAVE

Small-scale Hotel

All Year [ECP] 1P: $129 2P: $139

Location: Sam Houston Pkwy (Beltway 8), exit Imperial Valley, 0.8 mi w on frontage road; exit Hardy Toll Rd, turn under parkway, 1.2 mi w on west frontage road eastbound. 300 Ronan Park Pl 77060. Fax: 281/820-6464. **Facility:** 127 one-bedroom standard units. 6 stories, interior corridors. *Bath:* combo or shower only. **Parking:** on-site. **Terms:** weekly rates available, package plans, small pets only. **Amenities:** video games (fee), voice mail, irons, hair dryers. *Some:* dual phone lines. **Pool(s):** heated outdoor. **Leisure Activities:** exercise room. **Guest Services:** valet and coin laundry, airport transportation-George Bush Intercontinental Airport, area transportation-within 3 mi. **Business Services:** meeting rooms, fax (fee). **Cards:** AX, CB, DC, DS, MC, VI. **Special Amenities: free continental breakfast and free newspaper.** *(See color ad p 391)*

SOME UNITS

VCR DATA PORT / /

(See map p. 382)

BAYMONT INN & SUITES HOUSTON-GREENSPOINT   Phone: (281)875-2000   197
AAA SAVE   All Year [ECP]   1P: $49-$69   2P: $49-$69
▽▽▽▽   **Location:** I-45, exit 61 (Greens Rd), on southbound frontage road; northbound, just w on Greens Rd, just n on North-
borough, then just e on Glenborough. 12701 North Frwy 77060. Fax: 281/875-3459. **Facility:** 101 units. 97 one-
Small-scale Hotel   bedroom standard units. 4 one-bedroom suites ($69-$119). 4 stories, interior corridors. *Bath:* combo or
shower only. **Parking:** on-site. **Terms:** small pets only ($50 deposit). **Amenities:** video games (fee), voice
mail, irons, hair dryers. **Pool(s):** outdoor. **Guest Services:** valet and coin laundry, airport transportation-
George Bush Intercontinental Airport. **Business Services:** fax (fee). **Cards:** AX, CB, DC, DS, MC, VI. **Special Amenities:** free
continental breakfast and free newspaper.
SOME UNITS
🔊 ✈ 🐕 🍴 🛁 ☕ ⊇ 🎥 [DATA PORT] 💻 / ✕ 🔒 🖥 /

BAYMONT INN & SUITES HOUSTON SOUTHWEST   Phone: (713)784-3838   130
AAA SAVE   All Year [ECP]   1P: $54-$64   2P: $54-$64
▽▽▽▽   **Location:** Southwest Frwy (US 59), exit Hillcroft St/W Park eastbound; exit Hillcroft St westbound. 6790 Southwest Frwy
77074. Fax: 713/784-3189. **Facility:** 119 units. 115 one-bedroom standard units. 4 one-bedroom suites ($59-
$79). 4 stories, interior corridors. *Bath:* combo or shower only. **Parking:** on-site. **Terms:** small pets only ($50
Small-scale Hotel   deposit, in designated units). **Amenities:** video games (fee), voice mail, irons, hair dryers. **Pool(s):** heated
outdoor. **Guest Services:** coin laundry. **Business Services:** meeting rooms, fax (fee). **Cards:** AX, CB, DC,
DS, MC, VI. **Special Amenities:** free continental breakfast and free newspaper.
SOME UNITS
🔊 🐕 🛁 ⊇ 🎥 [DATA PORT] 💻 / ✕ 🔒 🖥

BEST WESTERN EXECUTIVE SUITES HOTEL   Phone: (281)866-0500   117
AAA SAVE   All Year [ECP]   1P: $62-$69   2P: $62-$69
▽▽▽▽   **Location:** Just e of jct with Veterans Memorial Dr. 4434 FM 1960 W 77068. Fax: 281/866-0599. **Facility:** 70 units.
69 one-bedroom standard units, some with whirlpools. 1 one-bedroom suite with kitchen. 3 stories, interior
corridors. *Bath:* combo or shower only. **Parking:** on-site. **Amenities:** irons, hair dryers. **Pool(s):** heated out-
Small-scale Hotel   door. **Leisure Activities:** whirlpool, exercise room. **Guest Services:** valet and coin laundry, area
transportation-within 5 mi. **Business Services:** meeting rooms, business center. **Cards:** AX, CB, DC, DS,
MC, VI. **Special Amenities:** free continental breakfast and free newspaper.
SOME UNITS
🔊 🛁 ⊇ 🎥 [DATA PORT] 🔒 🖥 💻 / ✕ [VCR] /

(See map p. 382)

BEST WESTERN GREENSPOINT INN & SUITES
Phone: (281)873-7575   190

(AAA) SAVE

Small-scale Hotel

All Year [ECP]   1P: $67-$115   2P: $69-$115
Location: I-45, exit 63 (Airtex Dr), on southbound frontage road. 14753 North Frwy 77090. Fax: 281/873-7594. **Facility:** 50 one-bedroom standard units, some with whirlpools. 3 stories, interior corridors. *Bath:* combo or shower only. **Parking:** on-site. **Amenities:** video library, high-speed Internet, voice mail, irons, hair dryers. *Some:* dual phone lines. **Pool(s):** outdoor. **Leisure Activities:** exercise room. **Guest Services:** complimentary evening beverages: Mon-Thurs, valet and coin laundry, airport transportation-George Bush Intercontinental Airport, area transportation-within 2 mi. **Business Services:** meeting rooms, business center. **Cards:** AX, CB, DC, DS, JC, MC, VI. **Special Amenities: free continental breakfast and free newspaper.**

SOME UNITS

BEST WESTERN WESTCHASE MINI SUITES
Phone: (713)782-1515   163

(AAA) SAVE

Small-scale Hotel

All Year [ECP]   1P: $79-$89   2P: $79-$89   XP: $10   F16
Location: Just w of Sam Houston Blvd and Westheimer Rd on southbound frontage road. 2950 W Sam Houston Pkwy S 77042. Fax: 713/782-9996. **Facility:** 61 units. 60 one-bedroom standard units. 1 one-bedroom suite ($109-$149) with whirlpool. 2 stories, interior corridors. *Bath:* combo or shower only. **Parking:** on-site. **Amenities:** high-speed Internet, dual phone lines, voice mail, irons, hair dryers. **Pool(s):** outdoor. **Leisure Activities:** whirlpool, exercise room. **Guest Services:** complimentary evening beverages: Mon-Thurs, valet laundry. **Business Services:** meeting rooms, fax (fee). **Cards:** AX, CB, DC, DS, JC, MC, VI.

SOME UNITS

BRADFORD HOMESUITES PARK 10 WEST
Phone: (281)646-9990   129

Small-scale Hotel

All Year [CP]   1P: $89   2P: $119
Location: I-10, just s to Grisby, then just w. 15405 Katy Frwy (I-10) 77094. Fax: 281/646-9984. **Facility:** 120 units. 99 one-bedroom standard units with efficiencies. 21 one-bedroom suites ($89-$119) with efficiencies. 3 stories, interior corridors. *Bath:* combo or shower only. **Parking:** on-site. **Terms:** cancellation fee imposed. **Amenities:** video games (fee), dual phone lines, voice mail, irons, hair dryers. **Pool(s):** outdoor. **Leisure Activities:** whirlpool, exercise room. **Guest Services:** sundries, complimentary evening beverages: Wed, valet and coin laundry. **Business Services:** meeting rooms, business center. **Cards:** AX, CB, DC, DS, JC, MC, VI.

SOME UNITS

CANDLEWOOD SUITES-HOUSTON-CLEAR LAKE
Phone: (281)461-3060   106

Small-scale Hotel

All Year   1P: $84-$104   2P: $103-$129
Location: I-45, exit 26, 3.7 mi e. 2737 Bay Area Blvd 77058. Fax: 281/461-6133. **Facility:** 122 units. 98 one-bedroom standard units with efficiencies. 24 one-bedroom suites with efficiencies. 3 stories, interior corridors. *Bath:* combo or shower only. **Parking:** on-site. **Terms:** cancellation fee imposed. **Amenities:** video library, CD players, dual phone lines, voice mail, irons, hair dryers. **Leisure Activities:** exercise room. **Guest Services:** complimentary laundry. **Business Services:** fax. **Cards:** AX, CB, DC, DS, JC, MC, VI.

SOME UNITS

CANDLEWOOD SUITES-TOWN & COUNTRY
Phone: 713/464-2677   108

Small-scale Hotel

All Year   1P: $109-$119   2P: $119-$129
Location: I-10, exit 755 eastbound, 1.1 mi on frontage road to Town & Country Blvd, 0.4 mi s; exit 756A westbound under I-10, just e to Town & Country Blvd, 0.4 mi s. 10503 Town & Country Way 77024. Fax: 713/464-1185. **Facility:** 122 units. 98 one-bedroom standard units with efficiencies. 24 one-bedroom suites with efficiencies. 3 stories, interior corridors. *Bath:* combo or shower only. **Parking:** on-site. **Amenities:** video library, CD players, dual phone lines, voice mail, irons, hair dryers. **Leisure Activities:** exercise room. **Guest Services:** sundries, valet and coin laundry. **Business Services:** fax. **Cards:** AX, CB, DC, DS, JC, MC, VI.

SOME UNITS

CANDLEWOOD SUITES-WESTCHASE
Phone: (713)780-7881   109

Small-scale Hotel

All Year   1P: $49-$129   2P: $49-$129
Location: Sam Houston Pkwy (Beltway 8), exit Westpark, southeast corner of Westpark and Beltway 8 on northbound frontage road. 4033 W Sam Houston Pkwy S 77042. Fax: 713/780-3550. **Facility:** 123 units. 101 one-bedroom standard units with efficiencies. 22 one-bedroom suites with efficiencies. 3 stories, interior corridors. *Bath:* combo or shower only. **Parking:** on-site. **Terms:** weekly rates available. **Amenities:** video library, CD players, dual phone lines, voice mail, irons, hair dryers. **Leisure Activities:** exercise room. **Guest Services:** sundries, valet and coin laundry. **Business Services:** fax (fee). **Cards:** AX, CB, DC, DS, JC, MC, VI.

SOME UNITS

CHAMPIONS LODGE MOTEL
Phone: (281)587-9171   202

Motel

All Year   1P: $39-$65   XP: $3   F16
Location: I-45, exit 66, 4.7 mi sw. 4726 FM 1960 W 77069. Fax: 281/587-0258. **Facility:** 67 one-bedroom standard units. 2 stories, exterior corridors. **Parking:** on-site. **Terms:** cancellation fee imposed, weekly rates available, package plans - seasonal, weekends. **Pool(s):** small outdoor. **Business Services:** meeting rooms. **Cards:** AX, DS, MC, VI.

SOME UNITS

CLARION INN INTERCONTINENTAL AIRPORT
Phone: (281)931-0101   142

SAVE

Large-scale Hotel

All Year   1P: $79-$109   2P: $79-$119   XP: $5   F19
Location: Beltway 8, 1.4 mi e of I-45, exit 60B (Hardy Toll Rd) eastbound; exit Imperial Valley Dr westbound. 500 N Sam Houston Pkwy 77060. Fax: 281/931-3523. **Facility:** 220 units. 216 one-bedroom standard units. 4 one-bedroom suites. 2 stories, interior corridors. **Parking:** on-site. **Amenities:** voice mail, irons. **Pool(s):** 2 outdoor. **Leisure Activities:** exercise room. *Fee:* game room. **Guest Services:** gift shop, valet and coin laundry, area transportation. **Business Services:** meeting rooms, PC, fax (fee). **Cards:** AX, CB, DC, DS, JC, MC, VI.

SOME UNITS

(See map p. 382)

COMFORT INN
AAA SAVE
▽▽ ▽▽
Small-scale Hotel

Phone: (713)783-1400 **172**
All Year [ECP] 1P: $69 2P: $79 XP: $10 F14
Location: Just w of jct Fondren. 9041 Westheimer Rd 77063. Fax: 713/783-8301. **Facility:** 74 units. 51 one-bedroom standard units, some with whirlpools. 23 one-bedroom suites ($89-$99). 2 stories, exterior corridors. **Parking:** on-site. **Terms:** small pets only ($25 fee). **Amenities:** voice mail, safes, irons, hair dryers. **Pool(s):** outdoor. **Leisure Activities:** exercise room. **Guest Services:** valet and coin laundry. **Business Services:** fax (fee). **Cards:** AX, CB, DC, DS, JC, MC, VI. **Special Amenities:** free continental breakfast and free local telephone calls.

SOME UNITS

COMFORT INN EAST HOUSTON
AAA SAVE
▽▽▽▽
Small-scale Hotel

Phone: (713)455-8888 **110**
All Year [ECP] 1P: $61-$86 2P: $66-$91 XP: $5 F18
Location: I-10, exit 778 (Normandy St/Federal Rd) westbound, 1.1 mi w; exit 778A eastbound, on westbound frontage road. 1016 Maxey Rd 77015. Fax: 713/451-1984. **Facility:** 59 one-bedroom standard units, some with whirlpools. 2 stories, interior corridors. *Bath:* combo or shower only. **Parking:** on-site. **Terms:** 7 day cancellation notice. **Amenities:** high-speed Internet, dual phone lines, voice mail, irons, hair dryers. **Pool(s):** outdoor. **Leisure Activities:** exercise room. **Guest Services:** valet and coin laundry. **Business Services:** meeting rooms, business center. **Cards:** AX, DC, DS, MC, VI. **Special Amenities:** free continental breakfast and free local telephone calls.

SOME UNITS

COMFORT INN HOUSTON WEST/ENERGY CORRIDOR
AAA SAVE
▽▽▽▽
Motel

Phone: (281)493-0444 **121**
All Year [ECP] 1P: $69-$74 2P: $79-$84
Location: I-10, exit 751 (Addicks/SR 6), 0.4 mi s. 715 Hwy 6 S 77079. Fax: 281/493-2377. **Facility:** 63 one-bedroom standard units, some with whirlpools. 2 stories, exterior corridors. *Bath:* combo or shower only. **Parking:** on-site. **Terms:** [CP] meal plan available. **Amenities:** voice mail, safes, irons, hair dryers. **Pool(s):** outdoor. **Leisure Activities:** whirlpool. **Guest Services:** coin laundry. **Business Services:** meeting rooms, fax (fee). **Cards:** AX, CB, DC, DS, JC, MC, VI. **Special Amenities:** free continental breakfast and free local telephone calls.

SOME UNITS
FEE

COMFORT SUITES
SAVE
▽▽▽▽
Small-scale Hotel

Phone: (713)856-5005 **185**
All Year 1P: $79-$150 2P: $89-$150 XP: $10 F14
Location: US 290, exit Jones Rd. 17550 Northwest Frwy 77065. Fax: 713/856-2221. **Facility:** 54 one-bedroom standard units, some with whirlpools. 3 stories, interior corridors. *Bath:* combo or shower only. **Parking:** on-site. **Amenities:** dual phone lines, voice mail, safes (fee), irons, hair dryers. **Pool(s):** outdoor. **Leisure Activities:** whirlpool, exercise room. **Guest Services:** coin laundry. **Business Services:** meeting rooms, fax (fee). **Cards:** AX, CB, DC, DS, MC, VI.

SOME UNITS

COMFORT SUITES
AAA SAVE
▽▽▽▽
Small-scale Hotel

Phone: (281)440-4448 **181**
All Year 1P: $69-$79 2P: $79-$89 XP: $10 F12
Location: I-45, exit 66 (CR 1960), on southbound frontage road. 150 Overland Trail 77090. Fax: 281/440-4492. **Facility:** 51 one-bedroom standard units, some with whirlpools. 2 stories, interior corridors. *Bath:* combo or shower only. **Parking:** on-site. **Terms:** 4 day cancellation notice, package plans. **Amenities:** voice mail, irons, hair dryers. **Pool(s):** outdoor. **Leisure Activities:** whirlpool, limited exercise equipment. **Guest Services:** coin laundry. **Business Services:** meeting rooms, fax (fee). **Cards:** AX, DC, DS, MC, VI. **Special Amenities:** free continental breakfast and free local telephone calls.

SOME UNITS

COMFORT SUITES INTERCONTINENTAL PLAZA
SAVE
▽▽▽▽
Small-scale Hotel

Phone: (281)442-0600 **153**
All Year [ECP] 1P: $69-$189 2P: $74-$194 XP: $5 F
Location: Beltway 8 (Sam Houston Pkwy), exit John F Kennedy Blvd, just n. 15555 John F Kennedy Blvd 77032. Fax: 281/442-0606. **Facility:** 57 units. 55 one-bedroom standard units, some with whirlpools. 2 one-bedroom suites with kitchens. 3 stories, interior corridors. *Bath:* combo or shower only. **Parking:** on-site. **Amenities:** voice mail, irons, hair dryers. **Pool(s):** indoor/outdoor. **Leisure Activities:** whirlpool, exercise room. **Guest Services:** coin laundry. **Business Services:** meeting rooms, fax (fee). **Cards:** AX, CB, DC, DS, JC, MC, VI.

SOME UNITS

COMFORT SUITES-WESTCHASE
AAA SAVE
▽▽▽▽
Small-scale Hotel

Phone: (713)334-8884 **196**
All Year 1P: $90-$100 2P: $90-$100 XP: $10 F12
Location: Jct Beltway 8 and Westheimer Rd, just w on Westheimer Rd, then just s. 2830 Wilcrest Rd 77042. Fax: 713/334-0011. **Facility:** 64 units. 63 one-bedroom standard units, some with whirlpools. 1 one-bedroom suite with whirlpool. 3 stories, interior corridors. *Bath:* combo or shower only. **Parking:** on-site. **Terms:** [ECP] meal plan available. **Amenities:** high-speed Internet, dual phone lines, voice mail, safes, irons, hair dryers. **Pool(s):** heated outdoor. **Leisure Activities:** whirlpool, exercise room. **Guest Services:** valet and coin laundry. **Business Services:** PC, fax (fee). **Cards:** AX, CB, DC, DS, JC, MC, VI. **Special Amenities:** free continental breakfast and free local telephone calls.

SOME UNITS

COMFORT SUITES-WILLOWBROOK
AAA SAVE
▽▽▽▽
Small-scale Hotel

Phone: 281/370-2727 **118**
All Year 1P: $89 2P: $159
Location: SR 249, jct with Louetta. 21222 Tomball Pkwy 77070. Fax: 281/370-7117. **Facility:** 64 units. 63 one-bedroom standard units, some with whirlpools. 1 one-bedroom suite with whirlpool. 3 stories, interior corridors. *Bath:* combo or shower only. **Parking:** on-site. **Terms:** [CP] meal plan available. **Amenities:** high-speed Internet, dual phone lines, voice mail, safes, irons, hair dryers. **Pool(s):** heated outdoor. **Leisure Activities:** whirlpool, exercise room. **Guest Services:** valet and coin laundry. **Business Services:** PC, fax (fee). **Cards:** AX, CB, DC, DS, JC, MC, VI. **Special Amenities:** free continental breakfast and free local telephone calls.

SOME UNITS

(See map p. 382)

COUNTRY INN & SUITES BY CARLSON   **Phone:** (281)987-2400   **145**
All Year [ECP]   1P: $69-$189   2P: $74-$194   XP: $5   F
Small-scale Hotel   **Location:** Beltway 8 (Sam Houston Pkwy), exit John F Kennedy Blvd/Vickery, just n. 15555B John F Kennedy Blvd 77032. Fax: 281/987-2424. **Facility:** 57 units. 41 one-bedroom standard units. 16 one-bedroom suites. 4 stories, interior corridors. *Bath:* combo or shower only. **Parking:** on-site. **Amenities:** voice mail, irons, hair dryers. **Pool(s):** outdoor. **Leisure Activities:** exercise room. **Guest Services:** valet and coin laundry. **Business Services:** fax (fee). **Cards:** AX, CB, DC, DS, JC, MC, VI. *(See color ad p 260)*

SOME UNITS

COUNTRY INN & SUITES HOUSTON AT SUGARLAND   **Phone:** (281)575-8283   **173**
4/1-8/31 [BP]   1P: $79-$89   2P: $79-$89   XP: $5   F12
2/1-3/31 & 9/1-1/31 [BP]   1P: $69-$79   2P: $69-$79   XP: $5   F12
Small-scale Hotel   **Location:** US 59, exit Wilcrest/Bellfort, on westbound frontage road. 11230 SW Frwy 77031. Fax: 281/933-0550. **Facility:** Designated smoking area. 80 one-bedroom standard units, some with efficiencies. 3 stories, interior corridors. *Bath:* combo or shower only. **Parking:** on-site. **Terms:** package plans, 17% service charge. **Amenities:** dual phone lines, voice mail, irons, hair dryers. **Pool(s):** small outdoor. **Leisure Activities:** whirlpool, exercise room. **Guest Services:** complimentary evening beverages: Wed, valet and coin laundry. **Business Services:** meeting rooms, fax (fee). **Cards:** AX, CB, DC, DS, JC, MC, VI. *(See color ad p 260)*

SOME UNITS

CROWNE PLAZA HOTEL AND RESORT BROOKHOLLOW HOTEL   **Phone:** (713)462-9977   **193**
All Year   1P: $149   2P: $149   XP: $10   F
Large-scale Hotel   **Location:** Nw on US 290, exit Hollister Rd, 0.7 mi e on south service road. 12801 Northwest Frwy 77040. Fax: 713/460-8725. **Facility:** 291 units. 289 one-bedroom standard units. 2 one-bedroom suites. 3-10 stories, interior/exterior corridors. *Bath:* combo or shower only. **Parking:** on-site. **Amenities:** video games (fee), dual phone lines, voice mail, irons, hair dryers. **Dining:** 6 am-2 & 5-10:30 pm, Sat & Sun from 7 am, cocktails, nightclub. **Pool(s):** outdoor. **Leisure Activities:** whirlpool. **Guest Services:** gift shop, valet and coin laundry, area transportation-within 5 mi. **Business Services:** conference facilities, business center. **Cards:** AX, CB, DC, DS, MC, VI.

SOME UNITS
FEE   FEE

DAYS INN & SUITES   **Phone:** 281/209-1400   **111**
All Year [ECP]   1P: $59   2P: $59   XP: $8   F12
Motel   **Location:** I-45 N, exit 66 (FM 1960), just e. 410 FM 1960 E 77073. Fax: 281/821-7175. **Facility:** 38 one-bedroom standard units, some with whirlpools. 2 stories, exterior corridors. *Bath:* combo or shower only. **Parking:** on-site. **Terms:** 30 day cancellation notice-fee imposed. **Amenities:** high-speed Internet, irons, hair dryers. **Pool(s):** heated outdoor. **Leisure Activities:** whirlpool, exercise room. **Guest Services:** coin laundry. **Business Services:** meeting rooms, fax. **Cards:** AX, DC, DS, MC, VI. **Special Amenities:** free continental breakfast and free local telephone calls.

SOME UNITS
FEE

DAYS INN-HOUSTON NORTH   **Phone:** (281)820-1500   **201**
All Year [CP]   1P: $44-$51   2P: $47-$61   XP: $6   F17
Motel   **Location:** I-45, exit 57A (Gulf Bank Rd). 9025 North Frwy 77037. Fax: 281/591-7731. **Facility:** 100 one-bedroom standard units. 2 stories, exterior corridors. **Parking:** on-site. **Terms:** small pets only ($20 deposit). **Amenities:** safes, hair dryers. **Pool(s):** outdoor. **Guest Services:** coin laundry. **Business Services:** fax (fee). **Cards:** AX, CB, DC, DS, MC, VI.

SOME UNITS

DRURY INN & SUITES HOUSTON WEST   **Phone:** (281)558-7007   **122**
9/1-1/31 [ECP]   1P: $75-$95   2P: $85-$105   XP: $10   F18
2/1-8/31 [ECP]   1P: $72-$92   2P: $82-$102   XP: $10   F18
Small-scale Hotel   **Location:** I-10, exit 751 (Addicks/SR 6), just n on SR 6. 1000 N Hwy 6 77079. Fax: 281/558-7007. **Facility:** 120 units. 106 one-bedroom standard units. 14 one-bedroom suites ($92-$115). 5 stories, interior corridors. *Bath:* combo or shower only. **Parking:** on-site. **Amenities:** voice mail, irons, hair dryers. **Pool(s):** heated indoor. **Leisure Activities:** whirlpool, exercise room. **Guest Services:** complimentary evening beverages: Mon-Thurs, valet and coin laundry. **Business Services:** meeting rooms, fax (fee). **Cards:** AX, CB, DC, DS, MC, VI. **Special Amenities:** free continental breakfast and free local telephone calls.

SOME UNITS

ECONO LODGE   **Phone:** (713)699-3800   **156**
All Year [CP]   1P: $55-$65   2P: $60-$65   XP: $5   F17
Motel   **Location:** I-45, exit 55A northbound; exit 56B southbound, 1.1 mi s on Frontage Rd. 7447 North Frwy 77076. Fax: 713/699-3349. **Facility:** 50 one-bedroom standard units, some with whirlpools. 2 stories, exterior corridors. *Bath:* combo or shower only. **Parking:** on-site. **Terms:** cancellation fee imposed, weekly rates available. **Amenities:** hair dryers. **Pool(s):** outdoor. **Guest Services:** coin laundry. **Business Services:** fax (fee). **Cards:** AX, CB, DC, DS, MC, VI. **Special Amenities:** free continental breakfast and free local telephone calls.

SOME UNITS

ECONO LODGE   **Phone:** (713)956-2828   **112**
All Year [CP]   1P: $47-$49   2P: $53-$55   XP: $6   F17
Motel   **Location:** US 290, exit Bingle Rd, just nw on Bingle Rd, then immediate turn ne. 6630 Hoover St 77092. Fax: 713/956-8866. **Facility:** 32 one-bedroom standard units. 2 stories, exterior corridors. **Parking:** on-site. **Amenities:** *Some:* irons, hair dryers. **Business Services:** fax (fee). **Cards:** AX, CB, DC, DS, MC, VI.

SOME UNITS

(See map p. 382)

EMBASSY SUITES HOTEL

| | Phone: (713)995-0123 | 166 |

SAVE

All Year   1P: $109-$139   2P: $109-$139   XP: $10   F18
Location: 10 mi sw on US 59, exit Gessner St/Beechnut. 9090 Southwest Frwy 77074. Fax: 713/779-0703.
Facility: 243 one-bedroom suites. 9 stories, interior corridors. **Parking:** on-site. **Terms:** [BP] meal plan avail-

Large-scale Hotel able. **Amenities:** dual phone lines, voice mail, irons, hair dryers. *Fee:* video games, high-speed Internet.
Pool(s): heated indoor. **Leisure Activities:** sauna, whirlpool, exercise room. *Fee:* game room. **Guest Services:** gift shop, complimentary evening beverages, valet and coin laundry. **Business Services:** meeting
rooms, fax (fee). **Cards:** AX, CB, DC, DS, JC, MC, VI.

SOME UNITS

FAIRFIELD INN

| | Phone: (281)646-0056 | 154 |

SAVE

All Year [ECP]   1P: $65-$85   2P: $65-$95   XP: $6   F18
Location: I-10, exit 748 (Baker Cypress Rd) eastbound; exit 751 (US 6) westbound, just s on US 6 to Grigsby Rd, 0.3
mi w. 15111 Katy Frwy 77094. Fax: 281/646-0056. **Facility:** 82 one-bedroom standard units. 3 stories, interior
corridors. *Bath:* combo or shower only. **Terms:** 14 day cancellation notice.

Small-scale Hotel **Amenities:** voice mail, irons. **Pool(s):** heated indoor. **Leisure Activities:** whirlpool. **Guest Services:** valet
laundry. **Business Services:** meeting rooms, fax (fee). **Cards:** AX, CB, DC, DS, MC, VI.

SOME UNITS

FAIRFIELD INN BY MARRIOTT

| | Phone: (281)895-8989 | 183 |

SAVE

All Year [ECP]   1P: $69-$89   2P: $69-$99   XP: $6   F18
Location: I-45, exit 66 (CR 1960), on southbound access road. 17617 North Frwy (I-45) 77090. Fax: 281/895-8989.
Facility: 64 one-bedroom standard units. 3 stories, interior corridors. *Bath:* combo or shower only. **Parking:**
on-site. **Terms:** 14 day cancellation notice. **Amenities:** irons. **Pool(s):** small heated indoor. **Leisure Activi-

Small-scale Hotel ties:** whirlpool. **Guest Services:** valet laundry. **Business Services:** fax (fee). **Cards:** AX, CB, DC, DS,
MC, VI.

SOME UNITS

FAIRFIELD INN BY MARRIOTT I-10 EAST

| | Phone: (713)675-2711 | 131 |

AAA SAVE

All Year [ECP]   1P: $72   2P: $72   F18
Location: I-10, exit 776A (Mercury), just nw. 10155 East Frwy 77029. Fax: 713/674-6853. **Facility:** 160 one-
bedroom standard units. 2 stories, exterior corridors. *Bath:* combo or shower only. **Parking:** on-site.
Amenities: video games (fee), irons. **Dining:** 11 am-11 pm, cocktails. **Pool(s):** outdoor, wading. **Guest Serv-

Small-scale Hotel ices:** valet and coin laundry. **Business Services:** meeting rooms, fax (fee). **Cards:** AX, DC, DS, MC, VI.
Special Amenities: free continental breakfast and free local telephone calls.

SOME UNITS

FEE   FEE

FAIRFIELD INN MARRIOTT-WESTCHASE

| | Phone: (713)334-2400 | 113 |

SAVE

All Year [ECP]   1P: $69-$89   2P: $69-$99   XP: $6   F18
Location: Sam Houston Pkwy, exit Westheimer Rd on southbound frontage road; nw of jct Sam Houston Pkwy and Westheimer Rd. 2400 W Sam Houston Pkwy S 77042. Fax: 713/334-2400. **Facility:** 82 one-bedroom standard units.
3 stories, interior corridors. *Bath:* combo or shower only. **Parking:** on-site. **Terms:** 14 day cancellation no-

Small-scale Hotel tice. **Amenities:** voice mail, irons. **Pool(s):** heated indoor. **Leisure Activities:** whirlpool. **Guest Services:**
valet laundry. **Business Services:** meeting rooms, fax (fee). **Cards:** AX, CB, DC, DS, MC, VI.

SOME UNITS

GUESTHOUSE INN & SUITES INTERCONTINENTAL

| | Phone: (281)876-7378 | 182 |

AAA SAVE

All Year   1P: $64-$89   2P: $64-$89   XP: $5   F18
Location: I-45, exit 63 (Airtex Dr), just w. 125 Airtex Dr 77090. Fax: 281/876-7379. **Facility:** 71 units. 50 one-
bedroom standard units. 21 one-bedroom suites, some with kitchens and/or whirlpools. 4 stories, interior corridors. *Bath:* combo or shower only. **Parking:** on-site. **Terms:** 3 day cancellation notice. **Amenities:** high-

Small-scale Hotel speed Internet, dual phone lines, voice mail, safes, irons, hair dryers. **Pool(s):** outdoor. **Leisure
Activities:** whirlpool, exercise room. **Guest Services:** complimentary evening beverages: Mon-Fri, valet and
coin laundry, airport transportation-George Bush Intercontinental Airport, area transportation-within 5 mi. **Business Services:**
meeting rooms, business center. **Cards:** AX, CB, DC, DS, MC, VI. **Special Amenities:** free continental breakfast and free
local telephone calls.

SOME UNITS

GUESTHOUSE INTERNATIONAL INN & SUITES

| | Phone: (713)690-1493 | 143 |

AAA SAVE

All Year   1P: $59-$89   2P: $65-$95   XP: $6   F18
Location: US 290 W, exit W Tidwell Rd, 0.3 mi on service road to W Tidwell Rd; on southeast corner of eastbound
service road and W Tidwell Rd. 7887 W Tidwell Rd 77040. Fax: 713/895-8674. **Facility:** 115 one-bedroom standard units. 5 stories, interior corridors. *Bath:* combo or shower only. **Parking:** on-site. **Terms:** [ECP] meal

Small-scale Hotel plan available, small pets only ($50 fee). **Amenities:** voice mail, irons, hair dryers. **Pool(s):** outdoor. **Guest
Services:** valet and coin laundry, area transportation-within 5 mi. **Business Services:** meeting rooms, fax
(fee). **Cards:** AX, CB, DC, DS, MC, VI. **Special Amenities:** free continental breakfast and free local telephone calls.

SOME UNITS

GUESTHOUSE INTERNATIONAL INN & SUITES

| | Phone: (713)776-2633 | 200 |

AAA SAVE

All Year [ECP]   1P: $59-$89   2P: $65-$95   XP: $6   F18
Location: US 59 N, exit Hillcroft Ave/West Park Dr, then just 0.7 mi eastbound; exit Hillcroft Ave westbound. 6687 South-
west Frwy 77074. Fax: 713/776-0326. **Facility:** 115 one-bedroom standard units. 5 stories, interior corridors.
Parking: on-site. **Terms:** small pets only ($25 fee). **Amenities:** voice mail, irons. *Some:* hair dryers. **Pool(s):**

Small-scale Hotel outdoor. **Guest Services:** valet and coin laundry, area transportation-within 3 mi. **Business Services:**
meeting rooms, fax (fee). **Cards:** AX, CB, DC, DS, MC, VI. **Special Amenities:** free continental breakfast
and free local telephone calls.

SOME UNITS

(See map p. 382)

GUESTHOUSE INTERNATIONAL INN & SUITES HOUSTON WEST
Phone: (281)493-5626   137

(AAA) (SAVE)   All Year [ECP]   1P: $59-$89   2P: $65-$95   XP: $6   F18

◆◆◆   **Location:** I-10, exit 753 (Dairy-Ashford Rd), on south service road. 12323 Katy Frwy 77079. Fax: 281/493-2907. **Facility:** 115 one-bedroom standard units. 5 stories, interior corridors. **Parking:** on-site. **Terms:** pets ($25 deposit). **Amenities:** voice mail, irons, hair dryers. **Pool(s):** outdoor. **Guest Services:** coin laundry, area

Small-scale Hotel   transportation-within 5 mi. **Business Services:** meeting rooms, fax (fee). **Cards:** AX, CB, DC, DS, MC, VI. **Special Amenities:** free continental breakfast and free local telephone calls.

SOME UNITS

[⑤] [🐕] [📶] [🛏] [➤] [📹] [DATA PORT] [🖥] / [✕] [🔒] [📷] /

HAMPTON INN-BROOKHOLLOW
Phone: (713)939-7100   205

(SAVE)   All Year [ECP]   1P: $81   2P: $85   XP: $4   F17

◆◆◆   **Location:** US 290, exit Hollister, on eastbound access road. 12909 Northwest Frwy 77040. Fax: 713/939-0088. **Facility:** 81 one-bedroom standard units, some with whirlpools. 3 stories, interior corridors. *Bath:* combo or shower only. **Parking:** on-site. **Amenities:** video games (fee), voice mail, irons, hair dryers. **Pool(s):** outdoor.

Small-scale Hotel   **Leisure Activities:** exercise room. **Guest Services:** valet and coin laundry. **Business Services:** meeting rooms, fax (fee). **Cards:** AX, CB, DC, DS, MC, VI.

SOME UNITS

[📶] [🛏] [➤] [📹] [DATA PORT] [🖥] / [✕] [🔒] [📷] /

HAMPTON INN-HOUSTON BUSH INTERCONTINENTAL AIRPORT
Phone: (281)820-2101   126

(SAVE)   All Year [ECP]   1P: $69-$89   2P: $69-$94

◆◆◆   **Location:** Off Beltway 8, 1.3 mi e of I-45, exit Hardy Toll Rd eastbound; exit Imperial Valley Dr westbound. 502 N Sam Houston Pkwy 77060. Fax: 281/820-9652. **Facility:** 157 units. 156 one-bedroom standard units, some with whirlpools. 1 one-bedroom suite ($115-$150). 2 stories, interior corridors. *Bath:* combo or shower only. **Parking:** on-site. **Amenities:** high-speed Internet (fee), voice mail, irons, hair dryers. **Pool(s):** indoor/outdoor. **Leisure Activities:** whirlpool, exercise room. **Guest Services:** valet and coin laundry, area

Small-scale Hotel   transportation. **Business Services:** meeting rooms, fax (fee). **Cards:** AX, DC, MC, VI.

SOME UNITS

[⑤] [✈] [🛏] [🔥M] [🐕] [📹] [➤] [📹] [DATA PORT] [🖥] / [✕] [🔒] [📷] /

HAMPTON INN- HOUSTON I-10 W
Phone: (713)935-0022   132

(SAVE)   All Year [ECP]   1P: $61-$97   2P: $65-$101

◆◆◆   **Location:** I-10, exit 754 (Kirkwood Rd), 0.5 mi e of Kirkwood Dr on eastbound frontage road. 11333 Katy Frwy 77079. Fax: 713/935-0989. **Facility:** 119 one-bedroom standard units. 4 stories, interior corridors. *Bath:* combo or shower only. **Parking:** on-site. **Amenities:** video games (fee), voice mail, irons, hair dryers. **Pool(s):** outdoor.

Small-scale Hotel   **Leisure Activities:** exercise room. **Guest Services:** valet laundry. **Business Services:** meeting rooms, business center. **Cards:** AX, CB, DC, DS, JC, MC, VI.

SOME UNITS

[⑤] [🛏] [🔥M] [🐕] [📹] [➤] [📹] [DATA PORT] [🖥] / [✕] [🔒] [📷] /
FEE   FEE

HAMPTON INN-HOUSTON NORTHWEST
Phone: (281)890-2299   189

(SAVE)   All Year [ECP]   1P: $81-$119   XP: $5   F18

◆◆◆   **Location:** SR 6, w of jct US 290 and FM 1960. 20035 Hwy 290 77065. Fax: 281/890-5046. **Facility:** 62 one-bedroom standard units. 3 stories, interior corridors. *Bath:* combo or shower only. **Parking:** on-site. **Amenities:** dual phone lines, voice mail, irons, hair dryers. **Pool(s):** outdoor. **Guest Services:** coin laundry.

Small-scale Hotel   **Business Services:** fax (fee). **Cards:** AX, CB, DC, DS, JC, MC, VI.

SOME UNITS

[⑤] [🛏] [🔥] [📹] [➤] [📶] [📹] [DATA PORT] [🖥] / [✕] [🔒] [📷] /

HAMPTON INN I-10 EAST
Phone: (713)673-4200   199

(SAVE)   All Year   1P: $87   2P: $87

◆◆◆   **Location:** I-10, exit 776A (Mercury Dr), just n. 828 Mercury Dr 77013. Fax: 713/674-6913. **Facility:** 90 one-bedroom standard units. 6 stories, interior corridors. **Parking:** on-site. **Terms:** [ECP] meal plan available, small pets only ($25 fee). **Amenities:** video games (fee), voice mail, irons. **Pool(s):** outdoor, wading. **Guest Services:**

Small-scale Hotel   valet laundry. **Business Services:** fax (fee). **Cards:** AX, DC, DS, MC, VI.

SOME UNITS

[⑤] [🐕] [🛏] [📹] [➤] [📶] [📹] [DATA PORT] [🖥] / [✕] [🔒] [📷] /
FEE

HAMPTON INN-WILLOWBROOK
Phone: (281)955-2400   114

(SAVE)   All Year [ECP]   1P: $99

◆◆◆   **Location:** Just e of jct SR 249 and FM 1960. Located in Willowbrook Mall. 7645 W FM 1960 77070. Fax: 281/955-6291. **Facility:** 75 one-bedroom standard units. 3 stories, interior corridors. *Bath:* combo or shower only. **Parking:** on-site. **Amenities:** voice mail, irons, hair dryers. **Pool(s):** small heated indoor. **Leisure Activities:** whirlpool. **Guest Services:** valet laundry. **Business Services:** fax (fee). **Cards:** AX, DC,

Small-scale Hotel   DS, MC, VI.

SOME UNITS

[⑤] [🛏] [🔥M] [🐕] [📹] [➤] [📹] [DATA PORT] [🖥] / [✕] [🔒] [📷] /

HAWTHORN SUITES
Phone: 281/999-9942   162

◆◆◆   All Year [CP]   1P: $50-$140   2P: $65-$155

Location: Beltway 8 (N Sam Houston Pkwy E), exit Imperial Valley westbound; exit Hardy Toll Rd eastbound, e on frontage road. 702 N Sam Houston Pkwy E 77060. Fax: 281/591-1215. **Facility:** 110 units. 8 one-bedroom stan-

Small-scale Hotel   dard units. 102 one-bedroom suites ($79-$149), some with efficiencies. 7 stories, interior/exterior corridors. **Parking:** on-site. **Terms:** [BP] meal plan available. **Amenities:** video games (fee), voice mail, irons, hair dryers. **Pool(s):** outdoor. **Leisure Activities:** exercise room. **Guest Services:** valet and coin laundry, area transportation. **Business Services:** meeting rooms, fax (fee). **Cards:** AX, CB, DC, DS, JC, MC, VI.

SOME UNITS

[✈] [➤] [📹] [DATA PORT] [🖥] / [✕] [🔒] [📷] /

(See map p. 382)

HILTON GARDEN INN HOUSTON/BUSH AIRPORT

SAVE
▼◆▼◆▼
Small-scale Hotel

Phone: (281)449-4148 〔151〕

All Year   1P: $149-$169   2P: $149-$169   XP: $10   F18
Location: Just n of jct Beltway 8. 15400 John F Kennedy Blvd 77032. Fax: 281/449-4713. **Facility:** 182 one-bedroom standard units. 6 stories, interior corridors. *Bath:* combo or shower only. **Parking:** on-site. **Amenities:** video games (fee), dual phone lines, voice mail, irons, hair dryers. **Pool(s):** heated outdoor. **Leisure Activities:** whirlpool, exercise room. **Guest Services:** sundries, valet and coin laundry, area transportation. **Business Services:** meeting rooms, business center. **Cards:** AX, CB, DC, DS, MC, VI.

SOME UNITS

HILTON GARDEN INN HOUSTON NORTHWEST

SAVE
▼◆▼◆▼
Small-scale Hotel

Phone: (832)912-1000 〔119〕

All Year   1P: $69-$219   2P: $69-$219   XP: $10   F18
Location: On SR 249, exit FM 1960, on northbound frontage road. 7979 Willow Chase Blvd 77070. Fax: 832/912-1025. **Facility:** 171 units. 162 one-bedroom standard units. 9 one-bedroom suites ($129-$399), some with whirlpools. 6 stories, interior corridors. *Bath:* combo or shower only. **Terms:** check-in 4 pm, cancellation fee imposed, package plans. **Amenities:** dual phone lines, voice mail, irons, hair dryers. *Fee:* video games, high-speed Internet. **Pool(s):** outdoor. **Leisure Activities:** whirlpool, exercise room. **Guest Services:** gift shop, valet and coin laundry, area transportation. **Business Services:** meeting rooms, business center. **Cards:** AX, CB, DC, DS, JC, MC, VI.

SOME UNITS

THE HILTON HOUSTON WESTCHASE & TOWERS

ⒶⒶⒶ **SAVE**
▼◆▼◆▼
Large-scale Hotel

Phone: (713)974-1000 〔171〕

All Year   1P: $89-$179   2P: $104-$194   XP: $10   F18
Location: Beltway 8, exit Westheimer Rd and Briar Forest Dr northbound; exit Westheimer Rd and Richmond Ave southbound, 0.5 mi e. 9999 Westheimer Rd 77042. Fax: 713/974-6866. **Facility:** 295 units. 275 one-bedroom standard units. 20 one-bedroom suites ($199-$1400), some with whirlpools. 12 stories, interior corridors. *Bath:* combo or shower only. **Parking:** on-site. **Terms:** cancellation fee imposed, 17% service charge. **Amenities:** high-speed Internet (fee), voice mail, honor bars, irons, hair dryers. *Some:* CD players. **Dining:** 6:30 am-10 pm, Fri & Sat-11 pm, Sat & Sun from 7 am, cocktails. **Pool(s):** heated outdoor. **Leisure Activities:** sauna, whirlpool, exercise room. **Guest Services:** gift shop, valet laundry, area transportation-within 5 mi. **Business Services:** conference facilities, business center. **Cards:** AX, CB, DC, DS, JC, MC, VI. *(See color ad below)*

SOME UNITS

(See map p. 382)

HOLIDAY INN EXPRESS-FM 1960
Phone: 281/444-5800 198

All Year 1P: $85-$119 2P: $85-$119

Small-scale Hotel

Location: I-45, exit 66, 3.5 mi w. Located next to the Walmart. 3555 FM 1960 W 77068. **Fax:** 281/444-6017. **Facility:** 56 one-bedroom standard units, some with whirlpools. 3 stories, interior corridors. *Bath:* combo or shower only. **Parking:** on-site. **Terms:** [CP] meal plan available. **Amenities:** irons, hair dryers. *Some:* dual phone lines. **Pool(s):** small heated outdoor. **Leisure Activities:** whirlpool, exercise room. **Guest Services:** valet and coin laundry. **Business Services:** meeting rooms, business center. **Cards:** AX, DC, DS, MC, VI.

SOME UNITS

ASK SO 📞 📧 🏊 📶 🖨 💻 🛗 🖥 /

HOLIDAY INN EXPRESS HOTEL & SUITES
Phone: (713)957-8222 194

All Year 1P: $95 2P: $95 XP: $5 F

Small-scale Hotel

Location: US 290, exit Bingle, on eastbound feeder. 12439 Northwest Frwy 77092. **Fax:** 713/957-8383. **Facility:** 62 units. 26 one-bedroom standard units. 36 one-bedroom suites ($95-$109), some with whirlpools. 3 stories, interior corridors. *Bath:* combo or shower only. **Parking:** on-site. **Terms:** cancellation fee imposed, [CP] meal plan available. **Amenities:** dual phone lines, voice mail, irons, hair dryers. **Pool(s):** outdoor. **Leisure Activities:** exercise room. **Guest Services:** valet and coin laundry. **Business Services:** meeting rooms, fax (fee). **Cards:** AX, DC, DS, MC, VI.

SOME UNITS

ASK SO ♿M 🏊 📶 🖨 🛗 💻 / 🖥 🖨 /

HOLIDAY INN EXPRESS HOTEL & SUITES-INTERCONTINENTAL
Phone: (281)372-1000 158

All Year 1P: $89 2P: $89 XP: $6 F21

Small-scale Hotel

Location: Off Beltway 8, exit Aldine Westfield eastbound, 0.8 mi e on service road; exit Hardy Toll road westbound, U-turn, then 1 mi e on service road. 1330 N Sam Houston Pkwy 77032. **Fax:** 281/372-1001. **Facility:** 59 one-bedroom standard units, some with whirlpools. 3 stories, interior corridors. *Bath:* combo or shower only. **Parking:** on-site. **Terms:** cancellation fee imposed, [ECP] meal plan available, small pets only ($25 fee). **Amenities:** dual phone lines, voice mail, irons, hair dryers. **Pool(s):** outdoor. **Leisure Activities:** whirlpool, exercise room. **Guest Services:** valet and coin laundry, area transportation. **Business Services:** meeting rooms, business center. **Cards:** AX, CB, DC, DS, MC, VI.

SOME UNITS

ASK SO 🔑 🐕 🛏 📧 🏊 📶 🖨 🛗 🖥 💻 / 🖥 /

HOLIDAY INN HOUSTON INTERCONTINENTAL AIRPORT
Phone: (281)449-2311 146

All Year 1P: $80-$150 2P: $80-$150

Large-scale Hotel

Location: Jct N Sam Houston Pkwy E and John F Kennedy Blvd. 15222 John F Kennedy Blvd 77032. **Fax:** 281/442-6833. **Facility:** 415 units. 414 one-bedroom standard units. 1 one-bedroom suite. 5 stories, interior corridors. *Bath:* combo or shower only. **Parking:** on-site. **Terms:** small pets only ($100 fee, $125 deposit). **Amenities:** video games (fee), voice mail, irons, hair dryers. **Pool(s):** outdoor, wading. **Leisure Activities:** 2 lighted tennis courts, exercise room, basketball, horseshoes, volleyball. **Guest Services:** gift shop, valet and coin laundry, area transportation. **Business Services:** meeting rooms, business center. **Cards:** AX, CB, DC, DS, JC, MC, VI. *(See color ad p 390)*

SOME UNITS

ASK SO 🔑 🐕 🛏 🍴 🍷 📧 🏊 🖥 📶 🖨 🛗 / 🖥 🖨 /
FEE FEE

HOLIDAY INN HOUSTON NORTH
Phone: (281)821-2570 176

All Year [BP] 1P: $99-$109 2P: $99-$109 XP: $10 F18

Small-scale Hotel

Location: I-45, exit 64 (Richey Rd), northbound service road, 0.8 mi n of jct I-45. 16510 I-45 N 77090. **Fax:** 281/821-1304. **Facility:** 230 units. 229 one-bedroom standard units. 1 one-bedroom suite. 2 stories, exterior corridors. **Parking:** on-site. **Terms:** weekly rates available. **Amenities:** voice mail, irons, hair dryers. **Pool(s):** outdoor, wading. **Leisure Activities:** exercise room. **Guest Services:** valet and coin laundry. **Business Services:** meeting rooms, fax (fee). **Cards:** AX, CB, DC, DS, JC, MC, VI. *(See color ad p 390)*

SOME UNITS

ASK SO 🔑 🍴 🍷 🏊 📶 🖨 🛗 💻 / 🖥 🖨 /

HOLIDAY INN HOUSTON SOUTHWEST/SUGAR LAND
Phone: (281)530-1400 167

All Year 1P: $76-$109 2P: $76-$109 XP: $10 F19

Small-scale Hotel

Location: US 59, exit West Belfort southbound; exit Bissonnet northbound (on southbound frontage road); northwest corner of intersection of Beltway 8 and US 59. 11160 Southwest Frwy 77031-3698. **Fax:** 281/530-2191. **Facility:** 238 units. 236 one-bedroom standard units. 2 two-bedroom suites with whirlpools. 2-6 stories, interior/exterior corridors. **Parking:** on-site. **Terms:** 3 day cancellation notice. **Amenities:** voice mail, irons, hair dryers. **Pool(s):** outdoor, heated indoor. **Leisure Activities:** whirlpool, playground, exercise room. **Guest Services:** gift shop, complimentary evening beverages: Tues, coin laundry, area transportation. **Business Services:** meeting rooms, PC, fax (fee). **Cards:** AX, CB, DC, DS, JC, MC, VI. *(See color ad p 390)*

SOME UNITS

ASK SO 🍴 🍷 📧 🏊 🖥 📶 🖨 🛗 💻 / 🖥 🖨 /
FEE FEE

HOLIDAY INN-NORTHWEST FREEWAY
Phone: (713)939-9955 192

All Year 1P: $69-$79 2P: $69-$79 XP: $10 F18

Motel

Location: Nw on US 290, exit W Little York/N Gessner rds, on westbound service road. 14996 Northwest Frwy 77040. **Fax:** 713/937-8121. **Facility:** 193 units. 190 one-bedroom standard units. 3 one-bedroom suites. 2-3 stories, exterior corridors. **Parking:** on-site. **Terms:** [AP] meal plan available. **Amenities:** video games, high-speed Internet, dual phone lines, voice mail, irons, hair dryers. *Some:* dual phone lines. **Pool(s):** outdoor. **Leisure Activities:** playground, exercise room. **Guest Services:** coin laundry. **Business Services:** meeting rooms, fax (fee). **Cards:** AX, CB, DC, DS, JC, MC, VI. *(See color ad p 390 & ad p 424)*

SOME UNITS

ASK SO 🍴 🍷 📧 🏊 🖥 📶 💻 / 🖥 VCR 🖨 🛗 /
FEE FEE FEE

HOLIDAY INN SELECT I-10
Phone: 281/558-5580 188

All Year 1P: $79-$122 2P: $79-$122

Large-scale Hotel

Location: I-10, exit 751 (Addicks Rd/SR 6), just n. 14703 Park Row 77079. **Fax:** 281/496-4150. **Facility:** 349 one-bedroom standard units. 19 stories, interior corridors. *Bath:* combo or shower only. **Parking:** on-site. **Terms:** cancellation fee imposed, small pets only ($100 deposit, $25 extra charge). **Amenities:** voice mail, irons, hair dryers. *Some:* fax. **Pool(s):** heated indoor. **Leisure Activities:** whirlpool, exercise room, basketball, volleyball. *Fee:* game room. **Guest Services:** gift shop, coin laundry, area transportation. **Business Services:** meeting rooms, business center. **Cards:** AX, CB, DC, DS, JC, MC, VI. *(See color ad p 390)*

SOME UNITS

ASK SO 🛏 🍴 🍷 📧 🏊 🖥 📶 🖨 🛗 💻 / 🖥 🖨 /
FEE FEE

(See map p. 382)

HOMESTEAD STUDIO SUITES HOTEL-HOUSTON/WILLOWBROOK　　　**Phone:** (281)397-9922　133
All Year　　　　1P: $75-$89　　　2P: $79-$94　　　XP: $5　　　　　F17
Location: Jct SR 249 and FM 1960 W, 0.9 mi e to Champion Center Dr, just n to Champion Center Plaza, just w. 13223
Small-scale Hotel　Champions Center Dr 77069. Fax: 281/397-8833. **Facility:** 137 one-bedroom standard units with efficiencies. 2
stories, exterior corridors. *Bath:* combo or shower only. **Parking:** on-site. **Terms:** pets ($100 fee).
Amenities: voice mail, irons. **Guest Services:** coin laundry. **Business Services:** fax (fee). **Cards:** AX, CB, DC, DS, JC,
MC, VI.

SOME UNITS
(ASK) (SØ) 🛏 (¶⬩) (Ṁ) (🗝) (🗲) (🛁⬩) (🎥) (DATA PORT) 🔲 🖥 🖵 / (✕) (VCR) /
　　　　　　　　　　　　FEE　　　　　　　　　　　　　　　　　　　　　　　　FEE

HOMEWOOD SUITES BY HILTON　　　　　　　　　　　　　　**Phone:** 281/486-7677　127
SAVE　　All Year [ECP]　　　　1P: $139-$179
　　　　Location: I-45, exit 26 (Bay Area Blvd), 1 mi e. 401 Bay Area Blvd 77058. Fax: 281/486-1665. **Facility:** 92 units. 86
　　　　one- and 6 two-bedroom suites with efficiencies. 3 stories, interior corridors. *Bath:* combo or shower only.
Motel　　**Parking:** on-site. **Terms:** small pets only ($100 fee). **Amenities:** video library, voice mail, irons, hair dryers.
　　　　Pool(s): outdoor. **Leisure Activities:** exercise room, sports court. **Guest Services:** complimentary evening
　　　　beverages: Mon-Thurs, valet and coin laundry. **Business Services:** meeting rooms, business center.
Cards: AX, DC, DS, MC, VI.

SOME UNITS
(SØ) 🛏 (¶⬩) (🗝) (🗲) (🏊) (VCR) (🎥) (DATA PORT) 🔲 🖥 🖵 / (✕) /

HOMEWOOD SUITES BY HILTON-WESTCHASE　　　　　　　**Phone:** 713/334-2424　179
SAVE　　All Year　　　　　1P: $112
　　　　Location: Beltway 8 (Sam Houston Pkwy), exit Westheimer Rd, just w to Rogerdale Rd, just n. 2424 Rogerdale Rd
　　　　77042. Fax: 713/787-6749. **Facility:** 96 units. 88 one- and 8 two-bedroom suites with kitchens. 3 stories, in-
Small-scale Hotel　terior corridors. *Bath:* combo or shower only. **Parking:** on-site. **Terms:** cancellation fee imposed.
　　　　Amenities: dual phone lines, voice mail, irons, hair dryers. **Pool(s):** heated indoor. **Leisure Activities:** whirl-
　　　　pool, exercise room, sports court. **Guest Services:** complimentary evening beverages: Mon-Thurs, coin
laundry. **Business Services:** meeting rooms, business center. **Cards:** AX, DC, DS, MC, VI.

SOME UNITS
(SØ) (Ṁ) (🗝) (🗲) (🏊) (✕) (🎥) (DATA PORT) 🔲 🖥 🖵 / (✕) /

HOMEWOOD SUITES HOTEL-WILLOWBROOK MALL　　　　　**Phone:** 281/955-5200　116
SAVE　　All Year [ECP]　　　　1P: $99-$169
　　　　Location: Just e jct SR 249 and FM 1960. Located in Willowbrook Mall. 7655 W FM 1960 77070. Fax: 281/890-8891.
　　　　Facility: 72 units. 65 one- and 7 two-bedroom suites, some with efficiencies or kitchens. 3 stories, interior
Small-scale Hotel　corridors. *Bath:* combo or shower only. **Parking:** on-site. **Terms:** pets ($100 fee). **Amenities:** voice mail,
　　　　irons, hair dryers. **Pool(s):** heated indoor. **Leisure Activities:** whirlpool, exercise room. **Guest Services:**
　　　　complimentary evening beverages: Mon-Thurs, coin laundry. **Business Services:** meeting rooms, business
center. **Cards:** AX, DC, DS, MC, VI.

SOME UNITS
(SØ) 🛏 (¶⬩) (Ṁ) (🗝) (🏊) (VCR) (🎥) (DATA PORT) 🔲 🖥 🖵 / (✕) /

HOUSTON AIRPORT MARRIOTT　　　　　　　　　　　　　**Phone:** (281)443-2310　141
SAVE　　All Year　　　　　1P: $89-$210　　　2P: $89-$210
　　　　Location: At the George Bush Intercontinental Airport. 18700 John F Kennedy Blvd 77032. Fax: 281/443-5294.
　　　　Facility: 565 units. 559 one-bedroom standard units. 6 one-bedroom suites. 7 stories, interior corridors. *Bath:*
Large-scale Hotel　combo or shower only. **Parking:** on-site and valet. **Terms:** 3 day cancellation notice. **Amenities:** voice mail,
　　　　irons, hair dryers. **Pool(s):** outdoor. **Leisure Activities:** whirlpool, jogging, exercise room. **Guest Services:**
　　　　gift shop. **Business Services:** conference facilities, business center. **Cards:** AX, CB, DC, DS, JC, MC, VI.

SOME UNITS
(SØ) (✚) 🍴 (Y) (Ṁ) (🗝) (🗲) (🏊) (✕) (🎥) (DATA PORT) 🖵 / (✕) (VCR) 🔲 /
　　　　　　　　　　　　　　　　　　　　　　　　　　　　　　　FEE

(See map p. 382)

HOUSTON MARRIOTT NORTH AT GREENSPOINT

Phone: (281)875-4000 **134**

SAVE

▽▼▽▼▽

Large-scale Hotel

All Year 1P: $200 2P: $200
Location: Off Beltway 8, exit Imperial Valley Dr, on westbound service road. 255 N Sam Houston Pkwy E 77060. Fax: 281/875-6208. **Facility:** 391 units. 388 one-bedroom standard units. 3 one-bedroom suites ($250-$350), some with efficiencies. 12 stories, interior corridors. *Bath:* combo or shower only. **Parking:** on-site. **Terms:** check-in 4 pm, 3 day cancellation notice-fee imposed, package plans - weekends. **Amenities:** voice mail, irons, hair dryers. *Fee:* video games, high-speed Internet. **Pool(s):** heated indoor/outdoor. **Leisure Activities:** sauna, whirlpool, exercise room. **Guest Services:** gift shop, area transportation. **Business Services:** conference facilities, business center. **Cards:** AX, DC, DS, MC, VI.

SOME UNITS

🅢💲 ✈ 🍴 ▽ 🛎 🕹 🏊 📶 🎥 📠 💻 / ✕ 🔒 /

HYATT REGENCY HOUSTON AIRPORT AT HOUSTON

INTERCONTINENTAL AIRPORT

Phone: (281)987-1234 **139**

AAA **SAVE**

▽▼▽▼▽

Large-scale Hotel

All Year 1P: $75-$195 2P: $75-$195 XP: $25 F18
Location: Just n of Beltway 8. 15747 John F Kennedy Blvd 77032. Fax: 281/590-8461. **Facility:** 314 units. 301 one-bedroom standard units, some with whirlpools. 13 one-bedroom suites. 7 stories, interior corridors. *Bath:* combo or shower only. **Parking:** on-site. **Terms:** cancellation fee imposed. **Amenities:** video games (fee), voice mail, irons, hair dryers. *Some:* fax. **Dining:** 2 restaurants, 6 am-2 & 5-11 pm, cocktails. **Pool(s):** outdoor. **Leisure Activities:** whirlpool, exercise room. **Guest Services:** gift shop, valet and coin laundry, airport transportation-George Bush Intercontinental Airport, area transportation-Deerbrook Mall. **Business Services:** conference facilities, business center. **Cards:** AX, CB, DC, DS, JC, MC, VI. *(See color ad inside front cover)*

SOME UNITS

✈ 🍴 ▽ 🛎M 🛎 🕹 🏊 📶 🎥 📠 💻 / ✕ 🔒 /
FEE

LA QUINTA INN & SUITES

Phone: (281)219-2000 **174**

AAA **SAVE**

▽▼▽▼▽

Small-scale Hotel

All Year 1P: $70-$110 2P: $75-$115 XP: $5 F18
Location: Beltway 8 (Sam Houston Pkwy), exit John F Kennedy Blvd/Vickery, just n. 15510 John F Kennedy Blvd 77032. Fax: 281/219-2325. **Facility:** 132 units. 114 one-bedroom standard units. 18 one-bedroom suites ($119-$159). 5 stories, interior corridors. *Bath:* combo or shower only. **Parking:** on-site. **Terms:** [ECP] meal plan available, small pets only. **Amenities:** video games (fee), voice mail, irons, hair dryers. *Some:* dual phone lines. **Pool(s):** outdoor. **Leisure Activities:** whirlpool, exercise room. **Guest Services:** valet and coin laundry, airport transportation-George Bush Intercontinental Airport, area transportation-within 5 mi. **Business Services:** meeting rooms, fax (fee). **Cards:** AX, CB, DC, DS, JC, MC, VI. **Special Amenities:** free continental breakfast and free local telephone calls. *(See color ad p 401)*

SOME UNITS

✈ 🐾 🛎M 🛎 🏊 📶 🎥 📠 💻 / ✕ 🔒 📺 /

LA QUINTA INN & SUITES PARK 10

Phone: (281)646-9200 **125**

AAA **SAVE**

▽▼▽▼▽

Small-scale Hotel

All Year 1P: $80-$90 2P: $90-$100 XP: $10 F18
Location: I-10, exit 748 (Barker-Cypress Rd) eastbound, 2.6 mi on eastbound service road; exit 751 (SR 6) westbound, just s to Grisby Rd, 0.5 mi w. 15225 Katy Frwy 77094. Fax: 281/646-9201. **Facility:** 117 units. 113 one-bedroom standard units. 4 one-bedroom suites ($119-$159). 4 stories, interior corridors. *Bath:* combo or shower only. **Parking:** on-site. **Terms:** [ECP] meal plan available, small pets only. **Amenities:** video games (fee), voice mail, irons, hair dryers. **Pool(s):** heated outdoor. **Leisure Activities:** whirlpool, exercise room. **Guest Services:** valet and coin laundry. **Business Services:** meeting rooms, fax (fee). **Cards:** AX, CB, DC, DS, JC, MC, VI. **Special Amenities:** free continental breakfast and free local telephone calls. *(See color ad p 401)*

SOME UNITS

🐾 🛎 🏊 📶 🎥 📠 💻 / ✕ 🔒 📺 /

LA QUINTA INN-GREENSPOINT

Phone: (281)447-6888 **203**

SAVE

▽▼▽▼▽

Small-scale Hotel

All Year 1P: $55-$63 2P: $55-$63
Location: I-45, exit 60A southbound; exit 60B northbound. 6 N Sam Houston Pkwy E 77060. Fax: 281/847-3921. **Facility:** 122 one-bedroom standard units. 2 stories, exterior corridors. *Bath:* combo or shower only. **Parking:** on-site. **Terms:** [ECP] meal plan available, small pets only. **Amenities:** video games (fee), voice mail. **Pool(s):** outdoor. **Guest Services:** valet laundry. **Business Services:** meeting rooms, fax (fee). **Cards:** AX, CB, DC, DS, JC, MC, VI. *(See color ad p 401)*

SOME UNITS

✈ 🐾 🍴 🛎M 🏊 📶 🎥 📠 💻 / ✕ /

LA QUINTA INN-HOUSTON-CY-FAIR

Phone: (281)469-4018 **191**

AAA **SAVE**

▽▼▽▼▽

Motel

All Year 1P: $73-$80 2P: $80-$87 XP: $7 F18
Location: SR 6, w of jct US 290 and FM 1960. 13290 FM 1960 W 77065-4005. Fax: 281/955-6350. **Facility:** 130 one-bedroom standard units. 3 stories, exterior corridors. **Parking:** on-site. **Terms:** [ECP] meal plan available, small pets only. **Amenities:** video games (fee), voice mail, irons, hair dryers. **Pool(s):** outdoor. **Guest Services:** coin laundry. **Business Services:** fax (fee). **Cards:** AX, CB, DC, DS, JC, MC, VI. **Special Amenities:** free continental breakfast and free local telephone calls. *(See color ad p 401)*

SOME UNITS

🐾 🍴 🛎 🕹 🏊 📶 🎥 📠 💻 / ✕ 🔒 /

LA QUINTA INN-HOUSTON EAST

Phone: (713)453-5425 **169**

AAA **SAVE**

▽▼▽▼▽

Motel

All Year 1P: $70-$76 2P: $70-$76
Location: I-10, exit 778A (Federal Rd) eastbound; exit 776B (Holland Ave) westbound, just n. Located adjacent to a truck parking area. 11999 E Frwy 77029-1932. Fax: 713/451-8374. **Facility:** 114 one-bedroom standard units. 2 stories, exterior corridors. *Bath:* combo or shower only. **Parking:** on-site. **Terms:** [ECP] meal plan available, small pets only. **Amenities:** video games (fee), voice mail, irons, hair dryers. **Pool(s):** outdoor. **Guest Services:** valet laundry. **Business Services:** meeting rooms, fax (fee). **Cards:** AX, CB, DC, DS, JC, MC, VI. **Special Amenities:** free continental breakfast and free local telephone calls. *(See color ad p 401)*

SOME UNITS

🐾 🍴 🛎 🕹 🏊 📶 🎥 📠 💻 / ✕ 🔒 📺 /

(See map p. 382)

LA QUINTA INN-HOUSTON-I-45 NORTH(LOOP 1960)
Phone: (281)444-7500 [195]

(AAA) (SAVE) ▼▼▼▼

Motel

All Year 1P: $60-$66 2P: $67-$73 XP: $7 F18
Location: I-45, exit 66, southbound service road, 0.4 mi s of jct FM 1960 and I-45. Truck parking located on premises. 17111 North Frwy 77090-5005. Fax: 281/893-6271. **Facility:** 138 one-bedroom standard units. 2 stories, interior corridors. **Parking:** on-site. **Terms:** [ECP] meal plan available, small pets only. **Amenities:** video games (fee), voice mail, irons, hair dryers. **Pool(s):** outdoor. **Guest Services:** valet and coin laundry. **Business Services:** meeting rooms, fax (fee). **Cards:** AX, CB, DC, DS, JC, MC, VI. **Special Amenities:** free continental breakfast and free local telephone calls. *(See color ad p 401)*

SOME UNITS
🛏 🍴 ⊿ 🛄 DATA PORT 💻 / ⊠ 🔌 / FEE

LA QUINTA INN-WILCREST
Phone: (713)932-0808 [177]

(AAA) (SAVE) ▼▼▼▼

Motel

All Year 1P: $50-$66 2P: $54-$70 XP: $4 F18
Location: I-10, exit 754 (Kirkwood Dr) westbound; exit 755 (Wilcrest Rd) eastbound, on eastbound service road. 11113 Katy Frwy (US 290) 77042. Fax: 713/973-2352. **Facility:** 176 one-bedroom standard units. 2 stories, exterior corridors. *Bath:* combo or shower only. **Parking:** on-site. **Terms:** [ECP] meal plan available, small pets only. **Amenities:** video games (fee), voice mail, irons, hair dryers. **Pool(s):** outdoor. **Guest Services:** coin laundry. **Business Services:** meeting rooms, fax (fee). **Cards:** AX, CB, DC, DS, JC, MC, VI. **Special Amenities:** free continental breakfast and free local telephone calls. *(See color ad p 401)*

SOME UNITS
🛏 🍴 ⑤ ⊘ ⊿ 🛄 DATA PORT 💻 / ⊠ 🔌 🖥 /

MAINSTAY SUITES-HOUSTON (NOW KNOWN AS TOWNEPLACE SUITES HOUSTON-NORTHWEST FREEWAY)
Phone: (713)690-4035 [160]

▼▼▼▼

Small-scale Hotel

All Year [CP] 1P: $49-$84 2P: $49-$84
Location: US 290, exit Bingle/43rd St eastbound; exit Bingle/Pinemont/43rd St westbound; on westbound feeder. 12820 Northwest Frwy (US 290) 77040. Fax: 713/690-1148. **Facility:** 85 units. 64 one-bedroom standard units with efficiencies. 21 one-bedroom suites with efficiencies. 3 stories, interior corridors. *Bath:* combo or shower only. **Parking:** on-site. **Terms:** 5 day cancellation notice, weekly rates available, pets ($75 fee, $10 extra charge). **Amenities:** voice mail, irons. **Leisure Activities:** whirlpool, exercise room. **Guest Services:** complimentary evening beverages: Mon-Wed, valet and coin laundry. **Business Services:** fax (fee). **Cards:** AX, DC, DS, MC, VI.

SOME UNITS
(ASK) 🅢🅓 🛏 🍴 ♿ ⑤ ⊿ 🛄 DATA PORT 🔌 🖥 💻 / ⊠ /

MICROTEL INN & SUITES
Phone: (281)335-0800 [202]

▼▼▼

Small-scale Hotel

All Year 1P: $50 2P: $60
Location: I-45, exit 25 (NASA Rd One), 3 mi e. Located across from NASA Johnson Space Center. 1620 NASA Rd One 77058. Fax: 281/335-7524. **Facility:** 55 one-bedroom standard units. 3 stories, interior corridors. *Bath:* combo or shower only. **Parking:** on-site. **Terms:** [CP] meal plan available. **Amenities:** voice mail, hair dryers. **Guest Services:** coin laundry. **Business Services:** meeting rooms, fax. **Cards:** AX, CB, DC, DS, MC, VI.

SOME UNITS
(ASK) 🅢🅓 🍴 ⑤ ➕ 🛄 DATA PORT / ⊠ 🔌 🖥 💻 /

MOTEL 6 - 1140
Phone: 713/937-7056 [155]

▼▼

Motel

5/22-1/31 1P: $41-$51 2P: $47-$57 XP: $3 F17
2/1-5/21 1P: $39-$49 2P: $45-$55 XP: $3 F17
Location: US 290, exit Jones Rd westbound; exit Senate Ave eastbound, on westbound frontage road. 16884 Northwest Frwy 77040. Fax: 713/849-5240. **Facility:** Designated smoking area. 119 one-bedroom standard units. 2 stories, exterior corridors. *Bath:* combo or shower only. **Parking:** on-site. **Terms:** small pets only. **Pool(s):** outdoor. **Guest Services:** coin laundry. **Business Services:** fax (fee). **Cards:** AX, CB, DC, DS, MC, VI.

SOME UNITS
🅢🅓 🛏 ⑤ ⊿ 🛄 DATA PORT / ⊠ /

MOTEL 6 - 1401
Phone: 713/334-9188 [150]

▼▼▼

Motel

5/22-1/31 1P: $43-$53 2P: $49-$59 XP: $3 F17
2/1-5/21 1P: $41-$51 2P: $47-$57 XP: $3 F17
Location: Sam Houston Pkwy (Beltway 8), exit Westheimer Rd. 2900 W Sam Houston Pkwy S 77042. Fax: 713/334-4470. **Facility:** 121 one-bedroom standard units. 3 stories, interior corridors. *Bath:* combo or shower only. **Parking:** on-site. **Terms:** small pets only. **Pool(s):** outdoor. **Guest Services:** coin laundry. **Business Services:** fax (fee). **Cards:** AX, CB, DC, DS, MC, VI.

SOME UNITS
🅢🅓 🛏 🍴 ♿ ⑤ ⊿ 🛄 DATA PORT / ⊠ /

NORTHWEST HOUSTON COURTYARD BY MARRIOTT
Phone: (281)374-6464 [123]

(SAVE) ▼▼▼

Small-scale Hotel

All Year 1P: $129 2P: $129
Location: SR 249, exit Louetta Rd, just w. 11050 Louetta Rd 77070. Fax: 281/374-6161. **Facility:** 126 units. 122 one-bedroom standard units, some with whirlpools. 4 one-bedroom suites ($139-$149). 4 stories, interior corridors. *Bath:* combo or shower only. **Parking:** on-site. **Terms:** 15% service charge. **Amenities:** high-speed Internet (fee), dual phone lines, voice mail, irons, hair dryers. **Pool(s):** outdoor. **Leisure Activities:** whirlpool, exercise room. **Guest Services:** valet and coin laundry. **Business Services:** meeting rooms, fax (fee). **Cards:** AX, CB, DC, DS, MC, VI.

SOME UNITS
🅢🅓 🍴 ♿ ⑤ ⊿ 🛄 DATA PORT 💻 / ⊠ VCR 🔌 / FEE

OMNI HOUSTON HOTEL WESTSIDE
Phone: (281)558-8338 [187]

▼▼▼

Large-scale Hotel

All Year 1P: $209-$229 2P: $219-$239 XP: $10 F17
Location: I-10, exit 753A (Eldridge St), just n. 13210 Katy Frwy 77079. Fax: 281/558-4028. **Facility:** 400 units. 396 one-bedroom standard units. 4 one-bedroom suites ($209-$999). 5 stories, interior corridors. **Parking:** on-site. **Terms:** cancellation fee imposed, small pets only ($25 extra charge). **Amenities:** voice mail, honor bars, irons, hair dryers. **Fee:** video games, high-speed Internet. **Pool(s):** heated outdoor. **Leisure Activities:** whirlpool, 2 lighted tennis courts, exercise room, sports court. **Guest Services:** gift shop, valet laundry, area transportation. **Business Services:** conference facilities, business center. **Cards:** AX, CB, DC, DS, JC, MC, VI.

SOME UNITS
(ASK) 🅢🅓 🛏 🍴 🍸 ⊘ ⊿ 🗙 🛄 DATA PORT / ⊠ VCR 🔌 🖥 / FEE

(See map p. 382)

QUALITY INN-NASA

[SAVE]

▼▼▼▼

Small-scale Hotel

Phone: (281)333-3737   **124**

All Year [CP]   1P: $59-$79   2P: $59-$79   XP: $6   F18
Location: I-45, exit 25 (NASA Rd One/Alvin), 1.5 mi e. 904 NASA Rd One 77058. Fax: 281/333-8354. **Facility:** 111 one-bedroom standard units. 2 stories, exterior corridors. *Bath:* combo or shower only. **Parking:** on-site. **Terms:** cancellation fee imposed. **Amenities:** irons, hair dryers. *Some:* dual phone lines. **Pool(s):** outdoor. **Leisure Activities:** exercise room. **Guest Services:** coin laundry. **Business Services:** fax (fee). **Cards:** AX, CB, DC, DS, JC, MC, VI.

SOME UNITS

(S⊘) (⊤⊥) (⏚) (⛿) (⟲) (⇌) (📷) (DATA PORT) (🛏) (🖨) (💻) / (⊠) /

QUALITY SUITES

[SAVE]

▼▼▼▼

Small-scale Hotel

Phone: (281)442-4444   **136**

All Year [ECP]   1P: $85-$95   2P: $95-$100   XP: $5   F12
Location: Beltway 8, exit Aldine Westfield, just nw on frontage road. 15321 Vantage Pkwy E 77032. Fax: 281/442-1231. **Facility:** 60 one-bedroom suites, some with whirlpools. 3 stories, interior corridors. *Bath:* combo or shower only. **Parking:** on-site. **Amenities:** irons, hair dryers. **Pool(s):** outdoor. **Leisure Activities:** whirlpool, exercise room. **Guest Services:** coin laundry. **Business Services:** meeting rooms, business center. **Cards:** AX, CB, DC, DS, JC, MC, VI.

SOME UNITS

(S⊘) (⛿) (⟲) (⇌) (VCR) (📷) (DATA PORT) (🛏) (🖨) (💻) / (⊠) /

RADISSON SUITE HOTEL HOUSTON WEST

(AAA) [SAVE]

▼▼▼▼

Large-scale Hotel

Phone: (713)461-6000   **135**

All Year [BP]   1P: $119   2P: $119   XP: $10   F17
Location: I-10, exit 756A westbound; exit 755 eastbound, southeast corner of I-10 and Beltway 8. 10655 Katy Frwy 77024. Fax: 713/467-2357. **Facility:** 173 units. 91 one-bedroom standard units. 82 one-bedroom suites ($139). 14 stories, interior/exterior corridors. *Bath:* combo or shower only. **Parking:** on-site. **Terms:** 3 day cancellation notice-fee imposed. **Amenities:** voice mail, irons, hair dryers. *Fee:* video games, high-speed Internet. **Pool(s):** outdoor. **Leisure Activities:** exercise room. **Guest Services:** gift shop, valet laundry, area transportation-within 3 mi. **Business Services:** meeting rooms, business center. **Cards:** AX, DC, DS, MC, VI. **Special Amenities:** free continental breakfast and free newspaper. *(See ad below)*

SOME UNITS

(S⊘) (⛿) (⟲) (⇌) (📷) (DATA PORT) (💻) / (⊠) (🛏) (🖨) /

RAMADA LIMITED

(AAA) [SAVE]

▼▼▼▼

Small-scale Hotel

Phone: (281)442-1830   **144**

All Year [ECP]   1P: $59-$99   2P: $64-$109   XP: $7   F17
Location: Beltway 8, exit John F Kennedy Blvd. 15350 John F Kennedy Blvd 77032. Fax: 281/987-8023. **Facility:** 126 one-bedroom standard units. 3 stories, interior corridors. **Parking:** on-site. **Amenities:** irons, hair dryers. **Pool(s):** outdoor. **Leisure Activities:** sauna, whirlpool, exercise room. **Guest Services:** valet laundry, airport transportation-George Bush Intercontinental Airport, area transportation-Deerbrook Mall. **Business Services:** fax (fee). **Cards:** AX, DC, DS, MC, VI. **Special Amenities:** free continental breakfast and free newspaper.

SOME UNITS

(S⊘) (➕) (⊤⊥) (⟲) (⇌) (⊠) (📷) (DATA PORT) (💻) / (⊠) (VCR) (🛏) /
FEE

RAMADA LTD/S.H. 249

▼▼ ▼▼

Motel

Phone: (281)970-5000   **107**

All Year   1P: $80-$90   2P: $90-$100   XP: $10   F18
Location: SR 249, exit Grant, on northbound frontage road. 18836 Tomball Pkwy 77070. Fax: 281/970-7300. **Facility:** 42 one-bedroom standard units, some with whirlpools. 2 stories, exterior corridors. **Parking:** on-site. **Terms:** [CP] meal plan available, pets ($10 extra charge). **Amenities:** dual phone lines, voice mail, safes, irons, hair dryers. **Pool(s):** outdoor. **Guest Services:** coin laundry. **Business Services:** fax (fee). **Cards:** AX, DC, DS, MC, VI.

SOME UNITS

(A$K) (S⊘) (🐾) (⇌) (📷) (DATA PORT) (🛏) (🖨) (💻) / (⊠) /

(See map p. 382)

RED ROOF INN HOUSTON WEST
Phone: (281)579-7200   **164**
CAAD **SAVE**   All Year   1P: $39-$56   2P: $44-$62   XP: $5   F18
▼▼ ▼▼   **Location:** I-10, exit 751 (Addicks Rd/SR 6), 0.8 mi on west frontage road. 15701 Park Ten Pl 77084.
Fax: 281/579-0732. **Facility:** 123 one-bedroom standard units. 3 stories, interior/exterior corridors. *Bath:*
combo or shower only. **Parking:** on-site. **Terms:** small pets only. **Amenities:** video games (fee), high-speed
Small-scale Hotel Internet, voice mail. **Guest Services:** valet laundry. **Business Services:** meeting rooms, fax (fee).
Cards: AX, CB, DC, DS, MC, VI. **Special Amenities: free local telephone calls and free newspaper.**

SOME UNITS
FEE   FEE

RED ROOF INNS
Phone: (713)939-0800   **128**
CAAD **SAVE**   All Year   1P: $39-$59   2P: $44-$64   XP: $5   F18
▼▼ ▼▼   **Location:** US 290, exit Hollister and Tidwell rds, on eastbound service road. 12929 Northwest Frwy 77040.
Fax: 713/939-0805. **Facility:** 122 one-bedroom standard units. 3 stories, interior/exterior corridors. *Bath:*
combo or shower only. **Parking:** on-site. **Terms:** small pets only. **Amenities:** video games, voice mail.
Small-scale Hotel **Pool(s):** outdoor. **Business Services:** meeting rooms, fax (fee). **Cards:** AX, CB, DC, DS, MC, VI.
Special Amenities: free local telephone calls and free newspaper.

SOME UNITS

RED ROOF INNS
Phone: (713)785-9909   **165**
CAAD **SAVE**   All Year   1P: $43-$59   2P: $48-$64   XP: $5   F18
▼▼ ▼▼   **Location:** SW Sam Houston Pkwy (Beltway 8), exit Westheimer Rd. 2960 W Sam Houston Pkwy S 77042.
Fax: 713/785-6162. **Facility:** 135 one-bedroom standard units. 3 stories, interior/exterior corridors. *Bath:*
combo or shower only. **Parking:** on-site. **Amenities:** video games (fee), voice mail. **Pool(s):** outdoor. **Guest**
Motel   **Services:** valet laundry. **Business Services:** meeting rooms, fax (fee). **Cards:** AX, CB, DC, DS, MC, VI.
Special Amenities: free local telephone calls and free newspaper.

SOME UNITS

RESIDENCE INN BY MARRIOTT HOUSTON WESTCHASE
Phone: (713)974-5454   **175**
SAVE   All Year [BP]   1P: $94-$204
▼▼ ▼▼ ▼▼   **Location:** Beltway 8 (Sam Houston Pkwy), exit Westheimer Rd, 0.7 mi e to Elmside Dr, just s. 9965 Westheimer Rd
77042. Fax: 713/974-5954. **Facility:** 120 units. 102 one- and 18 two-bedroom standard units. 3 stories, interior corridors. *Bath:* combo or shower only. **Parking:** on-site. **Terms:** small pets only ($50 fee, $5 extra
Small-scale Hotel charge). **Amenities:** high-speed Internet, dual phone lines, voice mail, irons, hair dryers. **Pool(s):** heated
outdoor. **Leisure Activities:** whirlpool, exercise room, sports court. **Guest Services:** complimentary evening
beverages: Mon-Thurs, coin laundry. **Business Services:** meeting rooms, fax (fee). **Cards:** AX, CB, DC, DS, JC, MC, VI.

SOME UNITS

RESIDENCE INN-HOUSTON CLEAR LAKE
Phone: (281)486-2424   **178**
SAVE   All Year [BP]   1P: $125-$175   2P: $125-$175
▼▼ ▼▼   **Location:** I-45 S, exit 26 (Bay Area Blvd), 1.2 mi e. 525 Bay Area Blvd 77058. Fax: 281/488-8179. **Facility:** 110 one-
bedroom standard units with kitchens. 2 stories, exterior corridors. *Bath:* combo or shower only. **Parking:** on-
site. **Terms:** pets ($50 fee, $6 extra charge). **Amenities:** voice mail, irons, hair dryers. **Pool(s):** heated
Small-scale Hotel outdoor. **Leisure Activities:** whirlpool, exercise room, sports court. **Guest Services:** complimentary evening
beverages: Mon-Wed, valet and coin laundry, area transportation. **Business Services:** meeting rooms, fax
(fee). **Cards:** AX, CB, DC, DS, JC, MC, VI.

SOME UNITS

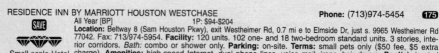

SLEEP INN
Phone: (281)442-7770   **138**
CAAD **SAVE**   All Year   1P: $66-$75   2P: $69-$79
▼▼ ▼▼   **Location:** Beltway 8, exit John F Kennedy Blvd, just n. 15675 John F Kennedy Blvd 77032. Fax: 281/442-6699.
Facility: 106 one-bedroom standard units. 3 stories, interior corridors. *Bath:* combo or shower only. **Parking:**
on-site. **Terms:** [CP] & [ECP] meal plans available. **Amenities:** video games (fee), irons, hair dryers.
Small-scale Hotel **Pool(s):** outdoor. **Guest Services:** valet laundry, airport transportation-George Bush Intercontinental Airport.
Business Services: fax (fee). **Cards:** AX, CB, DC, DS, JC, MC, VI. **Special Amenities: free continental
breakfast and free local telephone calls.**

SOME UNITS

STAR INN & SUITES
Phone: (713)695-5552   **115**
▼▼ ▼▼   All Year   1P: $49-$55   2P: $54-$60   XP: $5   F12
Motel   **Location:** I-45, exit 53 (Airline Dr), just w. 4515 Airline Dr 77022. Fax: 713/884-1612. **Facility:** 32 one-bedroom
standard units, some with whirlpools. 2 stories, exterior corridors. **Parking:** on-site. **Terms:** weekly rates
DS, MC, VI.   available, pets ($5 deposit). **Amenities:** CD players, voice mail. **Business Services:** fax (fee). **Cards:** AX,

SOME UNITS

STUDIO 6
Phone: 281/579-6959   **149**
▼▼ ▼▼   All Year   1P: $43-$53   2P: $47-$57   XP: $4   F17
Motel   **Location:** I-10, exit 751 (Addicks Rd), just n. 1255 Hwy 6 N 77084. Fax: 281/579-2404. **Facility:** 134 one-bedroom
standard units with efficiencies. 2 stories, exterior corridors. *Bath:* combo or shower only. **Parking:** on-site.
Terms: weekly rates available, small pets only. **Amenities:** voice mail, irons. **Guest Services:** coin laundry.
Business Services: fax (fee). **Cards:** AX, CB, DC, DS, MC, VI.

SOME UNITS

(See map p. 382)

STUDIO 6-CYPRESS STATION #6037
Motel
All Year   1P: $41-$51   2P: $45-$55   XP: $4
Phone: 281/580-2221   180   F17
Location: I-45, exit 66, southbound frontage road, then just n. 220 Bammel-Westfield Rd 77090. **Fax:** 281/580-2881. **Facility:** 134 one-bedroom standard units with efficiencies. 2 stories, exterior corridors. *Bath:* combo or shower only. **Parking:** on-site. **Terms:** weekly rates available, pets ($50 fee). **Amenities:** voice mail, irons. **Guest Services:** coin laundry. **Business Services:** fax (fee). **Cards:** AX, CB, DC, DS, MC, VI.

SOME UNITS

STUDIO 6-HOUSTON HOBBY SOUTH #6039
Small-scale Hotel
All Year   1P: $46-$56   2P: $50-$60   XP: $3
Phone: 281/929-5400   157   F17
Location: I-45, exit 33 (Fugua St) southbound, stay in right lane and cross over I-45, just e to Featherwood, then just s. 12700 Featherwood 77034. **Fax:** 281/929-5500. **Facility:** 133 one-bedroom standard units with efficiencies. 2 stories, exterior corridors. *Bath:* combo or shower only. **Parking:** on-site. **Terms:** weekly rates available, small pets only ($25-$50 fee). **Amenities:** voice mail, irons. **Guest Services:** coin laundry. **Business Services:** fax (fee). **Cards:** AX, CB, DC, DS, MC, VI.

SOME UNITS

SUPER 8-HOUSTON-GESSNER
Motel
All Year [CP]   1P: $45   2P: $49   XP: $5
Phone: (713)772-3626   148   F18
Location: Sw on US 59, exit Gessner St. Located within easy access to Southwest Medical Center. 8201 Southwest Frwy 77074-1707. **Fax:** 713/995-1270. **Facility:** 130 units. 129 one-bedroom standard units. 1 one-bedroom suite. 2 stories, exterior corridors. *Bath:* combo or shower only. **Parking:** on-site. **Terms:** small pets only. **Amenities:** video games, voice mail, hair dryers. **Pool(s):** outdoor. **Guest Services:** valet laundry. **Business Services:** meeting rooms, fax (fee). **Cards:** AX, CB, DC, DS, MC, VI.

SOME UNITS

SUPER 8 MOTEL
Motel
All Year   1P: $60-$65   2P: $70
Phone: 281/866-8686   186
Location: I-45, exit 66 southbound; exit 66A northbound, just w. 609 W FM 1960 77090. **Fax:** 281/866-7600. **Facility:** 49 one-bedroom standard units with whirlpools. 3 stories, interior corridors. *Bath:* combo or shower only. **Parking:** on-site. **Terms:** [CP] meal plan available, small pets only ($25 deposit). **Amenities:** irons, hair dryers. **Pool(s):** small indoor. **Leisure Activities:** whirlpool. **Guest Services:** coin laundry. **Business Services:** meeting rooms, fax (fee). **Cards:** AX, CB, DC, DS, MC, VI.

SOME UNITS

(See map p. 382)

TOWNEPLACE SUITES BY MARRIOTT-WESTLAKE
Phone: (281)646-0058 ⬛161
SAVE
All Year 1P: $90-$140
Location: I-10, exit 751, just s on SR 6 to Grisby Rd, then w. 15155 Katy Frwy 77094. Fax: 281/646-0386.
Facility: 95 units. 68 one-bedroom standard units with kitchens. 4 one- and 23 two-bedroom suites with kitchens. 3 stories, interior corridors. *Bath:* combo or shower only. **Parking:** on-site. **Terms:** cancellation fee
Small-scale Hotel imposed, small pets only ($100 fee). **Amenities:** dual phone lines, voice mail, irons. **Pool(s):** heated outdoor.
Leisure Activities: exercise room. **Guest Services:** valet and coin laundry. **Business Services:** fax.
Cards: AX, DC, DS, MC, VI.

SOME UNITS

TRAVELODGE SOUTHWEST FRWY
Phone: (713)270-9559 ⬛147
All Year [CP] 1P: $45 2P: $49 XP: $5 F12
Location: Sw on US 59, 1 mi sw of Bissonnet St exit. 10552 Southwest Frwy 77074-7499. Fax: 713/270-0219.
Facility: 114 units. 113 one-bedroom standard units. 1 one-bedroom suite ($79). 3 stories, interior/exterior
Motel corridors. **Parking:** on-site. **Terms:** small pets only ($25 fee). **Amenities:** video games (fee), voice mail.
Pool(s): outdoor. **Leisure Activities:** whirlpool. **Guest Services:** valet laundry. **Business Services:** meeting rooms, fax (fee).
Cards: AX, CB, DC, DS, MC, VI.

SOME UNITS
FEE FEE

WINGATE INN-HOUSTON
Phone: 281/987-8777 ⬛140
All Year [ECP] 1P: $87-$95 2P: $93-$101 XP: $6 F18
Location: Just n of Beltway 8, exit John F Kennedy Blvd. 15615 John F Kennedy Blvd 77032. Fax: 281/987-9317.
Small-scale Hotel **Facility:** 101 one-bedroom standard units, some with whirlpools. 3 stories, interior corridors. *Bath:* combo or
shower only. **Parking:** on-site. **Amenities:** video games (fee), high-speed Internet, dual phone lines, voice
mail, safes, irons, hair dryers. **Pool(s):** outdoor. **Leisure Activities:** whirlpool, exercise room. **Guest Services:** valet and coin
laundry, area transportation. **Business Services:** meeting rooms, business center. **Cards:** AX, CB, DC, DS, JC, MC, VI.

SOME UNITS

WINGATE INN SOUTHWEST
Phone: (281)568-6969 ⬛152
AAA SAVE
All Year 1P: $89-$99 2P: $99-$109 XP: $10 F18
Location: On US 59, exit Beltway 8 Frontage Rd southbound, then 0.6 mi s; then U-turn under highway. 11050 South-
west Frwy 77040. Fax: 281/568-6901. **Facility:** 82 units. 76 one-bedroom standard units. 6 one-bedroom
suites ($109-$129), some with whirlpools. 3 stories, interior corridors. *Bath:* combo or shower only. **Parking:**
Small-scale Hotel on-site. **Terms:** cancellation fee imposed, [BP] meal plan available. **Amenities:** video games (fee), high-
speed Internet, dual phone lines, voice mail, safes, irons. **Pool(s):** outdoor. **Leisure Activities:** whirlpool, exercise room. **Guest Services:** valet laundry, area transportation-within 5 mi. **Business Services:** meeting rooms, business
center. **Cards:** AX, DC, DS, MC, VI. **Special Amenities:** free continental breakfast and free local telephone calls.

SOME UNITS

WYNDHAM GREENSPOINT
Phone: (281)875-2222 ⬛120
AAA SAVE
All Year 1P: $99-$169 2P: $109-$179 XP: $10 F17
Location: I-45, exit 61 (Greens Rd), 0.5 mi e. Located across from mall. 12400 Greenspoint Dr 77060.
Fax: 281/875-0099. **Facility:** 472 units. 459 one-bedroom standard units. 13 one-bedroom suites. 15 stories,
interior corridors. **Parking:** on-site. **Terms:** cancellation fee imposed. **Amenities:** high-speed Internet (fee),
Large-scale Hotel dual phone lines, voice mail, irons, hair dryers. **Dining:** 2 restaurants, 6 am-11 pm, cocktails. **Pool(s):** heated
outdoor. **Leisure Activities:** saunas, exercise room. **Guest Services:** gift shop, valet laundry, airport
transportation-George Bush Intercontinental Airport, area transportation-within 3 mi. **Business Services:** conference facilities,
business center. **Cards:** AX, DC, DS, MC, VI.

SOME UNITS
FEE

---

*The following lodgings were either not evaluated or did not
meet AAA rating requirements but are listed for your information only.*

BEST VALUE PLATINUM INN
fyi Under construction, scheduled to open February 2003. **Location:** I-45, jct West Rd and Greens Landing. I-45 &
West Rd.
Small-scale Hotel

COUNTRY INN & SUITES BY CARLSON
Phone: 713/943-2700
fyi Not evaluated. **Location:** 8778 Airport Blvd 77061. Facilities, services, and decor characterize a mid-range property.

HOTEL SOFITEL HOUSTON
Phone: (281)445-9000 ⬛159
fyi All Year 1P: $199-$229 2P: $199-$229 XP: $10 F12
Under major renovation, scheduled to be completed November 2001. Last rated: ▽▽▽ **Location:** Beltway
Large-scale Hotel 8 (Sam Houston Pkwy), exit Imperial Valley westbound; exit Hardy Toll Rd eastbound, on westbound frontage road. Located in Greenspoint Business District. 425 N Sam Houston Pkwy E 77060. Fax: 281/445-9826. **Facility:** 334 units.
332 one-bedroom standard units. 2 one-bedroom suites ($199-$299). 8 stories, interior corridors. **Parking:** on-site and valet.
Terms: weekly rates available, [BP] & [CP] meal plans available, package plans - weekends, 20% service charge, small pets
only ($50 deposit). **Amenities:** dual phone lines, voice mail, irons, hair dryers. **Dining:** Le Cafe Royal, see separate listing.
Pool(s): outdoor. **Leisure Activities:** whirlpools. *Fee:* massage. **Guest Services:** gift shop, valet laundry, area transportation.
Business Services: conference facilities, business center. **Cards:** AX, CB, DC, DS, JC, MC, VI.

SOME UNITS
FEE FEE FEE

(See map p. 382)

─────── WHERE TO DINE ───────

BISTRO PROVENCE   **Lunch:** $10-$22   **Dinner:** $10-$22   **Phone:** 281/497-1122   (179)
♦♦♦ ♦♦♦   **Location:** Sam Houston Pkwy (Beltway 8), exit Westheimer Rd, 2.3 mi w, just n on Kirkwood. 11920-J Westheimer Rd
77077. **Hours:** 11 am-2:30 & 5-10 pm, Fri-11 pm, Sat 5 pm-11 pm. Closed: Sun & Mon.
French   **Features:** Relaxing, inviting and pleasant, the quaint bistro has a colorful dining room, including an open
kitchen with a wood-burning oven. Mediterranean influences are evident in creative Provence France
entrees that center on seafood, rabbit and Cornish game hen. Gourmet pizzas also are good. Casual dress; cocktails.
Parking: on-site. **Cards:** AX, DS, MC, VI.

BRENNER'S STEAKHOUSE   **Lunch:** $25-$33   **Dinner:** $25-$33   **Phone:** 713/465-2901   (161)
♦♦♦ ♦♦♦   **Location:** I-10 and US 90, exit 755 (Wilcrest Dr), just se of exit on service road. 10911 Katy Frwy 77079.
Hours: 11:30 am-2 & 5:30-10 pm, Mon & Sat from 5:30 pm, Sun noon-9 pm. Closed major holidays.
Steak & Seafood   **Reservations:** suggested. **Features:** Overlooking a beautiful garden with pools, waterfalls and a water
wheel, this dining room has been the setting for cozy meals since 1936. A limited menu recited by the wait
staff features prime steaks such as the char-grilled filet wrapped in bacon. Semi-formal attire; cocktails. **Parking:** on-site.
Cards: AX, DC, MC, VI.

CARMELO'S ITALIAN RESTAURANT   **Lunch:** $9-$15   **Dinner:** $14-$32   **Phone:** 281/531-0696   (162)
♦♦♦ ♦♦♦ ♦♦♦   **Location:** W on I-10, s on Dairy-Ashford Rd exit, to Memorial Dr, 0.3 mi w. 14795 Memorial Dr 77079. **Hours:** 11
am-2:30 & 5-10:30 pm, Fri & Sat 5 pm-11 pm. Closed major holidays. **Reservations:** suggested.
Italian   **Features:** Owner-operated since 1981, this eatery presents upscale dining with a good variety of freshly
prepared dishes that feature beef, chicken and seafood options. For a nice, light meal, try the grilled
chicken over pasta served with fresh steamed vegetables. Casual dress; cocktails; entertainment. **Parking:** valet. **Cards:** AX,
CB, DC, DS, MC, VI.

CATTLEGUARD RESTAURANT & BAR   **Lunch:** $12-$25   **Dinner:** $12-$25   **Phone:** 281/493-5094   (154)
♦♦♦ ♦♦♦   **Location:** I-10, exit 751 (Addicks Rd/SR 6), just n. 1010 N Hwy 6 77079. **Hours:** 11 am-10 pm, Sun-9 pm.
Closed: 11/27, 12/25. **Features:** Patrons can unwind in a casually rustic atmosphere to savor premium
gold Angus beef and award-winning chicken fried steak. Burgers and Tex-Mex round out the menu. Casual
American   dress; cocktails. **Parking:** on-site. **Cards:** AX, DC, DS, MC, VI.

CHRIS' TEXAS CHEESECAKE & GRILL   **Lunch:** $5-$22   **Dinner:** $5-$22   **Phone:** 713/946-1475   (182)
♦♦♦   **Location:** I-45, exit 34 (Almeda-Genoa), 1.1 mi w, then just s. 9880 Windmill Lakes Blvd 77075. **Hours:** 11
am-10:30 pm, Sun noon-10 pm. Closed: 12/25. **Features:** "No New York stuff" is the motto at the
restaurant, which is known for its down-home cooking. Among menu choices are half-pound burgers,
American   chicken-fried steak and baby back ribs, as well as a few salads. Don't leave without devouring the owner's
own signature cheesecake. Casual dress. **Parking:** on-site. **Cards:** AX, DS, MC, VI.

CHURRASCO'S-WEST CHASE   **Lunch:** $7-$19   **Dinner:** $12-$26   **Phone:** 713/952-1988   (177)
♦♦♦ ♦♦♦   **Location:** Just w of jct S Gessner Rd. 9705 Westheimer Rd 77042. **Hours:** 11 am-10 pm, Fri-11 pm, Sat 5 pm-11
pm. Closed major holidays; also Sun. **Reservations:** suggested. **Features:** Among South American
Ethnic   specialties are charcoal-grilled steak, seafood and the delicious grilled tenderloin that shares the
restaurant's name. Plantain chips are an addictive appetizer, and tres leches, or three-milk cake, sweetly
ends a meal. This location offers valet parking and slightly more sophisticated surroundings. Dressy casual; cocktails. **Parking:**
on-site. **Cards:** AX, CB, DC, DS, MC, VI.

THE COUNTY LINE BARBEQUE   **Lunch:** $6-$14   **Dinner:** $8-$20   **Phone:** 281/537-2454   (164)
♦♦♦   **Location:** Jct I-45 and FM 1960, exit 66, 7 mi w to Cutten Rd, 0.7 mi n. 13850 Cutten Rd 77069. **Hours:** 11:30
am-2 & 5:30-9 pm, Fri-10 pm, Sat 11:30 am-10 pm, Sun 11:30 am-9 pm. Closed: 1/1, 11/27, 12/25, 12/26;
Barbecue   also Mon. **Features:** Nestled in a natural landscape that provides a haven from the bustle of everyday life,
the family restaurant dishes up helpings of mouthwatering barbecue and down-home side dishes. Baby
back ribs are especially good with creamy potato salad. Casual dress; cocktails. **Parking:** on-site. **Cards:** AX, DC, DS,
MC, VI.

DONERAKI MEXICAN RESTAURANT   **Lunch:** $6-$12   **Dinner:** $8-$19   **Phone:** 281/893-1400   (150)
♦♦♦   **Location:** Jct FM 1960 W and Champion Forest Rd. 5505 FM 1960 W 77069. **Hours:** 8 am-10:30 pm, Fri &
Sat-midnight, Sun-11 pm. **Reservations:** suggested. **Features:** Patrons can relax on the covered patio to
feast on traditional cuisine, including enchiladas, tacos and fajitas. A strolling trio provides musical
Mexican   entertainment Thursday through Sunday evenings. Casual dress; cocktails; entertainment. **Parking:**
on-site. **Cards:** AX, CB, DC, DS, MC, VI.

ELVIA'S MEXICAN PUB   **Dinner:** $8-$18   **Phone:** 713/266-9631   (165)
♦♦♦   **Location:** Southeast corner of Fondren and Westheimer Rd, exit Fondren on US 59, n to Westheimer Rd. 2727
Fondren Rd, Suite 2A 77063. **Hours:** 6 pm-2 am. Closed: 12/25; also Sun-Tues. **Reservations:** suggested.
Mexican   **Features:** The lighthearted Latin music club offers a small menu of traditional Mexican offerings, including
fajitas and chicken empanadas. Casual dress; cocktails; entertainment. **Parking:** on-site. **Cards:** AX, DC,
DS, MC, VI.

EL YUCATAN MEXICAN RESTAURANT   **Lunch:** $6-$9   **Dinner:** $9-$20   **Phone:** 281/870-0079   (157)
♦♦♦ ♦♦♦   **Location:** I-10, exit 751 (Addicks Rd/SR 6), just s on SR 6 S. 410 S Hwy 6 77079. **Hours:** 11 am-10 pm, Fri-11
pm, Sat 9 am-11 pm, Sun 9 am-10 pm. Closed: 11/27, 12/25. **Features:** Just south of I-10, the relaxed,
family-owned Mexican restaurant features multiflavored dishes from Mexico's Yucatan Peninsula.
Mexican   Especially worthwhile are cochinita pibil (baked pork) and seafood enchiladas. Casual dress; cocktails.
Parking: on-site. **Cards:** AX, CB, DC, DS, MC, VI.

(See map p. 382)

EMPRESS
◆◆◆ ◆◆◆
Chinese

Lunch: $7-$20   **Dinner:** $15-$70   **Phone:** 281/583-8021   155
Location: Jct FM 1960 W and Champion Forest Dr. 5419-A FM 1960 W, Suite A 77069. **Hours:** 11 am-2:30 & 5-10 pm, Fri-10:30 pm, Sat 5 pm-10:30 pm. Closed major holidays; also Sun. **Reservations:** suggested. **Features:** Blending French, Asian and Pacific Rim elements creates an inventive, occasionally sublime menu. For example, try the salmon filet steamed with ginger, topped with a tangle of shredded scallions, and accompanied by a selection from an ambitious wine list. Casual dress; beer & wine only. **Parking:** on-site. **Cards:** AX, DC, DS, MC, VI.

❌

HARRIS COUNTRY SMOKEHOUSE
◆
Barbecue

Lunch: $4-$15   **Dinner:** $4-$15   **Phone:** 281/890-5735   184
Location: Jct US 290 and FM 1960 W. 13280 FM 1960 W 77065. **Hours:** 7 am-10 pm. Closed: 11/27, 12/25. **Features:** The family-owned restaurant builds its menu on classic Texas food, meaning smoked meats, T-bone steak, sausage links, grilled chicken breast and tasty sides. If a table is available, give the home-cooked breakfast a try. Casual dress; beer & wine only. **Parking:** on-site. **Cards:** AX, DS, MC, VI.

❌

HOUSE OF CREOLE
◆◆◆ ◆◆◆
Regional Cajun

Lunch: $7-$15   **Dinner:** $7-$15   **Phone:** 281/875-2260   170
Location: I-45, exit 64 (77090), on southbound frontage road. 15335 N I-45 77090. **Hours:** 11 am-10 pm, Fri & Sat-11 pm. Closed: 11/27, 12/25; also 1/1 for lunch. **Features:** Comfortable warm atmosphere with the feel of a New Orleans courtyard with a huge oak tree in the center of the restaurant. Collection of 750 hot sauces on display at the entrance. Enjoy Cajun seafood. Start out with Cajun seafood nachos, work your way to flame grilled chicken breast and for dessert try their homemade chocolate mile high cake. Casual dress; cocktails. **Parking:** on-site. **Cards:** AX, CB, DC, DS, MC, VI.

🍸 ❌

JIMMY G'S SEAFOOD CAJUN RESTAURANT
◆
Regional American

Lunch: $13-$20   **Dinner:** $13-$20   **Phone:** 281/931-7654   167
Location: Sam Houston Pkwy (Beltway 8), exit Imperial Valley westbound, 0.8 mi on west frontage road; exit Hardy Toll Rd eastbound, turn under parkway, 1.2 mi on west frontage road. 307 N Sam Houston Pkwy E 77060. **Hours:** 11 am-10 pm, Sat & Sun from noon. Closed major holidays. **Reservations:** accepted. **Features:** Locally owned and operated, it specializes in Cajun-style cooking. At the center of the restaurant is an oyster bar, with two private banquet rooms off to the side. Casual dress; cocktails. **Parking:** on-site. **Cards:** AX, CB, DC, DS, MC, VI.

❌

LE CAFE ROYAL
◆◆◆ ◆◆◆
French

Lunch: $17-$20   **Dinner:** $18-$40   **Phone:** 281/445-9000   166
Location: Beltway 8 (Sam Houston Pkwy), exit Imperial Valley westbound; exit Hardy Toll Rd eastbound, on westbound frontage road; in Hotel Sofitel Houston. 425 N Sam Houston Pkwy E 77060. **Hours:** 11:30 am-2 & 6-10 pm. Closed major holidays; also Sat & Sun. **Reservations:** suggested. **Features:** Expect old-fashioned dining in a quiet, intimate atmosphere accented by candlelight, soothing classical music, and excellent service. Provincial cuisine features seafood, chicken and lamb, with freshly baked bread and pastries as menu highlights. Casual dress; cocktails. **Parking:** on-site. **Cards:** AX, CB, DC, DS, MC, VI.

🍸 ❌

LUPE TORTILLAS
◆
Mexican

Lunch: $6-$16   **Dinner:** $6-$16   **Phone:** 281/496-7580   159
Location: I-10, exit 751 (Addicks Rd/SR 6), just s to Grisby Rd, then just e of jct Grisby Rd and SR 6. 318 Stafford 77079. **Hours:** 11 am-2 & 5:30-8:30 pm, Fri-9:30 pm, Sat 5:30 pm-9:30 pm, Sun 5:30 pm-8:30 pm. Closed major holidays. **Features:** Featuring an early Tex-Mex decor, the eatery pokes fun at itself with statements such as, "Es preety goood." However, the atypically good Mexican fare is nothing to laugh at. Unpretentious tacos, flautas, enchiladas, burritos, chiles rellenos and chalupas are made from original recipes. Casual dress; cocktails. **Parking:** on-site. **Cards:** AX, DC, DS, MC, VI.

🍸 ❌

LUTHER'S BAR-B-Q
◆
Barbecue

Lunch: $5-$11   **Dinner:** $5-$11   **Phone:** 713/465-7251   160
Location: I-10, exit 757 (Gessner Rd). 1001 Gessner Rd 77055. **Hours:** 11 am-10 pm, Fri & Sat-11 pm. Closed: 11/27, 12/25. **Features:** This busy establishment offers a good introduction to Texas-style barbecue. Walk through a cafeteria-style line and help yourself to sliced beef, brisket, sausages and ribs, as well as hearty side dishes like potato salad, baked beans and home fries. Casual dress; beer only. **Parking:** on-site. **Cards:** AX, DS, MC, VI.

❌

LYNN'S STEAKHOUSE
◆◆◆ ◆◆◆
Steak & Seafood

Lunch: $19-$40   **Dinner:** $19-$40   **Phone:** 281/870-0807   163
Location: I-10, exit 753, 0.5 mi s. 955 Dairy-Ashford Rd 77079. **Hours:** 11 am-2 & 5-10 pm, Sat from 6 pm; Sat 5 pm-10 pm in winter. Closed major holidays; also Sun. **Reservations:** suggested. **Features:** Sip from a glass of award-winning wine selected from an extensive list. The dimly-lit dining room is intimate and rustic. Thick steaks, rack of lamb and Australian rock lobster are favorites at this steakhouse. Casual dress; cocktails. **Parking:** on-site. **Cards:** AX, CB, DC, DS, MC, VI.

❌

MATSU JAPANESE RESTAURANT
◆◆◆ ◆◆◆
Japanese

Lunch: $7-$18   **Dinner:** $11-$18   **Phone:** 281/893-8700   158
Location: I-45, exit 66, 5.2 mi w of jct I-45 and FM 1960. 4855 FM 1960 W 77069. **Hours:** 11 am-2:30 & 5-10 pm, Sat noon-10 pm, Sun noon-9 pm. Closed major holidays. **Features:** The traditional restaurant serves sashimi, tempura and teriyaki dishes, and for lunch, the traditional bento meal. Lone diners will appreciate the many preparations displayed on the sushi bar. For a relaxing treat, enjoy a meal in the tatami room. Casual dress; beer & wine only. **Parking:** on-site. **Cards:** AX, DS, MC, VI.

❌

OLD SAN FRANCISCO STEAK HOUSE
◆◆◆ ◆◆◆
Steak & Seafood

Dinner: $15-$37   **Phone:** 713/783-5990   174
Location: W on FM 1093; 3 mi w I-610, exit 8C northbound (Westheimer Rd); exit 9A (San Felipe/Westheimer rds) southbound. 8611 Westheimer Rd 77063. **Hours:** 5 pm-10 pm, Fri-11 pm, Sat 4 pm-11 pm, Sun 4 pm-10 pm. **Reservations:** suggested. **Features:** Enjoy your meal in this Barbary Coast restaurant while waitress and piano players in "gay 90s costumes" sing and play "turn-of-the-century" songs. The highlight of the entertainment is a woman on a red velvet swing ringing cow bells hanging from the high ceiling with her feet. Tradtional American cuisine includes juicy filets, chicken and seafood selections. Casual dress; cocktails; entertainment. **Parking:** on-site. **Cards:** AX, CB, DC, DS, MC, VI.

❌

(See map p. 382)

PAPPASITO'S
Mexican
Lunch: $8-$21 **Dinner:** $9-$21 **Phone:** 281/893-5030 (181)
Location: I-45, exit 66, 6.6 mi w. 7050 FM 1960 W 77069. **Hours:** 11 am-10 pm, Fri & Sat-11 pm. Closed: 11/27, 12/25. **Features:** The rustic Tex-Mex cafe often is crowded during peak hours. In addition to the requisite fajitas and enchiladas, the menu lists some shrimp specialties. Tables in the large dining room are closely spaced. Casual dress; cocktails. **Parking:** on-site. **Cards:** AX, DC, DS, MC, VI.

PAPPAS SEAFOOD HOUSE AND OYSTER BAR
Seafood
Lunch: $13-$23 **Dinner:** $13-$23 **Phone:** 281/999-9928 (168)
Location: I-45, exit 60 (Aldine-Bender Rd), on west service road. 11301 I-45 N 77037. **Hours:** 11 am-10 pm, Fri-11 pm, Sat 11:30 am-11 pm, Sun 11:30 am-10 pm. Closed: 11/27, 12/25. **Features:** Friendly, energetic and fun perfectly describes this family favorite, with candlelight and large windows opening on a lovely scenic view. Cajun cooking is the menu's focus, including a savory array of entrees like crawfish etoufee and spicy jambalaya. Casual dress; cocktails. **Parking:** on-site. **Cards:** AX, DC, DS, MC, VI.

RESA'S PRIME STEAKHOUSE
Steak House
Dinner: $18-$36 **Phone:** 281/893-3339 (169)
Location: 4 mi sw on FM 1960 from jct I-45 and exit 66, just n. 14641 Gladebrook 77068. **Hours:** 5 pm-10:30 pm. Closed major holidays. **Reservations:** suggested. **Features:** Located off busy FM 1960 in far north Houston in a small strip center. Just look for the cars as this is one of the more popular restaurants in the area. The dining room's lighting is subdued, setting the mood for a romantic dining experience. Piano music is also provided for your nightly enjoyment. The knowledgeable waiters bring a tray displaying the various cuts of meats to your table and provide you with a brief explanation of the types of cuts to help you in making your selections. Dressy casual; cocktails; entertainment. **Parking:** on-site. **Cards:** AX, DC, DS, MC, VI.

ROTISSERIE FOR BEEF & BIRD
Continental
Lunch: $10-$16 **Dinner:** $19-$39 **Phone:** 713/977-9524 (171)
Location: Beltway 8 (Sam Houston S Pkwy), exit Westheimer Rd, 1.1 mi w on Westheimer Rd to jct Wilcrest Dr, 0.4 mi n. 2200 Wilcrest Dr 77042. **Hours:** 11:30 am-2 & 6-10 pm, Sat from 6 pm. Closed major holidays; also 12/24 & Sun except 5/12. **Reservations:** required. **Features:** Owner/chef Joe Mannke has collected accolades for the formal, white-tablecloth eatery. American heritage cuisine, such as duck and goose, is served in a tasteful, albeit tight-knit, dining area. Interesting artwork depicting the first Thanksgiving adorns the walls. Smoke free premises. Dressy casual; cocktails. **Parking:** on-site. **Cards:** AX, CB, DC, DS, MC, VI.

TASTE OF TEXAS
Steak House
Lunch: $10-$37 **Dinner:** $10-$37 **Phone:** 713/932-6901 (178)
Location: I-10, exit 756A (Frontage Rd) westbound; exit 755 (Beltway 8) eastbound, 1.8 mi w on east service road. 10505 Katy Frwy 77024. **Hours:** 11 am-10 pm, Fri-11 pm, Sat 3:30 pm-11 pm, Sun 3 pm-10 pm. Closed: 11/27, 12/25. **Features:** The family restaurant's extensive menu and wine list appeals to diners of different tastes. Chargrilled filet melts in the mouth, and the salad bar lines up plenty of variety. Casual dress; cocktails. **Parking:** on-site. **Cards:** AX, CB, DC, DS, MC, VI.

TOMMY'S PATIO CAFE
Creole
Lunch: $7-$12 **Dinner:** $12-$24 **Phone:** 281/480-2221 (183)
Location: I-45, exit 26, 3.1 mi e. 2555 Bay Area Blvd 77058. **Hours:** 11 am-10 pm, Fri-11 pm, Sat 4 pm-11 pm, Sun noon-10 pm. Closed major holidays. **Reservations:** suggested. **Features:** Because the restaurant shares space with a business center, it can be difficult to spot right away. Patio seating is arranged outside the main entrance. The creatively painted interior houses rich woods, upholstered chairs and carpeted dining rooms. The menu lists numerous seafood choices, in addition to chicken, beef, pasta and "heart healthy" items. Casual dress; cocktails. **Parking:** on-site. **Cards:** AX, CB, DC, DS, MC, VI.

TUBTIM SIAM THAI RESTAURANT
Thai
Lunch: $5 **Dinner:** $8-$13 **Phone:** 281/893-8889 (172)
Location: 1.5 mi e of jct SR 249 and 1960 W. 6488 FM 1960 W 77069. **Hours:** 11 am-2 & 5-9 pm, Fri-10 pm, Sat noon-3 & 5-10 pm. Closed major holidays; also Sun. **Features:** Varied beef and chicken dishes are prepared in the Thai tradition, some with enough zing to require liquid refreshment. Also on the menu are noodles, shrimp and other traditional dishes. Smoke free premises. Casual dress; beer & wine only. **Parking:** on-site. **Cards:** AX, CB, DC, DS, MC, VI.

VARGO'S
Continental
Lunch: $15-$25 **Dinner:** $20-$30 **Phone:** 713/782-3888 (175)
Location: 0.3 mi n Westheimer Rd, 3 mi n from US 59, exit Fondren Rd. 2401 Fondren Rd 77063. **Hours:** 5 pm-9:30 pm, Fri & Sat-10:30 pm, Sun 11 am-2:30 & 5-10:30 pm. Closed: 12/25; also Mon. **Reservations:** suggested. **Features:** On beautifully landscaped grounds, delightful peacocks preen and graceful swans glide as you take in a view of the bayou from an old-fashioned wedding gazebo. Feast on dishes like double French lamb chops and Long Island duck with bing cherry sauce. Semi-formal attire; cocktails. **Parking:** on-site and valet. **Cards:** AX, CB, DC, DS, MC, VI.

WOODLANDS HOUSE CHINESE RESTAURANT
Chinese
Lunch: $6-$9 **Dinner:** $7-$10 **Phone:** 281/880-8808 (173)
Location: I-45, exit 66 (Adicks-Humble FM 1960), 2.2 mi w; on FM 1960 between Sugar Pine Dr and Kuykendahl Rd. 2103 FM 1960 77090. **Hours:** 11 am-10 pm, Sat & Sun 11:30 am-10 pm. Closed: 11/27, 12/25. **Features:** This family-oriented Chinese restaurant specializes in a well-stocked, all-day buffet from which you may sample such varied cuisine as lomein, chicken, shrimp, egg rolls, roast beef and even french fries. All items are neatly labeled for easy selection. Casual dress; beer & wine only. **Parking:** on-site. **Cards:** AX, DS, MC, VI.

The following restaurant has not been evaluated by AAA
but is listed for your information only.

MOM'S KITCHEN
(fyi)
free premises.
Phone: 713/622-7290
Not evaluated. **Location:** 2620 Joanel St 77027. **Features:** Housed in the back of an antique store, Mom's Kitchen serves home-style food; specials include rice and beans, lasagna and King Ranch chicken. Smoke free premises.

(See map p. 382)

The Houston Vicinity

BAYTOWN pop. 66,430

──── WHERE TO STAY ────

BAYMONT INN & SUITES HOUSTON-BAYTOWN
(AAA) (SAVE)
◊◊◊◊ ◊◊◊◊

Small-scale Hotel

All Year [ECP]   1P: $49-$59   2P: $49-$59   **Phone: (281)421-7300**
Location: I-10, exit 792 (Garth Rd). 5215 I-10 E 77521. Fax: 281/421-7700. **Facility:** 104 units. 103 one-bedroom standard units. 1 one-bedroom suite ($64-$89) with kitchen. 4 stories, interior corridors. *Bath:* combo or shower only. **Parking:** on-site. **Terms:** small pets only ($50 deposit). **Amenities:** video games (fee), voice mail, irons, hair dryers. **Pool(s):** heated outdoor. **Leisure Activities:** whirlpool. **Guest Services:** coin laundry. **Business Services:** fax (fee). **Cards:** AX, CB, DC, DS, MC, VI. **Special Amenities:** free continental breakfast and free newspaper. *(See color ad p 416)*

SOME UNITS

BEST WESTERN BAYTOWN INN
(AAA) (SAVE)
◊◊◊ ◊◊◊

Motel

All Year [ECP]   1P: $55-$100   2P: $62-$115   XP: $5   F17   **Phone: (281)421-2233**
Location: I-10, exit 792 (Garth Rd). 5021 I-10 E 77521. Fax: 281/421-2215. **Facility:** 50 units. 46 one-bedroom standard units. 4 one-bedroom suites, some with whirlpools. 2 stories, exterior corridors. **Parking:** on-site. **Amenities:** irons, hair dryers. *Some:* safes. **Pool(s):** outdoor. **Business Services:** meeting rooms, fax (fee). **Cards:** AX, CB, DC, DS, JC, MC, VI. **Special Amenities:** free continental breakfast and free newspaper.

SOME UNITS

HAMPTON INN
(SAVE)
◊◊◊◊

Small-scale Hotel

All Year   1P: $74   2P: $79   **Phone: 281/421-1234**
Location: I-10, exit 792 (Garth Rd). 7211 Garth Rd 77521. Fax: 281/421-9825. **Facility:** 70 one-bedroom standard units, some with whirlpools. 3 stories, interior corridors. *Bath:* combo or shower only. **Parking:** on-site. **Terms:** [CP] meal plan available. **Amenities:** voice mail, irons, hair dryers. **Pool(s):** outdoor. **Leisure Activities:** whirlpool, exercise room. **Guest Services:** coin laundry. **Business Services:** meeting rooms, fax (fee). **Cards:** AX, CB, DC, DS, JC, MC, VI.

SOME UNITS

HOLIDAY INN EXPRESS
(AAA) (SAVE)
◊◊◊ ◊◊◊

Small-scale Hotel

All Year [ECP]   1P: $50-$80   2P: $63-$85   **Phone: (281)421-7200**
Location: I-10, exit 792 (Garth Rd). 5222 I-10 E 77521. Fax: 281/421-7209. **Facility:** 62 one-bedroom standard units. 3 stories, interior corridors. *Bath:* combo or shower only. **Parking:** on-site. **Terms:** pets ($10 fee). **Amenities:** irons, hair dryers. **Pool(s):** outdoor. **Guest Services:** valet laundry. **Business Services:** fax (fee). **Cards:** AX, CB, DC, DS, JC, MC, VI.

SOME UNITS

LA QUINTA INN-BAYTOWN
(AAA) (SAVE)
◊◊◊◊ ◊◊◊◊

Motel

All Year   1P: $66-$73   2P: $73-$80   XP: $7   F18   **Phone: (281)421-5566**
Location: I-10, exit 792 (Garth Rd). 4911 I-10 E 77521. Fax: 281/421-4009. **Facility:** 130 units. 128 one-bedroom standard units. 2 one-bedroom suites ($99-$149). 2 stories, exterior corridors. **Parking:** on-site. **Terms:** [ECP] meal plan available, small pets only. **Amenities:** video games, voice mail, irons, hair dryers. **Pool(s):** outdoor. **Guest Services:** valet laundry. **Business Services:** fax (fee). **Cards:** AX, CB, DC, DS, JC, MC, VI. **Special Amenities:** free continental breakfast and free local telephone calls.

(See color ad p 401)

SOME UNITS

MOTEL 6 - 1136
◊◊◊

Motel

2/1-5/21   1P: $39-$49   2P: $45-$59   XP: $3   F17   **Phone: 281/576-5777**
5/22-1/31   1P: $41-$51   2P: $47-$57   XP: $3   F17
Location: I-10, exit 797 (SR 146). 8911 Hwy 146 77520. Fax: 281/576-2351. **Facility:** 124 one-bedroom standard units. 2 stories, exterior corridors. *Bath:* combo or shower only. **Parking:** on-site. **Terms:** small pets only. **Pool(s):** outdoor. **Guest Services:** coin laundry. **Business Services:** meeting rooms, fax (fee). **Cards:** AX, CB, DC, DS, MC, VI.

SOME UNITS

QUALITY INN BAYTOWN
(SAVE)
◊◊◊ ◊◊◊

Small-scale Hotel

All Year   1P: $50   2P: $53   XP: $5   F16   **Phone: 281/427-7481**
Location: I-10, exit 797 (SR 146), 5 mi sw, 2.2 mi s on Business 146 (Alexander Rd). 300 S Hwy 146 business 77520. Fax: 281/427-7877. **Facility:** 173 units. 170 one-bedroom standard units. 3 one-bedroom suites. 2 stories (no elevator), exterior corridors. **Parking:** on-site. **Terms:** 7 day cancellation notice, weekly rates available, [AP] meal plan available, small pets only. **Amenities:** *Some:* irons, hair dryers. **Pool(s):** outdoor. **Leisure Activities:** exercise room. **Guest Services:** coin laundry. **Business Services:** meeting rooms, fax (fee). **Cards:** AX, CB, DC, DS, MC, VI.

SOME UNITS

SUPER 8 MOTEL
AAA SAVE
WWW WW
Motel

Phone: (281)843-6200

All Year [BP]   1P: $49-$59   2P: $59-$69   XP: $10   F16
Location: I-10, exit 789. 1931 I-10 E Frwy 77521. Fax: 281/426-1839. **Facility:** 56 one-bedroom standard units, some with whirlpools. 2 stories, exterior corridors. *Bath:* combo or shower only. **Parking:** on-site. **Terms:** weekly rates available, [ECP] meal plan available, package plans. **Amenities:** irons, hair dryers. **Guest Services:** coin laundry. **Business Services:** fax (fee). **Cards:** AX, DC, DS, MC, VI. **Special Amenities:** free continental breakfast and free local telephone calls.

SOME UNITS
[icons]

——— **WHERE TO DINE** ———

TIA MARIA'S
WWW WW
Tex-Mex

Lunch: $6-$7   Dinner: $6-$12   Phone: 281/427-8666
Location: I-10, exit 792 (Garth Rd), 4 mi s. 1711 Garth Rd 77520. **Hours:** 11 am-10 pm, Fri & Sat-11 pm. Closed: 11/27, 12/25. **Features:** Definitely not chain Tex-Mex, the family restaurant has deep roots. Some booths display name plaques for the regulars who frequently venture "south of the border." The food is good and flavorful. Casual dress; cocktails. **Parking:** on-site. **Cards:** AX, MC, VI.

[icons]

THE VERANDA CAFE
WWW WW
Italian

Lunch: $6-$13   Dinner: $9-$22   Phone: 281/427-1705
Location: I-10, exit 793, 4.5 mi s to W Texas Ave, then just w. 214 W Texas Ave 77520. **Hours:** 11 am-10 pm. Closed major holidays; also Sun. **Features:** In an original downtown building, the restaurant has become a favorite for diners looking for a casual dinner out. Among popular dishes are seafood pasta and the Mona Lisa, which features artichoke hearts, dried tomatoes and grilled chicken over pasta and in a white wine sauce. Jalapenos give Southwestern pasta a spicy, uncharacteristic taste. Casual dress; cocktails. **Parking:** street. **Cards:** AX, CB, CD, DC, DS, MC, VI.

[icon]

——— *The following restaurant has not been evaluated by AAA but is listed for your information only.* ———

GOING'S BARBEQUE & STEAK CO
[fyi]

Phone: 281/422-4600
Not evaluated. **Location:** I-10, exit 293 (Main St), 4 mi s. 1007 N Main St 77520. **Features:** Bring an apitite to this cafeteria style restaurant. The meat is pilled high on the sandwiches and portions of most offerings are generous. Order from a bill-board menu of over 40 items.

CHANNELVIEW pop. 29,685   (See map p. 382; index p. 388)

——— **WHERE TO STAY** ———

BEST WESTERN HOUSTON EAST
SAVE
WWW WW
Motel

Phone: (281)452-1000   215

3/17-4/30 [BP]   1P: $70   2P: $74
2/1-3/16 & 5/1-1/31 [BP]   1P: $40   2P: $46   XP: $4   F17
Location: I-10, exit 783 westbound; exit 784 eastbound. 15919 I-10 E 77530. Fax: 281/452-0467. **Facility:** 98 one-bedroom standard units. 2 stories, exterior corridors. **Parking:** on-site. **Terms:** small pets only ($10 fee, $10 deposit). **Amenities:** irons, hair dryers. **Pool(s):** outdoor. **Guest Services:** coin laundry. **Business Services:** fax (fee). **Cards:** AX, CB, DC, DS, MC, VI.

SOME UNITS
[icons]

HOLIDAY INN HOUSTON EAST
WWW WW
Small-scale Hotel

Phone: (281)452-7304   213

All Year   1P: $95-$150
Location: I-10, exit 783 (Sheldon Rd) eastbound; exit 782 (Dell Dale Ave) westbound, on west service road. 15157 I-10 E 77530. Fax: 281/452-4694. **Facility:** 177 units. 176 one-bedroom standard units. 1 one-bedroom suite. 2-3 stories, exterior corridors. **Parking:** on-site. **Amenities:** voice mail, irons, hair dryers. **Pool(s):** outdoor. **Leisure Activities:** jogging, playground, exercise room. **Guest Services:** valet and coin laundry. **Business Services:** meeting rooms, fax (fee). **Cards:** AX, CB, DC, DS, JC, MC, VI. *(See color ad p 390)*

SOME UNITS
[icons]

TRAVELODGE SUITES
WWW WW
Motel

Phone: (281)862-0222   212

All Year [CP]   1P: $60   2P: $65   XP: $5   F16
Location: I-10, exit 783 (Sheldon Rd) eastbound, just n, then just e on 2nd St; exit 783 (Sheldon Rd) westbound, 0.8 mi on Frontage Rd. 15831 2nd St 77530. Fax: 281/862-9264. **Facility:** 34 one-bedroom standard units, some with whirlpools. 2 stories, exterior corridors. **Parking:** on-site. **Terms:** small pets only ($15 fee). **Amenities:** hair dryers. **Pool(s):** outdoor. **Leisure Activities:** whirlpool. **Guest Services:** coin laundry. **Cards:** AX, CB, DS, MC, VI.

SOME UNITS
[icons]

CONROE pop. 36,811

——— **WHERE TO STAY** ———

BAYMONT INN-CONROE
AAA SAVE
WWW WW
Small-scale Hotel

Phone: (936)539-5100

All Year [CP]   1P: $69-$75   2P: $69-$75
Location: I-45, exit 85 (Gladstell St) northbound; exit 84 (Frazier St) southbound. 1506 I-45 77304. Fax: 936/539-4888. **Facility:** 91 one-bedroom standard units. 4 stories, interior corridors. *Bath:* combo or shower only. **Parking:** on-site. **Terms:** 30 day cancellation notice, [ECP] meal plan available, small pets only ($10 fee, $50 deposit). **Amenities:** video games (fee), voice mail, irons, hair dryers. **Pool(s):** outdoor. **Leisure Activities:** exercise room. **Guest Services:** coin laundry. **Business Services:** fax (fee). **Cards:** AX, CB, DC, DS, MC, VI. **Special Amenities:** free continental breakfast and free newspaper.

SOME UNITS
[icons]

COMFORT INN-CONROE

AAA [SAVE]

Small-scale Hotel

Phone: (936)890-2811

All Year   1P: $70-$80   2P: $75-$85   XP: $5   F18
Location: I-45, exit 91, just e. 1115 League Line Rd 77303. Fax: 936/890-0720. **Facility:** 57 one-bedroom standard units, some with efficiencies (no utensils) and/or whirlpools. 2 stories, interior corridors. *Bath:* combo or shower only. **Parking:** on-site. **Terms:** 7 day cancellation notice, [CP] meal plan available. **Amenities:** hair dryers. *Some:* irons. **Pool(s):** heated outdoor. **Leisure Activities:** whirlpool, exercise room. **Business Services:** meeting rooms, fax (fee). **Cards:** AX, CB, DC, DS, MC, VI. **Special Amenities:** free continental breakfast and free local telephone calls.

SOME UNITS

[icons] / [X] /

COUNTRY INN & SUITES BY CARLSON

Small-scale Hotel

Phone: (936)271-0110

All Year [ECP]   1P: $59-$79   2P: $59-$89   F18
Location: I-45, exit 79 (SR 242). 16850 I-45 S 77384. Fax: 936/271-0110. **Facility:** 83 units. 59 one-bedroom standard units. 24 one-bedroom suites. 3 stories, interior corridors. *Bath:* combo or shower only. **Parking:** on-site. **Terms:** 14 day cancellation notice. **Amenities:** voice mail, irons, hair dryers. *Some:* dual phone lines. **Pool(s):** heated indoor. **Leisure Activities:** whirlpool, exercise room. **Guest Services:** valet and coin laundry. **Business Services:** fax (fee). **Cards:** AX, CB, DC, DS, MC, VI. *(See color ad p 260)*

SOME UNITS

[A$K] [icons] / [X] [icons] /

HAMPTON INN-SERVING THE WOODLANDS & NORTH HOUSTON SUBURBS

[SAVE]

Small-scale Hotel

Phone: (936)273-3400

All Year [ECP]   1P: $69-$85   2P: $75-$95
Location: I-45, exit 78 southbound; exit 79 northbound. 18484 I-45 S 77384 (PO Box 8105, THE WOODLANDS, 77387-8105). Fax: 936/273-3460. **Facility:** 80 one-bedroom standard units. 2 stories, exterior corridors. *Bath:* combo or shower only. **Parking:** on-site. **Terms:** 2 night minimum stay - weekends. **Amenities:** dual phone lines, voice mail, irons, hair dryers. **Pool(s):** heated outdoor. **Leisure Activities:** whirlpool, exercise room. **Guest Services:** complimentary evening beverages: Tues & Thurs, valet and coin laundry. **Business Services:** meeting rooms, fax (fee). **Cards:** AX, CB, DC, DS, MC, VI.

SOME UNITS

[icons] / [X] /

HOLIDAY INN

Small-scale Hotel

Phone: (936)756-8941

All Year   1P: $69   2P: $79   XP: $10   F
Location: I-45, exit 84. 1601 I-45 S 77301. Fax: 936/756-8984. **Facility:** 137 units. 136 one-bedroom standard units. 1 one-bedroom suite. 2 stories, exterior corridors. **Parking:** on-site. **Terms:** small pets only ($15 fee). **Amenities:** voice mail, irons, hair dryers. **Pool(s):** outdoor, wading. **Leisure Activities:** exercise room. **Guest Services:** valet and coin laundry. **Business Services:** meeting rooms, fax (fee). **Cards:** AX, DC, DS, MC, VI.

SOME UNITS

[A$K] [icons] / [X] [icons] /
FEE FEE

——— *The following lodging was either not evaluated or did not* ———
meet AAA rating requirements but is listed for your information only.

SILVERLEAF'S PINEY SHORES RESORT **Phone:** 409/856-4692
(fyi) Not evaluated. **Location:** 8350 Piney Shores Dr 77304. Facilities, services, and decor characterize a mid-range property.

DEER PARK pop. 28,520 (See map p. 382; index p. 389)

——— **WHERE TO STAY** ———

BEST WESTERN DEER PARK INN & SUITES **Phone:** (281)476-1900 **296**
(SAVE) All Year 1P: $72-$95 2P: $78-$95 XP: $6 F12
Location: SR 225 (La Porte Rd), exit Center St, 0.9 mi s. Located in a busy commercial area. 1401 Center St 77536. Fax: 281/476-5447. **Facility:** 54 one-bedroom standard units, some with whirlpools. 2 stories (no elevator),
Motel exterior corridors. *Bath:* combo or shower only. **Parking:** on-site. **Terms:** cancellation fee imposed, [ECP] meal plan available. **Amenities:** high-speed Internet, voice mail, irons, hair dryers. **Pool(s):** small outdoor. **Leisure Activities:** whirlpool, exercise room. **Guest Services:** valet and coin laundry. **Business Services:** meeting rooms, PC, fax (fee). **Cards:** AX, CB, DC, DS, JC, MC, VI.

SOME UNITS

$\boxed{S_D}$ $\boxed{\text{\tt !!}}$ $\boxed{}$ $\boxed{}$ $\boxed{}$ $\boxed{\text{DATA PORT}}$ $\boxed{}$ $\boxed{}$ $\boxed{}$ / $\boxed{\times}$ /

HUMBLE pop. 14,579 (See map p. 382; index p. 389)

——— **WHERE TO STAY** ———

BEST WESTERN INTERCONTINENTAL AIRPORT INN **Phone:** (281)548-1402 **286**
(AAA) (SAVE) All Year [ECP] 1P: $70-$112 2P: $70-$112 XP: $6 F12
Location: US 59, exit Will Clayton Pkwy, just w. 7114 Will Clayton Pkwy 77338. Fax: 281/548-1404. **Facility:** 78 units. 75 one-bedroom standard units. 3 one-bedroom suites ($76-$112) with whirlpools. 3 stories, interior corridors. *Bath:* combo or shower only. **Parking:** on-site. **Amenities:** voice mail, irons, hair dryers. *Some:*
Small-scale Hotel DVD players. **Pool(s):** outdoor. **Leisure Activities:** whirlpool, exercise room. **Guest Services:** valet and coin laundry, airport transportation-George Bush Intercontinental Airport, area transportation-within 3 mi. **Business Services:** meeting rooms, fax (fee). **Cards:** AX, CB, DC, DS, JC, MC, VI. **Special Amenities: free continental breakfast and free room upgrade (subject to availability with advanced reservations).** *(See color ad below)*

SOME UNITS

$\boxed{S_D}$ $\boxed{\text{\tt +}}$ $\boxed{\text{\tt !!}}$ $\boxed{\text{\tt &M}}$ $\boxed{}$ $\boxed{}$ $\boxed{}$ $\boxed{}$ $\boxed{\text{DATA PORT}}$ $\boxed{}$ $\boxed{}$ $\boxed{}$ / $\boxed{\times}$ $\boxed{\text{VCR}}$ /

COUNTRY INN & SUITES BY CARLSON-HOUSTON
INTERCONTINENTAL AIRPORT EAST **Phone:** (281)446-4977 **285**
(AAA) (SAVE) All Year [ECP] 1P: $74 2P: $74 XP: $5 F
Location: US 59, exit Townsen Blvd on southbound access road. 20611 Hwy 59 N 77338. Fax: 281/446-7758.
Facility: 62 units. 25 one-bedroom standard units, some with whirlpools. 37 one-bedroom suites ($79). 3 stories, interior corridors. *Bath:* combo or shower only. **Parking:** on-site. **Terms:** package plans - weekends.
Small-scale Hotel **Amenities:** high-speed Internet, dual phone lines, voice mail, irons, hair dryers. **Pool(s):** heated indoor. **Leisure Activities:** whirlpool, exercise room. **Guest Services:** valet and coin laundry, airport transportation-George Bush Intercontinental Airport, area transportation-within 10 mi. **Business Services:** meeting rooms, fax (fee). **Cards:** AX, DC, DS, MC, VI. **Special Amenities: free continental breakfast and free newspaper.** *(See color ad p 260)*

SOME UNITS

$\boxed{S_D}$ $\boxed{\text{\tt +}}$ $\boxed{\text{\tt &M}}$ $\boxed{}$ $\boxed{}$ $\boxed{}$ $\boxed{\text{DATA PORT}}$ $\boxed{}$ $\boxed{}$ $\boxed{}$ / $\boxed{\times}$ /

ECONO LODGE **Phone:** (281)548-2900 **284**
(AAA) (SAVE) All Year [CP] 1P: $50-$59 2P: $57-$64 XP: $6 F18
Location: US 59, exit Business 1960 W, just w. 9821 W FM 1960 (Business) Rd 77338. Fax: 281/540-2224.
Facility: 36 one-bedroom standard units, some with whirlpools. 2 stories, exterior corridors. *Bath:* combo or shower only. **Parking:** on-site. **Terms:** weekly rates available. **Amenities:** hair dryers. **Pool(s):** small out-
Motel door. **Guest Services:** coin laundry. **Business Services:** fax (fee). **Cards:** AX, DS, MC, VI. **Special Amenities: free continental breakfast and free local telephone calls.**

SOME UNITS

$\boxed{S_D}$ $\boxed{\text{\tt !!}}$ $\boxed{}$ $\boxed{}$ $\boxed{}$ $\boxed{\text{DATA PORT}}$ $\boxed{}$ $\boxed{}$ / $\boxed{\times}$ $\boxed{}$ /

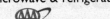

(See map p. 382)

FAIRFIELD INN BY MARRIOTT-HUMBLE   Phone: (281)540-3311   [287]
SAVE   All Year [ECP]   1P: $69-$89   2P: $69-$99   XP: $6   F
              Location: US 59, exit Townsend Rd on southbound access road. 20525 Hwy 59 77338. Fax: 281/540-3311.
▼▼▼▼   **Facility:** 64 one-bedroom standard units. 3 stories, interior corridors. *Bath:* combo or shower only. **Parking:**
              on-site. **Amenities:** irons. **Pool(s):** small heated indoor. **Leisure Activities:** whirlpool. **Guest Services:** valet
Small-scale Hotel laundry. **Business Services:** fax (fee). **Cards:** AX, CB, DC, DS, MC, VI.
                                                                                                          SOME UNITS

HAMPTON INN HUMBLE   Phone: (281)446-4800   [289]
SAVE   All Year [ECP]   1P: $80   2P: $78-$85
              Location: US 59, exit (Townsen Rd), on southbound access road. 20515 Hwy 59 N 77338. Fax: 281/446-4803.
▼▼▼▼   **Facility:** 81 one-bedroom standard units, some with whirlpools. 4 stories, interior corridors. *Bath:* combo or
Small-scale Hotel shower only. **Parking:** on-site. **Terms:** cancellation fee imposed. **Amenities:** video games (fee), dual phone
              lines, voice mail, irons, hair dryers. **Pool(s):** small heated indoor. **Leisure Activities:** exercise room. **Guest
              Services:** valet and coin laundry, area transportation. **Business Services:** meeting rooms, business center.
Cards: AX, CB, DC, DS, JC, MC, VI.
                                                                                                          SOME UNITS

──────── The following lodging was either not evaluated or did not ────────
meet AAA rating requirements but is listed for your information only.

HAWTHORN SUITES   Phone: 281/446-9997
[fyi]   All Year [BP]   1P: $119-$129   2P: $119-$129
              Too new to rate. Location: 7014 Will Clayton Pkwy 77338. Fax: 281/446-9998. **Amenities:** coffeemakers, micro-
Small-scale Hotel waves, refrigerators, pool. **Terms:** cancellation fee imposed. **Cards:** AX, DC, MC, VI. *(See color ad p 429)*

"It's making a'thumping' sound."

AAA
⌒ **Approved Auto Repair**

A curious "thumping" sound coming from your car usually makes your heart start thumping! AAA Approved Auto Repair facilities have ASE-certified technicians who are experts in vehicle repair and maintenance. AAA members receive a free safety inspection(on request during a service visit), a 12-month/12,000-mile warranty and the peace of mind that comes from knowing the facility meets AAA's standards. So look for the AAR sign–it'll do your heart good!

(See map p. 382)

——— WHERE TO DINE ———

CHEZ NOUS
▽▽▽▽
Provincial French

Location: US 59, exit FM 1960, 0.6 mi to N Houston Ave, 0.6 mi s to Main St, just w, then s on Main St. 217 S Ave G 77338. **Hours:** 5:30 pm-10 pm. Closed major holidays; also Sun. **Reservations:** suggested. **Features:** A charming French country inn located in a modest residential area, it serves reliable, classic dishes with tasty sauces, and offers a generous wine list from which to select the perfect vintage. Recommended are steak marchand de vin and shrimp Provencal. Smoke free premises. Semi-formal attire; cocktails. **Parking:** on-site. **Cards:** AX, CB, DC, MC, VI.

Dinner: $19-$31   **Phone:** 281/446-6717   (200)

🍽 ✕

KATY pop. 11,775

——— WHERE TO STAY ———

BEST WESTERN-HOUSTON WEST
ⒶⒶⒶ (SAVE)
▽▽▽▽
Motel

Phone: (281)392-9800

1/1-1/31 [CP]	1P: $69-$79	2P: $79-$89	XP: $10 F16
2/1-7/31 [CP]	1P: $62-$72	2P: $68-$78	XP: $10 F16
11/1-12/31 [CP]	1P: $60-$70	2P: $65-$75	XP: $10 F16
8/1-10/31 [CP]	1P: $59-$69	2P: $59-$69	XP: $10 F16

Location: I-10, exit 743 (Grand Pkwy), just e on eastbound service road. 22455 I-10 (Katy Frwy) 77450. Fax: 281/392-1818. **Facility:** 104 units. 103 one-bedroom standard units. 1 one-bedroom suite. 2 stories, exterior corridors. **Parking:** on-site. **Terms:** 7 day cancellation notice, package plans, small pets only ($10 extra charge). **Amenities:** video games (fee), voice mail, irons, hair dryers. **Pool(s):** outdoor. **Guest Services:** coin laundry. **Business Services:** meeting rooms, fax (fee). **Cards:** AX, DC, DS, MC, VI. **Special Amenities:** free continental breakfast and free newspaper.

SOME UNITS

(S🅳) 🐕 🍽️ 🏊 🐾 [DATA PORT] 💻 / ✕ 📶 📺 /

COMFORT INN & SUITES-WEST
(SAVE)
▽▽▽▽
Small-scale Hotel

Phone: (281)392-8700

12/21-1/31	1P: $120-$210	XP: $10 F17
4/30-8/31	1P: $99-$114	XP: $10 F17
2/1-4/29 & 9/1-12/20	1P: $89-$110	XP: $10 F17

Location: I-10, exit 745 (Mason Rd), just s to Provencial Blvd, just w to Applewhite Dr, then just n. 22025 I-10 W (Katy Frwy) 77450. Fax: 281/392-2883. **Facility:** 89 one-bedroom standard units, some with whirlpools. 2 stories, interior corridors. *Bath:* combo or shower only. **Parking:** on-site. **Terms:** 7 day cancellation notice-fee imposed. **Amenities:** dual phone lines, voice mail, irons, hair dryers. **Pool(s):** heated indoor. **Leisure Activities:** whirlpool, exercise room. **Guest Services:** coin laundry. **Business Services:** meeting rooms, fax (fee). **Cards:** AX, CB, DC, DS, JC, MC, VI.

SOME UNITS

(S🅳) 🍽️ 🚫M 🐾 🏊 🐾 [DATA PORT] 📶 📺 💻 / ✕ /

KEMAH pop. 2,330

——— WHERE TO DINE ———

CADILLAC BAR-KEMAH
▽▽
Mexican

Lunch: $7-$15   **Dinner:** $8-$19   **Phone:** 281/334-9049

Location: I-45 S, exit 24 (NASA Rd One), 7 mi e to SR 146, then 0.8 mi s over bridge, e to Kemah Waterfront. 7 Waterfront 77565. **Hours:** 11 am-10 pm, Fri-midnight, Sat 8 am-midnight, Sun 8 am-10 pm. Closed: 11/27, 12/25; also Mon. **Features:** The restaurant offers a nice place to look out over the marina. Graffiti covers the walls, chairs, tables and ceilings, everywhere but the restroom. On the menu are large portions of Mexican cuisine, including mesquite-grilled cabrito (baby goat). Casual dress; cocktails. **Parking:** on-site. **Cards:** AX, DC, DS, MC, VI.

🍽 ✕

THE FLYING DUTCHMAN
▽▽▽
Seafood

Lunch: $16-$22   **Dinner:** $10-$22   **Phone:** 281/334-7575

Location: I-45 S, exit 24 (Nasa Rd One), 7 mi e to SR 146, then s over bridge 0.8 mi, e to Kemah Waterfront. 9 Boardwalk 77565. **Hours:** 5 pm-11:30 pm, Sat from 4 pm, Sun from 11 am; downstairs dining area 11 am-10 pm. Closed: 11/27, 12/25. **Reservations:** accepted. **Features:** This establishment is really two restaurants in one. Upstairs you'll find friendly, efficient and attentive servers who know their way around the Dutchman's extensive wine list and seafood-dominated menu. Downstairs is reserved for more casual dining. Casual dress; cocktails. **Parking:** on-site. **Cards:** AX, CB, DC, DS, MC, VI.

🍽 ✕

KINGWOOD (See map p. 382; index p. 389)

——— WHERE TO STAY ———

COMFORT SUITES KINGWOOD
(SAVE)
▽▽▽▽
Small-scale Hotel

Phone: 281/359-4448   (299)

All Year [BP]   1P: $90   2P: $100   XP: $10   F12

Location: US 59, exit Kingwood Dr. 22223 Eastex Frwy 77339. Fax: 281/359-9990. **Facility:** 56 one-bedroom standard units, some with whirlpools. 3 stories, interior corridors. *Bath:* combo or shower only. **Parking:** on-site. **Amenities:** high-speed Internet, voice mail, irons, hair dryers. **Pool(s):** outdoor. **Leisure Activities:** whirlpool, exercise room. **Guest Services:** sundries, valet and coin laundry, area transportation. **Business Services:** meeting rooms, business center. **Cards:** AX, DC, DS, MC, VI.

SOME UNITS

LA PORTE pop. 31,880

─────── WHERE TO STAY ───────

BEST WESTERN LA PORTE INN

AAA SAVE

Motel

with advanced reservations).

All Year	1P: $60-$80	2P: $65-$90

Phone: (281)471-4040
XP: $8   F12

Location: SR 146, exit Fairmont Pkwy. 705 Hwy 146 S 77571. Fax: 281/470-9191. **Facility:** 49 one-bedroom standard units, some with whirlpools. 2 stories, exterior corridors. *Bath:* combo or shower only. **Parking:** on-site. **Terms:** [CP] meal plan available. **Amenities:** high-speed Internet, irons, hair dryers. **Pool(s):** heated outdoor. **Guest Services:** coin laundry. **Business Services:** meeting rooms, PC, fax (fee). **Cards:** AX, DC, DS, MC, VI. **Special Amenities: free continental breakfast and free room upgrade (subject to availability with advanced reservations).**

SOME UNITS
🖥️ 🛋️ 🏊 📷 DATA PORT 🛗 📠 🖨️ / ❌ /

COMFORT SUITES

SAVE

Small-scale Hotel

All Year [BP]	1P: $59-$99	2P: $69-$109

Phone: (281)842-9200
XP: $5   F18

Location: SR 146, exit Fairmont Pkwy, just e to S 8th, then just n. Located in a commercial area. 902 S 8th 77571. Fax: 281/471-5555. **Facility:** 67 units. 63 one-bedroom standard units, some with whirlpools. 3 one- and 1 two-bedroom suites. 3 stories, interior corridors. *Bath:* combo or shower only. **Parking:** on-site. **Amenities:** high-speed Internet, dual phone lines, voice mail, irons, hair dryers. **Pool(s):** outdoor. **Leisure Activities:** whirlpool, exercise room. **Guest Services:** valet and coin laundry. **Business Services:** meeting rooms, business center. **Cards:** AX, CB, DC, DS, MC, VI.

SOME UNITS
🖥️ 🍽️ 🛋️ 🏊 📷 DATA PORT 🛗 📠 🖨️ / ❌ /

LA QUINTA INN-LA PORTE

AAA SAVE

Small-scale Hotel

All Year	1P: $66-$76	2P: $73-$83

Phone: (281)470-0760
XP: $7   F18

Location: Jct SR 146, exit Fairmont Pkwy. 1105 Hwy 146 S 77571-6119. Fax: 281/471-2116. **Facility:** 114 one-bedroom standard units. 2 stories, exterior corridors. **Parking:** on-site. **Terms:** [ECP] meal plan available, small pets only. **Amenities:** video games (fee), voice mail, irons, hair dryers. **Pool(s):** outdoor. **Guest Services:** valet laundry. **Business Services:** meeting rooms, fax. **Cards:** AX, CB, DC, DS, JC, MC, VI. **Special Amenities: free continental breakfast and free local telephone calls.** *(See color ad p 401)*

SOME UNITS
🐕 🍽️ 📶 🏊 ♿ 📷 DATA PORT 🖨️ / ❌ 🛗 📠 /
FEE

MONTGOMERY pop. 489

─────── WHERE TO STAY ───────

─────── *The following lodgings were either not evaluated or did not* ───────
meet AAA rating requirements but are listed for your information only.

FIRST FAIRWAY AT WALDEN

fyi

Phone: 936/582-4477

Not evaluated. **Location:** 13151 Walden Rd 77356. Facilities, services, and decor characterize a mid-range property.

IVERNESS AT DEL LAGO

fyi

Phone: 936/582-4442

Not evaluated. **Location:** 100 Lacosta Dr 77356. Facilities, services, and decor characterize a mid-range property.

NASSAU BAY pop. 4,170   (See map p. 382; index p. 388)

─────── WHERE TO STAY ───────

HILTON HOUSTON NASA CLEAR LAKE

SAVE

Large-scale Hotel

All Year	1P: $189	2P: $189

Phone: (281)333-9300   240
XP: $25

Location: I-45, exit 25, 3.8 mi e. 3000 NASA Rd One 77058. Fax: 281/333-3750. **Facility:** 243 units. 241 one-bedroom standard units, some with whirlpools. 2 one-bedroom suites ($795-$1550). 13 stories, interior corridors. **Parking:** on-site. **Terms:** [CP] meal plan available. **Amenities:** dual phone lines, voice mail, irons, hair dryers. *Some:* CD players. **Pool(s):** outdoor. **Leisure Activities:** marina, fishing, exercise room. *Fee:* boats, canoes, sailboats, waterskiing, charter fishing. **Guest Services:** gift shop, valet laundry, area transportation. **Business Services:** conference facilities, business center. **Cards:** AX, DC, DS, MC, VI.

SOME UNITS
🖥️ ♿ 🍽️ 📺 📶 🏊 ❌ ♿ DATA PORT 🖨️ / ❌ 🛗 📠
FEE   FEE FEE

HOLIDAY INN HOUSTON/NASA

♦♦♦

Small-scale Hotel

All Year	1P: $99-$109

Phone: (281)333-2500   238

Location: I-45, exit 25, 2.5 mi e. 1300 NASA Rd One 77058. Fax: 281/335-1578. **Facility:** 222 units. 220 one-bedroom standard units. 2 one-bedroom suites ($139-$159). 2-4 stories, interior/exterior corridors. **Parking:** on-site. **Terms:** cancellation fee imposed, weekly rates available, [BP], [CP], [ECP] & [MAP] meal plans available, 18% service charge, small pets only ($50 fee). **Amenities:** voice mail, irons, hair dryers. **Pool(s):** outdoor. **Leisure Activities:** playground, exercise room. **Guest Services:** valet and coin laundry. **Business Services:** conference facilities, fax. **Cards:** AX, CB, DC, DS, JC, MC, VI. *(See color ad p 390)*

SOME UNITS
ASK 🖥️ ♿ 🐕 🍽️ 24📶 📺 📶 🏊 📷 DATA PORT 🖨️ / ❌ VCR 🛗 📠 /
FEE   FEE

OAK RIDGE NORTH pop. 2,991

―――― WHERE TO DINE ――――

SGHETTIES
♦♦ ♦♦
Italian
Lunch: $9-$10   **Dinner:** $10-$20   **Phone:** 281/364-9555
Location: I-45, exit 76 (Robinson Rd/Woodlands Pkwy) southbound; exit 77 (Research Forest Dr/Tamina Rd) northbound; in Woodridge Plaza North Service Rd. 27606 I-45 N 77385. **Hours:** 11 am-10 pm, Sun-9 pm. Closed major holidays. **Features:** Casual, upscale and professional, this family-owned and operated eatery surrounds their guests with an elegant, artsy decor that resounds with fine jazz music. Try the house specialty, chicken a la Talotta in a rich Colombian cream and mushroom sauce. Casual dress; cocktails. **Parking:** on-site.
Cards: AX, DC, DS, MC, VI.

PASADENA pop. 141,674   (See map p. 382; index p. 388)

―――― WHERE TO STAY ――――

ECONO LODGE
SAVE
♦♦ ♦♦
Motel
Phone: (713)477-4266   222
All Year   **1P:** $50-$65   **2P:** $55-$70   **XP:** $5   F12
Location: SR 225 (Pasadena Frwy), exit Richey St. 823 W Pasadena Frwy 77506. **Fax:** 713/477-4266. **Facility:** 40 one-bedroom standard units. 2 stories, exterior corridors. **Parking:** on-site. **Business Services:** fax (fee).
Cards: AX, CB, DC, DS, JC, MC, VI.

RICHMOND pop. 11,081

―――― WHERE TO DINE ――――

SWINGING DOOR
♦♦
American
Lunch: $12-$15   **Dinner:** $12-$15   **Phone:** 281/342-4758
Location: Jct Loop 762 and Alternate US 90 (at Brazos River Bridge), 1.3 mi e to FM 359, 3.7 mi nw. 3714 FM 359 77469. **Hours:** 11 am-9 pm, Fri & Sat-10 pm. Closed major holidays; also Mon, Tues & first week of Sept. **Reservations:** required; weekends. **Features:** Family owned and operated restaurant located "in the country" outside of Richmond. They specialize in Texas style barbecue serving large portions of beef, chicken, turkey, and pork. An extensive wine list includes several choices made in Texas. Casual dress; beer & wine only. **Parking:** on-site. **Cards:** AX, DC, DS, MC, VI.

ROSENBERG pop. 24,043

―――― WHERE TO STAY ――――

COMFORT INN
AAA SAVE
♦♦♦
Motel
Phone: (281)232-7300
All Year [ECP]   **1P:** $70-$75   **2P:** $75-$85   **XP:** $6   F12
Location: US 59, exit SR 36, just s. 3555 Hwy 36 S 77471. **Fax:** 281/232-3709. **Facility:** 49 one-bedroom standard units. 2 stories, interior corridors. *Bath:* combo or shower only. **Parking:** on-site. **Amenities:** irons, hair dryers. **Pool(s):** outdoor. **Guest Services:** coin laundry. **Business Services:** meeting rooms, fax (fee). **Cards:** AX, CB, DC, DS, MC, VI. **Special Amenities:** free continental breakfast and free local telephone calls.

HOLIDAY INN EXPRESS HOTEL & SUITES
♦♦♦♦
Small-scale Hotel
Phone: (281)342-7888
All Year   **1P:** $89   **2P:** $89
Location: US 59, exit SR 36, just se of jct. 27927 SW Frwy 77471. **Fax:** 832/595-0601. **Facility:** 67 units. 63 one-bedroom standard units, some with whirlpools. 4 one-bedroom suites ($100-$150) with whirlpools. 3 stories, interior corridors. *Bath:* combo or shower only. **Parking:** on-site. **Terms:** [CP] meal plan available, package plans, pets ($10 extra charge). **Amenities:** dual phone lines, voice mail, irons, hair dryers. **Pool(s):** outdoor. **Leisure Activities:** exercise room. **Guest Services:** valet and coin laundry. **Business Services:** meeting rooms, fax (fee). **Cards:** AX, DC, DS, JC, MC, VI.

SEABROOK pop. 9,443

―――― WHERE TO STAY ――――

HOLIDAY INN EXPRESS HOTEL & SUITES
♦♦♦♦
Small-scale Hotel
Phone: (281)326-7200
All Year   **1P:** $90-$100   **2P:** $110-$120   **XP:** $10   F19
Location: Jct SR 146 and NASA Rd One, 0.6 mi w. 2720 NASA Rd One 77586. **Fax:** 281/326-5871. **Facility:** 60 one-bedroom standard units. 2 stories, interior corridors. *Bath:* combo or shower only. **Parking:** on-site. **Terms:** 1-2 night minimum stay - seasonal, 30 day cancellation notice-fee imposed, [ECP] meal plan available. **Amenities:** dual phone lines, voice mail, safes, irons, hair dryers. **Pool(s):** outdoor. **Leisure Activities:** exercise room. **Guest Services:** coin laundry. **Business Services:** meeting rooms, fax (fee). **Cards:** AX, CB, DC, DS, JC, MC, VI.

——— **WHERE TO DINE** ———

SONNY'S CRAZY CAJUN FOOD FACTORY   Lunch: $8-$16   Dinner: $13-$25   Phone: 281/326-6055
▽▽
Cajun
Location: 0.8 mi w of SR 146. 2825 NASA Rd One 77586. **Hours:** 11 am-10 pm, Fri & Sat-11 pm, Sun from 11:30. Closed: 11/27, 12/25. **Features:** Old license plates and signs cover the walls of this rustic eatery. The Cajun cuisine will put a jump in your step! Spicy gumbo, catfish and stir fried jalapeno will please your palate. Colorful lights and fans hang from the metal ceiling. Casual dress; beer & wine only. **Parking:** on-site. **Cards:** AX, CB, DC, DS, MC, VI.   ☒

TOOKIE'S RESTAURANT   Lunch: $4-$6   Dinner: $4-$6   Phone: 281/474-3444
ⒶⒶⒶ
▽▽
American
Location: Just s jct SR 146 and NASA Rd One, on SR 146. 1202 Bayport Blvd 77586. **Hours:** 11 am-9 pm, Fri & Sat-10 pm. Closed major holidays. **Features:** With its bright green and yellow exterior, this place is hard to miss. Burgers "creations" are the specialty, made fresh in house with the normal accompaniments such as fries and onion rings. Try the "Squealer", a bacon cheeseburger with a twist. The portions are generous and maybe even a bit messy, a fact endorsed by the roll of paper towels placed at each table. The servers are friendly but if you go in the middle of peak times you may find the service to be a little frenetic. Casual dress; beer only. **Parking:** on-site. **Cards:** MC, VI.   ☒

VILLA CAPRI   Lunch: $5-$11   Dinner: $9-$28   Phone: 281/326-2373
▽▽ ▽▽
Italian
Location: 1.5 mi w of SR 146. 3713 NASA Rd One 77586. **Hours:** 11 am-10 pm, Fri & Sat-11 pm; 11 am-2 & 5-10 pm, Fri & Sat-11 pm 11/1-5/31. Closed: 11/27, 12/25; also Mon. **Reservations:** suggested. **Features:** This renovated home is set among a boat dock and a Roman-style garden. The seafood entrees include stuffed ravioli in a savory crabmeat sauce, and the scampi piccata is soaked in a buttery garlic herb sauce. Casual dress; cocktails. **Parking:** on-site. **Cards:** AX, CB, DC, MC, VI.   ☒

SHENANDOAH pop. 1,503

——— **WHERE TO DINE** ———

ALPENHAUS RESTAURANT & BEERGARTEN   Lunch: $5-$7   Dinner: $7-$16   Phone: 409/321-4416
▽▽ ▽▽
German
Location: I-45, exit 78 southbound; exit 79 northbound. 18450 I-45 N 77380. **Hours:** 11 am-9 pm, Fri & Sat-10 pm. Closed: 1/1, 11/27, 12/25. **Features:** Family-owned and operated, this German bistro has dining room walls painted with Alpine scenes. The veal is lightly breaded, pan-fried and smothered in a spicy sauce. For dessert, treat yourself to the sweet apple strudel. Casual dress; cocktails. **Parking:** on-site. **Cards:** AX, DS, MC, VI.   ☒ ☒

SPRING pop. 36,385   (See map p. 382; index p. 389)

——— **WHERE TO DINE** ———

AMERIGO'S SEAFOOD & PASTA   Lunch: $8-$13   Dinner: $11-$23   Phone: 281/370-8888   ⓸⓪⑨
▽▽ ▽▽
Italian
Location: Just w on jct Kvyken Dahl and Louetta Rd. 5010 Louetta Rd, Suite P 77379. **Hours:** 11:30 am-2 & 5-10 pm, Sat noon-10 pm, Sun 11 am-9 pm. Closed major holidays. **Features:** Classic cuisine is served at this small, family-oriented, neighborhood restaurant. The juicy chicken marsala is accented with a medley of steamed vegetables. Don't forget to have a glass of wine and the homemade tiramisu after your meal. Casual dress; beer & wine only. **Parking:** on-site. **Cards:** AX, CB, DC, DS, MC, VI.   ☒

WOODLANDS HOUSE CHINESE RESTAURANT   Lunch: $6-$9   Dinner: $7-$10   Phone: 281/367-4308   ②①③
▽▽
Chinese
Location: I-45, exit 73 (Rayford/Sawdust) northbound; exit 74 (Rayford/Sawdust) southbound, just w. 355 Sawdust 77380. **Hours:** 11 am-10 pm, Sat & Sun from 11:30 am. Closed: 11/27, 12/25. **Features:** Family-oriented, this Chinese-style cafe specializes in an all day buffet. The cuisine includes seafood, beef, veggies, fried rice and egg rolls. Attentive servers deliver menu items as well. The busy dining room resembles a cafeteria. Casual dress; beer & wine only. **Parking:** on-site. **Cards:** AX, DS, MC, VI.   ☒

WUNSCHE BROS CAFE   Lunch: $7-$11   Dinner: $7-$11   Phone: 281/350-1902   ②⓪⑦
▽▽
American
Location: I-45, exit 70A (Spring-Cypress Rd), 0.9 mi e to jct Gentry/Midway and Spring-Cypress, just e. 103 Midway 77373. **Hours:** 11 am-10 pm, Fri & Sat-11 pm, Sun-8 pm, Mon-3 pm. Closed major holidays. **Features:** In a wood-frame house built in 1902, you'll find a popular honky tonk that presents live musical entertainment nightly, and also offers excellent comfort foods like famous fried chicken, luscious bread pudding, sausage crumb salad and homemade beer bread. Smoke free premises. Casual dress; cocktails; entertainment. **Parking:** on-site. **Cards:** AX, DS, MC, VI.   ☒

STAFFORD pop. 1,991   (See map p. 382; index p. 389)

——— **WHERE TO STAY** ———

BEST WESTERN FORT BEND INN & SUITES   Phone: (281)575-6060   ②⑤⑥
ⒶⒶⒶ SAVE
▽▽▽▽
Motel

All Year [CP]	1P: $49-$129	2P: $59-$129	XP: $5 F12

Location: US 59, exit Kirkwood Rd/Airport Blvd, just s. 11206 W Airport Blvd 77477. Fax: 281/575-1122. **Facility:** 55 one-bedroom standard units, some with whirlpools. 2 stories, exterior corridors. **Bath:** combo or shower only. **Parking:** on-site. **Amenities:** irons, hair dryers. **Pool(s):** outdoor. **Leisure Activities:** whirlpool, exercise room. **Guest Services:** coin laundry. **Business Services:** meeting rooms, fax (fee). **Cards:** AX, DC, MC, VI. **Special Amenities:** early check-in/late check-out and free continental breakfast.

SOME UNITS

⦿ 🛗 ⅋ 🏊 ✷ 🖧 🖥 🖨 💳 / ☒ /

(See map p. 382)

COMFORT SUITES

AAA SAVE
▼▼▼▼
Small-scale Hotel

Phone: (281)565-5566 252 F

All Year   1P: $95   2P: $100   XP: $10

Location: US 59 service road, exit Corporate Dr southbound; exit Airport Blvd/Kirkwood Rd northbound. 4820 Techniplex Dr 77477. Fax: 281/565-5050. **Facility:** 53 one-bedroom standard units, some with whirlpools. 3 stories, interior corridors. *Bath:* combo or shower only. **Terms:** [ECP] meal plan available. **Amenities:** voice mail, irons, hair dryers. **Pool(s):** outdoor. **Leisure Activities:** whirlpool, exercise room. **Guest Services:** coin laundry. **Business Services:** meeting rooms, fax (fee). **Cards:** AX, CB, DC, DS, MC, VI.

SOME UNITS

COURTYARD BY MARRIOTT-HOUSTON/SUGARLAND

SAVE
▼▼▼▼
Small-scale Hotel

Phone: (281)491-7700 250

All Year   1P: $59-$119   2P: $59-$119

Location: US 59, exit Corporate Dr southbound; exit Kirkwood Rd/Airport Blvd northbound, on eastbound frontage road. 12655 Southwest Frwy 77477. Fax: 281/491-7733. **Facility:** 112 units. 108 one-bedroom standard units, some with whirlpools. 4 one-bedroom suites ($129). 4 stories, interior corridors. *Bath:* combo or shower only. **Parking:** on-site. **Terms:** cancellation fee imposed. **Amenities:** video games (fee), voice mail, irons, hair dryers. **Pool(s):** heated outdoor. **Leisure Activities:** whirlpool, exercise room. **Guest Services:** complimentary evening beverages: Mon-Thurs, coin laundry. **Business Services:** meeting rooms, business center. **Cards:** AX, CB, DC, DS, MC, VI.

SOME UNITS

DAYS INN

SAVE
▼▼
Small-scale Hotel

Phone: 281/240-8100 254 F16

All Year   2P: $50-$60   XP: $5

Location: US 59, exit Kirkwood Rd, just s to Techniplex Dr. 4630 Techniplex Dr 77477. Fax: 281/240-3232. **Facility:** 69 one-bedroom standard units. 2 stories (no elevator), interior corridors. *Bath:* combo or shower only. **Parking:** on-site. **Terms:** weekly rates available, [CP] meal plan available, small pets only ($5 fee). **Amenities:** safes, hair dryers. **Guest Services:** coin laundry. **Business Services:** fax (fee). **Cards:** AX, DC, DS, MC, VI.

SOME UNITS

HAMPTON INN-STAFFORD

SAVE
▼▼▼▼
Small-scale Hotel

Phone: (281)565-0559 248 F18

All Year [ECP]   1P: $65-$85   2P: $65-$95   XP: $6

Location: US 59 eastbound service road, exit Corporate Dr southbound; exit Airport Blvd/Kirkwood Rd northbound. 4714 Techniplex Dr 77477. Fax: 281/565-7096. **Facility:** 86 one-bedroom standard units. 3 stories, interior corridors. *Bath:* combo or shower only. **Parking:** on-site. **Terms:** 14 day cancellation notice. **Amenities:** voice mail, irons. **Pool(s):** heated indoor. **Leisure Activities:** whirlpool. **Guest Services:** valet laundry. **Business Services:** fax (fee). **Cards:** AX, CB, DC, DS, MC, VI.

SOME UNITS
FEE

LA QUINTA INN-STAFFORD

AAA SAVE
▼▼▼▼
Motel

Phone: (281)240-2300 253 F18

All Year   1P: $60-$76   2P: $66-$82   XP: $6

Location: US 59 eastbound service road, exit Corporate Dr southbound; exit Airport Blvd/Kirkwood Rd northbound. 12727 Southwest Frwy 77477. Fax: 281/240-6677. **Facility:** 129 one-bedroom standard units. 4 stories, interior corridors. **Parking:** on-site. **Terms:** [ECP] meal plan available, small pets only. **Amenities:** video games (fee), voice mail, irons, hair dryers. **Pool(s):** outdoor. **Guest Services:** valet and coin laundry. **Business Services:** meeting rooms, fax (fee). **Cards:** AX, CB, DC, DS, JC, MC, VI. **Special Amenities:** free continental breakfast and free local telephone calls. *(See color ad p 401)*

SOME UNITS

RESIDENCE INN BY MARRIOTT SUGARLAND

SAVE
▼▼▼▼
Small-scale Hotel

Phone: (281)277-0770 265

All Year [ECP]   1P: $129

Location: US 59, exit Corporate Dr southbound; exit Airport Blvd/Kirkwood Rd northbound. Located in the business district. 12703 Southwest Frwy 77477. Fax: 281/277-1440. **Facility:** 78 units. 36 one-bedroom standard units with kitchens. 30 one- and 12 two-bedroom suites ($129-$189) with kitchens. 3 stories, interior corridors. *Bath:* combo or shower only. **Parking:** on-site. **Terms:** pets ($25 fee, $5 extra charge). **Amenities:** video games, dual phone lines, voice mail, irons, hair dryers. **Pool(s):** heated outdoor. **Leisure Activities:** whirlpool, exercise room, sports court. **Guest Services:** complimentary evening beverages: Mon-Thurs, valet and coin laundry. **Business Services:** PC, fax (fee). **Cards:** AX, DC, DS, MC, VI.

SOME UNITS

STUDIO 6 #6044

▼▼▼
Motel

Phone: 281/240-6900 257 F17

All Year   1P: $46-$56   2P: $50-$60   XP: $4

Location: US 59, exit US 90 and SR 41 alternate northbound, following frontage road; exit Corporate Dr southbound, follow frontage road. 12827 Southwest Frwy 77477. Fax: 281/240-8222. **Facility:** 133 one-bedroom standard units with efficiencies. 2 stories, exterior corridors. *Bath:* combo or shower only. **Parking:** on-site. **Terms:** weekly rates available, pets ($50 fee). **Amenities:** voice mail, irons. **Guest Services:** coin laundry. **Business Services:** fax (fee). **Cards:** AX, CB, DC, DS, MC, VI.

SOME UNITS

WELLESLEY INN & SUITES (HOUSTON/STAFFORD)

AAA SAVE
▼▼▼▼
Motel

Phone: (281)240-0025 249 F17

All Year [ECP]   1P: $85-$115   XP: $10

Location: US 59, exit W Airport Blvd/Kirkwood Dr, just w on Frontage Rd to Sugar Grove Blvd, just n. 4726 Sugar Grove Blvd 77477. Fax: 281/240-0206. **Facility:** 80 one-bedroom standard units with efficiencies. 2 stories, exterior corridors. *Bath:* combo or shower only. **Parking:** on-site. **Terms:** small pets only. **Amenities:** high-speed Internet, dual phone lines, voice mail, irons, hair dryers. **Pool(s):** outdoor. **Leisure Activities:** exercise room. **Guest Services:** coin laundry. **Business Services:** fax (fee). **Cards:** AX, DC, DS, JC, MC, VI. **Special Amenities:** free continental breakfast and free newspaper.

SOME UNITS

SUGAR LAND pop. 63,328 (See map p. 382; index p. 389)

———— WHERE TO STAY ————

DRURY INN & SUITES-HOUSTON/SUGAR LAND
Phone: (281)277-9700   **266**

(AAA) (SAVE)

9/1-1/31 [ECP]	1P: $79-$99	2P: $89-$109	XP: $10 F18
2/1-8/31 [ECP]	1P: $76-$96	2P: $86-$106	XP: $10 F18

Location: Sw on US 59, exit Sugar Land/Alternate 90/Spur 41 (Dairy Ashford/Sugar Creek Blvd). 13770 Southwest Frwy 77478. Fax: 281/277-9700. **Facility:** 134 units. 121 one-bedroom standard units. 13 one-bedroom suites **Small-scale Hotel** ($96-$126). 5 stories, interior corridors. *Bath:* combo or shower only. **Parking:** on-site. **Terms:** small pets only. **Amenities:** voice mail, irons, hair dryers. **Pool(s):** heated indoor/outdoor. **Leisure Activities:** whirlpool, exercise room. **Guest Services:** valet and coin laundry. **Business Services:** meeting rooms, fax (fee). **Cards:** AX, CB, DC, DS, MC, VI. **Special Amenities:** free continental breakfast and free local telephone calls.

SOME UNITS

SHONEY'S INN & SUITES HOUSTON-SUGAR LAND
Phone: (281)565-6655   **268**

All Year [ECP]	1P: $52-$58	2P: $57-$63	XP: $6 F17

Location: Sw on US 59, exit Stafford/Sugar Land (Dairy Ashford/Sugar Creek Blvd). 14444 Southwest Frwy 77478. **Small-scale Hotel** Fax: 281/565-6670. **Facility:** 114 one-bedroom standard units. 5 stories, interior corridors. **Parking:** on-site. **Terms:** small pets only ($25 fee). **Amenities:** high-speed Internet (fee), voice mail, irons, hair dryers. **Pool(s):** outdoor. **Guest Services:** complimentary evening beverages: Wed, valet and coin laundry, area transportation. **Business Services:** meeting rooms, fax (fee). **Cards:** AX, CB, DC, DS, JC, MC, VI.

SOME UNITS

TOMBALL pop. 9,089 (See map p. 382; index p. 389)

———— WHERE TO STAY ————

HOLIDAY INN EXPRESS
Phone: (281)351-4114   **302**

All Year	1P: $85	2P: $85	XP: $10 F19

Location: SR 249 and FM 2920, northeast corner. 1437 Keefer St 77375. Fax: 281/255-9504. **Facility:** 40 one-**Small-scale Hotel** bedroom standard units, some with whirlpools. 2 stories, interior corridors. **Parking:** on-site. **Terms:** [CP] meal plan available. **Amenities:** irons, hair dryers. **Pool(s):** outdoor. **Leisure Activities:** whirlpool. **Guest Services:** valet laundry. **Business Services:** fax (fee). **Cards:** AX, DC, DS, JC, MC, VI.

SOME UNITS

WEBSTER pop. 9,083 (See map p. 382; index p. 388)

———— WHERE TO STAY ————

BEST WESTERN-NASA
Phone: (281)338-6000   **231**

(AAA) (SAVE)

All Year [ECP]	1P: $49-$99	2P: $49-$109	XP: $6 F12

Location: I-45, exit 26 (Bay Area Blvd), 0.3 mi e. 889 W Bay Area Blvd 77598. Fax: 281/338-2834. **Facility:** 80 units. 79 one-bedroom standard units. 1 one-bedroom suite with kitchen. 2 stories, interior corridors. **Parking:** on-**Small-scale Hotel** site. **Amenities:** voice mail, irons, hair dryers. **Pool(s):** outdoor. **Guest Services:** valet laundry, airport transportation-William P Hobby Airport. **Business Services:** meeting rooms, fax (fee). **Cards:** AX, CB, DC, DS, JC, MC, VI. **Special Amenities:** free continental breakfast and free room upgrade (subject to availability with advanced reservations).

SOME UNITS

HAMPTON INN & SUITES CLEAR LAKE/NASA
Phone: (281)332-7952   **229**

(SAVE)

All Year [CP]	1P: $82-$132	2P: $82-$132

Location: I-45 S, exit 27, 0.5 mi e. 506 W Bay Area Blvd 77598. Fax: 281/332-2989. **Facility:** 108 units. 79 one-bedroom standard units. 29 one-bedroom suites ($122-$132) with efficiencies. 3 stories, interior corridors. *Bath:* combo or shower only. **Parking:** on-site. **Amenities:** video games (fee), high-speed Internet, dual **Small-scale Hotel** phone lines, voice mail, irons, hair dryers. **Pool(s):** outdoor. **Leisure Activities:** whirlpool, exercise room. **Guest Services:** sundries, complimentary evening beverages: Tues & Wed, valet and coin laundry. **Business Services:** meeting rooms, fax (fee). **Cards:** AX, CB, DC, DS, MC, VI.

SOME UNITS

HOWARD JOHNSON EXPRESS INN-NASA
Phone: 281/316-2003   **227**

(AAA) (SAVE)

6/1-9/30 [CP]	1P: $55-$75	2P: $55-$75	XP: $5 F12
2/1-5/31 & 10/1-1/31 [CP]	1P: $49-$65	2P: $49-$65	XP: $5 F12

Location: I-45, exit 25, just e. 915 W NASA Rd One 77598. Fax: 281/338-0364. **Facility:** 45 one-bedroom standard units. 2 stories, exterior corridors. **Parking:** on-site. **Terms:** weekly rates available. **Amenities:** hair **Small-scale Hotel** dryers. *Some:* irons. **Pool(s):** heated outdoor. **Leisure Activities:** whirlpool. **Guest Services:** coin laundry. **Business Services:** fax (fee). **Cards:** AX, DS, MC, VI. **Special Amenities:** free continental breakfast and free local telephone calls.

SOME UNITS

MOTEL 6 HOUSTON NASA/CLEAR LAKE #551
Phone: 281/332-4581   **228**

5/22-1/31	1P: $41-$51	2P: $47-$57	XP: $3 F17
2/1-5/21	1P: $39-$49	2P: $45-$55	XP: $3 F17

Motel **Location:** I-45, exit 25, just e. 1001 W NASA Rd One 77598. Fax: 281/332-0341. **Facility:** 122 one-bedroom standard units. 2 stories, exterior corridors. *Bath:* combo or shower only. **Parking:** on-site. **Terms:** small pets only. **Pool(s):** outdoor. **Guest Services:** coin laundry. **Business Services:** fax (fee). **Cards:** AX, CB, DC, DS, MC, VI.

SOME UNITS

(See map p. 382)

WELLESLEY INN & SUITES (HOUSTON/NASA CLEAR LAKE)
Phone: (281)338-7711 230
AAA SAVE
All Year   1P: $81-$101   2P: $101   XP: $10   F17
Location: I-45, exit 26 (Bay Area Blvd), just e. 720 W Bay Area Blvd 77598. **Fax:** 281/338-7722. **Facility:** 86 units. 66 one-bedroom standard units with efficiencies. 20 one-bedroom suites, some with efficiencies or kitchens. 3 stories, interior corridors. *Bath:* combo or shower only. **Parking:** on-site. **Terms:** [ECP] meal plan available, small pets only. **Amenities:** dual phone lines, voice mail, irons, hair dryers. **Pool(s):** outdoor. **Leisure Activities:** exercise room. **Guest Services:** valet and coin laundry. **Business Services:** fax (fee). **Cards:** AX, DS, JC, MC, VI. **Special Amenities:** free continental breakfast and free newspaper.

Motel

SOME UNITS

[icons]

------- **WHERE TO DINE** -------

LUPE TORTILLA
Lunch: $6-$10   Dinner: $6-$10   Phone: 281/338-2711 186
Tex-Mex
Location: I-45, exit 26, just e. 891 W Bay Area Blvd 77598. **Hours:** 11 am-2:30 & 5-8:30 pm, Fri-9:30 pm, Sat 5 pm-9:30 pm, Sun 5 pm-8:30 pm. Closed major holidays. **Features:** Not every enchilada tastes the same. Here, green chicken enchiladas with tomatilla sauce have a great flavor, and the flan dessert is right on the mark. The environment is lively, sparked by cantina decor, background music and energetic service. Casual dress. **Parking:** on-site. **Cards:** AX, CB, DC, DS, MC, VI.

[icons]

ZIO'S ITALIAN KITCHEN
Lunch: $6-$10   Dinner: $6-$10   Phone: 281/338-7800 187
Italian
Location: I-45, exit 26 (Bay Area Blvd), just e. 820 W Bay Area Blvd 77598. **Hours:** 11 am-10 pm, Fri & Sat-11 pm. Closed: 11/27, 12/25. **Reservations:** accepted. **Features:** The small chain specializes in Italian cuisine, including oven-baked pizzas and pasta dishes. Guests are encouraged to get creative with their pizzas by mixing and matching from a list of 24 toppings. Particularly tempting dishes are chicken parmigiana and seven-layer lasagna. Smoke free premises. Casual dress; cocktails. **Parking:** on-site. **Cards:** AX, DC, DS, MC, VI.

[icons]

WILLIS pop. 3,985

------- **WHERE TO STAY** -------

BEST WESTERN-WILLIS
Phone: (936)856-1906
AAA SAVE
All Year   1P: $59-$125   2P: $150   XP: $5   F17
Location: I-45, exit 94, just s on frontage road to Old Montgomery Hwy, just sw to Western Rd, then just s. 12323 IH 45 N 77318. **Fax:** 936/856-0910. **Facility:** 48 one-bedroom standard units, some with whirlpools. 2 stories, exterior corridors. *Bath:* combo or shower only. **Parking:** on-site. **Terms:** 7 day cancellation notice.
Small-scale Hotel **Amenities:** irons, hair dryers. **Pool(s):** outdoor. **Business Services:** fax (fee). **Cards:** AX, DC, DS, MC, VI. **Special Amenities:** free continental breakfast and free newspaper.

SOME UNITS

[icons]

WINNIE pop. 2,914

------- **WHERE TO STAY** -------

HOLIDAY INN EXPRESS
Phone: (409)296-2866
Motel
All Year   1P: $64-$69   2P: $64-$69   XP: $5   F18
Location: I-10, exit 829, just n. 14932 FM 1663 77665. **Fax:** 409/296-9832. **Facility:** 43 units. 40 one- and 3 two-bedroom standard units, some with kitchens. 2 stories (no elevator), exterior corridors. *Bath:* combo or shower only. **Parking:** on-site. **Terms:** [ECP] meal plan available. **Amenities:** dual phone lines, voice mail, irons, hair dryers. **Pool(s):** small outdoor. **Leisure Activities:** whirlpool. **Guest Services:** coin laundry. **Business Services:** meeting rooms, fax (fee). **Cards:** AX, CB, DC, DS, MC, VI.

SOME UNITS

[icons]

THE WOODLANDS pop. 55,649

------- **WHERE TO STAY** -------

COMFORT SUITES
Phone: (936)273-1500
SAVE
All Year [CP]   1P: $65-$150   2P: $65-$150   XP: $5   F17
Location: I-45, exit 79 northbound; exit 78 southbound. 18456 I-45 S 77384. **Fax:** 936/273-2496. **Facility:** 64 units. 63 one-bedroom standard units, some with whirlpools. 1 one-bedroom suite with whirlpool. 3 stories, interior corridors. *Bath:* combo or shower only. **Parking:** on-site. **Terms:** check-in 4 pm. **Amenities:** voice mail, irons, hair dryers. *Some:* high-speed Internet. **Pool(s):** outdoor. **Leisure Activities:** whirlpool, exercise room. **Guest Services:** coin laundry. **Business Services:** meeting rooms, fax (fee). **Cards:** AX, CB, DC, DS, JC, MC, VI.

Small-scale Hotel

SOME UNITS

[icons]

COURTYARD BY MARRIOTT-HOUSTON (WOODLANDS)
Phone: (281)292-3262
SAVE
All Year   1P: $69-$109   2P: $69-$109
Location: I-45, exit 78 southbound; exit 77 northbound, 0.8 mi s jct I-45 and Research Forest Dr, just w. 1020 Lake Front Cir 77380. **Fax:** 281/292-3262. **Facility:** 90 units. 87 one-bedroom standard units. 3 one-bedroom suites. 3 stories, interior corridors. *Bath:* combo or shower only. **Parking:** on-site. **Terms:** [BP] meal plan available, $8 service charge. **Amenities:** voice mail, irons, hair dryers. **Pool(s):** heated indoor. **Leisure Activities:** whirlpool, exercise room. **Guest Services:** valet laundry. **Business Services:** meeting rooms, fax (fee).
Small-scale Hotel
Cards: AX, CB, DC, DS, JC, MC, VI.

SOME UNITS

[icons]

DRURY INN & SUITES-HOUSTON THE WOODLANDS

AAA SAVE
WWWW

Phone: (281)362-7222

9/1-1/31 [ECP]	1P: $73-$93	2P: $83-$103	XP: $10	F18
2/1-8/31 [ECP]	1P: $70-$90	2P: $80-$100	XP: $10	F18

Small-scale Hotel

Location: I-45, exit 78 southbound; exit 77 northbound on west service road. 28099 I-45 N 77380. **Fax:** 281/362-7222. **Facility:** 152 units. 128 one-bedroom standard units. 24 one-bedroom suites ($90-$113). 7 stories, interior corridors. *Bath:* combo or shower only. **Parking:** on-site. **Amenities:** voice mail, irons, hair dryers. **Pool(s):** heated indoor/outdoor. **Leisure Activities:** whirlpool, exercise room. **Guest Services:** complimentary evening beverages: Mon-Thurs, coin laundry. **Business Services:** meeting rooms, fax (fee). **Cards:** AX, CB, DC, DS, MC, VI. **Special Amenities:** free continental breakfast and free local telephone calls.

SOME UNITS

HOLIDAY INN EXPRESS HOTEL & SUITES

WWWW

Phone: (281)681-8088

All Year	1P: $80-$129	XP: $5	F

Small-scale Hotel

Location: I-45, exit 73 (Rayford/Sawdust Rd), on northbound access road. 24888 I-45 N 77386. **Fax:** 281/681-8168. **Facility:** 120 one-bedroom standard units, some with whirlpools. 3 stories, interior corridors. *Bath:* combo or shower only. **Parking:** on-site. **Terms:** cancellation fee imposed, [ECP] meal plan available. **Amenities:** *Some:* voice mail, irons, hair dryers. **Pool(s):** outdoor. **Leisure Activities:** sauna, whirlpool, steamroom, exercise room. **Guest Services:** valet and coin laundry. **Business Services:** meeting rooms, fax (fee). **Cards:** AX, CB, DC, DS, MC, VI.

SOME UNITS

LA QUINTA INN-HOUSTON-WOODLANDS

AAA SAVE
WWW

Phone: (281)367-7722

All Year	1P: $60-$70	2P: $67-$77	XP: $7	F18

Small-scale Hotel

Location: I-45, exit 78 southbound; exit 79 northbound on southbound frontage road. 28673 I-45 N 77381. **Fax:** 281/367-9054. **Facility:** 116 one-bedroom standard units. 3 stories, interior/exterior corridors. *Bath:* combo or shower only. **Parking:** on-site. **Terms:** [ECP] meal plan available, small pets only. **Amenities:** video games (fee), voice mail, irons, hair dryers. **Pool(s):** outdoor. **Leisure Activities:** exercise room. **Guest Services:** valet laundry. **Business Services:** meeting rooms, fax (fee). **Cards:** AX, CB, DC, DS, JC, MC, VI. **Special Amenities:** free continental breakfast and free local telephone calls. *(See color ad p 401)*

SOME UNITS

RESIDENCE INN-THE WOODLANDS

SAVE
WWW

Phone: (281)292-3252

All Year [BP]	1P: $85-$120	2P: $85-$120

Small-scale Hotel

Location: I-45, exit 78 southbound; exit 79 northbound, 0.8 mi s of jct I-45 and Research Forest, just w. 1040 Lake Front Cr 77380. **Fax:** 281/292-3252. **Facility:** 90 units. 78 one- and 12 two-bedroom suites, some with efficiencies or kitchens. 3 stories, interior corridors. *Bath:* combo or shower only. **Parking:** on-site. **Terms:** cancellation fee imposed, pets ($75 fee, $10 extra charge). **Amenities:** voice mail, irons, hair dryers. **Pool(s):** heated indoor. **Leisure Activities:** whirlpool, exercise room, sports court. **Guest Services:** complimentary evening beverages: Mon-Thurs, valet and coin laundry. **Business Services:** meeting rooms, fax (fee). **Cards:** AX, CB, DC, DS, MC, VI.

SOME UNITS

HE WOODLANDS RESORT & CONFERENCE CENTER　　　　　　Phone: (281)367-1100

▽▽▽▽　All Year　　　　1P: $139-$349

Resort
Large-scale Hotel

Location: I-45, exit 73 (Rayford/Sawdust Rd), 0.4 mi w on Sawdust Rd to Grogan's Mill Rd, 1.8 mi w on Grogan's Mill Rd to N Millbend Dr, just s. 2301 N Millbend Dr 77380. Fax: 281/364-6345. **Facility:** Hidden in the woods just north of sprawling downtown Houston, the resort offers ample conference and recreational facilities. 412 units. 338 one-bedroom standard units, some with kitchens and/or whirlpools. 58 one- and 16 two-bedroom suites $349-$1200), some with kitchens and/or whirlpools. 3 stories, interior/exterior corridors. **Parking:** on-site and valet. **Terms:** 3 ight minimum stay - seasonal, weekends, cancellation fee imposed, [BP] meal plan available, 19% service charge. **Amenities:** voice mail. *Some:* CD players, dual phone lines, fax, irons, hair dryers. **Pool(s):** 6 outdoor, heated outdoor, heated ndoor, wading. **Leisure Activities:** recreation programs, hiking trails. *Fee:* sauna, whirlpool, golf-54 holes, 24 tennis courts (5 ndoor, 24 lighted), bicycles, massage. **Guest Services:** gift shop, valet laundry, area transportation (fee). **Business Services:** onference facilities, business center. **Cards:** AX, MC, VI.

SOME UNITS

ASK SD ⊞ ⊞ ⊞ ⊞ ⊡ ⊡ ⊞ ⊠ ⊞ DATA/⊠ VCR ⊞ ⊞ ⊞/
　　　　FEE　　　　　　　　　　　　　　　　　　PORT　　　　FEE

──────── **WHERE TO DINE** ────────

AMERIGO'S GRILL　　　Lunch: $9-$16　　　Dinner: $12-$37　　　Phone: 281/362-0808

▽▽ ▽▽

Italian

Location: I-45, exit 73 (Rayford/Sawdust Rd), 0.8 mi w on Grogans Mill Rd/Sawdust; in Gorgan's Mill Mall. 25250 Grogan's Park Dr 77380. **Hours:** 11 am-2 & 5-10 pm, Fri & Sat-11 pm, Sun 5 pm-10 pm. Closed: 1/1, 11/27, 12/25. **Features:** Sit on the patio and enjoy an original Italian specialty. Begin with the shrimp cocktail appetizer. Savor the veal marsala with penne pasta, a hearty Caesar salad and a glass of wine. For essert, the moist tiramisu is a must. Casual dress; cocktails. **Parking:** on-site. **Cards:** AX, CB, DC, DS, MC, VI.　⊠ ⊠

CARRABBA'S ITALIAN GRILL　　　Lunch: $10-$20　　　Dinner: $10-$20　　　Phone: 281/367-9423

▽▽ ▽▽

Italian

Location: I-45, exit 73 (Rayford/Sawdust Rd), on service road southbound. 25665 I-45 N Hwy 77380. **Hours:** 4:30 pm-10 pm, Fri & Sat-11 pm, Sun noon-10 pm. Closed major holidays. **Features:** An open kitchen is in full view of guests. The dining room is decorated with Italian artifacts and has a fun and very loud atmosphere. Try the sirloin marsala with sauteed spinach. The popular tiramisu is a tasty item for dessert. Casual dress; cocktails. **Parking:** on-site. **Cards:** AX, DC, DS, MC, VI.　⊠

GUADALAJARA MEXICAN GRILLE & BAR　　　Lunch: $9-$18　　　Dinner: $9-$18　　　Phone: 281/362-0774

▽▽ ▽▽

Mexican

Location: I-45, exit 78 southbound; exit 79 northbound. 27885 I-45 N 77381. **Hours:** 11 am-10 pm, Fri & Sat-11 pm. Closed: 11/27, 12/25. **Features:** Savor Tex-Mex cuisine in a Mexican market interior. Murals, plants and Mexican writing cover the plastered walls. Try something different like stuffed camarones—shrimp wrapped in crispy bacon. This eatery makes a nice addition to the area. Casual dress; cocktails. **Parking:** on-site. **Cards:** AX, DS, MC, VI.　⊠ ⊠

KYOTO JAPANESE RESTAURANT　　　Lunch: $6-$10　　　Dinner: $9-$25　　　Phone: 281/363-9400

▽▽ ▽▽

Japanese

Location: I-45, exit 73 (Rayford/Sawdust Rd); on southbound service road. 25701 I-45 N 77380. **Hours:** 11 am-2:30 & 5-10 pm, Sat & Sun noon-3 & 5-9 pm. Closed major holidays. **Reservations:** suggested; weekends. **Features:** This small neighborhood restaurant features scrumptious Japanese cuisine served by a kimono-clad wait staff. Sushi, sashimi and tempura are all delicious. The Kyoto Bento contains sashimi, eef rolls and steamed rice. Casual dress; beer & wine only. **Parking:** on-site. **Cards:** AX, DS, MC, VI.　⊠

This ends listings for the Houston Vicinity.
The following page resumes the alphabetical listings of
cities in Texas.

HUMBLE —*See Houston p. 437.*

HUNTSVILLE pop. 35,078

──────── **WHERE TO STAY** ────────

COMFORT INN & SUITES
[SAVE] Small-scale Hotel
Phone: (936)438-8400
All Year — 1P: $55-$99 — 2P: $60-$105 — XP: $6 — F18
Location: I-45, exit 114 northbound; exit 116 southbound. 160 I-45 S 77340. Fax: 936/438-8007. **Facility:** 48 one-bedroom standard units. 2 stories, exterior corridors. **Parking:** on-site. **Terms:** [ECP] meal plan available. **Amenities:** irons, hair dryers. **Pool(s):** outdoor. **Guest Services:** valet laundry. **Business Services:** meeting rooms, fax (fee). **Cards:** AX, CB, DC, DS, MC, VI.
SOME UNITS

HOLIDAY INN EXPRESS (SAM HOUSTON)
Small-scale Hotel
Phone: (936)293-8800
All Year [ECP] — 1P: $74-$99 — 2P: $84-$109 — F18
Location: I-45, exit 116, just w on US 190. 201 West Hill Park Cir 77340. Fax: 936/293-8989. **Facility:** 52 one-bedroom standard units, some with whirlpools. 2 stories, exterior corridors. *Bath:* combo or shower only. **Parking:** on-site. **Terms:** pets ($10 fee). **Amenities:** dual phone lines, voice mail, irons, hair dryers. **Pool(s):** heated outdoor. **Leisure Activities:** whirlpool. **Guest Services:** valet and coin laundry. **Business Services:** meeting rooms, fax (fee). **Cards:** AX, CB, DC, DS, MC, VI. *(See ad below)*
SOME UNITS

LA QUINTA INN-HUNTSVILLE
[AAA] [SAVE] Small-scale Hotel
Phone: (936)295-6454
All Year — 1P: $60-$69 — 2P: $66-$75 — XP: $6 — F18
Location: I-45, exit 116. 124 I-45 N 77340. Fax: 936/295-9245. **Facility:** 120 one-bedroom standard units. 2 stories, exterior corridors. **Parking:** on-site. **Terms:** [ECP] meal plan available, small pets only. **Amenities:** video games (fee), voice mail, irons, hair dryers. **Pool(s):** outdoor, wading. **Leisure Activities:** exercise room. **Business Services:** meeting rooms, fax (fee). **Cards:** AX, CB, DC, DS, JC, MC, VI. **Special Amenities: free continental breakfast and free local telephone calls.**
SOME UNITS

──────── **WHERE TO DINE** ────────

THE JUNCTION
American
Lunch: $6-$10 — Dinner: $9-$19 — Phone: 409/291-2183
Location: I-45, exit 116, e on US 190 and SR 30. 2641 11th St 77340. **Hours:** 11 am-9:30 pm, Fri & Sat-10:30 pm. Closed major holidays; also 12/24. **Reservations:** accepted. **Features:** Quartered in a restored, antebellum plantation house—one of the four oldest standing homes in town—this unique blend of antiques and contemporary music provides a quiet, laid-back ambience in which to enjoy prime rib and all-you-can-eat shrimp. Casual dress; cocktails. **Parking:** on-site. **Cards:** AX, DC, DS, MC, VI.

HURST pop. 36,273 (See map p. 343; index p. 346)

──────── **WHERE TO STAY** ────────

AMERISUITES (FT WORTH/HURST)
[AAA] [SAVE] Small-scale Hotel
Phone: (817)577-3003 [90]
All Year [ECP] — 1P: $99-$114 — 2P: $99-$114 — XP: $10 — F18
Location: SR 183, exit Precinct Line Rd, just n to Thousand Oaks, just w. 1601 Hurst Town Center Dr 76054. Fax: 817/577-8388. **Facility:** 128 one-bedroom standard units. 6 stories, interior corridors. *Bath:* combo or shower only. **Parking:** on-site. **Terms:** small pets only. **Amenities:** video games (fee), voice mail, irons, hair dryers. *Some:* dual phone lines. **Pool(s):** heated outdoor. **Leisure Activities:** exercise room. **Guest Services:** valet and coin laundry, area transportation-within 5 mi. **Business Services:** meeting rooms, fax (fee). **Cards:** AX, CB, DC, DS, MC, VI. **Special Amenities: free continental breakfast and free newspaper.** *(See color ad p 347)*
SOME UNITS

INGLESIDE pop. 9,388

------ WHERE TO STAY ------

COMFORT INN
(AAA) [SAVE]
▽▽▽▽▽
Motel

			Phone: 361/775-2700
5/16-8/31	1P: $79-$118	2P: $84-$129	XP: $5 F12
2/1-5/15	1P: $69-$99	2P: $74-$104	XP: $5 F12
9/1-1/31	1P: $64-$94	2P: $69-$99	XP: $5 F12

Location: On SR 361. Located in a quiet, rural area. 2800 Hwy 361 78362. Fax: 361/775-1220. **Facility:** 40 one-bedroom standard units. 2 stories, interior corridors. **Parking:** on-site. **Terms:** [ECP] meal plan available. **Amenities:** irons, hair dryers. **Pool(s):** outdoor. **Leisure Activities:** sauna, whirlpool, exercise room. **Guest Services:** complimentary evening beverages: Mon-Thurs, coin laundry. **Business Services:** fax (fee). **Cards:** AX, DC, DS, MC, VI.

SOME UNITS

🏊 ⊠ 📹 [DATA PORT] 🔒 📺 💻 / ⊠ /

INGRAM pop. 1,740

------ WHERE TO STAY ------

LAZY HILLS GUEST RANCH
▽
Ranch

			Phone: (830)367-5600
5/16-8/15 [AP]	1P: $120	2P: $190	XP: $50
2/1-5/15 & 8/16-1/31 [AP]	1P: $110	2P: $170	XP: $50

Location: I-10, exit 488 (SR 27 E), 11.5 mi to Henderson Branch Rd, 1.2 mi n to ranch entrance. 373 Henderson Branch Rd 78025 (PO Box A). Fax: 830/367-5667. **Facility:** 25 one-bedroom standard units. 1 story, exterior corridors. *Bath:* shower only. **Parking:** on-site. **Terms:** check-in 4 pm, 15 day cancellation notice. **Pool(s):** outdoor, wading. **Leisure Activities:** whirlpool, fishing, 2 lighted tennis courts, recreation programs, playground, basketball, shuffleboard. *Fee:* horseback riding. **Guest Services:** gift shop, coin laundry. **Business Services:** meeting rooms, fax (fee). **Cards:** AX, DS, MC, VI.

🍴 🏊 ⊠ 📹 🆉

IRVING —See Dallas p. 297.

JACKSONVILLE pop. 13,868

------ WHERE TO STAY ------

HOLIDAY INN EXPRESS
▽▽▽▽
Small-scale Hotel

			Phone: 903/589-8500
All Year	1P: $73	2P: $73	XP: $10 F

Location: 2 mi s of jct US 69 and 79, on US 69. 1848 S Jackson 75766. Fax: 903/589-0800. **Facility:** 48 one-bedroom standard units. 2 stories, interior corridors. *Bath:* combo or shower only. **Parking:** on-site. **Terms:** [CP] meal plan available. **Amenities:** dual phone lines, voice mail, irons, hair dryers. **Pool(s):** outdoor. **Guest Services:** valet and coin laundry. **Business Services:** meeting rooms, business center. **Cards:** AX, CB, DC, DS, JC, MC, VI.

SOME UNITS

[ASK] [S/D] 🍴 [M] 🏊 📹 [DATA PORT] 🔒 📺 💻 / ⊠ /

JASPER pop. 8,247

------ WHERE TO STAY ------

BEST WESTERN INN OF JASPER
(AAA) [SAVE]
▽▽▽▽
Motel

			Phone: (409)384-7767
All Year	1P: $48-$52	2P: $52-$56	XP: $4 F19

Location: US 190 and SR 63, 0.5 mi w of jct US 96. 205 W Gibson 75951. Fax: 409/384-7665. **Facility:** 59 one-bedroom standard units. 1-2 stories, exterior corridors. **Parking:** on-site. **Terms:** [CP] meal plan available, small pets only ($10 fee). **Amenities:** irons, hair dryers. **Pool(s):** outdoor. **Leisure Activities:** whirlpool. **Guest Services:** valet laundry. **Business Services:** meeting rooms, fax (fee). **Cards:** AX, CB, DC, DS, MC, VI. **Special Amenities:** free continental breakfast.

SOME UNITS

[S/D] 🛏 🍴 🏊 📹 [DATA PORT] 💻 / ⊠ 🔒 📺 /
FEE FEE

HOLIDAY INN EXPRESS
▽▽▽▽
Motel

		Phone: (409)384-8600
All Year [ECP]	1P: $80-$100	

Location: US 96, 1.8 mi n of jct US 190. 2100 N Wheeler 75951. Fax: 409/384-9551. **Facility:** 57 units. 55 one- and 2 two-bedroom standard units. 2 stories, exterior corridors. **Parking:** on-site. **Terms:** small pets only. **Amenities:** irons, hair dryers. **Pool(s):** outdoor. **Leisure Activities:** exercise room. **Guest Services:** coin laundry. **Business Services:** meeting rooms, fax. **Cards:** AX, CB, DC, DS, JC, MC, VI.

SOME UNITS

[ASK] [S/D] 🛏 🍴 🏊 📹 [DATA PORT] 💻 / ⊠ [VCR] 🔒 📺 /
FEE FEE FEE

RAMADA INN JASPER
▽▽▽
Motel

			Phone: (409)384-9021
All Year [BP]	1P: $55-$75	2P: $58-$79	XP: $5 F17

Location: US 190 and SR 63, just w of jct US 96. 239 E Gibson (US 190) 75951. Fax: 409/481-1181. **Facility:** 100 one-bedroom standard units. 2 stories, exterior corridors. **Parking:** on-site. **Terms:** small pets only. **Amenities:** voice mail, irons, hair dryers. **Pool(s):** outdoor. **Guest Services:** coin laundry. **Business Services:** meeting rooms, fax (fee). **Cards:** AX, CB, DC, DS, JC, MC, VI.

SOME UNITS

[ASK] [S/D] 🛏 🍴 🍸 🏊 📹 [DATA PORT] 💻 / ⊠ 🔒 📺 /

——— **WHERE TO DINE** ———

ELIJAH'S CAFE
American
Lunch: $7-$12   **Dinner:** $7-$12   **Phone:** 409/384-9000
Location: US 190 and SR 63, 0.5 mi w of jct US 96. 201 W Gibson 75951. **Hours:** 11 am-9 pm, Fri & Sat-10 pm. Closed: 11/27, 12/25. **Features:** The family-oriented restaurant is known for such home-cooked staples as chicken-fried steak, pot roast, hamburgers and cobblers. Casual dress. **Parking:** on-site. **Cards:** AX, DC, DS, MC, VI.

JEFFERSON pop. 2,024

——— **WHERE TO STAY** ———

THE CLAIBORNE HOUSE
Bed & Breakfast
11/1-12/31 [BP]   2P: $130-$250   XP: $30
2/1-10/31 & 1/1-1/31 [BP]   2P: $100-$175   XP: $30
Phone: (903)665-8800
Location: Just e of jct US 59 and SR 49 to S Alley St, then just s. Located in a quiet, residential area. 312 S Alley St 75657. Fax: 903/665-9335. **Facility:** Original heart-pine floors are featured in this restored 1872 home decorated with antique furniture. Designated smoking area. 6 one-bedroom standard units, some with whirlpools. 2 stories (no elevator), interior/exterior corridors. *Bath:* combo or shower only. **Parking:** street. **Terms:** 2 night minimum stay - weekends, age restrictions may apply, 14 day cancellation notice-fee imposed. **Leisure Activities:** Fee: massage. **Cards:** AX, DS, MC, VI.

OLD MULBERRY INN
Bed & Breakfast
All Year [BP]   2P: $89-$155
Phone: (903)665-1945
Location: 0.3 mi s of jct US 59 and SR 49, just e. Located in a quiet, residential area. 209 Jefferson St 75657. Fax: 903/665-9123. **Facility:** This large, Greek Revival-style home mingles modern amenities with vintage touches such as antique claw-foot tubs. Smoke free premises. 5 one-bedroom standard units, some with whirlpools. 1 story, interior/exterior corridors. *Bath:* combo or shower only. **Parking:** on-site. **Terms:** age restrictions may apply, 7 day cancellation notice-fee imposed. **Amenities:** video library. **Cards:** AX, DS, MC, VI.

——— **WHERE TO DINE** ———

STILLWATER INN DINING ROOM   Historic
American
Dinner: $11-$23   **Phone:** 903/665-8415
Location: Just e of jct US 59 and SR 49. 203 E Broadway 75657. **Hours:** 6 pm-9 pm, Fri & Sat-10 pm. Closed: 12/25; also Sun. **Reservations:** suggested; weekends. **Features:** Restored turn-of-the-century home and inn. Furnished with some antique pieces. Unique tables in sun porch made of treadle sewing machines. Beef, poultry and seafood items offered on a limited menu. Smoke free premises. Casual dress; cocktails. **Parking:** street. **Cards:** AX, MC, VI.

JUNCTION pop. 2,618

——— **WHERE TO STAY** ———

COMFORT INN   (AAA) (SAVE)
Small-scale Hotel
All Year   1P: $79-$89   2P: $89-$100   XP: $10   F
Phone: (325)446-3572
Location: I-10, exit 456. 200 I-10 W 76849. Fax: 325/446-3888. **Facility:** 48 one-bedroom standard units, some with whirlpools. 2 stories (no elevator), exterior corridors. **Parking:** on-site. **Terms:** [CP] meal plan available. **Amenities:** irons, hair dryers. **Pool(s):** heated indoor. **Leisure Activities:** whirlpool. **Business Services:** fax (fee). **Cards:** AX, CB, DC, DS, MC, VI. **Special Amenities:** free continental breakfast and free local telephone calls. *(See color ad below)*

SOME UNITS

DAYS INN

SAVE

▼▼▼▼

Small-scale Hotel

Phone: (325)446-3730

All Year [CP]   1P: $60-$70   2P: $64-$74   XP: $4   F12
Location: I-10, exit 457, 0.3 mi s. 111 S Martinez St 76849. Fax: 325/446-3730. **Facility:** 48 one-bedroom standard units. 3 stories, exterior corridors. **Parking:** on-site. **Terms:** 14 day cancellation notice, pets ($5 extra charge). **Amenities:** hair dryers. **Pool(s):** outdoor. **Leisure Activities:** whirlpool. **Business Services:** fax (fee). **Cards:** AX, DC, DS, MC, VI.

SOME UNITS

🅂🄳 🐾 🚲 📠 ☕ / ✕ 🔋 📺 /

THE HILLS MOTEL

▼▼▼

Motel

Phone: (325)446-2567

All Year   1P: $32   2P: $40   XP: $5
Location: I-10, exit 456, 1.3 mi s on US 377. 1520 N Main St 76849. Fax: 325/446-8842. **Facility:** 27 one-bedroom standard units. 1 story, exterior corridors. **Parking:** on-site. **Terms:** 3 day cancellation notice, small pets only. **Pool(s):** outdoor. **Business Services:** fax (fee). **Cards:** AX, CB, DC, DS, MC, VI.

SOME UNITS

ASK 🅂🄳 🐾 🍴 🚲 📺 / ✕ 🔋 /

LA VISTA MOTEL

▼▼

Motel

Phone: 325/446-2191

All Year   1P: $30-$34   2P: $34-$38   XP: $5   F10
Location: I-10, exit 456, 0.8 mi s. 2040 N Main St 76849. **Facility:** 8 one-bedroom standard units. 1 story, exterior corridors. **Parking:** on-site. **Terms:** pets ($5 extra charge). **Amenities:** hair dryers. **Cards:** AX, DS, MC, VI.

SOME UNITS

ASK 🅂🄳 🐾 📺 🔋 ☕ / ✕ /

KATY —See Houston p. 439.

KEMAH —See Houston p. 439.

KERRVILLE pop. 20,425

——— **WHERE TO STAY** ———

BEST WESTERN SUNDAY HOUSE INN

🆎🆎🆎 **SAVE**

▼▼▼▼

Small-scale Hotel

Phone: (830)896-1313

All Year [BP]   1P: $59-$120   2P: $64-$120   XP: $6   F12
Location: I-10, exit 508 (SR 16), just s. 2124 Sidney Baker St 78028. Fax: 830/896-1336. **Facility:** 97 one-bedroom standard units. 2 stories, exterior corridors. **Parking:** on-site. **Terms:** cancellation fee imposed, pets ($10 extra charge). **Amenities:** irons, hair dryers. **Dining:** 7 am-2 & 5-9 pm; closed Sun & Mon. **Pool(s):** outdoor. **Guest Services:** valet laundry. **Business Services:** meeting rooms, fax (fee). **Cards:** AX, CB, DC, DS, JC, MC, VI. **Special Amenities:** early check-in/late check-out.

SOME UNITS

🅂🄳 🐾 🍴 🚲 📺 📠 ☕ / ✕ /

BUDGET INN

🆎🆎🆎 **SAVE**

▼▼

Motel

Phone: 830/896-8200

3/1-9/15   1P: $45-$55   2P: $55-$65   XP: $5
2/1-2/28 & 9/16-1/31   1P: $40-$45   2P: $45-$55   XP: $5
Location: I-10, exit 508, 0.5 mi s on SR 16. 1804 Sidney Baker St 78028. Fax: 830/792-3592. **Facility:** 45 one-bedroom standard units. 1-2 stories, exterior corridors. **Parking:** on-site. **Terms:** [CP] meal plan available, small pets only ($5 extra charge). **Pool(s):** outdoor. **Guest Services:** coin laundry. **Business Services:** fax (fee). **Cards:** AX, CB, DC, DS, MC, VI. **Special Amenities:** free continental breakfast and free local telephone calls. *(See color ad below)*

SOME UNITS

🐾 🍴 🚲 📺 📠 / ✕ 🔋 📺 /

DAYS INN OF KERRVILLE

SAVE

▼▼▼▼

Motel

Phone: 830/896-1000

3/1-7/31 [CP]   1P: $46-$90   2P: $56-$100   XP: $5   F15
2/1-2/28 & 8/1-1/31 [CP]   1P: $46-$70   2P: $56-$80   XP: $5   F15
Location: I-10, exit 508 (SR 16), 0.5 mi s. 2000 Sidney Baker St 78028. Fax: 830/896-3786. **Facility:** 40 one-bedroom standard units, some with whirlpools. 2 stories, exterior corridors. *Bath:* combo or shower only. **Parking:** on-site. **Terms:** pets ($5 extra charge). **Amenities:** hair dryers. **Pool(s):** outdoor. **Leisure Activities:** whirlpool. **Business Services:** fax (fee). **Cards:** AX, MC, VI.

SOME UNITS

🅂🄳 🐾 🍴 🛒 🚲 📺 📠 ☕ / ✕ 🔋 📺 /

ECONO LODGE OF KERRVILLE

SAVE

Small-scale Hotel

Phone: (830)896-1711

| All Year [CP] | 1P: $35-$125 | 2P: $39-$129 | XP: $10 | F |

Location: I-10, exit 505, just s on SR 16. Located in a busy commercial area. 2145 Sidney Baker 78028. **Fax:** 830/257-4375. **Facility:** 98 units. 95 one-bedroom standard units. 3 one-bedroom suites. 2 stories, interior corridors. **Parking:** on-site. **Terms:** small pets only ($15 extra charge). **Amenities:** Some: hair dryers. **Pool(s):** outdoor. **Guest Services:** coin laundry. **Business Services:** meeting rooms, fax (fee). **Cards:** AX, CB, DC, DS, JC, MC, VI.

SOME UNITS

HAMPTON INN OF KERRVILLE

SAVE

Small-scale Hotel

Phone: (830)257-0600

| 5/26-9/5 [CP] | 1P: $66-$110 | 2P: $76-$120 | XP: $5 | F15 |
| 2/1-5/25 & 9/6-1/31 [CP] | 1P: $56-$100 | 2P: $56-$110 | XP: $5 | F15 |

Location: I-10, exit 508, 0.5 mi s on SR 16. 2038 Sidney Baker 78028. **Fax:** 830/257-7406. **Facility:** 60 one-bedroom standard units, some with whirlpools. 3 stories, interior corridors. Bath: combo or shower only. **Parking:** on-site. **Terms:** cancellation fee imposed. **Amenities:** dual phone lines, voice mail, irons, hair dryers. **Pool(s):** outdoor. **Leisure Activities:** sauna, whirlpool, exercise room. **Guest Services:** valet and coin laundry. **Business Services:** fax (fee). **Cards:** AX, CB, DC, DS, MC, VI.

SOME UNITS

INN OF THE HILLS CONFERENCE RESORT

AAA SAVE

Large-scale Hotel

Phone: (830)895-5000

| All Year [CP] | 1P: $89-$129 | 2P: $89-$129 | XP: $10 | F |

Location: I-10, exit 505, 1.5 mi nw on SR 27. 1001 Junction Hwy 78028. **Fax:** 830/895-6020. **Facility:** 200 units. 193 one-bedroom standard units. 7 one-bedroom suites ($165-$250), some with kitchens and/or whirlpools. 2 stories, exterior corridors. Bath: combo or shower only. **Parking:** on-site. **Terms:** check-in 4 pm, 15% service charge. **Amenities:** video games (fee), voice mail, irons, hair dryers. **Dining:** 2 restaurants, 6 am-10 pm, Sun-9 pm, cocktails, nightclub, entertainment. **Pool(s):** 3 outdoor, 2 heated indoor, wading. **Leisure Activities:** sauna, whirlpool, fishing, putting green, 3 lighted tennis courts, jogging, playground, basketball, shuffleboard, volleyball. Fee: racquetball courts, aerobics, bowling, massage. **Guest Services:** valet and coin laundry, airport transportation (fee)-San Antonio Airport, area transportation. **Business Services:** conference facilities, fax (fee). **Cards:** AX, CB, DC, DS, MC, VI. **Special Amenities:** free continental breakfast and preferred room (subject to availability with advanced reservations).

SOME UNITS

FEE

Y. O. RANCH RESORT HOTEL & CONFERENCE CENTER

Small-scale Hotel

Phone: (830)257-4440

| 5/24-10/31 | 1P: $79-$109 | 2P: $79-$119 | XP: $10 | F18 |
| 2/1-5/23 & 11/1-1/31 | 1P: $69-$99 | 2P: $69-$99 | XP: $10 | F18 |

Location: I-10, exit 508 (SR 16), 0.3 mi s. 2033 Sidney Baker St 78028. **Fax:** 830/896-8189. **Facility:** 200 units. 192 one-bedroom standard units. 8 one-bedroom suites ($175-$250). 2 stories, interior/exterior corridors. **Parking:** on-site. **Terms:** check-in 4 pm, small pets only. **Amenities:** video games (fee), irons, hair dryers. **Dining:** Sam Houston's, see separate listing. **Pool(s):** outdoor, wading. **Leisure Activities:** whirlpool, lighted tennis court, jogging, playground. **Guest Services:** valet laundry. **Business Services:** conference facilities, fax (fee). **Cards:** AX, CB, DC, MC, VI.

SOME UNITS

---------- **WHERE TO DINE** ----------

SAM HOUSTON'S

American

| **Lunch:** $5-$7 | **Dinner:** $7-$22 | **Phone:** 830/257-4440 |

Location: I-10, exit 508 (SR 16), 0.3 mi s; in Y. O. Ranch Resort Hotel & Conference Center. 2033 Sidney Baker St 78028. **Hours:** 6:30 am-2 & 5-10 pm. **Reservations:** accepted. **Features:** This Old West-style dining room is decked out in red velour tapestries and features chandeliers and a marble bar. Country music plays in the background. Try the smoked prime rib and the juicy, baby back ribs. Casual dress; cocktails. **Parking:** on-site. **Cards:** AX, DC, DS, MC, VI.

KILGORE pop. 11,301

---------- **WHERE TO STAY** ----------

DAYS INN

SAVE

Motel

Phone: (903)983-2975

| All Year | 1P: $46-$50 | 2P: $50-$56 | XP: $5 | F12 |

Location: I-20, exit 589, 1.2 mi s on US 259. 3505 Hwy 259 N 75662. **Fax:** 903/983-2975. **Facility:** 51 one-bedroom standard units, some with whirlpools. 2 stories, exterior corridors. **Parking:** on-site. **Terms:** weekly rates available. **Amenities:** hair dryers. **Business Services:** fax (fee). **Cards:** AX, CB, DC, DS, MC, VI.

SOME UNITS

KILLEEN pop. 86,911

---------- **WHERE TO STAY** ----------

BEST WESTERN KILLEEN

AAA SAVE

Small-scale Hotel

Phone: (254)526-6651

| All Year [ECP] | 1P: $52-$55 | 2P: $53-$56 | XP: $3 | F12 |

Location: US 190 Bypass, exit W S Young, 1.3 mi n to E Veteran's Memorial Blvd, just e. 2709 E Veteran's Memorial Blvd 76543. **Fax:** 254/526-8622. **Facility:** 66 one-bedroom standard units, some with kitchens. 2 stories, exterior corridors. **Parking:** on-site. **Amenities:** irons, hair dryers. **Pool(s):** outdoor. **Guest Services:** valet laundry. **Business Services:** fax (fee). **Cards:** AX, DC, DS, MC, VI. **Special Amenities:** free continental breakfast and free newspaper.

SOME UNITS

HAWTHORN SUITES

Phone: (254)634-7795

▼▼▼▼

Small-scale Hotel

All Year [BP]   1P: $69-$79   2P: $69-$79

Location: US 190, exit Trimmier Rd. 1502 E Central Texas Expwy 76541. Fax: 254/634-1943. **Facility:** 63 one-bedroom standard units, some with efficiencies. 3 stories, interior corridors. *Bath:* combo or shower only. **Parking:** on-site. **Amenities:** voice mail, irons, hair dryers. **Leisure Activities:** exercise room. **Guest Services:** complimentary evening beverages: Wed, valet and coin laundry. **Business Services:** fax (fee). **Cards:** AX, CB, DC, DS, MC, VI.

SOME UNITS

ASK SD &' 🎥 DATA PORT 🛏 🖥 🖵 /✕/

HOLIDAY INN EXPRESS

Phone: (254)554-2727

ⒶⒶⒶ SAVE

▼▼▼ ▼▼▼

Small-scale Hotel

All Year   1P: $60   2P: $80

Location: US 190, exit Trimmier Rd. 1602 E Center Expwy 76541. Fax: 254/554-9980. **Facility:** 68 one-bedroom standard units. 2 stories, exterior corridors. **Parking:** on-site. **Terms:** [CP] meal plan available. **Amenities:** irons, hair dryers. **Guest Services:** valet laundry. **Business Services:** meeting rooms, fax (fee). **Cards:** AX, CB, DC, DS, JC, MC, VI. **Special Amenities:** early check-in/late check-out and free continental breakfast.

SOME UNITS

SD 🐄 🎥 DATA PORT 🛏 🖥 🖵 /✕/

LA QUINTA INN-KILLEEN

Phone: (254)526-8331

SAVE

▼▼▼▼

Small-scale Hotel

All Year   1P: $69-$89   2P: $79-$99   XP: $10   F18

Location: 1.3 mi sw on FM 439 at jct US 190. 1112 Fort Hood St 76541-7493. Fax: 254/526-0394. **Facility:** 106 units. 102 one-bedroom standard units. 4 one-bedroom suites, some with kitchens. 3 stories (no elevator), exterior corridors. **Parking:** on-site. **Terms:** [ECP] meal plan available, small pets only. **Amenities:** video games (fee), voice mail, irons, hair dryers. **Pool(s):** outdoor. **Guest Services:** valet laundry, area transportation. **Business Services:** fax (fee). **Cards:** AX, CB, DC, DS, JC, MC, VI.

SOME UNITS

SD ➡️ 🐄 🍴 🏊 🏊 ⛱ 🎥 DATA PORT 🛏 🖥 🖵 /✕/

KINGSLAND pop. 4,584

------ WHERE TO STAY ------

THE ANTLERS HOTEL

Phone: 325/388-4411

▼▼▼▼

Classic Historic Country Inn

All Year   1P: $110-$150   2P: $110-$150   XP: $10

Location: On FM 1431; center. 1001 King St 78639. Fax: 325/388-6488. **Facility:** An early 1900s railroad hotel, the property today offers lodgings in the main building as well as in cabins, converted cabooses and coach cars. Designated smoking area. 16 units. 5 one-bedroom standard units, some with efficiencies. 5 one-bedroom suites, some with efficiencies. 6 cabins. 2 stories (no elevator), exterior corridors. *Bath:* combo or shower only. **Parking:** on-site. **Terms:** cancellation fee imposed. **Leisure Activities:** canoeing, paddleboats, boat dock, fishing, game room. **Guest Services:** gift shop. **Business Services:** meeting rooms, fax (fee). **Cards:** AX, DS, MC, VI.

SOME UNITS

🍴 &' ✕ ✕ / 📺 VCR 🛏 🖥 🖵 /

KINGSVILLE pop. 25,575

------ WHERE TO STAY ------

BEST WESTERN KINGSVILLE INN

Phone: (361)595-5656

ⒶⒶⒶ SAVE

▼▼▼▼

Motel

All Year [ECP]   1P: $55-$75   2P: $59-$79   XP: $6   F12

Location: 1.5 mi e on US 77 Bypass; opposite jct SR 141. Rural surroundings. 2402 E King Ave 78363. Fax: 361/595-5000. **Facility:** 50 one-bedroom standard units. 2 stories, exterior corridors. **Parking:** on-site. **Amenities:** irons, hair dryers. **Pool(s):** outdoor, wading. **Leisure Activities:** whirlpool. **Guest Services:** coin laundry. **Cards:** AX, CB, DC, DS, MC, VI. **Special Amenities:** free continental breakfast.

SOME UNITS

SD 🍴 🐄 🎥 DATA PORT 🛏 🖥 🖵 /✕/

COMFORT INN

Phone: 361/516-1120

ⒶⒶⒶ SAVE

▼▼▼▼

Small-scale Hotel

4/1-8/15	1P: $74-$89	2P: $84-$99	XP: $10 F18
2/1-3/31	1P: $69-$89	2P: $79-$99	XP: $10 F18
8/16-1/31	1P: $69	2P: $79	XP: $10 F18

Location: Just off US 77. 505 N Hwy 77 Bypass 78363. Fax: 361/516-0353. **Facility:** 47 units. 45 one-bedroom standard units, some with whirlpools. 2 one-bedroom suites ($110-$135). 3 stories, interior corridors. *Bath:* combo or shower only. **Parking:** on-site. **Terms:** 3 day cancellation notice, [CP] meal plan available. **Amenities:** irons, hair dryers. **Pool(s):** outdoor. **Leisure Activities:** exercise room. **Guest Services:** coin laundry. **Business Services:** meeting rooms, business center. **Cards:** AX, CB, DC, DS, MC, VI. **Special Amenities:** free continental breakfast and free local telephone calls.

SOME UNITS

SD 🍴 🐄 🎥 DATA PORT 🛏 🖥 🖵 /✕/

HOLIDAY INN

Phone: (361)595-5753

▼▼ ▼▼

Motel

All Year   1P: $60   2P: $65   XP: $5   F18

Location: 1.5 mi s on US 77. Located in the Get-N-Go Travel Center. 3430 Hwy 77 S 78363. Fax: 361/595-4513. **Facility:** 75 one-bedroom standard units. 2 stories, exterior corridors. *Bath:* combo or shower only. **Parking:** on-site. **Terms:** [AP] meal plan available, small pets only. **Amenities:** voice mail, irons, hair dryers. **Pool(s):** outdoor, wading. **Leisure Activities:** exercise room. **Guest Services:** coin laundry. **Business Services:** meeting rooms, fax (fee). **Cards:** AX, DS, MC, VI.

SOME UNITS

ASK SD 🐄 🍴 🍽 🐄 ⛱ DATA PORT 🖵 /✕/

HOWARD JOHNSON
Phone: (361)592-6471
AAA SAVE Motel
All Year [ECP] 1P: $49-$55 2P: $55-$65 XP: $5 F18
Location: 0.8 mi e on US 77. 105 S 77 Bypass 78363. Fax: 361/592-4177. **Facility:** 87 one-bedroom standard units. 2 stories, exterior corridors. **Parking:** on-site. **Terms:** [CP] meal plan available, small pets only. **Pool(s):** outdoor. **Guest Services:** coin laundry. **Cards:** AX, CB, DC, DS, MC, VI. **Special Amenities:** free continental breakfast and free local telephone calls.

SOME UNITS

KINGWOOD —See Houston p. 439.

LAJITAS

——— WHERE TO STAY ———

——— *The following lodging was either not evaluated or did not* ———
meet AAA rating requirements but is listed for your information only.

LAJITAS ON THE RIO GRANDE
Phone: 432/424-3471
[fyi] Motel
2/1-5/31 & 10/1-1/31 1P: $125 2P: $125 XP: $10 F12
6/1-9/30 1P: $95 2P: $95 XP: $10 F12
Under major renovation, scheduled to be completed March 2003. **Last rated:** ▽▽ **Location:** Center. 1 Main Pl 79852 (Star Rt 70, Box 400, TERLINGUA). Fax: 432/424-3277. **Facility:** 100 one-bedroom standard units. 2 stories (no elevator), interior/exterior corridors. **Parking:** on-site. **Terms:** 14 day cancellation notice-fee imposed, [AP] meal plan available, small pets only ($10 extra charge). **Pool(s):** outdoor. **Leisure Activities:** 2 lighted tennis courts. *Fee:* golf-18 holes. **Guest Services:** gift shop, coin laundry. **Business Services:** meeting rooms, fax (fee). **Cards:** AX, DS, MC, VI.

SOME UNITS

LAKE JACKSON pop. 26,386

——— WHERE TO STAY ———

RAMADA INN LAKE JACKSON
Phone: (979)297-1161
▽▽▽ Small-scale Hotel
All Year 1P: $104-$130 2P: $104-$130 XP: $10 F18
Location: 2.8 mi e of jct SR 288 and 332. Located in a commercial area. 925 Hwy 332 77566. Fax: 979/297-1249. **Facility:** 143 units. 142 one-bedroom standard units. 1 one-bedroom suite. 2 stories, interior corridors. **Parking:** on-site. **Terms:** package plans, pets ($100 deposit). **Amenities:** voice mail, irons, hair dryers. **Pool(s):** heated outdoor. **Leisure Activities:** exercise room. **Guest Services:** valet laundry. **Business Services:** conference facilities, PC, fax (fee). **Cards:** AX, DC, DS, MC, VI.

SOME UNITS

SUPER 8 MOTEL LAKE JACKSON
Phone: (979)297-3031
AAA SAVE Motel
All Year 1P: $55 2P: $55 XP: $5 F13
Location: 3 mi e jct SR 288 and 332. Located in a commercial area. 915 Hwy 332 77566. Fax: 979/297-9875. **Facility:** 109 one-bedroom standard units. 2 stories, exterior corridors. **Parking:** on-site. **Terms:** [ECP] meal plan available, package plans, pets ($10 extra charge). **Pool(s):** outdoor, wading. **Guest Services:** coin laundry. **Business Services:** meeting rooms, fax (fee). **Cards:** AX, DC, DS, MC, VI. **Special Amenities:** free continental breakfast and free newspaper.

SOME UNITS

LAKE WORTH pop. 4,618 (See map p. 343; index p. 346)

——— WHERE TO STAY ———

BEST WESTERN INN & SUITES
Phone: (817)238-1199 [99]
AAA SAVE Small-scale Hotel
5/1-12/31 [ECP] 1P: $79-$84 2P: $84-$89
2/1-4/30 & 1/1-1/31 [ECP] 1P: $74-$79 2P: $79-$84 XP: $5 F17
Location: I-820, exit 10A (SR 199/Jacksboro Hwy), just w. 3920 Boat Club Rd 76135. Fax: 817/238-1133. **Facility:** 50 one-bedroom standard units, some with whirlpools. 2 stories, interior corridors. *Bath:* combo or shower only. **Parking:** on-site. **Terms:** weekly rates available. **Amenities:** high-speed Internet, dual phone lines, voice mail, irons, hair dryers. **Pool(s):** small outdoor. **Leisure Activities:** whirlpool, exercise room. **Guest Services:** valet and coin laundry. **Business Services:** meeting rooms, fax (fee). **Cards:** AX, CB, DC, DS, MC, VI. **Special Amenities:** free continental breakfast and free newspaper.

SOME UNITS

LAMESA pop. 9,952

——— WHERE TO STAY ———

BUDGET HOST INN
Phone: (806)872-2118
AAA SAVE Motel
All Year 1P: $32-$35 2P: $44 XP: $5 F12
Location: Jct US 87 and 180, 0.7 mi s. 901 S Dallas Ave (US 87) 79331. Fax: 806/872-3971. **Facility:** 30 one-bedroom standard units. 1 story, exterior corridors. *Bath:* combo or shower only. **Parking:** on-site. **Terms:** 3 day cancellation notice, small pets only. **Pool(s):** small outdoor. **Business Services:** fax (fee). **Cards:** AX, DS, MC, VI. **Special Amenities:** free local telephone calls. *(See color ad p 162)*

SOME UNITS

SHILOH INN

Motel

All Year   1P: $37-$43   2P: $42-$48   XP: $6

Phone: 806/872-6721
F12

Location: Jct US 87 and 180, 1 mi n. 1707 Lubbock Hwy 79331. Fax: 806/872-6721. **Facility:** 50 one-bedroom standard units. 2 stories (no elevator), exterior corridors. **Parking:** on-site. **Terms:** 3 day cancellation notice, small pets only. **Pool(s):** small outdoor. **Business Services:** fax (fee). **Cards:** AX, DC, DS, MC, VI.

SOME UNITS

LA PORTE —See Houston p. 440.

LAREDO pop. 176,576

──────── **WHERE TO STAY** ────────

COURTYARD BY MARRIOTT

Small-scale Hotel

All Year   1P: $114-$149   2P: $114-$149   XP: $10

Phone: 956/725-5555
F18

Location: I-35, exit 3, just s. Located close to Mexico border. 2410 Santa Ursula Ave 78040. Fax: 956/724-8848. **Facility:** 110 units. 100 one-bedroom standard units. 10 one-bedroom suites ($119-$149). 5 stories, interior corridors. *Bath:* combo or shower only. *Some:* fax. **Dining:** 6:30-10 am, Sat & Sun 7 am-noon. **Pool(s):** small outdoor. **Leisure Activities:** whirlpool, exercise room. **Guest Services:** valet and coin laundry, area transportation-mall & border. **Business Services:** meeting rooms, fax. **Cards:** AX, CB, DC, DS, MC, VI. **Special Amenities:** early check-in/late check-out and free newspaper.

SOME UNITS

FIESTA INN

Motel

All Year   1P: $74   2P: $77   XP: $3

Phone: (956)723-3603
F18

Location: I-35, exit 3B, on southbound access road. 5240 San Bernardo Ave 78041. Fax: 956/724-7697. **Facility:** 151 one-bedroom standard units, some with kitchens. 2 stories, exterior corridors. **Parking:** on-site. **Terms:** [ECP] meal plan available. **Pool(s):** outdoor. **Guest Services:** complimentary evening beverages: Tues-Fri, coin laundry. **Business Services:** meeting rooms, fax (fee). **Cards:** AX, DC, DS, MC, VI.

SOME UNITS

HAMPTON INN

Small-scale Hotel

All Year [ECP]   1P: $71-$101   2P: $71-$101

Phone: 956/717-8888

Location: I-35, exit 4, on northbound access road. Located in a commercial area. 7903 San Dario 78045. Fax: 956/717-8391. **Facility:** 120 one-bedroom standard units. 5 stories, interior corridors. *Bath:* combo or shower only. **Parking:** on-site. **Amenities:** video games (fee), voice mail, irons. *Some:* hair dryers. **Pool(s):** outdoor. **Leisure Activities:** whirlpool. **Guest Services:** valet laundry. **Business Services:** meeting rooms, fax (fee). **Cards:** AX, DC, DS, MC, VI. **Special Amenities:** free continental breakfast and free local telephone calls.** *(See color ad below)*

SOME UNITS

HOLIDAY INN CIVIC CENTER

Small-scale Hotel

All Year   1P: $85   2P: $90

Phone: (956)727-5800

Location: I-35, exit 2 (US 59), 2.3 mi n on US 81 and 83. 800 Garden St 78040. Fax: 956/727-0278. **Facility:** 203 one-bedroom standard units. 14 stories, interior corridors. **Parking:** on-site. **Terms:** 7 day cancellation notice. **Amenities:** voice mail, irons, hair dryers. **Pool(s):** outdoor. **Leisure Activities:** whirlpool, exercise room. **Guest Services:** valet and coin laundry, area transportation. **Business Services:** meeting rooms, business center. **Cards:** AX, CB, DC, DS, MC, VI.

SOME UNITS

LA POSADA HOTEL & SUITES
Phone: 956/722-1701

⬥⬥⬥ SAVE

All Year   1P: $109-$159   XP: $10   F12

Location: I-35 exit downtown, just e of International Bridge. Located opposite San Augustin Plaza. 1000 Zaragoza St 78040. Fax: 956/726-8524. **Facility:** 208 units. 151 one-bedroom standard units. 57 one-bedroom suites ($159-$249). 3-4 stories, interior/exterior corridors. *Bath:* combo or shower only. **Parking:** on-site (fee) and

Small-scale Hotel   valet. **Terms:** check-in 4 pm, cancellation fee imposed. **Amenities:** irons, hair dryers. **Dining:** 3 restaurants, 6:30 am-11 pm, cocktails, also, The Tack Room, see separate listing, entertainment. **Pool(s):** 2 outdoor. **Leisure Activities:** exercise room. **Guest Services:** gift shop, valet laundry. **Business Services:** meeting rooms, fax (fee). **Cards:** AX, DC, DS, MC, VI. *(See ad below)*

SOME UNITS

LA QUINTA INN-LAREDO
Phone: (956)722-0511

SAVE

All Year   1P: $79-$99   2P: $85-$105

⬥⬥⬥

Location: I-35, exit 2 (US 59). 3610 Santa Ursula Ave 78041-4453. Fax: 956/723-6642. **Facility:** 152 one-bedroom standard units. 2 stories, exterior corridors. **Parking:** on-site. **Terms:** [ECP] meal plan available, small pets only. **Amenities:** video games (fee), voice mail, irons, hair dryers. **Pool(s):** outdoor. **Guest Services:** valet

Small-scale Hotel   laundry. **Business Services:** meeting rooms, fax (fee). **Cards:** AX, CB, DC, DS, JC, MC, VI.

SOME UNITS

MOTEL 6 - 1107
Phone: 956/722-8133

⬥⬥

5/22-1/31   1P: $49-$59   2P: $55-$65   XP: $3   F17
2/1-5/21   1P: $45-$55   2P: $51-$61   XP: $3   F17

Motel   **Location:** I-35, exit 4 (Del Mar Blvd/Santa Maria Ave). 5920 San Bernardo Ave 78041. Fax: 956/725-8212. **Facility:** 109 one-bedroom standard units. 2 stories, interior/exterior corridors. *Bath:* combo or shower only. **Parking:** on-site. **Terms:** small pets only. **Pool(s):** outdoor. **Guest Services:** coin laundry. **Business Services:** fax (fee). **Cards:** AX, CB, DC, DS, MC, VI.

SOME UNITS

MOTEL 6 SOUTH-142
Phone: 956/725-8187

⬥⬥

5/21-1/31   1P: $46-$56   2P: $52-$62   XP: $3   F17
2/1-5/20   1P: $44-$54   2P: $50-$60   XP: $3   F17

Motel   **Location:** I-35, exit 3B (Mann Rd). 5310 San Bernardo Ave 78041. Fax: 956/725-0424. **Facility:** 94 one-bedroom standard units. 2 stories, exterior corridors. *Bath:* shower only. **Parking:** on-site. **Terms:** small pets only (with prior approval). **Pool(s):** small outdoor. **Business Services:** fax (fee). **Cards:** AX, CB, DC, DS, MC, VI.

SOME UNITS

RED ROOF INN LAREDO
Phone: (956)712-0733

⬥⬥⬥ SAVE

All Year   1P: $49-$63   2P: $54-$68   XP: $5   F18

Location: I-35, exit 3A, 0.3 mi w. Located in a commercial area. 1006 W Calton Rd 78041. Fax: 956/712-4337. **Facility:** 150 one-bedroom standard units. 4 stories, interior/exterior corridors. *Bath:* combo or shower only. **Parking:** on-site. **Terms:** small pets only. **Amenities:** voice mail. **Pool(s):** outdoor. **Business Services:** fax

Motel   (fee). **Cards:** AX, CB, DC, DS, MC, VI. **Special Amenities:** free local telephone calls and free newspaper.

SOME UNITS

RIO GRANDE PLAZA HOTEL
Phone: (956)722-2411

⬥⬥⬥

All Year   1P: $79-$89   2P: $89-$99   XP: $6   F16

Location: I-35, exit 1, just w of International Bridge. Located adjacent to River Drive Mall. One S Main Ave 78040.

Small-scale Hotel   Fax: 956/722-4578. **Facility:** 203 one-bedroom standard units. 15 stories, interior corridors. **Parking:** on-site. **Terms:** [CP] meal plan available, 15% service charge, small pets only ($50 deposit). **Amenities:** *Some:* irons, hair dryers. **Pool(s):** outdoor. **Leisure Activities:** exercise room. **Guest Services:** gift shop, coin laundry, area transportation. **Business Services:** meeting rooms, fax (fee). **Cards:** AX, CB, DC, DS, MC, VI.

SOME UNITS

——— WHERE TO DINE ———

PELICAN'S WHARF
♦♦♦ ♦♦♦
Steak & Seafood

Dinner: $7-$17
Phone: 956/727-5070
Location: I-35, exit 2, then w to Chicago St. 619 Chicago St 78040. **Hours:** 11 am-11 pm, Fri-midnight, Sat 5 pm-midnight, Sun noon-10 pm. Closed: 11/27, 12/25. **Reservations:** accepted. **Features:** This Caribbean-style cafe is decorated in tropical colors. Large windows and wood floors complete the attractive dining room. Savor the succulent slow-roasted prime rib and afterwards indulge in the creamy mud pie. Casual dress; cocktails. **Parking:** on-site. **Cards:** AX, CB, DC, DS, MC, VI.

📺 ✕

THE TACK ROOM
♦♦♦ ♦♦♦
Steak House

Dinner: $11-$32
Phone: 956/722-1701
Location: I-35, exit downtown; just e of International Bridge; in La Posada Hotel & Suites. 1000 Zaragoza St 78040. **Hours:** 5 pm-10 pm, Fri & Sat-11 pm. Closed: Sun. **Features:** Hear the sound of sizzling meat in the open kitchen mix with the sensual energy of live Spanish music, and your taste buds will practically dance with anticipation. Try the churrasco, an Argentine classic with tenderloin marinated in chimichurri sauce. Casual dress; cocktails. **Parking:** on-site. **Cards:** AX, CB, DC, MC, VI. *(See ad p 456)*

📺 ✕

LEAGUE CITY pop. 45,444   (See map p. 382; index p. 389)

——— WHERE TO STAY ———

SOUTH SHORE HARBOUR RESORT & CONFERENCE CENTER
♦♦♦ ♦♦♦
Resort
Large-scale Hotel

All Year   1P: $140-$200   2P: $150-$210
Phone: (281)334-1000   277
XP: $10   F14
Location: I-45, exit 23, 2.5 mi e on FM 518, 1.8 mi ne on FM 2094; on Clear Lake. 2500 S Shore Blvd 77573. Fax: 281/334-1157. **Facility:** Extensive recreational facilities are featured at this sprawling property. 242 units. 232 one-bedroom standard units. 10 one-bedroom suites with whirlpools. 11 stories, interior corridors. **Parking:** on-site. **Terms:** package plans. **Amenities:** video games (fee), dual phone lines, voice mail, irons, hair dryers. **Pool(s):** heated outdoor. **Leisure Activities:** sauna, whirlpool, rental boats, rental sailboats, marina, jogging, basketball, volleyball. *Fee:* charter fishing, golf-27 holes, 5 tennis courts (2 indoor, 3 lighted), racquetball courts, massage. **Guest Services:** gift shop, valet laundry. **Business Services:** conference facilities, business center. **Cards:** AX, CB, DC, DS, MC, VI.

SOME UNITS
(A$K) 🅂🄳 ➕ 🍽 📺 📷 🏊 🎣 ✕ 📹 DATA PORT 💻 / ✕ VCR 🛏 🖨 /
FEE   FEE   FEE

SUPER 8 MOTEL
♦♦ ♦♦
Small-scale Hotel

All Year [CP]   1P: $50-$55   2P: $55-$60
Phone: (281)338-0800   279
XP: $5   F12
Location: I-45, exit 23, just w to Hobbs Rd, just s. 102 Hobbs Rd 77573. Fax: 281/332-7723. **Facility:** 43 one-bedroom standard units. 2 stories, interior corridors. *Bath:* combo or shower only. **Parking:** on-site. **Terms:** small pets only (with prior approval). **Amenities:** irons, hair dryers. **Pool(s):** small heated indoor. **Leisure Activities:** whirlpool. **Guest Services:** coin laundry. **Business Services:** fax (fee). **Cards:** AX, DC, DS, MC, VI.

SOME UNITS
(A$K) 🅂🄳 🛏 🍽 📷 🏊 📷 DATA PORT 🖨 🖨 / ✕ /

LEON SPRINGS —See San Antonio p. 545.

LEWISVILLE —See Dallas p. 305.

LINDALE pop. 2,954

——— WHERE TO STAY ———

COMFORT INN
SAVE
♦♦ ♦♦ ♦♦
Small-scale Hotel

All Year   1P: $65-$73   2P: $75-$84
Phone: 903/882-8884
XP: $5   F18
Location: I-20, exit 556, just n. 3501 S Main St 75771. Fax: 903/882-1181. **Facility:** 56 one-bedroom standard units, some with whirlpools. 2 stories, exterior corridors. *Bath:* combo or shower only. **Parking:** on-site. **Amenities:** video library (fee), irons, hair dryers. **Pool(s):** outdoor. **Business Services:** fax (fee). **Cards:** AX, CB, DC, DS, JC, MC, VI.

SOME UNITS
🍽 🔧 ♿ 📷 🏊 VCR 📷 DATA PORT 🖨 🖨 🖨 / ✕ /

HAMPTON INN
SAVE
♦♦♦ ♦♦
Small-scale Hotel

All Year [ECP]   1P: $63-$79   2P: $73-$89
Phone: (903)882-1002
Location: I-20, exit 556. 3505 S Main St 75771. Fax: 903/881-8780. **Facility:** 62 one-bedroom standard units, some with whirlpools. 3 stories, interior corridors. *Bath:* combo or shower only. **Parking:** on-site. **Terms:** 3 day cancellation notice. **Amenities:** video games (fee), high-speed Internet, dual phone lines, voice mail, irons, hair dryers. **Pool(s):** small outdoor. **Leisure Activities:** whirlpool, exercise room. **Guest Services:** coin laundry. **Business Services:** fax (fee). **Cards:** AX, CB, DC, DS, JC, MC, VI.

SOME UNITS
🅂🄳 🔧 ♿ 🏊 📷 DATA PORT 🖨 🖨 🖨 / ✕ /

LITTLEFIELD pop. 6,507

——— WHERE TO STAY ———

CRESCENT PARK MOTEL
(AAA) SAVE
♦♦♦
Motel

All Year   1P: $36-$42   2P: $47-$52
Phone: 806/385-4464
XP: $5
Location: Jct US 84, 0.3 mi n on SR 385. 2000 Hall Ave 79339 (PO Box 909). Fax: 806/385-3281. **Facility:** 46 units. 45 one-bedroom standard units, some with efficiencies. 1 two-bedroom suite ($55-$75) with efficiency. 1 story, exterior corridors. *Bath:* combo or shower only. **Parking:** on-site. **Terms:** weekly rates available, pets ($5 extra charge). **Business Services:** fax (fee). **Cards:** AX, DS, MC, VI.

SOME UNITS
🛏 🖨 🖨 🖨 / ✕ /

LIVE OAK —See San Antonio p. 545.

LIVINGSTON pop. 5,433

———— WHERE TO STAY ————

ECONO LODGE
SAVE

Motel

Phone: (936)327-2451
All Year   1P: $55   2P: $58   XP: $6   F12
Location: US 59 at jct US 190 on southwest service road. 117 US 59 at Loop S & US 190 77351. Fax: 936/327-1254.
Facility: 55 one-bedroom standard units, some with kitchens (no utensils). 2 stories, exterior corridors.
Parking: on-site. **Terms:** cancellation fee imposed, weekly rates available. **Pool(s):** outdoor. **Guest Services:** coin laundry. **Business Services:** fax (fee). **Cards:** AX, CB, DC, DS, MC, VI.

SOME UNITS
FEE

HOLIDAY INN EXPRESS HOTEL & SUITES

Small-scale Hotel

Phone: (936)327-9600
All Year [ECP]   1P: $74   2P: $144   XP: $5   F18
Location: US 59 southbound, exit SR 1988, just s to Business Rt 59, just e to Southpoint Ln, then just n; exit Business Rt 59 northbound, just e to Southpoint Ln, then just n. 120 Southpoint Ln 77351. Fax: 936/327-9605. **Facility:** 60 one-bedroom standard units, some with whirlpools. 3 stories, interior corridors. *Bath:* combo or shower only.
Parking: on-site. **Amenities:** high-speed Internet, dual phone lines, voice mail, irons, hair dryers. **Pool(s):** outdoor. **Guest Services:** coin laundry. **Business Services:** meeting rooms, fax. **Cards:** AX, CB, DC, DS, MC, VI.

SOME UNITS

LLANO pop. 3,325

———— WHERE TO STAY ————

BEST WESTERN
AAA **SAVE**

Small-scale Hotel

Phone: (325)247-4101
All Year [ECP]   1P: $50-$84   2P: $56-$84   XP: $5   F17
Location: 1 mi w on SR 71 and 29. 901 W Young St 78643. Fax: 325/247-4104. **Facility:** 40 one-bedroom standard units. 2 stories (no elevator), exterior corridors. **Parking:** on-site. **Terms:** small pets only. **Amenities:** irons, hair dryers. **Pool(s):** small outdoor. **Business Services:** fax (fee). **Cards:** AX, CB, DC, DS, MC, VI. **Special Amenities:** free continental breakfast and free newspaper.

SOME UNITS

LOCKHART pop. 11,615

———— WHERE TO STAY ————

THE BEST WESTERN PLUM CREEK INN
AAA **SAVE**

Motel

Phone: (512)398-4911
4/1-9/1 [CP]   1P: $75-$80   2P: $75-$80   XP: $10   F12
2/1-3/31 & 9/2-1/31 [CP] 1P: $70-$75   2P: $70-$75   XP: $10   F12
Location: US 183 S, 1 mi s. 2001 Hwy 183 S 78644. Fax: 512/398-4175. **Facility:** 55 one-bedroom standard units, some with whirlpools. 1 story, exterior corridors. *Bath:* combo or shower only. **Parking:** on-site. **Terms:** small pets only ($10 fee). **Amenities:** irons, hair dryers. **Dining:** 9 am-9 pm; closed Mon. **Pool(s):** outdoor. **Guest Services:** coin laundry. **Business Services:** fax (fee). **Cards:** AX, DC, DS, JC, MC, VI. **Special Amenities:** early check-in/late check-out and free room upgrade (subject to availability with advanced reservations).

SOME UNITS

LONGVIEW pop. 73,344

———— WHERE TO STAY ————

BEST WESTERN INN & CONFERENCE CENTER
SAVE

Small-scale Hotel

Phone: (903)758-0700
All Year   1P: $62   2P: $62
Location: I-20, exit 595, just n. 3119 Estes Pkwy 75602. Fax: 903/758-8705. **Facility:** 178 one-bedroom standard units. 4 stories, interior/exterior corridors. **Parking:** on-site. **Amenities:** irons, hair dryers. **Pool(s):** heated indoor/outdoor. **Leisure Activities:** whirlpool, limited exercise equipment. **Guest Services:** valet and coin laundry. **Business Services:** conference facilities, business center. **Cards:** AX, CB, DC, DS, MC, VI.

SOME UNITS

COMFORT INN
AAA **SAVE**

Motel

Phone: (903)757-7858
All Year [BP]   1P: $60-$70   2P: $65-$75   XP: $6   F16
Location: Just n of jct US 80. 203 N Spur 63 75601. Fax: 903/757-7031. **Facility:** 63 one-bedroom standard units. 2 stories, exterior corridors. **Parking:** on-site. **Terms:** [ECP] meal plan available. **Amenities:** irons, hair dryers. **Pool(s):** outdoor. **Business Services:** fax (fee). **Cards:** AX, CB, DC, DS, MC, VI. **Special Amenities:** free continental breakfast and free local telephone calls.

SOME UNITS

COMFORT SUITES

SAVE

Small-scale Hotel

Phone: (903)663-4991

All Year [ECP]   1P: $69-$89   2P: $69-$99   XP: $6   F18
Location: Loop 281, just w of jct US 259. 3307 N 4th St 75605. Fax: 903/663-4991. **Facility:** 60 one-bedroom standard units. 3 stories, interior corridors. *Bath:* combo or shower only. **Parking:** on-site. **Terms:** 14 day cancellation notice. **Amenities:** *Some:* irons, hair dryers. **Pool(s):** small heated indoor. **Leisure Activities:** whirlpool. **Guest Services:** valet laundry. **Business Services:** meeting rooms, fax (fee). **Cards:** AX, CB, DC, DS, MC, VI.

SOME UNITS

DAYS INN OF LONGVIEW

AAA **SAVE**

Motel

Phone: (903)758-1113

All Year   1P: $50-$65   2P: $55-$70   XP: $5   F14
Location: I-20, exit 595, 0.3 mi n. 3103 Estes Pkwy 75602. Fax: 903/236-7726. **Facility:** 40 one-bedroom standard units, some with kitchens. 2 stories, interior/exterior corridors. **Parking:** on-site. **Terms:** [CP] meal plan available, small pets only ($10 fee). **Amenities:** *Some:* hair dryers. **Pool(s):** outdoor. **Leisure Activities:** whirlpool. **Guest Services:** coin laundry. **Business Services:** fax (fee). **Cards:** AX, CB, DC, DS, MC, VI. **Special Amenities:** free continental breakfast and free newspaper.

SOME UNITS

EXECUTIVE INN & SUITES

Motel

Phone: (903)234-2920

All Year   1P: $39-$45   2P: $42-$48   XP: $5   F10
Location: I-20, exit 596, 3.6 mi n on US 259 (Eastman Rd) to US 80 (Marshall Ave), then just w. 1905 E Marshall Ave 75601. Fax: 903/234-2920. **Facility:** 31 one-bedroom standard units, some with efficiencies. 2 stories, exterior corridors. *Bath:* combo or shower only. **Parking:** on-site. **Terms:** cancellation fee imposed, [CP] meal plan available. **Business Services:** fax (fee). **Cards:** AX, DS, MC, VI.

SOME UNITS

FAIRFIELD INN

SAVE

Small-scale Hotel

Phone: (903)663-1995

All Year [ECP]   1P: $69-$89   2P: $69-$99   XP: $6   F18
Location: Loop 281, just w of jct US 259. 3305 N 4th St 75605. Fax: 903/663-1995. **Facility:** 64 one-bedroom standard units. 3 stories, interior corridors. *Bath:* combo or shower only. **Parking:** on-site. **Terms:** 14 day cancellation notice. **Amenities:** irons. **Pool(s):** small heated indoor. **Leisure Activities:** whirlpool. **Guest Services:** valet laundry. **Business Services:** fax (fee). **Cards:** AX, CB, DC, DS, MC, VI.

SOME UNITS

HOMEWOOD SUITES BY HILTON

SAVE

Small-scale Hotel

Phone: (903)234-0214

All Year [ECP]   1P: $109   2P: $149
Location: Just n of jct US 80. 205 N Spur 63 75601. Fax: 903/758-6464. **Facility:** 75 units. 67 one- and 8 two-bedroom suites with efficiencies, some with whirlpools. 3 stories, interior corridors. *Bath:* combo or shower only. **Parking:** on-site. **Terms:** cancellation fee imposed. **Amenities:** video library (fee), dual phone lines, voice mail, irons, hair dryers. **Pool(s):** outdoor. **Leisure Activities:** whirlpool, exercise room, sports court. **Guest Services:** sundries, complimentary evening beverages: Mon-Thurs, valet and coin laundry. **Business Services:** meeting rooms, business center. **Cards:** AX, CB, DC, DS, MC, VI.

SOME UNITS

LA QUINTA INN

AAA **SAVE**

Motel

Phone: (903)757-3663

All Year   1P: $64-$79   2P: $74-$89   XP: $10   F18
Location: Jct Estes Pkwy and I-20, exit 595. 502 S Access Rd 75602-4202. Fax: 903/753-3780. **Facility:** 105 units. 104 one-bedroom standard units. 1 one-bedroom suite. 2 stories, exterior corridors. **Parking:** on-site. **Terms:** [ECP] meal plan available, small pets only. **Amenities:** video games (fee), voice mail, irons, hair dryers. **Pool(s):** outdoor. **Guest Services:** valet laundry. **Business Services:** meeting rooms, fax (fee). **Cards:** AX, CB, DC, DS, JC, MC, VI. **Special Amenities:** free continental breakfast and free local telephone calls.

SOME UNITS

WINGATE INN

Small-scale Hotel

Phone: 903/663-3196

All Year [CP]   1P: $75   2P: $85
Location: Loop 281, just w of jct US 259. 431 N Loop 281 75605 (112 S Access Rd, 75603). Fax: 903/663-3596. **Facility:** 80 one-bedroom standard units, some with whirlpools. 4 stories, interior corridors. *Bath:* combo or shower only. **Parking:** on-site. **Amenities:** video games (fee), high-speed Internet, dual phone lines, voice mail, safes, irons, hair dryers. **Pool(s):** heated indoor. **Leisure Activities:** sauna, whirlpool, exercise room. **Guest Services:** valet and coin laundry. **Business Services:** meeting rooms, business center. **Cards:** AX, DC, DS, MC, VI.

SOME UNITS

—— WHERE TO DINE ——

JOHNNY CACE'S SEAFOOD & STEAK HOUSE

AAA

Steak & Seafood

Lunch: $5-$8   **Dinner:** $10-$23   **Phone:** 903/753-7691

Location: US 80, 0.5 mi w of US 80 and 259 crossing. 1501 E Marshall Ave 75601. **Hours:** 11 am-10 pm, Mon from 5 pm, Fri & Sat-11 pm, Sun 3 pm-10 pm. Closed major holidays. **Features:** Celebrating 51 years, this dining experience features a New Orleans-style decor with chandeliers, blue drapery and a lovely courtyard. Broiled snapper, stuffed shrimp, flavorful fried catfish and delicious steaks, cut in-house, are just a few of the specialties that await. Casual dress; cocktails. **Parking:** on-site. **Cards:** AX, DC, DS, MC, VI.

OXFORD STREET RESTAURANT   **Lunch:** $6-$12   **Dinner:** $10-$22   **Phone:** 903/758-9130

American

Location: 1.3 mi nw on Spur 63; 0.3 mi n of jct US 80. 421 N Spur 63 75601. **Hours:** 11 am-2 & 5-9 pm, Fri-10 pm, Sat 5 pm-10 pm, Sun 11:30 am-9 pm. Closed: 12/25. **Reservations:** accepted. **Features:** Pleasant and quiet, this steakhouse offers thick, marinated filets grilled to perfection. Seafood entrees include stuffed shrimp and blackened red snapper. The pub-like dining room is dimly-lit and has a full-service bar. Casual dress; cocktails. **Parking:** on-site. **Cards:** AX, DC, DS, MC, VI.

LUBBOCK pop. 199,564

—— **WHERE TO STAY** ——

ASHMORE INN & SUITES   **Phone:** (806)785-0060

Motel

All Year [ECP]   1P: $75-$95   2P: $75-$95   XP: $5   F16
Location: Loop 289, exit Quaker St, 3 mi s. 4019 S Loop 289 79423. Fax: 806/785-6001. **Facility:** 124 units. 108 one-bedroom standard units, some with efficiencies. 16 one-bedroom suites ($85-$95), some with kitchens. 2-3 stories, interior corridors. *Bath:* combo or shower only. **Parking:** on-site. **Amenities:** high-speed Internet, voice mail, irons, hair dryers. **Pool(s):** heated outdoor. **Leisure Activities:** whirlpool, exercise room. **Guest Services:** valet and coin laundry. **Business Services:** meeting rooms, business center. **Cards:** AX, CB, DC, DS, JC, MC, VI. **Special Amenities:** free continental breakfast and free local telephone calls.

SOME UNITS

BEST WESTERN LUBBOCK WINDSOR INN   **Phone:** (806)762-8400

Motel

All Year [ECP]   1P: $59-$89   2P: $59-$89   F10
Location: 3.5 mi s on I-27, exit 1B southbound; U-turn at exit 1A (50th St) northbound. 5410 I-27 79412 (PO Box 3190, 79452). Fax: 806/762-8400. **Facility:** 64 one-bedroom standard units, some with whirlpools. 2 stories (no elevator), interior corridors. *Bath:* combo or shower only. **Parking:** on-site. **Terms:** 7 day cancellation notice, small pets only ($25 deposit, $6 extra charge). **Amenities:** voice mail, irons, hair dryers. **Pool(s):** small heated indoor. **Leisure Activities:** whirlpool, exercise room. **Guest Services:** coin laundry. **Business Services:** meeting rooms, fax (fee). **Cards:** AX, CB, DC, DS, MC, VI. **Special Amenities:** early check-in/late check-out and free continental breakfast. *(See color ad below)*

SOME UNITS

COMFORT INN & SUITES   **Phone:** 806/763-6500

Motel

All Year [ECP]   1P: $60-$72   2P: $70-$90   XP: $5   F17
Location: I-27, exit 1B, just s. 5828 I-27 S 79404. Fax: 806/763-0080. **Facility:** 66 units. 64 one-bedroom standard units, some with whirlpools. 2 one-bedroom suites. 2 stories, interior corridors. *Bath:* combo or shower only. **Parking:** on-site. **Amenities:** high-speed Internet, dual phone lines, voice mail, irons, hair dryers. **Pool(s):** heated indoor. **Leisure Activities:** whirlpool, exercise room. **Guest Services:** valet and coin laundry. **Business Services:** meeting rooms, business center. **Cards:** AX, DC, DS, MC, VI.

SOME UNITS
FEE

COMFORT SUITES   **Phone:** (806)798-0002

Motel

All Year [ECP]   1P: $65-$99   2P: $69-$109   XP: $10   F16
Location: S on Loop 289, exit Slide Rd, on south service road. 5113 S Loop 289 79424. Fax: 806/798-0035. **Facility:** 65 one-bedroom standard units, some with whirlpools. 2 stories (no elevator), interior corridors. *Bath:* combo or shower only. **Parking:** on-site. **Terms:** check-in 4 pm. **Amenities:** dual phone lines, voice mail, irons, hair dryers. **Pool(s):** small outdoor. **Guest Services:** valet and coin laundry. **Business Services:** meeting rooms, fax (fee). **Cards:** AX, CB, DC, DS, JC, MC, VI.

SOME UNITS

COURTYARD BY MARRIOTT   **Phone:** 806/795-1633

Motel

All Year   1P: $79-$129   2P: $84-$129
Location: Loop 289, exit Quarter Ave, 5 mi s. 4011 S Loop 289 79423. Fax: 806/795-1633. **Facility:** 78 units. 75 one-bedroom standard units. 3 one-bedroom suites ($119-$150). 3 stories, interior corridors. *Bath:* combo or shower only. **Parking:** on-site. **Terms:** [BP] meal plan available. **Amenities:** voice mail, irons, hair dryers. **Pool(s):** heated indoor. **Leisure Activities:** whirlpool, exercise room. **Guest Services:** valet and coin laundry. **Business Services:** meeting rooms, fax (fee). **Cards:** AX, CB, DC, DS, JC, MC, VI.

SOME UNITS

DAYS INN TEXAS TECH

Phone: (806)747-7111

	8/26-1/31 [ECP]	1P: $45-$89	2P: $49-$89	XP: $10	F12
	3/21-8/25 [ECP]	1P: $49-$65	2P: $54-$75	XP: $5	F12
	2/1-3/20 [ECP]	1P: $45-$54	2P: $49-$64	XP: $5	F12

Motel
Location: I-27, exit 4 (4th St), 1.5 mi w. 2401 4th St 79415. Fax: 806/747-9749. **Facility:** 91 one-bedroom standard units. 3 stories, exterior corridors. **Parking:** on-site. **Terms:** check-in 4 pm, 2 night minimum stay - seasonal, 7 day cancellation notice-fee imposed. **Amenities:** voice mail, hair dryers. *Some:* irons. **Pool(s):** small outdoor. **Business Services:** fax (fee). **Cards:** AX, CB, DC, DS, JC, MC, VI. **Special Amenities: free continental breakfast and free local telephone calls.**

SOME UNITS

FAIRFIELD INN BY MARRIOTT

Phone: (806)795-1288

All Year [ECP] 1P: $65-$85 2P: $65-$95 XP: $6 F18

Motel
Location: Loop 289, exit Quaker Ave. 4007 S Loop 289 79423. Fax: 806/795-1288. **Facility:** 64 one-bedroom standard units. 3 stories, interior corridors. *Bath:* combo or shower only. **Parking:** on-site. **Terms:** 14 day cancellation notice. **Amenities:** irons. **Pool(s):** small heated indoor. **Leisure Activities:** whirlpool. **Guest Services:** valet laundry. **Business Services:** meeting rooms, fax (fee). **Cards:** AX, CB, DC, DS, MC, VI.

SOME UNITS

FOUR POINTS SHERATON HOTEL

Phone: (806)747-0171

All Year 1P: $79-$89 2P: $89-$99 XP: $10 F18

Small-scale Hotel
Location: I-27, exit 4, 0.9 mi w to US 84, then just s. 505 Ave Q (US 84) 79401. Fax: 806/747-9243. **Facility:** 145 units. 141 one-bedroom standard units. 4 one-bedroom suites ($139-$200), some with efficiencies (no utensils). 6 stories, interior corridors. *Bath:* combo or shower only. **Parking:** on-site. **Terms:** 7 day cancellation notice, [AP], [BP] & [CP] meal plans available, package plans, 18% service charge, small pets only ($50 deposit). **Amenities:** video games (fee), voice mail, irons, hair dryers. **Pool(s):** heated indoor. **Leisure Activities:** exercise room. **Guest Services:** valet laundry, area transportation. **Business Services:** conference facilities, fax (fee). **Cards:** AX, CB, DC, DS, MC, VI.

SOME UNITS

HAMPTON INN

Phone: (806)795-1080

All Year [ECP] 1P: $69-$89 2P: $69-$99 XP: $6 F18

Motel
Location: Loop 289, exit Quarter Ave. 4003 S Loop 289 79423. Fax: 806/795-1376. **Facility:** 81 one-bedroom standard units. 3 stories, interior corridors. *Bath:* combo or shower only. **Parking:** on-site. **Terms:** 14 day cancellation notice. **Amenities:** voice mail, irons, hair dryers. **Pool(s):** small heated indoor. **Leisure Activities:** whirlpool. **Guest Services:** valet laundry. **Business Services:** fax (fee). **Cards:** AX, CB, DC, DS, MC, VI.

SOME UNITS

HOLIDAY INN HOTEL & TOWERS LUBBOCK CIVIC CENTER

Phone: 806/763-1200

All Year 1P: $99-$109 2P: $99-$109

Small-scale Hotel
Location: 0.8 mi nw on US 84. 801 Ave Q 79401. Fax: 806/763-2656. **Facility:** 293 units. 222 one-bedroom standard units. 71 one-bedroom suites ($109-$149). 6 stories, interior corridors. *Bath:* combo or shower only. **Parking:** on-site. **Amenities:** voice mail, irons, hair dryers. **Pool(s):** small heated indoor. **Leisure Activities:** saunas, whirlpool, exercise room. **Guest Services:** valet and coin laundry, area transportation. **Business Services:** conference facilities, fax (fee). **Cards:** AX, CB, DC, DS, MC, VI.

SOME UNITS

HOLIDAY INN PARK PLAZA

Phone: 806/797-3241

All Year 1P: $99-$109 2P: $99-$109

Motel
Location: 5 mi s on Loop 289, exit Indiana, south frontage road. 3201 S Loop 289 79423. Fax: 806/793-1203. **Facility:** 201 units. 197 one-bedroom standard units. 4 one-bedroom suites. 2 stories, interior/exterior corridors. *Bath:* combo or shower only. **Parking:** on-site. **Amenities:** voice mail, irons, hair dryers. **Pool(s):** heated indoor, wading. **Leisure Activities:** sauna, whirlpool, exercise room. **Guest Services:** valet and coin laundry, area transportation. **Business Services:** conference facilities, fax (fee). **Cards:** AX, CB, DC, DS, MC, VI.

SOME UNITS

HOWARD JOHNSON EXPRESS INN

Phone: (806)747-1671

All Year 1P: $45-$95 2P: $50-$100 XP: $5 F17

Motel
Location: I-27, exit 50th St, 0.5 mi w to US 84 (Ave Q), just n. 4801 Ave Q 79412. Fax: 806/747-4265. **Facility:** 54 one-bedroom standard units. 2 stories (no elevator), exterior corridors. *Bath:* combo or shower only. **Parking:** on-site. **Terms:** [CP] & [ECP] meal plans available. **Amenities:** hair dryers. *Some:* irons. **Pool(s):** outdoor. **Leisure Activities:** whirlpool. **Guest Services:** coin laundry. **Business Services:** fax (fee). **Cards:** AX, CB, DC, DS, MC, VI.

SOME UNITS

FEE

LA QUINTA INN-LUBBOCK-CIVIC CENTER

Phone: (806)763-9441

All Year 1P: $69-$80 2P: $75-$95

Motel
Location: 0.8 mi nw on US 84. 601 Ave Q 79401-2613. Fax: 806/747-9325. **Facility:** 137 units. 136 one-bedroom standard units. 1 one-bedroom suite. 2 stories, exterior corridors. *Bath:* combo or shower only. **Parking:** on-site. **Terms:** [ECP] meal plan available, small pets only. **Amenities:** video games (fee), voice mail, irons, hair dryers. **Pool(s):** outdoor. **Guest Services:** valet laundry. **Business Services:** meeting rooms, fax (fee). **Cards:** AX, CB, DC, DS, JC, MC, VI. **Special Amenities: free continental breakfast and free local telephone calls.**

SOME UNITS

LA QUINTA INN-LUBBOCK-MEDICAL CENTER **Phone:** (806)792-0065

AAA SAVE

Motel

All Year 1P: $75-$95 2P: $81-$101

Location: 3.3 mi sw; 2.5 mi ne of Loop 289 on US 62 and 82. 4115 Brownfield Hwy 79407. Fax: 806/792-0178. **Facility:** 130 units. 124 one-bedroom standard units. 6 one-bedroom suites. 6 stories, interior corridors. *Bath:* combo or shower only. **Parking:** on-site. **Terms:** [ECP] meal plan available, small pets only. **Amenities:** video games (fee), voice mail, irons, hair dryers. **Pool(s):** outdoor. **Leisure Activities:** exercise room. **Guest Services:** valet laundry. **Business Services:** meeting rooms, fax. **Cards:** AX, CB, DC, DS, JC, MC, VI. **Special Amenities: free continental breakfast and free local telephone calls.**

SOME UNITS

DATA PORT / /

LUBBOCK SUPER 8 MOTEL **Phone:** (806)762-8726

Motel

4/1-9/30	1P: $48-$60	2P: $53-$70	XP: $6	F12
10/1-12/31	1P: $46-$53	2P: $50-$70	XP: $6	F12
2/1-3/31 & 1/1-1/31	1P: $43-$48	2P: $46-$50	XP: $6	F12

Location: 1 mi nw on US 84. 501 Ave Q 79401. Fax: 806/762-8726. **Facility:** 35 one-bedroom standard units. 2 stories (no elevator), exterior corridors. **Parking:** on-site. **Terms:** 1-10 night minimum stay - seasonal, 7 day cancellation notice, package plans, small pets only ($25 fee, $6 extra charge). **Business Services:** fax (fee). **Cards:** AX, DC, DS, MC, VI.

SOME UNITS

ASK / /

RAMADA INN REGENCY HOTEL **Phone:** (806)745-2208

Motel

All Year 1P: $69-$99 2P: $79-$99 XP: $10 F17

Location: 3.8 mi s on I-27 and US 87; just w of jct Loop 289, exit 1B southbound. 6624 I-27 79404. Fax: 806/745-1265. **Facility:** 160 units. 157 one-bedroom standard units. 3 one-bedroom suites ($99-$200), some with whirlpools. 3 stories, interior corridors. **Parking:** on-site. **Terms:** 7 day cancellation notice, small pets only ($15 deposit). **Amenities:** voice mail, irons, hair dryers. **Pool(s):** heated indoor. **Leisure Activities:** sauna, whirlpool, limited exercise equipment. **Guest Services:** valet and coin laundry. **Business Services:** meeting rooms, fax (fee). **Cards:** AX, CB, DC, DS, MC, VI.

SOME UNITS

ASK DATA PORT / /

RESIDENCE INN BY MARRIOTT **Phone:** (806)745-1963

SAVE

Motel

All Year 1P: $112

Location: Loop 289, exit University, 3 mi s, south frontage road. 2551 S Loop 289 79423. Fax: 806/748-1183. **Facility:** 80 units. 74 one-bedroom standard units, some with kitchens. 6 one-bedroom suites with kitchens. 2 stories (no elevator), exterior corridors. *Bath:* combo or shower only. **Parking:** on-site. **Terms:** [ECP] meal plan available, pets ($50 fee). **Amenities:** voice mail, irons, hair dryers. **Pool(s):** heated outdoor. **Leisure Activities:** whirlpools, limited exercise equipment, sports court. **Guest Services:** complimentary evening beverages: Mon-Thurs, valet and coin laundry. **Business Services:** meeting rooms, business center. **Cards:** AX, CB, DC, DS, JC, MC, VI.

SOME UNITS

DATA PORT / VCR /

WHERE TO DINE

CATTLE BARON STEAK & SEAFOOD RESTAURANT **Lunch:** $6-$11 **Dinner:** $10-$28 **Phone:** 806/798-7033

American

Location: Jct of Quaker Ave and 82nd St, southeast corner. 8201 Quaker Ave 79423. **Hours:** 11 am-9:30 pm, Fri & Sat-10 pm. Closed: 12/25. **Reservations:** accepted. **Features:** Upscale Western decor is complete with wood trim and distinctive chandeliers made from deer antlers. A scrumptious array of menu selections includes steak, seafood, chicken and prime rib, as well as such desserts as caramel apple pie. Casual dress; cocktails. **Parking:** on-site. **Cards:** AX, CB, DC, DS, MC, VI.

CHEZ SUZETTE **Lunch:** $7-$15 **Dinner:** $11-$18 **Phone:** 806/795-6796

French

Location: 5.5 mi sw; in Quaker Square Shopping Center. 4423 50th St 79414. **Hours:** 11:30 am-2 & 5:30-10 pm, Mon, Fri & Sat from 5:30 pm. Closed major holidays; also Sun. **Reservations:** accepted. **Features:** Awnings and candlelit tables add to the romantic atmosphere. The escargot appetizer is a savory start, and French and Italian entrees reflect an American flair. Juicy beef filets are served with a variety of sauces, including bearnaise and Dijonnaise. Casual dress; cocktails. **Parking:** on-site. **Cards:** AX, DC, DS, MC, VI.

THE COUNTY LINE **Lunch:** $6-$20 **Dinner:** $9-$20 **Phone:** 806/763-6001

Southwest American

Location: I-27, exit 8 (Regis St), 4 mi n, then 0.5 mi w on FM 2641. **Hours:** 11 am-2 & 5-9 pm, Fri-10 pm, Sat 5 pm-10 pm. Closed: 11/27, 12/24, 12/25. **Features:** The bustling dining room is distinguished by 1940s decor and large windows that offer a splendid view of the lake. Ducks and peacocks stroll along the water's edge. Satisfying portions of barbecue ribs and prime rib are the house specialties. Casual dress; cocktails. **Parking:** on-site. **Cards:** AX, CB, DC, DS, MC, VI.

LUFKIN pop. 32,709

WHERE TO STAY

COMFORT SUITES **Phone:** 936/632-4949

SAVE

Small-scale Hotel

All Year 1P: $72 XP: $10 F18

Location: 2.2 mi s of jct US 59 and E Loop 287. 4402 S 1st St 75901. Fax: 936/632-4925. **Facility:** 65 units. 64 one-bedroom standard units, some with whirlpools. 1 one-bedroom suite with kitchen. 3 stories, interior corridors. *Bath:* combo or shower only. **Parking:** on-site. **Terms:** small pets only ($10 fee). **Amenities:** dual phone lines, voice mail, irons, hair dryers. *Some:* fax. **Pool(s):** heated indoor. **Leisure Activities:** whirlpool, exercise room. **Guest Services:** valet and coin laundry. **Business Services:** meeting rooms, business center. **Cards:** AX, DC, DS, MC, VI.

SOME UNITS

DATA PORT / VCR /

DAY'S INN

SAVE
Motel

Phone: (936)639-3301
All Year   1P: $58-$80   2P: $64-$84   XP: $5   F17
Location: 0.3 mi s of jct US 59 and Loop 287. 2130 S 1st St 75901. Fax: 936/634-4266. **Facility:** 124 one-bedroom standard units, some with whirlpools. 2 stories, interior/exterior corridors. **Parking:** on-site. **Terms:** weekly rates available, [ECP] meal plan available, package plans, small pets only. **Amenities:** hair dryers. *Some:* irons. **Pool(s):** outdoor, wading. **Guest Services:** valet and coin laundry. **Business Services:** meeting rooms, fax (fee). **Cards:** AX, CB, DC, DS, MC, VI.

SOME UNITS
🛎️🖥️ ✈️ 🏩 🍴 🍸 ➿ 🎦 💻 / ⊠ VCR DATA PORT ▯ 🖼️ /
FEE

LA QUINTA INN-LUFKIN

AAA SAVE
Motel

Phone: (936)634-3351
All Year   1P: $65-$75   2P: $75-$85   XP: $10   F18
Location: US 59, exit Carriageway northbound, 0.3 mi s of jct S Loop 287 and US 59 business route. 2119 S 1st St 75901-5902. Fax: 936/634-9475. **Facility:** 106 units. 105 one-bedroom standard units. 1 one-bedroom suite. 2 stories, exterior corridors. **Parking:** on-site. **Terms:** [ECP] meal plan available, small pets only. **Amenities:** video games (fee), voice mail, irons, hair dryers. **Pool(s):** outdoor. **Guest Services:** valet laundry. **Business Services:** meeting rooms, fax (fee). **Cards:** AX, CB, DC, DS, JC, MC, VI.
Special Amenities: free continental breakfast and free local telephone calls.

SOME UNITS
🛎️🖥️ 🏩 🍴 🎨 ➿ 🎦 🎥 DATA PORT 💻 / ⊠ ▯ 🖼️ /

SUPER 8 MOTEL-LUFKIN

AAA SAVE
Small-scale Hotel

Phone: (936)632-8885
All Year   1P: $55   2P: $65   XP: $5   F12
Location: US 59, exit Brentwood Dr/Daniel McCall Dr. 2216 S 1st St 75904. Fax: 936/632-8980. **Facility:** 43 one-bedroom standard units. 2 stories, interior corridors. *Bath:* combo or shower only. **Parking:** on-site. **Amenities:** hair dryers. **Pool(s):** small heated indoor. **Leisure Activities:** whirlpool. **Guest Services:** coin laundry. **Business Services:** fax (fee). **Cards:** AX, CB, DC, DS, JC, MC, VI.

SOME UNITS
🛎️🖥️ 🍴 🔲M 🎨 🎨 ➿ 🎥 DATA PORT ▯ 🖼️ 💻 / ⊠ /

── WHERE TO DINE ──

THE BRAZOS CATTLE COMPANY

American

Lunch: $7-$19   **Dinner:** $7-$19   **Phone:** 736/632-6969
Location: US 59, exit Carriageway northbound, 0.3 mi s of jct s Loop 287 and US 59 business route. 2115 S 1st St 75901. **Hours:** 11 am-10 pm, Fri & Sat-11 pm. Closed: 12/25. **Features:** A unique Southwestern decor with pine divider rails and ceiling beams and two fireplaces gives the impression of a Texas bunkhouse. A delicious home-style menu features steaks, chicken, and some seafood choices, plus desserts like brownies a la mode. Casual dress; cocktails. **Parking:** on-site. **Cards:** AX, CB, DC, DS, MC, VI.
🍸 ⊠

MABANK —*See Dallas p. 308.*

MADISONVILLE pop. 4,159

── WHERE TO STAY ──

WESTERN LODGE

AAA SAVE
Motel

Phone: 936/348-7654
All Year [CP]   1P: $40-$45   2P: $45-$50   XP: $55   F
Location: I-45, exit 142, 0.3 mi w. 2007 E Main St 77864. Fax: 936/348-7661. **Facility:** 62 units. 60 one-bedroom standard units. 2 one-bedroom suites. 1 story, exterior corridors. **Parking:** on-site. **Terms:** weekly rates available, small pets only ($10 extra charge). **Dining:** 6 am-10 pm. **Pool(s):** small outdoor. **Business Services:** fax (fee). **Cards:** AX, DC, DS, MC, VI. **Special Amenities:** free continental breakfast and free local telephone calls.

SOME UNITS
🏩 🍴 ➿ 🎥 DATA PORT / ⊠ ▯ 🖼️ /

WOODBINE HOTEL

Classic Historic Country Inn

Phone: (936)348-3333
All Year [BP]   1P: $75-$150   2P: $75-$150   XP: $15
Location: I-45, exit 142, 2.2 mi w to town square, 2 blks n on Madison St. 209 N Madison St 77864. Fax: 936/348-6268. **Facility:** 8 units. 7 one-bedroom standard units, some with whirlpools. 1 one-bedroom suite with whirlpool. 3 stories (no elevator), interior/exterior corridors. *Bath:* combo or shower only. **Parking:** on-site. **Terms:** 14 day cancellation notice-fee imposed. **Leisure Activities:** horseshoes, game room. **Business Services:** meeting rooms, fax (fee). **Cards:** AX, MC, VI.

SOME UNITS
ASK 🍴 🍸 ⊠ 🎥 / ▯ /

MARATHON pop. 455

── WHERE TO STAY ──

─── *The following lodging was either not evaluated or did not* ───
meet AAA rating requirements but is listed for your information only.

THE GAGE HOTEL

fyi
Classic Historic Country Inn

Phone: 432/386-4205
Did not meet all AAA rating requirements for locking devices in some guest rooms at time of last evaluation on 02/28/2002. **Location:** US 90; center. Hwy 90 79842 (PO Box 46). Facilities, services, and decor characterize a mid-range property.

—— WHERE TO DINE ——

CENIZO BAR & GRILL
ᗺᗺᗺᗺᗺ
Continental

Dinner: $13-$26

Phone: 432/386-4437

Location: US 90; center; in The Gage Hotel. US 90 79842. **Hours:** 7 am-10 & 6-9 pm, Fri-10 pm, Sat 7 am-11 & 6-10 pm, Sun 7 am-1 & 6-9 pm. **Reservations:** required. **Features:** In a restored historic ranch headquarters and hotel, the eatery serves eclectic Texas cuisine in four themed rooms: Native American, horns, skulls and the main 1800s Texas ranch. Smoke free premises. Casual dress; cocktails. **Parking:** on-site. **Cards:** AX, DS, MC, VI.

MARBLE FALLS pop. 4,959

—— WHERE TO STAY ——

BEST WESTERN MARBLE FALLS INN
ⒶⒶⒶ ⓢᴬᵛᴱ
ᗺᗺᗺ◊◊
Small-scale Hotel

3/2-9/1 [ECP]	1P: $59-$109	2P: $69-$119	XP: $10	F18
2/1-3/1 & 9/2-1/31 [ECP]	1P: $59-$89	2P: $69-$89	XP: $10	F18

Phone: (830)693-5122

Location: 0.4 mi n of jct SR 281 and FM 1431. 1403 Hwy 281 N 78654. Fax: 830/693-3108. **Facility:** 62 one-bedroom standard units, some with whirlpools. 2 stories (no elevator), interior/exterior corridors. **Bath:** combo or shower only. **Parking:** on-site. **Terms:** check-in 3:30 pm, 3 day cancellation notice, small pets only (in smoking units). **Amenities:** irons, hair dryers. **Pool(s):** small outdoor. **Leisure Activities:** whirlpool, limited exercise equipment. **Guest Services:** coin laundry. **Business Services:** meeting rooms, fax (fee). **Cards:** AX, CB, DC, DS, JC, MC, VI. **Special Amenities:** free continental breakfast and free newspaper.

SOME UNITS

HAMPTON INN ON THE LAKE—MARBLE FALLS
ⓢᴬᵛᴱ
ᗺᗺᗺ◊
Small-scale Hotel

All Year [ECP]

2P: $79-$129

XP: $10   F18

Phone: 830/798-1895

Location: Jct US 281 and FM 1831, 0.5 mi s, on Lake Marble Falls. 704 First St 78654. Fax: 830/798-1897. **Facility:** 64 one-bedroom standard units. 3 stories, interior corridors. **Bath:** combo or shower only. **Parking:** on-site. **Terms:** 2 night minimum stay - weekends, 5 day cancellation notice. **Amenities:** high-speed Internet, dual phone lines, voice mail, irons, hair dryers. **Pool(s):** outdoor. **Leisure Activities:** whirlpool. **Guest Services:** coin laundry. **Business Services:** meeting rooms, fax (fee). **Cards:** AX, CB, DC, DS, MC, VI.

SOME UNITS

HILL COUNTRY MOTEL
ⒶⒶⒶ ⓢᴬᵛᴱ
ᗺᗺ◊ᗺᗺ
Motel

All Year [CP]

1P: $59-$125

2P: $59-$125

XP: $5   F18

Phone: 830/693-3637

Location: Just n of jct SR 281 and FM 1431. 1101 Hwy 281 N 78654. Fax: 830/693-6028. **Facility:** 69 units. 68 one-bedroom standard units. 1 one-bedroom suite ($69-$145). 2 stories (no elevator), exterior corridors. **Parking:** on-site. **Terms:** small pets only ($25 deposit). **Amenities:** Some: irons, hair dryers. **Pool(s):** small outdoor. **Business Services:** fax (fee). **Cards:** AX, CB, DC, DS, MC, VI. **Special Amenities:** free continental breakfast and free local telephone calls.

SOME UNITS

RAMADA LTD
ᗺᗺ ᗺᗺ
Small-scale Hotel

3/2-9/30 [ECP]	1P: $59-$149	2P: $59-$149	XP: $5	F18
2/1-3/1 & 10/1-1/31 [ECP]	1P: $55-$149	2P: $55-$149	XP: $5	F18

Phone: (830)693-7531

Location: 0.3 mi n of jct SR 281 and FM 1431. 1206 Hwy 281 N 78654. Fax: 830/693-7080. **Facility:** 49 units. 48 one-bedroom standard units. 1 one-bedroom suite. 2 stories (no elevator), exterior corridors. **Bath:** combo or shower only. **Parking:** on-site. **Amenities:** voice mail, irons, hair dryers. **Pool(s):** small outdoor. **Leisure Activities:** whirlpool. **Business Services:** fax (fee). **Cards:** AX, CB, DC, DS, MC, VI.

SOME UNITS

—— WHERE TO DINE ——

JAMIN HOUSE CAFE
ᗺᗺ ᗺᗺᗺ
Caribbean

Lunch: $5-$20

Dinner: $5-$20

Phone: 830/693-3979

Location: Jct US 281 and FM 1431, 0.5 mi s; at the bridge. 700 First St 78764. **Hours:** 11 am-9 pm, Fri & Sat-9:30 pm. **Closed:** 11/27, 12/25. **Reservations:** accepted. **Features:** A Caribbean flair touches everything from the atmosphere to the flavorful food, which includes catfish, shrimp, seafood, jerk barbecue and steak entrees. Try toffee pie for dessert. Smoke free premises. Casual dress; cocktails. **Parking:** on-site. **Cards:** AX, DS, MC, VI.

RUSSO'S CAFE
ⒶⒶⒶ
ᗺᗺᗺ◊
Italian

Lunch: $6-$13

Dinner: $10-$24

Phone: 830/693-7091

Location: Just s of Marble Falls Bridge; jct US 281 and FM 2147. 602 Steve Hawkins Pkwy 78654. **Hours:** 11:30 am-2 & 5-9:30 pm, Fri & Sat-10 pm. Closed major holidays; also Sun & Mon. **Reservations:** accepted. **Features:** Atop a hill overlooking a lake, the modern establishment serves traditional Italian dishes. Casual dress; cocktails. **Parking:** on-site. **Cards:** AX, DS, MC, VI.

MARSHALL pop. 23,935

—— WHERE TO STAY ——

BEST WESTERN EXECUTIVE INN
ⒶⒶⒶ ⓢᴬᵛᴱ
ᗺᗺ ᗺᗺ
Small-scale Hotel

4/1-8/31 & 11/16-1/31	1P: $69-$79	2P: $79-$89	XP: $6	F
2/1-3/31 & 9/1-11/15	1P: $59-$69	2P: $69-$79	XP: $6	F

Phone: 903/935-0707

Location: I-20, exit 617, just n on US 59. 5201 E End Blvd S 75672 (PO Box 548, 75671). Fax: 903/935-1617. **Facility:** 40 one-bedroom standard units, some with whirlpools. 2 stories, exterior corridors. **Parking:** on-site. **Terms:** 7 day cancellation notice-fee imposed, [CP] meal plan available, small pets only ($7 extra charge). **Amenities:** irons, hair dryers. **Pool(s):** outdoor. **Guest Services:** coin laundry. **Business Services:** fax (fee). **Cards:** AX, CB, DC, DS, JC, MC, VI. **Special Amenities:** free continental breakfast and free local telephone calls.

SOME UNITS

HAMPTON INN MARSHALL

Phone: (903)927-0079

AAA SAVE
Motel

All Year [ECP]   1P: $75-$99   2P: $79-$99
Location: I-20, exit 617, 0.5 mi n on US 59. 5100 SE End Blvd 75672. Fax: 903/927-0080. **Facility:** 68 one-bedroom standard units, some with whirlpools. 3 stories, interior corridors. *Bath:* combo or shower only. **Parking:** on-site. **Amenities:** video games (fee), dual phone lines, voice mail, irons, hair dryers. **Pool(s):** heated outdoor. **Leisure Activities:** whirlpool, limited exercise equipment. **Guest Services:** valet laundry. **Business Services:** meeting rooms, fax (fee). **Cards:** AX, CB, DC, DS, MC, VI. **Special Amenities:** free continental breakfast and free local telephone calls.

SOME UNITS

HOLIDAY INN EXPRESS

Phone: (903)935-7923

Motel

All Year [ECP]   1P: $75-$79
Location: I-20, exit 617, 0.3 mi n on US 59. 4911 E End Blvd S 75672. Fax: 903/938-2675. **Facility:** 58 one-bedroom standard units, some with whirlpools. 2 stories, exterior corridors. *Bath:* combo or shower only. **Parking:** on-site. **Amenities:** irons, hair dryers. **Pool(s):** outdoor. **Guest Services:** valet and coin laundry. **Business Services:** fax (fee). **Cards:** AX, DC, DS, MC, VI.

SOME UNITS

MCALLEN pop. 106,414

------- WHERE TO STAY -------

BEST WESTERN ROSE GARDEN INN & SUITES

Phone: (956)630-3333

SAVE

All Year   1P: $59-$64   2P: $59-$64   XP: $7   F18
Location: 0.5 mi e of jct US 83, exit 2nd St. 300 E Expwy 83 78503. Fax: 956/687-9550. **Facility:** 92 units. 69 one-bedroom standard units. 23 one-bedroom suites ($68-$74). 2 stories, exterior corridors. **Parking:** on-site, winter plug-ins. **Terms:** [BP] meal plan available. **Amenities:** irons, hair dryers. **Pool(s):** outdoor. **Guest Services:** coin laundry. **Business Services:** meeting rooms, fax (fee). **Cards:** AX, CB, DS, MC, VI.

SOME UNITS

COUNTRY INN & SUITES BY CARLSON

Phone: (956)618-2424

Small-scale Hotel

All Year [ECP]   1P: $98-$109   2P: $98-$109   XP: $10   F18
Location: 1.8 mi s on SR 336 (S 10th St); just s of US 83 Expwy. Located in a commercial area. 1921 S 10th St 78503. Fax: 956/618-2736. **Facility:** 193 units. 110 one-bedroom standard units. 83 two-bedroom suites ($107-$119). 6 stories, interior/exterior corridors. *Bath:* combo or shower only. **Parking:** on-site. **Terms:** cancellation fee imposed. **Amenities:** voice mail, irons, hair dryers. **Pool(s):** heated indoor/outdoor. **Leisure Activities:** whirlpools, exercise room. **Guest Services:** valet and coin laundry, area transportation. **Business Services:** meeting rooms, business center. **Cards:** AX, CB, DC, DS, MC. *(See color ad p 260)*

SOME UNITS

COURTYARD BY MARRIOTT

Phone: 956/668-7800

SAVE
Small-scale Hotel

All Year   1P: $89   2P: $89   XP: $10   F17
Location: 0.3 mi s US 83, just off S 10th St. 2131 S 10th St 78503. Fax: 956/668-7801. **Facility:** 110 one-bedroom standard units. 3 stories, interior corridors. *Bath:* combo or shower only. **Parking:** on-site. **Terms:** [BP] meal plan available. **Amenities:** voice mail, irons, hair dryers. **Pool(s):** heated outdoor. **Leisure Activities:** whirlpool, exercise room. **Guest Services:** coin laundry. **Business Services:** meeting rooms, fax (fee). **Cards:** AX, CB, DC, DS, MC, VI.

SOME UNITS

DRURY INN

Phone: (956)687-5100

AAA SAVE
Small-scale Hotel

9/1-1/31 [ECP]   1P: $73-$86   2P: $83-$96   XP: $10   F18
2/1-8/31 [ECP]   1P: $70-$83   2P: $80-$93   XP: $10   F18
Location: US 83 Expwy, exit 2nd St, northwest frontage road. 612 W Expwy 83 78501. Fax: 956/687-5100. **Facility:** 89 one-bedroom standard units. 3 stories, interior corridors. **Parking:** on-site. **Amenities:** voice mail, irons, hair dryers. **Pool(s):** outdoor. **Guest Services:** complimentary evening beverages: Mon-Thurs, coin laundry. **Business Services:** meeting rooms, fax (fee). **Cards:** AX, CB, DC, DS, MC, VI. **Special Amenities:** free continental breakfast and free local telephone calls.

SOME UNITS

DRURY SUITES-MCALLEN

Phone: (956)682-3222

AAA SAVE
Small-scale Hotel

9/1-1/31 [BP]   1P: $95-$115   2P: $105-$125   XP: $10   F18
2/1-8/31 [BP]   1P: $90-$110   2P: $100-$120   XP: $10   F18
Location: At US 83 and 6th St. Located close to medical center. 228 W Expressway 83 78501. Fax: 956/682-3222. **Facility:** 90 units. 22 one-bedroom standard units with efficiencies, some with whirlpools. 64 one- and 4 two-bedroom suites ($105-$195) with kitchens, some with whirlpools. 6 stories, interior corridors. **Parking:** on-site. **Amenities:** voice mail, irons, hair dryers. **Pool(s):** outdoor. **Leisure Activities:** exercise room. **Guest Services:** complimentary evening beverages: Mon-Thurs, coin laundry. **Business Services:** meeting rooms, business center. **Cards:** AX, CB, DC, DS, MC, VI. **Special Amenities:** free continental breakfast and free local telephone calls.

SOME UNITS

EMBASSY SUITES

Phone: (956)686-3000

SAVE
Small-scale Hotel

All Year [BP]   1P: $130-$145   2P: $145-$160   XP: $15   F18
Location: US 83 Expwy, exit 2nd St. 1800 S 2nd St 78503. Fax: 956/631-8362. **Facility:** 252 one-bedroom suites. 9 stories, interior corridors. **Parking:** on-site. **Terms:** cancellation fee imposed. **Amenities:** video games, voice mail, irons, hair dryers. **Pool(s):** heated indoor, wading. **Leisure Activities:** whirlpool, steamroom, exercise room. **Guest Services:** gift shop, complimentary evening beverages, coin laundry, area transportation. **Business Services:** meeting rooms, fax (fee). **Cards:** AX, CB, DC, DS, MC, VI.

SOME UNITS

FAIRFIELD INN AND SUITES

Phone: 956/971-9444

SAVE

All Year [CP]   2P: $65-$74

Location: 0.3 mi s on US 83; just off S 10th St. Located opposite the airport. 2117 S 10th St 78503. Fax: 956/971-9424. **Facility:** 68 one-bedroom standard units, some with whirlpools. 3 stories, interior corridors. *Bath:* combo or shower only. **Parking:** on-site. **Amenities:** irons, hair dryers. *Some:* CD players. **Pool(s):** heated indoor.

Small-scale Hotel **Leisure Activities:** whirlpool, exercise room. **Guest Services:** valet and coin laundry. **Business Services:** fax (fee). **Cards:** AX, DC, DS, MC, VI.

SOME UNITS

FOUR POINTS HOTEL BY SHERATON

Phone: (956)984-7900

All Year [ECP]   1P: $69-$119   2P: $69-$129   XP: $10   F19

Location: 2.5 mi s on SR 336 (S 10th St). Located opposite the airport. 2721 S 10th St 78503. Fax: 956/984-7997.

Small-scale Hotel **Facility:** 148 units. 147 one-bedroom standard units. 1 one-bedroom suite. 5 stories, interior corridors. *Bath:* combo or shower only. **Parking:** on-site. **Terms:** cancellation fee imposed, [AP], [BP] & [CP] meal plans available, package plans - weekends, 17% service charge. **Amenities:** voice mail, irons, hair dryers. *Fee:* video games, high-speed Internet. **Pool(s):** outdoor, wading. **Leisure Activities:** whirlpool, lighted tennis court, exercise room. **Guest Services:** valet and coin laundry, area transportation. **Business Services:** conference facilities, business center. **Cards:** AX, CB, DC, DS, MC, VI.

SOME UNITS

HAMPTON INN-MCALLEN

Phone: (956)682-4900

SAVE

9/1-1/31 [ECP]   1P: $83-$102   2P: $93-$111   XP: $10   F18
2/1-8/31 [ECP]   1P: $80-$98   2P: $90-$108   XP: $10   F18

Location: US 83 Expwy, exit 2nd St, northwest frontage road. 300 W Expressway 83 78501. Fax: 956/682-6823.

Small-scale Hotel **Facility:** 91 one-bedroom standard units. 4 stories, interior corridors. **Parking:** on-site. **Terms:** small pets only. **Amenities:** irons. **Pool(s):** outdoor. **Guest Services:** valet laundry. **Business Services:** meeting rooms, fax (fee). **Cards:** AX, CB, DC, DS, MC, VI.

SOME UNITS

HOLIDAY INN CIVIC CENTER

Phone: (956)686-2471

All Year   1P: $89   2P: $94

Location: US 83 Expwy, exit 2nd St. 200 W Expressway 83 78501. Fax: 956/686-2038. **Facility:** 173 one-bedroom standard units. 2 stories, interior/exterior corridors. **Parking:** on-site. **Amenities:** voice mail, irons, hair

Small-scale Hotel dryers. **Pool(s):** outdoor, heated indoor, wading. **Leisure Activities:** sauna, whirlpool, exercise room. **Guest Services:** complimentary evening beverages, valet and coin laundry, area transportation. **Business Services:** conference facilities, business center. **Cards:** AX, CB, DC, DS, MC, VI.

SOME UNITS

HOLIDAY INN EXPRESS

Phone: (956)686-1741

7/1-9/30 [ECP]   2P: $79-$89
2/1-3/31 & 10/1-1/31 [ECP]   2P: $69-$89
4/1-6/30 [ECP]   2P: $59-$79

Small-scale Hotel **Location:** 1.8 mi s on SR 336 (S 10th St); just s of US 83 Expwy. 2000 S 10th St 78503. Fax: 956/682-7187. **Facility:** 150 one-bedroom standard units. 2 stories, exterior corridors. **Parking:** on-site. **Terms:** cancellation fee imposed, weekly rates available, [CP] meal plan available. **Amenities:** voice mail, irons, hair dryers. **Pool(s):** outdoor, wading. **Leisure Activities:** exercise room. **Guest Services:** valet and coin laundry, area transportation. **Business Services:** meeting rooms, business center. **Cards:** AX, CB, DC, DS, JC, MC, VI.

SOME UNITS

LA QUINTA INN-MCALLEN

Phone: (956)687-1101

AAA SAVE

All Year [CP]   1P: $73   2P: $78   XP: $5   F18

Location: 1.5 mi s on SR 336 (S 10th St); just n of jct US 83 Expwy. Located in a commercial area. 1100 S 10th St 78501. Fax: 956/687-9265. **Facility:** 120 one-bedroom standard units. 3 stories, exterior corridors. *Bath:* combo or shower only. **Parking:** on-site. **Terms:** small pets only. **Amenities:** video games (fee), voice mail, irons, hair

Small-scale Hotel dryers. **Pool(s):** outdoor. **Guest Services:** valet laundry. **Business Services:** meeting rooms, fax (fee). **Cards:** AX, CB, DC, DS, MC, VI. **Special Amenities:** free continental breakfast and free local telephone calls.

SOME UNITS

MICROTEL INN

Phone: (956)630-2727

AAA SAVE

All Year   1P: $55-$65   2P: $60-$70   XP: $5   F18

Location: US 83 Expwy, exit Jackson Ave, just nw. 801 E Expressway 83 78501. Fax: 956/630-0666. **Facility:** 102 one-bedroom standard units. 3 stories, interior corridors. *Bath:* combo or shower only. **Parking:** on-site. **Amenities:** video games (fee). **Pool(s):** outdoor. **Guest Services:** valet laundry. **Business Services:** fax

Small-scale Hotel (fee). **Cards:** AX, CB, DC, DS, JC, MC, VI. **Special Amenities:** free continental breakfast and free local telephone calls.

SOME UNITS

RENAISSANCE CASA DE PALMAS

Phone: (956)631-1101

SAVE

7/1-1/31   1P: $90   2P: $90   XP: $10   F12
2/1-6/30   1P: $85   2P: $85   XP: $10   F12

Location: On N Main St, just north of US Business 83. 101 N Main St 78501. Fax: 956/631-7934. **Facility:** 165 units. 144 one-bedroom standard units. 21 one-bedroom suites ($149-$200). 3 stories, interior corridors. *Bath:*

Historic   combo or shower only. **Parking:** on-site. **Terms:** cancellation fee imposed. **Amenities:** dual phone lines,

Large-scale Hotel voice mail, honor bars, irons, hair dryers. **Pool(s):** outdoor. **Leisure Activities:** exercise room. **Guest Services:** valet laundry, area transportation. **Business Services:** conference facilities, business center. **Cards:** AX, CB, DC, DS, MC, VI.

SOME UNITS

RESIDENCE INN BY MARRIOTT
Phone: (956)994-8626

[SAVE]

Small-scale Hotel

All Year [BP]   1P: $114   2P: $114
Location: US 83 Expwy, exit 2nd St, just w, then just n on 2nd St. 220 W Expressway 83 78501. Fax: 956/994-8627. **Facility:** 78 units. 18 one-bedroom standard units, some with efficiencies or kitchens. 48 one- and 12 two-bedroom suites, some with efficiencies or kitchens. 3 stories, interior corridors. *Bath:* combo or shower only. **Parking:** on-site. **Terms:** small pets only ($60 fee, $5 extra charge). **Amenities:** dual phone lines, voice mail, irons, hair dryers. **Pool(s):** outdoor. **Leisure Activities:** whirlpool, lighted tennis court, exercise room, sports court, basketball, volleyball. **Guest Services:** area transportation. **Business Services:** meeting rooms, fax (fee). **Cards:** AX, DC, DS, MC, VI.

SOME UNITS

THRIFTY-INN-MCALLEN
Phone: (956)631-6700

[AAA] [SAVE]

Small-scale Hotel

9/1-1/31 [CP]   1P: $53-$63   2P: $63-$73   XP: $10   F18
2/1-8/31 [CP]   1P: $51-$61   2P: $61-$71   XP: $10   F18
Location: US 83 Expwy, exit 2nd St, northwest frontage road. 620 W Expressway 83 78501. Fax: 956/631-6700. **Facility:** 93 one-bedroom standard units. 3 stories, interior corridors. **Parking:** on-site. **Leisure Activities:** off-site pool privileges. **Guest Services:** valet laundry. **Business Services:** fax (fee). **Cards:** AX, CB, DC, DS, MC, VI. **Special Amenities:** free continental breakfast and free local telephone calls.

SOME UNITS

——— **WHERE TO DINE** ———

CHINA INN SOUTH
Lunch: $4-$8   Dinner: $8-$20   Phone: 956/686-2328

Chinese

Location: 2 mi s on SR 336. 2001 S 10th St 78503. **Hours:** 11:30 am-10 pm, Fri-10:30 pm, Sat noon-10:30 pm, Sun noon-9:30 pm. **Reservations:** suggested. **Features:** Hunan, Szechuan, and Mandarin cuisines are served in an elegant setting of Oriental murals, umbrella lamp shades and framed artwork. Well-prepared specialties include general's chicken in a dark, spicy-sweet sauce, fried bananas, and sweet and sour shrimp. Casual dress; cocktails. **Parking:** on-site. **Cards:** AX, DC, DS, MC, VI.

MCKINNEY — *See Dallas p. 308.*

MEMPHIS pop. 2,479

——— **WHERE TO STAY** ———

EXECUTIVE INN
Phone: (806)259-3583

[AAA] [SAVE]

Motel

All Year   1P: $50   2P: $54   XP: $5   F13
Location: On US 287, 1.3 mi n of jct SR 256. 1600 Boykin Dr 79245. Fax: 806/259-3904. **Facility:** 37 one-bedroom standard units. 2 stories (no elevator), exterior corridors. **Parking:** on-site, winter plug-ins. **Terms:** cancellation fee imposed, small pets only. **Amenities:** hair dryers. *Some:* irons. **Dining:** 6 am-10 pm. **Pool(s):** outdoor. **Business Services:** meeting rooms. **Cards:** AX, CB, DC, DS, JC, MC, VI.

SOME UNITS

MESQUITE — *See Dallas p. 309.*

MIDLAND pop. 94,996

✈ **Airport Accommodations**

Spotter/Map Page Number	OA	MIDLAND INTERNATIONAL	Diamond Rating	Rate Range High Season	Listing Page
N/A		Ramada Inn Midland Airport, 1 mi s of airport terminal	▽▽▽	$63-$79	469

——— **WHERE TO STAY** ———

BEST INN & SUITES
Phone: (432)699-4144

[AAA] [SAVE]

Motel

All Year   1P: $49-$59   2P: $49-$59   XP: $7   F12
Location: 2 mi w on I-20 business loop. 3100 W Wall St 79701. Fax: 432/699-7639. **Facility:** 125 units. 117 one-bedroom standard units, some with whirlpools. 8 one-bedroom suites ($79-$179), some with whirlpools. 2 stories, interior corridors. **Parking:** on-site. **Terms:** [ECP] meal plan available, small pets only ($7 fee). **Amenities:** hair dryers. **Pool(s):** heated indoor. **Leisure Activities:** saunas. **Guest Services:** valet laundry. **Business Services:** meeting rooms, fax (fee). **Cards:** AX, CB, DC, DS, MC, VI. **Special Amenities:** free continental breakfast and free local telephone calls.

SOME UNITS

FEE

BEST WESTERN ATRIUM INN
Phone: (432)694-7774

[AAA] [SAVE]

Motel

All Year [ECP]   1P: $59-$89   2P: $59-$89   XP: $5   F18
Location: I-20, exit 134, 1 mi n on Midkiff Rd, 0.3 mi w on I-20 business route. 3904 W Wall St 79703. Fax: 432/694-0134. **Facility:** 109 one-bedroom standard units, some with whirlpools. 2 stories (no elevator), interior/exterior corridors. **Parking:** on-site. **Amenities:** irons, hair dryers. **Pool(s):** heated outdoor. **Leisure Activities:** sauna, whirlpool. **Guest Services:** valet laundry. **Business Services:** meeting rooms, fax (fee). **Cards:** AX, CB, DC, DS, MC, VI. **Special Amenities:** early check-in/late check-out and free continental breakfast.

SOME UNITS

COMFORT SUITES

AAA SAVE

▽▽▽▽

Motel

Phone: 432/620-9191

All Year
1P: $84-$89
2P: $89-$94
XP: $5
F18

Location: Loop 250, exit Garfield St, just n. 4706 N Garfield St 79705. Fax: 432/620-9292. **Facility:** 63 units. 62 one-bedroom standard units, some with whirlpools. 1 one-bedroom suite. 2 stories, interior corridors. *Bath:* combo or shower only. **Parking:** on-site. **Amenities:** voice mail, irons, hair dryers. **Pool(s):** outdoor. **Leisure Activities:** whirlpool, limited exercise equipment. **Guest Services:** valet and coin laundry. **Business Services:** meeting rooms, business center. **Cards:** AX, DC, DS, MC, VI. **Special Amenities:** free continental breakfast and free local telephone calls.

SOME UNITS

[icons] / X /

DAYS INN

SAVE

▽▽▽

Motel

Phone: 432/697-3155

All Year [ECP]
1P: $54
2P: $60
XP: $6
F12

Location: I-20, exit 134, 1 mi n. 1003 S Midkiff Rd 79701. Fax: 432/699-2017. **Facility:** 82 units. 57 one-bedroom standard units with kitchens. 15 one- and 10 two-bedroom suites with kitchens. 3 stories, exterior corridors. **Parking:** on-site. **Terms:** 3 day cancellation notice, pets ($10 fee). **Amenities:** voice mail, hair dryers. **Pool(s):** small outdoor. **Leisure Activities:** whirlpool. **Guest Services:** coin laundry. **Business Services:** meeting rooms, fax (fee). **Cards:** AX, CB, DC, DS, JC, MC, VI.

SOME UNITS

[icons] / X /

FAIRFIELD INN

SAVE

▽▽▽

Motel

Phone: (432)570-7155

All Year [ECP]
1P: $69-$89
2P: $69-$99
XP: $6
F18

Location: I-20, exit Loop 250, 7 mi to Garfield St. 2300 Faulkner Dr 79102. Fax: 432/570-7155. **Facility:** 71 one-bedroom standard units. 2 stories, interior corridors. *Bath:* combo or shower only. **Parking:** on-site. **Terms:** 14 day cancellation notice. **Amenities:** voice mail, irons. **Pool(s):** heated indoor. **Leisure Activities:** whirlpool. **Guest Services:** valet laundry. **Business Services:** meeting rooms, fax (fee). **Cards:** AX, CB, DC, DS, MC, VI.

SOME UNITS

[icons] / X /

HOLIDAY INN

▽▽▽▽

Motel

Phone: (432)697-3181

All Year
1P: $60-$64
2P: $60-$64

Location: I-20, exit 134 (Midkiff Rd), 1 mi n to I-20 business loop, 0.7 mi w. 4300 W Wall St 79703. Fax: 432/694-7754. **Facility:** 250 units. 219 one-bedroom standard units. 31 one-bedroom suites ($89-$129), some with whirlpools. 2 stories (no elevator), interior/exterior corridors. **Parking:** on-site. **Terms:** 7 day cancellation notice, pets (in designated units). **Amenities:** video games (fee), voice mail, irons, hair dryers. **Pool(s):** heated indoor. **Leisure Activities:** saunas, whirlpool, miniature golf, limited exercise equipment. **Guest Services:** valet and coin laundry. **Business Services:** conference facilities, fax (fee). **Cards:** AX, CB, DC, DS, JC, MC, VI.

SOME UNITS

ASK [icons] / X /

HOWARD JOHNSON EXPRESS INN

AAA SAVE

▽▽▽▽

Motel

Phone: (432)683-1111

All Year [ECP]
1P: $60-$65
2P: $60-$65
XP: $6
F19

Location: I-20, exit 136. 902 I-20 W 79701. Fax: 432/683-1122. **Facility:** 67 one-bedroom standard units, some with whirlpools. 2 stories, interior corridors. *Bath:* combo or shower only. **Parking:** on-site. **Terms:** cancellation fee imposed. **Amenities:** irons, hair dryers. **Pool(s):** heated indoor. **Leisure Activities:** sauna, whirlpool, limited exercise equipment. **Guest Services:** valet and coin laundry. **Business Services:** meeting rooms, fax (fee). **Cards:** AX, CB, DC, DS, JC, MC, VI. **Special Amenities:** free continental breakfast and free local telephone calls. *(See ad below)*

SOME UNITS

[icons] / X /

LA QUINTA INN-MIDLAND

Phone: (432)697-9900

AAA SAVE

Motel

All Year   1P: $59-$79   2P: $65-$85
Location: I-20, exit 131, 0.9 mi n on SR 250 Loop to exit 1A; 1.2 mi e on I-20 business route. 4130 W Wall St 79703-7718. Fax: 432/689-0617. **Facility:** 146 units. 144 one-bedroom standard units. 2 one-bedroom suites. 2 stories, exterior corridors. **Parking:** on-site. **Terms:** [ECP] meal plan available, small pets only. **Amenities:** video games (fee), voice mail, irons, hair dryers. **Pool(s):** outdoor. **Guest Services:** valet and coin laundry. **Business Services:** fax (fee). **Cards:** AX, CB, DC, DS, JC, MC, VI. **Special Amenities:** free continental breakfast and free local telephone calls.

SOME UNITS

MIDLAND HILTON & TOWERS

Phone: (432)683-6131

AAA SAVE

Large-scale Hotel

All Year   1P: $79-$159   2P: $89-$169   XP: $10   F18
Location: Jct Wall and Loraine sts; downtown. 117 W Wall St 79701. Fax: 432/683-0958. **Facility:** 249 one-bedroom standard units, some with whirlpools. 11 stories, interior corridors. *Bath:* combo or shower only. **Parking:** on-site. **Terms:** cancellation fee imposed, small pets only ($25 fee, in kennel). **Amenities:** high-speed Internet, voice mail, irons, hair dryers. **Dining:** 2 restaurants, 6:30 am-2 & 5-10 pm, cocktails. **Pool(s):** outdoor. **Leisure Activities:** whirlpools, exercise room. **Guest Services:** gift shop, valet laundry, area transportation-within 5 mi. **Business Services:** conference facilities, fax (fee). **Cards:** AX, CB, DC, DS, JC, MC, VI. **Special Amenities:** free newspaper. *(See ad below)*

SOME UNITS

FEE

PLAZA INN

Phone: (432)686-8733

Motel

All Year [CP]   1P: $70-$78   2P: $78-$86   XP: $8   F16
Location: I-20, exit 144, 6.1 mi on SR 349 to SR 349 (Big Spring St), just s on SR 349. 4108 N Big Spring St 79705. Fax: 432/685-0530. **Facility:** 114 one-bedroom standard units. 3 stories, exterior corridors. **Parking:** on-site. **Terms:** cancellation fee imposed, small pets only ($10 fee, in kennel). **Amenities:** voice mail. *Some:* irons, hair dryers. **Pool(s):** outdoor. **Leisure Activities:** whirlpool. **Guest Services:** valet laundry. **Business Services:** meeting rooms, fax (fee). **Cards:** AX, CB, DC, DS, JC, MC, VI.

SOME UNITS

ASK

RAMADA INN MIDLAND AIRPORT

Phone: (432)561-8000

Motel

All Year   1P: $63-$70   2P: $71-$79   XP: $8   F18
Location: I-20, exit 126, 0.8 mi n on I-20 business route to W CR 117, 0.4 mi e. 3312 S CR 1276 79711 (PO Box 60017). Fax: 432/561-5243. **Facility:** 97 units. 96 one-bedroom standard units. 1 one-bedroom suite ($89-$125). 2-3 stories, interior corridors. *Bath:* combo or shower only. **Parking:** on-site. **Amenities:** voice mail, irons, hair dryers. **Pool(s):** outdoor. **Leisure Activities:** limited exercise equipment. **Guest Services:** valet and coin laundry, area transportation. **Business Services:** meeting rooms, business center. **Cards:** AX, CB, DC, DS, JC, MC, VI.

SOME UNITS

ASK

Get the Complete Picture. AAA

When making travel plans online at **aaa.com**, look for lodgings and attractions with an online photo listing. The photographs and descriptive text not contained in standard listings allow you to "virtually" experience the property or attraction prior to making your reservations or buying your tickets. Properties with photo listings are easily located in the TourBook search section of AAA online. Simply begin your search by entering your trip criteria such as destination, and then look for the listings featuring the camera icon.

So, the next time you're making travel plans online at aaa.com, be sure to look at the photo listings prior to making your lodging decisions!

SLEEP INN
[SAVE]
Motel

All Year [ECP] 1P: $71 2P: $71 XP: $5 F12
Location: I-20, exit 134 (Midkiff Rd), 1 mi n to Wall St, just w. 3828 W Wall 79703. Fax: 432/689-8508. **Facility:** 42 one-bedroom standard units. 2 stories (no elevator), interior corridors. *Bath:* combo or shower only. **Parking:** on-site. **Terms:** cancellation fee imposed, small pets only ($20 deposit, in kennel). **Amenities:** *Some:* irons, hair dryers. **Pool(s):** outdoor. **Leisure Activities:** whirlpool. **Guest Services:** valet laundry. **Business Services:** fax (fee). **Cards:** AX, CB, DC, DS, MC, VI.

SOME UNITS

------- WHERE TO DINE -------

CATTLE BARON STEAK & SEAFOOD RESTAURANT Lunch: $6-$9 Dinner: $10-$21 Phone: 432/683-2334
American

Location: Loop 250, exit N Big Spring, s to Wadley, then 1 blk w. 418 W Wadley 79705. **Hours:** 11 am-9:30 pm, Fri-10 pm, Sat noon-10 pm, Sun 11 am-9 pm. Closed: 11/27, 12/25. **Reservations:** accepted. **Features:** Ample selections please nearly any diner at the upscale establishment. In addition to a dozen beef entrees and 10 seafood selections, the menu lists chicken, pork and combination dinners. Casual dress; cocktails. **Parking:** on-site. **Cards:** AX, CB, DC, DS, MC, VI.

LUIGI'S ITALIAN RESTAURANT Lunch: $5-$14 Dinner: $5-$14 Phone: 432/683-6363
Italian

Location: Just n of Wall St; downtown. 111 N Big Spring St 79701. **Hours:** 11 am-2:30 & 5-10 pm, Sat from 5 pm. Closed major holidays; also Sun. **Reservations:** accepted. **Features:** Pizza and pasta dishes mingle with sandwiches and other wholesome foods on the tried-and-true menu. A casual, bistro-like ambience, decent portions and friendly servers distinguish the restaurant. Casual dress; cocktails. **Parking:** on-site. **Cards:** AX, CB, DC, DS, MC, VI.

WALL STREET BAR & GRILL Lunch: $4-$18 Dinner: $4-$18 Phone: 432/684-8686
Steak & Seafood

Location: Jct Wall St at Main; downtown. 115 E Wall St 79701. **Hours:** 11 am-2:30 & 5:30-10 pm, Fri-11 pm, Sat 5:30 pm-11 pm, Sun 10:30 am-2:30 & 5:30-10 pm. Closed major holidays. **Reservations:** accepted. **Features:** The nostalgic bistro features late-19th-century decor, including a bar built in 1867. The menu comprises beef, chicken and seafood dishes, all homemade using fresh ingredients and meats cut on the premises. Savory crawfish etouffee is a house favorite. Casual dress; cocktails. **Parking:** on-site. **Cards:** AX, CB, DC, DS, MC, VI.

MIDLOTHIAN —See Dallas p. 310.

MILAM pop. 1,329

------- WHERE TO STAY -------

SUPER 8
Small-scale Hotel

All Year [CP] 1P: $60-$76 2P: $63-$79 XP: $10 F12
Location: 6.5 mi e on E SR 21 from jct SR 21 and 87. Hwy 21 E Pendleton Bridge 75948 (RR 1 Box 1502-8, HEMP-HILL). Fax: 409/625-3753. **Facility:** 44 one-bedroom standard units, some with kitchens. 2 stories, interior corridors. *Bath:* combo or shower only. **Parking:** on-site. **Pool(s):** small heated indoor. **Leisure Activities:** whirlpool, boat ramp. **Guest Services:** coin laundry. **Business Services:** fax (fee). **Cards:** AX, CB, DC, DS, JC, MC, VI.

SOME UNITS

MILFORD —See Dallas p. 310.

MINERAL WELLS pop. 16,946

------- WHERE TO STAY -------

BEST WESTERN CLUBHOUSE INN & SUITES Phone: (940)325-2270
[AAA] [SAVE]
Small-scale Hotel

All Year [ECP] 1P: $75-$99 2P: $75-$99
Location: Jct of US 180 and SR 1195; in East Mineral Wells. 4410 Hwy 180 E 76067. Fax: 940/325-1088. **Facility:** 50 one-bedroom standard units, some with whirlpools. 2 stories, interior corridors. *Bath:* combo or shower only. **Parking:** on-site. **Terms:** pets ($15 extra charge). **Amenities:** high-speed Internet, voice mail, irons, hair dryers. **Pool(s):** outdoor. **Leisure Activities:** whirlpool, exercise room. **Guest Services:** coin laundry. **Business Services:** meeting rooms, fax (fee). **Cards:** AX, CB, DC, DS, JC, MC, VI. **Special Amenities:** free continental breakfast and free room upgrade (subject to availability with advanced reservations).

SOME UNITS

MISSION pop. 45,408

------- WHERE TO STAY -------

BEST WESTERN LAS PALMAS Phone: 956/583-9290
[AAA] [SAVE]
Small-scale Hotel

All Year [ECP] 1P: $75-$85 2P: $75-$95 XP: $10 F12
Location: Off US 83, exit Conway Ave. 609 E Expwy 83 78572. Fax: 956/583-9292. **Facility:** 54 one-bedroom standard units, some with whirlpools. 2 stories (no elevator), exterior corridors. **Parking:** on-site. **Terms:** cancellation fee imposed, weekly rates available. **Amenities:** irons, hair dryers. **Pool(s):** outdoor. **Leisure Activities:** whirlpool, exercise room. **Guest Services:** valet and coin laundry. **Business Services:** meeting rooms, business center. **Cards:** AX, DC, DS, MC, VI. **Special Amenities:** free continental breakfast.

SOME UNITS

HOLIDAY INN EXPRESS HOTEL & SUITES
Property failed to provide current rates
Phone: 956/424-7788
▼▼▼
Small-scale Hotel
Location: Off US 83, exit Shary Rd. 901 S Shary Rd 78572. Fax: 956/424-7799. **Facility:** 85 units. 69 one-bedroom standard units. 16 one-bedroom suites. 2 stories, interior corridors. *Bath:* combo or shower only. **Parking:** on-site. **Amenities:** video games, voice mail, irons, hair dryers. **Pool(s):** outdoor. **Leisure Activities:** whirlpool, exercise room. **Guest Services:** coin laundry. **Business Services:** meeting rooms, business center.

SOME UNITS

MONAHANS pop. 6,821

——— **WHERE TO STAY** ———

BEST WESTERN COLONIAL INN
Phone: (432)943-4345
All Year   1P: $44-$54   2P: $50-$60   XP: $6   F12

Motel
Location: I-20, exit 80, just s. 702 W I-20 79756. Fax: 432/943-3627. **Facility:** 90 one-bedroom standard units. 1 story, interior/exterior corridors. **Parking:** on-site. **Terms:** small pets only. **Amenities:** irons, hair dryers. **Dining:** 6 am-8 pm. **Pool(s):** outdoor. **Guest Services:** coin laundry. **Business Services:** meeting rooms, fax (fee). **Cards:** AX, CB, DC, DS, MC, VI. *(See color ad below)*

SOME UNITS
FEE

MONTGOMERY —*See Houston p. 440.*

MOUNT PLEASANT pop. 13,935

——— **WHERE TO STAY** ———

BEST WESTERN MT. PLEASANT INN
Phone: (903)572-5051
All Year   1P: $65-$70   2P: $69-$74   XP: $6   F16

Small-scale Hotel
Location: I-30 and Business Rt US 271, exit 162. 102 Burton St 75455. Fax: 903/577-0401. **Facility:** 56 one-bedroom standard units, some with whirlpools. 2 stories, exterior corridors. *Bath:* combo or shower only. **Parking:** on-site. **Terms:** [ECP] meal plan available, pets ($10 extra charge, small dogs only). **Amenities:** irons, hair dryers. *Some:* dual phone lines. **Pool(s):** outdoor. **Leisure Activities:** exercise room. **Guest Services:** valet and coin laundry, airport transportation-Mount Pleasant Airport. **Business Services:** meeting rooms, fax (fee). **Cards:** AX, CB, DC, DS, MC, VI. **Special Amenities:** free continental breakfast and free newspaper.

SOME UNITS

COMFORT INN
Phone: (903)577-7553
5/1-8/31 [ECP]   1P: $65-$85   2P: $67-$90   XP: $5   F18
9/1-1/31 [ECP]   1P: $57-$75   2P: $67-$90   XP: $5   F18
2/1-4/30 [ECP]   1P: $57-$75   2P: $65-$80   XP: $5   F18

Small-scale Hotel
Location: I-30, exit 160. 2515 W Ferguson Rd 75455. Fax: 903/577-0546. **Facility:** 59 one-bedroom standard units, some with whirlpools. 2 stories, exterior corridors. *Bath:* combo or shower only. **Parking:** on-site. **Amenities:** irons, hair dryers. **Pool(s):** outdoor. **Leisure Activities:** exercise room. **Guest Services:** valet laundry. **Business Services:** fax (fee). **Cards:** AX, DC, DS, MC, VI. **Special Amenities:** free continental breakfast and free local telephone calls.

SOME UNITS

RAMADA INN-MT. PLEASANT
Phone: (903)572-6611
All Year   1P: $60   2P: $60   XP: $10   F16

Small-scale Hotel
Location: I-30, exit 160. 2502 W Ferguson Rd 75455. Fax: 903/572-6640. **Facility:** 103 units. 95 one-bedroom standard units. 8 one-bedroom suites ($103). 2 stories, exterior corridors. **Parking:** on-site. **Terms:** small pets only ($10 fee). **Amenities:** voice mail, irons, hair dryers. **Pool(s):** outdoor. **Leisure Activities:** fishing. **Guest Services:** valet and coin laundry. **Business Services:** fax (fee). **Cards:** AX, CB, DC, DS, MC, VI.

SOME UNITS

SUPER 8
(AAA) (SAVE)
Motel

All Year   1P: $45-$55   2P: $55-$59   XP: $5   F14
Location: I-30, exit 162 eastbound; exit 162A westbound. 204 Lakewood Dr 75455. Fax: 903/572-1485. **Facility:** 65 one-bedroom standard units. 2 stories, exterior corridors. **Parking:** on-site. **Terms:** [CP] meal plan available, pets ($5 extra charge). **Amenities:** *Some:* irons, hair dryers. **Pool(s):** outdoor. **Guest Services:** coin laundry. **Business Services:** fax (fee). **Cards:** AX, CB, DC, DS, MC, VI. **Special Amenities:** free continental breakfast and free local telephone calls.
Phone: 903/572-9808

SOME UNITS

MOUNT VERNON pop. 2,286

—— WHERE TO STAY ——

SUPER 8 MOTEL OF MOUNT VERNON
(AAA) (SAVE)
Small-scale Hotel

All Year [CP]   1P: $40-$45   2P: $45-$49   XP: $5   F12
Location: I-30, exit 146 (SR 37). 401 W I-30 75457. Fax: 903/588-2844. **Facility:** 43 one-bedroom standard units. 2 stories, exterior corridors. *Bath:* combo or shower only. **Parking:** on-site. **Terms:** small pets only ($5 extra charge). **Amenities:** hair dryers. *Some:* irons. **Business Services:** fax (fee). **Cards:** AX, CB, DS, MC, VI. **Special Amenities:** free continental breakfast and free local telephone calls.
Phone: (903)588-2882

SOME UNITS

MUENSTER pop. 1,556

—— WHERE TO DINE ——

THE CENTER RESTAURANT & TAVERN   **Lunch:** $8-$13   **Dinner:** $8-$13   Phone: 940/759-2910
German

Location: E on US 82; between Mesquite and Sycamore sts. 603 E Hwy 82 76252. **Hours:** 10:30 am-9 pm, Fri-10 pm, Sat 8 am-10 pm, Sun 8 am-9 pm. Closed: 11/27, 12/25; also Mon. **Features:** You're craving German sausages, your spouse is in the mood for Mexican, and the kids are chanting for pizza. The solution? You'll find it here with a menu that, while focusing on German cuisine, also features Mexican dishes as well as homemade pizza. Casual dress; cocktails. **Parking:** on-site. **Cards:** AX, DC, DS, MC, VI.

NACOGDOCHES pop. 29,914

—— WHERE TO STAY ——

BEST WESTERN INN OF NACOGDOCHES
(AAA) (SAVE)
Motel

All Year   1P: $55-$65   2P: $55-$95   XP: $5   F17
Location: US 59, just s of s jct Loop 224 and US 59 business route. 3428 South St 75964. Fax: 936/569-9752. **Facility:** 60 one-bedroom standard units, some with whirlpools. 2 stories, exterior corridors. *Bath:* combo or shower only. **Parking:** on-site. **Terms:** [ECP] meal plan available. **Amenities:** irons, hair dryers. **Pool(s):** outdoor. **Guest Services:** coin laundry. **Business Services:** fax (fee). **Cards:** AX, CB, DC, DS, MC, VI. **Special Amenities:** free continental breakfast and free newspaper.
Phone: (936)560-4900

SOME UNITS

BEST WESTERN NORTHPARK INN
(AAA) (SAVE)
Motel

All Year [ECP]   1P: $49-$69   2P: $49-$69   XP: $5   F12
Location: Jct of US 59 N and Loop 224, exit Westward Dr. 4809 NW Stallings Dr 75964. Fax: 936/560-1906. **Facility:** 71 one-bedroom standard units. 2 stories, exterior corridors. **Parking:** on-site. **Amenities:** irons, hair dryers. **Pool(s):** outdoor. **Guest Services:** coin laundry. **Business Services:** fax (fee). **Cards:** AX, CB, DC, DS, JC, MC, VI. **Special Amenities:** free continental breakfast.
Phone: (936)560-1906

SOME UNITS

COMFORT INN
(SAVE)
Small-scale Hotel

All Year [CP]   1P: $49-$79   2P: $49-$79   XP: $5   F
Location: US 59, just s of jct S Loop 224 and US 59 business route. 3400 South St 75964. Fax: 936/569-0332. **Facility:** 126 units. 122 one-bedroom standard units, some with whirlpools. 4 one-bedroom suites ($89-$159), some with whirlpools. 2 stories, interior corridors. *Bath:* combo or shower only. **Parking:** on-site. **Terms:** pets ($10 fee). **Amenities:** dual phone lines, voice mail, irons, hair dryers. **Pool(s):** heated indoor/outdoor. **Leisure Activities:** whirlpool, exercise room, sports court. **Guest Services:** coin laundry. **Business Services:** meeting rooms, fax (fee). **Cards:** AX, CB, DC, DS, MC, VI.
Phone: 936/569-8100

SOME UNITS

FEE

DAYS INN & SUITES
(AAA) (SAVE)
Motel

All Year [CP]   1P: $64-$119   2P: $69-$139   XP: $5   F12
Location: On US 59 business route (North St), 0.6 mi n of Stephen F Austin University's main entrance (Griffith Blvd). 2724 North St 75961. Fax: 936/560-6640. **Facility:** 39 one-bedroom standard units, some with whirlpools. 2 stories, exterior corridors. **Parking:** on-site. **Terms:** small pets only ($10 fee, in smoking units). **Amenities:** irons, hair dryers. **Pool(s):** outdoor. **Business Services:** fax (fee). **Cards:** AX, DC, DS, JC, MC, VI. **Special Amenities:** free continental breakfast and free newspaper.
Phone: (936)715-0005

SOME UNITS

LA QUINTA INN-NACOGDOCHES
AAA SAVE
VVVV
Motel
Phone: (936)560-5453
All Year 1P: $59-$69 2P: $69-$79 XP: $10 F18
Location: US 59 at S jct Loop 224 and US 59 business route. 3215 South St 75961-7212. Fax: 936/560-4372.
Facility: 106 units. 105 one-bedroom standard units. 1 one-bedroom suite. 2 stories, exterior corridors.
Parking: on-site. Terms: [ECP] meal plan available, small pets only. Amenities: video games (fee), voice
mail, irons, hair dryers. Pool(s): outdoor. Guest Services: valet laundry. Business Services: meeting
rooms, fax (fee). Cards: AX, CB, DC, DS, JC, MC, VI. Special Amenities: free continental breakfast and
free local telephone calls.
SOME UNITS

NASSAU BAY —See Houston p. 440.

NEDERLAND pop. 17,422

——— WHERE TO STAY ———

BEST WESTERN-AIRPORT INN
SAVE
VVVV
Motel
Phone: (409)727-1631
All Year [ECP] 1P: $46-$53 2P: $54-$62 XP: $6 F18
Location: US 69, 96 and 287, exit Nederland Ave. 200 Memorial Hwy 69 77627. Fax: 409/727-1546. Facility: 115
one-bedroom standard units. 2 stories, exterior corridors. Parking: on-site. Terms: [CP] meal plan available,
small pets only ($20 deposit). Amenities: irons, hair dryers. Pool(s): outdoor, wading. Guest Services: valet
laundry. Business Services: meeting rooms, fax (fee). Cards: AX, CB, DC, DS, MC, VI.
SOME UNITS

NEW BOSTON pop. 4,808

——— WHERE TO STAY ———

BEST WESTERN INN OF NEW BOSTON
AAA SAVE
VVVV
Motel
Phone: (903)628-6999
All Year 1P: $69-$89 2P: $74-$94 XP: $5 F12
Location: I-30 at jct SR 8, exit 201. 1024 N Center 75570. Fax: 903/628-6999. Facility: 49 one-bedroom standard
units, some with whirlpools. 2 stories, exterior corridors. Parking: on-site. Terms: 3 day cancellation notice,
[CP] meal plan available, small pets only ($20 deposit). Amenities: irons, hair dryers. Pool(s): outdoor.
Guest Services: coin laundry. Business Services: meeting rooms, fax (fee). Cards: AX, DC, DS, MC, VI.
Special Amenities: free continental breakfast.
SOME UNITS

NEW BRAUNFELS —See San Antonio p. 545.

NOCONA pop. 3,198

——— WHERE TO STAY ———

NOCONA HILLS MOTEL AND RESORT
VV
Motel
Phone: 940/825-3161
All Year 1P: $34-$40 2P: $40-$46 XP: $5 F5
Location: 6 mi w of St Jo, TX on US 82 to jct SR 1815, 4 mi n on SR 1815 to SR 1956; 2 mi w on SR 1956 to SR 3301.
Located in Nocona Hills via security entrance station. 100 E Huron Cir 76255. Fax: 940/825-4568. Facility: 17 one-
bedroom standard units, some with efficiencies (utensils extra charge). 1 story, exterior corridors. Parking:
on-site. Terms: small pets only ($5 extra charge). Leisure Activities: fishing, hiking trails, playground, basketball, horseshoes,
volleyball. Business Services: fax (fee). Cards: AX, DS, JC, MC, VI.
SOME UNITS

NORTH RICHLAND HILLS pop. 55,635 (See map p. 343; index p. 345)

——— WHERE TO STAY ———

COUNTRY INN & SUITES BY CARLSON
VVV
Small-scale Hotel
Phone: (817)268-6879 43
All Year [ECP] 1P: $68-$129 2P: $79-$142 XP: $17 F17
Location: I-820, exit 21 (Holiday Ln), 0.5 mi w on north access road. 5151 Thaxton Pkwy 76180. Fax: 817/428-9061.
Facility: 44 units. 38 one-bedroom standard units, some with whirlpools. 6 one-bedroom suites ($75-$150).
2 stories, interior corridors. Parking: on-site. Terms: weekly rates available, package plans.
Amenities: voice mail, irons, hair dryers. Pool(s): small outdoor. Guest Services: valet and coin laundry. Business Services:
fax (fee). Cards: AX, CB, DC, DS, MC, VI. (See color ad p 260)
SOME UNITS
FEE

MOTEL 6 - 1336
V
Small-scale Hotel
Phone: 817/485-3000 46
5/22-1/31 1P: $35-$45 2P: $41-$51 XP: $3 F1
2/1-5/21 1P: $33-$43 2P: $39-$49 XP: $3 F17
Location: I-820, exit 22A (Grapevine Rd), 0.5 mi e. 7804 Bedford Euless Rd N 76180. Fax: 817/485-8936.
Facility: 82 one-bedroom standard units. 2 stories, exterior corridors. Bath: combo or shower only. Parking:
on-site. Pool(s): outdoor. Business Services: fax (fee). Cards: AX, CB, DC, DS, MC, VI.
SOME UNITS

(See map p. 343)

RAMADA LIMITED   Phone: (817)485-2750   **45**

(AAA) [SAVE]   All Year [CP]   1P: $40-$60   2P: $40-$60
▼▼▼▼   Location: I-820, exit 22 A (Grapevine Rd), just e. 7920 Bedford-Euless Rd 76180. Fax: 817/656-8977. Facility: 101
Small-scale Hotel   units. 100 one-bedroom standard units. 1 one-bedroom suite ($70-$100). 2 stories, exterior corridors.
Parking: on-site. Terms: 30 day cancellation notice, weekly rates available, small pets only ($10 extra
free local telephone calls.   charge). Amenities: video games (fee), voice mail, irons, hair dryers. Pool(s): outdoor. Business Services:
meeting rooms, fax (fee). Cards: AX, DC, DS, MC, VI. Special Amenities: free continental breakfast and

SOME UNITS
[SD] [⌂] [⑪] [⟲] [⤲] [⚒] [DATA PORT] [▣] ··· [✕] [☎] [⌷] /

STUDIO 6 #6034   Phone: 817/788-6000   **44**
▼▼   All Year   1P: $39-$49   2P: $43-$53   XP: $17   F17
Location: I-820, exit 21 (Holiday Ln), 0.3 mi e on south access road. 7450 NE Loop 820 76180. Fax: 817/788-6100.
Small-scale Hotel   Facility: 133 one-bedroom standard units with efficiencies. 2 stories, exterior corridors. Bath: combo or
shower only. Parking: on-site. Terms: weekly rates available, pets ($10 extra charge). Amenities: voice
mail, irons. Guest Services: valet and coin laundry. Business Services: fax (fee). Cards: AX, CB, DC, DS, MC, VI.

SOME UNITS
[SD] [⌖] [⟲] [⚒] [DATA PORT] [☎] [⌷] [⌷] /[✕]/

OAK RIDGE NORTH — *See Houston p. 441.*

ODEM pop. 2,499

─────── **WHERE TO STAY** ───────

DAYS INN-ODEM   Phone: (361)368-2166
(AAA) [SAVE]   All Year   1P: $50-$110   2P: $60-$110   XP: $5   F12
▼▼ ▼▼   Location: US 77, 1 mi s of jct 631. 1505 Voss Ave (US 77) 78370 (PO Box 1296). Fax: 361/368-2678. Facility: 24
one-bedroom standard units. 1 story, exterior corridors. Parking: on-site. Terms: 3 day cancellation notice,
Motel   weekly rates available, small pets only. Amenities: hair dryers. Pool(s): outdoor. Business Services: fax
(fee). Cards: AX, CB, DC, DS, MC, VI. Special Amenities: free continental breakfast and free local telephone calls.

SOME UNITS
[SD] [⌂] [⑪] [⤲] [⚒] [☎] [⌷] /[✕]/

ODESSA pop. 90,943

─────── **WHERE TO STAY** ───────

BEST WESTERN GARDEN OASIS   Phone: (432)337-3006
[SAVE]   All Year [ECP]   1P: $63-$73   2P: $68-$78   XP: $6   F12
Location: Jct I-20 and US 385, exit 116. 110 W I-20 79761-6838. Fax: 432/332-1956. Facility: 118 units. 116 one-
▼▼ ▼▼   bedroom standard units. 2 one-bedroom suites ($125-$145). 2 stories (no elevator), interior/exterior corridors.
Motel   Parking: on-site. Terms: [MAP] meal plan available, pets (in designated units). Amenities: irons, hair dryers.
Pool(s): heated indoor. Leisure Activities: sauna, whirlpool. Guest Services: valet and coin laundry. Busi-
ness Services: meeting rooms, fax (fee). Cards: AX, CB, DC, DS, JC, MC, VI.

SOME UNITS
[SD] [✦] [⌂] [⑪] [⟲] [⤲] [⚒+] [⚒] [DATA PORT] [▣] /[✕] [VCR] [☎] /
FEE

DAYS INN   Phone: (432)335-8000
[SAVE]   All Year [CP]   1P: $43   2P: $49   XP: $4   F17
Location: I-20, exit 121, 0.7 mi n on Loop 338, then 0.5 mi w. 3075 E Business Loop 20 79761. Fax: 432/335-9562.
▼▼ ▼▼   Facility: 96 one-bedroom standard units. 3 stories, interior corridors. Parking: on-site. Terms: 7 day cancel-
lation notice. Amenities: irons, hair dryers. Pool(s): outdoor. Guest Services: valet laundry. Business
Small-scale Hotel   Services: meeting rooms, fax (fee). Cards: AX, CB, DC, DS, MC, VI.

SOME UNITS
[SD] [⌂] [⊻] [⤲] [⚒] /[✕] [☎] [⌷] /

HOLIDAY INN EXPRESS HOTEL & SUITES   Phone: (432)333-3931
▼▼ ▼▼   All Year [ECP]   1P: $70-$80   2P: $70-$80   XP: $5   F18
Location: I-20, exit 121, 0.7 mi n on Loop 338, then 0.5 mi w. 3001 E Business I-20 79761. Fax: 432/333-9961.
Motel   Facility: 186 one-bedroom standard units. 2 stories (no elevator), interior/exterior corridors. Parking: on-site.
Terms: small pets only. Amenities: video games (fee), voice mail, irons, hair dryers. Pool(s): heated indoor.
Leisure Activities: sauna, whirlpool, steamroom, miniature golf. Guest Services: valet and coin laundry. Business Services:
meeting rooms, fax (fee). Cards: AX, CB, DC, DS, JC, MC, VI. *(See color ad p 475)*

SOME UNITS
[ASK] [SD] [✦] [⌂] [⑪] [⤲] [⚒+] [✕] [▣] /[✕] [DATA PORT] [☎] [⌷] /

HOLIDAY INN HOTEL & SUITES   Phone: (432)362-2311
▼▼▼▼   All Year   1P: $69   2P: $69
Location: I-20, exit 121, 0.8 mi n on Loop 338, then 1 mi e. 6201 E Business I-20 79762. Fax: 432/362-9810.
Motel   Facility: 245 units. 210 one-bedroom standard units. 35 one-bedroom suites ($85-$110), some with whirl-
pools. 2-3 stories, interior/exterior corridors. Parking: on-site. Terms: small pets only. Amenities: video
games (fee), voice mail, irons, hair dryers. Pool(s): heated indoor/outdoor. Leisure Activities: sauna, whirlpool, miniature golf.
limited exercise equipment. Guest Services: valet and coin laundry. Business Services: meeting rooms, business center.
Cards: AX, CB, DC, DS, MC, VI. *(See color ad p 475)*

SOME UNITS
[ASK] [SD] [✦] [⌂] [⑪] [⊻] [⟲] [⤲] [✕] [⚒] [DATA PORT] [▣] /[✕] [☎] [⌷] /

LA QUINTA INN-ODESSA
Phone: (432)333-2820

AAA SAVE

◆◆◆◆◆

Motel

All Year 1P: $64-$84 2P: $70-$90
Location: I-20, exit 121, 0.8 mi n on Loop 338, then just w. 5001 E Business Loop I-20 79761-3510.
Fax: 432/333-4208. **Facility:** 122 units. 120 one-bedroom standard units. 2 one-bedroom suites. 2 stories (no elevator), exterior corridors. **Parking:** on-site. **Terms:** [ECP] meal plan available, small pets only.
Amenities: video games, voice mail, irons, hair dryers. **Pool(s):** outdoor. **Guest Services:** valet and coin laundry. **Business Services:** fax (fee). **Cards:** AX, CB, DC, DS, JC, MC, VI. **Special Amenities:** free continental breakfast and free local telephone calls.

SOME UNITS

🛏 📶 ⊷ 🐕 DATA/PORT 🖥 / ⊠ 🔌 🖨 /

MCM ELEGANTE HOTEL & CONFERENCE CENTER
Phone: (432)368-5885

AAA SAVE

◆◆◆◆◆

Large-scale Hotel

All Year 1P: $79 2P: $79
Location: I-20, exit 121, 1.3 mi n on Loop 338. 5200 E University Blvd 79762. Fax: 432/362-8958. **Facility:** 192 units. 188 one-bedroom standard units. 4 one-bedroom suites ($119-$250), some with whirlpools. 8 stories, interior corridors. *Bath:* combo or shower only. **Parking:** on-site. **Terms:** 15% service charge. **Dining:** 6:30 am-2 & 5-10 pm, cocktails. **Pool(s):** outdoor. **Leisure Activities:** whirlpool, exercise room. **Guest Services:** gift shop, valet laundry, area transportation-within 5 mi. **Business Services:** conference facilities, fax (fee).
Cards: AX, CB, DC, DS, MC, VI. **Special Amenities:** free newspaper.

SOME UNITS

🅂🄳 ✈ 🍽 🏋 📺 📶 ⊷ 🐕 DATA/PORT / ⊠ 🔌 🖨 /

VILLA WEST INN
Phone: (432)335-5055

AAA SAVE

◆◆◆

Motel

All Year 1P: $29-$33 2P: $35-$40 XP: $4 F12
Location: I-20, exit 116, just w on frontage road. 300 W Pool Rd 79763 (PO Box 2265, 79760). Fax: 432/335-9437.
Facility: 40 one-bedroom standard units. 2 stories (no elevator), exterior corridors. **Parking:** on-site.
Terms: [CP] meal plan available, small pets only. **Business Services:** fax (fee). **Cards:** AX, CB, DC, DS, JC, MC, VI. **Special Amenities:** free continental breakfast and free local telephone calls.

SOME UNITS

🅂🄳 🛏 📶 🐕 / ⊠ 🔌 🖨 /

———— **WHERE TO DINE** ————

THE BARN DOOR   **Lunch:** $6-$22   **Dinner:** $6-$22   **Phone:** 432/337-4142
  (AAA)   **Location:** I-20, exit 116, 4 mi n on US 385 (Andrews Hwy). 2140 N Andrews Hwy 79761. **Hours:** 11 am-9:30 pm,
              Fri-10:30 pm, Sat 4 pm-10 pm, Sun 11 am-3 pm. Closed major holidays. **Reservations:** accepted.
  ▼▼ ▼▼   **Features:** Built in 1963, the newly remodeled building, which resembles a rustic barn, adjoins a historic
              train depot that serves as a bar. Complimentary homemade soup and bread are served with lunch in the
  American   saloon-style dining room. Casual dress; cocktails. **Parking:** on-site. **Cards:** AX, MC, VI.   🔥M 🍸 ✕

ZUCCHI'S RISTORANTE ITALIANO   **Lunch:** $6-$12   **Dinner:** $10-$16   **Phone:** 432/550-7443
  ▼▼▼▼   **Location:** I-20, exit 121, n to business I-20, 0.4 mi w to JBS Pkwy, then 0.8 mi n; in Old Town Shopping Center. 1541
              JBS Pkwy 79761. **Hours:** 11:30 am-2 & 5:15-9:30 pm, Fri & Sat-10 pm. Closed major holidays.
  Northern   **Reservations:** accepted. **Features:** Diners can taste the treats of Northern Italy from a nice selection of
  Italian   antipasto, gourmet pizzas, pasta dishes and entrees featuring chicken, salmon, filet of beef and veal.
              Casual dress; cocktails. **Parking:** on-site. **Cards:** AX, DC, DS, MC, VI.   🔥M 🍸 ✕

OZONA pop. 3,436

———— **WHERE TO STAY** ————

BEST VALUE INN   **Phone:** 325/392-2631
  (AAA) [SAVE]   All Year   1P: $39-$49   2P: $45-$59
                 Location: I-10, exit 365 westbound to SR 163, 1 mi n; exit 363 eastbound to Loop 466, 2 mi s. Located next to the shop-
  ▼▼ ▼▼   ping center. 820 11th St 76943 (PO Box 70). Fax: 325/392-2633. **Facility:** 24 one-bedroom standard units. 1
                 story, exterior corridors. *Bath:* shower only. **Parking:** on-site. **Terms:** pets ($10 extra charge, in smoking
  Motel   units). **Amenities:** irons. **Guest Services:** coin laundry. **Business Services:** fax (fee). **Special Amenities:**
                 free local telephone calls.
                                                                              SOME UNITS
                                                         🆘 🐾 🍽 📷 DATA PORT / ✕ /

BEST WESTERN OZONA INN   **Phone:** (325)392-3791
  (AAA) [SAVE]   11/1-1/31 [ECP]   1P: $82-$92   2P: $92-$110   XP: $10   F16
                 2/1-10/31 [ECP]   1P: $75-$80   2P: $82-$100   XP: $10   F16
  ▼▼▼▼   **Location:** I-10, exit 365. 1307 Ave A 76943 (PO Box 28). Fax: 325/392-5277. **Facility:** 50 one-bedroom standard
                 units. 2 stories (no elevator), interior/exterior corridors. **Parking:** on-site. **Terms:** 7 day cancellation notice-fee
  Motel   imposed. **Amenities:** irons, hair dryers. **Pool(s):** outdoor. **Guest Services:** coin laundry. **Business Serv-
                 ices:** meeting rooms, fax (fee). **Cards:** AX, CB, DC, DS, MC, VI. **Special Amenities: free continental
breakfast and free newspaper.** *(See color ad below)*
                                                                              SOME UNITS
                                                 🆘 🍽 🚗 📷 DATA PORT 📺 / ✕ 🔒 📠 /

TRAVELODGE   **Phone:** 325/392-2656
  (AAA) [SAVE]   All Year   1P: $40-$50   2P: $50-$60   XP: $5   F
                 Location: I-10 W, exit 368, 2 mi w; I-10 E, exit 365 to Loop 466, 1 mi e. Located in a quiet area. 8 11th St 76943.
  ▼▼▼   Fax: 325/392-4152. **Facility:** 40 one-bedroom standard units. 1 story, exterior corridors. *Bath:* combo or
                 shower only. **Parking:** on-site. **Terms:** [CP] meal plan available, pets ($10 deposit). **Pool(s):** outdoor.
  Motel   **Leisure Activities:** playground. **Cards:** AX, DS, MC, VI. **Special Amenities: free continental breakfast
                 and free local telephone calls.**
                                                                              SOME UNITS
                                                 🆘 🐾 🚗 📷 DATA PORT 📺 / ✕ 🔒 📠 /

PALESTINE pop. 17,598

------ **WHERE TO STAY** ------

BEST WESTERN PALESTINE INN

Phone: (903)723-4655

(AAA) (SAVE)

Motel

All Year [BP]   1P: $52-$57   2P: $55-$60   XP: $5   F12
Location: 0.7 mi sw jct US 287/SR 19 on US 79. 1601 W Palestine Ave 75801. Fax: 903/723-2519. **Facility:** 66 one-bedroom standard units. 2 stories, exterior corridors. *Bath:* combo or shower only. **Parking:** on-site. **Terms:** weekly rates available, package plans. **Amenities:** irons, hair dryers. **Dining:** 6 am-9 pm. **Pool(s):** outdoor. **Guest Services:** valet laundry, airport transportation-Anderson County Airport. **Business Services:** meeting rooms, fax (fee). **Cards:** AX, CB, DC, DS, MC, VI.

SOME UNITS

HOLIDAY INN EXPRESS

Phone: (903)723-4884

(AAA) (SAVE)

Small-scale Hotel

All Year   1P: $70-$80   2P: $80-$85   XP: $5   F17
Location: 0.3 mi s of jct US 79 and Loop 256 on US 79. 1030 E Palestine Ave 75801. Fax: 903/723-4885. **Facility:** 62 one-bedroom standard units, some with whirlpools. 3 stories, interior corridors. *Bath:* combo or shower only. **Parking:** on-site. **Terms:** 3 day cancellation notice. **Amenities:** dual phone lines, voice mail, irons, hair dryers. **Pool(s):** outdoor. **Leisure Activities:** whirlpool, picnic area, exercise room. **Guest Services:** valet and coin laundry. **Business Services:** meeting rooms, business center. **Cards:** AX, DC, DS, MC, VI. **Special Amenities:** free continental breakfast and free newspaper.

SOME UNITS

PARIS pop. 25,898

------ **WHERE TO STAY** ------

BEST WESTERN INN OF PARIS

Phone: (903)785-5566

(AAA) (SAVE)

Small-scale Hotel

All Year   1P: $49-$53   2P: $54-$65   XP: $5   F16
Location: Jct US 82 and E Loop 286, just n. Located in a commercial area. 3755 NE Loop 286 75460. Fax: 903/783-0418. **Facility:** 80 one-bedroom standard units, some with kitchens and/or whirlpools. 2 stories, exterior corridors. *Bath:* combo or shower only. **Parking:** on-site. **Terms:** [ECP] meal plan available, small pets only. **Amenities:** voice mail, irons, hair dryers. *Some:* high-speed Internet (fee). **Pool(s):** outdoor. **Guest Services:** valet and coin laundry. **Business Services:** meeting rooms, fax (fee). **Cards:** AX, CB, DC, DS, MC, VI. **Special Amenities:** early check-in/late check-out and free continental breakfast.

SOME UNITS
FEE FEE

COMFORT INN

Phone: (903)784-7481

(AAA) (SAVE)

Small-scale Hotel

All Year   1P: $65-$70   2P: $69-$74   XP: $5   F18
Location: 0.5 mi n of jct US 82 and Loop E 286. 3505 NE Loop 286 75460. Fax: 903/784-0231. **Facility:** 62 one-bedroom standard units. 2 stories, exterior corridors. **Parking:** on-site. **Amenities:** irons, hair dryers. **Pool(s):** outdoor. **Business Services:** fax (fee). **Cards:** AX, CB, DC, DS, JC, MC, VI.

SOME UNITS

HAMPTON INN OF PARIS

Phone: (903)784-6536

(AAA) (SAVE)

Small-scale Hotel

All Year [ECP]   1P: $80-$105   2P: $89-$110
Location: Just n of jct US 82 and E Loop 286. 3563 NE Loop 286 75460. Fax: 903/784-6546. **Facility:** 67 one-bedroom standard units, some with whirlpools. 3 stories, interior corridors. *Bath:* combo or shower only. **Parking:** on-site. **Terms:** 14 day cancellation notice. **Amenities:** high-speed Internet (fee), dual phone lines, voice mail, irons, hair dryers. **Pool(s):** outdoor. **Leisure Activities:** whirlpool, limited exercise equipment. **Guest Services:** valet laundry. **Business Services:** meeting rooms, business center. **Cards:** AX, CB, DC, DS, MC, VI. **Special Amenities:** free continental breakfast and free newspaper.

SOME UNITS

HOLIDAY INN

Phone: (903)785-5545

(AAA) (SAVE)

Small-scale Hotel

All Year [CP]   1P: $55-$80   XP: $6   F
Location: E Loop 286, 0.3 mi n of jct US 82. 3560 NE Loop 286 75460. Fax: 903/785-9510. **Facility:** 114 units. 104 one-bedroom standard units. 10 one-bedroom suites ($119) with efficiencies. 2 stories, exterior corridors. *Bath:* combo or shower only. **Parking:** on-site. **Amenities:** video games (fee), dual phone lines, voice mail, safes, irons, hair dryers. **Dining:** 24 hours, cocktails. **Pool(s):** outdoor. **Leisure Activities:** exercise room. **Guest Services:** valet and coin laundry, airport transportation-Paris Airport. **Business Services:** meeting rooms, business center. **Cards:** AX, DC, DS, MC, VI. **Special Amenities:** free local telephone calls and free newspaper.

SOME UNITS
FEE FEE

------ **WHERE TO DINE** ------

GOLDEN CHINA

Chinese

Lunch: $8   **Dinner:** $10   **Phone:** 903-739-8860
Location: Just e of jct Loop 286 and US 82. 3755 Lamar Ave 75462. **Hours:** 11 am-9 pm, Fri & Sat-9:30 pm. Closed: 11/27. **Features:** This family owned and operated Chinese restaurant is a gem in this small Texas town. Lunch and dinner buffets offer a wide selection of traditional Chinese cuisine. There are also a few American dishes available as well. Casual dress. **Parking:** on-site. **Cards:** AX, DS, MC, VI.

PASADENA —*See Houston p. 441.*

PEARSALL pop. 7,157

------ **WHERE TO STAY** ------

EXECUTIVE INN
Phone: 830/334-3693
(AAA) [SAVE] All Year   1P: $35-$45   2P: $45-$55   XP: $5   F12
Location: 3 mi e of jct I-35 and Business 35, exit 104. 613 N Oak 78061. Fax: 830/334-4188. **Facility:** 19 one-bedroom standard units. 1 story, exterior corridors. *Bath:* combo or shower only. **Parking:** on-site.
Motel **Terms:** pets ($5 extra charge). **Amenities:** irons, hair dryers. **Business Services:** fax (fee). **Cards:** AX, CB, DC, DS, MC, VI. **Special Amenities:** free local telephone calls and preferred room (subject to availability with advanced reservations).

SOME UNITS

PECOS pop. 9,501

------ **WHERE TO STAY** ------

BEST WESTERN SWISS CLOCK INN
Phone: (432)447-2215
(AAA) [SAVE] All Year [BP]   1P: $59-$79   2P: $69-$89   XP: $10   F12
Location: 1 mi w of jct US 285; 1 mi e of jct I-20 and SR 17, exit 40. 133 S Frontage Rd, I-20 W 79772. Fax: 432/447-4463. **Facility:** 104 one-bedroom standard units. 1 story, exterior corridors. *Bath:* combo or shower only. **Parking:** on-site. **Terms:** small pets only. **Amenities:** irons, hair dryers. **Dining:** 6 am-10 & 6-9
Motel pm, Sun-2 pm. **Pool(s):** outdoor. **Guest Services:** complimentary laundry. **Business Services:** meeting rooms, fax (fee). **Cards:** AX, CB, DC, DS, MC, VI. **Special Amenities:** early check-in/late check-out and free continental breakfast.

SOME UNITS

LAURA LODGE
Phone: (432)445-4924
(AAA) [SAVE] All Year   1P: $35-$45   2P: $40-$48   XP: $5   F12
Location: I-20, exit 42 (US 285), 1 mi e to Business 20. 1000 E Business 20 79772. Fax: 432/445-4193. **Facility:** 28 one-bedroom standard units. 2 stories (no elevator), exterior corridors. *Bath:* combo or shower only. **Parking:** on-site. **Terms:** 5 day cancellation notice-fee imposed, package plans, small pets only ($10 fee).
Motel **Amenities:** hair dryers. **Pool(s):** outdoor. **Guest Services:** coin laundry. **Business Services:** fax (fee). **Cards:** AX, CB, DC, DS, JC, MC, VI. **Special Amenities:** free local telephone calls and free room upgrade (subject to availability with advanced reservations).

SOME UNITS

OAK TREE INN
Phone: (432)447-0180
(AAA) [SAVE] 6/30-1/31   1P: $55-$66   2P: $60-$71   XP: $5   F14
2/1-6/29   1P: $50-$61   2P: $55-$66   XP: $5   F14
Location: I-20, exit 42, just w on north access road. 22 N Frontage Rd 79772 (8110 E 32nd St N, Suite 100, WICHITA, KS, 67226). Fax: 432/445-1638. **Facility:** Designated smoking area. 40 one-bedroom standard units. 2 stories
Motel (no elevator), interior corridors. *Bath:* combo or shower only. **Parking:** on-site. **Terms:** small pets only ($10 extra charge). **Leisure Activities:** whirlpool, exercise room. **Guest Services:** valet and coin laundry. **Business Services:** meeting rooms, fax (fee). **Cards:** AX, CB, DC, DS, MC, VI. **Special Amenities:** early check-in/late check-out and free local telephone calls.

SOME UNITS

QUALITY INN
Phone: (432)445-5404
[SAVE] All Year   1P: $56-$81   2P: $61-$86   XP: $5   F12
Location: Jct I-20 and US 285. 4002 S Cedar St 79772. Fax: 432/445-2484. **Facility:** 96 one-bedroom standard units. 2 stories (no elevator), interior corridors. **Parking:** on-site. **Terms:** 7 day cancellation notice, pets ($10
Motel extra charge, in smoking units). **Amenities:** safes (fee), irons, hair dryers. **Pool(s):** outdoor, wading. **Guest Services:** coin laundry. **Business Services:** meeting rooms, fax (fee). **Cards:** AX, CB, DC, DS, JC, MC, VI.

SOME UNITS

PHARR pop. 46,660

------ **WHERE TO STAY** ------

RAMADA LIMITED SUITES
Phone: (956)702-3330
(AAA) [SAVE] All Year [CP]   1P: $70   2P: $75   XP: $7   F18
Location: Jct US 83 Expwy, exit I Rd. 1130 E Expwy 83 78577. Fax: 956/702-7358. **Facility:** 51 units. 47 one-bedroom standard units. 4 one-bedroom suites with whirlpools. 2 stories, exterior corridors. *Bath:* combo or shower only. **Parking:** on-site. **Terms:** small pets only ($10 deposit). **Amenities:** voice mail, irons, hair
Small-scale Hotel dryers. **Pool(s):** outdoor. **Guest Services:** valet and coin laundry. **Business Services:** fax (fee). **Cards:** AX, DC, DS, MC, VI. **Special Amenities:** free continental breakfast and free local telephone calls.

SOME UNITS

PITTSBURG pop. 4,347

------ **WHERE TO DINE** ------

CARSON HOUSE INN & GRILLE   Lunch: $7-$10   Dinner: $11-$25   Phone: 903/856-2468
Location: I-30, exit 160, 12.1 mi s on US 271 to Loop 238, 1 mi on right. 302 Mount Pleasant St 75686. **Hours:** 11 am-2 & 5-9 pm, Fri & Sat-10 pm. Closed major holidays; also Sun. **Reservations:** suggested; major
American holidays. **Features:** The turn-of-the-20th-century restored home affords visitors a delightful dining experience. Lunches feature freshly prepared sandwiches and homemade soups. Casual dress; cocktails.
Parking: on-site. **Cards:** AX, CB, DS, MC, VI.

PLAINVIEW pop. 22,336

———— WHERE TO STAY ————

BEST WESTERN CONESTOGA INN

Phone: (806)293-9454

(AAA) (SAVE)

All Year 1P: $50-$100 XP: $10 F17

Location: I-27, exit 49, just s of US 70 on east access road. 600 N I-27 79072. **Fax:** 806/293-9454. **Facility:** 82 units. 77 one-bedroom standard units. 5 one-bedroom suites ($69-$89). 2 stories (no elevator), exterior corridors. **Parking:** on-site. **Terms:** 4 day cancellation notice, small pets only ($10 fee). **Amenities:** video library (fee), irons, hair dryers. **Dining:** nightclub. **Pool(s):** outdoor. **Guest Services:** valet laundry. **Business Services:** meeting rooms, fax (fee). **Cards:** AX, CB, DC, DS, JC, MC, VI. **Special Amenities:** free continental break-fast and free newspaper.

Motel

SOME UNITS

FEE

RAMADA, LIMITED

Phone: (806)293-4181

All Year [ECP] 1P: $55-$65 2P: $60-$70 F17

Motel

Location: I-27, exit 49. 4005 Olton Rd 79072. **Fax:** 806/293-2565. **Facility:** 95 units. 93 one-bedroom standard units. 2 one-bedroom suites ($79-$99) with efficiencies. 2 stories (no elevator), interior/exterior corridors. **Parking:** on-site. **Terms:** pets ($10 fee). **Amenities:** voice mail, irons, hair dryers. **Pool(s):** outdoor. **Guest Services:** valet and coin laundry. **Business Services:** meeting rooms, fax (fee). **Cards:** AX, CB, DC, DS, MC, VI.

SOME UNITS

———— The following lodging was either not evaluated or did not meet AAA rating requirements but is listed for your information only. ————

COMFORT SUITES

Phone: 806/293-7700

(fyi)

All Year 1P: $79-$109 2P: $79-$109 XP: $5 F16

Small-scale Hotel

Location: I-27, exit 49. 3615 Grandview Dr 79072. **Fax:** 806/293-7708. **Amenities:** coffee-makers, microwaves, refrigerators, pool. **Cards:** AX, DC, DS, JC, MC, VI.

Too new to rate.

PLANO —See Dallas p. 310.

PONDER —See Dallas p. 314.

PORT ARANSAS pop. 3,370

———— WHERE TO STAY ————

BEACHGATE CONDOSUITES & MOTEL

Phone: 361/749-5900

3/9-9/5	1P: $80-$90	2P: $80-$90	XP: $5
9/6-10/31	1P: $75-$80	2P: $75-$80	XP: $5
2/1-3/8 & 11/1-1/31	1P: $70-$75	2P: $70-$75	XP: $5

Condominium

Location: Beach access between markers 8 and 9; street access on Anchor Rd off 11th St. 2000 On the Beach 78373. **Fax:** 361/749-3072. **Facility:** 32 units. 22 one-bedroom standard units, some with kitchens. 9 one- and 1 two-bedroom suites ($110-$325) with kitchens. 1-3 stories (no elevator), interior/exterior corridors. **Parking:** on-site. **Terms:** check-in 4 pm, 2-3 night minimum stay - weekends, 7 day cancellation notice-fee imposed, package plans. **Pool(s):** heated outdoor. **Leisure Activities:** whirlpool, fishing. **Guest Services:** coin laundry. **Business Services:** fax (fee). **Cards:** AX, DS, MC, VI.

SOME UNITS

CORAL CAY CONDOMINIUMS

Phone: (361)749-5111

(AAA) (SAVE)

5/23-9/1	1P: $129-$179	2P: $199-$269	XP: $5 F12
3/7-5/22	1P: $119-$159	2P: $169-$219	XP: $5 F12
9/2-1/31	1P: $89-$129	2P: $139-$179	XP: $5 F12
2/1-3/6	1P: $79-$119	2P: $129-$169	XP: $5 F12

Condominium

Location: Off 11th St. 1419 S 11th St 78373 (PO Box 448). **Fax:** 361/749-1490. **Facility:** 54 units. 48 one-, 3 two- and 3 three-bedroom suites with kitchens. 2-3 stories, exterior corridors. **Parking:** on-site. **Terms:** check-in 4 pm, 7 day cancellation notice, weekly rates available. **Pool(s):** outdoor, heated outdoor. **Leisure Activities:** fishing, 4 lighted tennis courts. **Guest Services:** coin laundry. **Business Services:** fax (fee). **Cards:** AX, DS, MC, VI. *(See color ad below)*

SOME UNITS

THE COURTYARD CONDOMINIUMS
Phone: 361/749-5243

▼▼ ▼▼

5/1-9/2	1P: $89-$196	2P: $89-$196	XP: $5	F5
2/1-4/30 & 9/3-10/31	1P: $65-$140	2P: $65-$140	XP: $5	F5
11/1-1/31	1P: $50-$118	2P: $52-$118	XP: $5	F5

Condominium

Location: 2.5 mi s on US 361. 622 Access Rd 1A 78373 (PO Box 249). Fax: 361/749-4132. **Facility:** 56 one-bedroom standard units with kitchens. 2 stories (no elevator), exterior corridors. **Parking:** on-site. **Terms:** check-in 4 pm, 2 night minimum stay, 3 day cancellation notice, weekly rates available. **Pool(s):** outdoor. **Leisure Activities:** 2 tennis courts, basketball, shuffleboard, volleyball. **Guest Services:** coin laundry. **Business Services:** fax (fee). **Cards:** DS, MC, VI.

SOME UNITS

🏊 ⊠ 🖥 📺 📼 / ⊠ /

THE DUNES CONDOMINIUMS
Phone: (361)749-5155

▼▼ ▼▼ ▼

3/1-3/31	1P: $180	2P: $245-$385
4/1-9/1	1P: $165-$180	2P: $220-$385
2/1-2/28 & 9/2-1/31	1P: $115	2P: $140-$250

Condominium

Location: SR 361, e on Beach, 1 blk s on Station St, just e. 1000 Lantana Dr 78373. Fax: 361/749-5930. **Facility:** 42 units. 6 one- and 2 two- and 4 three-bedroom suites with kitchens. 9 stories, exterior corridors. **Parking:** on-site. **Terms:** check-in 4 pm, 4 day cancellation notice. **Amenities:** hair dryers. **Pool(s):** heated outdoor. **Leisure Activities:** whirlpool, fishing, 2 lighted tennis courts, exercise room, basketball, horseshoes, shuffleboard, volleyball. **Guest Services:** coin laundry. **Business Services:** meeting rooms, fax (fee). **Cards:** AX, DC, DS, MC, VI.

(ASK) 🍴 🏊 ⊠ 📶 🖥 📺 📼

EXECUTIVE KEYS
Phone: 361/749-6272

▼▼ ▼▼

5/1-9/2	1P: $87-$225	2P: $87-$225	XP: $5	F5
2/1-4/30 & 9/3-11/30	1P: $65-$150	2P: $65-$150	XP: $5	F5
12/1-1/31	1P: $50-$128	2P: $50-$128	XP: $5	F5

Condominium

Location: 2.5 mi s on SR 361. 820 Access Rd 1A 78373 (PO Box 1087). **Facility:** 51 units. 16 one-bedroom standard units with efficiencies. 25 two- and 10 three-bedroom suites with kitchens. 2-3 stories (no elevator), exterior corridors. **Parking:** on-site. **Terms:** check-in 4 pm, 2-3 night minimum stay, 5 day cancellation notice, weekly rates available. **Pool(s):** outdoor. **Leisure Activities:** fishing. **Guest Services:** coin laundry. **Business Services:** fax (fee). **Cards:** DS, MC, VI.

🏊 🖥 📺 📼

PLANTATION SUITES
Phone: (361)749-3866

(AAA) (SAVE)

6/1-8/31 [ECP]		2P: $89-$199
2/1-5/31 & 9/1-1/31 [ECP]		2P: $59-$199

▼▼ ▼▼ ▼

Motel

Location: Just s on SR 361. Located on Mustang Island. 1909 Hwy 361 78373. Fax: 361/749-7873. **Facility:** Smoke free premises. 50 one-bedroom standard units, some with whirlpools. 2 stories, exterior corridors. **Bath:** combo or shower only. **Parking:** on-site. **Terms:** 2 night minimum stay - weekends, weekly rates available. **Amenities:** voice mail. **Pool(s):** heated outdoor. **Leisure Activities:** whirlpool. **Guest Services:** coin laundry. **Business Services:** meeting rooms, fax (fee). **Cards:** AX, DC, DS, MC, VI. **Special Amenities:** free continental breakfast and free local telephone calls.

(S/D) 🏊 ⊠ 🐾 📶 🖥 📺

PORT ROYAL OCEAN RESORT
Phone: (361)749-5011

▼▼ ▼▼ ▼

5/22-9/9	1P: $175-$505	2P: $175-$505	XP: $25	F16
2/1-5/21 & 9/10-1/31	1P: $110-$285	2P: $110-$285	XP: $25	F16

Small-scale Hotel

Location: 7.8 mi s on SR 361. Located on Mustang Island. 6317 State Hwy 361 78373. Fax: 361/749-5806. **Facility:** 176 units. 49 one-, 110 two- and 17 three-bedroom suites with kitchens, some with whirlpools. 3 stories, exterior corridors. **Parking:** on-site. **Terms:** check-in 4 pm, 2-4 night minimum stay - seasonal, 3 day cancellation notice-fee imposed. **Amenities:** video library. **Pool(s):** 4 outdoor. **Leisure Activities:** whirlpools, 2 lighted tennis courts. **Guest Services:** gift shop. **Business Services:** meeting rooms, fax (fee). **Cards:** AX, DS, MC, VI.

(ASK) (S/D) 🍴 🍸 🏊 📺 📼

The following lodging was either not evaluated or did not meet AAA rating requirements but is listed for your information only.

MUSTANG ISLAND BEACH CLUB
Phone: 361/749-5446

(fyi)

Not evaluated. **Location:** SR 361; Located on Mustang Island. 6275 SR 361 78373. Facilities, services, and decor characterize a mid-range property.

——— **WHERE TO DINE** ———

TROUT STREET BAR & GRILL **Lunch:** $15 **Dinner:** $25 **Phone:** 361/749-7800
▽▽ ▽▽ **Location:** Facing the marina, just n of ferry landing. 104 W Cotter St 78373. **Hours:** 11 am-8:30 pm, Fri & Sat-10
Seafood pm, Sun 11:45 am-8 pm. **Reservations:** accepted. **Features:** On the waterfront near the ferry landing, the
landmark restaurant plies diners with deliciously prepared fresh seafood. Casual dress; cocktails. **Parking:**
on-site. **Cards:** AX, MC, VI.

PORT ARTHUR pop. 57,755

——— **WHERE TO STAY** ———

COMFORT INN **Phone:** (409)729-3434
[SAVE] All Year [CP] 1P: $58-$85 2P: $58-$85 XP: $5 F12
▽▽ ▽▽ **Location:** US 69, exit Jimmy Johnson Blvd. 8040 Memorial Blvd. **Fax:** 409/729-1243. **Facility:** 44 one-
Motel bedroom standard units, some with kitchens and/or whirlpools. 2 stories, exterior corridors. **Parking:** on-site.
Terms: cancellation fee imposed. **Amenities:** *Some:* irons, hair dryers. **Pool(s):** small outdoor. **Leisure Ac-**
tivities: whirlpool, exercise room. **Guest Services:** valet laundry. **Business Services:** fax (fee). **Cards:** AX,
DC, DS, MC, VI.
SOME UNITS

HOLIDAY INN PARK CENTRAL **Phone:** (409)724-5000
▽▽▽ ▽ All Year 1P: $69-$84 2P: $69-$84
Small-scale Hotel **Location:** US 69, exit Jimmy Johnson Blvd. 2929 Jimmy Johnson Blvd 77642. **Fax:** 409/724-7644. **Facility:** 164 one-
bedroom standard units. 4 stories, interior/exterior corridors. *Bath:* combo or shower only. **Parking:** on-site.
Terms: [AP] meal plan available, 17% service charge. **Amenities:** high-speed Internet (fee), voice mail,
irons, hair dryers. **Pool(s):** outdoor. **Leisure Activities:** exercise room. **Guest Services:** valet and coin laundry, area transportation. **Business Services:** meeting rooms, fax (fee). **Cards:** AX, CB, DC, DS, JC, MC, VI.
SOME UNITS

SUPER 8 MOTEL & SUITES **Phone:** 409/722-1012
▽▽▽ ▽ Property failed to provide current rates
Small-scale Hotel **Location:** US 69, exit Jimmy Johnson Blvd. 7700 Memorial Blvd 77642. **Fax:** 409/722-0105. **Facility:** 51 units. 48
one-bedroom standard units, some with whirlpools. 3 one-bedroom suites. 3 stories, interior corridors. *Bath:*
combo or shower only. **Parking:** on-site. **Amenities:** dual phone lines, irons, hair dryers. **Pool(s):** small
heated indoor. **Leisure Activities:** whirlpool. **Guest Services:** valet and coin laundry. **Business Services:** meeting rooms.
SOME UNITS

PORT ISABEL pop. 4,865

——— **WHERE TO STAY** ———

SOUTHWIND INN **Phone:** 956/943-3392
[AAA] [SAVE] 2/1-3/31 1P: $40-$120 2P: $40-$120 XP: $10 F12
4/1-9/4 1P: $45-$99 2P: $45-$99 XP: $10 F12
▽▽ ▽▽ 9/5-12/31 1P: $35-$50 2P: $35-$50 XP: $10 F12
Motel 1/1-1/31 1P: $35-$45 2P: $35-$45 XP: $10 F12
Location: Queen Isabella Cswy to Musina, then 3 blks n. 600 Davis St 78578. **Fax:** 956/943-6000. **Facility:** 17 one-
bedroom standard units, some with efficiencies. 2 stories, exterior corridors. **Parking:** on-site. **Terms:** 3 day
cancellation notice, weekly rates available, pets ($5 extra charge). **Pool(s):** outdoor. **Business Services:** fax (fee). **Cards:** AX,
DS, MC, VI. **Special Amenities:** early check-in/late check-out and free local telephone calls.
SOME UNITS

——— **WHERE TO DINE** ———

——— *The following restaurant has not been evaluated by AAA* ———
but is listed for your information only.

MARCELLO'S ITALIAN RESTAURANT & LIGHTHOUSE PUB **Phone:** 956/943-7611
[fyi] Not evaluated. **Location:** Queen Isabella Cswy to Lighthouse Sq. 110 N Tarnava 78578. **Features:** Serving Italian
food in a casual atmosphere.

PORTLAND pop. 14,827

——— **WHERE TO STAY** ———

COMFORT INN **Phone:** (361)643-2222
[AAA] [SAVE] 5/16-9/5 1P: $84-$99 2P: $94-$124 XP: $6 F17
2/1-5/15 & 9/6-1/31 1P: $69-$114 2P: $79-$124 XP: $6 F17
▽▽ ▽▽ **Location:** US 181 W access road, exit FM 3239 northbound; exit Lang St southbound. 1703 N Hwy 181 78374.
Small-scale Hotel **Fax:** 361/643-1925. **Facility:** 40 one-bedroom standard units. 2 stories, exterior corridors. **Parking:** on-site.
Terms: cancellation fee imposed, [ECP] meal plan available, small pets only ($5 extra charge).
Amenities: voice mail, irons, hair dryers. **Pool(s):** outdoor. **Leisure Activities:** sauna, whirlpool. **Guest**
Services: coin laundry. **Business Services:** fax (fee). **Cards:** AX, CB, DC, DS, MC, VI. **Special Amenities:** free continental
breakfast and free local telephone calls.
SOME UNITS

HAMPTON INN

[SAVE]

| | 4/1-7/31 [ECP] | 1P: $89-$119 | 2P: $89-$129 |
| | 2/1-3/31 & 8/1-1/31 [ECP] | 1P: $79 | 2P: $84 |

Phone: (361)777-1500

Small-scale Hotel

DS, JC, MC, VI.

Location: US 181 W access road, exit Lang St. 1705 N Hwy 181 78374. **Fax:** 361/777-1600. **Facility:** 54 one-bedroom standard units. 3 stories, interior corridors. *Bath:* combo or shower only. **Parking:** on-site. **Amenities:** voice mail, irons, hair dryers. **Pool(s):** outdoor. **Leisure Activities:** sauna, whirlpools, exercise room. **Guest Services:** valet and coin laundry. **Business Services:** business center. **Cards:** AX, CB, DC,

SOME UNITS

QUANAH pop. 3,022

------ WHERE TO DINE ------

MEDICINE MOUND DEPOT RESTAURANT   **Lunch:** $4-$15   **Dinner:** $4-$15   **Phone:** 940/663-5619

American

Location: On US 287, 1 mi e of jct US 287 and SR 6. 1802 US 287 E 79252. **Hours:** 11 am-8 pm, Fri & Sat-9 pm. Closed: 11/27, 12/25. **Reservations:** accepted. **Features:** Housed in a historic railroad station, the rustic eatery sports such decor as a model train that runs high above the dining room's peanut-strewn floor. Among menu favorites is made-from-scratch chicken-fried steak. Casual dress. **Parking:** on-site. **Cards:** AX, DS, MC, VI.

RANCHO VIEJO

------ WHERE TO STAY ------

RANCHO VIEJO RESORT & COUNTRY CLUB

| | All Year | 1P: $88-$128 | 2P: $88-$236 | XP: $10 |

Phone: (956)350-4000

F14

Resort
Small-scale Hotel

Location: US 77/83, exit Rancho Viejo. 1 Rancho Viejo Dr 78575. **Fax:** 956/350-9681. **Facility:** The resort is on beautifully manicured grounds, including an 18 hole golf course, a landscaped 6,000 square foot pool and villa-style guest units. 63 units. 41 one-bedroom standard units. 22 one-bedroom suites with kitchens, some with whirlpools. 1-2 stories, exterior corridors. **Parking:** on-site. **Terms:** check-in 4 pm, 5 day cancellation notice, 17% service charge. **Amenities:** *Some:* honor bars, irons. **Pool(s):** outdoor, wading. **Leisure Activities:** whirlpool, boat dock, fishing, exercise room. **Fee:** golf-36 holes. **Guest Services:** gift shop, valet laundry. **Business Services:** conference facilities. **Cards:** AX, DC, MC, VI.

SOME UNITS

RED OAK —See Dallas p. 314.

RICHARDSON —See Dallas p. 314.

RICHMOND —See Houston p. 441.

ROANOKE —See Dallas p. 316.

ROBSTOWN pop. 12,727

------ WHERE TO STAY ------

DAYS INN

[SAVE]

| | All Year [CP] | 1P: $45-$95 | 2P: $55-$100 | XP: $7 |

Phone: (361)387-9416

F12

Small-scale Hotel

Location: 1 mi s on US 77. Located in a quiet, rural area. 320 Hwy 77 S 78380. **Fax:** 361/387-9416. **Facility:** 24 one-bedroom standard units. 1 story, exterior corridors. **Parking:** on-site. **Terms:** small pets only. **Amenities:** irons, hair dryers. **Pool(s):** outdoor. **Business Services:** fax (fee). **Cards:** AX, CB, DC, DS, MC, VI. **Special Amenities:** free continental breakfast and free newspaper.

SOME UNITS

------ WHERE TO DINE ------

JOE COTTEN'S BARBEQUE   **Lunch:** $6-$8   **Dinner:** $8-$10   **Phone:** 361/387-9273

American

Location: 1 mi s. US 77 S 78380. **Hours:** 10 am-10 pm. Closed: 11/27, 12/25; also Sun. **Features:** This rustic, Texas-style barbecue restaurant takes a unique approach to its operation. You may sit anywhere you please, but don't look for a menu. Just simply tell the server which plate of beef, pork, chicken, sausage or ribs you would like, and enjoy. Casual dress; beer only. **Parking:** on-site.

ROCKPORT pop. 7,385

------ WHERE TO STAY ------

DAYS INN

[SAVE]

| | All Year | 1P: $56-$110 | 2P: $56-$125 | XP: $8 |

Phone: (361)729-6379

F12

Small-scale Hotel

Location: Center. 1212 Laurel St @ 35 Hwy 78382. **Fax:** 361/729-5162. **Facility:** 28 one-bedroom standard units. 3 stories (no elevator), exterior corridors. *Bath:* combo or shower only. **Parking:** on-site. **Terms:** 2-3 night minimum stay - summer, [CP] meal plan available. **Amenities:** hair dryers. **Pool(s):** outdoor. **Business Services:** fax (fee). **Cards:** AX, CB, DC, DS, MC, VI.

SOME UNITS

HOLIDAY INN EXPRESS ROCKPORT
Phone: 361/727-0283

▼▼▼
All Year [CP]   1P: $55-$140   2P: $55-$140   XP: $10   F13
Location: Just s of downtown historic area on SR 35. 901 Hwy 35 N 78382. Fax: 361/727-0024. **Facility:** 50 one-
Small-scale Hotel bedroom standard units. 2 stories, exterior corridors. *Bath:* combo or shower only. **Parking:** on-site.
Amenities: voice mail, irons, hair dryers. **Pool(s):** outdoor. **Guest Services:** coin laundry. **Business Serv-**
ices: meeting rooms, fax (fee). **Cards:** AX, CB, DC, DS, MC, VI.

SOME UNITS

(ASK) (SD) (🍴) (🏊) (🎬) (DATA PORT) (📶) (📺) / (✕) /

LAGUNA REEF HOTEL
Phone: (361)729-1742

(AAA) (SAVE)
5/23-8/17 [ECP]   1P: $75-$290   2P: $75-$290   XP: $5
2/1-5/22 & 8/18-1/31 [ECP]   1P: $70-$260   2P: $70-$260   XP: $5
▼▼▼
Location: 0.5 mi s, just e of Business Rt 35; entrance on S Austin St. Located in a residential area. 1021 Water St 78382.
Condominium Fax: 361/729-7231. **Facility:** 71 units. 21 one-bedroom standard units. 38 one- and 12 two-bedroom suites
($120-$300) with kitchens. 4 stories, exterior corridors. **Parking:** on-site. **Terms:** weekly rates available,
small pets only ($40 deposit, $10 extra charge). **Amenities:** voice mail, hair dryers. *Some:* irons. **Pool(s):**
outdoor. **Leisure Activities:** 1000 foot lighted fishing pier, playground, horseshoes, volleyball. **Guest Services:** coin laundry.
Business Services: meeting rooms, fax (fee). **Cards:** AX, DS, MC, VI. **Special Amenities: free continental breakfast and free**
local telephone calls.

SOME UNITS

(SD) (🐕) (🏊) (✕) (🎬) / (✕) (📶) (📺) (💻) /

THE VILLAGE INN
Phone: (361)729-6370

(AAA) (SAVE)
2/1-10/15   1P: $60-$70   2P: $60-$70   XP: $5   F12
10/16-1/31   1P: $55-$65   2P: $55-$65   XP: $5   F12
▼▼▼
Location: Just w of jct SR 35 and Business Rt 35. 503 N Austin St 78382. Fax: 361/729-8925. **Facility:** 26 units. 22
Motel one-bedroom standard units, some with efficiencies. 4 two-bedroom suites ($100-$115) with efficiencies. 2
stories, exterior corridors. *Bath:* combo or shower only. **Parking:** on-site. **Terms:** 2-4 night minimum stay -
summer weekends, pets ($10 extra charge). **Pool(s):** outdoor. **Guest Services:** coin laundry. **Business**
Services: fax (fee). **Cards:** AX, DC, DS, MC, VI. **Special Amenities: free local telephone calls.**

SOME UNITS

(SD) (🐕) (🏊) / (✕) (📶) (📺) (💻) /

ROCKWALL —*See Dallas p. 317.*

ROSENBERG —*See Houston p. 441.*

ROUND ROCK pop. 61,136

——— WHERE TO STAY ———

AUSTIN MARRIOTT NORTH
Phone: (512)733-6767
(AAA) (SAVE)
▼▼▼▼ All Year 1P: $99-$169
Location: I-35, exit 251, 0.6 mi w to LaFrontera Blvd. 2600 LaFrontera Blvd 78681. Fax: 512/733-6868. **Facility:** 295
units. 291 one-bedroom standard units. 4 one-bedroom suites ($259). 8 stories, interior corridors. **Bath:**
combo or shower only. **Parking:** on-site. **Terms:** [BP] meal plan available, 19% service charge.
Small-scale Hotel **Amenities:** high-speed Internet, dual phone lines, voice mail, irons, hair dryers. **Dining:** 6 am-10 pm, Sat &
Sun from 6:30 am, cocktails. **Pool(s):** heated indoor. **Leisure Activities:** exercise room. **Guest Services:**
valet and coin laundry. **Business Services:** meeting rooms, business center. **Cards:** AX, CB, DC, DS, JC, MC, VI.
Special Amenities: free newspaper. *(See color ad below)*

SOME UNITS

BEST WESTERN EXECUTIVE INN
Phone: (512)255-3222
(AAA) (SAVE)
▼▼▼▼ All Year [ECP] 1P: $55-$79 2P: $55-$79 XP: $5 F12
Location: I-35, exit 253 northbound; exit 253A U-turn southbound. 1851 N I-35 78664. Fax: 512/255-9273.
Facility: 68 one-bedroom standard units. 2 stories (no elevator), exterior corridors. **Bath:** combo or shower
Motel only. **Parking:** on-site. **Terms:** weekly rates available, small pets only. **Amenities:** voice mail, irons, hair
dryers. **Pool(s):** outdoor. **Leisure Activities:** whirlpool, limited exercise equipment. **Guest Services:** valet
and coin laundry. **Business Services:** meeting rooms, fax. **Cards:** AX, CB, DC, DS, JC, MC, VI.
Special Amenities: free continental breakfast and free newspaper.

SOME UNITS

CANDLEWOOD SUITES
Phone: (512)828-0899
▼▼▼▼ All Year 1P: $67-$77
Location: I-35, exit 252A, just north on northbound frontage road. 521 S I-35 78664. Fax: 512/828-0897. **Facility:** 98
Small-scale Hotel units. 74 one-bedroom standard units with efficiencies. 24 one-bedroom suites with efficiencies. 3 stories, in-
terior corridors. **Bath:** combo or shower only. **Parking:** on-site. **Terms:** weekly rates available, small pets only
($75 fee). **Amenities:** video library, CD players, dual phone lines, voice mail, irons, hair dryers. **Leisure Activities:** exercise
room. **Business Services:** fax. **Cards:** AX, DC, DS, JC, MC, VI.

SOME UNITS

COMFORT SUITES
Phone: (512)244-2700
(SAVE)
2/1-9/30 [ECP] 1P: $74-$99 2P: $84-$109 XP: $10 F14
▼▼▼ 10/1-1/31 [ECP] 1P: $69-$99 2P: $79-$99 XP: $10 F14
Location: I-35, exit 252B northbound; exit 252AB southbound, just w. 609 Chisholm Trail 78681. Fax: 512/244-2246.
Motel **Facility:** 63 units. 62 one-bedroom standard units, some with whirlpools. 1 two-bedroom suite with kitchen.
3 stories, interior corridors. **Parking:** on-site. **Amenities:** dual phone lines, voice mail, irons, hair dryers.
Pool(s): heated outdoor. **Leisure Activities:** whirlpool, exercise room. **Guest Services:** valet and coin
laundry. **Business Services:** meeting rooms, business center. **Cards:** AX, DC, DS, MC, VI.

SOME UNITS

DAYS INN AND SUITES
Phone: (512)246-0055
(SAVE)
All Year 1P: $49-$69 2P: $59-$79 XP: $6 F17
▼▼▼ **Location:** I-35, exit 251, just s. 1801 S I-35 78681. Fax: 512/246-0345. **Facility:** 49 one-bedroom standard units.
2 stories (no elevator), interior/exterior corridors. **Bath:** combo or shower only. **Parking:** on-site.
Motel **Amenities:** high-speed Internet, hair dryers. *Some:* irons. **Pool(s):** outdoor. **Leisure Activities:** whirlpool.
Guest Services: complimentary evening beverages, coin laundry. **Business Services:** meeting rooms, fax
(fee). **Cards:** AX, CB, DC, DS, JC, MC, VI. *(See color ad p 485)*

SOME UNITS

HAMPTON INN AUSTIN-ROUND ROCK

Small-scale Hotel

Phone: (512)248-9100
XP: $10   F18
All Year [ECP]   1P: $79-$109   2P: $79-$109
Location: I-35, exit 251, on east frontage road. 110 Dell Way 78664. Fax: 512/248-9440. **Facility:** 93 one-bedroom standard units. 6 stories, interior corridors. *Bath:* combo or shower only. **Parking:** on-site. **Amenities:** high-speed Internet, dual phone lines, voice mail, irons, hair dryers. **Pool(s):** outdoor. **Leisure Activities:** whirl-pool, limited exercise equipment. **Guest Services:** valet laundry. **Business Services:** meeting rooms, fax (fee). **Cards:** AX, CB, DC, DS, JC, MC, VI.

SOME UNITS

HILTON GARDEN INN

Small-scale Hotel

Phone: (512)341-8200
XP: $10   F18
All Year   1P: $69-$99
Location: I-35, exit 254, on southbound access road. 2310 N I-35 78681. Fax: 512/238-8989. **Facility:** 122 one-bedroom standard units. 3 stories, interior corridors. *Bath:* combo or shower only. **Parking:** on-site. **Terms:** [BP], [CP] & [ECP] meal plans available, package plans. **Amenities:** dual phone lines, voice mail, irons, hair dryers. *Fee:* video games, high-speed Internet. **Pool(s):** outdoor. **Leisure Activities:** whirlpool, limited exercise equipment. **Guest Services:** valet and coin laundry. **Business Services:** meeting rooms, business center. **Cards:** AX, DC, DS, MC, VI.

SOME UNITS

LA QUINTA INN-AUSTIN-ROUND ROCK

Small-scale Hotel

Phone: (512)255-6666
XP: $10   F18
All Year   1P: $69-$89   2P: $79-$99
Location: I-35, exit 254, on west road. 2004 I-35 S 78681. Fax: 512/388-3635. **Facility:** 116 one-bedroom stan-dard units, some with whirlpools. 3 stories, interior corridors. **Parking:** on-site. **Terms:** [ECP] meal plan avail-able, small pets only. **Amenities:** video games (fee), voice mail, irons, hair dryers. **Pool(s):** small outdoor. **Leisure Activities:** whirlpool, exercise room. **Guest Services:** valet laundry. **Business Services:** meeting rooms, fax (fee). **Cards:** AX, CB, DC, DS, JC, MC, VI. **Special Amenities:** free continental breakfast and free local telephone calls. *(See color ad p 187)*

SOME UNITS

RED ROOF INN

Small-scale Hotel

Phone: (512)310-1111
XP: $5   F18
All Year   1P: $39-$59   2P: $44-$64
Location: I-35, exit 254, on west frontage road. 1990 I-35 N 78681. Fax: 512/310-1613. **Facility:** 107 one-bedroom standard units. 3 stories, interior corridors. *Bath:* combo or shower only. **Parking:** on-site. **Terms:** small pets only. **Amenities:** video games (fee), voice mail. **Pool(s):** small outdoor. **Guest Services:** coin laundry. **Busi-ness Services:** fax (fee). **Cards:** AX, CB, DC, DS, MC, VI. **Special Amenities:** free local telephone calls and free newspaper.

SOME UNITS
FEE   FEE

RESIDENCE INN BY MARRIOTT

Small-scale Hotel

Phone: (512)733-2400
All Year [ECP]   1P: $107-$116
Location: I-35, exit 250 southbound; exit 251 northbound, on east frontage road. 2505 S I-35 78664. Fax: 512/733-2500. **Facility:** 96 units. 85 one- and 11 two-bedroom standard units, some with efficiencies or kitchens. 3 stories, interior corridors. *Bath:* combo or shower only. **Parking:** on-site. **Terms:** cancellation fee imposed, small pets only ($75 fee, $5 extra charge). **Amenities:** video games (fee), dual phone lines, voice mail, irons, hair dryers. **Pool(s):** heated outdoor. **Leisure Activities:** whirlpool, limited exercise equipment, sports court. **Guest Services:** complimentary evening beverages: Mon-Thurs, valet and coin laundry. **Business Services:** meeting rooms, fax (fee). **Cards:** AX, CB, DC, DS, JC, MC, VI.

SOME UNITS

STAYBRIDGE SUITES AUSTIN-ROUND ROCK

Phone: (512)733-0942

▽▽▽▽▽
All Year [ECP]   1P: $99-$179   2P: $99-$179
Location: I-35, exit 252B northbound; exit 252AB southbound; on west frontage road. 520 I-35 S 78681.
Small-scale Hotel   **Fax:** 512/733-6139. **Facility:** 81 units. 71 one- and 10 two-bedroom standard units with efficiencies. 4 stories, interior corridors. *Bath:* combo or shower only. **Parking:** on-site. **Terms:** pets ($12 extra charge).
Amenities: video library (fee), high-speed Internet, dual phone lines, voice mail, irons, hair dryers. **Pool(s):** heated outdoor.
Leisure Activities: exercise room. **Guest Services:** sundries, complimentary evening beverages: Tues-Thurs, valet and coin laundry. **Business Services:** meeting rooms, business center. **Cards:** AX, CB, DC, DS, JC, MC, VI.

SOME UNITS

(A$K) (S❤) (🔓 FEE) (🐾) (🔥M) (💺) (📷) (🏊) (VCR) (🍴) (DATA PORT) (🛗) (🖥) (📠) /(✕)/

WINGATE INN & WILLIAMSON CONFERENCE CENTER

Phone: (512)341-7000

(AAA) (SAVE)
▽▽▽▽▽
All Year [ECP]   1P: $69
Location: I-35, exit 253, just e. 1209 N I-35 78664. Fax: 512/341-7011. **Facility:** 100 units. 97 one-bedroom standard units. 3 one-bedroom suites, some with whirlpools. 3 stories, interior corridors. *Bath:* combo or shower only. **Parking:** on-site. **Terms:** weekly rates available. **Amenities:** video games (fee), high-speed Internet,
Small-scale Hotel   dual phone lines, voice mail, safes, irons, hair dryers. **Pool(s):** small outdoor. **Leisure Activities:** whirlpool, exercise room. **Guest Services:** valet laundry, airport transportation (fee)-Austin Airport. **Business Services:** meeting rooms, business center. **Cards:** AX, CB, DC, DS, MC, VI. **Special Amenities: free continental breakfast and free newspaper.**

SOME UNITS

(S❤) (🔓 FEE) (🐾) (🍴) (🔥M) (💺) (📷) (🏊) (🍴) (DATA PORT) (🛗) (🖥) (📠) /(✕)/

The following lodging was either not evaluated or did not meet AAA rating requirements but is listed for your information only.

AMERISUITES

Phone: 512/733-2599

[fyi]
All Year   1P: $79-$109   2P: $79-$109   XP: $10   F17
Too new to rate. **Location:** I-35. 2340 I-35 N 78681. Fax: 512/733-1809. **Amenities:** pets, coffeemakers, micro-
Small-scale Hotel   waves, refrigerators, pool. **Cards:** AX, DS, JC, MC, VI.

WHERE TO DINE

SALTGRASS STEAK HOUSE

Lunch: $7-$26   **Dinner:** $10-$26   Phone: 512/238-0091

▽▽▽ ▽▽▽
Location: I-35, exit 254, on west frontage road. 2300 N I-35 78681. **Hours:** 11 am-10 pm, Fri & Sat-11 pm.
Closed: 11/27, 12/25. **Reservations:** accepted. **Features:** Born from the spirit of Texas cattle drives, the
West Steak House   restaurant presents a menu of hearty steaks, prime rib, chicken, seafood and baby back ribs. Save room for one of the yummy desserts. Casual dress; cocktails. **Parking:** on-site. **Cards:** AX, CB, DC, DS, MC, VI.

(🔥M) (✕)

ROUND TOP pop. 77

WHERE TO STAY

HEART OF MY HEART RANCH B & B

Phone: (979)249-3171

▽▽▽▽▽
All Year [BP]   1P: $115-$205   2P: $135-$225   XP: $20
Location: Jct SR 237 and 1457, 1.8 mi s on SR 237 to Florida Chapel Rd, 0.3 mi e. 403 Florida Chapel Rd 78954 (PO
Bed & Breakfast   Box 106). Fax: 979/249-3193. **Facility:** Spacious rooms decorated in period pieces on this 110 acre property offer fine accomodations with a variety of recreational opportunities. 12 units. 8 one-bedroom standard units.
2 one- and 2 two-bedroom suites ($135-$225). 2 stories (no elevator), interior/exterior corridors. *Bath:* combo or shower only.
Parking: on-site. **Terms:** 2 night minimum stay - weekends. **Amenities:** video library. **Pool(s):** outdoor. **Leisure Activities:** whirlpool, boating, canoeing, paddleboats, fishing, bicycles, hiking trails, horseback riding. **Guest Services:** complimentary evening beverages. **Business Services:** meeting rooms, fax. **Cards:** AX, DS, MC, VI.

SOME UNITS

(🏊) (🍴) (✕) (VCR) /(🛗) (🖥) (📠)/

OUTPOST @ CEDAR CREEK

Phone: 979/836-4975

▽▽▽▽▽
All Year [BP]   1P: $120-$300   2P: $120-$300   XP: $25
Location: Jct SR 237 and 1457, 5.4 mi e to Neumann Rd, just n. 5808 Wagner Rd 78954. Fax: 979/836-7577.
Classic Bed   **Facility:** Many types of rooms await the traveller at this reconstructed farm from the 1890 era including main
& Breakfast   house rooms, log cabins, Barn and Prarie cottages. Designated smoking area. 7 units. 3 one- and 2 two-
bedroom standard units, some with kitchens and/or whirlpools. 1 one- and 1 two-bedroom suites ($170-
$240), some with kitchens. 1-2 stories (no elevator), interior/exterior corridors. *Bath:* some shared or private. **Parking:** on-site.
Terms: 2 night minimum stay - weekends, 8 day cancellation notice-fee imposed. **Amenities:** video library. *Some:* CD players.
Leisure Activities: fishing, bicycles, hiking trails, jogging, horseback riding, game room. **Business Services:** fax. **Cards:** AX, MC, VI.

SOME UNITS

(🍴) (✕) (🏊) /(🏧) (VCR) (🛗) (🖥) (📠)/

WHERE TO DINE

ROYER'S CAFE

Lunch: $10-$29   **Dinner:** $10-$29   Phone: 979/249-3611

▽▽▽ ▽▽▽
Location: Just e of jct SR 237 and 1457. 105 Main St 78954. **Hours:** 11 am-9 pm, Fri & Sat-9:30 pm, Sun
noon-7 pm. Closed major holidays; also Mon-Wed & 1/1-1/7. **Features:** The family-owned cafe features
American   great regional American cuisine and wonderful pies. Smoke free premises. Casual dress; beer & wine only.
Parking: street.

(✕)

ROWLETT —*See Dallas p. 317.*
ROWLETT —*See Dallas p. 317.*

SALADO pop. 3,475

———— **WHERE TO STAY** ————

STAGECOACH INN   Phone: 254/947-5111
(AAA) [SAVE]   All Year   1P: $65-$76   2P: $72-$83   XP: $5   F12
▼▼▼▼   **Location:** I-35 and US 81, exit 284 southbound; exit 283 northbound. 1 Main St 76571 (PO Box 97).
                  Fax: 254/947-0671. **Facility:** 82 units. 80 one-bedroom standard units. 2 one-bedroom suites ($94-$104). 2
                  stories, exterior corridors. *Bath:* combo or shower only. **Parking:** on-site. **Amenities:** irons. *Some:* hair
Small-scale Hotel dryers. **Dining:** 2 restaurants, 6:30 am-9 pm, dining room, see separate listing. **Pool(s):** outdoor. **Leisure
                  Activities:** whirlpool, 2 lighted tennis courts, playground. **Business Services:** meeting rooms, fax (fee).
Cards: AX, DC, MC, VI. **Special Amenities: free local telephone calls.**

SOME UNITS

(icons)

SUPER 8 MOTEL   Phone: 254/947-5000
(AAA) [SAVE]   All Year [CP]   1P: $55-$60   2P: $60-$70   XP: $5   F12
▼▼▼▼   **Location:** I-35, exit 284 northbound; exit 285 southbound. 290 N Robertson Rd 76571. Fax: 254/947-5000.
                  Facility: 42 one-bedroom standard units. 2 stories, exterior corridors. **Parking:** on-site. **Amenities:** hair
                  dryers. **Pool(s):** small outdoor. **Business Services:** fax (fee). **Cards:** AX, CB, DC, DS, MC, VI.
Small-scale Hotel **Special Amenities: free continental breakfast and free local telephone calls.**

SOME UNITS

(icons)

———— **WHERE TO DINE** ————

STAGECOACH INN DINING ROOM   Historic   **Lunch:** $11-$14   **Dinner:** $14-$20   Phone: 254/947-9400
(AAA)   **Location:** I-35 and US 81, exit 284 southbound; exit 283 northbound; in Stagecoach Inn. 1 Main St 76571. **Hours:** 11
▼▼▼   am-4 & 5-9 pm. **Reservations:** suggested. **Features:** Relax and dine where the early pioneers once
                  stopped in their stagecoaches to rest and replenish for the next leg of their journey. Roasted prime rib,
                  hushpuppies and rich desserts are all served from a verbal menu in this restored stagecoach station.
American   Smoke free premises. Casual dress; cocktails. **Parking:** on-site. **Cards:** AX, DC, DS, MC, VI.   (icons)

SAN ANGELO pop. 88,439

———— **WHERE TO STAY** ————

BENCHMARK COMFORT INN   Phone: 325/944-2578
[SAVE]   All Year [CP]   1P: $60   2P: $60   XP: $5
▼▼▼ ▼▼▼   **Location:** Loop 306, exit Knickerbocker Rd. 2502 Loop 306 76904. Fax: 325/944-4373. **Facility:** 101 units. 99 one-
Motel   bedroom standard units. 2 one-bedroom suites. 2 stories (no elevator), exterior corridors. **Parking:** on-site.
                  Pool(s): outdoor. **Leisure Activities:** whirlpool. **Guest Services:** area transportation. **Business Services:**
                  meeting rooms, fax (fee). **Cards:** AX, DC, DS, MC, VI.

SOME UNITS

 (icons)

BEST WESTERN SAN ANGELO   Phone: (325)223-1273
(AAA) [SAVE]   All Year [CP]   1P: $65-$70   2P: $70-$75   XP: $5   F12
▼▼▼▼   **Location:** Loop 306, exit College Hills Blvd, just s. 3017 W Loop 306 76904. Fax: 800/995-1572. **Facility:** 55 one-
                  bedroom standard units. 2 stories (no elevator), exterior corridors. *Bath:* combo or shower only. **Parking:** on-
                  site. **Terms:** small pets only ($50 deposit). **Amenities:** irons, hair dryers. **Pool(s):** outdoor. **Leisure
Small-scale Hotel Activities:** whirlpool. **Guest Services:** airport transportation-San Angelo Airport. **Business Services:**
                  meeting rooms, fax. **Cards:** AX, CB, DC, DS, MC, VI. **Special Amenities: early check-in/late check-out
and free continental breakfast.**

SOME UNITS

(icons)

DAYS INN   Phone: (325)658-6594
[SAVE]   All Year [BP]   1P: $50   2P: $56   XP: $5   F12
▼▼▼ ▼▼▼   **Location:** 2.8 mi s on US 87 and 277. 4613 S Jackson 76904. Fax: 325/658-6594. **Facility:** 113 one-bedroom stan-
Motel   dard units. 2 stories (no elevator), exterior corridors. **Parking:** on-site. **Terms:** small pets only.
                  Amenities: hair dryers. **Pool(s):** outdoor. **Business Services:** meeting rooms, fax (tee). **Cards:** AX, DC, DS,
                  MC, VI.

SOME UNITS

 (icons)

EXECUTIVE INN   Phone: 325/653-6966
(AAA) [SAVE]   All Year   1P: $40-$50   2P: $45-$55   XP: $5   F
▼▼ ▼▼   **Location:** 3.2 mi s on US 87/277. 4205 S Bryant Blvd 76903. Fax: 325/659-6607. **Facility:** 78 one-bedroom stan-
Motel   dard units. 2 stories (no elevator), exterior corridors. **Parking:** on-site. **Terms:** weekly rates available, [CP]
                  meal plan available. **Amenities:** *Some:* irons, hair dryers. **Dining:** nightclub. **Pool(s):** outdoor. **Business
                  Services:** meeting rooms, fax. **Cards:** AX, DC, MC, VI.

SOME UNITS

(icons)

HAMPTON INN   Phone: (325)942-9622
[SAVE]   All Year [ECP]   1P: $75-$95   2P: $75-$105   XP: $6   F18
▼▼▼▼   **Location:** Loop 306, exit College Hills Blvd, just s. 2959 W Loop 306 76904. Fax: 325/947-8123. **Facility:** 64 one-
                  bedroom standard units. 3 stories, interior corridors. *Bath:* combo or shower only. **Parking:** on-site.
                  Terms: 14 day cancellation notice. **Amenities:** voice mail, irons. *Some:* hair dryers. **Pool(s):** heated indoor.
Small-scale Hotel **Leisure Activities:** whirlpool. **Guest Services:** valet laundry. **Business Services:** fax (fee). **Cards:** AX, CB,
                  DC, DS, MC, VI.

SOME UNITS

 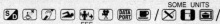 (icons)

HAWTHORN INN & SUITES
　　　　Phone: (325)653-1500
All Year [BP]　　　　1P: $79-$139　　　2P: $79-$139　　　XP: $10　　　　F12
Motel　　Location: US 87 S, 1 mi w. 1355 Knickerbocker Rd 76903. Fax: 325/653-1501. **Facility:** 80 units. 55 one-bedroom standard units, some with efficiencies. 25 one-bedroom suites ($99-$139) with efficiencies. 3 stories, interior corridors. *Bath:* combo or shower only. **Parking:** on-site. **Amenities:** video library (fee), dual phone lines, voice mail, irons, hair dryers. **Pool(s):** outdoor. **Leisure Activities:** whirlpool, limited exercise equipment. **Guest Services:** valet and coin laundry. **Business Services:** meeting rooms, fax (fee). **Cards:** AX, CB, DC, DS, MC, VI.　　SOME UNITS

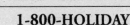

HOLIDAY INN CONVENTION CENTER HOTEL　　　　Phone: (325)658-2828
All Year　　　　1P: $109-$169　　　2P: $109-$169
Small-scale Hotel　**Location:** US 87 to Concho Ave, 0.5 mi e; downtown. Located adjacent to convention center. 441 Rio Concho Dr 76903. Fax: 325/658-8741. **Facility:** 148 units. 147 one-bedroom standard units. 1 one-bedroom suite ($119-$169). 6 stories, interior corridors. **Parking:** on-site. **Terms:** pets ($10 fee). **Amenities:** video games (fee), high-speed Internet, dual phone lines, irons, hair dryers. *Some:* voice mail. **Pool(s):** heated indoor. **Leisure Activities:** whirlpool, limited exercise equipment. **Guest Services:** valet laundry. **Business Services:** conference facilities, fax (fee). **Cards:** AX, CB, DC, DS, JC, MC, VI. *(See ad below)*　　SOME UNITS

HOWARD JOHNSON SAN ANGELO

AAA SAVE
▽▽▽▽ ▽▽▽▽
Small-scale Hotel

Phone: (325)653-2995

All Year | 1P: $53-$58 | 2P: $59-$64 | XP: $6 | F12
Location: Just w on US 67 business route at jct US 87 southbound. 415 W Beauregard 76903. Fax: 325/659-4393. **Facility:** 75 one-bedroom standard units. 3 stories, interior/exterior corridors. **Parking:** on-site. **Terms:** small pets only. **Dining:** 6 am-2 pm, cocktails. **Pool(s):** small heated indoor. **Leisure Activities:** sun deck. **Business Services:** meeting rooms, fax (fee). **Cards:** AX, CB, DC, MC, VI. **Special Amenities:** free local telephone calls and free newspaper.

SOME UNITS

INN OF THE CONCHOS

AAA SAVE
▽▽▽▽ ▽▽▽▽
Motel

Phone: (325)658-2811

All Year [CP] | 1P: $49-$69 | 2P: $57-$69 | XP: $10 | F18
Location: 2 mi n on US 87. 2021 N Bryant Blvd 76903. Fax: 325/653-7560. **Facility:** 125 one-bedroom standard units. 2 stories (no elevator), exterior corridors. **Parking:** on-site. **Terms:** cancellation fee imposed, weekly rates available. **Amenities:** voice mail. **Dining:** 6 am-9 pm, Sat & Sun from 7 am, cocktails, nightclub. **Pool(s):** outdoor. **Leisure Activities:** whirlpool. **Business Services:** meeting rooms, fax (fee). **Cards:** AX, CB, DC, DS, MC, VI. **Special Amenities:** free continental breakfast and free local telephone calls.

SOME UNITS

LA QUINTA INN-SAN ANGELO

AAA SAVE
▽▽▽▽ ▽▽▽▽
Motel

Phone: (325)949-0515

All Year | 1P: $69-$89 | 2P: $75-$95
Location: Loop 306, exit Knickerbocker Rd, just s. 2307 Loop 306 76904-6663. Fax: 325/944-1187. **Facility:** 171 units. 169 one-bedroom standard units. 2 one-bedroom suites. 2 stories (no elevator), exterior corridors. **Parking:** on-site. **Terms:** [ECP] meal plan available, small pets only. **Amenities:** video games (fee), voice mail, irons, hair dryers. **Pool(s):** outdoor. **Leisure Activities:** whirlpool. **Guest Services:** valet and coin laundry. **Business Services:** conference facilities, fax (fee). **Cards:** AX, CB, DC, DS, JC, MC, VI. **Special Amenities: free continental breakfast and free local telephone calls.**

SOME UNITS

FEE

RAMADA LIMITED

▽▽▽▽ ▽▽▽▽
Motel

Phone: (325)653-8442

All Year [CP] | 1P: $55-$80 | 2P: $58-$75 | XP: $5 | F17
Location: 2.1 mi n on US 87 at jct N 23rd St. 2201 N Bryant Blvd 76903. Fax: 325/653-4482. **Facility:** 39 one-bedroom standard units. 2 stories (no elevator), exterior corridors. **Parking:** on-site. **Terms:** pets ($10 fee). **Amenities:** voice mail, irons, hair dryers. **Pool(s):** outdoor. **Guest Services:** coin laundry. **Business Services:** meeting rooms, fax. **Cards:** AX, DC, DS, MC, VI.

SOME UNITS

──────── *The following lodging was either not evaluated or did not* ────────
meet AAA rating requirements but is listed for your information only.

CLARION INN & SUITES

fyi
Small-scale Hotel

Phone: 325/655-8000

7/2-1/31 | 1P: $99-$105 | 2P: $99-$105 | XP: $10 | F10
3/2-7/1 | 1P: $89-$105 | 2P: $99-$105 | XP: $10 | F10
2/1-3/1 | 1P: $79-$105 | 2P: $84-$105 | XP: $10 | F10
Too new to rate. **Location:** I-87, exit Concho Ave. 333 Rio Concho 76901. Fax: 325/655-8888. **Amenities:** coffeemakers, microwaves, refrigerators, pool. **Terms:** 7 day cancellation notice-fee imposed. **Cards:** AX, CB, DC, DS, MC, VI.

──────── **WHERE TO DINE** ────────

CHINA GARDEN RESTAURANT

▽▽▽▽ ▽▽▽▽
Chinese

Lunch: $4-$7 | **Dinner:** $6-$17 | **Phone:** 325/949-2838
Location: Loop 306, exit College Hills Blvd, 4.5 mi sw. 4217 College Hills Blvd 76904. **Hours:** 11 am-10 pm, Fri & Sat-10:30 pm. Closed major holidays. **Features:** Lovely Chinese appointments are drawn in soothing shades of green at the eatery, which features two dining areas separated by a large buffet room with two serving islands. Large, tasty portions characterize the food, from egg rolls to spicy chicken to desserts. Casual dress; cocktails. **Parking:** on-site. **Cards:** AX, DC, DS, MC, VI.

MEJOR QUE NADA (BETTER THAN NOTHING)

▽▽▽▽
Mexican

Lunch: $5-$12 | **Dinner:** $5-$12 | **Phone:** 325/655-3553
Location: 1.5 mi s on US 87 and 277. 1911 S Bryant Blvd 76903. **Hours:** 11 am-10 pm, Fri & Sat-11 pm, Sun-8 pm. Closed: 1/1, 11/27, 12/25. **Reservations:** accepted. **Features:** Pictures of celebrity guests, Mexican artifacts and imported planters mix in an eclectic decor that also features lovely fountains and lush gardens both inside and out. Guests can savor tacos and enchiladas, as well as good steaks. Casual dress; cocktails; entertainment. **Parking:** on-site. **Cards:** AX, DS, MC, VI.

Destination San Antonio
pop. 1,144,646

A city that tantalizes visitors with endless fun, San Antonio is made up of a vibrant cultural heritage blended with a cosmopolitan twist.

*F*estivals—ranging from Cinco de Mayo and Fiestas Navideñas to the Texas Folklife Festival and Greek Funstival—all represent the area's diversity. There's always a celebration in the Fiesta City. Olé!

The Alamo, San Antonio.
The symbol of Texas' pride lies in the heart of downtown surrounded by modern structures. (See listing page 139)

Market Square, San Antonio.
Local crafts and fresh-baked treats have tempted bargain-hunters for more than a century. (See listing page 141)

Brackenridge Park, San Antonio.
Nature trails, a zoo and a Japanese tea garden are among the urban wonders of this 343-acre park. (See listing page 140)

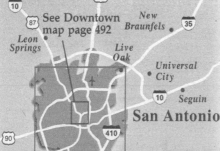

See Downtown map page 492

See Vicinity map page 496

*P*laces included in this AAA Destination City:

Tex-Mex Cuisine, San Antonio.
It started with the "Chili-Queens" dishing up the spicy stuff in the 1870s and continues with restaurateurs serving sizzling fajitas and hot tamales.

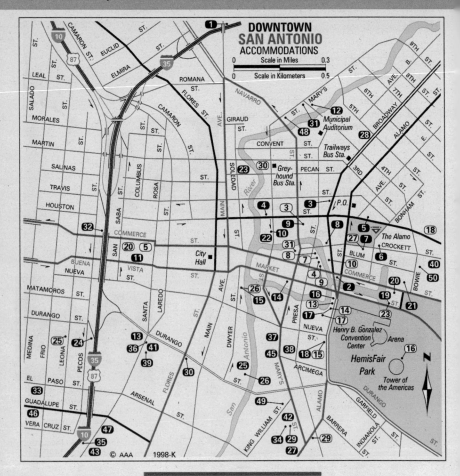

DOWNTOWN SAN ANTONIO ACCOMMODATIONS

Scale in Miles   0   0.3
Scale in Kilometers   0   0.5

© AAA   1998-K

Quality Repair Ahead

AAA
Approved Auto Repair

You can count on AAA's Approved Auto Repair providers to manage your vehicle's repair and maintenance needs. The providers meet strict standards for technician training and customer service. And, when you use an Approved Auto Repair provider, you get a 12-month/12,000-mile warranty. When you need a trusted resource for repair or maintenance services, just follow the signs.

Look for the Signs Along the Way

*W*hen selecting a place to dine while traveling, look for Official Appointment restaurants that display the AAA Approved sign. It's the only sign you need to be assured of an enjoyable dining experience.

As a member, you already know the AAA sign indicates quality establishments. So, when you don't have advance dining reservations, look for the AAA Approved sign along the way, for a meal you'll long remember!

Downtown San Antonio

This index helps you "spot" where approved accommodations and restaurants are located on the corresponding detailed maps. Lodging rate ranges are for comparison only and show the property's high season; rates are per night, unless only weekly (W) rates are available. Restaurant rate range is for dinner, unless only lunch (L) is served. Turn to the listing page for more detailed rate information and consult display ads for special promotions.

Spotter/Map Page Number	OA	DOWNTOWN SAN ANTONIO - Lodgings	Diamond Rating	Rate Range High Season	Listing Page
1 / p. 492	AAA	Rodeway Inn Downtown	◆◆	$62-$102 [SAVE]	514
2 / p. 492		Riverwalk Vista	◆◆◆	$140-$180	514
3 / p. 492	AAA	The St. Anthony-A Wyndham Historic Hotel	◆◆◆	$149-$169 [SAVE]	514
4 / p. 492		Sheraton Gunter - see color ad p 515	◆◆◆	$190-$223	515
5 / p. 492		Emily Morgan Hotel	◆◆◆	$149-$300	508
6 / p. 492	AAA	Holiday Inn Crockett Hotel	◆◆◆	$169-$199 [SAVE]	509
7 / p. 492	AAA	Menger Hotel - see ad p 511	◆◆◆	$195-$215 [SAVE]	511
8 / p. 492	AAA	Hyatt Regency San Antonio - see color ad inside front cover	◆◆◆	$149-$285 [SAVE]	510
9 / p. 492	AAA	La Mansion del Rio	◆◆◆◆	$209-$359 [SAVE]	510
10 / p. 492		Holiday Inn Riverwalk	◆◆◆	$119-$325	509
11 / p. 492		La Quinta Inn Market Square - see color ad p 510	◆◆◆	$89-$125	511
12 / p. 492		Four Points Sheraton Riverwalk North Hotel	◆◆◆	$89	508
13 / p. 492		Holiday Inn-Downtown-Market Square	◆◆	$79-$159	509
14 / p. 492		Homewood Suites Riverwalk by Hilton	◆◆◆	$159-$269	509
15 / p. 492	AAA	Howard Johnson Riverwalk Plaza Hotel - see color ad p 493	◆◆◆	$89-$199 [SAVE]	510
16 / p. 492	AAA	Hilton Palacio del Rio	◆◆◆	$150-$320 [SAVE]	509
17 / p. 492	AAA	The Fairmount-A Wyndham Historic Hotel	◆◆◆	$149-$174 [SAVE]	508
18 / p. 492	AAA	Plaza San Antonio, A Marriott Hotel - see color ad p 147 & p 507	◆◆◆◆	$169-$279 [SAVE]	512
19 / p. 492		Marriott Riverwalk - see color ad p 507	◆◆◆◆	$119-$304	511
20 / p. 492		La Quinta Inn-Convention Center - see color ad p 510	◆◆◆	$109-$145	511
21 / p. 492		San Antonio Marriott Rivercenter - see color ad p 507	◆◆◆◆	$119-$304	514
22 / p. 492	AAA	Drury Inn & Suites Riverwalk	◆◆◆	$136-$185 [SAVE]	507
23 / p. 492	AAA	Adam's Mark San Antonio Riverwalk Hotel	◆◆◆◆	$135-$209 [SAVE]	504
24 / p. 492	AAA	Radisson Downtown Market Square - see color ad p 513	◆◆◆	$85-$169 [SAVE]	513
25 / p. 492		Inn on the River	◆◆	$69-$175	510
26 / p. 492		Riverwalk Inn	◆◆◆	$130-$175	514
27 / p. 492	AAA	The Columns on Alamo	◆◆◆◆	$92-$230 [SAVE]	506
28 / p. 492	AAA	Alamo Travelodge	◆◆	$49-$149 [SAVE]	504
29 / p. 492		A Yellow Rose Bed & Breakfast	◆◆◆	$100-$200	505
30 / p. 492	AAA	Woodfield Suites San Antonio-Downtown - see color ad p 515	◆◆◆	$79-$99 [SAVE]	515
31 / p. 492		Hawthorn Suites Riverwalk	◆◆◆	$119-$189	509
32 / p. 492		Motel 6 - 1122	◆◆	$57-$73	512
33 / p. 492	AAA	Best Western Alamo Suites - see color ad p 520	◆◆◆	$89-$150 [SAVE]	505

Spotter/Map Page Number	OA	DOWNTOWN SAN ANTONIO - Lodgings (continued)	Diamond Rating	Rate Range High Season	Listing Page
34 / p. 492	AAA	Brackenridge House B & B	◆◆◆	$110-$200 SAVE	505
35 / p. 492		Ramada Limited Downtown	◆◆	$65-$125	513
36 / p. 492		Residence Inn by Marriott - see color ad p 507	◆◆◆	$139-$159	514
37 / p. 492	AAA	Holiday Inn Express Hotel & Suites	◆◆◆	$159-$339 SAVE	509
38 / p. 492	AAA	Arbor House Suites Bed & Breakfast	◆◆◆	$125-$175 SAVE	504
39 / p. 492		Fairfield Inn by Marriott - see color ad p 507	◆◆◆	$89-$109	508
40 / p. 492		Hampton Inn Downtown - see color ad p 508	◆◆◆	$99-$129	508
41 / p. 492		Courtyard by Marriott-Downtown - see color ad p 507	◆◆◆	Failed to provide	506
42 / p. 492	AAA	Noble Inns-The Jackson House - see color ad p 512	◆◆◆◆	$120-$200 SAVE	512
43 / p. 492		Days Inn-Downtown Laredo St	◆◆	$45-$109	506
45 / p. 492	AAA	AmeriSuites (San Antonio/Riverwalk) - see color ad p 504	◆◆◆	$109-$169 SAVE	504
46 / p. 492		Microtel Inn & Suites	◆◆	$44-$99	512
47 / p. 492	AAA	Comfort Suites Downtown - see color ad p 506	◆◆◆	$89-$150 SAVE	506
48 / p. 492		The Havana Riverwalk Inn	◆◆◆	$109-$215	509
49 / p. 492	AAA	Beauregard House	◆◆◆	$105-$190 SAVE	505
50 / p. 492		Residence Inn Alamo Plaza	◆◆◆	$109-$189	514
		DOWNTOWN SAN ANTONIO - Restaurants			
3 / p. 492		Las Canarias Restaurant	◆◆◆◆	$15-$30	517
4 / p. 492		Boudro's on the Riverwalk	◆◆◆	$14-$30	516
5 / p. 492		La Margarita	◆	$7-$12	517
7 / p. 492		Kangaroo Court	◆	$9-$15	516
8 / p. 492		Hunan River Garden	◆◆	$7-$14	516
9 / p. 492		Casa Rio Mexican Restaurant	◆	$5-$10	516
10 / p. 492		Rio Rio Cantina	◆◆	$7-$19	517
13 / p. 492		Little Rhein Steak House	◆◆	$28-$33	517
14 / p. 492		Polo's	◆◆◆◆	$16-$35	517
15 / p. 492		The Anaqua Room	◆◆◆	$16-$25	516
16 / p. 492		Tower of the Americas Restaurant	◆◆	$16-$30	517
17 / p. 492		Fig Tree Restaurant	◆◆◆◆	$24-$38	516
18 / p. 492		Barron's	◆◆◆	$8-$15	516
20 / p. 492		Mi Tierra Cafe Y Panaderia	◆◆	$6-$17	517
23 / p. 492		The Cactus Flower	◆◆◆	$10-$20	516
25 / p. 492		Pico de Gallo	◆◆	$8-$14	517
26 / p. 492		Cascades by the River-Steaks & Fine International Cuisine - see color ad p 493	◆◆◆	$21-$40	516
27 / p. 492		The Colonial Room	◆◆◆	$25-$30	516
29 / p. 492		La Focaccia Italian Grill	◆◆	$4-$15	517
30 / p. 492		Pecan Street Delicatessen	◆◆	$6-$10	517
31 / p. 492		Presidio	◆◆◆	$15-$30	517

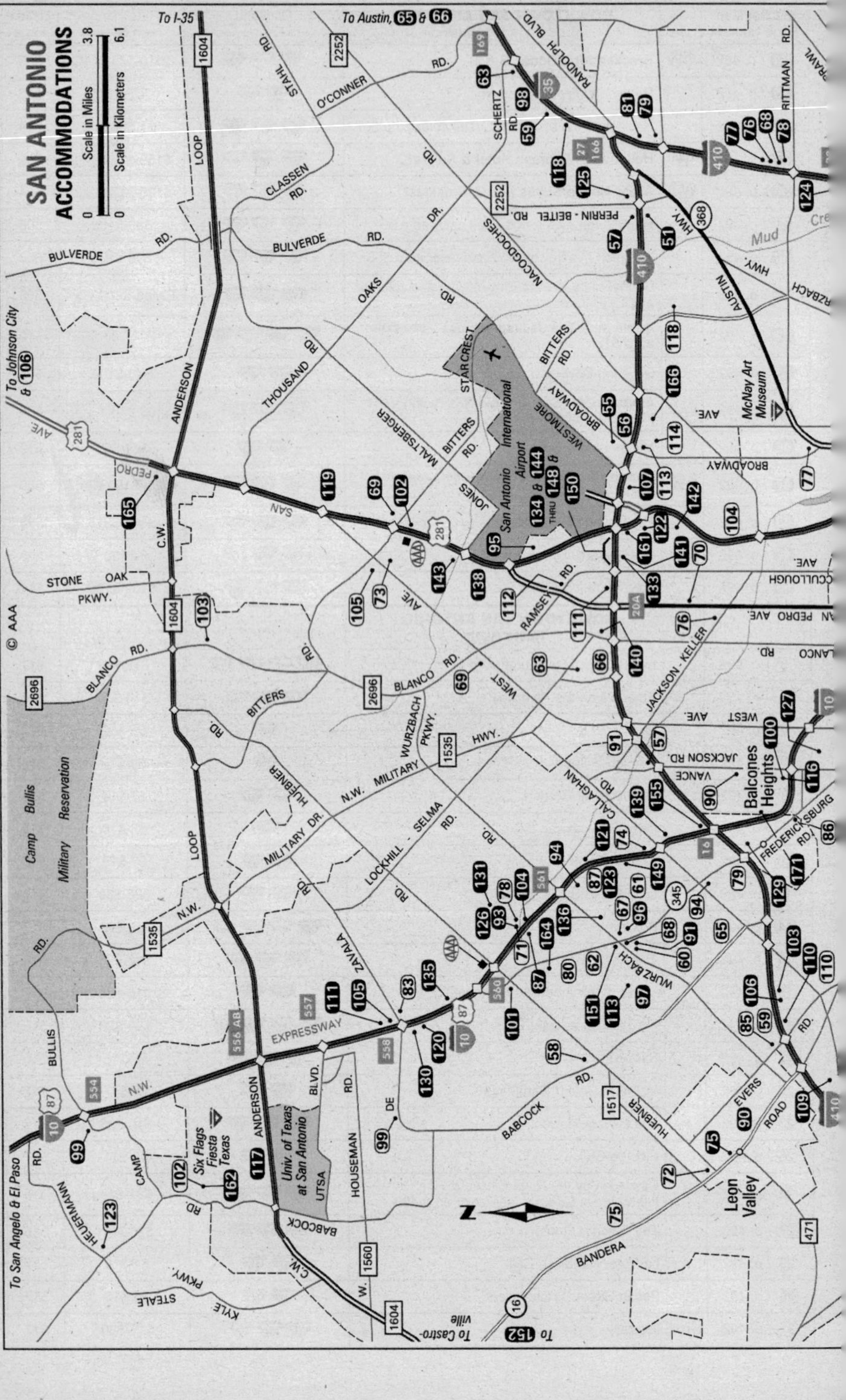

SAN ANTONIO
ACCOMMODATIONS

Scale in Miles
0   3.8

Scale in Kilometers
0   6.1

To I-35

To Austin, 65 & 66

1604

1604

LOOP

To Johnson City & 106

To San Angelo & El Paso

To Castroville

To 152

STAHL RD.
O'CONNER
CLASSEN RD.
BULVERDE RD.
BULVERDE RD.
ANDERSON
THOUSAND OAKS
2252
2252
SCHERTZ RD.
RANDOLPH BLVD.
PERRIN - BEITEL RD.
NACOGDOCHES RD.
AUSTIN HWY.
RZBACH
Mud Creek
McNay Art Museum
BROADWAY
STARCREST
WESTMORE
BITTERS RD.
JONES - MALTSBERGER
RD.
San Antonio International Airport
281
PEDRO
C.W.
STONE OAK PKWY.
1604
BLANCO RD.
2696
2696
BITTERS RD.
HUEBNER RD.
BLANCO RD.
WURZBACH PKWY.
1535 HWY.
N.W. MILITARY
MILITARY DR.
LOCKHILL - SELMA RD.
CALLAGHAN RD.
Camp Bullis Military Reservation
1535
N.W. LOOP
BULLIS RD.
354
CAMP BULLIS RD.
HEUERMANN
KYLE SEALE PKWY.
ZAVALA RD.
557
EXPRESSWAY
536
ANDERSON BLVD.
HOUSEMAN RD.
BABCOCK
1560
1604
16
471
BANDERA
Leon Valley
75
EVERS ROAD
1517
HUEBNER RD.
BABCOCK RD.
WURZBACH
WEST AVE.
SAN PEDRO AVE.
JACKSON - KELLER RD.
VANCE JACKSON RD.
Balcones Heights
FREDERICKSBURG RD.
10
410
CULLOUGH AVE.
BROADWAY
BITTERS
SAN
JONES

Six Flags Fiesta Texas
Univ. of Texas at San Antonio
UTSA

© AAA

N

SAN ANTONIO International Airport

Numbered location markers: 1604, 2252, 169, 63, 98, 35, 81, 79, 59, 27, 77, 76, 68, 78, 118, 125, 124, 57, 51, 410, 118, 166, 55, 56, 114, 77, 107, 113, 142, 104, 161, 122, 141, 70, 133, 76, 140, 127, 100, 116, 86, 119, 69, 102, 165, 73, 105, 103, 143, 138, 95, 134, 144, 148, 150, 112, 111, 66, 63, 69, 91, 57, 139, 155, 90, 79, 171, 129, 94, 121, 74, 149, 87, 123, 67, 61, 96, 345, 94, 103, 110, 131, 78, 104, 126, 93, 136, 68, 60, 91, 65, 85, 59, 106, 71, 164, 80, 62, 97, 151, 113, 58, 101, 120, 130, 83, 135, 105, 111, 87, 99, 102, 117, 162, 123, 99, 87, 72, 75, 90, 109

✈ Airport Accommodations

Spotter/Map Page Number	OA	SAN ANTONIO INTERNATIONAL	Diamond Rating	Rate Range High Season	Listing Page
122 / p. 496	AAA	Best Western-Posada Ana Airport, 0.5 mi w of terminal	◈◈◈	$64-$91 SAVE	521
69 / p. 496		Clarion Hotel San Antonio Airport, 4 mi nw	◈◈◈	$109-$129	523
55 / p. 496		Courtyard by Marriott-Airport, 2.5 mi e of terminal on I-410	◈◈◈	$89-$109	525
107 / p. 496		Days Inn Airport, 0.5 mi s	◈◈◈	$59-$149	525
56 / p. 496		Doubletree Club Hotel San Antonio Airport, 0.5 mi se of terminal	◈◈◈	$69-$119	527
148 / p. 496	AAA	Drury Inn & Suites Airport, 1.8 mi w of airport	◈◈◈	$69-$99 SAVE	527
95 / p. 496		Embassy Suites Hotel-Airport, 0.5 mi nw of terminal	◈◈◈	$159-$199	528
147 / p. 496		Hampton Inn-Airport, 0.8 mi w of terminal	◈◈◈	$79-$103	528
140 / p. 496	AAA	Hilton San Antonio Airport, 2.3 mi w of terminal	◈◈◈	$89-$149 SAVE	530
150 / p. 496		Holiday Inn Express-Airport, 1.8 mi w of airport	◈◈◈	$103-$129	530
145 / p. 496		Holiday Inn Select, 1 mi w of terminal	◈◈◈	$129	530
143 / p. 496		HomeGate Studios & Suites, 3 mi nw	◈◈	$69-$79	531
161 / p. 496	AAA	La Quinta Inns-San Antonio Airport, 1.8 mi s of main terminal	◈◈◈	$89-$135 SAVE	532
146 / p. 496	AAA	Pear Tree Inn Airport, 0.8 mi w	◈◈◈	$64-$91 SAVE	534
134 / p. 496		Staybridge Suites San Antonio-Airport, 1 mi w of terminal	◈◈◈	$149-$169	538

San Antonio and Vicinity

This index helps you "spot" where approved accommodations and restaurants are located on the corresponding detailed maps. Lodging rate ranges are for comparison only and show the property's high season; rates are per night, unless only weekly (W) rates are available. Restaurant rate range is for dinner, unless only lunch (L) is served. Turn to the listing page for more detailed rate information and consult display ads for special promotions.

Spotter/Map Page Number	OA	SAN ANTONIO - Lodgings	Diamond Rating	Rate Range High Season	Listing Page
51 / p. 496		Econo Lodge Airport	◈◈	$54-$74	528
52 / p. 496		Microtel Inn & Suites	◈◈	$79-$109	533
53 / p. 496	AAA	Quality Inn & Suites Coliseum - see color ad p 506	◈◈◈	$55-$120 SAVE	535
54 / p. 496	AAA	Rodeway Inn Lackland AFB	◈◈	$65-$80 SAVE	537
55 / p. 496	AAA	Courtyard by Marriott-Airport - see color ad p 507	◈◈◈	$89-$109	525
56 / p. 496		Doubletree Club Hotel San Antonio Airport - see color ad p 526	◈◈◈	$69-$119	527
57 / p. 496		Comfort Inn Airport	◈◈	$59-$89	523
58 / p. 496	AAA	Holiday Inn Lackland	◈◈◈	$79-$135 SAVE	530
59 / p. 496	AAA	Best Western Continental Inn	◈◈◈	$69-$119 SAVE	519
60 / p. 496	AAA	Econo Lodge-East	◈◈◈	$35-$139 SAVE	528
61 / p. 496	AAA	Hyatt Regency Hill Country Resort - see color ad inside front cover	◈◈◈◈	$185-$320 SAVE	531
62 / p. 496	AAA	Holiday Inn Express South	◈◈◈	$99-$104 SAVE	530

Spotter/Map Page Number	OA	SAN ANTONIO - Lodgings (continued)	Diamond Rating	Rate Range High Season	Listing Page
63 / p. 496		Super 8 Motel of San Antonio Airport	◆◆	$35-$80	539
64 / p. 496	AAA	Best Western Sunset Suites-Riverwalk - see color ad p 522	◆◆◆	$89-$155 [SAVE]	522
65 / p. 496		Days Inn Northside	◆◆◆	$45-$130	526
66 / p. 496		Holiday Inn Express	◆◆◆	$79-$109	530
67 / p. 496		A Beckmann Inn & Carriage House Bed and Breakfast	◆◆◆	$110-$150	518
68 / p. 496	AAA	Comfort Suites - see color ad p 525	◆◆◆	$70-$160 [SAVE]	524
69 / p. 496		Clarion Hotel San Antonio Airport	◆◆◆	$109-$129	523
70 / p. 496	AAA	Super 8 Motel- IH 10 East	◆◆	$39-$129 [SAVE]	539
71 / p. 496		Days Inn Coliseum	◆◆	$50-$110	526
72 / p. 496		Howard Johnson Coliseum	◆◆	$50-$110	531
73 / p. 496		Adams House Bed & Breakfast	◆◆◆	$109-$169	518
74 / p. 496	AAA	Holiday Inn-Northeast	◆◆◆	$95 [SAVE]	530
75 / p. 496		Suburban Lodge	◆◆	Failed to provide	538
76 / p. 496	AAA	La Quinta Inn-San Antonio-Windsor Park - see color ad p 510	◆◆◆	$69-$105 [SAVE]	532
77 / p. 496	AAA	Knights Inn Windsor Park	◆◆	$59-$89 [SAVE]	532
78 / p. 496		Super 8 Motel	◆◆	$49-$99	538
79 / p. 496	AAA	Drury Inn Northeast	◆◆◆	$74-$100 [SAVE]	527
80 / p. 496		Comfort Inn-East	◆◆◆	$54-$99	523
81 / p. 496		Hampton Inn-Northeast	◆◆◆	$91-$111	528
82 / p. 496	AAA	La Quinta Inn-San Antonio-South - see color ad p 510	◆◆◆	$69-$105 [SAVE]	532
83 / p. 496	AAA	Best Western Ingram Park Inn - see color ad p 520	◆◆◆	$80-$130 [SAVE]	521
84 / p. 496		La Quinta Inn-San Antonio-Lackland - see color ad p 510	◆◆◆	$69-$105	532
85 / p. 496	AAA	Best Western Lackland Inn & Suites	◆◆◆	$62-$99 [SAVE]	521
86 / p. 496	AAA	La Quinta Inn-San Antonio-Ingram Park - see color ad p 510	◆◆◆	$89-$125 [SAVE]	532
87 / p. 496		Residence Inn NW/Six Flags	◆◆◆	$119-$159	536
88 / p. 496		Christmas House Bed & Breakfast	◆◆	$85-$125	522
89 / p. 496	AAA	Red Roof Inn Lackland	◆◆	$40-$63 [SAVE]	536
90 / p. 496	AAA	Sierra Royale All Suite Hotel - see color ad p 537	◆◆◆	$105-$135 [SAVE]	537
91 / p. 496		Studio 6 #6047	◆◆	$57-$76	538
92 / p. 496		Bonner Garden Bed & Breakfast	◆◆◆	$85-$135	522

Spotter/Map Page Number	OA	SAN ANTONIO - Lodgings (continued)	Diamond Rating	Rate Range High Season	Listing Page
93 / p. 496	AAA	**Omni San Antonio Hotel -** see color ad p 534	▽▽▽▽	$149-$169 SAVE	534
94 / p. 496		La Quinta Inn-San Antonio-Wurzbach - see color ad p 510	▽▽▽	$69-$105	532
95 / p. 496		Embassy Suites Hotel-Airport	▽▽▽	$159-$199	528
96 / p. 496		Courtyard by Marriott-Medical Center - see color ad p 507	▽▽▽	$84-$109	525
97 / p. 496		Howard Johnson Inn & Suites Medical Center	▽▽▽	$69-$79	531
98 / p. 496		Park Inn	▽▽	$69	534
99 / p. 496	AAA	**Rodeway Inn-Six Flags Fiesta**	▽▽	$36-$125 SAVE	537
100 / p. 496		Quality Inn Northwest	▽▽	$39-$99	535
101 / p. 496	AAA	**Hampton Inn Six Flags Area -** see color ad p 529	▽▽▽	$79-$99 SAVE	529
102 / p. 496		Homestead Studio Suites Hotel-San Antonio/Airport	▽▽	$65-$80	531
103 / p. 496	AAA	**Hampton Inn Northwest-Sea World Area**	▽▽▽	$64-$104 SAVE	529
104 / p. 496		Homewood Suites by Hilton	▽▽▽	$109-$129	531
105 / p. 496	AAA	**Best Western Fiesta Inn -** see color ad p 520	▽▽▽	$80-$130 SAVE	520
106 / p. 496	AAA	**Comfort Inn Sea World -** see color ad p 524	▽▽▽	$59-$139 SAVE	524
107 / p. 496		Days Inn Airport	▽▽▽	$59-$149	525
109 / p. 496	AAA	**Days Inn Seaworld**	▽▽▽	$65-$115 SAVE	526
110 / p. 496	AAA	**Travelodge Suites**	▽▽	$49-$119 SAVE	539
111 / p. 496	AAA	**Super 8 Motel-Six Flags Fiesta**	▽▽	$60-$80 SAVE	539
112 / p. 496		Ramada Limited	▽▽	$100	535
113 / p. 496	AAA	**Best Western Posada Ana San Antonio Medical Center**	▽▽▽	$102-$132 SAVE	521
114 / p. 496		Holiday Inn Express Seaworld	▽▽▽	$79-$124	530
115 / p. 496		Motel 6 - 651	▽▽	$51-$67	533
116 / p. 496	AAA	**Econo Lodge**	▽▽	$35-$110 SAVE	527
117 / p. 496	AAA	**Comfort Inn-Fiesta -** see color ad p 523	▽▽▽	$89-$129 SAVE	523
118 / p. 496		Days Inn	▽▽▽	$60-$150	525
119 / p. 496		Comfort Suites Airport North	▽▽▽	$89-$99	524
120 / p. 496		Days Inn-Fiesta Park	▽▽▽	$59-$129	526
121 / p. 496	AAA	**Ramada Limited Northwest**	▽▽▽	$59-$109 SAVE	536
122 / p. 496	AAA	**Best Western-Posada Ana Airport**	▽▽▽	$64-$91 SAVE	521
123 / p. 496	AAA	**Sleep Inn San Antonio -** see color ad p 538	▽▽	$50-$120 SAVE	537
124 / p. 496		Super 8 Motel Downtown North	▽▽	$42-$68	539

Spotter/Map Page Number	OA	SAN ANTONIO - Lodgings (continued)	Diamond Rating	Rate Range High Season	Listing Page
125 / p. 496		Hill Country Inn & Suites	◆◆◆	$50-$70	529
126 / p. 496	AAA	AmeriSuites (San Antonio/Northwest) - see color ad p 504	◆◆◆	$105 [SAVE]	518
127 / p. 496	AAA	La Quinta Inn-San Antonio-Vance Jackson - see color ad p 510	◆◆◆	$69-$105 [SAVE]	532
128 / p. 496	AAA	Galaxy Inn Motel	◆◆	$45-$95 [SAVE]	528
129 / p. 496	AAA	AmeriSuites (San Antonio/Crossroads) - see color ad p 504	◆◆◆	$95 [SAVE]	518
130 / p. 496		Studio 6 #6046	◆◆	$45-$63	538
131 / p. 496		Staybridge Suites by Holiday Inn San Antonio NW-Colonnade	◆◆◆	$93-$202	538
132 / p. 496	AAA	Alamo Inn	◆◆	$50-$110 [SAVE]	518
133 / p. 496		Fairfield Inn by Marriott-San Antonio Airport - see color ad p 507	◆◆◆	$89	528
134 / p. 496		Staybridge Suites San Antonio-Airport	◆◆◆	$149-$169	538
135 / p. 496		Howard Johnson Express Inn Fiesta	◆◆	$69-$99	531
136 / p. 496		Motel 6 - 134	◆	$35-$51	533
137 / p. 496		Motel 6 - 183	◆◆	$35-$51	533
138 / p. 496	AAA	Red Roof Inn-San Antonio Airport	◆◆	$39-$61 [SAVE]	536
139 / p. 496		Embassy Suites Northwest	◆◆◆	$144-$164	528
140 / p. 496	AAA	Hilton San Antonio Airport - see ad p 529	◆◆◆	$89-$149 [SAVE]	530
141 / p. 496		Courtyard Airport at Northstar - see color ad p 507	◆◆◆	$129	525
142 / p. 496	AAA	AmeriSuites (San Antonio/Airport) - see color ad p 504	◆◆◆	$99-$129 [SAVE]	518
143 / p. 496		HomeGate Studios & Suites	◆◆	$69-$79	531
144 / p. 496		Doubletree Hotel	◆◆◆	$109-$139	527
145 / p. 496		Holiday Inn Select	◆◆	$129	530
146 / p. 496	AAA	Pear Tree Inn Airport	◆◆◆	$64-$91 [SAVE]	534
147 / p. 496		Hampton Inn-Airport	◆◆◆	$70-$103	528
148 / p. 496	AAA	Drury Inn & Suites Airport	◆◆◆	$69-$99 [SAVE]	527
149 / p. 496		Candlewood Suites Hotel	◆◆◆	$79-$109	522
150 / p. 496		Holiday Inn Express-Airport	◆◆◆	$103-$129	530
151 / p. 496		Drury Inn & Suites-San Antonio Northwest	◆◆◆	$65-$95	527
152 / p. 496		Radisson Resort Hill Country - see color ad p 535	◆◆◆	$199-$249	535
153 / p. 496		Econo Lodge	◆◆	$69-$84	527
155 / p. 496		San Antonio Marriott Northwest - see color ad p 507	◆◆◆	$129-$185	537

Spotter/Map Page Number	OA	SAN ANTONIO - Lodgings (continued)	Diamond Rating	Rate Range High Season	Listing Page
156 / p. 496	AAA	Red Roof Inn San Antonio (NW-SeaWorld)	◆◆	$52-$78 SAVE	536
157 / p. 496		A Victorian Lady Inn	◆◆◆	$89-$135	519
159 / p. 496		Days Inn South	◆◆	$40-$89	526
160 / p. 496	AAA	Red Roof Inn San Antonio (Downtown)	◆◆◆	$69-$89 SAVE	536
161 / p. 496	AAA	La Quinta Inns-San Antonio Airport - see color ad p 510	◆◆	$89-$135 SAVE	532
162 / p. 496		The Westin La Cantera Resort	◆◆◆◆	$189-$284	539
163 / p. 496		Quality Inn & Suites	◆◆◆	$45-$99	534
164 / p. 496	AAA	Regency Inn & Suites	◆◆	$49-$99 SAVE	533
165 / p. 496	AAA	Best Western Hill Country Suites	◆◆◆	$89-$139 SAVE	521
166 / p. 496		Residence Inn San Antonio-Airport - see color ad p 507	◆◆◆	$134	536
168 / p. 496		Super 8 Motel Downtown	◆◆	$45-$100	539
171 / p. 496		Comfort Suites	◆◆◆	$99-$139	524
		SAN ANTONIO - Restaurants			
55 / p. 496		Acapulco Seafood Restaurant	◆	$8-$11	540
56 / p. 496	AAA	Asia Kitchen	◆◆	$11-$18	540
57 / p. 496		Tom's Ribs	◆	$13	544
58 / p. 496		Regent Hunan Chinese Restaurant	◆	$6-$8	544
59 / p. 496		Cha-Cha's	◆◆◆	$7-$11	540
60 / p. 496		Golden Wok Chinese Restaurant	◆◆	$8-$13	541
61 / p. 496		Alamo Cafe	◆◆	$6-$10	540
62 / p. 496		Aldo's Ristorante Italiano	◆◆	$8-$13	540
63 / p. 496		La Scala	◆◆◆	$9-$13	542
64 / p. 496		Acadiana Cafe	◆	$8-$15	539
65 / p. 496		Old World German Restaurant-Delicatessen & Konditorei	◆◆	$6-$14	543
66 / p. 496		Los Patios	◆◆◆	$12-$28	542
67 / p. 496		Dry Dock Seafood Oyster Bar	◆	$8-$20	541
68 / p. 496		Mencui's Chinese Restaurnat	◆◆◆	$7-$18	543
69 / p. 496		India Oven	◆◆	$12-$25	542
70 / p. 496		The Sea Island Shrimp House	◆◆	$8-$12	544
71 / p. 496	AAA	Bolo's Rotisserie-Grille	◆◆◆◆	$8-$12	540
72 / p. 496		China Swan Chinese & Seafood Restaurant	◆◆	$9-$18	541
73 / p. 496		El Jarro de Arturo	◆◆	$7-$16	541
74 / p. 496		Fratelli's Caffe Italiano	◆◆	$8-$14	541

Spotter/Map Page Number	OA	SAN ANTONIO - Restaurants (continued)	Diamond Rating	Rate Range High Season	Listing Page
75 / p. 496		Cafe Milano	◆◆	$10-$16	540
76 / p. 496		Kiran Indian Restaurant	◆◆	$7-$12	542
77 / p. 496		Tomatillos Mexican Restaurant	◆◆	$5-$14	544
78 / p. 496		Pappasito's Cantina Restaurant	◆◆	$8-$12	543
79 / p. 496		Mario's Restaurant	◆◆	$8-$10	543
80 / p. 496		Saigon Elite	◆◆	$10-$14	544
81 / p. 496		Liberty Bar	◆◆◆	$10-$26	542
82 / p. 496	AAA	**Mina & Dimi's Greek House Restaurant**	◆	$8-$12	543
83 / p. 496		Barnacle Bill's	◆	$14	540
85 / p. 496		U. R. Cooks	◆◆	$10-$15	544
86 / p. 496		Grady's Bar-B-Que	◆	$6-$9	542
87 / p. 496		Ristorante Italiano Grissini	◆◆	$9-$24	544
90 / p. 496		La Fogata Restaurant	◆◆	$10-$22	542
91 / p. 496		Ernesto's Restaurant	◆◆◆	$9-$20	541
94 / p. 496		Bistro Time	◆◆◆	$10-$20	540
99 / p. 496		Meson European Dining	◆◆	$12-$24	543
101 / p. 496		Piedras Negras de Noche	◆◆	$9-$20	543
102 / p. 496		Francesca's at Sunset	◆◆◆	$20-$40	541
103 / p. 496		Boccone's Italian Restaurant-Bakery & Music Emporium	◆◆	$12-$18	540
104 / p. 496		Stone Werks Caffe & Bar	◆◆	$8-$10	544
105 / p. 496		Taste of Asia	◆	$9-$19	544
106 / p. 496		Mouse's Smokehouse Bar-B-Que	◆◆	$4-$11	543
107 / p. 496		Van's Chinese Seafood Restaurant	◆	$8-$19	544
110 / p. 496		Fatso's Barbeque & Sports Bar	◆	$7-$12	541
111 / p. 496		Tokyo Steak House	◆◆	$13-$47	544
112 / p. 496		Old San Francisco Steak House	◆◆◆	$11-$30	543
113 / p. 496		Magic Time Machine	◆◆	$15-$35	543
114 / p. 496	AAA	**The Barn Door Restaurant**	◆◆	$8-$25	540
117 / p. 496		Jacala Mexican Restaurant	◆◆	$6-$9	542
118 / p. 496		Crumpets Restaurant & Bakery	◆◆	$10-$26	541
120 / p. 496	AAA	**Earl Abel's Restaurant**	◆	$6-$19	541
121 / p. 496		La Calesa	◆◆	$6-$12	542
123 / p. 496		Grey Moss Inn	◆◆◆	$17-$40	542
124 / p. 496		La Fonda Mexican Restaurant	◆◆	$5-$8	542

DOWNTOWN SAN ANTONIO   (See map p. 492; index p. 494)

———— WHERE TO STAY ————

ADAM'S MARK SAN ANTONIO RIVERWALK HOTEL
Phone: (210)354-2800   **23**
AAA SAVE
2/1-5/31 & 9/7-11/22   1P: $135-$209   2P: $135-$209   XP: $20   F18
6/1-9/6 & 11/23-1/31   1P: $125-$199   2P: $125-$199   XP: $20   F18
Location: Corner of Pecan and Soledad sts. 111 Pecan St E 78205. Fax: 210/354-2700. **Facility:** 410 units. 406 one-bedroom standard units. 4 one-bedroom suites ($450-$900). 21 stories, interior corridors. *Bath:* combo **Large-scale Hotel** or shower only. **Parking:** valet. **Terms:** cancellation fee imposed, package plans - weekends. **Amenities:** video games, irons, hair dryers. **Dining:** 6:30 am-10 pm. **Pool(s):** heated outdoor. **Leisure Activities:** exercise room. **Guest Services:** gift shop, valet laundry. **Business Services:** conference facilities, business center. **Cards:** AX, CB, DC, DS, MC, VI. **Special Amenities:** early check-in/late check-out and preferred room (subject to availability with advanced reservations).

SOME UNITS

⑤ ➕ ⑪ ②④ ✆ ➷ ✳ 🖧 💻 / ✕ 🔌 /
FEE

ALAMO TRAVELODGE
Phone: (210)222-1000   **28**
AAA SAVE
All Year [BP]   1P: $49-$149   2P: $49-$149   XP: $5   F16
Location: US 281, exit Broadway. 405 Broadway 78205. Fax: 210/229-9744. **Facility:** 82 one-bedroom standard units. 2-3 stories, exterior corridors. *Bath:* combo or shower only. **Parking:** on-site. **Terms:** check-in 4 pm. **Amenities:** video games. **Dining:** 6 am-4 pm. **Pool(s):** outdoor. **Guest Services:** coin laundry. **Business Services:** fax (fee). **Cards:** AX, DC, DS, MC, VI. **Special Amenities:** free local telephone calls and free newspaper.
Small-scale Hotel

SOME UNITS

⑤ ⑪ ➷ ✳ 🖧 💻 / ✕ 🔌 🖼 /

AMERISUITES (SAN ANTONIO/RIVERWALK)
Phone: (210)227-6854   **45**
AAA SAVE
All Year [ECP]   1P: $109-$159   2P: $119-$169   XP: $10   F18
Location: I-35, exit Durango St, 0.9 mi e. 601 S St Mary's St 78205. Fax: 210/227-1247. **Facility:** 132 one-bedroom standard units. 7 stories, interior corridors. *Bath:* combo or shower only. **Parking:** on-site. **Terms:** cancellation fee imposed, small pets only. **Amenities:** voice mail, irons, hair dryers. **Pool(s):** heated outdoor. **Leisure Activities:** exercise room. **Small-scale Hotel Guest Services:** valet and coin laundry. **Business Services:** meeting rooms. **Cards:** AX, DC, DS, JC, MC, VI. **Special Amenities:** free continental breakfast and free newspaper. *(See color ad below)*

SOME UNITS

⑤ 🐾 ⑪ ➷ ✳ 🖧 🔌 🖼 💻 / ✕ /

ARBOR HOUSE SUITES BED & BREAKFAST
Phone: 210/472-2005   **38**
AAA SAVE
All Year   2P: $125-$175   XP: $15   F
Location: Near La Villita; just n of Durango St. 540 S Saint Mary's St 78205. Fax: 210/472-2007. **Facility:** Dating from 1903, this village of five houses features tranquil courtyards; the varied-size accommodations are individually decorated. Smoke free premises. 18 one-bedroom suites with kitchens. 2 stories (no elevator), interior/exterior corridors. *Bath:* combo or shower only. **Parking:** on-site. **Terms:** 3 day cancellation notice, **Historic Bed** [ECP] meal plan available, small pets only (with prior approval). **Amenities:** voice mail. **Leisure Activities: & Breakfast** guest access to nearby pool. *Fee:* nearby tennis court. **Guest Services:** valet laundry. **Business Services:** fax. **Cards:** AX, MC, VI. **Special Amenities:** free continental breakfast and free local telephone calls.

SOME UNITS

⑤ 🐾 ⑪ ✕ 🖧 💻 / 🔌 🖼 /

(See map p. 492)

A YELLOW ROSE BED & BREAKFAST
Phone: (210)229-9903   **29**

All Year [BP]   2P: $100-$200   XP: $15
Bed & Breakfast   **Location:** Just s of S St Marys at Durango St. Located in the King William Historic District. 229 Madison 78204. Fax: 210/229-1691. **Facility:** Porches with rocking chairs adjoin some accommodations at this restored property featuring spacious common areas; all rooms have private entrances. Smoke free premises. 5 units. 4 one-bedroom standard units, some with whirlpools. 1 one-bedroom suite with kitchen. 2 stories (no elevator), exterior corridors. *Bath:* combo or shower only. **Parking:** on-site. **Terms:** 2-4 night minimum stay - weekends, age restrictions may apply, 14 day cancellation notice-fee imposed, weekly rates available. **Amenities:** irons, hair dryers. *Some:* CD players. **Guest Services:** complimentary evening beverages, complimentary laundry, area transportation. **Cards:** AX, DS, MC, VI.

SOME UNITS
(A$K) (🛏) (✕) (🎦) (🔌) (💻) / (VCR) /

BEAUREGARD HOUSE
Phone: (210)222-1198   **49**

(AAA) (SAVE)   All Year [BP]   1P: $105-$180   2P: $125-$190   XP: $30
Bed & Breakfast   **Location:** 215 Beauregard St 78204. Fax: 210/222-9338. **Facility:** Smoke free premises. 5 one-bedroom standard units. 3 stories (no elevator), interior/exterior corridors. *Bath:* combo or shower only. **Parking:** on-site. **Terms:** 2 night minimum stay - weekends, 14 day cancellation notice-fee imposed, weekly rates available, package plans. **Amenities:** hair dryers. **Leisure Activities:** Fee: bicycles. **Cards:** AX, DS, MC, VI. **Special Amenities: free continental breakfast and free local telephone calls.**

SOME UNITS
(✕) (🎦) (🚭) (💻) (💻) / (VCR) (📠) /

BEST WESTERN ALAMO SUITES
Phone: (210)271-1000   **33**

(AAA) (SAVE)   3/28-8/16 [ECP]   1P: $89-$150   2P: $89-$150   XP: $6   F12
2/1-3/27 & 8/17-1/31 [ECP].   1P: $70-$150   2P: $70-$150   XP: $6   F12
Small-scale Hotel   **Location:** I-35, exit 155B, jct Fria St. 102 El Paso St 78204. Fax: 210/299-4473. **Facility:** 65 one-bedroom suites ($89-$150). 2 stories, interior corridors. *Bath:* combo or shower only. **Parking:** on-site. **Terms:** 2 night minimum stay - weekends 5/23-8/16. **Amenities:** high-speed Internet, voice mail, irons, hair dryers. **Pool(s):** heated outdoor. **Leisure Activities:** exercise room. **Business Services:** fax (fee). **Cards:** AX, DC, DS, MC, VI. **Special Amenities: free continental breakfast.** *(See color ad p 520)*

SOME UNITS
(S/D) (🏊) (🎦) (DATA PORT) (💻) (📠) (💻) / (✕) /

BRACKENRIDGE HOUSE B & B
Phone: (210)271-3442   **34**

(AAA) (SAVE)   All Year [BP]   1P: $110-$175   2P: $110-$200   XP: $25   F12
Bed & Breakfast   **Location:** King William Historic District. 230 Madison 78204. Fax: 210/226-3139. **Facility:** This B&B includes a carriage-house suite in addition to guest rooms in the main house; all have televisions. Smoke free premises. 6 units. 2 one-bedroom standard units. 3 one-bedroom suites ($125-$200). 1 cottage ($125-$250). 2 stories (no elevator), interior/exterior corridors. *Bath:* combo or shower only. **Parking:** on-site. **Terms:** 2 night minimum stay - weekends, age restrictions may apply, 14 day cancellation notice-fee imposed, pets (in carriage house). **Amenities:** irons, hair dryers. **Leisure Activities:** whirlpool. **Cards:** AX, DC, DS, MC, VI. **Special Amenities: early check-in/late check-out and free local telephone calls.**

SOME UNITS
(🐾) (✕) (🎦) (💻) (📠) (💻) / (DATA PORT) /

(See map p. 492)

THE COLUMNS ON ALAMO
[AAA] [SAVE]
[Bed & Breakfast]

Phone: (210)271-3245 **27**

All Year [BP] 1P: $92-$230   2P: $92-$230   XP: $20   D12
Location: 0.5 mi s of jct St Marys St. Located in the King William Historic District. 1037 S Alamo St 78210. Fax: 210/271-3245. **Facility:** This 1892 Greek Revival inn is furnished with antiques and reproductions. Smoke free premises. 13 one-bedroom standard units, some with whirlpools. 2 stories (no elevator), interior/exterior corridors. *Bath:* combo or shower only. **Parking:** on-site. **Terms:** 2 night minimum stay - weekends, age restrictions may apply, 8 day cancellation notice-fee imposed. **Amenities:** voice mail, irons, hair dryers. **Cards:** AX, CB, DC, DS, MC, VI.

COMFORT SUITES DOWNTOWN
[AAA] [SAVE]
[Small-scale Hotel]

Phone: (210)472-1002 **47**

3/28-8/16 [ECP]   1P: $89-$150   2P: $89-$150   XP: $6   F18
2/1-3/27 & 8/17-1/31 [ECP]   1P: $70-$150   2P: $70-$150   XP: $6   F18
Location: I-35/10, exit 155A (Alamo St), 0.5 mi s. 1002 S Laredo 78204. Fax: 210/227-4680. **Facility:** 63 one-bedroom standard units, some with whirlpools. 3 stories, interior corridors. **Parking:** on-site. **Terms:** 2 night minimum stay - weekends 5/23-8/16. **Amenities:** irons, hair dryers. **Pool(s):** indoor. **Leisure Activities:** whirlpool. **Guest Services:** coin laundry. **Cards:** AX, DC, DS, MC, VI. **Special Amenities:** free continental breakfast and free local telephone calls. *(See color ad below)*

SOME UNITS

COURTYARD BY MARRIOTT-DOWNTOWN
[Small-scale Hotel]

Phone: 210/229-9449 **41**

Property failed to provide current rates
Location: 0.5 mi e jct I-35 and Durango St. 600 S Santa Rosa 78204. Fax: 210/229-1853. **Facility:** 149 units. 137 one-bedroom standard units. 12 one-bedroom suites. 3 stories, interior corridors. *Bath:* combo or shower only. **Parking:** on-site. **Amenities:** voice mail, irons, hair dryers. **Pool(s):** heated outdoor. **Leisure Activities:** whirlpool, exercise room. **Guest Services:** valet and coin laundry. **Business Services:** meeting rooms, fax (fee). **Cards:** AX, CB, DC, DS, MC, VI. *(See color ad p 507)*

SOME UNITS

DAYS INN-DOWNTOWN LAREDO ST
[SAVE]
[Small-scale Hotel]

Phone: (210)271-3334 **43**

4/28-8/16 [ECP]   1P: $45-$109   2P: $45-$109   XP: $6   F18
3/28-4/27 [ECP]   1P: $45-$99   2P: $45-$99   XP: $6   F18
2/1-3/27 & 8/17-1/31 [ECP]   1P: $40-$90   2P: $40-$90   XP: $6   F18
Location: I-10/35, exit 154 (Laredo St). 1500 I-35 S 78204. Fax: 210/271-3306. **Facility:** 90 one-bedroom standard units. 2 stories (no elevator), interior/exterior corridors. *Bath:* combo or shower only. **Parking:** on-site. **Terms:** small pets only ($25 fee). **Amenities:** safes (fee), hair dryers. *Some:* honor bars. **Pool(s):** outdoor. **Guest Services:** coin laundry. **Business Services:** fax (fee). **Cards:** AX, DC, DS, MC, VI.

SOME UNITS

(See map p. 492)

DRURY INN & SUITES RIVERWALK

AAA SAVE

6/1-8/31 [BP]	1P: $136-$175	2P: $146-$185	XP: $10 F18
9/1-1/31 [BP]	1P: $132-$151	2P: $142-$161	XP: $10 F18
2/1-5/31 [BP]	1P: $130-$149	2P: $140-$159	XP: $10 F18

Phone: (210)212-5200 **22**

Large-scale Hotel **Location:** Just s of College St. 201 N St. Mary's St 78205. **Fax:** 210/352-9939. **Facility:** 150 units. 100 one-bedroom standard units. 50 one-bedroom suites ($149-$171). 7 stories, interior corridors. *Bath:* combo or shower only. **Parking:** on-site (fee). **Amenities:** dual phone lines, voice mail, irons, hair dryers. **Dining:** 11 am-10 pm, cocktails. **Pool(s):** outdoor. **Leisure Activities:** whirlpool, exercise room. **Guest Services:** complimentary evening beverages: Mon-Thurs, valet and coin laundry. **Business Services:** meeting rooms, business center. **Cards:** AX, CB, DC, DS, MC, VI. **Special Amenities:** free continental breakfast and free local telephone calls.

SOME UNITS

(See map p. 492)

EMILY MORGAN HOTEL   Phone: (210)225-8486 **5**

2/1-4/30	1P: $149-$289	2P: $159-$300	XP: $10 F17
9/1-1/31	1P: $139-$259	2P: $159-$289	XP: $10 F17
5/1-8/31	1P: $99-$219	2P: $109-$229	XP: $10 F17

Historic
Large-scale Hotel   **Location:** On Houston St, just n of Bonham St. Located opposite the Alamo. 705 E Houston St 78205. Fax: 210/225-7227. **Facility:** 177 units. 176 one-bedroom standard units, some with whirlpools. 1 one-bedroom suite ($289-$350). 12 stories, interior corridors. **Parking:** on-site (fee). **Amenities:** video games, voice mail, irons, hair dryers. **Pool(s):** heated outdoor. **Leisure Activities:** saunas, whirlpool, exercise room. **Guest Services:** valet laundry. **Business Services:** meeting rooms, business center. **Cards:** AX, CB, DC, DS, MC, VI.

SOME UNITS

(ASK) (SD) (TI) (Y) (&M) (video) (swim) (X) (VCR) (T) (DATA PORT) (L) / (X) /

FAIRFIELD INN BY MARRIOTT   Phone: (210)299-1000 **39**

(SAVE)

All Year [CP]	1P: $89-$109	2P: $89-$109

Small-scale Hotel   **Location:** I-35, exit Durango St, 0.5 mi e. 620 S Santa Rosa Blvd 78204. Fax: 210/299-1030. **Facility:** 110 one-bedroom standard units, some with whirlpools. 4 stories, interior corridors. *Bath:* combo or shower only. **Parking:** on-site. **Terms:** cancellation fee imposed. **Amenities:** video games, irons, hair dryers. **Pool(s):** heated indoor. **Leisure Activities:** exercise room. **Guest Services:** valet and coin laundry. **Business Services:** fax (fee). **Cards:** AX, CB, DC, DS, MC, VI. *(See color ad p 507)*

SOME UNITS

(SD) (TI) (&) (video) (swim) (T) (DATA PORT) / (X) (bed) (L) /

THE FAIRMOUNT-A WYNDHAM HISTORIC HOTEL   Phone: (210)224-8800 **17**

(AAA) (SAVE)

All Year	1P: $149-$164	2P: $159-$174 XP: $10 F17

Historic
Small-scale Hotel   **Location:** Opposite convention center and Hemisfair Plaza. Located adjacent to La Villita Historic District. 401 S Alamo St 78205. Fax: 210/475-0082. **Facility:** 37 units. 25 one-bedroom standard units. 12 one-bedroom suites ($359-$1000), some with whirlpools. 4 stories, interior/exterior corridors. *Bath:* combo or shower only. **Parking:** valet. **Terms:** cancellation fee imposed. **Amenities:** video library, irons, hair dryers. *Some:* CD players. **Dining:** 7 am-11 pm, Sun-2 pm, cocktails, also, Polo's, see separate listing. **Guest Services:** valet laundry. **Business Services:** conference facilities. **Cards:** AX, DC, DS, MC, VI.

SOME UNITS

(SD) (TI) (24↑) (Y) (video) (swim handicap) (VCR) (T) (DATA PORT) / (X) /
FEE

FOUR POINTS SHERATON RIVERWALK NORTH HOTEL   Phone: (210)223-9461 **12**

All Year	1P: $89	2P: $89 XP: $10 F

Large-scale Hotel   **Location:** 0.3 mi s of jct Lexington Ave and I-35. 110 Lexington Ave 78205. Fax: 210/223-9267. **Facility:** 324 units. 316 one-bedroom standard units. 7 one- and 1 two-bedroom suites. 3-9 stories, interior corridors. **Parking:** on-site (fee) and valet. **Terms:** 3 day cancellation notice-fee imposed. **Amenities:** video games (fee), dual phone lines, voice mail, irons, hair dryers. **Pool(s):** outdoor. **Leisure Activities:** exercise room. **Guest Services:** gift shop, valet laundry, area transportation. **Business Services:** conference facilities, business center. **Cards:** AX, DC, DS, MC, VI.

SOME UNITS

(ASK) (SD) (TI) (Y) (swim) (T) (DATA PORT) (L) / (X) (bed) /

HAMPTON INN DOWNTOWN   Phone: (210)225-8500 **40**

(SAVE)

All Year [CP]	1P: $99-$129	2P: $99-$129

Small-scale Hotel   **Location:** Just nw of I-37 at Commerce St. 414 Bowie St 78205. Fax: 210/225-8526. **Facility:** 169 one-bedroom standard units. 6 stories, interior corridors. **Parking:** on-site. **Terms:** check-in 4 pm. **Amenities:** voice mail, irons. **Pool(s):** outdoor. **Guest Services:** coin laundry. **Business Services:** meeting rooms, fax (fee). **Cards:** AX, CB, DC, DS, MC, VI. *(See color ad below)*

SOME UNITS

(SD) (TI) (&M) (&) (swim) (T) (DATA PORT) (L) / (X) /

(See map p. 492)

THE HAVANA RIVERWALK INN

Phone: (210)222-2008   48

Country Inn

All Year   1P: $109-$215   2P: $109-$215
Location: Located in a quiet area. 1015 Navarro St 78205. Fax: 210/222-2717. **Facility:** Smoke free premises. 27 one-bedroom standard units. Interior corridors. **Parking:** on-site (fee). **Amenities:** irons, hair dryers. **Guest Services:** valet laundry. **Business Services:** meeting rooms, fax. **Cards:** AX, CB, DC, DS, MC, VI.

HAWTHORN SUITES RIVERWALK

Phone: (210)527-1900   31

Small-scale Hotel

All Year [ECP]   1P: $119-$179   2P: $129-$189   XP: $10   F18
Location: Just n of Navarro St. 830 N Saint Marys St 78205. Fax: 210/527-9969. **Facility:** 149 one-bedroom standard units, some with whirlpools. 3 stories, interior corridors. *Bath:* combo or shower only. **Parking:** on-site (fee), dual phone lines, voice mail, irons, hair dryers. **Pool(s):** outdoor. 22 stories, interior corridors. **Leisure Activities:** exercise room. **Guest Services:** valet and coin laundry. **Business Services:** meeting rooms, fax (fee). **Cards:** AX, CB, DC, DS, MC, VI.

SOME UNITS

HILTON PALACIO DEL RIO

Phone: (210)222-1400   16

Large-scale Hotel

All Year   1P: $150-$300   2P: $170-$320   XP: $20   F18
Location: Adjacent to convention center. Located on the Riverwalk. 200 S Alamo St 78205. Fax: 210/270-0761. **Facility:** This hotel, overlooking Hemisfair Plaza and San Antonio River, displays a collection of Western riding saddles donated by celebrities; bathrooms feature granite counters. 483 units. 473 one-bedroom standard units. 6 one- and 4 two-bedroom suites. 22 stories, interior corridors. **Parking:** on-site (fee) and valet. **Terms:** small pets only ($25 extra charge). **Amenities:** *Some:* video games (fee), dual phone lines, voice mail, irons, hair dryers. **Dining:** 2 restaurants, 6:30 am-11 pm, Fri & Sat-midnight, cocktails, entertainment. **Pool(s):** outdoor. **Leisure Activities:** whirlpool, exercise room. **Guest Services:** gift shop, valet and coin laundry. **Business Services:** meeting rooms, business center. **Cards:** AX, CB, DC, DS, JC, MC, VI.

SOME UNITS

HOLIDAY INN CROCKETT HOTEL

Phone: (210)225-6500   6

Large-scale Hotel

All Year   1P: $169-$199   2P: $179-$199   XP: $10   F17
Location: Center. Located across from the Alamo. 320 Bonham St 78205. Fax: 210/225-6251. **Facility:** 206 units. 204 one-bedroom standard units, some with whirlpools. 2 one-bedroom suites. 3-7 stories, interior/exterior corridors. *Bath:* combo or shower only. **Parking:** on-site. **Terms:** pets ($50 fee, $100 extra charge). **Amenities:** video games, voice mail, irons, hair dryers. **Dining:** 6:30 am-10 pm, cocktails. **Pool(s):** outdoor. **Leisure Activities:** whirlpools. **Guest Services:** valet and coin laundry. **Business Services:** meeting rooms, fax. **Cards:** AX, CB, DC, DS, JC, MC, VI. **Special Amenities: free room upgrade and preferred room (each subject to availability with advanced reservations).**

SOME UNITS

HOLIDAY INN-DOWNTOWN-MARKET SQUARE

Phone: (210)225-3211   13

Small-scale Hotel

All Year   1P: $79-$159   2P: $79-$159
Location: I-35, exit Durango St. 318 W Durango St 78204. Fax: 210/225-1125. **Facility:** 315 one-bedroom standard units. 4 stories, interior corridors. **Parking:** on-site. **Terms:** cancellation fee imposed, [BP] meal plan available, small pets only. **Amenities:** voice mail, irons, hair dryers. **Pool(s):** outdoor, wading. **Leisure Activities:** whirlpool, exercise room, sports court. **Guest Services:** gift shop, coin laundry, area transportation. **Business Services:** meeting rooms, fax (fee). **Cards:** AX, CB, DC, DS, JC, MC, VI.

SOME UNITS

HOLIDAY INN EXPRESS HOTEL & SUITES

Phone: (210)354-1333   37

Small-scale Hotel

All Year   1P: $159-$339   2P: $159-$339   XP: $10   F18
Location: Just n of Durango St. 524 S St Mary's St 78205. Fax: 210/354-2888. **Facility:** 116 units. 115 one- and 1 two-bedroom suites, some with kitchens (no utensils). 4 stories, interior corridors. **Parking:** on-site (fee). **Amenities:** dual phone lines, voice mail, irons, hair dryers. **Pool(s):** outdoor. **Leisure Activities:** whirlpool, exercise room. **Guest Services:** coin laundry. **Business Services:** meeting rooms, business center. **Cards:** AX, CB, DC, DS, JC, MC, VI.

SOME UNITS

HOLIDAY INN RIVERWALK

Phone: (210)224-2500   10

Small-scale Hotel

All Year   1P: $119-$325
Location: By the San Antonio River; from Houston St, just s. 217 N Saint Mary's St 78205. Fax: 210/223-1302. **Facility:** 313 units. 301 one-bedroom standard units. 12 one-bedroom suites ($325-$325). 23 stories, interior corridors. *Bath:* combo or shower only. **Parking:** on-site (fee) and valet. **Terms:** small pets only. **Amenities:** voice mail, irons, hair dryers. **Pool(s):** heated outdoor. **Leisure Activities:** whirlpool, exercise room. **Guest Services:** gift shop, valet laundry. **Business Services:** conference facilities, fax (fee). **Cards:** AX, CB, DC, DS, JC, MC, VI.

SOME UNITS

HOMEWOOD SUITES RIVERWALK BY HILTON

Phone: (210)222-1515   14

Small-scale Hotel

All Year [ECP]   1P: $159-$249   2P: $169-$269   XP: $20   F18
Location: Corner of St. Mary's and West Market sts; center. 432 W Market St 78205. Fax: 210/222-1575. **Facility:** 146 units. 138 one- and 8 two-bedroom suites with kitchens. 10 stories, interior corridors. *Bath:* combo or shower only. **Parking:** valet. **Amenities:** video games, high-speed Internet, voice mail, irons, hair dryers. **Pool(s):** small heated outdoor. **Leisure Activities:** whirlpool, exercise room. **Guest Services:** gift shop, complimentary evening beverages: Mon-Sat, valet and coin laundry. **Business Services:** meeting rooms, business center. **Cards:** AX, CB, DC, DS, MC, VI.

SOME UNITS

FEE

(See map p. 492)

HOWARD JOHNSON RIVERWALK PLAZA HOTEL
Phone: (210)226-2271 〔15〕
AAA (SAVE) All Year   1P: $89-$189   2P: $109-$199   XP: $10   F17
Location: Just e of I-35; center. Located on the Riverwalk. 100 Villita St 78205. **Fax:** 210/226-9453. **Facility:** 132 one-bedroom standard units. 6 stories, interior/exterior corridors. **Parking:** on-site (fee). **Terms:** cancellation fee imposed, package plans. **Amenities:** voice mail, safes (fee), irons, hair dryers. **Dining:** 6 am-2:30 & 5:30-10:30 pm, Fri-midnight, Sat 7 am-2:30 & 5:30-midnight, Sun from 7 am, cocktails, also, Cascades by the River-Steaks & Fine International Cuisine, see separate listing, entertainment. **Pool(s):** heated outdoor.
Large-scale Hotel
Guest Services: gift shop, valet laundry. **Business Services:** meeting rooms, fax (fee). **Cards:** AX, DC, DS, JC, MC, VI.
Special Amenities: early check-in/late check-out and free newspaper. *(See color ad p 493)*

SOME UNITS
(icons) FEE / FEE FEE FEE

HYATT REGENCY SAN ANTONIO
Phone: (210)222-1234 〔8〕
AAA (SAVE) All Year   1P: $149-$285   2P: $149-$285   XP: $25   F18
Location: Between College and Crockett. Located on the Riverwalk at Paseo del Alamo. 123 Losoya St 78205.
Fax: 210/227-4925. **Facility:** Southwestern styling creates a casual ambience at this hotel. 632 units. 604 one-bedroom standard units. 28 one-bedroom suites. 14 stories, interior corridors. *Bath:* combo or shower only. **Parking:** on-site (fee) and valet. **Terms:** cancellation fee imposed. **Amenities:** dual phone lines, voice mail, honor bars, irons, hair dryers. *Some:* CD players, fax. **Dining:** 6:30 am-10 pm, cocktails. **Pool(s):** heated outdoor. **Leisure Activities:** whirlpool, exercise room. **Guest Services:** gift shop, valet laundry. **Business Services:** conference facilities, business center. **Cards:** AX, CB, DC, DS, JC, MC, VI. *(See color ad inside front cover)*
Large-scale Hotel

SOME UNITS
(icons) /

INN ON THE RIVER
Phone: (210)225-6333 〔25〕
All Year [BP]   2P: $69-$175
Location: Just n of W Durango St. 129 Woodward Pl 78204. **Fax:** 210/271-3992. **Facility:** Smoke free premises. 12 one-bedroom standard units. 3 stories (no elevator), interior/exterior corridors. *Bath:* combo or shower only. **Parking:** on-site. **Terms:** 7 day cancellation notice-fee imposed, package plans. **Business Services:** fax (fee). **Cards:** AX, CB, DC, DS, JC, MC, VI.
Bed & Breakfast

SOME UNITS
(icons) /

LA MANSION DEL RIO
Phone: (210)518-1000 〔9〕
AAA (SAVE) 2/1-5/31 & 9/1-1/31   1P: $209-$359   XP: $25   F18
6/1-8/31   1P: $179-$299   XP: $25   F18
Location: Just s on the riverwalk. 112 College St 78205. **Fax:** 210/226-1365. **Facility:** Spanish-style decor enhances this property offering many accommodations with balconies overlooking the San Antonio River. 337 units. 326 one-bedroom standard units, some with kitchens and/or whirlpools. 11 one-bedroom suites. 7 stories, interior/exterior corridors. *Bath:* combo or shower only. **Parking:** valet. **Terms:** 3 day cancellation notice-fee imposed, pets (sign a waiver). **Amenities:** video games, dual phone lines, voice mail, honor bars, irons, hair dryers. **Dining:** 6:30 am-10:30 pm, Fri & Sat-11 pm, Sunday brunch, cocktails, also, Las Canarias Restaurant, see separate listing, entertainment. **Pool(s):** heated outdoor. **Leisure Activities:** exercise room. **Guest Services:** gift shop, valet laundry, area transportation (fee)-within 10 mi. **Business Services:** meeting rooms, business center. **Cards:** AX, CB, DC, DS, JC, MC, VI. Affiliated with A Preferred Hotel.
Large-scale Hotel

SOME UNITS
(icons) / FEE

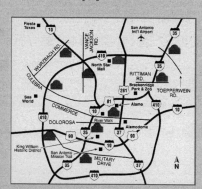

(See map p. 492)

LA QUINTA INN-CONVENTION CENTER   Phone: (210)222-9181   [20]

SAVE

Small-scale Hotel

All Year   1P: $109-$139   2P: $115-$145
Location: 0.5 mi ne; opposite Hemisfair site, within walking distance of the Alamo. Located opposite the convention center. 1001 E Commerce St 78205. Fax: 210/228-9816. **Facility:** 190 one-bedroom standard units. 3-5 stories, interior/exterior corridors. **Parking:** on-site. **Terms:** [ECP] meal plan available, small pets only. **Amenities:** video games, voice mail, irons, hair dryers. **Pool(s):** outdoor. **Guest Services:** valet laundry. **Business Services:** meeting rooms. *Fee:* PC, fax. **Cards:** AX, CB, DC, DS, JC, MC, VI.
(See color ad p 510)

SOME UNITS

LA QUINTA INN MARKET SQUARE   Phone: (210)271-0001   [11]

SAVE

Small-scale Hotel

2/1-9/7   1P: $89-$119   2P: $95-$125
9/8-1/31   1P: $79-$99   2P: $85-$105
Location: I-10/35, exit Durango St, just n on Santa Rosa St, then just w on Nueva St. 900 Dolorosa 78207-4540. Fax: 210/228-0663. **Facility:** 124 one-bedroom standard units. 2 stories, exterior corridors. **Parking:** on-site. **Terms:** [ECP] meal plan available, small pets only. **Amenities:** video games (fee), voice mail, irons, hair dryers. **Pool(s):** outdoor. **Business Services:** fax (fee). **Cards:** AX, CB, DC, DS, JC, MC, VI.
(See color ad p 510)

FEE   SOME UNITS

MARRIOTT RIVERWALK   Phone: (210)224-4555   [19]

SAVE

Large-scale Hotel

All Year   1P: $119-$284   2P: $119-$304
Location: Opposite convention center and Hemisfair Plaza. 711 E Riverwalk 78205. Fax: 210/224-2754. **Facility:** Accommodations overlooking downtown and the Riverwalk are offered at this property. 512 units. 507 one-bedroom standard units. 5 one-bedroom suites. 30 stories, interior corridors. *Bath:* combo or shower only. **Parking:** on-site (fee) and valet. **Terms:** check-in 4 pm, cancellation fee imposed, pets ($25 deposit). **Amenities:** high-speed Internet (fee), voice mail, irons, hair dryers. **Dining:** The Cactus Flower, see separate listing. **Pool(s):** heated indoor/outdoor. **Leisure Activities:** sauna, whirlpool, exercise room. *Fee:* massage. **Guest Services:** gift shop, valet and coin laundry. **Business Services:** conference facilities, business center. **Cards:** AX, CB, DC, DS, MC, VI. *(See color ad p 507)*

SOME UNITS

MENGER HOTEL   Phone: (210)223-4361   [7]
                                                                      XP: $10   F17

(AAA) SAVE

Historic
Large-scale Hotel

All Year   1P: $195   2P: $215
Location: Located opposite the Alamo. 204 Alamo Plaza 78205. Fax: 210/228-0022. **Facility:** 316 one-bedroom standard units. 4-5 stories, interior corridors. **Parking:** on-site (fee). **Terms:** 3 day cancellation notice-fee imposed, package plans, 16% service charge. **Amenities:** video games, voice mail, irons, hair dryers. **Dining:** The Colonial Room, see separate listing, entertainment. **Pool(s):** heated outdoor. **Leisure Activities:** sauna, whirlpool, exercise room. *Fee:* massage. **Guest Services:** gift shop, valet laundry. **Business Services:** meeting rooms, fax. **Cards:** AX, CB, DC, DS, JC, MC, VI. *(See ad below)*

FEE   FEE   FEE
SOME UNITS

(See map p. 492)

MICROTEL INN & SUITES   Phone: (210)226-8666   46
◆◆◆ All Year [CP].   1P: $44-$99   2P: $44-$99
Small-scale Hotel   **Location:** Just w of I-35/10. 1025 S Frio St 78207. Fax: 210/226-4440. **Facility:** 85 units. 73 one-bedroom standard units. 12 one-bedroom suites. 3 stories, interior corridors. **Parking:** on-site. **Amenities:** safes (fee). **Pool(s):** outdoor. **Leisure Activities:** whirlpool. **Guest Services:** coin laundry. **Business Services:** meeting rooms, fax (fee). **Cards:** AX, DC, DS, MC, VI.

SOME UNITS

MOTEL 6 - 1122   Phone: 210/225-1111   32
◆◆   6/26-8/9   1P: $57-$67   2P: $63-$73   XP: $3   F17
5/22-6/25   1P: $53-$63   2P: $59-$69   XP: $3   F17
Motel   2/1-5/21 & 8/10-1/31   1P: $47-$57   2P: $53-$63   XP: $3   F17
Location: I-10/35, exit 155 B (Pecos St). 211 N Pecos St 78207. Fax: 210/222-1134. **Facility:** 119 one-bedroom standard units. 2 stories (no elevator), exterior corridors. **Bath:** combo or shower only. **Parking:** on-site. **Terms:** small pets only. **Pool(s):** outdoor. **Guest Services:** coin laundry. **Business Services:** fax (fee). **Cards:** AX, CB, DC, DS, MC, VI.

SOME UNITS
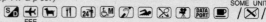

NOBLE INNS-THE JACKSON HOUSE   Phone: (210)225-4045   42
[AAA] [SAVE]   All Year [BP]   1P: $120-$200   2P: $130-$200   XP: $40
◆◆◆ ◆◆◆   **Location:** Just s jct Durango and St Mary's sts. Located in the King William Historic District. 107 Madison St 78204.
Historic Bed   Fax: 210/227-0877. **Facility:** Gas fireplaces and period antiques are featured in all guest rooms at this 1894
& Breakfast   home. Smoke free premises. 6 units. 5 one-bedroom standard units, some with whirlpools. 1 one-bedroom
suite ($185-$250). 2 stories, interior corridors. **Bath:** combo or shower only. **Parking:** on-site. **Terms:** 2 night
minimum stay - weekends, age restrictions may apply, 14 day cancellation notice-fee imposed, [CP] & [ECP]
meal plans available. **Amenities:** voice mail, hair dryers. **Leisure Activities:** whirlpool, pool privileges.
Guest Services: valet laundry. **Cards:** AX, CB, DC, DS, JC, MC, VI. **Special Amenities:** free continental breakfast and free
local telephone calls. *(See color ad below)*

PLAZA SAN ANTONIO, A MARRIOTT HOTEL   Phone: (210)229-1000   18
[AAA] [SAVE]   All Year   1P: $169-$279   2P: $169-$279
◆◆◆ ◆◆◆   **Location:** Opposite convention center and Hemisfair Plaza. Located adjacent to La Villita. 555 S Alamo St 78205.
Fax: 210/229-1418. **Facility:** This property includes a garden courtyard. 252 one-bedroom standard units.
5-7 stories, interior corridors. **Parking:** on-site (fee) and valet. **Terms:** cancellation fee imposed, small pets
Large-scale Hotel   only. **Amenities:** voice mail, irons, hair dryers. **Dining:** The Anaqua Room, see separate listing. **Pool(s):**
heated outdoor. **Leisure Activities:** saunas, whirlpool, 2 lighted tennis courts, bicycles, exercise room.
Guest Services: gift shop, valet laundry, area transportation (fee). **Business Services:** conference facilities, business center.
Cards: AX, CB, DC, DS, MC, VI. **Special Amenities:** free newspaper and free room upgrade (subject to availability with
advanced reservations). *(See color ad belowp 147 & p 507)*

SOME UNITS

FEE

(See map p. 492)

RADISSON DOWNTOWN MARKET SQUARE

Large-scale Hotel

All Year · 1P: $85-$169 · 2P: $85-$169 · XP: $10 · Phone: (210)224-7155 · **24** · F17
Location: I-35, exit Durango St. 502 W Durango St 78207. Fax: 210/224-9130. **Facility:** 250 one-bedroom standard units. 6 stories, interior corridors. **Parking:** on-site. **Terms:** cancellation fee imposed. **Amenities:** video games, voice mail, irons, hair dryers. **Dining:** 6:30 am-10 pm, cocktails. **Pool(s):** outdoor. **Leisure Activities:** whirlpool, exercise room. **Guest Services:** gift shop, valet and coin laundry, area transportation-downtown & Market Square. **Business Services:** conference facilities, business center. **Cards:** AX, CB, DC, DS, JC, MC, VI. **Special Amenities:** early check-in/late check-out and free newspaper. *(See color ad below)*

SOME UNITS

RAMADA LIMITED DOWNTOWN · Phone: (210)229-1133 · **35**

Small-scale Hotel

5/1-8/15 [CP]	1P: $65-$125	2P: $75-$125	XP: $10 · F18
3/16-4/30 [CP]	1P: $65-$99	2P: $75-$99	XP: $10 · F18
8/16-1/31 [CP]	1P: $65-$85	2P: $75-$95	XP: $10 · F18
2/1-3/15 [CP]	1P: $65-$85	2P: $65-$95	XP: $10 · F18

Location: I-35/10, exit 155A (Alamo St). 1122 S Laredo St 78204. Fax: 210/229-1023. **Facility:** 50 one-bedroom standard units, some with whirlpools. 2 stories (no elevator), exterior corridors. *Bath:* combo or shower only. **Parking:** on-site. **Amenities:** voice mail, safes (fee). **Pool(s):** outdoor. **Guest Services:** coin laundry. **Business Services:** meeting rooms, fax (fee). **Cards:** AX, CB, DC, DS, JC, MC, VI.

SOME UNITS

(See map p. 492)

RESIDENCE INN ALAMO PLAZA
Phone: (210)212-5555 **50**

SAVE

Small-scale Hotel

All Year [BP]   1P: $109-$189   2P: $109-$189
Location: I-37/281, exit Commerce St, just w to Bowie, 4 blks n; downtown. 425 Bonham 78205. Fax: 210/212-5554. **Facility:** 220 units. 99 one-bedroom standard units with efficiencies. 88 one- and 33 two-bedroom suites, some with efficiencies or kitchens. 13 stories, interior corridors. *Bath:* combo or shower only. **Parking:** on-site (fee). **Terms:** pets ($20 extra charge). **Amenities:** voice mail, irons, hair dryers. **Pool(s):** small heated outdoor. **Leisure Activities:** whirlpool, exercise room. **Guest Services:** complimentary evening beverages: Mon-Thurs, valet and coin laundry. **Business Services:** meeting rooms, fax (fee). **Cards:** AX, CB, DC, DS, JC, MC, VI.

SOME UNITS

RESIDENCE INN BY MARRIOTT
Phone: (210)231-6000 **36**

SAVE

Small-scale Hotel

All Year [BP]   1P: $139-$159
Location: I-35, exit Durango St, 0.5 mi e. 628 S Santa Rosa 78204. Fax: 210/231-6001. **Facility:** 95 units. 79 one- and 16 two-bedroom suites. 3 stories, interior corridors. **Parking:** on-site. **Terms:** weekly rates available, package plans, small pets only ($50 deposit, $5 extra charge). **Amenities:** video games, voice mail, irons, hair dryers. **Pool(s):** heated outdoor. **Leisure Activities:** whirlpool, exercise room, sports court. **Guest Services:** complimentary evening beverages: Mon-Thurs, coin laundry. **Business Services:** fax (fee). **Cards:** AX, CB, DC, DS, JC, MC, VI. *(See color ad p 507)*

SOME UNITS

RIVERWALK INN
Phone: (210)212-8300 **26**

Historic Bed
& Breakfast

MC, VI.

All Year [ECP]   1P: $130-$175   2P: $130-$175
Location: Just n of W Durango St. 329 Old Guilbeau 78204. Fax: 210/229-9422. **Facility:** Rustic decor. Smoke free premises. 11 one-bedroom standard units. 2 stories (no elevator), interior/exterior corridors. *Bath:* shower only. **Parking:** on-site. **Terms:** 2-3 night minimum stay - weekends, 10 day cancellation notice-fee imposed. **Amenities:** voice mail. **Business Services:** conference facilities, fax (fee). **Cards:** AX, DS, MC, VI.

SOME UNITS

RIVERWALK VISTA
Phone: (210)223-3200 **2**

Bed & Breakfast

All Year [ECP]   1P: $140-$180
Location: Jct Losoya St at Commerce St. Located in a converted historic building. 262 Losoya St 78205. Fax: 210/223-4278. **Facility:** 17 one-bedroom standard units. 3 stories, interior corridors. *Bath:* shower only. **Parking:** no self-parking. **Terms:** 2 night minimum stay - weekends, age restrictions may apply, 10 day cancellation notice-fee imposed. **Amenities:** video library, DVD players, CD players, high-speed Internet, voice mail, safes, irons, hair dryers. **Guest Services:** valet laundry. **Business Services:** meeting rooms, business center. **Cards:** AX, DC, MC, VI.

SOME UNITS

RODEWAY INN DOWNTOWN
Phone: (210)223-2951 **1**

AAA SAVE

Small-scale Hotel

3/7-11/29 [CP]	1P: $62-$92	2P: $72-$102	XP: $10	F17
2/1-3/6 & 11/30-1/31 [CP]	1P: $48-$78	2P: $54-$84	XP: $10	F17

Location: I-35, exit San Pedro. 900 N Main Ave 78212. Fax: 210/223-9064. **Facility:** 125 one-bedroom standard units. 2 stories (no elevator), exterior corridors. **Parking:** on-site. **Pool(s):** outdoor. **Guest Services:** coin laundry, area transportation (fee). **Business Services:** meeting rooms, fax (fee). **Cards:** AX, DC, MC. **Special Amenities:** free continental breakfast and free local telephone calls.

SOME UNITS

THE ST. ANTHONY-A WYNDHAM HISTORIC HOTEL
Phone: (210)227-4392 **3**

AAA SAVE

Historic
Large-scale Hotel

All Year   1P: $149-$159   2P: $159-$169   XP: $10
Location: Corner of Travis St and Jefferson. 300 E Travis St 78205. Fax: 210/227-0915. **Facility:** 352 units. 312 one-bedroom standard units. 40 one-bedroom suites ($259-$1000). 10 stories, interior corridors. *Bath:* combo or shower only. **Parking:** on-site (fee) and valet. **Terms:** cancellation fee imposed. **Amenities:** video games (fee), voice mail, irons, hair dryers. *Some:* high-speed Internet (fee). **Dining:** 6:30 am-10 pm, cocktails. **Pool(s):** heated outdoor. **Leisure Activities:** whirlpool, exercise room. **Guest Services:** gift shop, valet laundry. **Business Services:** conference facilities, business center. **Cards:** AX, DC, DS, MC, VI.

SOME UNITS

SAN ANTONIO MARRIOTT RIVERCENTER
Phone: (210)223-1000 **21**

SAVE

Large-scale Hotel

All Year   1P: $119-$284   2P: $119-$304
Location: Corner of Bowie and Commerce sts. Located adjacent to Rivercenter Mall, on the Riverwalk. 101 Bowie St 78205. Fax: 210/223-6239. **Facility:** 1001 units. 954 one-bedroom standard units. 47 one-bedroom suites. 38 stories, interior corridors. **Parking:** on-site (fee) and valet. **Terms:** check-in 4 pm, cancellation fee imposed. [MAP] meal plan available. **Amenities:** high-speed Internet (fee), voice mail, irons, hair dryers. **Pool(s):** heated indoor/outdoor. **Leisure Activities:** saunas, whirlpools, exercise room. *Fee:* massage. **Guest Services:** gift shop, complimentary laundry. **Business Services:** conference facilities, business center. **Cards:** AX, DC, DS, JC, MC, VI. *(See color ad p 507)*

SOME UNITS

FEE

(See map p. 492)

SHERATON GUNTER
Phone: (210)227-3241 **4**

1/1-1/31	1P: $190-$213	2P: $202-$223	XP: $20	F18
2/1-12/31	1P: $181-$203	2P: $193-$213	XP: $20	F18

Historic
Small-scale Hotel
Location: Center. Located one block from river. 205 E Houston St 78205. **Fax:** 210/227-9305. **Facility:** 322 units. 314 one-bedroom standard units. 8 one-bedroom suites. 12 stories, interior corridors. **Parking:** valet. phone lines, voice mail, irons, hair dryers. *Some:* high-speed Internet (fee), fax. **Dining:** Barron's, see separate listing. **Pool(s):** heated outdoor. **Leisure Activities:** sauna, exercise room. **Guest Services:** gift shop, valet laundry. **Business Services:** conference facilities, fax (fee). **Cards:** AX, DC, DS, MC, VI. *(See color ad below)*

SOME UNITS

 DATA PORT / ✕ /

WOODFIELD SUITES SAN ANTONIO-DOWNTOWN
Phone: (210)212-5400 **30**

All Year [ECP]   1P: $79-$99   2P: $79-$99

Small-scale Hotel
Location: I-35, exit 155B (Durango Blvd). 100 W Durango Blvd 78204. **Fax:** 210/212-5407. **Facility:** 151 units. 140 one-bedroom standard units. 11 one-bedroom suites ($149), some with whirlpools. 6 stories, interior corridors. *Bath:* combo or shower only. **Parking:** on-site. **Terms:** pets ($10 extra charge). **Amenities:** video games, voice mail, irons, hair dryers. **Pool(s):** heated outdoor. **Leisure Activities:** whirlpool, playroom, exercise room. **Guest Services:** gift shop, complimentary evening beverages, valet and coin laundry. **Business Services:** meeting rooms, business center. **Cards:** AX, CB, DC, DS, MC, VI. **Special Amenities:** free continental breakfast and free newspaper. *(See color ad below)*

SOME UNITS

DATA PORT / ✕ /

(See map p. 492)

──────── **WHERE TO DINE** ────────

THE ANAQUA ROOM   Lunch: $9-$13   Dinner: $16-$25   Phone: 210/229-1000   ⑮
▼▼▼▼▼   **Location:** Opposite convention center and Hemisfair Plaza; in Plaza San Antonio, A Marriott Hotel. 555 S Alamo St
American   78205. **Hours:** 6:30 am-2 & 6-10 pm, Fri & Sat-11 pm. **Reservations:** suggested. **Features:** Overlooking a
hotel garden, the dining room has fountains and Mediterranean-style decor. The Southwestern cuisine
includes tender filet covered in crawfish ragu. Make sure you have plenty to drink when you try the spicy
twisted pasta with mushrooms. Casual dress; cocktails. **Parking:** on-site (fee) and valet. **Cards:** AX, DC, DS, MC, VI.

BARRON'S   Lunch: $8-$15   Dinner: $8-$15   Phone: 210/227-3241   ⑱
▼▼▼▼   **Location:** Center; in Sheraton Gunter. 205 E Houston 78205. **Hours:** 6 am-2 & 5-10:30 pm. **Features:** A
American   resplendent dining room features lovely paintings and hotel memorabilia, and showcases an impressive
display of wines. Shrimp cocktail, crab cakes and decadent offerings like German chocolate cake and
DS, MC, VI.   eclairs are house specialties not to be missed. Casual dress; cocktails. **Parking:** valet. **Cards:** AX, DC,

BOUDRO'S ON THE RIVERWALK   Lunch: $6-$11   Dinner: $14-$30   Phone: 210/224-8484   ④
▼▼▼▼   **Location:** Just w of jct Commerce and Alamo sts. 421 E Commerce St 78205. **Hours:** 11 am-11 pm, Fri &
Southwestern   Sat-midnight. **Reservations:** suggested. **Features:** Enjoy a view of the river and wildlife from the dining
area at this waterfront restaurant. Steel pictographs hang from the limestone walls. The blackened prime
self-parking. **Cards:** AX, DC, DS, MC, VI.   rib is seared in Cajun spices, and the seafood has a Southern flair. Casual dress; cocktails. **Parking:** no

THE CACTUS FLOWER   Lunch: $8-$12   Dinner: $10-$20   Phone: 210/224-4555   ㉓
▼▼▼▼   **Location:** Opposite convention center and Hemisfair Plaza; in Marriott Riverwalk. 711 E Riverwalk 78205.
Hours: 6:30 am-2 & 5-11 pm, Sat & Sun 6:30 am-2 & 5:30-11 pm. **Reservations:** accepted.
American   **Features:** Located near the Alamo, this Southwestern cafe has a splendid view overlooking the river.
Mexican cuisine like tortilla soup is loaded with seasonings and monterey jack cheese. Don't leave until
you've tried the fried ice cream topped with strawberries. Casual dress; cocktails. **Parking:** on-site (fee) and valet. **Cards:** AX,
DC, DS, MC, VI.

CASA RIO MEXICAN RESTAURANT   Lunch: $5-$10   Dinner: $5-$10   Phone: 210/225-6718   ⑨
◆◆◆   **Location:** 1 blk from Hemisfair Plaza, on Riverwalk. 430 E Commerce St 78205. **Hours:** 11 am-11 pm. Closed:
1/1, 11/27, 12/25. **Features:** Tables with colorful umbrellas are lined along the San Antonio Riverwalk. This
Mexican   is a popular place for couples to dine. The green-chicken enchiladas are made with fresh, homemade
tortillas. Be sure to sip on a margarita with fresh lime juice. Casual dress; cocktails. **Parking:** on-site.
Cards: AX, CB, DC, DS, MC, VI.

CASCADES BY THE RIVER-STEAKS &
FINE INTERNATIONAL CUISINE   Dinner: $21-$40   Phone: 210/226-2970   ㉖
▼▼▼▼   **Location:** Just e of I-35; center; in Howard Johnson Riverwalk Plaza Hotel. 100 Villita St 78205. **Hours:** 6:30
Continental   am-10:30 & 6-9 pm, Sat & Sun 7 am-11:30 & 6-9 pm. **Reservations:** accepted. **Features:** Inside a
downtown HoJo, this restaurant's Mediterranean-style decor is done in pink and green tones. The exotic
menu features quesadillas filled with chunks of crabmeat topped with artichokes, and the buffalo entree is
prepared with a special sauce. Dressy casual. **Parking:** street. **Cards:** AX, CB, DC, DS, JC, MC, VI. *(See color ad p 493)*

THE COLONIAL ROOM   Lunch: $8-$15   Dinner: $25-$30   Phone: 210/223-4361   ㉗
▼▼▼▼   **Location:** In the Menger Hotel. 204 Alamo Plaza 78205. **Hours:** 6:30 am-10 pm, Fri & Sat-11 pm.
Reservations: suggested. **Features:** The Colonial Room's famous mango ice cream was served at
Continental   President Clinton's inauguration. Designed in 1909, the light-colored dining room has attractive archways
and a fireplace. Fill your plate at the breakfast and lunch buffets. Casual dress; cocktails. **Parking:** on-site
and valet. **Cards:** AX, CB, DC, DS, MC, VI.

FIG TREE RESTAURANT   Dinner: $24-$38   Phone: 210/224-1976   ⑰
▼▼▼▼ ▼▼▼▼   **Location:** In La Villita Historic Complex; just e of S Presa St. 515 Villita St 78205. **Hours:** 6 pm-9:30 pm.
Reservations: suggested. **Features:** Savor beef Wellington with a bodied cabernet in this cozy New
Traditional   England-style cottage. Elegant tables, classic Continental dishes and a flawless dining room staff make for
Continental   a memorable dining experience. Dressy casual; cocktails. **Parking:** no self-parking. **Cards:** AX, DS,
MC, VI.

HUNAN RIVER GARDEN   Lunch: $7-$8   Dinner: $7-$14   Phone: 210/222-0808   ⑧
◆◆◆ ◆◆◆   **Location:** On Riverwalk. 506 Riverwalk 78205. **Hours:** 11 am-10:30 pm, Fri-11 pm, Sat-11:30 am-11 pm, Sun
11:30 am-10:30 pm. **Features:** The attractive dining room is illuminated by Chinese lanterns. Enjoy a
Chinese   relaxing meal overlooking the Riverwalk. The sesame chicken is tender and smothered with delicious
seasonings. The duck entree is a favorite house specialty. Casual dress; cocktails. **Parking:** no
self-parking. **Cards:** AX, DC, MC, VI.

KANGAROO COURT   Lunch: $5-$11   Dinner: $9-$15   Phone: 210/224-6821   ⑦
◆◆◆   **Location:** Near Hemisfair Plaza; on Riverwalk. 516 N Presa St 78205. **Hours:** 9 am-11 pm, Fri & Sat-midnight.
Reservations: suggested. **Features:** Located on the Riverwalk, this pub-style eatery has fixtures and
American   furnishings from the late 1700s. The oysters Rockefeller are topped with spinach and melted cheese.
Delicious desserts like the secret recipe cheesecake are famous. Casual dress; cocktails; entertainment.
Parking: on-site. **Cards:** AX, DC, DS, MC, VI.

(See map p. 492)

LA FOCACCIA ITALIAN GRILL Lunch: $4-$8 Dinner: $4-$15 Phone: 210/223-5353 29
Italian
Location: Near King William Historic District, S Alamo jct at S Presa St. 800 S Alamo St 78205. **Hours:** 11:30 am-2:30 & 5-10 pm, Fri-11 pm, Sat from noon. Closed: Sun. **Reservations:** accepted. **Features:** The focaccia is great for dipping in olive oil. The antipasto is loaded with cold cuts, artichokes, olives, mozzarella and bean salad. Meatball parmigiana is covered in thick cheese on garlic toast. The wood-burning oven makes fresh pizza. Casual dress; beer & wine only; entertainment. **Parking:** on-site. **Cards:** AX, CB, DC, DS, MC, VI.

LA MARGARITA Lunch: $5-$10 Dinner: $7-$12 Phone: 210/227-7140 5
Tex-Mex
Location: I-35, exit 155B (Durango St); in Market Square. 120 Produce Row 78207. **Hours:** 11 am-10 pm, Fri & Sat-midnight. Closed: 11/27. **Reservations:** accepted. **Features:** Munch on a never-ending bowl of chips and salsa as you admire the Mexican paintings hanging on this restaurant's brick walls. Begin with the fajita and shrimp cocktail or oysters on ice. Spicy mole is served over chicken with a side of rice and beans. Casual dress; cocktails; entertainment. **Parking:** on-site. **Cards:** AX, DC, DS, MC, VI.

LAS CANARIAS RESTAURANT Lunch: $8-$14 Dinner: $15-$30 Phone: 210/518-1000 3
Continental
Location: Just s on the riverwalk; in La Mansion del Rio. 112 College St 78205. **Hours:** 6:30 am-10:30 pm, Fri & Sat-11 pm, Sun-2:30 pm. **Reservations:** suggested. **Features:** This eatery is within walking distance to the famous Alamo. Sit on the outdoor terrace and dine on unusual cuisine with a Spanish flair. Try the potato-crusted halibut with fermented black bean sauce. Satisfy your sweet tooth with banana cream pie. Casual dress; cocktails; entertainment. **Parking:** on-site (fee) and valet. **Cards:** AX, CB, DC, MC, VI.

LITTLE RHEIN STEAK HOUSE Historic Dinner: $28-$33 Phone: 210/225-2111 13
Steak House
Location: Opposite convention center and Hemisfair Plaza. 231 S Alamo St 78205. **Hours:** 5 pm-10 pm. Closed major holidays; also 12/24. **Reservations:** suggested. **Features:** Tender prime rib and lobster are house specialties. The Little Rhein dessert is an ice cream ball rolled in crushed Oreo cookies, topped with hot fudge, strawberries and whipped cream. The historic dining room is filled with antiques. Casual dress; cocktails. **Parking:** no self-parking. **Cards:** AX, CB, DC, DS, MC, VI.

MI TIERRA CAFE Y PANADERIA Lunch: $6-$9 Dinner: $6-$17 Phone: 210/225-1262 20
Mexican
Location: In Market Square. 218 Produce Row 78207. **Hours:** 24 hours. **Reservations:** required. **Features:** Photographs of long-time customers hang in the lobby of this Tex-Mex cafe which opened in 1941. A three-dimensional clay mural covers one wall. Juicy fajitas are seasoned to perfection, and the flan is coated with caramel. Casual dress; cocktails. **Parking:** on-site. **Cards:** AX, CB, DC, MC, VI.

PECAN STREET DELICATESSEN Lunch: $6-$10 Dinner: $6-$10 Phone: 210/227-3226 30
Deli/Subs/Sandwiches
Location: Between Soledad and N St. Marys St. 152 E Pecan 78205. **Hours:** 10 am-3 pm. Closed major holidays; also Sat & Sun. **Reservations:** accepted. **Features:** Located in a former loft apartment building, this downtown eatery offers great views through its large, plate-glass windows. Any sandwich you create from the Mediterranean-style deli counter should satisfy, but try the Greek gyros, hummus and tabbouleh. Casual dress. **Parking:** no self-parking. **Cards:** AX, DC, DS, MC, VI.

PICO DE GALLO Lunch: $4-$8 Dinner: $8-$14 Phone: 210/225-6060 25
Tex-Mex
Location: At Buena Vista, just w of Commerce at I-10. 111 S Leona 78207. **Hours:** 7 am-10 pm, Fri & Sat-2 am, Sun 8 am-10 pm. Closed major holidays. **Reservations:** accepted; 2 week notice. **Features:** Family-owned for three generations, this Mexican restaurant seats guests at unique, hand-painted tables. Savor the original recipe pepper steak entree. For dessert, try the bola bola with ice cream covered with coconut and chocolate. Casual dress; cocktails; entertainment. **Parking:** on-site. **Cards:** AX, DC, DS, MC, VI.

POLO'S Historic Lunch: $8-$20 Dinner: $16-$35 Phone: 210/224-8800 14
American
Location: Opposite convention center and Hemisfair Plaza; in The Fairmount-A Wyndham Historic Hotel. 401 S Alamo St 78205. **Hours:** 6:30-10:30 am, 11:30-2 & 6-10 pm, Fri & Sat-10:30 pm, Sun 7 am-noon. **Reservations:** suggested. **Features:** Located in the historic 1906 Fairmount Hotel, this restaurant offers an intimate courtyard setting. The Argentine beef and coastal seafood are delicious regional specialties, and the oak-fired oven bakes crispy pizzas you won't want to say no to. Dressy casual; cocktails. **Parking:** valet. **Cards:** AX, CB, DC, DS, JC, MC, VI.

PRESIDIO Lunch: $7-$11 Dinner: $15-$30 Phone: 210/472-2265 31
Regional American
Location: On the Riverwalk; across from La Mansion Hotel. 245 E Commerce St 78205. **Hours:** 11:30 am-10 pm, Fri & Sat-11 pm. Closed: 1/1, 11/27, 12/25. **Reservations:** accepted. **Features:** Treat yourself to trendy dining on the Riverwalk. The work of local artists drape the dining room walls. The Southwest marinated pork chops are filled with juice and will impress your taste buds. For dessert try the Southwestern key lime pie. Casual dress; cocktails. **Parking:** on-site. **Cards:** AX, DC, DS, MC, VI.

RIO RIO CANTINA Lunch: $5-$7 Dinner: $7-$19 Phone: 210/226-8462 10
Regional Mexican
Location: Between S Presa and Losoya sts. 421 E Commerce St 78205. **Hours:** 11 am-11 pm, Fri & Sat-midnight. **Features:** Overlooking the Riverwalk, this informal eatery offers outdoor seating. The rellenos, made with shredded beef, raisins and nuts, are an excellent choice. You definitely won't leave hungry after chowing down on the restaurant's large botana platter. Casual dress; cocktails. **Parking:** on-site. **Cards:** AX, DC, DS, MC, VI.

TOWER OF THE AMERICAS RESTAURANT Lunch: $8-$15 Dinner: $16-$30 Phone: 210/223-3101 16
American
Location: In Hemisfair Plaza. 701 S Bowie St 78205. **Hours:** 11 am-2 & 5:30-10 pm, Fri & Sat-10:30 pm. Closed: 12/25. **Reservations:** suggested. **Features:** Catch a spectacular view of San Antonio from the revolving dining room 600 feet in the air. You can dine on an array of seafood like grilled salmon and sea bass, or try the homemade tortilla soup. The hot fudge Oreo cheesecake is topped with strawberries. Downtown area pick-up is available. Casual dress; cocktails. **Parking:** on-site. **Cards:** AX, CB, DC, DS, MC, VI.

(See map p. 492)

─────── *The following restaurant has not been evaluated by AAA* ───────
but is listed for your information only.

LE REVE

[fyi]   Not evaluated. **Location:** Just e of St Mary's St. 152 E Pecan, Suite 100 78205. **Features:** The dining room is cozy and has a view of the kitchen. The crabcake appetizer is loaded with chunks of fresh, white crabmeat. Entrees include tender gnocchi with steamed asparagus spears drizzled with butter. The tempting desserts are included.

Phone: 210/212-2221

SAN ANTONIO pop. 1,144,646 (See map p. 496; index p. 498)

──────── **WHERE TO STAY** ────────

A BECKMANN INN & CARRIAGE HOUSE BED AND BREAKFAST   **Phone:** 210/229-1449   [67]
▼▼▼▼   All Year   2P: $110-$150
Historic Bed   **Location:** 0.5 mi s from downtown, just w of S Alamo St. Located in the historic district. 222 E Guenther St 78204.
& Breakfast   **Fax:** 210/229-1061. **Facility:** This restored 1886 Victorian features burled-pine doors, 14-foot ceilings and a wraparound porch furnished with wicker. Smoke free premises. 5 one-bedroom standard units. 1-2 stories (no elevator), interior/exterior corridors. *Bath:* combo or shower only. **Parking:** on-site. **Terms:** check-in 4 pm, 2-4 night minimum stay - seasonal, weekends, age restrictions may apply, 14 day cancellation notice-fee imposed, [BP] meal plan available. **Amenities:** irons, hair dryers. **Business Services:** fax. **Cards:** AX, DC, DS, MC, VI.

[⊣⊩] [✕] [DATA PORT] [🔒]

ADAMS HOUSE BED & BREAKFAST   **Phone:** (210)224-4791   [73]
▼▼▼▼   All Year   1P: $109-$149   2P: $119-$169   XP: $30   F10
Bed & Breakfast   **Location:** Just s of South Alamo St. Located in King William Historic District. 231 Adams St 78210. **Fax:** 210/223-5125. **Facility:** This 1905 inn features Victorian Italianate styling and period decor mingled with modern conveniences, such as in-room televisions. Smoke free premises. 4 one-bedroom standard units, some with whirlpools. 2 stories (no elevator), interior/exterior corridors. *Bath:* combo or shower only. **Parking:** on-site. **Terms:** 2 night minimum stay - weekends, age restrictions may apply, 14 day cancellation notice-fee imposed, [BP] meal plan available, package plans. **Amenities:** hair dryers. *Some:* irons. **Cards:** AX, DC, DS, MC, VI.

SOME UNITS
[ASK] [S🔊] [✕] [🐾] / [VCR] [🔒] [🖥] [🍴] /

ALAMO INN   **Phone:** 210/227-2203   [132]
🔺🔺🔺 [SAVE]   All Year [CP]   1P: $50-$110   2P: $55-$110   XP: $10   F12
▼▼ ▼▼   **Location:** I-37, exit 141A, 1.2 mi e. 2203 E Commerce St 78203. **Fax:** 210/222-2860. **Facility:** 15 one-bedroom standard units, some with kitchens. 1 story, exterior corridors. **Parking:** on-site. **Terms:** cancellation fee imposed. **Amenities:** irons, hair dryers. **Guest Services:** valet laundry, area transportation-downtown attractions. **Business Services:** fax (fee). **Cards:** AX, CB, DC, DS, JC, MC, VI. **Special Amenities:** free continental breakfast and free newspaper.
Motel

SOME UNITS
[✈] [🐾] [DATA PORT] [🔒] [🖥] [🍴] / [✕] /

AMERISUITES (SAN ANTONIO/AIRPORT)   **Phone:** (210)930-2333   [142]
🔺🔺🔺 [SAVE]   All Year   1P: $99-$119   2P: $109-$129   XP: $10   F
▼▼▼▼   **Location:** US 281, exit Jones Maltsberger Rd, inside Loop 410. 7615 Jones Maltberger Rd 78216. **Fax:** 210/930-2336. **Facility:** 128 one-bedroom standard units. 6 stories, interior corridors. *Bath:* combo or shower only. **Parking:** on-site. **Terms:** [CP] meal plan available, small pets only. **Amenities:** voice mail, irons, hair dryers. *Some:* dual phone lines. **Pool(s):** heated outdoor. **Leisure Activities:** exercise room. **Guest Services:** valet and coin laundry, area transportation-within 3 mi. **Business Services:** meeting rooms, fax. **Cards:** AX, DS, MC, VI. **Special Amenities:** free continental breakfast and free newspaper. *(See color ad p 504)*
Small-scale Hotel

SOME UNITS
[S🔊] [✈] [🐕] [⊣⊩] [🛋] [➰] [🐾] [DATA PORT] [🔒] [🖥] [🍴] / [✕] [VCR] /

AMERISUITES (SAN ANTONIO/CROSSROADS)   **Phone:** (210)737-6086   [129]
🔺🔺🔺 [SAVE]   All Year   1P: $95   XP: $10   F17
▼▼▼▼   **Location:** I-410, Loop 345, exit Fredericksburg Rd. Located next to Crossroads Mall. 3636 NW Loop 410 78201. **Fax:** 210/737-6170. **Facility:** 112 one-bedroom suites. 5 stories, interior corridors. *Bath:* combo or shower only. **Parking:** on-site. **Terms:** [ECP] meal plan available. **Amenities:** high-speed Internet, voice mail, irons, hair dryers. **Pool(s):** outdoor. **Leisure Activities:** exercise room. **Guest Services:** coin laundry, area transportation-limited areas. **Business Services:** meeting rooms, fax (fee). **Cards:** AX, DS, JC, MC, VI. **Special Amenities:** free continental breakfast and free newspaper.** *(See color ad p 504)*
Small-scale Hotel

SOME UNITS
[S🔊] [✈] [⊣⊩] [&M] [🛋] [➰] [🐾] [DATA PORT] [🔒] [🖥] [🍴] / [✕] /

AMERISUITES (SAN ANTONIO/NORTHWEST)   **Phone:** (210)561-0099   [126]
🔺🔺🔺 [SAVE]   3/1-8/16   1P: $105   XP: $10   F17
▼▼▼▼   2/1-2/28 & 8/17-1/31   1P: $99   XP: $10   F17
Small-scale Hotel   **Location:** I-10, exit Wurzbach Rd, 0.3 mi w on west side of frontage road. 4325 AmeriSuites Dr 78230. **Fax:** 210/561-0513. **Facility:** 128 units. 80 one-bedroom standard units. 48 one-bedroom suites. 6 stories, interior corridors. *Bath:* combo or shower only. **Parking:** on-site. **Terms:** check-in 4 pm, [ECP] meal plan available. **Amenities:** high-speed Internet, voice mail, irons, hair dryers. **Pool(s):** heated outdoor. **Leisure Activities:** exercise room. **Guest Services:** coin laundry, area transportation-within 5 mi. **Business Services:** meeting rooms, business center. **Cards:** AX, DS, JC, MC, VI. **Special Amenities:** free continental breakfast and free newspaper. *(See color ad p 504)*

SOME UNITS
[S🔊] [⊣⊩] [&M] [🛋] [➰] [🐾] [VCR] [🐕] [DATA PORT] [🔒] [🖥] [🍴] / [✕] /

(See map p. 496)

A VICTORIAN LADY INN
Phone: (210)224-2524 **157**

🔻🔻🔻 All Year　　　　1P: $89-$135　　　2P: $99-$135　　　XP: $10

Bed & Breakfast
Location: Just n of downtown; just n of The Alamo at the jct of W Cypress. Located in a residential area; on the trolley line. 421 Howard St 78212. Fax: 210/224-5123. **Facility:** This restored 1898 Victorian mansion is north of downtown; guest rooms include televisions. Smoke free premises. 10 one-bedroom standard units, some with whirlpools. 3 stories (no elevator), interior corridors. *Bath:* combo or shower only. **Parking:** on-site. **Terms:** age restrictions may apply, 14 day cancellation notice-fee imposed, [BP] meal plan available. **Pool(s):** outdoor. **Cards:** AX, DS, MC, VI.

SOME UNITS

(ASK) (S🔒) 🍴 🛏 ✖ / 🛗 🖥 🖨 /

BEST WESTERN CONTINENTAL INN
Phone: (210)655-3510 **59**

(AAA) (SAVE)　All Year　　　1P: $69-$99　　　2P: $79-$119　　　XP: $10　　　F18

🔻🔻🔻
Location: I-35, exit 167 (Starlight Terr) northbound; exit 167A (Randolph Blvd) southbound; just n of Loop 410 NE; on southbound access road. 9735 I-35 N 78233-6648. Fax: 210/655-0778. **Facility:** 160 one-bedroom standard units. 2 stories (no elevator), exterior corridors. **Parking:** on-site. **Terms:** [BP] meal plan available.

Small-scale Hotel　**Amenities:** voice mail, irons, hair dryers. **Dining:** 6 am-10 pm, cocktails. **Pool(s):** outdoor, wading. **Leisure Activities:** whirlpools, playground. **Guest Services:** coin laundry, area transportation (fee)-downtown. **Business Services:** meeting rooms, fax (fee). **Cards:** AX, CB, DC, DS, MC, VI. **Special Amenities:** early check-in/late check-out and free continental breakfast.

SOME UNITS

(S🔒) ➡ 🍴 (&M) 📷 🛏 🐾 (DATA PORT) 🖥 / ✖ 🛏 🖨 /

Do you know the facts?

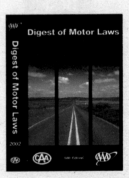

AAA publishes the Digest of Motor Laws to assist traveling motorists. Filled with facts and information, this one-of-a-kind compilation includes a comprehensive description of the laws that govern motor vehicle registration and operation in the United States and Canada. This sixty-eighth edition guide has a new, easy-to-read format with graphics, state-by-state tax summary tables and detailed information on occupant protection laws, driver licensing laws, automated enforcement laws and motor vehicle fees and taxes.

You can easily locate various licensing and motor laws governing the states in which you are traveling. In addition to vehicle registration and operation laws, the Digest contains information and facts about alcohol laws, traffic safety laws and more.

Call your local club or 1-877-AAA-BOOK to obtain a copy of the Digest.

The book retails for $13.95.

(See map p. 496)

BEST WESTERN FIESTA INN   Phone: (210)696-2400   [105]

4/28-8/16 [ECP]	1P: $80-$130	2P: $80-$130	XP: $6	F12
3/28-4/27 [ECP]	1P: $70-$110	2P: $70-$110	XP: $6	F12
2/1-3/27 & 8/17-1/31 [ECP]	1P: $50-$110	2P: $50-$110	XP: $6	F12

Location: I-10, exit 557 westbound; exit 558 eastbound, on westbound access road. 13535 I-10 W 78249. Small-scale Hotel **Fax:** 210/699-0251. **Facility:** 60 units. 56 one-bedroom standard units, some with whirlpools. 4 one-bedroom suites. Exterior corridors. *Bath:* combo or shower only. **Parking:** on-site. **Terms:** 2 night minimum stay - weekends 5/23-8/16, small pets only. **Amenities:** irons, hair dryers. **Pool(s):** outdoor. **Leisure Activities:** whirlpool, exercise room. **Guest Services:** coin laundry. **Business Services:** meeting rooms, fax (fee). **Cards:** AX, DC, DS, MC, VI. **Special Amenities:** free continental breakfast. *(See color ad below)*

SOME UNITS

(See map p. 496)

BEST WESTERN HILL COUNTRY SUITES
Phone: (210)490-9191   **165**

(AAA) (SAVE) All Year   1P: $89-$139   2P: $89-$139   XP: $10   F12

Location: Just n of jct Loop 1604, on southbound access lane. 18555 US Hwy 281 N 78258. Fax: 210/490-3465. **Facility:** 76 one-bedroom suites, some with efficiencies and/or whirlpools. 3 stories, interior corridors. *Bath:* combo or shower only. **Parking:** on-site. **Terms:** 3 day cancellation notice, [BP] meal plan available.

Small-scale Hotel **Amenities:** high-speed Internet, voice mail, irons, hair dryers. **Pool(s):** outdoor. **Leisure Activities:** whirlpool, exercise room. **Guest Services:** valet and coin laundry. **Business Services:** meeting rooms, business center. **Cards:** AX, DC, DS, JC, MC, VI. **Special Amenities: free continental breakfast.**

SOME UNITS

BEST WESTERN INGRAM PARK INN
Phone: (210)520-8080   **83**

(AAA) (SAVE)
4/28-8/16 [ECP]	1P: $80-$130	2P: $80-$130	XP: $6 F12
3/28-4/27 [ECP]	1P: $70-$110	2P: $70-$110	XP: $6 F12
2/1-3/27 & 8/17-1/31 [ECP]	1P: $50-$110	2P: $50-$110	XP: $6 F12

Location: I-410, exit 10 westbound; exit 11 eastbound; on westbound access road. 6855 NW Loop 410 78238. **Small-scale Hotel** Fax: 210/522-0892. **Facility:** 78 units. 62 one-bedroom standard units, some with whirlpools. 8 one- and 8 two-bedroom suites ($89-$229). 2 stories (no elevator), exterior corridors. **Parking:** on-site. **Terms:** 2 night minimum stay - weekends 5/23-8/16, small pets only. **Amenities:** high-speed Internet, irons, hair dryers. **Guest Services:** coin laundry. **Business Services:** meeting rooms, fax (fee). **Cards:** AX, DC, DS, MC, VI. *(See color ad p 520)*

SOME UNITS

BEST WESTERN LACKLAND INN & SUITES
Phone: (210)675-9690   **85**

(AAA) (SAVE) All Year   1P: $62-$90   2P: $68-$99   XP: $6   F18

Location: Jct US 90 and Military Dr, 1.5 mi e of Loop 410. 6815 Hwy 90 W 78227. Fax: 210/670-9471. **Facility:** 184 units. 130 one- and 54 two-bedroom standard units. 2-3 stories (no elevator), exterior corridors. **Parking:** on-site. **Terms:** 5 day cancellation notice, small pets only. **Amenities:** irons, hair dryers. **Pool(s):** 2 outdoor.

Small-scale Hotel **Guest Services:** coin laundry. **Business Services:** meeting rooms, fax (fee). **Cards:** AX, CB, DC, DS, MC, VI. **Special Amenities: early check-in/late check-out and free continental breakfast.**

SOME UNITS

BEST WESTERN-POSADA ANA AIRPORT
Phone: (210)342-1400   **122**

(AAA) (SAVE)
6/1-8/31 [CP]	1P: $64-$81	2P: $74-$91	XP: $10 F18
9/1-1/31 [CP]	1P: $61-$78	2P: $71-$88	XP: $10 F18
2/1-5/31 [CP]	1P: $59-$76	2P: $69-$86	XP: $10 F18

Location: I-410, exit 21A (Jones Maltsberger Rd), 0.5 mi s. 8600 Jones Maltsberger Rd 78216. Fax: 210/342-0905. **Small-scale Hotel** **Facility:** 59 one-bedroom standard units. 2 stories, interior corridors. **Parking:** on-site. **Amenities:** hair dryers. *Some:* irons. **Pool(s):** outdoor. **Guest Services:** valet laundry, area transportation-North Star Mall. **Business Services:** fax (fee). **Cards:** AX, CB, DC, DS, MC, VI. **Special Amenities: free continental breakfast and free local telephone calls.**

SOME UNITS

BEST WESTERN POSADA ANA SAN ANTONIO MEDICAL CENTER
Phone: (210)691-9550   **113**

(AAA) (SAVE)
5/1-8/31 [CP]	1P: $102-$122	2P: $112-$132	XP: $10 F18
9/1-1/31 [CP]	1P: $75-$95	2P: $85-$105	XP: $10 F18
2/1-4/30 [CP]	1P: $74-$94	2P: $84-$104	XP: $10 F18

Location: I-10 NW, exit 561 (Huebner Rd). 9411 Wurzbach Rd 78240. Fax: 210/561-9300. **Facility:** 79 one-**Small-scale Hotel** bedroom standard units. 4 stories, interior corridors. **Parking:** on-site. **Terms:** small pets only. **Amenities:** irons, hair dryers. **Pool(s):** outdoor. **Guest Services:** valet laundry. **Business Services:** meeting rooms. **Cards:** AX, CB, DC, DS, MC, VI. **Special Amenities: free continental breakfast and free local telephone calls.**

SOME UNITS

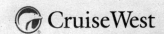

(See map p. 496)

BEST WESTERN SUNSET SUITES-RIVERWALK Phone: (210)223-4400 64

(AAA) (SAVE) | 5/24-8/19 | 1P: $89-$155 | 2P: $89-$155 | XP: $10 | F18
▼▼▼ | 2/1-5/23 & 10/3-1/31 | 1P: $79-$149 | 2P: $79-$149 | XP: $10 | F18
 | 8/20-10/2 | 1P: $79-$135 | 2P: $79-$135 | XP: $10 | F18

Historic **Location:** I-37, exit Commerce St, just e of I-37; in historic Sunset Station. 1103 E Commerce St 78205.
Small-scale Hotel Fax: 210/223-4402. **Facility:** 64 one-bedroom standard units. 4 stories, interior corridors. *Bath:* combo or shower only. **Parking:** on-site. **Terms:** cancellation fee imposed, [BP] meal plan available. **Amenities:** high-speed Internet, voice mail, irons, hair dryers. **Leisure Activities:** exercise room. **Guest Services:** gift shop, valet and coin laundry. **Business Services:** meeting rooms, business center. **Cards:** AX, DC, DS, MC, VI. **Special Amenities:** free newspaper and free room upgrade (subject to availability with advanced reservations). *(See color ad below)*

SOME UNITS

[S▲] [†|+] [🐾] [DATA PORT] [▣] / [✕] /

BONNER GARDEN BED & BREAKFAST Phone: (210)733-4222 92

▼▼▼ | All Year | 1P: $85-$135 | 2P: $85-$135 | XP: $10 | F12

Historic Bed **Location:** Corner of McCullough and E Agarita. Located in Monte Vista Historic District. 145 E Agarita Ave 78212.
& Breakfast Fax: 210/733-6129. **Facility:** This restored, Italian-style 1910 villa features a rooftop terrace offering expansive views of downtown San Antonio. 6 one-bedroom standard units, some with whirlpools. 2 stories (no elevator), interior/exterior corridors. *Bath:* combo or shower only. **Parking:** on-site. **Terms:** 2 night minimum stay - weekends, age restrictions may apply, 3 day cancellation notice-fee imposed, [BP] meal plan available. **Amenities:** video library. **Pool(s):** outdoor. **Business Services:** fax. **Cards:** AX, CB, DC, MC, VI.

[ASK] [S▲] [🏊] [✕] [VCR] [🐾]

CANDLEWOOD SUITES HOTEL Phone: (210)615-0550 149

▼▼▼ | All Year | 1P: $79-$109 | 2P: $79-$109 | XP: $10 | F18

Small-scale Hotel **Location:** I-10 W, eastbound access road between Warzbach Rd and Callaghan. 9350 I-10 W 78230.
Fax: 210/615-1185. **Facility:** 112 units. 48 one-bedroom standard units. 64 one-bedroom suites with efficiencies. 4 stories, interior corridors. *Bath:* combo or shower only. **Parking:** on-site. **Terms:** cancellation fee imposed, small pets only ($75 fee). **Amenities:** video library, CD players, voice mail, irons, hair dryers. **Pool(s):** outdoor. **Leisure Activities:** exercise room. **Guest Services:** complimentary laundry. **Business Services:** business center. **Cards:** AX, DC, DS, MC, VI.

[ASK] [S▲] [🛏] [†|+] [✎] [🏊] [VCR] [🐾] [DATA PORT] [▤] [▦] [▣]

CHRISTMAS HOUSE BED & BREAKFAST Phone: 210/737-2786 88

▼▼ | All Year | 1P: $85-$125 | 2P: $85-$125 | XP: $10 | F10

Bed & Breakfast **Location:** On McCullough Ave at corner of W Craig Pl. 2307 McCullough 78212. Fax: 210/734-5712. **Facility:** Smoke free premises. 5 units. 4 one-bedroom standard units. 1 one-bedroom suite. 2 stories, interior corridors. *Bath:* shower only. **Parking:** on-site. **Terms:** 2 night minimum stay - weekends, age restrictions may apply, 10 day cancellation notice-fee imposed, [BP] & [ECP] meal plans available, no pets allowed (owner's pet on premises). **Amenities:** hair dryers. **Cards:** MC, VI.

[ASK] [S▲] [✎] [✕] [W] [☎]

(See map p. 496)

CLARION HOTEL SAN ANTONIO AIRPORT
[SAVE]
▽▽▽▽
Small-scale Hotel

Phone: (210)494-7600 [69]
All Year [BP]   1P: $109-$119   2P: $119-$129   XP: $10   F18
Location: 2 mi n of airport on US 281; entrance at Countryside. Located in a commercial area. 12828 US Hwy 281 N 78216. Fax: 210/545-4314. Facility: 125 one-bedroom standard units, some with whirlpools. 4 stories, interior corridors. Parking: on-site. Terms: pets ($25 fee, $25 deposit). Amenities: voice mail, irons, hair dryers. Pool(s): small heated indoor. Leisure Activities: sauna. Guest Services: complimentary evening beverages, valet laundry, area transportation. Business Services: meeting rooms, business center. Cards: AX, CB, DC, DS, MC, VI.

SOME UNITS

[icons] / [X] /

COMFORT INN AIRPORT
[SAVE]
▽▽ ▽▽
Small-scale Hotel

Phone: 210/653-9110 [57]
4/1-8/31 [CP]   1P: $59-$69   2P: $79-$89
2/1-3/31 & 9/1-1/31 [CP]   1P: $52-$69   2P: $57-$79
Location: Jct Loop 410 and Perrin-Beitel Rd. 2635 NE Loop 410 78217. Fax: 210/653-8615. Facility: 141 one-bedroom standard units. 6 stories, interior/exterior corridors. Parking: on-site. Terms: small pets only ($25 deposit). Amenities: hair dryers. Fee: video games, safes. Some: irons. Pool(s): outdoor. Guest Services: coin laundry, area transportation. Business Services: fax (fee). Cards: AX, CB, DC, DS, MC, VI.

SOME UNITS

[icons] / [X] [icons] /

COMFORT INN-EAST
[SAVE]
▽▽▽▽
Small-scale Hotel

Phone: (210)333-9430 [80]
All Year   1P: $54   2P: $99   F17
Location: I-10, exit 580 (W W White Rd), on westbound access road. 4403 I-10 E 78219. Fax: 210/359-7201. Facility: 120 one-bedroom standard units. 2-3 stories (no elevator), exterior corridors. Parking: on-site. Terms: [ECP] meal plan available. Amenities: high-speed Internet, safes (fee). Some: irons, hair dryers. Pool(s): outdoor. Guest Services: coin laundry. Business Services: meeting rooms, fax (fee). Cards: AX, CB, DC, DS, JC, MC, VI.

SOME UNITS

[icons] / [X] [icons] /

COMFORT INN-FIESTA
[AAA] [SAVE]
▽▽▽▽
Motel

Phone: (210)696-4766 [117]
5/23-8/9 [ECP]   1P: $89-$109   2P: $99-$129   XP: $10   F18
2/1-5/22 & 8/10-1/31 [ECP]   1P: $49-$79   2P: $59-$89   XP: $10   F18
Location: I-10, exit CR 1604 W, 0.5 mi w La Cantera Blvd. Located opposite the University of Texas at San Antonio. 6755 N Loop 1604 W 78249. Fax: 210/696-4766. Facility: 124 one-bedroom standard units. 4 stories, interior corridors. Parking: on-site. Amenities: Some: irons, hair dryers. Pool(s): outdoor. Leisure Activities: exercise room. Business Services: meeting rooms, fax (fee). Cards: AX, CB, DC, DS, JC, MC, VI.
Special Amenities: free continental breakfast and free local telephone calls. (See color ad below)

SOME UNITS

[icons] / [X] /

(See map p. 496)

COMFORT INN SEA WORLD

Phone: (210)684-8606 **106**

AAA SAVE All Year [CP]   1P: $59-$139   2P: $64-$139   XP: $5   F18

Location: I-410, 0.5 mi e jct Evers Rd, eastbound access road. 4 Piano Pl 78228. Fax: 210/647-4225. **Facility:** 55 one-bedroom standard units. 2 stories, exterior corridors. *Bath:* combo or shower only. **Parking:** on-site.

Small-scale Hotel **Terms:** small pets only ($10 extra charge, with prior approval). **Amenities:** irons, hair dryers. **Pool(s):** outdoor. **Leisure Activities:** whirlpool. **Guest Services:** coin laundry. **Business Services:** meeting rooms, fax. **Cards:** AX, CB, DC, DS, JC, MC, VI. **Special Amenities:** free continental breakfast and free local telephone calls. *(See color ad below)*

SOME UNITS

COMFORT SUITES

Phone: (210)738-1100 **171**

SAVE 3/1-9/7 [ECP]   1P: $99-$129   2P: $109-$139   XP: $5   F18
2/1-2/28 [ECP]   1P: $69-$99   2P: $74-$109   XP: $5   F18
9/8-1/31 [ECP]   1P: $59-$99   2P: $59-$99   XP: $5   F18

Location: I-10, exit 565A (Crossroads), on westbound access road. 6901 I-10 W 78213. Fax: 210/738-1230.

Small-scale Hotel **Facility:** 74 units. 72 one-bedroom standard units. 2 one-bedroom suites with whirlpools. 2 stories, exterior corridors. *Bath:* combo or shower only. **Parking:** on-site. **Amenities:** dual phone lines, safes, irons, hair dryers. **Pool(s):** heated outdoor. **Leisure Activities:** whirlpool. **Guest Services:** coin laundry. **Business Services:** meeting rooms, fax (fee). **Cards:** AX, CB, DC, DS, MC, VI.

SOME UNITS

COMFORT SUITES

Phone: (210)646-6600 **68**

AAA SAVE All Year   1P: $70-$130   2P: $80-$160   XP: $5   F18

Location: I-35, exit 163B (Rittiman Rd) northbound, on northbound access road; exit 163 (Rittiman Rd) southbound. 6350 I 35 N 78218. Fax: 210/646-9800. **Facility:** 105 one-bedroom suites ($110-$160). 3 stories, interior corridors. *Bath:* combo or shower only. **Terms:** [ECP] meal plan available. **Amenities:** voice

Small-scale Hotel mail, irons, hair dryers. **Pool(s):** outdoor. **Leisure Activities:** whirlpool, exercise room. **Guest Services:** coin laundry. **Business Services:** meeting rooms, fax (fee). **Cards:** AX, CB, DC, DS, JC, MC, VI. **Special Amenities:** free continental breakfast and free local telephone calls. *(See color ad p 525)*

SOME UNITS

COMFORT SUITES AIRPORT NORTH

Phone: (210)494-9000 **119**

SAVE All Year [BP]   1P: $89-$99   XP: $10   F18

Location: US 281 N, exit Oak Shadows Dr and Winding Way Dr; from US 281 S, use Bitters exit to turn around, then 0.3 mi on frontage road. 14202 US Hwy 281 N 78232. Fax: 210/494-7200. **Facility:** 65 units. 50 one-bedroom standard units. 15 one-bedroom suites with whirlpools. 3 stories, interior corridors. *Bath:* combo or shower

Small-scale Hotel only. **Parking:** on-site. **Amenities:** high-speed Internet, voice mail, irons, hair dryers. **Pool(s):** small outdoor. **Leisure Activities:** whirlpool, exercise room. **Guest Services:** valet and coin laundry. **Business Services:** meeting rooms, business center. **Cards:** AX, CB, DC, DS, MC, VI.

SOME UNITS

(See map p. 496)

COURTYARD AIRPORT AT NORTHSTAR
Phone: 210/530-9881 [141]
SAVE
All Year — 1P: $129
Location: Loop 410, eastbound access road at exit 21A (Jones Maltsberger Rd). 80 Loop 410 NE 78216.
Fax: 210/530-0873. **Facility:** 78 one-bedroom standard units. 2 stories, interior corridors. **Parking:** on-site.
Amenities: dual phone lines, irons, hair dryers. **Pool(s):** heated indoor. **Leisure Activities:** whirlpool, exer-
Small-scale Hotel cise room. **Guest Services:** valet and coin laundry, area transportation. **Business Services:** meeting rooms.
Cards: AX, DC, DS, MC, VI. *(See color ad p 507)*

SOME UNITS

COURTYARD BY MARRIOTT-AIRPORT
Phone: (210)828-7200 [55]
SAVE
All Year — 1P: $89-$109
Location: Jct of I-410 and Broadway St, just n. Located in a quiet area. 8615 Broadway St 78217. Fax: 210/828-9003.
Facility: 145 units. 137 one-bedroom standard units. 8 one-bedroom suites ($149). 4 stories, interior corri-
dors. **Parking:** on-site. **Terms:** [BP] meal plan available. **Amenities:** high-speed Internet (fee), voice mail,
Small-scale Hotel irons, hair dryers. **Pool(s):** heated indoor. **Leisure Activities:** whirlpool, exercise room. **Guest Services:**
coin laundry, area transportation. **Business Services:** meeting rooms, fax. **Cards:** AX, DC, DS, JC,
MC, VI. *(See color ad p 507)*

SOME UNITS

COURTYARD BY MARRIOTT-MEDICAL CENTER
Phone: (210)614-7100 [96]
SAVE
All Year — 1P: $84-$99 — 2P: $89-$109
Location: Off Fredericksburg Rd, 5 mi n, jct I-410. 8585 Marriott Dr 78229. Fax: 210/614-7110. **Facility:** 146 units.
134 one-bedroom standard units. 12 one-bedroom suites. 3 stories, interior corridors. **Parking:** on-site.
Terms: check-in 4 pm, [BP] meal plan available. **Amenities:** voice mail, irons, hair dryers. **Pool(s):** heated
Small-scale Hotel outdoor. **Leisure Activities:** whirlpool, exercise room. **Guest Services:** coin laundry. **Business Services:**
meeting rooms. **Fee:** PC, fax. **Cards:** AX, CB, DC, DS, MC, VI. *(See color ad p 507)*

SOME UNITS

DAYS INN
Phone: (210)650-9779 [118]
SAVE

5/16-8/15 [ECP]	1P: $60-$150	2P: $60-$150	XP: $5	F16
2/1-5/15 & 8/16-1/31 [ECP]	1P: $45-$80	2P: $45-$80	XP: $5	F16

Location: I-35, exit 167 (Randolf Blvd), on northbound access road. 9401 I-35 N 78233. Fax: 210/599-3173.
Facility: 61 one-bedroom standard units, some with whirlpools. 2 stories (no elevator), exterior corridors.
Small-scale Hotel *Bath:* combo or shower only. **Parking:** on-site. **Terms:** cancellation fee imposed, pets ($10 extra charge).
Amenities: safes (fee), hair dryers. **Pool(s):** outdoor. **Guest Services:** coin laundry. **Business Services:** fax
(fee). **Cards:** AX, CB, DC, DS, JC, MC, VI.

SOME UNITS

DAYS INN AIRPORT
Phone: 210/930-3300 [107]
SAVE

6/1-8/31	1P: $59-$99	2P: $64-$149	XP: $6	F12
3/1-5/31	1P: $54-$99	2P: $59-$149	XP: $6	F12
2/1-2/28 & 9/1-1/31	1P: $49-$69	2P: $54-$74	XP: $6	F12

Motel **Location:** Loop 410 eastbound access road between Airport Blvd and Wetmore Rd. 542 NE Loop 410 78216.
Fax: 210/930-3259. **Facility:** 49 one-bedroom standard units. 2 stories, interior corridors. **Parking:** on-site.
Terms: [CP] meal plan available. **Pool(s):** outdoor. **Leisure Activities:** whirlpool. **Business Services:** fax
(fee). **Cards:** AX, DC, DS, MC, VI.

SOME UNITS

(See map p. 496)

DAYS INN COLISEUM
SAVE
Phone: (210)225-4040 **71**

4/28-8/16 [ECP]	1P: $50-$110	2P: $50-$110	XP: $6	F18
2/1-3/27 & 8/17-1/31 [ECP]	1P: $45-$110	2P: $45-$110	XP: $6	F18
3/28-4/27 [ECP]	1P: $50-$99	2P: $50-$99	XP: $6	F18

Small-scale Hotel **Location:** I-35, exit 160 (Splashtown), on southbound access road. 3443 I-35 N 78219. **Fax:** 210/225-4389. **Facility:** 122 units. 116 one-bedroom standard units. 6 one-bedroom suites ($70-$120) with whirlpools. 2 stories (no elevator), exterior corridors. **Parking:** on-site. **Amenities:** safes (fee). *Some:* irons, hair dryers. **Pool(s):** outdoor. **Business Services:** meeting rooms, fax (fee). **Cards:** AX, DC, DS, MC, VI.

SOME UNITS

DAYS INN-FIESTA PARK
SAVE
Phone: (210)696-7922 **120**

3/1-8/11 [CP]	1P: $59-$99	2P: $69-$129	XP: $10	F12
2/1-2/28 & 8/12-1/31 [CP]	1P: $49-$69	2P: $59-$79	XP: $10	F12

Location: I-10, exit 558 (De Zavala), on eastbound access road. 11790 I-10 W 78230. **Fax:** 210/696-8288. Small-scale Hotel **Facility:** 62 one-bedroom standard units. 2 stories (no elevator), exterior corridors. **Terms:** cancellation fee imposed. **Amenities:** hair dryers. **Pool(s):** outdoor. **Leisure Activities:** whirlpool. **Guest Services:** complimentary laundry. **Business Services:** conference facilities, fax (fee). **Cards:** AX, CB, DC, DS, JC, MC, VI.

SOME UNITS

DAYS INN NORTHSIDE
SAVE
Phone: (210)655-4311 **65**

2/1-9/3 [CP]	1P: $45-$100	2P: $50-$130	XP: $5	F15
9/4-1/31 [CP]	1P: $35-$60	2P: $40-$70	XP: $5	F15

Location: I-35, exit 168 (Weidner Rd), on northbound access road, just n on Weidner Rd. 11202 I-35 N 78233. **Fax:** 210/655-0665. **Facility:** 59 units. 58 one-bedroom standard units. 1 one-bedroom suite ($70-$120) with Small-scale Hotel whirlpool. 2 stories (no elevator), exterior corridors. **Parking:** on-site. **Amenities:** hair dryers. *Some:* irons. **Pool(s):** small outdoor. **Guest Services:** coin laundry. **Business Services:** fax (fee). **Cards:** AX, CB, DC, DS, JC, MC, VI.

SOME UNITS

DAYS INN SEAWORLD
AAA SAVE
Phone: (210)522-1995 **109**

3/7-9/3 [CP]	1P: $65-$95	2P: $75-$115	XP: $5	F12
9/4-11/30 [CP]	1P: $55-$75	2P: $65-$85	XP: $5	F12
12/1-1/31 [CP]	1P: $45-$50	2P: $50-$55	XP: $5	F12
2/1-3/6 [CP]	1P: $40-$50	2P: $45-$55	XP: $5	F12

Small-scale Hotel **Location:** I-410, exit 11 (Ingram Rd), 0.7 mi eastbound on access road. 6010 NW Loop 410 78238. **Fax:** 210/522-1106. **Facility:** 67 one-bedroom standard units. 2 stories, exterior corridors. *Bath:* combo or shower only. **Parking:** on-site. **Amenities:** voice mail, safes, hair dryers. **Pool(s):** small outdoor. **Guest Services:** coin laundry. **Business Services:** meeting rooms, fax (fee). **Cards:** AX, CB, DC, DS, JC, MC, VI. **Special Amenities:** free continental breakfast and free local telephone calls.

SOME UNITS

DAYS INN SOUTH
SAVE
Phone: 210/923-2361 **159**

All Year	1P: $40-$89	2P: $40-$89	XP: $5	F12

Motel **Location:** 0.3 mi s of jct Military Hwy. Located in a quiet area. 3760 Roosevelt Ave 78214. **Fax:** 210/923-2398. **Facility:** 30 one-bedroom standard units. 1-2 stories (no elevator). **Parking:** on-site. **Terms:** [CP] meal plan available. **Amenities:** hair dryers. **Business Services:** fax (fee). **Cards:** AX, DS, MC, VI.

SOME UNITS

(See map p. 496)

DOUBLETREE CLUB HOTEL SAN ANTONIO AIRPORT
Phone: (210)828-9031 **56**

[SAVE]

[diamond diamond diamond]

Large-scale Hotel

(See color ad p 526)

All Year 1P: $69-$119 2P: $69-$119
Location: Loop 410, exit Nacogdoches. 1111 NE Loop 410 78209. Fax: 210/828-3066. **Facility:** 227 one-bedroom standard units. 10 stories, interior corridors. *Bath:* combo or shower only. **Parking:** on-site. **Terms:** package plans. **Amenities:** dual phone lines, voice mail, irons. *Fee:* video games, high-speed Internet. **Pool(s):** outdoor. **Leisure Activities:** whirlpool, exercise room. **Guest Services:** valet laundry, area transportation. **Business Services:** meeting rooms, business center. **Cards:** AX, CB, DC, DS, JC, MC, VI.

SOME UNITS

[icons] / [icons] /

DOUBLETREE HOTEL
Phone: (210)366-2424 **144**
F18

[SAVE]

[diamond diamond diamond]

Large-scale Hotel

All Year 1P: $109-$129 2P: $119-$139 XP: $10
Location: I-410, exit 20B (McCullough Ave), on westbound access road. Located adjacent to North Star Mall. 37 NE Loop 410 78216. Fax: 210/341-0410. **Facility:** 290 units. 284 one-bedroom standard units. 6 one-bedroom suites ($209-$239). 5 stories, interior/exterior corridors. **Parking:** on-site. **Terms:** 3 day cancellation notice-fee imposed. **Amenities:** video games (fee), dual phone lines, voice mail, safes, irons, hair dryers. **Pool(s):** outdoor. **Leisure Activities:** sauna, whirlpool, exercise room. **Guest Services:** gift shop, valet laundry, area transportation. **Business Services:** conference facilities, business center. **Cards:** AX, DC, DS, MC, VI.

SOME UNITS

[icons] / [icons] /
FEE

DRURY INN & SUITES AIRPORT
Phone: (210)308-8100 **148**

[AAA] [SAVE]

[diamond diamond diamond]

Small-scale Hotel

9/1-1/31 [BP] 1P: $69-$89 2P: $79-$99 XP: $10 F18
2/1-8/31 [BP] 1P: $66-$86 2P: $76-$96 XP: $10 F18
Location: Jct Jones Maltsberger Rd at Loop 410, 1.8 mi w of airport. 95 NE Loop 410 78216. Fax: 210/341-6758. **Facility:** 284 units. 100 one-bedroom standard units. 184 one-bedroom suites ($86-$113). 6 stories, interior corridors. **Parking:** on-site. **Terms:** small pets only (in smoking units). **Amenities:** voice mail, irons, hair dryers. **Pool(s):** outdoor. **Leisure Activities:** whirlpool, exercise room. **Guest Services:** complimentary evening beverages: Mon-Thurs, valet and coin laundry, area transportation-North Star Mall. **Business Services:** meeting rooms, fax. **Cards:** AX, CB, DC, DS, MC, VI. **Special Amenities:** free continental breakfast and free local telephone calls.

SOME UNITS

[icons] / [icons] /

DRURY INN & SUITES-SAN ANTONIO NORTHWEST
Phone: (210)561-2510 **151**

[diamond diamond diamond]

Small-scale Hotel

6/1-1/31 [ECP] 1P: $65-$85 2P: $75-$95 XP: $10 F18
2/1-5/31 [ECP] 1P: $63-$83 2P: $73-$93 XP: $10 F18
Location: I-10, exit Wurzbach Rd. 9806 I-10 W 78230. Fax: 210/561-2510. **Facility:** 213 units. 113 one-bedroom standard units. 100 one-bedroom suites ($83-$155). 5 stories, interior corridors. *Bath:* combo or shower only. **Parking:** on-site. **Amenities:** voice mail, irons, hair dryers. **Pool(s):** outdoor. **Leisure Activities:** exercise room. **Guest Services:** valet and coin laundry. **Business Services:** meeting rooms, business center. **Cards:** AX, CB, DC, DS, MC, VI.

SOME UNITS

[ASK] [icons] / [icons] /

DRURY INN NORTHEAST
Phone: (210)654-1144 **79**

[AAA] [SAVE]

[diamond diamond diamond]

Small-scale Hotel

9/1-1/31 [ECP] 1P: $74-$90 2P: $84-$100 XP: $10 F18
2/1-8/31 [ECP] 1P: $72-$88 2P: $82-$98 XP: $10 F18
Location: I-35, exit 165 (Walzem Rd), northbound access road. 8300 I-35 N 78239. Fax: 210/654-1144. **Facility:** 105 one-bedroom standard units. 4 stories, interior/exterior corridors. **Parking:** on-site. **Terms:** small pets only. **Amenities:** voice mail, irons, hair dryers. **Pool(s):** outdoor. **Leisure Activities:** exercise room. **Guest Services:** complimentary evening beverages: Mon-Thurs, coin laundry. **Business Services:** meeting rooms, fax (fee). **Cards:** AX, CB, DC, DS, MC, VI. **Special Amenities:** free continental breakfast and free local telephone calls.

SOME UNITS

[icons] / [icons] /

ECONO LODGE
Phone: (210)737-1855 **116**
F17

[AAA] [SAVE]

[diamond diamond diamond]

Small-scale Hotel

All Year [CP] 1P: $35-$105 2P: $40-$110 XP: $5
Location: I-10, exit 565B eastbound; 565C westbound (Vance Jackson Rd), just n of I-10. 6023 I-10 W 78201. Fax: 210/737-6111. **Facility:** 57 one-bedroom standard units. 2 stories, exterior corridors. **Parking:** on-site. **Terms:** 7 day cancellation notice. **Guest Services:** coin laundry. **Business Services:** fax (fee). **Cards:** AX, DC, DS, MC, VI. **Special Amenities:** early check-in/late check-out and free local telephone calls.

SOME UNITS

[icons] / [icons] /

ECONO LODGE
Phone: (210)647-8000 **153**

[SAVE]

[diamond diamond]

Motel

5/23-9/1 [CP] 1P: $69-$79 2P: $74-$84 XP: $10 F17
3/1-5/22 [CP] 1P: $59-$69 2P: $64-$74 XP: $10 F17
9/2-1/31 [CP] 1P: $49-$59 2P: $59-$64 XP: $10 F17
2/1-2/28 [CP] 1P: $49-$59 2P: $49-$59 XP: $10 F17
Location: I-410, exit 11 (Ingram Rd), on eastbound access road. 6360 NW Loop 410 78238. Fax: 210/681-8118. **Facility:** 40 one-bedroom standard units. 2 stories (no elevator), exterior corridors. **Parking:** on-site. **Terms:** cancellation fee imposed. **Business Services:** fax (fee). **Cards:** AX, DC, DS, MC, VI.

SOME UNITS

[icons] / [icons] /

(See map p. 496)

ECONO LODGE AIRPORT
Phone: 210/247-4774 🔢51

[SAVE]

4/1-8/31 [CP]	1P: $54-$64	2P: $69-$74
9/1-1/31 [CP]	1P: $47-$69	2P: $57-$69
2/1-3/31 [CP]	1P: $47-$65	2P: $57-$69

▼▼▼ Motel

Location: Jct Loop 410 and Perrin-Beitel Rd. 2635 NE Loop 410 78217. Fax: 210/247-0005. **Facility:** 59 one-bedroom standard units. 3 stories, interior corridors. **Parking:** on-site. **Terms:** [CP] meal plan available, small pets only ($25 deposit). **Amenities:** hair dryers. **Pool(s):** outdoor. **Guest Services:** coin laundry, area transportation. **Business Services:** fax (fee). **Cards:** AX, CB, DC, DS, JC, MC, VI.

SOME UNITS

ECONO LODGE-EAST
Phone: (210)333-3346 🔢60

[AAA] [SAVE]

2/1-8/31 [CP]	1P: $35-$129	2P: $37-$139	XP: $5	F18
9/1-1/31 [CP]	1P: $32-$99	2P: $35-$109	XP: $5	F18

▼▼▼▼ Motel

Location: I-10, exit 580, 0.3 mi s of jct W W White Rd. 218 S W W White Rd 78219. Fax: 210/333-7564. **Facility:** 40 one-bedroom standard units. 2 stories, exterior corridors. **Parking:** on-site. **Amenities:** voice mail, irons, hair dryers. **Pool(s):** outdoor. **Guest Services:** coin laundry. **Business Services:** meeting rooms, fax (fee). **Cards:** AX, CB, DC, DS, JC, MC, VI. **Special Amenities:** free continental breakfast and free local telephone calls.

SOME UNITS

EMBASSY SUITES HOTEL-AIRPORT
Phone: (210)525-9999 🔢95

[SAVE]

1/1-1/31	1P: $159-$199	2P: $159-$199	XP: $20	F18
2/1-12/31	1P: $149-$189	2P: $149-$189	XP: $20	F18

▼▼▼ Large-scale Hotel

Location: US 281 Expwy, exit Jones Maltsberger Rd. Located just north of the airport. 10110 Hwy 281 N 78216. Fax: 210/525-0626. **Facility:** 261 one-bedroom suites. 9 stories, interior corridors. **Parking:** on-site. **Terms:** [BP] meal plan available, package plans. **Amenities:** video games, voice mail, irons, hair dryers. *Some:* dual phone lines. **Pool(s):** heated indoor. **Leisure Activities:** sauna, whirlpool, playground, exercise room. **Guest Services:** gift shop, complimentary evening beverages, valet and coin laundry, area transportation. **Business Services:** meeting rooms, business center. **Cards:** AX, CB, DC, DS, JC, MC, VI.

SOME UNITS

EMBASSY SUITES NORTHWEST
Phone: (210)340-5421 🔢139

[SAVE]

3/1-8/31 [BP]	1P: $144-$164	2P: $164	XP: $10	F18
2/1-2/28 & 9/1-1/31 [BP]	1P: $124-$144	2P: $144	XP: $10	F18

▼▼▼ Small-scale Hotel

Location: I-10, just n of Loop 410 via Callaghan Rd exit, n to Pinebrooke, then 0.3 mi e. 7750 Briaridge 78230. Fax: 210/340-1843. **Facility:** 216 one-bedroom suites. 8 stories, interior corridors. **Parking:** on-site. **Terms:** check-in 4 pm. **Amenities:** video games, voice mail, irons, hair dryers. **Pool(s):** heated indoor. **Leisure Activities:** sauna, whirlpool. **Guest Services:** gift shop, coin laundry, area transportation. **Business Services:** meeting rooms, business center. **Cards:** AX, DC, DS, MC, VI.

SOME UNITS

FAIRFIELD INN BY MARRIOTT-SAN ANTONIO AIRPORT
Phone: 210/530-9899 🔢133

[SAVE]

All Year — 1P: $89

▼▼▼ Small-scale Hotel

Location: Loop 410 eastbound access road, exit 21A (Jones Maltsberger Rd), between San Pedro Ave and Jones Maltsberger Rd. 88 Loop 410 NE 78216. Fax: 210/530-0394. **Facility:** 120 units. 91 one-bedroom standard units. 29 one-bedroom suites. 5 stories, interior corridors. **Parking:** on-site. **Terms:** [CP] meal plan available. **Amenities:** video games, irons. **Pool(s):** heated indoor. **Leisure Activities:** exercise room. **Guest Services:** coin laundry, area transportation. **Business Services:** meeting rooms, fax (fee). **Cards:** AX, DC, DS, MC, VI. *(See color ad p 507)*

SOME UNITS

GALAXY INN MOTEL
Phone: 210/732-5800 🔢128

[AAA] [SAVE]

All Year — 1P: $45-$90 — 2P: $50-$95 — XP: $5 — F7

▼▼▼ Motel

Location: I-10, exit 566B eastbound; exit 567A westbound, on eastbound access road. 1242 W Hollywood 78201. Fax: 210/738-0029. **Facility:** 18 one-bedroom standard units. 1 story, exterior corridors. **Parking:** on-site. **Amenities:** hair dryers. **Business Services:** fax (fee). **Cards:** AX, CB, DC, DS, MC, VI.

SOME UNITS

HAMPTON INN-AIRPORT
Phone: (210)366-1800 🔢147

[SAVE]

9/1-1/31 [ECP]	1P: $79-$93	2P: $89-$103	XP: $10	F18
2/1-8/31 [ECP]	1P: $77-$91	2P: $87-$101	XP: $10	F18

▼▼▼ Small-scale Hotel

Location: I-410, exit 21B (Jones Maltsberger Rd). 8818 Jones Maltsberger Rd 78216. Fax: 210/342-9694. **Facility:** 120 one-bedroom standard units. 5 stories, interior corridors. **Parking:** on-site. **Terms:** small pets only. **Amenities:** voice mail, irons. **Pool(s):** outdoor. **Guest Services:** valet laundry, area transportation. **Business Services:** meeting rooms, fax (fee). **Cards:** AX, CB, DC, DS, MC, VI.

SOME UNITS

HAMPTON INN-NORTHEAST
Phone: (210)657-1107 🔢81

[SAVE]

6/1-8/31 [ECP]	1P: $91-$101	2P: $101-$111	XP: $10	F18
9/1-1/31 [ECP]	1P: $81-$91	2P: $91-$101	XP: $10	F18
2/1-5/31 [ECP]	1P: $79-$89	2P: $89-$99	XP: $10	F18

▼▼▼ Small-scale Hotel

Location: I-35, exit 165 (Walzem Rd). 4900 Crestwind Dr 78239. Fax: 210/599-7172. **Facility:** 80 units. 40 one-bedroom standard units. 40 one-bedroom suites. 4 stories, interior corridors. **Parking:** on-site. **Amenities:** voice mail, irons. **Pool(s):** outdoor. **Leisure Activities:** exercise room. **Guest Services:** complimentary evening beverages: Mon-Thurs, valet and coin laundry. **Business Services:** meeting rooms, fax (fee). **Cards:** AX, CB, DC, DS, MC, VI.

SOME UNITS

(See map p. 496)

HAMPTON INN NORTHWEST-SEA WORLD AREA   Phone: (210)684-9966   103

(AAA) [SAVE]
▼▼▼▼▼

5/30-8/9 [ECP]   1P: $64-$104   2P: $64-$104
2/1-5/29 & 8/10-1/31 [ECP]   1P: $49-$89   2P: $49-$89

Small-scale Hotel   **Location:** I-410, exit Callaghon Rd eastbound; exit Ever Rd westbound, take turn around. 4803 Manitou Dr 78228. Fax: 210/684-6211. **Facility:** 123 one-bedroom standard units. 5 stories, interior corridors. **Parking:** on-site. **Terms:** cancellation fee imposed. **Amenities:** video games, voice mail, irons. **Pool(s):** outdoor. **Guest Services:** complimentary evening beverages: Wed, valet laundry. **Business Services:** meeting rooms, fax (fee). **Cards:** AX, CB, DC, DS, MC, VI. **Special Amenities:** free continental breakfast and free newspaper.

SOME UNITS

[S/D] [†|†] [⟋] [⇌] [†⟋†] [☆] [DATA PORT] [▭] / [✕] /

HAMPTON INN SIX FLAGS AREA   Phone: (210)561-9058   101

(AAA) [SAVE]
▼▼▼▼▼

All Year [ECP]   1P: $79-$89   2P: $89-$99   XP: $10   F18

Small-scale Hotel   **Location:** I-10, exit 560 westbound; exit 559 (Huebner Rd) eastbound. 11010 I-10 W 78230. Fax: 210/690-5566. **Facility:** 121 one-bedroom standard units. 6 stories, interior corridors. **Parking:** on-site. **Terms:** pets ($10 extra charge). **Amenities:** video games (fee), voice mail, irons, hair dryers. **Pool(s):** outdoor. **Leisure Activities:** exercise room. **Guest Services:** valet and coin laundry, area transportation-within 5 mi. **Business Services:** meeting rooms, business center. **Cards:** AX, CB, DC, DS, MC, VI. **Special Amenities:** free continental breakfast and free local telephone calls. *(See color ad below)*

SOME UNITS

[S/D] [🐾] [†|†] [⟋] [⇌] [☆] [DATA PORT] [▭] / [✕] [🛏] [▭] /

HILL COUNTRY INN & SUITES   Phone: (210)599-4204   125

▼▼▼
Small-scale Hotel

All Year   1P: $50-$60   2P: $60-$70

Location: Loop 410 W access road at Starcrest exit. 2383 NE Loop 410 78217-0867. Fax: 210/599-0356. **Facility:** 190 one-bedroom suites with efficiencies. 1 story, exterior corridors. **Parking:** on-site. **Terms:** weekly rates available, [CP] meal plan available, package plans, small pets only ($75 extra charge, limit 2). **Amenities:** voice mail, irons. **Pool(s):** outdoor, wading. **Leisure Activities:** whirlpools, playground. **Guest Services:** gift shop, coin laundry, area transportation. **Business Services:** meeting rooms, business center. **Cards:** AX, DS, MC, VI.

SOME UNITS

[ASK] [S/D] [✛] [🐾] [&M] [⟋] [⇌] [†⟋†] [☆] [DATA PORT] [🛏] [▭] [▭] / [✕] /

(See map p. 496)

HILTON SAN ANTONIO AIRPORT
Phone: (210)340-6060 140
(AAA) (SAVE)
WWWW
Large-scale Hotel

All Year 1P: $89-$149 2P: $89-$149 XP: $15 F18
Location: Jct Loop 410, exit US 281 N (San Pedro Ave). 611 NW Loop 410 78216. Fax: 210/377-4674. **Facility:** 386 units. 384 one-bedroom standard units. 2 one-bedroom suites. 13 stories, interior corridors. *Bath:* combo or shower only. **Parking:** on-site. **Terms:** cancellation fee imposed, [AP] meal plan available, 15% service charge, small pets only. **Amenities:** dual phone lines, voice mail, irons, hair dryers. **Dining:** 6:30 am-11 pm, cocktails. **Pool(s):** heated outdoor. **Leisure Activities:** saunas, whirlpool, putting green, exercise room. **Guest Services:** gift shop, valet and coin laundry, area transportation-within 2 mi. **Business Services:** conference facilities, business center. **Cards:** AX, CB, DC, DS, MC, VI. *(See ad p 529)*

HOLIDAY INN EXPRESS
Phone: (210)599-0999 66
WWW
Small-scale Hotel

All Year [CP] 1P: $79-$99 2P: $89-$109 XP: $10 F17
Location: I-35, exit 170, on southbound access road, 0.5 mi s to Judson Rd exit. 11939 N I-35 78237. Fax: 210/599-6980. **Facility:** 71 one-bedroom standard units. 2 stories, exterior corridors. **Parking:** on-site. **Terms:** small pets only ($10 extra charge). **Amenities:** voice mail, irons, hair dryers. **Pool(s):** outdoor. **Leisure Activities:** whirlpool. **Guest Services:** coin laundry. **Business Services:** fax (fee). **Cards:** AX, CB, DC, DS, JC, MC, VI.

HOLIDAY INN EXPRESS-AIRPORT
Phone: (210)308-6700 150
WWW
Small-scale Hotel

6/1-8/31 [CP] 1P: $103-$119 2P: $113-$129 XP: $10 F18
2/1-5/31 & 9/1-1/31 [CP] 1P: $85-$101 2P: $95-$111 XP: $10 F18
Location: Loop 410, exit 21A eastbound; exit 20B westbound, on eastbound access road between San Pedro Ave and Jones Maltsberger Rd. 91 NE Loop 410 78216. Fax: 210/308-6700. **Facility:** 154 one-bedroom standard units. 10 stories, interior corridors. **Parking:** on-site. **Amenities:** irons, hair dryers. **Pool(s):** outdoor. **Leisure Activities:** exercise room. **Guest Services:** coin laundry, area transportation. **Business Services:** meeting rooms, business center. **Cards:** AX, CB, DC, DS, MC, VI.

HOLIDAY INN EXPRESS SEAWORLD
Phone: (210)521-1485 114
WWW
Small-scale Hotel

3/1-8/15 [ECP] 1P: $79-$119 2P: $84-$124 XP: $5 F18
2/1-2/28 & 8/16-1/31 [ECP] 1P: $69-$89 2P: $74-$94 XP: $5 F18
Location: I-410, exit 10 (Culebra Rd), on eastbound access road. 7043 Culebra Rd 78238. Fax: 210/520-5924. **Facility:** 72 one-bedroom standard units. 2 stories (no elevator), exterior corridors. *Bath:* combo or shower only. **Parking:** on-site. **Amenities:** high-speed Internet, voice mail, irons, hair dryers. **Pool(s):** outdoor. **Guest Services:** coin laundry. **Business Services:** meeting rooms, fax (fee). **Cards:** AX, CB, DC, DS, JC, MC, VI.

HOLIDAY INN EXPRESS SOUTH
Phone: (210)927-4800 62
(AAA) (SAVE)
WWW
Motel

2/1-8/15 [ECP] 1P: $99-$104 2P: $99-$104 XP: $5
8/16-1/31 [ECP] 1P: $89-$99 2P: $89-$99
Location: I-35, exit 152 (Division Ave), on northbound access road. 606 Division Ave 78214. Fax: 210/927-5060. **Facility:** 69 one-bedroom standard units. 2 stories, exterior corridors. *Bath:* combo or shower only. **Parking:** on-site. **Amenities:** irons, hair dryers. **Pool(s):** outdoor. **Guest Services:** coin laundry. **Business Services:** meeting rooms, fax. **Cards:** AX, CB, DC, DS, MC, VI. **Special Amenities:** free local telephone calls and free newspaper.

HOLIDAY INN LACKLAND
Phone: (210)678-0444 58
(AAA) (SAVE)
WWW
Small-scale Hotel

6/1-8/20 1P: $79-$135 2P: $79-$135 XP: $5 F17
8/21-10/31 1P: $79-$109 2P: $79-$109 XP: $5 F17
2/1-5/31 1P: $69-$104 2P: $69-$104 XP: $5 F17
11/1-1/31 1P: $69-$99 2P: $69-$99 XP: $5 F17
Location: US 90, exit Old US 90, then 0.3 mi ne. Located in a quiet area. 6502 Old Hwy 90 W 78227. Fax: 210/678-9026. **Facility:** 74 units. 72 one-bedroom standard units. 2 one-bedroom suites ($125-$160) with efficiencies. 2 stories, interior corridors. *Bath:* combo or shower only. **Parking:** on-site. **Terms:** [AP], [BP], [CP] & [MAP] meal plans available. **Amenities:** video games, voice mail, irons, hair dryers. **Dining:** 7 am-2 & 5-9 pm. **Pool(s):** outdoor. **Leisure Activities:** whirlpool, exercise room. **Guest Services:** coin laundry. **Business Services:** meeting rooms. *Fee:* PC, fax. **Cards:** AX, CB, DC, DS, MC, VI. **Special Amenities:** free local telephone calls and free newspaper.

HOLIDAY INN-NORTHEAST
Phone: (210)226-4361 74
(AAA) (SAVE)
WWW
Small-scale Hotel

All Year 1P: $95 2P: $95
Location: I-35, exit 162 (Binz-Engleman Rd) southbound; exit 161 northbound on southbound access road. 3855 I-35 N 78219. Fax: 210/226-6909. **Facility:** 183 units. 160 one-bedroom standard units. 23 one-bedroom suites ($139), some with kitchens. 2 stories, exterior corridors. **Parking:** on-site. **Terms:** small pets only ($10 deposit). **Amenities:** voice mail, irons, hair dryers. **Dining:** 6 am-2 & 5-10 pm, cocktails. **Pool(s):** outdoor, wading. **Leisure Activities:** exercise room. **Guest Services:** coin laundry. **Business Services:** meeting rooms, fax (fee). **Cards:** AX, CB, DC, DS, MC, VI.

HOLIDAY INN SELECT
Phone: (210)349-9900 145
WWW
Small-scale Hotel

All Year 1P: $129 2P: $129 XP: $10 F18
Location: I-410, exit 20B (McCullough St), on westbound access road. 77 NE Loop 410 78216. Fax: 210/349-4660. **Facility:** 397 units. 391 one-bedroom standard units. 6 one-bedroom suites ($149). 11 stories, interior corridors. *Bath:* combo or shower only. **Parking:** on-site. **Terms:** pets ($25 fee, $150 deposit). **Amenities:** video games, voice mail, irons, hair dryers. **Pool(s):** outdoor. **Leisure Activities:** whirlpool, exercise room. **Guest Services:** gift shop, coin laundry. **Business Services:** meeting rooms, business center. **Cards:** AX, CB, DC, DS, MC, VI.

See map p. 496)

HOMEGATE STUDIOS & SUITES
Phone: 210/342-4800 **143**

| | 3/1-8/31 [CP] | 1P: $69-$79 | 2P: $69-$79 |
| | 2/1-2/28 & 9/1-1/31 [CP] | 1P: $59-$69 | 2P: $59-$69 |

Small-scale Hotel **Location:** US 281 N, exit Nakoma, on west frontage road. 11221 San Pedro Ave 78216. Fax: 210/342-1110. **Facility:** 115 one-bedroom standard units with kitchens. 3 stories, exterior corridors. **Parking:** on-site. **Terms:** pets ($100 fee). **Amenities:** voice mail, irons. **Pool(s):** outdoor. **Leisure Activities:** whirlpool, exercise room. **Guest Services:** coin laundry. **Business Services:** meeting rooms, fax (fee). **Cards:** AX, CB, DC, DS, MC, VI.

SOME UNITS

HOMESTEAD STUDIO SUITES HOTEL-SAN ANTONIO/AIRPORT
Phone: (210)491-9009 **102**

| | 5/2-9/6 | 1P: $65-$75 | 2P: $70-$80 | XP: $5 | F17 |
| | 2/1-5/1 & 9/7-1/31 | 1P: $55-$65 | 2P: $60-$70 | XP: $5 | F17 |

Motel **Location:** Loop 410, 4 mi w on US 281, exit Bitters Rd. 1015 Central Pkwy S 78232. Fax: 210/491-9033. **Facility:** 153 one-bedroom standard units with kitchens. 2 stories, exterior corridors. **Parking:** on-site. **Terms:** pets ($75 fee). **Amenities:** voice mail, irons. **Guest Services:** coin laundry. **Cards:** AX, CB, DC, DS, JC, MC, VI.

SOME UNITS

HOMEWOOD SUITES BY HILTON
Phone: (210)696-5400 **104**

SAVE

	6/6-8/9 [ECP]	1P: $109-$129	2P: $109-$129
	2/1-3/31 [ECP]	1P: $99-$129	2P: $99-$129
	4/1-6/5 & 8/10-1/31 [ECP]	1P: $99-$109	2P: $99-$109

Small-scale Hotel **Location:** I-10, exit Colonade. 4323 Spectrum One 78230. Fax: 210/696-8899. **Facility:** 123 units. 116 one- and 7 two-bedroom suites. 4 stories, interior corridors. **Parking:** on-site. **Amenities:** voice mail, irons, hair dryers. **Pool(s):** outdoor. **Leisure Activities:** exercise room, sports court. **Guest Services:** complimentary evening beverages: Mon-Thurs, valet and coin laundry, area transportation. **Business Services:** meeting rooms, business center. **Cards:** AX, CB, DC, DS, MC, VI.

SOME UNITS

HOWARD JOHNSON COLISEUM
Phone: (210)229-9220 **72**

	4/28-8/16 [ECP]	1P: $50-$110	2P: $50-$110	XP: $6	F18
	2/1-3/27 & 8/17-1/31 [ECP]	1P: $45-$110	2P: $45-$110	XP: $6	F18
	3/28-4/27 [ECP]	1P: $50-$99	2P: $50-$99	XP: $6	F18

Small-scale Hotel **Location:** I-35, exit 159B (Walters Ave), southbound access road. 2755 I-35 N 78208. Fax: 210/229-1242. **Facility:** 49 one-bedroom standard units. 2 stories (no elevator), exterior corridors. **Parking:** on-site. **Terms:** small pets only. **Amenities:** Some: irons, hair dryers. **Pool(s):** outdoor. **Business Services:** fax (fee). **Cards:** AX, DC, DS, MC, VI.

SOME UNITS

HOWARD JOHNSON EXPRESS INN FIESTA
Phone: (210)558-7152 **135**

	5/23-8/16	1P: $69-$89	2P: $79-$99	XP: $10	F17
	3/7-5/22	1P: $59-$69	2P: $69-$79	XP: $10	F17
	2/1-3/6 & 8/17-1/31	1P: $49-$59	2P: $59-$69	XP: $10	F17

Small-scale Hotel **Location:** I-10 NW, exit 557 westbound; exit 558 eastbound, on westbound access road. 13279 I-10 W 78249. Fax: 210/558-7228. **Facility:** 53 one-bedroom standard units. 2 stories, exterior corridors. **Parking:** on-site. **Terms:** [CP] meal plan available, small pets only (with prior approval). **Amenities:** voice mail, safes (fee). **Pool(s):** small outdoor. **Business Services:** meeting rooms, fax (fee). **Cards:** AX, CB, DC, DS, MC, VI.

SOME UNITS

HOWARD JOHNSON INN & SUITES MEDICAL CENTER
Phone: 210/614-9900 **97**

| | 2/1-9/2 [BP] | 1P: $69-$79 | 2P: $69-$79 | XP: $10 | F16 |
| | 9/3-1/31 [BP] | 1P: $59-$69 | 2P: $59-$69 | XP: $10 | F16 |

Small-scale Hotel **Location:** 1.5 mi s of jct I-10 and Wurzbach Rd, just ne of Babcock Rd. Located across from South Texas Medical Center. 7401 Wurzbach Rd 78229. Fax: 210/614-2105. **Facility:** 194 units. 169 one-bedroom standard units, some with whirlpools. 25 one-bedroom suites ($79-$119). 2-4 stories, interior/exterior corridors. **Parking:** on-site. **Terms:** weekly rates available, [AP] & [ECP] meal plans available, package plans. **Amenities:** voice mail. Some: irons, hair dryers. **Pool(s):** outdoor, wading. **Guest Services:** valet laundry, area transportation **Business Services:** meeting rooms, fax (fee). **Cards:** AX, DS, MC, VI.

SOME UNITS

FEE FEE

HYATT REGENCY HILL COUNTRY RESORT
Phone: (210)647-1234 **61**

AAA SAVE

| | 3/1-11/18 | 1P: $185-$320 | 2P: $185-$320 | XP: $25 | F18 |
| | 2/1-2/28 & 11/19-1/31 | 1P: $105-$240 | 2P: $105-$240 | XP: $25 | F18 |

Resort
Large-scale Hotel **Location:** Between Loop 410 and I-604. 9800 Hyatt Resort Dr 78251. Fax: 210/681-9681. **Facility:** Wood-trimmed porches and walls of regionally quarried limestone distinguish this property 1.5 miles from Sea World San Antonio. 500 units. 470 one-bedroom standard units. 30 one-bedroom suites. 5 stories, interior corridors. **Parking:** on-site and valet. **Terms:** check-in 4 pm, 3 day cancellation notice-fee imposed, $10 service charge. **Amenities:** voice mail, irons, hair dryers. Some: CD players, safes. **Dining:** 3 restaurants, 6 am-10 pm, Fri & Sat-11 pm, Sunday brunch, cocktails. **Pool(s):** 2 outdoor, 2 wading. **Leisure Activities:** sauna, whirlpool, 3 tennis courts (1 lighted), recreation programs, 4-acre water park, bicycles, jogging, playground, spa. Fee: golf-18 holes. **Guest Services:** gift shop, valet laundry, area transportation (fee)-Sea World. **Business Services:** conference facilities, business center. **Cards:** AX, CB, DC, DS, JC, MC, VI *(See color ad inside front cover)*

SOME UNITS

FEE

(See map p. 496)

KNIGHTS INN WINDSOR PARK　　　　　　　　　　　　　**Phone:** (210)646-6336　⑦
AAA SAVE　5/19-8/31　　　　1P: $59-$79　　2P: $69-$89　　XP: $6　　　F12
▼▼▼▼　2/1-5/18 & 9/1-1/31　1P: $49-$69　　2P: $59-$79　　XP: $6　　　F12
Location: Just off Loop 410/I-35, exit Rittiman Rd, northbound access road. 6370 I-35 N 78218. Fax: 210/599-7885.
Small-scale Hotel **Facility:** 85 one-bedroom standard units. 3 stories, exterior corridors. **Parking:** on-site. **Terms:** small pets only ($10 extra charge). **Pool(s):** small outdoor. **Guest Services:** coin laundry. **Business Services:** fax (fee). **Cards:** AX, CB, DC, DS, JC, MC, VI. **Special Amenities:** free continental breakfast and free local telephone calls.

SOME UNITS

LA QUINTA INN-SAN ANTONIO-INGRAM PARK　　　　　　**Phone:** (210)680-8883　⑧⑥
AAA SAVE　5/26-8/31　　　　1P: $89-$119　　2P: $95-$125
▼▼▼▼　2/1-5/25 & 9/1-1/31　1P: $69-$89　　2P: $75-$95
Location: Loop 410, exit 10 (Culebra Rd), eastbound access road. 7134 NW Loop 410 78238-4116.
Small-scale Hotel ridors. **Parking:** on-site. **Terms:** [ECP] meal plan available, small pets only. **Amenities:** video games, voice mail, irons, hair dryers. **Pool(s):** outdoor. **Guest Services:** valet laundry. **Business Services:** meeting rooms, fax (fee). **Cards:** AX, CB, DC, DS, JC, MC, VI. **Special Amenities:** free continental breakfast and free local telephone calls. *(See color ad p 510)*

SOME UNITS

LA QUINTA INN-SAN ANTONIO-LACKLAND　　　　　　　**Phone:** (210)674-3200　⑧④
SAVE　All Year　　　　1P: $69-$99　　2P: $75-$105
Location: Southwest jct of US 90 and Military Dr W; entrance on Military Dr. 6511 Military Dr W 78227-3615.
▼▼▼▼　Fax: 210/673-6015. **Facility:** 176 one-bedroom standard units. 2 stories (no elevator), exterior corridors.
Small-scale Hotel *Bath:* combo or shower only. **Parking:** on-site. **Terms:** [ECP] meal plan available, small pets only. **Amenities:** video games, voice mail, irons, hair dryers. **Pool(s):** 2 outdoor. **Guest Services:** coin laundry. **Business Services:** meeting rooms, fax (fee). **Cards:** AX, CB, DC, DS, JC, MC, VI. *(See color ad p 510)*

SOME UNITS

LA QUINTA INN-SAN ANTONIO-SOUTH　　　　　　　　**Phone:** (210)922-2111　⑧②
AAA SAVE　All Year　　　　1P: $69-$99　　2P: $75-$105
▼▼▼▼　**Location:** I-35, exit 150A (Military Dr) northbound; exit 150B southbound, southeast of jct I-35 and Military Dr SW. 7202 S Pan American Expwy 78224-1415. Fax: 210/923-7979. **Facility:** 122 one-bedroom standard units. 2 stories (no elevator), exterior corridors. **Parking:** on-site. **Terms:** [ECP] meal plan available. **Amenities:** video Small-scale Hotel games, voice mail, irons, hair dryers. **Pool(s):** outdoor. **Guest Services:** coin laundry. **Business Services:** fax (fee). **Cards:** AX, CB, DC, DS, JC, MC, VI. **Special Amenities:** free continental breakfast and free local telephone calls. *(See color ad p 510)*

SOME UNITS

LA QUINTA INN-SAN ANTONIO-VANCE JACKSON　　　　**Phone:** (210)734-7931　⑫⑦
AAA SAVE　All Year　　　　1P: $69-$99　　2P: $75-$105
▼▼▼▼　**Location:** I-10, exit 565B eastbound; exit 565C (Vance Jackson Rd) westbound, on eastbound access road. 5922 NW Expwy 78201-2814. Fax: 210/733-6039. **Facility:** 111 one-bedroom standard units. 2 stories, exterior corridors.
Small-scale Hotel **Parking:** on-site. **Terms:** [ECP] meal plan available, small pets only. **Amenities:** video games, voice mail. **Pool(s):** outdoor. **Guest Services:** valet laundry. **Business Services:** meeting rooms, fax (fee). **Cards:** AX, CB, DC, DS, JC, MC, VI. **Special Amenities:** free continental breakfast and free local telephone calls. *(See color ad p 510)*

SOME UNITS

LA QUINTA INN-SAN ANTONIO-WINDSOR PARK　　　　　**Phone:** (210)653-6619　⑦⑥
AAA SAVE　All Year　　　　1P: $69-$99　　2P: $75-$105
▼▼▼▼　**Location:** I-35, exit 163B northbound, on I-35 northbound access road between Rittiman and Eisenhauer rds; exit 163 (Rittiman Rd) southbound. 6410 I-35 N 78218-4405. Fax: 210/590-3359. **Facility:** 130 units. 129 one-bedroom standard units. 1 one-bedroom suite. 2 stories, exterior corridors. **Parking:** on-site. **Terms:** [ECP] meal plan
Small-scale Hotel available, small pets only. **Amenities:** video games, voice mail, irons, hair dryers. **Pool(s):** outdoor. **Guest Services:** coin laundry. **Business Services:** fax (fee). **Cards:** AX, CB, DC, DS, JC, MC, VI. **Special Amenities:** free continental breakfast and free local telephone calls. *(See color ad p 510)*

SOME UNITS

LA QUINTA INN-SAN ANTONIO-WURZBACH　　　　　　**Phone:** (210)593-0338　⑨④
SAVE　All Year　　　　1P: $69-$99　　2P: $75-$105
Location: I-10, exit Wurzbach Rd, just e on eastbound access road. 9542 I-10 W 78230. Fax: 210/593-0838.
▼▼▼▼　**Facility:** 106 units. 103 one-bedroom standard units. 1 one- and 2 two-bedroom suites. 2 stories (no elevator), exterior corridors. **Parking:** on-site. **Terms:** [ECP] meal plan available, small pets only. **Amenities:** video
Small-scale Hotel games, irons, hair dryers. **Pool(s):** outdoor. **Guest Services:** valet laundry. **Business Services:** meeting rooms, fax (fee). **Cards:** AX, CB, DC, DS, JC, MC, VI. *(See color ad p 510)*

SOME UNITS

LA QUINTA INNS-SAN ANTONIO AIRPORT　　　　　　**Phone:** (210)342-3738　⑯①
AAA SAVE　All Year　　　　1P: $89-$129　　2P: $95-$135
▼▼▼▼　**Location:** I-410, exit US 281 S, southeast corner Loop 410 jct US 281 S. Located near the San Antonio International Airport. 850 Halm 78216. Fax: 210/348-9666. **Facility:** 276 units. 224 one-bedroom standard units. 52 one-bedroom suites. 8 stories, interior corridors. *Bath:* combo or shower only. **Parking:** on-site. **Terms:** [ECP]
Small-scale Hotel meal plan available, pets (with prior approval). **Amenities:** video games, voice mail, irons, hair dryers. **Pool(s):** heated outdoor. **Leisure Activities:** whirlpool, exercise room. **Guest Services:** valet and coin laundry, area transportation-within 2 mi. **Business Services:** meeting rooms, business center. **Cards:** AX, CB, DC, DS, JC, MC, VI. **Special Amenities:** free continental breakfast and free local telephone calls. *(See color ad p 510)*

SOME UNITS

(See map p. 496)

REGENCY INN & SUITES

⬥⬥⬥ SAVE

⬥⬥ ⬥⬥

Motel

All Year   1P: $49-$89   2P: $55-$99   Phone: 210/690-2255   **164**

    XP: $10   F18

Location: Across from USAA, 0.3 mi s of Huebner Rd. 9727 Fredericksburg Rd 78240. Fax: 210/690-2329. **Facility:** 33 one-bedroom standard units. 2 stories (no elevator), exterior corridors. **Parking:** on-site. **Terms:** [ECP] meal plan available. **Amenities:** hair dryers. **Guest Services:** coin laundry. **Business Services:** fax (fee). **Cards:** AX, DC, DS, MC, VI. **Special Amenities:** free continental breakfast and free local telephone calls.

SOME UNITS

MICROTEL INN & SUITES

⬥⬥ ⬥⬥

Small-scale Hotel

			Phone: (210)231-0123	**52**
6/1-9/15 [CP]	1P: $79-$99	2P: $89-$109	XP: $5	F16
2/1-4/30 [CP]	1P: $59-$89	2P: $69-$99	XP: $5	F16
9/16-1/31 [CP]	1P: $49-$79	2P: $59-$89	XP: $5	F16
5/1-5/31 [CP]	1P: $49-$69	2P: $59-$79	XP: $5	F16

Location: I-35, exit 162 (Binz Engleman Rd) southbound; exit 161 (Binz Engleman Rd) northbound, on southbound access road. 3911 I-35 N 78219. Fax: 210/231-0089. **Facility:** 50 units. 27 one-bedroom standard units. 23 one-bedroom suites ($69-$149). 2 stories, interior corridors. **Parking:** on-site. **Terms:** 4 day cancellation notice. **Amenities:** safes (fee). **Pool(s):** outdoor. **Leisure Activities:** exercise room. **Guest Services:** coin laundry. **Business Services:** meeting rooms, fax (fee). **Cards:** AX, DS, MC, VI.

SOME UNITS

ASK SD ... (icons)

MOTEL 6 - 134

⬥⬥

Motel

			Phone: 210/650-4419	**136**
5/22-8/16	1P: $35-$45	2P: $41-$51	XP: $3	F17
8/17-1/31	1P: $31-$41	2P: $37-$47	XP: $3	F17
2/1-5/21	1P: $29-$39	2P: $35-$45	XP: $3	F17

Fax: 210/650-0118. **Location:** I-35, exit 167A (Randolf Blvd) southbound; exit 167 (Starlight Terrace) northbound. 9503 I-35 N 78233. **Facility:** 113 one-bedroom standard units. 2 stories (no elevator), exterior corridors. **Bath:** shower only. **Parking:** on-site. **Terms:** small pets only (with prior approval). **Pool(s):** outdoor. **Guest Services:** coin laundry. **Business Services:** fax (fee). **Cards:** AX, CB, DC, DS, MC, VI.

SOME UNITS

MOTEL 6 - 183

⬥⬥ ⬥⬥

Small-scale Hotel

			Phone: 210/333-1850	**137**
5/22-8/16	1P: $35-$45	2P: $41-$51	XP: $3	F17
8/17-1/31	1P: $31-$41	2P: $37-$47	XP: $3	F17
2/1-5/21	1P: $29-$39	2P: $35-$45	XP: $3	F17

Fax: 210/333-1408. **Location:** I-10, exit 580 (W W White Rd), just off westbound access road. 138 N W W White Rd 78219. **Facility:** 101 one-bedroom standard units. 2 stories (no elevator), exterior corridors. **Bath:** shower only. **Parking:** on-site. **Terms:** small pets only. **Pool(s):** outdoor. **Guest Services:** coin laundry. **Business Services:** fax (fee). **Cards:** AX, CB, DC, DS, MC, VI.

SOME UNITS

(icons) SD ... /X/

MOTEL 6 - 651

⬥⬥ ⬥⬥

Motel

			Phone: 210/673-9020	**115**
6/12-8/9	1P: $51-$61	2P: $57-$67	XP: $3	F17
5/22-6/11	1P: $47-$57	2P: $53-$63	XP: $3	F17
8/10-1/31	1P: $37-$47	2P: $43-$53	XP: $3	F17
2/1-5/21	1P: $36-$46	2P: $42-$52	XP: $3	F17

Location: I-410, exit 7 (Marbach Rd), on westbound access road. 2185 SW Loop 410 78227. Fax: 210/673-1546. **Facility:** 122 one-bedroom standard units. 3 stories (no elevator), exterior corridors. **Bath:** combo or shower only. **Parking:** on-site. **Terms:** small pets only. **Pool(s):** outdoor. **Guest Services:** coin laundry. **Business Services:** fax (fee). **Cards:** AX, CB, DC, DS, MC, VI.

SOME UNITS

(icons) SD ... /X/ ...

(See map p. 496)

OMNI SAN ANTONIO HOTEL

Phone: 210/691-8888   93

AAA SAVE

All Year   1P: $149-$169   2P: $149-$169

Location: I-10, exit Wurzbach Rd, 12 mi nw on westbound access road; in the Colonnade Mall. 9821 Colonnade Blvd 78230. Fax: 210/691-1128. **Facility:** The use of Texas granite on various surfaces within the hotel serves to unify the decor of this modern facility. 326 one-bedroom standard units. 20 stories, interior corridors. **Parking:** Large-scale Hotel on-site. **Amenities:** honor bars. **Dining:** Bolo's Rotisserie-Grille, see separate listing. **Pool(s):** heated indoor, indoor/outdoor. **Leisure Activities:** sauna, whirlpools, exercise room. **Guest Services:** gift shop, valet laundry, area transportation-within 5 mi. **Business Services:** conference facilities, business center. **Cards:** AX, CB, DC, DS, JC, MC, VI. **Special Amenities:** early check-in/late check-out and free newspaper. *(See color ad below)*

PARK INN

Phone: (210)590-4646   98
F18

All Year   1P: $69   2P: $69   XP: $5

Location: I-35, exit 168 (Weidner Rd), 0.5 mi s. 10811 I-35 N 78233. Fax: 210/590-2464. **Facility:** 161 one-bedroom standard units. 2 stories (no elevator), interior corridors. **Parking:** on-site. **Terms:** 3 day cancellation notice, [CP] meal plan available. **Amenities:** *Some:* hair dryers. **Pool(s):** outdoor. **Leisure Activities:** whirlpool. **Guest Services:** coin laundry. **Business Services:** conference facilities, fax (fee). **Cards:** AX, DC, DS, MC, VI.

Small-scale Hotel

SOME UNITS

PEAR TREE INN AIRPORT

Phone: (210)366-9300   146

AAA SAVE

6/1-8/1 [ECP]	1P: $64-$81	2P: $74-$91	XP: $10 F18
8/2-1/31 [ECP]	1P: $61-$78	2P: $71-$88	XP: $10 F18
2/1-5/31 [ECP]	1P: $59-$76	2P: $69-$86	XP: $10 F18

Location: Loop 410 W, exit 21 (Jones-Maltsberger Rd), on westbound access road, between San Pedro Ave and Jones-Small-scale Hotel Maltsberger Rd. 143 NE Loop 410 78216. Fax: 210/366-9300. **Facility:** 125 one-bedroom standard units. 4 stories, interior corridors. **Parking:** on-site. **Terms:** small pets only (in smoking units). **Amenities:** irons, hair dryers. **Pool(s):** outdoor. **Leisure Activities:** exercise room. **Guest Services:** complimentary evening beverages, coin laundry. **Business Services:** meeting rooms, fax (fee). **Cards:** AX, CB, DC, DS, MC, VI. **Special Amenities:** free continental breakfast and free local telephone calls.

SOME UNITS

QUALITY INN & SUITES

Phone: (210)359-7200   163
F

SAVE

All Year   1P: $45-$99   2P: $45-$99   XP: $5

Location: I-10, exit 580 (W W White Rd), 0.4 mi s. 222 S W W White Rd 78219. Fax: 210/359-1516. **Facility:** 54 one-bedroom standard units, some with whirlpools. 2 stories (no elevator), exterior corridors. *Bath:* combo or shower only. **Parking:** on-site. **Terms:** [CP] meal plan available, small pets only ($25 deposit). Small-scale Hotel **Amenities:** *Some:* irons, hair dryers. **Pool(s):** outdoor. **Guest Services:** coin laundry. **Business Services:** fax (fee). **Cards:** AX, CB, DC, DS, JC, MC, VI.

SOME UNITS

(See map p. 496)

QUALITY INN & SUITES COLISEUM
Phone: (210)224-3030 🆔53

AAA SAVE
▼▼▼▼
Small-scale Hotel

3/28-8/16 [BP]   1P: $55-$120   2P: $55-$120   XP: $6   F18
2/1-3/27 & 8/17-1/31 [BP]   1P: $50-$110   2P: $50-$110   XP: $6   F18

Location: I-35, exit Binz-Engleman Rd, follow signs to I-35 S access road northbound, exit Binz-Engleman Rd, continue straight southbound. 3817 I-35 N 78219. Fax: 210/228-0895. **Facility:** 124 units. 62 one-bedroom standard units. 62 one-bedroom suites ($70-$149). 2 stories (no elevator), interior corridors. **Parking:** on-site. **Terms:** 2 night minimum stay - weekends 5/23-8/16, pets ($25 deposit). **Amenities:** hair dryers. **Leisure Activities:** whirlpool. **Guest Services:** coin laundry. **Cards:** AX, DC, DS, MC, VI. **Special Amenities:** free continental breakfast and free local telephone calls. *(See color ad p 506)*

SOME UNITS

QUALITY INN NORTHWEST
Phone: (210)736-1900 🆔100

SAVE
▼▼
Small-scale Hotel

All Year   1P: $39-$99   2P: $39-$99   XP: $6   F16

Location: I-10, exit 565B eastbound; exit 565C (Vance Jackson Rd) westbound, just n. 6023 NW I-10 W 78201. Fax: 210/737-0981. **Facility:** 140 one-bedroom standard units. 2 stories, exterior corridors. **Parking:** on-site. **Terms:** 7 day cancellation notice, [CP] & [ECP] meal plans available, small pets only ($25 fee). **Pool(s):** outdoor, wading. **Leisure Activities:** exercise room. *Fee:* game room. **Guest Services:** coin laundry, area transportation. **Business Services:** meeting rooms, fax (fee). **Cards:** AX, CB, DC, DS, MC, VI.

SOME UNITS

RADISSON RESORT HILL COUNTRY
Phone: (210)509-9800 🆔152

▼▼▼
Resort
Large-scale Hotel

All Year   1P: $199-$249

Location: I-410, exit 9A (SR 151), 3.5 mi w to Westover Hills Blvd, just n. 9800 Westover Hills Blvd 78251. Fax: 210/509-9814. **Facility:** This up-to-date ranch-style resort nestled on 27 rolling acres features guest rooms with designer touches; suites have scenic views. 227 units. 174 one-bedroom standard units. 53 one-bedroom suites ($289-$399) with whirlpools. 5 stories, interior corridors. *Bath:* combo or shower only. **Parking:** on-site and valet. **Terms:** small pets only ($50 deposit). **Amenities:** video games (fee), dual phone lines, voice mail, irons, hair dryers. *Some:* high-speed Internet, safes. **Pool(s):** 3 heated outdoor, wading. **Leisure Activities:** whirlpool, playground, spa, fire pits, basketball. **Guest Services:** gift shop, valet and coin laundry, area transportation. **Business Services:** conference facilities, business center. **Cards:** AX, DC, MC, VI. *(See color ad below)*

SOME UNITS

RAMADA LIMITED
Phone: 210/359-1111 🆔112

▼▼
Small-scale Hotel

2/1-2/28 [CP]   1P: $100   2P: $100   XP: $5   F17
3/1-6/30 [CP]   1P: $89   2P: $99   XP: $5   F17
7/1-8/31 [CP]   1P: $65   2P: $75   XP: $5   F17
9/1-1/31 [CP]   1P: $39   2P: $59   XP: $5   F17

Location: I-10 E, exit 579 (Houston St). 3939 E Houston St 78220. Fax: 210/359-6939. **Facility:** 60 one-bedroom standard units. 2 stories (no elevator), exterior corridors. **Parking:** on-site. **Amenities:** safes (fee), hair dryers. **Pool(s):** small outdoor. **Guest Services:** coin laundry. **Business Services:** meeting rooms, fax (fee). **Cards:** AX, DC, DS, MC, VI.

SOME UNITS

(See map p. 496)

RAMADA LIMITED NORTHWEST
Phone: (210)558-9070 **121**

AAA SAVE
⬇⬇⬇⬇

Small-scale Hotel

All Year [CP]   1P: $59-$99   2P: $69-$109   XP: $10   F17
Location: I-10, exit Wuzbach Rd westbound; exit Callaghan Rd and circle back eastbound. 9447 I-10 W 78230. Fax: 210/558-4604. **Facility:** 76 one-bedroom standard units. 2 stories (no elevator), exterior corridors. *Bath:* combo or shower only. **Parking:** on-site. **Amenities:** voice mail. *Some:* irons, hair dryers. **Pool(s):** outdoor. **Leisure Activities:** whirlpool. **Guest Services:** coin laundry. **Business Services:** fax (fee). **Cards:** AX, DC, DS, MC, VI. **Special Amenities:** free continental breakfast and free local telephone calls.

SOME UNITS

RED ROOF INN LACKLAND
Phone: (210)675-4120 **89**

AAA SAVE
⬇⬇⬇

Small-scale Hotel

All Year [CP]   1P: $40-$59   2P: $45-$63   XP: $5   F18
Location: Ne jct of US 90 and Military Dr W; access via Renwick St, off Military Dr, just n of jct US 90. 6861 Hwy 90 W 78227. Fax: 210/670-1890. **Facility:** 156 one-bedroom standard units. 2 stories, exterior corridors. **Parking:** on-site. **Terms:** small pets only (with prior approval). **Amenities:** video games (fee). *Some:* hair dryers. **Pool(s):** heated outdoor. **Guest Services:** coin laundry. **Business Services:** fax (fee). **Cards:** AX, CB, DC, DS, MC, VI. **Special Amenities:** free local telephone calls and free newspaper.

SOME UNITS

RED ROOF INN-SAN ANTONIO AIRPORT
Phone: (210)340-4055 **138**

AAA SAVE
⬇⬇

Motel

All Year   1P: $39-$56   2P: $44-$61   XP: $5   F18
Location: On southbound access road, just s of US 281 at Isom Rd. 333 Wolfe Rd 78216. Fax: 210/340-4031. **Facility:** 135 one-bedroom standard units. 3 stories, interior/exterior corridors. **Parking:** on-site. **Amenities:** video games, voice mail. **Guest Services:** valet laundry. **Business Services:** fax (fee). **Cards:** AX, CB, DC, DS, MC, VI. **Special Amenities:** free local telephone calls and free newspaper.

SOME UNITS

RED ROOF INN SAN ANTONIO (DOWNTOWN)
Phone: (210)229-9973 **160**

AAA SAVE
⬇⬇⬇

Motel

5/24-8/17   1P: $69-$84   2P: $74-$89
8/18-1/31   1P: $46-$79   2P: $51-$84
2/1-5/23   1P: $46-$69   2P: $51-$74   XP: $5
Location: I-37, exit 141 northbound; exit 141B southbound. 1011 E Houston St 78205. Fax: 210/224-9975. **Facility:** 215 one-bedroom standard units. 6 stories, interior corridors. *Bath:* combo or shower only. **Parking:** on-site. **Amenities:** video games, voice mail. **Pool(s):** outdoor. **Business Services:** meeting rooms, fax (fee). **Cards:** AX, CB, DC, DS, MC, VI. **Special Amenities:** free local telephone calls and free newspaper.

SOME UNITS

RED ROOF INN SAN ANTONIO (NW-SEAWORLD)
Phone: (210)509-3434 **156**

AAA SAVE
⬇⬇⬇

Small-scale Hotel

5/18-8/16   1P: $52-$72   2P: $58-$78   XP: $6   F18
2/1-5/17   1P: $38-$47   2P: $44-$53   XP: $6   F18
8/17-1/31   1P: $39-$43   2P: $45-$49   XP: $6   F18
Location: I-410, exit 10B (Alamo Downs Pkwy), on eastbound access road. 6880 NW Loop 410 78238. Fax: 210/509-9898. **Facility:** 123 one-bedroom standard units. 3 stories, interior/exterior corridors. *Bath:* combo or shower only. **Parking:** on-site. **Terms:** small pets only. **Amenities:** video games. **Pool(s):** outdoor. **Business Services:** fax (fee). **Cards:** AX, CB, DC, DS, MC, VI. **Special Amenities:** free local telephone calls and free newspaper.

SOME UNITS

RESIDENCE INN NW/SIX FLAGS
Phone: (210)561-9660 **87**

SAVE
⬇⬇⬇

Small-scale Hotel

5/30-8/31 [BP]   1P: $119-$159
2/28-5/29 [BP]   1P: $109-$159
2/1-2/27 & 9/1-1/31 [BP]   1P: $99-$129
Location: I-10, exit Wurzbach Rd, 0.3 mi w. 4041 Bluemel Rd 78240. Fax: 210/561-9663. **Facility:** 128 units. 96 one-bedroom standard units with efficiencies. 32 one-bedroom suites with kitchens. 2 stories (no elevator), exterior corridors. **Parking:** on-site. **Terms:** weekly rates available, pets ($50 extra charge). **Amenities:** video games, voice mail, irons, hair dryers. **Pool(s):** outdoor. **Leisure Activities:** whirlpool, sports court. **Guest Services:** complimentary evening beverages: Mon-Thurs, coin laundry. **Business Services:** fax (fee). **Cards:** AX, MC, VI.

SOME UNITS

RESIDENCE INN SAN ANTONIO-AIRPORT
Phone: 210/805-8118 **166**

SAVE
⬇⬇⬇

Small-scale Hotel

All Year [ECP]   2P: $134
Location: On Loop 410, exit Broadway St, 0.4 mi e on access road. 1014 NE Loop 410 78209-0000. Fax: 210/805-9226. **Facility:** 120 units. 100 one-bedroom standard units with kitchens. 20 two-bedroom suites ($134) with kitchens. 2-3 stories, exterior corridors. *Bath:* combo or shower only. **Parking:** on-site. **Terms:** cancellation fee imposed, small pets only (with prior approval). **Amenities:** voice mail, irons, hair dryers. **Pool(s):** outdoor. **Leisure Activities:** whirlpool, racquetball court, exercise room, sports court. **Guest Services:** complimentary evening beverages: Mon-Thurs, coin laundry, area transportation. **Business Services:** meeting rooms, fax (fee). **Cards:** AX, DC, DS, MC, VI. *(See color ad p 507)*

SOME UNITS

(See map p. 496)

RODEWAY INN LACKLAND AFB

AAA SAVE

Motel

			Phone: (210)674-1511	**54**
6/1-8/31 [CP]	1P: $65-$69	2P: $75-$80	XP: $5	F18
9/1-11/30 [CP]	1P: $55-$65	2P: $60-$70	XP: $5	F18
2/1-5/31 [CP]	1P: $55-$59	2P: $60-$70	XP: $5	F18
12/1-1/31 [CP]	1P: $55-$59	2P: $60-$65	XP: $5	F18

Location: US 90, exit Old US 90, then 0.3 mi ne. 6500 Old Hwy 90 W 78227. Fax: 210/674-6059. **Facility:** 40 one-bedroom standard units. 1 story, exterior corridors. **Parking:** on-site. **Terms:** 2 night minimum stay - weekends 6/1-8/15. **Business Services:** fax (fee). **Cards:** AX, DC, DS, MC, VI. **Special Amenities:** free continental breakfast and free local telephone calls.

SOME UNITS

RODEWAY INN-SIX FLAGS FIESTA

AAA SAVE

Small-scale Hotel

			Phone: (210)698-3991	**99**
2/1-8/16 [CP]	1P: $36-$120	2P: $40-$125	XP: $6	F16
8/17-10/31 [CP]	1P: $32-$80	2P: $36-$89	XP: $6	F16
11/1-12/31 [CP]	1P: $32-$59	2P: $36-$65	XP: $6	F16
1/1-1/31 [CP]	1P: $32-$59	2P: $36-$59	XP: $6	F16

Location: I-10, exit 554 (Camp Bullis), on eastbound access road. 19793 I-10 W 78257. Fax: 210/698-1438. **Facility:** 73 one-bedroom standard units. 2 stories (no elevator), exterior corridors. **Parking:** on-site. **Terms:** small pets only ($20 fee). **Pool(s):** outdoor. **Guest Services:** coin laundry. **Business Services:** fax (fee). **Cards:** AX, DC, DS, MC, VI. **Special Amenities:** free continental breakfast and free local telephone calls.

SOME UNITS

SAN ANTONIO MARRIOTT NORTHWEST

SAVE

Large-scale Hotel

			Phone: (210)377-3900	**155**
All Year	1P: $129-$185	2P: $129-$185		

Location: I-410, exit 17 (Vance Jackson/Cherry Ridge), 1 mi on westbound access road. 3233 NW Loop 410 78213. Fax: 210/377-0120. **Facility:** 296 units. 1 one- and two-bedroom suites. 11 stories, interior corridors. *Bath:* combo or shower only. **Parking:** on-site. **Terms:** cancellation fee imposed. [AP], [BP], [CP] & [ECP] meal plans available, 20% service charge. **Amenities:** video games (fee), dual phone lines, voice mail, irons, hair dryers. **Pool(s):** heated outdoor. **Leisure Activities:** whirlpool, exercise room. **Guest Services:** valet and coin laundry, area transportation. **Business Services:** conference facilities, business center. **Cards:** AX, DC, DS, MC, VI. *(See color ad p 507)*

SOME UNITS

SIERRA ROYALE ALL SUITE HOTEL

AAA SAVE

Condominium

			Phone: (210)647-0041	**90**
2/1-8/11	1P: $105	2P: $135	XP: $10	F12
8/12-1/31	1P: $95	2P: $115	XP: $10	F12

Location: I-410, exit 13A (Bandera Rd), 0.5 mi n, just e. 6300 Rue Marielyne 78238. Fax: 210/647-4442. **Facility:** 91 units. 22 one- and 69 two-bedroom suites ($130-$160) with kitchens. 2 stories, interior corridors. **Parking:** on-site. **Terms:** cancellation fee imposed, package plans. **Amenities:** irons, hair dryers. *Some:* CD players. **Pool(s):** outdoor. **Leisure Activities:** whirlpool. **Guest Services:** complimentary evening beverages: Mon-Thurs, complimentary laundry. **Business Services:** fax (fee). **Cards:** AX, MC, VI. *(See color ad below)*

SOME UNITS

SLEEP INN SAN ANTONIO

AAA SAVE

Small-scale Hotel

			Phone: 210/344-5400	**123**
All Year [ECP]	1P: $50-$85	2P: $75-$120	XP: $10	F12

Location: I-10, exit 561 (Callaghan Rd), on eastbound access road. 8318 I-10 W 78230. Fax: 210/340-2666. **Facility:** 107 one-bedroom standard units. 3 stories, interior corridors. *Bath:* combo, shower or tub only. **Parking:** on-site. **Terms:** check-in 4 pm, small pets only ($25 fee). **Amenities:** video games, irons. *Some:* hair dryers. **Pool(s):** outdoor. **Guest Services:** coin laundry. **Business Services:** fax (fee). **Cards:** AX, DC, DS, MC, VI. **Special Amenities:** free continental breakfast and free local telephone calls.

(See color ad p 538)

SOME UNITS

(See map p. 496)

STAYBRIDGE SUITES BY HOLIDAY INN SAN ANTONIO NW-COLONNADE   Phone: (210)558-9009   131
▼▼▼▼   All Year   1P: $93-$202
     Location: I-10 W, exit 560 (Wurzbach Rd), follow access road through light, then right. 4320 Spectrum One 78230.
Small-scale Hotel   **Fax:** 210/558-9339. **Facility:** 118 units. 35 one-bedroom standard units. 60 one- and 23 two-bedroom suites.
3 stories, interior corridors. **Parking:** on-site. **Terms:** cancellation fee imposed. [ECP] meal plan available,
small pets only ($75 fee). **Amenities:** dual phone lines, voice mail, irons, hair dryers. *Some:* high-speed Internet (fee). **Pool(s):**
heated outdoor. **Leisure Activities:** exercise room, sports court. **Guest Services:** complimentary evening beverages: Tues-
Thurs, valet and coin laundry. **Business Services:** business center. **Cards:** AX, DC, DS, MC, VI.

SOME UNITS

(ASK) (S_D) (🐾) (&) (🚲) (VCR) (🎙) (DATA PORT) (🖥) (📠) (💻) / (✕) /

STAYBRIDGE SUITES SAN ANTONIO-AIRPORT   Phone: (210)341-3220   134
▼▼▼   5/2-8/31 [BP]   1P: $149-$159   2P: $159-$169   XP: $10   F18
     2/1-5/1 & 9/1-1/31 [BP]   1P: $137-$147   2P: $147-$157   XP: $10   F18
Large-scale Hotel   **Location:** 66 NE Loop 410 78216. **Fax:** 210/377-1030. **Facility:** 136 units. 41 one-bedroom standard units with
kitchens. 80 one- and 15 two-bedroom suites ($150-$275) with kitchens. 9 stories, interior corridors. **Parking:**
on-site. **Terms:** pets ($75 extra charge). **Amenities:** video library, high-speed Internet (fee), dual phone lines, voice mail, irons,
hair dryers. **Pool(s):** heated outdoor. **Leisure Activities:** limited exercise equipment. **Guest Services:** complimentary evening
beverages: Tues-Thurs. **Business Services:** meeting rooms, business center. **Cards:** AX, CB, DC, DS, MC, VI.

SOME UNITS

(ASK) (✈) (🐾) (🍴+) (&M) (🚲) (VCR) (🎙) (DATA PORT) (🖥) (📠) (💻) / (✕) /

STUDIO 6 #6046   Phone: 210/691-0121   130
▼▼▼   All Year   1P: $45-$59   2P: $49-$63   XP: $4   F17
Motel   **Location:** I-10, exit 558 (De Zavala), on eastbound access road. 11802 I-10 W 78230. **Fax:** 210/691-1617.
     Facility: 131 units. 121 one-bedroom standard units with kitchens. 10 one-bedroom suites with kitchens. 2
stories (no elevator), exterior corridors. **Bath:** combo or shower only. **Parking:** on-site. **Terms:** weekly rates
available, pets ($75 fee). **Amenities:** voice mail, irons. *Some:* hair dryers. **Guest Services:** coin laundry. **Business Services:**
fax (fee). **Cards:** AX, CB, DC, DS, MC, VI.

SOME UNITS

(🐾) (&) (🍴+) (🎙) (DATA PORT) (📠) (💻) / (✕) /

STUDIO 6 #6047   Phone: (210)349-3100   91
▼▼▼   3/20-1/31   1P: $57-$72   2P: $61-$76   XP: $4   F17
     2/1-3/19   1P: $45-$55   2P: $49-$59   XP: $3   F17
Motel   **Location:** Loop 410, 1.5 mi nw on Fredericksburg Rd to Louis Pasteur Ct. 7719 Louis Pasteur Ct 78229.
     Fax: 210/349-3676. **Facility:** 135 one-bedroom standard units with efficiencies. 2 stories (no elevator), ex-
terior corridors. **Parking:** on-site. **Terms:** weekly rates available, pets ($75 extra charge). **Amenities:** voice mail, irons. **Guest
Services:** coin laundry, area transportation (fee). **Business Services:** fax (fee). **Cards:** DC, DS, MC, VI.

SOME UNITS

(🐾) (🍴+) (&) (🎙) (DATA PORT) (📠) (💻) / (✕) /

SUBURBAN LODGE   Phone: 210/684-9085   75
▼▼   Property failed to provide current rates
     Location: Loop 410, exit 13A (Bandera Rd), 0.7 mi n of Loop 410. 6451 Bandera Rd 78238. **Fax:** 210/684-9733.
Small-scale Hotel   **Facility:** 132 one-bedroom standard units with kitchens. 3 stories, exterior corridors. **Bath:** combo or shower
only. **Parking:** on-site. **Amenities:** *Some:* video games. **Guest Services:** coin laundry. **Business Services:**
fax (fee). **Cards:** AX, MC, VI.

SOME UNITS

(🍴+) (🐾) (🎙) (🖥) (📠) (💻) / (✕) (VCR) /

SUPER 8 MOTEL   Phone: (210)657-0808   78
▼▼   All Year   1P: $49-$89   2P: $59-$99   XP: $10   F14
     Location: I-35, exit 163B (Rittiman Rd) northbound, on northbound access road; exit 163 (Rittiman Rd) southbound.
Small-scale Hotel   6364 I-35 N 78218. **Fax:** 210/657-3211. **Facility:** 40 one-bedroom standard units with whirlpools. 1-3 stories,
exterior corridors. **Parking:** on-site. **Terms:** 7 day cancellation notice. **Business Services:** fax (fee).
Cards: AX, DC, DS, JC, MC, VI.

SOME UNITS

(ASK) (S_D) (🎙) / (✕) /

(See map p. 496)

SUPER 8 MOTEL DOWNTOWN
Phone: (210)222-8833   168

Motel

	2/1-8/15	1P: $45-$100	2P: $45-$100	XP: $5	F15
	8/16-12/31	1P: $35-$100	2P: $45-$100	XP: $5	F15
	1/1-1/31	1P: $41-$100	2P: $41-$100	XP: $5	F15

Location: I-35, exit 157B (Brooklyn/McCullough St) to Quincey, e on Quincey. 1614 N St Mary's St 78215.
Fax: 210/354-2882. **Facility:** 62 one-bedroom standard units. 2 stories (no elevator), exterior corridors. *Bath:* combo or shower only. **Parking:** on-site. **Terms:** [CP] meal plan available. **Amenities:** safes (fee). **Pool(s):** small outdoor. **Guest Services:** coin laundry. **Business Services:** fax (fee). **Cards:** AX, DC, DS, MC, VI.

SOME UNITS

(ASK) (S/D) (TI+) (&M) (E) (≈) (★) (DATA PORT) / (X) (■) (▭) (▯) /
                                                      FEE FEE

SUPER 8 MOTEL DOWNTOWN NORTH
Phone: (210)227-8888   124

Motel

| | 2/1-7/31 [BP] | 1P: $42-$62 | 2P: $48-$68 | XP: $8 | F12 |
| | 8/1-1/31 [BP] | 1P: $38-$58 | 2P: $42-$52 | XP: $8 | F12 |

Location: I-35, exit 160 (Splashtown), on southbound access road. 3617 N PanAm Expwy 78219. Fax: 210/224-2092.
Facility: 91 one-bedroom standard units. 2 stories (no elevator), exterior corridors. **Parking:** on-site.
Terms: small pets only (not in summer). **Amenities:** safes (fee). **Pool(s):** outdoor. **Guest Services:** coin laundry. **Business Services:** fax (fee). **Cards:** AX, CB, DC, DS, MC, VI.

SOME UNITS

(ASK) (S/D) (🛏) (TI+) (&M) (≈) (★) / (X) (■) (▭) /

SUPER 8 MOTEL- IH 10 EAST
Phone: (210)359-8080   70

Small-scale Hotel

| | All Year | 1P: $39-$89 | 2P: $49-$129 | XP: $5 | F12 |

Location: I-10, exit 580 (W W White Rd), just s. 170 S W W White Rd 78219. Fax: 210/359-8080. **Facility:** 42 one-bedroom standard units, some with kitchens (no utensils). 2 stories, exterior corridors. *Bath:* combo or shower only. **Parking:** on-site. **Terms:** cancellation fee imposed. **Amenities:** irons, hair dryers. **Pool(s):** outdoor. **Guest Services:** coin laundry. **Business Services:** fax (fee). **Cards:** AX, CB, DC, DS, JC, MC, VI.
Special Amenities: free continental breakfast and free local telephone calls.

SOME UNITS

(S/D) (TI+) (&M) (E) (≈) (★) (■) (▭) / (X) /

SUPER 8 MOTEL OF SAN ANTONIO AIRPORT
Phone: (210)637-1033   63

Small-scale Hotel

| | All Year | 1P: $35-$75 | 2P: $40-$80 | XP: $6 | F12 |

Location: I-35, exit 168 (Weidner Rd), southbound access road. 11027 I-35 N 78233. Fax: 210/637-1033. **Facility:** 62 one-bedroom standard units. 3 stories (no elevator), interior corridors. **Parking:** on-site. **Pool(s):** small outdoor. **Business Services:** fax (fee). **Cards:** AX, DC, DS, MC, VI.

SOME UNITS

(ASK) (S/D) (🛏) (≈) (★) / (X) /

SUPER 8 MOTEL-SIX FLAGS FIESTA
Phone: (210)696-6916   111

Small-scale Hotel

	4/1-7/31 [CP]	1P: $60-$70	2P: $70-$80	XP: $5	F
	11/1-1/31 [CP]	1P: $50-$60	2P: $70	XP: $5	F
	2/1-3/31 & 8/1-10/31 [CP]	1P: $39-$59	2P: $49-$69	XP: $5	F

Location: I-10, exit 557 westbound; exit 558 eastbound on westbound access road. 5319 Casa Bella 78249. Fax: 210/696-4321. **Facility:** 71 one-bedroom standard units. 3 stories, interior corridors. **Parking:** on-site. **Terms:** pets ($5 extra charge). **Pool(s):** outdoor. **Guest Services:** coin laundry. **Business Services:** fax (fee). **Cards:** AX, DS, MC. **Special Amenities:** free continental breakfast and free local telephone calls.

SOME UNITS

(S/D) (🛏) (E) (≈) (★) / (X) /

TRAVELODGE SUITES
Phone: (210)680-3351   110

Small-scale Hotel

| | All Year [CP] | 1P: $49-$89 | 2P: $59-$119 | XP: $5 | F18 |

Location: I-410, exit Evers Rd, on eastbound access road. 4934 NW Loop 410 78229. Fax: 210/680-3709. **Facility:** 201 units. 180 one- and 21 two-bedroom suites with kitchens. 3 stories, exterior corridors. **Parking:** on-site. **Terms:** check-in 4 pm. **Amenities:** voice mail, hair dryers. **Pool(s):** heated outdoor. **Guest Services:** coin laundry, area transportation-theme parks, riverwalk. **Business Services:** meeting rooms, fax (fee). **Cards:** AX, DC, DS, MC, VI. **Special Amenities:** free continental breakfast and free local telephone calls.

SOME UNITS

(S/D) (✈) (TI+) (≈) (👥+) (★) (DATA PORT) (▭) (▯) / (X) /

THE WESTIN LA CANTERA RESORT
Phone: (210)558-6500   162

Resort
Large-scale Hotel

| | 2/28-11/30 | 1P: $189-$284 | 2P: $189-$284 | | |
| | 2/1-2/27 & 12/1-1/31 | 1P: $139-$234 | 2P: $139-$234 | | |

Location: I-10, exit La Cantera Pkwy, access also via Loop 1604 at La Cantera Pkwy. 16641 La Cantera Pkwy 78256. Fax: 210/558-2400. **Facility:** Overlooking San Antonio, this elegant, expansive resort features design details that embody the South Texas Hill Country style. 508 units. 484 one-bedroom standard units. 24 one-bedroom suites ($380-$1800), some with whirlpools. 3 stories, interior corridors. *Bath:* combo or shower only. **Parking:** on-site. **Terms:** 3 day cancellation fee imposed, $10 service charge. **Amenities:** video games, dual phone lines, voice mail, safes, honor bars, irons, hair dryers. *Some:* fax. **Dining:** Francesca's at Sunset, see separate listing. **Pool(s):** outdoor, 5 heated outdoor, wading. **Leisure Activities:** 2 lighted tennis courts, spa, Westin kids club. *Fee:* golf-36 holes. **Guest Services:** gift shop, valet laundry. **Business Services:** conference facilities, business center. **Cards:** AX, CB, DC, DS, JC, MC, VI.

SOME UNITS

(ASK) (S/D) (TI) (24TI) (ff) (&M) (E) (≈) (👥+) (X) (★) (DATA PORT) (▭) / (X) (■) /

───────── **WHERE TO DINE** ─────────

ACADIANA CAFE
Lunch: $6-$12   Dinner: $8-$15   Phone: 210/674-0019   64

Regional Cajun

Location: Jct Loop 410 at Marbach Rd. 1289 SW Loop 410 78227. **Hours:** 11 am-10 pm, Fri & Sat-11 pm. Closed: 11/27, 12/25. **Features:** Cajun-style cuisine served in a modest, down home atmosphere is what this restaurant is all about. Delicious food served hot and well-seasoned includes crisp salad, spicy gumbo, fried oysters with French fries, and warm, homemade peach cobbler. Casual dress; cocktails. **Parking:** on-site. **Cards:** AX, DC, DS, MC, VI.

(X)

(See map p. 496)

ACAPULCO SEAFOOD RESTAURANT   Lunch: $5-$8   Dinner: $8-$11   Phone: 210/432-1366   ⑤⑤
Mexican
Location: Near west side, just w of Zarzamora St. 2918 W Commerce 78207. **Hours:** 10 am-9 pm, Fri & Sat-10 pm. **Features:** The Mexican seafood entrees give this little cafe an Acapulco feel. The seafood cocktail includes squid, octopus, marinated fish and oysters served with a tangy sauce. The seafood soup has a clear broth with a tomato sheen. Casual dress. **Parking:** on-site. **Cards:** AX, CB, DC, DS, MC, VI.

ALAMO CAFE   Lunch: $4-$7   Dinner: $6-$10   Phone: 210/691-8827   ⑥①
Southwest American
Location: I-10, exit Wurzbach Rd, east access road between Huebner and Wurzbach rds. 10060 W I-10 78216. **Hours:** 10:45 am-11 pm, Fri & Sat-midnight. Closed: 11/27, 12/25. **Features:** Southwestern cuisine like chicken-fried steak and fajitas are served here by a cordial wait staff. The hamburgers are loaded with the works. This large and noisy dining establishment is a good family eating spot, and the margarita pie has a kick to it. Casual dress; cocktails. **Parking:** on-site. **Cards:** AX, DC, DS, MC, VI.   ✕

ALDO'S RISTORANTE ITALIANO   Lunch: $6-$9   Dinner: $8-$13   Phone: 210/696-2536   ⑥②
Italian
Location: Jct of Wurzbach and Fredericksburg rds. 8539 Fredericksburg Rd 78229. **Hours:** 11 am-10 pm, Fri-11 pm, Sat 5:30 pm-11 pm, Sun 5 pm-10 pm. **Features:** Set inside a 100-year-old Italian-style villa, this romantic bistro boasts a relaxing garden surrounded by tall oak trees. Try the snapper di aldo—sauteed filet with crabmeat, artichoke hearts and white wine basil sauce. Casual dress; cocktails. **Parking:** on-site.
Cards: AX, DC, DS, MC, VI.   Y ✕

ASIA KITCHEN   Lunch: $4-$5   Dinner: $11-$18   Phone: 210/673-0662   ⑤⑥
Ethnic
Location: On southbound access road, just s of jct SW Loop 410 and Marbach Rd; next to Super K-Mart. 1739 SW Loop 410 78227. **Hours:** 11 am-3 & 5-9 pm, Fri & Sat-10 pm. Closed major holidays; also Sun. **Reservations:** accepted. **Features:** White rattan chairs and glass tabletops draped with linen characterize the dining room at this restaurant. The two-entree plate with rice and spring rolls is tasty, as is the Filipino coconut ice cream, which is filled with coconut chunks and jackfruit. Casual dress; beer & wine only. **Parking:** on-site. **Cards:** AX, CB, DC, DS, MC, VI.   ✕

BARNACLE BILL'S   Lunch: $9   Dinner: $14   Phone: 210/641-7655   ⑧③
Seafood
Location: I-10, exit 558 (DeZavala Rd). 5258 DeZavala Rd. **Hours:** 10:30 am-9 pm, Fri & Sat-10 pm. Closed major holidays. **Features:** Down-home dishes are made from the freshest seafood found this side of the Texas coast. Watch out for the dinghy hanging from the ceiling. Casual dress; beer & wine only. **Parking:** on-site. **Cards:** AX, MC, VI.   ✕

THE BARN DOOR RESTAURANT   Lunch: $5-$10   Dinner: $8-$25   Phone: 210/824-0116   ①①④
Steak House
Location: Loop 410, exit Broadway, 0.3 mi s. 8400 N New Braunfels 78209. **Hours:** 11 am-2 & 5-10 pm, Fri-10:30 pm, Sat 5 pm-10:30 pm, Sun 4 pm-9 pm. Closed major holidays. **Reservations:** suggested. **Features:** This barn-like structure is noted for its rustic, Western decor. Various photographs and store memorabilia decorate the walls. Charcoal-broiled steaks are a specialty. Casual dress; cocktails. **Parking:** on-site. **Cards:** AX, DS, MC, VI.   Y ✕

BISTRO TIME   Lunch: $6-$9   Dinner: $10-$20   Phone: 210/344-6626   ⑨④
Continental
Location: Jct Fredericksburg Rd and Callaghan Ave. 5137 Fredericksburg Rd 78229. **Hours:** 11 am-2 & 5-9 pm, Fri & Sat-10 pm. Closed: Sun. **Reservations:** suggested. **Features:** You'll enjoy haute cuisine served in a casual bistro setting. Start with the salmon croquette with caviar and wild greens. The beef Wellington and fresh crab cakes are served with a special house sauce. Dressy casual; beer & wine only. **Parking:** on-site. **Cards:** AX, DC, MC, VI.   ✕

BOCCONE'S ITALIAN RESTAURANT-BAKERY &
MUSIC EMPORIUM   Lunch: $7-$12   Dinner: $12-$18   Phone: 210/492-2996   ①⓪③
Italian
Location: Just s of jct Loop 1604. 17776 Blanco Rd 78232. **Hours:** 11 am-3 & 5-10 pm, Sat 11 am-10:30 pm, Sun 11 am-3 & 5-9 pm. Closed: 1/1, 12/25. **Features:** The dining room becomes lively at night, as homespun arias are served alongside classic selections. Casual dress; entertainment. **Parking:** on-site. **Cards:** AX, CB, DC, DS, MC, VI.   Ⓚ ✕

BOLO'S ROTISSERIE-GRILLE   Lunch: $5-$9   Dinner: $8-$12   Phone: 210/691-8888   ⑦①
Regional American
Location: I-10, exit Wurzbach Rd, 12 mi nw on westbound access road; in the Colonnade Mall; in Omni San Antonio Hotel. 9821 Colonnade St 78230. **Hours:** 6 am-2 & 5-10 pm, Sat & Sun from 6:30 am. **Reservations:** suggested. **Features:** Perceptive staff fulfill your every wish as you sample culinary delights from deep in the heart of Texas. Evidence of the chef's artistic talents are a fried parmesan basket filled with exotic greens, and rack of lamb flavored with mango-cilantro pico. Casual dress; cocktails. **Parking:** on-site. **Cards:** AX, DC, DS, MC, VI.   ✕

CAFE MILANO   Lunch: $6-$8   Dinner: $10-$16   Phone: 210/680-8111   ⑦⑤
Italian
Location: Ne jct Bandera Rd (SR 16) at Eckert Rd. 7530 Bandera Rd 78238. **Hours:** 11 am-10 pm, Fri-11 pm, Sat 5 pm-11 pm, Sun 11 am-9 pm. Closed major holidays. **Reservations:** accepted. **Features:** An attentive staff, a unique Old World decor and authentic Milano dishes make this cheerful eatery a very pleasant place to visit. Servers work in teams to present baskets of fresh, hot rolls, a delicious antipasto, fresh seafood and flavorful vegetables. Casual dress; beer & wine only. **Parking:** on-site. **Cards:** AX, DS, MC, VI.   ✕

CHA-CHA'S   Lunch: $4-$8   Dinner: $7-$11   Phone: 210/615-7000   ⑤⑨
Mexican
Location: Just ne of Babcock at Louis Pasteur D; medical center area. 2026 Babcock 78229. **Hours:** 11 am-10 pm, Fri-11 pm, Sat from noon. Closed major holidays; also Sun. **Features:** Known for its extensive selection of margaritas, Cha-Cha's offers 52 different flavors to choose from including one that honors the 1999 NBA Champions. Spanish-style artwork decorates the dining room. Try the Cha-Cha Trio with fajitas and veggies. Casual dress; cocktails. **Parking:** on-site. **Cards:** AX, DC, DS, MC, VI.   Y ✕

(See map p. 496)

CHINA SWAN CHINESE & SEAFOOD RESTAURANT   **Lunch:** $6-$9   **Dinner:** $9-$18   **Phone:** 210/681-5111   72
Chinese
Location: Just n of jct Huebner Rd; in Lim's Village complex. 7015 Bandera 78238. **Hours:** 11 am-2:30 & 4:30-9:30 pm, Sat & Sun from 11:30 am. **Features:** Cantonese and Hong Kong specialties with lots of seafood fill the menu. The triple delight with crunchy vegetables has hearty cuts of chicken, beef and shrimp. The jellyfish salad is tossed with marinated cucumbers and carrots. Casual dress; beer & wine only. **Parking:** on-site. **Cards:** AX, DS, MC, VI.

CRUMPETS RESTAURANT & BAKERY   **Lunch:** $6-$12   **Dinner:** $10-$26   **Phone:** 210/821-5454   118
Continental
Location: 0.8 mi s of Loop 410, jct Harry Wurzbach Rd and Oakwell Dr. 3920 Harry Wurzbach Rd 78209-2410. **Hours:** 11 am-2:30 & 5:30-10 pm, Fri-11 pm, Sat 11 am-3 & 5:30-11 pm, Sun 11 am-3 & 5-9 pm. Closed: 1/1, 12/25. **Reservations:** accepted. **Features:** Floor-to-ceiling windows let guests enjoy the surroundings, which include woods and a waterfall. The aroma of luscious cakes and pastries wafts from the in-house bakery, and homemade whipped cream over strawberries is a favorite. Casual dress; cocktails; entertainment. **Parking:** on-site. **Cards:** AX, DC, DS, MC, VI.

DRY DOCK SEAFOOD OYSTER BAR   **Lunch:** $5-$8   **Dinner:** $8-$20   **Phone:** 210/692-3959   67
Seafood
Location: 3.5 mi w of jct Loop 410. 8522 Fredericksburg Rd 78240. **Hours:** 11 am-11 pm, Sun noon-10 pm. Closed: 1/1, 12/25. **Reservations:** accepted. **Features:** Fresh seafood is served Cajun-style in simple, nautical surroundings housed in a landmark, boat-shaped building. Enjoy seasonal crawfish specialties and fresh, cold oysters served on the half shell with all the trimmings in a relaxed neighborhood setting. Casual dress; beer & wine only. **Parking:** on-site. **Cards:** AX, MC, VI.

EARL ABEL'S RESTAURANT   **Lunch:** $5-$10   **Dinner:** $6-$19   **Phone:** 210/822-3358   120
American
Location: Broadway and Hildebrand aves. 4210 Broadway Ave 78209. **Hours:** 6:30 am-1 am. Closed: 12/25. **Reservations:** accepted. **Features:** This well-established restaurant has been family owned since 1933, passed along through three generations of restaurateurs. Southern comfort foods like fried chicken and homemade desserts are the specialty, with service designed to make you feel at home. Casual dress; cocktails. **Parking:** on-site. **Cards:** AX, DC, MC, VI.

EL JARRO DE ARTURO   **Lunch:** $5-$8   **Dinner:** $7-$16   **Phone:** 210/494-5084   73
Mexican
Location: Southwest corner jct US 281 at Bitters Rd. 13421 San Pedro Ave 78216. **Hours:** 11 am-10 pm, Fri & Sat-11:30 pm. Closed: 11/27, 12/25. **Reservations:** suggested; for dinner. **Features:** You can watch while cooks prepare tortillas which arrive at your table soft and fresh. The staff knows their Mexican cuisine, and the hand-painted tiles and other decorating touches provide the perfect setting for sampling it. Casual dress; cocktails. **Parking:** on-site. **Cards:** AX, DC, DS, MC, VI.

ERNESTO'S RESTAURANT   **Lunch:** $5-$11   **Dinner:** $9-$20   **Phone:** 210/344-1248   91
Regional Seafood
Location: I-410, exit Vance Jackson Rd, 0.3 mi n to Jackson-Keller Rd; in the "Corner's at Jackson" shopping complex. 2559 Jackson-Keller Rd 78230. **Hours:** 11:30 am-2 & 5:30-10 pm, Fri-10:30 pm, Sat 5:30 pm-10:30 pm. Closed major holidays; also Sun. **Reservations:** suggested. **Features:** Cozy like a neighborhood tea room, this cafe has candle-lit dining. Feast on imaginative blends of French and Mexican cuisine. Grilled seafood dishes are brushed with one of nine specialty butter sauces. Shrimp nachos and seafood crepes are tasty. Casual dress; cocktails. **Parking:** on-site. **Cards:** AX, CB, DC, MC, VI.

FATSO'S BARBEQUE & SPORTS BAR   **Lunch:** $6-$9   **Dinner:** $7-$12   **Phone:** 210/432-0121   110
Barbecue
Location: 1.5 mi s of jct Loop 410. 1704 Bandera Rd 78228. **Hours:** 11 am-midnight, Wed-Sat to 2 am. Closed: 12/25; also 12/31. **Features:** Texas-style hot wings are smothered in original wing sauce. The baby back ribs are baked in beer and then placed on a mesquite grill. The barbecue ribs are delicious. Watch a volleyball tournament from the huge outdoor deck. Casual dress; cocktails. **Parking:** on-site. **Cards:** AX, DC, DS, MC, VI.

FRANCESCA'S AT SUNSET   **Dinner:** $20-$40   **Phone:** 210/558-6500   102
Regional American
Location: I-10, access also via Loop 1604 at La Cantera Pkwy; in The Westin La Cantera Resort. 16641 La Cantera Pkwy 78256. **Hours:** 6 pm-10 pm. Closed: Sun & Mon. **Reservations:** suggested. **Features:** In the Westin La Cantera resort, the restaurant blends fresh ingredients into dramatic, distinctive dishes. Service is equally flawless and attentive. Dressy casual; cocktails. **Parking:** on-site. **Cards:** AX, CB, DC, DS, JC, MC, VI.

FRATELLI'S CAFFE ITALIANO   **Lunch:** $6-$10   **Dinner:** $8-$14   **Phone:** 210/349-7997   74
Italian
Location: I-10, exit Callaghan Rd, westbound access road. 8085 Callaghan Rd 78230. **Hours:** 11 am-10 pm, Fri & Sat-11 pm, Sun from noon. Closed: 12/25. **Reservations:** accepted. **Features:** An extensive selection of Italian specialties are served in a light and airy dining room enhanced with romantic touches like Italian tapestries. Be sure to meet Sweet Lolita, a cheesecake filling in an Oreo cookie crust topped with Ghiradelli chocolate. Casual dress; cocktails. **Parking:** on-site. **Cards:** AX, DS, MC, VI.

GOLDEN WOK CHINESE RESTAURANT   **Lunch:** $5-$7   **Dinner:** $8-$13   **Phone:** 210/615-8282   60
Chinese
Location: Just e of Babcock Rd. 8822 Wurzbach Rd 78240. **Hours:** 11 am-10 pm, Sat from 11:30 am, Sun 11:30 am-9 pm. Closed: 11/27, 12/25. **Reservations:** accepted. **Features:** The dramatic decor includes huge mirrors bordered with ornate dragons like those in Hong Kong. Known for the large portions, the restaurant features a chicken supreme dish which is filled with yellow corn and colored mushrooms in a wine sauce. Casual dress; cocktails. **Parking:** on-site. **Cards:** AX, MC, VI.

(See map p. 496)

GRADY'S BAR-B-QUE
Lunch: $5-$7   **Dinner:** $6-$9   **Phone:** 210/732-3644   86

Barbecue

Location: Between Vance Jackson Rd and Loop 410. 4109 Fredericksburg Rd 78201. **Hours:** 10:30 am-8:30 pm, Fri & Sat-9:30 pm, Sun-8 pm. Closed major holidays. **Features:** Try one of Grady's combo plates, like sausage, brisket and ham with fresh pintos and south Texas style potato salad. Casual dress; beer only. **Parking:** on-site. **Cards:** AX, MC, VI.

GREY MOSS INN
Dinner: $17-$40   **Phone:** 210/695-8301   123

American

Location: 12 mi n of Loop 1604 on Babcock Rd to Scenic Loop Rd, 2 mi w. 19010 Scenic Loop Rd 78023. **Hours:** 5 pm-10 pm. Closed major holidays. **Reservations:** suggested. **Features:** Leave the city behind and relish the country inn ambience nestled in oak-studded Texas hill country. Most entrees are mesquite grilled like lamb chop T-bones with a rosemary wine sauce. A selection from the lengthy wine list enhances the relaxed mood. Cocktails. **Parking:** on-site. **Cards:** AX, DC, DS, MC, VI.

INDIA OVEN
Lunch: $6-$7   **Dinner:** $12-$25   **Phone:** 210/366-1030   69

Ethnic

Location: Near Blanco and West Ave. 1031 Patricia 78213. **Hours:** 11 am-2:30 & 5-10 pm, Fri & Sat-10 pm, Sun 11 am-3 & 5-10 pm. Closed: 1/1, 11/27, 12/25. **Reservations:** accepted. **Features:** At this restaurant you'll find flavorful Northern Indian cuisine bursting with spices. The mint chutney with katti-kabab is basically a soft taco filled with strips of spicy lamb. The tomato and coconut soup from the buffet will make you want seconds. Smoke free premises. Casual dress; beer & wine only. **Parking:** on-site. **Cards:** AX, DS, MC, VI.

JACALA MEXICAN RESTAURANT
Lunch: $4-$6   **Dinner:** $6-$9   **Phone:** 210/732-5222   117

Mexican

Location: I-10, exit West Ave, 0.5 mi s. 606 West Ave 78201. **Hours:** 11 am-9:45 pm, Fri & Sat-10:45 pm. Closed: 11/27, 12/25. **Reservations:** accepted. **Features:** This is one of the oldest, originally-owned Mexican restaurants in San Antonio. A mural of the San Antonio River decorates the dining room. Spicy salsa is perfect for dipping crunchy tortilla chips. The chicken tacos with mole are flavorful. Casual dress; cocktails. **Parking:** on-site. **Cards:** AX, CB, DC, DS, JC, MC, VI.

KIRAN INDIAN RESTAURANT
Lunch: $6-$8   **Dinner:** $7-$12   **Phone:** 210/349-6600   76

Ethnic

Location: 0.5 mi s of Loop 410. 7075 San Pedro 78216. **Hours:** 11 am-2 & 5:30-10 pm, Fri & Sat-10:30 pm, Sun noon-8 pm. Closed: 11/27, 12/25. **Features:** Specializing mainly in Northern Indian dishes, this restaurant offers its delicious South Asian fare in a colorfully decorated dining room. The moist yogurt-marinated chicken is served over aromatic basmati rice. Casual dress; beer & wine only. **Parking:** on-site. **Cards:** AX, CB, DC, DS, MC, VI.

LA CALESA
Lunch: $4-$7   **Dinner:** $6-$12   **Phone:** 210/822-4475   121

Regional Mexican

Location: US 281, exit Hildebrand Ave, 0.5 mi e. 2103 E Hildebrand Ave 78209. **Hours:** 11 am-9:30 pm, Fri-10:30 pm, Sat 11:30 am-10:30 pm, Sun 11:30 am-9 pm. Closed: 11/27, 12/25. **Reservations:** suggested; dinner. **Features:** Upscale Mexican cuisine is served in a candle-lit dining room. Attractive artwork decorates the walls. Multi-regional cuisine fills the menu. Try the scrumptious pork entree drenched in a savory marinade. End your meal with sponge cake covered in milk. Casual dress; cocktails. **Parking:** on-site. **Cards:** AX, CB, DC, MC, VI.

LA FOGATA RESTAURANT
Lunch: $8-$18   **Dinner:** $10-$22   **Phone:** 210/340-1337   90

Mexican

Location: 1.5 mi s of jct Loop 410 and Vance Jackson Rd exit. 2427 Vance Jackson Rd 78213. **Hours:** 11 am-10 pm, Thurs-Sat 8 am-midnight, Sun 8 am-10 pm. Closed: 11/27, 12/25. **Features:** The outdoor patio is surrounded by beautiful landscaping. Indoors you will find an attractive, brightly-colored dining room with metal chairs. Try the hearty stuffed peppers or soft enchiladas filled with gooey cheese. Casual dress; cocktails. **Parking:** on-site. **Cards:** AX, DC, DS, MC, VI.

LA FONDA MEXICAN RESTAURANT
Lunch: $5-$8   **Dinner:** $5-$8   **Phone:** 210/733-0621   124

Mexican

Location: Just s of Woodlawn. 2415 N Main Ave 78212. **Hours:** 11 am-3 & 5-9:30 pm, Fri & Sat-10 pm, Sun 11 am-3 pm. Closed major holidays. **Reservations:** required. **Features:** Since 1939, this inviting eatery has been serving fine Mexican food including fish served with pineapple and South American plantains. Kick back, relax and enjoy your meal on the outdoor patio next to a huge 300-year-old oak tree. Casual dress; cocktails. **Parking:** on-site. **Cards:** AX, CB, DC, DS, MC, VI.

LA SCALA
Lunch: $7-$10   **Dinner:** $9-$13   **Phone:** 210/366-1515   63

Italian

Location: NW Military Hwy at West Ave, 0.5 mi n of jct Loop 410; in Westoak Shopping Center. 2177 NW Military Hwy 78231. **Hours:** 11 am-10 pm. **Reservations:** suggested. **Features:** An attentive wait staff delivers fettuccine with colorful vegetables. Sip on a glass of fine wine with your meal. Sophisticated decorations and twin-colored linens accent the softly-lit dining room. Complete your meal with a rich dessert. Dressy casual; cocktails. **Parking:** on-site. **Cards:** AX, DC, DS, MC, VI.

LIBERTY BAR
Lunch: $7-$11   **Dinner:** $10-$26   **Phone:** 210/227-1187   81

Regional American

Location: At US 281, 328 E Josephine St 78215. **Hours:** 11:30 am-10:30 pm, Sun from 10:30 am, Fri & Sat-midnight. **Reservations:** suggested. **Features:** A celebration of unpretentious Texas and Mexican cooking is served here. The cordial wait staff delivers grilled portobello sandwiches with smoked gouda and grainy mustard. The tuna wrapped in anise-scented hoja santa leaves is unforgettable. Casual dress; cocktails. **Parking:** on-site. **Cards:** AX, MC, VI.

LOS PATIOS
Lunch: $7-$10   **Dinner:** $12-$28   **Phone:** 210/655-6171   66

Mexican

Location: Loop 410 to exit Starcrest, 0.3 mi w on westbound access road. 2015 NE Loop 410 78217. **Hours:** 11:30 am-2:30 & 6:30-9:30 pm. Closed: 1/1, 12/25. **Reservations:** suggested. **Features:** Set amid a canopy of oak trees, the Spanish architecture includes a gazebo with airy dining rooms. Buttery, homemade biscuits accompany such delicious entrees as Los Patios shrimp and crepes. Huge, homemade desserts are to die for. Dressy casual; cocktails. **Parking:** on-site. **Cards:** AX, DC, DS, MC, VI.

(See map p. 496)

MAGIC TIME MACHINE   **Lunch:** $9-$14   **Dinner:** $15-$35   **Phone:** 210/828-1478   113

American   **Location:** 6.3 mi n off Loop 410 at Broadway exit. 902 NE Loop 410 78209. **Hours:** 5:30-9 pm, Fri 5-10:30 pm, Sat 11 am-10:30 pm, Sun 11 am-9 pm. Closed: 11/27, 12/25. **Reservations:** accepted; Mon-Thurs. **Features:** A costumed staff creates a boisterous party atmosphere more suited to special occasion dinners. Superman and Catwoman prance around the dining room while you enjoy prime rib and other specialties. This is a great place for the young at heart! Casual dress; cocktails. **Parking:** on-site. **Cards:** AX, CB, DC, DS, MC, VI.

MARIO'S RESTAURANT   **Lunch:** $5-$8   **Dinner:** $8-$10   **Phone:** 210/349-0188   79

Regional Mexican   **Location:** Fredericksberg Rd at Lake Ridge St; in the Woodlake Plaza Mall. 4841 Fredricksburg Rd 78229. **Hours:** 11 am-10 pm, Fri & Sat-11 pm. Closed: 11/27. **Reservations:** suggested. **Features:** There is always a party happening inside this resurrected city landmark. The festive atmosphere will put a smile on your face. Dig into the tender filet sauteed in a chili sauce. A mariachi trio wanders the dining room nightly, entertaining guests. Casual dress; cocktails. **Parking:** on-site. **Cards:** AX, DC, MC, VI.

MENCUI'S CHINESE RESTAURNAT   **Lunch:** $5-$10   **Dinner:** $7-$18   **Phone:** 210/615-1288   68

Continental   **Location:** Southwest corner jct Fredericksburg Rd at Warzbach St. 7959 Fredericksburg Rd 78229. **Hours:** 11 am-2:15 & 5-10 pm, Sun-Tues to 9 pm. **Features:** Oriental sauces are served in attractive ceramic dishes and the dining room features black lacquer tables. The triple delight consists of shrimp, chicken and beef with stir fry vegetables. Finish your meal with an exotic Asian dessert. Casual dress; cocktails. **Parking:** on-site. **Cards:** AX, CB, DC, DS, JC, MC, VI.

MESON EUROPEAN DINING   **Lunch:** $8-$12   **Dinner:** $12-$24   **Phone:** 210/690-5811   99

Continental   **Location:** Sw on De Zavala, 0.7 mi w of I-10. 5999 De Zavala, Suite 150 78249. **Hours:** 11 am-2:30 & 5:30-10 pm, Fri & Sat-10:30 pm, Sun 5 pm-9:30 pm. **Reservations:** accepted. **Features:** Enjoy the freshest salmon you've ever tasted at this upbeat eatery. The potato soup is creamy and tasty. The grilled fish entree is served with a variety of perfectly steamed vegetables. The bananas foster is prepared table-side. Casual dress; cocktails. **Parking:** on-site. **Cards:** AX, DC, DS, MC, VI.

MINA & DIMI'S GREEK HOUSE RESTAURANT   **Lunch:** $6-$9   **Dinner:** $8-$12   **Phone:** 210/674-3464   82

Greek   **Location:** W across from Lackland AFB at Military Dr W and US 90. 7159 W Hwy 90 78227. **Hours:** 11 am-8 pm, Fri & Sat-9 pm. Closed major holidays; also Sun. **Features:** Zesty Greek cuisine is served by a cordial staff. A charming dining room has homemade decorations hanging on the wall. Crisp salads are covered with oils and feta. The gyro has a soft, fresh pita with tangy sauce and tender cuts of beef. Casual dress; beer & wine only. **Parking:** on-site. **Cards:** AX, DS, MC, VI.

MOUSE'S SMOKEHOUSE BAR-B-QUE   **Lunch:** $4-$11   **Dinner:** $4-$11   **Phone:** 830/980-2526   106

Regional Barbecue   **Location:** On US 281 N, 5.5 mi in jct SR 1604. 26098 US 281 N 78217. **Hours:** 8:30 am-8:30 pm, Fri & Sat-9 pm, Sun-5 pm. Closed: Mon. **Features:** Located in San Antonio's northern approach to the Texas Hill Country and the Canyon Lake recreational area, this long time family-owned smokehouse is a must for tender, moist barbecue enhanced with fresh homemade side dishes. Casual dress. **Parking:** on-site. **Cards:** AX, DC, MC, VI.

OLD SAN FRANCISCO STEAK HOUSE   **Dinner:** $11-$30   **Phone:** 210/342-2321   112

American   **Location:** 0.8 mi n of jct Loop 410 and San Pedro Ave. 10223 Sahara Dr 78216. **Hours:** 5 pm-10 pm, Fri & Sat-11 pm, Sun 5 pm-10 pm. Closed: 12/25. **Reservations:** suggested. **Features:** Enjoy the high-energy atmosphere in a Barbary Coast dance hall setting of the 1800s. A woman swings above the cavern-like dining room. Fresh baked rolls and the tender, moist chicken breast are delicious. Casual dress; cocktails; entertainment. **Parking:** on-site. **Cards:** AX, DC, DS, MC, VI.

OLD WORLD GERMAN RESTAURANT-DELICATESSEN & KONDITOREI   **Lunch:** $5-$12   **Dinner:** $6-$14   **Phone:** 210/366-9523   65

German   **Location:** I-410, exit Babcock Rd, 0.3 mi w of jct Babcock Rd and Loop 410. 1546 Babcock Rd 78229. **Hours:** 9 am-9 pm, Fri & Sat-10 pm, Sun 11 am-4 pm. Closed: 7/4, 11/27, 12/25. **Features:** An accordion player saunters through the oak wood dining room, which is accented by deer horns and German photographs on the walls. Hanging flowers drape the balcony. Devour Wiener schnitzel and finish your meal with homemade apple strudel. Casual dress; beer & wine only; entertainment. **Parking:** on-site. **Cards:** AX, DC, DS, MC, VI.

PAPPASITO'S CANTINA RESTAURANT   **Lunch:** $6-$10   **Dinner:** $8-$12   **Phone:** 210/691-8974   78

Mexican   **Location:** On I-10 westbound access road; between Wurzbach and Huebner rds. 10501 I-10 W 78230. **Hours:** 11 am-10 pm, Fri & Sat-11 pm, Sun 10:30 am-10 pm. Closed: 11/27, 12/25. **Features:** Like a rustic cantina, this cafe has a beautiful tile fountain, exposed brickwork and a bustling dining room. The homemade tamales are served with a spicy meat gravy topping. Mexican favorites like fajitas are delivered to your table sizzling. Casual dress; cocktails. **Parking:** on-site. **Cards:** AX, MC, VI.

PIEDRAS NEGRAS DE NOCHE   **Lunch:** $9-$14   **Dinner:** $9-$20   **Phone:** 210/227-7777   101

Mexican   **Location:** I-35, exit S Laredo St, just n of Cevallos St. 1312 S Laredo St 78204. **Hours:** 11 am-10 pm, Fri & Sat-1 am. Closed: Sun. **Reservations:** accepted. **Features:** You'll find unforgettable Tex-Mex cuisine inside this restaurant resembling an old, rickety house. The queso flameado con chorizo is flamed at the table. The fried avocado sticks are a healthy choice. Try one of the Mexican desserts. Casual dress. **Parking:** on-site. **Cards:** AX, CB, DC, DS, MC, VI.

(See map p. 496)

REGENT HUNAN CHINESE RESTAURANT Lunch: $4-$6 Dinner: $6-$8 Phone: 210/690-8499 58
Chinese
Location: Just n of Huebhner Rd. 5865 Babcock Rd 78240. **Hours:** 11 am-9:30 pm. Closed: 12/25. **Features:** Casual decor, low prices and a varied menu make the neighborhood favorite worth the visit. Casual dress; beer & wine only. **Parking:** on-site. **Cards:** AX, MC, VI.

RISTORANTE ITALIANO GRISSINI Lunch: $6-$10 Dinner: $9-$24 Phone: 210/615-7270 87
Italian
Location: Jct Fredericksburg Rd at Wurzbach Rd. 8498 Fredericksburg Rd 78229. **Hours:** 11:30 am-2 & 5-10 pm. Closed: Sun. **Reservations:** suggested. **Features:** This comfortable, pleasantly appointed restaurant features fresh salads and seafood served by an attentive and courteous staff. Choose beef, chicken or seafood and then select from a list of pasta and sauces to create your own delicious entree. Casual dress; beer & wine only. **Parking:** on-site. **Cards:** AX, DC, DS, MC, VI.

SAIGON ELITE Lunch: $6-$10 Dinner: $10-$14 Phone: 210/696-7712 80
Vietnamese
Location: Loop 410, 2.3 mi n. 9425 Fredericksburg Rd 78240. **Hours:** 11 am-2:30 & 5-9:30 pm. Closed: Sun. **Reservations:** accepted. **Features:** Chandeliers, red table cloths and mother of pearl furnishings create a very attractive, Vietnamese dining room. The crepes are filled with meat, shrimp, bean sprouts, onions and mushrooms and served with a tasty fish sauce and leaves of romaine. Casual dress; beer & wine only. **Parking:** on-site. **Cards:** AX, DS, MC, VI.

THE SEA ISLAND SHRIMP HOUSE Lunch: $5-$8 Dinner: $8-$12 Phone: 210/342-7771 70
Seafood
Location: Rector St at San Pedro, 0.4 mi s Loop 410. 322 W Rector St 78216. **Hours:** 10:45 am-9:30 pm, Sun 11 am-8:30 pm. Closed major holidays. **Features:** A local favorite, this appropriately decorated restaurant serves simply prepared seafood including charbroiled or grilled shrimp, lemon pepper shrimp and crab cakes. The energetic wait staff will no doubt recommend the delicious cheesecake for dessert. Smoke free premises. Casual dress; beer & wine only. **Parking:** on-site. **Cards:** AX, DS, MC, VI.

STONE WERKS CAFFE & BAR Lunch: $7-$8 Dinner: $8-$10 Phone: 210/828-3508 104
American
Location: At corner of Jones Maltsberger and Basse rds; opposite Quarry Market Mall. 7300 Jones Maltsberger Rd 78209. **Hours:** 11 am-midnight, Thurs-Sat to 2 am. **Features:** This is one of the few structures left of the old Alamo Cement Company complex. It sports natural-looking forms molded from concrete. The large hamburgers served here are smothered with blue cheese, and the giant quesadillas are over-stuffed. Outdoor seating under the stars or inside in the office. Casual dress; cocktails. **Parking:** on-site. **Cards:** AX, DS, MC, VI.

TASTE OF ASIA Lunch: $4-$5 Dinner: $9-$19 Phone: 210/496-6266 105
Chinese
Location: 300 W Bitters Rd, Suite 120 78216. **Hours:** 11 am-3 & 5-10 pm, Sat & Sun 11 am-10 pm. Closed: 7/4, 11/27, 12/25. **Features:** Two connecting restaurants, one Chinese, the other Vietnamese, serve homemade cuisine. You can use chopsticks to dig into mounds of Vietnamese noodles mixed with shredded chicken. On the Chinese side, crunchy sesame seeds cover sweet-and-sour chicken. Cocktails. **Parking:** on-site. **Cards:** AX, DS, MC, VI.

TOKYO STEAK HOUSE Dinner: $13-$47 Phone: 210/341-4461 111
Ethnic
Location: Loop 410, exit San Pedro Ave N, 0.3 mi n. 9405 San Pedro Ave 78216. **Hours:** 5:30 pm-9:30 pm, Fri & Sat-11 pm. Closed major holidays. **Reservations:** suggested. **Features:** You will get your share of food and entertainment at this restaurant. A quirky, talented chef cooks large portions of fried rice, shrimp, chicken and beef at your table. The full sushi bar offers colorful entrees of fresh seafood and shrimp stir fry. Casual dress; cocktails. **Parking:** on-site. **Cards:** AX, DC, DS, MC, VI.

TOMATILLOS MEXICAN RESTAURANT Lunch: $5-$10 Dinner: $5-$14 Phone: 210/824-3005 77
Mexican
Location: US 281, exit Hildrebrand, 0.5 mi e to Broadway, 0.3 mi s. 3210 Broadway 78209. **Hours:** 11 am-10 pm, Fri & Sat-11 pm. Closed: 11/27, 12/24, 12/25. **Reservations:** accepted. **Features:** Tomatillos makes all of their Tex-Mex cuisine from scratch. The interior is brightly colored like a Mexican fiesta. While you wait for your meal, munch on chips and spicy salsa. The specialty quesadillas are filled with fresh meat, chicken and cheese. Casual dress; cocktails. **Parking:** on-site. **Cards:** AX, DC, DS, MC, VI.

TOM'S RIBS Lunch: $6 Dinner: $13 Phone: 210/344-7427 57
Southwest Barbecue
Location: I-410, exit 17 (Vance Jackson Rd), nw Loop 410 at Vance Jackson Rd. 2535 NW Loop 410 78230. **Hours:** 11 am-10 pm, Fri & Sat-11 pm. Closed: 1/1, 12/25. **Features:** A longtime area favorite, the smokehouse provides fast service, quality barbecue and fresh, homemade side dishes. Casual dress; cocktails. **Parking:** on-site. **Cards:** AX, MC, VI.

U. R. COOKS Dinner: $10-$15 Phone: 210/647-4846 85
Steak House
Location: Loop 410 W access road at Summit Pkwy; in Loehmann's Village Mall (east end). 4907 NW Loop 410 78229. **Hours:** 4 pm-11 pm, Fri & Sat from 11:30 am, Sun 11:30 am-10 pm, Mon 4 pm-10 pm. Closed: 11/27, 12/25. **Reservations:** required. **Features:** Here your food is cooked just as you want it—by you! Three large grills sit in the middle of the contemporary dining room for you to grill your choice of beef, chicken and seafood. All you can eat potatoes, salad and Texas toast accompany your meal. Casual dress; cocktails. **Parking:** on-site. **Cards:** AX, CB, DC, DS, MC, VI.

VAN'S CHINESE SEAFOOD RESTAURANT Lunch: $4-$8 Dinner: $8-$19 Phone: 210/828-8449 107
Chinese
Location: Opposite Brackenridge City Park. 3214 Broadway 78209. **Hours:** 11 am-9:45 pm. Closed major holidays. **Features:** Dine in this friendly environment and savor the homemade Chinese and Vietnamese cuisine. The garlic chicken is very sweet and served with white rice. The egg drop soup is very spicy. Sip on a glass of wine from the extensive list. Casual dress. **Parking:** on-site. **Cards:** AX, DC, DS, MC, VI.

(See map p. 496)

The San Antonio Vicinity

FLORESVILLE pop. 5,868

——— WHERE TO STAY ———

BEST WESTERN FLORESVILLE INN   Phone: (830)393-0443
(AAA) [SAVE]   6/1-10/31 [ECP]   1P: $55-$75   2P: $62-$85   XP: $5   F16
                  2/1-5/31 & 11/1-1/31 [ECP]   1P: $52-$70   2P: $56-$80   XP: $5   F16
▽▽▽▽   **Location:** US 181, just s of downtown. 1720 S 10th St 78114. Fax: 830/393-1900. **Facility:** 42 one-bedroom stan-
dard units. 2 stories (no elevator), exterior corridors. **Parking:** on-site. **Terms:** cancellation fee imposed.
Small-scale Hotel   **Amenities:** irons, hair dryers. **Pool(s):** outdoor. **Business Services:** meeting rooms, fax (fee). **Cards:** AX,
CB, DC, DS, MC, VI. **Special Amenities:** early check-in/late check-out and free continental breakfast.
(See color ad below)   SOME UNITS

[icons]

LEON SPRINGS

——— WHERE TO DINE ———

RUDY'S COUNTRY STORE & BAR-B-QUE   **Lunch:** $6   **Dinner:** $10   **Phone:** 210/698-2141
▽▽▽   **Location:** I-10, exit Boerne Stage Rd. 24152 I-410 W 78006. **Hours:** 10 am-9:30 pm, Fri & Sat-10 pm. Closed:
1/1, 12/25. **Features:** On the city's outskirts, the traditional barbecue restaurant serves moist, tender
Southwest   brisket, sausages and ribs with all the down-home fixin's. Casual dress; beer & wine only. **Parking:** on-site.
Barbecue   **Cards:** AX, MC, VI.

LIVE OAK pop. 9,156

——— WHERE TO STAY ———

LA QUINTA-INN-SAN ANTONIO-TOEPPERWEIN   Phone: (210)657-5500
(AAA) [SAVE]   2/1-8/31   1P: $75-$99   2P: $86-$105
                  9/1-1/31   1P: $69-$89   2P: $75-$95
▽▽▽▽   **Location:** I-35, exit 170B (Toepperwein), northbound access road. 12822 I-35 N 78233. Fax: 210/590-3640. **Facility:** 136 units. 124 one-bedroom standard units. 12 one-bedroom suites. 3-4 stories, interior/exterior cor-
Small-scale Hotel   ridors. **Parking:** on-site. **Terms:** [ECP] meal plan available, small pets only. **Amenities:** video games, voice
mail, irons, hair dryers. **Pool(s):** outdoor. **Guest Services:** valet and coin laundry. **Business Services:**
meeting rooms, fax (fee). **Cards:** AX, CB, DC, DS, JC, MC, VI. **Special Amenities:** free continental breakfast and free local
telephone calls. *(See color ad p 510)*   SOME UNITS

[icons]

NEW BRAUNFELS pop. 36,494

——— WHERE TO STAY ———

BEST WESTERN INN & SUITES   Phone: (830)625-7337
(AAA) [SAVE]   5/16-9/1 [ECP]   1P: $79-$149   2P: $79-$149   XP: $10   F17
                  2/1-5/15 & 9/2-1/31 [ECP]   1P: $44-$94   2P: $44-$94   XP: $10   F17
▽▽▽▽   **Location:** I-35, exit 190, On southbound access lane. Located in a quiet area. 1493 I-35 N 78130. Fax: 830/625-7337.
Facility: 60 units. 30 one-bedroom standard units. 30 one-bedroom suites. 2 stories, interior/exterior corri-
Small-scale Hotel   dors. *Bath:* combo or shower only. **Parking:** on-site. **Terms:** 14 day cancellation notice, weekly rates available, pets (with prior approval). **Amenities:** irons, hair dryers. **Leisure Activities:** whirlpool. **Guest Services:**
coin laundry. **Business Services:** meeting rooms, fax (fee). **Cards:** AX, CB, DC, DS, MC, VI. **Special Amenities:** free continental breakfast and free newspaper.   SOME UNITS

[icons]

COMFORT SUITES

Phone: (830)643-1100

All Year [ECP]	1P: $59-$199	2P: $69-$199	XP: $10	F17

Location: I-35, exit 190, on the southbound access road. Located in a quiet area. 1489 I-35 N 78130. Fax: 830/643-1112. **Facility:** 62 one-bedroom standard units. 2 stories, interior corridors. *Bath:* combo or shower only. **Parking:** on-site. **Amenities:** high-speed Internet, voice mail, irons, hair dryers. **Pool(s):** outdoor. **Leisure Activities:** whirlpool, exercise room. **Guest Services:** coin laundry. **Business Services:** meeting rooms, business center. **Cards:** AX, CB, DC, DS, JC, MC, VI. **Special Amenities:** free continental breakfast and free local telephone calls.

Small-scale Hotel

SOME UNITS

DAYS INN

Phone: (830)608-0004

5/24-9/2	1P: $109-$119	2P: $109-$129
3/1-5/23	1P: $59-$79	2P: $65-$79
9/3-1/31	1P: $59-$69	2P: $65-$79
2/1-2/28	1P: $59-$69	2P: $59-$69

Motel

Location: I-35, exit 189, southbound access road. 963 I-35 N 78130. Fax: 830/608-1120. **Facility:** 60 one-bedroom standard units, some with whirlpools. 2 stories, exterior corridors. **Parking:** on-site. **Amenities:** hair dryers. **Pool(s):** outdoor. **Leisure Activities:** whirlpool. **Guest Services:** coin laundry. **Business Services:** fax (fee). **Cards:** AX, DC, DS, MC, VI.

SOME UNITS

GRUENE APPLE BED & BREAKFAST

Phone: 830/643-1234

All Year [BP]	1P: $155-$205	2P: $155-$205

Bed & Breakfast

Location: I-35, exit 189, 1.6 mi w to Common St, just n to Gruene Rd, 1.3 mi w. Located in a rural area. 1235 Gruene Rd 78130. Fax: 830/609-4449. **Facility:** On a bluff overlooking the Guadalupe River, this B&B offers luxurious accommodations as well as an on-site movie theater. Smoke free premises. 14 one-bedroom standard units, some with whirlpools. 3 stories, interior corridors. *Bath:* combo or shower only. **Parking:** on-site. **Terms:** check-in 4 pm, cancellation fee imposed. **Amenities:** voice mail, irons, hair dryers. **Pool(s):** heated outdoor. **Leisure Activities:** whirlpool, fishing. **Guest Services:** complimentary evening beverages. **Business Services:** conference facilities, business center. **Cards:** AX, MC, VI.

HAMPTON INN

Phone: (830)608-0123

5/24-9/2	1P: $109-$139	2P: $119-$139
3/1-5/23	1P: $84-$89	2P: $89-$99
9/3-1/31	1P: $79-$84	2P: $79-$89
2/1-2/28	1P: $79-$84	2P: $79-$84

Small-scale Hotel

Location: I-35, exit 189, southbound access road. 979 I-35 N 78130. Fax: 830/608-0121. **Facility:** 61 one-bedroom standard units. 2 stories, interior corridors. *Bath:* combo or shower only. **Parking:** on-site. **Amenities:** voice mail, irons, hair dryers. **Pool(s):** outdoor. **Leisure Activities:** whirlpool, exercise room. **Guest Services:** coin laundry. **Business Services:** meeting rooms, fax (fee). **Cards:** AX, DC, DS, MC, VI.

SOME UNITS

HOLIDAY INN

Phone: (830)625-8017

5/23-8/31	1P: $149-$179	2P: $149-$179	XP: $5	F12
2/1-5/22 & 9/1-1/31	1P: $109-$179	2P: $109-$179	XP: $5	F12

Location: I-35, exit 189, on southbound access road. 1051 I-35 E 78130. Fax: 830/625-3130. **Facility:** 140 units. 138 one-bedroom standard units. 2 stories, exterior corridors. *Bath:* combo or shower only. **Parking:** on-site. **Terms:** 2 night minimum stay - summer weekends, pets ($15 extra charge). **Amenities:** voice mail, irons, hair dryers. **Dining:** 7 am-11 & 5:30-9:30 pm, cocktails. **Pool(s):** outdoor. **Leisure Activities:** barbecue area, exercise room. **Guest Services:** valet and coin laundry. **Business Services:** meeting rooms, fax (fee). **Cards:** AX, CB, DC, DS, JC, MC, VI.

Small-scale Hotel

SOME UNITS

THE LAMB'S REST INN

Phone: 830/609-3932

All Year [BP]	1P: $125-$250	2P: $125-$250	XP: $25

Bed & Breakfast

Location: I-35, exit 189 (SR 46), 3 mi w to River Rd, 0.4 mi n to Edwards Blvd, then 1.2 mi e. Located in a rural area. 1385 Edwards Blvd 78132. Fax: 830/620-0864. **Facility:** Bathrobes are among the in-room amenities at this property located on the banks of the Guadalupe River. Smoke free premises. 6 units. 4 one-bedroom standard units. 1 two-bedroom suite with kitchen. 1 cottage with whirlpool. 2 stories, interior/exterior corridors. *Bath:* combo or shower only. **Parking:** on-site. **Terms:** check-in 4 pm, 2 night minimum stay - weekends, 7 day cancellation notice. **Amenities:** video library, irons, hair dryers. *Some:* CD players. **Pool(s):** outdoor. **Leisure Activities:** whirlpool, boat dock, fishing. **Guest Services:** complimentary evening beverages. **Business Services:** fax (fee). **Cards:** DS, MC, VI.

SOME UNITS

RODEWAY INN

Phone: (830)629-6991

5/23-8/31	1P: $59-$139	2P: $59-$139	XP: $6	F18
2/1-5/22 & 9/1-1/31	1P: $39-$89	2P: $39-$89	XP: $6	F18

Location: I-35, exit 189, southbound access lane. 1209 I-35 E 78130. Fax: 830/629-0754. **Facility:** 130 one-bedroom standard units, some with kitchens (no utensils). 2 stories (no elevator), exterior corridors. **Parking:** on-site. **Terms:** [CP] meal plan available, small pets only. **Amenities:** voice mail. **Pool(s):** outdoor. **Leisure Activities:** whirlpool. **Guest Services:** coin laundry. **Business Services:** meeting rooms, fax (fee). **Cards:** AX, DC, DS, MC, VI. **Special Amenities:** free continental breakfast and free local telephone calls.

Small-scale Hotel

SOME UNITS

SUPER 8 MOTEL-NEW BRAUNFELS

Phone: (830)629-1155

All Year [ECP]	1P: $44-$109	2P: $49-$129	XP: $5

Motel

Location: I-35, exit 189 (SR 46), just e. 510 Hwy 46 S 78130. Fax: 830/629-1155. **Facility:** 50 one-bedroom standard units. 2 stories, exterior corridors. **Parking:** on-site. **Terms:** pets ($5 extra charge). **Pool(s):** outdoor. **Leisure Activities:** whirlpool. **Guest Services:** coin laundry. **Business Services:** fax (fee). **Cards:** AX, CB, DC, DS, MC, VI.

SOME UNITS

———— WHERE TO DINE ————

GRIST MILL
American

Lunch: $5-$15   **Dinner:** $9-$20   **Phone:** 830/625-0684
Location: In Historic Gruene Township; I-35, exit 188, 2 mi e, follow signs. 1287 Gruene Rd 78130. **Hours:** 11 am-9 pm, Fri & Sat-10 pm. **Features:** Located in Historic Gruene Township inside a 19th-century grist mill, this eatery serves traditional foods like beef, chicken and fish. Chopped steak con queso and the slab-cut fries are the house specialty. The courtyard is perfect for sunset dining. Casual dress; cocktails. **Parking:** on-site. **Cards:** AX, DC, DS, MC, VI.

HUISACHE GRILL
American

Dinner: $6-$15   **Phone:** 830/620-9001
Location: Just s of main plaza. 303 W San Antonio St 78130. **Hours:** 11 am-10 pm. **Features:** This eatery's influences can be seen in offerings such as Tuscan-style T-bone steak, charbroiled chicken merida, and grilled portabello mushroom sandwich. Casual dress; cocktails. **Parking:** on-site. **Cards:** AX, CB, DC, MC, VI.

SEGUIN pop. 22,011

———— WHERE TO STAY ————

BEST WESTERN OF SEGUIN
Small-scale Hotel

| | 4/1-9/2 | 1P: $69-$79 | 2P: $79-$99 | XP: $10 | F12 |
| 2/1-3/31 & 9/3-1/31 | 1P: $50-$65 | 2P: $55-$69 | XP: $7 | F12 |

Phone: (830)379-9631

Location: I-10, exit 607 (SR 46). 1603 I-10 & Hwy 46 78155. Fax: 830/379-9631. **Facility:** 79 one-bedroom standard units. 2 stories, exterior corridors. **Parking:** on-site. **Terms:** [ECP] meal plan available, small pets only. **Amenities:** irons, hair dryers. **Pool(s):** outdoor. **Business Services:** fax (fee). **Cards:** AX, CB, DC, DS, JC, MC, VI. **Special Amenities:** early check-in/late check-out and free continental breakfast.

SOME UNITS

COMFORT INN & SUITES
Small-scale Hotel

All Year [ECP]   1P: $49-$125   2P: $49-$125   XP: $8   F18
Phone: (830)372-3990
Location: I-10, exit 610 (SR 123). Located in a rural area. 3013 N SR 123 Bypass 78155. Fax: 830/372-5382. **Facility:** 72 units. 62 one-bedroom standard units. 10 one-bedroom suites. Interior corridors. *Bath:* combo or shower only. **Parking:** on-site. **Amenities:** voice mail, irons, hair dryers. **Pool(s):** outdoor. **Guest Services:** coin laundry. **Business Services:** fax (fee). **Cards:** AX, CB, DC, DS, JC, MC, VI.

SOME UNITS

HOLIDAY INN SEGUIN

Phone: (830)372-0860

| | 5/18-9/2 | 1P: $98-$111 | 2P: $98-$111 | XP: $8 | F16 |
| | 2/1-5/17 & 9/3-1/31 | 1P: $85-$101 | 2P: $85-$101 | XP: $8 | F16 |

Small-scale Hotel   **Location:** I-10, exit 610 (SR 123). Located in a rural area. 2950 N 123 Bypass 78155. **Fax:** 830/372-3020. **Facility:** 139 one-bedroom standard units. 2 stories, exterior corridors. *Bath:* combo or shower only. **Parking:** on-site. **Terms:** 13% service charge, small pets only ($25 deposit). **Amenities:** dual phone lines, voice mail, irons, hair dryers. **Pool(s):** outdoor. **Leisure Activities:** exercise room. **Guest Services:** coin laundry. **Business Services:** meeting rooms, fax (fee). **Cards:** AX, CB, DC, DS, JC, MC, VI.

SOME UNITS

SUPER 8 MOTEL OF SEGUIN

Phone: 830/379-6888

| | 6/1-8/31 | 1P: $55-$99 | 2P: $59-$109 | XP: $6 | F12 |
| | 2/1-5/31 & 9/1-1/31 | 1P: $50-$69 | 2P: $59-$69 | XP: $6 | F12 |

Small-scale Hotel   **Location:** I-10, exit 607 (SR 46). Located in a quiet, rural area. 1525 N Hwy 46 78155. **Fax:** 830/379-3800. **Facility:** 49 one-bedroom standard units, some with whirlpools. 2 stories, exterior corridors. **Parking:** on-site. **Terms:** [CP] meal plan available, pets (with prior approval). **Business Services:** fax (fee). **Cards:** AX, CB, DC, DS, MC, VI.

SOME UNITS

UNIVERSAL CITY pop. 14,849

——— **WHERE TO STAY** ———

CLARION SUITES HOTEL

Phone: (210)655-9491

All Year [ECP]   1P: $79-$109   2P: $89-$159   XP: $10   F18

Location: Loop 1604 at Pat Booker Rd; 0.8 mi e of I-35. 13101 E Loop, 1604 N 78233. **Fax:** 210/655-8940. **Facility:** 102 units. 66 one- and 36 two-bedroom suites. 2 stories (no elevator), exterior corridors. **Parking:** on-site. **Terms:** pets ($25 extra charge). **Amenities:** irons, hair dryers. **Pool(s):** heated outdoor. **Leisure Activities:** whirlpool. **Guest Services:** coin laundry. **Business Services:** fax (fee). **Cards:** AX, CB, DC, DS, MC, VI. **Special Amenities:** free continental breakfast and free local telephone calls.

Small-scale Hotel

SOME UNITS

COMFORT INN-UNIVERSAL CITY

Phone: (210)659-5851

All Year   1P: $39-$120   2P: $45-$125   XP: $5

Location: I-35 N, exit Loop 1604, 1 mi e. Located in a quiet area. 200 Palisades Dr 78148. **Fax:** 210/659-3686. **Facility:** 119 one-bedroom standard units. 2 stories, exterior corridors. **Parking:** on-site. **Terms:** [CP] & [ECP] meal plans available. **Amenities:** *Some:* irons, hair dryers. **Pool(s):** outdoor. **Leisure Activities:** playground. **Guest Services:** coin laundry. **Business Services:** meeting rooms, fax (fee). **Cards:** AX, DC, DS, MC, VI. **Special Amenities:** free continental breakfast and free local telephone calls.

Small-scale Hotel

SOME UNITS

This ends listings for the San Antonio Vicinity.
The following page resumes the alphabetical listings of
cities in Texas.

SAN BENITO pop. 23,444

------ WHERE TO DINE ------

LONGHORN CATTLE COMPANY BARBEQUE & STEAK RESTAURANT   **Lunch:** $4-$12   **Dinner:** $7-$22   **Phone:** 956/399-4400

Southwest Steak House

Location: US 83 eastbound access road, 0.5 mi e, exit Helen Moore. 3055 W Expwy 83 78586. **Hours:** 11 am-9 pm, Fri & Sat-10 pm. Closed: 4/20, 11/27, 12/25; also Mon. **Features:** Visit the enormous screened porch decorated with mounted longhorns. Western relics cover the walls, and ceiling fans twirl above. Guests are greeted with a spicy cup of pintos at their table. Texas barbecue is the specialty at this bustling eatery. Casual dress; beer & wine only. **Parking:** on-site. **Cards:** AX, DS, MC, VI.

SANDERSON pop. 861

------ WHERE TO STAY ------

BUDGET INN   **Phone:** (432)345-2541

Motel

All Year   1P: $30-$36   2P: $35-$42   XP: $5   D5
Location: Just e of center. Hwy 90 E 79848 (PO Box 338). **Fax:** 432/345-2541. **Facility:** 16 one-bedroom standard units. 1 story, exterior corridors. **Parking:** on-site. **Terms:** package plans, small pets only ($10 deposit). **Business Services:** fax (fee). **Cards:** AX, CB, DC, DS, JC, MC, VI.

SOME UNITS

DESERT AIR MOTEL   **Phone:** (432)345-2572

Motel

All Year   1P: $30-$36   2P: $34-$39   XP: $4
Location: 0.5 mi w on US 90, just e of jct US 285. 806 W Oak 79848 (PO Box 326). **Fax:** 432/345-2572. **Facility:** 16 one-bedroom standard units. 1 story, exterior corridors. **Bath:** combo or shower only. **Parking:** on-site. **Terms:** weekly rates available. **Business Services:** fax (fee). **Cards:** MC, VI. **Special Amenities:** free local telephone calls.

SOME UNITS
FEE

SAN JUAN pop. 26,229

------ WHERE TO STAY ------

DAYS INN SAN JUAN   **Phone:** (956)782-1510

Small-scale Hotel

All Year [BP]   1P: $56-$67   2P: $65-$72   XP: $5   F12
Location: US 281 S and 83 S, exit Paul Longoria; from US 83 N, exit Paul Longoria. 112 W Expwy 83 78589. **Fax:** 956/782-1885. **Facility:** 90 units. 78 one-bedroom standard units. 12 one-bedroom suites ($112-$122). 2 stories (no elevator), exterior corridors. **Bath:** combo or shower only. **Parking:** on-site. **Amenities:** hair dryers. *Some:* irons. **Pool(s):** outdoor. **Guest Services:** coin laundry. **Business Services:** meeting rooms, fax (fee). **Cards:** AX, CB, DC, DS, MC, VI.

SOME UNITS

SAN MARCOS pop. 34,733

------ WHERE TO STAY ------

AMERIHOST INN & SUITES-SAN MARCOS   **Phone:** (512)392-6800

Small-scale Hotel

All Year   1P: $76-$83   2P: $83-$89   XP: $7   F18
Location: I-35, exit 200 (Center Point Rd), on frontage road. 4210 I-35 S 78666. **Fax:** 512/392-6847. **Facility:** 61 one-bedroom standard units, some with whirlpools. 2 stories (no elevator), interior corridors. **Bath:** combo or shower only. **Parking:** on-site. **Terms:** [ECP] meal plan available. **Amenities:** safes, irons, hair dryers. **Pool(s):** heated indoor. **Leisure Activities:** sauna, whirlpool, exercise room. **Guest Services:** valet laundry. **Business Services:** meeting rooms, fax (fee). **Cards:** AX, CB, DC, DS, JC, MC, VI. **Special Amenities:** free continental breakfast and free newspaper.

SOME UNITS

BEST WESTERN SAN MARCOS   **Phone:** (512)754-7557

Small-scale Hotel

6/1-9/1 [ECP]   1P: $69-$119   2P: $69-$119
2/1-5/31 & 9/2-1/31 [ECP]   1P: $45-$85   2P: $45-$85
Location: I-35, exit 204B, on westside access road. 917 I-35 N 78666. **Fax:** 512/754-7557. **Facility:** 52 one-bedroom standard units. 2 stories (no elevator), interior corridors. **Parking:** on-site. **Terms:** small pets only ($10 extra charge). **Amenities:** dual phone lines, irons, hair dryers. **Pool(s):** outdoor. **Leisure Activities:** whirlpool. **Guest Services:** coin laundry. **Business Services:** meeting rooms, fax (fee). **Cards:** AX, CB, DC, DS, MC, VI. **Special Amenities:** free continental breakfast and free newspaper.

SOME UNITS

COMFORT INN   **Phone:** (512)396-5665

Small-scale Hotel

All Year [ECP]   1P: $45-$150   2P: $45-$150   XP: $10   F10
Location: I-35, exit 206, on southbound frontage road. 1611 I-35 N 78666. **Fax:** 512/390-5092. **Facility:** 54 units. 51 one-bedroom standard units, some with whirlpools. 3 one-bedroom suites ($69-$179). 2 stories (no elevator), exterior corridors. **Bath:** combo or shower only. **Parking:** on-site. **Terms:** cancellation fee imposed, package plans. **Amenities:** hair dryers. *Some:* irons. **Pool(s):** small outdoor. **Leisure Activities:** whirlpool. **Guest Services:** complimentary evening beverages: Sun-Thurs. **Business Services:** fax (fee). **Cards:** AX, DC, DS, MC, VI.

SOME UNITS

DAYS INN

AAA SAVE ◆◆ ◆◆

Small-scale Hotel

Phone: (512)353-5050

All Year — 1P: $35-$100 — 2P: $40-$115 — XP: $5 — F12
Location: I-35, exit 205 northbound; exit 204B southbound; on southbound frontage road, at jct I-35 and SR 80. 1005 I-35 N 78666. Fax: 512/353-5050. **Facility:** 62 one-bedroom standard units, some with efficiencies. 2 stories (no elevator), exterior corridors. **Parking:** on-site. **Terms:** [CP] meal plan available, small pets only. **Amenities:** hair dryers. **Pool(s):** small outdoor. **Business Services:** fax (fee). **Cards:** AX, CB, DS, MC, VI.
Special Amenities: free continental breakfast and free newspaper.

SOME UNITS

ECONO LODGE

AAA SAVE ◆◆ ◆◆

Small-scale Hotel

Phone: (512)353-5300

3/1-9/30 & 1/1-1/31	1P: $50-$90	2P: $60-$100	XP: $6	F16
10/1-12/31	1P: $50-$90	2P: $50-$100	XP: $6	F16
2/1-2/28	1P: $45-$90	2P: $50-$100	XP: $6	F16

Location: I-35, exit 204 northbound; exit 204A southbound, on southbound access road. 811 S Guadalupe St 78666. Fax: 512/353-8010. **Facility:** 54 one-bedroom standard units, some with kitchens (no utensils). 2 stories (no elevator), exterior corridors. **Parking:** on-site. **Pool(s):** small outdoor. **Business Services:** fax (fee). **Cards:** AX, DC, DS, MC, VI.

SOME UNITS

HOLIDAY INN EXPRESS HOTEL & SUITES

◆◆◆ ◆◆◆

Small-scale Hotel

Phone: (512)754-6621

All Year — 1P: $79-$129 — 2P: $79-$129
Location: I-35, exit 204A southbound; exit 204 northbound, on east side of interstate. 108 I-35 N 78666. Fax: 512/754-6946. **Facility:** 105 one-bedroom standard units. 3 stories, interior corridors. *Bath:* combo or shower only. **Parking:** on-site. **Terms:** [ECP] meal plan available. **Amenities:** voice mail, irons, hair dryers. *Some:* dual phone lines. **Pool(s):** heated outdoor. **Leisure Activities:** limited exercise equipment. **Guest Services:** valet and coin laundry. **Business Services:** meeting rooms, fax (fee). **Cards:** AX, CB, DC, DS, MC, VI.

SOME UNITS

LA QUINTA INN-SAN MARCOS

AAA SAVE ◆◆◆ ◆◆◆

Small-scale Hotel

Phone: (512)392-8800

All Year — 1P: $69-$99 — 2P: $79-$109 — XP: $10 — F18
Location: I-35, exit 206. 1619 I-35 N 78666. Fax: 512/392-0324. **Facility:** 117 units. 116 one-bedroom standard units. 1 one-bedroom suite ($129-$179). 2 stories, interior/exterior corridors. *Bath:* combo or shower only. **Parking:** on-site. **Terms:** age restrictions may apply, [ECP] meal plan available, small pets only. **Amenities:** video games (fee), voice mail, irons, hair dryers. **Pool(s):** outdoor, wading. **Guest Services:** valet laundry. **Business Services:** meeting rooms, fax (fee). **Cards:** AX, CB, DC, DS, JC, MC, VI.
Special Amenities: free continental breakfast and free local telephone calls.

SOME UNITS

QUALITY INN

SAVE ◆◆◆ ◆◆◆

Small-scale Hotel

Phone: (512)353-7770

| 5/1-12/31 [BP] | 1P: $60-$109 | 2P: $69-$119 | XP: $5 | F8 |
| 2/1-4/30 & 1/1-1/31 [BP] | 1P: $60-$100 | 2P: $65-$110 | XP: $5 | F8 |

Location: I-35, exit 206, on southbound frontage road. 1433 I-35 N 78666. Fax: 512/353-7774. **Facility:** 92 one-bedroom standard units, some with whirlpools. 2 stories, exterior corridors. *Bath:* combo or shower only. **Parking:** on-site. **Amenities:** high-speed Internet, voice mail, irons, hair dryers. **Pool(s):** outdoor. **Leisure Activities:** whirlpool, limited exercise equipment. **Guest Services:** valet and coin laundry. **Business Services:** meeting rooms, business center. **Cards:** AX, CB, DC, DS, JC, MC, VI.

SOME UNITS

RAMADA LIMITED

AAA SAVE ◆◆ ◆◆

Motel

Phone: (512)395-8000

All Year [ECP] — 1P: $33-$149 — 2P: $33-$149
Location: I-35, exit 206 (Aquarina Spring). 1701 I-35 N 78666. Fax: 512/395-8006. **Facility:** 38 one-bedroom standard units, some with whirlpools. 2 stories (no elevator), exterior corridors. **Parking:** on-site. **Terms:** small pets only. **Amenities:** voice mail, irons, hair dryers. **Pool(s):** small outdoor. **Guest Services:** valet laundry. **Business Services:** fax (fee). **Cards:** AX, DC, DS, MC, VI. **Special Amenities:** free continental breakfast and free local telephone calls.

SOME UNITS

RED ROOF INN

◆◆ ◆◆

Small-scale Hotel

Phone: (512)754-8899

6/1-8/31	1P: $70-$110	2P: $70-$130	XP: $6	F17
2/1-5/31	1P: $50-$100	2P: $59-$100	XP: $6	F17
9/1-11/30	1P: $50-$80	2P: $55-$90	XP: $6	F17
12/1-1/31	1P: $40-$60	2P: $50-$70	XP: $6	F17

Location: I-35, exit 204B southbound; exit 205 northbound on westside access road. 817 I-35 N 78666. Fax: 512/369-2169. **Facility:** 50 one-bedroom standard units. 2 stories (no elevator), interior corridors. *Bath:* combo or shower only. **Parking:** on-site. **Terms:** cancellation fee imposed, small pets only. **Amenities:** high-speed Internet, dual phone lines, voice mail, irons, hair dryers. **Pool(s):** outdoor. **Leisure Activities:** whirlpool. **Guest Services:** coin laundry. **Business Services:** fax. **Cards:** AX, CB, DC, DS, MC, VI.

SOME UNITS

SAN MARCOS MICROTEL INN

◆◆◆ ◆◆◆

Small-scale Hotel

Phone: 512/754-7766

5/16-8/15 [CP]	1P: $55-$85	2P: $60-$95	XP: $5	F12
2/1-5/15 & 8/16-10/15 [CP]	1P: $45-$65	2P: $50-$80	XP: $5	F12
10/16-1/31 [CP]	1P: $40-$50	2P: $45-$60	XP: $5	F12

Location: I-35, exit 205, on southbound access road. 921 I-35 N 78666. Fax: 512/392-7714. **Facility:** 32 one-bedroom standard units. 2 stories (no elevator), interior corridors. *Bath:* combo or shower only. **Parking:** on-site. **Pool(s):** small outdoor. **Business Services:** fax (fee). **Cards:** AX, DC, DS, MC, VI.

SOME UNITS

--------- WHERE TO DINE ---------

PALMER'S RESTAURANT BAR & COURTYARD **Lunch:** $6-$20 **Dinner:** $7-$20 **Phone:** 512/353-3500
American
Location: I-35, exit 205, 1.6 mi w on CR 12 to Hutchinson St. 218 W Moore 78666. **Hours:** 11 am-10 pm, Sat & Sun-11 pm. Closed major holidays; also 12/24. **Reservations:** accepted. **Features:** The dining room has a rustic, homey atmosphere, while the courtyard has a comfortable, breezy feel. On the varied menu are pasta, Tex-Mex, seafood and premium Angus beef dishes. Smoke free premises. Casual dress; cocktails.
Parking: on-site. **Cards:** AX, MC, VI.

SAN MARCOS RIVER PUB & GRILL **Lunch:** $6-$16 **Dinner:** $6-$16 **Phone:** 512/353-3747
American
Location: I-35, exit 204, 0.3 mi w on 82/12 to Cheatham St, 0.6 mi e. 701 Cheatham St 78660. **Hours:** 11 am-10 pm, Fri & Sat-11 pm. Closed: 11/27, 12/24, 12/25. **Features:** The rustic, riverfront restaurant offers indoor and outdoor seating. The menu lists a good selection of appetizers, salads, steaks, seafood, chicken and pasta, as well as such lighter fare as burgers, chicken and club sandwiches and tacos. Portions are generous. Casual dress; cocktails. **Parking:** on-site. **Cards:** AX, CB, DC, DS, MC, VI.

SEABROOK —See Houston p. 441.

SEALY pop. 5,248

--------- WHERE TO STAY ---------

BEST WESTERN INN OF SEALY **Phone:** (979)885-3707
Motel
All Year [CP] 1P: $63-$69 2P: $69-$72 XP: $7 F12
Location: I-10, exit 720. 2107 Hwy 36 S 77474 (PO Box 510). Fax: 979/885-4201. **Facility:** 66 one-bedroom standard units. 2 stories, exterior corridors. *Bath:* combo or shower only. **Parking:** on-site. **Amenities:** irons, hair dryers. **Pool(s):** outdoor. **Leisure Activities:** whirlpool. **Business Services:** meeting rooms, fax (fee). **Cards:** AX, DC, DS, MC, VI. **Special Amenities:** early check-in/late check-out and free continental breakfast.

SOME UNITS

HOLIDAY INN EXPRESS **Phone:** (979)885-2121
Motel
All Year [ECP] 1P: $62-$84 2P: $67-$89 XP: $5 F18
Location: I-10, exit 720. 231 Gebhard Rd 77474. Fax: 979/885-4242. **Facility:** 50 one-bedroom standard units, some with whirlpools. 2 stories, exterior corridors. *Bath:* combo or shower only. **Parking:** on-site. **Amenities:** irons, hair dryers. **Pool(s):** outdoor. **Leisure Activities:** whirlpool. **Guest Services:** coin laundry. **Business Services:** meeting rooms, fax (fee). **Cards:** AX, CB, DC, DS, JC, MC, VI. **Special Amenities:** free continental breakfast and free local telephone calls. *(See color ad below)*

SOME UNITS

--------- WHERE TO DINE ---------

HINZE'S BAR-B-QUE **Lunch:** $5-$11 **Dinner:** $5-$11 **Phone:** 979/885-7808
Barbecue
Location: I-10, exit 720. 2101 Hwy 36 S 77474. **Hours:** 10:30 am-9 pm, Fri-10 pm, Sat 10:30 am-9:30 pm. Closed major holidays. **Features:** The homey eatery is a great place to stop for a fast, but mouthwatering, meal of pork ribs, bacon cheeseburger or fried catfish. Lighter eaters will appreciate the numerous vegetable sides. Homemade pies melt in the mouth. Casual dress; beer & wine only. **Parking:** on-site.
Cards: AX, DC, DS, MC, VI.

SEGUIN —See San Antonio p. 547.

SEMINOLE pop. 5,910

──── WHERE TO STAY ────

RAYMOND MOTOR INN   Phone: (432)758-3653
(AAA) [SAVE]   All Year   1P: $34-$35   2P: $40-$45   XP: $4   F12
▼▼▼   Location: 0.3 mi w on US 62 and 180. 301 W Ave A 79360. Fax: 432/758-5703. **Facility:** 37 one-bedroom stan-
            dard units, some with efficiencies. 1 story, exterior corridors. *Bath:* combo or shower only. **Parking:** on-site.
Motel   **Terms:** package plans, small pets only ($5 fee). **Business Services:** fax (fee). **Cards:** AX, DC, DS, JC,
            MC, VI. **Special Amenities: early check-in/late check-out and free local telephone calls.**

SOME UNITS
[S D] [🐾] [🍽+] [▤] / [✕] [VCR] [DATA PORT] [▣] /
FEE

SEMINOLE INN   Phone: 432/758-9881
▼▼ ▼▼   All Year   1P: $36-$39   2P: $39-$42   XP: $5   F12
Motel   Location: 1.5 mi w on US 62 and 180. 2200 Hobbs Hwy 79360. Fax: 432/758-9865. **Facility:** 40 one-bedroom
            standard units. 1 story, exterior corridors. **Parking:** on-site. **Terms:** 3 day cancellation notice. **Pool(s):** small
            outdoor. **Business Services:** fax (fee). **Cards:** AX, DS, MC, VI.

SOME UNITS
[🛬] / [✕] [▤] [▣] /

SHAMROCK pop. 2,029

──── WHERE TO STAY ────

BEST WESTERN SHAMROCK INN & SUITES   Phone: (806)256-1001
(AAA) [SAVE]   All Year [ECP]   1P: $79-$89   2P: $89-$109   XP: $5   F12
▼▼▼ ▼▼▼   Location: I-40, exit 163, just n. 1802 N Main St 79079. Fax: 806/256-1006. **Facility:** 47 one-bedroom standard
            units, some with kitchens (no utensils) and/or whirlpools. 3 stories, interior corridors. *Bath:* combo or shower
            only. **Parking:** on-site. **Terms:** cancellation fee imposed. **Amenities:** voice mail, irons, hair dryers. **Pool(s):**
Small-scale Hotel   heated indoor. **Leisure Activities:** whirlpool, limited exercise equipment. **Business Services:** fax (fee).
            Cards: AX, DC, DS, MC, VI. **Special Amenities: free continental breakfast and free room upgrade (sub-**
ject to availability with advanced reservations).

SOME UNITS
[S D] [🍽+] [♿] [🛬] [📶] [DATA PORT] [�] / [✕] [▤] [▣] /

BUDGET HOST-BLARNEY INN   Phone: (806)256-2101
(AAA) [SAVE]   All Year   1P: $28-$35   2P: $35-$45   XP: $4   F12
▼▼   Location: I-40, exit 164 westbound; exit 161 or 163 eastbound, just e of US 83. 402 E 12th St, Rt 66 79079.
            Fax: 806/256-8923. **Facility:** 20 one-bedroom standard units. 1 story, exterior corridors. *Bath:* combo or
            shower only. **Parking:** on-site. **Terms:** weekly rates available, [CP] meal plan available, small pets only ($3
Motel   extra charge). **Leisure Activities:** golf privileges. **Guest Services:** complimentary laundry. **Business Serv-**
            ices: fax (fee). **Cards:** AX, DS, MC, VI. **Special Amenities: free continental breakfast and free local tele-**
phone calls. *(See color ad p 162)*

SOME UNITS
[S D] [🐾] [DATA PORT] / [✕] [▤] [▣] /

ECONO LODGE   Phone: 806/256-2111
(AAA) [SAVE]   All Year   1P: $40-$50   2P: $48-$65   XP: $5   F14
▼▼ ▼▼   Location: I-40, exit 164 westbound; exit 161 or 163 eastbound, just e of US 83. 1006 E 12th St 79079.
            Fax: 806/256-2302. **Facility:** 71 one-bedroom standard units. 2 stories (no elevator), exterior corridors.
            Parking: on-site. **Terms:** [CP] meal plan available, small pets only ($5 fee). **Pool(s):** outdoor. **Leisure Ac-**
Small-scale Hotel   tivities: golf privileges. **Business Services:** meeting rooms, fax (fee). **Cards:** AX, CB, DC, DS, JC, MC, VI.
            Special Amenities: free continental breakfast and free local telephone calls.

SOME UNITS
[S D] [🐾] [🛬] [📶] / [✕] [▤] [▣] [merge] /

IRISH INN MOTEL   Phone: (806)256-2106
(AAA) [SAVE]   All Year [BP]   1P: $45-$58   2P: $49-$58   XP: $4   F12
▼▼▼ ▼▼▼   Location: I-40, exit 163, 0.3 mi e on north service road. 301 I-40 E 79079. Fax: 806/256-5472. **Facility:** 160 one-
            bedroom standard units. 2 stories (no elevator), interior/exterior corridors. **Parking:** on-site. **Amenities:** voice
            mail. **Dining:** 24 hours, cocktails. **Pool(s):** heated indoor. **Leisure Activities:** whirlpool, golf privileges.
Small-scale Hotel   **Guest Services:** gift shop, coin laundry, area transportation. **Business Services:** meeting rooms, fax (fee).
            Cards: AX, CB, DC, DS, MC, VI. **Special Amenities: free continental breakfast and free local telephone**
calls.

SOME UNITS
[S D] [❄] [🐾] [🍽] [Y] [⊘] [🛬] [📶] [DATA PORT] [merge] / [✕] [VCR] [▤] /
FEE

THE WESTERN MOTEL   Phone: (806)256-3244
(AAA) [SAVE]   All Year   1P: $39-$49   2P: $39-$59   XP: $5   D12
▼▼   Location: Business I-40 and US 83. 104 E 12th St 79079. Fax: 806/256-3244. **Facility:** 24 one-bedroom standard
            units. 2 stories, exterior corridors. **Parking:** on-site. **Terms:** 3 day cancellation notice, small pets only ($3
            extra charge). **Dining:** 6 am-9:30 pm. **Leisure Activities:** golf privileges. **Business Services:** fax (fee).
Motel   **Cards:** AX, DC, DS, MC, VI. **Special Amenities: free local telephone calls and free room upgrade (sub-**
ject to availability with advanced reservations).

SOME UNITS
[S D] [🐾] [🍽] [📶] [DATA PORT] / [✕] /

------ **WHERE TO DINE** ------

MITCHELL FAMILY RESTAURANT   **Lunch:** $5-$12   **Dinner:** $5-$12   **Phone:** 806/256-1900
American
Location: I-40, exit 163, just e on north service road. I-40 & Hwy 83 79079. **Hours:** 6 am-9:30 pm. Closed: 11/27, 12/25. **Features:** Fishing and hunting antiques surround the nostalgic eatery, where families are welcomed to try well-prepared American dishes, most of which include the well-stocked salad bar. Casual dress. **Parking:** on-site. **Cards:** AX, DC, DS, MC, VI.

SHENANDOAH —*See Houston p. 442.*

SHERMAN pop. 35,082

------ **WHERE TO STAY** ------

COMFORT SUITES OF SHERMAN   **Phone:** (903)893-0499
SAVE
Small-scale Hotel
All Year [ECP]   1P: $79   2P: $129   XP: $8   F18
Location: US 75, exit 63, 0.3 mi s of jct US 82, exit 20A. 2900 US Hwy 75 N 75090. Fax: 903/891-3685. **Facility:** 67 one-bedroom standard units, some with whirlpools. 2 stories, interior corridors. *Bath:* combo or shower only. **Parking:** on-site. **Terms:** small pets only ($10 fee). **Amenities:** dual phone lines, voice mail, irons, hair dryers. **Pool(s):** outdoor. **Leisure Activities:** whirlpool, exercise room. **Guest Services:** valet and coin laundry. **Business Services:** meeting rooms, fax (fee). **Cards:** AX, CB, DC, DS, MC, VI.

SOME UNITS

DAYS INN-SHERMAN   **Phone:** (903)892-0433
AAA SAVE
Motel
All Year [CP]   1P: $44-$50   2P: $50-$59   XP: $5   F
Location: US 75, exit 61, just n on SR 91. 1831 Texoma Pkwy 75090. Fax: 903/893-8199. **Facility:** 87 units. 82 one- and 3 two-bedroom standard units. 2 one-bedroom suites ($65-$70). 2 stories, exterior corridors. *Bath:* combo or shower only. **Parking:** on-site. **Terms:** pets ($5 extra charge). **Amenities:** hair dryers. **Pool(s):** outdoor. **Guest Services:** coin laundry. **Business Services:** meeting rooms, fax (fee). **Cards:** AX, CB, DC, DS, MC, VI. **Special Amenities:** free continental breakfast and free newspaper.

SOME UNITS

HAMPTON INN   **Phone:** (903)893-9333
SAVE
Small-scale Hotel
All Year [ECP]   1P: $74   2P: $84
Location: US 75, exit 63, 0.3 mi s of jct US 82. 2904 Michelle Dr 75090. Fax: 903/891-8812. **Facility:** 69 one-bedroom standard units. 3 stories, interior corridors. *Bath:* combo or shower only. **Parking:** on-site. **Amenities:** dual phone lines, voice mail, irons, hair dryers. **Pool(s):** heated indoor. **Leisure Activities:** whirlpool, limited exercise equipment. **Guest Services:** valet and coin laundry. **Business Services:** meeting rooms, fax (fee). **Cards:** AX, CB, DC, DS, MC, VI.

SOME UNITS

LA QUINTA INN & SUITES SHERMAN   **Phone:** (903)870-1122
AAA SAVE
Small-scale Hotel
All Year   1P: $75-$95   2P: $85-$105   XP: $10   F18
Location: US 75, exit 63, jct US 82, just sw. 2912 US 75 N 75090. Fax: 903/870-1132. **Facility:** 115 units. 111 one-bedroom standard units, some with whirlpools. 4 one-bedroom suites ($119-$169). 4 stories, interior corridors. *Bath:* combo or shower only. **Parking:** on-site. **Terms:** [ECP] meal plan available, small pets only. **Amenities:** video games (fee), dual phone lines, voice mail, irons, hair dryers. **Pool(s):** heated outdoor. **Leisure Activities:** whirlpool, exercise room. **Guest Services:** valet and coin laundry. **Business Services:** meeting rooms, fax (fee). **Cards:** AX, CB, DC, DS, JC, MC, VI. **Special Amenities:** free continental breakfast and free local telephone calls.

SOME UNITS

SHERMAN, SUPER 8 MOTEL   **Phone:** 903/868-9325
Motel
All Year   1P: $36-$46   2P: $41-$50   XP: $5   F12
Location: 3 mi s on US 75, exit 56. 111 E Hwy 1417 75090. Fax: 903/870-0114. **Facility:** 47 one-bedroom standard units. 2 stories, interior corridors. **Parking:** on-site. **Terms:** 3-7 night minimum stay - seasonal, package plans, pets ($5 extra charge). **Amenities:** safes. **Business Services:** fax (fee). **Cards:** AX, DC, DS, MC, VI.

SOME UNITS

SNYDER pop. 10,783

──── **WHERE TO STAY** ────

BEST WESTERN SNYDER INN   Phone: (325)574-2200
◆◆◆ [SAVE]   All Year   1P: $65-$75   2P: $65-$75   XP: $5   F
♦♦♦ ♦♦♦   **Location:** 1.5 mi w of US 84/80. 810 E Coliseum Dr 79549. Fax: 325/574-2201. **Facility:** 39 one-bedroom stan-
           dard units. 1 story, exterior corridors. **Parking:** on-site. **Terms:** pets ($25 fee). **Amenities:** voice mail, irons,
Motel   hair dryers. **Pool(s):** outdoor. **Leisure Activities:** limited exercise equipment. **Business Services:** fax (fee).
           Cards: AX, CB, DC, DS, JC, MC, VI. **Special Amenities: free continental breakfast and free news-
           paper.** *(See ad below)*

                                                                              SOME UNITS
[icons] / ⊠ /

DAYS INN   Phone: (325)573-1166
◆◆◆ [SAVE]   All Year [ECP]   1P: $50-$55   2P: $55-$60   XP: $6   F12
♦♦♦ ♦♦♦   **Location:** 1.5 mi w on US 180 from jct US 84. 800 E Coliseum Dr 79549. Fax: 325/573-1166. **Facility:** 56 one-
           bedroom standard units. 2 stories (no elevator), exterior corridors. *Bath:* combo or shower only. **Parking:** on-
Motel   site. **Terms:** cancellation fee imposed, [CP] meal plan available. **Amenities:** irons, hair dryers. **Pool(s):**
           outdoor. **Business Services:** fax (fee). **Cards:** AX, CB, DC, DS, MC, VI. **Special Amenities: free conti-
           nental breakfast and free local telephone calls.**

                                                                              SOME UNITS
[icons] / ⊠ /

PURPLE SAGE MOTEL   Phone: (325)573-5491
◆◆◆ [SAVE]   9/1-1/31   1P: $47-$57   2P: $51-$69   XP: $5   F12
♦♦♦ ♦♦♦   2/1-8/31   1P: $46-$56   2P: $50-$68   XP: $5   F12
           Location: 1 mi w on US 180 from jct US 84. 1501 E Coliseum 79549. Fax: 325/573-9027. **Facility:** 44 one-bedroom
           standard units, some with efficiencies. 1 story, exterior corridors. **Parking:** on-site. **Terms:** [ECP] meal plan
Motel   available, small pets only. **Amenities:** *Some:* irons, hair dryers. **Pool(s):** outdoor. **Business Services:** fax
           (fee). **Cards:** AX, CB, DC, DS, MC, VI. **Special Amenities: free local telephone calls and free news-
paper.**

                                                                              SOME UNITS
[icons] / ⊠ [VCR] /

SONORA pop. 2,924

──── **WHERE TO STAY** ────

BEST WESTERN SONORA INN   Phone: (325)387-9111
[SAVE]   1/1-1/31 [CP]   1P: $69-$89   2P: $74-$89   XP: $5   F12
♦♦♦ ♦♦♦   2/1-12/31 [CP]   1P: $65-$85   2P: $70-$85   XP: $5   F12
           Location: I-10, exit 400. 270 Hwy 277 N 76950. Fax: 325/387-9221. **Facility:** 54 one-bedroom standard units. 2
Small-scale Hotel stories (no elevator), exterior corridors. *Bath:* combo or shower only. **Parking:** on-site. **Terms:** cancellation
           fee imposed, pets ($10 fee). **Amenities:** irons, hair dryers. **Pool(s):** outdoor. **Leisure Activities:** limited ex-
MC, VI.   ercise equipment. **Guest Services:** coin laundry. **Business Services:** fax (fee). **Cards:** AX, CB, DC, DS,

                                                                              SOME UNITS
[icons] / ⊠ /

DAYS INN   Phone: (325)387-3516
◆◆◆ [SAVE]   All Year   1P: $40-$50   2P: $55-$65   XP: $4   F18
♦♦♦ ♦♦♦   **Location:** I-10, exit 400, just n. 1312 N Service Rd 76950. Fax: 325/387-2854. **Facility:** 99 one-bedroom standard
           units. 1 story, exterior corridors. **Parking:** on-site. **Terms:** 7 day cancellation notice, [CP] meal plan available,
Motel   pets ($2 extra charge). **Amenities:** hair dryers. **Dining:** 6 am-2 & 5-9:30 pm, cocktails. **Pool(s):** outdoor.
           Guest Services: valet and coin laundry. **Business Services:** meeting rooms, fax (fee). **Cards:** AX, CB, DC,
           DS, MC, VI. **Special Amenities: free continental breakfast and free local telephone calls.**

                                                                              SOME UNITS
[icons] / ⊠ /
                                                                              FEE FEE

HOLIDAY HOST MOTEL

(AAA) (SAVE)
◆◆◆
Motel

All Year   1P: $34-$40   2P: $40-$50   XP: $3

Phone: (325)387-2532
          D5

Location: Loop 467, exit 404 westbound, 3 mi w; exit 399 eastbound, 3 mi e. 127 Loop 467 (Hwy 290) 76950. **Fax:** 325/387-6180. **Facility:** 20 one-bedroom standard units. 1 story, exterior corridors. *Bath:* combo or shower only. **Parking:** on-site. **Terms:** small pets only. **Pool(s):** outdoor. **Business Services:** fax. **Cards:** AX, CB, DC, DS, MC, VI. **Special Amenities: free local telephone calls.** *(See color ad below)*

SOME UNITS

🛏 🥤 🎥 / ✕ 🗄 📺 /

TWIN OAKS MOTEL

(AAA) (SAVE)
◆◆◆
Motel

All Year [CP]   1P: $35-$40   2P: $40-$50   XP: $5

Phone: 325/387-2551
         F10

Location: I-10, exit 400 westbound; exit 399 eastbound, 0.5 mi e, then 0.3 mi s on US 277. 907 N Crockett Ave 76950. **Fax:** 325/387-3670. **Facility:** 53 one-bedroom standard units. 1 story, exterior corridors. **Parking:** on-site. **Terms:** 3 day cancellation notice-fee imposed, small pets only. **Business Services:** fax (fee). **Cards:** AX, CB, DC, DS, JC, MC, VI. **Special Amenities: free continental breakfast and free local telephone calls.**

SOME UNITS

[SD] 🛏 [¶¶] / ✕ /

SOUTH PADRE ISLAND pop. 2,422

—— **WHERE TO STAY** ——

BAHIA MAR RESORT

◆◆◆◆
Small-scale Hotel

3/2-5/22	1P: $90-$395	XP: $10 F17
2/1-3/1 & 9/2-1/31	1P: $90-$225	XP: $10 F17
5/23-9/1	1P: $144	XP: $10 F17

Phone: (956)761-1343

Location: 3.5 mi n of Queen Isabella Cswy. 6300 Padre Blvd 78597. **Fax:** 956/761-6287. **Facility:** 236 units. 194 one-bedroom standard units. 30 two- and 12 three-bedroom suites with kitchens. 2-12 stories, interior/exterior corridors. **Parking:** on-site. **Terms:** 3 day cancellation notice-fee imposed, package plans. **Amenities:** voice mail, irons, hair dryers. **Pool(s):** outdoor, heated outdoor, wading. **Leisure Activities:** whirlpool, putting green, 2 lighted tennis courts, exercise room, sports court, shuffleboard. **Guest Services:** gift shop, coin laundry. **Business Services:** meeting rooms, fax (fee). **Cards:** AX, CB, DC, DS, MC, VI.

SOME UNITS

(ASK) [SD] [¶¶] 🍸 📷 🥤 ✕ 🎥 [DATA PORT] 🗄 📺 💻 / ✕ /

BEST WESTERN FIESTA ISLES HOTEL

(AAA) (SAVE)
◆◆◆◆
Small-scale Hotel

3/7-3/29 [CP]	1P: $149-$249	2P: $149-$249
3/30-8/31 [CP]	1P: $59-$119	2P: $59-$119
2/1-3/6 [CP]	1P: $49-$69	2P: $49-$69
9/1-1/31 [CP]	1P: $39-$69	2P: $39-$69

Phone: (956)761-4913

Location: 3 mi n of Queen Isabella Cswy. Located on the waterfront. 5701 Padre Blvd 78597 (PO Box 3079). **Fax:** 956/761-2719. **Facility:** 58 units. 40 one-bedroom standard units. 18 one-bedroom suites. 3 stories, exterior corridors. **Parking:** on-site. **Terms:** pets ($25 deposit). **Amenities:** voice mail. *Some:* safes. **Pool(s):** outdoor. **Leisure Activities:** whirlpool, fishing. **Guest Services:** coin laundry. **Cards:** AX, CB, DC, DS, MC, VI. **Special Amenities: free continental breakfast and free newspaper.**

SOME UNITS

[SD] 🛏 [¶¶] 🥤 🎥 [DATA PORT] 🗄 📺 💻 / ✕ /

COMFORT SUITES

(SAVE)
◆◆◆◆
Small-scale Hotel

3/1-4/20	1P: $259-$329	2P: $259-$329
4/21-9/6	1P: $179-$209	2P: $179-$209
2/1-2/28 & 9/7-1/31	1P: $69-$139	2P: $69-$139

Phone: (956)772-9020
XP: $10 F16
XP: $10 F16
XP: $10 F16

Location: Opposite Queen Isabela Causeway. Located behind the McDonalds. 912 Padre Blvd 78597. **Fax:** 956/772-9022. **Facility:** 74 one-bedroom suites, some with whirlpools. 3 stories, interior corridors. *Bath:* combo or shower only. **Parking:** on-site. **Terms:** 3 day cancellation notice-fee imposed, [BP] meal plan available. **Amenities:** video games, high-speed Internet, voice mail, irons, hair dryers. **Pool(s):** outdoor. **Leisure Activities:** whirlpool, exercise room. **Guest Services:** coin laundry. **Business Services:** meeting rooms, fax (fee). **Cards:** AX, CB, DC, DS, MC, VI.

SOME UNITS

[SD] [¶¶] 🥤 🎥 [DATA PORT] 🗄 📺 💻 / ✕ /

DAYS INN
Phone: 956/761-7831

▽▽ ▽▽
Small-scale Hotel

Property failed to provide current rates
Location: 2.6 mi n of Queen Isabella Cswy. 3913 Padre Blvd 78597. Fax: 956/761-2033. **Facility:** 58 one-bedroom standard units. 2-3 stories (no elevator), exterior corridors. *Bath:* combo or shower only. **Parking:** on-site. **Terms:** pets ($25 deposit). **Amenities:** hair dryers. **Pool(s):** outdoor. **Leisure Activities:** whirlpool. **Guest Services:** coin laundry. **Business Services:** fax (fee). **Cards:** AX, CB, DC, DS, MC, VI.

SOME UNITS
🛏 🍴 ➷ 🎦 🖥 / ⊠ /

ECONO LODGE
Phone: (956)761-8500

🆔 SAVE
▽▽ ▽▽▽

2/28-8/16 [CP]	1P: $99-$249	2P: $99-$249	XP: $20	F14
8/17-1/31 [CP]	1P: $39-$69	2P: $39-$89	XP: $5	F14
2/1-2/27 [CP]	1P: $39-$59	2P: $39-$69	XP: $5	F14

Small-scale Hotel
Location: 2.6 mi n of Queen Isabella Cswy. 3813 Padre Blvd 78597. Fax: 956/761-5131. **Facility:** 64 one-bedroom standard units, some with efficiencies (no utensils) and/or whirlpools. 2 stories, interior corridors. *Bath:* combo or shower only. **Parking:** on-site. **Terms:** 7 day cancellation notice-fee imposed, pets ($5 extra charge). **Amenities:** hair dryers. *Some:* irons. **Pool(s):** outdoor. **Leisure Activities:** whirlpool. **Guest Services:** coin laundry. **Business Services:** fax (fee). **Cards:** AX, CB, DC, DS, JC, MC, VI. **Special Amenities: free continental breakfast and free local telephone calls.**

SOME UNITS
🆂 🛏 🍴 ➷ 🎦 [DATA PORT] 🖥 / ⊠ 📺

HOLIDAY INN-SUNSPREE RESORT
Phone: (956)761-5401

🆔 SAVE
▽▽▽▽▽

3/8-4/20	1P: $109-$259
4/21-8/21	1P: $119-$229
8/22-1/31	1P: $79-$199
2/1-3/7	1P: $89-$149

Small-scale Hotel **Location:** Just s of Queen Isabella Cswy. 100 Padre Blvd 78597. Fax: 956/761-1560. **Facility:** 227 units. 219 one-bedroom standard units. 8 one-bedroom suites ($129-$299). 6 stories, interior corridors. **Parking:** on-site. **Terms:** 3 day cancellation notice-fee imposed, [BP] meal plan available. **Amenities:** voice mail, safes, irons, hair dryers. **Dining:** 2 restaurants, 6:30 am-2 & 5-10 pm, cocktails. **Pool(s):** outdoor, heated outdoor, wading. **Leisure Activities:** whirlpool, 2 lighted tennis courts, recreation programs, playground, exercise room. **Guest Services:** gift shop, valet and coin laundry. **Business Services:** meeting rooms, fax (fee). *(See color ad below)*

SOME UNITS
🍴 🍸 ➷ 🗙 🎦 [DATA PORT] 🖥 📠 💻 / ⊠ 📺

HOWARD JOHNSON INN-RESORT
Phone: (956)761-5658

▽▽ ▽▽▽

4/1-8/31 [CP]	1P: $59-$259	2P: $69-$329	XP: $10	F12
3/1-3/31 [CP]	1P: $200	2P: $250	XP: $10	F12
2/1-2/28 [CP]	1P: $49-$59	2P: $49-$79	XP: $10	F12
9/1-1/31 [CP]	1P: $49	2P: $49	XP: $10	F12

Small-scale Hotel
Location: SR 100, 0.9 mi n at corner of W Palm St. 1709 Padre Blvd 78597. Fax: 956/761-5520. **Facility:** 89 one-bedroom standard units, some with efficiencies and/or whirlpools. 3 stories, interior corridors. *Bath:* combo or shower only. **Parking:** on-site. **Terms:** cancellation fee imposed. **Amenities:** dual phone lines, voice mail, safes (fee), irons, hair dryers. **Pool(s):** outdoor. **Leisure Activities:** whirlpool, exercise room. **Guest Services:** coin laundry. **Business Services:** meeting rooms. **Cards:** AX, CB, DC, DS, MC, VI.

SOME UNITS
(ASK) 🆂 🍴 ♿M 🖥 ➷ 🎦 [DATA PORT] 🖥 📠 / ⊠ 📺 /
FEE

RADISSON RESORT SOUTH PADRE ISLAND
Phone: (956)761-6511

🆔 SAVE
▽▽▽▽▽

3/1-9/1	1P: $220-$405	2P: $220-$405	XP: $10	F17
10/26-1/31	1P: $105-$335	2P: $105-$335	XP: $10	F17
2/1-2/28 & 9/2-10/25	1P: $145-$265	2P: $145-$265	XP: $10	F17

Resort
Large-scale Hotel
Location: 0.3 mi n of Queen Isabella Cswy. Located on the beach. 500 Padre Blvd 78597. Fax: 956/761-1602. **Facility:** Featuring an eye-catching lobby, this property is located on a notable beach. 190 units. 128 one-bedroom standard units. 12 one- and 50 two-bedroom suites with kitchens. 2-12 stories, interior/exterior corridors. **Parking:** on-site. **Terms:** 3 day cancellation notice-fee imposed. **Amenities:** video games, dual phone lines, voice mail, irons, hair dryers. **Dining:** 6:30 am-10 pm, Fri & Sat-11 pm, cocktails, entertainment. **Pool(s):** outdoor, heated outdoor. **Leisure Activities:** whirlpools, 4 lighted tennis courts, beach volleyball. **Guest Services:** gift shop, valet and coin laundry. **Business Services:** meeting rooms, fax (fee). **Cards:** AX, CB, DC, DS, MC, VI.

SOME UNITS
🆂 🍴 📶 ➷ 🗙 🎦 [DATA PORT] / ⊠ 🖥 📠 💻 /

ROYALE BEACH & TENNIS CLUB
Phone: (956)761-1166

AAA [SAVE] ▼▼▼▼

Condominium

3/1-3/31	1P: $180-$450
2/1-2/28 & 4/1-1/31	1P: $138-$300

Location: Just s of SR 100. 400 Padre Blvd 78597 (PO Box 2809). Fax: 956/761-5808. **Facility:** 143 units. 70 one-bedroom standard units, some with kitchens. 70 one- and 3 two-bedroom suites with kitchens. 14 stories, exterior corridors. **Parking:** on-site. **Terms:** check-in 4 pm, 3 day cancellation notice-fee imposed. **Amenities:** voice mail, irons. *Some:* CD players. **Pool(s):** 3 outdoor. **Leisure Activities:** whirlpools, 4 tennis courts. **Guest Services:** complimentary laundry. **Business Services:** fax (fee). **Cards:** AX, DC, MC, VI.

SHERATON FIESTA
Phone: (956)761-6551

AAA [SAVE] ▼▼▼▼

Resort
Large-scale Hotel

3/1-3/29	1P: $129-$470	2P: $129-$470
3/30-9/30	1P: $119-$470	2P: $119-$470
10/1-1/31	1P: $79-$470	2P: $79-$470
2/1-2/28	1P: $79-$380	2P: $79-$380

Location: Just s of Queen Isabella Cswy. Located on the beach. 310 Padre Blvd 78597. Fax: 956/761-4181. **Facility:** All rooms at this property on the gulf have balconies overlooking the water. 256 units. 200 one- and 56 two-bedroom standard units. 12 stories, interior corridors. **Parking:** on-site. **Terms:** 3 day cancellation notice-fee imposed, package plans. **Amenities:** video games, voice mail, irons, hair dryers. **Dining:** 6 am-10 pm, Fri & Sat-11 pm, cocktails, nightclub, entertainment. **Pool(s):** outdoor, heated outdoor, wading. **Leisure Activities:** whirlpool, fishing, 4 lighted tennis courts, exercise room. **Guest Services:** gift shop, coin laundry, area transportation (fee). **Business Services:** meeting rooms, fax (fee). **Cards:** AX, DC, DS, JC, MC, VI.

SOME UNITS

SUNCHASE IV CONDOMINIUMS BY SOUTH PADRE RESORT
Phone: (956)761-6818

▼▼▼ ▼▼▼

Condominium

All Year	1P: $115-$395	2P: $115-$395

Location: Queen Isabella Cswy, 0.6 mi n turn left; just before Sunchase Mall. 1000 Padre Blvd 78597 (1004 Padre Blvd, Suite #K1). Fax: 956/761-1537. **Facility:** 72 units. 10 one-, 50 two- and 12 three-bedroom suites with kitchens, some with whirlpools. 14 stories, interior corridors. **Parking:** on-site. **Terms:** off-site registration, 3-7 night minimum stay - seasonal, 30 day cancellation notice-fee imposed, weekly rates available, $25 service charge. **Amenities:** irons. **Pool(s):** outdoor, heated outdoor, wading. **Leisure Activities:** sauna, whirlpool, steamroom, fishing, 4 tennis courts, racquetball courts, exercise room, basketball. **Guest Services:** complimentary laundry. **Business Services:** fax (fee). **Cards:** AX, MC, VI.

SOME UNITS

SUPER 8 MOTEL
Phone: 956/761-6300

▼▼▼ ▼▼▼

Small-scale Hotel

3/1-3/31 [ECP]	1P: $225-$275	2P: $250-$320	XP: $10 F12
4/1-8/13 [ECP]	1P: $45-$199	2P: $45-$199	XP: $10 F12
8/14-1/31 [ECP]	1P: $39-$99	2P: $39-$99	XP: $10 F12
2/1-2/28 [ECP]	1P: $35-$45	2P: $35-$45	XP: $10 F12

Location: 2.7 mi n of Queen Isabella Cswy. 4205 Padre Blvd 78597. Fax: 956/761-6300. **Facility:** 65 one-bedroom standard units, some with efficiencies and/or kitchens. 2 stories (no elevator), exterior corridors. *Bath:* combo or shower only. **Parking:** on-site. **Terms:** pets ($10 extra charge, dogs only). **Amenities:** hair dryers. **Pool(s):** outdoor. **Leisure Activities:** whirlpool. **Guest Services:** coin laundry. **Business Services:** meeting rooms, fax (fee). **Cards:** AX, DC, DS, MC, VI.

SOME UNITS

THE TIKI CONDOMINIUM HOTEL
Phone: 956/761-2694

▼▼▼ ▼

Condominium

5/24-9/4	1P: $150-$350	2P: $150-$350	XP: $7 F6
9/5-12/23	1P: $90-$170	2P: $90-$170	XP: $7 F6
2/1-5/23 & 12/24-1/31	1P: $96-$160	2P: $96-$160	XP: $7 F6

Location: 3.8 mi n of Queen Isabella Cswy. 6608 Padre Blvd 78597. Fax: 956/761-7538. **Facility:** 144 units. 120 one-, 16 two- and 8 three-bedroom suites with kitchens. 2-3 stories (no elevator), exterior corridors. **Parking:** on-site. **Terms:** 7 day cancellation notice, weekly rates available, small pets only ($2-$35 extra charge). **Amenities:** voice mail. **Pool(s):** 2 heated outdoor. **Leisure Activities:** sauna, whirlpool, fishing. **Guest Services:** coin laundry. **Business Services:** meeting rooms, fax (fee). **Cards:** AX, CB, DC, DS, MC, VI.

SOME UNITS

————— **The following lodgings were either not evaluated or did not** —————
meet AAA rating requirements but are listed for your information only.

GALLEON BAY CLUB   **Phone: 956/761-7808**
[fyi]   Not evaluated. **Location:** Jct Capricorn St. 4901 Laguna Blvd 78597. Facilities, services, and decor characterize a mid-range property.

SEASCAPE CONDOMINIUMS   **Phone: 956/761-7168**
[fyi]   Not evaluated. **Location:** 117 E Verna Jean 78597. Facilities, services, and decor characterize a mid-range property.

——————— **WHERE TO DINE** ———————

LOUIE'S BACKYARD   **Dinner:** $15-$18   **Phone: 956/761-6406**
Location: 1.5 mi n of Queen Isabella Cswy at corner Ling and Laguna Blvd. 2305 Laguna Blvd 78597. **Hours:** 5 pm-10 pm. **Features:** The waterfront dining area is the perfect place to watch a splendid sunset and to catch a tropical breeze. Seafood and hand-cut steaks are served by a friendly wait staff. The upstairs
Seafood   sports bar has 14 televisions to satisfy even the biggest sports fan! Casual dress; cocktails; entertainment.
Parking: on-site. **Cards:** AX, DS, MC, VI.

SCAMPI'S   **Dinner:** $12-$24   **Phone: 956/761-1755**
Location: On bay; 3 mi n of Queen Isabella Cswy. 206 N Aries St 78597. **Hours:** 5 pm-10 pm, Fri & Sat-11 pm. Closed: 11/27; also 12/20-12/25; also Super Bowl Sun. **Features:** Experience an unforgettable panoramic view of the bay at this quaint restaurant. The primavera shrimp is served with a baked potato and
Seafood   seasoned, steamed vegetables. The Key lime pie is tangy and has a homemade taste like no other.
Cocktails. **Parking:** on-site. **Cards:** AX, CB, DC, DS, MC, VI.

SPRING —See Houston p. 442.

STAFFORD —See Houston p. 442.

STEPHENVILLE pop. 14,921

——————— **WHERE TO STAY** ———————

DAYS INN   **Phone: (254)968-3392**
[SAVE]   All Year   1P: $48-$58   2P: $56-$66   XP: $7   F12
Location: On US 377, just s of jct US 281. 701 South E Loop 76401. Fax: 254/968-3527. **Facility:** 60 one-bedroom standard units. 2 stories, exterior corridors. **Parking:** on-site. **Terms:** [CP] meal plan available, small pets
Small-scale Hotel   only (no puppies). **Amenities:** hair dryers. **Pool(s):** outdoor. **Business Services:** meeting rooms, fax.
Cards: AX, CB, DC, DS, JC, MC, VI.
SOME UNITS

HOLIDAY INN STEPHENVILLE   **Phone: (254)968-5256**
All Year   1P: $73-$93   2P: $78-$98   XP: $5   F18
Location: 1.5 mi s on US 377/167. 2865 W Washington St 76401. Fax: 254/968-4255. **Facility:** 100 one-bedroom standard units. 2 stories, exterior corridors. **Parking:** on-site. **Terms:** small pets only ($100 deposit).
Small-scale Hotel   **Amenities:** irons, hair dryers. **Pool(s):** outdoor. **Leisure Activities:** whirlpool. **Guest Services:** valet
laundry. **Business Services:** meeting rooms, fax (fee). **Cards:** AX, CB, DC, DS, MC, VI.
SOME UNITS

——————— **WHERE TO DINE** ———————

MONTANA RESTAURANT   **Lunch:** $7-$16   **Dinner:** $7-$16   **Phone: 254/968-5707**
Location: 0.9 mi s of Courthouse Square; between Lillian and McIlhaney sts. 1376 W Washington St 76401. **Hours:** 11 am-11 pm. Closed: 11/27, 12/25. **Features:** Rustic decor furnishes the cozy restaurant, which is
American   across from Tarleton State University near downtown. The menu lists simply prepared American and Mexican favorites. Casual dress; cocktails. **Parking:** on-site. **Cards:** AX, DC, DS, MC, VI.

SUGAR LAND —See Houston p. 444.

SULPHUR SPRINGS pop. 14,551

——————— **WHERE TO STAY** ———————

BEST WESTERN TRAIL DUST INN   **Phone: (903)885-7515**
[SAVE]   All Year [ECP]   1P: $59-$69   2P: $59-$69   XP: $5   F18
Location: Jct I-30 and Loop 301, exit 127. 1521 Shannon Rd 75482 (PO Box 789, 75483). Fax: 903/885-7515. **Facility:** 101 units. 87 one-bedroom standard units. 14 one-bedroom suites ($74-$84), some with whirlpools. 2 stories, interior/exterior corridors. *Bath:* combo or shower only. **Parking:** on-site. **Terms:** 3 day cancellation
Small-scale Hotel   notice, small pets only. **Amenities:** video games (fee), irons, hair dryers. **Pool(s):** outdoor. **Guest Services:** valet and coin laundry. **Business Services:** meeting rooms, fax (fee). **Cards:** AX, CB, DC, DS, MC, VI.
SOME UNITS

COMFORT SUITES

Phone: (903)438-0918

AAA [SAVE]

All Year [ECP]   1P: $74-$99   2P: $74-$99   XP: $5   F18
Location: I-30, exit 127, just n. 1521 E Industrial 75482-0789 (PO Box 789, 75483-0789). Fax: 903/438-0329. **Facility:** 60 units. 58 one-bedroom standard units. 2 one-bedroom suites. 3 stories, interior corridors. *Bath:* combo or shower only. **Parking:** on-site. **Terms:** pets (in smoking units). **Amenities:** video library (fee), dual

Small-scale Hotel   phone lines, voice mail, irons, hair dryers. **Pool(s):** outdoor. **Leisure Activities:** exercise room. **Guest Services:** valet and coin laundry, airport transportation-Sulphur Springs Airport. **Business Services:** meeting rooms, fax (fee). **Cards:** AX, CB, DC, DS, MC, VI. **Special Amenities:** free continental breakfast and free local telephone calls.

SOME UNITS

HOLIDAY INN

Phone: (903)885-0562

All Year   1P: $64   2P: $74   XP: $5   F18
Location: I-30, exit 127. 1495 E Industrial Dr 75482. Fax: 903/885-0562. **Facility:** 97 units. 95 one-bedroom standard units. 2 one-bedroom suites ($84-$94). 2 stories, interior/exterior corridors. **Parking:** on-site. **Terms:** 3

Small-scale Hotel   day cancellation notice, small pets only. **Amenities:** video games (fee), dual phone lines, voice mail, irons, hair dryers. **Pool(s):** outdoor. **Leisure Activities:** exercise room. **Guest Services:** valet and coin laundry. **Business Services:** meeting rooms, fax (fee). **Cards:** AX, CB, DC, DS, JC, MC, VI.

SOME UNITS

SWEETWATER pop. 11,415

——— WHERE TO STAY ———

COMFORT INN

Phone: (325)235-5234

AAA [SAVE]

6/1-8/31	1P: $62-$82	2P: $62-$89	XP: $10 F18
2/1-5/31	1P: $59-$79	2P: $59-$79	XP: $10 F18
9/1-1/31	1P: $59-$69	2P: $59-$79	XP: $10 F18

Location: I-20, exit 244. 216 SE Georgia Ave 79556. Fax: 325/235-5395. **Facility:** 44 one-bedroom standard

Motel   units. 2 stories (no elevator), exterior corridors. *Bath:* combo or shower only. **Parking:** on-site. **Terms:** [ECP] meal plan available, small pets only. **Amenities:** irons, hair dryers. **Pool(s):** outdoor. **Leisure Activities:** limited exercise equipment. **Business Services:** meeting rooms, fax (fee). **Cards:** AX, CB, DC, DS, MC, VI. **Special Amenities:** free continental breakfast and free local telephone calls.

SOME UNITS

HOLIDAY INN

Phone: (325)236-6887

All Year   1P: $59-$99   XP: $10   F
Location: I-20, exit 244, just w of jct SR 70 on north access road. 500 NW Georgia St 79556 (PO Box 157). Fax: 325/236-6887. **Facility:** 110 units. 108 one-bedroom standard units. 2 one-bedroom suites ($89-$149). 2 stories (no elevator), interior/exterior corridors. **Parking:** on-site. **Terms:** check-in 4 pm, pets ($25 fee).

Small-scale Hotel   **Amenities:** *Some:* irons, hair dryers. **Pool(s):** outdoor. **Leisure Activities:** limited exercise equipment. **Guest Services:** coin laundry, airport transportation-Abilene Airport, area transportation-within 6 mi. **Business Services:** meeting rooms, fax (fee). **Cards:** AX, DC, DS, MC, VI. **Special Amenities:** free local telephone calls and free newspaper.

SOME UNITS

MULBERRY MANSION

Phone: (325)235-3811

All Year [BP]   1P: $70-$225   2P: $70-$225   XP: $15   F18
Location: I-20, exit 244, 0.4 mi n on Lamar St to Texas Ave, then 0.3 mi w. 1400 Sam Houston St 79556. Fax: 325/235-4701. **Facility:** This restored 1913 home of 10,000 square feet features Spanish Revival archi-

Historic Bed & Breakfast   tecture and a distinctive atrium room; guest rooms are spacious. 7 units. 6 one- and 1 two-bedroom standard units. 2 stories (no elevator), interior/exterior corridors. *Bath:* combo or shower only. **Parking:** on-site. **Terms:** weekly rates available, package plans. **Amenities:** CD players, hair dryers. **Leisure Activities:** exercise room. **Business Services:** business center. **Cards:** AX, CB, DC, DS, JC, MC, VI.

SOME UNITS

RANCH HOUSE MOTEL & RESTAURANT

Phone: 325/236-6341

AAA [SAVE]

All Year [BP]   1P: $37-$53   2P: $49-$62   XP: $6   F12
Location: I-20, exit 244, just w of jct SR 70 on south access road. 301 SW Georgia Ave 79556. Fax: 325/235-1536. **Facility:** 49 one-bedroom standard units. 2 stories (no elevator), interior/exterior corridors. **Parking:** on-site. **Terms:** package plans, pets (in smoking units). **Amenities:** *Some:* irons, hair dryers. **Dining:** 6 am-2 pm.

Motel   **Pool(s):** outdoor, wading. **Leisure Activities:** horse stables. **Business Services:** fax (fee). **Cards:** AX, DC, DS, MC, VI. **Special Amenities:** early check-in/late check-out and free continental breakfast.

SOME UNITS

——— WHERE TO DINE ———

BUCK'S STEAKS & BBQ

Lunch: $4-$25   **Dinner:** $4-$25   **Phone:** 325/235-4049
Location: I-20, exit 244. 103 SW Georgia 79556. **Hours:** 11 am-9 pm, Fri & Sat-10 pm. Closed: 11/27, 12/25.

American   **Features:** The rustic family restaurant serves steaks, pork chops, chicken, quail and a barbecue buffet, including brisket, ham, sausage and ribs. Burgers and a children's menu are also available. Casual dress. **Parking:** on-site. **Cards:** AX, DS, MC, VI.

TAYLOR pop. 13,575

———— **WHERE TO STAY** ————

REGENCY INN

Motel

Phone: 512/352-2666

All Year   1P: $47-$49   2P: $52-$57   XP: $5   F13
Location: 1.3 mi n on SR 95. 2007 N Main 76574. Fax: 512/352-5002. **Facility:** 25 one-bedroom standard units. 2 stories, exterior corridors. **Parking:** on-site. **Terms:** cancellation fee imposed, weekly rates available, pets ($50 deposit). **Business Services:** fax (fee). **Cards:** AX, CB, DC, DS, MC, VI.

SOME UNITS

TEMPLE pop. 54,514

———— **WHERE TO STAY** ————

COMFORT SUITES

SAVE

Small-scale Hotel

Phone: (254)770-0300

All Year [CP]   1P: $55-$79   2P: $60-$89   XP: $6   F17
Location: I-35, exit 302. 1415 N General Bruce Dr 76504. Fax: 254/770-0110. **Facility:** 58 one-bedroom standard units. 2 stories, interior corridors. *Bath:* combo or shower only. **Parking:** on-site. **Amenities:** high-speed Internet, voice mail, irons, hair dryers. **Pool(s):** outdoor. **Guest Services:** coin laundry. **Business Services:** meeting rooms; fax (fee). **Cards:** AX, CB, DC, DS, JC, MC, VI.

SOME UNITS

DAYS INN

SAVE

Small-scale Hotel

Phone: (254)774-9223

All Year   1P: $49   2P: $69   XP: $5   F12
Location: I-35, exit 302 (Nugent Ave). 1104 N General Bruce Dr 76504. Fax: 254/774-7568. **Facility:** 58 one-bedroom standard units. 2 stories, exterior corridors. *Bath:* combo or shower only. **Parking:** on-site. **Terms:** [ECP] meal plan available, small pets only ($7 extra charge). **Amenities:** irons, hair dryers. **Pool(s):** outdoor. **Guest Services:** coin laundry. **Business Services:** meeting rooms, fax (fee). **Cards:** AX, DC, DS, MC, VI.

SOME UNITS

FAIRFIELD INN BY MARRIOTT

SAVE

Small-scale Hotel

Phone: (254)771-3030

All Year [ECP]   1P: $64-$79   2P: $64-$89   XP: $6   F18
Location: 0.5 mi s on Loop 363, US 190 at jct SR 36. 1402 SW H K Dodgen Loop 76504. Fax: 254/771-3030. **Facility:** 62 one-bedroom standard units. 3 stories, interior corridors. *Bath:* combo or shower only. **Parking:** on-site. **Terms:** 14 day cancellation notice. **Amenities:** irons. *Some:* hair dryers. **Pool(s):** small heated indoor. **Leisure Activities:** whirlpool. **Guest Services:** valet laundry. **Business Services:** fax (fee). **Cards:** AX, CB, DC, DS, MC, VI.

SOME UNITS

HAMPTON INN

SAVE

Small-scale Hotel

Phone: (254)778-6700

All Year [ECP]   1P: $65-$85   2P: $65-$95   XP: $6   F18
Location: 1.5 mi s on Loop 363, US 190 at jct SR 36. 1414 SW H K Dodgen Loop 76504. Fax: 254/778-4044. **Facility:** 62 one-bedroom standard units. 3 stories, interior corridors. *Bath:* combo or shower only. **Parking:** on-site. **Terms:** 14 day cancellation notice. **Amenities:** voice mail, irons, hair dryers. **Pool(s):** heated indoor. **Leisure Activities:** whirlpool. **Guest Services:** valet laundry. **Business Services:** fax (fee). **Cards:** AX, CB, DC, DS, MC, VI.

SOME UNITS

HOLIDAY INN EXPRESS

Small-scale Hotel

Phone: (254)770-1100

All Year   1P: $75   2P: $75   XP: $5
Location: I-35, exit 302 (Nugent Ave). 1610 W Nugent Ave 76504. Fax: 254/770-1500. **Facility:** 61 one-bedroom standard units. 3 stories, interior corridors. *Bath:* combo or shower only. **Parking:** on-site. **Amenities:** high-speed Internet, voice mail, irons, hair dryers. **Pool(s):** outdoor. **Leisure Activities:** exercise room. **Guest Services:** valet and coin laundry. **Business Services:** meeting rooms, fax (fee). **Cards:** AX, CB, DC, DS, MC, VI.

SOME UNITS

HOWARD JOHNSON EXPRESS INN & SUITES

Small-scale Hotel

Phone: (254)778-5521

All Year [CP]   1P: $55   2P: $59   XP: $3
Location: 0.4 mi ne jct Loop 363, US 190 and SR 36. 1912 S 31st St 76504. Fax: 254/770-3211. **Facility:** 50 one-bedroom standard units. 2 stories, exterior corridors. **Parking:** on-site. **Terms:** [ECP] meal plan available, package plans, small pets only ($5 extra charge). **Amenities:** hair dryers. *Some:* irons. **Guest Services:** coin laundry. **Business Services:** fax (fee). **Cards:** AX, DC, DS, MC, VI.

SOME UNITS

THE INN AT SCOTT AND WHITE

(AAA) SAVE

Small-scale Hotel

Phone: (254)778-5511

All Year   1P: $66-$76   2P: $86   XP: $9   F12
Location: 3 mi sw on FM 1741, 0.3 mi ne jct Loop 363, US 190 and SR 36. Located adjacent to Scott and White Memorial Hospital. 2625 S 31st St 76504. Fax: 254/773-3161. **Facility:** 129 units. 125 one-bedroom standard units. 4 one-bedroom suites ($125-$135). 2 stories, interior/exterior corridors. **Parking:** on-site. **Terms:** [BP] meal plan available, 15% service charge, small pets only. **Amenities:** voice mail, irons, hair dryers. **Dining:** 6:30 am-2 & 4-9 pm, Fri-Sun to 2 pm. **Pool(s):** outdoor. **Guest Services:** gift shop, valet laundry, airport transportation-Draughn-Miller Airport. **Business Services:** meeting rooms, fax (fee). **Cards:** AX, CB, DC, MC, VI. **Special Amenities:** free local telephone calls and free newspaper.

SOME UNITS

LA QUINTA INN-TEMPLE

SAVE

Small-scale Hotel

Phone: (254)771-2980

All Year   1P: $59-$79   2P: $69-$89   XP: $10   F18

Location: SR 53, just e, jct I-35 and US 81, exit 301. 1604 W Barton Ave 76501-2457. **Fax:** 254/778-7565. **Facility:** 106 units. 104 one-bedroom standard units. 2 one-bedroom suites. 3 stories, interior/exterior corridors. **Parking:** on-site. **Terms:** [ECP] meal plan available, small pets only. **Amenities:** video games (fee), voice mail, irons, hair dryers. **Pool(s):** outdoor. **Guest Services:** area transportation. **Business Services:** fax (fee). **Cards:** AX, CB, DC, DS, JC, MC, VI.

SOME UNITS

MOTEL 6 - 257

Small-scale Hotel

Phone: 254/778-0272

5/22-1/31   1P: $31-$41   2P: $37-$47   XP: $3   F17
2/1-5/21   1P: $29-$39   2P: $35-$45   XP: $3   F17

Location: I-35, exit 302 (Nugent Ave), just s on access, follow signs. 1100 N General Bruce Dr 76504. **Fax:** 254/778-1839. **Facility:** 95 one-bedroom standard units. 2 stories, exterior corridors. *Bath:* shower only. **Parking:** on-site. **Terms:** small pets only. **Pool(s):** outdoor. **Guest Services:** coin laundry. **Business Services:** fax (fee). **Cards:** AX, CB, DC, DS, MC, VI.

SOME UNITS

SUPER 8 MOTEL

AAA **SAVE**

Small-scale Hotel

Phone: 254/778-0962

All Year   1P: $45-$60   2P: $50-$70   XP: $6   F12

Location: I-35, exit 297 (Midway Dr). 5505 S General Bruce Dr 76502. **Fax:** 254/778-1527. **Facility:** 96 one-bedroom standard units. 2 stories, exterior corridors. **Parking:** on-site. **Terms:** 7 day cancellation notice, [CP] meal plan available, small pets only ($5 extra charge). **Pool(s):** outdoor. **Guest Services:** valet and coin laundry. **Business Services:** meeting rooms, fax (fee). **Cards:** AX, CB, DC, DS, MC, VI. **Special Amenities:** free continental breakfast and free local telephone calls.

SOME UNITS

------- WHERE TO DINE -------

EMPEROR'S OF CHINA

Chinese

Lunch: $7-$14   **Dinner:** $7-$14   **Phone:** 254/774-7955

Location: I-35, exit 299 (Loop 363), e on SW H K Dodgen (Loop 363), 2.4 mi. 220 SW H K Dodgen Loop 76504. **Hours:** 11 am-10 pm, Fri & Sat-10:30 pm. **Closed:** 11/27, 12/25. **Reservations:** accepted. **Features:** Casual dress; cocktails. **Parking:** on-site. **Cards:** AX, CB, DC, DS, MC, VI.

MONTEREY'S LITTLE MEXICO

Tex-Mex

Lunch: $7-$10   **Dinner:** $7-$10   **Phone:** 254/778-9212

Location: 0.7 mi s on Loop 363, US 190 at jct SR 36. 1712 SW Dodgen Loop 76504. **Hours:** 11 am-10 pm, Fri & Sat-11 pm. **Closed:** 11/27, 12/25. **Features:** Serving traditional Tex-Mex cuisine since 1955, the family-friendly restaurant serves up a festive mercado atmosphere and tasty fajitas. Casual dress; cocktails. **Parking:** on-site. **Cards:** AX, DS, MC, VI.

TERLINGUA

------- WHERE TO STAY -------

BIG BEND MOTOR INN

AAA **SAVE**

Motel

Phone: (432)371-2218

2/1-7/6 & 9/1-1/31   1P: $75-$82   2P: $85-$87   XP: $5   F6
7/7-8/31   1P: $70-$77   2P: $75-$82   XP: $5   F6

Location: SR 118, 2 mi from entrance of Big Bend National Park. 79852 (PO Box 336). **Fax:** 432/371-2555. **Facility:** 50 units. 45 one-bedroom standard units, some with efficiencies (no utensils). 5 two-bedroom suites with kitchens (no utensils). 1 story, exterior corridors. **Parking:** on-site. **Terms:** 7 day cancellation notice-fee imposed, pets (in smoking units). **Guest Services:** gift shop, coin laundry. **Business Services:** fax. **Cards:** AX, DC, DS, MC, VI.

SOME UNITS

TERRELL —See Dallas p. 317.

TEXARKANA pop. 34,782

------- WHERE TO STAY -------

BEST WESTERN NORTHGATE INN

AAA **SAVE**

Small-scale Hotel

Phone: (903)793-6565

All Year [CP]   1P: $50-$60   2P: $55-$65   XP: $5   F12

Location: I-30, exit 223B, on northwest frontage road. 400 W 53rd St 75503. **Fax:** 903/793-3171. **Facility:** 64 one-bedroom standard units. 2 stories, interior corridors. **Parking:** on-site. **Terms:** 14 day cancellation notice, small pets only ($20 fee). **Amenities:** irons, hair dryers. **Pool(s):** outdoor. **Leisure Activities:** putting green. **Guest Services:** valet and coin laundry. **Business Services:** fax (fee). **Cards:** AX, CB, DC, DS, MC, VI. **Special Amenities:** free continental breakfast.

SOME UNITS

COMFORT SUITES

SAVE

Small-scale Hotel

Phone: (903)223-0951

All Year   1P: $89-$120   2P: $89-$129   XP: $10   F18

Location: I-30, exit 220B. 215 Richill Dr 75503 (1920 N Washington, MAGNOLIA, AR, 71753). **Fax:** 903/223-0729. **Facility:** 70 units. 68 one- and 2 two-bedroom standard units. 3 stories, interior corridors. *Bath:* combo or shower only. **Parking:** on-site. **Terms:** cancellation fee imposed, [CP] meal plan available. **Amenities:** dual phone lines, voice mail, irons, hair dryers. *Some:* safes. **Pool(s):** outdoor, heated indoor. **Leisure Activities:** putting green, exercise room. **Guest Services:** valet and coin laundry, area transportation. **Business Services:** meeting rooms, business center. **Cards:** AX, CB, DC, DS, JC, MC, VI.

SOME UNITS

FOUR POINTS HOTEL SHERATON TEXARKANA

Phone: (903)792-3222

All Year   1P: $75-$105   2P: $75-$105   XP: $10   F12

Location: I-30, exit 223B. 5301 N State Line Ave 75503. Fax: 903/793-3930. **Facility:** 147 one-bedroom standard units, some with whirlpools. 6 stories, interior corridors. **Parking:** on-site. **Terms:** cancellation fee imposed, pets ($25 extra charge). **Amenities:** voice mail, irons, hair dryers. **Dining:** 5 pm-10 pm; closed Sun & Mon, Small-scale Hotel cocktails. **Pool(s):** heated indoor. **Leisure Activities:** whirlpool, limited exercise equipment. **Guest Services:** valet laundry, airport transportation-Texarkana Municipal Airport. area transportation-within 5 mi. **Business Services:** meeting rooms, fax (fee). **Cards:** AX, DC, DS, MC, VI. **Special Amenities:** early check-in/late check-out and free newspaper.

SOME UNITS

HOLIDAY INN EXPRESS

Phone: 903/792-3366

All Year   1P: $79-$129   2P: $79-$129   F

Location: I-30, exit 223B, 0.3 mi n on US 71. 5401 N State Line Ave 75503. Fax: 903/792-5649. **Facility:** 120 one-Small-scale Hotel bedroom standard units, some with whirlpools. 3 stories, interior corridors. **Parking:** on-site. **Terms:** small pets only ($25 fee, $100 deposit). **Amenities:** dual phone lines, voice mail, irons, hair dryers. **Pool(s):** outdoor. **Leisure Activities:** whirlpool. **Guest Services:** valet and coin laundry. **Business Services:** fax (fee). **Cards:** AX, DC, DS, MC, VI.

SOME UNITS

LA QUINTA INN-TEXARKANA

Phone: (903)794-1900

All Year   1P: $65-$75   2P: $75-$85   XP: $10   F18

Location: I-30, exit 223A, sw of jct US 59 and 71. 5201 State Line Ave 75503. Fax: 903/792-5506. **Facility:** 130 units. 128 one-bedroom standard units. 2 one-bedroom suites. 2 stories, exterior corridors. **Parking:** on-site. **Terms:** [ECP] meal plan available, small pets only. **Amenities:** video games (fee), voice mail, irons, hair Small-scale Hotel dryers. **Pool(s):** outdoor. **Guest Services:** valet laundry, airport transportation-Texarkana Municipal Airport. **Business Services:** fax (fee). **Cards:** AX, CB, DC, DS, JC, MC, VI. **Special Amenities:** free continental breakfast and free local telephone calls.

SOME UNITS

FEE

MOTEL 6 - 201

Phone: 903/793-1413

All Year   1P: $33   2P: $36

Motel

Location: I-30, exit 222 (Summerhill Rd). 1924 Hampton Rd 75503. Fax: 903/793-5831. **Facility:** 100 one-bedroom standard units. 2 stories, exterior corridors. **Bath:** shower only. **Parking:** on-site. **Terms:** weekly rates available. **Pool(s):** outdoor. **Guest Services:** coin laundry. **Business Services:** fax (fee). **Cards:** AX, DC, DS, MC, VI.

SOME UNITS

——— WHERE TO DINE ———

BRYCE'S CAFETERIA

Lunch: $8-$12   **Dinner:** $8-$12   **Phone:** 903/792-1611

American

Location: I-30, exit 222 (Summerhill Rd). 0.3 mi sw. 2021 Mall Dr 75503. **Hours:** 11 am-2 & 5-8 pm, Sat & Sun from 11 am. Closed: 1/1, 12/25. **Features:** Classic American favorites are offered at the traditional cafeteria, a great place for diners who are looking for generous portions of hearty comfort food. Casual dress. **Parking:** on-site. **Cards:** AX, DS, MC, VI.

TEXARKANA, AR

——— WHERE TO STAY ———

BAYMONT INN & SUITES TEXARKANA

Phone: (870)773-1000

All Year [ECP]   1P: $64-$74   2P: $64-$74

Location: I-30, exit 223B, just n. 5102 N State Line Ave 71854. Fax: 870/773-5000. **Facility:** 103 units. 99 one-bedroom standard units. 4 one-bedroom suites ($74-$119), some with kitchens. 4 stories, interior corridors. **Parking:** on-site. **Terms:** small pets only. **Amenities:** video games (fee), voice mail, irons, hair dryers. Small-scale Hotel **Pool(s):** outdoor. **Guest Services:** valet and coin laundry. **Cards:** AX, CB, DC, DS, MC, VI. **Special Amenities:** free continental breakfast and free newspaper.

SOME UNITS

BEST WESTERN KINGS ROW INN & SUITES

Phone: (870)774-3851

(AAA) [SAVE]

All Year [ECP]   1P: $60-$65   2P: $65-$70   XP: $5   F12

Location: I-30, exit 223A, just s. 4200 N State Line Ave 71854. Fax: 870/772-8440. **Facility:** 114 one-bedroom standard units. 2 stories (no elevator), interior/exterior corridors. *Bath:* combo or shower only. **Parking:** on-site. **Terms:** small pets only ($20 deposit). **Amenities:** irons, hair dryers. **Dining:** 6 am-2 & 5-10 pm. **Pool(s):** outdoor. **Guest Services:** valet and coin laundry, airport transportation-Texarkana Municipal Airport. **Business Services:** meeting rooms. **Cards:** AX, CB, DC, DS, MC, VI.

Small-scale Hotel

SOME UNITS

HOLIDAY INN TEXARKANA

Phone: (870)774-3521

All Year   1P: $88   2P: $88

Location: I-30, exit 223B, just n. 5100 N State Line Ave 71854. Fax: 870/772-3068. **Facility:** 210 one-bedroom standard units. 4 stories, interior corridors. *Bath:* combo or shower only. **Parking:** on-site. **Terms:** 7 day cancellation notice, small pets only ($25 fee). **Amenities:** voice mail, irons, hair dryers. **Pool(s):** indoor. **Leisure Activities:** sauna, whirlpool, exercise room. **Guest Services:** valet and coin laundry. **Business Services:** meeting rooms. **Cards:** AX, CB, DC, DS, JC, MC, VI.

Small-scale Hotel

SOME UNITS

QUALITY INN

Phone: (870)772-0070

(AAA) [SAVE]

All Year   1P: $69-$122   2P: $69-$122   XP: $5   F16

Location: I-30, exit 223B, just n. 5210 N State Line Ave 71854. Fax: 870/773-1408. **Facility:** 72 units. 71 one-bedroom standard units, some with whirlpools. 1 one-bedroom suite with kitchen. 2 stories, exterior corridors. **Parking:** on-site. **Terms:** [BP] meal plan available, small pets only ($25 extra charge). **Amenities:** irons, hair dryers. **Pool(s):** outdoor. **Leisure Activities:** exercise room. **Guest Services:** valet and coin laundry, airport transportation-Texarkana Municipal Airport. **Business Services:** meeting rooms. **Cards:** AX, CB, DC, DS, MC, VI.

Small-scale Hotel

SOME UNITS

------- WHERE TO DINE -------

CATTLEMANS STEAKHOUSE

Dinner: $13-$24   **Phone:** 870/774-4481

Steak House

Location: I-30, exit 223A, 0.5 mi s. 4018 State Line Ave 72632. **Hours:** 5:30 pm-10 pm, Fri & Sat-11 pm. Closed: 1/1, 11/27, 12/25; also Sun. **Reservations:** accepted. **Features:** Cattlemen's features the traditional steak dishes with basic presentation and preparation methods, but they also serve a nice variety of chicken and fried, broiled or blackened seafood. You'll find the service friendly and attentive. Casual dress; cocktails. **Parking:** on-site. **Cards:** AX, DS, MC, VI.

TEXAS CITY pop. 41,521

------- WHERE TO STAY -------

HAMPTON INN

Phone: (409)986-6686

[SAVE]

All Year [ECP]   1P: $65-$85   2P: $65-$95   XP: $6   F18

Location: I-45, exit 15 (Hitchcock FM 2004), just e. 2320 FM 2004 77591. Fax: 409/986-1267. **Facility:** 64 one-bedroom standard units. 3 stories, interior corridors. *Bath:* combo or shower only. **Parking:** on-site. **Terms:** 14 day cancellation notice. **Amenities:** voice mail, irons. **Pool(s):** heated indoor. **Leisure Activities:** whirlpool. **Guest Services:** valet laundry. **Business Services:** fax. **Cards:** AX, CB, DC, DS, MC, VI.

Small-scale Hotel

SOME UNITS

FEE

LA QUINTA INN

Phone: (409)948-3101

(AAA) [SAVE]

All Year   1P: $63-$75   2P: $68-$80   XP: $5   F18

Location: Jct SR 146 S and FM 1764, 5 mi se of I-45, exit 16 southbound; exit 15 northbound. 1121 Hwy 146 N 77590-6505. Fax: 400/945-4412. **Facility:** 121 one-bedroom standard units. 2 stories, exterior corridors. **Parking:** on-site. **Terms:** [ECP] meal plan available, small pets only. **Amenities:** video games (fee), voice mail, irons, hair dryers. **Pool(s):** outdoor. **Guest Services:** valet and coin laundry. **Business Services:** meeting rooms, fax (fee). **Cards:** AX, CB, DC, DS, JC, MC, VI. **Special Amenities:** free continental breakfast and free local telephone calls.

Small-scale Hotel

SOME UNITS

FEE

THREE RIVERS pop. 1,878

------- WHERE TO STAY -------

BASS INN

Phone: 361/786-3521

Motel

All Year   1P: $37   2P: $48   XP: $5   F12

Location: SR 72, 7.5 mi w of jct US 281. Located adjacent to Choke Canyon Lake. Hwy 72 W 78071 (Box 3349 Hwy 72 W). Fax: 361/786-4357. **Facility:** 31 units. 30 one-bedroom standard units. 1 one-bedroom suite ($75-$80) with kitchen (no utensils). 1 story, exterior corridors. **Parking:** on-site. **Terms:** small pets only. **Pool(s):** outdoor. **Business Services:** fax (fee). **Cards:** AX, DC, DS, MC, VI.

SOME UNITS

TOMBALL —*See Houston p. 444.*

TULIA pop. 5,117

——— WHERE TO STAY ———

SELECT INN OF TULIA
▼▼ ▼▼
Motel
MC, VI.

Phone: (806)995-3248
All Year   1P: $49-$59   2P: $54-$64   XP: $5   F12
Location: I-27, exit 74. Rt 1, Box 60 79088. **Fax:** 806/995-3106. **Facility:** 37 one-bedroom standard units, some with whirlpools. 1 story, exterior corridors. **Parking:** on-site. **Terms:** [CP] meal plan available, small pets only ($5 extra charge, in smoking units). **Pool(s):** outdoor. **Guest Services:** coin laundry. **Cards:** AX, DC, DS,

SOME UNITS
[ASK] [S/D] [🐾] [🍴] [&M] [🛥] [📽] [DATA PORT] [💻] / [✕] [🔒] [📠] /

TYLER pop. 83,650

——— WHERE TO STAY ———

BEST WESTERN INN & SUITES
AAA [SAVE]
▼▼ ▼▼
Small-scale Hotel

Phone: (903)595-2681
All Year   1P: $59-$99   2P: $59-$99   XP: $5   F14
Location: Jct US 69 N and Loop 323. 2828 W NW Loop 323 75702. **Fax:** 903/592-5672. **Facility:** 90 units. 80 one-bedroom standard units, some with whirlpools. 10 one-bedroom suites ($69-$99), some with efficiencies and/or whirlpools. 2 stories, exterior corridors. *Bath:* combo or shower only. **Parking:** on-site. **Terms:** weekly rates available, [BP] meal plan available, pets ($10 extra charge). **Amenities:** irons, hair dryers. *Some:* high-speed Internet. **Pool(s):** outdoor, wading. **Leisure Activities:** exercise room. **Guest Services:** complimentary evening beverages: Mon-Thurs, valet and coin laundry, airport transportation-Tyler Pounds Field Airport. **Business Services:** meeting rooms, fax (fee). **Cards:** AX, CB, DC, DS, JC, MC, VI. **Special Amenities:** free continental breakfast and free room upgrade (subject to availability with advanced reservations).

SOME UNITS
[S/D] [✛] [🐾] [🍴] [🛥] [📽] [DATA PORT] [🔒] [💻] / [✕] [📠] /

FAIRFIELD INN
[SAVE]
▼▼▼ ▼▼
Small-scale Hotel

Phone: (903)561-2535
All Year [ECP]   1P: $64-$79   2P: $64-$89   XP: $6   F18
Location: 1.5 mi w of S US 69 on W Loop 323. 1945 W SW Loop 323 75701. **Fax:** 903/561-2535. **Facility:** 64 one-bedroom standard units. 3 stories, interior corridors. *Bath:* combo or shower only. **Parking:** on-site. **Terms:** 14 day cancellation notice. **Amenities:** irons. **Pool(s):** small heated indoor. **Leisure Activities:** whirlpool. **Guest Services:** valet and coin laundry. **Business Services:** fax (fee). **Cards:** AX, CB, DC, DS, MC, VI.

SOME UNITS
[S/D] [🍴] [&] [🛥] [📶] [📽] [DATA PORT] / [✕] [🔒] [📠] [💻] /

HAMPTON INN
[SAVE]
▼▼▼ ▼▼
Small-scale Hotel

Phone: (903)596-7752
All Year [CP]   1P: $72-$115   2P: $77-$115
Location: 3.5 mi se on SR 110, 0.3 mi n of jct E Loop 323. 3130 Troup Hwy 75701. **Fax:** 903/596-7765. **Facility:** 78 one-bedroom standard units, some with whirlpools. 3 stories, exterior corridors. *Bath:* combo or shower only. **Parking:** on-site. **Amenities:** voice mail, irons, hair dryers. **Pool(s):** heated indoor. **Leisure Activities:** whirlpool, exercise room. **Guest Services:** valet laundry. **Business Services:** meeting rooms, fax. **Cards:** AX, DC, DS, MC, VI.

SOME UNITS
[S/D] [🍴] [&] [🛥] [VCR] [📽] [DATA PORT] [🔒] [📠] [💻] / [✕] /

HOLIDAY INN EXPRESS HOTEL & SUITES
▼▼▼ ▼▼
Small-scale Hotel

Phone: (903)533-0214
All Year   1P: $76-$120   2P: $84-$130   XP: $6   F16
Location: Northeast corner of Loop 323 and US 69. 3247 W Gentry Pkwy 75702. **Fax:** 903/533-0083. **Facility:** 67 one-bedroom standard units, some with whirlpools. 3 stories, interior corridors. *Bath:* combo or shower only. **Parking:** on-site. **Terms:** 7 day cancellation notice, [CP] & [ECP] meal plans available. **Amenities:** high-speed Internet, dual phone lines, voice mail, irons, hair dryers. **Pool(s):** outdoor. **Leisure Activities:** whirlpool, exercise room. **Guest Services:** valet laundry. **Business Services:** meeting rooms, PC, fax (fee). **Cards:** AX, CB, DC, DS, MC, VI.

SOME UNITS
[ASK] [S/D] [&M] [🛥] [📽] [DATA PORT] [💻] / [✕] [🔒] [📠] /

HOLIDAY INN-SOUTHEAST CROSSING
▼▼▼ ▼▼
Small-scale Hotel

Phone: (903)593-3600
All Year   1P: $84   2P: $84   XP: $10   F18
Location: 3.5 mi se on SR 110, 0.3 mi n of jct E Loop 323. 3310 Troup Hwy 75701. **Fax:** 903/533-9571. **Facility:** 160 one-bedroom standard units. 2 stories, exterior corridors. **Parking:** on-site. **Terms:** 7 day cancellation notice, pets ($10 extra charge). **Amenities:** video games (fee), voice mail, irons, hair dryers. **Pool(s):** outdoor. **Guest Services:** valet and coin laundry. **Business Services:** meeting rooms, fax (fee). **Cards:** AX, DC, DS, JC, MC, VI.

SOME UNITS
[ASK] [S/D] [✛] [🐾] [🍴] [&] [🛥] [📶] [📽] [DATA PORT] [💻] / [✕] [🔒] [📠] /

LA QUINTA INN
AAA [SAVE]
▼▼▼ ▼▼
Motel

Phone: (903)561-2223
All Year   1P: $69-$84   2P: $79-$94   XP: $10   F18
Location: 1 mi w of S US 69 on W Loop 323. 1601 W SW Loop 323 75701-8533. **Fax:** 903/581-5708. **Facility:** 130 one-bedroom standard units. 2 stories, exterior corridors. **Parking:** on-site. **Terms:** [ECP] meal plan available, small pets only. **Amenities:** video games (fee), voice mail, irons, hair dryers. **Pool(s):** outdoor. **Guest Services:** valet laundry. **Business Services:** meeting rooms, fax (fee). **Cards:** AX, CB, DC, DS, JC, MC, VI. **Special Amenities:** free continental breakfast and free local telephone calls.

SOME UNITS
[S/D] [🐾] [🍴] [📄] [🛥] [📶] [📽] [DATA PORT] [💻] / [✕] /

RADISSON HOTEL TYLER

Phone: (903)597-1301

All Year [BP]   1P: $89-$109   2P: $89-$109   XP: $10   F17

Small-scale Hotel   **Location:** On Loop 323, just w of jct US 69. 2843 W NW Loop 323 75702-1333. Fax: 903/597-9437. **Facility:** 140 one-bedroom standard units, some with whirlpools. 4 stories, interior corridors. **Parking:** on-site. **Terms:** cancellation fee imposed, small pets only ($25 fee). **Amenities:** voice mail, safes (fee), irons, hair dryers. *Some:* fax. **Pool(s):** outdoor. **Leisure Activities:** exercise room. **Guest Services:** valet and coin laundry, area transportation. **Business Services:** conference facilities, fax. **Cards:** AX, DC, DS, MC, VI.

SOME UNITS

RESIDENCE INN BY MARRIOTT

Phone: 903/595-5188

SAVE

All Year [BP]   1P: $77   2P: $113

Small-scale Hotel   **Location:** 3.5 mi se on SR 110, 0.3 mi e E Loop 323. 3303 Troup Hwy 75701. Fax: 903/595-5719. **Facility:** 128 units. 96 one-bedroom standard units with kitchens. 32 one-bedroom suites ($71-$113) with kitchens. 2 stories, exterior corridors. *Bath:* combo or shower only. **Parking:** on-site. **Terms:** cancellation fee imposed, pets ($50 fee). **Amenities:** voice mail, irons, hair dryers. **Pool(s):** heated outdoor. **Leisure Activities:** whirlpool, sports court. **Guest Services:** complimentary evening beverages: Mon-Thurs, valet and coin laundry. **Business Services:** meeting rooms, fax (fee). **Cards:** AX, CB, DC, DS, JC, MC, VI.

SOME UNITS

SHERATON TYLER HOTEL

Phone: (903)561-5800

All Year   1P: $85   2P: $85

Small-scale Hotel   **Location:** 1.1 mi s of jct Loop 323 and US 69 (S Broadway). 5701 S Broadway 75703. Fax: 903/561-9916. **Facility:** 183 units. 178 one-bedroom standard units. 5 one-bedroom suites. 8 stories, interior corridors. *Bath:* combo or shower only. **Terms:** [AP] meal plan available, small pets only ($25 extra charge). **Amenities:** video games (fee), voice mail, irons, hair dryers. *Some:* fax. **Pool(s):** outdoor, wading. **Leisure Activities:** whirlpool, exercise room. **Guest Services:** sundries, valet laundry, area transportation. **Business Services:** meeting rooms, fax (fee). **Cards:** AX, CB, DC, DS, JC, MC, VI.

SOME UNITS

WINGATE INN

Phone: 903/566-0600

All Year [ECP]   1P: $77   2P: $87

Small-scale Hotel   **Location:** 0.3 mi e of SR 110, between SR 110 and Spur 248. 2421 East SE Loop 323 75701. Fax: 903/565-4049. **Facility:** 88 one-bedroom standard units, some with whirlpools. 4 stories, interior corridors. *Bath:* combo or shower only. **Parking:** on-site. **Amenities:** video games (fee), high-speed Internet, dual phone lines, voice mail, safes, irons, hair dryers. **Pool(s):** heated indoor. **Leisure Activities:** whirlpool, exercise room. **Guest Services:** coin laundry. **Business Services:** meeting rooms, business center. **Cards:** AX, DC, DS, MC, VI.

SOME UNITS

——— **WHERE TO DINE** ———

CACE'S SEAFOOD

Lunch: $5-$14   Dinner: $8-$16   Phone: 903/581-0744

Seafood   **Location:** 2.1 mi s on US 69 from jct Loop 323 and US 69. 7011 S Broadway 75703. **Hours:** 11 am-10 pm, Fri & Sat-10:30 pm, Sun 11 am-9 pm. Closed major holidays; also Mon. **Features:** Pictures of historic riverboats decorate the dark walls of this restaurant that has a warm, old-parlor feel. Heavy curtains drape the windows. Dig into generous portions of crisp salads, blackened fish and desserts. Casual dress; cocktails. **Parking:** on-site. **Cards:** AX, CB, DC, DS, MC, VI.

OXFORD STREET RESTAURANT

Lunch: $7-$14   Dinner: $11-$20   Phone: 903/593-2655

American   **Location:** 3.5 mi se on SR 110, 0.3 mi n of jct E Loop 323. 3300 Troup Hwy 75701. **Hours:** 11 am-2 & 5-9 pm, Sat 5 pm-10 pm, Sun 11 am-9 pm. Closed: 12/25. **Reservations:** accepted. **Features:** Subdued lighting creates a relaxing atmosphere at this candle-lit, classic cafe. Booths are separated by stained-glass dividers. The savory prime rib is tender and juicy. Smother the loaf of whole grain bread that accompanies your meal with butter. Casual dress; cocktails. **Parking:** on-site. **Cards:** AX, DC, DS, JC, MC, VI.

SWEET SUE'S RESTAURANT & BUFFET

Lunch: $3-$7   Dinner: $3-$7   Phone: 903/581-5464

American   **Location:** 4 mi sw of downtown and just w of SR 155 S on Loop 323. 3350 S SW Loop 323 75701. **Hours:** 6 am-9 pm, Sun-3 pm. Closed: 1/1, 7/4, 12/25. **Features:** Just minutes away from a lovely rose garden, this cafe offers a tasty buffet. The catfish, chicken-fried steak and meatloaf are homemade. The sweet cobblers are famous! Antique pictures of babies and lots of greenery decorate the dining room. Casual dress. **Parking:** on-site. **Cards:** AX, DS, MC, VI.

UNIVERSAL CITY —*See San Antonio p. 548.*

UTOPIA pop. 241

——— **WHERE TO DINE** ———

THE GARDEN OF EAT'N

Lunch: $2-$8   Dinner: $10-$18   Phone: 830/966-3391

Deli/Subs/ Sandwiches   **Location:** On SR 187; in center of town. 301 Main St 78884. **Hours:** Open 2/1-12/31; 9 am-5 pm, Sat 9 am-4 & 6-9 pm, Sun 11 am-2 pm. **Features:** "Down-home simple and down-home fresh" is the catch phrase at the small, family-operated delicatessen in the heart of Texas hill country. In addition to tried-and-true American favorites, the menu lists limited breakfast selections. Smoke free premises. Casual dress. **Parking:** street. **Cards:** DS, MC, VI.

UVALDE pop. 14,929

------ WHERE TO STAY ------

BEST WESTERN CONTINENTAL INN
Phone: 830/278-5671

[SAVE]

Motel

All Year — 1P: $56-$66 — 2P: $63-$78 — XP: $10 — F12
Location: 0.5 mi e on US 90. 701 E Main St 78801. Fax: 830/278-6351. **Facility:** 87 one-bedroom standard units. 1-2 stories, exterior corridors. **Parking:** on-site. **Terms:** small pets only (in smoking units). **Amenities:** irons, hair dryers. **Pool(s):** outdoor. **Guest Services:** valet laundry. **Business Services:** fax (fee). **Cards:** AX, DC, DS, MC, VI.

SOME UNITS

🛏 🛎 🐾 🛢 [DATA PORT] 💻 / ✕ 🖥 / FEE

HOLIDAY INN
Phone: (830)278-4511

Small-scale Hotel

All Year — 1P: $72-$86 — 2P: $72-$86 — XP: $8 — F18
Location: 0.5 mi e on US 90. 920 E Main St 78801. Fax: 830/591-0413. **Facility:** 114 one-bedroom standard units. 2 stories (no elevator), exterior corridors. **Parking:** on-site. **Terms:** small pets only. **Amenities:** irons, hair dryers. **Pool(s):** outdoor. **Guest Services:** valet and coin laundry. **Business Services:** meeting rooms, fax (fee). **Cards:** AX, CB, DC, DS, JC, MC, VI.

SOME UNITS

[ASK] [S/D] 🛏 🍴 🍷 🐾 🛢 [DATA PORT] 💻 / ✕ 🖥 📠 /

VANDERPOOL

------ WHERE TO STAY ------

------ *The following lodgings were either not evaluated or did not meet AAA rating requirements but are listed for your information only.* ------

THE LODGES AT LOST MAPLES
Phone: 830/966-5178

[fyi]

Cabin

Did not meet all AAA rating requirements for locking devices in some guest rooms at time of last evaluation on 04/08/2002. **Location:** Jct FM 187 and 337, 4 mi w. Lower Sabinal River Rd 78885 (PO Box 215). Facilities, services, and decor characterize a mid-range property.

TEXAS STAGECOACH INN
Phone: 830/966-6272

[fyi]

Bed & Breakfast

Did not meet all AAA rating requirements for locking devices in some guest rooms at time of last evaluation on 04/08/2002. **Location:** On FM 187, 4 mi s. Located on Sabinal River. TX 187 S 78885. Facilities, services, and decor characterize a mid-range property.

VAN HORN pop. 2,435

------ WHERE TO STAY ------

BEST WESTERN AMERICAN INN
Phone: (432)283-2030

[AAA] [SAVE]

Motel

All Year — 1P: $49-$69 — 2P: $55-$85 — XP: $8 — F12
Location: I-10, exit 138, 1 mi e. 1309 W Broadway 79855 (PO Box 626). Fax: 432/283-2779. **Facility:** 33 units. 31 one- and 2 two-bedroom standard units. 1 story, exterior corridors. **Parking:** on-site. **Terms:** [CP] meal plan available. **Amenities:** irons, hair dryers. **Pool(s):** outdoor. **Guest Services:** coin laundry. **Business Services:** fax (fee). **Cards:** AX, CB, DC, DS, MC, VI. **Special Amenities:** free continental breakfast and free newspaper. *(See color ad below)*

SOME UNITS

[S/D] 🛏 🍴 🐾 🛢 [DATA PORT] 🛢 💻 / ✕ [VCR] 📠 / FEE

BEST WESTERN INN OF VAN HORN

AAA SAVE

Motel

All Year [ECP]

Phone: 432/283-2410

| 1P: $39-$59 | 2P: $49-$79 | XP: $6 | F13 |

Location: I-10, exit 138, 0.3 mi e, 1 mi w on US 80. 1705 W Broadway 79855 (PO Box 309). **Fax:** 432/283-2143. **Facility:** 60 one-bedroom standard units. 1 story, exterior corridors. **Parking:** on-site. **Terms:** [CP] meal plan available. **Amenities:** irons, hair dryers. **Pool(s):** heated outdoor. **Guest Services:** coin laundry. **Business Services:** fax (fee). **Cards:** AX, CB, DC, DS, MC, VI. **Special Amenities:** early check-in/late check-out and free continental breakfast.

SOME UNITS

BUDGET INN

AAA SAVE

Motel

All Year

Phone: 432/283-2019

| 1P: $25-$40 | 2P: $30-$45 | XP: $3 |

Location: I-10, exit 138, 0.7 mi e. 1303 W Broadway 79855 (PO Box 734). **Fax:** 432/283-8058. **Facility:** 14 one-bedroom standard units. 1 story, exterior corridors. *Bath:* combo or shower only. **Parking:** on-site. **Terms:** small pets only ($3 extra charge). **Business Services:** fax (fee). **Cards:** AX, DC, DS, MC, VI.

SOME UNITS

DAYS INN

AAA SAVE

Motel

12/15-1/15
2/1-12/14 & 1/16-1/31

Phone: (432)283-1007

| 1P: $68-$78 | 2P: $75-$99 | XP: $6 | F12 |
| 1P: $52-$60 | 2P: $58-$70 | XP: $6 | F12 |

Location: I-10, exit 140B, just w. 600 E Broadway St 79855 (PO Box 128). **Fax:** 432/283-1189. **Facility:** 58 one-bedroom standard units. 1 story, exterior corridors. **Terms:** pets ($4-$8 extra charge). **Amenities:** hair dryers. **Pool(s):** outdoor. **Business Services:** fax (fee). **Cards:** AX, CB, DC, DS, MC, VI. **Special Amenities:** free continental breakfast and free local telephone calls.

SOME UNITS

ECONOMY INN

AAA SAVE

Motel

All Year

Phone: (432)283-2754

| 1P: $25-$28 | 2P: $30-$32 | XP: $40 |

Location: I-10, exit 138, 0.5 mi e on US 80. 1500 W Broadway St 79855 (PO Box 622). **Facility:** 16 one-bedroom standard units. 1 story, exterior corridors. **Parking:** on-site. **Terms:** 10 day cancellation notice, weekly rates available, [CP] meal plan available. **Cards:** AX, DC, DS, MC, VI. **Special Amenities:** free continental breakfast and free local telephone calls.

SOME UNITS

HOLIDAY INN EXPRESS

AAA SAVE

Small-scale Hotel

All Year [ECP]

Phone: (432)283-7444

| 1P: $69-$99 | 2P: $69-$99 |

Location: I-10, exit 138 (Golf Course Dr). 1905 SW Frontage Rd 79855 (PO Box 69). **Fax:** 432/283-7234. **Facility:** 45 one-bedroom standard units. 2 stories (no elevator), exterior corridors. **Parking:** on-site. **Terms:** small pets only. **Amenities:** irons, hair dryers. **Pool(s):** outdoor. **Business Services:** fax (fee). **Cards:** AX, CB, DC, DS, JC, MC, VI. **Special Amenities:** free continental breakfast and free local telephone calls. *(See color ad below)*

SOME UNITS

MOTEL 6 - 4024

AAA SAVE

Motel

All Year

Phone: 432/283-2992

| 1P: $45-$51 | 2P: $51-$55 | XP: $4 | F17 |

Location: I-10, exit 138. 1805 W Broadway St 79855 (PO Box 821). **Fax:** 432/283-2111. **Facility:** 40 one-bedroom standard units. 1 story, exterior corridors. **Parking:** on-site. **Pool(s):** heated outdoor. **Business Services:** fax (fee). **Cards:** AX, DC, DS, MC, VI. **Special Amenities:** free local telephone calls.

SOME UNITS

RAMADA LIMITED   Phone: (432)283-2780

⚑⚑ [SAVE]   All Year   1P: $48-$68   2P: $68-$88
⚑⚑⚑   Location: I-10, exit 138 (Golf Course Dr). 200 Golf Course Dr 79855 (PO Box 1568). Fax: 432/283-2804. **Facility:** 68
one-bedroom standard units. 2 stories, interior/exterior corridors. **Parking:** on-site. **Terms:** [BP] meal plan
available, small pets only ($6 extra charge). **Amenities:** voice mail. **Pool(s):** outdoor, wading. **Leisure Ac-**
Small-scale Hotel **tivities:** complimentary 9 hole greens fee. **Guest Services:** coin laundry. **Business Services:** meeting
rooms, fax (fee). **Cards:** AX, CB, DC, DS, MC, VI. **Special Amenities: free continental breakfast and free**
local telephone calls.

SOME UNITS
[S/D] [🐾] [🐕] [🍴] [DATA PORT] / [✕] [🛗] [🖥] [🖥] /

VAN HORN SUPER 8   Phone: (432)283-2282

⚑⚑ [SAVE]   12/15-1/15   1P: $68-$78   2P: $75-$99   XP: $6   F12
⚑⚑⚑   2/1-12/14 & 1/16-1/31   1P: $52-$60   2P: $58-$70   XP: $6   F12
Location: I-10, exit 138 (Golf Course Dr). 1807 E Service Rd 79855 (PO Box 189). Fax: 432/283-2292. **Facility:** 41
one-bedroom standard units. 2 stories (no elevator), exterior corridors. *Bath:* combo or shower only. **Parking:**
Small-scale Hotel on-site. **Terms:** pets ($5 extra charge). **Guest Services:** coin laundry. **Business Services:** fax (fee).
Cards: AX, CB, DC, DS, MC, VI. **Special Amenities: free continental breakfast and free local telephone**
calls.

SOME UNITS
[S/D] [🐾] [🍴] [🛗] [🐕] / [✕] [🛗] [🖥] /

─────── **WHERE TO DINE** ───────

CHUY'S RESTAURANT   Lunch: $4-$13   Dinner: $4-$13   Phone: 432/283-2066

⚑⚑   **Location:** I-10, exit 138. 1200 W Broadway St 79855. **Hours:** Closed: 4/20, 11/27, 12/25.
⚑⚑⚑   **Reservations:** accepted. **Features:** Fun and family-operated, the unpretentious cafe prepares requisite
Mexican dishes—such as tacos and enchiladas—as well as seafood, steak and chicken selections. Juicy
fajitas are served with new potatoes. Casual dress; beer & wine only. **Parking:** on-site. **Cards:** AX, DC,
Mexican   DS, MC, VI.
[✕]

SMOKE HOUSE RESTAURANT & AUTO MUSEUM   Lunch: $4-$13   Dinner: $6-$14   Phone: 432/283-2453

⚑⚑⚑   **Location:** I-10, exit 138. 905 W Broadway St 79855. **Hours:** 6 am-10 pm. Closed: 4/20, 11/27, 12/25.
Reservations: accepted. **Features:** The eatery shows off professionally restored cars and gas station
American   memorabilia. Smoked meats—such as ham, sausage and pork—are the specialty, and hearty hamburgers
are piled with lettuce and tomato. Sandwiches are stacked with fresh deli meats. Smoke free premises.
Casual dress. **Parking:** on-site. **Cards:** AX, DC, DS, MC, VI.
[✕]

VEGA pop. 936

─────── **WHERE TO STAY** ───────

BEST WESTERN COUNTRY INN   Phone: (806)267-2131

⚑⚑ [SAVE]   All Year   1P: $59-$79   2P: $69-$89   XP: $10   F18
⚑⚑⚑   **Location:** 0.5 mi w on US 40 business loop. 1800 W Vega Blvd 79092 (PO Box 350). Fax: 806/267-2134.
Facility: Designated smoking area. 41 one-bedroom standard units. 1 story, exterior corridors. **Parking:** on-
site. **Terms:** [ECP] meal plan available, small pets only. **Pool(s):** heated outdoor. **Business Services:**
Motel   meeting rooms, fax (fee). **Cards:** AX, CB, DC, DS, MC, VI. **Special Amenities: early check-in/late**
check-out and free continental breakfast.

SOME UNITS
[S/D] [🐾] [🐕] [🍴] [DATA PORT] [🖥] / [✕] /

COMFORT INN   Phone: (806)267-0126

⚑⚑ [SAVE]   All Year [CP]   1P: $69-$99   2P: $79-$120   XP: $5   F12
⚑⚑⚑   **Location:** I-40, exit 36. 1005 S Main 79092 (PO Box 690). Fax: 806/267-0126. **Facility:** 41 one-bedroom standard
units. 2 stories (no elevator), interior corridors. **Parking:** on-site. **Terms:** 14 day cancellation notice-fee im-
posed. **Amenities:** irons, hair dryers. **Pool(s):** small heated indoor. **Leisure Activities:** whirlpool, limited ex-
Motel   ercise equipment. **Guest Services:** coin laundry. **Business Services:** fax (fee). **Cards:** AX, CB, DC, DS, JC,
MC, VI. **Special Amenities: free continental breakfast and free local telephone calls.**

SOME UNITS
[S/D] [🐕] [🍴] [DATA PORT] [🛗] / [✕] [🖥] /

VERNON pop. 11,660

─────── **WHERE TO STAY** ───────

BEST WESTERN VILLAGE INN   Phone: (940)552-5417

[SAVE]   All Year   1P: $59-$64   2P: $59-$64   XP: $5   F17
⚑⚑⚑   **Location:** US 287, exit Main St, just w. 1615 Expwy 76384. Fax: 940/552-5417. **Facility:** 46 one-bedroom standard units. 2 stories (no elevator), interior/exterior corridors. **Parking:** on-site, winter plug-ins. **Terms:** small
pets only. **Amenities:** irons, hair dryers. **Pool(s):** heated outdoor. **Guest Services:** valet laundry. **Business**
Motel   **Services:** meeting rooms, fax (fee). **Cards:** AX, CB, DC, DS, JC, MC, VI.

SOME UNITS
[S/D] [➕] [🐕] [🍴] [🍷] [🐾] [🐾] [🍴] [DATA PORT] [🖥] / [✕] [🛗] [🖥] /

GREENTREE INN   Phone: (940)552-5421

⚑⚑⚑   3/1-8/15   1P: $49-$54   2P: $54-$69   XP: $5   F12
⚑⚑⚑   8/16-12/31   1P: $44-$49   2P: $49-$59   XP: $5   F12
Motel   2/1-2/28 & 1/1-1/31   1P: $44-$49   2P: $49-$54   XP: $5   F12
Location: US 287, exit Bentley St, just w. 3029 Morton St 76384. Fax: 940/552-5421. **Facility:** 30 one-bedroom
standard units. 1 story, exterior corridors. **Parking:** on-site, winter plug-ins. **Terms:** cancellation fee imposed. [CP] meal plan
available, small pets only ($5 extra charge). **Pool(s):** small outdoor. **Business Services:** fax (fee). **Cards:** AX, DS, MC, VI.

SOME UNITS
[ASK] [S/D] [🐕] [🍴] [🐾] [🐾] [DATA PORT] / [✕] /

VICTORIA pop. 60,603

-------- WHERE TO STAY --------

COMFORT INN
AAA SAVE
▼▼▼▼▼
Small-scale Hotel

Phone: 361/574-9393
All Year [CP]　　1P: $69-$80　　2P: $75-$85　　XP: $6　　F18
Location: 3.5 mi ne on US 59. 1906 Houston Hwy 77901. Fax: 361/574-9529. **Facility:** 50 one-bedroom standard units, some with whirlpools. 2 stories (no elevator), exterior corridors. **Parking:** on-site. **Terms:** 30 day cancellation notice-fee imposed, small pets only ($25 deposit). **Amenities:** hair dryers. *Some:* irons. **Pool(s):** outdoor. **Guest Services:** valet laundry. **Business Services:** fax (fee). **Cards:** AX, CB, DC, DS, JC, MC, VI. **Special Amenities: free continental breakfast and free local telephone calls.**

SOME UNITS

FAIRFIELD INN BY MARRIOTT
SAVE
▼▼▼▼
Small-scale Hotel

Phone: (361)582-0660
All Year [ECP]　　1P: $59-$79　　2P: $59-$89　　XP: $6　　F18
Location: US 77 at Loop 463. 7502 N Navarro St 77904. Fax: 361/582-0660. **Facility:** 64 one-bedroom standard units. 3 stories, interior corridors. *Bath:* combo or shower only. **Parking:** on-site. **Terms:** 14 day cancellation notice. **Amenities:** irons. **Pool(s):** small indoor. **Leisure Activities:** whirlpool. **Guest Services:** valet laundry. **Business Services:** fax (fee). **Cards:** AX, CB, DC, DS, MC, VI.

SOME UNITS

FRIENDLY OAKS BED AND BREAKFAST
▼▼▼▼
Historic Bed
& Breakfast

MC, VI.

Phone: 361/575-0000
All Year [BP]　　　　2P: $55-$80　　XP: $15　　F12
Location: Jct US 77 and Main St, 0.7 mi s on Main, just n. Located in a quiet neighborhood. 210 E Juan Linn St 77901. **Facility:** Individually themed rooms are featured at this B&B close to the town square. Smoke free premises. 4 one-bedroom standard units. 2 stories, interior corridors. *Bath:* combo or shower only. **Parking:** on-site. **Terms:** check-in 4 pm, age restrictions may apply, 3 day cancellation notice-fee imposed. **Cards:** AX, DC,

SOME UNITS

HAMPTON INN
SAVE
▼▼▼▼
Motel

Phone: 361/578-2030
All Year [CP]　　1P: $61　　2P: $67
Location: 2 mi ne on US 59. 3112 E Houston Hwy (Business Rt 59) 77901. Fax: 361/573-1238. **Facility:** 100 one-bedroom standard units. 2 stories (no elevator), exterior corridors. **Parking:** on-site. **Amenities:** voice mail, irons, hair dryers. **Pool(s):** outdoor. **Guest Services:** valet laundry, area transportation. **Business Services:** meeting rooms, fax (fee). **Cards:** AX, CB, DC, DS, MC, VI.

SOME UNITS
FEE FEE

HOLIDAY INN HOLIDOME
▼▼▼▼
Small-scale Hotel

hair dryers.
Guest Services:
MC, VI.

Phone: (361)575-0251
All Year　　1P: $90-$160　　2P: $90-$160　　XP: $10　　F18
Location: 2.5 mi ne on Business Rt US 59. 2705 E Houston Hwy (Business Rt 59) 77901. Fax: 361/575-8362. **Facility:** 226 one-bedroom standard units, some with whirlpools. 2 stories (no elevator), interior/exterior corridors. **Parking:** on-site. **Terms:** check-in 4 pm, small pets only ($150 deposit). **Amenities:** voice mail, irons, hair dryers. **Pool(s):** heated indoor/outdoor. **Leisure Activities:** sauna, whirlpool, limited exercise equipment. *Fee:* game room. **Guest Services:** valet and coin laundry. **Business Services:** meeting rooms, business center. **Cards:** AX, CB, DC, DS, JC, MC, VI.

SOME UNITS

LA QUINTA INN-VICTORIA
SAVE
▼▼▼▼
Motel

Phone: (361)572-3585
All Year　　1P: $65-$85　　2P: $71-$91
Location: 4 mi n on US 77 at jct Loop 463. Truck parking on premises. 7603 N Navarro (US 77 N) St 77904. Fax: 361/576-4617. **Facility:** 130 one-bedroom standard units. 2 stories (no elevator), exterior corridors. **Parking:** on-site. **Terms:** [ECP] meal plan available, small pets only. **Amenities:** video games (fee), voice mail, irons, hair dryers. **Pool(s):** outdoor. **Guest Services:** valet laundry. **Business Services:** meeting rooms, fax (fee). **Cards:** AX, CB, DC, DS, JC, MC, VI.

SOME UNITS

RAMADA INN
▼▼▼▼
Motel

pets only. **Amenities:**
ices: valet laundry. **Business Services:**

Phone: 361/578-2723
All Year　　1P: $69　　2P: $69　　XP: $10　　F18
Location: US 59 business route, 2.3 mi ne of jct US 77. Truck parking on premises. 3901 E Houston Hwy (Business Rt 59) 77901. Fax: 361/578-2723. **Facility:** 126 one-bedroom standard units, some with whirlpools. 2 stories (no elevator), exterior corridors. **Parking:** on-site. **Terms:** weekly rates available, [CP] meal plan available, small pets only. **Amenities:** voice mail. *Some:* irons, hair dryers. **Pool(s):** outdoor. **Leisure Activities:** sauna, whirlpool. **Guest Services:** valet laundry. **Business Services:** meeting rooms, fax (fee). **Cards:** AX, CB, DC, DS, JC, MC, VI.

SOME UNITS

-------- WHERE TO DINE --------

OLDE VICTORIA RESTAURANT
▼▼▼
Continental

Lunch: $7-$13　　Dinner: $10-$21　　Phone: 361/572-8840
Location: Jct US 77, 0.5 mi s. 207 N Navarro 77901. **Hours:** 11 am-2 & 5-10 pm, Sat 5 pm-10 pm. Closed major holidays; also Sun. **Reservations:** suggested. **Features:** On the perimeter of Old Town, the old house was converted to accommodate the restaurant. Intercontinental cuisine is well-prepared, and the menu offers good variety. The surroundings, which include white tablecloths and moderately sophisticated food presentations, hint at fine dining, but the service is casual and the experience stays away from coat-and-tie territory. Casual dress; cocktails. **Parking:** on-site. **Cards:** AX, DC, DS, MC, VI.

——— *The following restaurants have not been evaluated by AAA* ———
but are listed for your information only.

PELICAN'S WHARF   **Phone:** 361/578-5253
[fyi]   Not evaluated. **Location:** 2912 Houston Hwy 77901. **Features:** This is the place in Victoria you go for oysters on the half shell. Seafood is the specialty.

ROSEBUD FOUNTAIN & GRILL   **Phone:** 361/573-5111
[fyi]   Not evaluated. **Location:** Just s of jct US 77. 102 S Main St 77901. **Features:** Have a hankering for real old fashion malted milks and a great hamburger? Located in a corner brick building of old town Victoria, this is the place to revisit mom and dad's soda fountain.

WACO pop. 113,726

——— **WHERE TO STAY** ———

BEST WESTERN OLD MAIN LODGE   **Phone:** (254)753-0316
AAA SAVE   All Year   1P: $66-$85   2P: $72-$95
♦♦ ♦♦   **Location:** I-35 and US 81, exit 335A (4th-5th St). Located within easy access to the university. I-35 & 4th St 76706 (PO Box 174, 76703). Fax: 254/753-3811. **Facility:** 84 one-bedroom standard units. 2 stories, exterior corridors.
Parking: on-site. **Terms:** [ECP] meal plan available, small pets only. **Amenities:** voice mail, irons, hair
Small-scale Hotel   dryers. *Some:* safes. **Pool(s):** outdoor. **Guest Services:** valet laundry. **Business Services:** meeting rooms, fax (fee). **Cards:** AX, CB, DC, DS, JC, MC, VI. **Special Amenities: free continental breakfast and free newspaper.**

SOME UNITS

BEST WESTERN WACO MALL   **Phone:** (254)776-3194
SAVE   All Year   1P: $59-$65   2P: $66-$70   XP: $5   F17
♦♦ ♦♦   **Location:** On US 84, 0.3 mi w of jct SR 6 and Loop 340. 6624 Hwy 84 W 76712. Fax: 254/772-6047. **Facility:** 55 one-bedroom standard units. 2 stories, exterior corridors. **Parking:** on-site. **Terms:** small pets only ($10 extra charge). **Amenities:** irons, hair dryers. **Pool(s):** small outdoor. **Leisure Activities:** whirlpool. **Guest Serv-**
Small-scale Hotel   **ices:** valet laundry. **Business Services:** fax (fee). **Cards:** AX, CB, DC, DS, MC, VI.

SOME UNITS

CLARION HOTEL   **Phone:** (254)757-2000
SAVE   3/1-12/8   1P: $69-$129
2/1-2/28 & 12/9-1/31   1P: $59-$109
♦♦ ♦♦   **Location:** I-35, exit 335A. 801 S 4th St 76706. Fax: 254/757-1110. **Facility:** 148 units. 146 one-bedroom stan-
Small-scale Hotel   dard units. 2 one-bedroom suites ($119-$169), some with kitchens. 2 stories, interior/exterior corridors.
Parking: on-site. **Terms:** [BP] meal plan available, small pets only ($100 deposit). **Amenities:** high-speed Internet, voice mail, irons, hair dryers. **Pool(s):** heated outdoor. **Leisure Activities:** exercise room. *Fee:* game room. **Guest Services:** complimentary evening beverages: Tues-Thurs, coin laundry, area transportation. **Business Serv-ices:** meeting rooms, business center. **Cards:** AX, CB, DC, DS, JC, MC, VI. *(See color ad below)*

SOME UNITS

COMFORT INN   **Phone:** (254)752-1991
SAVE   All Year [ECP]   1P: $64-$185   2P: $64-$185   XP: $7   F17
♦♦ ♦♦   **Location:** I-35, exit 334, on northbound access road. 1430 I-35 S 76706. Fax: 254/752-2084. **Facility:** 53 one-bedroom standard units. 2 stories, exterior corridors. **Parking:** on-site. **Amenities:** high-speed Internet, voice mail, irons. *Some:* hair dryers. **Pool(s):** outdoor. **Business Services:** fax (fee). **Cards:** AX, CB, DC, DS, JC,
Small-scale Hotel   MC, VI.

SOME UNITS

COUNTRY INN & SUITES BY CARLSON, WACO

Phone: (254)799-1766

AAA SAVE

All Year [CP]   1P: $89-$155   2P: $89-$155   XP: $5   F18
Location: I-35, exit 338B. 1502 N I-35 76705. Fax: 254/799-1702. **Facility:** 63 units. 42 one-bedroom standard units, some with whirlpools. 21 one-bedroom suites, some with kitchens and/or whirlpools. 3 stories, interior corridors. *Bath:* combo or shower only. **Parking:** on-site. **Terms:** 1% service charge. **Amenities:** high-speed Internet, voice mail, irons, hair dryers. *Some:* dual phone lines. **Pool(s):** small outdoor. **Leisure Activities:** exercise room. **Guest Services:** valet and coin laundry. **Business Services:** meeting rooms, business center. **Cards:** AX, DS, MC, VI. **Special Amenities:** free continental breakfast and free newspaper. *(See color ad p 260)*

Small-scale Hotel

SOME UNITS

COURTYARD BY MARRIOTT

Phone: (254)752-8686

SAVE

All Year   1P: $79-$155   2P: $89-$155   XP: $10   F17
Location: I-35, exit 335B, 0.6 mi w on University Parks Dr. 101 Washington Ave 76701. Fax: 254/752-1011. **Facility:** 153 units. 147 one-bedroom standard units. 6 one-bedroom suites ($129-$205). 3 stories, interior corridors. *Bath:* combo or shower only. **Parking:** on-site. **Terms:** cancellation fee imposed. **Amenities:** voice mail, irons, hair dryers. **Pool(s):** heated outdoor. **Leisure Activities:** whirlpool, exercise room. **Guest Services:** valet and coin laundry. **Business Services:** meeting rooms, fax (fee). **Cards:** AX, DC, DS, MC, VI.

Small-scale Hotel

SOME UNITS

DAYS INN

Phone: (254)799-8585

AAA SAVE

All Year [ECP]   1P: $62-$72   2P: $62-$82   XP: $6   F16
Location: I-35, exit 338B (Behrens Cir), just n. 1504 I-35 76705. Fax: 254/799-3031. **Facility:** 60 one-bedroom standard units, some with whirlpools. 2 stories, exterior corridors. **Parking:** on-site. **Terms:** small pets only ($30 deposit, $10 extra charge). **Amenities:** hair dryers. **Pool(s):** outdoor. **Business Services:** fax (fee). **Cards:** AX, CB, DC, DS, MC, VI. **Special Amenities:** free continental breakfast and free local telephone calls.

Small-scale Hotel

SOME UNITS

HILTON-WACO

Phone: (254)754-8484

SAVE

All Year   1P: $89-$139   2P: $89-$149   XP: $10   F18
Location: I-35, exit 335B, 0.5 mi w. 113 S University Parks Dr 76701. Fax: 254/752-2214. **Facility:** 196 units. 193 one-bedroom standard units. 3 one-bedroom suites. 11 stories, interior corridors. **Parking:** on-site. **Terms:** cancellation fee imposed. **Amenities:** dual phone lines, voice mail, irons, hair dryers. **Pool(s):** outdoor. **Leisure Activities:** whirlpool, tennis court, exercise room. **Guest Services:** valet laundry. **Business Services:** meeting rooms, business center. **Cards:** AX, CB, DC, DS, JC, MC, VI.

Large-scale Hotel

SOME UNITS
FEE

HOLIDAY INN-WACO I-35

Phone: (254)753-0261

All Year   1P: $85-$100   2P: $95-$110   XP: $10   F17
Location: I-35, exit 335C (Lake Brazos Dr), just n. 1001 Martin Luther King Blvd 76704. Fax: 254/753-0227. **Facility:** 170 one-bedroom standard units. 4 stories, interior corridors. *Bath:* combo or shower only. **Parking:** on-site. **Terms:** check-in 4 pm, pets ($25 fee, $100 deposit). **Amenities:** voice mail, irons, hair dryers. **Pool(s):** outdoor. **Leisure Activities:** exercise room. **Guest Services:** valet and coin laundry. **Business Services:** meeting rooms, business center. **Cards:** AX, CB, DC, DS, MC, VI.

Small-scale Hotel

SOME UNITS

LA QUINTA INN-WACO

Phone: (254)752-9741

SAVE

All Year   1P: $69-$89   2P: $79-$99   XP: $10   F18
Location: E off I-35, exit 334 (17th St) southbound; exit 334A (18th St) northbound. 1110 S 9th St 76706-2399. Fax: 254/757-1600. **Facility:** 102 units. 100 one-bedroom standard units. 2 one-bedroom suites. 2 stories, exterior corridors. **Parking:** on-site. **Terms:** [ECP] meal plan available, small pets only. **Amenities:** video games (fee), voice mail, irons, hair dryers. **Pool(s):** outdoor. **Guest Services:** valet laundry. **Business Services:** fax (fee). **Cards:** AX, CB, DC, DS, JC, MC, VI.

Small-scale Hotel

SOME UNITS

RESIDENCE INN-WACO

Phone: (254)714-1386

SAVE

All Year [BP]   1P: $95-$100   2P: $130
Location: I-35, exit 335B, 0.3 mi w. 501 S University Park Dr 76706. Fax: 254/714-1386. **Facility:** 78 units. 36 one-bedroom standard units with efficiencies. 30 one- and 12 two-bedroom suites, some with efficiencies or kitchens. 3 stories, interior corridors. *Bath:* combo or shower only. **Parking:** on-site. **Terms:** pets ($75 fee, $10 extra charge). **Amenities:** dual phone lines, voice mail, irons, hair dryers. **Pool(s):** heated indoor. **Leisure Activities:** whirlpool, exercise room. **Guest Services:** complimentary evening beverages: Wed, valet and coin laundry. **Business Services:** meeting rooms, fax (fee). **Cards:** AX, CB, DC, DS, MC, VI.

Small-scale Hotel

SOME UNITS

SUPER 8 MOTEL-WACO

Phone: (254)754-1023

All Year [CP]   1P: $49-$69   2P: $49-$69   XP: $5   F12
Location: I-35, exit 334, just e. 1320 S Jack Kultgen Frwy 76706. Fax: 254/754-0127. **Facility:** 78 one-bedroom standard units. 3 stories, interior corridors. **Parking:** on-site. **Terms:** pets ($25 fee). **Amenities:** safes. **Business Services:** fax (fee). **Cards:** AX, CB, DC, DS, MC, VI.

Small-scale Hotel

SOME UNITS

──────── *The following lodging was either not evaluated or did not* ────────
meet AAA rating requirements but is listed for your information only.

QUALITY INN & SUITES   **Phone:** 254/296-0550
[fyi]   All Year [ECP]   1P: $79-$109   2P: $89-$119   XP: $5   F14
             Too new to rate. **Location:** I-35, exit 331. 2410 S New Rd 76716. **Fax:** 254/296-0417. **Amenities:** coffeemakers,
Motel   microwaves, refrigerators, pool. **Cards:** AX, DC, DS, MC, VI.

──────── **WHERE TO DINE** ────────

ELITE CAFE   **Lunch:** $5-$14   **Dinner:** $7-$17   **Phone:** 254/754-4941
▽▽ ▽▽   **Location:** I-35, exit 333A, just e on Waco Cir. 2132 S Valley Mills Dr 76706. **Hours:** 11 am-10 pm, Fri & Sat-11
             pm. Closed: 11/27, 12/25. **Reservations:** suggested; Fri. **Features:** Take a walk back in time to the 40s
American   and 50s at this cafe. Pictures of locals on motorcycles hang in the colorful dining room. Home-style
             cooking features chicken-fried steak, juicy burgers, sandwiches and steak. Casual dress; cocktails.
Parking: on-site. **Cards:** AX, DC, DS, MC, VI.   [X]

FRANKLIN'S SEAFOOD GRILL   **Dinner:** $9-$15   **Phone:** 254/754-3474
▽▽ ▽▽   **Location:** I-35, exit 335B, 0.5 mi w; in The Shops of River Square Center. 215 S 2nd St 76701. **Hours:** 5 pm-10
             pm. Closed major holidays; also 12/24. **Reservations:** accepted. **Features:** This seafood restaurant is
Seafood   located in "The Shops of River Square Mall", a historic downtown warehouse known for it's unique style
             shops and eateries. Enjoy fresh fish entrees skillfully cooked on a hardwood-burning grill or try your hand
at grilled to perfection steak, ribeye or filet. The high wood beamed ceilings, seafaring decor and a light blue painted interior
sets the tone for an inviting and enjoyable meal. Casual dress; cocktails. **Parking:** on-site. **Cards:** AX, DC, DS, MC, VI.
                                                                                                       [Y] [X]

LA FIESTA RESTAURANT AND CANTINA   **Lunch:** $6-$8   **Dinner:** $7-$15   **Phone:** 254/756-4701
▽▽ ▽▽   **Location:** I-35, exit 333A, 2.2 mi w on Valleymills Rd to Franklin Ave exit. 3815 Franklin Ave 76710. **Hours:** 11
             am-10 pm, Fri-midnight, Sat 9 am-midnight, Sun 9 am-10 pm. Closed: 11/27, 12/25. **Features:** The smell
Tex-Mex   of sizzling onions, green peppers, grilled beef and chicken fill the air. Fajitas are a speciality here. Seafood
             lovers try the tasty shrimp fajitas sauteed over roasted potatoes. There is a wide selection of enchiladas,
burritos, tacos and chimichangas to satisfy everyone's cravings. Casual dress; cocktails. **Parking:** on-site. **Cards:** AX, DS,
MC, VI.
                                                                                                       [Y] [X]

PEKING CHINESE RESTAURANT   **Lunch:** $6-$12   **Dinner:** $6-$12   **Phone:** 254/776-2468
▽▽ ▽▽   **Location:** I-35, exit 333A, 3.3 mi w. 1420 N Valley Mills Dr 76710. **Hours:** 11 am-10 pm. Closed: 11/27; also
             Mon. **Features:** The family-owned and operated Chinese restaurant lays out Sunday and lunch buffets.
Chinese   The menu lists a wide selection of traditional dishes, as well as a few American selections. Casual dress;
             cocktails. **Parking:** on-site. **Cards:** AX, DC, DS, MC, VI.
                                                                                                       [X]

Look for a SAVE Place to Stay!

UNCLE DAN'S RIB HOUSE   **Lunch: $5-$8**   **Dinner: $5-$8**   **Phone:** 254/772-3532
    Location: I-35, exit 333A, 3 mi w on Valley Mills Rd, then just s. 1001 Lake Air Dr 76710. **Hours:** 11 am-8:30 pm.
    Closed: 9/1, 11/27; also Sun & 12/25-1/1. **Features:** If you are in the mood for Texas style barbecue, you
Barbecue   have to stop by Uncle Dan's. They serve a variety of mouth watering barbecue items made to satisfy any
    appetite. Place you order and then stroll down a buffet line filled with tasty side dishes. Casual dress; beer
only. **Parking:** on-site. **Cards:** AX, DS, MC, VI.

WAXAHACHIE —See Dallas p. 318.

WEATHERFORD pop. 19,000

——— WHERE TO STAY ———

BEST WESTERN SANTA FE INN   **Phone:** 817/594-7401
  All Year   1P: $69-$79   2P: $69-$89   XP: $5   F12
  Location: I-20, exit 409 (Clear Lake Rd/FM 2552), 0.3 mi nw. Located in a semi-rural area. 1927 Santa Fe Dr 76086.
  Fax: 817/594-5542. **Facility:** 45 one-bedroom standard units. 2 stories, exterior corridors. **Parking:** on-site.
  Terms: [CP] meal plan available, small pets only ($5 extra charge). **Amenities:** irons, hair dryers. **Pool(s):**
Small-scale Hotel outdoor. **Guest Services:** coin laundry. **Business Services:** meeting rooms, fax (fee). **Cards:** AX, CB, DC,
  DS, MC, VI.

SOME UNITS

HAMPTON INN   **Phone:** (817)599-4800
  All Year [CP]   1P: $80-$120   2P: $90-$130
  Location: I-20, exit 408. 2524 S Main St 76087. Fax: 817/599-4040. **Facility:** 56 one-bedroom standard units,
  some with whirlpools. 3 stories, interior corridors. *Bath:* combo or shower only. **Parking:** on-site. **Terms:** cancellation fee imposed, weekly rates available, pets ($10 extra charge). **Amenities:** voice mail, irons, hair
Small-scale Hotel dryers. **Pool(s):** outdoor. **Leisure Activities:** whirlpool, exercise room. **Guest Services:** valet and coin
  laundry. **Business Services:** fax (fee). **Cards:** AX, CB, DC, DS, JC, MC, VI.

SOME UNITS

HOLIDAY INN EXPRESS   **Phone:** (817)599-3700
  All Year [CP]   1P: $74-$110   2P: $84-$120
  Location: I-20, exit 408. 2500 S Main St 76087. Fax: 817/613-0790. **Facility:** 45 one-bedroom standard units,
  some with whirlpools. 2 stories, exterior corridors. **Parking:** on-site. **Terms:** cancellation fee imposed, weekly
  rates available, pets ($10 extra charge). **Amenities:** irons, hair dryers. **Pool(s):** outdoor. **Leisure Activi-**
Small-scale Hotel **ties:** whirlpool. **Guest Services:** valet and coin laundry. **Business Services:** meeting rooms, fax (fee).
  Cards: AX, CB, DC, DS, JC, MC, VI. **Special Amenities: free continental breakfast and free local tele-**
phone calls.

SOME UNITS

——— *The following lodging was either not evaluated or did not* ———
meet AAA rating requirements but is listed for your information only.

COMFORT SUITES   **Phone:** 817/599-3300
  fyi   4/1-10/31 [ECP]   1P: $85-$159   2P: $85-$159   XP: $10   F17
      2/1-3/31 & 11/1-1/31 [ECP]   1P: $75-$159   2P: $85-$159   XP: $10   F17
Motel Too new to rate, opening scheduled for September 2002. **Location:** I-20, exit 408, on SR 171, FM 51. 210 Alford
Dr 76086. Fax: 817/599-5342. **Amenities:** pets, coffeemakers, microwaves, refrigerators, pool. **Terms:** 3 day
cancellation notice-fee imposed. **Cards:** AX, CB, DC, DS, MC, VI. *(See color ad below)*

------ WHERE TO DINE ------

MONTANA RESTAURANT   **Lunch:** $7-$13   **Dinner:** $7-$13   **Phone:** 817/341-3444
▽▽ ▽▽   **Location:** I-20, exit 408. 1910 S Main St 76086. **Hours:** 11 am-11 pm. Closed: 12/25. **Features:** Rustic decor
          characterizes this restaurant offering specialties such as simply prepared American and Mexican cuisine.
American   Casual dress; cocktails. **Parking:** on-site. **Cards:** AX, DC, DS, MC, VI.   ⊠

WEBSTER —See Houston p. 444.

WELLINGTON pop. 2,275

------ WHERE TO STAY ------

CHEROKEE INN & RESTAURANT   **Phone:** (806)447-2508
▽▽   All Year   1P: $32-$38   2P: $34-$48   XP: $3   F16
       Location: US 83, just n of jct FM 338. 1105 Houston 79095. Fax: 806/447-1017. **Facility:** 21 one-bedroom stan-
Motel   dard units. 1 story, exterior corridors. *Bath:* combo or shower only. **Parking:** on-site. **Terms:** small pets only.
       Cards: AX, DS, MC, VI.
                                                                       SOME UNITS
                                          (ASK) (S🇩) �面 (📅) / ⊠ /

WESLACO pop. 26,935

------ WHERE TO STAY ------

BEST WESTERN PALM AIRE MOTOR INN & SUITES   **Phone:** (956)969-2411
(AAA) (SAVE)   2/1-3/23 & 1/16-1/31 [BP]   1P: $59-$105   2P: $65-$111   XP: $6   F17
              3/24-1/15 [BP]   1P: $48-$80   2P: $54-$86   XP: $6   F17
▽▽▽▽   **Location:** US 83 Expwy, exit International Blvd. 415 S International Blvd 78596. Fax: 956/969-2211. **Facility:** 193
Small-scale Hotel   units. 119 one-bedroom standard units, some with whirlpools. 74 one-bedroom suites ($67-$112), some with
              whirlpools. 2 stories, exterior corridors. **Parking:** on-site. **Terms:** check-in 4 pm, small pets only.
              Amenities: voice mail, irons, hair dryers. **Dining:** 6:30 am-10 pm, Sat from 7 am, Sun 7 am-1 pm, entertain-
ment. **Pool(s):** 3 outdoor. **Leisure Activities:** sauna, whirlpools, steamroom, lighted tennis court, racquetball courts, exercise
room. **Guest Services:** gift shop, coin laundry. **Business Services:** meeting rooms, fax (fee). **Cards:** AX, CB, DC, DS, JC,
MC, VI. **Special Amenities:** early check-in/late check-out.   SOME UNITS
                    (S🇩) 🐂 (📅) (🍷) (📶) 🐾 ⊠ (📹) (DATA PORT) (💻) / ⊠ 🔋 (📶) /

SUPER 8 MOTEL   **Phone:** 956/969-9920
▽▽▽▽   All Year [CP]   1P: $45-$59   2P: $50-$69   XP: $5   F12
         Location: US 83, exit Airport Dr. 1702 E Expwy 83 78596. Fax: 956/969-9920. **Facility:** 52 one-bedroom standard
Small-scale Hotel   units, some with whirlpools. 2 stories, exterior corridors. *Bath:* combo or shower only. **Parking:** on-site.
         Amenities: irons, hair dryers. **Pool(s):** outdoor. **Leisure Activities:** whirlpool. **Guest Services:** coin laundry.
Business Services: meeting rooms, fax (fee). **Cards:** AX, CB, DC, DS, MC, VI.
                                                                       SOME UNITS
                          (ASK) (S🇩) 🐂 🐾 (📹) (DATA PORT) 🔋 (📶) / ⊠ /

WESTLAKE

------ WHERE TO STAY ------

DALLAS-FORT WORTH MARRIOTT SOLANA   **Phone:** (817)430-3848
(SAVE)   All Year   1P: $159   2P: $159
          Location: SR 114, exit Kirkwood Blvd, just s. 5 Village Cir 76262. Fax: 817/430-4870. **Facility:** 198 units. 195 one-
▽▽▽▽   bedroom standard units. 3 one-bedroom suites. 7 stories, interior corridors. **Parking:** on-site.
          Terms: package plans, 13% service charge, small pets only. **Amenities:** high-speed Internet (fee), voice
Small-scale Hotel   mail, irons, hair dryers. **Pool(s):** outdoor. **Leisure Activities:** whirlpool, exercise room. **Guest Services:** gift
          shop, valet and coin laundry. **Business Services:** conference facilities, fax (fee). **Cards:** AX, DC, DS, JC,
MC, VI.
                                                                       SOME UNITS
                    🐂 (🍴) (🍷) (♿M) 🐾 (📹) (DATA PORT) (💻) / ⊠ 🔋 /

WICHITA FALLS pop. 104,197

------ WHERE TO STAY ------

COMFORT INN   **Phone:** 940/322-2477
▽▽▽▽   Property failed to provide current rates
         Location: I-44, exit 2, just e. 1750 Maurine St 76306. Fax: 940/322-3866. **Facility:** 67 one-bedroom standard
Motel   units, some with whirlpools. 2 stories (no elevator), interior corridors. *Bath:* combo or shower only. **Parking:**
         on-site. **Terms:** pets ($10 extra charge). **Amenities:** safes (fee). *Some:* hair dryers. **Pool(s):** small indoor.
Leisure Activities: whirlpool, limited exercise equipment. **Guest Services:** valet laundry. **Business Services:** fax (fee).
Cards: AX, CB, DC, DS, MC, VI.
                                                                       SOME UNITS
                    🐂 (♿M) (🔣) 🐾 (📹) (DATA PORT) (💻) / ⊠ 🔋 (📶) /

FAIRFIELD INN   **Phone:** (940)691-1066
(SAVE)   All Year [ECP]   1P: $69-$89   2P: $69-$99   XP: $6   F18
          Location: US 281, exit Southwest Pkwy (CR 369), 2.3 mi w, just n on Kemp Blvd, then just w. 4414 Westgate Dr 76308.
▽▽▽▽   Fax: 940/691-1066. **Facility:** 64 one-bedroom standard units. 3 stories, interior corridors. *Bath:* combo or
          shower only. **Parking:** on-site. **Terms:** 14 day cancellation notice. **Amenities:** irons, hair dryers. **Pool(s):**
Small-scale Hotel   small heated indoor. **Leisure Activities:** whirlpool. **Guest Services:** valet laundry. **Business Services:**
          meeting rooms, fax (fee). **Cards:** AX, CB, DC, DS, MC, VI.
                                                                       SOME UNITS
                    (S🇩) (🍴) (♿M) (🔣) (📹) 🐾 (📹) (DATA PORT) / ⊠ 🔋 (📶) /

HAMPTON INN
SAVE

Small-scale Hotel

Phone: (940)766-3300

All Year [ECP]   1P: $69-$89   2P: $69-$89
Location: I-44, exit 2, just w. 1317 Kenley Ave 76305. Fax: 940/723-8226. **Facility:** 119 one-bedroom standard units. 4 stories, interior corridors. **Parking:** on-site. **Terms:** small pets only ($30 fee). **Amenities:** voice mail, irons, hair dryers. **Pool(s):** outdoor. **Guest Services:** valet and coin laundry. **Business Services:** meeting rooms, fax (fee). **Cards:** AX, CB, DC, DS, MC, VI.

SOME UNITS

LA QUINTA INN-WICHITA FALLS
SAVE

Motel

Phone: (940)322-6971

All Year   1P: $69-$89   2P: $79-$99   XP: $10   F18
Location: I-44, exit 2, just w. 1128 Central Frwy N 76306. Fax: 940/723-2573. **Facility:** 139 units. 134 one-bedroom standard units. 5 one-bedroom suites. 2 stories, exterior corridors. **Parking:** on-site. **Terms:** [ECP] meal plan available, small pets only. **Amenities:** video games (fee), voice mail, irons, hair dryers. **Pool(s):** outdoor. **Guest Services:** valet and coin laundry. **Business Services:** fax (fee). **Cards:** AX, CB, DC, DS, JC, MC, VI.

SOME UNITS

MOTEL 6

Motel

Phone: 940/322-8817

All Year   1P: $40   2P: $50   XP: $3   F17
Location: I-44, exit 2, just e. 1812 Maurine St 76306. Fax: 940/322-5944. **Facility:** 81 one-bedroom standard units. 2 stories (no elevator), exterior corridors. *Bath:* combo or shower only. **Parking:** on-site. **Pool(s):** small outdoor. **Guest Services:** coin laundry. **Business Services:** fax (fee). **Cards:** AX, DC, DS, MC, VI.

SOME UNITS

RADISSON HOTEL

Large-scale Hotel

Phone: (940)761-6000

All Year [BP]   1P: $69-$78   2P: $69-$78   XP: $8   F17
Location: I-287, exit 1C, on westside access road. 100 Central Frwy 76306. Fax: 904/766-1730. **Facility:** 167 units. 161 one-bedroom standard units. 6 one-bedroom suites. 6 stories, interior corridors. **Parking:** on-site. **Terms:** small pets only ($5 extra charge). **Amenities:** video games (fee), dual phone lines, voice mail, irons, hair dryers. **Pool(s):** heated indoor. **Leisure Activities:** whirlpool, exercise room. **Guest Services:** gift shop, valet laundry. **Business Services:** conference facilities, business center. **Cards:** AX, CB, DC, DS, MC, VI.

SOME UNITS

RAMADA LIMITED
AAA **SAVE**

Motel

Phone: (940)855-0085

All Year   1P: $46   2P: $46   XP: $5   F14
Location: US 287, exit Beverly (CR 11), just w. 3209 Northwest Frwy (US 287) 76305. Fax: 940/855-0040. **Facility:** 59 one-bedroom standard units. 2 stories (no elevator), exterior corridors. *Bath:* combo or shower only. **Parking:** on-site. **Terms:** 10 day cancellation notice, [CP] meal plan available, package plans, pets ($10 extra charge). **Amenities:** voice mail, irons, hair dryers. **Pool(s):** outdoor. **Guest Services:** coin laundry. **Business Services:** fax (fee). **Cards:** AX, CB, DC, DS, JC, MC, VI. **Special Amenities:** early check-in/late check-out and free continental breakfast.

SOME UNITS

SUPER 8 MOTEL-WICHITA FALLS

Small-scale Hotel

Phone: (940)322-8880

All Year   1P: $48-$60   2P: $53-$65
Location: I-44, exit 2, just w. 1307 Kenley Ave 76305. Fax: 940/767-8880. **Facility:** 104 one-bedroom standard units. 3 stories, interior corridors. *Bath:* combo or shower only. **Parking:** on-site. **Terms:** [CP] & [ECP] meal plans available, pets ($10 fee). **Business Services:** meeting rooms, fax. **Cards:** AX, DC, DS, MC, VI.

SOME UNITS

TOWNE CREST INN

Motel

Phone: (940)322-1182

All Year   1P: $37-$45   2P: $41-$49   XP: $4   F16
Location: US 287, exit Broad St/Business, w on 9th St to Brook, 1 blk n on Brook to 8th St, then just e. Located across from United Regional Hospital. 1601 8th St 76301. Fax: 940/322-3457. **Facility:** 42 one-bedroom standard units. 2 stories (no elevator), exterior corridors. **Parking:** on-site. **Terms:** cancellation fee imposed, weekly rates available, pets ($5 extra charge). **Business Services:** fax (fee). **Cards:** AX, DS, MC, VI.

SOME UNITS

TRAVELERS INN
AAA **SAVE**

Small-scale Hotel

Phone: (940)766-6881

4/1-8/31   1P: $46-$60   2P: $46-$60
2/1-3/31 & 9/1-1/31   1P: $40-$50   2P: $40-$50
Location: I-44, exit 2, just w. 1032 Central Frwy 76306. Fax: 940/723-2957. **Facility:** 111 units. 108 one-bedroom standard units. 3 one-bedroom suites ($89-$99). 3 stories, exterior corridors. **Parking:** on-site. **Terms:** [CP] meal plan available, pets ($7 extra charge). **Amenities:** video games (fee), irons. **Pool(s):** heated outdoor. **Leisure Activities:** whirlpool, exercise room. **Guest Services:** valet and coin laundry. **Business Services:** meeting rooms, fax (fee). **Cards:** AX, CB, DC, DS, MC, VI. **Special Amenities:** free continental breakfast and free newspaper.

SOME UNITS

——— WHERE TO DINE ———

MCBRIDE LAND & CATTLE COMPANY

Steak House

Lunch: $6-$19   **Dinner:** $9-$19   **Phone:** 940/322-2516
Location: At jct 5th St; downtown. 501 Scott St 76301. **Hours:** 11 am-1:30 & 5-10 pm, Sat & Sun 5 pm-9 pm. Closed: 1/1, 12/25. **Features:** Family owned and operated since 1975, the restaurant sports a rustic exterior and a log cabin-like dining room with a large, stone fireplace as its centerpiece. The professional, uniformed staff is welcoming and offers friendly service. The menu lists appetizers, several steak choices and desserts. Dive into thick and juicy filet mignon wrapped with bacon and served with a baked potato. Smoke free premises. Casual dress; cocktails. **Parking:** on-site. **Cards:** AX, DC, DS, MC, VI.

OXFORD STREET RESTAURANT AND PUB   **Lunch:** $6-$19   **Dinner:** $9-$19   **Phone:** 940/692-9888

American

Location: 3 mi sw; in Century Plaza (opposite Sikes Center Mall). 2611 Plaza Pkwy, Suite 101 76308. **Hours:** 11 am-10 pm, Fri-10:30 pm, Sat 5 pm-10:30 pm, Sun-11:30 am-9 pm. Closed: 12/25. **Features:** The intimate restaurant's feel is evocative of an English pub, with several rooms decorated in dark woods, cozy leather chairs and pictures with scenes of England. Servers are cordial and efficient. On the menu are prime rib, sirloin, tenderloin medallions, rib eye, filet, New York strip, stuffed shrimp, grilled salmon, lobster a la Oxford, pork chops and chicken. Casual dress; cocktails. **Parking:** on-site. **Cards:** AX, CB, DC, DS, MC, VI.

WILLIS —See Houston p. 445.

WILLOW PARK pop. 2,849

——— **WHERE TO STAY** ———

RAMADA LIMITED-WILLOW PARK   **Phone:** (817)441-5443

Small-scale Hotel

All Year [CP]   1P: $59   2P: $59   XP: $5   F17
Location: I-20, exit 418 (Ranch House Rd). 5080 E I-20 76087. Fax: 817/441-5041. **Facility:** 62 one-bedroom standard units, some with whirlpools. 2 stories, exterior corridors. *Bath:* combo or shower only. **Parking:** on-site. **Amenities:** voice mail, irons, hair dryers. **Pool(s):** small outdoor. **Business Services:** fax (fee). **Cards:** AX, DC, DS, MC, VI.

SOME UNITS

WIMBERLEY pop. 3,797

——— **WHERE TO STAY** ———

BLAIR HOUSE INN   **Phone:** (512)847-1111

Bed & Breakfast

All Year   1P: $145-$280
Location: Jct of Ranch Rd 32 and 12, 2.4 mi s of downtown on Ranch Rd 12. 100 Spoke Hill Rd 78676. Fax: 512/847-8820. **Facility:** Wildflowers, towering oak trees and a hammock make the inn's 85-acre grounds well-suited for long walks or lounging. Designated smoking area. 9 one-bedroom standard units, some with whirlpools. 1 story, interior/exterior corridors. *Bath:* combo or shower only. **Parking:** on-site. **Terms:** 2 night minimum stay - weekends, 30 day cancellation notice-fee imposed, [BP] meal plan available, $10 service charge. **Amenities:** video library, CD players, hair dryers. **Leisure Activities:** sauna, bicycles, hiking trails, jogging. *Fee:* massage. **Guest Services:** complimentary laundry. **Business Services:** fax. **Cards:** AX, DS, MC, VI.

SOME UNITS

WINNIE —See Houston p. 445.

THE WOODLANDS —See Houston p. 445.

WOODVILLE pop. 2,415

——— **WHERE TO DINE** ———

THE PICKETT HOUSE   Historic   **Lunch:** $4-$10   **Dinner:** $10   **Phone:** 409/283-3371

American

Location: 1.5 mi w on US 190; in Heritage Village. Hwy 190 W 75979. **Hours:** 11 am-2 pm, Sat & Sun-6 pm; Fri 11 am-8 pm in summer. Closed major holidays. **Features:** Located inside an old, restored schoolhouse, this cute restaurant serves tasty American cuisine. Fried chicken dinners are served boarding-house style. Corn bread and fresh vegetables in season are favorites. The peach cobbler is the perfect way to end your meal. Smoke free premises. Casual dress. **Parking:** on-site. **Cards:** AX, DS, MC, VI.

WOODWAY pop. 8,733

——— **WHERE TO STAY** ———

FAIRFIELD INN   **Phone:** (254)776-7821

SAVE

Small-scale Hotel

All Year [ECP]   1P: $69-$89   2P: $69-$99   XP: $6   F18
Location: I-35, exit 330 (SR 6), 5 mi w; Loop 340, exit 330 to jct SR 84. 5805 N Woodway Dr 76712. Fax: 254/776-7821. **Facility:** 64 one-bedroom standard units. 3 stories, interior corridors. *Bath:* combo or shower only. **Parking:** on-site. **Terms:** 14 day cancellation notice. **Amenities:** *Some:* hair dryers. **Pool(s):** small heated indoor. **Leisure Activities:** whirlpool. **Guest Services:** valet laundry. **Business Services:** fax (fee). **Cards:** AX, CB, DC, DS, MC, VI.

SOME UNITS

RAMADA LTD & SUITES WACO   **Phone:** (254)751-7400

Small-scale Hotel

All Year [ECP]   1P: $63-$73   2P: $69-$79   XP: $6   F
Location: I-35, exit 330 (SR 6 N), 2.4 mi w to exit US 84, 1.1 mi s. 7007 Woodway Dr 76712 (7007 Woodway Dr, WACO). Fax: 254/751-7553. **Facility:** 49 one-bedroom standard units. 3 stories, interior corridors. **Parking:** on-site. **Terms:** 14 day cancellation notice. **Amenities:** voice mail, irons, hair dryers. **Pool(s):** small heated indoor. **Leisure Activities:** whirlpool. **Guest Services:** valet and coin laundry. **Business Services:** fax (fee). **Cards:** AX, CB, DC, DS, MC, VI.

SOME UNITS

ZAPATA pop. 4,856

—— WHERE TO STAY ——

BEST WESTERN INN BY THE LAKE   **Phone:** (956)765-8403

All Year   1P: $59   2P: $65   XP: $8   F15
Location: 0.5 mi se on US 83. Star Rt 1, Box 252 78076. **Fax:** 956/765-8071. **Facility:** 56 one-bedroom standard
units. 1 story, exterior corridors. **Parking:** on-site, winter plug-ins. **Terms:** [CP] meal plan available, small
pets only. **Amenities:** irons, hair dryers. **Pool(s):** small outdoor. **Guest Services:** coin laundry. **Business**
Small-scale Hotel   **Services:** meeting rooms, fax (fee). **Cards:** AX, DS, MC, VI. **Special Amenities:** early check-in/late
check-out and free continental breakfast.

SOME UNITS

578

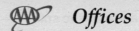 **Offices**

Cities with main offices are listed in **BOLD TYPE** and toll-free member service numbers in *ITALIC TYPE*.
All are closed Saturdays, Sundays and holidays unless otherwise indicated.
The type of service provided is designated below the name of the city where the office is located:

➕ Auto travel services, including books/maps, marked maps and on-demand Triptik maps
⬤ Auto travel services, including books/maps, marked maps, but no on-demand Triptik maps
◼ Provides books/maps only. No marked maps or on-demand Triptik maps available
▲ Travel agency services

NATIONAL OFFICE: 1000 AAA DRIVE, HEATHROW, FLORIDA 32746-5063, (407) 444-7000

TEXAS

AMARILLO—AAA TEXAS, 2607 WOLFLIN VILLAGE #4, 79109-1838. MON-FRI 9-6, SAT 9-1. (806) 354-8288, *(800) 765-0766.*➕▲

ARLINGTON—AAA TEXAS, 4634 S COOPER #176, 76017. MON-FRI 9-6, SAT 9-1. (817) 417-5636.➕▲

AUSTIN—AAA TEXAS, 13376 RESEARCH BLVD #124, 78750. MON-FRI 9-6, SAT 9-1. (512) 335-5222, *(800) 765-0766.*➕▲

AUSTIN—AAA TEXAS, 4970 HWY 290 WEST #310, 78735. MON-FRI 9-6, SAT 9-1. (512) 444-4757, *(800) 765-0766.*➕▲

BEDFORD—AAA TEXAS, 2220 AIRPORT FWY #410, 76022. MON-FRI 9-6, SAT 9-1. (817) 354-8484, *(800) 765-0766.*➕▲

CONROE—AAA TEXAS, 27726 I-45 N, 77385. MON-FRI 9-6, SAT 9-1. (713) 834-3200.➕▲

DALLAS—AAA TEXAS, 4425 N CENTRAL EXPY, 75205. MON-FRI 9-6, SAT 9-1. (214) 526-7911, *(800) 765-0766.*➕▲

DALLAS—AAA TEXAS, 5445 BELTLINE RD, 75240. MON-FRI 9-6, SAT 9-1. (214) 526-7911, *(800) 765-0766.*➕▲

EL PASO—AAA TEXAS, 1201 AIRWAY BLVD #A-1, 79925. MON-FRI 9-6, SAT 9-1. (915) 778-9521, *(800) 765-0766.*➕▲

FORT WORTH—AAA TEXAS, 5431 S HULEN, 76132. MON-FRI 9-6, SAT 9-1. (817) 370-3000, *(800) 765-0766.*➕▲

GARLAND—AAA TEXAS, 1237 NORTHWEST HWY, 75041-5835. MON-FRI 9-6, SAT 9-1. (972) 926-1535.➕▲

HOUSTON—AAA TEXAS, 8508 HIGHWAY 6 N, 77095. MON-FRI 9-6, SAT 9-1. (281) 859-4188, *(800) 765-0766.*➕▲

HOUSTON—AAA TEXAS, 16921 EL CAMINO REAL, 77058. MON-FRI 9-6, SAT 9-1. (281) 480-5059, *(800) 765-0766.*➕▲

HOUSTON—AAA TEXAS, 3307 SAGE RD, 77056. MON-FRI 9-6, SAT 9-1. (713) 284-6335.➕▲

HOUSTON—AAA TEXAS, 9311 KATY FWY #E, 77024. MON-FRI 9-6, SAT 9-1. (713) 284-6489, *(800) 765-0766.*➕▲

HOUSTON—AAA TEXAS, 2234 FM 1960 W SUITE E, 77090. MON-FRI 9-6, SAT 9-1. (713) 284-6450, *(800) 765-0766.*➕▲

MISSOURI CITY—AAA TEXAS, 4729 HWY 6, 77459. MON-FRI 9-6, SAT 9-1. (713) 284-6494, *(800) 765-0766.*➕▲

PLANO—AAA TEXAS, 7200 INDEPENDENCE PKY 224, 75025. MON-FRI 10-7, SAT 9-1. (972) 661-3300, *(800) 765-0766.*➕▲

SAN ANTONIO—AAA TEXAS, 11075 I-H 10 WEST STE 309, 78230-1057. MON-FRI 9-6, SAT 9-1. (210) 403-5080, *(800) 765-0766.*➕▲

SAN ANTONIO—AAA TEXAS, 13415 SAN PEDRO, 78216. MON-FRI 9-6, SAT 9-1. (210) 499-0222, *(800) 765-0766.*➕▲

The One That Does It All

For years, people have turned to AAA for their emergency road service needs. But AAA is more than just towing. Access to AAA's travel services can give you the world. Its financial services can help you pay for it. And AAA insurance can give you the peace of mind to enjoy the ride.

Plus, AAA gives you exclusive Show Your Card & Save® offers, bail bond benefits, and much more.

Discover the ways AAA can simplify your life. Call or stop by your nearest AAA office today to find out about the specific products and services they offer.

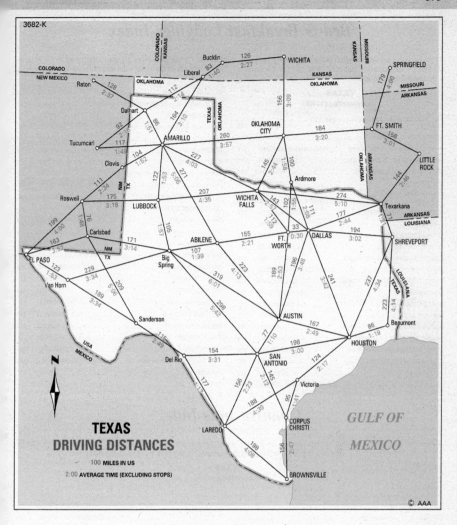

TEXAS
DRIVING DISTANCES

100 MILES IN US
2:00 AVERAGE TIME (EXCLUDING STOPS)

© AAA

Camper Sweet Camper

If camping is where your heart is, then **AAA CampBook® guides** are for you. With information about campgrounds throughout North America, **CampBooks** provide campers valuable details on camping facilities. From rate information to site descriptions to recreational activities, these guides give campers all the information they need before hitting the trail.

Travel With Someone You Trust®

*To get your **CampBook guide**, call or visit your local AAA office today.*

Bed & Breakfast Lodgings Index

Some bed and breakfasts listed below might have historical significance. Those properties are also referenced in the Historical index. The indication that continental [CP] or full breakfast [BP] is included in the room rate reflects whether a property is a Bed-and-Breakfast facility.

TEXAS
ACCOMMODATIONS

Country Inns Index

Some of the following country inns can also be considered as bed-and-breakfast operations. The indication that continental [CP] or full breakfast [BP] is included in the room rate reflects whether a property is a Bed-and-Breakfast facility.

TEXAS
ACCOMMODATIONS

RESTAURANT

Historical Lodgings & Restaurants Index

Some of the following historical lodgings can also be considered as bed-and-breakfast operations. The indication that continental [CP] or full breakfast [BP] is included in the room rate reflects whether a property is a Bed-and-Breakfast facility.

TEXAS
ACCOMMODATIONS

HISTORICAL LODGINGS & RESTAURANTS (CONT'D)

RESTAURANTS

Resorts Index

Many establishments are located in resort areas; however, the following places have extensive on-premises recreational facilities:

Points of Interest Index

MUSIC HALLS & OPERA HOUSES

NATURAL BRIDGES

NATURAL PHENOMENA

NATURE CENTERS

NATURE TRAILS

OBSERVATORIES

WALKING TOURS

WATERFALLS

WATER PARKS

WAX MUSEUMS

WILDERNESS AREAS

WILDLIFE SANCTUARIES

SAVE *Attraction Admission Discount Index*

Comprehensive City Index

Here is an alphabetical list of all cities appearing in this TourBook® guide. Cities are presented by state/province. Page numbers under the POI column indicate where points of interest text begins. Page numbers under the L&R column indicate where lodging and restaurant listings begin.

Photo Credit Index

For nearly 100 years members have counted on AAA for their emergency road service needs, maps, TripTiks and travel information & services.

$\mathcal{B}$ut did you know...

'Due to state regulations and local restrictions, insurance is not available through all AAA clubs.

you can also trust AAA to provide you with insurance protection. Most[1] AAA clubs provide a variety of insurance products for all phases of your life, at competitive rates from leading companies in their markets. Policies most often available include coverage for your:

- Automobile
- Home
- Life
- Boat
- RV
- Trip Cancellation
- Travel Delay/Lost Baggage

Call your local AAA office today and ask one of our knowledgeable insurance representatives to help you with your insurance needs.

Insure With Someone You Trust®

One Perfect Gift

Give the gift of security, service, and savings—buy someone you care about a AAA gift membership. AAA memberships provide your loved ones more than emergency road service.

AAA members also have access to travel services, insurance, financial services, exclusive Show Your Card & Save® discounts, bail bond services, and more.

Give them more than a gift. Give them AAA. And let them discover how AAA can simplify their lives. Call or stop by your nearest AAA office today. And make AAA the one for you.

AAA Travel ... for Those On the Go.

Travel

G oing on a trip? Whether you let AAA handle the planning or do it yourself, trust us to steer you right with reliable information and valuable guidance. We'll help you:

- Choose the best **travel route**, whether it's scenic, direct, or somewhere in between.
- Select **accommodations**, from pampered luxury to clean and practical.
- Explore your **dining** options, whether it's a night on the town to a bite on the run.
- Get the inside scoop on **attractions**, from neon lights to natural sights.

Prefer personal assistance? Enjoy the complimentary services of a AAA/CAA auto travel professional at your local club office or by phone. Just tell us what you have in mind and we'll design your route, book your reservations, and offer you exclusive travel materials to enhance your trip.

Rather do it yourself? Choose from a flexible array of travel resources. Use *Traveler*, the Internet TripTik on aaa.com, to create your ultimate route, complete with driving distances and stops at AAA Approved hotels, restaurants, and attractions. Book your stays using the Online TourBook. And explore your destination using detailed TourBook guides and handy sheet maps.

Whichever way you go ... go with AAA Travel! Contact your nearest AAA/CAA service office to speak with a travel professional and pick up valuable travel materials. Or, access AAA's renowned travel services online at www.aaa.com!

Travel With Someone You Trust®

See for yourself why Holiday Inn® is *America's hotel*

For good reasons, travelers have chosen Holiday Inn® hotels for over fifty years. Comfort, value, convenient locations… and a great place to create family memories.

Here's what you can expect at every Holiday Inn hotel:*
• Kids Eat & Stay Free
• Swimming pools
• Restaurant, lounge, room service, and fitness center
• In-room amenities, including: dataport, iron/ironing board, coffeemaker, and hair dryer.

Holiday Inn hotels across the nation offer special AAA rates.

For Reservations:
Call **1-800-734-4275**,
your AAA Travel Professional
or visit **holiday-inn.com/aaa**